Independent Traveller's

EUROPE
2003

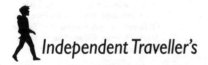

Independent Traveller's

EUROPE
2003

The INTER-RAILER'S and EURAILER'S GUIDE

Edited by Tim Locke

Thomas Cook

Publishing

Published by Thomas Cook Publishing
A division of Thomas Cook Holdings Ltd
PO Box 227, Units 19–21
The Thomas Cook Business Park
Peterborough PE3 8XX
United Kingdom

Telephone: 01733 416477
E-mail: books@thomascook.com

Text:
© 2003 Thomas Cook Publishing

Maps and diagrams:
© 2003 Thomas Cook Publishing

Transport maps © TCS, Aldershot
London Underground map
© London Regional Transport
London city map, 2001 © Lovell Johns, Witney,
  Oxon
Route maps prepared by Pixel Cartography,
  Henley-on-Thames
Country maps prepared by Polly Senior

ISBN 1 841573 03 5

Publisher: Donald Greig
Project Editor: Edith Summerhayes
Text design: Tina West

Cover design: Pumpkin House, Cambridge, and
  Wiz Graphics, Rockland St Mary, Norfolk
Cover layout: Studio 183, Peterborough
Proofreader: Colin Follett
Text update editors: Susie Behar, Peter Cooling,
  Patsy North

Text typeset in Book Antiqua and Gill Sans
  using QuarkXPress
Picture research: Michelle Warrington
Imagesetting: Z2 Reprographics, Thetford,
  Norfolk
Text revisions: Cooling Brown,
  Hampton-upon-Thames, Middlesex
Printed and bound in Italy by Rotolito
  Lombarda SpA

First edition (1999) written and
researched by:
**Ethel Davies; Sevil Delin; Jane Foster;
Will Hardie; Dr Annie Kay; Susie
Lunt; Jennifer Morris; Caroline
Oldfield; Jeremy Smith; Dan Taylor;
Mark Thomas; Wendy Wood; Barry
Worthington**

Update research for 2003:
**Colin Follett
Mark Corner
Tim Locke
The compilers of the**
Thomas Cook European Timetable:
**Brendan Fox (Editor), Kevin Flynn,
John Potter, Dave Turpie and Chris
Woodcock**

Book Editor:
Tim Locke

ACKNOWLEDGEMENTS

The authors and Thomas Cook Publishing would like to thank the following for their help during the production of this book:

Jenny Alexander, for all her excellent tips on Berlin, Amsterdam, the Baltics, Istanbul and elsewhere
Ognian Avgarski, Balkania Travel Ltd
Personnel (official and non official) involved in the tourist industry of the Baltic States
Beatrice at the Hotel Miramar in Cap d'Ail
Bernd Buhmann
Klara Burianova
Leszek Butowski
Eva Draxler, Vienna tourist board
Jela Faltanyova, Slovak tourist board
Barry Fiedler
Jaroslav Flak, Torun tourist board
Elizabeth Harney
Hotel Ibis, Krakow
Natascha Kompatzki
Peter Kozyrev of the *St Petersburg Times*
Sara Malamunic, Split and Dalmatia County Tourist Board
The exceptionally helpful tourist office in Nice
Charles Page, Rail Europe
Marie-Hélène Piani and the Corsican tourist offices
Janina Pizlo, Krakow tourist information
Alenka Rebec, Ljubljana Promotion Centre
Clare Ring
The Romanian National Tourist Office
Tourist offices at Brno, Czech Rep; Dresden; Innsbruck; Kitzbuhel; Linz, Salzburg, Austria; Zakopane, Poland and throughout Europe.

PHOTOGRAPHS

Thomas Cook Publishing would like to thank Spectrum Colour Library, Neil Setchfield and Tim Locke for supplying the photographs (and to whom the copyright belongs):

pp. 96/97 Spectrum Colour Library except Eurostar train, Paris, Neil Setchfield; Sagrada Família, Barcelona, Tim Locke
pp. 224/225 Spectrum Colour Library except tram in narrow street, Lisbon, Tim Locke; Douro river, Portugal, Neil Setchfield
pp. 352/353 Spectrum Colour Library except Milan central railway station, Neil Setchfield
pp. 480/481 Spectrum Colour Library except tramcars, Stockholm, Neil Setchfield

COVER PHOTOGRAPHS

Louvre, Paris, Caroline Jones
Cyclists, Ibiza, Stockfile/Steven Behr
Tram on Damrak, Amsterdam, Jon Arnold/jonarnold.com

The Authors

Tim Locke is an editor and guidebook writer who has journeyed over much of Europe including backpacking over the Alps and cycling in France. He is the author of several walking and general guides to Britain, as well as guides to Germany, New England and Thailand. He wishes to dedicate this guide to Ronald Locke (1921–1999) who enthused him with his passion for rail travel and discovering new places.

Ethel Davies is a freelance photographer and journalist who makes her living travelling around the globe. Rail travel remains one of her favourite modes of getting around.

Sevil Delin is an Oxford graduate working as a writer in Istanbul. A contributor to previous Thomas Cook guides, she can ask directions to the train station fluently in five languages.

Jane Foster lives in Split on the Dalmatian coast, where she works as a freelance travel writer. She contributes to a number of British and American publications and websites, concentrating primarily on Croatia, Slovenia and Italy.

Will Hardie has travelled through the Indian subcontinent and the Americas as well as extensively in Europe, where he wrote the Spain and Portugal sections of a previous Thomas Cook guide. He is now a reporter at Reuters news agency.

Dr Annie Kay, freelance travel writer and journalist specialising in Bulgaria. Winner of the Bulgarian Rose International Award for Journalists. Organiser of special interest tours to Bulgaria.

Susie Lunt is a freelance writer based in Prague, where she has lived off and on since 1991. She specialises in writing about Central and East European travel, culture and food, and has travelled extensively throughout the region.

Jennifer Morris studied at Oxford where she edited a number of student publications including *Oxford Student* and *Isis*. She has travelled widely throughout Europe and America and has worked in France for several years. She winters in the Alps as a ski representative.

Caroline Oldfield has travelled extensively throughout Europe, edited student publications before gaining BA (Hons) Journalism, written for various publications; and is currently a Trinity Newspapers reporter and travel writer.

J J Smith and Dan Taylor were recently released from university and survived in the wild by preying on doughnuts. They now haunt the Oxford Media Underground. Dan would like to express no thanks at all to the Mannekin-Pis.

Mark Thomas took a year-out from managing his own PR consultancy to tour Europe with his family. The former journalist is also a freelance travel writer.

Wendy Wood studied at Oxford and has travelled extensively in Europe, most recently France and Spain. She has contributed to several Thomas Cook publications and revised the *Thomas Cook European 12-Language Phrasebook*.

Barry Worthington, lecturer in Tourism at Bolton Institute of Higher Education, travelled extensively over the last few years in the Baltic States and is in the process of completing a doctoral thesis on the Estonian Tourism Industry. He is a rail enthusiast.

7

'Ever since childhood ... I have seldom heard a train go by and not wished I was on it. Those whistles sing bewitchment: railways are irresistible bazaars, snaking along perfectly level no matter what the landscape, improving your mood with speed, and never upsetting your drink. The train can reassure you in awful places – a far cry from the anxious sweats of doom aeroplanes inspire, or the nauseating gas-sickness of the long-distance bus, or the paralysis that afflicts the car passenger. If a train is large and comfortable you don't even need a destination; a corner seat is enough, and you can be one of those travellers who stay in motion, straddling the tracks, and never arrive or feel they ought to.'

Paul Theroux, *The Great Railway Bazaar*
(1975, published by Penguin Books)

CONTENTS

CONTENTS

INTRODUCTION

I first got the Inter-rail/Eurail bug when a 19-year-old student. It's an exciting but also quite a daunting feeling: you buy this ticket, and the whole of Europe is yours.

For a glorious month, the train became my way of life: I was glued to the constantly changing views outside. Europe was more startlingly varied than I could ever have believed.

The main problem was information: there wasn't a guidebook like this in those days, and it wasn't that easy to work out where to go. I ended up sleeping in a field one night because that promising-sounding seaside town in Yugoslavia turned out to have no accommodation whatsoever. And I had the nagging feeling I was missing out; as my homeward-bound night train glided through stations whose names promised so much – among them Venice, Verona, Arles and Orange – I realised how much there was to come back and see. And somewhere to the north were supposed to be some amazing mountain railway lines through the Alps – but where exactly?

What I've sought to do in this book is to help you make the choices. It's all too easy to fall in the trap of trying to do too much. Then eventually Europe becomes one confused blur of cathedrals, railway stations and youth hostels. Instead, well it might have been nicer to have mixed things up more – a few great cities, some smaller towns, and maybe the chance to relax on a beach or hike into the mountains.

After all, it's the diversity of Europe that is the key to its enduring appeal. Architecture, people, language, culture, food, drink and landscapes vary with bewildering rapidity as you cross the continent – whether from the old baroque cities of eastern and northern Europe to the rugged, parched sierras of inland Spain, or from the wildflower-speckled meadows of the Alps and Pyrenees to the astonishing ancient ruins of Greece and Italy.

With all this in mind I have arranged the bulk of this book into rail tours that really take in the cream, and with the expert help of the European Railway Timetable team at Thomas Cook have worked out all the logistics of rail travel – connections, where to go next, how long trips take and so on. So those great trans-Alpine routes are in the book, together with the amazing trips up through Scandinavia and up to the Arctic Circle. I've also pieced together routes that are really memorable for their cultural attractions and for their sheer contrasts. To get you started, I have highlighted some routes through Europe on pp. 41–42, but of course there are many more. No other guidebook to Europe has ever been published in this rail tour format; to avoid overwhelming you with information and ensure that the book is reasonably portable, I've endeavoured to keep descriptions concise.

The book is arranged into countries, so that it can be used if you're travelling with a regional or country pass. For those who are heading across the border, I have put in links to other countries. Major cities such as Barcelona, Berlin and Munich get their own sections at the beginning of each country section, although all of these also feature on the rail tours that follow.

As Paul Theroux succinctly suggests on p. 9, rail travel is an experience in itself. Trains are great for meeting other travellers, and they're generally safer and more comfortable than buses. Once you get into the swing of them they're ten times less hassle than navigating your way around by car. Often they get you right into city centres (where driving can be a nightmare), right where you want to be. And usefully the cheap hotel area in much of Europe often happens to be right next to the main station itself.

The rail network is impressively dense, and on the whole the trains work pretty well. Plan things carefully and you can even save money and time by sleeping on the train.

Do buy the latest *Thomas Cook European Timetable* (published monthly). This masterpiece of compression gives all the main rail routes in Europe, and lots of minor ones. It also has rail maps for each country, showing corresponding table numbers for each route. If you are just visiting one or two countries and want to cut out the relevant bits to save carrying the rest, don't forget to take the list of standard symbols at the front. Be careful to read all the footnotes to the train you want to take: some trains require supplements, and some don't run every day. Also useful is the *Thomas Cook Rail Map of Europe*, which highlights scenic routes and shows Europe all in one go – handy for planning trips across borders.

Europe can be an expensive place to visit but you can keep costs down appreciably by staying at youth hostels and budget hotels (often called pensions), having picnic lunches and sticking to cheaper countries such as those in eastern Europe – Prague, for instance, is still a bargain – or those in the south such as Spain and Portugal. Although it might be tempting to save on travel insurance, it's still a good idea in case disaster strikes. Europe is pretty safe and hassle-free, but petty crime is a fact of life in some places.

During the course of your travels, you'll inevitably gather your own views on what you visit. I'd very much appreciate feedback on anything we cover, either as a short e-mail (books@thomascook.com) or as a completed form: see the back of this book. So whether you like or don't like something we describe, or like something we haven't included, please tell us.

Have a great trip.

Tim Locke

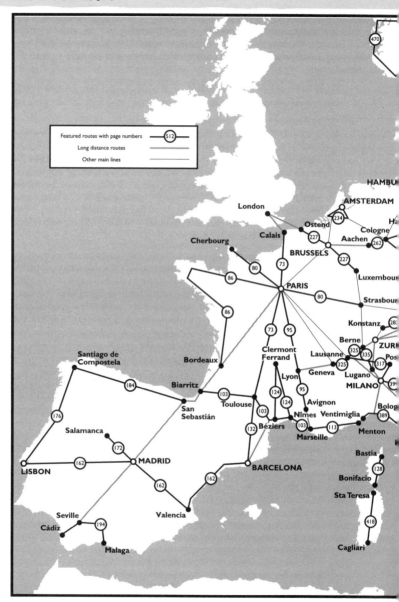

Featured routes with page numbers — 512
Long distance routes
Other main lines

London
Cherbourg
Calais
Ostend
AMSTERDAM
HAMBU
234
Cologne
Aachen
227
262
BRUSSELS
227
80
73
Luxembou
PARIS
80
Strasbour
86
86
Konstanz
28
73
95
Berne
ZUR
Clermont
Ferrand
Lausanne
325
335
Pos
317
Santiago de
Compostela
Bordeaux
Lyon
Geneva
Lugano
325
39
184
Biarritz
95
MILANO
Avignon
103
San
Sebastián
Toulouse
124
124
176
Bolog
103
Nîmes
Ventimiglia
389
Salamanca
132
Béziers
103
113
Menton
172
Marseille
Bastia
162
LISBON
MADRID
128
162
Bonifacio
162
BARCELONA
Sta Teresa
162
Seville
Valencia
194
418
Cádiz
Malaga
Cagliari

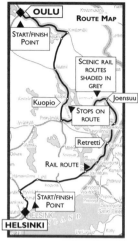

ROUTE DETAIL

Helsinki–Oulu		ETT table 794
Type	Frequency	Journey Time
Train	5–10 daily	7 hrs

Helsinki–Parikkala		ETT table 797
Type	Frequency	Journey Time
Train	4–5 daily	4 hrs 10 mins

▲

ROUTE DETAIL

Helsinki–Oulu:
direct journey details
Helsinki–Parikkala:
point to point information

Mode of travel, typical journey time,
frequency of service and *ETT* table
numbers are given.

KEY TO ICONS

📞 Telephone

🚌 Bus

🚉 Rail Stations

🚍 Public Transport

⛴ Ferry Services

✈ Airports

ℹ Information

🏨 Accommodation

🍽 Food and Drink

Independent Traveller's Europe is divided into country, city and route chapters. City and route chapters fall within sections that cover one country, or a group of countries where we link areas of Europe, such as Spain and Portugal, South-East Europe.

Many travellers will start their journey in London and head to Paris and beyond, and the format of this guide reflects this. So, the United Kingdom is followed by France, Spain, Portugal, Central Europe, Scandinavia, the Baltic States, Eastern Europe and finally South-East Europe. The routes are chosen for their interest and do not all link together, but using suggestions in this book and a copy of the *Thomas Cook European Timetable* they form a menu from which you can plan a rail tour.

Country introductory sections concentrate on accommodation and food and drink within that country. Each Country introduction ends with Editor's Choice, listing some of the best areas to head for if time is limited, and Beyond the Border, giving you pointers to train trips into adjacent countries. Country-specific details, national rail information and local rail passes are given within the **Directory**, pp. 586–617. **City chapters** cover the major centres within each country section. The 'Highlights' featured are a selective choice of attractions.

Route chapters start with a map plotting the route and possible stopping points (featured within that chapter), combined with route details and any 'notes' that may help the rail traveller. Places given in a plain type (rather than bold) in the route details are included as a transfer point en route. Within route and city chapters, day trips are suggested. Where Next? features further places and attractions to explore, or links to other routes.

The **route map** on pp. 14–15 gives a summary of the routes covered in this book; **Travelling Around Europe** gives basic travel advice; and **Rail Passes** and **Rail Travel** concentrate on aspects of rail touring. **International Routes** details journeys that will take you across the continent. At the back of this guide is a selection of colour city and transport maps.

Travellers are strongly advised to purchase the *Thomas Cook European Timetable*, referred to as the *ETT*, published monthly (p. 25). You will see ETT numbers throughout this guide, but note that table numbers do change and services are altered. Don't forget also to check local station timetables as you travel, as the ETT has insufficient space to show every short-distance rail service.

Accommodation price bands reflect relative costs within a country (not given for hostels and campsites, which all fall into the € band):

€	budget
€€	moderate
€€€	expensive

This chapter is full of helpful tips for anyone planning to travel around Europe. For information covering specific countries, see under individual countries in the Directory section (pp. 586–617).

ACCOMMODATION Europe offers an excellent choice, from five-star hotels to room only. Your main problem may lie in finding something to suit your budget. Rooms in private houses can be a good, inexpensive and friendly option (local tourist offices often have lists), but you may be expected to stay for more than one night. The quality of cheaper hotels in Eastern Europe may still be less than inspiring and you could do better with a private room. Local tourist offices are almost always your best starting point if you haven't pre-booked. If they don't handle bookings themselves (there's usually a small charge), they will re-direct you to someone who does and/or supply you with the information to do it yourself – tell them your price horizons.

Hostels: For those on a tight budget, the best bet is to join HI (Hostelling International); there's no age limit. Membership of a national association will entitle you to use over 5000 HI hostels in 60 different countries and, apart from camping, they often provide the cheapest accommodation. The norm is dormitory-style, but many hostels also have single and family rooms. Many offer excellent-value dining and many have self-catering and/or laundry facilities. Some hostels are open 24 hours, but most have lock-out times and reception's hours are usually limited – check what they are and advise them if you are arriving out of hours. Reservation is advisable – especially in summer, when many hostels fill well in advance and even those with space are likely to limit your stay to three nights if you just turn up without booking. In winter (except around Christmas) you may be able to get special price deals. Buy the HI's directory Europe, which lists hostel addresses, contact numbers, locations and facilities; the HI website is www.iyhf.org. Free online booking is available through the HI web-based system at www.hostelbooking.com. A useful independent website is www.hostels.com, which has lists of private as well as HI hostels. For information, to join, and to book international accommodation in advance: Australia, ☎(02) 9565 1699; Canada, ☎(613) 237 7844; England and Wales, ☎0870 870 8808; Republic of Ireland, ☎(01) 830 4555; New Zealand, ☎(03) 379 9970; Northern Ireland, ☎(028) 9031 5435; Scotland, ☎(01786) 891400; South Africa, ☎(021) 424 2511; USA, ☎(202) 783 6161.

Camping: This is obviously the cheapest accommodation if you're prepared to carry the equipment. There are campsites right across Europe, from basic (just toilets and showers) to luxury family-oriented sites with dining-rooms, swimming pools and complexes of permanent tents. The drawback is that sites are often miles from the city centres. There's no really good pan-European guide to campsites, but most tourist offices can provide a directory for their country.

BORDERS Land borders between the EU (European Union) countries are virtually non-existent and it's only if you arrive/leave by air or sea that you're likely to encounter any formalities. Checks between the EU and other West European countries are seldom more than perfunctory. Most former Eastern bloc countries, however, still go through the full routine and you should be prepared for delays when crossing between East and West.

CHILDREN Most children find train travel a great novelty and thoroughly enjoy themselves. However, they can get bored on long journeys. Most tourist destinations in Europe are reasonably well adapted for children and babysitters are not hard to find (ask at the local tourist office). Many hotels offer family rooms or provide a cot in a normal double. Many sights and forms of transport accept babies for free, and children under 12 for half price. For useful reading try: Maureen Wheeler, *Travel with Children* (Lonely Planet, £8.99).

CLIMATE The climate in Europe is affected by three main factors: latitude (Scandinavia is colder than Spain); altitude (the Alps are colder than Belgium); and distance from the sea (the Central European countries, such as the Czech Republic, can suffer surprisingly harsh winters and unexpectedly hot summers). That said, most of Europe has a relatively gentle climate. Rain is common throughout the year, except along some stretches of the Mediterranean. The summer temperature rarely exceeds 28°C (see the temperature chart, for centigrade and fahrenheit equivalents on p. 618), except in the far south (the Mediterranean area), where it can be agonisingly hot (occasionally even 40°C) in high summer. Winter tends to be grey and wet, with temperatures hovering around -5/+5°C and relatively little snow, except in Scandinavia, the high mountains and parts of central Europe. In the far north, midsummer is the best time to travel, to take advantage of the ultra-long days. Almost everywhere else, May and September are the best months, and have the added advantage of avoiding school holiday crowds.

CONSULAR SERVICES/EMBASSIES Most embassies/consulates/high commissions will lend a helping hand if their nationals have real problems – and charge a small fee for any services rendered. Help should be available if: your passport is stolen (or a travel document that will get you home); there's a death or serious accident (advice on procedures, next of kin notified – probably also sympathetic help); you go to jail – don't expect sympathy, nor direct intervention, but they will explain your rights and tell you how to get a lawyer. Should something happen to make the area dangerous (an act of God, local rebellion, etc), contact your embassy to register your presence and ask for advice. In case of real financial trouble, embassies may agree to make a small loan or contact next of kin with a request for help, but they do not look kindly on people who have simply overspent. Do not expect them to act as surrogate travel agents, banks, interpreters, etc. If your own country has no representation, get advice from one with which it has ties, e.g. Commonwealth citizens can try the British Embassy.

CURRENCY The Euro (€) has replaced the currencies in Austria, Belgium, Finland, France, Germany, Greece, the Republic of Ireland, Italy, Luxembourg, the Netherlands, Portugal and Spain; although the coins and notes issued by each country differ slightly in appearance, they can be spent in any of the other Euro countries. This is good news for travellers, making European trips that much easier. Most

European countries place no limit on the import/export of currencies. However, almost all the former Eastern bloc countries state that the amount taken out must not exceed the amount taken in (and checks are made on your departure), so always declare large amounts of cash on arrival.

Carry credit cards (which can be used in cash machines, but don't rely too heavily on them; note you are charged per transaction made, and pay interest from the time you make the withdrawal) and travellers' cheques (usually best in the local currency; if you're travelling through several countries, cheques in sterling or US dollars will probably suffice; keep the counterfoil separate from the cheques, as you can be reimbursed if you lose the cheques; record which cheques you have cashed). Eurocheques are only semi-useful: many establishments charge a hefty fee for dealing with them, and others don't take them at all.

Though it's obviously risky to carry wads of banknotes, you should always try to obtain some local currency before you enter a new country. If you are unable to do so and arrive outside banking hours, the best bet (albeit an expensive option) is to ask the receptionist at a big hotel to change some for you. Try to ensure you always carry one or two coins of each denomination for use in slot machines.

There is no black market in currency in Western Europe. You may find people eager to trade in some Eastern European countries, but you could face heavy penalties if caught. You may also be ripped off by those making the exchange.

In border towns and on cross-border transport, you can almost always use either of the relevant currencies (a good way to dispose of excess coins), but you generally pay less if you choose the one in which prices are marked.

CUSTOMS Importing narcotics and offensive weapons is banned throughout Europe, and pornography is banned in many countries. Never carry luggage across borders for other people. If you have to take a prescribed drug on a regular basis, carry a doctor's letter to prove it's legitimate.

There are often restrictions on the import and export of plants and fresh foodstuffs (particularly meat and meat products), as well as certain souvenirs (such as those made of tortoiseshell) and you might be asked to abandon them at borders.

CUSTOMS ALLOWANCES IN THE EU European Union member states (Austria, Belgium, Denmark, Finland, France, Germany, Greece, the Republic of Ireland, Italy, Luxembourg, the Netherlands, Portugal, Spain, Sweden and the UK) have set the purchase of tobacco, alcohol and perfume at the same basic allowance for each country, and the tobacco and alcohol allowances apply to anyone aged 17 or over.

There are no restrictions between the EU countries for goods bought in ordinary shops and including local taxes, but you may be questioned if you have excessive amounts. Allowances are:

> 800 cigarettes, 200 cigars, 400 cigarillos and 1 kg tobacco
> + 90 litres wine (maximum 60 litres sparkling)
> + 10 litres alcohol over 22% volume (e.g. most spirits)
> + 20 litres alcohol under 22% volume (e.g. port and sherry)
> +110 litres beer.

TRAVELLING AROUND EUROPE

The allowances for goods bought outside the EU are:

> 200 cigarettes or 50 cigars or 100 cigarillos or 250 g tobacco*
> + 2 litres still table wine
> + 1 litre spirits or 2 litres sparkling or fortified wine
> + 50 g/60 ml perfume
> + 0.25 l/250 ml toilet water.
> Other goods (including gifts/souvenirs) up to the value of £145

*Some EU countries have more generous tobacco allowances for non-Europeans arriving from outside Europe, so check in the duty-free shop or with your carrier.

Allowances for those returning home:

> **Australia**: goods to the value of Aust$400 (half for those under 18) plus 250 cigarettes or 250 g tobacco and 1 litre alcohol.
>
> **Canada**: allowances apply to anyone aged 19 or more (a year younger if you are entering AL, MN or QU). You are allowed 50 cigars and 200 cigarettes and 400 g tobacco plus 1.1 litre alcohol or 24 x 355 ml bottles/tins beer, as well as gifts not exceeding Can$60 each in value.
>
> **New Zealand**: goods to the value of NZ$700. Anyone over 17 may also take 200 cigarettes or 250 g tobacco or 50 cigars or a combination of tobacco products not exceeding 250 g in all plus 4.5 litres of beer or wine and 1.125 litres spirits.
>
> **South Africa**: goods to a total value of 500 Rand. Those aged 18 or more are allowed 400 cigarettes and 50 cigars and 250 g tobacco plus 2 litres wine and 1 litre spirits plus 50 ml perfume and 250 ml toilet water.
>
> **Republic of Ireland and UK**: standard EU regulations apply (see foregoing notes and above).
>
> **USA**: goods to the value of US$400 as long as you have been out of the country for at least 48 hrs and only use your allowance once every 30 days. Anyone over 21 is also allowed 1 litre alcohol plus 100 (non-Cuban) cigars and 200 cigarettes and a reasonable quantity of tobacco.

DISABILITIES, TRAVELLERS WITH Usually only the more modern trains and more upmarket hotels cater for travellers with disabilities, who need to reserve and ensure there is someone on hand to help. The amount of advance warning required for trains varies; Austrian State Railways ask for three days' notice, while the ever-efficient Swiss need only one day. In many European stations the platforms are quite low and passengers have to climb steep steps to board trains. Once aboard, only the more modern carriages provide space for a wheelchair; otherwise, space will be provided in the baggage car. Express services, such as the French TGV and the Spanish AVE, have good facilities, while some Scandinavian trains have adapted hydraulic lifts, accessible toilets and spacious compartments. Some national rail offices and tourist offices have leaflets about rail travel for the disabled. A few national networks offer discount passes for the disabled. The best routes to travel include the main lines in Scandinavia, Switzerland, Germany, the Netherlands and France. The worst facilities are in Turkey, Spain, Hungary, Greece, Bulgaria, the Czech Republic and Slovakia. UK information: **RADAR**, Unit 12, City Forum, 250 City Rd, London EC1V 8AF; ☎(020) 7250 3222 (www.radar.org.uk) can help with information on rail stations, airports, seaports and other transport matters across Europe concerning travellers with disabilities. US information: **SATH** (Society for the Advancement of Travel for the Handicapped), 347 5th Ave, Suite 610, New York NY 10016; ☎ (212) 447 7284.

DISCOUNTS In many countries reductions are available on public transport and on entrance fees for senior citizens, students and the young. Carry proof of your status, e.g. an official document that shows your age or an International Student Identity Card (ISIC; see p. 24) from your student union or travel agents such as, STA and Campus Travel. Some destinations offer (for a small fee) a book of discount vouchers covering anything from museums to restaurants. Many discount passes for tourists, including some rail passes, must be purchased before you leave home as they are not available in the country itself.

DRIVING If you want to hire a motor vehicle while you are away, check requirements with the AA/RAC, or your own national motoring organisation, well before you leave, so that you have time to get any necessary documentation and additional insurance cover. To hire a vehicle (except a moped), you usually have to be over 21, with two years' driving experience. In most European countries your national licence is valid for up to six months, but you may need a translation as well and it can be easier to get an international licence. Always check that the vehicle is in good condition before you set out, with special attention to brakes, lights and tyres (including the spare). Most road signs are standardised throughout Europe, but the quality of signposting varies dramatically, as do speed limits. Check for local peculiarities before you set out. Except in the British Isles, Europeans drive on the right. There is a network of motor-rail services across Europe, for those who wish to take their own cars across Europe by train.

ELECTRICITY With a few exceptions (notably the UK, which uses 230/240V), the European countries use 220V. The shape of plugs varies and, if you are taking any sort of electrical gadget, you should take a travel adaptor.

FLYING TO EUROPE FROM BRITAIN Budget flights make crossing Europe easy and not that expensive. The leading ones bookable online are Buzz (www.buzzaway.com), easyJet (easyjet.com), Go (www.go-fly.com), Ryanair (www.ryanair.ie) and Virgin Express (www.virgin-exp.com). Go, Buzz and Ryanair flights go from Stansted, easyJet mostly go from Luton and Gatwick; Virgin Express uses Heathrow and Gatwick, but flights go via Brussels. Note that Go is now owned by easyJet, and the name Go will disapear during 2003. The earlier you book, the cheaper the tickets, though some are sold off cheaply later on; it's also less expensive if you fly and return midweek.

These were the main destinations available from Britain in 2002; however things are always changing, so it's worth browsing the websites to see what's new. These airlines also fly to and from a number of regional airports in the UK, with flights from Belfast, Edinburgh, Glasgow and elsewhere.

Austria: Graz, Klagenfurt, Salzburg (all Ryanair). **Belgium**: Brussels (Ryanair, Virgin

TRAVELLING AROUND EUROPE

Express). **Czech Republic**: Prague (Go). **Denmark**: Aarhus (Ryanair), Copenhagen (Go, Virgin Express), Esbjerg (Ryanair). **France**: Bergerac (Buzz), Biarritz (Ryanair), Bordeaux (Buzz), Brest (Buzz), Brittany/Dinard (Ryanair), Caen (Buzz), Carcassone (Ryanair), Dijon (Buzz), Grenoble (Buzz), La Rochelle (Buzz), Limoges (Buzz), Lyon (Buzz, Go), Marseille (Buzz), Montpellier (Ryanair), Nice (easyJet, Go, Virgin Express), Nîmes (Ryanair), Paris (Buzz, Ryanair to Glasgow), Perpignan (Ryanair), Poitiers (Buzz), Rouen (Buzz), St Etienne (Ryanair),Toulon (Buzz), Toulouse (Buzz), Tours (Buzz). **Germany**: Berlin (Buzz), Düsseldorf (Buzz), Frankfurt (Buzz, Ryanair), Hamburg (Ryanair), Munich (Go). **Greece**: Athens (easyJet, Virgin Express). **Iceland**: Reykjavik (Go). **Ireland**: Belfast (easyJet), Cork, Derry, Dublin, Kerry, Knock, Shannon (all Ryanair). **Italy**: Alghero/Sardinia (Ryanair), Ancona (Ryanair), Bologna (Go, Ryanair), Brescia (Ryanair), Genoa (Ryanair), Milan (Buzz, Go, Ryanair, Virgin Express), Naples (Go), Pescara (Ryanair), Pisa (Ryanair), Rome (Go, Ryanair, Virgin Express), Trieste (Ryanair), Turin (Ryanair), Venice (Go, Ryanair). **Netherlands**: Amsterdam (easyJet), Eindhoven (Ryanair). **Norway**: Oslo (Ryanair). **Portugal**: Faro (Go, Virgin Express). **Spain**: Alicante (Go), Barcelona (easyJet, Go, Virgin Express), Bilbao (Go), Gerona (Buzz), Ibiza (Go), Jerez (Buzz), Madrid (easyJet, Virgin Express), Malaga (easyJet, Go), Murcia (Buzz), Palma/Majorca (easyJet, Go). **Sweden**: Gothenburg (Ryanair, Virgin Express), Malmö (Ryanair), Stockholm (Ryanair, Virgin Express). **Switzerland**: Geneva (easyJet, Virgin Express), Zurich (easyJet, Virgin Express).

HEALTH There are no compulsory vaccination requirements. However, it is always advisable to keep your tetanus protection up to date and vaccination against typhoid and hepatitis A is also a good idea. You must be able to produce a certificate against yellow fever if you have been in a yellow fever endemic zone in the six days before entering Europe. UK citizens should fill in Form E111 (available free from post offices) before leaving, allowing access to treatment across most of Europe (you may have to pay up-front and reclaim the cost when you return home). It's worth visiting a pharmacy before consulting a doctor: European pharmacists tend to be well trained and may well save you medical bills.

Although most of Europe is temperate, there is a definite risk of sunburn in the south and in high mountain areas. Don't spend hours outdoors without using a high-factor sunblock. If casual sex is your scene, fine, but do take precautions against AIDS and other unpleasant sexually-transmitted diseases; bring condoms with you if travelling to Eastern Europe. Rabies risk is very small, but be wary of stray and wild animals. Lyme disease – caught from ticks in undergrowth – is present in Central European forests (long trousers and long-sleeved shirts are a useful method of avoidance); symptoms are similar to arthritis and if they show up within three months of possible exposure ask your doctor for a blood test – early treatment is nearly always effective. Most tap water in Western Europe is safe. Boil or sterilise all tap water (including the water you use to brush your teeth) if you think there may be cause for concern.

HITCHHIKING What used to be fun and a good way to meet local people is now too risky. However, in a few countries, such as Poland, there are official schemes for getting drivers and hitchers together, so that both can feel safe.

TRAVELLING AROUND EUROPE

INSURANCE Take out travel insurance that covers your health as well as your belongings. It should also give cancellation cover and include an emergency flight home if something goes really wrong. If you are likely to do something that might be classified as risky (e.g. ski, drive a moped, dive), make sure your policy does not exclude that risk. Annual travel insurance policies are often good value if you're planning more than one trip a year.

LANGUAGE The *Thomas Cook European 12-Language Phrasebook* (£4.99) contains over 300 phrases, each translated (with phonetic spellings) into: French, German, Italian, Czech, Hungarian, Polish, Bulgarian, Romanian, Portuguese, Spanish, Greek and Turkish. Keep a pen and paper handy at all times, then you can ask people to write down such figures as times and prices, and so you can write down words if others can't understand your pronunciation.

PASSPORTS AND VISAS Ensure that your identity document is valid well beyond the end of your stay. EU citizens can travel to other EU countries with a National Identity Card instead of a full passport. Those not citizens of western Europe, Australia, Canada, New Zealand, South Africa or the USA should check about visas with the relevant embassies. Anyone planning to stay more than 90 days in a single country may need a visa. There are no border controls between countries party to the **Schengen Agreement** (Austria, Belgium, Denmark, Finland, France, Germany, Greece, Iceland, Luxembourg, the Netherlands, Norway, Portugal, Spain and Sweden). Some countries will refuse entry if you don't have an onward/return ticket and enough money to cover the cost of food, accommodation and other expenses during your stay. A credit card is a practical way of avoiding precise cash requirements. Even if you can theoretically obtain a visa at the border, it may be easier to get it in advance. Allow plenty of time, especially if you need to get several. You'll need a stack of passport photos and may have to pay in cash or by postal order.

SALES TAX Value Added Tax (known as VAT in the UK) is automatically added to most goods in Western European countries. The level is usually 10–20%. In most countries (except Greece), non-residents can reclaim the tax on major spending; each country sets a different minimum. The refund is also intended to apply to only one article, but if you buy several things in the same shop on the same day, the authorities seldom argue. Ask the shop assistant to fill in a tax refund form for you. Show the form, the receipt and the goods to customs on leaving the country and they will give you an official export certificate. This can sometimes be exchanged on the spot (necessary in Scandinavia); alternatively, post the certificate back to the shop (within a month) and they should send the refund. Many shops will send the goods directly to your home, but anything you save in paperwork at the time is likely to be offset by customs formalities in your own country.

SECURITY Things can certainly go wrong for any traveller, but don't get paranoid: Europe's still generally safe and fear of crime should not spoil your trip. Travel insurance softens the blow if you have possessions stolen (in which case be sure to get the required paperwork from the police as proof for your claim). You can cut the chances of being ripped off by carrying valuables in a money belt or in a pouch concealed under your shirt, and by being extra-vigilant about bags at stations and airports.

SMOKING Banned in many public places and, even where it is allowed, there may be a special area for smokers. In some countries, such as France, Italy and Spain, the prohibitions are often ignored by the locals, but play safe if in doubt and ask before lighting up.

STUDENT TRAVEL Before leaving home consider buying an International Students' Identity Card (ISIC) if you are a full-time student in the present academic year. The card costs £6 from student travel offices or £6.50 from ISIC Mail Order, Dernier ID, Unit 192, Louis Pearlman Centre, Goulten St, Hull HU3 4DL, UK; enclose a passport photo and proof of full-time education (such as a letter from your college or university), together with a completed form which can be downloaded from www.isiccard.com (which gives full details of the card). The card entitles you to a range of discounts on accommodation, museums, theatres etc, with wide-ranging discounts offered in 'gateway cities' (which include Amsterdam, Athens, Barcelona, Berlin, Edinburgh, Frankfurt, Glasgow, Liverpool, London, Madrid, Manchester, Munich, Paris, Prague and Rome); it also gives access to a 24-hour helpline. If you are not a full-time student but are under 26, you can still qualify for a Youth Travel Card (from ISIC Mail Order).

TELEPHONES You should have few problems finding a phone in European towns and everywhere is on direct-dial. In EU countries you have an extra option: ☎112 for all emergency services. Avoid phones in hotel rooms: they invariably cost exorbitantly.

TIME ZONES United Kingdom, Ireland and Portugal: Greenwich Mean Time in winter, and GMT+1 hr in summer. GMT+1 hr in winter, GMT+2 hrs in summer: Austria, Belgium, the Czech Republic, Denmark, France, Germany, Hungary, Italy, the Netherlands, Norway, Poland, Slovakia, Spain, Sweden and Switzerland. GMT+2 hrs in winter, GMT+3 hrs in summer: Bulgaria, Estonia, Finland, Greece, Latvia, Romania and Turkey. Lithuania: GMT+2 hrs all year. Clocks change on the last weekend of March and October.

TIPPING Not usually necessary in Continental Europe. You can leave small change on bar counters; otherwise tips are generally not expected. In Britain you should tip 10 per cent at restaurants and in taxis (but never in pubs).

WHAT TO TAKE Travel as light as possible is the golden rule.

Luggage: Backpack and day sack; sort your luggage into see-through polythene bags (makes fishing out your socks from the backpack much easier), plus take plastic bags for dirty clothes etc, and elastic bands for sealing them.

Clothing: Lightweight clothing, preferably of a type that doesn't need ironing; smart casual clothes for evening wear, at least three sets of underwear, swimsuit, sun hat, long-sleeved garment to cover shoulders (essential in some churches/temples; women may need head-scarves); non-slip foot-wear. All purpose hiking boots useful for big walks around cities – or rubber sandals with chunky soles good when it's hot; flip flops for the shower etc.

First aid/medical: Insect repellent and antihistamine cream, sun-screen cream, after-sun lotion, something for headaches and tummy troubles, prescription medicines, antiseptic spray or cream, medicated wet-wipes, plasters for blisters, bandage, contraceptives and tampons (especially if visiting Eastern Europe, where they can be difficult to get. Spare spectacles/contact lenses and a copy of your prescription. Take a completed and stamped E111 form if you are from the EU and travelling in EU countries; available free from post offices in the UK, the form gives you free medical cover in those countries.

THOMAS COOK PUBLICATIONS

The *Thomas Cook European Timetable (ETT)*, published monthly at £9.50, has up-to-date details of most rail services and many shipping services throughout Europe. It is essential both for pre-planning and for making on-the-spot decisions about independent rail travel around Europe. A useful companion to it is the *Thomas Cook Rail Map of Europe* (£6.95), with scenic lines shown in green (see advertisement, p. 161). Both of these publications are obtainable by phoning (01733) 416477 in the UK; in North America, contact the Forsyth Travel Library Inc., Westchester 1, 44 South Broadway, White Plains, New York 10601; ☎ 1-800/367 7984.

Thomas Cook Travellers (£7.99/£8.99), cover a number of European cities and countries. If you plan on going as far as Athens and then seeing some of the Greek islands, you will find the *Thomas Cook Independent Traveller's Greek Island Hopping* invaluable; as well as covering (literally) every island, it provides detailed, essential information on the complex ferry schedules.

These guides and the *Thomas Cook European 12-Language Phrasebook* (£4.99) are available from many bookshops in the UK and the USA (publisher: Passport Books) and from UK branches of Thomas Cook.

Overnight equipment: Lightweight sleeping-bag (optional), sheet liner (for hostelling), inflatable travel pillow, earplugs, and eyemask.

Documents: Passport, tickets, photocopies of passport/visas (helps if you lose the passport itself) and travel insurance, travellers' cheques counterfoil, passport photos, student card, numbers of credit cards and where to phone if you lose them.

Other items: A couple of lightweight towels, small bar of soap, water-bottle, pocket knife, torch (flashlight), sewing kit, padlock and chain (for anchoring your luggage), safety matches, mug and basic cutlery, toothbrush, Travel Wash, string (for a washing-line), travel adapter, universal bath plug (often missing from wash-basins), sunglasses, alarm clock, notepad and pen, pocket calculator (to convert money), a contact list of important phone numbers (e.g. for lost credit cards and travel insurance claims), a money-belt and a good book/game (for long journeys).

RAIL PASSES

Rail passes represent excellent value for train travellers and, if you are taking a number of journeys, usually allow you to make substantial savings over point-to-point tickets. Passes may cover most of the continent, a specific 'zone' of Europe or a regional group of countries. Passes for travel within a specific country are detailed within the Directory (pp. 586–617). You should get details of any extras when you buy the pass. An annual feature on rail passes appears in the May edition of the *Thomas Cook European Timetable*.

BOOKING RAIL PASSES

IN THE UK Sources of international rail tickets, passes and information about rail travel include: **Rail Pass Direct**, which can provide UK travellers with Inter-Rail passes, guidebooks and maps, delivered direct to their home address, ☎(01733) 402001; fax: (01733) 416688 (www.railpassdirect.com). **Rail Europe**, 34 Tower View, Kings Hill, West Malling, Kent ME19 4ED, ☎0870 584 8848 (www.raileurope.co.uk). **Deutsche Bahn UK** (German Railways), ☎0870 243 5363. **European Rail**, ☎(020) 7387 0444 (www.europeanrail.com). **Ffestiniog Travel,** Porthmadog, Gwynedd LL49 9NF, Wales; ☎(01766) 512340. **International Rail**, Chase House, Gilbert Street, Ropley, Hampshire SO24 0BY; ☎0870 120 1606 (www.hollandrail.com). **RailChoice**, ☎(020) 8659 7300 (www.railchoice.com). **Freedom Rail**, ☎(01252) 728506 (www.freedomrail.co.uk). **Stephen Walker Travel**, ☎0870 746 6400. **Trainseurope**, ☎0900 195 0101 (60p/min) (www.trainseurope.co.uk). For a copy of the Inter-Railer's brochure, ☎0870 502 4000.

IN THE USA **Rail Europe Group**, Westchester 1, 44 South Broadway, White Plains, New York, NY 10601 (www.raileurope.com); ☎1-800/438-7245 (1-800/4-EURAIL) or, for Eurostar, ☎1-800/EUROSTAR. Also **DER** ☎1-800/782-2424. Mexico toll free ☎001-800-726-1936.

ELSEWHERE International rail information and tickets in Australia, Canada and New Zealand are obtainable from Thomas Cook branches (and branches of Marlin Travel in Canada). To contact Rail Europe in Canada, ☎1-800/361-RAIL (www.raileurope.com/canada). In South Africa, international rail information and tickets are available from branches of Rennies Travel.

EUROPEAN RAIL PASSES

Most countries offer **domestic rail passes** valid only for travel within that country. They are better value than zonal or European passes if you are only travelling in one country. We have listed many of these in the Directory (pp. 586–617); they are mostly sold at any branch of the national railway or its agents. To purchase almost any pass you'll need your passport. Generally rail passes cover the national rail services, but you have to pay extra supplements for high-speed and certain other services; some private lines are not covered. A few passes, such as Eurailpass, cover most supplements. If you're visiting more than one country, consider one of the following international passes.

INTER-RAIL PASS It still comes as a surprise to many people over 26 that nowadays people of all ages can travel on an Inter-Rail Pass – the under-26 rule has been scrapped. But you can get a discount on the pass if you're under 26 on the first day on which it's valid. You must have lived for at least six months in one of the European countries where the pass is valid (see list below), or are a national of that country and hold a valid passport. It can be purchased up to two months before travel begins. The current cost

Note Prices quoted in this chapter were correct at time of going to press. However, rail pass prices are liable to fluctuate so check prices with the organisations listed on p. 26.

of the **all-zones under-26 version** is £249 for a month and you can buy consecutive passes for longer journeys. You will not get free travel in the country where you buy the pass, but you may be eligible for some discount. The **Inter-Rail 26+ Pass** offers all the benefits of the Inter-Rail Pass except that discounts are not available for travel in the country of purchase. The current cost is £355 for an all-zones pass. Child passes (age 4–11) are now available at half the 26+ price for all-zones and for zonal passes.

Inter-Rail provides unlimited second-class rail travel for a month on the national railways of: Austria, Belgium, Bulgaria, Croatia, the Czech Republic, Denmark, Finland, France, Germany, Greece, Hungary, the Republic of Ireland, Italy, Luxembourg, Macedonia, Morocco, the Netherlands, Norway, Poland, Portugal, Romania, Slovakia, Slovenia, Spain, Sweden, Switzerland, Turkey and Yugoslavia. It also includes a free crossing on the Hellenic Mediterranean, Blue Star or Superfast Ferries shipping lines between Italy and Greece (you will have to pay port tax). There are free or discounted crossings on other ferries, so check. The Inter-Rail ticket does not include high-speed train supplements, seat reservations, or couchette or sleeper charges. On trains with 'global' prices, the Inter-Rail only entitles you to a discount; this includes most international trains from France, and high-quality night trains such as CityNightLine. Reductions of between 10% and 50% are available on various ferry services; the discount only applies to the basic ferry fare. Some ferries require compulsory accommodation. If you purchase an under-26 Inter-Rail Pass in the UK, you are entitled to a 34% reduction on most UK fares. Eurostar offers a special 'Passholder Fare' to Lille, Brussels or Paris.

Zonal Inter-Rail Passes: These regional variations on the Inter-Rail Pass now apply for those over 26 as well as for those under 26. The same eligibility rules apply.

For zonal passes, Europe has been divided into eight geographical zones:

A United Kingdom and the Republic of Ireland.
B Sweden, Norway and Finland.
C Denmark, Switzerland, Germany and Austria.
D Poland, the Czech Republic, Slovakia, Hungary and Croatia.
E France, Belgium, the Netherlands and Luxembourg.
F Spain, Portugal and Morocco.
G Italy, Slovenia, Greece and Turkey (including certain shipping lines between Italy and Greece).
H Bulgaria, Romania, Yugoslavia and Macedonia.

Rail Passes

Passes are available for 1 zone (12 days: under-26 £119, 26+ £169. 22 days: under-26 £139, 26+ £209); 2 zones (1 month: under-26 £189, 26+ £265); and 3 zones (1 month: under-26 £209, 26+ £299). If you have a definite route in mind, these can offer savings over the standard Europe-wide pass. For instance, if you're under 26 and a UK resident you could buy a 2-zone pass for zones E and G, and could travel through France into Italy and on to Greece and Turkey for only £189 (plus supplements), with a side trip through the Benelux countries on the way home.

EURAILPASS These are available only to people living outside Europe and North Africa and can be obtained up to six months in advance from the agents listed (under 'In the USA' and 'Elsewhere') on p. 26. You can also get the passes once you've arrived (from Rail Europe, see p. 26), but at much higher prices.

Eurailpass offers unlimited travel on the national railways of: Austria, Belgium, Denmark, Finland, France, Germany, Greece, Hungary, the Republic of Ireland, Italy, Luxembourg, the Netherlands, Norway, Portugal, Spain, Sweden and Switzerland. It also covers some private railways and a few selected ferries, such as Hellenic Mediterranean and Blue Star shipping lines between Brindisi in Italy and Patras in Greece (although, as with the Inter-Rail Pass, you will have to pay the port tax). In addition to this, Eurailpass holders must pay a high-season (June to October) supplement.

> ### CHILDREN
>
> Although there are exceptions, the norm is for children aged 4–11 to pay approximately 50% of the adult fare and for babies under 4 to travel free – but babies are not entitled to a seat in crowded trains. Childrens fares can vary from country to country, anywhere between 4–6 and 11–17.

The basic **Eurailpass** has no age limit. It provides first-class travel on all services and covers most of the supplements for travelling on express and high-speed trains. It also gives free or reduced travel on many lake steamers, ferries and buses. There are several versions, valid for 15 days, 21 days, 1 month, 2 months or 3 months. Current prices range from US$572 for 15 days to US$1606 for 3 months. The **Eurailpass Youth** is much the same, but cheaper, as it is designed for those under 26 and is based on second-class travel. There are versions valid for 15 days (US$401), 21 days (US$518), 1 month (US$644) and 2 months (US$910). The **Eurailpass Flexi** is similar to the basic Eurailpass, but allows you to travel (first class) for any 10 days (US$674) or any 15 days (US$888) within a 2-month period. The under-26 second-class version is the **Eurailpass Youth Flexi** (US$473 for 10 days in 2 months, US$622 for 15 days in 2 months). You can also choose three adjoining countries from the above and buy a **Eurail Selectpass**, valid for 5, 6, 8 or 10 days in a 2 month period (US$346–502). The second-class **Youth** version costs US$243–352. Prices will be revised after this book has gone to print; for latest prices check www.raileurope.com.

All of the Eurailpass, Eurailpass Flexi and Eurail Selectpass tickets (but not youth passes) are available in **Saver** versions if you are travelling in a group of 2 to 5 persons – prices for each person are approximately 15% lower. All passes (including Saver passes) are available to children aged 4–11, who pay half the adult (not youth) fare.

EURO DOMINO PASS This is a catch-all title for a whole series of passes allowing unlimited travel on the national railway of an individual country (but not if you are a resident of that country). Conditions of use are the same everywhere and the options available are for any 3–8 days within a period of 1 month. The passes can only be purchased by persons who have lived at least 6 months in Europe, Morocco, Algeria or Tunisia. They cover many of the fast-train supplements.

There is no age limit, but the price depends on age. Those under 26 pay less but are restricted to second class, while those over 26 can opt for either class. The price varies according to the size of the railway network in the country chosen. Your ticket includes all high-speed train supplements (except on certain 'Global Price' trains – a discount fare is usually available). Seat reservations, couchettes and sleepers are extra. If you are travelling overnight or are to connect with an overnight service, you may commence your journey after 1900. The next day's date must be entered on your ticket. Your Euro Domino Pass is valid to the frontier; only in a few cases does your ticket allow you to cross into a different country.

Passes can be purchased up to two months before travel begins. They are available for the following countries: Austria, Belgium, Bulgaria, Croatia, the Czech Republic, Denmark, Finland, France, Germany, Greece, Hungary, the Republic of Ireland, Italy, Luxembourg, Macedonia, Morocco, the Netherlands, Norway, Poland, Portugal, Romania, Slovakia, Slovenia, Spain, Sweden, Switzerland, Turkey and Yugoslavia. There is also a pass covering several Italy–Greece ferry routes. Prices vary widely: typical second-class prices include £36 for 3 days' travel in Poland, £115 for 3 days in France (8 days £217) and £119 for 3 days in Germany (8 days £176). Youth fares (under 26) are 25–35% lower. The Euro Domino Pass entitles the holder to a special 25% discount fare from his or her home country to the country of visitation. However, this option is not available from the UK, where residents can buy the Eurostar 'Passholder' ticket. Other ferry discounts are also available.

EUROPASS The Europass is designed for non-Europeans who only want to visit a few countries in Europe. Available in the USA or from Rail Europe, London, Europass is valid for first-class rail travel in France, Germany, Italy, Spain and Switzerland. Passes are available for 5, 6, 8, 10 or 15 days' travel over a 2-month period. The 5-day pass costs US$422. Other examples are 8 days, US$536, and 15 days, US$772. Saver rates are available for 2–5 people travelling together, at a discount of 15% per person. Associate countries can be added for US$62 (US$102 for two) to extend the geographic reach of the pass. There are four to choose from: Austria/Hungary, Belgium/Netherlands/Luxembourg, Greece and Portugal.

For those under 26 the **Europass Youth** is available for second-class travel. Prices are: 5 days (US$253), 6 days (US$282), 8 days (US$332), 10 days (US$382) or 15 days (US$497). One associate country can be added for US$43, two for US$72. Various bonuses are available and are listed on the map that accompanies the rail pass.

Rail Passes

Senior Pass The **RailPlus Senior Card**, priced at £12, gives cardholders 25% discount on international journeys between: Belgium, Croatia, the Czech Republic, Denmark, Finland, France, Germany, Greece, Hungary, the Republic of Ireland, Italy, Latvia, Lithuania, Luxembourg, the Netherlands, Norway, Poland, Portugal, Romania, Slovakia, Slovenia, Spain, Sweden, Switzerland, the UK (including Northern Ireland), Ukraine and Yugoslavia.

> For information on **passes to individual countries**, see the Directory on pp. 586–617.

Residents of Britain are eligible for a RailPlus Senior Card provided they also hold a British Senior Railcard, cost £18 p.a. The RailPlus card will expire on the same day as the Senior Railcard. No discount is available on Eurostar services.

Regional European Rail Passes

Balkan Flexipass Available in the USA, this pass offers unlimited first-class travel in Greece, Bulgaria, Romania, Macedonia, Yugoslavia and Turkey for any 5 days in one month (US$152), any 10 days in 1 month (US$264) or any 15 days in 1 month (US$317). A youth version for under 26s is also available: 5, 10 or 15 days in 1 month costs US$90/156/190. It will often be cheaper to buy single tickets, however.

Scanrail Pass This is available in both the UK and the USA and gives unlimited travel on the national rail networks of Denmark, Finland, Norway and Sweden (including all local railways except Inlandsbanan and Stockholm Landstrafik), plus the following ferry services: Helsingsør–Helsingborg, Kalundborg–Århus, Rødby–Puttgarten and Trelleborg–Sassnitz. Several bus routes in Norway, Sweden and Finland are also included.

Supplements are payable to use X2000 (Sweden), Signatur (Norway), Pendolino S220 and IC+ (Finland) services, as well as the Flåm Railway in Norway. Seat reservations are compulsory on most expresses and InterScandinavian services. Couchettes and sleepers are extra. Journeys may commence 1900 for long-distance overnight travel; the next day's date is written on the flexi pass. Scanrail is available as a consecutive pass, which offers unlimited rail travel over a 21-day period, or a flexi pass, valid for 5 or 10 days' travel in a 2-month period. Youth (12–25) and Senior (60+) versions are also available.

Scanrail also offers additional discounts on many ferries and boats, long-distance buses and private railways, and discounts at over 100 Best Western hotels. It is possible to get Scanrail for first-class travel, but second-class seating is almost as comfortable and second-class seats are far more likely to be available.

In the UK Scanrail is available from Deutsche Bahn UK, ☎0870 243 5363, and Rail Europe, ☎0870 584 8848.

Typical UK prices for 5 days in 2 months: adult second class £139, first class £189; senior (second class) £123; youth £105. Any 10 days within a 2-month period: adult second class £187, first class £252; senior (second class) £166; youth £140. For 21 consecutive days: adult second class £216, first class £291; senior (second class) £192; youth £162. Children (4–11) half price. Senior and youth first-class tickets are available at about 35% more.

In the USA Scanrail passes are available from Forsyth Travel Library (see p. 25) or Rail Europe (see p. 26): 5 days in a 2-month period costs US$214 (US$290 first class), 10 days in 2 months US$288 (US$388 first class) and 21 consecutive days US$332 (US$448 first class).

Scanrail passes are obtainable inside Scandinavia, but the validity is different and those passes bought prior to arrival are far better value.

BENELUX TOURRAIL PASS This is available in the UK and the USA, and from train stations in Belgium and Luxembourg (but not in the Netherlands) to residents living outside the Benelux countries. It provides unlimited rail travel throughout Belgium, Luxembourg and the Netherlands for any 5 days in a month. UK/Belgian prices are £132/€174 in first class, £88/€116 in second class, and under 26 (second class only) is £66/€87 in the UK. Not valid on Thalys trains.

EUROPEAN EAST PASS This is available in the USA only and provides unlimited rail travel throughout Austria, the Czech Republic, Hungary, Poland and Slovakia for any 5 days within a month. The pass is available for first-class travel (US$220, extra days US$25) or second-class travel (US$154, extra days US$18). Children aged 4–11 pay half price. Discounts are available on certain Austrian steamers and rack railways.

YOUTH PASSES For those under 26, there are many other discounted tickets and passes available. Some are to single destinations or for travel in single countries, others (like the examples above) to whole groups of countries. Passes come under many different names, such as Euro-Youth, Explorer Pass and BIJ (Billets International de Jeunesse).

RAIL TRAVEL

This chapter provides general information about travelling by train around Europe. Information about rail travel for individual countries is given in the Directory, pp. 586–617, towards the back of this book.

TICKETS It's generally safest to buy your ticket before travelling (from a station or travel agent) as passengers found without tickets can face heavy penalties or criminal prosecution; however, if boarding at a station that has no ticket office or machine, pay on the train. Always ask about discounts (e.g. for travel outside the rush hour and at weekends) before you buy a ticket. Most countries have discounts for children; the age limits vary from country to country, but commonly children under 4 travel free and those under 12 at half price.

ADVANCE RESERVATIONS There's no firm rule as to whether it's worth reserving (and it isn't always possible to do so anyway); some trains never get busy (especially many leisurely back-country routes), while others (such as some InterCity expresses) are packed in high season and around public holidays , and you could spend hours standing in a crowded corridor. In some cases, you may be refused permission to board at all if there are no seats available. There's normally a small fee for reservations. If you are travelling during the busy summer period and have no reservation, board your train as early as possible.

Some of the major express trains (usually marked in timetables by an 'R' in a box) are restricted to passengers with reservations, and you can usually make a reservation about two months in advance. You should book if you want sleeping accommodation, though you can chance your luck and just turn up in the hope that a couchette will be available; in this case pay the supplement to the attendant.

SUPPLEMENTS If you are travelling with certain types of rail pass you'll be exempt from many routine surcharges made on express trains, but sometimes you'll have to pay a little more (so always travel with some local currency); ask if you're uncertain – there's often a surcharge-free slower service. Some special high-speed services (such as the French TGV, the German ICE, the Swedish X2000, Eurostar Italia, Eurostar trains and Spanish AVE services) invariably require a supplement. Holders of a first-class Eurailpass can use most of the special services without paying extra, but even they should check its validity if they want to use certain luxury trains – for example, InterCityNight (Germany) or Trenhotel (Spain).

The fee for reserving seats is normally included in the supplementary payments for faster trains. Sleeping accommodation (see pp. 34–35) always attracts charges. Sort out the extras before you start your journey. You may be able to pay the supplements on the train, but it almost always costs more than doing so in advance.

TYPES OF TRAIN Many of the best daytime international trains are branded EuroCity (or EC) and all have names. To qualify, trains have to be fast and offer a certain standard of service, such as food and drink during the journey. Eurostar trains are the only trains in operation through the Channel Tunnel between

Britain and France, apart from the Eurotunnel shuttle trains carrying vehicles from one side of the tunnel to the other. Most overnight services use ordinary trains, but there is a breed of high-quality night service known as EuroNight (EN) with air-conditioned coaches and extras such as evening drinks and breakfast, available even to couchette passengers.

The IC or InterCity label is applied by many countries to the fast long-distance trains, although there are slight variations in what they provide. The ICE (InterCity Express) designation also crops up in several countries, but is mostly applied to the latest high-speed trains in Germany. IR is the classification for inter-regional express services, which make more stops than InterCity services; it is used mainly in Germany (where it stands for 'Inter-Regio') and in Italy (where it's short for 'Interregionale'). These names are all used to distinguish the faster long-distance trains from local or stopping trains.

Most longer-distance trains in Europe offer both first- and second-class travel, but second class is the norm for local stopping services. Where overnight trains offer seating accommodation, this is usually second class only. As a rule in Western Europe, second class is perfectly adequate for all but the most ardent comfort-seeker. A few Eastern European services still leave a lot to be desired (and information is often hard to obtain), but as tickets are so cheap it's worth paying the extra to upgrade to first class.

FINDING YOUR TRAIN Larger stations have potential for confusion. Look for the electronic departure boards or large paper timetables (often yellow for departures and white for arrivals) that list the routes, the times of departure and arrival, and the relevant platforms; double-check footnotes and symbols – that seemingly ideal train may in fact turn out to run only on the third Sunday in August. In some stations, the platforms are also labelled with details of regular trains or the next departure and may even give the location of specific carriages and the facilities on board. If you have a reservation, board your allocated carriage (they are all numbered, usually by the entrance).

Look for destination boards or displays on each carriage: even if you've found the right platform you might end up in the wrong place. Make sure you board in the right place: some long platforms serve more than one train at a time, and quite a few trains split en route, with only some carriages going the full distance.

First-class coaches usually have a yellow stripe above the windows and large number '1s' on the side of the coach, on the door or on the windows. No-smoking coaches (the majority) display clear signs. A sign near the compartment door often gives seat numbers and sometimes indicates which are reserved. In open carriages (without compartments) seats are usually numbered individually (on the back or on the luggage rack) and reserved seats may have labels attached to their head-rests (or the luggage racks). In some countries, however, reserved seats are not marked – so be prepared to move if someone who has booked boards the train.

Rail Travel

OVERNIGHT TRAINS A night on the train, being rocked to sleep, soothed by the clatter of the wheels, is not to be missed. Sleeping cars can cost about the same as a hotel but have the advantage of covering large distances as you rest and you won't waste precious time in transit. Couchettes are more crowded bunk-type arrangements, but are reasonably comfortable and inexpensive. You can save quite a bit of money if you are prepared to curl up on the ordinary seats (don't do this too often without a break, however, or you will end up exhausted; the chatter of other passengers and regular checks to make sure you still have all your bags can lead to a disturbed night). Take earplugs and possibly an eyemask, and, as there are often no refreshment facilities, plenty of water and a supply of food. In Eastern Europe, you may be woken for Customs and Immigration checks, which can involve a search of luggage or the compartment/berth. Within Western Europe, it's unlikely you'll notice the borders, even if you're awake.

If you have a rail pass and the night train is due to reach your next destination too early in the morning, consider booking to a town an hour or so further along the line; you can then get some extra sleep and backtrack to your intended destination (assuming there's a suitable early train back).

SLEEPING ACCOMMODATION Sleeping cars have bedroom-style compartments with limited washing facilities (usually just a wash-basin) and full bedding. WCs are located at the end of the coach. An attendant travels with each car, or pair of cars, and there are sometimes facilities for drinks and/or breakfast – but be prepared to pay extra.

First-class sleeping compartments usually have one or two berths while second-class compartments have two or three berths. However, there are some special sleeping cars (described as 'T2' in schedules) that have only one berth in first class and two in second class. An exception to the norm is Spain: their T2 cars are first class and their Talgo trains have four berths in second class. Compartments are allocated to a single sex and small unaccompanied children are placed in female compartments. In Estonia, Latvia and Lithuania berths are allocated on a first-come, first-served basis without regard to sex. Claim your berth within 15 minutes of boarding the train or it may be reallocated.

Couchettes are more basic – and much cheaper. They consist of simple bunk beds with a sheet, blanket and pillow. They are converted from the ordinary seats at night and there are usually four berths in first class and six in second class, with washing facilities and WCs at the end of each coach. Males and females are booked into the same compartment and are expected to sleep in their daytime clothes. In a few cases (notably Italy), overnight trains have airline-style reclining seats, which are allocated automatically when you make a seat reservation. These are sometimes free if you have a rail pass.

Couchette/sleeping-car attendants will often keep your ticket overnight, and return it prior to your stop. Attendants will give you an alarm call if you tell them you are leaving the train before the final destination – specify the stop rather than the time, so you can sleep longer if the train runs late. If you want to go to sleep before other passengers have arrived, switch on their berth lights and switch off the main overhead light. Before boarding, sort out the things you will need for the night and put them somewhere easily accessible (preferably in a small separate bag), as busy compartments don't allow much room for searching through luggage. Sleepers and couchettes can usually be reserved up to three months in advance; early booking is recommended as space is limited. If you don't have a booking, it's still worth asking the conductor once you are on board. Keep some local currency handy to pay him/her.

WASHING Showers are generally restricted to a few luxury-class compartments (notably Gran Clase cars on the overnight Spanish Talgos; Intercity Natt cars in Sweden; CityNightLine trains in Germany/Austria/Switzerland and InterCityNight trains in Germany). A few large rail stations have showers for public use.

EATING Many long-distance trains in Europe have dining cars serving full meals and/or buffet cars selling drinks and snacks. There is an increasing tendency for refreshments to be served from a trolley wheeled through the train. Dining cars are sometimes red or indicated by a red band above the windows and doors. Quite a few services offer full meals only to first-class passengers. In some cases, especially in Spain, the cost of a meal is included in the first-class fare. Dining cars often have set times for full meals. Buffets are usually open to both classes and are served for longer periods, but even they may not be available for the whole journey. Train food and drink is not generally good value, so save money by bringing your own. Even if money is no object it's always sensible to carry a full water bottle and some food. Long stops at East European frontiers may tempt you to get out and buy food and drink: always get permission from the control officers, and check that you have the right currency and enough time.

BAGGAGE Lockers are invaluable if you want to look round a place without carrying heavy baggage, and most stations (and other transport hubs) have them; sometimes it's cheaper to use a manned left-luggage office (which will be subject to opening hours). The initial payment generally covers 24 hours, but you are allowed to return after a longer period (usually up to a week, but check). The newest lockers have display panels and are automatic: you simply pay any excess when you return. With older lockers, you have to pay the excess to station staff (at the left-luggage office, if there is one). Baggage trolleys (where available) are usually free, but often supermarket-style: you need a coin to release them, which you get back when you return them to a stand.

BUSES To most people, buses simply aren't as much fun as trains for exploring Europe. However in parts of southern Europe (such as Spain, Portugal and Greece) the bus is the more convenient option – making life easier where the train journeys are rather convoluted. For bargain-price long-distance bus travel in most of Europe, contact **Eurolines** (www.gobycoach.com).

Busabout Europe offers private coach service for backpackers and independent travellers. Interlinking 15 countries and 66 destinations, it allows you to start and finish where you want and there is no restriction on how long you stay in any one place. Drivers and on-board-guides can make reservations (at no charge) and also assist in arranging hostel beds en-route. Bus stops are at the hostels, so very often you're dropped off right at the door. They sell flexipasses allowing a certain number of days' travel over a period (one, two or three months, or a whole season) as well as passes for consecutive days of travel. Busabout takes the hassles out of travel without compromising your independence. For more info check out the website, www.busabout.com. For details: **Busabout**, 258 Vauxhall Bridge Rd, London, SW1V 1BS (underground: VICTORIA); ☎(020) 7950 1661.

FLYING If time is short, you might prefer flying within Europe and focusing on one or two countries. London's a good place to start, with plenty of inexpensive flights on offer through travel agencies advertising in newspapers and elsewhere. Business-only destinations tend to be less good value than holiday areas. Budget airlines such as easyJet offer some very cheap no-frills deals: For example from Amsterdam you can fly to and from Geneva and Nice, and Geneva is served with flights to Nice and Barcelona; online bookings are available. For details of all budget flights to Continental Europe from Britain, see pp. 21–22.

CARS If you're starting from London and intend to hire a car elsewhere in Europe, you may get the best deals by booking from Britain (it pays to phone around). Holiday Autos, ☎0870 400 0099 (www.holidayautos.com) often have good deals, and easyJet run a bargain car rental agency with online bookings (easyrentacar.com) with locations at Amsterdam, Barcelona, Madrid, Malaga, Nice and Paris as well as major British cities. Check you're insured if the car gets damaged, and inspect the vehicle thoroughly before you drive off; some Mediterranean resorts have a notorious reputation for dodgy vehicles. The same goes for motorbikes (some hirers won't give you any insurance cover at all). Driving laws, standards and styles vary greatly within Europe. Britain, for example is often congested, and traffic drives on the left. Brussels can be terrifying, with poor lane discipline and frequent minor collisions, and Spain's Costa del Sol has Europe's most accident-ridden road, while France is generally pleasant, with long, empty roads, good toll autoroutes and clear signposting.

Many of the rail journeys in this book traverse superlatively alluring scenery. If you want to immerse yourself in it all, there's no better way than walking, be it a couple of hours strolling round a lake or a fully kitted-out trek across the mountains.

PRACTICALITIES

PATHS The availability of walks varies hugely across the continent. In some countries, particularly Germany, Switzerland and Austria, walking is super-organised, with paths very clearly marked; conversely, in parts of southern Europe, including Greece and much of Spain, you've got to know what you're doing as the mapping can be pretty useless and the paths can be hard to follow. France is covered by a dense network of Sentiers de Grande Randonnée (GRs) – long-distance paths – each with a number (such as GR10). A great thing about Alpine and other ski areas is that in summer many lifts stay open for walkers, cutting out many massive ascents and descents.

WHEN TO GO In mountain areas such as the Alps and the Pyrenees you're more or less restricted to going between June and August as the weather can get wintry outside that time (which does mean some areas get pretty crowded). The famous Alpine meadows give glorious displays of wild flowers before the grass is cut for hay in early to mid-July.

ACCOMMODATION Don't assume you can necessarily camp anywhere in mountain areas. The major mountain areas are dotted with manned huts that provide dormitory accommodation and food. The huts are marked on maps and there's often a small discount if you are a member of the national hut association. At peak times you should book ahead.

MAPS AND GUIDES These can usually be picked up locally, but if you want to get them before you go, **Edward Stanford**, 12–14 Long Acre, London WC2E 9LP; ☎(020) 7836 1321, stocks virtually everything.

EQUIPMENT Walking boots with ankle support are essential in any rough terrain. You'll need a compass, a whistle (six blasts once a minute is the distress signal), waterproof clothing, a first-aid kit, plus plenty of spare food and drink; a ski stick is useful. It's obviously wise to go with a companion, and to choose routes well within your capabilities.

AREAS TO VISIT

This is a selection of areas you can reach by rail or bus. In major mountain areas such as the Alps, Dolomites, High Tatra and Pyrenees, things are well set up for walkers, with large-scale maps on sale locally and a range of accommodation available.

ITALIAN DOLOMITES AND LAKES The scenery in the Dolomites near Bolzano (Bozen) is stupendous, with vast pastures interrupted by improbable rocky peaks. There's a huge amount of potential around such resorts as

Ortisei (St Ulrich; buses from Bolzano) and Cortina, where you can take chair lifts and cable cars. The rail line from Fortezza to Lienz (ETT table 596) gives access to some good areas around Innichen. There's scope for lift-assisted walks above the Italian Lakes near Como; trains and ferries make the area easy to reach.

GERMAN AND AUSTRIAN ALPS From Garmisch-Partenkirchen take the chair lift up Eckbauer, and walk down from the hilltop café into the Partnachklamm, a tremendous rocky gorge that leads you back into town. There are many other similar half-day walks here, with lifts up to the summits. The highest summit in Germany, Zugspitze (shared with Austria), is reached by rack railway from Eibsee (itself a delightful lake, easily walked from Garmisch). Good Austrian bases are Kitzbühel and Salzburg (with rail access to the Salzkammergut area and the German mountain resort of Berchtesgaden).

THE FRENCH AND SWISS ALPS Annecy, a pretty lakeside town with a rail station, is right in the centre of things, with walks from the town. Travel east by rail to Chamonix-Mont Blanc for the celebrated (and crowded) Mont Blanc area – the circuit of Mont Blanc is a hugely popular hut-to-hut trek. Into Switzerland, obvious starting points include Interlaken, St Moritz, Davos and Zermatt, the latter close to the Matterhorn, one of the best-known Alpine peaks; Kandersteg lies in a plum position for walking in the heart of the Bernese Oberland.

THE PYRENEES Unfortunately access without a car is tricky, as the best parts lie up dead-end valleys such as the Cirque de Gavarnie, a huge glacial hollow south of Lourdes, and the grand canyon scenery of Ordesa on the Spanish side. The rail line south-east from Foix gives some useful starting points from such towns as Ax-les-Thermes and Prades (the latter near the summit of Pic du Canigou).

THE MASSIF CENTRAL These central French highlands are not on the scale of the Alps or Pyrenees, but they are extremely varied, with timeless villages, limestone gorges and volcanic crags. The Béziers–Clermont-Ferrand–Nîmes rail route takes in part of the region (immortalised by Robert Louis Stevenson in *Travels with a Donkey in the Cévennes*). West of Clermont-Ferrand, Le Mont-Dore is an excellent centre for hill walks up Puy de Sancy and the Monts Dore.

THE NEAPOLITAN RIVIERA For some absolutely stunning coastal scenery with walks on stepped paths through lemon groves, head for the towering limestone cliffs and spectacularly steep villages around Amalfi, Ravello and Capri near Naples (see pp. 373–375).

THE HIGH TATRA Well-served by lifts, this fine chain of jagged mountains extends along the Polish/Slovakian border, with Zakopane and Starý Smokovec (rail stations) within walking distance. It's compact enough to explore within a few days, though it does get crowded in summer.

If you want to get to the parts of Europe trains don't reach, then a bicycle may be your answer, taking you via quiet roads and tracks into the heart of the countryside. First, though, you need to consider whether it's worth taking a bicycle with you or hiring one once you're there. Unless you are very keen on having your own machine and plan to do a lot of cycling, hiring will save you hassle. Another option is to carry a folding bike as luggage.

TAKING YOUR BIKE ABROAD You can still take bikes for free on many trains in Britain, though some routes require a £3 advance reservation, and bikes are barred from certain rush-hour services. On some ferries you can take the bike free as a foot passenger (but check with the ferry company first). For inland destinations in France and beyond you generally need to send a bike ahead separately as unaccompanied baggage and hope that your machine is there when you arrive.

European Bike Express, ☎(01642) 251440 (www.bike-express.co.uk; bike@bike-express.co.uk), operates cycle-carrying buses that head down from northern England to Dover, and into Europe by four routes into France, Spain, Italy and the Alps. You can join or leave at numerous points; you can also travel on one route and cycle across to meet the returning bus on another. Fares in 2002 were £159–179 return.

Budget and charter airlines may charge for carrying cycles, while many scheduled carriers don't. Flying can be the quickest and easiest way of reaching an inland starting point, but some baggage handlers aren't that careful with bikes; it's probably safest to wrap your machine in heavy duty plastic so that they can see what it is, and have it well insured. Get a detailed map of the airport area before you go: cycling out of a major European airport can be a nerve-wracking affair. Look for cycle paths and small back routes, or try to get your bike on a local train or bus to escape the congestion.

TRANSPORTING A BIKE IN EUROPE You can usually travel with your bike on local train services; you may need to buy a separate ticket for it. Typically on long-distance routes there are only occasional baggage trains, often indicated on the timetable by a bicycle symbol. You can travel with your bike on these services, but may have to send it separately as registered luggage at other times.

Long-distance buses, particularly in Southern Europe, will often take bikes for a small fee if they have a baggage compartment underneath.

For further information about cycling matters (including taking bikes on ferries, European trains and planes, and routes abroad), join the **Cyclists' Touring Club (CTC)**, 69 Meadrow, Godalming, Surrey GU7 3HS, UK; ☎(01483) 417217 (www.ctc.org.uk). Membership entitles you to a range of fact sheets.

Cycling in Europe

Hiring a bike In France and many parts of northern Europe, cycles can easily be hired at major stations and bike shops. Belgium, Denmark and the Netherlands are very well provided for cyclists. To check about availability of cycle hire, try e-mailing the tourist office for the area you want to see (we give websites and e-mail addresses for most of the towns and cities in this book, under Tourist Offices). Try asking for a discount if you want the bike for a week or so.

Where to cycle Much of rural Europe has a good network of back roads ideal for cycling. They go through the centre of historic towns and villages where modern routes pass by: it is worth seeking them out with the help of a large-scale map. Belgium, the Netherlands, Denmark and Sweden have much flat country and are rarely too hot for cycling in summer. France has something for everyone: deep countryside and a spectacular coast in Brittany (accessible directly by ferry from Britain), sleepy southern villages and long but well-graded climbs and descents in the Alps and Pyrenees following Tour de France routes. Cycling facilities are less well developed in southern and eastern Europe but cycling is reportedly becoming more popular. Bike-borne travellers generally get a friendly welcome.

Selected routes In **Belgium** you can tour the country by the well-signposted 750-km **Vlaanderen Fietsroute** (Flanders Cycle Route), which keeps away from the traffic – either on special cycle paths or along designated cycle-only parts of the road. You can join the route by taking the train to Antwerp, Lier and Bruges; Mechelen, Leuven and Ghent lie close to the route. There is simple self-catering accommodation at 'Trekkershutten' along the way.

The Danube Bike Trail from Passau to Vienna: This 197-mile trail is Austria's most famous bike route, 90% traffic-free and mostly flat or slightly downhill. Starting at Passau on the German border (p. 282), the trail follows the Danube River (Europe's second largest) into Vienna. For details see the national tourist website (www.austria-tourism.at/us), which also details three other celebrated cycle routes in superb lake and forest scenery. Bikes can be transported on most Austrian trains, and cycle hire is widely available.

Switzerland is admirably geared-up for cycling, with special carriages on trains for taking your bike, and 3300 km of signed bike routes all over the country. The national rail organisation SBB publish a leaflet giving routes, station links and train times; bike hire is available at 140 stations (www.rent-a-bike.ch).

Germany is also very cyclist-friendly, with plenty of dedicated cycle routes. The Elbe Radweg (www.elberadweg.de) follows the Elbe 260 km from Dessau to Bad Schandau (via Dresden), with plenty of rail links and some beautiful towns and river scenery along the way. At Dessau it links with the Muldentalradweg (www.multentalradweg.de), heading along the river to Colditz.

The following are some suggestions for long rail routes that cross several frontiers; each of them would make a superb holiday in itself. All the main places of interest and many of the lines travelled are covered in this book.

Some routes in the main text of the book also cross international borders, for example Munich to Verona (p. 306) and Copenhagen to Stockholm (p. 483).

Ferry routes are outlined on pp. 57–58.

LONDON–PARIS–MARSEILLE–NICE–PISA–BOLOGNA–VENICE

ETT TABLES

10 · 350 · 360 · 580 · 610 · 614 · 620

The two great cities of London and Paris are the prelude to the trip down to the Mediterranean, for and exploration of the French and Italian rivieras, then through the historic cities of northern Italy to romantic Venice.

BERLIN–DRESDEN–PRAGUE–VIENNA

ETT TABLES

60 · 843 · 1100 · 1150

From Berlin, one of Europe's great cultural centres, through the resurrected city of Dresden in former East Germany, to Prague and Vienna, two wonderfully unspoilt old capitals.

PARIS–BORDEAUX–BURGOS–MADRID–GRANADA

ETT TABLES

300 · 46 · 689 · 671

Heads down via the castles of the Loire and the Futuroscope theme park near Poitiers to France's south-western corner and into Spain's Basque country, past the cathedral at Burgos and the Spanish capital to end in the heart of Andalucía, with its Moorish monuments as reminders that Africa is not far away.

LONDON–OSTEND–BRUSSELS–BERLIN

ETT TABLES

12 · 20 · 400 · 800 · 810

The ferry leaves Dover's white cliffs behind for the Belgian coast, then the train passes the beautiful old cities of Bruges and Ghent, entering Germany near Aachen and passing the great cathedral spires of Cologne; optional diversions to the Harz Mountains before reaching the German capital.

PARIS–MILAN–FLORENCE–ROME

ETT TABLES

44 · 620

Four strongly contrasting cities, with a magnificent scenic experience through the Swiss Alps, via Lausanne and Brig, to Milan, followed by a journey through Tuscany to the Italian capital.

LYON–ZÜRICH–INNSBRUCK–VIENNA

ETT TABLES

348 · 500 · 86 · 950

An Alpine traverse from west to east, passing Geneva and Berne (both convenient for excursions into the Swiss Alps), then virtually through the entire length of Austria to its very different capital city.

STOCKHOLM–COPENHAGEN–HAMBURG–WÜRZBURG–MUNICH–VERONA–VENICE

ETT TABLES

730 · 50 · 900 · 70 · 600

A display of Europe in all its moods, from the watery northern beauty of Stockholm, Copenhagen and Hamburg, through the heart of Bavaria, through the Alps, to the sunny climes of northern Italy, with the Roman amphitheatre at Verona and the canals of Venice.

PRAGUE–MUNICH–ZURICH–MILAN–NICE–MARSEILLE–BARCELONA–MADRID–LISBON

ETT TABLES

57 · 75 · 82 · 90 · 355
650 · 677

An epic voyage from the Czech Republic, through Bavaria and the Alps, across southern France to Perpignan, and over the eastern end of the Pyrénées to Barcelona, the capital of Catalan, then crosses Spain and Portugal to end near Europe's southwestern corner.

BERLIN–POZNAŃ–WARSAW–VILNIUS–RIGA–TALLIN–HELSINKI

ETT TABLES

1001 · 1005 · 1040 · 1850
1845 · 2410 · 1800

Through the former Eastern Bloc, taking in Poland, with an optional detour south from Warsaw to Kraków, and by train and bus through the Baltic states of Lithuania, Latvia and Estonia, to finish with a ferry across to the Finnish capital (or optional extension to St Petersburg; visa required).

ATLANTIC
OCEAN

Wick
Ullapool
Inverness
Oban
Fort
William   SCOTLAND
Aberdeen
Dundee

NORTH
SEA

Glasgow   Edinburgh
Berwick-on-Tweed

Londonderry   NORTHERN
IRELAND
Omagh   Dumfries
Carlisle   Newcastle
Sligo
Belfast
Newry

Scarborough
Athlone
Leeds   York   Hull
Galway   IRELAND   Dublin
Liverpool
Holyhead   Manchester
Limerick
Chester   ENGLAND
Nottingham
Wexford
Aberystwyth
Waterford
Bantry   Cork   Fishguard   WALES   Birmingham   Norwich
Stratford-
upon-Avon   Cambridge
Swansea   Ipswich
Oxford
Bristol   Bath   London
Barnstaple   Canterbury
Southampton   Dover
Exeter   Brighton   Rye   Calais
Plymouth   Portsmouth   Boulogne   Brugg
Lille

English Channel
Cherbourg   Dieppe
Guernsey   Amiens
Le Havre   Rouen
Jersey   Caen
N   Brest
St Malo   Paris
0   200 km   Seine
0   100 miles   Quimper   Rennes   FRANCE

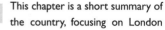

(for Directory information, see p. 616).

This chapter is a short summary of the country, focusing on London and some of the places within easy reach of the capital. The *Independent Traveller's Guide to Britain and Ireland* (Thomas Cook Publishing) goes into much more detail.

Made up of **Great Britain (England, Wales and Scotland)** and **Northern Ireland**, this once mighty power formerly commanded a huge empire. Although its insular qualities are being eroded to an extent by the rapidly growing status of the European Union, there is plenty that is quintessentially British, and a lot is carefully preserved. Regional variation surprises many visitors, with an eye-opening range of traditional building styles, plus some astonishing changes in scenery – from the flat marshes of East Anglia to the rugged cliffs of the south-west, from the domesticated landscapes of the south-east to the

remote hills of northern England and the majestic peaks of the Scottish Highlands. Even regional accents have survived – voices sound very different in south Wales, north-east England, Glasgow and London, for example.

It does pay to be selective when touring the UK: a lot of the big cities of the Midlands are not holiday territory, the scenery in parts of east and central England is unspectacular, and some seaside resorts are well past their prime.

For a varied sample of the country, visit **London** plus one or two of the great historic cities such as **York, Canterbury, Norwich, Durham, Edinburgh, Glasgow, Oxford, Cambridge, Bath** and **Lincoln**. Seek out the coastal heritage, both in seaside resorts such as **Brighton, Broadstairs** or **Scarborough**, and the naval history chronicled in **Portsmouth**, and look out for the many reminders of early industrialisation (there are many excellent museums on the subject). If it's scenery you're after, head for one of the ten national parks (the **Lake District** is the star of them all, a great place for walking – **Windermere** is a useful rail station to start from), or **western Scotland**.

ACCOMMODATION

Except in some resorts in high summer, there should rarely be a problem finding somewhere to stay. At the cheapest level are **campsites** and **youth hostels**.

Bed and breakfast (or **'B and B'**) is the next level up, and not the cheapest, but often fair value, with prices around £15–25 per person plus a generous cooked breakfast: smaller places that are effectively a few spare rooms in someone's home or

YOUTH HOSTELS

**Head office for
England and Wales:**
YHA, Trevelyan House, Dimple
Road, Matlock, Derbyshire DE4 3YH,
☎ 0870 870 8808
(www.yha.org.uk)

Scotland:
SYHA, 7 Glebe Crescent, Stirling,
FK8 2JA, Scotland,
☎ (01786) 891400
(www.syha.org.uk).

farmhouse are often the most comfortable and friendly. **Tourist offices** can usually book in the area, sometimes for a small deposit that is refunded when you pay your bill. Alternatively, in tourist areas it's usually easy to find places to stay just by strolling likely-looking streets. Some pubs have inexpensive accommodation, though they can be noisy.

Large **hotels** are often expensive. There's a wide choice of country-house-style hotels in historic buildings, often in remote locations. The **BTA (British Tourist Authority), AA (Automobile Association), RAC (Royal Automobile Club)** and other organisations each publish guides with different rating systems.

FOOD AND DRINK

Eating out has progressed immeasurably in the last 20 years, with an explosion in variety and quality, with international, specialised ethnic (particularly **Italian, Hong Kong Chinese, Indian** and **Thai**), **whole food/vegetarian** and **fast food** available in most medium-sized and larger towns. Famously British, **fish and chips** are still going strong, and feature thickly sliced chips (fries). **Pub food** is generally the best-value sit-down fare, though some of it is pre-cooked and frozen by distributors and bought in by the pubs. Naturally conditioned brown 'real ale' is served in pubs from long wooden handpumps that sit on the counter, or is dispensed direct from the barrel. It's slightly less chilled than pasteurised beer or lager; it varies greatly in taste and character, and there's an increasing amount of choice. 'Bitter' is the most popular of these brown beers. Many pubs are now open all day. 'Cider' is an alcoholic apple drink, stronger than beer and occasionally available in 'real' draught form, which can be sweet or acidically dry.

Usual eating hours are:
breakfast 0730–0900,
lunch 1200–1400,
afternoon tea
1330–1700, **dinner**
1930–2130.

EDITOR'S CHOICE

Bath; Brighton's Royal Pavilion; Cambridge; Canterbury Cathedral; London; Oxford; Portsmouth Historic Dockyard; York. Scenic rail journeys: Settle–Carlisle (ETT table 174); Glasgow–Mallaig (table 217); Inverness–Kyle of Lochalsh (table 226).

BEYOND THE BORDER

from LONDON

Paris or Brussels by Eurostar (ETT table 10, 12), via Dover (visit Dover Castle) for ferries to Calais or Ostend (tables 100, 101, 2110, 2112); Newhaven (visit Lewes on the way) for ferry to Dieppe and train to Paris via Rouen (tables 103, 104, 2125, 270); Portsmouth (visit Historic Dockyard) for ferry to Cherbourg (tables 107, 2160) to join Cherbourg–Paris–Strasbourg route (p. 80); Harwich for ferry to Hook of Holland (tables 15a, 207, 2235). For ferry information see also pp 57–58.

UNITED KINGDOM: LONDON

Its gateway airports and rail links to the Continent, reinforced by the direct **Eurostar** services through the Channel Tunnel to Paris and Brussels, make **London** a natural starting point for overseas visitors embarking on a rail tour of Europe. Though it can't compete in terms of sustained physical beauty with, say, Paris or Rome, London is undoubtedly one of the world's great cities – with a huge amount of indoor attractions, concerts and theatres. It's an expensive place to stay, but this can be offset by visiting the many free museums and exploring on foot.

There's an excellent range of possible day trips by rail, some of which are listed here.

46 AREAS FOR WALKING
include St James's/ Westminster, the Inns of Court/City, the South Bank, Hampstead, Richmond and the Regent's Canal between Camden and Little Venice.

Central London is pretty safe (although be wary of thieves in crowded places). Women on their own should avoid the King's Cross area.

ARRIVAL AND DEPARTURE

There are 16 main-line rail stations (all linked by Underground trains) in central London. The most important are **Victoria**, for trains to Gatwick and the south coast (Tourist Office and accommodation desk); **Waterloo** (south-west, including Portsmouth for ferries to France and Spain (see p. 57); Eurostar trains (see p. 58) for Paris and Brussels; **Liverpool Street** (eastern England, including services to Harwich for ferries to the Netherlands and Scandinavia); **King's Cross** (north-east and Scotland); **Euston** (West Midlands, north-west and Scotland); **Paddington** (west and Wales); and **St Pancras** (Sheffield and East Midlands). For information about trains to Continental Europe, contact Rail Europe, ☎ 0870 584 8848.

Buses: **Victoria Coach Station**, Buckingham Palace Rd, ☎ (020) 7730 3499, is the main London terminal for long-distance buses; the main operator is **National Express**, ☎ 08705 808080 (or book online at www.gobycoach.com); tourist and other passes available.

Heathrow Airport, ☎ (020) 8759 4321, is 24 km west of central London. The PICCADILLY LINE UNDERGROUND (£3.60 one-way; journey time 50 mins) serves all four terminals. The **Heathrow Express** is more expensive, at £12 single (rail passes not valid), but takes 15 mins to reach Paddington and runs every 15 mins (0500–2345 approximately). A **taxi** to the centre costs about £40–50, cheaper if you share with someone in the queue. The **tourist information desk** at Heathrow is located at the underground station for Terminals 1, 2 and 3; open daily 0830–1800.

Gatwick Airport, ☎ 0870 000 2468, is 43 km south of London. **Gatwick Express** trains run every 15 mins during the day (rail passes not valid), and every 30 mins at night from London Victoria, taking 30 mins; other trains (not called Gatwick Express) are slightly slower and cheaper. **Speedlink** coach service, **Flightline 777**, ☎ 08705 747777 runs approximately hourly 0500–1740, then 2010 (£7.50 one-way): allow 70–75 mins for the journey. Taxis will set you

TOURIST OFFICES

The main tourist information centre is in **Victoria Station** and usually very crowded; allow plenty of time; hotel booking service for whole of UK.

The British Travel Centre (BTC), 12 Lower Regent St, London SW1 (UNDERGROUND: **PICCADILLY CIRCUS**, local **Bed and Breakfast** and **Book a Bed Ahead** services (£5 booking fee, plus redeemable deposit of first night); booking service for guided tours and theatres; transport passes; and comprehensive multi-lingual information; last bookings 30 mins before closing. Website: www.londontouristboard.com

back £70–80 to central London. There's a **tourist information desk** on the arrivals concourse of the South Terminal.

Other international airports are: Stansted (trains to London Liverpool Street), **City** (airport shuttle 10 mins to Canary Wharf on the Docklands Light Railway) and **Luton** (shuttle bus to Luton Airport Parkway rail station for services to London St Pancras).

INFORMATION

CITY AND TRANSPORT MAP – inside back cover

MONEY   Banks and bureaux de change in virtually every main street.

POST AND PHONES   The **post office** near Trafalgar Sq. (24/28 William IV St, WC2 4DL) has poste restante (Mon–Fri 0830–1830).

London is covered by the 020 **phone code** followed by an eight-figure number (beginning with 7 for central London and 8 for outer London). You need to dial 020 if you're calling from outside London; within London, just dial the eight-figure number, including the initial 7 or 8.

PUBLIC TRANSPORT

Travel during rush hour (primarily Mon–Fri 0800–0930 and 1700–1900) is no fun at all. Free bus and Underground maps and other information about London Transport (LT), including tickets, are available in most Underground stations. The main LT office on the ground level of **ST JAMES'S PARK** UNDERGROUND station, ☎ (020) 7222 1234 – 24 hours a day. As for street maps, the *A–Z Map of London* covers the central area, while the full London A–Z or *Nicholson Street Guides* include the whole city and its suburbs.

Underground trains: London Underground ('the Tube'), the world's oldest and deepest **metro** (subway) is extensive, efficient and usually the quickest way to get around, but can be impossibly crowded during rush hours. Most lines operate Mon–Sat from 0530 to around midnight, Sun 0700–2330. Smoking anywhere in the system is forbidden. Each line is colour-coded and named. Boards on the platforms and the front of the trains show the destination. Keep your ticket

REQUEST STOPS

The red signs are request stops and the buses halt at them only if you signal: by raising your arm if you are at a stop or ringing the bell (once only) if you are on board.

handy: there are occasional inspections and it must be passed through the turnstile machine at the beginning and end of your journey.

Buses: London's bright red double-decker buses have become a tourist attraction in their own right, but others run by private companies now vie for business on some routes and single-deckers are fairly common. The roads are often congested and travel can be slow, but some routes (e.g. 🚌 nos. 11/15/38) are excellent for sightseeing and the view from the top deck is always great. Most services run Mon–Sat 0600–2400, Sun 0730–2300. Restricted (often hourly) services radiate from TRAFALGAR SQ. throughout the night: night bus numbers are prefixed by 'N'. Keep your ticket until you reach your destination as there are random checks. Buses sometimes cover only part of the route, so check the final destination board on the front or back. There are bus stops every few hundred metres, showing the relevant bus numbers.

Taxis: The famous 'black cabs' may be painted in other colours, but their shape remains distinctive. Fares are metered and not cheap; there are extra (metered) charges for baggage, for more than one passenger, and for travelling in the evening (after 2000) or at weekends; drivers expect a tip of 10% of the fare (but you don't need to tip minicabs that you order by phone). There are taxi ranks at key positions, but you can also hail them in the street. When a taxi is available, the roof-light at the front is on.

ACCOMMODATION

London has an enormous range of accommodation, from world-renowned hotels with sky-high prices to bed and breakfast establishments. The best value for **cheap accommodation** are the seven **Hostelling International youth hostels** in London; main office, ☎ (020) 7373 3400, fax (020) 7373 3455 (lonres@yha.org.uk). The **Paddington, Victoria** and **Earls Court** areas, in particular, have a good range of **bed and breakfast** at around £30 per person. **LTB (London Tourist Board)**, ☎ (020) 7604 2890 (for bookings only), will take hotel bookings by phone up to six weeks in advance if you have MasterCard or Visa. Alternatively, for a small fee, you can book at the

TICKETS
Underground fares depend on the number of zones travelled: zone 1 is the centre and may well be all you need. **Single tickets** are purchased in the station and allow you to change lines as often as necessary. One-zone tickets are £1.60; carnets of ten tickets are £11.50. **Bus fares** are determined by fare stages and not easy to define, but a **single ticket** (purchased when you board) is valid only for that vehicle, so you must get another ticket if you change.

TRAVELCARDS
Available from most rail and tube stations and many newsagents, these are much better value than single tickets. They cover all London's public transport systems (except Airbuses), giving you the freedom to hop on and off LT buses, the Underground, the Docklands Light Railway and suburban trains. **One-day Travelcards** (£4.50 all zones; less for fewer zones) are valid at weekends and after 0930 Mon–Fri. Peak versions are also available.

Thomas Cook desks at Charing Cross, St Pancras, Paddington, Victoria, Euston and King's Cross stations, and at Gatwick Airport. The London School of Economics, ☎(020) 7955 7370 (www.lse.ac.uk/vacations) lets out rooms in centrally located student halls of residence in Bloomsbury, Islington and the South Bank during Easter and summer vacations, and you don't have to be a student to stay there; triples, twins and singles are available. Singles are about £24–36, twins £40–58 (more expensive with bathroom), with breakfast; you can prepare your own food in the kitchens.

Camping in central London is not possible. The parks are locked around midnight and patrolled until they re-open. The city spreads for miles in every direction and the nearest campsites are some way out of town. Crystal Palace Caravan Club Site ☎(020) 8778 7155 is pleasantly placed in the southern suburbs (🚌no. 3 from Oxford Circus/Trafalgar Sq., or rail to Crystal Palace station from Victoria), with prices in high summer at £2 per tent pitch plus £4.50 per adult.

FOOD AND DRINK

London is a superb hunting ground for food, with restaurants of every conceivable type, from traditional British to those of countries few could pin point on a map. The cost is equally varied: from fast food chains, where you can get something filling for about £3, to places with no prices on the menu that cost more than some would spend on food in a year.

The Covent Garden and Soho districts (there's an endless choice of Chinese places in the GERRARD ST/WARDOUR ST area of Soho) offer the best array of West End restaurants. The Queensway, Victoria, Leicester Sq., Panton St and Earls Court areas are very lively, especially in the evenings, with innumerable cheap eateries of all types, including some of the eat-your-fill variety.

Italian, Chinese, Indian, Greek and Turkish restaurants are common and many are excellent, with a wide range of cheap dishes on offer. Many do takeaways and there are still plenty of fish and chip shops. Food in pubs and wine bars is usually good value though pubs in the centre are often unpleasantly crowded. Sandwich bars are a good alternative for a light lunch. For food shopping, visit Fortnum and Masons, PICCADILLY, and the Food Hall in Harrods, KNIGHTSBRIDGE. There are pubs on virtually every street, including historic inns reputed to have been frequented by everyone from Ben Jonson to Charles Dickens.

HIGHLIGHTS

It's possible to take in a lot of the most famous landmarks in a couple of days. From Big Ben (UNDERGROUND: WESTMINSTER), the famous Gothic clock tower of the Houses of Parliament (where you can hear parliamentary debate if you're prepared to queue), there's a splendid walk over **Westminster Bridge**, after which you turn left along the **Thames** embankment, enjoying river views from the **South Bank**, where you'll see the transition from the **West End** to the **City**, with domed **St Paul's Cathedral** rising spectacularly; on the South Bank is the thatched **Shakespeare's Globe Theatre**, a faithful 1990s replica of the place where many of Shakespeare's plays were performed in his lifetime. Around **London Bridge** there are some atmospheric (converted) Victorian warehouses, with high catwalks; then comes **Tower Bridge**, the best known Thames span, which is still raised to allow tall ships through; cross to the north bank here to the **Tower of London**, one of Britain's best-preserved Norman castles, where many famous and notorious prisoners of the Crown met a grisly end. It's home to the Crown Jewels and is guarded by Beefeaters attired in medieval uniform.

In the other direction from Big Ben you can delve into the best of the **West End**. In **Parliament Square** is **Westminster Abbey**, crammed with memorials and famed as the crowning place of British monarchs. Along WHITEHALL, with its limestone-fronted government buildings, the **Banqueting House** is a remnant of the otherwise vanished **Palace of Whitehall**, and the breastplated Horse Guards keep watch in HORSE GUARDS PARADE. TRAFALGAR SQUARE is London's big set piece, with **Nelson's Column** flanked by a quartet of lions and looked over by **St Martin's-in-the-Fields Church** and the **National Gallery**. From the **Admiralty Arch** runs THE MALL, a Parisian boulevard lined by Regency terraces on one side and the greenery of **St James's Park** (a lovely spot with a lake and bandstand) on the other; at the end is **Buckingham Palace** (the Queen's main residence), rather cold and austere (its state rooms are open Aug–Sep: you can also visit the Queen's Gallery and Royal Mews collection of state coaches). In ugly Victoria Street, the 19th-century **Westminster (Catholic) Cathedral** has a cavernous interior. A lift whisks you up the tower for £2.

For the new millennium, London added a host of attractions. Along Millennium Mile (the South Bank between Westminster and Tower bridges) are the **BA London Eye** (a 150m ferris wheel), the **Tate Modern** (free; in the old Bankside power station, with the **Millennium Footbridge** over the river to St Paul's) and the huge **BFI London Imax Cinema** (with Britain's largest screen).

The **City of London** (the east part of the centre) houses such venerable and ancient City institutions such as the **Guildhall**, the **Inns of Court** (the heart of legal London) and the **Bank of England**. The 17th-century architect Sir Christopher Wren built numerous City churches, most famously **St Paul's Cathedral**, with its **Whispering Gallery** providing remarkable acoustics. Buildings to look out for near FENCHURCH ST include **Leadenhall Market** (exuberantly Victorian) and the **Lloyd's Building** (provocatively high-tech).

MUSEUMS AND GALLERIES Most museums and galleries open daily, year round, but check before you go. The following listing is only the briefest indication of the cream.

Of the countless art galleries, three are outstanding – and admission is free, except for special exhibitions. **The National Gallery**, TRAFALGAR SQ., displays 12th–19th-century art, with a superb cross-section of Impressionists and post-Impressionists (try to catch one of the free gallery tours), and the neighbouring **National Portrait Gallery** offers a comprehensive display (entrance free; UNDERGROUND: **CHARING CROSS/LEICESTER SQ.**). The **Tate Britain** (incorporating the **Clore Gallery**), MILLBANK (UNDERGROUND: **WESTMINSTER/PIMLICO**) is another free gallery, with some outstanding Turners among its all-British collection. For the wonderful **Tate Modern** see p. 50.

The **British Museum**, GREAT RUSSELL ST (UNDERGROUND: **RUSSELL SQ.**), is a treasure trove (entrance free); it's daunting in scale – many come in just to see the **Elgin Marbles** (originally the frieze of the **Parthenon** in Athens) and the ancient Egyptian section. The **Museum of London**, LONDON WALL (UNDERGROUND: **BARBICAN/ST PAUL'S MOORGATE**), offers a beautifully displayed history of the city with an excellent Roman section and a reconstruction of a Victorian street of shops. Most visitors enjoy **London's Transport Museum**, COVENT GARDEN. Don't miss the free and wonderfully eccentric **Sir John Soane's Museum**, Lincoln's Inn Fields (UNDERGROUND: HOLBORN) a bizarre Georgian house stashed with Soane's 'museum' objects. The free **Imperial War Museum** (UNDER-GROUND: **LAMBETH NORTH**) looks at modern warfare since 1914, with lots on social history and how wars affect our lives – so you don't need to be turned on by guns to get a lot out of a visit; there are brilliant re-creations of a blitzed London street and a First World War trench, and often highly worthwhile temporary exhibitions. Clustered together (UNDERGROUND: **SOUTH KENSINGTON**) are three other truly great museums (entrance free). The **Science Museum**, EXHIBITION RD, has an array of hands-on exhibits demonstrating all things scientific. The adjacent **Natural History Museum** has many interactive exhibits, and there's a wonderful section on dinosaurs. Across the road is the **Victoria and Albert Museum**, CROMWELL RD, a vast treasure house of arts and crafts. **Madame Tussaud's** (UNDERGROUND: **BAKER STREET**) has the famous waxworks, plus the **Spirit of London** ride through London's history; fun but expensive, and often a big queue to get in.

> At £22 for one day the **London Pass** is pricey but might be worthwhile if you're visiting lots of places; it includes boat trips and attractions (some outside London). For information 📞(01644) 500107 (www.londonpass.com).

OUT OF THE CENTRE A distinguishing feature of the suburbs are the old villages incorporated into the cityscape but still with attractive old centres. Along the Thames to the west there are delightful riverside walks from **Richmond** (UNDERGROUND: **RICHMOND**) and up to **Richmond Park**, a huge deer park; within reach are CHISWICK MALL, just west of **Hammersmith Bridge** and with several old waterside pubs and imposing Georgian houses, and **Kew Gardens (Royal Botanic Gardens)** (UNDERGROUND: **KEW GARDENS**), one of the greatest plant collections in the world. A bit further out is Henry VIII's superb **Hampton Court Palace** (famous for its maze) and **Windsor Castle** (still a royal residence, but parts of it are open); both are accessible by suburban train from **Waterloo** station – these and Kew Gardens can be reached by boat (see Tours, p. 52).

East from the centre, **Greenwich** was once the hub of nautical Britain and is still the definitive Meridian, or 0 degrees longitude. In **Greenwich Park** and towards the river are the **National Maritime Museum, Old Royal Naval College, Royal Observatory,** and the refurbished **Queen's House** (free entrance to all these). From Greenwich a slightly creepy tiled foot tunnel (free) under the Thames leads to ISLAND GARDENS station on the elevated **Docklands Light Railway**, which gives a futuristic ride north from here, past **Canary Wharf** (London's tallest building) in the heart of redeveloped Docklands to **West India Quay**, where you can carry on to TOWER GATEWAY near the **Tower of London** to finish a memorable day at Tower Bridge.

Another great place to explore is **Hampstead** (UNDERGROUND: **HAMPSTEAD**), a haunt of artists, writers and the simply wealthy; it's a knot of old cottages, Georgian terraces, pretty pubs and stately villas fringing **Hampstead Heath**, a surprisingly large and countrified expanse of unkempt woodland and heath; places to seek out are CHURCH ROW (the finest Georgian street), **Fenton House** (Hampstead's oldest house, home to a keyboard instrument collection) and **Kenwood House** (a stately home with an outstanding art collection, free entry).

NIGHT-TIME AND EVENTS

There are several publications listing London's entertainments, of which the best are the weekly magazine *Time Out*, the daily *Evening Standard* and the free *TNT Magazine* (help yourself from special stands in central areas).

CLUBS, DISCOS, PUBS Almost everything is on offer in terms of nightlife, including casinos, jazz clubs, discos, straight and gay clubs and pub entertainment. Most clubs offer one-night membership at the door and often have

---

TOURS

The **Original London Sightseeing Tour**, ☎ (020) 8877 1722, runs special tourist buses, some open-topped, which take in the major sights and provide a multi-lingual commentary via headphones during the journey. **Departure points** are PICCADILLY CIRCUS, MARBLE ARCH, VICTORIA and BAKER ST; a day ticket allows you to board and get off as often as you like. Several companies operate daily **themed walking tours**, usually from underground stations; one of the best is **Original London Walks**, ☎ (020) 7642 3978; no booking, cost around £5.

For **river tours**, buy tickets on the day at the pier (no need to book): cruises run from around 1030–1530 with the last boat back about an hour later; return prices vary from around £6 from Westminster or the Embankment to the Tower, and £8 to Greenwich; services run every 40–45 minutes. Or head west (up-river) from Westminster to Richmond, Kew and Hampton Court. The **London Bicycle Tour Company**, 1A GABRIEL'S WHARF, 56 UPPER GROUND, LONDON SE1; ☎ (020) 7928 6838 (www.londonbicycle.com), offers **bike hire** and **guided bicycle tours** of the capital.

a dress code, which might be a jacket and tie or could just depend on whether you look trendy enough. Jeans and trainers are usually out. The larger **rock venues** (such as the **Fridge** in **Brixton** and the **Hammersmith Odeon**) are all a little way from the centre, as are many of the **pubs with live entertainment**.

THEATRE, CINEMA AND MUSIC London is one of the world's greatest centres of theatre and music. In addition to the **National Theatre** (**South Bank Centre** – see below) and the **Royal Shakespeare Company** (**Barbican Centre**), there are about 50 theatres in central London. West End theatre tickets are expensive, but there is a **half-price ticket kiosk**, LEICESTER SQ. (the south side), for same-day performances. **To book ahead**, go to the theatre itself – most agents charge a hefty fee. Seats for big musicals and other hits are hard to get, but it's always worth queuing for returns.

> Most of London shuts by midnight. Those places that do stay open late usually increase their entrance charges at around 2200 and many places charge more at weekends.

There's a wide range of classical music, from free lunchtime performances in churches to major symphonies in famous venues. **The Proms** are a huge summer-long festival of concerts held at the **Royal Albert Hall**, with the cheapest tickets sold on the day to 'Promenaders' who stand at floor level; the flag-waving 'Last Night' is massively popular.

Other major classical music venues are the **Barbican Concert Hall** and the **Royal Festival Hall**. The latter, part of the South Bank Centre (UNDERGROUND: EMBANKMENT, then walk over Hungerford Bridge) is a stylish 1950s hall where there's lots going on in the daytime in the way of free foyer concerts, jazz and exhibitions, and there's an inexpensive self-service restaurant downstairs. The cheapest tickets for concerts are in the 'choir' behind the orchestra, where the sound's a bit distorted but you are really close to the musicians.

Also on the South Bank are the **National Theatre**, **National Film Theatre** (where you can get temporary membership if you just want to see one film) and the **BFI London IMAX Cinema** (imax.cinema@bfi.org.uk), boasting a gigantic screen (Britain's largest). It's also well worth catching a play at **Shakespeare's Globe Theatre** (see p. 50), where it's very cheap to get a ticket for standing space (or 'groundling').

EVENTS It's not difficult to see British pageantry if you time your visit to coincide with one of the many traditional annual events. These include **Trooping the Colour** (second Sat June), the **State Opening of Parliament** (early Nov) and the **Lord Mayor's Show** (second Sat Nov). Other free spectacles include: the **London Marathon** (Apr: the world's largest, truly international); the **University Boat Race** (Sat near Easter: a traditional contest between Oxford and Cambridge Universities); and the **Notting Hill Carnival** (which takes over a wide area for two days late Aug – the largest of its type in Europe, noisy and fun, but don't take any valuables).

SHOPPING

The West End is full of famous shopping areas. For serious shopping, including many department stores, try OXFORD ST and REGENT ST (home to Hamleys toy shop). For designer clothes and upmarket window shopping, try BOND ST, SOUTH MOLTON ST, BEAUCHAMP PLACE and BROMPTON RD (home of Harrods; UNDERGROUND: **KNIGHTSBRIDGE**). For **books**: CHARING CROSS RD. For **trendy boutiques**: Covent Garden and KINGS RD (Chelsea). For **electronic goods**: TOTTENHAM COURT RD. **London-related souvenirs** don't extend much beyond ephemeral tat; a better bet are items on sale at museum shops such as the **Museum of London, British Museum, National Gallery** and **London's Transport Museum**.

Some of London's **street markets** are tourist attractions in themselves. Amongst the best are **Portobello Rd** (UNDERGROUND: **LADBROKE GROVE** OR **NOTTING HILL GATE**), Mon–Sat (best Sat morning; antiques and junk) and **Camden Lock**, all week, but best on Sun, with antiques and crafts (UNDERGROUND: **CHALK FARM**): you can tie a visit in with a walk westwards along the Regent's Canal, passing **Regent's Park**, the Zoo and leading to a pretty canal basin at **Little Venice**. For sheer East-end atmosphere seek out **Brick Lane** on a Sun morning (much better than the touristy **Petticoat Lane** nearby), with some real bargains among piles of cheap junk (UNDERGROUND: **SHOREDITCH**).

DAY TRIPS FROM LONDON

BATH (1 hr 20 mins from **Paddington**; ETT table 133): A fine Georgian town, at the height of fashion in the 18th and early 19th centuries, began life as a Roman spa, and the original **Roman baths** are impressively intact next to the **18th-century pump room**, where you can sip tea to the accompaniment of chamber music; adjacent **Bath Abbey** was known as the 'Lantern of the West' for its display of stained glass. Among some of the masterpieces of Georgian town planning are the **Royal Crescent** (No.1 is open as a museum house) and **The Circus**, built like much of the rest in mellow Bath stone. Pick of the museums are the **Museum of Costume** at the Assembly Rooms, the **Building of Bath Museum** (explaining how John Wood transformed the city), the **Industrial Museum** and the **American Museum**. There are **river cruises** from Pulteney Bridge. [i]Tourist office: ☎(01225) 477101 (www.cityofbath.co.uk).

BRIGHTON (1 hr from **Victoria**; ETT table 103): Still the best place to go to experience the English seaside resort, though it's past its prime as a bathing spot. George IV made sea-bathing fashionable when he erected his **Royal Pavilion**, an Indian fantasy Regency mansion sprouting domes and minarets, as astonishing inside as out. Virtually contemporary are the imposing stucco crescents and terraces lining the front; below are numerous booths offering palm-reading and tattooing, and two magnificent 19th-century piers – **Brighton Pier** very much alive with tacky amusements, and the wrecked **West Pier,** in the process of restoration. The maze-like old fishing quarter, now full of eateries, boutiques and antique shops, is known as the LANES – not to be confused with the NORTH LAINE, a line of pedestrianised shopping streets at the heart of trendy, alternative Brighton. You can return to London by way of **Lewes**, a handsome and surprisingly untouristy town on a ridge between the chalky **South Downs**, with views of the rooftops and coast from its **Norman castle**, and lots of second-hand bookshops and ancient alleys (known as 'twittens'). [i] Tourist office: ☎0906 711 255 (calls charged at 50p/minute; www.brighton.co.uk).

CAMBRIDGE (1 hr; quickest service from **King's Cross**; ETT table 199): With Oxford, one of Britain's two oldest universities, with colleges scattered around the city (there are very few university buildings as such). Richly varied architecturally, the colleges have a cloistered tranquillity of the colleges themselves, and there are lovely walks along the river (popular for punting – an 'Oxbridge' boating tradition). Many colleges charge for entry and some close to the public in term time., with the chapel at **King's** (a superb example of Perpendicular Gothic) and the main courtyard and library at **Trinity** among its treasures. The **Fitzwilliam Museum** (free) is a magnificent general museum with some choice art collections. The station is a 15–20 min walk, but there are frequent bus services from Victoria Coach Station in London getting you closer to the centre. [i] Tourist office: ☎(01223) 322640 (www.cambridge.gov.uk).

CANTERBURY (1 hr 25–40 mins from **Victoria**; ETT table 100): Seat of the premier church of England, **Canterbury** has some gems, notably the **cathedral** (with medieval stained glass, Norman crypt and cloister) and its precincts, which miraculously escaped wartime bombing that obliterated part of the centre (unimaginatively rebuilt) but left some old streets intact. You can walk round the remaining city walls past whirling traffic, and pass under the medieval **Christ Church and Westgate**; one of the former pilgrims' hostels, **Poor Priests' Hospital** now houses a good museum covering the city's heritage. **St Augustine's Church** is the oldest church in England, in use since the 6th century. [i] Tourist office: ☎(01227) 766567 (www.canterbury.co.uk).

DOVER (1hr 45mins from London Victoria; 30 mins from Canterbury East; ETT table 100): The main channel port, Dover was sadly bashed about by wartime bombing and town planners. However it does have a tremendous setting, with sheer chalk cliffs (the famous 'white cliffs') giving great coastal walks in either direction (to Folkestone or Deal; both have rail services to Dover), and looking across the Channel to France. **Dover Castle** is one of the best-preserved Norman keeps in the country and you can visit the miles of secret tunnels that in the World War II housed the HQ for the Dunkirk evacuation and a military hospital; the site also includes a Roman lighthouse and a Saxon church. [i] Tourist office: ☎(01304) 205108 (www.whitecliffscountry.org.uk).

OXFORD (1 hr from Paddington; ETT table 150): In many ways Oxford is similar to Cambridge, with a river to explore and many ancient-feeling colleges with pretty gardens. It's virtually all built in honey-coloured Cotswold stone. Of the colleges, **Christ Church** and **Magdalene** are among the finest. Seek out the free **Ashmolean Museum**, with a superb collection of art and artefacts. The station is a 15–20 min walk, but there are frequent bus services from Victoria Coach Station in London getting you closer to the centre. ⓘ Tourist office: ☎(01865) 726871 (www.oxford.gov.uk).

RYE (1 hr 45 mins from **Charing Cross**; change at **Ashford**; ETT tables 101, 109): One of the **Cinque Ports**, which in medieval times supplied men and ships to defend the coast and received special privileges, **Rye** has survived as one of the best-preserved small towns in England, though the sea that brought fame and fortune has receded. The town is full of quaint alleys and cobbled lanes, MERMAID STREET being the best-known. Take the train one stop to **Winchelsea** – another lapsed port, laid out as a medieval town but now a handsome, French-looking hilltop village. Further on is the resort of **Hastings**, a bit run down but with a fascinating and extensive hilly old town of former fishermen's cottages, with walks eastward along the tops of sandstone cliffs. ⓘ Tourist office: ☎(01797) 226696 (www.rye-tourism.co.uk).

STRATFORD-UPON-AVON (2 hrs 10 mins from **Paddington**; ETT table 127): famous as Shakespeare's birthplace, the main places connected with the Bard are **Shakespeare's Birthplace Museum** (within a small timber-framed house), **Anne Hathaway's Cottage** (the thatched cottage of his wife), **Mary Arden's House** (his mother's childhood home) and the **Royal Shakespeare Theatre** (productions by the Royal Shakespeare Company; excellent backstage tours). Shakespeare aside, it's an agreeable town but extremely touristy, and if you're not into literary pilgrimage you might want to give it a miss. ⓘ Tourist office: ☎(01789) 293127 (www.warwickshire.gov.uk/tourism).

YORK (2 hrs from **King's Cross**; ETT table 185): The most satisfying English medieval city, encircled by impressively preserved walls (with extensive walks along the top of them), and graced with the magnificent **Minster** (Britain's largest medieval cathedral, renowned for the quality of its stained glass). Close by **Clifford's Tower** (a 14th-century castle) is the **Castle Museum**, with a reconstructed street of shops among its excellent displays of social history, while **Jorvik, The Viking City** is a remarkable time journey back to 10th-century York. Foremost among the rest of an excellent set of museums is the **National Railway Museum**, with Queen Victoria's royal carriage as well as the record-breaking *Mallard* locomotive. The centre is enjoyably traffic free, and full of buskers and street life; the **Shambles**, with its jettied, overhanging houses, and the **Merchant Adventurers' Hall** are among the best medieval timber-frame survivals. ⓘ Tourist office: ☎ (01904) 554488 (www.york-tourism.co.uk).

CROSSING TO CONTINENTAL EUROPE

This section details how travellers can reach mainland Europe from Britain and Ireland. Frequencies and journey times are given for the summer season. Please note that the services and timings listed below are always subject to alteration as ferry operators alter their routes and services. Refer to the shipping section of the current edition of the *Thomas Cook European Timetable* for the latest details.

From...To	Sailings	Journey Time	Operator	☎ for details
DOVER to				
Calais (SeaCat)	11–13 per day	60 mins	Hoverspeed	0870 524 0241
Calais	23–35 per day	75–90 mins	P&O	0870 600 0600
Calais	17 per day	90 mins	SeaFrance	0870 571 1711
Ostend	2 per day	2 hrs	Hoverspeed	0870 524 0241
HARWICH to				
Cuxhaven	3 per week	16 hrs 45 mins	DFDS Seaways	0870 533 3000
Esbjerg	3 per week	22 hrs	DFDS Seaways	0870 533 3000
Hook of Holland (fast ferry)	2 per day	3 hrs 40 mins	Stena Line	0870 570 7070
HULL to				
Rotterdam Europoort	1 per day	10 hrs	P&O North Sea Ferries	0870 129 6002
Zeebrugge	1 per day	13 hrs	P&O North Sea Ferries	0870 129 6002
NEWCASTLE to				
Amsterdam	1 per day	15 hrs	DFDS Seaways	0870 533 3000
Bergen	3 per week	21–25 hrs	Fjord Line	(0191) 296 1313
Gothenburg	2 per week	25 hrs	DFDS Seaways	0870 533 3000
Kristiansand	2 per week	17 hrs	DFDS Seaways	0870 533 3000
Stavanger	3 per week	18–26 hrs	Fjord Line	(0191) 296 1313
NEWHAVEN to				
Dieppe (SeaCat)	2–3 per day	2 hrs	Hoverspeed	0870 524 0241
Dieppe (ship)	1–2 per day	4 hrs	Transmanche Ferries	0800 917 1201
PLYMOUTH to				
Roscoff	1–3 per day	6 hrs	Brittany Ferries	0870 536 0360
Santander	2 per week	24 hrs	Brittany Ferries	0870 536 0360
POOLE to				
Cherbourg (fast ferry)	1 per day	2 hrs 15 mins	Brittany Ferries/ Condor Ferries	(01305) 761551
Cherbourg (ship)	2–3 per day	4 hrs 15 mins– 5 hrs 45 mins	Brittany Ferries	0870 536 0360
PORTSMOUTH to				
Bilbao	2 per week	35 hrs	P&O Portsmouth	0870 242 4999
Cherbourg (ship)	1 per week	5 hrs	Condor Ferries	(01305) 761551
Cherbourg (ship)	3–4 per day	5–7 hrs	P&O Portsmouth	0870 242 4999
Cherbourg (fast ferry)	2 per day	2 hrs 45 mins	P&O Portsmouth	0870 242 4999
Le Havre	3 per day	5 hrs 30 mins	P&O Portsmouth	0870 242 4999
Ouistreham (Caen)	2–3 per day	6 hrs	Brittany Ferries	0870 536 0360
St Malo	1 per day	9 hrs– 10 hrs 30 mins	Brittany Ferries	0870 536 0360

From...To	Sailings	Journey Time	Operator	☎ for details
CORK to				
Roscoff	1 per week	14 hrs 30 mins	Brittany Ferries	0870 536 0360
ROSSLARE to				
Cherbourg	1–2 per week	18 hrs	Irish Ferries	0870 517 1717
Roscoff	1–2 per week	17 hrs	Irish Ferries	0870 517 1717

THE CHANNEL TUNNEL

The idea of a cross-Channel tunnel was first proposed as long ago as as 1802. Early attempts were stopped for fear of invasion and the project finally got the green light in 1985. This extraordinary feat of engineering actually consists of three tunnels (two for trains, one for services and emergency use), each one 50 km long. Eurostar rail services began in late 1994 and is now one of the easiest ways of reaching Continental Europe.

The advantage Eurostar has over ferry services, for many travellers, is that the journey is from city centre to city centre. Waterloo International is served by the London Underground and by domestic rail services (see p. 46). From Waterloo, up to 18 trains each day take 3 hrs to reach Paris Gare du Nord, whilst 10 services take just 2 hrs 40 mins to reach Brussels Midi, and from late 2003 it will be 15 mins quicker still. Some trains stop at Ashford International (for south-east England), Lille (for connections with TGV services across France) or Calais, and there are services direct to Disneyland Paris. Waterloo International is more like an airport than a typical London rail terminus. Facilities at the modern, purpose-built terminal include shops, cafés and bars. There is an automated check-in system at all Eurostar terminals, and passengers have to check in up to 30 mins before departure. Passengers clear customs before boarding; passport and immigration checks take place during the journey.

The sleek Eurostar trains look incongruous amongst London's commuter services. Each train, a quarter-mile long, provides two classes of travel – first-class offers complimentary meals and drinks, and standard-class usually provides an at-seat trolley service. There are also two buffet cars on each train. Discounted tickets are available to most rail pass holders, and there are often special offers (particularly off season).

The 20-minute trip through the Channel Tunnel seems just like travelling on any metro system. The thrill comes as you emerge in France and the train accelerates to over 180 mph across the Pas de Calais. Both Paris Gare du Nord (p. 63) and Brussels Midi (p. 222) have been altered to accommodate the Eurostar trains. For details and bookings, ☎0870 518 6186 (www.eurostar.com).

Eurotunnel, which runs from Folkestone to Calais, is the car transporter service. Trains run up to 4 times per hour and journey time is about 35 mins during the day. Tickets are bought at the terminal or given in exchange for vouchers. The carriages have toilet facilities, but little by way of refreshments and no seats – passengers remain in or near their car. For details and bookings; ☎0870 535 3535.

FRANCE

(for Directory information, see p. 594). Many people holiday nowhere else but France. It has a lifetime's worth of historic towns, cities and other heritage, food and wine that can verge on the wonderful, and both scenery and architecture of astonishing variety. To top that, **Paris** is one of the world's most romantic capitals, with a streetscape familiar from a thousand movies.

In the north-west, **Normandy** is a land of half-timbered farms and graceful old manor houses; vast war cemeteries and numerous rebuilt towns that suffered massive bombing are sobering reminders of the toll inflicted by the 20th century's two World Wars. **Brittany** has the best scenery on France's Atlantic coast, with fishing villages and sweeping sandy bays, and inland lies the **Loire valley** – scenically undramatic, but remarkable for its châteaux that span the ages from feudal times.

Despite the impressive legacy of medieval towns and cities (including some superb cathedrals), much of inland northern France is pretty humdrum scenically, with endless cornfields and long straight roads. It is in the **Massif Central**, the volcanic upland covering much of southern central France, that the scenery becomes wilder. Heading south towards the Spanish border down through western France, after the gentle hills of the **Dordogne**, studded with prehistoric sights and many pretty (if sometimes over-discovered) villages, you reach the Pyrénées which offer an excellent range of walks. Between the Massif Central and the Alps, **Provence** is really Mediterranean, with red tiled roofs, vineyards and cypress trees under the harsh summer sun. Known as the **Riviera**, the south-east coast boasts glamorous resorts (good for people-watching) and fine (but packed) beaches. North of the Alps, the areas of **Burgundy** and **Alsace** – the latter distinctly German in appearance – have attractive landscapes and rewarding territory for pottering round villages and vineyards.

Trains are fast, comfortable and usually reliable. The French are proud of the **TGV** (*Train à Grande-Vitesse*), among the fastest in the world, with speeds of up to 300 km/h. Most of the scenic routes are in the south – in the **Massif Central**, through the **Pyrénées**, in **Provence** and through the **Alps**.

ACCOMMODATION

HOTELS If you're staying at hotels, it's much cheaper if you share rather than go single, as prices are often per room. Half-board (i.e. breakfast and evening meal included) can be excellent value in smaller towns and villages. As elsewhere in Europe, budget hotels are often clustered near stations. In summer, it is advisable to book in larger towns and resort areas. *Offices de Tourisme* or *Syndicats d'Initiative* (Tourist Offices) provide lists of local accommodation alternatives, generally for free; they also often book for you for a small charge. **Gîtes de France** produces catalogues of B&Bs, *gîtes d'étape*, farm accommodation and holiday house rentals for each *département*, available from certain retail outlets or **Maison des Gîtes de France**, 59 r. St Lazare, 75009 Paris; ☎01 49 70 75 75, fax 01 42 81 28 53 (www.gites-de-france.fr). Accommodation tax (around €1/person/day) may be charged by the owner in addition to the price.

Hotels are graded from 1 (basic) to 5 (luxury) stars. Paris is expensive: a comfortable double room in most places would average €35–40; in Paris it would be more like €70. Hotels in large towns and/or tourist areas are also more expensive, but always try to bargain: owners everywhere are often ready to drop their prices. Hotel prices quoted never include breakfast – which is generally continental (coffee, bread/croissant and jam) and expensive compared to picking up a local speciality and eating it in a nearby café (just ask first). Room prices are displayed at hotel entrances and in each room.

CHAMBRES D'HÔTES *Chambres d'Hôtes* are bedrooms, and often more , in private homes, from farms to village houses to châteaux, and the price always includes breakfast. *Table d'hôte* (evening meal) is often available. A useful travelling companion is the detailed Thomas Cook *Selected Bed & Breakfast France 2003* (£11.99 plus p&p), available from **Thomas Cook Publishing**, PO Box 227, Units 19–21, The Thomas Cook Business Park, Coningsby Rd, Peterborough PE3 6XX, UK; ☎(01733) 416477.

GÎTES D'ÉTAPE These are rural hostels, usually with private rooms as well as dormitories, and are mainly used by groups. It is advisable to book.

YOUTH HOSTELS Most **Auberges de Jeunesse** belong to the Hostelling International (HI) organisation, but whether they do or not, their prices generally range from about €7–18 for the only 3 Paris hostels (all HI), depending on whether sheets and breakfast are included. They all have kitchen facilities and some serve meals. **Fédération Unie des Auberges de Jeunesse** (FUAJ) (HI), 27 r. Pajol, 75018 Paris; ☎01 44 89 87 27, fax 01 44 89 87 10 (www.fuaj.org); **Ligue des Auberges de Jeunesse**, 67 r. Vergniaud, 75013 Paris; ☎01 44 16 78 78, fax 01 44 16 78 80 (www.auberges-de-jeunesse.com).

CAMPING This is virtually a national pastime, and you'll have no problem finding a site; most towns and larger villages will have signposts to the nearest, commonly the 1- or 2-star *Camping Municipal* (fairly basic but very cheap). High-grade sites (4 & 5 star) provide entertainment and facilities such as watersports, but can get very crowded in season. The most comprehensive guides, by **Michelin** or the **Fédération Française de Camping et de Caravaning** are widely available (or contact the **Michelin** shop at 32 blvd de l'Opéra, 75002 Paris; ☎ 01 72 68 05 00 (www.michelin-travel.com). The *Accueil à la Ferme* brochure, available from Tourist Offices, lists farms with serviced campsites.

REFUGE HUTS In mountain areas, a chain of refuge huts is run by **Club Alpin Français**, 24 av. de Laumière, 75019 Paris; ☎01 53 72 87 04, fax 01 42 03 55 60 (www.clubalpin.com).

FOOD AND DRINK

France has a gastronomic reputation that frequently lives up to reality, providing you're prepared to look beyond the ubiquitous *steak frites* (steak and chips). The regional variations are vast, and exploring them is part of the French experience. In general, north-west France tends towards butter-based cooking, with meat and cream much in evidence, while the south is dominated by Mediterranean influences such as olive oil, fish, wine and herbs; in the mountainous areas the cuisine is more rustic, based on home-cured hams and cheeses. In restaurants, *à la carte* can be expensive, but the *menu* (set menu, of which there may be several) or the *plat du jour* (today's special), can be superb value, especially at lunch time. Purely **vegetarian** restaurants are rare, but most places will have salads, variations on an omelette or possibly a veggie tart.

Coffees and beers can run up your expenses: wine is invariably cheaper – order a *pichet* of house red *(rouge)*, white *(blanc)* or rosé, all usually palatable. If you ask for *café*, you'll get a small black coffee; *café crème*, with hot milk, can be small or larger. To be sure to get the larger, order *un grand crème*. You need to specify *thé au lait* (tea with milk) or *thé citron* (tea with a slice of lemon), or your tea will be served black. Herbal teas, especially *tilleul* (lime-flower) and *verveine* (verbena) are widely available. *Thé à la menthe* (mint tea) is generally the sweet Arab speciality. **Beer** is mostly yellow, cold, French and fizzy, though gourmet and foreign beers are becoming popular. *Une pression* is the same as a *demi*: draught beer, better value than bottled. Places in the north of France have the best selection of beers. Ask about the local specialities for **liqueurs** and **apéritifs** – but beware of prices; and avoid mixed drinks for the same reason. *Baguettes* (french bread sticks) with a variety of fillings from cafés and stalls are cheap – as are *crêpes* and *galettes* (sweet and savoury pancakes). Morning markets are excellent for stocking up on picnic items. Buy your food before noon as shops can be closed for hours at lunchtime.

EDITOR'S CHOICE

Annecy; Bayeux (for the Tapestry); Brittany (especially Carnac); Carcassonne; Chartres Cathedral; Corsica; Poitiers ('Futuroscope'); Mont St Michel; Loire Valley (Amboise to Angers); Nancy; Nice; Paris; Provence (including Avignon; Arles; Nîmes; Orange; Pont du Gard; Strasbourg. Scenic rail journeys: French Alps (especially Lyon or Marseille–Turin via Chambéry, and Aix les Bains–Chamonix–Mont Blanc; ETT tables 44, 362, 365, 367, 369, 572; and Where Next from Sion?, p. 331); Béziers–Clermont-Ferrand–Nîmes (p. 124); Marseille–Menton (French Riviera p. 113); Bastia–Ajaccio (p. 128); Toulouse–Barcelona via Perpignan and the Pyrénées (p. 132).

Paris has always held great romantic allure for travellers. It has been a byword for style, glamour and romance since railway tourism began and the British started to go there for weekends in the 19th century. Everyone is familiar with Paris through films, paintings and songs to the accordeon celebrating everything about it from its bridges to its womenfolk. In the 19th century Baron Haussmann created a grand defensive plan for Napoleon III, with **boulevards** punctuated by imposing **monuments**. The idea was to prevent any more uprisings and stop the Parisians from creating barricades as the new boulevards were so wide. The dignified uniformity of Haussman's grey-roofed, tall cream shuttered houses compounds the sense of cohesion the plan created.

The geometrical layout and long vistas make it generally an easy place to get your bearings. Stand amid a nonstop whirl of traffic at the **Arc de Triomphe** and you can see far along the main axis: in one direction is the modern arch of **La Défense**, while in the other you look past the obelisk in the **Place de la Concorde** to the **Jardin des Tuileries**, where old ladies toss crumbs to plump pigeons within sight of the **Louvre**, one of the world's biggest and best art museums, ensconced on the north bank of the **Seine**.

Paris, though, is now very much a city for young people. Even the Rue de Rivoli next to the Louvre has a trendy air these days. Students traditionally hang out in the **Latin Quarter** on the Left Bank, so-called because the students originally studied everything in Latin. The older quarters such as **Le Marais** and **Montmartre** are warrens of picturesque old streets. Parisian night views (notably from a **river boat**, the top of **Eiffel Tower** and from the steps in front of **Sacré-Coeur**) are part of the experience too. Strangely, the high holiday season of August finds Paris rather empty and low key during the mass exodus south.

ARRIVAL AND DEPARTURE

There are six main rail stations in Paris, all with tourist information and left luggage etc. Each has its own métro stop; Gare du Nord, Gare d'Austerlitz and Gare de Lyon are also served by express RER trains. SNCF enquiries for the whole country are handled centrally: ☎08 36 35 35 35; premium-rate number. **Paris–Nord** (or **Gare du Nord**): for Scandinavia, Belgium, the Netherlands and the UK (via Boulogne/Calais ferries and Eurostar Channel Tunnel services). **Paris–Est** (**Gare de l'Est**): north-east France, Luxembourg, Germany, Austria and Switzerland. **Gare–St–Lazare**: Normandy and the UK (via Dieppe). **Gare–Montparnasse**: Brittany, Versailles, Chartres and TGV services to the south-west. **Gare d'Austerlitz**: Loire Valley, south and south-west France and Spain. **Gare de Lyon**: south-eastern France, the Auvergne, Provence, the Alps and Italy. Night trains to the south leave from **Gare d'Austerlitz**; night trains to Italy leave from **Bercy**. Travellers by high-speed TGV trains through France may not need to pass through Paris; there's also a TGV station at Roissy-Charles-de-Gaulle airport.

FRANCE

✈ **Roissy-Charles-de-Gaulle** is 23 km north-east of the city: flight times, ☎01 48 62 22 80 (24-hr) (www.adp.fr); three main terminals, bureaux de change, cashpoints, tourist information and hotel booking desk. Links to the city. **Roissyrail trains** to GARE DU NORD and on to CHÂTELET-LES-HALLES every 15 mins, taking 45 mins (RER B3); **Roissybus** (☎08 36 68 77 14; premium-rate number) to RUE SCRIBE near L'OPÉRA 0545–2300 every 15 mins, taking 45 mins (more if the traffic is heavy). **Air France coaches** (☎01 41 56 89 00) to the ARC DE TRIOMPHE and PORTE MAILLOT, 0600–2300 every 12–20 mins, taking 35–50 mins and to GARE DE LYON and GARE MONTPARNASSE 0700–2100 every 30 mins, taking 45–60 mins. Regular buses are slower but cost less – 🚌no. 350 serves GARE DU NORD and GARE DE L'EST, and 🚌no. 351 serves PL. DE LA NATION. A taxi to the centre (30 mins–1 hour) should cost around €50.

Orly is 14 km south; information service, ☎01 49 75 15 15; two terminals (*Sud* and *Ouest*), each with a tourist information booth and bureau de change. City transport roughly 0600–midnight (takes about 30 mins): **Orlyrail** (RER C2) to GARE D'AUSTERLITZ, 0545–2310 every 15 mins, taking 50 mins; **shuttle service, Orlyval**, to RER ANTONY every 7 mins and on to CHÂTELET-LES-HALLES or DENFERT-ROCHEREAU, taking 30 mins; **RATP Orlybus** to DENFERT-ROCHEREAU métro station, 0600–2330 every 15 mins, taking 30 mins; **Air France coaches** (☎01 41 56 89 00) to GARE MONTPARNASSE and GARE DES INVALIDES every 12 mins or so, 0600–2300 daily. A **taxi** to the centre (20–40 mins) should cost around €50.

TOURIST INFORMATION

Office de Tourisme de Paris, 127 av. des Champs-Elysées, ☎08 36 68 31 12 (premium-rate number; 24-hr recorded information in English and French; www.paris.org) (métro: CHARLES DE GAULLE-ÉTOILE/GEORGE V). Covers **Paris** and the surrounding **Île de France**, a booking service for **excursions**, a France-wide **hotel reservation** desk, desks for **SNCF** and **Disneyland Paris**.
Branches: **Gare de Lyon**, ☎01 43 43 33 24; **Eiffel Tower** (summer only), ☎01 45 51 22 15.

INFORMATION

CITY AND METRO MAP – inside back cover

MONEY The exchange office at **Gare de Lyon** stays open until 2330, and there are plenty of late-opening private bureaux de change and also lots of automatic machines (which take credit cards) at transport terminals etc.

POST AND PHONES Main post office, 52 R. DU LOUVRE, open 24 hrs for *poste restante*, telephones, Fax, telegrams and stamps; other services close at 1900. All French **telephone numbers** have 10 digits (there is no code); in Paris and the Ile de France numbers begin with 01 (or 08 for free-phone and premium-rate numbers). From anywhere in France the full 10-digit number must be dialled; from outside France drop the initial '0' of the number.

PUBLIC TRANSPORT

You can see Paris on foot, but it's worth taking advantage of the efficient and well co-ordinated public transport, made up of the **métro** (subway) and **buses of RATP** (*Régie autonome des Transport Parisiens*) and **RER** (*Réseau Express Régional*) **trains**.

Free **maps** of the networks are available from métro and bus stations (plus many hotels and big stores): the *Petit Plan de Paris* covers the centre; the *Grand Plan de Paris* is more extensive.

Métro: The impressive métro system runs every few mins 0530–0100. Lines are coded by colour and number and named after their final destination. A recent addition is the driver-less Météor line 14 linking the Madeleine with the new National Library. Maps of the whole system are at all stations and signs on platforms indicate connecting lines (*correspondances*). To reach the platform, slot your ticket into an automatic barrier, then retrieve it.

RER: This system, running 0530–0100, consists of five rail lines (A, B, C, D – plus the new 'E'), which are basically **express services** between the city and the suburbs. They form a cross through Paris and have a few central stops. The numbers following the letters (usually in the suburbs) indicate a branch from the main line. There are **computerised route-finders** at the RER stations. These give you alternative ways to reach your destination – on foot, as well as by public transport.

RATP, 53 bis quai des Grands-Augustins and opposite Gare de Lyon at 54 Quai de la Rapée, have an **information line** (in English), manned 0600–2100, ☎08 36 68 41 14 (premium-rate number). Bus-stops show the numbers of the routes using them and display route maps. On some there are on-board announcements of the next stop. **Tickets** must be validated when you board, but **passes** are just shown to the driver. Most buses run 0630–2030, but some lines continue until 0030. Services on Sundays and bank holidays (*jours feriés*) are infrequent.

Night buses (*Noctambus*) are hourly 0130–0500 and have 18 suburban routes fanning out from PL. DU CHÂTELET.

Good bus routes for **seeing the city** are nos. 24, 47, 67, 69 and 73.

TICKETS

The same tickets are used in the métro, bus and RER systems. The network is divided into five zones: green tickets are used in the two central zones, Paris proper; others, usually yellow, are used as you get further out. Outside the central zone, buy a ticket from an automatic machine or the ticket office (*guichet*). Bus tickets are valid for the whole journey in the central zone. Passes are sold at airports, stations, Tourist Offices and some tobacconists (*tabacs*). The best value for a short stay is probably the *carnet* (a book of ten tickets). The **Mobilis** pass gives one day unlimited city travel over 1–2 zones, 1–5 zones and 1–8 zones, but excludes the airports. The **Paris Visite** pass for zones 1–3 is valid for three or five consecutive days and can be extended to cover other zones; it also gives you discounts at some tourist attractions. You can also get a **Carte Orange** (weekly or monthly pass; passport photo needed). The **weekly** (*Coupon Hebdomadaire*) is valid Mon–Sun (price depends on the number of zones you require). The **monthly** (*Coupon Mensuel*) is valid from the first day of the month (price depends on the number of zones you require).

Tickets cont'd.

Ticket Jeune allows student-card holders under 26 to travel in zones 1–3 or zones 1–5 but only at weekends and holidays (fares usually increase July–Aug).

Taxis: Flagging them down in the street is rarely successful. **Licensed taxis** have roof lights; white indicates that the taxi is free, orange means it is occupied. **Fares** are determined by three time zones and a host of extras, but they are regulated. Major companies include **Alpha**, ☎01 45 85 85 85, **Taxis Bleus**, ☎01 49 36 10 10, **G7**, ☎01 47 39 47 39. **Avoid unofficial taxis**. **Tips** are expected (say 10%).

ACCOMMODATION

Whatever your price range (except rock-bottom), a lot of options are available, and finding suitable accommodation is a problem only in the busiest months (usually May, June, Sept and Oct). Bureaux d'Accueil at the main Tourist Office and main-line stations offer a **room-finding service** for hostels or hotels and there are auto-mated room-finding machines at airports. Try Budget Hotels and Accommodation (BHA), ☎01 43 57 37 33 (www.bha.fr). If you can afford it, stay in a hotel on St-Louis-en-Île.

Very central and fairly quiet medium-price options are: **Le Pavillon**, 54 R. ST-DOMINIQUE, 7E, ☎01 45 51 42 87 (patrickpavillon@aol.com), €€ (former convent with a peaceful courtyard), and **Thoumieux**, 79 R. ST-DOMINIQUE, 7E, ☎01 47 05 49 75, fax 01 47 05 36 96, €€€ (with good bistro). Other good options for hotels include **Henri IV**, 25 PL. DAUPHINE, ÎLE DE LA CITÉ, 1E, ☎01 43 54 44 53, €, and **Castex**, 5 R. CASTEX, 4E, ☎01 42 72 31 52 (www.castexhotel.com; info@castexhotel.com), €€.

Cheaper accommodation is not hard to find. Quartier Latin (Latin Quarter) and St-Germain-des-Prés, on the Left Bank, have a good range of low- to medium-price hotels; there are a few places in Le Marais, a quiet and characterful area in which to stay; a well-located inexpensive hotel is the **Pratic**, 9 R. D'ORMESSON, 4E, ☎01 48 87 80 47 (pratic.hotel@wanadoo.fr), €€. Many budget hotels are clustered round Faubourg Montmartre, in the 9th arrondissement, and there's plenty of cheap accommodation around the GARE DU NORD, though it's a somewhat sleazy area. Another really cheap place is **Hotel Tiquetonne**, 6 R. TIQUETONNE, 2E, ☎01 42 36 94 58, €, centrally sited near Les Halles (métro: LES HALLES). Close by between LES HALLES and LOUVRE stations is **Hotel Vauvilliers**, 6 R. VAUVILLIERS, 1E, ☎01 42 36 89 08 (métro: LOUVRE-RIVOLI/CHÂTELET, €–€€. Near the Pompidou Centre, the **Hôtel du Séjour**, 36 R. DU GRENIER ST LAZARE, ☎01 48 87 40 36, €, is only slightly dearer and offers very good value comfort. A pleasant hotel in a colourful pedestrian street in a southern district near Montparnasse is the **Hotel du Lionceau**, 22 R. DAGUERRE, 14E (métro: DENFERT-ROCHEREAU), ☎01 43 21 08 20, fax 01 43 21 08 21, €–€€. **Self-catering apartments** are arranged by **Paris Séjour Réservation**, 90 AV. DES CHAMPS ÉLYSÉES, ☎01 53 89 10 50 (reservation@psrparis.com). **Tourisme chez l'Habitant**, 15 R. DES PAS PERDUS, 95804 CERGY SAINT-CHRISTOPHE, ☎01 34 25 44 44, fax: 01 34 25 44 45 (www.tch-voyage.fr; resa@tch-voyage.fr), covers bed and breakfast.

Fédération Unie des Auberges de Jeunesse, 27 R. PAJOL, 18E, ☎01 44 89 87 27 (centre-national@fuaj.org), has a list of youth hostels in France. AJF (Accueil des Jeunes de France), 119 R. ST-MARTIN, 4E, ☎01 42 77 87 80, and 139 BLVD ST-MICHEL, 5E, ☎01 43 54 95 86, find beds (often cheap ones) for people aged 18-30. HI youth hostels: Le d'Artagnan, 80 R. VITRUVE, 20E, ☎01 40 32 34 56 (métro: PORTE-DE-BAGNOLET); Cité des Sciences, 1 R. JEAN-BAPTISTE CLEMENT, LE PRÉ ST-GERVAIS, 19E, ☎01 48 43 24 11 (métro: HOCHE, PORTE DE PANTIN); Jules-Ferry, 8 BLVD JULES FERRY, 11E, ☎01 43 57 55 60 (métro: RÉPUBLIQUE); Léo Lagrange, 107 R. MARTRE, 92110 CLICHY, ☎01 41 27 26 90 (métro: MAIRIE DE CLICHY). The Woodstock Hostel, 48 R. RODIER, 9E, ☎01 48 78 87 76 (métro: ANVERS), has young, friendly staff and is 10 mins walk from Gare du Nord.

Easily the most central campsite is Camping du Bois de Boulogne, 2, ALLÉE DU BORD-DE-L'EAU, 16E, ☎01 45 24 30 00 (métro: PORTE MAILLOT). Next to the Seine and very popular, so book well in advance.

FOOD AND DRINK

Paris is still a great place to eat, with many fabulous restaurants, both French and exotic, at relatively cheap prices. Cafés and bars are the cheapest, and brasseries and *salons de thé* are more expensive. The closer to the bar you stand, the less you pay. Self-service restaurants are usually fine, if a little institutional, and a snack at a crêperie will usually keep hunger at bay. Set lunches tend to be much better value than the evening equivalents. A trip to the supermarket and an hour's picnic in the Tuileries gardens of the Palais Royal are also a lovely way to lunch.

For evening meals, study the set menus outside most restaurants; these often provide a reasonable choice at affordable prices. The Latin Quarter, Marais, Montmartre and Montparnasse are good areas for cheap eating and multi-ethnic cuisine, especially Greek, North African, East European and Vietnamese. For kosher food, try R. DES ROSIERS and R. XAVIER PRIVAS. The weekly listings magazine, *Pariscope*, provides a guide to Paris restaurants.

If you fancy eating *al fresco*, make an early evening visit to R. MOUFFETARD (métro: MONGE/CENSIER DAUBETON) or R. DE BUCI (métro: ST-GERMAIN-DES-PRÉS/MABILLON), where a range of mouth-watering delicacies is on offer; or try the organic products market, BLVD RASPAIL, on Sun morning (métro: RENNES). Around BLVD DE LA CHAPELLE on Sat morning there is a huge exotic food market.

HIGHLIGHTS

Almost everything in Paris has an entrance fee, and this can be quite steep. Some places give you up to 50% discount if you are under 25 and have an ISIC card. Paris Visite gives discounts on some major attractions. Much more comprehensive is the *Carte Musées et Monuments* (Museums and Monuments Card), which offers entrance and reductions to some 70 museums and monuments in and around Paris for 1, 3 or 5 days; available from participating museums and monuments, tourist offices, principal métro and RER stations, FNAC ticket counters and Batobus stops.

Unmissable freebies include **Père Lachaise Cemetery**, the view from the **Pompidou Centre**, **Notre-Dame** and **Sacré-Coeur**; there are **reduced entry fees** on **Suns** to the **Musée d'Orsay**, the **Musée Rodin** and the **Louvre** (which is free on the first Sun of the month and cheaper on other days after 1500).

Most monuments are on the **Right Bank**, while the islands in the middle of the River Seine are where the city began and offer some of the best architecture. The **Left Bank** is more laid-back, traditionally popular with artists and the Bohemian crowd.

THE ISLANDS (LES ÎLES) Take time out just to wander round the largely 17th-century Île St-Louis, as well as the major sights on **Île de la Cité**, which is linked to it by a footbridge (métro: CITÉ). The great twin-towered cathedral of **Notre Dame**, built between 1163 and 1345, is one of the world's finest Gothic buildings. The tiny **Ste-Chapelle** (in the courtyard of the Palais de Justice) has acres of stunningly beautiful stained glass – on a sunny day, it's like standing in a kaleidoscope. The **Conciergerie**, once a prison for those awaiting the guillotine, is also worth a look.

THE RIGHT BANK (LA RIVE DROITE) Just over the bridge from the islands, the Hôtel de Ville marks the start of the **Marais**, a Jewish district filled with charming small streets and squares (make a point of seeing the exceptionally beautiful Renaissance PL. DES VOSGES, a prime picnic spot; the **Maison Victor Hugo**, where the novelist resided, occupies a corner), as well as several fine museums. The cream are probably **Musée Carnavalet**, 23 R. DE SEVIGNE, 3E, dedicated to the history of Paris, and **Musée Picasso**, 5 R. DE THORIGNY, 4E (closed Tues), which has an excellent selection of the artist's work (métro for both: ST-PAUL/CHEMIN VERT).

Just outside the area is the unmistakable **Centre Pompidou** (also known as Beaubourg; Wed–Mon 1100–2200, closed Tues), R. ST MARTIN (métro: RAMBUTEAU), a high-tech metal and glass shopping mall. It's thumpingly provocative (with its ducts and pipes stuck on the outside) though showing signs of wear, but it's impossible not to be drawn up the escalator for the view; inside there's a wonderful cross-section of art in the **Musée National d'Art Moderne** (closed Tues). Outside are humorously eccentric fountains by the modern Swiss sculptor, Tinguely.

Back beside the river is the **Louvre** (métro: PALAIS-ROYAL; enter via métro to avoid long queues; Thurs–Mon 0900–1800, Wed 0900–2145; closed Tues). From here, the formal **Jardins des Tuileries** lead along the river to the PL. DE LA CONCORDE. At the far end **Jeu de Paume**, 20 R. ROYALE (métro: CONCORDE/TUILERIES) hosts changing exhibitions of modern art, while the **Orangerie**, PL. CARROUSEL, is devoted to the Impressionists and post-Impressionists, notably Renoir, Matisse and Picasso – it was created largely as a show-place for eight of Monet's large waterlily paintings, which have two oval rooms to themselves.

From PL. DE LA CONCORDE the AV. DES CHAMPS-ELYSÉES leads up towards the **Arc de Triomphe**, PL. CHARLES-DE-GAULLE (métro: CHARLES DE GAULLE-ÉTOILE); open 0930–2300 Apr–Oct; 1000–2230 Nov–Mar. Near the river south of the Arc de Triomphe, the PL. DE L'ALMA is immediately above the road tunnel where Princess Diana fatally crashed in 1997 and has become an unofficial memorial to her.

THE LEFT BANK (LA RIVE GAUCHE) Go up the **Eiffel Tower**, CHAMP DE MARS (métro: BIR-HAKEIM); open 0930–2300, 0900–2400 mid June–Aug) – either take the lift to the highest level or (much cheaper) climb 700 steps to the second level. Then head towards the magnificent 17th-century **Les Invalides**, AV. DE TOURVILLE (métro: LATOUR-MAUBOURG/VARENNE), to see Napoleon's tomb and the **Musée de l'Armée** (Army Museum), with its many Napoleonic exhibits. Behind this is the **Musée Rodin**, 77 R. DE VARENNE; (métro: VARENNE), a magnificent house and garden, is full of the sculptor's works (0930–1745; closed Mon).

Continuing along the river, the **Musée d'Orsay**, 1 R. DE BELLECHASSE, 7E (métro: SOLFÉRINO), open Tues, Wed, Fri and Sat 1000–1800, Thurs 1000–2130, Sun 0900–1800, closed Mon), is a converted railway station that houses a spectacular collection of 19th- and early 20th-century art, including works by Monet, Manet, Van Gogh and Delacroix.

Beyond this are the narrow medieval streets of the Latin Quarter, home of the **Sorbonne University** and two great parks: **Jardins du Luxembourg** and **Jardin des Plantes**, PL. VALHUBERT. Between them is the Panthéon, PL. DU PANTHÉON, France's hall of fame, full of the remains of and memorials to the great and the glorious. **Musée National du Moyen-Age**, 6 PL. PAUL-PAINLEVÉ (métro: CLUNY-LA SORBONNE/ST MICHEL/ODEON), in a 16th-century monastery, contains a vast number of wonderful medieval tapestries and other works of art.

FURTHER OUT North of the river **Montmartre**, once the haunt of artists, offers the most accessible views of the city. Topping the hill are the overblown white cupolas of the basilica of **Sacré-Coeur**, built at the turn of the 20th century. The area is now besieged by tourists and touts, yet somehow the charm of the place outweighs the kitsch as portrait artists await custom at their easels in the nearby PL. DU TERTRE.

On the north-eastern edge of the city, **Parc de la Villette** (metro: PORTE DE LA VILLETTE) offers a range of attractions. The main one is the vast **Cité des Sciences et de l'Industrie**, a state-of-the-art science museum, both in its architecture and in its contents. The Parc de la Villette can be reached by canal each Sun from Bastille; boats leave BASSIN DE L'ARSENAL in front of the Bastille column and take a leisurely 2 hrs through tunnels and up the Canal St Martin.

The city's largest park, **Bois de Boulogne** (métro: PORTE-DAUPHINE), is a big Sunday strolling ground, fun for observing Parisian life, and looking at some of the most elegant of the city's suburbs; after dark it's a very different place – famous for its transvestite nightlife and not that safe. Nearby is the **Musée Marmottan** (R. LOUIS-BOILLY; métro: LA MUETTE; closed Mon), housing a choice collection of Monet paintings, including

TOURS

Paris Vision, 214 R. DE RIVOLI, 📞01 42 60 30 01, offer **recorded commentary multilingal bus tours**, all the main sights in about two hours. **Caisse Nationale des Monuments Historiques et des Sites**, HÔTEL DE SULLY, 62 R. ST-ANTOINE, 📞01 44 61 20 00, operate **daily walking tours** with specific themes. **Maison Roue Libre**, 95 BIS R. RAMBUTEAU, 📞01 53 46 43 77, and **Paris à vélo, c'est sympa!**, 37 BLVD BOURDON, 📞01 48 87 60 01, offer **cycling tours** of Paris and also rent scooters. Most of the **boat companies** operate half-hourly departures, with multilingual commentaries and some offer evening **dinner cruises**. The glass-topped **Bateaux-Mouches** have frequent departures from PONT DE L'ALMA, 📞01 40 76 99 99 (recorded info). For bookings, 📞01 42 25 96 10. Other companies include **Bateaux Vedettes de Paris**, 📞01 47 05 71 29, from PORT DE SUFFREN, and **Bateaux Parisiens**, 📞01 44 11 33 44, from PORT DE LA BOURDONNAIS. Buy a ticket before boarding. The **Batobus**, 📞01 44 11 33 99, is a water-bus (without commentary) every 25 mins 1000–1900 (Apr–Oct), stopping at the Eiffel Tower, the Musée d'Orsay, St Germain, Notre-Dame, the Hôtel de Ville, the Louvre and Champs Elysées. You can pay per stop or get a day-ticket or two-day ticket.

several water lilies and scenes of the garden at Giverny.

The **Cimetière Père Lachaise** (métro: PÈRE LACHAISE) is the most aristocratic of cemeteries, a fantastically atmospheric place both for the quality of the monuments and the people who are buried there (who include Bizet, Chopin, Oscar Wilde, Edith Piaf, Balzac, Corot and, most famously of all, Jim Morrison.

A little way out of town to the south west is the royal palace of **Versailles**, an unmissable attraction because of its sheer scale and luxury. Built in the 17th century by Louis XIV it was designed to dazzle all comers and to show the pre-eminence of the Sun King. The doomed Marie Antoinette, Queen of his grandson Louis XVI, used to play at milkmaids in her fake farmhouse 'Le Petit Trianon' in the palace grounds, in the days before she was captured and guillotined by the mob in the French Revolution at the end of the 18th century. Fontainebleau is the other famous royal palace to the south. Dating from a century earlier it was the home of François I.

> **THE LOUVRE**
> is one of the greatest art museums in the world. Housed in a former palace, it's a sightseeing marathon, with miles of corridors. Its most famous exhibits, the **Mona Lisa** (*La Joconde* in French) and the **Venus de Milo**, are always surrounded by vast crowds. I M Pei's glass pyramid has formed the startling entrance since 1989.

NIGHT-TIME AND EVENTS

The monthly *Paris Sélection* and annual *Saisons de Paris* listings are available (free) from Tourist Offices. There's also a 24-hr information line, 📞08 36 68 31 12 (premium rate). Two weekly listings are *l'Officiel des Spectacles* and *Pariscope*, the latter of which has an 8-page English language section (*Time Out Paris*), both on sale at newsagents.

Half-price theatre tickets can be purchased for same-day performances from the kiosks at 15 PL. DE LA MADELEINE and PARVIS DE LA GARE

Montparnasse, 15e (métro: Montparnasse Bienvenue). Both open Tues–Sat 1230–2000 and Sun 1230–1600; credit cards are not accepted.

Paris is famous for the **huge revues** staged (mainly) in Montmartre, notably **Bal du Moulin Rouge**, the **Lido de Paris** and the **Crazy Horse Saloon**, 12 av. George V. The best one and most Parisian is **Le Paradis Latin**. The famous **Folies-Bergère** is no longer a revue. Be warned – these shows are exorbitantly expensive.

There are regular seasons of both ballet and opera at **Opéra-Bastille**, 120 r. de Lyon, **Opéra-Garnier**, 8 r. Scribe (which sells cheap stand-by tickets on the day of the performance), and **Opéra-Comique**, Salle Favart, 5 r. Favart. There are also numerous concerts, held everywhere from purpose-built auditoria to museums, with a variety of free performances in several churches (including Notre Dame, every Sun evening).

Jazz is so popular that it has a special information service: **Centre d'Information du Jazz**, 22 r. Soleillet, 20e, ☎01 43 15 11 11 (www.irma.asso.fr/cij). Other live music (especially rock) is also easy to find, and there's no shortage of discos and other places to dance.

At cinemas, there are often discounts on Sun morning. VO (*Version Originale*) means the film is in the original language, while VF (*Version Française*) means it's been dubbed.

The most famous annual celebration is **Bastille Day** (13–14 July), when fireworks and parades mark the anniversary of the storming of the city prison in 1789.

Other major events include **Mardi Gras** (Feb); **May Day workers' marches** (1 May); the **French Open Tennis Championships** (late May–early June); **Fête de la Musique** (June); the final stage of the **Tour de France** cycle race along the Champs Elysées (last or second to last Sun July); and **Festival de Jazz** (late Oct).

SHOPPING

You can get everything you may want, but don't expect bargains. To admire designer styles, head for r. de Faubourg St-Honoré, av. Montaigne and r. de Rivoli. More reasonable prices can be tracked down at **Les Halles**, **St-Germain-des-Près** and the r. de Rennes. The most famous department stores are **Galeries Lafayette**, 40 blvd Haussmann, **Printemps**, 64 blvd Haussmann, and, on the Left Bank, and **Au Bon Marché**, 24 r. de Sèvres.

Markets (specialist and otherwise) are big business in Paris (both covered and open-air), so the Tourist Office produces a free list.

The best-known flea-market is **St Ouen** (métro: St Ouen/Porte de Clignancourt), held Sat–Mon 0730–1800, which consists of 16 separate markets, including **Jules-Vallès** (curios, lace and postcards), **Marché Paul-Bert** (second-hand goods), **Marché Serpette** (products from the 1900s–1930s) and **Marché Malik** (second-hand clothes and records). Bargains are hard to find. You might do better at Porte de Montreuil (métro: Porte de Montreuil), held Sat–Sun 0700–1930.

SIDE TRIPS FROM PARIS

VERSAILLES (RER line C to Versailles-Rive Gauche, then walk through the town.) Versailles was the pride and joy of Louis XIV, the long-reigning 'Sun King' who in 1668 transformed his father's hunting lodge to this stupendous palace. Most famous of all are the dazzling Galerie des Glaces (Hall of Mirrors) and the Petit Trianon and Grand Trianon – two elegant pavilions built for the king's mistresses – but also seek out Marie Antionette's dairy where she used to milk cows and act the part of a peasant. At the height of summer the crowds can make it a bit hard-going, but the huge grounds, with their statuary, topiary and water parterres, are always rewarding. Open daily.

FONTAINEBLEAU (Frequent suburban trains from Gare de Lyon to Fontainebleau-Avon.) This sumptuous palace represents one of the pinnacles of French renaissance architecture (closed Tues), and has gardens by the great 18th-century landscaper Le Nôtre; the adjacent Fontainebleau Forest is a good place for stretching your legs.

DISNEYLAND PARIS (RER line A to Marne-la-Vallée/Chessy takes you to the gates.) Disney's first incursion into Europe is as big as its American counterparts – including Main Street, USA (a period re-creation), a Wild West experience in Frontierland, the favourite Disney characters at Fantasyland, a look at the future in Discoveryland, and everything from the jungle to the Far East at Adventureland. Open daily (www.disneylandparis.com).

PARC ASTÉRIX (RER line B3 to Roissy-Charles de Gaulle, then shuttle bus.) The plucky Roman-hating Gallic cartoon hero Astérix is immortalised in this theme park (which is much more French than Disneyland Paris), with heart-stopping rides, acrobats, duels, dolphins and a Roman arena. The shows are easy for non-French speakers to follow (closed some Mondays and Fridays; phone 03 36 68 30 10 to check; www.parcasterix.com).

WHERE NEXT FROM PARIS?

Gare de Lyon is the Parisian station for the south and is served by the high-speed TGV trains (small supplement payable for rail pass holders; reservation required, but often possible to make a few minutes beforehand). These trains get you down to southern France in 3–4 hrs (5½ to Nice), with services to Marseille, Nice, Aix-en-Provence, Perpignan, Béziers and elsewhere, via Lyon and Avignon. (If you want to use the TGV to get to southern France without going through Paris, you can start your journey at Lille-Europe, especially if you are coming from London.)

*Additionally you can take direct services to join routes in other countries, including **Amsterdam, Barcelona, Basel, Berlin, Brussels, Cologne, Dresden, Frankfurt, Lausanne, Madrid, Milan, Prague, Rome, Vienna**; see also International Routes (pp. 41–42).*

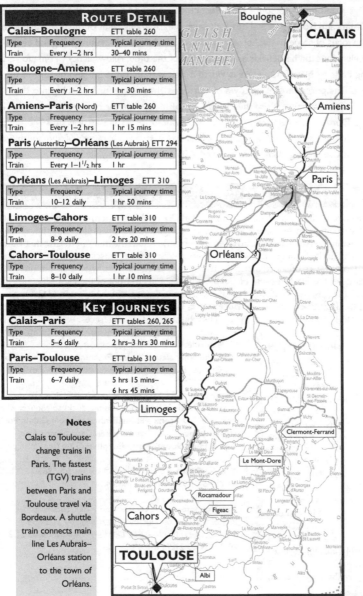

ROUTE DETAIL

Calais–Boulogne   ETT table 260

Type	Frequency	Typical journey time
Train	Every 1–2 hrs	30–40 mins

Boulogne–Amiens   ETT table 260

Type	Frequency	Typical journey time
Train	Every 1–2 hrs	1 hr 30 mins

Amiens–Paris (Nord)   ETT table 260

Type	Frequency	Typical journey time
Train	Every 1–2 hrs	1 hr 15 mins

Paris (Austerlitz)–Orléans (Les Aubrais) ETT 294

Type	Frequency	Typical journey time
Train	Every 1–1¹/₂ hrs	1 hr

Orléans (Les Aubrais)–Limoges   ETT 310

Type	Frequency	Typical journey time
Train	10–12 daily	1 hr 50 mins

Limoges–Cahors   ETT table 310

Type	Frequency	Typical journey time
Train	8–9 daily	2 hrs 20 mins

Cahors–Toulouse   ETT table 310

Type	Frequency	Typical journey time
Train	8–10 daily	1 hr 10 mins

KEY JOURNEYS

Calais–Paris   ETT tables 260, 265

Type	Frequency	Typical journey time
Train	5–6 daily	2 hrs–3 hrs 30 mins

Paris–Toulouse   ETT table 310

Type	Frequency	Typical journey time
Train	6–7 daily	5 hrs 15 mins– 6 hrs 45 mins

Notes

Calais to Toulouse: change trains in Paris. The fastest (TGV) trains between Paris and Toulouse travel via Bordeaux. A shuttle train connects main line Les Aubrais–Orléans station to the town of Orléans.

FRANCE

This grand north to south cross-section of France begins from the Channel ports of **Calais** and **Boulogne** and heads through the flat arable lands of the north that formed the focus of some of the fiercest fighting of World War I. **Amiens** is a good centre for seeking out the battlefields and memorials of the time. Allow plenty of time for crossing Paris by Métro. **Orléans** is worth a stay, with its cathedral and history of Joan of Arc. The porcelain-making town of **Limoges** gives scope for branching into the more out-of-the-way uplands of the Massif Central; meanwhile the main route continues into the Dordogne, a rural region that's much visited for its prehistoric sites and unspoilt old towns, castles and villages. **Cahors** has a strong character of the south, while **Toulouse** is a big, demanding city and **Albi** a highly worthwhile detour.

CALAIS

Just under 40 km from the English coast at Dover, this busy cross-channel port is not a place to linger in, as it gets brisk trade from English daytrippers stocking up with cheap booze at the **Auchan** and **Carrefour** hypermarkets and the mammoth **Cité de l'Europe** mall near the Channel Tunnel loading area, west of town (buses available). There's also a decent range of shops along the main roads from the port, where the famous Rodin statue of the **Six Burghers of Calais**, which stands in front of the Flemish-style **Hôtel de Ville** (town hall), commemorates the English capture of the town in 1347. Opposite, in the **Parc St-Pierre**, is the **Musée de la Guerre**, devoted to a more recent conflict – World War II – and originally used as a bunker by German forces.

INFORMATION

P&O
(Dover)
📱 (44) (0)870 600 0600, fax (44) ((0)1304) 863464
(www.posl.com);
SeaFrance
(Dover)
📱 (44) (0)870 571 1711, fax (44) ((0)1304) 240033
(www.seafrance.com);
Hoverspeed
(Dover)
📱 (44) (0)870 524 0241, fax (44) ((0)1304) 865203
(www.hoverspeed.co.uk)

🚆 **Calais-Ville**, the main station, is almost opposite the Hôtel de Ville. The other station, **Calais-Fréthun**, near the mouth of the Channel Tunnel, serves the Eurostar (London–Paris).

🚢 All the companies run free shuttles, for valid ticket holders, between **Calais-Ville** station and the docks to connect with sailings. **P&O Stena** and **SeaFrance** sail from **Calais Port**; **Hoverspeed** (SeaCats and SuperSeaCats) departs from **Calais High-Speed Ferry Terminal** (3 km from main port).

ℹ️ **Tourist Office**: 12 BLVD. CLEMENCEAU; 📱 03 21 96 62 40, fax 03 21 96 01 92 (www.ot-calais.fr).

🏨 Plenty of hotels in the centre. Good value rooms at the Bristol, 13–15 R. DU DUC DE GUISE, 📱/fax 03 21 34 53 24, €. **Hostel**: AV. DU MARÉCHAL DE LATTRE DE TASSIGNY, 📱 03 21 34 70 20, fax 03 21 96 87 80.

BOULOGNE

The **Vieille Ville** (Old Town) sits above the largely unremarkable modern part of Boulogne. If you've just stepped off the ferry, the walk around the 13th-century city walls immediately transports you into the real France, and provides views of the harbour. Within these ramparts, the 19th-century **Basilique Notre-Dame** draws together elements from St Paul's in London and St Peter's in Rome. The premier modern addition to Boulogne's tourist attractions is **Nausicaä**, on the seafront at BLVD. SAINTE BEUVE, one of the largest aquariums in France, equipped with under-water observation tanks. **La Matelote** (opposite Nausicaä), is one of the best fish restaurants in town.

Boulogne-Ville, 1 km south of the centre; all buses stopping here go to the centre.

Buses leave the BLVD F. MITTERRAND for weekend return trips to Folkestone or Canterbury (G.B.) via the Channel Tunnel in Calais.

Tourist Office: 24 BLVD GAMBETTA, 📞03 21 10 88 10, fax 03 21 10 88 11. There is also a branch (summer only) on PARVIS DE NAUSICAÄ, 📞03 21 33 95 51. From the station, take BLVD DAUNOU to the port and keep following the port around to the fish stalls: the Tourist Office is opposite.

Boulogne has good value hotels right in the heart of town. Try the reasonably priced **Hôtel de Lorraine**, PL. DE LORRAINE, 📞03 21 31 34 78, fax 03 21 32 91 42, €–€€, or **Hôtel de Londres**, 22 PL. DE FRANCE, 📞03 21 31 35 63, fax 03 21 83 50 07, €€, both 2-star and central. **Hôtel au Sleeping**, 18 BLVD DANOU, 📞03 21 80 62 79, fax 03 21 10 63 97, €–€€, is convenient and cheap. **Youth Hostel** (HI): PL. ROUGET-DE-LISLE, 📞03 21 99 15 30, fax 03 21 99 15 39, is 100m from the station.

AMIENS

Two world wars did great damage to what was a major industrial centre, sparing only the **Cathédrale de Notre-Dame** which survives as the largest in Europe and arguably France's purest example of Gothic architecture. The west doorway lingers in the memory, a 'book in stone' featuring the famed *Beau Dieu* portal. Restored in keeping with its original character, the winding streets of the **St-Leu** district, straddling the Somme just north of the cathedral, date from medieval times. In summer, take a boat trip on the tiny canals criss-crossing the 'Hortillonnages' (market gardens), just beyond the cathedral.

The main station is about 500 m south-east of the cathedral. The grim concrete **Tour Perret** provides a prominent landmark for your return to the station. To reach the cathedral from the station, turn right on BLVD D'ALSACE LORRAINE and then second left on R. GLORIETTE. Certain buses are allowed into the pedestrianised centre, but it is usually much faster to walk – and certainly the best way to explore.

Tourist Office: 6 BIS R. DUSEVEL, 📞03 22 71 60 50, fax 03 22 71 60 51 (www.amiens.com/tourisme).

FRANCE

PARIS

See p. 63.

Trains from **Calais** arrive at **Paris Nord** station. Ask at Information (*Renseignements/Accueil*) which station your connection leaves from, and allow 1 hr to cross Paris via métro.

ORLÉANS

Strategically sited in the middle of Ancient Gaul, Orléans has been attacked from Roman times to World War II, yet much of the rather austere historic centre has survived, including a number of Renaissance mansions. Taking pride of place in the spacious PL. DU MARTROI is a statue of **Jeanne d'Arc** (Joan of Arc or the 'Maid of Orléans'), who saved Orléans from the English in 1429 before they burnt her at the stake as a witch. The nearby **Maison de Jeanne d'Arc**, PL. DU GÉNÉRAL DE GAULLE, is a reconstruction of the house where she stayed, and houses a museum recounting her life and the story of the events of 1429. The annual **Fête de Jeanne d'Arc** (Apr 29, May 1 and 7–8) features a 'real' Jeanne riding through the streets.

Jeanne celebrated her triumph at the city's most impressive monument, the **Cathédrale Sainte-Croix** (Holy Cross Cathedral), where she is commemorated by a series of 19th-century stained glass windows. A guided tour visits the impressive roof structure before taking in the panoramic view over the city.

Gare d'Orléans is on the northern edge of the centre, right by the **pl. d'Arc** shopping complex; R. DE LA RÉPUBLIQUE runs straight ahead to PL. DU MARTROI, in the heart of town. Gare d'Orléans is actually on a short spur, just off the main rail line, and through-services stop only at nearby **Les-Aubrais-Orléans** station. A train shuttle service (*navette*) linking the two stations connects with every through-train; there is also a tram service.

R. M-PROUST, ☎02 38 53 94 75, a block from Gare d'Orléans (connected by a covered passage).

☐ **Tourist Office**: 6 R. ALBERT 1ER; ☎02 38 24 05 05, fax 02 38 54 49 84.

Advance booking is recommended. For reasonably priced places, try around R. DU FG-BANNIER and PL. GAMBETTA. The 2-star **Hôtel Le St-Aignan**, 3 PL. GAMBETTA, ☎02 38 53 15 35, fax 02 38 77 02 36, €€, and the small **Hotel Saint Martin**, 52 BLVD ALEXANDRE MARTIN, ☎02 38 62 47 47, fax 02 38 81 13 28, €, are good value. The central **Le Brin de Zinc**, 3 R. SAINT PIERRE DU MARTROI has a restaurant, ☎02 38 53 38 77, fax 02 38 62 81 18, €; also central and cheap is the **Sauvage**, 71 R. DE BOURGOGNE, ☎02 38 62 42 31, fax 02 38 77 17 74, €. **Hostel**: 1 BLVD DE LA MOTTE SANGUIN, ☎02 38 53 60 06, fax 02 38 52 96 39, 10 mins from the cathedral (☐ G or SY).

WHERE NEXT FROM ORLÉANS?

*Train it down to Tours (pp. 91–92; journey time 1 hr, frequent services, ETT table 296) to pick up the Paris–Bordeaux line. On the way stop off at **Blois**, with its superb château where the Duc de Guise and his brother were murdered on the orders of Henri III in 1588, and then visit the 440-room Château de Chambord nearby.*

LIMOGES

Capital of the Limousin region, Limoges is a large industrial city, renowned for producing high-quality enamel and (to some, often overly frilly) porcelain, but it has a delightful old centre, dating in part from the 11th and 13th centuries, comprising a web of dark, narrow streets filled with half-timbered houses, small boutiques, antique and china shops. Surrounded by well-maintained botanical gardens and overlooking the River Vienne is the Gothic **Cathédrale de St-Etienne** (St Stephen's). One of the world's best collection of Limoges porcelain and faïence is on show at the **Musée Adrien-Dubouché**, PL. WINSTON-CHURCHILL, with over 12,000 pieces.

Gare des Bénédictins, 500 m north-east of the old town. Walk straight along AV. DU GÉN. DE GAULLE, across PL. JOURDAN and into BLVD DE FLEURUS – or take 🚌 nos. 8 /10 to PL. JOURDAN.

Tourist Offices: BLVD DE FLEURUS, ☎05 55 34 46 87, fax: 05 55 34 19 12.

Cheap accommodation can be found around the train station.

There are well-priced ethnic restaurants at the southern end of R. CHARLES MICHELS. For an al fresco eating alternative, stock up at the **Halles Centrales** (covered market), open daily until 1300. The **Jardin de L'Eveche** by the cathedral makes a charming picnic area.

WHERE NEXT FROM LIMOGES?

Trains head east to Clermont-Ferrand (ETT table 326) with optional detour to Le Mont-Dore; see p. 127.

CAHORS

An important Roman base on the tortuously winding river Lot, Cahors became famous for wine that was at times considered to be finer than that of Bordeaux. Its major monument, frequently depicted on wine labels, is the 14th-century **Pont Valentré**, west of the centre – take the R. DU PRÉSIDENT WILSON to get to it – a six-arched fortified bridge with three towers. Gallo-Roman remains dot the town, and medieval houses are grouped around the cathedral.

10-mins walk west of the centre: leave PL. GAMBETTA by AV. J-JAURÈS (to the right) and turn left on R. DU PRÉSIDENT WILSON. At BLVD GAMBETTA, turn right and then right again onto PL. F-MITTERAND for the **Tourist Office**.

Tourist Office: PL. F-MITTERAND, ☎05 65 53 20 65, fax 05 65 53 20 74.

Hôtel de la Paix, 30 PL. ST MAURICE, ☎05 65 35 03 40, fax 03 65 35 40 88, €, and the 8-room **Hôtel La Bourse**, 7 PL. CLAUDE ROUSSEAU, ☎/fax 03 65 35 17 78, €, are both on small squares in the old centre. **Hostels**: 20 R. FRÉDÉRIC SUISSE, ☎05 65 35 64 71, fax 05 65 35 95 92; former convent, 500 m from the station; (non-HI), 129 R. FONDUE HAUTE, ☎05 65 35 29 32.

WHERE NEXT FROM CAHORS?

SNCF buses heading east from Cahors snake along one of the most beautifully sinuous sections of the Lot valley to **Figeac**, a likeable old town that makes a pleasant base for a day or two. The bus carries on to Conduché, from where it's a walk of just over 5km past Cabrerets to **La Grotte du Pech-Merle**. This cave is one of Europe's great underground sights, not only for its stalactites and stalagmites, but also for the abundant Stone-Age art, including paintings of horses and bison, ochre-outlined 'signatures' of human hands, and fossilised footprints of a man and a child. Also on the way are **Saint-Cirq-Lapopie** and **Carjac**, quaint medieval villages well-worth visiting.

On the rail line north from Figeac to Brive la Gaillarde, **Rocamadour** is the stunningly situated village (4 km from Rocamadour station) set on narrow ledges of a cliff face, where the famous Black Virgin has drawn pilgrims since the 12th century. The village actually looks more impressive from a distance. Wall-to-wall kitsch shops pander to the tourists and the devout who pack its main street for much of the year, and the atmosphere is not a little surreal.

TOULOUSE

Now a lively university city and cultural centre, the capital of the Midi region is one of France's largest cities, not consistently attractive but with a wealth of medieval religious art. The pinky-red brick of many of the grandiose town houses has earned the city the epithet of the *Ville Rose*.

The centre is walkable, but there is also an efficient bus service, run by **SEMVAT** (7 PL. ESQUIROL) and a modern one-line métro. Tickets cover both, the best value being the *carnet* (pack) of ten, available from ticket booths or the main office: buses only sell single tickets. Maps of the bus network are available from the Tourist Office, SEMVAT and ticket booths.

Many of the main attractions are in the old town, centred on **pl. du Capitole**, dominated by the 18th-century **Le Capitole** (town hall); most of the best-value restaurants are here. The town's liveliest part is **pl. St Georges**, which is usually covered with café tables.

The superb **Basilique St-Sernin** is the sole survivor of an 11th-century Benedictine monastery established to assist pilgrims en route to Santiago de Compostela (p. 191). The **Musée des Augustins** has an exceptional show of medieval sculptures rescued from long-gone city churches.

🚉 **Toulouse–Gare Matabiau**, north-east of the city; 15–20- min walk from PL. DU CAPITOLE – or take the métro (the station stop is **MARENGO–SNCF**). The railway station has baths and showers.

ℹ️ **Tourist Office**: DONJON DU CAPITOLE, PL. CHARLES DE GAULLE, ☎ 05 61 11 02 22, fax 05 61 22 03 63 (www.ot-toulouse.fr).

A wide range of hotels means finding space is seldom a problem. Get the (free) *Hôtels Restaurants* booklet from the Tourist Office. Budget places can be found in the centre, around PL. WILSON (R. ST-ANTOINE) and PL. DE CAPITOLE (R. DU TOUR and R. ROMIGUIÈRES). There are cheap hotels around the station, but the area is quite unpleasant. The **Hôtel du Grand Balcon**, 8 R. ROMIGUIÈRES, 🖃 05 61 21 48 08, fax 05 61 21 59 98, €€, is famous as having been where Antoine Saint-Exupéry, the author of *Le Petit Prince*, stayed on several occasions. The **Beauséjour**, 4 R. CAFFARELLI, 🖃/fax 05 61 62 77 59, €, and the **Hôtel des Arts**, 1BIS R. CANTEGRIL, 🖃 05 61 23 36 21, fax 05 61 12 22 37, €, are both budget and right in the centre of town. Further out, the **Hôtel de l'Université**, 26 R. EMILE CARTAILHAC, 🖃/fax 05 61 21 35 69, €, is in a quiet student quarter, near the St Sernin Basilica. **Hostel**: 3 R. DES GALLOIS, 🖃 05 61 52 29 56. **Campsites**: all four are on the outskirts of the town, but accessible by bus (information from the Tourist Office).

LA CITÉ DE L'ESPACE

A recent newcomer is **La Cité de l'Espace**, east of **Toulouse** and reached by 🚌 no. 19. Situated in a large park, there are exhibitions on a multitude of space themes, a planetarium and the 'Terradome': learn how our earth was formed. The rocket *Ariane 5* stands in its own purpose-built garden. Open daily Apr–Oct.

WHERE NEXT FROM TOULOUSE?

Albi (about an hour from Toulouse; ETT table 323), another city of pink-red brick, has one of the strangest cathedrals in Christendom: from outside it resembles a fortress (erected by crusading bishops in the wake of their systematic slaughter of the peaceable Cathar sect in the 14th century), its interior completely covered with murals, including a depiction of Heaven and Hell intended to strike terror and unswerving faith into the hearts of the congregation. It's a scene that was familiar to Henri Toulouse-Lautrec, the city's best-known son, many of whose most famous works are displayed in the adjacent Musée Toulouse-Lautrec. He emerged as one of the great portrait artists; he chose to depict prostitutes for the reason that brothels gave him a unique opportunity to observe women at their most unaffected and unposed. For an explanation of the major pictures, rent the multi-lingual audio tour.

Alternatively join the **Biarritz–Marseille** route (p. 103) or continue from Toulouse over the Pyrénées on the **Toulouse–Barcelona** route (p. 132).

CHERBOURG

Bayeux

Dieppe

Rouen

Paris

Lunéville

Nancy

STRASBOURG

ROUTE DETAIL

Cherbourg–Bayeux   ETT table 275

Type	Frequency	Typical journey time
Train	11 daily	1 hr

Bayeux–Rouen   ETT table 275

Type	Frequency	Typical journey time
Train	4 daily	3 hrs

Rouen–Paris   ETT table 270

Type	Frequency	Typical journey time
Train	Every 1–2 hrs	1 hr 20 mins

Paris–Nancy   ETT table 390

Type	Frequency	Typical journey time
Train	13 daily	2 hrs 50 mins

Nancy–Lunéville   ETT table 390

Type	Frequency	Typical journey time
Train	Every 1–2 hrs	20 mins

Lunéville–Strasbourg   ETT table 390

Type	Frequency	Typical journey time
Train	5 daily	1 hr 8 mins

Notes

Bayeux to Rouen: change at Caen. Cherbourg to Strasbourg: change trains in Paris.

KEY JOURNEYS

Cherbourg–Paris   ETT table 275

Type	Frequency	Typical journey time
Train	4–7 daily	3 hrs–3 hrs 30 mins

Paris–Strasbourg   ETT table 390

Type	Frequency	Typical journey time
Train	6–7 daily	4 hrs

RAIL TOUR: CHERBOURG – PARIS – STRASBOURG

The prelude to Paris is a trip through **Normandy** (*Normandie*), named after the invading Norsemen who settled in the Seine valley in the Dark Ages. To the north are some of the most attractive chalklands of the region, dotted with gracious manors and half-timbered farmhouses and culminating in great white cliffs around **Dieppe**. It was on the beaches of Normandy that the Allied invasion began in June 1944; many larger towns were badly bombed and have been reconstructed with varying standards of skill. East of Paris, the route crosses the unspectacular **Champagne** region, Épernay being the industry's headquarters (where you can tour champagne cellars by underground train and often enjoy free samples afterwards). Next is **Nancy** with its monumental architecture, indisputably the star of Lorraine, a region separated by the Vosges hills from Alsace, where the architecture, dialect and place names are distinctly Germanic. On the French side of the Rhineland plain, **Strasbourg** leads you into Germany.

CHERBOURG

Essentially just a commercial and military port, Cherbourg is more a convenient resting place than a base for exploration of the coast. It was liberated by American troops three weeks after the landings on Utah beach to give the Allies a deep-water port for bringing in heavy vehicles. One point of interest is the **Fort du Roule**, which overlooks the town and port. Inside, the **Musée de la Libération** commemorates the Allied landings and the liberation of Cherbourg and the Cotentin peninsula.

PL. JEAN JAURÈS, at the south end of Bassin du Commerce (harbour). The Gare-Maritime (ferry port) is northeast of the town centre; a shuttle bus runs between the two.

DAY TRIP FROM CHERBOURG

A bus service (the bus station is opposite the rail station) heads down the Cotentin peninsula to the hilltop town of **Coutances**, via the villages of Martinvast and medieval Bricquebec, whose ancient fortress has a mighty keep housing a tiny museum.

There are cross-channel ferry services to the UK: Poole (ETT table 2145), Portsmouth (table 2160) and Rosslare (table 2010).

i **Tourist Office:** 2 QUAI ALEXANDRE III, 02 33 93 52 02; fax: 02 33 53 66 97. On the far side of Bassin du Commerce, between the lifting bridge and R. MARÉCHAL FOCH. An office also opens at the Gare-Maritime on ferry arrivals and departures, 02 33 44 39 92.

The area north of the Tourist Office offers some cheap lodging options. Try the **Hôtel de la Renaissance**, 4 R. DE L'ÉGLISE 02 33 43 23 90, fax 02 33 43 96 10, €–€€, with views of the sea; or **Hôtel de la Gare**, opposite the station, 02 33 43 06 81, fax 02 33 43 12 20, €–€€. **Hostel:** 55 R. DE L'ABBAYE, 02 33 78 15 15, fax 02 33 78 15 16, 3 km from the station by nos. 3/5 to 'Chantier'.

BAYEUX

One of the first towns liberated by the Allies after World War II, Bayeux escaped any damage to its fine medieval centre, which is still dominated by the spires of the magnificent **Cathédrale Notre-Dame**, a marriage of Norman, Roman and Gothic styles.

One of the most remarkable historical records in the world is the **Bayeux tapestry**: 70 m of linen embroidered in the 11th century, illustrating the Norman Conquest of England (famously portraying the Battle of Hastings) – thought to have been commissioned by the Bishop of Bayeux from an Anglo-Saxon workshop run by monks. Despite the passage of time, the colours are bright and the design is amazingly detailed. The historical explanations and displays in the **Musée de la Tapisserie**, where it is housed, are essential to interpreting the real thing fully; but do hire an audio-guide as well.

DAY TRIP FROM BAYEUX

Low tide at **Arromanches** (about 10 km from Bayeux, 🚌 no. 74), reveals the remains of Mulberry Harbour – the artificial port and floating landing-stage for transporting troops and vehicles from GB during D-Day operations. Visit the **Musée du Débarquement** for a comprehensive panorama of the events leading up to and during D-Day.

The **Musée Mémorial de la Bataille de Normandie**, 1944 BLVD FABIAN WARE, is probably the best museum in the area for its explanations and depictions of the World War II Normandy landings.

🚊 PL DE LA GARE, 10–15 mins walk south-east of the centre; turn left on BLVD SADI CARNOT, bearing right until it becomes R. LARCHER. Continue to R. ST-MARTIN on the left: the Tourist Office is on the right. There are also buses into the centre from the bus station right by the train station.

ⓘ **Tourist Office:** PONT ST-JEAN, ☎ 02 31 51 28 28, fax 02 31 51 28 29 (www.bayeux.tourism.com).

WHERE NEXT FROM BAYEUX?

A neat way of avoiding Paris is by changing at Caen for trains to Le Mans and Tours (ETT tables 275 and 271), both on the Paris–Bordeaux route (see p. 86).

ROUEN

Your first stop in Rouen should be the **Cathédrale Notre-Dame**, the subject of a series of Monet's paintings. An example of his work showing the west front can be seen at the attractively restored **Musée des Beaux Arts**, PL. VERDREL.

The old city was considerably damaged during World War II but has been well restored, with a wealth of colourful half-timbered buildings gracing the centre. Wander from the cathedral down the main street, R. DU GROS HORLOGE. Here a 16th-century gatehouse supports the equally ancient *Gros Horloge* itself, with its traditional Renaissance single hand. At the end of the road, in PL. DU VIEUX MARCHÉ, a 20-m high cross by the church dedicated to Saint Joan of Arc marks the spot where she was burned at the stake.

La Tour Jeanne d'Arc, R. DU DONJON, is the only remaining tower of the castle where Joan of Arc was imprisoned just before her execution. Entrance is free for students.

🚉 R. JEANNE D'ARC, 1 km north of the centre. Either walk down into town (10–15 mins) or take the métro. The centre is pedestrians only, with all the sights within walking distance of each other, so avoid the bus and métro day-pass unless you plan on leaving the city centre.

ℹ️ **Tourist Office:** 25 PL. DE LA CATHÉDRALE, ☎ 02 32 08 32 40; fax 02 32 08 32 44, right in front of the cathedral.

🛏️ There are many affordable hotels in town, most in the north, but there are also some in the old city. Try **Hôtel Bristol**, 46 R. AUX JUIFS, ☎ 02 35 71 54 21, fax 02 35 52 06 33, €€, close to the cathedral; or two-star **Hotel des Carmes**, 33 PL. DES CARMES, ☎ 02 35 71 92 31, fax 02 35 71 76 96, situated in one of the liveliest squares and part of the 'Hôtels de Charme' association. Round the corner at 52 R. DES CARMES is **Hôtel des Arcades**, ☎ 02 35 70 10 30, fax 02 35 70 08 91, with comfortable rooms and a friendly owner. Near the train station **Hôtel Normandya**, 32 R. DU CORDIER, ☎ 02 35 71 46 15, has rooms with fine views of the city.

DIEPPE

Dieppe, reached in just over an hour from Rouen by train (ETT table 270) and with ferries to Newhaven in England, is an attractive coastal town, with lofty white cliffs rising either side of the resort and bathing beach, and a flint and sandstone château-museum perched up high. Down below in the harbour, a renowned Saturday market (PL. NATIONALE/ GRANDE RUE/R. ST JACQUES) draws people from afar. The long-distance walkers' path GR21 follows the clifftops north to Le Tréport and south to Etretât, but has slid away in several places. Various guidebooks detailing local walks are available from the **Tourist Office**, PONT JEHAN ANGO, ☎ 02 32 14 40 60, fax 02 32 14 40 61. Accommodation includes **Le Grand Duquesne**, 15 PL. ST JACQUES, ☎ 02 32 14 61 10, fax 02 35 84 29 83, €€, right by the market; and **Le Pontoise** 10 R. THIERS, ☎ 02 35 84 14 57, €€. **Youth hostel:** 48 R. LOUIS FROMAGER, ☎ 02 35 84 85 73, fax 02 35 84 89 62 (4 km from rail station).

PARIS

See p. 63.

Trains from Cherbourg/Rouen arrive at **Paris St Lazare** station, while trains for the Strasbourg direction leave from **Paris-Est** station. Allow 1 hr to cross Paris via the métro (lines 3 and 7, changing at OPÉRA) or use the new RER line E from HAUSSMANN ST LAZARE to MAGENTA, close to **Paris-Est**.

NANCY

The historical capital of Lorraine is a stylish town, though surprisingly little known for its architectural treasures. Three squares, each World Heritage Sites, combine to make one of the greatest architectural set pieces in France: cream stone, ornate gateways and stately arches characterise the 18th-century **place Stanislas**, constructed by ex-King Stanislas Leszcynski of Poland, and with its entire south side taken up by the palatial **Hôtel de Ville** (town hall), behind which is the PL. D'ALLIANCE, and to the north, through the Arc de Triomphe, the 15th-century PL. DE LA CARRIÈRE.

In the early 1900s art nouveau made its mark on the city. You can pick up leaflets of walking tours taking in the best examples from the Tourist Office, or visit the **Musée de l'École de Nancy**, 36 R. DU SERGENT BLANDAN (🚌 no. 123 to Painlevé or Thermal) for fine exhibits of the style.

🚊 PL. THIERS; a 10-min walk from the town centre along R. STANISLAS.

ℹ️ **Tourist Office:** PL. STANISLAS, ☎03 83 35 22 41, fax 03 83 35 90 10.

🏨 If you fancy staying in an official historic monument, **Grand Hôtel de la Reine**, 2 PL. STANISLAS, ☎03 83 35 03 01, fax 03 83 32 86 04, €€–€€€, fits the bill, but nearby **Hôtel Stanislas**, 22 R. SAINTE CATHERINE, ☎03 83 37 23 88, fax 03 83 32 31 02, €€, is far more affordable. The nearest (HI) **hostel** is 15th-century **Château de Rémicourt**, 149 R. DE VANDOEUVRE, VILLERS-LÈS-NANCY, ☎03 83 27 73 67, fax 03 83 41 41 35, 4 km west of Nancy station (🚌no. 26 to ST FIACRE). Close by is **Camping de Brabois,** AV. P-MULLER, VILLERS-LÈS-NANCY, ☎03 83 27 18 28, fax 03 83 40 06 43 (open Apr–Oct; 🚌nos. 122/125 from the station to Camping).

🍴 Try PL. STANISLAS and R. DES MARÉCHAUX for cheap and lively restaurants: don't forget to sample some *macarons* (almond biscuits), the town's speciality.

LUNÉVILLE

Lunéville's chief glory is its massive 18th-century **château,** built by duke Leopold of Lorraine in imitation of Versailles and graced with magnificent gardens. Inside, two museums exhibit the local traditional specialties of fine embroidered tulle (silk) and porcelain, while the Galérie Militaire details the history of the château as a military barracks. The rococo church of **St-Jacques**, PL. ST-RÉMY, has a unique baroque organ with no visible pipes.

🚊 15-min walk from the centre.

ℹ️ **Tourist Office:** AILE SUD DU CHÂTEAU DE LUNÉVILLE, ☎03 83 74 06 55, fax 03 83 73 57 95.

🏨 **Hôtel de l'Europe,** 53 R. D'ALSACE, ☎03 83 74 12 34, fax 03 83 74 54 27, €.

STRASBOURG

The old capital of Alsace, which began life as a Celtic fishing village, has grown into a most attractive city, successfully combining old with new, business with tourism. It's best known today as the seat of the **European Parliament**, housed in an imposing new building on the edge of the city. Conspicuously photogenic is the **Petite-France** quarter, a former tanning and milling quarter, with its 16th- and 17th-century houses crowded around narrow alleys and streams. The river itself is spanned by the **Ponts Couverts**, a trio of covered bridges with square towers, remnants of 14th-century fortifications. Boat trips are operated by **Strasbourg Fluvial**, ☎03 88 84 13 13. The **Cathédrale Notre-Dame**, built over three centuries, is a Gothic triumph, with its elaborately carved western façade. Highlights inside include the 13th-century **Pilier des Anges** (Angels' Pillar) and the astonishingly complicated-looking 19th-century **Horloge Astronomique** (Astronomical clock), which strikes noon at 1230 each day. The tower, a 330-step climb, provides a good view over all the city.

PL. DE LA GARE: 10-min walk to the centre (which is on an island in the River Ill) straight along R. DU MAIRE KUSS or by tram (direction Illkirch).

i **Tourist Office:** 17 PL. DE LA CATHÉDRALE, ☎03 88 52 28 28, fax 03 88 52 28 29 (www.strasbourg.com), with a branch at PL. DE LA GARE, ☎03 88 32 51 49 and at PONT DE L'EUROPE, ☎03 88 61 39 23. The Tourist Offices sell a good-value 3-day Strasbourg Pass, which covers admission to one museum (a second museum is half price), the cathedral tower, a boat trip, use of a bicycle and some half-price tours.

There's a good choice of hotels in every grade, including a clutch in the wide semi-circle of buildings around PL. DE LA GARE opposite the station, such as **Victoria**, 7 R. MAIRE KUSS, ☎03 88 32 13 06, fax 03 88 32 69 78, €€€. More reasonable and in the old centre by the cathedral, is **Patricia**, 10 R. DU PUITS, ☎03 88 32 14 60, fax 03 88 32 19 08, €€. **Hostels: René Cassin**, 9 R. DE L'AUBERGE DE JEUNESSE, ☎03 88 30 26 46, fax 03 88 30 35 16, 2 km from the station (🚌no. 2: Auberge de Jeunesse, or tram B/C to Montagne Verte) and there's an associated campsite next door; **Parc du Rhin**, R. DES CAVALIERS, ☎03 88 45 54 20; 4 km from the station (🚌nos. 2/21 to Parc du Rhin); and also (non-HI) 8 R. SOLEURE, ☎03 88 36 15 28, fax 03 88 36 71 92 (🚌nos. 10/20).

There are plenty of wholesome restaurants along R. DU MAROQUIN (near the cathedral), R. DES TONNELIERS and in the Petite France quarter.

WHERE NEXT FROM STRASBOURG?

Continue east over the border into Germany, to Offenburg or Baden-Baden (ETT table 910) on the Munich–Konstanz route (p. 283). You can also continue through Alsace to enter Switzerland at Basel (p. 317) on the Lausanne–Milan route.

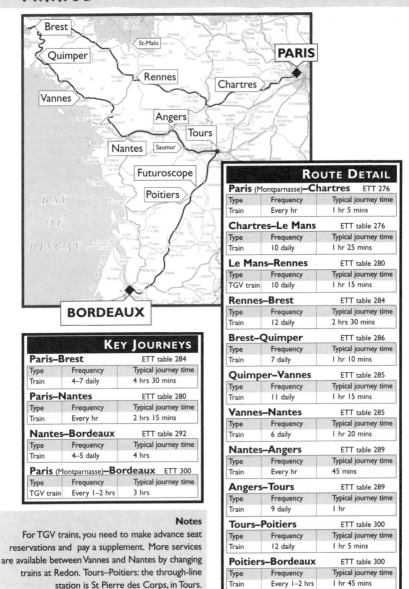

KEY JOURNEYS

Paris–Brest — ETT table 284

Type	Frequency	Typical journey time
Train	4–7 daily	4 hrs 30 mins

Paris–Nantes — ETT table 280

Type	Frequency	Typical journey time
Train	Every hr	2 hrs 15 mins

Nantes–Bordeaux — ETT table 292

Type	Frequency	Typical journey time
Train	4–5 daily	4 hrs

Paris (Montparnasse)–Bordeaux — ETT 300

Type	Frequency	Typical journey time
TGV train	Every 1–2 hrs	3 hrs

ROUTE DETAIL

Paris (Montparnasse)–Chartres — ETT 276

Type	Frequency	Typical journey time
Train	Every hr	1 hr 5 mins

Chartres–Le Mans — ETT table 276

Type	Frequency	Typical journey time
Train	10 daily	1 hr 25 mins

Le Mans–Rennes — ETT table 280

Type	Frequency	Typical journey time
TGV train	10 daily	1 hr 15 mins

Rennes–Brest — ETT table 284

Type	Frequency	Typical journey time
Train	12 daily	2 hrs 30 mins

Brest–Quimper — ETT table 286

Type	Frequency	Typical journey time
Train	7 daily	1 hr 10 mins

Quimper–Vannes — ETT table 285

Type	Frequency	Typical journey time
Train	11 daily	1 hr 15 mins

Vannes–Nantes — ETT table 285

Type	Frequency	Typical journey time
Train	6 daily	1 hr 20 mins

Nantes–Angers — ETT table 289

Type	Frequency	Typical journey time
Train	Every hr	45 mins

Angers–Tours — ETT table 289

Type	Frequency	Typical journey time
Train	9 daily	1 hr

Tours–Poitiers — ETT table 300

Type	Frequency	Typical journey time
Train	12 daily	1 hr 5 mins

Poitiers–Bordeaux — ETT table 300

Type	Frequency	Typical journey time
Train	Every 1–2 hrs	1 hr 45 mins

Notes

For TGV trains, you need to make advance seat reservations and pay a supplement. More services are available between Vannes and Nantes by changing trains at Redon. Tours–Poitiers: the through-line station is St Pierre des Corps, in Tours.

Western France offers a heady mix of wine and brandy, cathedrals, châteaux, long beaches and rocky coastlines. Beyond **Chartres** you enter **Brittany** (*Bretagne*), where regional identity is still strong and in evidence in the Breton dialect (similar to Welsh), the cuisine (featuring crêpes in particular) and numerous summer festivals in which villagers don traditional costumes. The three peninsulas on Brittany's west coast make up **Finistère** (*Finis Terrae*, the end of the earth), buffeted by the gusts of the Atlantic, which has claimed many shipwrecks. The region also abounds in quaint fishing villages, prehistoric remains, resorts and superb beaches – only the fickle climate might dampen your enthusiasm for a seaside holiday here. Just to the east, **Roscoff** is an attractive Channel port with services to **Plymouth** (England).

At **Nantes** the route joins the **Loire**, famous for its abundant châteaux and high-quality wines. Further south lies **Poitiers**. **Angoulême** stands at the eastern end of the cognac region, while **Bordeaux** is the capital of one of the world's greatest wine-producing areas.

It's also feasible to shorten the route by omitting the Loire and heading directly down from Nantes to Bordeaux via **La Rochelle**. This journey forms part of the **Paris–Granada** route (p. 41).

PARIS

See p. 63.

CHARTRES

Its spires visible from afar dominating the cornfields of the Beauce plain, and arguably the world's greatest example of the Gothic style, the **Cathédrale Notre-Dame** replaced an earlier building destroyed by fire in 1194. It's known especially for the quality and brilliance of its 13th-century stained glass, dazzling even on the dullest of days, and the wealth of carved stone, notably around the west doorways.

After the cathedral, the rest of Chartres seems somewhat insignificant, but it's an enjoyable enough place with winding streets and a pleasant riverside area by the **Eure**, which encompasses the old town and gives some choice views of the cathedral.

🚉 PL. PIERRE SÉMARD. Follow the signs to the cathedral to reach the centre.

i **Tourist Office:** PL. DE LA CATHÉDRALE, ☎ 02 37 18 26 26, fax 02 37 21 51 91 (www.chartres.com).

🏨 Chartres has a fine selection of hotels: Try the 8-room **Chêne Fleuri**, 14 R. DE LA PORTE MORARD, ☎/fax 02 37 35 25 70, €, with its 2 restaurants, log fire and shady patio by the Eure River; or closer to the station is the 2-star **Jehan de Beauce**, 19 AV JEHAN DE BEAUCE, ☎ 02 37 21 01 41, fax 02 37 21 59 10, €€. **Hostel:** 23 AV NEIGRE, ☎ 02 37 34 27 64, fax 02 37 35 75 85, 🚐 minibus service from by the Tourist Office.

RENNES

A useful base for day and longer trips, the commercial and administrative capital of Brittany is not really a place to spend a lot of time in, except on Saturday mornings for the market (stock up on Breton food specialties) and in the first week of July, when the **Festival des Tombées de la Nuit** (Festival of Nightfall) takes over the town, with street theatre, music and costumed events celebrating different folk cultures. Following a huge fire in 1720, Rennes was largely rebuilt in stone, but many of the pretty half-timbered houses do remain.

The 17th-century **Parlement de Bretagne** was one of the few major structures to survive the first fire, but was less lucky when another fire broke out in 1994. The nearby 18th-century **Hôtel de Ville** (Town Hall), PL. DE LA MAIRIE, contains some fine Flemish tapestries. The **Musée de Bretagne**, 20 QUAI EMILE-ZOLA, gives an excellent background to Brittany, while the **Musée des Beaux Arts** (above it) houses a collection of French art from the 14th century onwards.

[RAIL] PL. DE LA GARE. About 15 mins' walk south-east of the centre or take the métro (VAL).

[i] **Tourist Office**: 11 r. St Yves, ☎02 99 67 11 11, fax 02 99 67 11 10 (www.bretagne35.com).

[📭] The best place to find hotels is in the area of the station. **Hôtel d'Angleterre**, 19 R. MARÉCHAL JOFFRE, ☎02 99 79 38 61, fax 02 99 79 43 85, €, is cheap and close to the station. The tiny 4-room **Rocher de Cancale**, 10 R. ST MICHEL, ☎02 99 79 20 83, €€, is more central, a stone's throw from the PL. DES LICES. **Youth hostel**: 10–12 CANAL ST-MARTIN, ☎02 99 33 22 33, fax 02 99 59 06 21, 2 km from the station (🚌no. 18 to Auberge de Jeunesse). **Campsite**: **Camping Municipal des Gayeulles**, R. DU PROFESSEUR M-AUDIN, ☎02 99 36 91 22, fax 02 23 20 06 34 (🚌 no. 3 to GAYEULLES); open Apr–Sept.

[🍴] PL. DES LICES following through R. ST MICHEL right to R. ST MELAINE; and R. ST GEORGES and R. DU CHAPITRE, are packed with a variety of multi-cultural restaurants.

SIDE TRIPS FROM RENNES There are regular buses linking Rennes to many other Breton towns. The long-distance bus station is at blvd Solférino (just near the station). Trains run from Rennes to St-Malo (every 1–2 hrs, journey time 1 hr; ETT table 281) and then on to Dol, where you should change for Dinan.

The romantically named **Côte d'Emeraude** (Emerald Coast) and **Côte de Granit Rose** (Coast of Pink Granite) are fringed with rugged cliffs and unspoilt sandy beaches, interspersed with sheltered fishing ports, many doubling as resorts.

St-Malo, beautifully poised at the mouth of the rock-girt Rance estuary and endowed with a fine white sand beach, has been carefully restored since wartime destruction and makes a good base for exploring the coastline by bus. [i]**Tourist Office**: Esplanade St Vincent, ☎02 99 56 64 48, fax 02 99 56 67 00 (www.ville-saint-malo.fr). [📭]**Hôtel Le Croiseur**, 2 pl. de la Poissonnerie, ☎02 99 40 80 40, fax 02 99 56 83 76,

€€: simply furnished rooms, in the old town; or if you want to be right opposite the beach try, in nearby Paramé, **Les Charmettes**, 64 blvd Hébert, ☎02 99 56 07 31, fax 02 99 56 85 96, €€. **Hostel**: 37 av. du RP Umbricht, ☎02 99 40 29 80, fax 02 99 40 29 02, 1.5 km from the station. Buses and ferries connect St-Malo with **Dinard**, an appealing resort of early 20th-century turreted villas with a beach.

East of St-Malo, the astonishing fortified abbey of **Le Mont St-Michel** perches on its craggy island; unfortunately, it is hideously over-run in high season. Despite the major alterations to the causeway access until 2007, this World Heritage site must not be missed; walk around the abbey, the village and the ramparts for sweeping views of the surrounding bay. The nearest rail station is at **Pontorson**, 9 km away, but more regular bus lines run from St-Malo as well as from Rennes (ETT table 273).

A little way inland, **Dol-de-Bretagne** was built mainly in the 13th century and, although now little more than a village, it has a fine Roman cathedral and arcaded timber-framed houses. At **Champ-dolent** is one of the finest *menhirs* (prehistoric standing stones) on the north coast, standing 9 m high. Not far away is **Dinan**, with a 16th-century castle, a Romano-Gothic basilica and cobbled streets of 15th-century houses.

QUIMPER

Quimper is a good base for exploring south-western Finistère. The Gothic **Cathédrale St-Corentin** features a strangely off-centre nave. Close by are the well-presented collections of **Musée Breton** and the outstanding **Musée des Beaux-Arts**, both of which capture the spirit of Brittany.

The **Musée de la Faïence** has an excellent collection of traditional Quimper porcelains; the porcelain factory next door has tours.

Av. DE LA GARE: east of town, 15 mins' walk to the centre; turn right along AV. DE LA GARE, cross the River Odet and turn left. For the Tourist Office, do not cross the river but follow it down to just past the cathedral.

Tourist Office: pl. de la Résistance, ☎02 98 53 04 05, fax 02 98 53 31 33.

Budget hotels by the station are **Le Derby**, 13 av. de la Gare, ☎02 98 52 06 91, fax 02 98 53 39 04, €, and **Le Pascal**, ☎02 98 90 00 81, fax 02 98 53 21 81, €€. **Hostel**: 6 av. des Oiseaux, ☎02 98 64 97 97, fax 02 98 55 38 37, 3km from the station (🚌 no. 1 to Chaptal).

Side Trips from Quimper **Douarnenez** (30 mins north-west by SNCF bus) is a working fishing port with lots of activity to watch on the harbour and quays. The major sight is **Le Port-Musée**, where you can explore a variety of vessels and watch demonstrations of skills such as boat-building and rope-making.

The **Crozon peninsula**, further north, is also reachable by bus (plan an overnight stop).

At the tip of the peninsula (forming part of the **Parc Naturel Régional d'Armorique**), **Camaret** is a small resort and lobster fishing port; a long sea wall leads to a huge 17th-century tower built by the military architect Vauban.

Boat trips down-river from Quimper lead to Benodet, from where other boats go to the **Îles de Glénan** (the path round the isle of St Nicolas makes a pleasant walk) – or to **Concarneau**, a busy fishing port with a medieval *Ville Close* (walled island town).

VANNES

Situated at the top of the **Gulf of Morbihan** – an inland sea strewn with over 40 islands, mostly private. **Vannes** makes a handy base for exploring south-eastern Brittany, and taking a boat trip around the Gulf. At the heart of the walled town, near the imposing **Cathédrale de St-Pierre**, the ancient covered market of **La Cohue** has been restored, with upstairs in the old courthouse an art gallery combined with exhibitions on Breton culture. Behind the cathedral, you can climb a short stretch of the old ramparts, where the Joliette watchtower gives a view over the long roof of the former wash-house.

🚋 A good distance north-east of the centre: turn right onto av. Favrel et Lincy and left along AV. VICTOR HUGO. Continue straight ahead for the old centre and the port.

ℹ️ **Tourist Office**: 1 r. Thiers, ☎02 97 47 24 34, fax 02 97 47 29 49, near the port.

🏨 The town gets crowded in season, and hotels are often booked up. On the harbour front is **Le Marina**, ☎02 97 47 22 81, fax 02 97 47 00 34, €€; or close to the station is **Le Cap**, ☎02 97 47 21 88, €.

SIDE TRIPS FROM VANNES Carnac (south-west of Vannes and reachable by bus) is a major resort, with numerous campsites and caravan parks and a long beach that is packed in summer. In the area are some 5000 *menhirs*. The most famous formation is the **Alignements du Ménec**, probably dating from 3000 BC and consisting of over 1000 megaliths stretching for more than 1 km. They are now fenced off, and although you can no longer just wander up to them (compulsory) guided visits in the high season do take you inside the fence, while off season you can visit at your own pace. There's an informative prehistory museum, explaining how these mysterious structures were erected, and displaying turquoise necklaces and other finds.

Several companies offer **boat tours** around the coast and islands, but to explore properly it's better to use the regular ferries – you can reach the various departure points by bus. **Belle-Île** is the largest of the islands and offers everything from fortifications, a citadel and wonderful scenery to beaches, good walking and picturesque villages. Another of Brittany's great ancient sites is the **Île de Gavrinis**, an islet only, reached by taking a guided boat trip (in season) from **Larmor-Baden** (south-west of Vannes). The amazingly numerous megalithic remains are definitely linked to the standing stones at the nearby village of **Locmariaquer**, on the nearby mainland.

ANGERS

Former capital of the Counts of Anjou (the Plantagenet ancestors of the British royal family), this attractive town stands in one of France's major wine-producing areas, in a land of black schist and slate quarries. It is dominated by the massive stone walls of the 13th-century **Château d'Angers**, the 17 towers of which stand to only half of their original height, while the moat has been converted into formal gardens. Inside is the great series of 14th-century tapestries depicting in astonishing graphic detail the *Apocalypse of St John*. The nearby **Cathédrale St-Maurice** has a medieval façade and Gothic vaulting over an unusually wide nave, lighted by stained glass dating from several different eras.

Across the river, the **Hôpital St-Jean** contains another spectacular tapestry, the 20th-century *Chant du Monde* (inspired by the *Apocalypse*) by Jean Lurçat.

About a 10-min walk south of the centre – or 🚌 no. 1.

Tourist Office: 7–9 pl. du Prés-Kennedy, 📞 02 41 23 50 00, fax 02 41 23 50 09 (www.angers-tourisme.com)

Side Trips from Angers Infrequent trains run from Angers (taking 20–25 mins; ETT table 289) to the town of **Saumur**, with its famous cavalry riding school (the *Cadre Noir*, which mounted a heroic defence of the town in 1940, though greatly outnumbered by the Germans). The 14th-century château has a fascinating history: from a fortress for Louis I, it became a country residence for the Dukes of Anjou, then a state prison, and it now houses two museums. There are tours in English in summer. Vineyards and mushroom caves surround the town.

Like Saumur, the châteaux of the 625-mile long **Loire Valley** were mostly medieval fortresses converted into luxurious country residences by 16th-century nobles. Although some are located within range of (often infrequent) train services (the Saumur–Tours line provides the best access), many are only easily reached by car. Another ideal way to explore is by bike – which can be put on certain trains for longer distances.

Villandry is famous for its magnificent terraced gardens, with formal box-hedged beds. The fortress-like **Langeais** and the more graceful **Montsoreau** and **Montreuil-Bellay** can be reached by SNCF bus from Saumur.

TOURS

Founded by the Romans on the banks of the Loire, Tours had, by the 8th century, become an important cultural centre and place of pilgrimage. Home to one of the oldest and most influential universities in France, the city also thrived during the 15th and 16th centuries when the French court and nobility streamed into the region. Today, it is the largest city on the Loire, and much has been sensitively restored after damage during World War II.

The flamboyant Gothic-style **Cathédrale St-Gatien** dates from the 13th to 16th centuries, and has some wonderful 13th-century stained glass; while the **Cloître de la Psalette,** to one side, has 13th- and 14th-century frescos. The 17th-century Archbishop's Palace is the **Musée des Beaux-Arts**; and the **Hôtel Goüin** and the **Historial de Touraine** offer different approaches to local history.

In the evening, head for the heart of the old town, around the PL. PLUMEREAU, which offers an excellent selection of cheap–moderate restaurants, many found in one of the carefully restored half-timbered houses that line this maze of mostly pedestrianised narrow streets. Walk east to R. COLBERT if you want an even greater choice.

🚉 Pl. du Maréchal Leclerc. Near the *Mairie* (Town Hall) in the city centre.

ⓘ **Tourist Office**: 78–82 r. Bernard Palissy (opposite the train station), 📠02 47 70 37 37, fax 02 47 61 14 22 (www.ligeris.com).

🏨 Many visitors prefer to stay in the small villages and towns around Tours. However, you can find a reasonable range of cheap hotels in the areas both around the station and the cathedral. There is a **youth hostel** in the Parc de Grandmont, av. d'Arsonval, 📠02 47 25 14 45, fax 02 47 48 26 59, 4 km from the station (🚌nos. 3/6/11 to Auberge de Jeunesse).

SIDE TRIPS FROM TOURS Right in the centre of the most château-laden part of France, Tours is an excellent place from which to explore the adjoining valleys of the **Loire**, **Loir**, **Cher** and **Indre**, strewn with such famous castles as **Amboise, Azay-le-Rideau, Chambord, Chenonceaux, Chinon, Loches** and **Blois**. Most are some distance apart, as well as from Tours, so take one of the many chartered bus trips, a regular bus line (info at the Tourist Office), or hire a car.

WHERE NEXT FROM TOURS?

There are train services to **Caen** *(3 hrs; ETT table 271)* *on the* **Cherbourg– Strasbourg** *route, (p. 80).*

FUTUROSCOPE

This massive theme park is dedicated to the moving image. The amazing series of pavilions – such as the one with a façade of cascading water, another like a giant rock crystal and yet another resembling organ pipes – has more than anyone could see in a day. The range of cinematic experiences – the less sedate ones have height and/or health restrictions – include a terrifying 3D projection of the world of the T Rex and a meeting with Miss Phig to combat evil in Cyber World. Liquid crystal glasses, gigantic screens and the most technologically advanced digital imaging processes are put to impressive use.

Admission rates are seasonal (from about €16 for a 4- or 6-hr evening ticket to lots more for 2-day passes with top-class accommodation, food and TGV travel) but the best option is a 2-day pass including on-site budget accommodation with breakfast (booking agency, ☎ 05 49 49 30 80). There is a forest of hotels around about, and the TGV station for Futuroscope has direct trains to Paris Montparnasse (about 1 hr 30 mins). Website for the theme park: www.futuroscope.org.

POITIERS

As one of the earliest Christian centres in France, Poitiers today boasts an impressive array of churches (though for many visitors it is just the nearest place to **Futuroscope**). The oldest, first built in 356, is the **Baptistère de Saint-Jean**, R. JEAN-JAURÈS. Almost next door is the 12th to 13th-century **Cathédrale Saint-Pierre**, R. DE LA CATHÉDRALE. Squat from the outside, inside the nave soars high, crowned by some lovely 13th-century stained glass and carved wooden choir stalls. Behind the cathedral is the **Église Ste-Radegonde**, R. DU PIGEON BLANC, first built in the 6th century with fine Romanesque and Gothic additions and alterations. Admire the former colours of the decorated façade of **Notre-Dame-la-Grande**, when they're spotlit on summer evenings. Outstanding among the secular buildings is the 13th-century **Salle des Pas Perdus** within the **Palais de Justice**.

Blvd du Grand Cerf, about 15 mins' walk from the centre; there is a pedestrian overpass shortcut.

Tourist Office: 8 r. Grandes-Écoles, ☎ 05 49 41 21 24, fax 05 49 88 65 84.

Plenty of hotels both around Futuroscope and in the town, but not easy to find budget bets. **Hostel**: I allée Roger Tagault, ☎ 05 49 30 09 70, fax 05 49 30 09 79 (🚌 no. 3 to Cap Sud or Pierre Loti).

Restaurants on R. CARNOT have regional specialties and tend to be up-market; the squares PL. DE MARÉCHAL LECLERC and PL. DE GAULLE have a wider choice. Poitiers is at the heart of a region noted for the best goats' cheeses in France.

DAY TRIP FROM POITIERS   Poitiers has a train service to the historic port of **La Rochelle** (ETT table 300), popular with the yachting set; it's an elegant place with gracious old squares, a fine old town hall, arcaded Renaissance houses and a good choice of fish restaurants. Two medieval towers preside over the harbour entrance.

BORDEAUX

Set on the **Garonne** River just before it joins the **Dordogne** and **Gironde** to travel out to sea, **Bordeaux** is the sixth largest port in France, a busy, working city with an 18th-century centre of monumental splendour surrounded by industrial gloom. But primarily the city is the commercial heart of one of the world's greatest wine-growing areas, surrounded by the vineyards of names such as **Graves**, **Médoc** and **Sauternes**.

Take a boat tour leaving from the ESPLANADE DE QUINCONCES, before strolling south to see the best of the city's historic buildings. On the way to the PL. DE LA COMÉDIE, on which stands the majestic neo classical **Grand Théâtre**, stop off en route at the **Maison du Vin**, 1 COURS DU 30 JUILLET, ☎05 56 00 22 66, for all kinds of wine information, and the Tourist Office opposite to arrange wine tours and tastings.

Most of the greatest sights of interest are within 1 square km, so you should be able to get around on foot. From the PL. DE LA COMÉDIE, the COURS DU CHAPEAU ROUGE leads to the PL. DE LA BOURSE, a pleasant square on which stand the **Musée Nationale des Douanes**, housed in the 18th-century **Customs House**, and the elegant (private) **Hôtel de la Bourse**. Just to the south of this begins the quartier **Saint-Pierre**, the bustling old town filled with small boutiques and cafés, and PL. DU PARLEMENT where restaurants abound.

About 1 km from here, along R. DES TROIS-CONILS, you come to the city's richest gathering of fine buildings and museums, including the 11th–15th-century **Cathédrale St-André** and the superb 18th-century **Hôtel de Ville** opposite, the **Musée des Beaux-Arts**, 9220 COURS D'ALBRET (nicely varied collection), and the **Musée des Arts Décoratifs**, R. BOUFFARD (furniture, silver, pottery etc.).

DAY TRIPS FROM BORDEAUX

Probably the main reason for coming to Bordeaux is to visit the great wineries spread out through the surrounding countryside. There are bus tours (ask at the Tourist Office), but also a local rail line to **Pointe-de-Grave** (ETT table 303), whose stations include such redolent names as **Château Margaux** and **Pauillac** (for **Château Mouton-Rothschild** and **Château Lafitte**). There are also services to **La Rochelle** (ETT table 292; takes 2 hrs 30 mins).

🚃 **Gare St-Jean**, R. CHARLES DOMERCQ. About 2 km from the south of the centre (🚌 nos. 1/7/8). The **Gare St Louis** serves local trains.

✈ **Bordeaux-Mérignac**, 12 km from the city, ☎05 56 34 50 50.

ℹ **Tourist Office**: 12 COURS DU 30 JUILLET, ☎05 56 00 66 00, fax 05 56 00 66 01; with an annexe at the station, ☎05 56 91 64 70 (www.bordeaux-tourisme.com)

🏨 The city has a wide range of accommodation, suitable for all pockets. As this is a port, many of the cheapest hotels, scattered around the grimy docks and the red-light district immediately around the railway station, can be rather basic. In a safer area, central but still budget, is **Le Choiseul**, 13 R. HUGUERIE, ☎05 56 52 71 24, fax 05 56 52 00 08, €€. **Hostel** (non-HI): 22 COURS BARBEY, ☎05 56 33 00 70, fax 05 56 33 00 71.

WHERE NEXT FROM BORDEAUX?

*Carry on to **Biarritz** to join the **Biarritz–Marseille** route (p. 103).*
*Alternatively carry on south over the Spanish border to **Seville** (p. 203).*

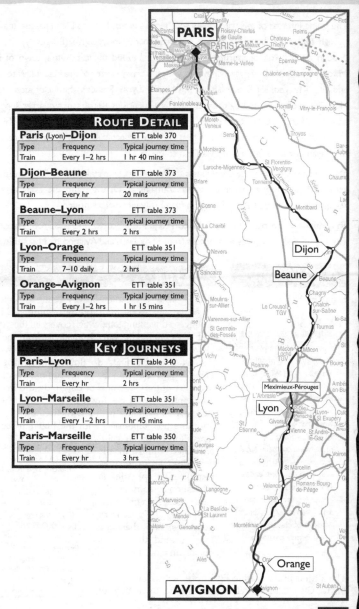

ROUTE DETAIL

Paris (Lyon)–Dijon — ETT table 370

Type	Frequency	Typical journey time
Train	Every 1–2 hrs	1 hr 40 mins

Dijon–Beaune — ETT table 373

Type	Frequency	Typical journey time
Train	Every hr	20 mins

Beaune–Lyon — ETT table 373

Type	Frequency	Typical journey time
Train	Every 2 hrs	2 hrs

Lyon–Orange — ETT table 351

Type	Frequency	Typical journey time
Train	7–10 daily	2 hrs

Orange–Avignon — ETT table 351

Type	Frequency	Typical journey time
Train	Every 1–2 hrs	1 hr 15 mins

KEY JOURNEYS

Paris–Lyon — ETT table 340

Type	Frequency	Typical journey time
Train	Every hr	2 hrs

Lyon–Marseille — ETT table 351

Type	Frequency	Typical journey time
Train	Every 1–2 hrs	1 hr 45 mins

Paris–Marseille — ETT table 350

Type	Frequency	Typical journey time
Train	Every hr	3 hrs

FRANCE

The prime interest of this trip is in its southern sections. Paris to Dijon passes uneventfully, though **Dijon**, at the heart of the wine region of **Bourgogne** (Burgundy) is appealing enough for a break of journey. Further south beyond the captivating town of Beaune, **Mâcon** is at the hub of more vineyards, with the classy whites of the Mâconnais to the west and the light reds of Beaujolais to the south. **Lyon**, France's third city after Paris and Marseille, is often missed by tourists but has a surprising Renaissance quarter, superb food and some evocative Roman remains; from there you can strike out east into the Savoie Alps into Switzerland via some of the highest and most spectacular railways in Europe, or cross the Italian border and carry on via Turin to Milan.

Meanwhile the main route continues into **Provence**, unmistakably Mediterranean in character, and harbouring the great Roman remains at **Orange** and the lively, arty city of **Avignon**, with its vast Papal Palace and famously incomplete bridge.

To continue south, travel on to **Tarascon** to join the Biarritz–Marseille route (see p. 103). The high-speed TGV gives easy access from Paris, Lyon and Avignon to **Marseille** itself.

PARIS

See p. 63.

MUSTARD AND CASSIS

In addition to the wines of Burgundy two products spring to mind when Dijon is mentioned: *moutarde* (mustard) and *crème de cassis*. The latter is the sweet blackcurrant liqueur that's often mixed with dry white wine to make *kir*, a cocktail named after a French resistance leader whose favourite tipple it was. A good *cassis* can make even a very ordinary bottle of cheap white extremely palatable.

DIJON

Dijon's partly pedestrianised city centre is dotted with attractive squares and 15th and 16th century architecture. A suggested walking tour, which covers all the main sites and takes around 90 mins, is available from the Tourist Office. The highlight is undoubtedly the massive **Palais des Ducs et des Etats de Bourgogne** which is best viewed from the PLACE DE LA LIBÉRATION. Formerly the residence of the Governors of Burgundy, this impressive palace now houses the **Town Hall** and the **Musée des Beaux Arts**, the latter with a rich ensemble of painting, sculpture and tapestries, with the highlight being the marvellously carved, gold-encrusted tombs in the Salle des Gardes (guards-room). The pl. de la Libération contains an elegant crescent of *hôtels particuliers* (17th-century mansions) and there are more behind the palace, notably in r. des Forges.

Colour Section
(i) The BA London Eye (p. 50); French TGV, Gare du Nord, Paris (p. 63)

(ii) La Grande Arche, La Défense, Paris (p. 63)

(iii) Cassis, Provence, France (p. 114); Calvi Beach, Corsica (p. 131)

(iv) Sagrada Família, Barcelona (p. 145); hanging house at Cuenca (p. 166); shepherd in front of the Alcázar, Segovia, Spain (p. 173)

The 13th-century Gothic **Eglise de Notre Dame**, in R. DE LA CHOUETTE, is celebrated for the three tiers of

SOUVENIR

arches adorning the façade. Numerous gargoyles add to the effect although these were made in 1881 by the sculptor Lagoule who apparently gave his imagination free reign in their design. High overhead, life-size figures on the 14th-century Horloge de Jacquemard (Jacquemard's clock) spring into action every quarter-hour. There are many attractive half timbered houses in R. VERRERIE as well as numerous antique shops. At the end of R. DE LA LIBERTÉ, Dijon's lively main street, stands **Porte Guillaume**, an Arc de Triomphe dedicated to the Princes de Condé, one-time Governors of Burgundy. The 6th-century Romanesque **Cathédrale de St Bénigne** has Gothic additions by Guilluame de Volpiano.

Many of Dijon's **museums** are free to students, and reduced rates are available for all by buying a special pass from the Tourist Office or from the first museum visited.

COURS DE LA GARE, 5 mins west of the centre. The station is at the end of AV. MARÉCHAL-FOCH, which leads to PL. DARCY.

Tourist Offices: PL. DARCY, ☎ 03 80 44 11 44, fax 03 80 42 18 83 and 34 R. DES FORGES, ☎ 03 80 44 11 44, fax 03 80 30 90 02 (www.ot-dijon.fr).

The lowest-priced hotels (mainly 2-star) tend to be in the old town; try the charming **Hostellerie 'Le Sauvage'**, 64 R. MONGE ☎ 03 80 41 31 21, fax 03 80 42 06 07, €€, a former staging inn. If you feel like sleeping in Napoleonic style go for the 4-star **Hostellerie du Chapeau Rouge**, 5 RUE MICHELET, ☎ 03 80 50 88 88, fax 03 80 50 88 89, €€€, built for the Emperor himself. The very central **Hôtel de la Poste le Grand Café**, 5 R. DE CHÂTEAU, ☎ 03 80 30 51 64, fax 03 80 30 77 44, is cheap with spacious rooms. **Hostels: Centre de Rencontres Internationales**, 1 BLVD. CHAMPOLLION, ☎ 03 80 72 95 20, fax 03 80 70 00 61, quite a way from the centre (🚌 no. 5 to Epirey from R. DES GODRANS; or night 🚌 A). Students could try **Foyer International d'Étudiants**, 4–6 R. MARÉCHAL LECLERC, ☎ 03 80 71 70 00, fax 03 80 71 60 48 (🚌 4/6 to Billardon). **Campsite: Camping Municipal du Lac**, 3 BLVD KIR, ☎/fax 03 80 43 54 72. By a lake about 1 km from the centre (🚌 no. 12 to CHS La Chartreuse).

There are lots of lively pizzerias and foreign restaurants, many with outside tables in summer, in the streets around PL. EMILE ZOLA. This is also the home of *bœuf bourguignonne* and *coq au vin* – well worth trying here.

WHERE NEXT FROM DIJON?

Four trains a day run to Nancy (taking 2 hrs 20 mins; ETT table 378), to join the Cherbourg–Strasbourg route (p. 80).

BEAUNE

Beaune is a charming old town of cobbled streets and fine mansions. The magnificent **Hôtel-Dieu**, R. DE L'HÔTEL-DIEU, was originally built in the 15th century as a hospital for the sick and needy. Don't miss its multi-coloured glazed roofs or the 15th-century *Polyptych of the Last Judgement*, showing sinners tumbling to an unpleasant fate. This is also the centre of the Côtes de Beaune and Côtes de Nuit vineyards, some of the finest in Burgundy; the Tourist Office lists local *caves* (wine

FRANCE

cellars) that offer tastings (*dégustations*). The old ducal palace houses a museum dedicated to the subject: **Musée du Vin**, R. D'ENFER.

Av. du 8 Septembre. East of town, just outside the old walls. For the Tourist Office, take AV. DU 8 SEPTEMBRE and follow the signs to the Hôtel-Dieu which is in the pedestrianised area. The Tourist Office is opposite (15 mins).

i **Tourist Office**: R. DE L'HÔTEL-DIEU, ☎ 03 80 26 21 30, fax 03 80 26 21 39 (www.ot-beaune.fr).

LYON

This big metropolis (population 1.5 million) at the junction of the Saône and the Rhône is not the best-known of French cities, but its old centre is really special, with a hive of charming streets and some wonderful restaurants; it's rated as one of France's gastronomic capitals. Nightlife is thriving too. The two rivers divide the city into thirds. On the west bank of the Saône is **Vieux Lyon**, the Renaissance quarter, while on the east bank of the Rhône is the business centre, the **Part-Dieu** rail station and high-rise offices and apartment blocks. In between is the partly-pedestrianised 17th- and 18th-century centre, running from PL. BELLECOUR, north to the old silk quarter of **La Croix-Rousse**.

Lyon is famous for its *traboules* – covered passageways between streets which once served as shortcuts for the silk traders and as protection from the weather for the silk they transported. Most *traboules* are in the preserved Vieux Lyon quarter and in La Croix-Rousse.

The Tourist Office in pl. Bellecour, between the two rivers, is central for exploring Lyon by foot. Head north to pl. des Terreaux to visit Lyon's best museum – the **Musée des Beaux Arts** (closed Tues). South of pl. Bellecour is the **Musée Historique des Tissus** (closed Mon), 34 R. DE LA CHARITÉ, a monument to the history of textile in general, and especially the 18th-century silk industry in Lyon. Old silk looms are still in use at **Maison des Canuts**, 10–12 R. D'IVRY, (closed Sun). Just across Pont Galliéni over the Rhône River from Perrache station is the poignant **Centre d'Histoire de la Résistance et de la Déportation**, 14 av. Berthelot (closed Mon, Tues).

PÉROUGES

Pérouges, 35 km east of Lyon, is a charming medieval hill-top village with narrow cobbled streets lined with 15th-century houses. In the centre of the main square is the Tree of Liberty, planted in 1792 to commemorate the Revolution. (Approx. 15 trains a day, fewer at weekends, taking 40 mins; trains stop at Meximieux-Pérouges, about 2 km away; you can see the village as you step off the train.)

Julius Caesar was responsible for developing the Roman town of Lugdunum, centred on the hillside of Fourvière above Vieux Lyon. Ride on the funicular railway which leaves from near the cathedral up to the **Basilique Notre Dame de Fourvière**, built in the 19th century by the people of Lyon after they had been saved from invasion, and from which there are spectacular views over the town. Then walk down to the **Musée Gallo-Romain**, 17 R. CLÉBERG (closed Mon, Tues), which has mosaics, coins and jewels, before admiring the main sight hereabouts: the neighbouring **Théâtre Romain**, R. DE L'ANTIQUAILLE, the oldest Roman amphitheatre in France (free). Take the other *funiculaire* back down to the riverside.

There are two mainline stations; many trains stop at both. **Lyon-Perrache**, pl. Carnot, is the more central. It provides left luggage facilities, 0530–2030, showers, money exchange offices, a restaurant and bar. For the Tourist Office, cross pl. Carnot, then follow r. Victor Hugo to pl. Bellecour (15 mins). **Lyon-Part-Dieu** (mainly TGVs) is on the east bank of the Rhône and serves the business district. It has similar facilities to Perrache.

i **Tourist Office:** pl. Bellecour, ☎ 04 72 77 69 69, fax 04 78 42 04 32 (www.lyon-france.com) (métro: BELLECOUR). Additional branch at 3 av. Aristide-Briand, Villeurbanne, ☎ 04 78 68 13 20, fax 04 78 37 73 74 (métro: GRATTE-CIEL).

Lyon-Saint Exupéry Airport: 32 km east of Lyon, ☎ 04 72 22 72 21. Buses every 20 mins between the airport and Perrache rail station (via Part-Dieu rail station); takes 45 mins.

There is a huge choice of hotels in every category and finding a room should not be difficult even at the height of summer. Try around the stations or in the Presqu'île quarter, north and south of the Tourist Office. **Hostels:** 41–45 montée du Chemin Neuf, ☎ 04 78 15 05 50, fax 04 78 15 05 51, ideally located in the old quarter and with local character (🚌 no. 28 from Part-Dieu rail station to Vieux Lyon quarter, then the funicular to Minimes); and 51 r. Roger Salengro, 5km to the south, ☎ 04 78 76 39 23, fax 04 78 77 51 11 (🚌 no. 35 from Bellecour to Auberge de Jeunesse). Also (non-HI): 164 r. Challemel-Lacour, ☎ 04 72 78 03 03, fax 04 78 09 16 45 (🚌 no. 12 to Moulin à Vent or 🚌 no. 32 to Challemel-Lacour). **Campsite:** Aire de la Porte de Lyon, 10 km northwest, ☎ 04 78 35 64 55, fax 04 72 17 04 26 (🚌 no. 89 from Gare de Vaise to Porte de Lyon).

Lyon is renowned for its cuisine and boasts some of the best restaurants in France serving fantastic food but often with prices to match. The most

Buses, funiculars, tramways and subway trains (métro) are run by **TCL** (*Transports en commun lyonnais*). Get the map (*plan de réseau*) from the Tourist Office or any TCL branch. The métro is modern, clean and safe. Four lines, A, B, C and D, criss-cross the city. It operates 0500–2400. The two *Funiculaires* (funicular trains) depart every 10 mins until 2200 from VIEUX LYON métro station to either the hill-top Basilique or the Roman ruins. Buses cover every corner of Lyon, generally 0500–2100, but check individual services. The two tram lines, T1 and T2, both leave from Perrache station.

NIGHT-TIME IN LYON

The weekly *Lyon Poche* lists the week's events (not in English). Clubs and discos abound, with the best areas near the Hôtel de Ville and QUAI PIERRE SCIZE in Vieux Lyon. The 1200-seat Lyon Opera House on PL. DE LA COMÉDIE is a surprising mix of 18th and 20th century architecture, with 18 storeys inside, and a glass cupola that glows red as it fills up with people. Lyon was birthplace of Guignol, the original 'Punch and Judy'. Shows for kids and adults alike are on either at the Guignol de Lyon theatre, 2 R. LOUIS CARRAND in Vieux Lyon, ☎ 04 78 28 92 57, or in the open air in the Parc de la Tête d'Or.

FRANCE

traditional restaurants are *bouchons*, mainly found in Presqu'île, the area to the north of the Tourist Office, and Vieux Lyon, where simple, and often very good-value, meals are served. The name *bouchon* dates from the time when inn keepers used to a hang a handful of straw outside so that travellers knew they could eat and drink there while their horses were being rubbed down *(bouchonner)*. Lyon has many specialities: *tablier de sapeur* are slices of tripe fried in breadcrumbs; *andouillette*, tripe sausages cooked in white or red wine; and *quenelles de brochet*, poached pike fish balls. Lyon has some wonderful street **markets**. There are food markets every day except Mon at **Les Halles** and **La Croix Rousse**. On Sun mornings don't miss the art and craft market, **Marché de la Création**, on the riverside by the cathedral in Vieux Lyon; and on the opposite bank, the *bouquinistes* stalls (old cards, maps and books) at QUAI DE LA PECHERIE.

WHERE NEXT FROM LYON?

Lyon is handily placed for exploring the Alps by rail. For a superb route into Switzerland, either to Geneva (p. 332) or to Martigny, go via Culoz, Aix-les Bains, Annecy and La Roche sur Foron, where you can either continue to Geneva or take the route via Chamonix-Mont Blanc to Martigny. There's also a (less interesting) direct line from Lyon to Geneva (ETT table 348; takes 2 hrs).

Culoz *is a gateway for the **Marais de Lavours**, a national park noted for its marshland habitats, while beyond the well-heeled lakeside spa of **Aix-les-Bains** (where excursion boats cross Lac du Bourget to the mystical monastery of L'Abbaye d'Hautecombe) is **Annecy**, an (upmarket) lakeside resort in the heart of the Savoie Alps. If you continue to Martigny, you switch to a metre-gauge line and climb into the mountains, with the option of a side-trip on the **Tramway du Mont Blanc** (ETT table 366a) from St-Gervais-le-Fayet to (summer only) the Nid d'Aigle (2386 m – and a 15-min stroll from the Bionnassay Glacier). Chamonix is placed beneath snow-capped Mt Blanc, the highest peak in the Alps; the **Montenvers rack railway** climbs 5 km to 1913 m, looking over the Mer de Glace, France's biggest glacier. A great way of venturing into Italy is by travelling to Turin via Chambéry, Modane and through the 12.8-km **Fréjus tunnel** and past the Italian ski resort of Bardonecchia.*

ORANGE

This northern gateway to Provence had a population of some 80,000 in Roman times and several sites have survived from the period. The **Arc de Triomphe** is the third largest Roman arch to have survived, and was originally in fact a gate to the ancient walled city. Dating from about 25BC, it is a majestic three-arched structure lavishly decorated with reliefs depicting battles, naval and military trophies and prisoners, honouring the victories of Augustus and the setting up of *Arausio* (Orange) as a colony.

Orange's most famous sight is its Roman **theatre**, dating from the 1st century AD and with the best preserved back wall in the Roman Empire, standing 37 m tall, a magnificent setting for the town's song and opera festival in summer. A museum opposite the amphitheatre has some unique local Roman finds as well as some intriguingly incongruous scenes of British life painted by the Welsh artist Frank Brangwyn, some 800 of his paintings having been donated to the town.

AV. F -MISTRAL, 1.5 km east of the centre; the main Tourist Office is across town, follow AV F. MISTRAL right, cross PL. DE LA RÉPUBLIQUE to R. ST MARTIN and straight on (15 mins).

Tourist Office: 5 COURS ARISTIDE BRIAND, ☎ 04 90 34 70 88, fax 04 90 34 99 22 (www.provence-orange.com). Another branch on PL. DES FRÈRES MOUNET (open Apr–Sept only).

Hôtel St Jean, 7 COURS POURTOULE, ☎ 04 90 51 15 16, fax 04 90 11 05 45, €€, the lobby is actually a cave. **Hôtel le Français**, at the station, ☎ 04 90 34 67 65, fax 04 90 51 89 50, €€, has a pool.

AVIGNON

In 1305, troubles in Rome caused the Pope to move his power base to Avignon. Wealth flowed into the town – and remained after the papacy moved back to Rome 70 years later. The city walls, built to protect the papal assets, still surround the city. Jutting from the north-western section is **Pont St-Bénézet**, the unfinished bridge famed in song (*Sur le pont d'Avignon*), inevitably a tourist trap (admission payable), but now with a museum and a restored rampart walk leading up to the **Rocher des Doms** garden with its great views over both the bridge and the nearby town of Villeneuve-lès-Avignon. Take the steps from the gardens down to the Romanesque cathedral, **Notre Dame des Doms**, dating from the 12th century and containing the tombs of Pope John XXII and Pope Benedict XII.

Adjacent is the most photographed sight in the city, the huge **Palais des Papes** (**Papal Palace**), boasting a 45m-long banqueting hall where cardinals would meet to elect a new Pope. In appearance it's more like a fortress than a palace and is still the most prominent landmark in the city. Its bleak walls are etched with arches and openings, and topped with castellations and a pair of pointy towers. You can wander by yourself or take a 90-minute guided tour in English. The popes acquired the dignified **Petit Palais** in 1335, and a couple of centuries later it was adapted into a sumptuous residence for Cardinal Giulio della Rovere, the future Pope Julius II, who took a lively interest in the arts; he began the collection of Renaissance treasures that has now made the building into an art museum. Contemporary art is to be found at the **Lambert Museum**, while several private mansions have **art collections** open to the public.

AVIGNON'S SUMMER FESTIVAL

From early July to early August, Avignon hosts one of Europe's largest drama festivals. Soak up the 'ambiance' generated by people and theatrical events of all dimensions, or watch the events themselves, held outdoors or in venues running from the majestic Palais des Papes to quaint courtyards to barn-like warehouses.

In the middle of the Rhône lies **Île de la Barthelasse**, a favourite picnic island, with its own summer swimming pool. Also try people-watching at **Place de l'Horloge**, popular for its street entertainment and outdoor cafés.

[RAIL] Avignon-Centre, just outside Porte de la République gateway in the city walls: head through this gateway and straight along COURS J-JAURÈS for the centre. Shuttle buses from this station link up to the new Avignon-TGV station, 5 km to the south.

[i] Tourist Office: 41 cours J-Jaurès, ☎04 32 74 32 74, fax 04 90 82 95 03 (www.ot-avignon.fr). Another branch at Pont d'Avignon (Apr–Oct only), ☎04 90 27 93 21.

[🏨] During the drama festival in July and August (see box p. 101) everywhere gets completely booked up and you'd do better to stay at Tarascon or elsewhere, and travel in. At other times, from Avignon-Centre head through the gateway into the old town, where you'll find a large number of reasonably priced pensions and hotels in the backstreets a few minutes away: try r. Joseph Vernet and r. Agricol Perdiguier (both off COURS J-JAURÈS). To step back to the future – just for a look as extremely expensive – visit **Cloître St Louis**, 20 r. Portail Boquier, ☎04 90 27 55 55, fax 04 90 82 24 01, €€€, a truly unique 4-star hotel. An oasis of calm just off Avignon's main street, it combines tradition and modernity; the old part is housed in original 16th-century cloisters and the new wing was designed by Jean Nouvel. The restaurant, overlooking the impressive courtyard, is particularly stunning in the evening when the cloisters are illuminated. **Hostels** (all non-HI): **Foyer Bagatelle**, Île de la Barthelasse, ☎04 90 86 30 39, fax 04 90 85 78 45 (🚌 nos. 10/11 from the post office opposite Avignon-Centre rail station to Barthelasse on bridge); also has all-year 3-star camping facilities. **Provence Accueil**, 33 av. Eisenhower, ☎04 90 85 35 02, fax 04 90 85 21 47, is close to the station but outside the city ramparts (🚌 nos. 1/2, from the post office opposite Avignon-Centre station to Champfleury). The **YMCA** is over the Rhône, in Villeneuve-lès-Avignon, 7 bis chemin de la Justice, ☎04 90 25 46 20, fax 04 90 25 30 64 (🚌 no. 10 from the post office opposite Avignon-Centre station to Monteau). **Campsites:** several on Île de la Barthelasse. Try 4-star **Camping du Pont d'Avignon**, ☎04 90 80 63 50, fax 04 90 85 22 12 (🚌 nos. 10/11, as for Foyer Bagatelle), open Mar–Oct; or 2-star **Camping les Deux Rhônes**, ☎04 90 85 49 70, fax 04 90 85 91 75 (🚌 no. 20 from Porte de l'Oulle; infrequent). Both have pools.

WHERE NEXT FROM AVIGNON?

Take the train to Tarascon (ETT table 355; 14 services a day; journey time 13 minutes) to join the Biarritz–Marseille route (p. 103). For Marseille and Nice you have a choice of direct trains – either the TGV trains (supplement payable and reservation required; ETT table 350) or the cheaper non-TGV trains (no supplement). Both are hourly; journey time by non-TGV is around 1 hr 10 mins to Marseille and about 4 hrs to Nice.

ROUTE DETAIL

Biarritz–Pau   ETT table 325

Type	Frequency	Typical journey time
Train	7 daily	1 hr 45 mins

Pau–Lourdes   ETT tables 305, 325

Type	Frequency	Typical journey time
Train	Every 2 hrs	30 mins

Lourdes–Toulouse   ETT table 325

Type	Frequency	Typical journey time
Train	9 daily	2 hr 10 mins

Toulouse–Carcassonne   ETT table 321

Type	Frequency	Typical journey time
Train	Every 2 hrs	50 mins

Carcassonne–Narbonne   ETT table 321

Type	Frequency	Typical journey time
Train	Every 2 hrs	30 mins

Narbonne–Béziers   ETT table 355

Type	Frequency	Typical journey time
Train	Every 1–2 hrs	15 mins

Béziers–Montpellier   ETT table 355

Type	Frequency	Typical journey time
Train	Every hour	45 mins

Montpellier–Nîmes   ETT table 355

Type	Frequency	Typical journey time
Train	Every hr	30 mins

Nîmes–Arles   ETT table 355

Type	Frequency	Typical journey time
Train	8 daily	25 mins

Arles–Marseille   ETT tables 351, 355

Type	Frequency	Typical journey time
Train	Every hr	50 mins

KEY JOURNEYS

Biarritz–Toulouse   ETT table 325

Type	Frequency	Typical journey time
Train	3 daily	4–5 hrs

Toulouse–Marseille   ETT table 355

Type	Frequency	Typical journey time
Train	8–9 daily	4 hrs

Toulouse–Nîmes   ETT table 355

Type	Frequency	Typical journey time
Train	7–8 daily	2 hrs 45 mins

FRANCE

From the Atlantic coast at **Biarritz**, the route edges along the plain to the vast mountain backdrops of the northern Pyrénées. The journey visits **Lourdes**, with its somewhat surreal, non-stop pilgrimage scene, **Carcassonne** with its massive fortifications, and **Montpellier**, the lively university town in Languedoc–Roussillon.

Nîmes and **Arles** are two of the great Roman sites of the Midi, and the finale, **Marseille**, is a big, bustling port, stronger in atmosphere than in sights. If you have time, stop off en route at **Tarascon** to admire the Château du Roi René, gloriously seated on the Rhône and impressively intact despite the heavy bombing of the surrounding town during World War II. You can lengthen and vary the journey by diverting onto the Béziers–Nîmes route (p. 124), heading up to Clermont-Ferrand before returning south through the Allier gorge.

BIARRITZ

The smart set have been coming to Biarritz since the splendid **beaches** and mild climate were 'discovered' in the mid-19th century by such visitors as Napoleon II and Queen Victoria. Although rather less grand now, it is still essentially a fairly upmarket coastal resort with a string of good sandy beaches, great surfing and a casino.

Gare de Biarritz-La Négresse, 3 km from the centre, along a winding road: about 40-mins walk. Left luggage facilities open daily 0900–1200 and 1415–1800. Take 🚌 no. 2 for a 15-min ride to the town hall – 🚌 no. 9 also goes there, but via a longer route.

i **Tourist Office:** 1 SQ. D'IXELLES, ☎05 59 22 37 00, fax 05 59 24 97 80 (biarritztourisme@biarritz.tm.fr). Open daily 0800–2000 (July–Aug); 0900–1800 (Sept–June). You can get free maps and information on the whole Basque region. There are branches open July–Aug at the station and at PL. CLÉMENCEAU.

Hostel: 8 R. CHIQITO DE CAMBO, ☎05 59 41 76 00.

WHERE NEXT FROM BIARRITZ?

Bayonne (bus or train from Biarritz) has better services to Toulouse.

PAU

This elegantly prosperous town is perched on a cliff above its river, providing panoramic views of the snow-capped Pyrénées. Pau's attractions are easily walkable and a free map is available from the tourist office. Its **château** (reached via R. HENRI IV from the PL. ROYALE) was the birthplace of the charismatic French monarch, Henri IV, and contains some of his personal possessions, as well as the **Musée Béarnais** (the provincial museum). Soak up more history at the **Musée Bernadotte**, 5 R. TRAN, the birthplace of one of Napoleon's marshals, whose descendants are today's Swedish royal family.

Av. Gaston Lacoste. On the southern edge of town. It's a tough 15-min uphill walk to the centre, but the funicular railway opposite the station will take you to PL. Royale for free. It operates every 3 minutes, Mon–Sat 0645-1230, 1255–1930 and 1955–2140; Sun 1330–1930 and 1955–2100.

Tourist Office: PL. Royale, ☎05 59 27 27 08, fax 05 59 27 03 21 (www.ville.pau.fr; smt@ville-pau.fr).

LOURDES

In a mountainous riverside setting, Lourdes is surrounded by natural beauty, but is overwhelmed by its status as a pilgrimage centre. The place swarms with visitors (over six million a year), and every other building is a shop overflowing with astonishingly kitsch religious souvenirs of the plastic Virgin genre.

DAY TRIPS FROM LOURDES

There are many regular bus excursions in and around the surrounding area, including **Parc National des Pyrénées**, which follows the Franco-Spanish border for 100 km, providing magnificent views; the Basque country; and the **Grottes de Bétharram**, vast underground caverns full of limestone formations.

It all began in 1858, when the 14-year-old Bernadette Soubirous claimed to have seen the Virgin Mary in a local grotto. After 17 further appearances, a spring appeared by the **grotto**, and once word spread that its waters had effected miraculous cures, there was no looking back: the spring still flows and its water supplies local baths and drinking fountains. The 19 baths (rebuilt in 1955) are open to sick and healthy alike and hundreds of people plunge into them daily. To discover more about Bernadette and her life, you can visit various key locations in the centre of town, including **Boly Mill**, where she was born, and the *cachot*, where she lived during the time of the apparitions. Obtain a free map of the grotto from the Forum information centre, St Joseph's Gate, off PL. Mgr Laurence.

Av. DE LA Gare. 10-mins' walk north-east of the centre. ▨ no. 1 (Apr–Oct only) goes to the centre and the Grotto. To reach the Tourist Office, turn right out of the station down Av. DE LA Gare, and then left at the end along Chaussée Maransin to PL. Peyramale.

Tourist Office: PL. Peyramale, ☎05 62 42 77 40, fax 05 62 94 60 95 (www.lourdes.edi.fr/lourdes; lourdes@sudfr.com).

Paris aside, Lourdes has more hotels than anywhere else in France, including a huge number of budget and moderate establishments close to the station and around the castle. The tourist office has an excellent list of all types of accommodation. Try the **Hôtel de l'Europe**, 38 Av. Peyramale, ☎05 62 94 01 50, fax 05 62 94 80 62, €€; or the **Hôtel Concorde**, 7 R. du Calvaire, ☎05 62 94 05 18, fax 05 62 42 22 06, €€, for moderate lodging. **Hostel** accommodation (non-HI) can be found at **Accueil International**, R. DE L'Arrouza, ☎05 62 94 34 54. There are 13 **campsites**, including two along the RTE DE LA Forêt: **Camping du Loup**, ☎05 62 94 23 60, and **Camping de la Fôret**, ☎05 62 94 04 38.

TOULOUSE

See p. 78.

CARCASSONNE

From the 13th century, Carcassonne was the greatest stronghold of the Cathars, a Christian sect ruthlessly annihilated by Albigensian crusaders sent out on the orders of Rome. The great **fortress** held out for only a month, but the structure survived for long afterwards, until being quarried for building materials. Most of what you now see was restored in the 19th century by the architect Viollet-le-Duc.

Today there are two distinct towns. On one side of the River Aude is the Ville Basse, (Lower Town), which although modern and grid-like, is in fact of 13th-century origins. The more impressive **Cité** perches on a crag on the other bank of the river and is entered by two gates – Porte d'Aude and Porte Narbonnaise. If you are walking up from Ville Basse, look for the footpath beside St-Gimer, which leads to the 12th-century Château Comtal (Counts' Castle) that dominates the centre – visits inside are by tour only.

Behind Jardin André Chenier, in the Ville Basse, on the north bank of the Canal du Midi. It's a long walk to La Cité – about 30 mins and the last part uphill; cross the bridge and head straight on R. G. CLEMENCEAU. Turn left onto R. DE LA LIBERTÉ and then right along BLVD JEAN JAURÈS. At SQ. GAMBETTA, take R. DU PORT-VIEUX and cross the old bridge, from where La Cité is signposted. 🚌 no. 4 goes from the station to SQ. GAMBETTA, then change and take 🚌 no. 2 to just outside the walls of La Cité.

i **Tourist Offices**: In the Ville Basse – 15 BLVD CAMILLE-PELLETAN, 📞04 68 10 24 30, fax 04 68 10 24 38 (www.tourisme.fr/carcassonne; carcassonne@fnotsi.net). In La Cité – **Tours Narbonnaise**, 📞04 68 10 24 36, fax 04 68 10 24 37.

🛏 The most picturesque area to stay is in the Cité but hotels can be extremely expensive. Best to find a hotel in the Ville Basse and 'commute': a couple of cheap options are **Hôtel Astoria**, 18 R. TOURTEL, 📞04 68 25 31 38, fax 04 68 71 34 14, €, and **Hôtel Le Cathare**, 53 R. J.-BRINGER, 📞04 68 25 65 92, €. **Hostel**: R. DU VICOMTE TRENCAVEL, 📞04 68 25 23 16, fax 04 68 71 14 84, though is in La Cité. **Camping: Camping de la Cité**, RTE DE ST-HILAIRE, 📞04 68 25 11 77, across the Aude, ask Tourist Office for bus routes (open Mar 1–early Oct).

NARBONNE

A fine Midi town, lapped by vineyards and good beaches, Narbonne is dominated by the magnificent Gothic **Cathédrale St-Juste-et-St-Sauveur**. It was originally designed to be one of the biggest churches in Christendom, but was never finished as the authorities would not allow the town walls to be pulled down to build the nave. It has some lovely stained glass and the views make it worth climbing the towers. Together with the adjacent **Palais des Archevêques** (archbishop's palace) this forms a remarkable group of civil, military and religious buildings. Entered between two medieval towers, the **Passage de l'Ancre** is a lovely cobbled, L-shaped way between the cathedral and the old and new palaces; the new palace contains archaeological and art museums.Below ground is **L'Horreum**, 16 R. ROUGET-DE-L'ISLE, a well-preserved Roman granary.

10-mins' walk north-east of the centre: turn right along BLVD F-MISTRAL to the river, and left along R. J-JAURÈS.

Tourist Office: PL. SALENGRO, ☎ 04 68 65 15 60, fax 04 68 65 59 12 (www.mairie.narbonne.fr; office.tourisme.narbonne@wanadoo.fr), is near the cathedral. Guided city tours (including museum admission) leave from here (July–Sept; fee payable).

Founded in 1648 and with a slightly faded air is the centrally located **La Dorade**, 44 R. J-JAURÈS, ☎ 04 68 32 65 95, €€. Virtually adjacent, across a back street is the less expensive **Hôtel de Paris**, ☎ 04 68 32 08 68, €.

WHERE NEXT FROM NARBONNE?

Trains to Perpignan take 50 minutes and run every 1–2 hrs (ETT table 355); from there you can join the Toulouse–Barcelona route (p. 132).

BÉZIERS

Vineyards spread from the outskirts of Béziers at the heart of the Languedoc wine country. Rising from the Pont-Vieux over the river Orb, the old town climbs to the 13th-century Gothic **Cathédrale de St-Nazaire**, which replaces an earlier cathedral that was burned down with 20,000 citizens locked inside during the Albigensian Crusade (1209).

DAY TRIP FROM BÉZIERS

West of town, the **Canal du Midi** leads from the Mediterranean to the Atlantic and there are day cruises through the locks and vineyards, while buses offer a way to reach the long, sandy beaches not far from town.

As an antedote to that bleak episode, the **Musée du Biterrois**, a wine/local history collection, is recommended for its entertainingly diverse exhibits.

For the centre of town, head straight up through the charming Plateau des Poètes. This is a lovely 19th-century park with statues and a dripping grotto topped by Atlas standing on two horses. When you reach the top, head along Allées Paul Ricquet, marked by an avenue of limes; the old town lies ahead and to the left.

i **Tourist Office**: PALAIS DES CONGRÈS, 29 AV. ST-SAËNS, ☎ 04 67 76 47 00; fax 04 67 76 50 80 (www.ville-beziers.fr; mairie.de.beziers@wanadoo.fr). Details of local wine festivals are available here.

There are hotels near the station, but it's more fun to stay in the centre of town. The budget hotel here is the **Cécil**, 5 PL. J. JAURÈS, ☎ 04 67 28 48 55, with basic rooms, €. For more comfort, try the **Angleterre**, 22 PL. J. JAURÈS, ☎ 04 67 28 48 55, €€.

FRANCE

MONTPELLIER

High-tech, young and trendy, Montpellier's attraction is that it's simply fun to spend time in. As a university town, with 55,000 students to feed, Montpellier abounds with inexpensive eating places, bars and hotels. The **Vieille Ville** (old town) mixes cobbled streets with many 17th- and 18th-century mansions. To the west side, the **Promenade de Peyrou** leads to an impressive monumental group, with a triumphal arch, a water tower in the form of a hexagonal pavilion and an equestrian statue of Louis XIV, all looking out to the Mediterranean. Just to the north is **Jardin des Plantes**, France's oldest botanical garden.

PL. A.-GIBERT. 5-mins' walk south-east of the Tourist Office.

i **Tourist Office:** TRIANGLE COMÉDIE, ALLÉE DU TOURISME, ☎ 04 67 60 60 60, fax 04 67 60 60 61 (www.ot-montpellier.fr; contact@ot.montpellier.fr).

For an inexpensive hotel in the historic centre, try **Hôtel du Palais**, 3 R. DU PALAIS, ☎ 04 67 60 47 38, €. **Youth hostel:** R. DES ECOLES LAÏQUES, ☎ 04 67 60 32 22; 1 km from the station (☐ nos. 2/3/5/6/7/9).

NÎMES

Nîmes has effectively become a household word, by virtue of being the origin of the **Serge de Nîmes**, now known as denim, which was manufactured here in the 18th Century and imported to California for Levi Strauss. However, its history stretches back as far as Roman times, and though much of the town is undistinguished there are several superb Roman buildings.

Les Arènes, seating 23,000 in 34 elliptical tiers, is reckoned to be the finest preserved Roman amphitheatre in the world, and still stages concerts, theatrical events and bullfights. **Maison Carrée**, an outstandingly well-preserved 1st-century AD temple, is now an exhibition centre. Next door is the futuristic **Carré d'Art**, designed by Norman Foster and containing wide-ranging displays of contemporary art forms. To the west, the 18th-century **Jardin de la Fontaine** (Garden of the Fountain), off AV. J-JAURÈS, features a romantic Temple of Diana.

PONT DU GARD

The **Pont du Gard** is a spectacular Roman aqueduct 48 m above the Gard river (at a popular swimming spot), accessible by bus eight times a day from Nîmes. The site attracts two million visitors a year. Water was brought to the aqueduct from **Uzès**, a medieval village centred on a formidable castle, where today waxworks and holographic ghosts entertain visitors.

BLVD TALABOT, 10-mins walk south-east of the centre: head down AV. FEUCHÈRES to ESPL. C DE-GAULLE, then along BLVD VICTOR HUGO.

i **Tourist Office:** 6 R. AUGUSTE, ☎ 04 66 58 38 00, fax 04 66 58 38 01 (www.ot-nimes.fr; info@ot-nimes.fr). Branch: in the station.

🏨 For budget hotels, try BLVD DES ARÈNES, or around BLVD AMIRAL COURBET such as **Hotel Terminus Audrans**, 23 AV. FEUCHERES, 📞04 66 29 20 14, fax 04 66 29 08 24, €. Or try the more expensive **Hôtel Majestic**, 10 R. PRADIER, 📞04 66 29 24 14, fax 04 66 29 77 33, €€. **Youth hostel**: CHEMIN DE LA CIGALE, 📞04 66 68 03 20, €, is about 4 km from the station, 🚌 no. 2; 500 m uphill walk from bus stop to hostel. **Campsite: Domaine de la Bastide,** RTE DE GÉNÉRAC, 📞04 66 38 09 21, 5 km to the south; cheap (🚌 D: La Bastide direction).

ARLES

Ancient Rome meets Van Gogh and black bulls in Arles, the spiritual heart of Provence and a great place to relax and absorb history. Most major sights and museums are tucked into a tiny old town and are easily accessible on foot.

Arles is one of the best-preserved Roman towns in the world. **Les Arènes** is a mini Colosseum, less intact than the Roman amphitheatre at Nîmes but still used for bullfights (Easter-Sept). Summer theatrical productions are still staged at the **Théâtre Antique**, and assorted Roman finds, including mosaics, are exhibited at the Musée Lapidaire Paien. Elsewhere in town are the 4th-century **Thermes** (baths) of the otherwise vanished palace of Emperor Constantine and the seating and columns of the **Théâtre Antique**. Built by a Roman racetrack, the modern **Musée de l'Arles Antique** (closed Tue) has some superb Roman sarcophagi, mosaics and statuary.

Art buffs should seek out the **Musée Réattu**, R. DU GRAND PRIEURÉ, which houses a collection of Picasso sketches, the **Espace Van Gogh**, an exhibition centre within the former hospital where the artist was treated after chopping off his ear, and **Alyscamps** (Elysian Fields), an ancient burial ground painted by Van Gogh and Gaugin. Unfortunately none of Van Gogh's works are still in the town, but the tourist office runs Van Gogh tours to some of the places that inspired his paintings.

The **Cathédrale St-Trophime** has a west front regarded as one of the pinnacles of Provençal medieval stonework, depicting the damned descending naked into the flames of Hell while the Heaven-bound and robed saved people smirk self-righteously. The airy cloisters blend Gothic and Romanesque styles.

Arles parties through the summer: in late June–early July, the *Fête de la Tradition* fills the streets with music, dance and theatre. In mid-July, the festival *Mosaique Gitane* celebrates gipsy music and way of life.

🚉 Av. P.-Talabot. A few blocks north of Les Arènes: walk down AV. P.-TALABOT and along R. LACLAVIÈRE.

ℹ️ **Tourist Office**: espl. Charles de Gaulle (🚌 no. 4 from rail station), 📞04 90 18 41 20, fax 04 90 18 41 29 (www.arles.org). Accommodation service. Differently themed walking tours and self-guided tours use symbols embedded in the pavement. The *Petit Train d'Arles* departs every day from Apr–mid-Oct between 1000–1200 and 1400–1900 from BLVD DES LICE and Sat 1000–1200 from LES ARENES 📞04 93 41 31 09.

FRANCE

For budget hotels look around PL. DU FORUM and PL. VOLTAIRE (also good for cafés and restaurants). Two elegant upmarket hotels are **Jules César**, 9 BLVD DES LICES, ☎04 90 52 52 52, fax 04 90 52 52 53, €€€, and **D'Arlatan**, 26 R. DU SAUVAGE, ☎04 90 93 56 66, fax 04 90 93 33 47, €€€. **Hôtel Gauguin**, 5 PL. VOLTAIRE, ☎04 90 96 14 35, fax 04 90 18 98 87, is one of the better moderate places. **Youth hostel**: 20 AV. MARÉCHAL FOCH, ☎04 90 96 18 25, is 1.8 km south-east of town, a 15-min walk from town centre or ☐ no. 8: FOURNIER. **Camping**: **Camping-City**, 67 RTE DE CRAU, ☎04 90 93 08 86 or 04 90 93 08 08, or **Les Rosiers**, PONT DE CRAU, ☎04 90 96 02 12, fax 04 90 93 36 72. Both to the south of the town.

SIDE TRIP TO THE CAMARGUE Hourly buses run between Arles and **Les-Stes-Maries-de-la-Mer**, on the coast. This is the site of an annual gypsy pilgrimage in late May and the main base for the **Camargue**. The Camargue is now a nature reserve, an area of marshland and rice fields where semi-wild white horses and black bulls roam free and lagoons are often pink with flamingos in summer. Horseback is the best way to get around; the **Stes-Maries Tourist Office**, 5 av. Van-Gogh, ☎04 90 97 82 55, fax 04 90 97 71 15 (www.saintesmairiesdelamer.com; saintes-mairies@enprovence.com) can supply a list of some thirty farms with horses for hire. Cycling is the best alternative: bikes can be hired either from Stes-Maries or from Arles (the Tourist Office, train station, or **Le Vélociste**, 7 av. de la République, ☎04 90 97 83 26).

MARSEILLE

France's second city is hectically vibrant. The busiest port in France, it is something of a melting pot as French and North African cultures intermingle and sometimes clash. Its residents eat, sleep and breath to the rhythm of the sea. The grubby, run-down character of Marseille appeals to some, while others will want to move on swiftly. The centre is mostly safe, although the St Charles area and 6th arrondissement can be dodgy; there's a good metro and bus system (regular buses stop running at 2100).

Full of small restaurants and street cafés, the **Vieux Port** (Old Port) is the hub of Marseille life and is guarded by the forts of St Jean and St Nicholas on either side of its entrance. From the Quai des Belges, the main boulevard of **La Canebière** extends back into the city.

Across the port from the dark narrow streets of **Le Panier** – the oldest part of Marseille – is the Notre Dame de la Garde and impressive 19th century Roman Byzantine basilica (take ☐ no. 60 or the tourist train). Affection-ately known to the Marseillais as *'la Bonne Mère'* the golden virgin

MARSEILLE'S MUSEUMS

The streets of Le Panier lead up to the **Vieille Charité**, 2 R. DE LA CHARITÉ, an erstwhile sanatorium now housing a science and arts centre and two museums covering African and American Indian art and medieval archaeology. Try **Musée Cantini** 19 R. GRIGNAN (métro: ESTRANGIN PRÉFECTURE) which houses a considerable collection of modern art, or the fascinating **Musée des Docks Romains** (Roman Docks Museum) PL. VIVAUX (métro: VIEUX PORT). All museums are open daily 1000–1700, 1100–1800 in summer, closed Mon.

Getting Around Marseille

The central (Vieux Port) area is walkable. Elsewhere, use the métro and buses, both run by **RTM** (*Réseau de Transport Marseillais*). Plan du Réseau (from the Tourist Office and RTM kiosks) covers the routes: the map looks complicated but the system is easy to use. Buses stop running at around 2100 and there is a reduced night service, Fluobus, until midnight. Eleven lines cover most of the city and most depart from La Canebière. Most of the city centre is safe but avoid wandering too far off the main streets at night particularly in the 6th arrondissement and around St Charles.

watches over all sailors and travellers and the interior decoration features paintings of their ordeals and models of the ships that went down. There are regular boat trips to the Iles de Frioul just outside the harbour. According to legend the Count of Monte Cristo was imprisoned in Chateau d'If on one of the smallest islands: the prison can be visited. Contact **GACM**, 1 quai des Belges, ☎04 91 55 50 09.

RAIL **Gare St-Charles**, pl. Victor Hugo, is the main station, 20 mins' walk north-east of the **Vieux Port** (Old Port): head down the steps and straight along blvd d'Athènes and blvd Dugommier to La Canebière, then turn right; or métro: Vieux Port – Hôtel de Ville. Facilities include showers, baths, left luggage; open daily 0715–2200 and **SOS Voyageurs**, ☎04 91 62 12 80. **Gare Maritime** is west of the old port: follow r. de la République.

For information on ferries to Corsica, Sardinia and North Africa, contact **SNCM**, 61 blvd des Dames, ☎08 36 67 95 00 (premium-rate number).

✈ **Marseille–Provence Airport**, ☎04 42 14 14 14; at Marignane, 25 km north-west. (Terminal 1 handles international flights.) An airport bus runs between Provence and St-Charles approximately every 20 mins 0615–2315, taking 25 mins. Buses run every 20 mins 0600–2150 in the other direction.

i **Tourist Office:** 4 La Canebière, ☎04 91 13 89 00, fax 04 91 13 89 20 (www.marseille-tourisme.com; info@marseille-tourisme.com). Branch: Gare St-Charles, ☎04 91 50 59 18. Student and youth information: **Centre d'Information Jeunesse**: 96 LA CANEBIÈRE, ☎04 91 24 33 50. Walking tours taking in the main sights depart from LA CANEBIÈRE at 1000 (June–Sept), 1400 (Oct–May).

The Tourist Office has a free accommodation booking service. For cheap, functional and tranquil hotels, try around allées L-Gambetta and r. Montgrand, but avoid the dodgy streets south-west of the station (roughly the area bounded by blvd d'Athènes, blvd Charles Nédélec, cours Belsunce and La Canebière). **Hôtel St Louis**, 2 r. de Récollettes, ☎04 91 54 02 74, €, is just behind the port, inexpensive and air-conditioned. A good budget hotel is the **Hotel Pavillon**, 27 R. PAVILLON, ☎04 91 33 76 90, €. Nearer to the port, rooms tend to be pricier. **Youth hostel: Château de Bois Luzy**, 76 av. de Bois Luzy, ☎04 91 49 06 18 (🚌 no. 8). You can also camp here Mar–Oct; **Bonneveine hostel**, 47 av. Joseph Vidal, ☎04 91 73 21 81, is 5 km south in a residential district near the beaches. (Take métro no. 2 to rond pont du Prado or 🚌 no. 41, then 🚌 no. 44 toward Roy d'Espagne, get off at Borely).

The harbour and the streets leading from it are lined with fish and North African restaurants: try PL. THIARS and PL. AUX HUILES. More opulent restaurants are found along CORNICHE J F

KENNEDY. Specialities of Marseille include *bouillabaisse* (literally meaning to boil slowly): the authentic version of this fish stew contains rascasse, an ugly red Mediterranean species, and is served with rouille, potatoes and croutons.

SIDE TRIP TO AIX-EN-PROVENCE Aix-en-Provence, the capital of Provence, and 30–40 mins from Marseille by train (ETT table 362), is a university town of culture, grace and charm; in term time, the distinctly well-groomed students are a feature of the town's street and café life.

Cours Mirabeau, flanked by plane trees and dotted with ancient fountains, forms the southern boundary of Vieil Aix, the old town, a maze of lively streets with elegant 17th- to 18th-century houses. The **Cathédrale St Sauveur** is an architectural mishmash, ranging from the 5th to the 17th century, but it has lovely Romanesque cloisters and contains some worthwhile medieval artefacts. The best of the museums is **Musée des Tapisseries** (Tapestry Museum).

Aix was the birthplace of Cézanne and inspired some of his work, although he despised the town, which ridiculed him and his art. Later it came to its senses and his studio, **Atelier Cézanne**, has been lovingly preserved, exactly as it was at his death. Using studs embedded in the pavement and a tourist guide you can follow a tour of the main stages of Cézanne's life.

Aix is also renowned for its **thermal springs** and a **thermal centre** is open to the public, ☎04 42 23 81 81.

The **station** is 5 mins south of the centre: take AV. V-HUGO to La Rotonde; the **Tourist Office** is on the left, at 2 PL. DU GÉNÉRAL-DE-GAULLE, ☎04 42 16 11 61, fax 04 42 16 11 62 (www.aixenprovencetourisme.com; infos@aixenprovencetourisme.com).

WHERE NEXT FROM MARSEILLE?

Marseille is a major rail junction, from which run some of the most scenic lines in France. In addition to exploring the Marseille–Menton route (p. 113) and perhaps continuing from Menton over the Italian border, you can take the slow train to Paris via the Allier gorge.

*Béziers-Nîmes, p. 124. The line through Aix-en-Provence continues round the hills of the **Lubéron** (the subject of Peter Mayle's book A Year in Provence), and then through increasingly dramatic limestone scenery as you enter the foothills of the Alps.*

*Beyond **Gap**, you're really into the Alps proper; you can continue on to **Briançon**, a major centre for the mountains, with a hilltop quarter fortified by the military architect Vauban. Alternatively, stop at **Montdauphin-Guillestre** (between Gap and Briançon); from here there are connecting minibuses to the **Parc Régional de Queyras**, one of the least developed and most rural parts of the French Alps. Good bases are St-Véran (at 2425 m, Europe's highest permanently inhabited village), and Ceillac.*

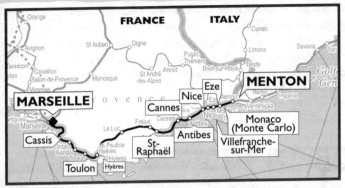

KEY JOURNEYS

Marseille–Nice   ETT table 360

Type	Frequency	Typical journey time
Train	Every 1–2 hrs	2 hrs 30 mins–2hrs 45 mins

Nice–Milan   ETT table 90

Type	Frequency	Typical journey time
Train	3 daily	4 hrs 45 mins

ROUTE DETAIL

Marseille–Cassis

Type	Frequency	Typical journey time
Train	Every 1–2 hrs	25 mins

Cassis–Toulon

Type	Frequency	Typical journey time
Train	1–2 hrs	35 mins

Toulon–St Raphaël   ETT table 360

Type	Frequency	Typical journey time
Train	12 daily	1 hr

St Raphaël–Cannes   ETT table 360

Type	Frequency	Typical journey time
Train	Every hr	22 mins

Cannes–Antibes   ETT table 360

Type	Frequency	Typical journey time
Train	1–2 every hr	12 mins

Antibes–Nice   ETT table 360

Type	Frequency	Typical journey time
Train	1–2 every hr	15–25 mins

Nice–Villefranche sur Mer   ETT 360

Type	Frequency	Typical journey time
Train	1–2 every hr	8 mins

Villefranche sur Mer–Eze   ETT 360

Type	Frequency	Journey Time
Train	1–2 every hr	7 mins

Eze–Monaco (Monte Carlo)   ETT 360

Type	Frequency	Typical journey time
Train	1–2 every hr	8 mins

Monaco (Monte Carlo)–Menton   ETT table 360

Type	Frequency	Typical journey time
Train	1–2 every hr	10 mins

FRANCE

This stretch of coast, the **Côte d'Azur**, became the haunt of British aristocrats in the 19th century, heralding its new status as a sophisticated playground for the famous, beautiful or just plain rich. Grand hotels and casinos sprung up to cater for their tastes, and although parts have declined into untidy sprawls there's still an enticing mix of ostentatious villas, pretty waterside towns and fine beaches. Sophisticated **Monaco**, a tiny country within France, and **Cannes** (marking the westward bounds of the glamorous Riviera) are hot spots for night life, while **Nice** is large and cosmopolitan. Inland the land rises abruptly and you're into a different world, of rugged mountains and ancient perched villages; much of it is difficult to reach without a car.

MARSEILLE

See p. 110.

CASSIS

Centred around a pretty, traditional fishing harbour and making an easy day trip from Marseille via bus or train, the town makes a handy base for seeing the spectacular *calanques*, rocky inlets that cut into the limestone cliffs. Coastal walks (including the long-distance path GR98 west to Cap Croisette) offer stunning views.

🚆 3.5km from town centre, on foot or by taxi (no buses from the station). Go along av. des Albizzi to av. Auguste Favier then av. Augustin Isnard which leads into town.

ℹ️ **Tourist Office**: Place Baragnon, ☎04 42 01 71 17, fax 04 42 01 28 31 (www.cassis.enprovence.com; omt-cassis@enprovence.com). There is a beachside branch open during summer, daily 1000–1300 and 1530–2230.

FRÉJUS AND ST-RAPHAËL

The two communities almost merge and, although each has its own station and tourist office, they are effectively one place with three areas. St-Raphaël is the upmarket end and the main transport hub, with spacious beaches, though it lacks real style. Fréjus-Plage is a strip of tacky bars and restaurants that lies between the sea and Fréjus town, the historic area.

Fréjus was a Roman port, created by Julius Caesar in 49 BC and there are quite a few Roman remains scattered around the town. The smallish amphitheatre, **Arènes**, R. HENRI-VADON, is still used for bullfights and rock concerts. Fréjus Cathedral, PL. FORMIGÉ, was Provence's first Gothic church, built around the time the Romans lost power, though little building from that time survives.

🚆 **Gare de St-Raphaël** is central: for the sea, head down R. JULY BARBIER to PROMENADE DE LA LIBERATION.

🚌 **St-Raphaël bus station**: behind the rail station, AV. VICTOR HUGO, ☎04 94 83 87 63.

ℹ️ **Tourist Offices: St-Raphaël**, r. W.-Rousseau, ☎04 94 19 52 52; fax 04 94 83 85 40 (www.saint-

raphael.com; sainte-raphael.information@wanadoo.fr), opposite the station. **Fréjus-Ville**, 325 R.
J-Jaurès, ☎04 94 51 83 83, fax 04 94 51 00 26 (www.ville-freju.fr; frejus.tourisme@wanadoo.fr),
dispenses a guide to the (widespread) Roman sites.

Youth hostel: chemin de Counillier, ☎04 94 53 18 75, in a large park 2 km from Fréjus town
along the RN7 road towards Cannes. **Campsites**: **Parc Camping Agay Soleil**, blvd de la
Plage, ☎04 94 82 00 79, fax 04 94 82 56 17; **St-Aygulf**, 270 av. Salvarelli, ☎04 94 17 62 49, fax
04 94 81 03 16, is 4 km from Fréjus station (☐no. 9 from St-Raphaël bus station to St-Aygulf).

Side Trips from St-Raphaël   **Hyères** makes a pleasant excursion from St-Raphaël
via Toulon; this charming old resort, with a medieval
walled core, first attracted winter visitors in the late 19th century: Tolstoy, Queen
Victoria and Robert Louis Stevenson enjoyed its mild climate.

From Hyères you can catch a ferry to offshore islands – Île de Porquerolles
(20 mins), **Île de Port-Cros** (1 hr) and Île du Levant (1 hr 30 mins) – which offer some
of the most beautiful beaches in the Mediterranean. Take a bus from the town to the
port at La Tour Fondue for the ferry to Île de Porquerolles (21 ferries a day in
summer, 6 a day off season) ferry information: ☎04 94 58 21 81), Port la Gavine for
Port-Cros and Île du Levant, ☎04 94 57 44 07 (5 ferries per day in summer, 3 per day
off season). **Hyères Tourist Office**: 3 ave Ambroise Thomas, ☎04 94 01 84 50, fax 04
94 01 84 51 (www.provence-azur.com; ot.hyeres@libertysurf.fr).

St-Tropez, a famously chic resort accessible by Sodetrav bus (10–15 a day in summer, from
St-Raphaël, ETTtables 358 and 359, ☎04 94 97 88 51), can be a disappointment. The best
way to get around the area (more rewarding than the town) is to cycle and you can hire
bikes or mopeds locally. There are two small beaches in town. Tahiti-Plage is the jet-set
hang-out and is at one end of Pampelonne, a 5-km stretch of sand that draws most of the
crowds and is credited with starting the fashion for topless bathing. **Tourist Office**: Quai J.-
Jaurès, ☎04 94 97 45 21, fax 04 94 97 82 66 (www.nova.fr/saint-tropez; tourisme@nova.fr).

CANNES

Cannes proudly upholds the Riviera's reputation as an overpriced, overcrowded fleshpot. Entertainment here consists of looking good, spending money and sleeping little.
Orientation is easy: the town stretches around the **Baie de Lérins**, the promenade being
called **La Croisette**. Everything is within walking distance and virtually all the cultural
activities (including the film festival) centre on the hideous concrete Palais des Festivals.

Cannes' nightlife can be fun. Twinned with Beverley Hills, glitzy Cannes is surprisingly
welcoming to those without MGM contracts or family jewels, especially if they wander
away from La Croisette to the small winding streets and hidden squares inland: try R.
Macé and R. F-Faure for some reasonably-priced bars. Cannes specialises in second-
hand glamour. Begin at the Palais des Festivals, built in 1982 and christened 'the
bunker'. Here the Rollers glide up, disgorging world-famous faces (and many that seem

not so familiar), while the world of cinema pats itself on the back. Glimpses of stars are frequent (practise climbing lampposts) and, when it's all over, you may find your favourite's handprint cast in the concrete around the festival hall.

There are few specific sights, but try climbing R. ST-ANTOINE to the hill of Le Suquet, the oldest quarter. The **Musée de la Castre**, housed in the old citadel here, displays antiquities from around the world and gives a history of the town.

EVENTS IN CANNES

With towns all along the coast competing for custom, Cannes keeps ahead of the game by organising an ever-increasing number of special events: barely a week goes by without some kind of conference or festival – concerts, jazz and blues galas, even chess tournaments.
'The' event, of course, is the prestigious **Cannes Film Festival**, which begins during the second week in May. Public tickets for films outside the main competition are sold daily from a special office next to the tourist office.

📶 250 m from the sea and the Palais de Festivals: head straight (south) down R. DES SERBES.

ⓘ **Tourist Offices**: PALAIS DE FESTIVALS, ESPLANADE GEORGES POMPIDOU, 📞04 93 39 24 53, fax 04 92 99 84 23 (www.cannes-on-line.com; semoftou@palais-festivals-cannes.fr). At the station: 1 R. J-JAURÈS, 📞04 93 99 19 77, fax 04 93 39 40 19.

🛏 Some of the most exclusive hotels in the world overlook the Croisette. Try the streets leading from the station towards the sea front for more reasonably priced rooms: R. DES SERBES, R. DE LA REPUBLIQUE or R. MARÉCHAL JOFFRE. Advance reservations recommended; during the festival rooms in Cannes are a highly prized commodity often booked from year to year. For celebrity spotting try the **Carlton Inter-Continental**, 58 BLVD CROISETTE, 📞04 93 06 40 06, fax 04 93 06 40 25, or the **Majestic**, 14 BLVD CROISETTE, 📞04 92 98 77 00, fax 04 93 38 97 90 (both €€€). If your budget won't stretch this far the **Atlantis**, 4 R. DU 24 AOÛT, 📞04 93 39 18 72, fax 04 93 68 37 65, €€, or the **Bourgogne**, 11 R. DU 24 AOÛT, 📞04 93 38 36 73, fax 04 92 99 28 41, €. Otherwise consider making one of the other towns along the coast your base. **Youth hostel** (in Le Trayas): 9 AV DE LA VÉRONÈSE, 📞04 93 75 40 23; closed Jan. **Camping**: **Cannes La Bocca** (reached by train from Cannes) is convenient for the wide sandy beaches to the west of the town but not really for the centre. **Parc Bellevue Camping**, 67 AV. M.-CHEVALIER, 📞04 93 47 28 97, fax 04 93 48 66 25 (🚌 nos. 2/10/11; open Apr–Sept).

DAY TRIP FROM CANNES

Off Cannes, the **Îles de Lérins** are an antidote to chic. **Île de Ste-Marguerite** is the larger of the two, and boasts the better beaches. At the north end, Fort Royal is an impressively stark fortress built by Vauban in 1712 – and the legendary home of the Man in the Iron Mask (whose identity is debated to this day). There are daily ferry departures from the quay next to the Palais des Festivals casino (📞04 93 39 11 82).

DAY TRIPS FROM ANTIBES

Juan-les-Pins, the playground of the coast, is where the Côte d'Azur originated one summer in 1921; it has beaches (many are private, but there is still some public space), bars, discos and in July, a jazz festival. Accessible by train from Antibes, it is a pleasant place to while away a few days. Just inland, to the west of Antibes and reachable by bus, **Vallauris**, meaning 'Valley of Gold', is pottery capital of the Riviera, famous for ceramics since 1500. Picasso came here in 1946 (to make pots) and was commissioned to paint a huge fresco, War and Peace, in a chapel which has become the small **Musée National Picasso**, PL. DE LA LIBÉRATION (closed Tues).

ANTIBES

Mixing chic and tackiness, Antibes is still home to the obscenely rich, but the town has a relaxed atmosphere. Take a walk along the port; the biggest boats in the northern Med moor here. Do not miss the **Musée Picasso**, looking over the sea from its home in the **Château Grimaldi**, PL. MARIJOL. Picasso worked here in 1946 and this excellent museum displays some of his most entertaining creations from that period.

🚃 For the centre, head down AV. ROBERT SOLEAU to PL. DE GAULLE. From here BLVD ALBERT IER leads to the sea.

ℹ️ **Tourist Office**: 11 PL. DU GÉN-DE-GAULLE, ☎ 04 92 90 53 00, fax 04 92 90 53 01 (www.antibes-juanlespins.com; accueil@antibes-juanlespins.com). There is a branch at the train station. Free maps and accommodation information. Free minibuses run between all the main sites 0700–1900, but most are within walking distance.

NICE

Nice has been the undisputed Queen of the Riviera ever since Russian princes and British royalty began to grace the opulent hotels along the **Promenade des Anglais** named in their honour. This thoroughfare runs along the seafront, still adorned with the ornate Art Nouveau lamp-posts of the city's heyday. Here are hotels such as the Negresco, still as luxurious and imposing as ever, and not excessively expensive for a snack or a drink to sample how the other half lives. Standing apart from the pastel-coloured villas of the rich, **Le Vieux Nice** (the Old Town) seems more Italian than French (which it was until 1860), and is one of the best places to shop at the outdoor markets.

NICE'S BEACHES

The beaches of Nice are pebbly, but this does not deter sun-worshippers from crowding onto the Baie des Anges, below the Promenade des Anglais. Whilst private beach clubs cover some of the central section, charging heftily for a day's hire of lounger and umbrella, most of the long beach is free. For less hectic sun-bathing, seek out the long beach between Cagnes-sur-Mer and Antibes to the west.

However, the prettiest beaches are to the east, at Villefranche (young, lively crowd), Beaulieu (elderly and sedate) and St-Jean Cap Ferrat (well-heeled and laid-back).

Nice boasts some of the best museums in France. Some are free; you can also purchase a pass from the Tourist Office. Most are easily accessible by local bus. Best of the bunch is the **Musée Matisse**, 164 AV. DES ARÈNES DE CIMIEZ, wonderfully set in a 17th-century villa amongst the Roman

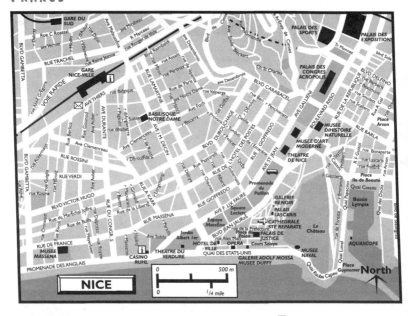

ruins of Cimiez. It houses Matisse's personal collection of paintings (🚌 nos. 15/17/20/22 from PL. MASSÉNA; daily except Tues). Next door **Musée et Site Archéologique de Cimiez**, 160 AV. DES ARÈNES DE CIMIEZ, exhibits the copious finds dug up while excavating the Roman arenas in Cimiez (🚌 nos. 15/17/20/22 to Arènes; 1000–1200, 1400–1800 or 1700 in winter; closed Mon). Matisse and fellow artist Raoul Dufy are buried in the neighbouring Couvent des Frères Mineurs.

Also in Cimiez, the **Musée Marc Chagall**, AV. DU DR. MÉNARD, is a graceful temple to Chagall's genius –

WHERE TO SHOP

Vieux Nice with its outdoor markets and small shops is a good place to start: head for the pedestrian area around R. MASSENA. **Cours Saleya** is the main market place and there is a colourful flower market here everyday except Mon when an antique and flea market replaces it. All the big department stores line AV. JEAN MÉDECIN, while luxury goods and designer boutiques are on R. PARADIS and R. SUÈDE.

GETTING AROUND NICE

The Old Town quarter is manageable on foot, but to get between the various museums and sights requires transport. Bus services are good, most radiating from PL. MASSÉNA.
Bus Information: 10 R. FÉLIX FAURE, 📞 04 93 13 53 13.
Renting a car or motor bike is a popular option, but the traffic is hectic and parking difficult. Rent motorbikes from **Nicea**, 9 AV. THIERS, near the station, 📞 04 93 82 42 71.
Taxis (📞 04 93 13 78 78) are expensive.

beautifully lit to display his huge biblical canvases (🖾 no. 15; closed Tues).

In the centre of town, the **Musée d'Art Moderne et d'Art Contemporain** (🖾 no. 5; closed Tues), Promenade des Arts, is unmistakable: a white marble cliff rising above the street, and filled with striking pop art. The **Musée d'Art et d'Histoire** in Palais Masséna (closed Mon), 65 R. de France, is in a splendid old Italianate villa adorned with antiques and decorated with paintings by Renoir and local artists. A Tourist Train visits the flower market, old town and castle hill during summer, from 1000–1900.

Nice-Ville, AV. Thiers. Information office. Frequent services to all resorts along the Côte d'Azur. Left luggage 0700–2200; baths and showers 0800–1900 in the basement. For the town centre, turn left from station to AV. Jean Médecin, the main thoroughfare, right down to PL. Masséna (300 m), right again to the sea, a 15-min walk. 🖾 no. 23 to the airport from outside the station, every 20 mins 0600–2100.

SNCM, Quai du Commerce (on the east side of the port), ☎ 04 93 13 66 66, fax 04 93 13 66 81. Regular crossings to Corsica.

Nice-Côte d'Azur: Promenade des Anglais, 7 km west of the city. Information: ☎ 04 93 21 30 12 (www.nice.aeroport.fr). Airport buses run along Promenade des Anglais to the Gare Routière (bus station) every 20 mins, and the journey takes 20 mins. 🖾 no. 23 to the rail station (marked 'Gare SNCF') also takes 20 mins.

Tourist Offices: AV. Thiers (on the left just outside the station), ☎ 04 92 14 48 00, fax 04 93 92 82 98 (www.nicetourism.com; info@nicetourism.com). Also 5 Promenade des Anglais; Airport, Terminal 1; and Ferber, near the airport.
Post Office: 23 AV. Thiers with poste restante, money transfer and fax. Open 0800–1900, 0800–1200 Sat.

For the budget conscious, good-value accommodation is available near the station – R. de Suisse, AV. Durante, R. d'Alsace-Lorraine – and in Old Nice, around PL. St François. Nice's **youth hostels** are all far from the centre. **Mt-Alban**: Rte de Mont-Alban, ☎ 04 93 89 23 64, 4 km out of town, uphill! (🖾 no. 5 from the station to Blvd Jean Jaurès, then 🖾 no. 14 to hostel.) No reservations; open 0800–1200 and 1700–2400. The **HI youth hostel** is on Route Forestière du Mont Alban, ☎ 04 93 89 23 64, fax 04 92 04 03 10; 4 km from the station (🖾 nos. 14/17). **Relais International de la Jeunesse Clairvallon**, 26 AV. Scudéri, ☎ 04 93 81 27 63, is up in Cimiez, north of the centre (🖾 nos 15/22, stop at Scudéri), located in a park with a pool. **Espace Magnan**, 31 R. Louis de Coppet, ☎ 04 93 86 28 75, fax 04 93 44 93 22 (open mid-June–mid-Sept). The nearest **campsite** is at St Laurent du Var at **Camping Magali**, 1814 Rte de la Barronne, ☎ 04 93 31 57 00, fax 04 92 12 01 33 (take the CP train from the Gare du Sud towards Plan du Var; get off at Saint Sauveur – last train 1915), open Feb–Oct. Sleeping on the beach is not recommended.

Something of a culinary paradise, Nice is influenced by its neighbour – Italy, and by the Mediterranean. The city has many specialities. *Pissaladière* is a Niçois onion tart, garnished with anchovies and olives; socca, a traditional lunchtime snack of flat bread made from crushed chick peas, served hot; and of course *salade niçoise*. Vieux Nice (the Old Town) is best for eating out – particularly COURS SALEYA, which is covered with open-air tables in summer, R. STE RÉPARARTE and the other narrow side-streets around the cathedral. North of the old town, PL. GARIBALDI boasts the best shellfish.

NIGHT-TIME Nice is the cultural and social capital of the South of France, offering a choice of opera, concerts and plays. **FNAC (Fédération Nationale d'Achats des Cadres)** in the Nice Étoile shopping mall, 24 av. Jean Médecin, supplies tickets, ☎04 92 17 77 74. In summer, Nice grinds on long after midnight, thanks to its many piano bars and nightclubs, though the younger generation gravitate to the beach. For many it is entertainment enough simply to stroll along the Promenade des Anglais or sit on the Cours Saleya and watch the world go by.

WHERE NEXT FROM NICE?

A superb route through the Alps to Lyon can be taken via the CP private narrow gauge line to Digne-les-Bains (ETT table 361); see Where Next From Lyon? on p. 100. Nice is also served by international trains to Milan, Venice and Rome (ETT table 90). There is a useful night train to Venice (departs around 2035, arrives 0715).

DAY TRIPS FROM NICE Renoir spent the last years of his life in **Cagnes sur Mer**, buying an isolated house overlooking the sea. Today this is **Musée Renoir**, chemin les Colettes, closed Tues), a tour of the artist's life, with rooms as he kept them 80 years ago (from the rail station, take the bus to Beal-Les Colettes). Above the town, the medieval citadel is now a museum: **Montée de la Bourgade**; Haut-de-Cagnes, entrance pl. Grimaldi, closed Tues).

There are hourly buses from Nice to **St Paul-de-Vence**, a picturesque village which houses one of the most interesting modern art museums in France, the **Fondation Maeght**, built by the Maeght family, friends of Matisse. The garden is a quirky sculpture park designed by Miró.

Vence, 3 km further up the valley, is another delightful little town. Here Matisse was nursed by local nuns and repaid them by designing a simple yet breathtakingly beautiful chapel – that he considered his masterpiece – **La Chapelle du Rosaire**, av. Henri Matisse; open Tues and Thur, 1000–1130, 1430–1730, also Wed, Fri and Sat in summer. A mosaic by Chagall enlivens the Romanesque church.

The old perfume town of **Grasse** is a 75-min bus journey from Nice. Here you can visit the original perfume factory and see the villa of the painter Fragonard, complete with cartoon frescoes and a collection of paintings, or shop and idle in the pl. aux Aires farmers' market and flower stalls.

VILLEFRANCHE-SUR-MER

The incredibly steep little resort of precariously tall ochre houses has one of the deepest ports on the coast, so it's a major stop for cruise ships and also has the liveliest beach in the region.

From Villefranche beach you can walk up to St-Jean Cap-Ferrat, a peninsula with gorgeous beaches plus some of the world's most expensive properties, where second-home owners include the likes of Elizabeth Taylor, Joan Collins and Mick Jagger. The port is lined with restaurants, tranquil even in high season and surprisingly inexpensive. If you make it to **St-Jean Cap-Ferrat**, don't miss the **Villa Rothschild**. Once owned by Beatrice de Rothschild, the house is a visual delight, but the exotica-filled gardens are stunning, with views down to Villefranche and Beaulieu. Open daily 1000–1800 summer; Mon–Fri 1400–1800 and weekends 1000–1800 in winter.

Access platform 2 to PROMENADE DES MARINIERES, turn right and follow signs to Vieille Ville (uphill).

Tourist Office: JARDINS FRANÇOIS BINON, ☎ 04 93 01 73 68, fax 04 93 76 63 65 (www.villefranche-sur-mer.com; ot-villefranchesurmer@rom.fr).

LA TURBIE

La Turbie, just above Monaco, is accessible from Monaco by bus (six times a day, but not Sun) – or a steep bicycle ride. The culminating point of the Roman road *Via Aurelia*, and marking the boundary between Italy and Gaul, La Turbie is renowned for the restored remnants of a huge statuesque tower of 6BC known as the Trophée des Alpes (in Latin: Tropaea Augusti). The only other Roman monument of its kind is in Romania. During the 13th century it was converted into a fortress, but was later blown up.

BEAULIEU-SUR-MER

'Beautiful place' (the name was bestowed by Napoleon) is a tranquil spot full of affluent retired people, and palms flourish profusely in its mild climate. Don't miss the **Villa Kérylos** – built by an archaeologist at the turn of the century, this is a faithful replication of a 5th-century BC Athenian home, complete with furnishings.

A few mins' walk north of the centre.

Tourist Office: PL. G-CLÉMENCEAU, ☎ 04 93 01 02 21, fax 04 93 01 44 04 (www.ot-beaulieu-sur-mer.fr; tourisme@ot.beaulieu-sur-mer.fr).

There's a decent range of one and two-star hotels at the back of the town; the waterfront is much pricier (the **Métropole** and **La Réserve de Beaulieu** are distinctly select).

EZE

The perched village of Eze (as opposed to the sea-level Eze-sur-Mer) is a stiff climb from the station. It's inevitably a tourist trap, but you're rewarded by arguably the best views on the Riviera; cacti flourish in the botanical gardens.

At sea-level in Eze-sur-Mer.

Tourist Office: PL. DE GAULLE, EZE-SUR-MER, ☎ 04 93 41 26 00, fax 04 93 41 04 80 (www.eze-riviera.com; eze@webstore.fr).

MONACO (MONTE CARLO)

Covering just a couple of square km this tiny principality has been a sovereign state ruled since 1308 by the Grimaldis, a family of Genoese descent. Later it grew rich on gambling and banking, and now high-rises crowd round the harbour, some built on man-made platforms that extend into the sea. Whatever the geographical and aesthetic limitations of the place, its curiosity value is undeniable.

Old Monaco is the extra-touristy part, with its narrow streets, the much-restored **Grimaldi Palace**, and the 19th-century **Cathédrale de Monaco**, containing the tombs of the royals, including Princess Grace. In AV. ST-MARTIN is the stimulating **Musée Océanographique**, in the basement of which is one of the world's great aquariums, developed by Jacques Cousteau.

The **Monte-Carlo Rally** (Jan) includes exciting stages in the hills behind Monaco, while the second week in May is a good time to avoid the town unless you are interested in watching the **Grand Prix** – which takes over the city streets.

[RAIL] AV. PRINCE PIERRE: head straight down past PL. D'ARMES to the port (with the palace off to the right), then turn left for the Tourist Office and casino (500 m); or take [bus] no. 4.

[i] **Tourist Office**: 2A BLVD DES MOULINS, [phone] (00 377) 92 16 61 16 (www.monaco-congres.com; dtc@monaco-congres.com).

[lodging] Budget accommodation is scarce but there are a number of 2-star establishments around the station, R. DE LA TURBIE being the best place to look for it – otherwise, make your base elsewhere. **Hôtel Cosmopolite**, 4 R. DE LA TURBIE, [phone] (00 377) 93 30 16 95, fax (00 377) 93 30 23 05, is relatively cheap, €€. **Hôtel Helvetia**, 1 BIS R. GRIMALDI, [phone] (00 377) 93 30 21 71, fax (00 377) 92 16 70 51, €€, is also reasonable. **Youth hostel** (non HI): **Centre de la Jeunesse Princesse-Stéphanie**, 24 AV. PRINCE-PIERRE, [phone] (00 377) 93 50 83 20, fax (00 377) 93 25 29 82 (100 m from the station) is open all year to 16–26 year olds and students up to the age of 31.

CASINOS IN MONACO

Monaco is synonymous with gambling and there are several casinos, but you must be over 21 (they check). Granddaddy of them all is the most famous casino in the world, the **Casino de Paris**, PL. DU CASINO, which is worth a look for the interior gilt alone. You can play the slot machines at the entrance, but to get any further you'll have to pay just for the pleasure of walking into the hallowed gaming rooms – and smart dress is required. The adjoining **Café de Paris** (opens 2200) has no entrance fee, but it's definitely less classy.

LONG-DISTANCE WALKS IN THE CÔTE D'AZUR

From Menton you can venture into the **Parc National du Mercantour**, in the French Alps, by following the waymarked long-distance path GR52. Another route, GR51 (forking from GR52 north of Menton), heads west parallel to the coast and over wild, broken country. Both paths require good levels of fitness.

Eating out in Monaco ranges from simple bistros and pizzerias (try around the station or the port) to some of the most decadent restaurants in the world. Expect to pay big money in any of the restaurants around the casino. There are also a number of take away establishments, particularly around LA PLACE D'ARMES from which you can sample typical snacks such as *socca* and *tourte*.

MENTON

Looking into Italy, Menton is a retirement town of ample Italianate charm, endowed with long stony beaches and full of lemon, orange and olive trees. Wander around the old town, constructed by the Grimaldis in the 15th-century. The baroque **Église St-Michel** (St Michael's), built in 1640, is an attractive structure. To the west, **Palais Carnolès** was the summer residence of the princes of Monaco and now houses an interesting art collection (mainly impressionists and modern). **Musée Jean-Cocteau**, 111 QUAI NAPOLÉON-III, was established by Cocteau himself and contains many of his works. In **Musée Municipale de Préhistoire Régionale** (City Museum of Regional Prehistory), R. LORÉDAN-LARCHEY, there are human remains some 80,000 years old.

PL. DE LA GARE. West of the centre. For the sea (about 300 m), head down AV. EDOUARD VII or R. MORGAN.

Tourist Office: 8 AV. BOYER, ☎04 92 41 76 76, fax 04 92 41 76 78 (www.villedementon.com; ot@villedementon.com). Turn left from the station for about 100 m, then right.

Plenty of undistinguished one- and two-star places in the town centre. Rather better is **Hôtel Chambourt**, 6 AV. BOYER, ☎04 93 35 94 19, fax 04 93 41 30 55, €€, with spacious rooms. **Youth hostel:** PLATEAU ST-MICHEL, ☎04 93 35 93 14; 2km from the station (closed Nov–Jan).

WHERE NEXT FROM MENTON?

*Continue to Ventimiglia in Italy (ETT table 360) and join the **Ventimiglia–Pisa** route (p. 389).*

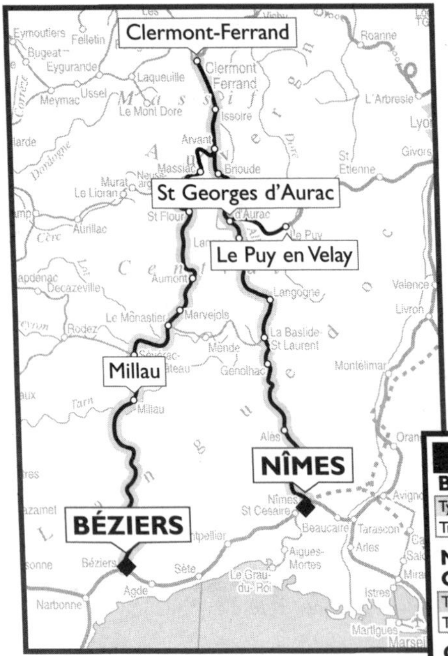

Notes

Infrequent services may mean that getting back to the main line out of Le Puy en Velay means returning to Brioude before heading south. Alternatively, there are a few buses from Le Puy to Langeac but connections are poor.

ROUTE DETAIL

Béziers–Millau ETT table 332

Type	Frequency	Typical journey time
Train	1–4 per day	1 hr 50 mins

Millau–Clermont-Ferrand ETT table 332

Type	Frequency	Typical journey time
Train	1–2 per day	4 hrs 25 mins

Clermont-Ferrand–St Georges d'Aurac ETT table 333

Type	Frequency	Typical journey time
Train	1–4 per day	1 hr 20 mins

St Georges d'Aurac–Le Puy en Velay ETT table 333

Type	Frequency	Typical journey time
Train	1–4 per day	50 mins

Le Puy en Velay–Nîmes ETT table 333

Type	Frequency	Typical journey time
Train	2–4 per day	7 hrs 45 mins

KEY JOURNEYS

Béziers–Clermont-Ferrand ETT table 332

Type	Frequency	Typical journey time
Train	2 per day	5 hrs 30 mins–6 hrs

Clermont-Ferrand–Nîmes ETT table 333

Type	Frequency	Typical journey time
Train	3 per day	5 hrs

Rural France doesn't come any better than this, as the train slices through the heart of the Massif Central, the vast upland area of extinct volcanoes in central southern France. The one drawback is the infrequency of services, so you would need several days to explore the area thoroughly – but the views from the window are reason enough to make the trip. On the northern leg towards Clermont-Ferrand you encounter the limestone heights of the Cévennes, a region of remote plateaux cut by huge gorges.

Though we haven't described them here, the intervening towns of **Marvejols** and **St Flour** are both characterful and well off the tourist circuit. Marvejols has a lively Saturday market and medieval buildings; St Flour has an extraordinary high town perched on volcanic crags (a good 20-min walk up from the station, where most of the hotels cluster) with a cathedral built of lava rocks that resemble breeze blocks.

There's accessible hiking west of Clermont-Ferrand where you can base yourself at **Le Mont-Dore** for a few days in the dramatic peaks of the Monts Dore. From Clermont, the route leads back south, through **Issoire** and **Brioude**, both of which have magnificent Romanesque churches. The city of **Le Puy en Velay** is off the main route, but well worth a stopover.

South of Langeac you travel through the spectacular **Allier gorge** amid the wild, volcanic scenery of the Auvergne. It's not a wealthy area, and some of the medieval red-roofed villages look distinctly depopulated.

BÉZIERS

See p. 107.

MILLAU

Prettily situated at a confluence of valleys, this town is a good base for the Cévennes, one of the most ruggedly remote parts of the Massif Central uplands. The historic centre is quietly attractive and almost traffic-free, with a spectacularly tall **belfry** (open July–Aug), the delightful arcaded **Place Foch**, and a **museum** chronicling Millau's former glove industry. Within the Parc de la Victoire is the **Jardin des Causses**, with flora typical of the neighbouring limestone plateaux. A 3-km walk on the far bank of the Tarn leads to **la Graufesenque**, a 1st-century AD Gallo-Roman settlement with a kiln site where vast quantities of pottery have been unearthed, now on display in the museum.

Much of the area is hard to explore without your own transport, so hire a car to visit stunning geological formations such as the impressive limestone gorges of the Tarn and the Jonte, the show cave of Aven Armand and the Chaos de Montpellier-le-Vieux. One word of warning, though: these sites get pretty packed in high summer, and you may do better to arm yourself with a detailed map and explore the top of the virtually empty windswept Causses (plateaux) above. For the very fit, hire a bike (from **Orts Cycle Espace**, 21 BLVD DE L'AYROLLE, ☎05 65 61 14 29) or take the long-distance marked walking paths GR62, GR71c or GR 71d, to get up there.

There are excursion buses (July and Aug) to the cheese-making village of Roquefort, to surrounding Knight Templar villages and to the Tarn Gorge, plus regular buses to Montpellier, Rodez and St Affrique.

🚆 10 mins' walk from the centre: walk along AV. A. MERLE, turn right at the T-junction.

i **Tourist information**: PL. DU BEFFROI (by the big belfry), ☎05 65 60 02 42, fax 05 65 60 95 08.

🏨 Hotels: nothing really in the historic core, but cheap and central is **Hôtel du Commerce**, 8 PL. DU MANDOUROUS, ☎05 65 60 00 56, fax 05 65 61 93 75, €; or central and with a pool is **Cévénol Hôtel**, 115 R. DU RAJOL, ☎05 65 60 74 44, fax 05 65 85 99, €€€. **Hostel: Sud Aveyron Accueil**, 26 R. LUCIEN COSTES, ☎05 65 61 27 74, fax 05 65 61 90 58, 1 km from the station (🚌 no. 1 to Cardabelles).

CLERMONT-FERRAND

Clermont, centre of the French rubber industry, and birthplace of Michelin tyres, is built of a dark volcanic stone, and is not exactly picturesque. But the centre has an absorbing maze of little lanes and alleys, dominated by the hilltop Gothic **cathedral**. The building to seek out is the 11th century church of **Notre-Dame-du-Port**, one of France's greatest examples of the local Romanesque style, displaying some wonderful stone carving inside and out.

🚆 **Station**: 1 km east of the old centre: turn left to PL. DE L'ESPLANADE and take either AV. DE GRANDE BRETAGNE or AV. CARNOT.

i **Tourist Office**: PL. DE LA VICTOIRE, ☎04 73 98 65 00, fax 04 73 98 64 98 (www.ot-clermont-ferrand.fr).

🏨 Most hotels are uninspiring, but by lively PL. JAUDE is **Hôtel Foch**, 22 R. MARÉCHAL FOCH, ☎04 73 93 48 40, fax 04 73 35 71 41, €€. **Hostels: Auberge du Cheval Blanc**, 55 AV. DE L'URSS, ☎04 73 92 26 39, fax 04 73 92 99 96, opposite the station (open May–Oct); **Corum St Jean** (non-HI), 17 R. GAULTIER DE BIAUZAT, ☎04 73 31 57 00, fax 04 73 31 59 99 (🚌no. 120 to PL. GAILLARD).

ST GEORGES D'AURAC

Change here for the connecting train to Le Puy en Velay. Other ways of getting to Le Puy include the SNCF bus from Langeac (the next stop on the main line).

WHERE NEXT FROM CLERMONT-FERRAND?

*To venture into the mountains, take the train south-west to **Le Mont-Dore**. This pretty spa and ski resort is ideally placed for walks into the Monts Dore, a volcanic mountain range laced with 650 km of marked paths, including long-distance Chemins de Grandes Randonnées – or GRs. For example from Mont-Dore you can head up to the 1373-m summit of Roc de Cuzeau via the GR4, then hike along the ridge to the Puy de Sancy (1885 m) before taking the GR30 back down to Mont Dore. It's quite tough walking, with appreciable slopes and (if you're lucky) far-ranging views. Tourist Office: AV. DE LA LIBÉRATION, ☎ 04 73 65 20 21, fax 04 73 65 05 71. **Hostel:** Le Grand Volcan, ☎ 04 73 65 03 53, fax 04 73 65 26 39. Trains continue west to join the **Calais–Toulouse route** (p. 73) at either **Brive-la-Gaillarde** (a scenic route skirting the Plateau des Millevaches, one of the major watersheds of France) or **Limoges**.*

LE PUY EN VELAY

With its cathedral, monumental statue and ancient chapel each capping a volcanic hill Le Puy is an enticing city with a memorable skyline; inevitably it's hard work to explore. On Rocher Corneille (Crow Rock) is the bizarre 19th-century red statue of **Notre-Dame-de-France** (Our Lady of France), a colossal 110-tonne figure fashioned from 213 melted-down cannons from the battle of Sébastopol. Walk up the internal staircase for stunning views over the town. The 11th-century chapel of **St-Michel d'Aiguilhe** can be reached by climbing 268 steps. The vast black-and-white striped **cathedral**, one of the great pilgrimage churches of France and reached by 134 steps from rue des Tables, has a lovely cloister and a carved grand entrance; its famous dark cedar Black Madonna on the high altar is a 19th-century copy of a figure reputedly brought back from the Crusades and burnt during the French Revolution.

Traditional lace-making is still a local industry and **Le Centre d'Enseignement de la Dentelle au Fuseau,** 38–40 R. RAPHAËL, has an exhibition and demonstration room. Bobbin lace-work from the 16th–20th centuries is on display at the **Musée Crozatier,** Jardin Henri Vinay.

15 mins from centre; turn left from station, follow AV. CHARLES DUPUY.

Tourist Office: PL. DU BREUIL, ☎ 04 71 09 38 41, fax 04 71 05 22 62 (www.ot-lepuyenvelay.fr).

Hostel: 9 R. JULES VALLÈS, ☎ 04 71 05 52 40, fax 04 71 05 61 24, 1 km (all uphill!) from the station. Check for closing periods.

NÎMES

See p. 108.

ROUTE DETAIL		
Bonifacio–Ajaccio		
Type	Frequency	Typical journey time
Bus	3 daily	4 hrs
Ajaccio–Corté		ETT table 393
Type	Frequency	Typical journey time
Train	4–5 daily	2 hrs
Corté–Bastia		ETT table 393
Type	Frequency	Typical journey time
Train	4–5 daily	1 hr 40 mins

In French hands since the 18th century, the island of *Corsica* offers an improbably dramatic combination of rugged coastlines, beaches (notably in the south-east) and huge mountains (crossed by the demanding GR20 path, running 200 km from **Conca** in the south-east to **Calenzana** in the north-west). This route uses bus services from **Bonifacio** (the port serving *Sardinia*) to **Ajaccio**, then uses splendidly scenic railways to **Bastia** in the far north. Fish and seafoods are a speciality around the coasts and hearty mountain sausages and strong goat and sheep's cheeses are a local treat.

Note that no rail passes are honoured in Corsica, as the *U Trinighellu* (small train) railway is a privatised service.

BONIFACIO – AJACCIO

Three scheduled bus services per day (Jul–Aug), and 2 a day rest of year, taking 3 hrs 30 mins. Buses are operated by **Eurocorse Voyage**, ☎ 04 95 70 13 83, and the long, slow bus journey presents an ideal opportunity to discover the vineyards, mountains and valleys of southern Corsica.

BONIFACIO

Seen from a ferry or one of the many boat trips that depart from here, **Bonifacio** looks most dramatic, with its characterful upper town and citadel clinging precariously to a spur overlooking the harbour. The hardy can save time climbing to the old city by using

PORTO VECCHIO

Porto Vecchio, accessible by frequent bus services (the closest being Bonifacio), lies to the South West of the island and has, arguably Corsica's best beaches. Looking more Caribbean than Mediterranean, Rondinara, Santa Giulia, Palombaggia, and Pinarello are protected stretches of white sand and phenomenally clear pale turquoise blue seas.

FERRIES TO CORSICA

Corsica is well served with ferries. For example, **Bonifacio**, at the southern end, has 2–10 sailings daily to **Santa Teresa di Gallura** in Sardinia (p. 422; crossing time 1 hr). Large ferries sail infrequently (not daily) from **Bastia** to **Marseille**. There are many other sailings to **Nice** and **Toulon** from most Corsican ports. Check locally for exact details. Reservations should be made well in advance for the large ferries during July/Aug and French school holiday periods. There's scope for a journey from Sicily, across Sardinia and Corsica and then on to mainland France or Italy. (See various ETT tables from 2635 to 2699).

the covered stairway inside the Genoese walls on the right after leaving the port. Inter-island buses depart from the end of the bay, about a 10-min walk along the quay from the port, past innumerable restaurants and cafés lining the anchorage.

Within the intriguing warren of narrow streets and alleys that makes up the upper town is a seemingly endless number of restaurants. Sights include the **Place du Marché**, the 12th-century Pisan **Eglise Sainte Marie Majeure** with its 14th-century white stone clock tower – the intricate buttresses along both sides contain an ingenious system of rain water canalisation. The 187-step **Staircase of the King of Aragon** is carved into the stone down to the water and is said to have been built one agited night in 1421. The massive 16th-century Genoese Gate with its drawbridge and moat open on to the medieval RUE LONGUE, where the house of Napoleon Bonaparte's ancestor stands.

i **Tourist Office**: 2 R. FRED SCAMARONI, ☎04 95 73 11 88, fax 04 95 73 14 97 (www.bonifacio.com); also a basic, seasonal office at the port.

🚢 **Moby Lines**, represented in Bonifacio by **Les Voyages Gazano**, ☎04 95 73 00 29, fax 04 95 73 05 50; **Saremar**, ☎04 95 73 00 96, fax 04 95 73 13 37.

🛏 **Hotels** of all categories abound. Five **campsites** are located in the brush beyond the car park bounding the bay: **L'Araguina**, AV. SYLVÈRE BOHN, ☎04 95 73 02 96, fax 04 95 73 01 62, is the closest to the bay and **Des Îles**, 5.5 km from town on Cap Petusato road, ☎04 95 73 11 89 (both open Apr–Oct) is closest to the beach.

AJACCIO

Palm trees shade the waterfront cafés of the most French settlement on the island, the birthplace of Napoleon Bonaparte. Like most Corsican cities, **Ajaccio** is compact and all points are easily accessible by foot or by bus. Bicycles and motorcycles can be rented from **Loca Corse**, 10 AV. BEVERINI VICO, ☎04 95 20 71 20.

The birth of local-boy-
made-good (or is it bad?)
Napoleon is
commemorated from
13–15 Aug with parades,
dances and pageants.

Foremost among the Napoleon-related sights is **La Maison Bonaparte**, R. SAINT CHARLES at the PL. LETIZIA, the great man's birthplace. His death mask can be seen in a special room in the town hall, while one of the best viewpoints in city is the monumental statue of Napoleon in the PL. D'AUSTERLITZ. looking over the Gulf. Housing works collected by Napoleon's mother's half-brother, Cardinal Fesch, the **Fesch Museum** (closed Tues; also Sun and Mon in winter) is Corsica's major art museum with works by Raphael, Titian and Botticelli making it France's best collection of early Italian paintings outside Paris; one wing of the building is the 1868 Public Library, a striking walnut and chestnut creation.

Maritime/Bus Station, on the QUAI L'HERMINIER, ☎04 95 51 55 45; also houses kiosks for inter-island buses. Open daily 0630 until departure of last ferry (usually 2000).

Rail station about 500 m north of the Maritime station along the BLVD SAMPIERO, an extension of the QUAI L'HERMINER.

ⓘ **Tourist Office:** 3 BLVD ROI JÉRÔME, ☎04 95 51 53 03, fax 04 95 51 53 01 (ajaccio.tourisme@ wanadoo.fr). A complete tourist desk is in the bus station, open from just before the first to just after the last sailing of the day. Main Corsica Tourism office, 17 BLVD DU ROI JÉRÔME, ☎04 95 51 00 00, fax 04 95 51 14 40. **Parc Naturel Regional de la Corse** has its main information centre at 2 R. MAJOR-LAMBROSCHINI, ☎04 95 51 79 10, fax 04 95 21 88 17.

A plethora of lodging of all categories is available. In the centre between the bus/maritime station and the rail station are many smaller **hotels**, while slightly further away are the more upmarket **Hotel Impérial**, ☎04 95 21 50 62, fax 04 95 21 15 20 and the **Hotel Fesch**, ☎04 95 51 62 62, fax 04 95 21 83 36. **Camping Les Mimosas**, ☎04 95 20 99 85, 3 km east of the city (☐ no. 4), is well equipped (open Apr–mid-Oct). The Corsican branch of **Gîtes de France**, 1 R. DU GENERAL FIORELLA, 20000 AJACCIO, ☎04 95 51 72 82, fax 04 95 51 72 89, provides information and a brochure on rural gîtes (self-catering accommodation) in the area.

The full range of Corsican and French cuisine is available and there are numerous Chinese, fast-food and Asian restaurants.

CORTÉ

Ringed by mountains, Corté perches on a huge outcrop, with cobblestone stairways threading between stone houses to a 15th-century citadel. The town is a good centre for exploring the regional natural park.

500 m south-east of the centre.

ⓘ **Tourist Office:** QUARTIER DES QUATRE FONTAINES, ☎04 95 46 26 70.

SIDE TRIP FROM PONTE LECCIA TO CALVI From **Ponte Leccia** (between Corté and Bastia) this exotic rail route takes a curving, mountainous passage through mostly deserted countryside to **l'Île Rousse**, and then hugs the seashore to **Calvi**. Direct narrow-gauge services run, two daily, via **l'Île Rousse**, journey taking 2 hrs. Between **l'Île Rousse** and **Calvi**, 10 additional services operate July–Sept (ETT table 393). **L'Île Rousse** takes its name from the nearby red granite isles joined to the mainland by a causeway. The town itself, the warmest place in Corsica, is handsomely compact but lively. **Tourist office**: 7 pl. Paoli, ☎04 95 60 04 35, fax 04 95 60 24 74. **Rail information**: ☎04 95 60 00 50; maritime information **CCR**, ☎04 95 60 09 56, representing **SNCM**, **CMN** and **Corsica Ferries**.

Calvi makes another excellent base, with a lively summer beach and the chance to discover the untouched hinterlands. Treks and camping tours can be organised through the tourist office. **Tourist Office**: Porte de Plaisance, ☎04 95 65 16 67, fax 04 95 65 14 09.

BASTIA

Bastia has a certain allure, especially around the old port and the citadel. Seek out the animated pl. St. Nicolas and the r. Napoleon that connects it with the atmospherically dilapidated, horseshoe-shaped Vieux Port (Old Port), with fishing boats creaking at anchor and flapping washing-lines strung over dark, shuttered alleys. The evening promenade seems to be the summer activity of many locals. The 17th-century **Église St-Marie** contains a 19th-century silver Virgin said to weigh one ton. Just beyond the Cathedral is the sumptuously baroque **Chapelle St-Croix**, containing the much venerated *Black Christ of Miracles* found in 1428 and now the patron of local fishermen.

🚆 Close to the centre and port. **Maritime Station**: in the new port area near the pl. St Nicolas.

ℹ️ **Tourist Office**: pl. St. Nicolas, ☎04 95 54 20 40, fax 04 95 54 20 41 (www.ville-bastia.fr; ot-bastia@wanadoo.fr), town plans available. **Objectif Nature**, ☎/fax 04 95 32 54 34, 3 r. Notre-Dame-de-Lourdes can assist campers and trekkers.

🚢 **SNCM**, ☎04 95 29 66 99; **Corsica Ferries**, ☎04 95 32 95 95; **Moby Lines**, ☎04 95 34 84 94.

🚌 **Buses**: Services for the Cap Corse peninsula – check with the municipal tourist office for details.

🛏️ A variety of accommodation can be found around the old city between the railway station and the maritime port along the av. Marechal Sebastiani. **Camping du Bois de San Damiano**, ☎04 95 33 68 02, fax 04 95 30 84 10 (open Apr–Oct) is 5 km south on the long Marana beach.

🍽️ The Old Port area contains a large number of **restaurants** ranging from Corsican seafood speciality to pizzerias to Tex-Mex establishments. The **daily market** in the square around the City Hall behind the St Jean Baptiste Church offers a delectable array of fresh, local produce.

ROUTE DETAIL

Toulouse–Foix ETT table 312

Type	Frequency	Typical journey time
Train	8–10 daily	1 hr 10 mins

Foix–Villefranche ETT tables 312, 356

Type	Frequency	Typical journey time
Train	3–4 daily	2 hrs 30 mins–4 hrs 30 mins

Villefranche–Perpignan ETT table 356

Type	Frequency	Typical journey time
Train	5–6 daily	50 mins

Perpignan–Collioure ETT table 355

Type	Frequency	Typical journey time
Train	11–13 daily	25 mins

Collioure–Figueres ETT tables 355, 662

Type	Frequency	Typical journey time
Train	6 daily	1 hr 40 mins

Figueres–Girona ETT table 662

Type	Frequency	Typical journey time
Train	Every hr	30 mins

Girona–Barcelona ETT table 662

Type	Frequency	Typical journey time
Train	Every hr	1 hr 20 mins

KEY JOURNEYS

Toulouse–Perpignan (change at Narbonne) ETT tables 321, 355

Type	Frequency	Typical journey time
Train	10–12 daily	2 hrs 30 mins–3 hrs

Perpignan–Barcelona ETT table 49

Type	Frequency	Typical journey time
Train	2 daily	3 hrs

Toulouse–Latour de Carol ETT table 312

Type	Frequency	Typical journey time
Train	4–5 daily	2 hrs 45 mins

Latour de Carol–Barcelona ETT table 654

Type	Frequency	Typical journey time
Train	5 daily	3 hrs 15 mins

Notes

Toulouse to Barcelona: for fastest journey change trains at Narbonne. Collioure to Figueras: change trains at the border. Toulouse or Foix to Villefranche: change trains at Latour de Carol.

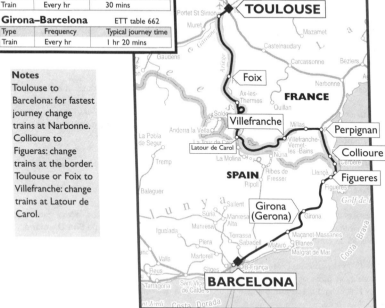

RAIL TOUR: TOULOUSE – PERPIGNAN – BARCELONA

The Pyrénées mountain chain is one of the world's most emphatic national boundaries, a great wall of snow-capped peaks separating France from Spain. Virtually any route over it is a thrilling encounter: here the journey rises up to **Latour de Carol** at 1250 m before either running straight south to Barcelona (sit on the right-hand side of the train for the best views), or twisting and turning down the mountains in the scenic narrow-gauge Petit Train Jaune (Little Yellow Train), which twists and turns its way through the mountains to **Villefranche-de-Conflent**, with the great summit of Canigou rising to the south. From **Perpignan** you are firmly in Catalunya (Catalonia), a distinctive region that strongly holds on to its regional identity. Beyond **Collioure**, the route heads close to the Mediterranean and into Spain, where the rugged coast of the Costa Brava (reached by bus from Gerona or **Figueras**) has been much developed for the package holiday industry, but has some pleasantly tranquil coves. **Barcelona** is covered on pp. 141–147.

TOULOUSE

See p. 78.

FOIX

This almost perfect looking medieval town stands just south of the Plantaurel hills at the meeting of two rivers, with the three towers of its castle dominating the scene from a lofty crag. About 6 km north-west, take a boat-trip (1 hr 30 mins) on the Labouiche, Europe's longest navigable underground river, and some 15 km south there are superb caves: admire 12,000-year-old cave paintings at the Grotte de Niaux, and majestic stalactites and stalagmites in the Grotte de Lombrives.

10 mins north-east of town: follow the Ariège river and cross the bridge to the centre.

Tourist Office: 29 R. DELCASSÉ, ☎ 05 61 65 12 12, fax 05 61 65 64 63.

The charming 2-star **Hôtel du Lac**, ☎ 05 61 65 17 17, fax 05 61 02 94 24, €€, by the lakeside, can be reached by bus from the centre. **Hostel: Leo Legrange**, 16 R. NOËL PEYREVIDAL, ☎ 05 61 65 09 04, fax 05 61 02 63 87.

VILLEFRANCHE-DE-CONFLENT

The tiny fortified village of Villefranche is riddled with narrow streets and seems almost to have been transported from the Middle Ages. It is dominated by the enormous 17th-century **Fort Liberia**: walk up to it (open all year) along the original soldiers' path (30 mins), coming back down via the 734 steps of the underground staircase that leads directly to Pont St Pierre, the medieval village bridge. For the less athletic, there is a minibus from the Porte de France gateway.

Villefranche-Vernet-les-Bains, 3 km from the village.

Tourist Office: PL. DE L'ÉGLISE, ☎ 04 68 96 22 96, fax 04 68 96 07 24.

PERPIGNAN

Unmistakably Spanish in character though unfortunately overrun in summer, Perpignan was formerly the mainland capital of Majorca and is now a vibrant, large city at the heart of French Catalonia. Catalan is spoken hereabouts, and the *sardane*, Catalonia's national dance, is performed to music a couple of times a week in summer in the 14th-century PL. DE LA LOGE, Perpignan's main square and still the hub of the city's life. A 15th-century fortified gatehouse, **Le Castillet**, QUAI SADI-CARNOT, houses Casa Païral (a museum of local folk traditions), while the **Cathédrale St-Jean**, PL. GAMBETTA, is Gothically grand. The imposing Citadelle, to the south, guards the 13th-century **Palais des Rois de Majorque** (Palace of the Kings of Majorca).

RAIL R. COURTELINE, 600 m from the centre: walk straight along AV. GÉN-DE-GAULLE to PL. CATALOGNE, and continue ahead to the centre; or take 🚌 nos. 2/19.

🚌 **Bus station**: AV. DU GÉN-LECLERC. There are regular services to the nearby beaches, especially in summer. 🚌 City bus no. I also goes to Canet beach.

i **Tourist Office**: PL. ARMAND-LANOUX, at the Congress Centre (Palais des Congrès), 📞04 68 66 30 30, fax 04 68 66 30 26 (www.little-france.com/perpignan); 30-min walk from the station.

🏨 Lots of one- and two-star establishments along and off AV. GÉNÉRAL DE GAULLE (leading from the station to the town centre). Actually on PL. DE LA LOGE, **Hôtel de la Loge**, I R. FABRIQUES-NABOT, 📞04 68 34 41 02, fax 04 68 34 25 13, €€€ is central. Less charming, but very inexpensive is **Le Métropole**, 3 R. DES CARDEURS, 📞04 68 34 43 34, €. **Hostel**: PARC DE LA PÉPINIÈRE, AV. DE GRANDE-BRETAGNE, 📞04 68 34 63 32, fax 04 68 51 16 02, 300 m from the station.

COLLIOURE

Easily visited as a day trip from Perpignan, this is the most picturesque of the local ex-fishing villages, on a knob of land between two bays, and overlooked by a 13th-century château. Matisse, Braque, Dufy and Picasso discovered Collioure, and artists still set up their easels here. The domed church steeple looks distinctly Arabic.

RAIL 300 m west of the centre.

i **Tourist Office**: PL. 18-JUIN, 📞04 68 82 15 47, fax 04 68 82 46 29 (www.collioure.com).

🏨 **Hôtel Madeloc**, R. ROMAIN ROLLAND, 📞04 68 82 07 56, fax 04 68 82 55 09, €€€, has a pool in a garden setting, but is pricey.

FIGUERES (FIGUERAS), SPAIN

The much-visited **Teatre-Museu Dalí** (www.salvador-dali.org; open daily in summer; Oct–May closed Mon) is the only real attraction, honouring the town's most famous son. Whether you consider Dalí a genius or a madman (or both), the museum is likely to confirm your views of the surrealist artist. Appropriately enough, it's a bizarre building, parts of which Dalí designed himself (including his own grave), a terracotta edifice sporting giant sculpted eggs. Inside are displays of his works, including the Mae West room and the Abraham Lincoln mural.

PLAZA DE LA ESTACIÓN. Central. Luggage lockers and cash machine.

Tourist Offices: PLAZA DEL SOL S/N, ☎972 50 31 55, fax 972 67 31 66 (www.figueras.org; fituris@ddgi.es). There is also a branch at the bus station across the Plaza from the train station.

GIRONA (GERONA)

The medieval part of the town stands on the east side of the River Onyar, connected by the Pont de Pedra to a prosperous new city in the west. From the bridge you can see the **Cases de l'Onyar** – a line of picturesque houses overhanging the river. In the heart of the labyrinthine old town is the superlative Gothic **cathedral**. Its interior has a single-naved vault with a 22 m span (the largest ever constructed). Buy a ticket for entry to the Romanesque cloister and the museum within the chapterhouse, containing the 15th-century **Tapis de la Creació** (Tapestry of the Creation).

Also seek out the **Banys Arabs** (Arab Baths), Romanesque with Moorish touches and dating from the 13th century. **Museu d'Art**, housed in a splendid Renaissance bishop's palace, displays a wealth of paintings and carvings from the Romanesque period to the 20th century. In the narrow streets of **El Call** (old Jewish quarter) is the **Bonastruc ça Porta Centre** (Centre Isaac el Cec), soon to become a Museum of Jewish Culture. The 11th–12th-century Benedictine **Monastery Sant Pere de Galligants** now houses the archaeological museum. The **Palau des Agullana** is a 14th–17th century town palace which, together with Sanxt Marti Sacosta Church, forms an attractive baroque group.

In the new town; 10-min walk from the river and Pont de Pedra.

Bus station: there is a linking door from the train station.

Tourist Offices: Rambla de la Llibertat 1, ☎972 22 65 75, fax 972 22 66 12 (www.ajuntament.gi), by the river, on the east bank. There's also an office at the train station in summer.

Try around the cathedral and C. SANTA CLARA, or head for the streets around PLAÇA DE LA CONSTITUTIÓ. **Youth hostel**: **Cerverí de Girona**, CARRER DELS CIUTADANS 9, ☎972 21 80 03, fax 972 21 20 23 (alberg_girona@tujuca.com).

BARCELONA

See p. 141.

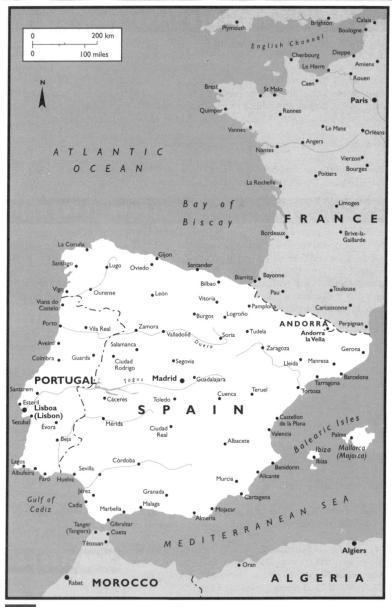

(for Directory information, see pp. 611 and 607).
Inexpensive to travel in and blessed with a warm climate, **Spain** is astonishingly varied, ranging from the fashion-conscious sophistication and pulsating atmospheres of Madrid and Barcelona to rural scenes that look as if they might belong to another continent, or another century. It's not consistently beautiful – views from the train might take in hideous high-rise developments or uneventful cereal plains, whilst much of the coast is taken up with concrete resorts that sprang up in the 1950s and 1960s to provide cheap package holidays. But the classic Spanish elements are there too – parched, empty landscapes dotted with cypresses and cacti and backed by rugged sierras, lines of poplars receding to hazy horizons and red-roofed fortified towns clustered round castles. Some scenes are peculiarly local: the luxuriant greenness of Galicia, the spectacular snowy pinnacles of the Picos de Europa, or the canyon-like badlands of Aragon on the southern fringes of the Pyrenees.

Although surrounded on the landward sides by Spain, **Portugal** contrasts strongly from its Iberian neighbour, with a different language and customs; indeed, for centuries the two countries were at war with one another. Portugal prospered as a great maritime power and ruled a far-flung empire across Africa, the Far East and South America. For some 500 years the Arabs held sway over the country, and you'll see Moorish buildings with low domes and flat roofs, although some of the architecture is uniquely Portuguese – such as the Manueline style (a flamboyant transition between Gothic and Renaissance). Landscapes look positively lush, with rolling hills dotted with orange, lemon and olive groves. Inland rises a chain of lowish mountains with some timeless fortified towns. Away from the touristy Algarve, there are plenty of smaller places awaiting discovery, and much of it is amazingly untouched and little-developed – you'll still see peasants with donkeys and find communities rich in rural customs. Low prices make it tempting to linger, and distances are small.

In Spain you must reserve and pay a reservation fee for all trains that have a train category shown in the timing column of the European timetable (IC, Talgo, Arco etc), even if you have a rail pass. You also have to reserve for AP and IC trains in Portugal.

SPAIN

ACCOMMODATION
There's generally no problem finding somewhere to stay, outside major festivals and other peak periods; however, some large cities (notably Madrid) can be problematic, with virtually everywhere booked up by 0900; accordingly, book ahead, for example through the **Hostelling International Booking Network (IBN)**.

BUDGET ACCOMMODATION
By strolling around, you'll often find budget places congregated near the station and around the main square. Thanks to a useful hierarchy imposed by regional tourist authorities, accommodation is graded according to facilities. Cheapest are the basic **boarding houses**, known variously as *fondas* (look for plaques marked F), *Pensiones* (P), *Posadas*, *Ventas* and *Casas de Huéspedes*; then come *Hostales* (HS) and *Hostales Residencias* (HR); generally higher in the pecking order are *hotels* (H), ranging from one to five stars. Note that there can be an overlap between different types of accommodation, e.g. the best *Hostales Residencias* are often more expensive than the low-grade (one- to two-star) hotels. If there is also an 'R' on the plaque, do not expect a full dining service.

HISTORIC ACCOMMODATION
There's also scope for staying in a number of castles, old monasteries and other historic buildings, converted to government-run hotels called *Paradores Nacionales* (or *paradors*); these tend to be very expensive, but the standard is extremely high. Central booking service in Madrid for *paradors* throughout the whole country: ☎ 91 516 66 66 (www.parador.es).

PRIVATE HOMES
Private homes that offer rooms are known as *Casas Particulares*. They seldom have much in the way of facilities, but are usually centrally located and almost invariably very cheap. *Casas rurales* are farmhouses and *Refugios* are mountain huts.

Tourist Offices will give you information about accommodation, but they are not allowed to make hotel reservations. In major cities, there are often hotel booking agencies at the airports and railway stations. Prices away from major resorts start at about €18 for a double room (€12 for a single). Double rooms usually have twin beds, so ask for *matrimonio* if you want a double bed. By law, places that officially provide accommodation must place a notice (updated annually) in every bedroom stating the maximum amount payable for that room. The price includes all taxes and service charges (but seldom breakfast), and you should pay no more than the stated amount (which is for the room, not per person). When paying for your room, it is a good idea to keep a copy of the quoted price or a copy of the accommodation guide handy as some places have a tendency to put the prices up for tourists. All hotels and hostels are listed in the *Guía de Hoteles*, an annual publication available from Tourist Offices.

YOUTH HOSTELS There are dozens of **HI** youth hostels around the country, and some universities offer accommodation in student dormitories *(Colegios Mayores)* when students are not in residence. Prices are €3–11 for those under 26 and €3.6–14 for 26 and over. Head office: RED ESPAÑOLA DE ALBERGUES JUVENILES, C JOSÉ ORTEGA Y GASSET 71, MADRID 28006, ☎91 347 77 00, fax 91 401 81 60 (www.mtas.es/injuve/intercambios/albergues/reaj).

CAMPING There are over 500 **campsites** (some open all year, others just in summer); the Spanish Tourist Office issues a list of the approved ones *(Guía de Campings)*, which are classified as luxury, first, second and third class. You can camp 'rough' in most suitable places, but not on tourist beaches. Book locally or through the **Federación Española de Empresarios de Campings**, SAN BERNARDO, 97/99, BUILDING COLOMINA, 5, 28015 MADRID, ☎91 448 12 34, fax 91 448 12 67.

FOOD AND DRINK The pattern is to have a light **breakfast**: coffee or hot chocolate with rolls or fritters *(churros)*. The main meal is **lunch** (1330–1500 – nearer 1500 on Sunday). Dinner is a little lighter, but can still consist of three courses, and is eaten at around 2200. Restaurants are open only for lunch and dinner, so go to *cafeterías* (usually open 0800–midnight) for breakfast and light meals/snacks. *Platos combinados* and *menú del día* are both good value. If you want an inexpensive light meal, ask for *raciones*, a larger portion of *tapas* (little more than nibbles, intended as aperitifs). The best-known Spanish dish is *paella*, which originated in Valencia; it is at its best when made to order – which takes about half an hour. Another famous dish is *gazpacho* (cold tomato soup), which originated in Andalucía and is found mainly in the south.

Choose your drinking place according to what you want to consume. For **beer**, you need a bar or *cervecería*, for wine a *taberna* or *bodega*. For **cider** (in the north), you need a *sidreria*. The custom is to pay for all your drinks at the end of the evening, although this is changing in some resort areas. Many drinking places have a dining-room *(comedor)* at the rear if you want a full meal, or you can go to a proper restaurant *(mesón)*. It is claimed that water is safe to drink, but check for a *'potable'* (drinking) notice above the tap. Mineral water is available everywhere. Coffee tends to be strong. There are some excellent **wines** (notably from the Rioja and Ribera de Duero regions) and Jerez is, of course, the home of sherry. *Sangría* is a sweet, light drink based on wine and fruit juice. Beer is generally yellow and weak, but amply thirst-quenching.

PORTUGAL

ACCOMMODATION A good bet in most places is to find a room *(quartos or dormidas)* in a private house, or in a pension *(pensão –* more of a business than a house, and graded from one to three stars). Other inexpensive places are boarding houses *(hospedarias/casas de hóspedes)* and one-star hotels.

Information

Tourist Offices will be able to give details of many of the available places to stay, and can make bookings.

Youth hostels

Hostels are mostly open 24 hrs and cost €6–14.5, including bed linen and breakfast; for details, contact **Movijovem**, Avda Duque d'Ávila 137, 1050 Lisbon, ☎21 359 60 00, fax 21 352 86 21.

Camping

For a national coverage of **campsites**, contact the **Portuguese Camping and Caravan Association**, Av Coronel Eduardo Galbardo 24, 1000 Lisbon; ☎21 812 68 90, fax 21 812 69 18.

Pousadas

Advance reservations are essential. For further information or to make a reservation, contact **Enatur**, Avda Santa Joana a Princesa 10, 1700 Lisbon, ☎21 844 20 00, fax 21 844 20 86

Pousadas are state-run establishments in three categories. Some are converted national historic monuments, others are modern buildings in historic locations: both these types are four- to five-star standard. The third category is composed of comfortable modern inns or lodges, built in locations chosen for their wild remoteness and fabulous views: these are three- to four-star.

Food and Drink

The Portuguese pattern of eating is to have a fairly frugal breakfast and two big main meals: **lunch** (1200–1500) and **dinner** (1930–2230). Places that have evening entertainment may stay open until around midnight and, if so, tend to offer a late supper. The **cafés** and **pastry shops** usually stay open all day.

Eating is not expensive but, if your budget is strained, go for the meal of the day, *prato do día* or *menú*. Eating is taken seriously, the cuisine flavoured with herbs rather than spices and rather heavy on olive oil. There is lots of delicious seafood, such as grilled sardines and several varieties of *caldeirada* (fish stew). Other local dishes are *bacalhau* (dried salted cod in various guises) and *leitão* (roasted suckling pig). The most popular pudding is a sweet egg custard.

Portugal is, of course, the home of **port**, but there are also several excellent (and often inexpensive) wines, such as the *vinho verde* whites and the rich reds of the Dão and Bairrada regions. Do not be surprised if you are charged for pre-dinner bread, olives or other nibbles that are brought to your table unordered. If you don't want them, say so.

EDITOR'S CHOICE

Ávila; Barcelona; Bilbao (Museo Guggenheim); Burgos Cathedral; Cáceres; Cádiz; Córdoba; Cuenca; El Escorial; Évora; Granada; Lisbon; Madrid (especially the Prado); Óbidos; Oporto; Picos de Europa; Salamanca; Santiago; Segovia; Seville; Sintra; Toledo. Scenic rail journeys: Lisbon–Santiago de Compostela (p. 176) and on via Ourense to León (p. 184); Douro valley from Oporto (see p. 180); Málaga–Ronda (p. 194); Granada–Almería (see Side Trips from Granada, p. 201); Madrid–Burgos (ETT table 689).

BEYOND THE BORDERS

Algeciras–Tangier (Morocco) by ferry (ETT table 2502); Madrid–Paris via San Sebastián (table 46); Barcelona–Paris (table 11); Barcelona–Milan via Montpellier and Nice (table 90).

Spain's second city, Barcelona, metropolis of the revolutionary and energetic Catalan people, has real style and demands a visit of at least a couple of days. The city is home to remarkable organic-looking Modernist (or Spanish art nouveau) buildings of Antoni Gaudí and wonderful specialist galleries displaying works by Picasso and Miró.

Barcelona is pretty spread out, and apart from the old Gothic quarter – known as the Barri Gòtic – it's best to use the metro or the Bus Turístic for getting about, as there are endless busy roads to cross and walking around is not that much fun in the large 19th-century grid of roads called the Eixample.

Since hosting the Olympic games in 1992, the Catalan capital has been transformed by large-scale urban renewal. It has now gained a cosmopolitan, prosperous air. Tourism has arrived here in a very big way, and in summer the whole place can seem oppressively crowded, especially around major attractions such as the Casa Milà (also known as La Pedrera) and the Sagrada Familia.

Another less appealing aspect of the city is its appreciable crime rate. In particular, beware of muggers at night in the Barri Gòtic and the red-light district in the lower part of the Ramblas.

ARRIVAL AND DEPARTURE

There are two main stations: the central **Estació de França**, AVDA MARQUÈS DE L'ARGENTERA ☎ 902 24 02 02 (Metro: BARCELONETA), for certain long-distance national services; and **Estació de Sants**, PLAÇA DELS PAÏSOS CATALANS, about 3.5 km from the old town (Metro: SANTS-ESTACIÓ), for suburban, regional and international trains as well as those to the airport. All trains to and from Estació de França also call at Estació de Sants.

Estació de Autobuses Barcelona Nord: CALLE ALI-BEI 80, ☎ 93 265 65 08 (Metro: ARC DE TRIOMF). **Estació de Sants**: PLAÇA DE LOS PAÏSOS CATALANS, ☎ 93 490 40 00 (Metro: SANTS-ESTACIÓ).

From the port, virtually next door to Estació de França, ferries leave for the Balearics and Sicily. For details, contact **Trasmediterránea**, ☎ 902 45 46 45 (www.trasmediterranea.com).

Aeroport del Prat is 12 km south-west of the city. Expanded and refurbished for the 1992 Olympic games, it now has three terminals. Airport information: ☎ 93 298 38 38. RENFE trains run every 30 mins, between about 0600 and 2300, to and from Estació de Sants (journey time: 16 mins) and Estació Plaça de Catalunya (21 mins).

The **aerobus** runs to and from Plaça de Catalunya every 15 mins. The service operates from the airport Mon–Fri 0600–2400, Sat and Sun 0630–2400; in the other direction, Mon–Fri 0530–2315, Sat and Sun 0600–2320. Additional stops are shown on the city map available from Tourist Offices. For information: ☎ 93 415 60 20.

TOURS

From the quay below the Columbus monument, at PLAÇA DEL PORTAL DE LA PAU, **Las Golondrinas** (pleasure boats) ferry visitors around the harbour or across to the Olympic Port. Round trips last 30 mins or 2 hrs.

INFORMATION

CITY MAP – inside back cover

For **city information** ☎ 906 30 12 82 (www.barcelonaturisme.com; teltur@barcelonaturisme.com). City tourist information centres at: PLAÇA DE CATALUNYA 17 (in the centre of the square, beneath street level); City Hall, CARRER CIUTAT 2; Estació de Sants (Sants Station) (www.gencat.es/probertt). **Regional tourist information** for Catalunya and the rest of Spain: at the airport; at PLAÇA PAÏSOS CATALANS; and Palau Robert, PASSEIG DE GRÀCIA 107, ☎ 93 238 40 00, fax 93 238 40 10. For an English phone information service run by Generalitat, dial 010. Also from late June to late Sept at PLAÇA DE LA SAGRADA FAMÍLIA. The Tourist Office also runs street information services during summer. Look for staff in red and white uniforms, with the standard 'i' symbol on their shirt sleeves.

There are two main youth information offices. **Centre d'Informació i Assessorament per a Joves**, CALLE FERRAN 32, ☎ 93 402 78 00/1, fax 93 402 78 01, and CALLE CALÀBRIA 147 (another entrance at CALLE ROCAFORT, 116–122), ☎ 93 483 83 63 (www.bcn.es/ciaj), gives information and assistance on cultural, sports and leisure facilities in the city. **Oficina de Turisme Juvenil** (www.tujuca.com), gives advice on the best travel prices and issues IYHF and ISIC cards, amongst other services.

MONEY There are several **Ultramar Express** locations acting as Thomas Cook Licensees around the city.

POST The main **post offices** are at PLAÇA ANTONIO LÓPEZ 1, RONDA UNIVERSITAT 23 and GRAN DE GRÀCIA 118.

PUBLIC TRANSPORT

METRO There are two fast and clean metro services. The **Metro**, run by the city (Ciutat), has five colour-coded lines. Trains are designated by the name of the last stop. The **Ferrocarrils de la Generalitat de Catalunya**, run by the Catalan State, serves fewer places in the centre, but can take you out into the suburbs and beyond. The same tickets are valid on Metro and Generalitat lines and there is a flat rate for all journeys, regardless of distance or location. You have to pay again if you transfer between the two lines. The Metro runs Mon–Thur 0500–2300, Fri, Sat and the day before holidays 0500–0200, Sun 0600–midnight.

TOURIST BUS The **Bus Turístic** (tourist bus) runs every day 0900–2130 for the whole year, except 1 Jan and 25 Dec, usually from late Mar to the following Jan. Pick up a map and guide, which outlines the monuments and sights, and ticket from the bus: the two routes start from Plaça de Catalunya, though to avoid the queues you might do better to walk on to the next stop and then pick up the bus from there. The northern (red) route takes in the Pedrera (Casa Milà), Sagrada

PASSES

The T10 pass is valid for 10 journeys by metro, Ferrocarrils de la Generalitat de Catalunya, bus or RENFE regional trains. Price depends which of the six zones you travel in.

FURTHER INFORMATION

Barcelona Hotel Association,
VIA LAIETANA 47,
📠 93 301 62 40
www.barcelonahotels.es;
mihotels@cambrabcn.es)

Youth Hostels
93 483 83 63, fax 93 483
3 50 (www.tujuca.com)

Camping
For more details:
sociació de Campings
e Barcelona, 📠 93 412
59 55, fax 93 302 13 36
(www.campingbcn.com;
info@campingbcn.com)

Família and Parc Güell, while the generally more scenic southern (blue) route heads past the Olympic Stadium, Montjuïc and the waterfront attractions. Tickets are available for one or two days and include a booklet giving reductions to most city sights; get on or off as you please.

TAXIS Yellow and black cabs can be hailed in the streets. Make sure you have change. To order a taxi: 📠 93 357 77 55, 93 433 10 20 or 93 300 11 00; or for 7-person taxis: 📠 39 303 30 33.

ACCOMMODATION

Barcelona has as wide a range of hotels as any major European city, but prices are pretty high compared to the rest of Spain; rates vary throughout the year, with high summer generally the peak time – when it's worth reserving well in advance or arriving early in the day as demand is high. The main area for inexpensive accommodation is around the Ramblas, particularly on the east side around CALLE FERRAN (take the metro to LICEU). *Pensiones* come as two- and one-star accommodation (generally €25–45 for a double with shared facilities). Here you'll find relatively inexpensive pensions and a few unofficial youth hostels, mostly €€.

In this area is the **Hostal Albergue Fernando**, CALLE FERRAN 31, 📠 93 301 7993 (www.barcelona-on-line.es/fernando), a popular backpackers' haunt with doubles and singles (shared bathroom). Just off this street is the **Hostal Canadiense**, BAJADA DE SAN MIGUEL 1, JUNTO A CALLE FERRÁN, 📠 93 301 7461, with doubles only (with bath), right opposite which is the quiet **Hostal Levante**, BAJADA DE SAN MIGUEL 2, JUNTO A CALLE FERRÁN, 📠 93 317 9565 (www.hostallevante.com; reservas@hostallevante.com). **Hostal Villanueva**, PLAZA REIAL 2, 📠 93 301 5084, has doubles and a few singles, with some cheaper rooms with shared bathroom. If this is full, try the adjacent and slightly pricier **Hostal Colón**, CALLE COLÓN 3, 📠 93 318 0631, where rooms at the front have balconies overlooking the square; laundry facilities; dormitories, singles, doubles and family rooms. Near the cathedral is the **Pensión Colmenero**, PETRITXOL 12, 📠 93 302 6634. Recently opened is **Backpackers BCN**, CALLE DIPUTACIÓN 323, PRINCIPAL 1A, 📠 93 488 0280 (www.backpackersbcn.com), with doubles and 4-bed dorms, €13–15.

About 15 **student halls of residence** become hostels for young people in summer. For details, contact a youth information centre (see p. 142). There are also four HI **youth hostels** (reservation highly recommended). The most central are: **Palau**, CALLE PALAU 6, 📠 93 412 50 80, fax 93 319 53 25 (Metro: LICEU/JAUME) and **Hostal de Joves**, PASSEIG PUJADES 29, 📠 93 300 31 04, fax 93 300 31 04; reduction for under 26s (Metro: ARC DE TRIOMF). There are also several private hostels, such as **Kabul**, PLAÇA REIAL 17, 📠 93 318 51 90, fax 93 301 40 34 (www.kabul-hostel.com; info@kabul-hostel.com), in the Gothic quarter (Metro: LICEU), and **Arco**, CALLE SANTE EULALIA 1, 📠 93 412 54 68, fax 93 302 40 02, with dorms only (booking up to 5 days ahead only; Metro: LICEU). **Hostal Palermo**, CALLE BOQUERÍA 21, 📠 93 302 40 02, fax 93 302 40 02, is around €35–60.

Campsites: there are 12 within easy reach of Barcelona, mostly on the coast south of the city. **El Toro Bravo**, Autovía de Castelldefels, Km 11, ☎93 637 34 62, fax 93 637 21 15 (www.eltorobravo.com; info@eltorobravo.com), is one of the closest. Take ☐no. 95 from Ronda Universitat, Rambla Catalunya or Plaça Espanya. **Filipinas**, ☎93 658 17 91, and **La Ballena Alegre**, ☎93 658 05 04, fax 93 658 05 75 (www.ballena-alegre.es; ballena1@ballena-alegre.es) are about 1 km further out on the same road. For more details, call the **Associació de Campings de Barcelona**, ☎93 412 59 55, fax 93 302 13 36 (www.campingbcn.com; info@campingbcn.com).

FOOD AND DRINK

Catalan cooking is known as good peasant fare, made from ingredients such as cuttlefish, serrano ham and salt cod. *Crema catalana* is a delicious local dessert, similar to crème brûlée. Catalunya is also famous for its champenoise sparkling wine, Cava. It is the speciality of establishments known as *Xampanyerías*, especially around **Gràcia**.

In the evenings, there are some good restaurants and tapas bars along Carrer de Avinyó and the streets leading off it or along Carrer de la Mercè; iced sherry and local Penedés wine are widely on offer. For seafood specialities, try around the Passeig de Colom, at the bottom of Las Ramblas. Away from the old town, the Olympic Village is packed with bars and restaurants. The *Guía del Ocio*, published weekly, has a good coverage of restaurants; it is available from most newsstands. Off Las Ramblas is **Boqueria** covered market, with an excellent selection of fruit, vegetables and meats.

HIGHLIGHTS

AQUARIUM AND ZOO

Barcelona has two notable animal collections: the **Aquarium** (www.aquariumbcn.com), on the harbour (by cable car to Montjuïc), where a moving walkway conveys you through a tunnel of tropical and Mediterranean marine life; and **Parc Zoològic**, Parc de la Ciutadella (www.zoobarcelona.com), Spain's foremost zoo.

Art goes hand in hand with architecture in Barcelona. In this deeply style-conscious city, there is always a brave juxtaposition of old and new. Further-flung sights can easily be reached using the efficient metro system.

Best seen on foot, the **Barri Gòtic** is an enchanting, if disorienting, Gothic quarter

DAY TRIP FROM BARCELONA

The best way to reach **Montserrat monastery** (www.abadiamontserrat.net; informacio@larsa-montserrat.com) is by train and then an exciting cable car. Trains depart from under the Plaça de Espanya, and connect at Montserrat Aeri with a cable car (leaves every 15 mins). Or take one of the regular tour buses that leave from the Plaça de la Universitat. For the devout, the attraction is the 12th-century Virgin of Montserrat, in the cavernous basilica, but despite the crowds the setting is in any case interestingly surreal, with formidable crags of the Montserrat ('serrated mountain') dwarfing the scene. Twice daily a boys' choir sings in the basilica itself. A funicular climbs the mountain to a lofty hermitage and gains sublime views, and there are museums with religious works by Catalan, Italian and other artists.

FOR FREE

Basílica de Santa Maria
del Mar

Olympic Stadium

Parc de la Ciutadella

Parc Güell

Cathedral del Plaça de
Sant Jaume

inhabited from Roman times. A web of tiny, dark streets radiates from **La Seu Cathedral**, a magnificent Gothic edifice, started in 1298 but only finished in 1892. The small Romanesque chapel of **Santa Llúcia** opens off the cathedral cloister, which encloses a lush central garden with palm trees, ducks and magnolias; on Sun mornings and Wed evenings, the *sardana*, a distinctively Catalan dance, is performed in the square outside the cathedral. Nearby, in **La Ribera**, is the 14th-century **Basílica of Santa Maria del Mar**, often regarded as one of the finest examples of Catalan Gothic.

Barcelona is famed for its Modernist architecture, the most eye-openingly innovative being in the hundred or so blocks around the PASSEIG DE GRÀCIA, the so-called **Quadrat d'Or** (Golden Square) in the **Eixample**. At the fore was Antoni Gaudí (1852–1926), who used the city as his canvas, leaving such extraordinary, swirling masterpieces as the wave-like **Casa Milà** (PASSEIG DE GRÀCIA) – also known as **La Pedrera**. It's worth buying the ticket for both

CAMP NOU

This vast 100,000-seater stadium is home to FC Barcelona, one of Spain's most successful soccer teams, whose arch rivals are Real Madrid. Fans unable to go to a match can visit the club museum and souvenir shop (Metro: MARIA CRISTINA).

parts of the building. Tour the apartment, set up as it might have looked in Gaudí's time with the latest kitchen equipment, electric light fittings and Modernist furniture. From the adjacent Espace Gaudí, a wonderful brick-vaulted attic housing an exhibition with models and photos of the architect's other works, a staircase gives access to the roof, whose twisted chimneys and weird ducts provide great photo opportunities. Gaudí's most famous building is the **Temple Expiatori de la Sagrada Família**, the astonishing cathedral to which he dedicated the last 43 years of his life, but which remains as yet unfinished and more of a building site than a cathedral. It's a synthesis of all his architectural styles, and incorporates complex religious symbolism and visual representations of the mysteries of faith. Since Gaudí's death in 1926, work has continued on the building, but progress has been slow and hampered by controversy. Those with a head for heights can climb up the 400-step winding staircases of the spires (of which a couple have lifts), rising to over 100 m; for an idea of what the final structure should look like, visit the cathedral museum in the crypt. The Quadrat d'Or isn't all Gaudí, however: for instance, the Illa de la Discòrdia, a block on PASSEIG DE GRÀCIA, contains a quartet of remarkable early 20th-century houses, including Domènech i Montaner's **Casa Lleó Morera**.

The recommendable tourist pamphlet *Gaudí* details other buildings by the architect and there is a museum dedicated to him, the **Casa-Museu Gaudí**, in the PARC GÜELL,

Museums
are closed
on Mon.

an area he designed himself as a decidedly eccentric residential garden city. Inside the park, a flight of steps, guarded by a brightly coloured salamander, lead up to a large pavilion supported by over 80 columns – the original marketplace of the development. Above the pavilion, a colourful mosaic twists and curves its way around the perimeter of an open terrace, from which there are superb views.

Another classic panorama of Barcelona is from **Montjuïc Castle**, now a military museum, which is reached by cable car from AVDA MIRAMAR in **Parc de Montjuïc**. The cable car stops halfway

SHOPPING

Barcelona is rapidly gaining ground as one of the great European centres of fashion and design. The main shopping streets are PASSEIG DE GRÀCIA, RAMBLA DE CATALUNYA and AVINGUDA DIAGONAL. Wandering off these streets sometimes pays dividends, and if you don't mind not being able to find the shop again the next day, try the streets in the Gothic quarter, near the cathedral. Barcelona's newest shopping centre, the **L'Illa Diagonal**, is in an attractive white building designed by Rafael Moreo, who won the Pritzeker Prize for architecture in 1996.

up at the **Parc d'Atraccions** fun fair; you can reach the cable car station by funicular railway from AVINGUDA DEL PARAL-LEL (Metro: PARAL-LEL), and there's also a cable car to **Montjuïc** from the harbour.

Also near here is the **Olympic Stadium**, while just across the hillside is **Poble Espanyol** (Spanish village), with miniature replicas of famous Spanish buildings and monuments.

You can also get good views from the **Columbus** monument at the bottom of the Ramblas. From the quay below the monument, Las Golondrinas (pleasure boats) ferry visitors around the harbour or across to the Olympic Port.

The **Picasso Museum**, CARRER DE MONTCADA, is formed from two Gothic palaces on a street just 3 m wide. The collection is largely made up of the artist's early work, but does include *Las Meninas*, a series of paintings inspired by Velázquez's famous work.

In Montjuïc is one of a number of museums in the city that merit a visit for their architecture alone: the **Fundació Joan Miró** at Parc de Montjuïc has paintings, sculptures, ceramics and tapestries by Miró, one of Catalonia's cultural giants, who died in 1983. Within a short walk, the **Museu d'Art de Catalunya** displays a superb collection of Romanesque art, much of it brought from country churches and now housed in the **Palau Nacional**, a former exhibition hall of the 1929 Universal Exhibition. Another Catalan artist, Antoni Tàpies, is given place of honour in a Modernist building housing the **Fundació Tàpies**, CALLE ARAGÓ 255 in the Eixample.

The **Ramblas** is a long street with an avenue of trees running along its spine; it's full of hawkers, tourists, buskers and strolling locals. Along it is the idiosyncratic **Museu de l'Eròtica**, devoted to fleshy delights through the ages and featuring a quite bizarre 'pleasure chair'. Just off the Ramblas is the beautiful **Plaça Reial**, whose lampposts were Gaudí's first commission in the city. Unfortunately, the square has acquired an unsavoury reputation as a haunt of drug dealers and petty thieves, so be extra careful here, especially after dark. In this square the **Museu d'Historia de la Ciutat** takes a look back at Barcelona from Roman times to the building of the Eixample. On the other side of the Ramblas is a turning leading past the **Palau Güell**, a Gaudí building which you can admire only from the outside. At the southern end of the Ramblas, the **Monument a Colom** is a monumental column to Columbus, which you can climb up for the view. Here you're close to the **harbour area**, where there's the **Aquarium**, **Imax cinema** and the **Rambla de Mar**, a wavy concrete pedestrian walkway over the water. Aptly housed within the ancient sheds where Barcelona's galleys of old were built, the **Museu Maritim**, PLAÇA PORTAL DE LA PAU, features a gilded replica of *La Real*, the flagship in the battle of Lepanto in 1571.

NIGHT-TIME AND EVENTS

Barcelona offers a superb range of clubs, bars and discos, catering for all musical tastes from rock to jazz; the busiest nights are Thur–Sat. Clubbing can be very expensive and there is often a high minimum drinks charge. However, it depends on where you go: there are plenty of 'pubs' (clubs) where there's no entrance charge.

The *Guía del Ocio* has comprehensive listings of what's on in the city. The **Eixample**, particularly the streets off AVDA DIAGONAL and PLAÇA REIAL, is reputedly the fashionable area for bars and clubs.

One of the world's most extraordinary concert halls, the **Palau de la Música Catalana**, is an astonishing Modernist building, resplendent in tiles and a huge stained-glass pendant-like dome, designed by Montaner and finished in 1908; tours are available, or you can attend a concert.

Nearly every district in Barcelona and every village and town has its own *festa*, or feast. The main ones in Barcelona are:
• **Festa mayor de Gràcia**: 1 week around 15 Aug. This is the big one, a quite spectacular event.
• **Festa mayor de Sants**: around 24 Aug.
• **Festes de Sarrià i de Les Corts**: 1st Sun of Oct.
• **Revetlla de Sant Joan**: 24 June – Midsummer's Eve, specially celebrated on Montjuïc and on the beaches.

WHERE NEXT FROM BARCELONA?

There are international services to Paris, Zurich, Montpellier, Geneva and Milan. Cross Spain to Vigo (ETT tables 681, 682) on the west coast, or escape to the isle of Mallorca by ferry to Palma (ETT table 2510; quickest crossing 3 hrs), itself a pleasant cathedral city with great beaches.

Side Trip to Majorca (Mallorca) Reached by ferry from Barcelona (ETT table 2510), this perennially popular island is one of the world's busiest package holiday regions for the sand and sun. It is the largest and most varied island in the Balearic group.

While Majorca is massively touristy, it has some surprisingly beautiful scenery and unspoilt villages, particularly in the rugged northern mountains, which rise to 1400 m. The island capital, **Palma**, is at the hub of a bay that has been densely developed with high-rise concrete, but the compact old city has some rewarding sights, including the gothic cathedral, the Moorish palace and the 10th-century Arab baths. There's no shortage of excellent sandy **beaches** around Palma and the other resorts (though some, notably Palma Nova, can get impossibly crowded), as well as water sports and other sports facilities. The big resorts of Palma Bay (Palma Nova, Magaluf, El Arenal, Paguera and Palma) are the best places for **nightlife**.

The island's two **railway lines** link Palma to Inca (35 mins, hourly) and Sóller (55 mins, 5 trains a day); trains leave from the two stations in Plaça d'Espanya – the trip to the old fishing village of Sóller is particularly recommended. There's rather more in the way of **buses**, which serve all the main towns and many villages; timetables from the tourist information kiosk on Plaça d'Espanya. Bono Bus travel cards give freedom of travel on city buses in Palma. **Boat trips** offer one of the most pleasant ways of seeing Majorca. A popular cruise heads around the north-west coast from Port de Sóller to Sa Calobra; for information contact Consselleria Transports, Plaza d'España, Palma, ☎971 75 34 45. There's plenty of sightseeing elsewhere on the island, including some fine **caves** on the east coast; the caves of Hams and Artá are very attractive, while the somewhat over-commercialised caves of Drach feature musicians performing on an underground lake. Another place to head for is the 14th-century **Monastery of Valldemosa** where Chopin and George Sand spent a somewhat miserable winter.

The majority of **accommodation** is in the form of large hotels built for the package industry, although Palma does have a number of inexpensive *hostales*, and there are two youth hostels – near Palma and outside Alcudia. You can also stay in monasteries inexpensively. The Palma **tourist offices** are at C. Santo Domingo 11, Plaça d'Espanya and Plaça de la Reina 2; ☎971 72 40 90, fax 971 72 02 40.

Ferries also serve the other Balearic islands, each of which has its own character. **Ibiza** is a brash nightlife haunt – a noisy, crowded playground that definitely won't appeal to those in search of a cultural island paradise. **Menorca** is much more low-key, and popular with families and older tourists; sightseeing and nightlife are distinctly limited, though you might like to seek out the island's intriguing Bronze Age sites. Tiny **Formantera** is fun to explore by bicycle; it's comparatively undeveloped, with some *hostal* accommodation in the port of La Sabina; Playa Illetas and Playa Levante are among the best beaches.

The Portuguese capital lies on seven low hills at the estuary of the River Tagus (Tejo). A massive earthquake in 1755 destroyed most of the city, but spared the Alfama quarter – a flower-bedecked labyrinth of cobbled alleys and balconied whitewashed houses – and, remarkably, the ancient 18 km-long aqueduct. The rest of Lisbon was redesigned on a grid system and rebuilt on a grand scale, with classical squares and wide esplanades paved with mosaics. It's a relatively small capital by European standards, but you need at least two to three days to explore it.

> **Lisbon** has an excellent range of day trips by rail, notably to the historic cities of **Évora** and **Óbidos**, and the palaces at **Sintra**.

ARRIVAL AND DEPARTURE

For general rail enquiries, ☎ 21 888 40 25. **Santa Apolónia Station**, on the banks of the Tagus near Alfama, is the main station, handling all international trains and those to east and north Portugal; accommodation desk, luggage lockers. All trains to and from Santa Apolónia also call at the Gare Intermodal do Oriente, where there is an interchange with the metro system. By 2003 the metro should have been extended to this station; in the meantime, take 🚌 nos. 9, 46 or 90 to Baixa and Rossio, the main areas for accommodation. **Rossio Station** serves the west. **Cais do Sodré Station** doubles as the quay for the Tagus ferries and as the station handling the local coastal services. **Terreiro do Paço Station** is the terminal for the ferries across the Tagus to **Barreiro**, the station for trains to southern Portugal. The 30-min ferry crossing costs about €1 single (free with some rail passes and tickets). There are ferry departures whenever trains are scheduled from Barreiro.

TOURIST INFORMATION

The main **Tourist Office** is in **Palácio Foz** (Praça dos Restauradores), ☎ 21 346 33 14 (daily 0900–2000); commission-free accommodation service. **Branch**: Rua Jardim Do Regedor 50, ☎ 21 343 36 72. **Municipal Office**: Av. 5 de Outubro 293, ☎ 21 799 61 00 (Mon–Fri 0930–1130, 1400–1700; Metro: Campo Pequeno).

🚌 Express **bus services** to the Algarve and Porto are run by Renex, ☎ 21 887 48 71, departing from Arco de Cego and Oriente. **Terminal Rodoviario Do Arco Do Cego**, Av Duque De Avila 12. **Taxis**: Inexpensive, ☎ 21 793 27 56 or 21 815 50 61.

✈ **Portela de Sacavém Airport** (☎ 21 80 20 60) is 7 km north of the city, with no train link; Tourist Office. 🚌 nos. 44/45/83 go to the centre, or take the Aero-bus (every 20 mins; daily 0700–2100; buy tickets from driver; tickets valid for any bus, tram or funicular that day), which stops at various points in the city, including Cais do Sodré station, Rossio and Restauradores.

CITY MAP
– inside back cover

INFORMATION

Thomas Cook Licensees: Star Viagens S.A., Travessa Escola Araujo 31, ☎ 21 314 24 25.

PORTUGAL

POST AND PHONES **Main post office**: PRAÇA DO COMÉRCIO. **International telephone calls**: from PRAÇA DOM PEDRO IV 68. You must dial the 21 code even when calling within Lisbon.

PUBLIC TRANSPORT

Public transport in Lisbon is cheap, efficient and varied, consisting of buses, trams, the metro and funiculars *(elevadores)* between different levels of the city. Make a point of getting a walking map of the labyrinthine Alfama district.

METRO AND TRAMS

TICKETS
Train: available from travel agencies or the **Rossio** and **Santa Apolónia** stations. **Buses and trams**: you can pay on board for each ride. If you're making more than two journeys in a day, go to the *Carris* yellow and green kiosk in PRAÇA DA FIGUEIRA or the kiosk by the Elevador Santa Jústa and get a day ticket or a 3-day ticket.

The **Metro** is fast and frequent, and is currently being extended. **Trams**: still an integral part of the city and easy to use. **Carris** offer tram and bus tours: a slow and picturesque way to see the city. Tours leave from PRAÇA DO COMÉRCIO and cost €15 for the tram and €10 for the bus; you can hop on and off the bus as you like, but have to stay on the tram for the whole trip. Buy tickets from the driver.

For intensive sightseeing, the **Lisboacard** (valid for 1, 2 or 3 days) gives unrestricted metro access and free travel on most buses, funiculars and trams, as well as free or discounted entry to 25 museums and monuments. Available from RUA JARDIM DO REGEDOR 50, **Jeronimos Monastery** and the **Museum of Ancient Art**. If you're only visiting a couple of sights a day, it probably isn't worth it.

ACCOMMODATION

Accommodation is scarcest and priciest at Easter and in summer; out of season you may be able to find a room for around €15–20, but around €25–30 at busier times. The vast majority of cheap places are in the centre of town, on and around AVDA LIBERDADE or the Baixa. In the latter, head for the three squares PRAÇA DA FIGUEIRA, PRAÇA DOS RESTAURADORES and PRAÇA DOM PEDRO IV. Reasonable no-frills places are **Pensão Ibérica**, PRAÇA DA FIGUEIRA 10, ☎21 886 74 12; **Pensão Residencial Praça da Figueira**, TRAVESSA NOVA DE SÃO DOMINGOS 9, ☎/fax 21 342 43 23 (rrcoelho@esoterica.pt), with Internet and laundry, plus a range of rooms; and **Pensão Beira Minho**, PRAÇA DA FIGUEIRA 6, ☎21 346 18 46. **Pensão Residencial Restauradores**, PRAÇA DOS RESTAURADORES 13, 4th floor, ☎21 347 56 60, is similar. If these are full, try the choice on AVDA ALMIRANTE REIS (to the east). The perenially popular **Duas Naçoes**, 41 RUA DA VITÓRIA, ☎21 346 07 10, is very good value, with breakfast and TV; one month advance booking is generally recommended but you might try your luck and just turn up.

Heading a short way north from Rossio, turn left just after the Elevador Glória: there are a number of possibilities in the backstreets here. The attractive and excellent value **Nova Avenida**, RUA DE SANTO ANTÓNIO DE GLÓRIA 87, ☎21 342 36 89, €, is friendly and quiet; English is spoken. Just round the corner, slightly pricier but both clean, are **Pensão Sevilha**, PRAÇA DA ALEGRIA 11, ☎21 346 95 79 (English spoken), and **Residencial Milanesa**, RUA DA ALEGRIA 25, ☎21 346 64 56, fax 21 342 09 45. If those are full you could try the nearby **Residencial Alegria**, PRAÇA DA ALEGRIA 12, ☎21 322 06 70, fax 21 347 80 70 (pensao.alegria@mail.telepac.pt).

Youth hostel: RUA ANDRADE CORVO 46, ☎21 353 26 96 (Metro: PICOAS); be careful with your belongings here, as there have been thefts from rooms. There are dorms as well as private rooms with own bathrooms at **Pensión Beira-Mar**, a '*hostal* backpacker's place' at LARGO TERRERIO DO TRIGO 16, ☎21 886 99 33, fax 21 887 15 28, in Alfama, near the waterfront and only 10 mins' walk from Santa Apolonia station (but they'll pick you up for free if you ring up and want to see a room); laundry, Internet, kitchen facilities, sea views, free transport to beach and nightlife.

Campsites: **Parque da Câmara Municipal de Lisboa–Monsanto** (on the road to Benfica), ☎21 762 31 00, fax 21 762 31 05, is very pleasant and inexpensive and has a pool (🚌no. 43 from Rossio to Parque Florestal Monsanto); **Clube de Campismo de Lisboa**, COSTA DA CAPARICA, ☎21 290 01 00, is 5 km out of town, with a beach (🚌 from PRAÇA DE ESPANHA metro station).

FOOD AND DRINK

Lisbon's restaurants are inexpensive and offer a wide choice. The bohemian **Bairro Alto** area is frequented by locals and particularly good value, as are the restaurants in **Alfama**. **Baixa** is aimed at tourists and more expensive, but still worthwhile. If you're really into cheap eats, there are food stalls in the market behind Cais do Sodré station. Students can also use the *cantinas* on the university campus.

HIGHLIGHTS

Obtainable from Tourist Offices, the free magazine *Follow Me Lisboa* is useful for opening times and events.

Lisbon is a wonderful place for exploring on foot, enjoying the many views and riding the old wooden trams. **Tram no. E28** is a great introduction to the city (beware pickpockets), and can be picked up from Martim Moniz (on the east side of the square); it squeals its way along a tortuous, hilly route, beneath the Castelo de São Jorge and above the cathedral in the Alfama district. Also ride an *elevador* (funicular);

the much-photographed **Elevador Glória** is really just a steep tram ride up to the Bairro Alto district, while the **Elevador Santa Justa** is an amazing 19th-century wooden lift within a startlingly odd iron tower – spiral steps lead from the upper exit to a viewing platform. For the best views of the waterfront ride the **ferry** to Barreiro and back.

> Most attractions are closed all day Mon and Tues, morning but are free on Sun morning.

The **Alfama** (Metro: ROSSIO) is the old Moorish quarter, little changed since the 12th century, with winding cobbled streets overhung with washing lines and flanked by whitewashed houses, and leading to lots of dead ends. One of the few areas to survive the earthquake of 1755, it's a marvellous place to explore on foot. The medieval **Castelo de São Jorge** (🚌no. 37 from PRAÇA DA FIGUERA) has ten towers linked by massive battlements and stands on one of the seven hills, giving superb views over the city. A royal residence for four centuries, later it served as a prison and houses the **Olissiponia Museum**, covering the history of Lisbon. The **Sé Patriarchal** (Cathedral), LARGO DA SÉ, was once a fortress. It contains some notable 14th-century tombs, a magnificent Romanesque screen and a fine collection of religious art, and exquisite cloisters.

> The **Torre de Belém**, with its lace-like loggia, is an exquisite example or Manueline architecture. This tower was built during 1512–21 to protect the harbour entrance, and the fifth floor has a great view across the estuary. The tower was restored in 1845 and is furnished in period style.

Adjoining the **Museu de Arte Sacra** is the **Church of São Roque**, with its marvellous 18th-century chapel dedicated to St John the Baptist, which was constructed in Rome, then shipped in its entirety to Lisbon.

The **Parque Eduardo VII** (Metro: PARQUE/ROTUNDA) is a landscaped park with a lake, a good view of lower Lisbon and some attractive tropical plants in its greenhouses.

The **Mosteiro dos Jerónimos** (Jerónimos Monastery; tram E15) began life as a chapel for Henry the Navigator's seamen. Vasco da Gama was royally received in the chapel when he returned from his triumphant voyages. The present building was designed by Boytac, the best of the Manueline architects, and construction began in 1502; its magnificent south door is often cited as the finest example of the style. Unfortunately, as Portugal's greatest church building it does get absolutely packed with tourists.

Lisbon's foremost museum, with a delightful park, is the **Calouste Gulbenkian Museum** (Metro: PRAÇA DE ESPANHA), housing the private collection of oil magnate Calouste Gulbenkian, with a superlative and all-embracing collection of art and applied art – from all ages and parts of the world, from Ancient Egypt to the French Impressionists. Next door is the **Centro de Arte Moderna Calouste Gulbenkian**, with exhibits by 20th-century Portuguese painters and sculptors. The **Museu Nacional de Arte Antiga** on RUA DAS JANELAS VERDES is home to a 15th-century polyptych, which is a masterpiece of Portuguese art. Other exhibits include tapestries, ceramics, ancient sculptures and oriental rugs. The **Museu Nacional do Azulejo** (National Painted Tile Museum), RUA DA MADRE DE DEUS 4, is in a 16th-century convent that was badly damaged in the 1755 earthquake, but restored in the original Manueline style. The cloister survived and the *azulejos* (decorative tiles) include a huge depiction of Lisbon before the earthquake.

There are **beaches** west of the city centre. Take a bus to Corcavelos or Oeiras from Cais do Sodré metro station.

SHOPPING

The **Baixa** and **Chiado** districts are good for shopping of all kinds, while RUA DO OURO is a centre for jewellery. The neo-modern **Amoreiras** shopping centre on AVENIDA ENGENHEIRO DUARTE PACHECO is a huge complex with over 300 shops. There's a dawn fish and flower market daily opposite **Cais do Sodré** station. **Feira da Ladro** flea market takes place in the CAMPO DE SANTA CLARA on Tues and Sat.

NIGHT-TIME

There are many bars, discos and nightclubs, the streets around RUA DIÁRIO DE NOTICIAS (in the **Bairro Alto**) being a particularly lively area. Lisbon also has a lot of bars that feature *fado* singing (a uniquely Portuguese melancholy chant) and guitar playing. The best places are in the **Bairro Alto**; there may be an entrance fee or cover charge. Performances usually begin around 2200 and it's quite common for them to continue until 0230 or later.

SIDE TRIPS FROM LISBON

ÓBIDOS An enchanting medieval walled town (formerly a coastal settlement, but the sea has receded 10 km) and designated a national monument, Óbidos has winding streets and small whitewashed houses, their balconies brimming with flowers. The many places of interest include the 12th–13th- century **castle** (now a hotel), the 15th–18th- century **Church of the Misericórdia**, the Renaissance **Church of Santa Maria** and the 18th-century **town gate**. There are trains from Lisbon Rossio station (change at Cacém); the journey takes about 2 hrs (ETT table 692). **Tourist Office**: RUA DIREITA, ☎262 95 92 31. **Accommodation: Pensão Martim de Freitas**, ESTRADA NACIONAL 8, ☎262 95 91 85.

QUELUZ AND SINTRA The trains to Queluz continue to Sintra (the full journey takes 45 mins; four trains an hour; ETT table 691), so both can be visited in one day trip.
Queluz is the home of an exquisite small, pink rococo palace that was inspired by Versailles, built in the 18th century for Dom Pedro III. It became the summer residence of the Bragança kings; the interior and the formal gardens have scarcely changed since; closed Tues.

Sintra (Tourist Office: Praça da República 23, ☎21 923 39 19, with a branch at the station; the station is a 15-min walk from town – turn left, then left at the junction by the turreted town hall) is a small town built up against the luxuriantly vegetated granite upland of the Serra de Sintra. In town is the **Palácio Real**, the royal summer palace – a mixture of architectural styles and with two remarkable conical chimneys. From here take ☐ no. 434 up to the architecturally eccentric **Pena Palace** (closed Mon), a hotchpotch of mock medievalism, porcelain pillars, Arabic motifs and baroque flourishes. It's more fun to walk up (ask the tourist office to mark up a map with the path for you) – this takes about an hour: turn uphill by the sign for the tourist office as you enter the town, follow the road past the Pensão Bristol, take the first right (marked by 'no entry' roadsigns), then turn left, up past a church, and right 50 m later on Rampa do Castelo; this becomes a path, and after a turnstile fork left at a mini castellated tower; to the right here you'll reach the rest of the **Moorish Castle**, with tremendous views from the restored ramparts.

There are several places to stay in Sintra: cheapies include **Casa Hósp. Adelaide**, ☎21 923 08 73, €, and **Pensão Nova Sintra**, ☎21 923 02 20, €€; the **youth hostel**, ☎/fax 21 924 12 10, is very pleasant but a taxi ride out.

From Sintra, you can take the bus (hourly services; a day pass lets you get on and off any bus in the area) to **Cabo de Roca**, the westernmost point on mainland Europe, with stunning clifftop views.

Évora This is a stupendous walled city south-east of Lisbon (ferry from Lisbon to Barreiro for train to Évora; ETT table 698; 2 hrs 30 mins). It's best known for the 2nd-century AD **Templo Romano** (Roman Temple; its Corinthian columns standing to their original height) in the square in front of the magnificent 12th–13th-century façade of the cathedral, while the cathedral museum's collection of sacred art is noted for its 13th-century ivory statue of the Virgin of Paradise. The **Museu de Évora** houses an all-embracing collection of art from Roman to modern times. Other highlights include the **Paço dos Duques de Cadaval** (Palace of the Dukes of Cadaval) and the **Igreja de São João Evangelista** (Church of St John the Evangelist), with its splendid painted azulejo tiles. **Tourist Office**: Rua De Aviz 90, ☎266 74 25 34. There's a pleasant **youth hostel**, Rua Miguel Bombarda 40, ☎266 74 48 48.

The Algarve The Algarve (Portugal's south-west coast), is served by trains to **Lagos**, **Albufeira** and **Faro** (ETT table 698/699), plus a good bus network. The area is renowned for the quality of its beaches, as well as its sports facilities and nightlife, but some of the resorts are hideously overdeveloped; June and Sept are less busy than July and Aug, and the climate's more bearable. Some places, such as **Carvoeiro**, **Luz** and **Ferragudo**, have kept their old fishing village character, while **Albufeira** and **Lagos** are busy night spots. There are fine coastal walks from **Lagos** to **Salema** and from **Carvoeiro** to **Armação de Pêra**. **Faro**, the capital of the Algarve, has an international airport (5 km west of **Faro**; ☐nos. 14/16). **Tourist Offices**: (regional) Avda 5 de Outubro 18,8001-902, ☎289 80 04 00 (www.rtalgarve.pt; rtalgarve@rtalgarve.pt); (municipal) Rua da Misericórdia 8, ☎289 80 36 04.

Chosen by Philip II in 1561 to avoid inflaming regional jealousies, the Spanish capital lies right in the geographical centre of Spain; indeed, the PUERTA DEL SOL is the point from which all distances in the country are measured. Beyond the compact old quarter, most of it looks 19th century or later, the grand boulevards punctuated with triumphal arches and lavish fountains; elsewhere, there's pretty much relentless high-rise, most of it fairly drab. Architecturally, it must be admitted, the city dwindles into insignificance besides the likes of Barcelona or Seville. What Madrid does score for, however, is its street and night life, with the smart, fun-loving Madrileños taking their evening *paseo* along Calle del Carmen and Calle de Preciados; thereafter the city keeps going late into the night.

Sightseeing is dominated by the Prado, one of the world's great art galleries, needing a couple of days to do it justice; the Royal Palace is similarly daunting in size, while the Parque del Retiro makes a handy escape from the hectic whirl of the city. Meanwhile, the almost equally unmissable Centro de Arte Reina Sofía boasts a choice selection of 20th-century Spanish art and is a bit more manageable than the Prado.

With so many railways fanning out from Madrid, the city makes a good base for trips to such places as Toledo (p. 167), El Escorial (p. 174) and Segovia (p. 173).

ARRIVAL AND DEPARTURE

Chamartín Station, AGUSTÍN DE FOXÁ, is in the northern suburbs. It is Madrid's main station (a modern place with a full range of facilities) and handles trains to the north, north-east and north-west, including those for France. It is also the terminal for some of the south-bound trains, but most of those stop at **Atocha** en route. All *cercanías* (commuter) trains stop at Chamartín. At Atocha there are accommodation services and a currency exchange that charges no commission. There are no showers at this station.

Part of **Atocha Station**, AVDA CIUDAD DE BARCELONA, is the main terminal for the southern, eastern and western services, and also for trains to Portugal. The older part of the station, **Puerta de Atocha**, GLORIETA EMPERADOR CARLOS V, is now the terminal for the AVE express service via Córdoba to Seville.

There are also two intermediate stations: **Recoletos**, PASEO DE RECOLETOS 4; and **Nuevos Ministerios** (on the corner of CALLE RAIMUNDO FERNÁNDEZ VILLAVERDE and PASEO DE LA CASTELLANA), but no trains originate from these. **Príncipe Pío Station** (formerly known as Norte) is to the west of town, south of PLAZA DE ESPAÑA, and has suburban services only. All the mainline railway stations are connected to the Metro. 🚌 no. 5 leaves the station every 5 mins until 2330. Luggage lockers are available.

Madrid Barajas Airport, ☎ 91 305 83 43/4, is 13 km north-east of town. There is a Tourist Office in the international arrivals hall. A **bus** (no. 89) operates every 10–15 mins between the airport and LA PLAZA DE COLÓN in the centre. The journey takes about 30 mins. **Metro** line 8 connects the airport to **Nuevos Ministerios** (20 mins), for train connections to Chamartín and Atocha (6–8 mins) or line 10 to **Alonso Martínez**.

SPAIN

RAIL INFORMATION

The main **RENFE office** is at CALLE ALCALÁ 44. For general RENFE information:
☎ 902 240 202
(www.renfe.es).

TOURIST INFORMATION

Websites:
www.tourspain.es
www.munimadrid.es.
Regional/provincial office:
MERCADO PUERTA DE TOLEDO,
RONDA DE TOLEDO 1,
☎ 91 364 18 76.
Branch office:
DUQUE DE MEDINACELI 2,
☎ 91 429 49 51.
Municipal office:
PLAZA MAYOR 3,
☎ 91 588 16 36.
Chamartín station:
OPPOSITE PLATFORMS 10/11.
Viajes TIVE:
CALLE FERNANDO EL CATÓLICO
(www.comadrid.es).
In summer, there are temporary tourist stands around the city.

INFORMATION

POST The main **post office** is in the **Palacio de Comunicaciones**, PLAZA DE CIBELES (Metro: BANCO DE ESPAÑA), and is worth a visit just to see the building.

INTERNET CAFÉS
These are springing up throughout Madrid and seem to be all the rage at the moment. Try **Zahara**, GRAN VÍA 31, ☎ 91 523 84 55 (Metro: CALLAO); cybercafé and restaurant.

PUBLIC TRANSPORT

METRO With services every 5 mins (0600–0130) and colour-coded lines marked according to the destination, the Metro (subway) is easy to use. Free maps are available from ticket offices, Tourist Offices and many hotels.

BUSES The bus system is comprehensive, efficient and the same price as the Metro, but not as easy to master. You can get a map of the whole system (*Plano de los Transportes*) from Tourist Offices, bookshops and the EMT booths on Plaza de la Cibeles or Plaza del Callao. There are also route plans on the bus stops (*paradas*). The regular city buses mostly operate 0600–midnight (there are a few night services from Puerta del Sol and Plaza de Cibeles, with stops marked 'N', which run every 30 mins to 0200 and then every hour until 0600, but late at night it's safer to use taxis). Metrobuses depart from Metro stations. All long-distance buses use the brand new state-of-the-art terminal at Méndez Alvaro (Metro: Méndez Alvaro). This has good facilities, including hot showers.

TAXIS An inexpensive way of getting around late at night; ☎ 91 547 82 00 or 91 371 21 31.

METROBUS TICKETS
There's a flat fare, but you save by buying **Metrobus tickets** (books of ten tickets). These give access to buses and the Metro; also sold in tobacconists and kiosks.

ACCOMMODATION

Your best bet may be to take the metro to Sol and then head south-east towards the PLAZA DE SANTA ANA, where there are a number of pleasant streets that are close to the action but less seedy and noisy than the other large accommodation area just north of Sol.

ACCOMMODATION SERVICE

Brujula is an accommodation service for the whole of Spain with offices at **Atocha station**, 91 539 11 73, fax 91 530 09 75 and **Chamartín station**, 91 315 78 94.

Just off Plaza Santa Ana is **Hostal Residencia Villar**, PRÍNCIPE 18; 91 531 6600, fax 91 521 50 73 (hvillar@arrakis.es), €, in a pleasant old-fashioned building, with several additional places on other floors, including the friendly **Hostal Regional** on the fourth floor, 91 522 33 73, €. Close by are the **Hostal Residencia Marina**, CARRETAS 27, 91 532 16 26, €; **Hostal Residencia Pan-América**, CARRETAS 27, /fax 91 522 36 11, €; and **Hostal Residencia Mocelo**, CALLE DEL PRADO 10, 91 429 49 63, €, (with English-speaking staff). A more luxurious three-star *hostal* here is **Hostal Lisboa**, VENTURA DE LA VEGA 17, 91 429 98 94, fax 91 429 46 76 (hostallisboa@inves.es), €€.

For cheap places around Sol itself, try **Hostal-Residencia María del Mar**, CALLE MARQUÉS VIUDO DE PONTEJOS 7 (2nd and 3rd floors), 91 531 90 64, €, or for one-star hotel comfort right next to Sol, try **Hotel Europa**, CARMEN 4, 91 521 29 00, fax 91 521 46 96 (info@hoteleuropa.net), €€. Nearby, CALLE ARENAL is virtually lined with reasonably priced accommodation. To the east of Puerta del Sol, good deals can be found on CARRERA DE SAN JERÓNIMO and its side streets. The GRAN VÍA is a hectic and noisy thoroughfare with a not unjustifiable reputation for prostitution; however, together with side streets such as CALLE DE FUENCARRAL, the area offers plenty of accommodation. CALLE DE LA MONTERA runs from Gran Vía to Sol. Although fairly seedy, it has a number of acceptable lodgings. There's also cheap accommodation around Atocha station, but it's a rather creepy area at night.

Youth hostels: **Santa Cruz de Marcenado**, CALLE SANTA CRUZ DE MARCENADO 28, 91 547 45 32, fax 91 548 11 96 (Metro: ARGÜELLES), gets heavily booked. **Richard Schirrmann**, CASA DE CAMPO, 91 463 56 99, fax 91 464 46 85 (Metro: LAGO); a long way out of the centre. A friendly private hostel in the centre is **Casa de Huéspedes Lutz**, CALLE FUENTES 10, 91 542 07 59, €, (Metro: SOL). **Campsites**: both are out of town, but compensate by having enough facilities to be self-contained. **Camping Madrid**, 91 302 28 35, is 11 km from town on the N1 road to Burgos, exit 10 (Metro: PLAZA DE CASTILLA, then no. 151 to Iglesia de los Dominicos). **Camping Osuna**, 91 741 05 10, fax 91 320 63 65, is 8 km from town on the Ajalvir–Vicálvaro road (Metro: CANILLEJAS, then no. 105 to Avda Logroño).

FOOD AND DRINK

Madrid offers a full range of regional dishes from all over Spain; local items include roast lamb and *sopa castellana*, a garlicky soup with a poached egg in it. Restaurants don't really get going until well after 2200, late even by Spanish standards. The old town, south-west of PLAZA MAYOR, is full of 'typical' Spanish bars and restaurants built in cellars and stone-walled caves, where *Madrileños* tend to head for after the evening *paseo* (stroll). However, as with the *tapas* bars surrounding PLAZA MAYOR, some of these tend to be touristy and overpriced.

A better area is around PLAZA DE SANTA ANA: CALLES ECHEGARAY, VENTURA DE LA VEGA and MANUEL FERNÁNDEZ GONZÁLEZ all host a number of quality budget restaurants, and PLAZA DE SANTA ANA itself is great for *tapas*. Pork lovers can't leave Madrid without visiting the **Museo del Jamón**. A restaurant, not a museum, its walls are covered in huge slabs of meat, and diners can feast on Iberian ham in any conceivable shape or form. There are several branches throughout the city, including **Carrera de San Jerónimo 8** (near PUERTA DEL SOL).

HIGHLIGHTS

Madrid's major sights occupy a relatively compact area, stretching from the PALACIO REAL to the west, to the PRADO and the PARQUE DEL RETIRO to the east. This historic core is pleasant and compact enough for walking, taking just half an hour or so to cross.

Plaza Mayor (Metro: SOL) is a stately square surrounded by neoclassical buildings dating from the 17th century, at which time it was a centre of Spanish society, where such dubious entertainments as bullfighting and the Inquisition's *autos-da-fé* were staged. Today's pleasures are more civilised: you can sit at a pavement café, admire the equestrian statue of King Philip III and watch the world go by. The old **Habsburg** area to the south-west of PLAZA MAYOR is the most attractive in Madrid.

FOR FREE

The **Prado** and **Centro de Arte Reina Sofía** are free on Sat afternoons and Sun mornings until 1400, though bear in mind that the queues to get in can be very long at these times (they only let in a certain number of people at a time). The **Congreso de los Diputados** (Parliament Building) is free on Sat morning. The **Palacio Real** is free on Wed to EU citizens.

The **Parque del Retiro** (Metro: RETIRO/ATOCHA) is a park that was laid out in the 17th century as the grounds of Felipe IV's palace; it's a cooling retreat from the summer heat of the city, with wooded corners, formal avenues, brilliant flowers and a large boating lake. At summer weekends half of Madrid seems to be here, and there are sometimes bandstand concerts as well as impromptu entertainments. Adjoining it is the **Jardín Botánico** (Metro: ATOCHA), with three separate terraces, some of which feature vegetables as well as shrubs, herbs and flowers, including many exotic species.

Bear in mind that practically all museums close all day on Mon, except (if there's a special event) the **Centro Reina Sofía**, also closed Tues (www.museoreinasofia.mcu.es), and the **Palacio Real** (www.patrimonionacional.es). The

Museo del Prado (Metro: ATOCHA/BANCO DE ESPAÑA; www.museoprado.mcu.es) is one of the world's greatest art galleries, with admission a bargain at just €3. Many of its paintings were collected by Spanish monarchs between the 16th and 18th centuries. Today there are individual sections devoted to Goya, Velázquez, Murillo, Zurbarán and El Greco. The Italian and Flemish schools are also well represented.

Picasso's masterpiece *Guernica* – showing the misery of a small Basque town bombed by the Germans during the Spanish Civil War – hangs in the art museum **Centro de Arte Reina Sofía** (Metro: ATOCHA), also home to a fabulous collection of other 20th-century Spanish works, including paintings by Miró and Dalí.

The **Museo Arqueológico Nacional** (National Archaeological Museum; Metro: SERRANO or COLÓN; www.mcu.es/nmuseos/man) contains a major collection of arte-facts from all over Spain, including stone-carved Iberian mother-goddesses from the 4th century BC. In the grounds is a full-scale reproduction of the **Altamira Caves**: they contain one of the world's greatest sets of early cave paintings.

The late-Renaissance **Palacio Real** (Metro: OPERA; www.patrimonionacional.es), or Royal Palace, is a vast 18th-century Italianate pile, with colonnaded arches and some 2,800 rooms; the Spanish Royal Family now live in Zarzuela Palace outside the city. The state rooms were decorated in the 18th and 19th centuries and are full of price-less treasures: Tiepolo frescos, magnificent tapestries, glittering chandeliers, decora-tive clocks, silverware, gilt ornamentation and works by a variety of famous artists – rather swamped by their surroundings. Other highlights are the king's entertain-ingly over-the-top dressing room, an 18th-century pharmacy, a huge hall lined by prancing horses and an armoury. It can all be a bit overwhelming, but the adjacent free **Jardines de Sabatini** make a relaxing escape, with views over the mountains giving the illusion that the palace is perched on the edge of the city.

Just opposite the palace is **Plaza de Oriente**, a small garden adorned with over 40 statues of Spanish royalty. For something distinctly different, visit the small **Convento de la Encarnación** (Convent of the Incarnation; Metro: SANTO DOMINGO/OPERA), with its astonishing collection of some 1500 reliquaries.

The 16th-century **Convento de las Descalzas Reales** (Metro: SOL) was a convent for noblewomen and was handsomely endowed by their families. It still houses a closed order, but parts of it are open: it has a superb collection of 16th- and 17th-century religious art (fittingly displayed in a series of shrines) and many other treasures, including a magnificent set of tapestries with Rubens designs.

The **Museo Thyssen-Bornemisza** (Metro: BANCO DE ESPAÑA; www.museothyssen.org) is one of Madrid's newer attractions. After lending the city his priceless 800-piece art collection for a limited period in 1992, Baron Thyssen decided it should be on permanent view and so sold it to the nation; it represents a complete chronology of Western art, from the Italian primitives and medieval German masters to 20th-century pop art.

SHOPPING

For window shopping, try any of the several main upmarket shopping streets off, or parallel to, CALLE SERRANO, which is the Spanish equivalent of Knightsbridge or Fifth Avenue.

Foodstuffs, including wine, hams, sausages, cheese and olive oil, are good value and high quality, and there are some splendid food emporia in Old Madrid. **El Rastro** (Metro: LA LATINA) is a huge flea market that is something of a Sunday-morning institution. It's best to go early because it can be impossibly crowded by midday and begins to pack up around 1400. Around **Plaza Mayor** is a huddle of specialist craft shops selling such items as fans, ceramics, lace and leather. The square itself hosts a collectors' market (coins, stamps, books, badges, etc.) on Sunday mornings.

NIGHT-TIME

Madrid has a pulsating nightlife, centred on its numerous restaurants, bars and dance venues. Live music can easily be found. At weekends, many bars stay open until 0300 and some close much later than that. Discos tend to have a cover charge, but bars with dance floors don't.

The **Malasaña** area (Metro: BILBAO/TRIBUNAL) is good for music and bars, and is popular with a wide range of age groups. It centres on PLAZA DOS DE MAYO, CALLE DE VELARDE and CALLE DE RUÍZ. Although flamenco guitar playing, dancing and singing belong to Andalucía, Madrid is said to have the best performers around, though some of it is aimed firmly at tourists with prices to match.

Huertas (Metro: ANTÓN MARTÍN) is the area around PLAZA DE SANTA ANA and has a huge variety of bars that stay open pretty much through the night. **Paseo del Prado** (Metro: ATOCHA/BANCO DE ESPAÑA) is rather more upmarket, with smart and expensive café-bars. The **Chueca** area has a lively gay scene, particularly along CALLE DE PELAYO.

The *Guía del Ocio* is a weekly Spanish-language publication with listings of what's on in Madrid, including details of theatre, opera and clubs; it is sold at newsstands. Useful free handouts from Tourist Offices and hotels include *Enjoy Madrid*, *En Madrid* and *What's On in Madrid*. The free magazine, *In Madrid*, in English, gives a monthly low-down on Madrid youth culture, including pubs, clubs and gigs, aimed at young travellers.

TOURS

Madrid Vision runs hop-on, hop-off **bus tours** of the city, taking in PLAZA MAYOR the PALACIO REAL and major museums such as the Prado. These give a feel for the monumental layout of Madrid, but in fact most of the sights of interest are walkable anyway. Services run about every 10 mins, and you pay on board for a day ticket (€10). Ask at the Tourist Office for details of English-speaking **walking tours**.

ROUTE DETAIL

Barcelona (Sants)– **Tarragona** ETT tables 650/660

Type	Frequency	Typical journey time
Train	1–3 per hr	1 hr 5 mins

Tarragona–Valencia ETT table 660

Type	Frequency	Typical journey time
Train	Every 1–2 hrs	2 hrs 20 mins

Valencia–Cuenca ETT table 668

Type	Frequency	Typical journey time
Train	4 daily	3 hrs 25 mins

Cuenca–Aranjuez ETT table 668

Type	Frequency	Typical journey time
Train	4–5 daily	2 hrs

Aranjuez– Madrid (Atocha) ETT tables 667/668/671/680

Type	Frequency	Typical journey time
Local Train	2–3 per hr	42 mins

Madrid (Atocha)–**Cáceres** ETT table 677

Type	Frequency	Typical journey time
Train	5–6 daily	4 hrs 15 mins

Cáceres–Mérida ETT table 677

Type	Frequency	Typical journey time
Train	4–5 daily	1 hr

Mérida–Badajoz ETT table 677

Type	Frequency	Typical journey time
Train	5–7 daily	50 mins

Badajoz–Lisbon ETT table 677

Type	Frequency	Typical journey time
Train	1 daily	5 hrs 05 mins

KEY JOURNEYS

Barcelona–Madrid ETT table 650

Type	Frequency	Typical journey time
Train	6–7 daily	6 hrs 45 mins (day) 9 hrs (night)

Madrid–Lisbon ETT table 677

Type	Frequency	Typical journey time
Train	1 daily	10 hrs

Notes

Most trains in Spain need advance reservations.

Barcelona to Lisbon: change trains at Madrid.

Badajoz to Lisbon: change trains at Abrantes.

Remember Spain's time is 1 hr ahead of Portugal's.

This trip across central Spain and Portugal links the three largest cities on the Iberian peninsula – **Barcelona** (p. 141), **Madrid** (p. 155), and **Lisbon** (p. 149). From the heart of Catalan-speaking Spain you head along the Costa Dorada – not Spain's most beautiful stretch of coast, but endowed with impressive Roman remains at **Tarragona** (where you can opt to head inland direct to Madrid via **Zaragoza**). Further down at the centre of the orange-and-vegetable-growing Levante region is **Valencia** – big, untidy-looking, but still rewarding to visit. Beyond the wine-making town of **Requena**, with its Moorish castle, extend the excitingly rugged sierras of the north-east corner of New Castile, where you encounter **Cuenca**, with its precariously perched houses beside a precipice. **Madrid** and **Toledo** give good reason for lingering in the very centre of Spain. Extremadura (meaning 'the land beyond the Duero') is the name given to west central Spain, a deeply rural region of vast rolling sierras, forests and landscapes rich in wildlife; there are also some deeply atmospheric settlements virtually untouched by the passage of time, notably **Cáceres** and the Roman remains at **Mérida**. Over the border into Portugal, **Abrantes** provides a base for visiting **Marvão**, an enchanting hilltop town in the wild Alentejo region.

BARCELONA

See p. 141.

DAY TRIP FROM TARRAGONA

Port Aventura is one of Spain's best adventure theme parks (mid-Mar–early Jan). There are at least 10 trains a day from Tarragona, taking about 10 mins. For further details ☎ 977 77 99 00 (www.portaventura.es).

TARRAGONA

With its ancient walled town above the modern settlement, Tarragona has dual attraction: its glorious cliff-top position and its rich heritage of **Roman sites**, including the remains of temples, a substantial **amphitheatre** and the Roman **forum**, which now abuts modern housing. There is also a **necropolis**, where early Christians were buried, and a well-preserved **aqueduct** out of town. Along the foot of the 3rd-century BC Roman walls extends the **Passeig Arqueològic**, an archeological walkway. Catalonia's foremost collection of Roman sculptures, temple friezes, bronzes and mosaics is housed in the high-tech **Museu Arqueològic**, PLAÇA DEL REI, while the neighbouring *Pretori*, a Roman palace, contains the **Museu de la Romanitat**, with historical displays ranging from Roman to medieval finds. **La Seu** (the cathedral) exemplifies the transition from Romanesque to Gothic and has a fine cloister.

🚉 PASSEIG DE ESPANYA. Taxis and 🚌 no. L2. It's a 10-min walk uphill to the old centre: take C. D'OROSI opposite, uphill; go right at the junction with C. D'APODACA, and carry on up to the main street (RAMBLA NOVA); the Tourist Office is left and immediately left again, while the old town lies ahead.

🛏 The best budget bets are in Plaça de la Font, a pleasant traffic-free square in the old town (also some good places to eat); here are two clean, adequate pensions – **Marsal**, 🕾 977 238 231, €, and **La Noria**, 🕾 977 238 717, €.

ℹ️ **Tourist Office: (Regional)** Carrer Fortuny 4, 🕾 977 23 34 15. **(Municipal)** Carrer Major 39, 🕾 977 24 50 64 (near the cathedral). Below the main town. For the centre, take C. d'Orosi opposite, uphill; go right at the junction with C. d'Apodaca, and carry on up to the main street (Rambla Nova); the Tourist Office is left and immediately left again, while the old town lies ahead.

Side Trip to Zaragoza   Zaragoza (ETT table 650) is on the direct line from Barcelona to Madrid (7 hrs; it is 1 hr 5 mins from Tarragona to Zaragoza; reservations needed). Although flanked by immense tower blocks and traffic-ridden *paseos*, the old town reveals a lively, historic centre. The station (where you can pick up a city map) is 3 km out; to avoid the 25-min walk, take 🚌 no. 22 into the centre.

There are two cathedrals: **La Seo** is Romanesque and Gothic, and contains fine Flemish tapestries and a Gothic reredos; more famous is the mosque-like 18th-century **Basílica de Nuestra Señora del Pilar**, with its domes of coloured tiles, named after the pillar bearing a tiny, much-venerated statue of the Virgin within the church (where the Virgin Mary is said to have descended from heaven in a vision of St James in AD 40). You get a good view from the tower (reached by lift, then stairs). The **Plaza del Pilar** features an interesting water monument of South America: stand at the closest point of the pool to theBasilica, crouch down, and you will see a clear outline of the continent. The **Museo Camón Aznar**, C. Espoz y Mina 23 (closed Mon), has a fine art collection assembled by a devotee of Goya. Zaragoza's most impressive sight, the **Aljafería**, is a stunning Moorish fortress-palace just outside the city centre; look out for the ornate stucco oratory in the northern portico. Tours also take in the Gothic quarters added by Fernando and Isabel.

A modern attraction is the theme **Parque Zaragoza**, 1 km north from the station on Duque Alba. Open Mar–Oct, there are ferris wheels, rollercoasters and houses of horror.

The **Tourist Office** is on Plaza del Pilar, 🕾 976 39 35 37, fax 976 20 06 35 (www.turismozaragoza.com; ofturismopilar@ayto-zaragoza.es), €€, and offers guided walking and bus tours. The **Hotel Las Torres**, pl. del Pilar 11, 🕾 976 39 42 50, fax 976 39 42 54, €€, gets a superb view of the Basilica. Alternatively, try the **Hostal Milmarcos**, C. Madre Sacramento 40, 🕾 976 28 46 18, fax 976 44 62 66, €€; or the **Posada de las Almas**, C. San Pablo 22, 🕾 976 43 97 00, fax 976 43 91 43, €.

VALENCIA

Lush parks and gardens and a sprinkling of orange trees redeem the general modernity of Spain's third city, known as the home of *paella* as well as a place of effervescent outdoor life. Many historical structures were destroyed by inept town planners; the Spanish Civil War put paid to most of the rest, but two medieval gateways survive (**Torres de Serranos** and **Torres de Quart**) and there is a large old quarter with some pleasant squares, characterful if run-down backstreets and crumbly baroque mansions. There's a sizeable student population, based on the university; nightlife tends to focus hereabouts.

HORCHATA
In summer, many cafés and bars in Valencia offer *horchata*, a sweet milky drink made from *chufas*, or earth almonds, and bread sticks (either chewy, sweet *fartons*, or more brittle *rosquilletas*). The place to drink it is the **Horchatería Santa Catalina**, in the PLAZA DE LA REINA.

The old town (containing the main sights) is easily walked. EMT buses operate throughout the city; most can be boarded in PLAZA AYUNTAMIENTO (tickets from tabacos and kiosks), a traffic-ridden triangle overlooked by the copper-domed town hall. Two towers preside over the PLAZA DE LA REINA: the baroque spire of **Santa Catalina** and the **Miguelete**, which is the bell tower of the cathedral; climb the spiral staircase to the top for a magnificent view. Valencia's key building is the cathedral, a mixture of styles ranging from Romanesque to Baroque. A 1st-century agate chalice adorned with gold and pearls is said to be the Holy Grail and is displayed behind the altar in a side chapel.

LAS FALLAS IN VALENCIA
Las Fallas, a week-long festival in mid-Mar, centres on a competition to produce the best *ninot* (papier mâché doll). Entries are paraded through the streets and (on the last night) ritually burned, to the accompaniment of a huge firework display.

The Gothic **Lonja de la Seda,** PLAZA DEL MERCADO, with its exquisite interior, is a legacy of the heady days of the 15th-century silk trade, while the nearby **Mercado Central** is a vast art nouveau market hall with a stained-glass ceiling and *azulejos* (coloured tiles).

The **Palacio del Marqués de Dos Aguas** is a baroque pile with an eye-catching alabaster door-way and home to the **Museo Nacional de Cerámica** (National Ceramics Museum; closed Sun and Mon), its displays ranging from ancient Greek vases to 20th-century creations by the likes of Picasso.

The main station is **Estació del Nord**, with its magnificent art nouveau entrance hall, centrally located (Metro: XÁTIVA; ⊟nos. 5/8/10/11/14/19; lockers),10 mins by rail from **Cabanyal** station (⊟no. 81), which serves the ferries. There is also an **FGV** station across the river from Torres Serranos, from which a network of narrow gauge railways radiates.

i **Tourist Offices: Regional**: C. DE LA PAZ 48, ☎ 96 398 64 22 (www.comunidad-valenciana.com) and at Estacio del Nord. **Municipal**: PLAZA AYUNTAMIENTO 1, ☎ 96 351 04 17, and AVDA CATALUÑA 1.

Good budget areas are around PLAZA AYUNTAMIENTO and PLAZA DEL MERCADO. **Hostal Moratín**, C. MORATÍN 15, ☎ 96 352 12 20 (hmoratin@tpi.infomail.es), €, is comfortable and cheap, if slightly airless. **Hostal-Residencia El Cid**, C. CERRAJEROS 12, ☎ 96 392 23 23, €, gives special deals for groups and, they say, *Independent Traveller* readers. **Youth hostel**: **La Paz**, AVDA DEL PUERTO 69, ☎ 96 369 01 52 (⊟no.19 from PLAZA AYUNTAMIENTO), is open Jan–Oct. The most convenient **campsite** is **Devesa Gardens**, CARRETERA DE EL SALER km13, ☎ 96 161 11 36, fax 96 161 11 05; ⊟ to El Saler-Valencia Centre, every 30 mins.

CUENCA

Finely carved wooden balconies, armorial bearings, impressive doorways and breathtaking views over two river gorges are keynotes to this delightful town. Especially striking are the **Casas Colgadas**, the 13th-century tiered houses that hang over a sheer chasm and form the city's emblem. Level ground is in pretty short supply, a notable exception being the arcaded **Plaza Mayor**, flanked by the cathedral, which dates from the 12th century. It's more refined inside than its unfinished exterior suggests, and houses an absorbing treasury with paintings by El Greco. The best museums are the **Diocesan Museum** and the **Museo de Arte Abstracto**, the latter within one of the hanging houses and displaying Spanish abstract art. An iron footbridge in one of the gorges provides a famous view of the hanging houses. Don't miss the very top of the town either: keep going right up, through an old gateway, for superlative views from the crags over the whole town: it's pretty astonishing, even by Spanish standards.

▓ C. MARIANO CATALINA, 10. It is a hard climb from the station to the old town and most prefer to take a bus 🚌 no.1. The walk takes 20–25 mins: take the street diagonally left from the station, past a sign for Hostal Cortes in Ramón y Cajal.

𝒊 **Tourist Office**: PLAZA MAYOR, 📞969 23 21 19 (www.cuenca.org or www.jccm.es).

🛏 Several cheap places are found between the station and the old town, including **Pensión Marin**, RAMÓN Y CAJAL 53, 2ND FLOOR📞969 22 19 78, €. A few doors up is the comfortable **Hostal Cortes**, RAMÓN Y CAJAL 49, 📞969 22 04 00, fax 969 22 04 06, €€. A nicely placed pension below the old town is **Tintes**, C. DE LOS TINTES 7, 📞969 21 23 98, fax 969 22 47 18, €. There are two pensions at the top of the old town (served by 🚌 no. 1): **La Tabanqueta**, TRABUCO 13, 📞969 21 12 90, €, dramatically perched by the edge of the gorge, while beyond the gateway and the very last building (with jaw-dropping views) is **Real**, LARGA 41, 📞969 22 99 77, €. For a treat in the old town, stay at the beautiful **Posada San José**, JULIÁN ROMERO 4, 📞969 21 13 00, fax 969 23 03 65 (psanjose@arrakis.es), €€.

🍴 Meaty variations occur on Cuenca's menus, most famously *morteruelo*, a spicy dish combining a multitude of meats, including game, chicken, pig's lard, cured ham and grated pig's liver, with the odd walnut thrown in for good measure. Something of an acquired taste, *zarajos* is roast lamb's guts, one of a number of local concoctions that are rolled on vine shoots, while *ajoarriero* is a more generally palatable dish of cod, eggs, parsley and potato; trout and crayfish are also on offer. *Resolí* is a liqueur made of orange peel, cinnamon and coffee.

ARANJUEZ

Change here for trains to **Toledo** (p. 167).

Situated on the south bank of the Tagus, Aranjuez has just one major attraction: the spectacular **Royal Palace** (closed Mon). This started life as a country house that was presented to Ferdinand VI and Isabella, but the present structure dates from the 18th century and is a succession of opulently furnished rooms with marble mosaics, crystal chandeliers, ornate clocks and the like. In the gardens are the **Casa del Labrador** (Farmer's Cottage; more like the *Petit Trianon* at Versailles than a humble workman's dwelling) and the **Casa de Marinos**, housing royal barges.

🚇 I km outside town and 10-min walk from the palace. As you exit the station, take the road to the right and then turn left at the end.

ℹ️ **Tourist Office**: PLAZA DE SAN ANTONIO 9, ☎ 91 891 04 27.

MADRID

See p. 155.

TOLEDO

A sense of history permeates every street of this famous walled city, perched on a hill and with the Río Tajo (River Tagus) forming a natural moat on three sides. Over the centuries Christian, Moorish and Jewish cultures have each left their mark on Toledo, which was a source of inspiration to El Greco, who lived and worked here for nearly 40 years. Although possible as a day trip (easy from Madrid), it's highly recommended that you stay longer. Only the sheer number of tourists detracts from the atmosphere.

As you walk from the **station** (itself an absolutely spectacular building with tiles, chandeliers, stained glass moorish windows and art nouveau signs) and cross the Tagus, you soon reach the **Alcázar** (old fortress). Aptly home to a military museum and on a site that's been fortified from Roman times, it has been repeatedly rebuilt, most recently following its near-total destruction in the Spanish Civil War; a monument to the Nationalists who perished in the fighting stands outside. Notable religious paintings and a 15th-century zodiacal Flemish tapestry hang in the **Museo de Santa Cruz**.

Built over some 250 years, the heavily buttressed **cathedral** is one of the wonders of Spain for its stained glass, for the sculpture in the choir, for the tombs within its chapels, and for its works of art, notably the **Transparente** – an extravagant baroque creation of paintings and marble sculptures which catches the light in a most dramatic way. In the Sacristy hang paintings by El Greco, Van Dyck, Goya and Velázquez, whilst in the treasury is a huge 16th-century monstrance of gold and silver which is still paraded through the town during the **Corpus Christi celebrations** (May/June), when the route is decked out with awnings, embroidered shawls, flags, lanterns and tapestries In the old **Jewish quarter** to the south are the two surviving synagogues. **El Tránsito** is a 14th-century Mudéjar edifice with a ceiling of carved cedarwood, now home to the **Museo Sefardí**, a museum about Jewish culture. The 12th-century synagogue of **Santa María la Blanca** is very different: its conversion into a Christian church did not affect the basic layout of the interior, with five aisles separated by horseshoe arches and supported by pillars with unusual capitals and stone carvings.

The **Iglesia de San Tomé** (Church of St Thomas), dates from the 14th century and houses El Greco's famous masterpiece *The Burial of Count Orgaz*. The **Museo de El Greco** is a small museum dedicated to the artist (though he didn't live there), with a number of his paintings as well as some of his personal effects.

Apart from Corpus Christi (see above) other **processions** take place in Holy Week, with the Procession of Christ the Redeemer on Wednesday, while on Thursday and Good Friday the 'men in armour' represent the Roman legion and there's a Burning of Judas. On 1 May is a pilgrimage to the shrine of the Virgen del Valle, while the Festival of the Patroness in mid Aug features sports, bullfights and shows.

PASEO DE LA ROSA, just east of the centre (nos. 5/6 to the PLAZA DE ZOCODOVER). It's more pleasant to take the 20-min walk in; cross the main road from the station, turn right and immediately fork left on a quiet road with no-entry road signs, then cross the 10th-century bridge known as the Puente de Alcántara, with the classic view of the town, and take the road rising opposite into town.

i **Tourist Offices**: the main office is at PUERTA DE BISAGRA, 925 22 08 43 (www.jccm.es). There is a branch in the town hall opposite the cathedral.

It can be difficult to find somewhere to stay for summer weekends. The best cheap lodgings are in the old town (try around C. DE JUAN LABRADOR or C. DE DESCALZOS), such as **Las Armas**, ARMAS 7, 925 22 16 68, €; **La Belviseña**, CUESTA DEL CAN 5, 925 22 00 67, €; and **Lumbreras**, JUAN LABRADOR 9, 925 22 15 71, €. There is a **youth hostel** on the outskirts of town in a medieval castle (near the station), the Castillo San Servando, 925 22 45 54. The university sometimes has rooms available. **Campsites: Circo Romano**, AVDA CARLOS III 19, 925 22 04 42, not very comfortable but only a 10-min walk from Puerta de Bisagra; and **El Greco**, /fax 925 22 00 90, which has much better facilities, but is 1.5 km out of town, on CTRA. TOLEDO-PUEBLA DE MONTALBÁN (no. 7 from PLAZA DE ZOCODOVER).

CÁCERES

Despite its abundant charms, huge concentration of monuments and World Heritage site status, the golden stone town of Cáceres is less known than it deserves to be, and visitors are still almost outnumbered by the storks that have built nests on every conceivable perch. In medieval times it prospered as a free trade town, and was largely rebuilt in the 15th and 16th centuries; thereafter, it fell into decline and very little was added, hence the time-warp quality. Ancient city walls surround a largely intact old town, with its Jewish quarter and numerous gargoyle-embellished palaces, displaying the heraldic shields of the status-conscious families who built them; the place particularly comes into its own after dark, when it's dramatically floodlit.

The obvious starting point is the cobbled, partially arcaded PLAZA MAYOR, from which the gateway of 1726 known as the **Arco de la Estrella** (Arch of the Star) leads into the compact old town (easily explored on foot). You immediately reach the Plaza de Santa María, abutted by the **Iglesia de Santa María** (with an interesting cedarwood retable), the **Palacio Episcopal,** and the **Casa de los Golfines de Abajo** (one of the two mansions of the Golfine family)

The **Palacio de Carvajal**, with its Moorish tower, houses the tourism and craft council, but you can visit the chapel and the first floor gallery (decorated in 19th-century style). On the top of the town's hill, the **Church of San Mateo** has a fine array of nobles' tombs, while the nearby **Casa de las Cigüeñas** (House of the Storks) was the only noble's house exempted from a royal decree and allowed to keep its fortifications. Home to a small provincial museum, the **Casa de las Veletas** (House of the Weathervanes) stands on the foundations of a Moorish citadel and contains an *Almohade* water cistern *(aljibe)*, with a vaulted ceiling supported by horseshoe arches. The **Casa-Museo Yusuf Al Burch**, Cuesta del Marqués, is a faithful recreation of a 12th-century Arabian residence.

Avda Alemania. **Bus Station:** Carretera De Merida. The bus and train stations are together, about 3 km from the centre. no.1 goes to Plaza Obispo Galarza, near the Plaza Mayor. From the station, cross the green footbridge over the road, then turn left 100 m for the bus stop (or walk up from here); a taxi to Plaza Mayor will cost about €5. Luggage lockers.

Tourist Office: Plaza Mayor, 927 62 50 47.

There's a good choice of hotels; the best area for both staying and eating cheaply is in the vicinity of Plaza Mayor. Cheapies (€ to €€) include **Hostal Princesa**, Camino Llano 34, 927 22 70 00, €€; **Hostal Almonte**, Gil Cordero 6, 927 24 09 25, fax 927 24 86 02, € (handy for the station); **Pensión Carretero**, Plaza Mayor 22, 927 24 74 82, fax 927 21 61 22, €; and **Pensión Castilla**, Rio Verde 3, €, central but budget-price and reasonably quiet (take the turning between the two main restaurants in Plaza Mayor and turn right).

Side Trip from Cáceres to Trujillo   Trujillo (47 km east of Cáceres; reached by bus; journey 40 mins), overlooked by a 10th-century Moorish castle, was built largely from the proceeds of the Peruvian conquests and known as the *Cradle of the Conquistadores*. From the bus station, a 15-min walk uphill leads to the **Plaza Mayor**, built on two different levels, connected by steps, and lined with once-magnificent palace-mansions, arcades and whitewashed houses. It is dominated in one corner by the **Iglesia de San Martín**, at the foot of which stands a bronze statue of conquistador Francisco Pizarro (who conquered the Inca empire in Peru), mounted and in full regalia. The Plateresque-style **Palacio de los Marqueses de la Conquista** was built by Hernando Pizarro (the elaborate window grilles and corner balcony are particularly attractive), and there are many other 16th- and 17th-century seigneurial mansions with lavish armorial bearings.

From Plaza Mayor, C. de Ballesteros leads up to the old walls, in which there is a gateway to the 13th-century Romanesque-Gothic church of **Santa María la Mayor**, which contains Roman sarcophagi as well as the tombs of the Pizarros and other Spanish heroes, and a winged retable by Fernando Gallego. A short distance away is the **Casa-Museo de Pizarro**, with a reconstruction of a 15th-century *hidalgo* (nobleman's house) and an exhibition of the life of Pizarro.

Tourist Office: PLAZA MAYOR, ☎927 65 90 39 (www.ayto-trujillo.com).

Accommodation: **Pensión Boni**, DOMINGO RAMOS 11, ☎927 32 16 04, €; **Hostal Nuria**, PLAZA MAYOR 27, ☎927 32 09 07, €; **Hostal Trujillo**, FRANCISCO PIZARRO 4, ☎927 32 26 61, fax 927 32 22 74 (hstruji@arrakis.es), €.

MÉRIDA

Around 25BC Mérida was one of the wealthiest and most important centres in Roman Spain. Today it's at first sight an unremarkable modern town, but look around and you'll find an impressive array of Roman monuments (open daily) that fully deserve most of a day. If you can only spare a few hours, head for the theatres, the Casa del Mitreo and the Roman bridge, and look in at the museum. It's worth buying the €5 ticket (www.mcu.es/nmuseos/mnar) covering all the sites apart from the Roman Museum: you can get this from any site. Notable free sites include the Roman bridge, the Forum Portico and the Temple of Diana.

As you arrive by train from Cáceres, the appreciable remains of the Roman **aqueduct** are visible immediately on the left (north) side. The bulk of the sites lie to the south of the station however. Head for the tourist office (see below) via José Ramon Melida, where you'll notice a number of shops selling replica Roman artefacts, including some quite convincing pots and oil lamps at pretty reasonable prices. By the tourist office is the entrance to the 14,000-seater **Anfiteatro** (**amphitheatre**), used by the Romans for 'entertainments' such as gladiatorial combat, and the acoustically perfect **Teatro** (**theatre**), still used for theatrical events, its magnificent collonades rising two storeys and enclosing the back of the stage. In the adjacent **Casa del Anfiteatro** (**House of the Amphitheatre**) look out for the mosaic depicting three men treading grapes. The nearby **Museo Nacional de Arte Romano** deserves a couple of hours, with exhibits ranged on three floors, and including some superb items such as a vast mosaic of a boar hunt and a statue of Chronos trapped by a snake.

Close to the bullring (which itself makes you realise that some things haven't changed that much since the days of amphitheatres) the **Casa del Mitreo** is a Roman house with a celebrated cosmological mosaic. Carry on past the **Alcazaba** – successively a Roman, Visigothic and Moorish fort – to the much-renewed **Roman bridge** over the Rio Guadiana, 792 m long and with 60 arches, within sight of the handsomely sleek modern concrete road bridge to the north.

Behind the main street, the **Temple of Diana** retains full-height columns. Near the station, the **Basílica de Santa Eulalia** is built over the remains of a 5th-century church built during the reign of Emperor Constantine; there's a museum and you can walk into the underground archaeological excavations.

From the station it is a 10-minute walk to the tourist office: take the street ahead from the station, go over the first road junction then fork left past Pensión El Arco into M. Cervantes to a roundabout; the Tourist Office is signposted ahead, at the end of José Ramon Melida.

Tourist Office: Avenida José Alvárez Saez de Buruaga (by the entrance to the Roman amphitheatre and theatres), 924 31 53 53. Pick up a map and a free English-language guide to the sites of Mérida here (the sites themselves have no information in English).

There's not a huge amount of budget accommodation in the town centre; good bets are **Pensión El Arco**, Cervantes 16, 924 31 83 21, €, and **Hostal Senero**, Holguín 12, 924 31 72 07, fax 924 31 60 67 (hostalsenero@oem.es), €.

ABRANTES, PORTUGAL

Sited high above the Tagus, the small hillside town of Abrantes originally defended the old Portuguese province of Beirã. Above the town, approached through a maze of flower-bedecked alleys, are the remains of a castle of uncertain, pre-12th-century origins, rebuilt by King Denis in the 14th century. The keep has been partially restored and is now a belvedere offering panoramic views of the town, the Tagus Valley and the mountains. The 13th-century **Church of Santa Maria do Castelo** (in the castle grounds) was restored in the 15th century and houses a museum containing Gothic works of art and *azulejos* (decorative blue and yellow tiles), and is also home to a trio of superb tombs of the Counts of Abrantes (the *Almeidas*).

No luggage lockers, but the Tourist Office sometimes lets visitors leave bags. The station is about 4 km south of the town centre, on the other side of the River Tagus. nos. 3/4/5 run from the station car park approximately every 30 mins.

Tourist Office: Largo 1° De Maio, 241 362 55. Turn left out of the small street at the station. Cross the bridge over the Tagus, follow the road round, then take the turning on your left-hand side and continue up the winding steep hill, past the hospital, to Abrantes; the Tourist Office is near the town's market and car park.

Pensão Alianca, Largo do Chafariz 50, 241 223 48, €; **Pensão Central**, Praça Raimundo Soares 15, 241 224 22, €; **Pensão Vera Cruz**, Av. Dr Augusto Silva Martins, Rossio ao Sul do Tejo, 241 312 50, €.

Budget places are around O Pelicano, Rúa Nossa Senhora de Conceição and Praça Raimundo Soares (pleasant for sitting outside one of the cafés by the fountains).

LISBON

See p. 149.

ROUTE DETAIL

Madrid (Chamartín)–
Salamanca ETT table 679

Type	Frequency	Typical journey time
Train	3–4 daily	2 hrs 40 mins

Madrid (Chamartín)–
Segovia ETT table 679

Type	Frequency	Typical journey time
Train	7–9 daily	I hr 50 mins

Segovia–Villalba

Type	Frequency	Typical journey time
Train	7–9 daily	65 mins

Villalba–El Escorial

Type	Frequency	Typical journey time
Local train	I–3 per hr	I I mins

El Escorial–Ávila

Type	Frequency	Typical journey time
Train	6–7 daily	I hr

Ávila–Salamanca ETT table 679

Type	Frequency	Typical journey time
Train	5 daily	I hr 20 mins

From **Madrid** an incongruously suburban-looking train climbs onto the **Sierra de Guadarrama** to **Segovia**, one of the most exciting places in Spain. At Segovia station there is no hint of the nearby old city, but it soon comes into view after a short bus journey. From here retrace the route over the Sierra to the junction at Villalba de Guadarrama (or else take the bus from Segovia to Salamanca), and change trains, soon passing close to the vast complex of **El Escorial**, seen on the right-hand side of the train. Beyond the walled pilgrimage town of **Ávila** lies **Salamanca**, an elegant old university city built in a gorgeous yellow stone.

MADRID

See p. 155.

This romantic walled hilltop city has a tremendous situation, perched above the **Río Eresma** and looking out to the heights of the Sierra de Guadarrama. The **cathedral**, which towers majestically above the rest of the town, dates from the 16th century and was the last Gothic church to be built in Spain. It's huge inside; one side chapel has great metal dragons supporting censers each side of a ceramic altar. Segovia also has a fine clutch of smaller medieval churches, notably **San Esteban**, with its 12th-century tower, **La Trinidad**, an exceptional Romanesque church; **Vera Cruz** (closed Mon and lunchtime), a remarkably interesting Templar church with a 12-sided nave and 15th-century murals; and the **Convent of S. Antonio de Real**, noted for its 15th-century portal and painted wooden Calvary of the Flemish school.

Heading down towards the gorge that cuts around the town, you reach the **Alcázar** (castle), an amazing pile bristling with spiky towers. A massive fire in 1862 destroyed much of it, and most of what you see today is architectural bravado dating from the 1882 restoration. Fake it may be, but it does make an entertaining visit, with quaintly undersize suits of armour dotted around the rooms, and dizzying views from the tower. It's also worth following the riverside path from just below the Alcázar – a delightful semi-rural walk with views up to the old town.

Believed to have been built by Augustus, the **aqueduct** is one of Spain's most magnificent Roman monuments, with 165 arches spanning 813 m. It was constructed without mortar – each granite block has a groove whereby the Roman machinery lifted it into place – and although partly repaired in the 15th century is still intact. The Plaza del Azoguejo, where the aqueduct is a double-decker construction, is the main viewing point, though it's fun to follow the structure as it runs along more obscure streets, where the arches get increasingly wonky and amateurish.

The railway station is in the new town; take 🚌 no. 3 (it's much too far to walk) to the PLAZA MAYOR in the old town, or get off just outside the walls. The **bus station** is a 15-min walk from the centre, or you can take the bus.

Tourist Office: PLAZA MAYOR 10, ☎ 921 46 03 34, fax 921 46 03 30 (www.jcyl.es). Another Tourist Office (in summer) is PLAZA DEL AZOGUEJO.

Stay in the old town. **Hostal El Hidalgo**, JOSÉ CANALEJAS 3–5, ☎ 921 46 35 29, fax 921 46 35 31 (rte-hostal-hidalgo@hotmail.com), €€, has a pleasantly old-fashioned restaurant (serving local specialities such as *judiones*, or huge white beans, and roast suckling pig). Slightly cheaper are the **Pensión San Justo**, CALLE OCHOA ONDATEGUI 15, ☎ 921 42 88 69, €, (central, near the aqueduct); the **Montero**, CTRA. VILLACASTÍN 2, 2ND FLOOR, ☎ 921 42 08 63, €; and the **Tagore**, SANTA ISABEL 15, ☎ 921 42 00 35 or 921 42 42 82, fax 921 44 24 96, €. The **youth hostel** is at AVDA. CONDE DE SEPÚLVEDA S/N, ☎ 921 44 11 11, open July and Aug only.

Reasonable bars, cafés and restaurants in and around Plaza Mayor, the attractive central square of the old town.

SPAIN

EL ESCORIAL

Although it's some way from the station, you can easily see this vast grey palace and monastery, set beneath a hillside, from the railway. El Escorial is a magnificent 16th-century complex that includes a monastery, where the kings of Spain are buried, and a library with nearly 3000 5th–18th-century documents. Many notable works of art are on display in the complex, some forming an intrinsic part of the décor. The **palace** is of particular interest. Closed Mon; free on Wed for EU nationals only.

About 2 km from town, uphill, so it's better to take a local shuttle bus to the centre.

[i] **Tourist Office**: C. FLORIDABLANCA 10, ☎91 890 15 54.

ÁVILA

The highest city in Spain, Ávila is encircled by **medieval walls** in such a perfect state of preservation that the whole place looks like a cardboard model from a distance. Much of the walled town is surprisingly neglected and underpopulated, though it's obviously the most atmospheric area to stay in. Throughout Spain and beyond pilgrims are drawn to Ávila, indelibly associated with its native mystic and reformer Santa Teresa de Jesús (now the city's patron saint), canonised in 1622 and who spent 30 years in a convent in the city. The **Sala de Reliquias** contains a variety of relics associated with the saint, including her finger, the sole of her sandal and her walking stick.

Apart from the **walls** (part of which you can walk along the top of), Ávila's main attractions are the cathedral the **Monastery of Santo Tomás**, the **Basilica of San Vincente** and a number of other buildings associated with Santa Teresa. The **cathedral** and **Basilica de San Vincente** each deserve a visit, while **El Real Monasterio de Santo Tomás** is a real time-warp of a monastery, which became the summer palace of Ferdinand and Isabella. There are three cloisters, in different styles, containing gardens graced with a romantic, overgrown air of repose; the monastic church has the tomb of Torquemada, the infamously nasty grand inquisitor.

Avenida José Antonio; luggage lockers. (The bus and train stations are about 2 km from the centre. ☐ nos. 1/3/LP run from Avda de José Antonio – opposite the train station – to within the city walls.)

[i] **Tourist Office**: PLAZA DE LA CATEDRAL 4, ☎920 21 13 87, fax 920 25 37 17 (www.jcyl.es).

Hostal Continental, ☎920 21 15 02, fax 920 25 16 91, €, facing the cathedral and next to the Tourist Office, is thick in faded grandeur, the rooms a strange blend of modern and antiquated, with period plumbing arrangements.

SALAMANCA

Salamanca is beautifully built in yellow stone and home to one of Spain's oldest universities. Virtually throughout the year there's a generous offering of concerts, exhibitions and other cultural events, many of them free.

Echoing to hundreds of footsteps, the PLAZA MAYOR is one of Spain's finest squares, a strikingly unified example of the baroque style. Walk south from here, past the **Casa de las Conchas** (House of Shells), a 15th-century mansion named after the carved shells embellishing its exterior, the motif of the Santiago pilgrimage. Dating from 1243, the main part of the **university** (at the south end of RÚA MAYOR) is the country's prime instance of the plateresque style, seen on the ornamental façade, with its carvings of floral themes, royal heraldry, children, women and beasts. Inside you can look round the cloister, off which lie some of the oldest rooms, giving an idea of the university in medieval times, notably a dimly lit lecture hall austerely furnished with narrow, backless benches, and with a pulpit for the lecturer; the temptation to nod off must have been great. The benches were installed in the 18th century – before that, students had to sit on the floor (richer ones employed servants to sit on the floor beforehand and warm up their spaces).

The two cathedrals stand side by side – the **Romanesque Catedral Vieja** (old cathedral), with wonderful frescos, cloisters and a 15th-century retable, and the **Catedral Nueva** (new cathedral), displaying ornate relief carvings in the so-called churrigueresque style. Nearby, the **Monastery of St Esteban** is highly atmospheric.

Just below the cathedrals, the **Casa Lis** (www.museocasalis.org) is a striking modernist edifice of glass and filigree ironwork, restored and now home to the city's collection of art nouveau, art deco and (for some reason) dolls. From here, you can walk down to the river and the 26-arch **Puente Romano**; the 15 arches on the city side are Roman.

PASEO DE LA ESTACIÓN. Luggage lockers; shopping and entertainment centre. Central. 🚌 nos. 1/1B.

Tourist Office: CASA DE LAS CONCHAS, ☎ 923 26 85 71, or PLAZA MAYOR 14, ☎ 923 21 83 42 (www.jcyl.es).

Accommodation is plentiful; head for the PLAZA MAYOR, around which numerous pensions are signposted at the foot of staircases. The **youth hostel** is at C. ESCOTO 13–15, ☎ 923 26 91 41, 1 km from the rail station. **Campsite: Regio**, CARRETERA SALAMANCA-MADRID KM. 4, ☎ 923 13 88 88, fax 923 13 80 44 (recepcion@campingregio.com), 4 km from to the city centre, buses every 30 mins.

ROUTE DETAIL

Lisbon (Sta Apolónia)–
Coimbra (B)   ETT table 690

Type	Frequency	Typical journey time
Train	16–18 daily	2 hrs 20 mins

Coimbra (B)–
Oporto (Campanha)   ETT table 690

Type	Frequency	Typical journey time
Train	21–33 daily	1 hr 40 mins

Oporto (Campanha)–
Viana do Castelo   ETT table 696

Type	Frequency	Typical journey time
Train	11 daily	1 hr 45 mins

Viana do Castelo–
Valença   ETT table 696

Type	Frequency	Typical journey time
Train	7–8 daily	1 hr

Valença–Tui   ETT table 696

Type	Frequency	Typical journey time
Train	2 daily	19 mins

Tui (Túy)–Vigo   ETT table 696

Type	Frequency	Typical journey time
Train	2 daily	51 mins

Vigo–Pontevedra   ETT table 681

Type	Frequency	Typical journey time
Train	16–18 daily	28 mins

Pontevedra–
Santiago de Compostela ETT table 681

Type	Frequency	Typical journey time
Train	11–17 daily	1 hr 5 mins

KEY JOURNEY

Lisbon–Porto   ETT table 690

Type	Frequency	Typical journey time
Train	10–13 daily	3 hrs 45 mins

Notes

Lisbon to Santiago: change trains at Porto and Vigo. Fast trains call at Coimbra B station. A frequent rail shuttle connects to Coimbra station a few mins later. There are also hourly local trains Coimbra–Oporto (journey time 1 hr 45 mins).

From the Portuguese capital the route heads north through a series of photogenic towns such as the old university town of **Coimbra**, the port-producing city of **Oporto** and the delightful coastal resort of Viano do Castelo, lying close to sweeping golden beaches.

You can add on **Tomar** (to visit the fortified Convent of Christ, one of the architectural pearls of Portugal; see below) by changing at Lamarosa. From **Oporto** it's worth spending a few days exploring the scenic and deeply rural Douro valley.

Between **Valença** and **Tui**, you cross the border into Spain, and enter **Galicia**, with its wild coastal inlets known as the Rías Bajas; the journey ends in the breathtaking pilgrimage city of **Santiago**.

> Remember Portugal's time zone is 1 hr behind Spain's.

LISBON

See p. 149.

TOMAR

Hourly trains from Lisbon serve Tomar (journey time 2 hrs, ETT table 694); these go via Entroncamento, itself halfway between Lisbon and Coimbra – so if you're heading north you can detour to Tomar, then retrace to Entroncamento, where you change for Coimbra.

On a wooded hill above the old town of cobbled streets is the 12th-century castle and subsequent monastery of the Order of the Knights Templar, the **Convento de Cristo** (open daily). The structure was erected in 1160 for the master of the Knights Templar (responsible for keeping open pilgrim routes to the Holy Land during the Crusades), but from the 1320s became the seat of the royally created Order of the Knights of Christ. Highlights include the Templars' Rotunda (the round chancel), modelled on the Holy Sepulchre in Jerusalem, and the magnificent Manueline-style window between the west end of the nave and Santa Barbara cloister. The window combines every maritime and nautical motif known to the Manueline style: ropes, shells, coral, fishing floats, seaweed, even an anchor chain.

The Convento parking terrace overlooks **Nossa Senhora da Conceição**, perhaps Portugal's finest early-Renaissance church. While the outside is plain, the beautifully proportioned interior has finely carved Corinthian columns and faces with acanthus-leaf beards flanking the sanctuary arch.

Other sights in the old town are the **Igreja de São João Baptista**, with two fine Manueline doorways and a richly carved altar covered in gold, and the 15th-century **Sinagoga**, housing the **Museu Luso-Hebraico**, a museum of Portuguese Judaism.

Change at Lamarosa for 22-min journey to Tomar; 1–2 trains per hour (ETT table 694).

i **Tourist Office:** AV DR CÂNDIDO MADUREIRA, ☎ 249 32 24 27.

THE KNIGHTS TEMPLAR

Begun as a military-religious order to guard pilgrim routes to the Holy Land, the Order of the Knights Templar had its own rules, its own confessors, and its own sizable wealth. Known for their military skill, if not piety (vows of chastity were not required), they were especially successful in driving Moorish conquerors from Iberia.

The king of France, badly in need of some money, coveted the order's wealth and convinced the Pope that they were not only too worldly, but dangerous. The order was abolished and Templar properties were distributed to the kings in whose countries they had holdings. But King Dinis remembered their bravery in ridding Portugal of the Moors and, with the Pope's approval, established a new Order of Christ. Without the Pope's blessing, he invited all former Templars to join, in effect restoring them to all their properties in Portugal.

COIMBRA

Coimbra was a centre of the Portuguese Renaissance and is the seat of one of the oldest universities in the world. Set on a hillside above the River Mondego, the town is packed with medieval character; in term time it has a lively, youthful air. Coimbra has its own version of the *fado*, a melancholy, monotonous and sentimental chant originally sung by sailors in the 18th century.

Although founded in 1290, the old university building is baroque, with a magnificent library resplendent in painted ceilings and gilded wood; you can also visit the grand **Graduates' Hall** and a small museum of sacred art (free to students with ISIC cards).

The 12th-century **Sé Velha** (cathedral) is a striking Romanesque building with a fine altarpiece and Gothic cloisters, while the **Monastery of Santa Cruz** contains a 16th-century Manueline cloister, an elaborately carved stone pulpit and the tombs of the first two kings of Portugal.

BOAT TRIPS

along the Mondego start from **Parque Doctor Manuel Braga** (trips take 75 mins), ☎ 239 404 135.

Machado de Castro Museum, a choice display of medieval and Renaissance art, is housed in a former bishop's palace, which still retains access to the old Roman forum underneath the building.

🚃 **Coimbra**, 10 mins' walk from centre or 🚌 nos. 1/7/11/24. **Coimbra B**, 3 km north-west of town, handles long-distance trains, including those from Lisbon; 🚌 nos. 5/33. Frequent trains between Coimbra and Coimbra B. For luggage lockers go to the Café Internacional near Coimbra. For the town centre, follow the road along by the river and fork left by the Tourist Office.

ℹ️ **Tourist Office: (Regional)** LARGO DA PORTAGEM, 📞 239 833 019 (Mon–Sun and holidays 0900–1800). **(Municipal)** LARGO DOM DINIS, 📞 239 83 25 91.

🛏️ Several cheap places near Coimbra, such as **Pensão Atlântico**, RUA SARGENTO MOR 42 (just behind the Hotel Astória), 📞239 826 469, €. **Youth hostel**: RUA ANTÓNIO HENRIQUES SECO 14, 📞239 82 29 55 (🚌nos. 7/8/29 from LARGO DA PORTAGEM). **Campsite**: the **Municipal Sports Complex**, 📞239 701 497 (🚌no. 7 from LARGO DA PORTAGEM).

🍴 Plenty of centrally placed cheap eateries, for example in the University Gardens and in BECO DO FORNO and RUA DOS GATOS (alleyways between LARGO DA PORTAGEM and RUA DO SOTO).

OPORTO (PORTO)

Portugal's seductive second city, spectacularly sited on the steep banks of the River Douro near its mouth, gives its name to the fortified wine the English-speaking world knows as port (fortuitously invented by two Englishmen who used brandy in an attempt to preserve some Portuguese wine).

Get your bearings by climbing the **Torre dos Clérigos**, Oporto's symbol, an 18th-century granite bell-tower that gives a magnificent view. Below, the characterfully shabby old town, with its pastel shades and changes in level, is strongly atmospheric, notably in the **Ribeira** riverside area. The **Soares dos Reis Museum**, housed in the Carrancas Palace, is acclaimed for its collection of the decorative arts, including Portuguese faïence.

For an astonishing temple to money-making, take the guided tour of the **Palácio da Bolsa** (former Stock Exchange, now headquarters of the Chamber of Commerce), rather grey and boring-looking from outside but revealing a lavish interior which includes the Arabian Hall, a 19th-century gilded evocation of the Alhambra in Granada (pp. 198–199). The nearby **Church of São Francisco** is a fine example of the Manueline style and with a dazzling baroque interior.

The vineyards themselves are a long way up river in the magnificently scenic Douro valley, but most of the port is aged in the numerous **port lodges** in the district of **Vila Nova de Gaia**, linked to the city centre by the double-decker coathanger-shaped Dom Luis I Bridge; walk over the top level for dizzying views. The lodges offer **free tours** with tastings (Sandeman and Offley charge admission) and booking is not generally necessary; Taylor's gives an authoritative tour of their 300-year-old lodges, don't miss the fabulous views from their terrace. Barros are particularly generous with the tastings. Moored on the river, small barrel-laden sailing craft (*barcos rabelos*), last used in 1967, serve as a reminder of how the young ports used to be brought down river from the vineyards. Porto's port days are probably limited: operations may all move upriver over the next couple of decades.

To the west of the town, amidst magnificent gardens, is the **Fundação de Serralves**, an art deco mansion with a fine collection of modern art.

Campanhã, RUA DA ESTAÇÃO, near the south-east edge of town, serves Lisbon trains (☐no. 35 to centre); luggage lockers and cash machine. **São Bento**, near PRAÇA DA LIBERDADE, much more central (wonderful tiling makes it a sight in itself), handles local/regional services. Frequent connections between the stations, taking 10 mins. Leave **São Bento** Station and turn right up PRAÇA DA LIBERDADE then go left to AVDA DOS ALIADOS; Tourist Office is on your left, towards the top of this large square.

i **Tourist Offices**: PRAÇA DOM JOÃO I 25, ☎22 205 75 14 (national office), and RUA CLUBE DOS FENIANOS 25, ☎22 339 34 70 (www.portoturismo.pt); branch at RUA INFANTE D HENRIQUE 63. The free city map shows four **walking tours**: Medieval, Baroque, Azulejos (tiles) and Neoclassical.

Francisco Sá Carneiro, ☎22 941 31 50/60 (☐no. 56 from PRAÇA DE LISBOA or Aero Bus from AVENIDA DOS ALIADOS); Tourist Office.

Day bus passes (about €2 – cheaper than three separate fares) for buses and trolley buses and **tourist passes** (4- or 7-day, for all transport) are sold at STCP kiosks. DIANA run hop-on-hop-off **bus tours** (€12.50; buy on board). The **Museu Carro Eléctrico** is a vintage tram that tours the city from near the Church of São Francisco.

50-min **boat trips** depart from CAIS DA ESITVA (Ribeira) and near the Sandeman port lodge and tour the river (€7.50).

For cheap lodgings, try the central area around AVDA DOS ALIADOS. Avoid the dockside RIBEIRA. A friendly place with a variety of rooms from budget singles and quads to more comfortable doubles with private bathrooms is the **Pensão Duas Nações**, PRAÇA G G FERNANDES 59, ☎/fax 22 208 16 16 (duasnacoes@mail.teleweb.pt), €–€€; inexpensive Internet access; laundry service. Other places close by are the **Residencial Portuguesa**, TRAVESSA CORONEL PACHECO 11, ☎22 200 41 74, €; **Pensão Estoril**, RUA DE CEDOFEITA 193, ☎22 200 27 51 (estoril@usa.net), €–€€; and **Pensão França**, PRAÇA GOMES TEIXEIRA 7, ☎22 200 27 91, €. **Youth hostel**: RUA P GAMA 551, ☎22 617 72 57, fax 22 617 72 47; a long way west by the mouth of the Douro, with beaches and a supermarket nearby; ☐nos. 35/78 from the city centre. **Campsites**: **Parque de Prelada**, RUA MONTE DOS BURGOS, ☎22 831 37 59 (☐no. 6 from PRAÇA DA LIBERDADE); two in VILA NOVA DE GAIA (**Salgueiros**, ☎22 781 05 00, and **Marisol**, ☎22 713 59 42).

SIDE TRIPS FROM OPORTO Allocate time to explore the mountain-backed **Douro valley** east of Oporto (ETT table 697), with its many vineyards as well as some enchanting places accessible by train. **Amarante**, memorably placed by the River Tâmega, has photogenic houses of wooden balconies and iron grilles, and a monastic church with gilded baroque woodwork. **Vila Real**, placed on Corgo gorge, has a host of 16th–18th-century patricians' houses.

North-east of Oporto, **Guimarães** was once the Portuguese capital and contains a rewarding medieval core within its industrial outskirts; **Paço dos Duques** (still used as the president's residence when visiting) includes a museum charting the town's former status, and there's a fine wooden ceiling within the Banqueting Hall.

Braga (Tourist Office: AVDA DA LIBERDADE 1, ☎253 262 550), the nation's religious capital, has more than 300 churches as well as Portugal's oldest cathedral; it's the site of massive celebrations in Holy Week, and 5 km east is the pilgrimage site of **Bom Jesus do Monte**, with a 116-m climb up the monumental 'Staircase of the Five Senses' to its Chapel of Miracles and massive reliquary. Some trains from Oporto to Braga require a change at Nine; there are also direct trains and buses from Lisbon.

VIANA DO CASTELO

This old fortress town doubles as the Costa Verde's most pleasant resort, with the beach on one side of the River Lima and the charming little town (noted for its Renaissance and Manueline architecture, which appeared when trade began with the great Hanseatic cities of northern Europe) on the other. It's also a centre of Portuguese folklore and famous for its handicrafts.

With the exception of **Santa Luzia** on the top of the **Monte de Santa Luzia** (accessible by funicular from AVDA 25 DE ABRIL; excellent view), interesting sights are walkable. The central square, **Praça da República**, has a 16th-century fountain that has been copied all over the region. Some choice examples of *azulejos* (tiles) can be seen in **Misericórdia Church** and the **Municipal Museum** (also showing glazed earthenware and furniture). Viana do Castelo's **Romaria** (in Aug) is the biggest festival in the country.

There are several spectacular sandy beaches accessible by train within half an hour, on the line to **Valença**.

AVDA DOS COMBATENTES near the town centre.

i **Tourist Office**: PRAÇA DA ERVA, ☎258 82 26 20 (www.rtam.pt).

Pensions are easy to find, but not that cheap; rooms in private houses are often a better bet (look for cards in windows). **Campsites: Orbitur**, ☎258 32 21 67, and **Inatel**, ☎258 32 20 42 (both by Cabedelo beach, about 2 km away; from AVDA 25 DE ABRIL and main bus station, plus seasonal ferry from LARGO 5 DE OUTUBRO).

VALENÇA

Unsightly modern sprawl has marred the approaches to this ancient town by the Minho river, but it still has its fortress-with-a-fortress guarding the border with Spain. Much survives of the 17th–18th-century walls and there are narrow old streets of white houses.

RAIL On the east side of the new town.

i **Tourist Office**: Avda de Espanha, ☎/fax 251 823 374.

TUI (TÚY), SPAIN

A bridge connects this tiered Spanish town to Portugal. Tui has grown around the lichen-encrusted **Cathedral of San Telmo**. This impressive, austere Romanesque and Gothic building has a 13th-century cloister, carved choir stalls, an ornate 14th-century porch and fine Gothic sepulchres. Visit the churches of **Santo Domingo** and **San Bartolomé** if time permits.

RAIL Central.

i **Tourist Office**: Calle Colón, ☎ 986 60 17 89.

🛏 **Argentino**, Bo de Baños 82, Caldelas, ☎ 986 62 90 11; **Generosa**, Calvo Sotelo 37, ☎ 986 60 00 55.

VIGO

Spain's major fishing port lies on a beautiful sheltered bay. It's a clamorous, busy place built of grey granite, not immediately attractive except in the old, sloping quarter near the seafront. Castro Castle, the ruined fort on a hill just above, provides a fine view. There are **beaches** and an **open-air pool** 2 km west at **Samil** (🚌 L15/L16/L27/LN).

The wonderfully unspoilt **Islas Cíes** archipelago, reached by ferry from Vigo from mid June to mid Sept, is the main reason for stopping here. Designated a national park, the islands have white sands and rugged hilltops, with enough trails to provide a day's walking on the main two isles (which are joined together by a sand bank). The third island is a bird sanctuary and is not open to visitors. Book ahead (☎ 986 43 83 58) to camp in summer. For ferry information ☎ 986 22 52 72; visitors are limited to 2,000 per day, so go early in the day if you haven't booked.

RAIL Plaza de la Estación. Station information counter has free city maps (10 mins from the quays/Tourist Office: turn right out of the station, along C. Alfonso XIII). Lockers and cash machine.

i **Tourist Office**: c. Cánovas del Castillo 22, ☎ 986 43 05 77.

🛏 **La Nueva Cubana**, c. Lepanto 15, ☎ 986 22 20 20, €. **Orensano**, c. Lepanto 9, ☎ 986 43 51 12, €. Pricier but nicely sited in a pretty cobbled alley near the ferry terminal in the old quarter is the **Continental**, Bajada a la Fuente 3, ☎ 986 22 07 64, fax 986 22 38 87, €€.

PONTEVEDRA

This typical old Galician town on the River Pontevedra began life as a port, but its importance dwindled as the old harbour silted up. Although surrounded by a new city, the compact old town is pretty much intact, with parts of the original walls still visible around a maze of cobbled streets, arcaded squares with carved stone crosses and low houses with flower-filled balconies. **La Peregrina**, an unusual chapel in the shape of a scallop shell, is situated by the partly arcaded main square, PLAZA DE LA FERRERÍA, on the boundary between the old and new towns. The Gothic façade of the **Convent of San Francisco** looks onto the Herrería. **Iglesia de Santa María la Mayor** has an impressive Plateresque façade, which is floodlit at night. The 13th-century Gothic **Convent of Santo Domingo** by the **Jardines de Vincenti** is now largely in ruins but still evokes a certain splendour. The surviving wing holds part of the **Provincial Museum**, other sections of which are at PLAZA DE LA LEÑA.

[ABS] PLAZA CALVO SOTELO, about 1 km from the centre; lockers.

i **Tourist Office**: C. CALLE GUTIÉRREZ MELLADO 1B, ☎/fax 986 85 08 14 (www.riasbaixas.org).

[⌂] Budget accommodation is limited; there are some *fondas* and *pensiones* in the streets around C. DE LA PEREGRINA and PLAZA DE GALICIA, for example at C. DE ANDRÉS MELLADO 7 and 11. **Casa Alicia**, AVDA DE SANTA MARIA 5, ☎ 986 85 70 79, €, is welcoming. Others include **Casa Maruja**, AVDA SANTA MARIA 2, ☎ 986 85 49 01, €, and **Pensão Michelena**, C. MICHELENA 11, 3RD FLOOR, ☎ 986 86 32 91, €.

SANTIAGO DE COMPOSTELA

See p. 191.

ROUTE DETAIL

San Sebastián–Vitoria   ETT table 689

Type	Frequency	Typical journey time
Train	9–10 daily	1 hr 40 mins

Vitoria–Burgos   ETT table 689

Type	Frequency	Typical journey time
Train	10–11 daily	1 hr 25 mins

Burgos–León   ETT table 682

Type	Frequency	Typical journey time
Train	3–4 daily	1 hr 50 mins

León–Astorga   ETT table 682

Type	Frequency	Typical journey time
Train	7–9 daily	34 mins

Astorga–Santiago de Compostela   ETT tables 681, 682

Type	Frequency	Typical journey time
Train	2 daily	5 hrs 25 mins

Notes

Reservations are needed on most services in Spain.
Astorga to Santiago: one direct train daily; one with change at Ourense.

KEY JOURNEYS

San Sebastián–Burgos   ETT table 689

Type	Frequency	Typical journey time
Train	1 daily	8 hrs

Burgos–Bilbao   ETT table 689

Type	Frequency	Typical journey time
Train	3–4 daily	2 hrs 55 mins

If it were ever possible to make a pilgrimage by rail, this is it, for **Santiago de Compostela** (or just plain Santiago to most) has been the objective for millions of pilgrims over many centuries, walking the routes from France and across northern Spain that have come to be known as the 'Camino de Santiago'. San Sebastián stands on the coast beneath the green, rainy foothills of the Pyrenees in the Basque province, known to the assertively independent Basque people as *Euskadi*. Never conquered either by the Romans or the Moors, the Basques suffered appalling repression during the Franco period and their language, one of Europe's oldest, was banned. This area has a reputation for the best cuisine in Spain.

Burgos and **León,** both with superlative cathedrals, lie in the great *meseta* (high plain) of Castilla y León (formerly known as Old Castile). To the north rise the Picos de Europa, not that well served by public transport, but offering some of the best mountain scenery in the country. By contrast, Galicia, comprising Spain's north-west corner, is lushly verdant and intricately hilly, with a complicated coastline buffeted by Atlantic gusts and characterised by fjord-like scenery.

This forms part of the Paris–Granada route (p. 41); for Madrid and Seville, change at Burgos.

SAN SEBASTIÁN (DONOSTIA)

Known as San Sebastián to the Spanish and as Donostia to the Basques, this is now an elegant resort, with tamarisks gracing the promenade that runs along a crescent-shaped bay. Formerly a whaling and deep-sea fishing port doubling as a stopover for pilgrims en route to Santiago de Compostela (p. 191), San Sebastián really came into its own in the mid 19th century, when someone recommended sea-bathing as a cure for Queen Isabel II's herpes. She arrived, along with a great retinue, and San Sebastián became fashionable.

Take time to wander the streets of the 'old' town, or *parte vieja*, nestled at the foot of Monte Urgull. Although mainly rebuilt in the 19th century, it retains a characterful maze of small streets, tiny darkened shops and bars, arcaded plazas like the **Plaza de la Constitución**, which used to serve as a bull ring, and churches such as the beautiful baroque **Basilica of Santa María del Coro**. Fishing is still much in evidence, with the daily catch on show on stalls in the fish market.

The **Museum of San Telmo** occupies a former Dominican monastery, with archaeological displays in the cloister and a

FESTIVALS IN SAN SEBASTIÁN

In Sept, the international San Sebastián Film Festival, which has been going strong ever since 1953, draws thousands into town; the best star wins the coveted Donostia Prize. July sees a pulsating jazz festival, while classical music is thick in the air in late August.

changing exhibition in the church. At the far end of the quay are the **Naval Museum** and the renovated **Aquarium**.

For superb views, climb **Monte Urgull** itself, topped by a much-rebuilt fort (the **Castillo de la Mota**; free tours in summer). Standing proudly near the top of the hill is the statue of the **Sagrado Corazón de Jesús**, which watches over the city.

RAIL **RENFE: Estación del Norte**, PASEO DE FRANCIA. Cross the ornate Maria-Cristina bridge, turn right, and it is a few mins' walk through the 19th-century area to the Old Town. **FV: Estación de Amara**, PLAZA DE EASO. Beware of being hounded by unregistered hotel owners who group outside the station. Luggage lockers.

i **Tourist Offices: (Regional)** PASEO DE LOS FUEROS 1, ☎ 943 02 31 50, fax 943 02 31 51 (www.sansebastianturismo.com). Outside each of the Tourist Offices are touch-screen kiosks that give print-outs of town information. **(Municipal)** CALLE DE LA REINA REGENTE 8, ☎ 943 48 11 66, fax 943 48 11 72. Leave the station by walking over the Maria Christina Bridge, then turn right and walk alongside the river up PASEO DE LOS FUEROS. The regional office is on the corner of the PLAZA DE ESPAÑA, on the left where PASEO DE LOS FUEROS reaches the Santa Catalina Bridge. The municipal office is a little further on: walk along PASEO DE LA REPÚBLICA ARGENTINA then left at Zurriola Bridge.

🛏 For budget accommodation head for the old town: hidden amongst the narrow streets are many pensiones. Try **Pensión Amalur**, CALLE. 31 DE AGOSTO, which offers spotless, comfortable rooms and a friendly welcome, or **La Perla**, LOIOLA 10, ☎ 943 42 81 23, €. Rooms can be difficult to find during July and Aug. **Youth hostels: Albergue La Sirena**, PASEO DE IGUELDO 25, ☎ 943 31 02 68 (udala.youthhostel@donostia.org), 3km to station, 🚌 nos. 5/6/15/16/22/24/25/27; **Ulia-Mendi** (same tel and e-mail as La Sirena above), 6 km from station. There is a **campsite**, **Camping Igueldo**, on the fringes of the city at PUEBLO DE IGUELDO, ☎ 943 21 45 02, fax 943 28 04 11 (🚌 no. 16 from ALAMEDA DEL BOULEVARD).

🍽 San Sebastián has a reputation for gourmet cuisine; there are many superb back-street tapas bars – monkfish kebabs, stuffed peppers and wild mushroom vol-au-vents may be on offer. There are two excellent markets: **La Bretxa**, on ALAMEDA DEL BOULEVARD, and **San Martin**, near the cathedral on C. LOIOLA. For the best small **restaurants**, try the old town and the fishing harbour at the north end of PLAYA DE LA CONCHA.

SIDE TRIPS TO BILBAO AND SANTANDER

These trips can be done by narrow-gauge railway or bus from San Sebastián (ETT tables 686, 688; alternatively there are trains from Zaragoza and Madrid/Ávila/Burgos, all via Miranda de Ebro; ETT tables 653, 689)

Bilbao, a sprawling industrial port, has been put firmly on the tourist map since 1997 with the opening of the **Museo Guggenheim Bilbao** (Tues–Sun, 1000–2000; www.guggenheimbilbao.es; ☎ 94 435 90 80, fax 94 435 90 10 for details of exhibitions). This stunning modern art gallery has changing exhibitions of part of the collections of the fabulously wealthy New York art collector Solomon R Guggenheim. It's one of the most talked-about examples of architecture that came out of the late

20th century, and its titanium-clad geometry looks different according to where you approach it from. Elsewhere the **Museo de Belles Artes** in Doña Casilda Iturriza park surveys early Spanish art up to the 17th century, and has collections of Basque, Dutch/Flemish and contemporary works. Bilbao's old town, on the right bank of the river and beneath the hillside, is pleasant for strolling around. **Tourist Office**: Plaza Arriaga 1, ☎94 479 5760; www.bilbao.net. The **HI hostel** is at Carretera Basurto-Kastrexana 70, ☎944 270054, fax 944 275479 (aterpe@albergue.bilbao.net); take ☎no. 58 from the rail station.

Santander, is an elegant, cosmopolitan resort and university town set in a beautiful bay and endowed with a fine sandy beaches. It has buses to the superb mountain scenery of the Picos de Europa (see p. 190). The town is quite modern, having been destroyed in 1941 not by bombing but by a tornado. **Tourist Office**: Estación Marítima, ☎942 310708; branch at Jardines de Pereda. A centrally located backpackers' hostel (non HI) is **Albergue El Elbaicín**, C. Francisco Palazuelos 21, ☎942 217753, fax 34 942 211452; dorms €12, doubles €20.

VITORIA (GASTEIZ)

Known by the Spanish as Vitoria and by the Basques as Gasteiz, the Basque capital is surprisingly little visited. Known for making playing cards and chocolate truffles, it also has considerable charm. Within ugly outskirts, the almost perfectly preserved medieval hill town focuses on handsomely arcaded squares; at the centre of **Plaza de la Virgen Blanca,** a monument commemorates a nearby battle of 1813 in which Napoleon's army was defeated by the Duke of Wellington. From here you can explore a tangled web of narrow dark streets, filled with inexpensive eateries as well as several fine churches and Renaissance palaces. Look out for the **Church of San Miguel**, beside the steps at the top of the large and open PLAZA DE LA VIRGEN BLANCA, and the 16th-century **Palacio de Escoriaza-Esquibel**, with its fine Plateresque-style patio. The **Catedral de Santa María** is currently closed for - renovations until further notice; its unfinished 20th-century replacement, the huge neo-Gothic **Cathedral of María Inmaculada** (open 1100–1400), stands amid parkland in the flat new town; from here you can stroll CALLE CORRERIA, a tree-lined promenade where a mansion houses the **Museo de Bellas Artes** (Museum of Fine Art), with sculpture lurking among the topiary outside, and the rooms containing works by Picasso and Miró.

RENFE. Off the CALLE EDUARDO DATO, about two blocks from the cathedral and Tourist Office. Left luggage lockers.

Tourist Office: (Regional) PARQUE DE LA FLORIDA, S/N, ☎945 13 13 21, fax 945 13 02 93. **(Municipal)** CALLE EDUARDO DATO 11, ☎945 16 15 98/9, fax 945 16 11 05 (www.vitoria-gasteiz.org/turismo).

Carlos Abaitua Aterpetxea, ESCULTOR ISAAC DIEZ ☎/fax 945 14 81 00.

BURGOS

In medieval times Burgos grew rich on the wool trade, and in the 11th century the city became the capital of Christian Spain as well as home of Rodrigo Díaz de Vivar, better known as El Cid, the romantic mercenary. During the Civil War in the 1930s, it again rose to fame as the Nationalist headquarters. It was here that Franco formed his Falangist government and (18 months later) declared a ceasefire that ended the war.

Burgos has now grown into a large and busy modern city, but its heart is the atmospheric old town around the ruined castle (itself of little interest apart from the views from it). The grand entrance to old Burgos is formed by the **Arco de Santa María**, a fortified 14th-century gateway, altered and decorated in 1536 to pacify Charles V, depicting his figure and those of the founder (Diego Porcelos) and El Cid (whose equestrian statue stands near the **Puente de San Pablo**).

From here, it's a short walk to the bulk of the main attractions, eating places and hotels. Foremost is the **cathedral**, consecrated in 1260 but not completed until the 18th century, making it the third largest cathedral in Spain (after Toledo and Seville), and also probably the richest. Amidst the splendour of the 19 chapels and 38 altars, positively dripping in gold leaf, is El Cid's unobtrusive tomb and a grotesquely real-looking crucifix, made in the 13th century with human hair, fingernails and a body of buffalo hide.

Evening sees everyone promenade along the **Paseo del Espolón**, graced with fountains and statues and stretching along the river, with cafés and restaurants making the most of the atmosphere.

Outside the old town, the 16th-century **Casa de Miranda** houses one of Spain's best archaeological museums, exhibiting finds from the Roman city of Clunia.

THE SAN PEDRO FESTIVAL IN BURGOS

The annual festival in Burgos, celebrating **San Pedro**, is held on the last Sun in June, when the old town is transformed with glorious floral displays, a procession with marching bands and street entertainment and fireworks in the evening. Watch out for ladies in traditional dress who tell you your fortune as you are walking along the street – and then try to remove it from you in reward for their efforts!

WHERE NEXT FROM BURGOS?

7–8 trains a day make the 3-hr 45-min journey from Burgos southwards to Madrid (ETT table 689), a beautiful route over the **Sierra de Guadarrama**, rising to over 1400 m. Alternatively, services to Salamanca (2 hrs 50 mins; ETT table 689) join the **Madrid–Salamanca** route (p. 172).

About 1 km south-west of the cathedral on the far side of the Arlanzon river. nos. 3/5/7.

Tourist Office: PLAZA DE ALONSO MARTÍNEZ 7, ☎ 947 20 31 25, fax 947 27 65 29 (www.patroturisbur.es and www.jcyl.es).

The **youth hostel, Gil de Siloe**, AVENIDA DE CANTABRIA, ☎/fax 947 22 03 62, opens from the beginning of July until mid-Aug only; 2.5 km from station.

LEÓN

Nestling between the Bernesga and Torío rivers and surrounded by rolling *meseta* (plains), León was founded by the Romans (the *Legio Septimo*, or Seventh Legion, gave its name to the city), and over the years was ruled by Visigoths, Moors and Christians. In 1188, Alfonso IX summoned his first Cortés (parliament) here – one of the earliest democratic governments in Europe – but the court moved away permanently in the 13th century, and León became little more than a trading centre until 1978, when it was made the capital of the province of León. Today it's thriving once again. The major monuments are within easy walking distance of each other in the old city.

Of all the city's buildings, the most spectacular from the outside is the 16th-century, Plateresque-style **Hostal de San Marcos** (now an upmarket *parador*, or state-run hotel), which was founded by Fernando and Isabel, the catholic monarchs, as a pilgrim hostel and was later rebuilt as the headquarters for the Knights of Santiago. What is left of the old city is still bounded by fragments of the 14th-century city walls, which followed the line of the original Roman (and medieval) fortifications. Thirty-one of the original 80 bastions are still standing, and are best seen around the cathedral and the **Royal Basílica of San Isidoro**. Much influenced by the cathedrals of France, the **cathedral** has some of the very finest medieval stained glass in Europe (even rivalling Chartres in brilliance), with 125 windows dappling the interior with coloured light. Meanwhile, the Royal Basílica possesses a magnificent Romanesque pantheon, where some 20 monarchs are laid to rest.

RENFE: El Norte, CALLE ASTORGA, on the west bank of the river. **FEVE**: AVDA DEL PADRE ISLA 48, near the Basilica de San Isidoro. Luggage lockers.

Tourist Office: PLAZA DE LA REGLA 4, ☎ 987 23 70 82, fax 987 27 33 91; next to the cathedral (turn right out of the station to reach it).

The city has a wide range of hotels and guesthouses, ranging downwards from the ultra-luxurious **San Marcos** (see above). The Tourist Office has a list of places to stay. A good area to find budget accommodation is on and around AVDA DE ROMA and AVDA DE ORDOÑO II. Budget places include **Pensión Avenida**, AVDA DE PALENCIA 4, 3RD FLOOR, ☎ 987 22 37 63, €. **Youth hostels**: SAN PELAYO 15, ☎/fax 987 23 30 10 (open July–Sept); C. CORREDERA 4, ☎ 987 20 34 14, fax 987 25 15 25 (July–mid-Aug); PASEO DEL PARQUE 2, ☎ 987 20 02 06, fax 987 25 14 53 (July–mid-Aug).

SPAIN

SIDE TRIP TO THE PICOS DE EUROPA From León you can head north by bus (to Posada de Valdeón via Riaño; other approaches include from **Santander** to **Potes** and **Fuente Dé**; services are infrequent and you should check with Tourist Offices what's running) into the high mountains of the **Picos de Europa**, a stunning (often snow-capped) cave-riddled karst limestone wilderness that still shelters a few wolves and bears. Said to have been the first sign of European land seen by sailors returning from the New World, the peaks rise almost vertically from the Bay of Biscay and offer magnificent views and walking, notably through gorges (such as the **Cares Gorge**). The scope for longer hut-to-hut walks is more limited, unless you're extremely fit and experienced in mountain walking; the area isn't huge (roughly 40 km across) but it's very easy to get lost in if you stray from the waymarked paths, and there are numerous sink holes and other hazards. Unreliable weather is a further drawback: for much of the time the peaks are swathed in mist. Summer is obviously the time to go, though rooms get heavily booked up from late July to the end of Aug.

ASTORGA

Described by the Roman historian Pliny in the 1st century AD as a 'magnificent city', this is now a small, gracefully decaying country town, capital of the bleak moorland region of La Maragatería. Sections of the 6-m Roman walls survive around the old town. Towering over it all, the 15th–17th-century **cathedral** displays an intriguing hotchpotch of late Gothic, Renaissance, baroque and Plateresque styles, with motley towers, one grey and the other pink (there wasn't enough stone to complete it all in the same material). It's a frequent visit for pilgrims on their way to Santiago; next door, the flamboyant **Palacio Episcopal** (Episcopal Palace), designed by Gaudí in 1889, now houses the **Museo de los Caminos** (Museum of the Pilgrims' Way). Smaller buildings of interest centre on the PLAZA MAYOR.

PLAZA DE LA ESTACIÓN, about 1 km east of the town centre. Lockers.

i **Tourist Office**: PLAZA EDUARDO CASTRO 5, ☎987 61 82 22. From the station head straight on up PEDRO DE CASTRO, across to ENFERMERAS, then right through PLAZA OBISPO ALCOLEA and up LOS SITIOS. The Tourist Office is on your left near the Episcopal Palace.

Budget options include **Delfin**, AVDA MADRID CORUNA, ☎/fax 987 61 50 16, €; **Pensión Garcia**, BAJADA DEL POSTIGO 3, ☎987 61 60 46, €; and **Ruta Leonesa**, CARRETERA DE LEÒN 82, ☎987 61 50 37, fax 987 61 70 21, €.

GETTING AROUND SANTIAGO

The old city is tiny and everything of interest is easily accessible on foot. A tourist train tours the sights of interest, leaving C. SAN FRANCISCO every 20 mins (July and Aug only).

A magnet for millions of pilgrims for the last thousand years, Santiago de Compostela hit the big time when the tomb of St James (*Sant' Iago*, Spain's patron saint) was discovered in AD 813, supposedly by a shepherd who was guided to the site by a star. Destroyed in 997 by the Moors, the town was rebuilt during the 11th century and began its golden age. In the 12th century, the Pope declared it a Holy City: for Catholics, only Jerusalem and Rome share this honour. The newer sections of the city do not have a great deal of charm, but the old town (contained within the medieval walls) is one of the most beautiful urban landscapes in Europe.

The 12th-century Colegiata de Santa María del Sar, about 2 km from the old town, has a beautiful Romanesque cloister with wild flowers sprouting from its crumbling stone walls; the pillars inside the church lean at such precarious angles that it's a wonder the building still stands. Alameda is a delightful park, with shady walkways, ancient oak trees and superb views of the cathedral and the surrounding countryside.

It's not entirely given over to the pilgrimage, endowed as it is with a theatre, a concert hall and plenty of bars and clubs offering dancing and late-night drinking. Around the old town, free entertainment in the form of music and singing is provided by *tunas* – groups of buskers dressed in medieval clothes. Souvenir shops do a roaring trade.

The old town contains a host of fine churches and monasteries as well as notable secular buildings tucked down the narrow side streets. The **cathedral** (started in 1075) is the obvious centre of attention. Its existing 18th-century baroque façade covers the original 12th-century façade, the *Pórtico de la Gloria* by Maestro Mateo, said to be the greatest single surviving work of Romanesque art in the world, with 200 exceptionally imaginative and detailed sculptures. To celebrate their arrival in the Holy City, pilgrims traditionally touch the base of the *Jesse tree* on the central column, accordingly known as the 'Pilgrim Pillar', and deeply worn down by millions of fingers over the centuries. On the other side of the pillar, facing the altar, is a figure of the sculptor Mateo, popularly known as the 'Saint of bumps on the head', as people knock heads with him in the belief that his talent is contagious. Pilgrims mark the end of their journey by climbing up behind the shiny statue of St James and kissing the scallop shell (the symbol of the pilgrimage) on the back of his gown. The interior is dominated by a silver Mexican altar and a dazzling 17th-century baroque altarpiece. The **museum** contains a valuable collection of tapestries, including a series based on cartoons by Goya, manuscripts from

ATLAS THE BALL BOY
In the **Praza Do Toral**, a little statue of **Atlas** stands on top of one of the buildings. Legend has it that if any female student in Santiago is still a virgin at graduation time, Atlas will drop his ball!

the *Codex Calixtus* and a huge silver *botafumeiro* (incense burner) that is spectacularly swung through the transept on special occasions, with eight men clinging to it.

Four plazas surround the cathedral, each architectural gems in themselves. On the largest, the pigeon-populated PLAZA DEL OBRADOIRO, stand the impressive **Hostal de los Reyes Católicos** (the former hospital for pilgrims) and the classical **Pazo de Raxoi** of 1772 (now the town hall). Along one side of PLAZA DE QUINTANA is the austere façade of the **Monasterio de San Pelayo de Antealtares**. Entrance to the church and the monastery's **Museum of Sacred Art** are via the steps at one end of the square. Another landmark is the 16th-century **Monastery of San Martín Pinario**, (whose monks used to give new clothes to pilgrims who looked worse for wear after their journey), though the interior is no longer open to the public.

RÚA DO HORREO, 1 km south of the old city. no. C2 goes into the centre, but it's quicker to walk. Luggage lockers, accommodation service and cash machine.

10 km from the centre, 981 54 75 01; takes 30 mins.

Bus station: **Estación Central de Autobuses**, PLAZA CAMILO DÍAZ BALIÑO, 30-min walk from the old town; no.10 runs every 20 mins from PLAZA DE GALICIA. There is a good local bus system and route plans are posted at most stops.

BUS TICKETS
Bus fares cost €0.60. There is also a €3 card for multi-use.

Taxis: There are taxi ranks at the bus and train stations; 981 59 59 64, 981 58 24 50 or 981 59 84 88, and at PLAZA DE GALICIA; 981 56 10 28 (24 hrs).

i **Tourist Offices: Regional office**: Rúa do Vilar 43, ☎ 981 58 40 81, fax 981 56 51 78. **Municipal office**: Plaza de Galicia, ☎ 981 57 39 90, fax 981 58 48 55. From the station turn right along Avenida De Lugo then left up Rúa do Horreo, to Plaza de Galicia. **Websites**: www.turgalicia.es and www.citcompostela.es/santiago/principal.

Post and phones: The main **post office** is at Travesía de Fonseca.

During the three weeks leading up to the feast of St James on 25 July, the town is absolutely packed and you should book well in advance. Accommodation ranges from the five-star **Hostal de los Reyes Católicos**, €€€, a magnificent 16th-century pilgrim hostel built by Fernando and Isabel, to an array of small, relatively inexpensive guesthouses in both the old and new parts of the city. For budget accommodation in the old town, try around Rúa do Vilar and C. Raíña. **Hospedaje Ramos**, C. Raíña 18, 2nd floor, ☎ 981 58 18 59, €, is very central, with small, basic rooms. Other good-value places are **Hospedaje Sofia**, C. del Cardenal Paya 16, ☎ 981 58 51 50, €; **Hospedaje Santa Cruz**, Rúa do Vilar, € (laundry service); **Barbantes**, Rúa do Franco, ☎ 981 58 10 77, €; **Hostal San Antonio**, Rúa do San Antonio 4, ☎ 981 57 00 51, €. C. de Montero Ríos (just outside the old town) has a number of reasonably priced **hostels**.

There are three large **campsites** outside the city. **Cancelas**, C. del 25 de Xulio 35, ☎ 981 58 02 66, is the best option, being only 2 km from the centre (🚌 no. 6 from Plaza de Galicia). **Campsites: Monte do Gozo**, Carretera del Aeropuerto km. 3, ☎ 981 55 89 42, fax 981 56 28 92 (comercial.mdg@ctv.es), 3 km from centre of Santiago, 🚌 nos. 7 and UN (open summer only); **Punta Batuda**, Playa de Ornanda-Gaviotas, Porto do Son (30 km from Santiago), ☎ 981 76 65 42 (www.puntabatuda.com), 🚌 Santiago-Noia, every 30 mins.

WHERE NEXT FROM SANTIAGO?

*Carry on to **Lisbon** by taking the **Lisbon–Santiago** route in reverse (p. 176).*

There are plenty of **budget restaurants** around the old town, especially on the streets leading south from the cathedral. Slightly further out of town, the Praza Roxa area, near the university, is very cheap.

Side Trip to A Coruña A Coruña (frequent rail services, taking about 1hr 5 mins) is a large maritime city, with its old town on an isthmus between the beach and the harbour. The town's main attractions (after its beaches) are the **Castelo de San Antón**, which now houses an Archaeology Museum, and the **Torre de Hércules**, a 2nd-century Roman lighthouse, restored in the 18th century and still in use today, standing at the extreme north of the isthmus. There are also a number of fine churches and gardens.

The rail station is 45 mins' walk from the centre; 🚌 nos. 5/5A go to the Tourist Office. The municipal office is at Jardines de Méndez Núñez, ☎ 981 21 61 61, fax 981 20 07 11. Budget accommodation includes **Muiños**, Santa Catalina 17, ☎ 981 22 28 79, €; **Palacio**, Plaza de Galicia 2, ☎ 981 12 23 38, €; and **Roma**, Rúa Nueva 3, ☎ 981 22 80 75, €.

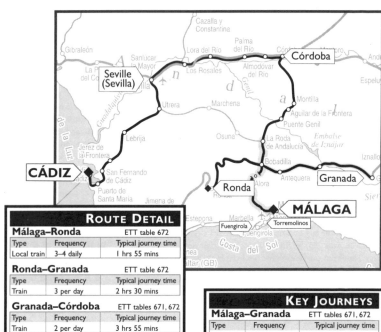

ROUTE DETAIL

Málaga–Ronda   ETT table 672

Type	Frequency	Typical journey time
Local train	3–4 daily	1 hrs 55 mins

Ronda–Granada   ETT table 672

Type	Frequency	Typical journey time
Train	3 per day	2 hrs 30 mins

Granada–Córdoba   ETT tables 671, 672

Type	Frequency	Typical journey time
Train	2 per day	3 hrs 55 mins

Córdoba–Seville   ETT table 670

Type	Frequency	Typical journey time
AVE	10–15 per day	44 mins

Seville–Cádiz   ETT table 670

Type	Frequency	Typical journey time
Train	9–14 per day	1 hr 40 mins

KEY JOURNEYS

Málaga–Granada   ETT tables 671, 672

Type	Frequency	Typical journey time
Train	3 daily	3 hrs 25 mins

Málaga–Córdoba   ETT table 671

Type	Frequency	Typical journey time
Train	9 daily	2 hrs 15 mins

Málaga–Seville   ETT tables 671, 672

Type	Frequency	Typical journey time
Train	5–6 daily	2 hrs 30 mins

Málaga–Algeciras   ETT tables 671, 672

Type	Frequency	Typical journey time
Train	5 daily	3 hrs 35 mins

Algeciras–Tangier   ETT table 2502

Type	Frequency	Typical journey time
Ship	30 daily	2 hrs 30 mins
Hydrofoil		1 hr 30 mins

Notes

AVE (Spanish TGV equivalent) runs Madrid –
Córdoba – Sevilla on high speed line. Special
fares apply and reservations are compulsory.

Málaga to Ronda: change at Bobadilla on
most services. Granada to Córdoba: change
at Bobadilla. Málaga to Granada: change at
Bobadilla. Málaga to Algeciras: change
at Bobadilla.

Andalucía (Andalusia) conjures up the classic images of Spain – with great parched plains dotted with cypresses and groves of olive trees, backdrops of rugged sierras, flamenco music, lively fiestas and timeless hilltop castles. The Moors left evidence of their occupation in the form of spectacular monuments such as the Alhambra in **Granada** and Mezquita in **Córdoba**, but there's also a rich Christian heritage.

Sit on the left-hand side of the train as you leave the port of **Málaga**, for the views soon become stupendous as you snake along the Garganta del Chorro, a huge chasm 180 m deep, and only visible from the train or by a rather dodgy-looking catwalk for walkers with a lot of nerve.

The scenery is less special after the little rail junction of Bobadilla, but westwards lies **Ronda**, one of the finest of the aptly named 'white towns' of Andalucía, perched improbably above a precipice. There's more of the same at **Arcos de la Frontera**, reachable by bus from Ronda and Cádiz. **Antequera** merits a stop for its remarkable prehistoric dolmens, but **Granada** easily outstrips it as a place to visit. From there, you could take a bus up to **Capiliera**, the highest village in the **Sierra Nevada** range that overlooks Granada. **Cádiz** is an atmospheric old port, but much of the rest of the coast is a mess.

For further information check out the websites www.junta-andalucia.es and www.andalucia.org.

A visit to the region can tie in with a ferry trip to Morocco (see pp. 207–209).

MÁLAGA

The fourth largest city in Spain and a busy working port, Málaga is the communications centre for the holiday coasts on either side. At first sight it isn't exactly pretty, with high-rise modern apartment blocks built up close together within close range of a dismal-looking canalised river. But the centre is a hundred times more cheerful and resolutely Spanish in character, with a tree-lined main boulevard, dark back alleys, a covered market, antique-looking pharmacies and dazzling flamenco dress shops; restaurants are inexpensive and lively, and the city has a real sense of place far removed from the tourist excesses of much of the rest of the Costa del Sol.

THEATRE IN THE OPEN

At **Paseo del Parque** there is an open-air theatre, which sometimes stages free productions in summer (ask at the Tourist Office for details).

Málaga's past is most evident in the area near the port. The long, shady walks of PASEO DEL PARQUE are overlooked by the **Alcazaba** (🚌 no. 35 from PASEO DEL PARQUE), a fort built by the Moors on Roman foundations; it's rather neglected, but you can walk around for free, and the views extend over the city to the coast (be careful if you're by yourself, as it's a crime hotspot).

Gibralfaro castle (now a *parador*), further up the hill, is of Phoenician origin, reconstructed later by the Moors.

Moorish influence can also be seen in the city centre, where the **Museo Arqueológico**, with its collection of neolithic pottery, is located. Just off the PASEO is the Cathedral, set in a secluded square and built between the 16th and 18th centuries. **Museo de Bellas Artes** houses a fine collection of mosaics, sculptures and paintings, including works by Picasso, Málaga's most famous son, as well as Murillo and Ribera. You can visit the house Picasso was born in for free; it's now the **Museo Casa Natal**, on the PLAZA DE LA MERCED (www.fundacionpicasso.es). The **Museo Picasso** (Picasso Museum) is in POSTIGO SAN AGUSTIN.

EXPLANADA DE LA ESTACIÓN (luggage lockers and accommodation services; for currency exchange go to the nearby bus station), a boring 20–30-min walk from the main part of town. 🚌 no. 3 goes to ALAMEDA PRINCIPAL and PASEO DEL PARQUE near the centre. Local trains for the coastal resorts leave from here as well (at a different level), and this line is also served by another more centrally located station, CENTRO ALAMEDA.

✈ 8 km from the city, 📞 952 04 88 38, fax 952 04 87 77. There is a Tourist Office in the main hall. Trains to Málaga run every 30 mins, taking about 10 mins. There is also a bus every 20 mins (🚌 no. 19), which stops near the cathedral and takes 20–25 mins.

ℹ **Tourist Offices: Municipal**: CASA DEL JARDINERO-PARK, AUDA-CERVANTES 1, 📞 95 260 44 10, fax 95 221 41 20 (www.malagaturismo.com); branch at PASEO DE LOS TILOS 21, plus information vans stationed throughout the city. **Regional**: PASAJE DE CHINITAS 4, 📞 95 221 34 45, fax 95 222 9421. There is a small municipal office in the bus station, PASEO DE LOS TILOS.

🏨 There is a good choice of hotels, including a small *parador* set in the gardens of the Gibralfaro castle (🚌 no. 35 from PASEO DEL PARQUE) above the town. Budget accommodation is functional, but lacking in any obvious regional charm. Good areas for cheap lodgings are around the PLAZA DE LA CONSTITUCIÓN (north-west of the cathedral) and immediately off either side of the ALAMEDA PRINCIPAL (although the south side is less salubrious). In high season, central Málaga is lively at night (all night); the only solution is to ask for a room away from the street, or buy earplugs. The **Pensión Rosa**, C. MARTÍNEZ 10, 📞 95 221 27 16, €, has reasonably sized rooms, some of which have balconies, and there are several other hostels on this street. **Hostal Córdoba** CALLE BOLSA 1, 📞 952 21 44 69, €, is very reasonable. **Hostal Juanita**, ALARCÓN LUJÁN 8, 4TH FLOOR, 📞/fax 95 221 35 86, €€, has a number of small, basic rooms. South of ALAMEDA PRINCIPAL, and slightly more expensive, are **Hostal-Residencia El Ruedo**, TRINIDAD GRUND 3, 📞 95 221 58 20, €, and **Hostal Castilla y Hostal Guerrero**, CÓRDOBA 7, 2ND FLOOR, 📞/fax 95 221 86 35, €€. **Youth hostel**: PLAZA PÍO XII 6, 📞 95 230 85 00, fax 952 30 85 04 (🚌 no. 18). **Campsite**: the nearest is 12 km away in **Torremolinos**, CTRA CÁDIZ KM 228, 📞 95 238 26 02, reached by 🚌 (Málaga-Benalmádena) or train.

🍽 There are several good **restaurants** around the cathedral, especially along C. CAÑÓN. Seafood and *gazpacho* are good bets. You do need to trawl through the usual tourist fare to find the really good places. **Paseo Marítimo** and the seafront in PEDREGALEJE are the best areas for bars and seafood restaurants. Málaga gives its name to an inexpensive sweet fortified red wine. *Convent dulces* are cakes made by nuns throughout Andalucía: in the morning nuns of **Santa Clara** at C. Cister 11 (just east of the cathedral) sell their goodies.

Side Trips to the Costa del Sol A frequent train service runs west from Málaga (Centro-Alameda and RENFE stations) along the **Costa del Sol**, connecting it to the airport and the busy resorts of Torremolinos, Benalmádena and Fuengirola. Once a fishing village, **Torremolinos** is a tacky, exuberant, fun-oriented, concrete high-rise resort, with a plethora of discos, fish and chip shops and bars, much of it run by a huge expatriate population. There are abundant beach facilities along the expansive stretch of grey sands. To the east, **Fuengirola** is another sun and sand haunt, more family-oriented and slightly calmer than Torremolinos, but equally ugly.

Málaga is also at the centre of a bus network reaching out to many smaller resorts. Eastwards, it is possible to reach Nerja and other assorted seaside towns all the way to Almeria. **Nerja** is a relatively peaceful resort, built around an old town that still feels distinctly Spanish, about 50 km from Málaga. Buses run approximately every hour, the journey taking 1 hr 30 mins. It is noted for its panoramic views of the coast, especially from the promenade known as the **Balcón de Europa**. Just east of the town is the **Cuevas de Nerja**, a series of large caverns full of breathtaking rock formations (Tourist Office: Puerta del Mar 2, ☎ 95 252 15 31; www.nerja.net).

RONDA

Ronda is a small town of pre-Roman origin set in the rugged Serranía de Ronda, and split in two by a dizzying gorge, with white houses clinging to the rim, and spanned in quite spectacular fashion by an 18th-century bridge known as the **Puente Nuevo**. The view from the bridge is hair-raising, even more so when you realise that it was from here that in 1936 during the Civil War 512 prisoners of the Republicans were hurled to their deaths, an incident adapted by Ernest Hemingway in *For Whom the Bell Tolls*. It was in Ronda that Pedro Romero invented the modern style of bullfighting – on foot rather than from horseback – and the bullring is one of the oldest in Spain. Near the bullring is the **Alameda**, a public garden beside the gorge, getting breathtaking views of the surrounding area, with olive groves stretching into the hilly distance.

On the other side of the bridge is the old Moorish quarter, with the attractive **Casa del Rey Moro** (House of the Moorish King), an early 18th-century mansion, now a hotel; you can visit the gardens, designed in 1912, and the mines, which provided Ronda with water as early as the 14th century and include the room of secrets, where it is fabled that what is said from one corner of the room to another cannot be heard in the centre. A path from this side of the bridge leads into the gorge for another interesting view, though the whiff of sewage can be a turn-off.

The *Baños Árabes* (Arab Baths) near **Puente San Miguel** were constructed in the late 13th and early 14th centuries and are thought to be the best-preserved baths in the Iberian peninsula. Entry is free.

Ronda is at its most charming during one of the many fiestas which occur throughout the year.

🚈 10–15-min walk to centre. Luggage lockers and accommodation service.

i **Tourist Office**: Plaza de España 9, ☎/fax 95 287 12 72 (otronda@andalucia.org).

🏠 You'll inevitably pass plenty of inexpensive places as you walk in from the station. Options include **Hostal San Francisco**, Calle Maria Cubrera 18, ☎ 95 287 32 99, €; **Hostal Virgen del Rocio**, Calle Nueva, ☎ 95 287 74 25, €; and **Hostal Biarritz**, Calle Cristo 7, ☎ 95 287 29 10, €.

> **DAY TRIP FROM RONDA**
>
> **Setenil**, reached by a handful of buses per day from Ronda bus station, is a bizarre village crammed into a gorge with houses built into overhanging rock ledges, a great place to walk round with a camera, or picnic on the hillside above. Other tourists are unlikely to be much in evidence.

GRANADA

Founded, according to legend, either by Noah's or Hercules's daughter, Granada was the last of the great Moorish cities to succumb to Fernando and Isabel's ferocious Christian Reconquest, in 1492. The main reason for visiting the city is to see the fortress-palace, the **Alhambra**, resplendent on its lush hilltop, and reachable by bus from PLAZA NUEVA (every 12 mins) if you don't fancy the pleasant but often hot walk up.

Most of the exterior of the Alhambra (see box on p. 199) dates from rebuilding in the 13th–14th centuries and is reasonably simple, giving no hint of the wealth of decoration inside. There are three sets of buildings: the **Alcazaba** (Fortress), the **Alcázar** (Palace) and the **Generalife** (Summer Palace and Gardens), with a combined entrance fee. The number of visitors to some areas of the Alhambra is now being limited to 8000 per day with timed tickets, so it is advisable to arrive in the morning (or reserve through any branch of Bilbao Vizcaya bank, €6.70 ☎ 902 22 44 60, or through www.alhambratickets.com) if you don't want to face a 2-hr wait to get in. The **Generalife** shelters a stunning garden with patios and running water; the Moors used their irrigational expertise to divert the River Darro to supply the pools and fountains. The main Christian edifice in the complex is the 16th-century **Palace of Charles V**, which houses the **Museum of Fine Arts** and the **National Museum of**

> **BEING PAMPERED IN GRANADA**
>
> If you're willing to splash out for the experience, **Al Andalus Baths**, CALLE SANTA ANA 16, ☎ 958 22 99 78, provide the chance to bathe in therapeutic waters for 2 hrs in Alhambra-like surroundings; massages are on offer for a very reasonable price.

Hispano-Islamic Art. Sat evenings see a surreal parade of newly married couples being photographed beside the ramparts.

In the city below the Alhambra, the **Capilla Real** (Royal Chapel) deserves a visit for the tombs of the Catholic monarchs, Ferdinand and Isabella, and their daughter and her husband; displayed in the Sacristy are some notable paintings from the private collection of Queen Isabella. Next door, the Cathedral was completed in the early 18th century, and has rather cold, gloomily impressive classical grandeur.

HIGHLIGHTS OF THE ALHAMBRA

The **Alcazaba** was predominantly used as a military outpost and is the oldest part of the present site. Its **Torre de la Vela** (watchtower), from where the Catholic flag was hoisted in 1492, commands panoramic views of Granada and the Sierra Nevada. The **Alcázar** was the main palace. Richly decorated and stunningly beautiful, with brilliant use of light and space, it was largely built in the 14th century. Of particular note are: the **Mexuar** (council chamber); the **Patio de los Arrayanes**, with an incredible honeycomb cupola made up of thousands of small cells; and the **Patio de los Leones**, so-named for the famous fountain in its centre. The **Sala de Embajadores** is the largest and most sumptuous room, its walls covered with inscriptions from the Koran, ornamental motifs, and brilliantly glazed tiles that glint metallically in light.

The **Albaicín** quarter, on the hill opposite the Alhambra, retains some Moorish atmosphere and is a rewarding and tranquil place for a stroll in its disorientating maze of stepped alleys, out from the hectic whirl of the city centre. Beware of bag-snatchers here. Close by you might stumble on CALLE CALDERERÍA NUEVA and CALLE CALDERERÍA VIEJA, a narrow street with rug-hung Moroccan teashops and eateries. Nearby, on the edge of town, are the gypsy cave-dwellings of **Sacromonte** (buses from GENERALIFE or PLAZA NUEVA; every 15 mins); note that the widely touted evening gypsy entertainments are a gross tourist trap.

AVDA DE LOS ANDALUCES. Lockers. No currency exchange or showers, but you can get information on accommodation. **Viajes Ronda**, ☎ 958 26 65 15, CAMINO DE RONDA 63, can provide cheap young-persons' rail passes.
From the station it's a 20-min walk to the centre. Walk straight out of the station and up AVENIDA DE LOS ANDALUCES. Turn right onto AVENIDA DE LA CONSTITUCIÓN, which becomes GRAN VÍA DE COLON. Turn off by REYES CATÓLICOS on your right; at PLAZA DEL CARMEN follow CALLE MARIANA PINEDA behind REYES CATÓLICOS. The **Tourist Office** is by the cathedral.

nos. 3/4/6/9 go to the GRAN VÍA and the centre from the main road up the hill from the station; they run every 20 minutes.

17 km from Granada on CTRA DE MÁLAGA, ☎ 958 24 52 00. Only 6 buses a day to the airport.

i **Tourist Offices: Regional:** PLAZA DE MARIANA PINEDA 1, ☎ 958 24 71 28 (www.granadatour.com).

GUADIX

Guadix (east of Granada) is an old walled town with a sandstone cathedral, and remarkable for its cave district, the **Barrio Santiago**. Some 10,000 live-in cave dwellings have been cut into pyramids of red rock – and electricity installed. Some inhabitants may demand rip-off fees to show you round their homes; you can find some deserted caves, and there's a **cave museum** near San Miguel Church. Frequent buses run from Granada to the town centre; there's a less good train service (with the station some way out). The journey by bus or train takes about 1hr 15 mins.

Municipal: CORRAL DEL CARBÓN, C. MARIANA PINEDA (by the cathedral), ☎958 22 59 90, fax 958 22 39 27. There is also a small Tourist Office in the Alhambra complex.

🏠 Budget accommodation (€) is plentiful, especially off PLAZA NUEVA, PLAZA DE LA TRINIDAD, GRAN VÍA DE COLÓN and on the streets north of PLAZA MARIANA PINEDA. CUESTA DE GOMÉREZ leads directly up to the Alhambra and is lined with hostals. **Hostal Gomérez**, CUESTA DE GOMÉREZ 10, ☎958 22 44 37, €; must be one of the cheapest places in town, and nearby is **Britz**, CUESTA DE GOMÉREZ 1, ☎/fax 958 22 36 52, €. GRAN VÍA is a busy street, so traffic noise may be a problem, but try **Hostal Gran Vía**, GRAN VÍA 17, ☎958 27 92 12, €. Around PLAZA MARIANA PINEDA, **Hostal Roma**, NAVAS 1, ☎958 22 62 77, €, has beautifully furnished rooms and spotless bathrooms. Near the university, **Hospedaje Almohada**, ☎958 20 74 46, €, is cheap, clean and homely.

At the top end of the scale, the *parador* is located in the former **Convent of San Francisco**, €€€, in the Alhambra complex. Also here is the small but good one-star **Hotel America**, REAL DE LA ALHAMBRA 53, ☎958 22 74 71, €€. **Youth hostels**: CAMINO DE RONDA 171, ☎958 27 26 38 (🚌 nos. 10/11 from ACERA DE DARRO in the centre); AVDA RAMON Y CAJAL 2, ☎958 28 43 06, fax 958 28 52 85 (www.inturjoven.com) 🚌 no. 11 from the station. **Campsite: Sierra Nevada**, AVDA DE MADRID 107, ☎958 15 00 62, fax 958 15 09 54 (www.andalucia.org/alojamiento), is the nearest; 🚌 no. 3 from ACERA DE DARRO. **Granada campsite** is 3 km away at CERRO DE LA CRUZ, PELIGROS, ☎958 34 05 48 (www.andalucia.org/alojamiento) 🚌 to PELIGROS every 20 mins.

🍴 PLAZA NUEVA and the streets around it are where the locals eat: not always cheap, but fair value. A cup of Arabian tea in one of the bars on CALDERERÍA NUEVA will help capture the Moorish spirit.

CÓRDOBA

Once the capital of the Moorish caliphate and one of the greatest cities in Europe, Córdoba is filled with a harmonious blend of Christian, Jewish and Moorish architecture. The main attraction is undoubtedly the **Mezquita**, the grandest and most beautiful mosque ever built in Spain. There's also a fascinating Jewish quarter.

The huge Mezquita (it's free to attend mass in the cathedral section of the building) was founded in the 8th century by Caliph Abd al Rahman I and was enlarged over the next 200 years. At the foot of the bell tower, the delicately carved **Puerta del Perdón** leads through the massive outer walls to the **Patio de los Naranjos**

SIDE TRIPS FROM GRANADA

The rail connections from Granada to Córdoba are not that good (though there is a direct bus taking 4 hrs, 3 services a day) and you could instead opt to take the train to **Linares-Baeza**, for the connecting bus to **Baeza** (ETT table 671), which has abundant dozy charm in its Renaissance squares and palaces; from there you can take a bus on to **Úbeda**, another stunning Renaissance town, linked by bus to Córdoba and Seville. You can also head on by train from Linares-Baeza through spectacular desert to **Almería**, a landscape that's been used for numerous movie locations.

Buses from Granada zigzag up onto the **Sierra Nevada**, the great mountain mass that looms over the city. A good place to stay here is **Capileira**, the highest village, with its flat-roofed whitewashed old houses; there are several places to stay, and spectacular views. Walking hereabouts is fun, but hit and miss; you can try following the many irrigation channels built by the Moors.

(Courtyard of the Orange Trees), a courtyard with fountains for ritual cleansing. Inside the mosque, the fantastic forest of 850 pillars, joined by two-tiered Moorish arches in stripes of red brick and white stone, extends over a vast area. The pillars are not identical: materials include alabaster, marble, jasper, onyx, granite and wood; some are smooth, others have ribs or spirals; most are Roman in origin and were shipped in from places as far apart as France and North Africa, then cut to size. The capitals are equally varied. After the Moors departed, the Christians added the cathedral within the complex, incongruous but stunning, and blocking out the light that was an integral part of the design. The Third Mihrab once housed the original copy of the Koran. Unlike the other two, it survived Christian vandalism and its walls are covered in mosaics of varied colours and friezes of texts from the Koran. Its unusual off-centre position in the *qibla* (the south-facing holy wall) is the result of the final enlargement of the mosque in the 10th century, which, because of the proximity of the river in the south and the palace in the west, had to be made on the east side.

The **Puente Romano** is a bridge of mainly Moorish construction, but the arches have Roman foundations. Downstream are the remains of an Arab waterwheel, which originally transported water to the grounds of the Alcázar. The **Torre de la Calahorra** (on the other side of the river) is a high-tech museum with a model of the Mezquita as it was before the Christians got to work on it.

The **Alcázar de los Reyes Catolicos,** on the north bank, retains the original Moorish terraced gardens and pools.

CÓRDOBA'S MUSEUMS

The grisly **Museo de Arte Taurino** on PLAZA DE MAIMÓNIDES is devoted to bullfighting. The **Museo Arqueológico**, PLAZA DE JERÓNIMO PÁEZ, is housed in a 16th-century mansion with visible Roman foundations. The **Museo Torre de la Calahorra** chronicles the occupation of Muslims in Córdoba from the 9th to the 13th centuries. Recorded information is given to you through headphones (various languages available) as you enter each room.

In August, these stay open until midnight, perfect for an evening stroll. Less gloriously, this was the headquarters of the Spanish Inquisition for over three centuries.

The **Judería** is the old Jewish quarter, a maze of lanes surrounding a tiny Synagogue in C. Judíos. Open doorways provide tantalising glimpses of chequered courtyards filled with flowers; to get a better look visit the town in May, when the **Festival de los Patios** (a type of best-kept patio competition) takes place.

GLORIETA DE LAS TRES CULTURAS. Tourist Office and taxis at the station. I km north of the main area of interest; 20–30 mins on foot, or take 🚌 no. 3 (every 15 mins). Luggage lockers and cash machine.

Tourist Offices: Provincial: C. TORRIJOS 10 (PALACIO DE CONGRESOS Y EXPOSICIONES), 📞 957 47 12 35, fax 957 49 17 78 (www.turiscordoba.es; otcordoba@andalucia.org). **Municipal:** PLAZA DE JUDÁ LEVÍ, 📞 957 20 05 22, fax 957 20 02 77 (www.ayuncordoba.es). To reach the municipal office from the station, go down AVENIDA DE AMÉRICA, turn right along it onto AVENIDA DE LOS MOZARABES then cross over to follow PASEO DE LA VICTORIA. Turn left onto CAIRUAN and walk onto CALLE JUDÍOS. Follow the road round, past PLAZA MAIMONIDES and bear left down ALBUCASIS; the Tourist Office is on your left at PLAZA J LEVÍ.

Cheap places are near the station, in and around the Judería (Jewish Quarter) and off PLAZA DE LAS TENDILLAS. PLAZA DE LA CORREDERA, although cheap, is a less savoury area. **Pensión Bagdad**, FERNÁNDEZ RUANO 11, 📞 957 20 28 54, €€, has a beautiful central courtyard. **Hostal Luis de Gongora**, HORNO DE LA TRINIDAD 7, 📞 957 29 53 99, fax 957 29 55 99, €€, is lacking in traditional charm, but is clean, quiet and comfortable. Other budget options include **Hostal Los Arcos**, C. ROMERO BARROS 14, 📞 957 48 56 43, fax 957 48 60 11; **Mary II**, HORNO DE PORRAS 6, 📞 957 48 60 04, €; **Maestre**, ROMERO BARROS 16–18, 📞 957 47 53 95, €; and **Hostal Ronda**, AVENIDA DE LAS OLLERÍAS 45, 📞 957 48 02 50, fax 957 48 02 68, €€. There is a **youth hostel** at PLAZA DE JUDÁ LEVÍ, 📞 957 29 01 66, fax 957 29 05 00 (www.inturjoven.com), and a **campsite**, **El Brillante**, at AVDA DEL BRILLANTE 50, 📞 957 40 38 36, fax 957 28 21 65 (about 2 km north of the train station; 🚌 nos. 10/11 from AVDA DE CERVANTES).

WALKING TOUR OF CÓRDOBA

This walk encompasses the main attractions of Córdoba in a couple of hours. Begin at the PLAZA DEL POTRO, see the fountain, the **Museo de Bellas Artes** and the inn, **La Posada del Potro**, where Cervantes is thought to have stayed. Walk down PASEO DE LA RIBERA, along the banks of the Rio Guadalquivir. Turn right down CANO QUEBRADO to take in Córdoba's most famous sight, the **Mezquita**. Carry on along to the riverside RONDA DE ISASA; on reaching an Arab waterwheel on your left, with the **Alcázar** off to your right, go down SANTA TERESA DE JORNET. Go back onto RONDA DE ISASA/ AVENIDA DEL ALCÁZAR and continue alongside the river. Turn left onto PUENTE SAN RAFAEL, cross the bridge, and turn left to head back in the direction you just came, but on the opposite side of the river. Call at the **Museo Torre de la Calahorra** and afterwards cross PUENTE ROMANO and continue straight ahead into the little shops and inexpensive cafés of the Judería.

There are a number of restaurants around the *Judería*. Budget eateries can be found along
C. Doctor Fleming or in the *Judería*.

SEVILLE (SEVILLA)

The capital of Andalucía is a romantic, theatrical place, with a captivating park, a
gigantic cathedral and such fiestas as the **April Feria** and the processions of **Holy
Week**. Columbus sailed from Seville to discover the New World, and *Don Giovanni,
Carmen, The Barber of Seville* and *The Marriage of Figaro* were all set here.

The downside is the high level of petty crime: be on the alert for bag-snatchers and
pickpockets, and never leave anything of value in your hotel room or your car.

The prime sights are in a very small area, but the secondary ones are quite widespread.
All but the keenest walkers will probably want to get a few buses along the way.

Most places of interest are in the Barrio de Santa Cruz. A pleasant place for a stroll,
it lives up to the idealised image of Spain; white and yellow houses with flower-
bedecked balconies and attractive patios. The focal point is the **Giralda**, a minaret
that has towered over the old city since the 12th century and which now serves as
belfry to the cathedral. Built by the Almohad rulers 50 years before Ferdinand and
Isabella's Christian Reconquest, it consists of a series of gentle ramps designed for
horsemen to ride up; it's in excellent condition and worth climbing for the views.

The **cathedral** is the largest Gothic structure in the world, simply groaning with gold
leaf. The **Capilla Mayor** has a vast gilded retable, which took 82 years to complete.
Sacristía Mayor houses the treasury and **Sacristía de los Cálices** contains Murillos
and a Goya. A huge memorial honours Christopher Columbus, while outside is the
pretty **Patio de los Naranjos** (orange-tree courtyard).

The **Alcázar** (closed Mon) was inspired by the Alhambra of Granada (see
pp. 198–199), but has been marred by later additions. Within is the **Salón de
Embajadores,** where Columbus was received by Ferdinand and Isabella on his
return from the Americas, and there are also shady, interconnected gardens separated by arched Moorish walls. The neighbouring **Casa Lonja** contains a collection
of documents relating to the discovery of the Americas.

Hospital de la Caridad, C. Temprado, was commissioned by a reformed rake,
reputed to have been the real-life inspiration for Don Juan. The church contains several works by Valdés Leal, depicting death in ghoulishly disturbing ways; there are
also paintings by Murillo.

Nowadays, the 18th-century *Fábrica de Tabacos* (on C. de San Fernando south of the
Alcázar) houses parts of the university, but it was once a tobacco factory, employing
over 10,000 women (supposedly including Carmen).

South-east of the factory is **María Luisa Park**, a delightful mixture of wilderness areas and formal gardens laid out for a trade fair in 1929 and shaded by trees from Latin America. It contains PLAZA DE ESPAÑA, which was the central pavilion, and PLAZA DE AMÉRICA, a peaceful place which is home to the **Archaeological Museum,** containing a famously rich Roman section (closed Mon). The Latin American countries that exhibited at the fair each built a pavilion in their own national style, most of which survive.

The **Museo de Bellas Artes** (closed Mon, free for EU nationals), PL. DEL MUSEO (between SANTA CRUZ and CARTUJA), has a collection of 13th–20th-century Spanish paintings, second only to that in the Prado in Madrid. The decorative **Maestranza** (bullring), near the river, dates from the 18th century. Fights are held every Thur Mar–Oct. A short way along the river bank is the 13th-century **Torre del Oro** (Golden Tower), named after the gold-coloured tiles that once covered its twelve sides. It now contains a small **naval museum** (free to EU citizens on Tues). **Cartuja Park** (across the river from the old town) was the site of Expo 92 and is due to reopen as a science and technology park, with theatres and concert halls for staging cultural events.

Estación Santa Justa, AVDA KANSAS CITY; 15-min walk from the centre. no. 27 goes from the station to PLAZA DE LA ENCARNACIÓN; no. 70 goes to PLAZA DE ESPAÑA. Tourist Office and taxis. Luggage lockers; the locker area is open 0600–2400. Currency exchange and cash machines.

There are two bus stations: **Prado de San Sebastián**, PLAZA PRADO DE SAN SEBASTIÁN, 95 441 71 11, is mainly for buses to Andalucía; PLAZA DE ARMAS, AVENIDA CRISTO DE LA EXPIRACIÓN, 95 490 77 37, is for buses elsewhere.
City buses: C1 and C2 are circular routes around the town. Many buses pass through PLAZA DE LA ENCARNACIÓN, PLAZA NUEVA and AVDA DE LA CONSTITUCIÓN. If you're making more than four trips, buy a **bónobus** ticket, valid for ten journeys.
Taxis: There's a rank on PLAZA NUEVA. To order a taxi 95 462 22 22 or 95 458 00 00.

San Pablo Airport, 12 km east of town, 95 444 90 23; tourist information desk, 95 444 91 28. Trains to Seville

DAY TRIP FROM SEVILLE

Itálica (closed Mon; free to EU nationals) is a substantial excavated Roman town at **Santiponce**, about 9 km from Seville, with remains of streets, baths and mosaics. The 25,000-seater amphitheatre is particularly interesting. Itálica was first founded by Publio Cornelio Escipion, and it was thought to be the home of Trajano and Hadrian in the 2nd century AD. Buses leave Seville bus station every 20 mins and cost €0.60.

TOURS OF SEVILLE

Bus tours depart every 45 mins touring the PLAZA DE ESPAÑA, TORRE DEL ORO, MONASTERIO DE LA CARTUJA and ISLA MAGICA (www.islamagica.es). The tours run from 1000–1900.
Tickets are a little expensive but they are valid all day and you can get on and off as you please.
Take a **boat tour** along the Rio Guadalquivir to see the sights of Seville. They embark at 1100, 1200, then every 30 mins until 2200; 95 456 16 92. City tours by **horse-drawn trap** leave from outside the cathedral.

RAIL TOUR: MÁLAGA – GRANADA – CÁDIZ

take 15 mins; taxis cost about €18. Express buses take 30 mins to the centre.

Tourist Offices: Regional: Avda de la Constitución 21B, ☎ 95 422 14 04, fax 95 422 97 53 (www.sevilla.org). **Municipal:** Paseo de las Delicias, ☎ 95 423 44 65 (otsevilla@andalucia.org). **Centro de Información de Sevilla**, C. de Arjona 28, ☎ 95 450 56 00. There are also tourist information booths in strategic locations, including the rail station.
Post and phones: The main **post office** is at Avda de la Constitución 32.

Accommodation is very difficult to obtain, unless pre-booked, during Holy Week and the April Fair. It also tends to be expensive. For the least expensive lodgings, try the **Barrio Santa Cruz**: C. Archeros, the streets around Plaza Nueva (C. Marqués de Paradas or C. Gravina), or the area west of Plaza Nueva towards the river. **Pensión Fabiola**, C. Fabiola 16 (in Santa Cruz), ☎ 95 421 83 46, €€, has basic rooms arranged around a central courtyard. **Hostal Aguilas**, C. Aguilas 15, ☎ 95 421 31 77, €, has a small number of clean, well-furnished rooms. **Pensión Alcázar**, C. Dean Miranda 12, ☎ 95 422 84 57, €€, is a pension right next to the Alcázar wall. The rooms are beautifully furnished and decorated, with ceiling fans or air-conditioning. **Hotel Simon** (1-star), García de Vinuesa 19, ☎ 95 422 66 60, fax 95 456 22 41 (info@hotelsimonsevilla.com), €€, is in a former 18th-century mansion. **Youth hostel**: C. Isaac Peral 2, ☎ 95 461 31 50 (www.inturjoven.com). All three **campsites** are about 12 km out of town. The main one is **Camping Sevilla**, Ctra Madrid-Cádiz km 534, ☎ 95 451 43 79, near the airport: take either **Empresa Casal** bus towards **Carmona** (hourly) or the 🚌 no. 70 to Parque Alcosa (800 m away). The other two sites are at **Dos Hermanas: Club de Campo**, Avda de la Libertad 13, ☎ 95 472 02 50, fax 95 472 63 08, and **Camping Villsom**, Ctra Seville-Cádiz km 554.8, ☎/fax 95 472 08 28, served by buses from Prado de San Sebastián every 30–45 mins.

Seville is probably the best place to sample such typical Andalusian dishes as *gazpacho* (chilled tomato and pepper soup) and *pescaíto frito* (deep-fried fish). Eating out can be expensive, but there are a few places with excellent menus for reasonable prices. The liveliest bars and restaurants, frequented by students, are in BARRIO SANTA CRUZ. For a meal with a view, try restaurants on the other side of the river by the Puente de San Telmo. Buying your own food is a cheap

SEVILLE'S NIGHTLIFE

Seville is the home of flamenco and it's easy to find, but you should be selective because it is often staged specially for tourists. If you ask around, you should be able to find more genuine (and cheaper) performances. There are various clubs with flamenco evenings, but they can be quite expensive, especially during festival time in the spring. An excellent one to try is **El Gallo** in BARRIO DE SANTA CRUZ.
Seville is packed with lively bars, clubs and discos, notably in the **Los Remedios** district in the south of the city and on C. BETIS next to the river, but little seems to happen until close to midnight. If you're looking for activity and atmosphere a little earlier in the evening, try the other side of the river, where there is a range of tapas bars, some of which have live music.

option and to be recommended if you go to the **Mercado del Arenal**, C. ARENAL and C. PASTOR, the town's largest market.

CÁDIZ

Like Venice, that other once-great naval city, Cádiz is approached by a causeway and all but surrounded by water. Its tight grid of streets, squares and crumbly ochre buildings exudes an atmosphere of gentle decay, but it's all the better for that, and really comes into its own during the huge **carnival** in Feb (one of the best in Spain) and in the evening, when the promenaders come out and the bars open.

Colourful tiling is a feature of the pavements, parks and even the **Catedral Nueva** (new cathedral), which was rebuilt, like much of the rest, in the city's 18th-century heyday.

However its origins go back to 1100 BC when it was founded by the Phoenicians; the port was of vital importance at the time of the conquest of the Americas (which was why Sir Francis Drake attacked it). You can get a panoramic view of it all from **Torre Tavira**, both from the top of the tower and in the camera obscura below, via a mirror and lens on the roof.

The **Museo Histórico Municipal** contains an 18th-century ivory and mahogany scale model of Cádiz, while **Museo de Cádiz** has an eclectic display of exhibits from sarcophagi to paintings by Murillo, Van Dyck and Rubens. The chapel of the **Hospital de Mujeres** houses El Greco's *St Francis in Ecstasy* and **Oratorio de la Santa Ceura** has, among other works, three Goya frescos.

The **main station** is at PLAZA DE SEVILLA.

i **Tourist Office**: AVENIDA RAMÒN DE CARRANZA. ☎ 956 25 86 46, fax 956 25 24 49 (www.infocadiz.com, www.cadizayto.es and www.fjate.com; otcadiz@andalucia.org).

España, MARQUES DE CADIZ 9, ☎ 956 28 55 00, €; **La Argentina**, CONDE DE O'REILLY 1, 1ST FLOOR, ☎ 956 22 33 10, €, is a bit cheaper; or **Hospederia del Mar**, PZA SAN LORENZO 2, EDF. CLUB NÁUTICO, ☎ 956 26 09 14, €.

JÉREZ DE LA FRONTERA

Just before you reach Cádiz on the train from Seville you pass through the station for Jérez. This town has given its name to sherry and the bodegas are the town's main attraction; it's also home to Spanish brandy. Here you will find such familiar names as Harvey. Most bodegas offer tours (of varying prices; reservations necessary for some; many close in Aug) that finish with a tasting for a small fee. Sherry also appears in the local cuisine; kidneys in sherry sauce is a speciality. The old town (to the west) is an attraction in itself, with palms and orange trees and some attractive old mansions. Other places of interest are the **Alcázar** and the **Plaza de la Asunción**.

VISITING MOROCCO

If you are visiting southern Spain, it is seriously worth considering taking the ferry over from there to Morocco. It's remarkably unlike anywhere in Europe and, despite some obvious French colonial hangovers and evidence of Roman occupation in the north, is unmistakably north African. It was invaded by Arabs from the east but the indigenous Berbers held on to much of their own traditions and culture that still survive today.

Morocco has great scenic variety, with the High Atlas Mountains rising to over 4000 m in the centre of the country – high enough to retain snow even in summer. In the south-east of the country is a vast desert of stony barrenness dotted with oases of palm trees and villages dominated by dried mud fortresses *(kasbahs)*. The cities and larger towns have wonderful markets *(souks)*.

There's a good network of trains (see map on p. 208), operated by Office National des Chemins de Fer (ONCF); additionally the bus network is excellent, though you would be wise to stick to air-conditioned services in the hot season. Some buses even penetrate the desert. For train times see the *Thomas Cook Overseas Timetable*.

The one downside of being a tourist in Morocco is the sheer amount of hassle you can get from touts, carpet sellers and guides. People do get ripped off, lone women may find themselves as an unwanted centre of attention, and such activities as haggling can test one's patience. However, many travellers find the locals extremely friendly and welcoming.

RAIL PASSES AND FERRIES

All-zone and zone F Inter-rail passes and Euro Domino passes cover Moroccan railways, and give 30% discounts on the ferries from Spain. The quickest way over is from Algeciras to Ceuta (Sebta), with frequent services by catamaran (30 mins), fast ferry (40 mins) and ship (1 hr 30 mins); see ETT table 2500. If you fancy a longer crossing you can sail from Algeciras to Tánger (Tangiers; 2 hrs 30 mins, 10 crossings daily Mon–Sat, ETT table 2502) or from Cádiz to Tánger (3 hrs, 2 crossings daily, ETT table 2667). From Almeria there's a night crossing to Melilla (7 hrs, not Sat, ETT table 2505) and one or two ferries a day to Nador (6–7 hrs, 1 Mar–15 June, ETT table 2507).

Algeciras, the main Spanish port for Morocco, is served by buses running every 30 mins from La Línea, from where there are 5 services a day to and from Malaga (ETT table 675), and there are buses from Cádiz; there is a train station serving Talgo 200 and Estrella trains running from Madrid and local trains from Granada. There's plenty of accommodation, though apart from the ferries there's no real reason to stop off here; the main restaurant area is around the harbour.

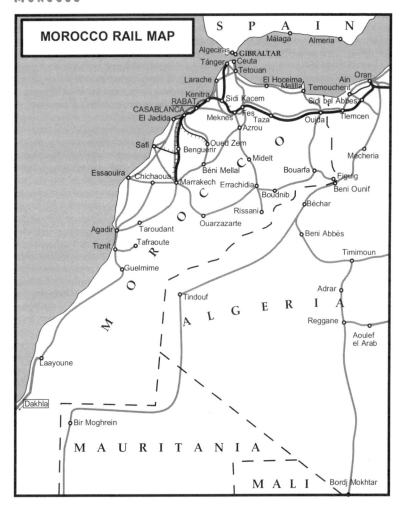

MOROCCO RAIL MAP

PRACTICALITIES

Citizens of the EU, USA, Canada, Australia, New Zealand and many other countries don't need a **visa** to enter Morocco. Standards of **health** are lower than in European countries. Polio and typhoid jabs and malaria pills are generally recommended, but check the latest health advice with your doctor. In high summer the temperatures can reach 40 degrees C; spring, winter and autumn are more pleasant times to travel.

The main **language** is Arabic, with some Berber. In the north, French is widely spoken, and Spanish and English are often understood.

The **currency** is the Dirham (Dr); £1=Dr16.35; €1=Dr10.26; $1=Dr11.46. Morocco is not an expensive country to visit. In cities, rooms in a pension or 1-star hotel start at around £5 ($8).

The **Moroccan National Tourist Office** has a UK branch at 205 Regent St, London W1B 4HB, ☎020 7437 0073, fax 020 7734 8172 (www.tourism-in-morocco.com).

HIGHLIGHTS

Most visitors start from Ceuta (Sebta) or Tánger (Tangiers). Although **Ceuta** is on the African continent, it belongs to Spain and has an unmistakable Andalusian character. **Tánger** is a lively place with great, bustling markets, and an interesting old quarter (*medina*) just above the port; the newer part of town looks European. The sandy beach is superb and very extensive.

If you only want to take in one Moroccan city, make it **Fes**, the former capital with a huge and remarkably timeless *medina* known as Fes el Bali – full of workshops and markets, while two hilltop castles (Borg Sud and Borg Nord) give fine views of the old city. Only Muslims may enter the mosques. From Fes you can visit the country's finest Roman remains out of town at **Volubis**.

Sited on the plain beneath the Atlas Mountains, **Marrakech** is Morocco's major southern city: surrounded by walls, it has pink-hued buildings. For sightseeing, head for the Saadian Tombs and the Koutoubia Minaret, or soak up the exotic atmosphere at the Djemaa el Fna, a vast public space crammed with tribespeople, snake-charmers and story-tellers. The road to **Taroudant** is a thrilling bus or car journey across the High Atlas, crossing the Tii n' Test pass at 2100 m.

Although movie buffs may well get a kick out of its name you'd do well to skip **Casablanca** – it's large and quite devoid of interest. Similarly, you can give **Agadir** a miss, unless you want to relax on the beach; the city was largely destroyed by an earthquake in 1962 and is now largely modern.

(for Directory information, see pp. 587, 603 and 602).
BELGIUM, THE NETHERLANDS & LUXEMBOURG

Also known collectively as the Low Countries, these small nations for the most part live up to their name: the land lies very low and flat. There are bits of pleasant dune-backed coast, notably in The Netherlands, and agreeably hilly terrain in the **Ardennes** of Belgium and Luxembourg, but essentially it's the places rather than the scenery that provide interest. Cycling is a national passion in the Netherlands and parts of Belgium, with an excellent network of cycle routes making it a feasible way to get around the cities and to tour larger areas. Cycle hire is available at many stations. In Belgium the **Vlaanderen Fietsroute** is a well-signposted and varied 750-km cycle route round the entire country, taking in **Bruges**, **Antwerp**, **Lier**, **Ghent**, **Leuven** and other cities.

BELGIUM

Belgium has found it hard to shake off a reputation for dullness. Certainly the coast – almost entirely built up – is undistinguished to the point of blandness, but elsewhere there are handsome brick-built cities with a great sense of history. **Bruges** is the most attractive of all, a canal-laced city dubbed the 'Venice of the North', graced with fine old merchants' houses. There's more fine waterside architecture and a notable cathedral at **Ghent**, while **Antwerp** is a lively cultural city with a medieval printing works. **Brussels**, the capital, has a magnificent central square as well as some surprises – including a legacy of art nouveau architecture that by far outstrips Paris.

For a country small in size and population, Belgium has a surprisingly diverse mix of **people** and **languages**. There are cultural as well as linguistic differences between the Flemish, who mostly live in the wealthier northern towns, and the poorer French-speaking parts of the country in the south. Bureaucracy, signposts and life in general are complicated by the need to produce all information in at least two languages (Dutch and French). In the northern towns of Flanders, the Flemish often prefer to be addressed in English rather than French.

BENELUX

ACCOMMODATION

The Benelux countries have a common hotel-rating system. The lowest is 'O' (accommodation only, but meeting minimum requirements of hygiene and comfort); the next is 'H' (moderately comfortable, with at least one bathroom per ten rooms). After that, you're on to the usual star system, one-star places being obliged (as a minimum) to have a washstand in every room and to serve breakfast.

HOTELS Hotels tend to be pricey, with city prices starting at around €30 for a double and €20 for a single. Tourist Offices charge a deposit for booking hotels (which is then deducted from your bill), and can often offer reduced rates. They sometimes agree to check availability of other accommodation. In summer, accommodation of all kinds can be hard to find and it's sensible to book, especially in Bruges and on the coast.

HOSTELS **Hostelling organisations**: **Vlaamse Jeugdherbergcentrale**, Van Stralenstraat 40, 2060 Antwerpen, ☎(03) 232 72 18, fax (03) 231 81 26 (www.vjh.be; info@vjh.be); **Les Auberges de Jeunesse**, rue de la Sablonnière 28, Zavelputstraat, B-1000 Brussels, ☎(02) 219 56 76, fax (02) 219 14 51 (www.laj.be; info@laj.be).

CAMPING Rough camping is not permitted, but some farmers may give you permission to use their land. A leaflet covering officially rated campsites should be available from your nearest Belgian Tourist Office.

FOOD AND DRINK

Most restaurants have good-value fixed-price menus (*plat du jour, tourist menu, dagschotel*). There's a wide variation in prices; establishments in the main squares can charge two or three times as much as similar places in nearby streets. Try **waffles** (*wafels/gaufres*) and sweet or savoury **pancakes** (*crêpes*), **mussels** (*moules*) and freshly baked pastries. The most common snacks are *fritures/frites* (french fries with mayonnaise or other sauce) and (delicious) ice-cream. Candies are ubiquitous, notably **nougat** and the deservedly famous **chocolates**, but be warned: the ones containing cream have a very short shelf-life. **Tea** comes as teabags with lemon, unless you specify milk (you'll get cream), and the **coffee** and **hot chocolate** are delicious. It's easy (though not cheap) to get freshly squeezed orange and lemon. Many bottled juices are refreshingly low on sugar. Belgium produces literally hundreds of beers (both dark and light); **wheat beer** (*blanche*) comes with a slice of lemon in it in the summer.

THE NETHERLANDS

Canals and 17th- and 18th-century gabled buildings are abiding memories of a visit to The Netherlands, whose numerous historic towns and cities have a strikingly uniform appearance. In between, the bulb fields and windmills lend the Dutch farmland a distinctive character. **Amsterdam**, sleazy and bustling at the same time, justifiably draws most visitors, and even the red-light area has become a tourist

INFORMATION

HOTELS

NRC (Netherlands Reservation Centre):
Nieuwe Gouw 1,
1442 Le Purmerend,
☎0299 6891 44,
fax 0299 6891 54
(www.hotelres.nl;
info@hotelres.nl).

HOSTELS

Dutch Youth Hostel Association (NJHC):
Postbus 9191,
1006 AD Amsterdam,
☎(010) 264 6064
(www.njhc.org).

BED AND BREAKFAST

Bed & Breakfast Holland:
Theophile de Bockstraat 3,
1058 TV Amsterdam,
☎(020) 615 7527,
fax (020) 669 1573
(www.bedandbreakfastholland
.com; bbrholland@hetnet.nl).

Holiday Link:
Postbus 70–177, 9704 AD
Groningen,
☎(050) 313 2424,
fax (050) 313 3177
(www.holidaylink.com;
b&b@holidaylink.com).

attraction. Elsewhere, **Delft**, **Haarlem**, **Leiden**, **Maastricht** and **Utrecht** are among many places with pretty centres, while **Rotterdam** has striking modern architecture. Cheese addicts should head for **Gouda**, **Edam** and **Alkmaar**. The inexpensive **Museum Card** gives you admission to 400 museums for a whole year across the entire country.

ACCOMMODATION Standards are high; lower prices reflect limited facilities rather than poor quality. Room rates start around €170 for a double, but most cost more. Booking is advisable: there's a free centralised booking service: **Netherlands Reservation Centre (NRC)**.

HOTELS VVV offices have listings of bed and breakfast accommodation in their area, where it exists, or you can book nationwide through **Bed & Breakfast Holland**. Bed & Breakfast in Holland + Amsterdam offers a similar service, and has a guide.

FOOD AND DRINK Dutch cuisine is mainly simple and substantial: fish or meat, potatoes and vegetables. Many Indonesian restaurants offer spicy food and in cities a good variety of international cuisine is available. Most eating places stay open all day but restaurants in small places take last orders by 2100. Look for boards saying *dagschotel* (a very economical 'special'). 'Brown cafés' (traditional pubs) also serve good-value food. **Mensas** are subsidised student canteens in university towns; very cheap and not restricted to students, but open only during term-time.

Specialities include apple pie (heavy on cinnamon and sultanas), herring marinated in brine, smoked eels (somewhat pricey), *poffertjes* (tiny puff-pancakes with icing sugar) and *pannekoeken* (pancakes: try bacon with syrup). Street stalls for snacks abound, options invariably including *frites/patates* (a cross between french fries and British chips) with mayonnaise or other sauces. In **Limburg**, try the regional (slightly sour) *zuurvlees*. Automats (also at stations) sell heated croquettes, the *bami* and *nasi* varieties being spicy.

Excellent coffee and hot chocolate are available everywhere, often topped with whipped cream – *slagroom*. Tea is hot water with a choice of teabags – ask if you want milk. Dutch beer is topped by two fingers of froth. Most local liqueurs are excellent. The main spirit is *jenever*, a strong, slightly oily gin made from juniper berries.

LUXEMBOURG

The Grand Duchy of Luxembourg covers some pretty terrain for hiking, with river valleys, forests and hills. Its eponymous capital has a fine setting straddling two gorges.

ACCOMMODATION The national Tourist Office has free brochures covering hotels (of all grades, plus restaurants), holiday apartments, farm holidays and camping in the Grand Duchy, plus a bed and breakfast booklet that covers all three Benelux countries.

HOSTELS There are 11 youth hostels. The price of bed and breakfast (including linen): €13.60 ('standard' category) and €15.50 ('confort' category). Extra charges: €2.50 per person (double room) and €7.50 per person (single room). Packed lunch is €3.80, light meal €5.40 and dinner €7.10.

INFORMATION
HOSTELS
Youth Hostelling organisation:
Centrale des Auberges de Jeunesse Luxembourgeoises, 24–26 Place de la Gare, Galerie Kons, L-1616 Luxembourg,
☎ 26 29 35 00,
fax 26 29 35 03
(www.youthhostels.lu;
information@youthhostels.lu).

FOOD AND DRINK Cuisine is pithily described as 'French quality, German quantity', but eating out is expensive. Keep costs down by making lunch your main meal and looking for the special deals: **plat du jour** (single course) or **menu** (2–3 courses). There are takeaways, pizzerias plus light meals are often available in pastry shops. Local specialities are: Ardennes ham, *treipen* (black pudding), *quenelles* (calf's liver dumplings), *thüringer* (standard local sausage), *gromperekichelcher* (fried potato patties) and (in Sept) *quetschentaart* (a flan featuring dark, violet plums).

Luxembourg produces a variety of lagers, liqueurs and white wines. Sugar may not be added while making wine, so the Moselles are drier and fruitier than their German equivalents.

EDITOR'S CHOICE
Amsterdam; Antwerp; Bruges; Brussels; Delft; Ghent; Gouda; The Hague; Kröller-Müller Museum (near Arnhem); Luxembourg; Maastricht; Rotterdam.

BEYOND THE BORDERS
Amsterdam–Paris via Brussels (ETT table 18); Amsterdam–Berlin (table 22); Amsterdam–Munich via Cologne (table 28); Brussels–Milan via Luxembourg and Strasbourg (table 43); Luxembourg–Cologne (table 915); Luxembourg–Nice via Avignon (table 47).

The Dutch say that they earn their money in Rotterdam, talk about it in The Hague and spend it in **Amsterdam**. Romantic and laid-back, Amsterdam combines the quintessential historic Dutch city features of tree-lined canals, bicycles and elegant gabled brick houses, with a vibrant, emphatically youthful streetlife. There's a strong seasonal contrast: in summer it's full of tourists, while in winter it's often shivery and shrouded in fog, the few visitors huddled in the famous 'brown cafés' over coffee and apple cake. In the 'Golden Age' of the revolutionary Dutch republic (the 17th century) Amsterdam followed only London and Paris in importance – and assumed its present cobweb-like shape with the building of three new canals. Allow a couple of days for casual exploration, plus plenty of time to visit the marvellously varied museums and galleries around the city, and to take in a canal cruise.

The city centre is wonderful for walking (especially along the canals), though you would do best to concentrate on one area at a time and use trams to cross the city. VVV, the Amsterdam Tourist Board, suggests walking routes, which are well signposted and colour-coordinated by city maps at strategic points. Amsterdam's layout can be confusing; bear in mind that *gracht* means 'canal' and that the centre follows the horseshoe shape dictated by the ring canals. The Singel canal confines the old centre, with the red-light district around the handsome Oude Kerk (Old Church), and the Royal Palace at the Dam. Seek out the Keizersgracht, the Herengracht and the houseboats along the Prinsengracht, and explore the Jordaan, an enticing area of quirky shops, bars and restaurants that lies to the west of the ring canals. At night Amsterdam can be magical (get hold of an entertainments listing, as there's lots going on). The canals seem to come alive, with the largest lit by twinkling lights and the glow from windows.

ARRIVAL AND DEPARTURE

Centraal (www.ns.nl) is the terminal for all the city's trains and 5 mins' walk north of Dam (the central area); beware of opportunistic thieves that hang around there. There's a manned left-luggage facility, as well as lockers, but the baggage area is closed 0100–0500. Shower facilities upstairs (extremely limited, often long queues of up to 3 hrs).

Amsterdam-Schiphol (020) 601 2182 (www.schiphol.nl) is about 14 km south-west of town. Transfers by train to/from Centraal are the cheapest: every 15 mins 0500–0100 (hourly 0100–0500); journey time 20 mins.

CITY AND TRANSPORT MAP
– inside back cover

INFORMATION

MONEY **Thomas Cook foreign exchanges**: Dam 23–25; Leidseplein 31 A; and next to Victoria Hotel, Damrak 1–5. Outside banking hours, the **GWK Bank** at Centraal and Schiphol Airport railway stations opens 24 hrs a day.

THE NETHERLANDS

TOURIST OFFICE

Amsterdam Tourist Board, Stationsplein 10 (immediately opposite Centraal, in a wooden building just beyond the tram terminal); invariably very busy; computerised system for last-minute availability of rooms nationwide. There's a booth in Centraal (in the international area, platform 2), and branches at Leidseplein 1 and Argonautenstraat 98. For all: ☎(020) 551 2525 or 0900 400 4040 (Mon–Fri 0900–1700; premium rate), fax (020) 625 2869 (www.amsterdamtourist.nl; info@amsterdamtourist.nl).

POST AND PHONES The main **post office**, SINGEL 250–256, open Mon–Wed, Fri 0900–1800, Thur 0900–2000, Sat 0900–1330, has poste restante. **Branch**: Oosterdokskade 3–5 (Mon–Fri 0830–2100, Sat 0900–1200). The telephone code for Amsterdam is 020. **Public phones**: in bright green booths; phone cards sold at post offices, stations, etc.

PUBLIC TRANSPORT

MAPS The free *Tourist Guide to Public Transport* shows how to use the city transport and how to reach the highlights; for details buy the *Public Transport Map*. Most tourist literature includes a small map of central Amsterdam.

TICKETS GVB (Amsterdam's public transport company: a few doors from VVV and easily identified by the large yellow signs in the windows) has a whole range. Worthwhile are day tickets and the *strippenkaart* (with 15 strips), which is also sold at post offices, rail stations and VVV. Besides VVV sells day tickets, and combination passes (transport and attractions). Paying on board of tram/bus is expensive, so buy your ticket in advance. Each journey requires one strip plus a strip for each zone you travel in; so if you travel in the centre of town, leave one strip blank and stamp the second; for two zones, leave two strips blank and stamp the third. The ticket lasts one hour, with as many changes of tram or bus as you like. For transport information ☎0900 9292 (premium rate), 0700–2100.

METRO Primarily for commuters; few central stops.

TRAMS The most efficient method of travel in the centre; the network is extensive and services frequent and fast from early morning to midnight. The terminal is just in front of Centraal. Pressure on the lowest step keeps the door open. The circle tram no. 20 runs around all the major tourist attractions, with a tram every 12 mins in each direction 0900–1900.

BUSES These begin/end just around the canal in front of Centraal (on the left side as you leave the station), but not all from the same terminal. They are less frequent than trams, but go further afield; limited night services (indicated by black square on bus-stops).

TAXIS Tip 10%. Taxis are not usually hailed: go to a rank. Main ranks are at Centraal, Dam, Rembrandtplein and Leidseplein, ☎0900 0724 (premium rate) or (020) 677 7777.

BICYCLES This is a quick and fun way of getting around. Bike paths are either separate or marked on the road (in red, or with lines). The brakes on some Dutch bikes are operated by back-pedalling. Hire shops require a deposit; there are many in the city, including **Bike City**, BLOEMGRACHT 68 ☎(020) 626 3721 (just west of Anne Frank's House)

ACCOMMODATION

It is best to reserve, particularly in the peak season through **Amsterdam Reservation Center**, Postbus 3901, NL–1001 As Amsterdam, ▣/fax 0777 000 888 (www.amsterdamtourist.nl; reservations@amsterdamtourist.nl); open Mon–Fri 0900–1700, or through the Amsterdam Tourist Service (both ask a small charge). Consider commuting from Zandvoort. You may encounter **accommodation touts** at Centraal station. Bear in mind they are illegal.

Cheaper 2-star (both €€) options are **Agora**, Singel 462, ▣(020) 627 2200 (www. hotelagora.nl; info@hotelagora.nl), and **Acro**, Jan Luijkenstr. 44, ▣(020) 662 5538 (www.acro-hotel.nl; info@acro-hotel.nl), while two good budget (1-star) establishments (both €€) are **Bema**, Concertgebouwplein 19ᵦ, ▣(020) 679 1396 (www.hotel-bema.demon.nl; postbus@hotel-bema.demon.nl), and **Pax**, Raadhuisstr. 37ᵦ, ▣(020) 624 9735. The Raadhuisstraat and Damrak areas have a plethora of cheap hotels.

Highly recommended are the two **Flying Pig private hostels** (www.flyingpig.nl) in Centrum. These are friendly and secure; cheap bars, free internet and e-mail, kitchens and breakfast. **Downtown Hostel**, Nieuwendijk 100, ▣(020) 420 6822 (downtown@flyingpig.nl) is well-placed, only 500 m from Centraal. **Palace Hostel**, Vossiusstr. 46, ▣(020) 400 4187 (palace@flyingpig.nl) is by Vondelpark (tram no. 1/2/5). Dorm accommodation is a good bet. There are two **HI youth hostels**, both in Centrum: **Vondelpark**, Zandpad 5, ▣(020) 589 8996, fax (020) 589 8955 (tram nos. 1/2/5: Leidseplein); **Stadsdoelen**, Kloveniersburgwal 97, ▣(020) 624 6832, fax (020) 639 1035 (tram nos. 4/9/16/20/24/25: Muntplein). If you don't mind a bit of religion, a good cheapie is **Shelter Jordan Christian Youth Hostel**, Bloemstr. 179, ▣(020) 624 4717 (www.shelter.nl; jordan@shelter.nl) (tram nos. 13/17/20: Marnixstr.).

Campsites: **Vliegenbos**, Meeuwenlaan 138, ▣(020) 636 8855 (www.citycamps.com/ho_vliegenbos) (10 mins from Centraal on ▣no. 32), open April–Sept. **Camping Zeeburg**, Zuider IJdijk 20, ▣(020) 694 4430, fax (020) 694 6238 (www.campingzeeburg.nl; info@campingzeeburg.nl), is on an island next to the A10 ringway; also has cabins; tram 14 from Dam to Flevopark (go past swimming pool and over bridge).

FOOD AND DRINK

Amsterdam is a good place to eat, with restaurants in every price range and a wide choice of international cuisine (especially Indonesian), though Dutch cuisine itself is not widely available (apart from pancakes). Note that many restaurants close fairly early. There's a concentration of eating places around the **Leidseplein**. Cheap food is easy to find, even in Centrum: the international fast-food chains are well represented and there are plenty of other takeaways. If you want to buy your own groceries there's a good **Albert Heijn** supermarket on the corner of Singel and Koningsplein (nicely situated for picnics next to the floating flower market). For a sit-down meal at a reasonable price, try one of the many traditional 'brown cafés'. Around **Spui** it's mega touristy; there are better places in backstreets and around quieter canals, while the areas around **Nieuwmarkt**, **Dam** and **De Pijp** (especially along Albert Cuypstr.) are the best for Eastern cuisine. Amsterdam has two *mensas* (student canteens): **Atrium** and **Agora**.

HIGHLIGHTS

Amsterdam has nearly 200 museums and art galleries. *Amsterdam Museums* is a helpful map (free from **Amsterdams Uit Bureau** – see p. 221). Particularly unmissable are the **Rijksmuseum** the **Van Gogh Museum** and the **Anne Frank House**. Others (in addition to the ones below) are devoted to such diverse subjects as torture, spectacles, coffee and tea, chess, trams, sex, pipes, pianolas, the Bible, cats and the Dutch Resistance.

THE CENTRE: DAM From Centraal, DAMRAK leads directly to **Dam**, site of the original dam, with its distinctive **war memorial**. **Koninklijk Paleis** (the Royal Palace) dominates the square. The interior reflects the glory of the Golden Age and much Empire furniture remains from the time of Louis Bonaparte. The Gothic **Nieuwe Kerk** (New Church) is used for exhibitions and state functions: the investiture of the Dutch rulers has taken place here since 1814. Also in Dam is the **Madame Tussaud's Scenerama** (Dam 7), where audio-animation techniques bring many waxworks to life.

AMSTERDAM PASS

This pass is good value. It gives 1, 2 or 3 days free or discounted admission to many museums (which might make the purchase of a Museum Card superfluous) and attractions, discounts on excursions and at restaurants, plus free city transport and a free canal cruise. It is available from Amsterdam Tourist Board offices, prices starting at €24.

CANAL TRIPS

The canals are an integral part of Amsterdam and provide an excellent way to appreciate the city: **boat trips** can be very cheap and have multilingual commentaries. Most people embark at Centraal, but you can board at any stop; there are quays in each area of interest – get tickets at any quay where Rondvaart/Rederij boats are moored.

Museumboats
(STATIONSPLEIN) every 30 mins (45 mins in winter), 1000–1700, with 5 intermediate stops convenient for 17 museums; day ticket includes several discounts; boats are turquoise and the stops have turquoise signs. **Canal Buses** (Weteringschans 24, ☎ (020 623 9886; www.canal.nl) operate Mon–Fri 1000–1800, Sat–Sun 1100–1700 (every 25–45 mins) and issue day tickets (valid until 1200 the following day), allowing you to get on or off as often as you like at the 11 stops along three different routes. There are regular (free) **ferries** across the River IJ, linking Centrum with northern Amsterdam, departures from de Ruijterkade (behind Centraal). For individual exploration, you can hire **Canal Bikes** (contact details as for Canal Buses), pedal-boats for two to four people (from Leidseplein, Leidsestraat, the Rijksmuseum and Westerkerk).

THE FRINGE

Amsterdam is renowned for its libertarian views on, among other things, marijuana and homosexuality, and there is a nationwide gay and lesbian organisation (☎(020)623 6565; manned 1000–2200; www.switchboard.nl) that gives information about gay venues nationwide. The city has many 'smoking' coffee-shops (often with such words as free, happy, high or space in their name) where hash and pot can be purchased and smoked (usually to the accompaniment of ear-shattering music). Though it's not legal, the police usually turn a blind eye. One reason for this tolerance is that it contains the problem, so do not assume it's OK to smoke elsewhere.

The red-light district, in and around Oude Zijdsachterburgwal, is always an eye-opener in the evening, with prostitutes posing in windows; the **Erotic Museum** makes the experience that much more memorable if you don't mind the sleazy exterior (well, you probably wouldn't be here if you did!). This area is supposedly a den of thieves, so be warned. Many habitués do not appreciate being photographed and your last sight of your camera might well be as it sinks into the nearest canal. Stick to the well-lit and crowded main streets.

WEST OF DAM The **Anne Frank Huis**, Prinsengracht 267 (boat: Prinsengracht; tram nos. 13/14/17/20: Westermarkt), is where two Jewish families hid from the Nazis for two years. They were betrayed in 1944 and only the father survived the concentration camps. Thirteen-year-old Anne recorded the family's ordeal in a moving diary that was discovered after the war. The house has been restored and the tour captures vividly what life must have been like in these cramped secret quarters. Not far away is the 17th-century **Westerkerk**, the largest Protestant church in the country, topped by the gold crown of the Austrian emperor Maximilian. The tower (Amsterdam's highest at 85 m) gives one of the few bird's-eye views of the city.

DAY TRIPS FROM AMSTERDAM

Amsterdamse Bos, Amstelveenseweg 264 (🚌 nos. 142/170/171/172 – or antique trams Apr–Oct), on the southern fringe of the city, is an 80-hectare park, pleasant for swimming, rowing, canoeing, cycling and walking (200 km of tracks). **Enkhuizen** (1 hour by train) was cut off from the sea when the Zuider Zee was dammed to create Lake IJsselmeer. The boat for the **Zuiderzee Museum** leaves from behind the station. On boarding you buy a ticket which includes both the boat and museum. The indoor section, Binnenmuseum, contains traditional costumes and historic fishing craft, while the open-air section, Buitenmuseum, consists of whole streets rescued from fishing villages that were destroyed. You can enter any house with an open door and ask questions if you find someone at home.

THE OLD CITY: EAST OF DAMRAK

Across the canal from Centraal is **Sint Nicolaaskerk**, with its largest dome featuring a cross donated by the prostitutes of the area. The notorious red-light district (*De Walletjes* – Little Walls) is (roughly) the area between Warmoesstr. and Gelderskade.

SOUTH OF DAM The most notable museum here is the

THE NETHERLANDS

Amsterdams Historisch Museum, Kalverstr. 92 (boat: Herengracht; tram nos. 1/2/4/5/9/11/16/20/24/25: Spui), where you can not only view, but also try your hand at bell-ringing. Turn right as you leave and signs lead to the **Begijnhof**, with its old almshouses (once home to pious upper-class women) and chapel surrounding a peaceful square and 15th-century church.

The highly fragrant **floating flower market**, Singel (between Muntplein and Koningsplein), takes place Mon–Sat 0830–1800, some stalls also open Sun. The backs of the stalls are on barges, but the fronts are squarely on terra firma.

Herengracht was the city's grandest canal and one stretch (between Vijzelstr. and Leidsestr.) is known as the 'Golden Bend'. This typifies the old architecture, when buildings were tall and thin (to minimise taxes based on width) and had protruding gables (still used) to winch up furniture too big for the narrow staircases.

THE MUSEUM QUARTER This district, south-west of the centre, contains museums of international status, well worth the short tram ride. Also seek out the Vondelpark – highly festive in summer, with café terraces, theatre and street artists. The **Rijksmuseum**, Stadhouderskade 42 (boat: Singelgracht; tram nos. 2/5/20: Hobbemastraat or tram no. 16: Museumplein), ranks as one of the world's great museums, with famous canvasses by Dutch and Flemish masters, including several by Vermeer and Rubens, and Rembrandt's celebrated *Night Watch*. A short walk away, the **Van Gogh Museum** (tram nos. 2/3/5/12/20: van Baerlestraat) displays some 200 paintings and 600 drawings by the great artist, spanning his entire career from his early works to his final, violently creative outbursts. Virtually next door, the **Stedelijk Museum** covers modern art from the mid-19th century to the present, including works by Picasso, Mondrian, Chagall, Monet and Cézanne.

THE JEWISH QUARTER This lies south-east of Dam (metro: Waterlooplein; boat: Muziektheater). The Jews played a very important part in the development of Amsterdam and formed 10% of the pre-war population. The **Rembrandthuis**, Jodenbreestr. 4 (tram nos. 9/14/20: Mr. Visserplein), is where Rembrandt lived between 1639 and 1659. It isn't that evocative, but does contain most of his engravings and a number of his drawings. Along the street is a gateway leading to the **Zuiderkerk** (South Church). The splendid spire (which you can climb) reputedly inspired Christopher Wren in his rebuilding of London.

THE PORT The **Scheepvaart Museum**, Kattenburgerplein 1 (boat: Oosterdok; nos. 22/28: Kattenburgerplein) is an exceptionally rich maritime museum housed in a 17th-century arsenal, with complete craft (you can go aboard an 18th-century East Indiaman, *The Amsterdam*, and watch costumed personnel performing shipboard duties). There's masses to take in at the ethnographical **Tropenmuseum**, Linnaeusstr. 2 (tram nos. 9/14: Mauritskade), with re-created Indian slums, Middle Eastern bazaars, South American rainforests and much more – all with appropriate background music.

SHOPPING

Leidsestraat, Kalverstraat, Nieuwendijk, Damrak and Rokin are the main shopping streets. For fun shopping, explore the small specialist shops in the alleys linking the main canals, especially in the area between Leidsegracht and Raadhuisstraat. The whole **Jordaan** area is scattered with second-hand shops and boutiques that offer the creations of up-and-coming designers. For antiques and art, look around the Spiegelkwartier. Amsterdam's great stores are the enormous **De Bijenkorf**, Damrak and **Magna Plaza**, Nieuwezijds Voorburgwal. Most shops in the centre of Amsterdam are open on Sunday.

The free VVV leaflet *Amsterdam Market City* lists the markets. The general market, **Albert Cuypmarkt**, Albert Cuypstr., is the largest in the country, held Mon–Sat 0900–1700 (tram nos. 4/16/20/24/25). The **flea market**, Waterlooplein (next to the **Muziektheater**), takes place Mon–Sat 0900–1700.

NIGHT-TIME AND EVENTS

The English-language magazine *Day by Day* (published monthly by the VVV), is the most comprehensive guide to events and useful addresses. You can buy it from VVV and bookshops, but it's sometimes free from good hotels. **Amsterdams Uit Bureau (AUB)**, Leidseplein 26 (www.aub.nl), also distributes information about the city's entertainments. AUB and VVV make bookings, but there is a charge.

The city's nightlife is both varied and affordable, with bars, live music, cinemas and classical concerts; use the *Day by Day* magazine to suit your taste. Lively areas include **Leidseplein**, **Rembrandtplein** and **Nieuwezijds Voorburgwal**. The **Jordaan** area is less hectic, and pleasant for a quiet evening.

Major venues for classical music and opera are the **Muziektheater** at Waterlooplein and the world-famous **Concertgebouw** on Museumplein (which has free lunchtime concerts on Wednesday).

Foreign movies are invariably subtitled, so there's a good choice of showings in English. There is a concentration of cinemas around the Leidseplein. Two spectacular art deco picture palaces are **Tuschinski** near the Rembrandtplein (screen 1 is the most impressive), and **The Movies** on the Haarlemmerstraat near the Jordaan.

Amsterdam has several water-related events and music festivals each year. The major arts event is the **Holland Festival** (June), which covers all the performing arts.

LIVE BANDS
Live music (including jazz and dance) can be heard at **Paradiso**, Weteringschans 6–8, ☎ (020) 626 4521, and **De Melkweg** (The Milky Way), Lijnbaansgracht 234A, ☎ (020) 531 8181. **Pompoen**, Spuistraat 2, ☎ (020) 521 3000, has live jazz almost every evening.

BELGIUM: BRUSSELS (BRUXELLES, BRUSSEL

Headquarters of the EU and NATO, Brussels is an exceptionally cosmopolitan city, as well as home to a sizeable number of immigrants from around the Mediterranean. Though it's not the most glamorous or romantic of European capitals – its two most famous monuments are a statue of a urinating boy (the Manneken-Pis) and an outsized 1950s atomic model (the Atomium) – it has some great art galleries, abundant greenery, a majestic central square and many excellent restaurants. There's also a wealth of art nouveau architecture which, for the most part, you have to look at from the outside. Streets to head for include the Square Ambiorix and Square Marie-Louise (both just north of Schuman station), and avenue Louise, with several houses by the great Victor Horta.

Brussels is well placed for journeys by rail into the Netherlands, Germany, France and the UK, and the most interesting Belgian cities are accessible by day trip. The city is officially bilingual and there's often little similarity between the two versions of street names (e.g. French *Arts-Loi* is Dutch *Kunst-Wet*); this chapter uses the French ones.

ARRIVAL AND DEPARTURE

Virtually all long-distance trains stop at both **Midi** and **Nord** (Metro no. 23: change at Rogier from no. 2 or at DE BROUCKÈRE from no. 1), but many omit **Centrale** (Metro no.1: Centrale, 5-min walk from GRAND-PLACE). The facilities at all three include baggage lockers, eating places and newsagents that sell English papers. Other main-line stations are for local journeys only.

Midi/Zuid (Metro nos. 2/23) is the terminal for Eurostar services from London (2 hrs 40 mins) and the Thalys train from Paris (1 hr 20 mins), although it's in an area best avoided at night; train information office (daily 0630–2230; www.sncb.be) with a Tourist Information desk (daily 0800–2000, except Fri to 2100 in summer; Tue–Fri 0800–1700, Sat 0900–1800, Sun 0900–1400 in winter); few other tourist facilities except bureau de change. Your best bet, unless just transferring, is to hop on a train to **Centrale** station as fast as possible.

Bruxelles Zaventem Airport, ☎0900 70000 (www.brusselsairport.be), is 14 km north-east of the centre; exchange offices, tourist information desk (daily 0600–2200). An express rail link operates from before 0500 until nearly midnight (every 20 mins or so to all three main stations; journey time approx 30 mins). A taxi should cost around €30.

INFORMATION

CITY AND TRANSPORT MAP
– inside back cover

The *Brussels Guide & Map* is the most comprehensive tourist leaflet; cheaper from the Tourist Office than from bookshops. The English-language weekly *The Bulletin* has a useful What's On supplement.

MONEY **Midi** station: currency exchange, daily 0700–2200; cash machine. Currency exchange offices at **Nord** (0700–2000) and **Centrale** (0700–1900).

TOURIST OFFICE

Brussels International – Tourism & Congress (BI-TC), Hôtel de Ville, Grand-Place, ☎ (02) 513 89 40, fax (02) 513 83 20 (www.tib.be; tourism.brussels@tib.be). If you make a hotel booking you will get free city and transport maps. Better is the **Belgian Tourist Information Centre**: r. du Marché-aux-Herbes 61, ☎ (02) 504 03 90, fax (02) 504 02 70 (www.belgium-tourism.net; info@opt.be). From Grand-Place, take the road to the right of the museum, opposite the Hôtel de Ville. It has information about the whole country (plus a free city map with points of interest marked); ask about the **Tourist Passport**, which offers free city transport and a range of discounts (also available from museums, metro stations and hotels). **Infor-Jeunes Centre**: r. Ste-Catherine 9A, ☎ (02) 514 41 11 (www.inforjeunes.be; bruxelles@inforjeunes.be), has information about special deals for young people.

TICKETS

Individual tickets can be purchased from drivers or in metro stations, and multi-ride tickets from STIB/MIVB kiosks, Tourist Offices, metro stations and some newsagents; 10-trip tickets are sold (€9). There's also a one-day travelcard (€3.59) for unlimited travel on all city transport for one calendar day. Stamp your ticket in the machine by the metro entrance or on board buses before travelling.

POST AND PHONES

Main post office: **Centre Monnaie**, pl. de Brouckère (upstairs). There's a 24-hr post office at **Midi** (av. Fonsny 1E/F), plus branches at **Centrale** and **Nord**, (Mon–Fri 0900–1700). The telephone code for Brussels is 02: the prefix has to be dialled within and outside the Brussels area.

PUBLIC TRANSPORT

The city centre is smaller than it looks on maps and walking is the best way to get around, though it can be confusing initially. Away from the centre, the metro and bus network is efficiently run.

MAPS

Free route maps from STIB/MIVB (www.stib.irisnet.be) kiosks, metro stations and Tourist Offices. De Rouck maps (www.de-rouck.be) are sold at newsagents.

METRO

Primarily for commuters; few central stops. The terms 'tram' and 'metro' are interchangeable here. Metro stations are indicated by a square white 'M' on a blue background. *Loket/guichet* booths for tickets are in all stations and the trams run 0530–0030. The system is comprehensive, efficient and easy to use: study the map before setting out. Lines are identified by number and colour (nos. 1/red and 2/orange are central). Routes of the relevant line are shown on all platforms and trams, and every platform has a city map with the metro system superimposed. Doors close automatically (don't use them after the warning buzzer sounds), but you have to open them yourself: by pressing a thin strip by the door. Smoking is prohibited throughout the system. Watch the escalators: they're pressure-activated, which is pretty smart until you miss the sign and try to walk up the down one.

BUSES

Buses also have a comprehensive network (approximately 0530–0030), and there's a very limited night service. If stops show *sur demande*, raise your hand to the driver as the vehicle approaches. If you want to get off, ring the bell.

TAXIS

Ranks are strategically positioned at all the stations and main squares. Don't tip the drivers.

BIKE HIRE

The streets are a bit crowded, but bikes can be hired from r. E. Solvay 32A, ☎ (02) 502 73 55, or **Vélo Cité**, ☎ (02) 241 36 35.

ACCOMMODATION

There's a fair choice of hotels in every grade, including plenty of budget establishments in the **Ixelles** and **pl. Ste-Catherine** areas, plus several hostels (HI and otherwise) and a number of bed and breakfasts. Nevertheless, advance booking is recommended – and essential in peak periods. Near Grand Place is **Arlequin**, r. de la Fourche 17–19, ☎ (02) 514 16 15, fax (02) 514 22 02, €€, is reasonably priced and pleasant (www.arlequin.be; reservation@arlequin.be).

At the bottom of the hotel price range are (both 1-star) **La Tasse d'Argent**, r. du Congres 48, ☎ (02) 217 32 74, fax (02) 218 83 75, €€ (Metro: MADOU) and **Saint Michel**, Grand Place 15, ☎ (02) 511 09 56, fax (02) 511 46 00, €€ (Metro: GARE CENTRALE).

Youth hostels: Auberge de Jeunesse Jacques Brel, r. de la Sablonnière 30, ☎ (02) 218 01 87 (brussels.brel@laj.be; Metro no. 2: MADOU, direction Simonis, i.e. away from the centre). A sign in the ticket hall indicates the exit: leave by the right-hand stairs and continue straight along the road to the second turning left. One of the cheapest places, within walking distance from Nord and Centrale stations, is **New Sleepwell** (non-HI), Auberge du Marais, r. du Damier 23, ☎ (02) 218 50 50, fax (02) 218 13 13 (www.sleepwell.be; info@sleepwell.be), €. **Jeugdherberg Bruegel**, r. du St-Esprit 2, ☎ (02) 511 04 36 (brussel@vjh.be), is 300 m from Centrale (behind Notre-Dame-de-la-Chapelle) and very modern. **Auberge de Jeunesse Generation Europe**, r. de l'Eléphant 4, ☎ (02) 410 38 58 (brussels.europe@laj.be), 2 km from Centrale (Metro: COMTE DE FLANDRE – 500 m). **CHAB–Centre Vincent van Gogh** (non-HI), r. Traversiére 8, ☎ (02) 217 01 58, fax (02) 219 79 95 (www.ping.be/chab; chab@ping.be), is the oldest youth hostel in Brussels and has the largest capacity.

Campsites: the nearest official campsite is **Camping Beersel**, 75 Steenweg, Op Urrel 1650, Beersel, ☎ (02) 331 05 61, 9 km to the south (tram no. 55: UCCLE). Another is **Espace International** at Chaussée de Wavre 205, ☎ (02) 644 16 81, fax (02) 648 97 87.

FOOD AND DRINK

The Belgians enjoy eating and there's a huge choice of restaurants serving excellent food, but prices tend to be high and it's advisable to book for the more upmarket restaurants. Many bars sell food and give better value than the restaurants. In the area surrounding GRAND-PLACE you can find every imaginable type of eating place, including fast-food chains.

AV. DE LA COURONNE, especially around Ixelles cemetery and CHAUSÉE DE WAVRE, offers several inexpensive establishments. One of the many bars is **La Fleur en Papier Doré**, once a favourite of the artist Magritte.

Colour Section

(i) Tram in narrow street, Lisbon (p. 150); Douro river, Portugal (p. 180)

(ii) Tulip fields at Lisse, The Netherlands (p. 236)

(iii) Quay of the Rosary, Bruges, Belgium (pp. 228–230); Old Town, Luxembourg (p. 233)

(iv) View of Heidelberg, Germany (pp. 288–290); Cologne Cathedral, Germany (p. 273)

RAIL TOUR: OSTEND – BRUSSELS – LUXEMBOURG

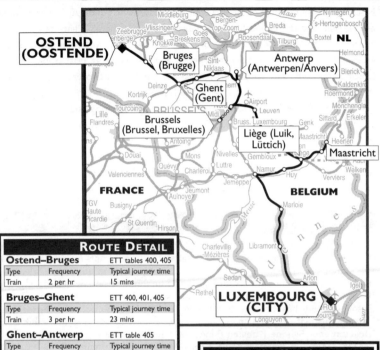

ROUTE DETAIL

Ostend–Bruges
ETT tables 400, 405

Type	Frequency	Typical journey time
Train	2 per hr	15 mins

Bruges–Ghent
ETT tables 400, 401, 405

Type	Frequency	Typical journey time
Train	3 per hr	23 mins

Ghent–Antwerp
ETT table 405

Type	Frequency	Typical journey time
Train	2 per hr	49 mins

Antwerp–Brussels
ETT table 410

Type	Frequency	Typical journey time
Train	2 per hr	41 mins

Brussels–Liège
ETT tables 400, 401

Type	Frequency	Typical journey time
Train	2 per hr	1 hr 20 mins

Liège–Maastricht
ETT table 403

Type	Frequency	Typical journey time
Train	Every hr	30 mins

Maastricht–Namur
ETT tables 403, 435

Type	Frequency	Typical journey time
Train	Every hr	1 hr 22 mins

Namur–Luxembourg
ETT table 430

Type	Frequency	Typical journey time
Train	Every hr	1 hr 57 mins

KEY JOURNEYS

Ostend–Brussels
ETT table 400

Type	Frequency	Typical journey time
Train	Every hr	1 hr 15 mins

Brussels–Paris
ETT table 18

Type	Frequency	Typical journey time
Train	1–2 per hr	1 hr 25 mins

Brussels–Amsterdam
ETT table 18

Type	Frequency	Typical journey time
Train	1–2 per hr	2 hrs 40 mins

Brussels–Cologne
ETT table 400

Type	Frequency	Typical journey time
Train	Every hr	2 hrs 30 mins

Note
Ostend to Luxembourg: change trains at Brussels Midi

BENELUX

Not a hill in sight for most of the way, until you cross the hills of the Ardennes in southern Belgium and the Grand Duchy of Luxembourg, but there's plenty of man-made interest, notably the handsome cities of **Bruges**, **Ghent** and **Antwerp**, each boasting impressive legacies of medieval prosperity, and deserving at least a night's stay; Luxembourg itself has a remarkable natural site, perched on two deep gorges. A trip to **Maastricht** (just over the border in the Netherlands) is recommended, while the journey from **Ostend** to **Brussels** makes a useful link for those starting a European journey from London via the Dover–Ostend Fast-Ferry sea crossing and venturing on to Germany (see International Routes, **London–Ostend**, p. 41). From the little capital of **Luxembourg** (Luxembourg City) it is only a short rail journey to the Roman town of **Trier** in Germany (p. 276) or southwards to **Metz** in France, where you can join the **Cherbourg–Strasbourg** route (p. 80).

OSTEND (OOSTENDE)

A fishing port, ferry port and seaside resort rolled into one, Ostend is not likely to detain you for long, but there are excellent seafood restaurants (oysters are a local speciality). The three-master *Mercator*, a training vessel in authentic style, now houses a maritime museum, **Noordzeeaquarium** (on the front), which displays the flora and fauna of the North Sea. The studio where the expressionist painter James Ensor worked has become a museum devoted to him (**James Ensorhuis**, Vlaanderenstraat 27), and many of his possessions are among the exhibits in **Museum voor Schone Kunsten** (Fine Arts Museum), Cultuurpaleis, Wapenplein. **PMMK** (**Museum voor Moderne Kunst**–Modern Art Museum), Romestraat 11, contains modern paintings and sculptures.

RAIL Adjacent to the port.

The Fast Ferries and trains share a building, 20 mins' walk from the Tourist Office (or no. 5).

i **Tourist Office**: Monacoplein 2, (059) 70 11 99, fax (059) 70 34 77 (www.oostende.be; info@toerisme-oostende.be). Walk right from the station and along the sea front, then take the last turning left before the front curves. Sells the A–Z brochure and town map.

Youth Hostel: De Ploate, Langestraat 82, (059) 80 52 97, fax (059) 80 92 74 (www.deploate.com; oostende@vjh.be), 1 km from train and bus stations and ferry terminal.

BRUGES (BRUGGE)

A powerful trading city 500 years ago, Bruges became an economic backwater and the industrial age largely passed it by. Placed at the heart of Flanders, it has survived as one of northern Europe's most impressive medieval cities and, despite the throngs of tourists, you still get the feeling of stepping back in time in its cobbled streets, although it's an expensive and affluent place and its worth getting away from the crowded main squares into the quieter back streets. A boat trip on the extensive and pretty canal system is a good introduction to the town, with frequent departures from quays along **Dijver**, which, along with **Groene Rei** and **Rozenhoedkaai**, provide some of the vintage views of Bruges. After that, explore on foot – the Tourist Office has an English 'Walkman' guide. Most places of interest are in a small area around **Markt** and **Burg**, and much of it is tranquil and traffic-free. Seek out the windmills on the old city ramparts near **Kruispoort** (east of the centre).

Markt, Bruges' large, lively and impressive main square, is surrounded by guild buildings, many of which have been converted into restaurants and bars. All around are shops selling those world-famous Belgian chocolates and truffles. **Belfort**, an octagonal 88-m belfry and a useful landmark, is mainly 13th century, but the top storey was added in the 15th century. There are 366 steps to the top.

The Burg, the other main square, features monumental buildings, notably the **Baziliek van Het Heilig Bloed** (Basilica of the Holy Blood), with an early 12th-century stone chapel below a 16th-century chapel. Other buildings around the square include the renaissance **Civiele Griffie** (Recorder's House) and the neoclassical **Gerectshof** (Court of Justice). The Gothic **Stadhuis** (Town Hall) has a magnificent hall with a vaulted ceiling and murals.

Dijver is the central canal; Dijverstraat (scene of a weekend antiques and flea market) is home to several museums. **Groeningemuseum** (closed Tues in winter) houses a fine collection of Flemish art from the 15th century to date, notably primitive and expressionist works. **Gruuthusemuseum** (closed Tues in winter), on the opposite side of the street, was a 16th-century palace and its décor reflects that time. **Brangwyn Museum** in Arenthuis is noted for its collection of lace, among other items. **Onze-Lieve Vrouwekerk** (Church of Our Lady), Mariastraat, has Belgium's highest spire (122 m). Among its treasures are a beautiful white marble Madonna and Child by Michelangelo. Not far away, the **Kathedraal St-Salvator** (St Saviour's Cathedral), Zuidzandst., contains Gobelin tapestries, a rood-loft organ, 15th-century carved stalls and a Louis XVI-style pulpit.

DAY TRIP FROM BRUGES

Quasimodo Tours, Leenhofweg 7, ☎ (050) 37 04 70, fax (050) 37 49 60, runs an English-language day trip in a minibus, which includes **Damme**, two castles, **Zeebrugge** harbour, waffle sampling, a visit to Chocolate World and a guided tour of a brewery and beer tasting. Departs Mon, Wed and Fri. Pick-ups at various hotels or the rail station.

BEGIJNHOF

A visit to Bruges would not be complete without a walk around the walled convent community of the Begijnhof. The houses where the Beguines once lived are neatly arranged near the **Minnewater**, a tranquil, swan-populated water known as 'Love Lake'.

20 mins' walk south of the centre; buses stop in front (tickets and a free route map from the De Lijn kiosk). To the right as you leave the station is a branch of the Tourist Office.

i **Tourist Office: Municipal**: Burg 11, ☎(050) 44 86 86, fax (050) 44 86 00 (www.brugge.be; toerisme@brugge.be). **Provincial** (West Flanders): Koning Albert I-Lann 120, Sint-Michels, ☎(050) 30 55 00, fax (050) 30 55 90 (www.westtoerisme.be; info@westtoer.be).

🛏 Book ahead. **Youth hostels: Europa**, Baron Ruzettelaan 143, Assebroek, ☎(050) 35 26 79, fax (050) 37 37 32 (brugge@vjh.be) is about 1.5 km east of the station (2 km south of Markt; 🚌no. 2: Steenbruges). **Herdersbrugge**, Louis Coiseaukaai 46, Dudzele, ☎(050) 59 93 21, fax (050) 59 93 49 (brugge.dudzele@vjb.be), is about 5 km from the station (🚌no. 788: Brugges/Knokke or no. 2: Breskens). **Private hostel: Bauhaus**, Langestraat 135–137, ☎(050) 34 10 93, fax (050) 33 41 80 (www.bauhaus.be); 🚌 nos. 6/16: Kruispoort. **Campsite: St-Michiel**, Tillegemstraat 55, Sint-Michiels, ☎(050) 38 08 19, fax (050) 80 68 24, 3 km south-west of the station (🚌no. 7).

🍽 Bruges is a great place to eat, drink and enjoy the Belgian lifestyle. The main square has many inexpensive pavement restaurants serving mussels and chips, but there's more sophisticated fare on offer too, in the side streets and along the canals. There's no shortage of bars offering excellent Belgian beers.

GHENT (GENT)

Ghent is a deeply Flemish town, steeped in culture, yet very lively during the university year. For ten days in July, **Gentse Feesten** (traditionally a holiday for factory workers) dominates the town, with lots of cheap food, high beer consumption and street entertainments, as well as a variety of more formal performances. The 12th–17th-century **guildhouses** along the **Graslei quay** and the old houses by the **Kraanlei quay** provide two of the city's classic views.

Sint-Baafskathedraal (St Bavo's Cathedral), resplendent with marble statuary and a baroque organ and pulpit, contains Van Eyck's multi-panelled masterpiece *The Adoration of the Mystic Lamb*, painted in 1432 and considered to be the most important work of church art in Belgium (entry fee payable); parts were repeatedly stolen through centuries of turbulence, and the Adam and Eve nude panels were at one stage replaced by bearskin-clad versions (since discarded, but on display), strangely reminiscent of the Flintstones. The Romanesque crypt contains medieval tombs, frescos and examples of local stonework. You can ascend the 90-m **Belfort** (belfry) by lift.

Gravensteen, Sint-Veerleplein, the 12th-century 'Castle of the Counts', has a museum that displays a selection of gruesome instruments of torture, with illustrations of how they were used. You can also walk round the ramparts and explore the castle grounds. Allow plenty of time for the fascinating **Museum Voor Volkskunde** (Museum of Folklore), Kraanlei 65 (closed Mon), which spreads through three converted almshouses. It portrays the town's lifestyle at the turn of the 20th century and is crammed with pleasingly unrelated everyday items – toys, flat irons, hats, etc.

🚈 **Gent-St-Pieters**: south of the centre (tram nos. 1/10/11/12: Korenmarkt). De Lijn bus/tram information to the left as you exit.

CARRIAGE TRIPS

These can be made through the city during summer holidays, weekends and public holidays, 1000–1800 (Apr–Nov). Depart from **Sint-Baafsplein**. There are summer boat trips on the River Leie, excursions including Bruges.

> i **Tourist Offices: Municipal:** Botermarkt 17A (in the crypt of the Belfry), ☎(09) 266 52 32–4, fax (09) 225 62 88 (www.gent.be; toerism@gent.be). **Provincial** (East Flanders): Woodrow Wilsonplein 3, ☎(09) 267 70 20, fax (09) 267 71 99 (www.oost-vlaanderen.be/toerisme; toerisme@oost-vlaanderen.be).

ANTWERP (ANTWERPEN/ANVERS)

Belgium's second city, Antwerp has enough for at least a couple of days' sightseeing, including an extensive old Flemish quarter, plus views over the **River Schelde** (or Scheldt), on which boat tours are available.

The medieval **Steen** (Castle), Steenplein 1, houses the **National Scheepvartmuseum** (National Maritime Museum), ☎(03) 232 08 50 (closed Mon), while the **Diamantmuseum**, Lange Herentalsestr. 31–33 (walkable from Centraal station), covers all aspects of the diamond trade, one of the cornerstones of Antwerp's appreciable fortunes.

The **cathedral** is Belgium's largest (free multilingual tours; entrance on Handschoenmarkt), built 1352–1521. Its 123-m tower would have been one of a pair had the money not run out. Highlights here are four enormous masterpieces by Rubens and some recently revealed 15th-century frescos.

PLANTIN-MORETUS MUSEUM

Perhaps Antwerp's most astonishing survival is the unique **Plantin-Moretus Museum/Stedelijk Prentenkabinet**, Vrijdagmarkt 22 (closed Mon), a perfectly preserved 16th–18th-century printer's works and home built by the famous printer Plantin; don't spend too long on the first few rooms – the most interesting parts come later on.

Grote Markt is home to the 19th-century **Brabo Fountain** (which depicts the legend of the city's founding), elaborately gabled guildhouses and the Renaissance **Stadhuis** (Town Hall). Not far away is the **Vleeshuis** (Butchers' Hall), Vleeshouwersstr. 38/40 (closed Mon), now an applied arts museum with woodcarvings, antique china, old musical instruments and lots of ticking grandfather clocks. On Sunday mornings, **Vogelmarkt** (Bird Market), Oude Vaartplaats, sells birds – plus almost everything else. The **Openluchtmuseum Voor Beeldhouwkunst** (Open-Air Sculpture Museum), Middelheim Park (🚌nos. 18/17), is dotted with sculptures, notably by Rodin and Moore.

🚆 **Antwerpen-Centraal**, 2 km east of the centre, linked by metro-tram. The marble- and gold-decorated station is worth a visit in its own right. The bookstand stocks UK newspapers and there's an exchange office. De Lijn's office is in Centraal's metro-tram stop, Diamant; you can get transport maps and tickets from them. Some international trains stop at **Berchem**, 2 km to the south; local services link it to Centraal.

$\boxed{i}$ **Tourist Office: Municipal**: Grote Markt 15, ☎(03) 232 01 03, fax (03) 231 19 37
(www.visitantwerpen.be; visit@antwerpen.be). From Centraal, take Metro nos. 2/15 to
Groenplaats (direction: Linkeroever), go past the cathedral and continue along the street ahead.
Provincial: Koningin Elisabethlei 16, ☎(03) 240 63 73, fax (03) 240 63 83
(www.tourproantwerp.be; tpa@tourproantwerp.be).

The Tourist Office gets good discounts. Some cheap places near Centraal (beware that some
rent by the hour). **Youth Hostel**: Op Sinjoorke, Eric Sasselaan 2, ☎(03) 238 02 73, fax (03)
248 19 32 (antwerpen@jeugdherbergen.be); 0.5 km from south station, 🚌 no. 2 to
Bouwcentrum or 🚌 no. 27. **Campsite**: **Camping Vogelzang,** Vogelzanlaan, ☎(03) 238 57 14,
fax (03) 216 91 17.

BRUSSELS (BRUXELLES, BRUSSEL)

See p. 222.

LIÈGE (LUIK/LÜTTICH)

Change here for the detour to **Maastricht**. Liège is an industrial, sprawling city; the
rail station is 2 km south of the centre.

MAASTRICHT, THE NETHERLANDS

Tucked into the southern, mildly hilly corner of the Netherlands, the provincial capital
of Limburg and busy university town has a captivating atmosphere in its lively squares
and precincts, in its Mosan-style stone houses and in its ebullient February carnival. You
can get a good view from the tower of **Sint Janskerk**, next to huge **Sint Servaasbasiliek**
(see the 11th- and 12th-century crypts). The most atmospheric church is the elaborately
decorated Romanesque **Onze-Lieve-Vrouwe Basiliek**, with a statue that is credited
with miraculous powers. At **Museumkelder Derlon**, there are *in situ* remnants of
Roman Maastricht, while centuries-old **fortifications** abound in and around the city,
notably at **Fort Sint Pieter**. **St Pietersberg Caves** are the result of centuries of excavation
of marl stone, which have left a labyrinth of more than 20,000 passages; you can visit two
sections (daily guided tours in English in July and August). The rocket-shaped
Bonnefantenmuseum is a fascinating structure containing three distinct sections: sculpture and religious/magical artefacts, Old Masters and contemporary works.

RAIL 10 mins' walk east of centre.

$\boxed{i}$ **Tourist Office: VVV Tourist Office**, Kleine staat 1, ☎(043) 325 2121, fax (043) 321 37 46
(www.vvvmaastricht.nl; info@vvvmaastricht.nl).

Cheap options round the station and in the Markt area. **Youth hostel: De Dousberg**, Dousbergweg
4, ☎(043) 34 66 777, fax (043) 34 66 755, 4 km from the station (🚌 nos. 55/56 to Dousberg,
the last stop, which is beside a swimming pool that is free to hostellers). **Campsite**: **Camping
Dousberg**, Dousbergweg 102, ☎(043) 34 32 171, fax (043) 34 30 556, 1 km from the hostel.

LUXEMBOURG (CITY)

Though not exactly Europe's most exciting city, Luxembourg is a pleasant enough place to pass a day in. The city was founded in Roman times and is dramatically sited on a gorge cut by the rivers **Alzette** and **Pétrusse**. It falls naturally into three sections: the **old centre** (north of the Pétrusse Valley and home to most of the sights); the **modern city** and **station** (south of the gorge); and **Grund** (the valley settlement), reachable by deep escalators or lift from the central part of town. Descending to the Grund ('the ground') is like entering a different, darker city, and it is this area that houses most of Luxembourg's racier nightlife. As well as the usual guided tours, you can 'Walk with a Walkman' (Apr–Oct) or take the **Pétrusse Express** (a misnomer: it's slow-moving; runs mid-Mar–Oct) from pl. de la Constitution.

DAY TRIPS FROM LUXEMBOURG

About 25 mins by train north of the capital, Ettelbrück is the base for visiting (by bus) **Echternach**, a 7th-century Benedictine abbey founded by St Willibrord, an English missionary monk.

One wing of the basilica houses the **Musée de l'Abbaye** (open Easter–Oct), with its display of **illuminated manuscripts**, including Codex Aureus, the gospels decorated in gold and bound in a 10th-century gold cover encrusted with enamel and gems.

The **Cathédrale Notre-Dame**, a 17th-century Jesuit church, contains the simple stone crypt that is the tomb of Duke John the Blind (King of Bohemia and Count of Luxembourg), backed by statues of mourners. Bronze lions flank a gate through which can be seen the burial chapel of the Grand-Ducal family. From PL. DE LA CONSTITUTION there is access to the **Pétrusse casemates**: the underground passages that formed part of the city's original defences (open Easter, Whitsun and school holidays). Tours take about 45 mins and you need to be reasonably fit. If you're in any doubt, opt for the similar casemates at **Rocher du Bock** (open Mar–Oct), which are easier. The entrance is on R. SIGEFROI, the site where Count Siegfried built the **original fortress**, later expanded, especially by the French in the 17th century.

Gare Centrale, 15 mins' walk south of the centre; showers.

i **Tourist Office: Municipal**: pl. d'Armes, ☎22 28 09, fax 46 70 70 (www.luxembourg-city.lu/touristinfo; touristinfo@luxembourg-city.lu) in the old town; also interactive computer kiosks in r. du Curé and at the railway station. **National**: 1 r. du Fort Thüngen, ☎42 82 82-1, fax 42 82 82-38 (www.ont.lu; info@ont.lu).

Most of the cheaper hotels are near the station. Two good moderately priced (€€) options: **Bristol**, 11 r. de Strasbourg, ☎48 58 29, fax 48 64 80, and **Carlton**, 9 r. de Strasbourg, ☎29 96 60, fax 29 96 64 (carlton@pt.lu). **Youth hostel**: 2 r. du Fort Olisy (3 km from the station), ☎22 68 89 and 22 19 20, fax 22 33 60, 🚌no. 9:Vallée d'Alzette (150 m from the stop, down a steep hill). **Campsite: Camping Kockelscheuer**, Rte de Bettembourg 22, Kockelscheuer, ☎47 18 15, fax 40 12 43, is south of the centre, 4 km from Gare Centrale and 500 m from the 🚌no. 2 stop; open Mar–Oct.

🍽 Avoid the tacky eating places in the station area – there are much better middle-range ones in the old centre. Pl. d'Armes is full of eateries, with open-air entertainment on most summer evenings. There's a regular food market in pl. Guillaume II (Wed and Sat 0800–1200).

ROUTE DETAIL		

Amsterdam–Haarlem ETT tables 450, 480		
Type	Frequency	Typical journey time
Train	8 per hour	15 mins

Haarlem–Leiden ETT tables 450, 465		
Type	Frequency	Typical journey time
Train	6 per hour	20 mins

Leiden–The Hague ETT tables 450, 465		
Type	Frequency	Typical journey time
Train	6 per hour	10 mins

The Hague–Delft ETT table 450		
Type	Frequency	Typical journey time
Train	5 per hour	9 mins

Delft–Rotterdam ETT table 450		
Type	Frequency	Typical journey time
Train	5 per hour	12 mins

Rotterdam–Gouda ETT tables 467, 491		
Type	Frequency	Typical journey time
Train	4 per hour	21 mins

Gouda–Utrecht ETT table 491		
Type	Frequency	Typical journey time
Train	3 per hour	23 mins

Utrecht–Arnhem ETT table 470		
Type	Frequency	Typical journey time
Train	4 per hour	36 mins

Arnhem–Apeldoorn ETT tables 485, 494		
Type	Frequency	Typical journey time
Train	2 per hour	43 mins

Apeldoorn–Amsterdam ETT tables 492, 490		
Type	Frequency	Typical journey time
Train	2 per hour	59 mins

Note
Arnhem to Apeldoorn:
change at Zutphen.

RAIL TOUR: AMSTERDAM – GOUDA – AMSTERDAM

This is a circular tour of much of the best of the Netherlands, through such classic canal-laced towns as **Delft** and **Gouda** (famous for porcelain and cheese respectively), across the **Bulb District** between **Haarlem** (worth a stop for the Frans Hals Museum) and the university town of **Leiden**, and past **Arnhem**. The round trip offers an impressive show of past and present, with some remarkable modern architecture, magnificent art collections and such oddities as **Rotterdam's** vertigo-inducing **Euromast**.

AMSTERDAM

See p. 215.

HAARLEM

The late Gothic **St Bavo/Grote-Kerk** (1370–1520), with its soaring 80-m wooden lantern tower, contains a notable 16th-century screen and the famous Christian Müller baroque pipe-organ (1738), on which both Handel and Mozart played; it's still used for regular concerts. The Antwerp-born painter Frans Hals is buried here. He spent most of his life in Haarlem, and much of his work is in the **Frans Hals Museum**, Groot Heiligland 62; the highlight of the collection is a group of his paintings depicting militia companies. The Netherlands' oldest public museum, which first went on view in 1784, is the **Teylers Museum**, Spaarne 16, an entertaining miscellany of old scientific instruments, fossils, gemstones, coins and above all a fine display of drawings (by Raphael, Michelangelo, Rembrandt and others).

Corrie ten Boom Museum, Barteljorisstr. 19, was founded by Willem ten Boom in 1837 as a clock shop; the family tradition of helping the needy extended to the Jews in World War II. The family were betrayed in 1944 and most perished in the camps, but the house is maintained as a monument to the family's courage and charity.

10 mins' walk north of the centre.

i **Tourist Office**: Stationsplein 1, ☎0900 616 1600 (www.vvvzk.nl; info@vvvzk.nl).

Youth Hostel: Jan Gijzenpad 3, ☎(023) 537 3793, fax (023) 537 1176. Accommodation generally is limited; better choice in Zandvoort (see below).

DAY TRIP FROM HAARLEM

Zandvoort (10 mins by train and frequent buses in summer) is a busy beach resort (casino; sandy beaches including nudist beach 200 m from station) and has plenty of cheap pensions. Tourist Office: VVV, Schoolplein 1, ☎(023) 571 7947, can supply information.

LEIDEN

Birthplace of Rembrandt, this delightful old university town has a medieval quarter, centred on the vast Pieterskerk, plenty of studenty haunts and some excellent museums, covering archaeology (**Rijksmuseum van Oudheden**, Rapenburg 28), local history and art (**De Lakenhal**, Oude Singel 32), changing exhibitions from around the world (**Voor Volkenkunde**, Steenstr. 1) and milling (within a windmill; **Molenmuseum de Valk**, Binnenvestgracht 1). In the **Boerhaave**, Lange St Agnietenstr. 10, is an anatomical theatre, complete with skeletons and displays of early medical paraphernalia. The university, founded in 1575, includes the world's oldest botanical garden (**Hortus Botanicus**).

> **DAY TRIP FROM LEIDEN**
> **Keukenhof Gardens**
> (near Lisse; ▤ no. 54 in season from Leiden): the showcase of the Dutch bulb industry (late Mar–late May; best in April), noted for tulips, narcissi and hyacinths; take a picnic because the cafés are invariably overcrowded.

 10 mins' walk north-west of the centre.

i **Tourist Office**: Stationsplein 210, ☎0900 222 2333 (www.leiden.nl; info@leiden.nl).

🛏 **Nieuw Minerva**, Boommarkt 23, ☎(071) 512 6358. Stylish 2-star canalside hotel in town centre.

THE HAGUE (DEN HAAG, 'S-GRAVENHAGE)

The administrative capital of the Netherlands is a pleasant town, spread over a wide area of parks and canals and centred around **Binnenhof**, the home of the **Dutch parliament** (tram nos. 1/ 2/3/6/7/8/9/10/16/17, ▤nos. 4/5/22). The 13th-century **Ridderzaal** (Knights' Hall) hosts official ceremonies.

> **GALLERY**
> One of the great galleries of the world, the **Mauritshuis**, Korte Vijverberg 8 (tram/bus: see Binnenhof, above; closed Mon), is a Renaissance mansion on the famous Hofvijver (Courtpond), housing much of the royal collection, with paintings by the major Flemish masters, including Rembrandt and Vermeer.

Installed in a rotunda, the remarkable **Panorama Mesdag**, Zeestr. 65 (tram nos. 7/8, ▤nos. 4/5/13/22), consists of a realistic circular view of the North Sea resort of **Scheveningen** painted by Hendrik Mesdag, his wife and some friends in 1881. The current equivalent might be the **Omniversum**, President Kennedylaan 5 (tram nos. 7/10, ▤nos. 4/14 – or through the small garden to the rear of **Gemeentemuseum**), a stunning spectacle with a wrap-around movie screen that makes you feel like a participant in the action: English headphones are available.

Most of the city's palaces can be viewed only from the outside. An exception is the huge **Vredespaleis** (Peace Palace), Carnegieplein 2 (tram nos. 3/7/8, 🚃 nos. 4/13), which houses the International Court of Justice and the Permanent Court of Arbitration; it is a strange architectural mishmash, with a display of items donated by world leaders. There are normally tours Mon–Fri.

🚉 **Centraal** is 5 mins' walk from the centre and serves most Dutch cities. Fast services for Amsterdam and Rotterdam use **HS** (Hollandse Spoor) station (1 km south). Centraal and HS are linked by frequent trains and by tram nos. 9/12.

ℹ️ **Tourist Office**: Koningin Julianaplein 30, 📞 0900 340 3505 (www.denhaag.com; info@denhaag.com), at the Babylon shopping centre. *Den Haag Info* is a free monthly covering everything of interest; for films, theatres and music consult leaflets and posters (around everywhere). Buy a proper street map, as the free small ones are deceptive in scale.

🚌 There is an excellent bus and tram network.

🏨 If money is a consideration, base yourself at **Scheveningen** or ask VVV about private rooms. **Youth Hostel: NJHC City Hostel Den Haag**, Scheepmakersstraat 27, 📞 (070) 315 7878; 10 km west of CS near Kijkduin beach (🚌 nos. 122/123/124 from CS, then 10 mins' walk: tell the driver you want the hostel). Close to it are a small cheap **hotel** and a **campsite**.

DELFT

Long famed for Delftware porcelain and birthplace of the artist Vermeer, Delft is an elegant town with old merchants' houses lining the canal. It has a number of porcelain factories where you can watch the traditional processes in action; the oldest is **De Koninklijke Porceleyne Fles** (Rotterdamseweg 196), but more central is **Aardewerk-atelier de Candelaer** (Kerkstr. 14).

Stedelijk Museum Het Prinsenhof (the Prince's Court), St Agathaplein 1, includes silverware, tapestries, paintings and Delftware. Across the road is **Nusantara Museum**, with a collection of art from the former Dutch East Indies.

Nieuwe Kerk (New Church) houses the huge black-and-white marble mausoleum of Prince William, and its 109-m spire provides great views.

A nice way to see Delft is by horse-drawn tram from Markt, or by canal cruise.

🚉 5 mins' walk south of the centre or 🚌 no. 60 to Markt.

ℹ️ **Tourist Office**: Markt 83–85, 📞 0900 335 3888, fax (015) 215 8695 (www.vvvdelft.nl).

ROTTERDAM

The city was virtually flattened in World War II, but much of its modern architecture is strikingly innovative (**Lijnbaan** was the European pioneer of shopping precincts, for example). Situated at the delta of the rivers **Rhine**, **Maas** and **Waal**, **Europoort** is the world's largest container port; **harbour tours** operated by Spido, Leuvehoofd, ☎(010) 413 5400 (Metro: Leuvehaven, tram nos. 8/20/22).

The **Museum Boijmans Van Beuningen**, Museumpark 18/20, ☎(010) 441 9400 (Metro: Eendrachtsplein, tram no. 5), is massive and high quality, with applied and fine art (including clocks, lace and paintings by Dali, Magritte, Rembrandt, Van Gogh and Bosch). **Maritiem Museum Rotterdam**, Leuvehaven 1 (Metro: Beurs, tram nos. 3/6/13/20, 🚌 nos. 8/20/22), is the country's oldest and biggest maritime museum.

The 185-m **Euromast**, Parkhaven 20 (Metro: DIJKZIGT, tram no. 8, 🚌 no. 39), towers over the trees in **Central Park**. This is the highest structure in the Netherlands. Even from the first platform you have panoramic views of the 37-km-long waterfront, but go right to the top on the **Space Adventure**, a simulated rocket flight: after blast-off you go into 'orbit' and have breathtaking views as the capsule ascends and revolves slowly to the top. **Abseiling** is available in summer.

The most striking modern buildings are located around **Erasmusbridge** (Metro: WILHELMINAPLEIN, tram nos. 20/22) and near metro station Blaak (tram no. 1, 🚌 nos. 32/49), with its futuristic cube houses (one is open to the public).

🚆 **Centraal**, on the northern edge of the centre (blue line metro).

i **Tourist Office**: Coolsingel 67 (5 mins' walk from Centraal; follow the signs), ☎0900 403 4065, fax (010) 413 3124 (www.vvv.rotterdam.nl; info@vvv.rotterdam.nl). *R'uit* is a free monthly listing. VVV sells advantageous combination tickets (travel and attractions and reduction in restaurants).

🚌 **RET**: Coolsingel 141, ☎0900 92 92, sells good-value tickets for unlimited city travel over 1, 2 or 3 days. Metro stations are indicated by a large yellow M. Only two lines matter for the centre: blue (north–south) and red (east–west), and they intersect at only one station, where you walk from BEURS platform to CHURCHILLPLEIN platform (or vice versa). Trams fill the gaps in the metro; summer-service tourist tram no. 10 visits all the main places of interest. Buses are more useful away from the centre.

🏨 Plenty of middle-range options. Cheap hotel areas: about 1 km south-west of CS (try Gravendijkwal and Heemraadsingel) and just north of CS (try Provenierssingel). **Youth hostel**: **NJHC City Hostel Rotterdam**, Rochussenstr. 107–109, ☎(010) 436 5763 (Metro: direction Marconiplein: Dijkzigt; tram no. 4; take the Nieuwbinnen exit, U-turn at top of steps and you're on Rochussenstr. – turn left and the hostel is 30 m away). **Campsite**: **Stadscamping Rotterdam**, Kanaalweg 84, ☎(010) 415 3440, west of CS (🚌 no. 33), is open all year. Usually cheap dormitory accommodation (mid-June–mid-Aug) is at **Sleep-In**, Mauritsweg 29, ☎(010) 412 1420, 5 mins' walk south of CS.

WHERE NEXT FROM ROTTERDAM?

*Head south to **Antwerp** (ETT table 450) to join the **Ostend–Brussels** route (p. 227).*

GOUDA

This quaint place exemplifies small-town Holland, with a ring of quiet canals around ancient buildings. The 15th-century **Stadhuis** (Town Hall) is the oldest Gothic municipal building in Holland, while **Sint Janskerk** (the Netherlands' longest church) is famed throughout the country for its 64 superb 16th-century stained-glass windows.

WAAG (WEIGH-HOUSE)

The old weigh-house in Marktplein (the market square) opens for trading on Thur morning (mid-June–Aug). Gouda cheese comes in several grades (the extra-mature is hard, dry and deliciously strong), while syrup waffles (or *goudse*) are another local speciality.

10-mins' walk north of the centre.

i **Tourist Office**: Markt 27, 0900 468 3288.

UTRECHT

Tree-lined canals encircle the old town at the heart of this sizeable city, not a major tourist destination but worth a brief visit. **Domtoren**, the 112-m cathedral tower (nos. 2/22, but the 10-min walk from CS takes less time), is the tallest in the Netherlands, and gives a marvellous view – if you can face 465 steps.

Utrecht is the headquarters of Dutch Railways (NS), and home to the **Nederlands Spoorwegmuseum** (Rail Museum), Maliebaanstation 16, no. 3. The highly entertaining **Nationaal Museum van Speelklok tot Pierement**, Buurkerkhof 10, nos. 2/22 (or 10-min walk), covers mechanical musical instruments from music boxes to barrel-organs, with demonstrations given. To the east of the centre, the **Rietveld Schröderhuis**, Prins Hendriklaan 50a (closed Mon and Tue), dates from 1924 and represents one of the most radical architectural designs of its day, with an open plan divided by internal sliding doors, and ingenious use of light and space.

Centraal: west of the centre, separated from the old quarter by the Hoog Catharijne indoor shopping centre. There are several outlying stations; don't get off until you reach Centraal.

i **Tourist Office**: Vinkenburgstraat 15 (10-min walk from Centraal Station; follow Smakkelaarsveld, then Vredenburg and right on Neude), 0900 414 1414 (www.vvvutrecht.nl).

ARNHEM

The attractions are scattered, but there's an excellent network of buses and reaching them is not difficult.

Attractions include **Burgers' Zoo**, Schelmseweg 85 (🚌 nos. 3/13 in summer), a zoo with safari park, pride of place going to a giant greenhouse; and **Nederlands Openluchtmuseum**, Schelmseweg 89, an extensive and delightful open-air museum.

At **Osterbeek**, the **Airborne Museum**, Hartenstein, Utrechtseweg 232 (8 km west of the centre – 🚌 no. 1), is devoted to Operation Market Garden, the Allied débâcle of Sept 1944 that was immortalised in the film *A Bridge Too Far*. You can find photographs, film footage, and weapons and equipment from both sides.

🚆 On the north-western edge of town.

ℹ️ **Tourist Office**: Willemsplein 8, ☎ 0900 202 4075 (www.vvvarnhem.nl; info@vvvarnhem.nl).

🏨 The 1-star **Hotel-Pension Parkzicht**, Apeldoornsestr. 16, ☎ (026) 442 0698, is walkable from the station. A good budget place is the **Rembrandt**, Patersstr. 1–3, ☎ (026) 442 0153 (in the city centre). **Youth hostel: Herberg Alteveer**, Diepenbrocklaan 27, ☎ (026) 442 0114, 4 km north of the station (🚌 no. 3 towards Alteveer: Ziekenhuis Rijnstaete). You'll see a sign with the HI logo; 30 m further on steps climb a forested hill to the hostel. Three **campsites**: **Camping Warnsborn**, Bakenbergseweg 257, ☎ (026) 442 3469, Apr–Oct (north-west of the centre, 🚌 no. 2); **Camping Arnhem**, Kemperbergerweg 771, ☎ (026) 443 1600, Apr–Oct (🚌 no. 2 towards Schaarsbergen); and **De Hooge Veluwe**, Koningsweg 14, ☎ (026) 443 2272, Apr–Oct, by the Hoenderloo entrance to the park.

AMSTERDAM

See p. 215.

THE KRÖLLER-MÜLLER MUSEUM

De Hoge Veluwe National Park: to the north-west of Arnhem, this expanse encompasses dunes, fens, heath, forest and added attractions. The visitors' centre in the park houses Museonder, an underground museum devoted to every form of subterranean life; 🚌 nos. 110 (Ede/Wageningen and Apeldoorn) and 12 (Arnhem, in summer). Entrances: Otterlo (🚌 nos. 12/107-Arnhem-/110), Hoenderloo (🚌 no. 110) and Schaarsbergen (🚌 no. 12). Once at a gate, buy a map and borrow a white bicycle (free) as there's a lot of ground to cover.

The **Kröller-Müller Museum**, Houtkampweg 6 (closed Mon; a good 35 mins' walk from the Otterlo entrance, but 🚌 nos. 12/110 stop there), has one of Europe's best modern art collections, notably 278 paintings by Van Gogh (including *The Potato Eaters* and *Café Terrace at Night*), although only 50 or so are on show at any one time. The adjacent **Sculpture Garden** and **Sculpture Forest** contain works by Rodin, Epstein and Moore, plus Dubuffet's extraordinary *Jardin d'Email*.

GERMANY

(for Directory information, see p. 595).

Germany has an immense historic heritage boasting such greats as Beethoven and Goethe. Famously, there's a wealth of castles, while church architecture ranges from the superb Gothic cathedrals of the north to the frothy baroque creations of **Bayern** (Bavaria). Even today, much of Germany is surprisingly little-frequented by outsiders.

All the major cities were bombed in World War II, but have been reconstructed with varying degrees of success, and showing very different characters. A plethora of small medieval towns escaped bombing and have survived the centuries impressively intact: **Rothenburg-ob-der-Tauber** is the touristy showpiece, but there are scores of lesser-known spots. You'll also find health resorts (often prefixed by 'Bad', denoting 'bath') where many Germans go for a *Kur* (cure).

Walking is a national pastime, whether in the **Harz Mountains** of central Germany, in the **Alps** near **Garmisch-Partenkirchen** or **Mittenwald,** or in the **Black Forest** *(Schwarzwald)*, with its rolling forests and neat pastures, dotted with huge-roofed old farmhouses.

The excellent network and services make it feasible to tour much of the country by train. It's easy to link the great historic cities and many smaller towns. Scenic routes proliferate in the south-west and the east. Rail travel is much less spectacular in central and northern Germany.

ACCOMMODATION

Prices vary enormously according to demand. The differences between west and east have steadily been eroded since reunification, but it's still cheaper in the east. Though there's no identifiable low season as such, rates are highest between Christmas and mid March in ski resorts and July and August nationwide. As a very rough guide, a budget room in the west might be around €15–20 in more remote areas, or €30 in cities. Try to avoid major trade fairs at such cities as **Frankfurt** and other special events, such as Munich's **Oktoberfest,** when prices are at their highest; consult the events calendar published by the **German National Tourist Office (GNTO)** – see pp. 596–597.

PENSIONS *Pensionen* or *Fremdenheime* and **private rooms** *(Privatzimmer)* represent particularly good value: they're nearly always meticulously kept, and many of the family-run establishments in the country and in small towns are very welcoming and comfortable. You may be required to stay at least two nights at pensions. Less wonderful in general are city hotels, which frequently border on the characterless; the cheapest places tend to be clustered near main railway stations. *Zimmer frei* and *zu vermieten* (posted in a window) indicate availability, while *besetzt* means a place is full. You can usually book through **Tourist Offices** (many of which have lists of places to stay posted in their windows, often with an indication of which places have rooms free). Note that many establishments don't supply soap. Be prepared to pay for pensions and private rooms in German cash, as credit cards and cheques are seldom accepted by small establishments.

YOUTH HOSTELS There are around 600 *Jugendherbergen*, **Deutsches Jugendherbergswerk (DJH)** in Germany (mostly affiliated with **Hostelling International**). You should book well ahead in peak season (cost €9–17 for under-27s and €12–20 for over-27s; reductions for those staying more than one night); self-catering is not usually available. Hostels have the emphasis firmly on youth (with an age limit of 26 in Bavaria, and preferential treatment given to under 27s elsewhere): they're often used by school parties. This has resulted in the introduction of a new category of accommodation, *Jugendgästehaus*, aimed more at young adults and mostly with 2–4-bedded rooms, costing €20–32 including breakfast and bed linen. Most offer meals; self-catering is uncommon. There are discounts if you stay several nights. Bookings can be made through: **Deutsches Jugendherbergswerk (DJH)**, Bismarckstr. 8, D-32756 Detmold, Germany, ☎(49) (5231) 7401-0, fax (49) (5231) 7401-74 (www.djh.de).

CAMPING The cheapest form of accommodation is camping and site facilities are generally excellent, though few sites are conveniently close to stations. **Deutscher Camping-Club (DCC)**, Mandlstr. 28, D-80802 München, Germany; ☎(40) (89) 380 14 20, publishes an annual list of 1600 sites. **The German National Tourist Office (GNTO)** publishes a free list and map showing more than 600 of the best sites nationwide. There are fewer sites in the east. Most sites open only May–Oct and it is advisable to book a few days in advance. A few are open all year and usually have space out of season.

FOOD AND DRINK Breakfast is any time from 0630 to 1000. Lunch is around 1200–1400 (from 1130 in rural areas) and dinner 1800–2130 (earlier in rural areas). Breakfast is often substantial (and often included in the price of a room), consisting of a variety of bread, cheese and cold meats and a boiled egg. Germans eat their main meal at midday, with a light supper in the evening, but restaurants and pubs also offer light lunches and cooked evening meals. For lunch, the best value is the daily menu *(Tageskarte)* in the country there's often a snack menu *(Vesperkarten)* from mid-afternoon onwards.

Traditional German cuisine is widespread, both in towns and rural areas, and age-old recipes are produced with pride. A lot of it tends towards the hearty, with satisfying portions, and often not pricey for what you get: home-made soups, high-quality meat, piquant marinated pot roasts (known as *Sauerbraten*) and creamy sauces commonly turn up on the menu. Service is included, but a 2–3% tip is normal. Regional variations are quite striking. In the south-west, cherries turn up famously in *Schwarzwälderkirschtorte* (the so-called Black Forest gateau found in Britain and elsewhere is a very distant relative), and in *Kirschwasser* (cherry brandy), while *Spätzle* are home-made flour noodles, delicious in soup or with meat. Bavarian cooking is emphatically wholesome and peasanty, with *knödel* (dumplings) and sausages such as *Nürnberger Bratwurst* (a dark, grilled sausage) and *Münchner Weisswurst* (a white sausage eaten with sweet mustard) making frequent appearances on the menu. In Lower Saxony (around Hannover and Bremen), eel is popular, and there's a tasty local mutton known as *Heidschnucke*. In the north, during the soft fruit season, look for *Rote Grütze*, a wonderful blend of vanilla cream and red fruits such as redcurrants and sour cherries – one of the best German desserts.

For really cheap but generally appetising eats, there are roadside *Imbisse* (stalls) serving a variety of snacks, especially *Kartoffelsalat* (potato salad) and *Wurst* (sausage) in its numerous variations, plus fish in the north.

German **beer** is famously varied in strength, sweetness, colour and character, with dozens of breweries in the great brewing centres like Dortmund and Cologne alone. At the lighter end of the scale are *Helles* (a term for any pale beer), *Weizenbier* (wheat beer, usually served with a slice of lemon in it) and *Berliner Weisse* (served with a dash of fruit syrup); stronger beers are *Bock*, *Doppelbock* (double strength) and *Starkbier*; *Dunkel* is any dark beer. Draught beer is known as *vom Fass*, and is normally a hoppy lager. Medium and medium-sweet white **wines** from the Mosel and Rhine regions are abundant; there are also dry *(trocken)* and semi-dry *(halbtrocken)* whites from Baden and Franconia, plus light reds from Baden and the Ahr Valley.

EDITOR'S CHOICE Aachen (Schatzkammer); Augsburg; Berlin; Bodensee (Konstanz area); Bonn (Beethoven's birthplace); Bremen; Cologne; Dachau; Dresden; Eisenach; Freiburg im Breisgau; Hamburg; Heidelberg; Lübeck; Mittenwald and Garmisch areas (German Alps); Munich; Neuschwanstein; Rothenburg ob der Tauber; Stuttgart (Staatsgalerie); Trier (Porta Nigra); Weimar. Scenic rail journeys: narrow-gauge lines in Harz Mountains (p. 267); Bonn–Mainz (Rhine gorge; p. 272); Offenburg–Konstanz (via Black Forest; p. 283); Stuttgart-Konstanz via Rottweil (see p. 288); Munich–Verona via Innsbruck (p. 306).

BEYOND THE BORDER Hamburg–Copenhagen via Lübeck (ETT table 50); Berlin–Warsaw (table 56); Berlin–Prague (table 60); Nuremburg–Vienna via Regensburg (table 66); Stuttgart–Zurich–Milan (table 82); Cologne–Brussels (table 20); Cologne–Amsterdam (table 28). Cologne–Nice via Avignon (table 47). See also Where Next from Munich? (p. 261) and Where Next from Frankfurt? (p. 278).

Unconventional and forward-thinking, Berlin is always an exciting place to visit. The rapid pace of reunification since the Berlin Wall – the hated symbol of the Iron Curtain – was torn down in 1989, the tremendous rebuilding efforts and the relocation of Germany's Parliament (Reichstag) and most of its civil service to Berlin from Bonn has seen the city re-emerge as one of Europe's great cities. Berlin aims to be at the heart of an ever expanding European Union and is fast becoming Germany's most important business and cultural centre.

Though no great beauty as a city, Berlin is rewarding for its modern architecture, its vibrant restaurant and cafe culture, its nightlife, and its breadth of excellent museums and galleries. There's a surprising amount of open space (a third of Berlin is made up of park-land, forest and water). Although there is little physical evidence of the Wall that divided the city from 1961, differences between the people and areas of West and East remain.

ARRIVAL AND DEPARTURE

Berlin's two major stations for long-distance main line trains are **Bahnhof Zoologischer Garten** (Zoo), Hardenbergpl. 11, in the western part of the city, and **Berlin Ostbahnhof**, STR. der Pariser Kommune 5, in the east. Zoo lands you right in the centre of former West Berlin. Kurfürstendamm (often shortened to Ku'damm), one of the main shopping streets, is a 2-min walk. Ostbahnhof is quieter, more spacious with a distinctly 1950s feel. There is little to do or see near to Ostbahnhof, so head instead to the S-Bahn platforms – any of four lines take you to the centre of the old east, Alexanderpl., just two stops away. Both Zoo and Ostbahnhof have a good range of facilities, including left-luggage lockers (up to 72 hrs).
Some main-line trains also stop at **Berlin Friedrichstrasse**, Friedrichstr. 142, midway between the two larger stations; **Berlin Alexanderplatz**, Dircksenstr., 5 mins' walk from Ostbahnhof; and **Berlin Lichtenberg**, Weitlingerstr., 7 km east of Ostbahnhof. Within Zoo station the **EurAide** office has useful information on places to stay and visits outside Berlin, and acts on behalf of the German railways; upstairs is a hotel reservation service.

(0180) 500 01 86 (all airports). Most flights from the West are to **Berlin-Tegel Otto Lilienthal Airport**, 8 km from the centre of town. For west city destinations, ☐ no. 109, which takes around 20–30 mins to Zoo station and ☐ no. X9 which takes around 30 mins to Kurfürstendamm. For north city destinations ☐ no. 128 connects with the U-Bahn at Kurt-Schumacher-Pl. (9 mins). The Jet Express TXL bus service takes 40 mins to Unter den Linden/Friedrichstr. Taxis to the centre cost around €16. **Schönefeld Airport** (18 km south-east) serves destinations in the East. The S-Bahn and regional trains (*Regionalverkehr*) run to the main rail stations: **Ostbahnhof** – this may appear as **Hauptbahnhof** on older maps – 30 mins by S-Bahn, 15 mins by the half-hourly AirportExpress train, **Zoo** (47 mins by S-Bahn, 29 mins by AirportExpress) and **Lichtenberg** (23 mins by regional train and 34 mins by U/S-Bahn). **Tempelhof Airport** is 6 km south of the city centre, 10–20 mins by U-Bahn.

Long-distance buses: These depart from the **ZOB (Central Bus Station)**, (030) 302 52 94 or (030) 301 80 28 (daily 0630–2100); (030) 302 52 61 or (030) 301 00 175 (24 hrs). The ZOB is at Masurenallee 4–6, Charlottenburg, opposite the International Conference Centre (U-Bahn: Kaiserdamm; S-Bahn: Witzleben). Buses run daily to all major cities and smaller towns.

INFORMATION CITY AND TRANSPORT MAP – inside back cover

Berlin Tourismus Marketing GmbH through its **Tourist Info Centers** offer accommodation and ticket reservation services. From these offices you can pick up a copy of *Berlin City Map*, *Hotels und Pensionen* (Hotel Guide), and the quarterly *Das Berlin Magazin*, with information and listings in English.

Money Cashpoints and bureaux de change are found throughout the city.

Post and phones There is a **post office** at Joachimstaler Str. 7, open Mon–Sat 0800–2400, Sun 1000–2400, where you can also collect mail. The post office at **Tegel Airport** is open Mon–Fri 0800–1800, Sat 0800–1300. **Post offices** are usually open Mon–Fri 0800–1800, Sat 0800–1200.

To phone **Berlin**, (international code) + 49 (Germany) + 30 (Berlin) + number; to phone Berlin from inside Germany, 030 + number.

PUBLIC TRANSPORT

Berlin's efficient public transport network combines buses, trams, underground and surface trains. Free photocopied maps showing public transport routes can be picked up from the Tourist Offices. More comprehensive versions, some with street indexes, are available from newsagents. Train maps are easy to find, but for **bus maps** you must go to the **BVG information centre**, in a separate building outside Zoo station; here you can get the *Region Berlin Linienplan* (large) and free smaller transport maps. For timetable and ticket enquiries 19449 (daily 0600–2300).

Taxis are plentiful, especially in the west, and relatively inexpensive; they can be flagged down on the street or from ranks at stations, the airport and other key points.

Metro: The 20 lines of the U-Bahn (underground) and S-Bahn (suburban surface trains) offer quick transport to most spots

TOURIST OFFICES

Main administrative office:
Berlin Tourismus Marketing GmbH, Am Karlsbad 11, D-10785 Berlin; reservations (030) 25 00 25, fax (030) 25 00 24 24, Information Hotline 0190 01 63 16 (premium rate) within Germany and 00 (011 from the US) 49 1805 75 40 40 (premium rate) from abroad (www.berlin-tourism.de).

Berlin Tourist Info Centers:
Europa-Center, Budapester Str. 45; 5 mins from Zoologischer Garten (Zoo) station (walk towards the Kaiser Wilhelm Memorial Church with its damaged spire), access only from Budapester Str.
Brandenburger Tor (Brandenburg Gate) Pariser Pl; 2 mins from Unter den Linden.
Fernsehturm (TV Tower), Alexanderpl., Panoramastr. 1.
Infopoint Flughafen Tegel (Tegel Airport), Haupthalle (Main Hall). **Infopoint KaDeWe** (KaDeWe department store, travel centre), Tauentzienstr. 21–24. and fax numbers as for **Berlin Tourismus Marketing GmbH**.

Tickets and passes

Get **tickets** for buses, trains and trams from automatic machines on station platforms, from bus drivers or from ticket offices; validate your ticket by punching it on the special machine once on board or on the platform.
Cont. p. 247

BOAT TRIPS

For daily boat trips along the **River Spree** and **Landwehr Canal** contact **Reederei Riedel**, ☎ (030) 691 37 82 (www.reederei-riedel.de).

within the 40-km diameter of Berlin. The stations are recognised by the white U on a blue square or white S on a green circle and lines are colour-coded and numbered. Direction is indicated by the name of the final destination. Trains run 0500–0030 but 24 hrs at weekends on U9 and U12 (U-Bahn) and S7 (S-Bahn).

Buses: Buses are also a convenient way to see the city. A good sightseeing route is no. 100, which runs from Zoo station through the **Tiergarten**, the **Brandenburg Gate** and along **Unter den Linden**; pick up a free guide brochure to this route from the BVG information centre. Bus-stops are indicated by a green H on a yellow background. There are plenty of night bus services.

ACCOMMODATION

Try to book well in advance, as demand for accommodation often outstrips supply. Most upmarket tourist accommodation is in the west, especially in the environs of Zoo, Kurfürstendamm and Charlottenburg, though more deluxe and tourist standard hotels have opened in the east of the city. There are a large number of moderate hotels, budget hotels and pensions in Charlottenburg (formerly West Berlin) and in the eastern part of central Berlin (the Mitte district) – a trendy and happening area, worth making for. Tourist Offices will make free **reservations** and give out accommodation lists. **Guest rooms** in private houses can be booked through **Bed & Breakfast in Berlin**, Ahlbeckerstr. 3, Berlin-Prenzlauer Berg, ☎ (030) 4405 0582 (www.members.aol.com/bedbreakfast; bedbreakfast@aol.com).

Relatively inexpensive **hotels** (under €160 for a double room) include: **Apart Hotel Hanse**, Jenaer Str. 2, Berlin-Wilmersdorf, ☎ (030) 211 9052 (www.hotel-hanse.com; info@hotel-hanse.com), €€; **Comfort Hotel Lichtenberg**, Rhinstr. 159, Berlin-Lichtenberg, ☎ (030) 549350 (www.comfort-hotel-berlin.de; reservierung@comfort-hotel-berlin.de), €€; and **Quality Hotel & Suites Wilhelmsberg**, Landsberger Allee 203, Berlin-Hohenschönhausen, ☎ (030) 978080 (www.quality-hotel-berlin.de; wilhelmsberg@quality-hotel-berlin.de), €€.

There are three **HI youth hostels** (www.djh.de) in Berlin (more are planned), all of which get heavily booked for much of the year. The most central is **JH Berlin International**, Kluckstr. 3, ☎ (030) 261 1097, fax (030) 265 0383 (djh-berlin-brandenburg-zr@jugendherberge.de), 3 km from the centre, 🚌 no. 129. The others are **JH Berlin Ernst Reuter**, Hermsdorfer Damm 48–50, ☎ (030) 404 1610, fax (030) 404 5972 (jh-ernst-reuter@jugendherberge.de), 15 km from Zoo station, 🚌 no. 125

Tickets and passes cont'd.

A **short-distance ticket** is for a short trip on any bus, train or tram. A **single** allows travel on any bus, train or tram for a period of two hours. A **day ticket** and a **7-day ticket** is for travel on all public transport during that period.

The **Berlin Welcome-Card** allows you unlimited free use of public transport throughout the city and its suburbs for 72 hrs. The card also entitles you to free admission and reductions on city tours, museums, theatres and tourist attractions in Berlin and Potsdam. Buy WelcomeCards for €18 at stations, bus ticket offices, hotels, or Tourist Offices.

and **JGH Berlin am Wannsee**, Badeweg 1, Ecke Kronprinzessinnenweg, ☎(030) 803 2034, fax (030) 803 5908 (jh-wannsee@jugendherberge.de), S-Bahn nos. S1/S3/S7 to Nikolassee (500 m away), or 🚌 no. 118 passes closer.

Private hostels and **other budget accommodation** (all €): **Haus Wichern**, Waldenser Str. 31, ☎(030) 395 4072, fax (030) 396 5092 (U-Bahn: TURMSTR); **Haus Sonnenland**, Gartenfelder Str. 1, ☎/fax (030) 334 4492 (U-Bahn: HASELHORST); **Jugendgästehaus Tegel**, Ziekowstr. 161 – Reinickendorf, ☎(030) 433 3046, fax (030) 434 5063 (🚌 no. 222); **Frederik's Hostel**, Str. der Pariser Kommune 35, ☎(030) 296 69450 (U-Bahn: WEBERWIESE); **The Clubhouse Hostel Berlin**, Kalkscheunenstr. 4–5, ☎(030) 2809 7979, fax (030) 2809 7977 (www.clubhouse-berlin.de; info@clubhouse-berlin.de), centrally located for restaurants and nightlife; **CVJM-Haus**, Einemstr. 10, ☎(030) 264 9100, fax (030) 230 05777 (U-Bahn: NOLLENDORFPLATZ); **Gästehaus Luftbrücke**, Kolonnenstr. 10, ☎(030) 7870 2130 (U-Bahn: KLEISTPARK); **Globetrotter Hostel Odyssee**, Grünberger Str. 23, ☎/fax (030) 2900 0081 (www.globetrotterhostel.de; odyssee@hostel-berlin.de); from Ostbahnhof 🚌 nos. 141/240; **Freiraum Guesthouse**, Wiener Str. 14, ☎(030) 618 2008, fax (030) 618 2006 (U-Bahn: GÖRLITZER BAHNHOF; singles up to 5 beds in a room); **Jugendgästehaus am Zoo**, Hardenbergstr. 9A, ☎(030) 312 9410, fax (030) 312 5430 (U-Bahn: ERNST-REUTER-PLATZ); **Jugendgästehaus Central**, Nikolsburger STR. 2–4, ☎(030) 873 0188, fax (030) 861 3485 (U-Bahn: HOHENZOLLERNPLATZ).

Most **campsites** are out of town. One of the most central is **Campingplatz Am Krossinsee**, Wernsdorfer Str. 38, Kopenick, ☎(030) 675 8638, fax (030) 675 9150 (🚌 nos. 134/X34).

FOOD AND DRINK

Around **Zoo** station, **Ku'damm** and the **Europa-Center** are plenty of fast-food snackeries and cafés. Just off Ku'damm is Meinekestr., which is much quieter and has a good selection of brasseries and German pubs. In the east of the city the past few years have seen an explosion of restaurants and cafes, many offering very reasonably-priced food in attractive and trendy surroundings. There are several areas to head to. The streets adjoining Gendarmenmarkt feature smart brasseries and cafes with pavement tables. Towards the north of the Mitte area in the streets around Hackescher Markt including the Oranienburger Str. there is a large choice of restaurants and bars from a wide range of cultures, some with an anarchic edge, and all packed out with young people in the evenings. For a treat, try the cakes at **coffee shops**, while for cheap food and a happy evening's drinking head for the *Kneipen* (pubs) around Prenzlauer Berg – particularly the side streets around Kollwitzpl., Savignypl. and Kreuzberg.

HIGHLIGHTS

There is almost too much to see in Berlin, and it is best to be selective or run the risk of sightseeing overload. Large parts of the city can be explored on foot though you'll need to use public transport, too.

On emerging from the Zoo station, you're in the heart of the former West Berlin with its wide, prosperous-looking boulevards. Just to the west is the **Kurfürstendamm**, Berlin's main shopping street, 3.5 km long and a glitzy showcase of high-rise and neon. Opposite the station is the **Kaiser-Wilhelm-Gedächtnis Kirche** (Kaiser Wilhelm Memorial Church), with its war-damaged tower left unrepaired as a symbol of World War II. The church, which is free to enter, is open daily 0900–1900, with **concerts** on Saturdays at 1800. Heading north from the station, you are soon in the **Tiergarten**, a large area of parkland in central Berlin with lakes and the English Garden: this was the former hunting ground of the kings of Prussia. A busy and wide main road runs through the Tiergarten to the grandiose **Brandenburg Gate**. The Tiergarten's other main attractions include **Schloss Bellevue**, residence of the Federal President, the 1960s **Kongresshalle** and just to the south the **Tiergarten Museum** complex (mainly art galleries).

Schloss Charlottenburg, which dates from 1695, was built to be Berlin's answer to the Palace of Versailles. Tours of the building (closed Mon) are available and the grounds are very attractive. Close by is the **Ägyptisches Museum** (Egyptian antiquities) and just over the road is the excellent art collection in the **Bröhan Museum** (both closed Mon). If you prefer to wander the streets, head for the roads named after famous philosophers (Goethe, Schiller, Leibnitz and others) in the Charlottenburg district – interesting for their small shops and cafes. Another top sight in former West Berlin is the **Olympiastadion**, built by Hitler to host the Olympic Games in 1936, which brings home how much of Berlin's architecture helped to reinforce the Nazi hold on power.

The towering **Brandenburger Tor** (Brandenburg Gate), which stands between Str. des 17 Juni and Unter den Linden, was built in 1788–91 as a triumphal arch for Prussia's victorious armies. The Gate became a symbol of the divided Germany and was reopened in December 1989. Another powerful symbol stands just to the north: the **Reichstag**, built 1884–94 to house the imperial parliament, reopened in 1999 after a stunning restoration by Norman Foster. It is now the seat of the *Bundestag*, the Lower House of Parliament for the reunited Germany. You can climb to the top of the glass dome (for free) and look down into the building; there are also highly recommended tours.

Sections of the **Wall** can still be seen in a number of places including: Mühlenstr., a 1300 m section along the **River Spree**, Bernauer Str. at the corner of Eberswalderstr., where you will find the entrance to **Berlin Wall Park,** and Niederkirchnerstr. at the **Martin Gropius Building,** where one of the most sensational escapes took place. **Checkpoint Charlie**, the Berlin Wall crossing point is close to the **Checkpoint Charlie Museum**, Friedrichstr. 44 (U-Bahn: KOCHSTR. or STADTMITTE), which relates the history of the Wall and the numerous attempts to escape.

TOURS

The **Original Berlin Walks**
☎ (030) 301 9194
(www.berlinwalks.com;
berlinwalks@berlin.de) run an excellent daily programme of walking tours with English-speaking guides, cost €10 or €15 depending on tour (discount with WelcomeCard; free for under 14s) and starting from the taxi rank at Zoo station (no booking required). The themes covered are Discover Berlin, Jewish Life in Berlin, Discover Potsdam, Infamous Third Reich Sites and the Sachsenhausen Concentration Camp.

GERMANY

East of the Brandenburg Gate stretches Unter den Linden, an attractive wide boule-vard which has regained its former status as one of Berlin's principal thoroughfares. It features a large number of well restored, monumental public buildings and smart shops and restaurants. Just beyond this street's eastern end is the **Berliner Dom**, the city's baroque cathedral. From here take the Rathausbrücke, past **Palast der Republik** to Rathausstr. On the right is the restored 15th-century twin-towered **Nikolaikirche**, Berlin's oldest building. The **Rotes Rathaus** (Red Town Hall, so-called on account of its bricks) leads to the base of the **Fernsehturm** (TV tower). This 368-m spike, Berlin's tallest building, includes a globe-shaped revolving restaurant and viewing gallery at 203 m.

'Museum Island' or **Museumsinsel**, on the **River Spree**, is home to outstanding museums, including the great archaeological collections at the **Pergamon-Museum** and the **Altes Museum**, and Expressionism and other 19th-century art at the **Alte National Galerie**. These close on Monday.

Heading north from Museum Island, you soon come to an area completely different in character to the prosperous wide roads of west Berlin. A stroll around the **north Mitte** area soon brings home the divisions between the two sides of Berlin in terms of prosperity and comfort. There are a number of sights of interest including the **Neue Synagogue** (not in fact new at all but dating from the 1860s) and the **Sophienkirche** but far more fascinating are the streets themselves which tell the story of how far Soviet-controlled East Germany was stripped of investment and progress. Meanwhile the **Jüdisches Museum Berlin** (**Berlin Jewish Museum**) Lindenstr. chronicles the tragic history of the German Jewish community (closed Jewish holidays).

Further flung sites worth heading for include the **Dahlem Museums** (U-Bahn: DAHLEM-DORF); closed Mon, a complex of seven quite outstanding fine art museums, including medieval and Renaissance works and oriental collections; and the lakes of the **Havel** and the forest of **Grunewald**, which offer plenty of scope for relaxation.

MUSEUM PASS
A three-day Museum Pass, **SchauLUST MuseenBERLIN** (from main Tourist Offices, €8) is valid for over 50 of Berlin's museums and collections, including all national and state museums.

DAY TRIP TO POTSDAM **Potsdam** is an eye-opening array of landscaped gardens and palaces, 30 km south-west of Berlin (S-Bahn: POTSDAM-HAUPTBAHNHOF from Zoo, Ostbahnhof or Friedrichstr., taking about 20 mins). The seat of the Hohenzollern kings in the late 17th century and now a UNESCO World Heritage Site, it is best known for the compact rococo **Sanssouci Palace** (1745–47) set in the huge Park Sanssouci. Arrive early to ensure a place on the guided tours. A leisurely walk through the park reveals the breathtaking **Chinese Tea House** (1754–57), the pagoda-like **Drachenhaus**, **Schloss Charlottenhof** and the so-called **Romische Bader** (Roman Baths).

SHOPPING

Berlin is becoming much better for shopping, though prices are generally high. The West still has greater variety and includes Berlin's chief shopping boulevard **Ku'damm**, 3.5 km of boutiques, department stores, cafés, shopping malls and the **Europa-Center** shopping complex. Some of the most expensive and chic fashion houses can be found on Ku'damm between Bleibtreustr. and Olivaer Pl. The giant **KaDeWe** on Wittenbergpl. has long been a temple to Berlin's consumer society, but the new **Arkaden** (The Arcades) shopping complex at Potsdamer Pl. is fast becoming another mecca for shopaholics. Friedrichstr. in the former East, historically the city's premier shopping street, has regained its former status as one of Berlin's premier shopping streets. However, also of appeal are the numerous small, innovative shops and galleries in the heart of the Mitte district around Hackeshe Höfe.

The central food market is at **Winterfeldtplatz**, Schöneberg (Wed and Sat, 0800–1400; U-Bahn: Nollendorfplatz). Covered markets can be found on **Marheinekeplatz**, Kreuzberg; **Ackerstr., Mitte** and **Arminiusstr.**, Tiergarten. On Saturday and Sunday between 1000 and 1700 the Strasse des 17 Juni becomes one long stretch of market stalls selling everything – antiques, cheap modern jewellery, CDs, books, snacks and clothes; it's a fun way to pass a weekend morning or afternoon.

NIGHT-TIME AND EVENTS

Berlin has a well-deserved reputation for diverse and non-stop entertainment. There are two listings magazines: *Zitty* and *Tip*, available from newsagents. The quarterly *Das Berlin Magazin*, available from tourist information offices and newsagents, also covers entertainment and events. **Oranienstrasse**, in the **Kreuzberg** district, is the heart of a busy **club and music bar scene**. East Berlin has become the centre of the vibrant youth culture of the city. The streets in the north of the Mitte host a wide selection of small clubs and bars often featuring live music. Berlin usually features on the tour schedules of most rock, pop and other modern music groups.

Berlin boasts a large number of cinemas ranging from multiplexes showing the latest Hollywood blockbusters to smaller venues with avant garde films. Check to see whether films are shown with subtitles or have been dubbed into German. Classical concerts are held at **Philharmonie und Kammermusiksaal der Philharmonie** (the home of the world-famous Berlin Philharmonic Orchestra, for which tickets are extremely hard to get), Herbert-von-Karajan-Str. 1, ☎ (030) 254 88-0 (www.berlin-philharmonic.com) and **Konzerthaus Berlin**, Gendarmenmarkt 2, ☎ (030) 2030 92101/2 (www.konzerthaus.de).

GERMANY: HAMBURG

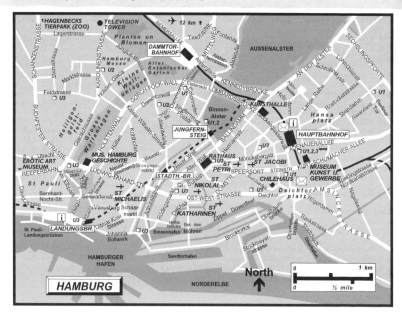

Germany's largest seaport and the country's media capital, Hamburg is one of the most sophisticated and cosmopolitan German cities and is an invigorating place to visit – both as a stopping-off point on the way to Scandinavia and in its own right. Although comprehensively destroyed in turn by fire in 1842 and by World War II bombing, it has a special watery character of its own, with some enjoyable boat trips on offer in the Binnenalster and Aussenalster lakes and into the massive working port area. One of the main streets, the Jungfernstieg, resembles something of a seaside promenade, while six soaring green copper spires impose themselves on the skyline over the rebuilt historic centre, the numerous parks and the canals. Entertainment and nightlife ranges from the famously sleazy Reeperbahn to the musical offerings of the opera company and the city's resident orchestras.

Hamburg is Germany's second largest city, after Berlin, and also a federal state with its own parliament. The city's prominence as a port dates from the 12th century, with Hamburg becoming a member of the Hanseatic League in 1321, making it one of the most powerful and wealthy free cities in Europe. Hamburg is also a gateway for onward travel by ferry to ports in the UK, Denmark, Sweden and Norway.

The **Hamburg Card** includes free travel on public transport, free or reduced admission to museums, and reductions of up to 30% on sightseeing, lake and harbour tours.

A **one-day card** and a **three-day card** are available. For under 30s there is the cheaper **Power Pass** (one-day plus up to seven additional days), offering similar deals as well as vouchers for free drinks and reductions at cinemas, pubs and discos.

TOURIST OFFICES

Main office: Steinstr. 7, 20095 Hamburg ☎ (040) 300 51-0, fax (040) 300 51-220 (www.hamburg-tourism.de; info@hamburg-tourism.de). Other Tourist Offices are at **Hauptbahnhof** (by the Kirchenallee exit), and at the Port, between Pier 4 and 5 on the **St-Pauli-Landungsbrücken**, at the **airport** (terminal 4 arrivals), at the **Hamburg Musikhalle** ticket office (Johannes-Brahms-Platz) and at **Dammtor** ticket office. A **hotline** for information, hotel reservations, tickets etc. operates daily throughout the year 0800–2000; ☎ (040) 300 51 300 or (040) 300 51 800.

ARRIVAL AND DEPARTURE

🚃 The **Hauptbahnhof** (**Hbf**) handles most long-distance trains. Huge, central and on the U-Bahn. Houses the main post office and a wonderfully cosmopolitan selection of eateries. The station's main exit is on Kirchenallee. **Altona**, in the west of the city, is the terminal for most trains serving **Schleswig-Holstein**. **Dammtor**, north of the centre, is mostly for convention traffic and is therefore unlikely to be of much interest to tourists. **Rail information:** ☎ (01805) 99 66 33 or (040) 19419. Frequent S-Bahn trains link the three stations.

🚢 **Landungsbrücken**, Brücke 9, ☎ (040) 38 90 30 (2 km from St Pauli), is the terminal for ferries from the UK (**DFDS Seaways**) and Scandinavia.

✈ **Hamburg-Fuhlsbüttel**, ☎ (040) 50 750, is 8 km from town centre. The **Airport Express** bus to the Hauptbahnhof takes 25 mins. It runs every 20 mins, 0630–2250. In the opposite direction it runs 0530–2120. The **HVV-Airport Express** bus 110 runs every 10 mins from U-Bahn station OHLSDORF.

INFORMATION

Get the free *City Map and Tips from A–Z*, also *St Pauli Tips from A-Z*, plus *Top Info* magazine, which include a map of the city rail system, full details of Hamburg travel cards and an outline guide to the city's attractions from the **main Tourist Office**.

POST AND PHONES The main post office is at Münzstr. 1, open Mon–Fri 0700–1900, Sat 0900–1200. At the main railway station, at Hachmannpl. 13, the post office is open Mon–Fri 0800–2000, Sat 0900–1800, Sun 1000–1800.

PUBLIC TRANSPORT

The main area of interest is small enough to be walkable. **HVV** (Hamburg Transit Authority) run efficient buses, U-Bahn (underground) and S-Bahn (urban trains), as well as a night bus service to most city districts.

ACCOMMODATION

Accommodation can be booked through the Tourist Office booking service: **Tourismus-Zentrale Hamburg GmbH**, Postfach 10 22 49, 20015 Hamburg, ☎(040) 300 51 351, or through the main website or hotline phone number (see p. 253). **Rooms in private homes** can be booked through **Privatzimmervermittlung** 'Bed & Breakfast', Müggenkampstr. 59, Hamburg 20257, ☎(040) 49 15 666, and **Agentur Zimmer Frei**, Semperstr. 16, ☎(040) 27 87 77 77.

Cheaper **hotel-pensions** in the central area include: **Von Blumfeld**, Lange Reihe 54, ☎(040) 245 860, €; **Sarah Petersen**, Lange Reihe 50, ☎(040) 249826, €€–€€€; **Schmidt**, Holzdamm 14, ☎(040) 2802119, €€; **Stern**, Reeperbahn 154, ☎(040) 317 69990, €; **Selig u. Abromeit**, Bremer Reihe 23, ☎(040) 24 4689, €; **Terminus**, Steindamm 5, ☎(040) 280 3144, €; **Annenhof**, Lange Reihe 23, ☎(040) 243 426, €; **Kieler Hof**, Bremer Reihe 15, ☎ (040) 24 3024, €.

The **HI youth hostels** are: **Jugendherberge Auf dem Stintfang**, Alfred-Wegener-Weg 5, ☎(040) 3134 88 (jh-stintfang@t-online.de), central (U/S-Bahn: Landungsbrücken); and **Jugendgästehaus Hamburg**, 'Horner Rennbahn', Rennbahnstr. 100, ☎(040) 6511671 (jgh-hamburg@t-online.de), in the eastern suburbs (U-Bahn: Horner Rennbahn).

There are several non-HI hostels. **CVJM Young Hotel (YMCA)**, Kurt-Schumacher-Allee 14, ☎(040) 419230 is near the station; proceeds go to funding social projects in the city. **Jugendgästehaus Woge in Ottensen**, Kleine Rainstr. 24–26, ☎(040) 31919191 (info@woge.net) is 500 m from Altona station; singles, doubles and quads. **Schanzenstern**, Bartelsstr. 12, ☎(040) 439 8441 (info@schanzenstern.de) has beds starting from around €17 (S-Bahn 21/31 to Sternschanze). In the lively Schanzenviertel area is **Backpacker Hostel Instant Sleep**, Max-Brauer-Allee 277, ☎ (040) 4318 2310 (backpackerhostel@instantsleep.de) has dorms from around €15 (open 24 hrs). Located by a park, **Europa Gästehaus**, Horner Landstr. 85, ☎(040) 659 0880 (europagh@t-online.de) in the Horn district (U-Bahn 3: Rauhes Haus).

FOOD AND DRINK

Hamburg's cosmopolitan nature is reflected in its restaurants, with some of the best fine dining in Germany. Seafood and fish are, of course, a speciality. Prices tend to reflect the areas in which they are located, but the places in **Rathausmarkt** are not exorbitant and it's a good place to watch the world go by. **Kirchenallee, Altona, Univiertel** and **Schanzenviertel** are cheap eating areas.

HIGHLIGHTS

The oldest part of the city, which survived the great fire of 1842 and carpet bombing

TOURS

The city is dominated by water and a boat-trip is part of the experience. **Hadag**, ☎(040) 311 70713, is one of the companies that run daily English-language harbour tours Mar–Oct/Nov, departing from St Pauli-Landungsbrücken, Brücke 1; ☎(040) 564 523. Divided into the Binnen-(inner) and Aussen- (outer) alster, this 455-hectare stretch of water contributes to the city's relaxed, open-air ambience. The shortest Alster cruise takes about an hour, looping through the inner and outer lakes, but there are longer inland voyages like the 3-hour trip to Bergedorf or the pretty summer twilight cruise through the backwater canals. For trips around the harbour and further afield, boats depart from Landungsbrücken piers 1–9, daily every 30 mins from 0900–1800 (Apr–Oct), and hourly from 1030–1630 (Nov–Mar). The **Hummelbahn Train** is a 1920s-style train with multilingual guides that covers the major sights (weekends only Nov–Mar); ☎(040) 792 8979. There are a number of walking tours in summer (ask at the Tourist Office for details). These feature the warehouse district, the St Pauli district, and a tour of the city highlights.

by the Allies in World War II, is around the harbour, where two **museum ships** are moored: the tall ship **Rickmer Rickmers** at **Pier 1** and the more modern **Cap San Diego** at the **Überseebrücke**. **Speicherstadt**, just east of the docks, is a district of early 20th-century red-brick gabled warehouses, between Deichtorhallen and Baumwall. **Blankenese**, reached from St Pauli by ferry, has something of the character of a fishing village with its maze of alleys and steps.

The neo-Renaissance **Rathaus** (Town Hall), Marktpl. (U-Bahn: RATHAUS), is a magnificent sandstone building constructed 1886–97. Some of its 647 rooms, which can be toured when government is not in session, are adorned with tapestries, chandeliers and paintings. Tours are conducted in English daily; for details ☎(040) 428 312 470. The **Rathaus Tower** is one of six towers dominating the city's skyline, the others belonging to churches, the most impressive of which is **St Michaelis**, Krayenkamp 4C (U- or S-Bahn: LANDUNGSBRÜCKEN), a 132-m high baroque structure with a crypt and a viewing level at 82 m, which gives panoramic views. This is the city's symbol and a trumpet solo is played from the tower every day.

Hamburg has a good range of museums, some of which are usually closed on Mon, with late night opening on Thur. Foremost is the **Kunsthalle**, Glockengiesserwall 1 (U- or S-Bahn: HBF) with a superb international art collection that dates from the Gothic period to the present day (Tues–Sun). It includes a choice selection of German works, including the Grabow Altarpiece of 1379, its 24 panels constituting one of the greatest triumphs of the North German Primitive style. This is complemented by the modern works in the **Kunstverein**, Klosterwall 23 (U-Bahn: STEINSTR.; Tues–Sun). **Museum für Kunst und Gewerbe**, Steintorpl. 1 (U- or S-Bahn: HBF), is the museum of arts and crafts with an excellent range of art from ancient Egypt, Greece and Rome, along with medieval works, art nouveau and modern art (Tues–Sun).

Elsewhere you can delve into the city's history at the **Museum für Hamburgische Geschichte**, Holstenwall 24 (U-Bahn: ST PAULI) or experience 500 years' worth of erotica at the **Erotic Art Museum**, Nobistor 10a (S-Bahn: REEPERBAHN).

Hamburg's tallest building, the 280-m **TV Tower**, Lagerstr. 2–8 (U-Bahn: MESSEHALLEN) has a viewing platform (open daily 1000–2300) and a revolving restaurant. Just below is **Planten un Blomen** (U-Bahn: STEPHANSPL.; S-Bahn: DAMMTOR), the city's largest park, with a vast Japanese garden and illuminated fountain displays and concerts on summer nights (May– Sept).

SHOPPING

Rathausmarkt and Gänsemarkt is the **main shopping area**, easily covered on foot. Shops along Neuer Wall specialise in furniture and interiors, while the **Quartier Satin**, on the ABC-Strasse, is the place for designer names and antiques. **Colonnaden**, a delightful pedestrianised colonnade just off Jungfernstieg, has pavement cafés alongside designer shops, together with specialist tobacco, tea and coffee shops. Leading east from Rathausmarkt is the city's longest shopping street, the Mönckebergstr.; a lively mix of small shops, cafés, noble restaurants and large department stores.

NIGHT-TIME AND EVENTS

Local nightlife is cosmopolitan, to say the least. In the **St Pauli** quarter, north of the Elbe riverfront, raunchy sex-show clubs tout their delights next to casinos, discos, tattoo parlours and some of Hamburg's best restaurants. The Reeperbahn, St Pauli's main drag, has been going strong for generations, though there is now an element of gentrification, with a growing number of bars popular with the bohemian and media set. The **DOM Amusement Fair** is open three times a year in the Heiligengeistfeld, from mid-Mar to mid-Apr, mid-July to mid-Aug, and early Nov to early Dec.

A good way to get to the city's various disco and club locations is on the **Nightcruiser** 🚌 lines 620 and 630. These special night buses run every 15 mins 2200–0400 from Fri to Sat, and Sat to Sun. They depart from Rathausmarkt and make a circuit via the Reeperbahn and Altona/Bahrenfeld. On the buses a genuine disco-feeling is provided by a stereo sound system, bar and light show.

WHERE NEXT FROM HAMBURG?

Onward travel by train to Denmark/Copenhagen (ETT table 50; 4 hrs 30 mins; 4 trains daily) is popular. Trains have a small number of carriages and limited places so early booking is advisable, especially at weekends in the summer. The train spends about 30 minutes of the journey loaded on a ferry.

Although there's virtually nothing medieval remaining in the centre, Bavaria's sophisticated and cosmopolitan capital is many people's favourite German city. It's easy to see why: the city exudes a sense of space and greenery, and you soon get caught up in its laid-back approach to life, noticeable particularly among the crowds of all ages out enjoying themselves in its many beer halls, pavement cafés and gardens, and in the student haunts and fringe theatres of the Schwabing area. Only the *Föhn*, a dry wind blowing from the mountains, tempers the local sense of fun.

TOURIST OFFICES

Administrative Office: **Fremdenverkehrsamt München**, SENDLINGER STR. 1, 80313 MÜNCHEN; ☎ (089) 233 03 00, fax (089) 23 33 02 33 (www.muenchen-tourist.de; tourismus@ ems.muenchen.de).
Main Tourist Office: BAHNHOFPL. 2, outside the main railway station.
Branch: City centre in the **Rathaus**, MARIENPL. 2. There is a central telephone number and fax number (as above for administrative office).

ARRIVAL AND DEPARTURE

[RAIL] **München Hauptbahnhof (Hbf)**, BAHNHOFPL. (about 15 mins' walk straight ahead to MARIENPL. in the centre) is Munich's main railway station, and southern Germany's most important rail junction, with connections into southern, central and south-east Europe. Timetable information: ☎ (01805) 99 66 33.

✈ Munich's ultra-modern **Franz Josef Strauss Airport** is Germany's second international hub (after Frankfurt). Flight information: ☎ (089) 97 52 1313. S-Bahn lines S1 and S8 run every 10 mins from the rail station via the Ostbahnhof and city centre to the airport. For the city centre, get off at MARIENPL. Journey time from MARIENPL. to the airport is 44 mins by S1 and 38 mins by S8. Buses also run every 20 mins 0520–1950 between the airport and the rail station; journey time about 45 mins.

CITY MAP – inside back cover

INFORMATION

The main Tourist Office offers an accommodation service, hotel listing, city map and theatre bookings. Useful publications include *In München*, a free fortnightly listings magazine, *Monatsprogramm*, a monthly listing, and *Infopool: Young People's Guide*, what it says.

Tourist Offices sell the **Münchner Schlüssel** (Munich Key), a book of coupons which allows reduced entrance charges to museums, theatres, cinemas, restaurants and special attractions, together with a hotel booking, city transport ticket and suggestions to help you plan your visit. Price per night depends on hotel.

POST AND PHONES   The **main post office** is at BAHNHOFSPL. 1, just across from the the main rail station, with poste restante, money exchange and long-distance telephone calling facilities, all open 24 hrs.

PUBLIC TRANSPORT

The city centre, pedestrianised apart from trams and cycles, is easy to explore on foot, being only a 20-min walk across. For trips further afield, use the excellent public transport system of buses, trams and trains: **S-Bahn** (overground) and **U-Bahn** (underground). Nowhere is more than a few mins' walk from a stop or station; all transport runs 0430–0200. Further information from **MVV** (city transport authority), THIERSCHSTR. 2, ☎(089) 41 42 43 44.

TICKETS

City transport tickets can be used on trains, buses or trams; they must be validated in the blue box the first time you board, or you are liable to be fined on the spot. Buy them at stations, newsagents, hotel desks and campsites (single and strip tickets can also be bought on board buses and trams). **Single ticket** price depends on the number of zones: short trip, I zone, 2 zones, 3 zones, 4 zones or 5 zones are available. A **Streifenkarte** (a strip of I0 tickets) is the best value. A **Tageskarte** (day trip ticket offering unlimited use of the system) for inner Munich is valid from the time it is stamped till 0600 the following morning.

Obtain information on S-Bahn routes, tickets and timetables from **MVV**. The city also has an impressive 11,000 km of cycle paths. Bicycle hire at Radius Radverleih at the rail station (platforms 30–36); ☎(089) 59 61 13 (Apr–Oct). Daily walking tours (in English) start from the rail station at 1000. For a tour with a knowledgeable English-speaking guide, try one of the **Original Munich Walks**, ☎0177 227 5901 (info@munichwalks.com).

Official taxis are cream-coloured, usually a Mercedes, and are plentiful and reliable; ☎(089) 21 61 0.

ACCOMMODATION

Finding accommodation is rarely a problem except during the city's biggest tourist attractions, the annual Oktoberfest beer festival (Sept–Oct) and Fasching, the Bacchanalian carnival which precedes Ash Wednesday.

The biggest choice of hotels is around the rail station in streets like SCHILLERSTR. and SENEFELDERSTR.; it's a rather drab area but handy for the centre. Mid-range ones there include **Hotel Haberstock**, SCHILLERSTR. 4, ☎(089) 557 855, €, and **Hotel Senefelder**, SENEFELDERSTR. 4, ☎(089) 551 540, €. Other moderately priced hotels include **Hotel Andi**, LANDWEHRSTR. 33, ☎(089) 552 5560, €€; **Hotel Arosa**, HOTTERSTR. 2, ☎(089) 267 087, €€; **Hotel Brunnenhof**, SCHILLERSTR. 36, ☎(089) 545 100, €€; and **Hotel Herzog**, HÄBERLSTR. 9, ☎(089) 530 495, €€.

Budget accommodation in Munich is in plentiful supply with several **youth hostels**, including **Jugendherberge München**, WENDL-DIETRICH-STR. 20, ☎(089) 131 156, fax (089) 167 8745, with 380 beds (U-Bahn 1 to ROTKREUZPL.) and **DJH-Jugendgästehaus**, MIESINGSTR. 4, ☎(089) 723 6550, fax (089) 724 2567. A useful non-HI option open 24 hrs and just 50 m from the main station is **Euro Youth Hostel**, Senefelderstr. 5, ☎(089) 5990 8811 (info@euro-youth-hotel.de), with singles, doubles and 3–5 bed rooms, some with private bathroom; breakfast buffet; prices range from €17.50 for a dorm to €45 for a single with private bathroom. There are also several hostels outside the city limits easily accessible by public transport. An interesting last resort in summer is **Das Zelt** ('The Tent'), KAPUZINERHÖLZL, IN DEN KIRSCHEN 30, ☎(089) 1414 300 (www.the-tent.de), a marquee in the Botanischer Garten, where €8 gets you floor space. Facilities include washing machines, lockers and bicycle rental.

The city's biggest **campsite** is **München Thalkirchen**, ZENTRALLANDSTR. 49, ☎(089) 723 17 07, open Mar–Oct (U-Bahn 3 to THALKIRCHEN).

FOOD AND DRINK

Good eating areas include SCHWABING, GÄRTNERPL. and, across the River Isar, HAIDHAUSEN. An entertaining place for cheap snacks is the open-air **Viktualienmarkt**, a food market where a score of traditional taverns dispense beer, schnapps, sausage and soup – look out particularly for the tasty *Schwarzwaldschinken* (Black Forest smoked ham), black on the outside and red inside. The city's favourite titbit, particularly popular for mid-morning second breakfast washed down with beer, is the *Weisswurst*, a boiled white sausage flavoured with herbs and spices.

Munich is famous for its bread, but even more for its **beers**. The main varieties are *Helles* (normal), *Dunkeles* (dark) and the cloudy orange-coloured *Weissbier* made from wheat instead of hops. There are beer halls and gardens all over the city; the touristy **Hofbräuhaus**, AM PLATZL 9, is where Hitler launched the Nazi party in 1920. **Augustiner Gaststätten**, NEUHAUSERSTR. 27, is the home of Munich's oldest brewery. In traditional beer gardens, you can bring your own food. (Two useful bits of trivia: first, beer gardens always have chestnut trees, and are shown on maps by tree symbols; second, beer gardens have tables with and without table cloths – you only get served at your table if it has a cloth.) Snacks at beer halls and beer gardens include salted mackerel, giant pretzels, radish spirals and cheese. The city's largest beer garden is by the Chinesischer Turm (Pagoda) in the Englischer Garten.

HIGHLIGHTS

Right at the hub of the pedestrianised city centre, the **Glockenspiel** (with its host of jousting knights, among others) of the clock of the **Neues Rathaus** (New Town Hall) performs (at 1100, 1200 and 1700) to the shoppers, buskers and sightseers on the MARIENPL. (U and S-Bahn: MARIENPL.), Munich's main square. And across MARIENPL., the less prominent medieval **Altes Rathaus** (Old Town Hall) houses a small toy museum, while just to the west rise the twin onion domes of the 15th-century **Frauenkirche** (cathedral), FRAUENPL. Facing the Altes Rathaus is **Alter Peter** (Old St Peter's church), inside which is the strange skeleton of St Munditia, wearing

GERMANY

MUNICH'S EVENTS

The world-famous **Oktoberfest** actually begins in Sept, and lasts 16 days, with beer and barbecued chicken the accompaniment to Bavarian band music, amusements and sideshows. It takes place in the THERESIENWIESE, south-west of the rail station (U-Bahn 4/5 to THERESIENWIESE). The year begins with a lively carnival known as the **Fasching**, with masked balls as well as dancing through the streets.

a jewel-laden shroud and bearing a quill pen.

From here, it's a very short stroll northwards into MAX-JOSEPHPL., to the vast **Residenz** (U-Bahn: ODEONSPL.), the baroque palace of Bavaria's Wittelsbach rulers – faithfully rebuilt after bomb destruction. As it's almost a bit too much to take in, different parts of the building are open in the morning and in the afternoon. The highlights include the vaulted, statue-filled Antiquarium, and the Schatzkammer (Treasury) with its dazzling collection of jewellery, gold and silver amassed by the Wittelsbachs. It ís worth the separate admission for the Cuvilliés Theater, a rococo gem that's still used for theatrical performances. A few steps on from here, ODEONSPL. is Munich's stateliest streetscape, an admirable example of post-war reconstruction. Beside ODEONSPL. are the manicured lawns and flowerbeds of the **Hofgarten** park. To the north-east, the **Englischer Garten** (named because of its informal landscaping) is Europe's biggest city park, popular for the beer garden at its **Chinesischer Turm** (Pagoda) and the naturist meadow beside the **River Isar**.

West of the city centre is **Schloss Nymphenburg** (U-Bahn: ROTKREUZPL. then change to tram 17), the summer palace of the Wittelsbachs. The wonder of it is its parkland, with numerous lakes, varied gardens, pavilions and hunting lodges, including the **Magdelenklause**, a folly built in the form of a hermit's grotto.

SHOPPING

The main shopping area is the wide traffic-free roadway from KARLSPL. to MARIENPL., a mixture of department stores, supermarkets and fashion shops, but the city's most elegant designer boutiques are along THEATINERSTR. and MAXIMILIANSTR.

From late Nov to Christmas Eve, the **Christkindlmarkt** (Christ-Child Market) is held on MARIENPL.

The collection of art in Munich's leading museum, the **Alte Pinakothek**, BARER-STR. 27 (U-Bahn: THERESIENSTR.), is among the world's top six. It includes 65 paintings by Rubens, a small but priceless collection of Italian works and an unrivalled collection of great German masters. For something specially Bavarian, seek out the **Bayerisches Nationalmuseum**, PRINZREGENTENSTR. (🚌 no. 53 from ODEONSPL.), with its carvings by the medieval master Tilman Riemenschneider, and an enchanting collection (the world's largest) of nativity tableaux in the basement.

NIGHT-TIME AND EVENTS

The monthly *Monatsprogramm* lists all kinds of events, from live music to art exhibitions. An English-language magazine *Munich Found*, published monthly, contains up-to-date news on entertainment, restaurants and the like.

The many **rock, jazz and blues bars** provide a venue for and visiting bands. The city's liveliest area is **Schwabing**, north of the university. Streets there such as LEOPOLDSTR., AMALIENSTR. and TÜRKENSTR. are famous for their many bars, cafés and jazz cellars. Plenty of discos can be found around **Gärtnerpl.**, which is also the city's gay area. At the **Kunstpark Ost**, near OSTBAHNHOF, old warehouses have been converted into bars and nightclubs.

Several cinemas show English-language films; these are advertised in newspapers as *OmU* films. The **Bavarian State Opera** performs at the **Nationaltheater**, MAX-JOSEPH-PL. 2; ☎2185 1919. **Staatstheater**, GÄRTNERPL. 3; ☎2185 1960, stages opera, ballet and classical concerts. The ultra-modern **Gasteig Kulturzentrum**, ROSENHEIMSTR. 5, ☎480 980, is three concert halls high on the right bank of the Isar.

WHERE NEXT FROM MUNICH?

In addition to following the routes to **Berlin** (p. 245), **Verona** (p. 400) and **Frankfurt** (p. 276), you can take international services to **Ostend** via **Brussels** (ETT table 21), **Amsterdam** (table 28), **Paris** (table 32), **Budapest** (table 61), **Bucharest** (table 61), **Belgrade** (table 61), **Ljubljana** (table 62), **Vienna** via **Salzburg** (table 67), **Rome** (table 70) and **Geneva** via **Zürich** (table 75).

DACHAU

Fourteen miles north-west of Munich, on the edge of the town of Dachau, the Nazis' first concentration camp has been turned into a memorial, known as the KZ Gedenkstätte (free entry). It commemorates the 35,000 inmates, mostly Jews, who died there between 1933 and 1945. Its former administration block is now a thought-provoking museum, with an audiovisual presentation, in English at certain times of day. (S-Bahn 2 from the rail station to DACHAU; then 🚌 no. 726 to the Memorial.) The town itself retains a surprisingly pleasant old centre with an attractive Hofgarten (castle garden) on a terrace high above the river.

NIGHT-TIME AND EVENTS   261

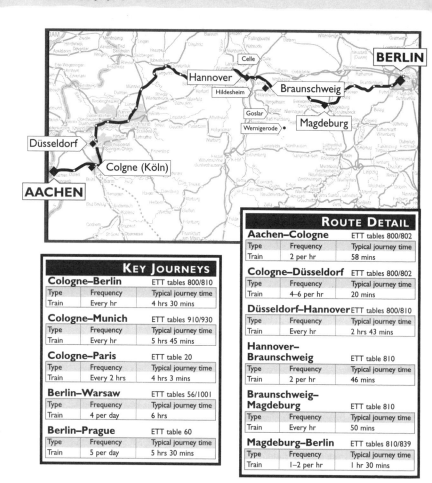

KEY JOURNEYS

Cologne–Berlin
ETT tables 800/810

Type	Frequency	Typical journey time
Train	Every hr	4 hrs 30 mins

Cologne–Munich
ETT tables 910/930

Type	Frequency	Typical journey time
Train	Every hr	5 hrs 45 mins

Cologne–Paris
ETT table 20

Type	Frequency	Typical journey time
Train	Every 2 hrs	4 hrs 3 mins

Berlin–Warsaw
ETT tables 56/1001

Type	Frequency	Typical journey time
Train	4 per day	6 hrs

Berlin–Prague
ETT table 60

Type	Frequency	Typical journey time
Train	5 per day	5 hrs 30 mins

ROUTE DETAIL

Aachen–Cologne
ETT tables 800/802

Type	Frequency	Typical journey time
Train	2 per hr	58 mins

Cologne–Düsseldorf
ETT tables 800/802

Type	Frequency	Typical journey time
Train	4–6 per hr	20 mins

Düsseldorf–Hannover
ETT tables 800/810

Type	Frequency	Typical journey time
Train	Every hr	2 hrs 43 mins

Hannover–Braunschweig
ETT table 810

Type	Frequency	Typical journey time
Train	2 per hr	46 mins

Braunschweig–Magdeburg
ETT table 810

Type	Frequency	Typical journey time
Train	Every hr	50 mins

Magdeburg–Berlin
ETT tables 810/839

Type	Frequency	Typical journey time
Train	1–2 per hr	1 hr 30 mins

For the most part, it's the man-made aspects that lend this journey its character, as for much of the way you're travelling over the flat farmlands of the north German plain. From the Belgian border to the German capital, the route heads out from the frontier post of Aachen, past Cologne with its great cathedral and through the industrial heartland of the Ruhr. At Osnabrück there is the option of striking out northwards to Bremen, Hamburg, Lübeck and into Denmark; otherwise carry on east through Hannover, diverting southwards to the old towns of Goslar and Wernigerode in the Harz Mountains – with the chance to ride the area's narrow-gauge railways.

AACHEN

Now important only as a frontier town between Belgium and Germany, Aachen was a great city more than 1000 years ago, when the Emperor Charlemagne the Great enjoyed the thermal springs and made it the capital of his revived empire. His octagonal chapel is now the heart of the **Dom** (cathedral), built on the site of the imperial palace. Some of the original structure survives and his successors added many embellishments. Charlemagne's gilded tomb is here and you can see the imperial throne by joining a guided tour.

The **Schatzkammer** (Treasury) is one of Europe's most dazzling, with such priceless objects as a gold bust of Charlemagne and a jewel-encrusted 10th-century cross. Statues of 50 Holy Roman Emperors adorn the façade of the 14th-century **Rathaus** (Town Hall), which incorporates two of the original palace towers. Inside are replicas of Charlemagne's crown jewels (the originals are in Vienna).

Three other indoor sights to seek out are the **Ludwig Forum für Internationale Kunst** (JÜLICHER STR.), with its excellent collection of **East European art**; the unique **International Press Museum** (PONTSTR. 13) that acts as the 'registry office' of the world's press (in that it contains not only specimen copies, but also first, jubilee and final editions from every publication of the international press): and the **Aachen Computer Museum** (SOMMERFELDSTR. 32; free entry) charts the evolution from the earliest data processing to modern PCs.

A spa town, Aachen also has several places to unwind in the thermal waters, including the new **Carolus Thermen**, PASSSTRASSE. 79, ☎ (0241) 182740, and the **Kurbad Quellenhof**, MONHEIMSALLEE 52, ☎ (0241) 180 29 22.

RAIL REUMONTSTR. 1, about 1 km from the city centre.

i **Tourist Office**: in the centre at ELISENBRUNNEN, FRIEDRICH WILHELM PL., ☎ (0241) 19433 (www.aachen-tourist.de; info@aachen-tourist.de). The tourist office operates a hotel booking service, ☎ (0241) 1 80 29 50 or (0241) 1 80 29 51, fax (0241) 1 80 29 30 (Mon–Fri 0900–1800, Sat 0900–1400). Daily guided tours throughout the year start from the Tourist Office.

🛏 Medium-priced **hotels** include **Hotel-Restaurant Forthaus Schöntal**, KORNELIMÜNSTERWEG 1, ☎(0241) 601 459, €€, with singles beginning at around €40, and the **Hotel Marx**, HUBERTUSSTR. 33–35, ☎(0241) 37 541, €. The **youth hostel** is out of town at MARIA-THERESIA ALLEE 260, ☎(0241) 71 1010, 🚌no. 2 from Aachen Central station, direction PREUSWALD, stop RHONHEIDE. The nearest **campsite** is **Camping Hoeve de Gastmolen**, 7 kms west of the centre at **Vaals** in the Netherlands, ☎(0031) (43) 306 5755.

COLOGNE (KÖLN)

See p. 273.

The 60,000-year-old skeleton of what has come to be known as **Neanderthal man** was found in the **Düssel Valley** (also known by the local name of Neandertal) outside Düsseldorf. The city has recently opened a **Neanderthal Museum**, TALSTR. 300, Mettmann (www.neanderthal.de.) – a communications and documentation centre delving into the early history of mankind.

DÜSSELDORF

Originally a centre of heavy industry, Düsseldorf is now decidedly upmarket, its transition exemplified by the KÖNIGSALLEE (generally termed the 'KÖ'), one of the most elegant shopping streets in Germany. Primarily Düsseldorf breathes money, and is aptly dominated by four modern monuments as testament to its commercial success: the new **Stadttor**, the **Thyssen Skyscraper**, **Mannesmann Haus** and the **Rhine Tower**.

Most of the areas of interest are along the Rhine, itself spanned by the graceful **Rheinkniebrücke** (bridge) and with the **Rhine Tower** prominent on the skyline. Marked by the SCHLOSS-

The Romantic poet **Heinrich Heine** is Düsseldorf's most famous son, and his works are commemorated in the **Heinrich-Heine-Haus**, BILKERSTR. 12–14.

TURM, all that remains of the original 14th-century castle, the **Altstadt** (Old Town), is small and walkable, covering no more than 1 square km. Almost wholly demolished during World War II, it has been skilfully reconstructed. Within it is **Flingerstr.,** a quaint pedestrianised shopping precinct, somewhat more affordable than KÖNIGSALLEE. One of the most attractive corners is the **Marktpl.,** brimming over with outdoor cafés and restaurants. A pedestrian zone that's a hive of entertainment around the clock, Altstadt has more than 200 bars crammed into its busy streets and claims to be 'the longest bar in the world'. At GRABBEPL. 5 is the **Kunstsammlung Nordrhein-Westfalen,** a museum of modern art with nearly 100 works by Paul Klee.

🚆 About 2 km from the east bank of the Rhine, where most places of interest are concentrated.

ⓘ **Tourist Office**: IMMERMANNHOF 65B, ☎(0211)172 020, fax (0211) 161 071 (opposite main rail station). Room booking service.

🛏 **Youth hostel**: DÜSSELDORFER STR. 1, ☎(0211) 557 310; 6 km from the station; 🚌nos. 725/835/836.

HANNOVER (HANOVER)

Hannover is the ancestral home of the first four King Georges of England and capital of Lower Saxony. The best way of getting to know the city is to follow the '**Der Rote Faden**' ('the Red Thread', a red line painted on the pavement that goes along a 4200-m (2-hr) path through the city centre and can be followed on foot; free maps of it from the Tourist Office. A huge **Schützenfest** (folk festival), featuring fireworks and parades, takes place in July.

From the station, BAHNHOFSTR. leads to the KRÖPCKE PIAZZA, in the heart of the largely reconstructed **Altstadt**; the **Kröpcke clock** is the most popular rendezvous in town. For shopping, head for GEORGSTRASSE, GALERIE LUISE and KRÖPCKE-PASSAGE.

The high-gabled, carefully restored **Altes Rathaus** is a splendid edifice with elaborate brickwork. Alongside is **Marktkirche**, with 14th–15th-century stained glass and a bulky tower that is the city's emblem.

Across town, over the FRIEDRICHSWALL, is the high-domed **Neues Rathaus** located in a pleasant garden and reflected in a small lake. Next door, the **Kestner Museum,** TRAMMPL. 3, contains 'Hannover's most expensive head' (a 3000-year-old Egyptian bust). The wide-ranging **Landesmuseum**, WILLY-BRANDT-ALLEE 5, includes a fascinating archaeological section.

The absolute must-see is the **Royal Herrenhausen Garden**, 10 mins from KRÖPCKE (U-Bahn: HERRENHAUSERGARTEN). It consists of four once-royal gardens, two of which are the English-style landscaped **Georgengarten** and the formal **Grosser Garten**, the scene of spectacular fountain displays in summer. Frequent musical and theatrical performances are staged in the palace and gardens.

Central location; follow the red line to the information office. The Ernst-August Statue in front is a well-known landmark and meeting place.

Tourist Office: In the **Post Building**, ERNST-AUGUST-PL. 2 (next to Hbf), ☎(0511) 1684 9700, fax (0511) 1684 9707. Also at the **Hannover Tourism Center**, THEODOR-HEUSS-PL. 1–3 (www.hannover.de; hcc@hannover.de).

The Tourist Office can make room reservations at all budget levels, ☎(0511) 1684 9716, fax (0511) 1684 9709. Or contact the Reservation and Information Service of the **Tourismusverband Hannover Region**, ☎(0511) 3661 990, fax (0511) 3661 997 (www.tourismus.hannover.de). Many conventions take place here, so cheap accommodation is hard to find, although prices drop further away from the centre. The **youth hostel** (reservations advisable) is at FERDINAND-WILHELM-FRICKE-WEG 1, ☎(0511) 131 7674 (U-bahn: 3/7/9 to FISCHERHOF). Youth hostel-style accommodation at **Naturfreundehaus Eilenriede**, HERMANN-BAHLSEN-ALLEE 8, ☎(0511) 691493, Line 3 direction LAHE or Line 7, towards FASANENKRUG; bus stop SPANNHAGENGARTEN. Also at **Naturfreundehaus Misburg**, AM FAHRHORSTFELDE 50, ☎(0511) 580537, Line 4, direction RODERBRUCH, bus stop MISBURGER STR. then 🚌 no. 124 to the end station (WALDFRIEDHOF).

SIDE TRIPS FROM HANNOVER Celle (41 km north-east of Hannover; hourly trains, 20 mins, ETT table 904), overlooked by a magnificent 16th-century castle, rates among the best-preserved medieval towns in northern Germany. The **youth hostel** is at WEGHAUSSTR. 2, ☎(05141) 53208, while other room reservations can be made through the **Tourist Office**, MARKT 14–16, ☎(05141) 1212, fax (05141) 12459 (www.celle.de).

Hildesheim (35 mins by train; hourly service, ETT table 860), 36 km south-east of Hannover, has the 11th-century **Dom** and **Michaelskirche** (St Michael's Church), both UNESCO World Heritage sites. The **Tourist Office** is at RATHAUSSTR. 18–20, ☎(05121) 17980 (www.hildesheim.de).

WHERE NEXT FROM HANNOVER?

You can join the **Hannover–Lübeck** route (p. 268) here. Express trains (ETT table 900, 1 per hr) from Hannover to **Munich** enable you to stop off at **Würzburg** and join the route to **Passau** (p. 272) or travel up the **Rhine** via **Mainz** and **Koblenz**.

BRAUNSCHWEIG

Change here for trains to Goslar (hourly trains, ETT table 903) and to Vienenburg for Wernigerode (tables 903, 860).

GOSLAR

Goslar has a handsome, labyrinthine centre characterised by half-timbered and stone houses, its sheer architectural diversity being the key to its appeal. It gained its prosperity through silver and lead mining in the Middle Ages, and is now a UNESCO World Heritage site. At its heart is the **Marktplatz**, presided over by the **Rathaus** and **Marktkirche**; on the 15th-century **Kaiserworth**, a statue of a boy on a gable illustrates the town's right to mint coinage by defecating a coin.

Goslar is also the centre of the **Harz**, one of Germany's most scenic mountain regions, the country's loftiest uplands outside the Alps. The highest peak, the Brocken, rises to 1142 m. The heart of the region is the **Hochharz National Park**, with a vast network of marked hiking trails.

[i] **Tourist Office**: MARKT 7 , ☎(05321) 78060, fax (05321) 780644 (www.goslarinfo.de).

MAGDEBURG

If coming from the east, change here for Wernigerode via Halberstadt (ETT tables 862, 860).

WERNIGERODE

Reached by direct trains from Hannover, or from Magdeburg or Braunschweig, Wernigerode is yet another historic half-timbered town. Some of it's a bit dour, but the **Rathausplatz** is charming, with the 13th-century **Rathaus** rated as one of the finest in Germany. Cafés, restaurants and horse-drawn carriages line the square, offering the standard tourist fare. Looming over the town is the Schloss – genuinely medieval, although owing much of its present appearance to 19th-century restoration. Wernigerode is an excellent base from which to explore the **Harz mountains**, with excursions, hikes, a free local animal zoo (**Wildpark Christianental**: 45-min walk) and even a steam railway, offering several options in which to explore the surrounding countryside.

i **Tourist Office**: Nicolaipl. 1, ☎ (03943) 633 035 (www.harztourist.de and www.wernigerode.de; wernigerode-tg@netco.de).

Pensions are the best bet for reasonably priced accommodation, including: **Fürsten-Grotte**, Burgberg 9b, ☎ (03943) 54590, €€; **Kristall**, Karl-Marx-Str. 12, Elbingerode, ☎ (039454) 41235, €; and **Landhaus-Pension Rohrbeck**, Unterengengasse 1, ☎ (03943) 604120, €. **Youth hostel**: Am Eichberg 5, ☎ (03943) 606176.

The Harz Mountain Railways

Wernigerode is the northern terminus of Europe's most extensive narrow-gauge steam railway network. The **Harzer Schmalspurbahnen**: 132 km of scenic lines winding through the picturesque Harz mountains. The longest section of the network is the **Harzquerbahn**, 61 km of track between Wernigerode and Nordhausen, traversed by three trains in summer, two in winter. Some are drawn by 1950s steam locomotives, but some older engines are used for special trips.

The Harzquerbahn connects at Eisfelder Talmühle with the 52 km of the **Selketalbahn**, which runs through the scenic Selke valley. A branch line, the **Brockenbahn**, reopened in 1992 for the first time since World War II, and connects with the Harzquerbahn at Drei-Annen-Hohne, from which it ascends 19 km to the summit of Brocken mountain.

For timetables and fares, contact: **Harzer Schmalspurbahnen GmbH**, Friedrichstr. 151, D-38855 Wernigerode, ☎ (03943) 5580 and 558151, fax (03943) 558148 (www.hsb-wr.de); see also ETT table 867.

Rail passes are not accepted on these lines.

BERLIN

See p. 245.

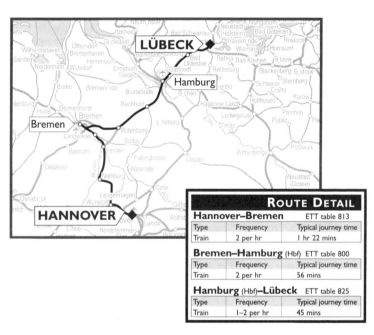

ROUTE DETAIL

Hannover–Bremen   ETT table 813

Type	Frequency	Typical journey time
Train	2 per hr	I hr 22 mins

Bremen–Hamburg (Hbf) ETT table 800

Type	Frequency	Typical journey time
Train	2 per hr	56 mins

Hamburg (Hbf)**–Lübeck**   ETT table 825

Type	Frequency	Typical journey time
Train	I–2 per hr	45 mins

KEY JOURNEYS

Hannover–Hamburg   ETT tables 900/904

Type	Frequency	Typical journey time
Train	2–3 per hr	I hr 15 mins

Hamburg–Berlin   ETT table 840

Type	Frequency	Typical journey time
Train	Every hr	2 hrs 23 mins

Hamburg–Copenhagen ETT table 50

Type	Frequency	Typical journey time
Train	4–6 per day	4 hrs 30 mins

Hannover, easily accessible from Amsterdam and on the Aachen–Berlin route (p. 262), is the starting point for a tour of three great cities that were members of the great 14th- to 16th-century trading association known as the Hanseatic League – Bremen, Hamburg (p. 252) and Lübeck. Beyond Lübeck you can continue by a train that boards a ferry for a memorable entry into Denmark.

BREMEN

Bremen was a Hanseatic city and much of its 15th- and 16th-century structure survives – much of it quite Dutch-looking. Together with Bremerhaven, its outer harbour at the mouth of the Weser river, Bremen is one of the Länder (states) which make up Germany, continuing a proud tradition of self-government which dates back to the Middle Ages.

The Altstadt, on the north-east bank of the river, is the main area of historical interest. MARKTPLATZ is dominated by the Rathaus, a 15th-century structure overlaid with a Renaissance façade. It's worth joining a tour to see the splendid interior. In MARKTPLATZ are two notable statues. One is a 15th-century, 10-m-high portrait of Roland (Charlemagne's nephew), which is a symbol of the town's independence; legend has it that Bremen will remain free as long as he is standing. The other (which is modern and much smaller) illustrates the Grimm Brothers' fairy-tale about the Four Musicians of Bremen – a donkey, a dog, a cat and a rooster.

The 11th-century twin-spired St Petri Dom, SANDSTR. 10–12, is beautiful in a sombre way. In the Bleikeller (basement: open May–Oct) are some perfectly preserved corpses, believed to be of men who fell from the roof during construction, and saved from corruption by the lack of air.

To the south side of MARKTPL. is Böttcherstr., a street that is an art deco fantasy from the 1920s. It houses craft workshops, restaurants, a casino and a musical clock that chimes three times a day: at 1200, 1500 and 1800. The Schnoorviertel area (between the Dom and the river) consists of well-preserved 16th–18th-century buildings, many of which are now craft shops. Just to the east is Kunsthalle, AM WALL 207 (closed Mon), which has an eclectic collection of paintings and sculptures dating from the Renaissance to the present day.

Among other highlights are Beck's Brewery, ☎ (0421) 5555, and the fascinating excursion into the realms of science at the recently opened Universum Science Center, WIENER STR. 2 (open daily).

🚉 Just north of the main area of interest.

ℹ️ Tourist Office: AM HAUPTBAHNHOF, ☎ (0421) 308 000 (www.bremen-tourism.de). Close to the station; open Mon–Wed 0930–1830, Thur–Fri 0930–2000, Sat–Sun 0930–1600. Other branches at LIEBFRAUENKIRCHHOF and on the WESERPROMENADE SCHLACHTE.

Hotel Ibis Bremen Altstadt, FAULENSTR. 45, (0421) 304 80, fax (0421) 304 8600, €€, offers doubles beginning at around €60. **Gästehaus Walter**, BUNTENTORSTEINWEG 86–88, (0421) 558 027, fax (0421) 558 029, €, has double rooms from around €38. The **youth hostel**, KALKSTR. 6, (0421) 171369, is on the western side of Altstadt; no. 26 or tram no. 1/8 to BRILL. **Campsite: Campingplatz Bremen** is at AM STADTWALDSEE 1, (0421) 212002, fax (0421) 219857.

The Ratskeller (in the Rathaus) has been a bar since the early 15th century and offers 600 different wines, although it is quite pricey. Cheap eating places can be found on and around OSTERTORSTEINWEG. **Lift-Internet Café**, WEBERSTR. 18 (hallo@brainlift.de), open Wed–Mon 1500–2400, nos. 2/3/3/10/N12 to S-bahn stop SIELWALL.

The **Bremer Kärtchen** gives one day's unlimited travel on all the city's buses and trams. With the exception of some museums, the places of interest cluster around MARKTPL. The **ErlebnisCARD Bremen**, available for 1 day or 2 days (1 adult and 2 children, or a more expensive version for up to 5 persons), provides free bus travel as well as significant discounts on the city's attractions.

SIDE TRIPS FROM BREMEN Located 110 km north of Bremen, **Cuxhaven** is Germany's favourite seaside health resort, with a long sandy beach and a small offshore island, **Neuwerk**, which you can visit at low tide by horse-drawn carriage. Trains from Bremen run take 1 hr 30 mins (every 2 hrs, ETT table 817). En route you pass through **Bremerhaven**, and it is worth stopping here for the fine **Deutsches Schiffahrtsmuseum** (German Ship Museum), open Apr–Oct: daily 1000–1800, Nov–Mar: Tues–Sun, where exhibits include square-riggers and a U-boat.

From Cuxhaven, ferries sail to the remote island of **Helgoland**, with pleasant walks above its red craggy cliffs – quite unusual in these parts. Once a British possession, it was swapped for (of all places) Zanzibar in 1890, and was nearly bombed to bits by RAF target practice in the immediate postwar years; it was reconstructed in 1952 and is now a busy little holiday resort. **Youth hostel: Haus der Jugend**, POSTFACH 580, 27487 HELGOLAND, (04725) 341, fax (04725) 7467; Apr–Oct.

HAMBURG

See p. 252.

LÜBECK

What's really impressive about **Lübeck** is the virtually seamless restoration of a large chunk of the old town: it's amazingly hard to spot what's rebuilt and what's original. Capital of the Hanseatic League, Lübeck has a striking range of architectural styles, but it's the stepped gables and tranquil, concealed courtyards that stay in the memory – there are fine old buildings on the waterfront. There's an excellent bus network, but most places of interest are in the 12th-century **Altstadt**, the moated old city.

Between the main station and Altstadt is Lübeck's emblem, the twin-towered **Holstentor**, which appears in motif form on the ubiquitous marzipan, the town's gastronomic speciality. It's a 15th-century structure, and now museum, that was one of the four city gates. The Altstadt, perched on an oval island, is a World Heritage Site. Get your bearings by taking the lift up the 50-m spire of the Gothic **Petrikirche** (itself now an art gallery). Nearby, **Museum für Puppentheater**, KLEINE PETERSGRUBE 4–6, is devoted to theatrical puppets from all over the world, while behind the façades of 22 handsome houses in GROSSE PETERSGRUBE is the **Music Academy**. Both places give regular public performances.

The Marktplatz is dominated by the striking L-shaped 13th- to 16th-century **Rathaus**, typical of Lübeck's architectural style of alternating red unglazed and black glazed bricks, a style copied by the Dutch and more common in Holland. Opposite the east wing is **Niederegger Haus**, BREITESTR., renowned for displays of **marzipan** (the town has been producing it since the Middle Ages and sells the sweet in an endless number of varieties). Opposite the north wing is the 13th-century **Marienkirche**, a brick-built Gothic church with square towers that was the model for many in the area. Later embellishments were damaged in the war and ignored in the restoration. It contains a magnificent gilded altarpiece dating from 1518.

Buddenbrookhaus, the inspiration for Thomas Mann's Lübeck-based saga of the same name, is a museum at MENGSTR. 4. To the south of Altstadt is the large brick-built **Dom**, which contains an allegorical triumphal arch and ornate rood screen.

WHERE NEXT FROM LÜBECK?

Carry on north-east into Denmark (ETT tables 720, 825), crossing the border in spectacular style beyond Puttgarden, where the trains follow the tracks onto ferries; continue on to Copenhagen (p. 438).

🚃 10 mins' walk west of Altstadt.

i **Tourist Offices:** There's a small office in the **station** which offers a room-booking service, ☎ (0451) 864675, fax (0451) 863024 (www.luebeck.de). The **main office**, though, is at BREITE STR. 62, ☎ (0451) 122 1925. Branches at BECKERGRUBE 95, in the HOLSTENTOR-PASSAGE and at HOLSTENSTR. 20.

🏨 There are several reasonably priced hotels around the main station **(Hbf)**. Private rooms are also available, e.g. **Fam. Zingel**, VERMEHRENRING 11A, ☎ (0451) 625029, €, non-smoking, or **Frau Andresen**, G. ALTEFÄHRE 17, ☎ (0451) 9308099, €. **Youth hostels:** AM GERTRUDENKIRCHHOF 4, ☎ (0451) 33433, north-east of **Burgtor** (🚌 nos.1/3 from Hbf to bus stop GUSTAV-RADBRUCH-PL.). There is also a **Jugendgästehaus** at MENGSTR. 33, ☎ (0451) 7020399. The YMCA (CVJM) runs a **Sleep-In**, GROSSE PETERSGRUBE 11, ☎ (0451) 71920.

GERMANY

KEY JOURNEYS

Cologne–Frankfurt ETT table 910

Type	Frequency	Typical journey time
Train	2–3 per hr	1 hr 12 mins

Frankfurt–Munich ETT table 930

Type	Frequency	Typical journey time
Train	Every hr	3 hrs 35 mins

ROUTE DETAIL

Cologne–Bonn ETT tables 802, 910

Type	Frequency	Typical journey time
Train	4 per hr	18 mins

Bonn–Koblenz ETT tables 802, 910

Type	Frequency	Typical journey time
Train	3–4 per hr	32 mins

Koblenz–Frankfurt ETT table 910

Type	Frequency	Typical journey time
Train	Every hr	1 hr 24 mins

Frankfurt–Würzburg ETT table 920

Type	Frequency	Typical journey time
Train	2 per hr	1 hr 10 mins

Würzburg–Nuremburg ETT tables 900, 920

Type	Frequency	Typical journey time
Train	2 per hr	52 mins

Nuremburg–Regensburg ETT table 920

Type	Frequency	Typical journey time
Train	Every hr	1 hr

Regensburg–Passau ETT table 920

Type	Frequency	Typical journey time
Train	Every 1–2 hrs	1 hr 5 mins

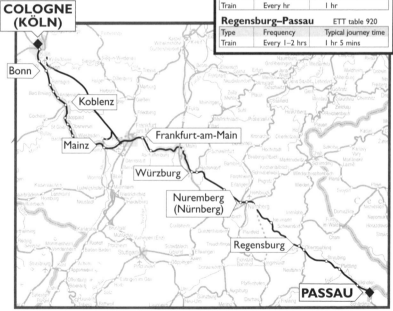

COLOGNE (KÖLN) · Bonn · Koblenz · Mainz · Frankfurt-am-Main · Würzburg · Nuremberg (Nürnberg) · Regensburg · PASSAU

Leaving **Cologne**, Germany's fourth city, the train takes you past **Bonn**, Beethoven's birthplace, and along the best of the **Rhine valley**, one of the country's classic rail journeys, with castles clinging to the slopes and a series of waterside towns and villages. Sit on the left (east) side for the best views. **Trier**, with its astonishing Roman remains, is a highly worthwhile side trip from Koblenz. **Mainz** was where in the 1450s Gutenberg invented the first printing press with moveable type and has the outstanding Gutenberg Museum. Beyond **Mainz** the scene briefly becomes less appealing, taking in the high-rise commercial centre of **Frankfurt**. This route enters **Bayern** (Bavaria) at **Aschaffenburg**. South-eastern Bavaria is a relatively little-visited corner of the country; **Passau** stands on a neck of land between two rivers, the **Ilz** and the **Danube**, and at the threshold of **Austria**.

COLOGNE (KÖLN)

During World War II, nine-tenths of what was Germany's largest Altstadt was flattened by bombing, and the quality of reconstruction has been patchy. But there's much to enjoy, in the cathedral, churches and museums, and Kölners themselves have an irresistible verve, exemplified in the city's Lent carnival. The twin spires of the **Dom** (**cathedral**), one of the world's greatest Gothic buildings, soar over the Rhineland capital, Germany's fourth city and busiest railway junction. The cathedral's highlights include the stained glass, the 9th-century Gero Crucifix in the north chapel and the 15th-century triptych of the Adoration of the Magi in the south chapel; you can climb the tower for a dizzying view.

The city's Roman traces include remnants of the original, 5th-century AD city wall. The superlative **Römisch-Germanisches Museum**, RONCALLIPL. 4, holds many of the finds of the ancient town, including an arched fortress gate and the famous Dionysus Mosaic. By the 13th century, Cologne was a thriving metropolis of 40,000 people, protected by Europe's longest city walls – a 6-km rampart pierced by 12 massive gates. Within the original city wall stand a dozen Romanesque churches, Germany's finest such architectural concentration. The most striking are Gross St Martin, overlooking the Rhine in the Altstadt, and St Aposteln.

From 321 until 1424, the city was home to one of the most important Jewish communities in Germany. The remains of a 'mikvah' (a Jewish ritual bath) dating from 1170 is preserved under a glass pyramid in the middle of the square of the City Hall. Nearby, in BISCHOFSGARTENSTR., is a modern complex incorporating the **Philharmonie Hall**, the **Agfa-Foto-Historama**,

> **NIGHT-TIME**
> Nightlife ranges from the latest dance clubs to cool jazz spots (the Altstadt is the best area for music). Cologne also has a strong reputation for classical music and opera, with hundreds of performances a year in top venues, including the modern Opera House and the fine Philharmonie concert house close to the cathedral.

covering all things photographic and the **Museum Ludwig**, housing 20th-century works including Kirchner, Beckmann and Dix. The outstanding **Wallraf-Richartz-Museum**, with superb 14th–16th-century paintings by the Cologne school recently reopened at MARTINSTR. 39 (www.museenkoeln.de) about 10 mins' walk from the **Dom**.

🚉 Centrally placed, right by the cathedral with a huge shopping centre, information desk, currency exchange and 24-hr service point; station closes 0100–0400; left luggage.

✈ **Flughafen Köln–Bonn**, south-east of the city. **Information** ☎ (02203) 404001. 🚌 no. 170 connects the airport with the rail station in 20 mins, running every 15 mins 0700–2000 (every 30 mins 0530–0700 and 2000–2345).

i **Tourist Office:** UNTER FETTENHENNEN 19, ☎ (0221) 2212 3345, fax (0221) 2212 3320 (www.koeln.de; koelntourismus@stadt-koeln.de) by the Dom. **Main post office:** BREITE STR. 2–26, in the WDR ARCADEN (Mon–Fri 0800–2000, Sat 0800–1600).

🛏 Central rooms are almost always at a premium and the cheap hotels are very scattered. Book ahead. The **Tourist Office** can book hotels on the day but also has a separate advance booking number, fax (0221) 2212 3320, and charges a reservation fee. **Cheaper hotels** include: **Am Rathaus**, BÜRGERSTR. 6, ☎ (0221) 257 7624, fax (0221) 258 2829, €; and **Brandenburger Hof**, BRANDENBURGER STR. 2–4, ☎ (0221) 122889, fax (0221) 135304, € and **Hotel Ariane**, HOHE PFORTE 19–21, ☎ (0221) 236033, €–€€. The more central of the two **youth hostels** is **Deutz**, SIEGESSTR. 5A, ☎ (0221) 814711, fax (0221) 884425, 15-min walk from the station, over the HOHENZOLLERNBRÜCKE, a couple of blocks south of Deutz station. The second hostel is at **Köln-Riehl**, AN DER SCHANZ 14, ☎ (0221) 767081, fax (0221) 761555. The most accessible **campsite** is POLL, ☎ (0221) 831966, fax (0221) 761555, south-east of ALTSTADT (tram 16: MARIENBURG).

🍴 Balanced between the beer-drinking north and the wine lands of the south, Cologne has the best of both worlds. A typical dish is *Sauerbraten*, a 'sour roast', with beef soaked in vinegar and stewed, served with *Kartoffelklöße Schrägschrift* (potato dumplings) and apple sauce. The local sweet Rhine wine is *suuren Hungk* ('sour dog'). *Blootwoosch* (blood sausage) makes a snack served with mustard on a bread roll, known as 'Cologne caviar'. This could be washed down with *Kölsch* (also the name of the local dialect), the local surface-fermented beer made with a special yeast, no less than 5% alcoholic content. The **Kvartier Lateng** (BARBAROSA PL.), Underground line 12 and 16, and the **Südstadt** are where most of the student hangouts are.

GETTING AROUND COLOGNE

The comprehensive public transport system includes U-Bahn (underground/subway), S-Bahn (surface suburban trains), trams and buses. The **24-hour ticket**: worthwhile if making more than four single trips.

KÖLNTOURISMUS CARD

The **Kölntourismus Card** (available from Tourist Offices and hotels) offers free public transport within Cologne, Bonn and Brühl for one day, a coach sightseeing trip and admission to nine museums, plus reductions on a Rhine boat trip, Rhine cable car, Cologne Cathedral, zoo, the opera and more.

BONN

For a couple of peaceful days in a pleasant German town, Bonn makes an ideal stopover. All the central areas are walkable, the pubs near the river do a roaring trade at night and are crowded with young people and students. Now that the capital status has reverted to Berlin, musical pilgrims beating a path to Beethoven's birthplace are likely to become the town's mainstay. The great composer is also remembered in the modern **Beethovenhalle**. The **Geburtshaus** (house of birth), where he spent the first 22 years of his life, is at BONNGASSE 20 and contains his instruments and a rather sad collection of ear trumpets as testament to his irreversible decline towards total deafness.

On the other side of the rail station, the **Rheinisches Landesmuseum,** COLMANTSTR. 14–16, exhibits a 60,000-year-old Neanderthal skull, discovered in 1856, as well as Celtic gold and superb Roman finds. The **Museum Meile** (Museum Mile) is a complex outside the city centre, easily reached by Underground lines 16, 63 or 66 (stop HEUSSALLEE/MUSEUMSMEILE) or nos. 610/630 (stop BUNDESKANZLERPL.). It includes the **Kunst- und Ausstellungshalle** (for art exhibitions), the **Kunstmuseum Bonn** (the city art gallery), the **Zoological Institute** and the **Haus der Geschichte**, WILLY-BRANDT-ALLEE 14, a new hi-tech museum on the history of Germany (free entry).

Beside the bus terminal and right in the centre, on the edge of the pedestrian precinct.

Tourist Office: WINDECKSTR.I/AM MÜNSTERPL., (0228) 775000, fax (0228) 775077 (www.bonn.de; bonninformation@bonn.de). There is a hotel booking service: (0228) 910 410, fax (0228) 910 4111 (www.bonn-region.de; info@tc-bonn.de).

Beethoven, RHEINGASSE 26, (0228) 631411, €–€€; **Bergmann** KASERNENSTR. 13, (0228) 633891, €. Nearby Bad Godesberg can be cheaper: **Gästehaus Scholz**, ANNETTENSTR. 16, (0228) 379363, €. **Youth hostel**: HAAGER WEG 42, (0228) 289970. **Campsite: Genienau**, FRANKENKELLER 49, (0228) 344949 is in Mehlem, part of Bad Godesberg.

KOBLENZ

The Mosel and Rhine rivers meet here at the **Deutsches Eck** (the German Corner), marked by a massive, heavy-handed monument to Kaiser Wilhelm I. Although originally a memorial to the Kaiser erected by his wife, the edifice was later to become a symbol of German unity. The significance increased at the time of reunification in 1989. The pleasant gardens along both rivers combine to provide an attractive 8 km stroll.

Ehrenbreitstein (across the Rhine, ferries in summer) is dominated by an enormous fortress, the **Festung**. Its earliest fortifications date from the 12th century, but it grew to its present size during the 16th century. The **Sesselbahn** (cable car) operates Easter–end Oct. As well as providing a fantastic view, the fortress contains two regional museums and a youth hostel (see p. 276). A big firework display (**Rhein in Flammen**) is staged here on the second Sat in Aug.

🚈BAHNHOFPL. 2. South-west of the centre, 25-min walk downhill (or 🚌no. 1) to the riverside area
from which cruises (*Rheinfähre*) depart.

ⓘ **Tourist Offices**: BAHNHOFSPL. 17 (opposite rail station), ☎(0261) 31304, fax (0261) 100 43 88
(www.koblenz.de; touristik@koblenz.de). It provides boat schedules and a city map that includes
listings. There is another **Tourist Office** in the historical Rathaus (town hall), AM JESUITENPL. 2–4.

🏨 **Hotel Jan van Werth**, V.-WERTH-STR. 9, ☎(0261) 36500, € (from €24), **Hotel-Garni
National**, ROONSTR. 47, ☎(0261) 14194, €, and **Am Sessellift**, OBERTAL 22, ☎(0261) 75256,
€, are reasonable. The **youth hostel** is housed in the **Festung** (see p. 275), ☎(0261) 972870,
and is popular, so book well ahead. The downside is that the ferry and chair lift both stop very
early so, after taking a bus (🚌nos. 7/8/9/10) to CHARLOTTENSTR., you end the day with a long
uphill climb. The **campsite** is at **Lutzel**, across the Mosel: **Campingplatz Rhein-Mosel**,
SCHARTWIESENWEG 6, ☎(0261) 82719. There's a ferry across during the day.

🍽 Some of the best bargains for food are to indulge in the *Stehcafés* (standing cafés) and
Biergartens on the banks of the Rhine, directly at the **Deutsches Eck**.

SIDE TRIP FROM KOBLENZ TO TRIER   Worth a substantial detour for its Roman
and early Christian remains, Trier (ETT
table 915; hourly rail services, taking 1 hr to 1 hr 24 mins) is Germany's oldest city,
dating back to 16 BC. The focal point is the **Porta Nigra** (Black Gate), one of the most
impressive Roman structures in northern Europe. You can also see Emperor
Constantine's throne room and part of a Roman street in the huge **Konstantin-
Basilika**, KONSTANTINPL., part of the imperial palace, and the largest surviving
single-hall structure of the ancient world. Backing onto it is the picture-perfect pink,
white and gold rococo **Kurfürstliches Palais** in gardens with fountains (and a café).
This area leads directly to the **Rheinisches Landesmuseum**, WEIMARER ALLEE 1 (at
the southern end of the pleasant and well-tended **Palastgarten**), which contains
Roman remains. Close by are the **Kaiserthermen**, a huge complex of well-preserved
imperial baths, and the **Amphitheatre** (c. AD100), where crowds of up to 20,000
watched gladiatorial combat. The **Bischofliches Museum**, WIND-STR., has statuary,
sacred art, models of the Roman cathedral and Roman frescos.

The **Karl-Marx-Haus Museum**, BRÜCKENSTR. 10, gives an exhibition on Marx's work
and life, in the house in which he was born. Trier's Renaissance **Marktplatz** is
outstanding even by German standards. **Tourist Office**: PORTA NIGRA, ☎(0651)
978080 (www.trier.de).

FRANKFURT-AM-MAIN

Frankfurt, the country's financial capital and major convention centre claims the
only skyline of Germany. While you're unlikely to succumb to love at first sight on
entering the modern city, where massive office blocks assert their presence, the
traffic-free boulevards with shops, parks and the leafy banks of the River Main,

which flows through the centre, make Frankfurt surprisingly pleasant for strolling around.

Affectionately known as the *gut Stubb* (front parlour), ROEMERBERG, a square of half-timbered and steeply gabled buildings, is at the heart of the *Altstadt* (old town). Along one side is the **Roemer,** the city's town hall, meticulously restored as it was in the Middle Ages. A short walk to the east leads to **Kaiserdom,** DOMSTR., the red-sandstone Gothic cathedral, with its dome and lantern tower, where the emperors were crowned.

Frankfurt was the birthplace of Germany's most famous writer, Goethe. The **Goethe Haus,** GROSSER HIRSCHGRABEN 23, is a careful post-war reconstruction of the house where he was born in 1749. It is furnished in period style and has a museum with manuscripts and documents next to it.

The old **Sachsenhausen** district, reached by crossing the Alte Brücke (Old Bridge) or the Eiserner Steg footbridge, has an almost village-like atmosphere. Its little square and cobbled alleys of half-timbered houses survived the World War II bombing more or less intact.

A recent addition to Frankfurt's famous zoo, **Zoologischer Garten,** ALFRED-BREHM-PL. 16 (U-Bahn 6 to Zoo), which was founded in 1858, is the **Grzimek-Haus,** where nocturnal animals can be observed in daytime. To the north (U-bahn 6/7 to WESTEND) are the botanical gardens, **Palmengarten,** ZEPPELIN ALLEE, with lily ponds and conservatories of orchids and cacti.

Twelve of the city's forty museums are gathered on the south bank of the river along SCHAUMAINKAI, known as **Museumsufer** (Museum Bank).

Hauptbahnhof (Hbf), Europe's busiest rail terminus, opens 24 hrs and has good cafés and shops. There's an airport-style lounge, with bar, armchairs and toys. The city centre is a 15-min walk straight ahead along KAISERSTR.

Flughafen Frankfurt-Main (9 km south-west of the city) is central Europe's busiest airport. ☎ (069) 6901 (www.frankfurt-airport.de). S-Bahn suburban trains (service S8) to Frankfurt Hbf, the city's main station, leave every 10 mins from 0430 to 0030; the journey takes 11 mins. InterCity rail services to Cologne, Dortmund, Hamburg and Nuremberg stop at the airport station hourly. Direct services are also available to Stuttgart, Freiburg and Basel.

NIGHT-TIME AND EVENTS

Frankfurt's entertainment spans everything from the latest dance craze to the best of classical concerts, opera, theatre, cinema and cabaret. For detailed information on the city's cultural scene consult the Info-Hotline: ☎ (069) 2123 8800 (www.rhein-main.net). The **Main Fair** (usually the first week in Aug) takes over the streets UNTERMAINKAI and MAINKAI, along the north bank of the river from the RÖEMERBERG to UNTERMAINKAIBRÜECKE. Its centrepiece is a big funfair surrounded by beer and wine stalls, and it ends with a huge firework display over the river. In Apr and Sept the **Dippemess**, a traditional folk fair, is in RATSWEG and FESTPL. Open-air concerts are part of the **Museumsuferfest** at the end of Aug.

| i | **Tourist Office: Tourismus+Congress GmbH**, |

Frankfurter Hauptbahnhof (Hbf) station, ☎(069) 2123
8800 (www.frankfurt-tourismus.de; info@tcf.frankfurt.de).
Hotel booking service: ☎(069) 2123 0808. **Other
branches**: in the city centre at Römerberg 27, and in the
Zeil (main shopping street) near Brockhausbrunnen.

🛏 Cheap, no-frills **pensions** are found around the rail
station. Inexpensive accommodation includes Europe's
biggest **youth hostel**, **Haus der Jugend**, by the river at
Deutschherrnufer 12, ☎(069) 6100150. Mid-range
accommodation can be in short supply during the main
trade fairs. The **Aller**, Gutleutstr. 94, ☎(069) 252596, €,
is near the rail station. The **Am Berg**, Grethenweg 23,
☎(069) 612021, €, is further away near the Südbahnhof,
rooms from around €40. **Campsite**: **City Camp
Frankfurt**, An der Sandelmühle 35, in Heddernheim,
☎(069) 570332, lines 1–3.

🍽 A range of national cuisines are represented; the city also
has a plentiful choice of *Lokale* (taverns) serving local and
regional treats like *Eisbein* (stewed pork knuckle), *Handkäse
mit Musik* (sour cheese garnished with chopped onions and
caraway seeds) and *Sauerkraut.* Above all, of course, there's
the original *frankfurter* – long, thin and at its tastiest eaten at
a *Schnell Imbiss* (street stall) in a really fresh roll. You'll find a
good selection of restaurants along Fressgasse and the
narrow streets running north off it. For the more informal
Lokale, head south of the river to the **Sachsenhausen**
district, particularly streets like Schweizerstr., or the
cobbled Grosse Rittergasse and Kleine Rittergasse. The
city's own beverage is apple wine, called *Apfelwein*
(nicknamed *Stoeffche)* a deceptively strong variety of cider.
Hocheimer (hock) is wine from municipal vineyards.

Getting Around Frankfurt

Travel within Frankfurt is easy,
with an efficient combination of
S-Bahn (overground) and U-Bahn
(underground) trains, trams and
buses all run by **RMV**, the
regional transport authority.
Directions to the system, in six
languages, including English, are on
the blue automatic ticket
machines at all bus stops, tram
stops and stations. **Transport
information**: ☎0180 2351451.
Buy **tickets** (valid for all RMV
transportation) at newspaper
booths and blue automat
machines. If you are making more
than two trips a day, it's worth
buying a day pass. The **Frankfurt
Card**, available from Tourist
Offices for one or two days, gives
unlimited travel on all public
transport, including local and S-
Bahn trains to the airport, as well
as half-price admission to 15
museums and the zoo. To book a
taxi, ☎230001, 250001, 230033
or 545011. A short city-centre
ride costs about six times as much
as a single RMV ticket. Bikes can
be hired at the rail station.

WHERE NEXT FROM FRANKFURT?

*Frankfurt is a major international rail junction and has services to **Amsterdam** (ETT table
28), **Vienna** (table 28), **Paris** (table 30), **Prague** (table 30), **Moscow** (table 55), **Warsaw**
and **Kraków** (table 55) and **Ventimiglia** via **Avignon**, **Marseille** and **Nice**
(table 47).*

WÜRZBURG

See p. 298.

NUREMBERG (NÜRNBERG)

Tragically Hitler chose Nuremberg, one of the greatest historical cities in all Europe, to hold his mass rallies. Post-war reconstruction has been piecemeal – in turns atmospheric and dully modern. Some of the most historic sites were re-created with meticulous care, and it's hard to tell that they're not original. Heading north from the station, you immediately enter the old town, which is surrounded by a 5-km **Stadtbefestigung** (city wall). Beyond the much-photographed **Schöner Brunnen** (Beautiful Fountain), the spacious **Hauptmarkt** (market square) makes a perfect setting for one of Germany's liveliest Christmas markets during Dec.

For a good view of the whole city, seek out the terraces of the **Kaiserburg** fortifications above the north-west corner of the old town. Just below it nestles Nuremberg's prettiest corner, including the gabled **Dürerhaus**. Here the artist Albrecht Dürer lived from 1509 until his death in 1528; it's now furnished in period style and contains several of his woodcuts. The **Germanisches Nationalmuseum**, KARTÄUSERGASSE 1, founded in 1852, houses the country's largest and choicest collection of German art and culture.

Hitler's mass rallies in the 1930s were held in the vast **Reichsparteitagsgelände** (in the Luitpoldhain, in the south-eastern suburbs), a huge area with a vast parade ground, stadium and the shell of a massive congress hall which was never completed. One of the parts that remain, the Zeppelin grandstand, ZEPPELINSTR. (S-Bahn: S2 to FRANKENSTADION), contains an exhibition called *Faszination und Gewalt* (Fascination and Terror), open May–Oct. After World War II, the surviving Nazi leaders were put on trial in the city's court, FÜRTHERSTR. 110, on the western outskirts (U-Bahn: U1 to BÄRENSCHANZE). The Tourist Office has a free brochure describing the *Nazionalsozialismus Movement* in Nuremberg.

On the southern edge of the old town centre, 5 mins to HAUPTMARKT via the underpass.

Tourist Office: FRAUENTORGRABEN 3/IV, ☎ (0911) 23360, fax (0911) 2336166, branches at the station (BAHNHOFSVORPL.) and at HAUPTMARKT, (www.nuernberg.de; tourismus @nuernberg.de). Free accommodation booking service.

Gasthof Zum Schwänlein, HINTERE STERNGASSE 11, ☎ (0911) 2251620, €, and **Vater Jahn**, JAHNSTR. 13, ☎ (0911) 444507, €. **Youth hostel:** BURG 2, ☎ (0911) 2309360 (U-Bahn to PLÄRRER, then tram no. 4), wonderfully sited in the castle and for many travellers it alone justifies staying in the city. **Campsite: Dutzendteich**, HANS KALBSTR. 56, ☎ (0911) 9812717 (U-Bahn U6 and S-Bahn S6 to FRANKENSTADION).

WHERE NEXT FROM NUREMBERG?

*Join the **Munich–Berlin** route (p. 295) by taking the scenic line north via **Jena**; through trains from **Nuremberg** to **Berlin** via **Leipzig** take 5 hrs (ETT table 850), and run every 2 hrs.*

🚆 The TIERGARTENPL. is a good place to go in the evenings, with music, night life and drinking. Don't forget to taste some *Lebkuchen* (spiced honey cakes), a local speciality that although imported throughout the world, is still best here. *Bratwurst* and cod typically appear on the menu in the city's restaurants.

BAMBERG

From Nuremberg you can join the Munich–Berlin route (p. 295) by taking the scenic line north via **Jena**; see Where Next from Nuremburg, p. 279.

This route passes through **Bamberg**, arguably the most beautiful of all medieval Bavarian cities, itself a feasible day trip from Nuremberg, being only 45 mins away. The old centre, steeply placed above the river Regnitz, is crowned by a four-towered Romanesque-Gothic cathedral, known as the Kaiserdom and filled with wonderful sculpture – notably the Bamberger Reiter (Bamberg Knight) and the 16th-century tomb of Henry II and his queen by Tilman Riemenschneider. Houses sport all manner of façades, and the particularly striking Rathaus displays a strange blend of half-timbering and refined Rococo. Tourist Office: www.bamberg.de; there's a youth hostel at OBERER LEINRITT 70, ☎(951) 56002.

REGENSBURG

Above the Danube, with the knobbly twin towers of the grey stone **cathedral** dominant on the skyline, and a cheerful huddle of stone houses and red roofs, Regensburg claims to be the largest city in Germany to have escaped bombing in World War II. Rather less manicured than the German norm, it has preserved its medieval character particularly well. Pretty pastel plasterwork, in pinks, yellows and greens, and decorative towers on many of the former patrician houses in the narrow streets lend it a southern feel. Originally the city was divided into three areas where, respectively, the princes, churchmen and merchants lived.

The town had strong trading links with Venice in the 13th century, when its merchants grew rich from the selling of silk, spices and slaves. They competed to have the biggest house (often incorporating its own chapel) in the style of an Italian fortified palace with the highest tower on top – these were never defensive, just status symbols. The most striking of the 20 surviving towers is the **Baumburger Turm,** WATMARKT, though the highest is the 9-storey **Goldener Turm,** WAHLENSTR. Some of the chapels have been turned into restaurants but the tiny **Maria-Läng Kapelle,** PFARRGASSE, is still in use.

Domstadt, the church area, centres on *Dom St Peter,* the magnificent gothic cathedral; started in the 13th century, its 105-m spires were completed six centuries later. It has fine stained-glass, medieval and modern, and its own interior well. Look out for quirky details such as the tiny stone carvings of the devil and his grandmother

Day Trips from Regensburg

In summer there are a variety of cruises on the Danube, departing from Steinerne Brücke. Destinations include **Walhalla**, where a 19th-century Greek temple modelled on the Parthenon and filled with busts of German heroes, gives a splendid view to reward the steep climb. The **Bayerisches Wald (Bavarian Forest)** is a traditional rural region encompassing wooded peaks, rivers, and tiny villages with churches and ruined castles; there aren't a lot of highlights – the emphasis is on the simple life. An hourly bus service goes round the Bavarian Forest National Park and there are many marked trails (www.nationalpark-bayerischer-wald.de).

just inside the main entrance – a warning to those stepping outside – and a laughing angel near the transept. The exterior of **Alte Kapelle**, ALTE KOMMARKT, belies the wealth of rococo decorations within, including a marble altar and superb frescoes. The **Porta Praetoria** archway, Unter den Schwibbögen, is part of 2nd-century Roman defences.

The south-western part of town was formerly the monastic quarter and many of the old buildings survive. At the far end, the former Benedictine monastery of **St Emmeran**, was once a great centre of learning. The 12th-century 14-arch **Steinerne Brücke** over the Danube gives the best view of the medieval spires, towers and battlements along the waterfront. **Schloss Thurn und Taxis**, EMMERAMSPL., consists of Benedictine buildings that were turned into luxurious residences in Napoleonic times. The state rooms are open to the public when the family are not in residence.

🚃 10 mins' walk from the historic centre, or take 🚌 nos. 1/2/6.

ℹ️ **Tourist Office**: ALTES RATHAUS, RATHAUSPL. 4, ☎ (0941) 507 4410, fax (0941) 507 4419 (www.regensburg.de; tourismus@regensburg.de). Located in a 14th-century building.

🛏️ **Münchner Hof**, TÄNDLERGASSE 9, ☎ (0941) 58440, fax (0941) 561709, €€, is centrally located near the cathedral. Cheaper alternatives include **Hotel Zum Fröhlichen Türken**, FRÖHLICHE TÜRKEN-STR. 11, ☎ (0941) 53651, fax (0941) 562256, €, and **Am Peterstor**, FRÖHLICHE TÜRKEN-STR. 12, ☎ (0941) 54545, fax (0941) 54542, €–€€. **Youth hostel**: WÖHRDSTR. 60, ☎ (0941) 57402, fax (0941) 52411, on an island in the Danube, 5-min walk from the centre (🚌 no. 3 to GRASS). **Campsite**: **Azur**, WEINWEG 40, ☎ (0941) 270025, fax (0941) 299432.

🍴 The town claims to have the highest proportion of restaurants and bars per head of population in Germany. Thanks to the presence of several student residences in the centre (a deliberate policy by the town council), many are reasonably priced. The 850-year-old **Historische Wurstküche**, WEIßE LAMM GASSE 3, beside the Danube, is Germany's oldest sausage house and sells nothing else; note the awesomely high flood-marks on the walls. **Alte Linde Biergarten**, MÜLLERSTR. 1, on an island in the river, is a lovely beer garden overlooking the old town.

PASSAU

'Living on three rivers' at the point where the Danube, Inn and Ilz come together, this captivating cathedral city on the Austrian border has plenty of scope for water-side walks and cruises on the Danube. With the exception of the **Veste Oberhaus**, a castle high on a hill across the Danube, everything of interest is within close range.

The oldest part lies between the Danube and Inn; most of it postdates a major 17th-century fire and is an enjoyable jumble of colour-washed stone walls, assorted towers, and baroque, rococo and neoclassical styles. Like Regensburg, it's rather Italian in feel. The lofty onion-domed **Stephansdom** (St Stephen's Cathedral) is home to the world's largest church organ (over 17,000 pipes); try to catch a concert (weekdays 1230, May–Oct).

Veste Oberhaus, the former palace of the bishops and a prison for their enemies, is on a peninsula between the Danube and the narrower River Ilz. To avoid the steep walk up, use the regular bus services from the rail station and RATHAUSPL. The stronghold, which offers good photo opportunities over the confluence of the rivers, now contains the **Cultural History Museum** (54 rooms of art and artefacts spanning two millennia) as well as changing exhibitions. Another, more accessible viewpoint is the **Fünfersteg** footbridge, looking over the Inn towards the **Innstadt** on the opposite bank. River ferries leave from the quayside, along Fritz-Schäffer-Promenade, in front of the Rathaus, and offer day and longer trips up and down the Danube.

🚉 West of the centre, a 10-min walk to the right along BAHNHOFSTR., or take 🚌 nos. 7/8/9.

ℹ️ **Tourist Offices**: **Main office**: RATHAUSPL. 3, ☎ (0851) 955980, fax (0851) 35107. **Branch**: BAHNHOFSTR. 36, opposite the rail station: turn left and cross the road. ☎ (0851) 955980, fax (0851) 57298 (www.passau.de; tourist-info@passau.de). Room reservation service.

🏠 The **Hotel Deutscher Kaiser**, BAHNHOFSTR. 30, ☎ (0851) 955 6615, fax (0851) 955 6670, €€, is opposite the station. The **Pension Rössner**, BRÄUGASSE 19, ☎ (0851) 931350, fax (0851) 931 3555, €, is much more interestingly sited, near the confluence with a pleasant terrace facing the castle across the Danube. There are also cheaper **guesthouses** and **private rooms** available (see Tourist Office brochure). **Youth hostel**: Veste Oberhaus, OBERHAUS 125, ☎ (0851) 493780, fax (0851) 493 7820, is in the castle across the Danube. Cross the bridge by the docks and be prepared for a steep climb, or take the bus from RATHAUSPL. to the door. **Campsite**: Campground Ilzstadt, HALSERSTR. 34, ☎ (0851) 41457, by the River Ilz (🚌 nos. 1/2/3/4).

🍴 Reasonably-priced restaurants spill out onto the promenades beside the Danube in summer, particularly around RATHAUSPL.

WHERE NEXT FROM PASSAU?

Continue into Austria from Passau to Linz (10 trains, taking 1 hr 15 mins; ETT table 920), joining the **Innsbruck–Vienna** route on p. 349.

ROUTE DETAIL

Munich–Augsburg
ETT tables 900, 930

Type	Frequency	Typical journey time
Train	4 per hr	35 mins

Augsburg–Ulm
ETT table 930

Type	Frequency	Typical journey time
Train	2 per hr	40 mins

Ulm–Stuttgart
ETT table 930

Type	Frequency	Typical journey time
Train	3–4 per hr	55 mins

Stuttgart–Heidelberg
ETT table 923

Type	Frequency	Typical journey time
Train	2 per hr	1 hr 55 mins

Heidelberg–Karlsruhe
ETT table 910

Type	Frequency	Typical journey time
Train	1–2 per hr	30 mins

Karlsruhe–Baden-Baden
ETT tables 910, 916

Type	Frequency	Typical journey time
Train	1–2 per hr	18 mins

Baden-Baden–Offenburg
ETT tables 910, 916

Type	Frequency	Typical journey time
Train	Every hr	29 mins

Offenburg–Freiburg
ETT table 910

Type	Frequency	Typical journey time
Train	1–2 per hr	29 mins

Offenburg–Triberg
ETT table 916

Type	Frequency	Typical journey time
Train	Every hr	40 mins

Triberg–Konstanz
ETT table 916

Type	Frequency	Typical journey time
Train	Every hr	1 hr 35 mins

KEY JOURNEYS

Konstanz–Heidelberg
ETT tables 916/930/940

Type	Frequency	Typical journey time
Train	Every 2 hrs	3 hrs 9 mins (via Singen/Stuttgart)

Heidelberg–Munich
ETT table 930

Type	Frequency	Typical journey time
Train	Every hr	3 hrs 6 mins

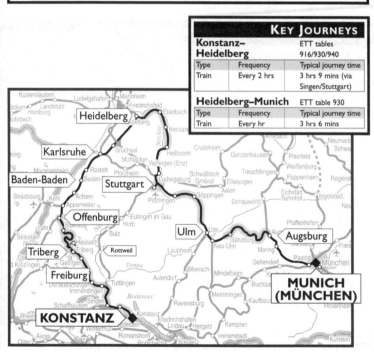

The scenic highpoint of this excursion to Germany's south-western corner is the **Schwarzwaldbahn**, the railway that crosses the lofty massif of the **Schwarzwald (Black Forest)**, climbing tortuously between Hornberg, Triberg and St Georgen and passing through a series of tunnels, before passing the source of the Danube at **Donaueschingen** and eventually reaching **Konstanz**, on the **Bodensee (Lake Constance)** at the border with Austria and Switzerland. The prelude is no less distinguished, leading out to the beautifully sited old university town of **Heidelberg** via **Augsburg** (a starting point for visiting the amazing **Ludwig II castles** near Füssen) and **Ulm** – with its stupendously tall cathedral spire. **Stuttgart** has one of the world's greatest modern buildings in the Neue Staatsgalerie. You can shorten the route by going directly from Stuttgart to Konstanz, taking in the improbably perfect-looking hill town of **Rottweil**.

MUNICH (MÜNCHEN)

See p. 257.

AUGSBURG

Within sprawling industrial outskirts is the attractive old heart of the city, originally fashioned in the 16th century by two wealthy trading and banking families, the Welsers and Fuggers. The main sights are within walking distance of the central pedestrianised RATHAUSPL, with its distinctive onion-domed **Rathaus** (painstakingly rebuilt after World War II). There's a great view from the adjoining **Perlachturm** (70 m), the tower of the **Peterskirche,** beside it.

A short stroll east down narrow alleys and over three small canals leads to the **Fuggerei**, a pioneering 'village' that the Fugger brothers built in 1516 as accommodation for the poor, who were requested to pray for the Fuggers in lieu of paying rent. You can see inside one small house that's been set up as a museum with furnishings of the period. The Fuggerei retains its four original gateways, which are still closed each night. By contrast, the city burghers lived in style in the stately mansions that still set the tone of MAXIMILIANSTR., where the **Schaezler Palace**, an 18th-century rococo edifice with a sumptuous ballroom, now houses the state art gallery.

On the hilly north side of the city centre, the lofty Gothic cathedral is striking for its imposing south doorway, 12th-century stained glass (the earliest in Germany), and paintings by Hans Holbein the Elder on the nave's four altars.

🚆 10 mins west of the city centre.

ℹ️ **Tourist Offices**: BAHNHOFSTR. 7, 5 mins from the rail station and RATHAUSPL. 10, ☎(0821) 502070, fax (0821) 502 0745 (www.regio-augsburg.de). Reservations for accommodation.

Within 0.5 km of the rail station is the **Lenzhalde**, Thelottstr. 2, ☎ (0821) 520745, fax (0821) 528761, €; a bit pricier is **Hennemann Stadthotel**, Gögginger Str. 39, ☎ (0821) 578077, fax (0821) 592600. **Youth hostel**: Beim Pfaffenkeller 3, ☎ (0821) 33909, fax (0821) 151149 (tram no. 2 to Stadtwerke). **Campsite: Campingplatz Augusta**, ABA Augsburg, Am Autobahnsee, ☎ (0821) 707575, 7 km from city centre (🚌 nos. 301/302/305 to Autobahnsee).

There's no shortage of places to eat in the old town centre, mostly offering hearty local Swabian or Bavarian dishes. Plenty of jolly beer cellars too.

Side Trips to the Royal Castles Bavaria's most famous attractions are the Royal Castles – Neuschwanstein, Hohenschwangau and Linderhof – built at preposterous expense by King Ludwig II in the 19th century.

The easiest way of getting to Neuschwanstein and Hohenschwangau is to take the train to **Füssen**, an attractive old town beneath the mountains, served by trains from Augsburg (2 hrs, ETT table 935). There's a youth hostel in Mariahilferstr. 5, ☎ (08362) 7754, fax (08362) 2770. From Füssen, numerous buses make the short journey to the castles.

For Linderhof, there are regular buses from **Oberammergau** (ETT tables 895, 897; reached from Munich via Murnau; hourly, 1 hr 45 mins), a touristy but attractive small Alpine town celebrated for its Passion Play and numerous painted houses; the play is performed only every ten years, but in the meantime you can visit the theatre and see the props and costumes.

Alternatively you can go by **Europabus**, which follows the celebrated Romantic Road from Frankfurt to Füssen via Würzburg, Rothenburg, Dinkelsbühl, Nördlingen, Augsburg and several other historic towns (60% discount for holders of Eurailpass, Europass, and DB Railcard; reservation strongly recommended, ☎ (069) 790350, fax (069) 7903219; one bus daily, Apr–Oct, ETT table 927; you can join at a number of points).

Just over the road from Schwangau (and 4 km from Füssen), Hohenschwangau and Neuschwanstein are within walking distance of each other (involving a modest climb). Tudor-style **Hohenschwangau,** built in the early 19th century by Maximilian II, was an attempt to recreate the romantic past and was adorned with Wagnerian references by his son, King Ludwig II. Ludwig surpassed his father by building the fairy-tale neo-Gothic **Neuschwanstein** on a rocky outcrop high above; it is best seen from the dizzying heights of the **Marienbrücke**, a bridge spanning a huge gorge. This most famous of his castles was never finished – hence the Throne Room without a throne, and doorways leading to suicidal drops.

The third castle, **Linderhof**, 20 km east, is a small French-style château, modelled on the Petit Trianon at Versailles. The outstanding oddity is the king's dining table, engineered to be lowered to the kitchens and then raised again for him to dine entirely alone.

GERMANY

A fourth Ludwig castle is **Herrenchiemsee** on a wooded island on the Chiemsee south-east of Munich. Built in the style of Versailles near Paris, this building has a hall of mirrors but remains unfinished (train from Munich to Prien am Chiemsee, hourly, 1 hr, then ferry). He lived here for only a week, before his body was found mysteriously drowned.

ULM

This endearing old town on the Danube has a quaint quarter known as **Fischer-und-Gerberviertel,** the old fishing and tanning district, with half-timbered houses beside the Blau, a rushing tributary. Most places of interest are on the north bank of the Danube and the main attractions are easily walkable.

You can hardly fail to notice the soaring spire of the **Münster** (cathedral), all 161 m of it, the tallest such structure in the world. Dominating a huge traffic-free square, the cathedral represents gothic architecture at its mightiest. Climb the 768 steps up the tower to survey the terrain, on a clear day, from the Black Forest to the Alps.

Many buildings that were hit in the bombing raid in 1944 have been carefully restored, including the 14th-century **Rathaus**, MARKTPLATZ, NEUE STR., with its intricate astronomical clock. One notably fine Renaissance building houses the **Ulmer Museum**, MARKTPL. 9, notable for its early Ulm paintings and an outstanding 20th-century collection.

INTERNET ACCESS
Albert's Café, KORNHAUSPL.; or at the public library, **Weinhof** in the Schworhaus; or **Connect**, FRAUENSTR. 25.

Ulm was the birthplace of Einstein, marked by a memorial opposite the rail station. It was also the place where Albrecht Ludwig Berblinger, the 'Tailor of Ulm', made one of man's first attempts to fly. In 1811, he took off from the Adlerbastei (town wall), but didn't make it across the Danube.

Towards the Danube, the **Metzgerturm** (Butchers' Tower), formerly a prison, is known as the leaning tower of Ulm (36 m high) as it's about 2 m off the vertical. Paths lead from it to a pleasant riverside walk dotted with sculptures or up onto a stretch of the old city walls.

RAIL 5 mins to centre through pedestrian zone.

i **Tourist Office**: Stadthaus, MÜNSTERPL. 50, ☎(0731) 161 2830, fax (0731) 161 1641 (www.tourismus.ulm.de; info@tourismus.ulm.de). There is a free accommodation booking service.

There are several reasonably priced central hotels, including **Münster-Hotel**, MÜNSTERPL. 14 (opposite the cathedral), ☎(0731) 64162, €–€€, and the **Pension Jäger**, SÖFLINGER STR. 210, ☎(0731) 389643, fax (0731) 9387295, €. **Youth hostel**: GRIMMELFINGERWEG 45, ☎(0731) 384455, fax (0731) 384511, 4 km south-west of the centre (🚌nos. 4/8 to SCHULZENTRUM).

The old fishermen's quarter near the Danube has a selection of restaurants in picturesque spots. The wood-panelled **Allgäuer Hof**, 'Ulm's First Pancake House', FISCHERGASSE 12, ☎ (0731) 67408, features traditional pancakes on large platters, with a choice of over 40 toppings.

STUTTGART

Surrounded by green hills, the capital of Baden-Württemberg is probably best known for its vibrant cultural activities and as the home of the Daimler-Benz and Porsche motor factories. But the traffic-free centre, radiating from the huge **Schlosspl**. – with its pavement cafés, buskers, fountains and gardens – is an inviting place to stroll. Along one side is the **Neues Schloss**, the former palace of the Württemberg kings, now offices. The **Württembergisches Landesmuseum**, SCHILLERPL., occupies the Altes Schloss opposite, an imposing Renaissance palace. Its exhibits range from 19th-century crown jewels and Swabian sculptures to an intact Celtic grave and Renaissance clocks. The nearby **Stiftskirche**, extensively rebuilt over the centuries, has remarkable modern windows and Renaissance carvings of 11 of the rulers of Württemberg around the choir.

Round the corner, the **Market Hall** groans with delicacies Mon–Fri from 0700-1830, and on Sat 0700–1600. A **flea market** is held on KARLSPL. on Sat. The **Schlossgarten** park stretches all along the city centre as far as the River Neckar and then joins the Rosensteinpark, with the Natural History Museum and the **Wilhelma**, a large zoological/botanical garden with about 9000 animals, buildings in Moorish style and a large lily pond.

The British architect James Stirling has firmly put the city on the map with his **Neue Staatsgalerie**, the post-modern wing of the **Staatsgalerie**, KONRAD- ADENAUER-STR. 30, with its audacious use of materials. It's the setting for one of the world's largest Picasso collections, as well as a comprehensive survey of 20th-century art. The adjoining **Alte Staatsgalarie** has earlier works, notably the superb *Herrenberg Altar* by Jorg Ratgeb.

Motor enthusiasts can head for the **Daimler-Benz Museum**, Mercedesstr. 137, Bad Cannstatt (S1 to GOTTLIEB-DAIMLER STADION), where 100 historic models are on show. Racing cars make up the bulk of the exhibits in the smaller **Porsche-Museum**, Porrschestr. 42, in the northern suburb of Zuffenhausen (S6 to NEUWIRTSHAUS).

STUTTCARD AND TRAVEL PASS

The **Stuttcard** (valid 3 days) allows free travel on public transport, free admission to nearly all state museums, reductions at other attractions including the zoo, planetarium, mineral baths, theatres and night clubs, plus savings on city tours. Available from Tourist Offices but only if you book a hotel room.

You can get a **pass** for three consecutive days' travel on Stuttgart's public transport system (rapid-transit railway, city trains and buses). For the inner zone or entire Stuttgart region. Available on proof of hotel reservation only.

GERMANY

RAIL 5 mins' walk from the centre, along SCHLOSSPL.

i **Tourist Office**: Directly on coming out from the rail station underpass, at KÖNIGSTR. IA, fax
(0711) 22280 (www.stuttgart-tourist.de; info@stuttgart-tourist.de). Free accommodation
booking service, ☎ (0711) 222 8233, fax (0711) 222 8251. They also sell tickets, ☎ (0711) 255
5555 (Mon–Fri 1000–1800).

🛏 **Hotel** prices around the station tend to be high as it is so central. Small **pensions**, such as the
Theaterpension, PFIZERSTR. 12, ☎ (0711) 240722, fax (0711) 236 00 97, €, **Schwarzwaldheim**,
FRITZ-ELSAS-STR 20, ☎ (0711) 296988, €, and **Alte Mira**, BUCHSENSTR. 24, ☎ 0711) 2229502, fax
(0711) 950329, €, begin at around €35, but without private bath or toilet. **Youth hostel**:
HAUSSMANNSTR. 27, ☎ (0711) 241583, a 15-min uphill walk from the rail station (tram no. 15 to
EUGENSPL.). **Campsite**: **Campingplatz Cannstatter Wasen**, MERCEDESSTR. 40, ☎ (0711)
556696, is beside the River Neckar (tram nos. 1/2). Open all year.

SIDE TRIP FROM
STUTTGART TO ROTTWEIL
From Stuttgart you can go south to Singen (1 hr 50 mins–
2 hrs 20 mins; ETT table 940) and change trains there to
Konstanz. This is a very pretty line through the **Neckar
valley**. On the way, **Rottweil** deserves a pause. It's a
delightful little market town, squeezed on a spur of the Neckar between the Black
Forest and the Schwäbische Alb (Swabian Jura), with tremendous views. Punctuated
by the medieval Schwarzes Tor (Black Tower), the pedestrianised Hauptstrasse has a
striking array of colourful Renaissance and baroque houses displaying a wealth of
carvings and murals, and sprouting projecting oriel windows.

The town is also the provenance of the ferocious Rottweiler dog, descended from
Roman guard-dog stock and formerly used by local butchers to pull carts (hence the
German name of Metzerhund – butcher's dog). **Tourist Office**: im Alten Rathaus,
Hauptstr. 21 ☎ (0741) 494280, fax (0741) 494373 (www.rottweil.de; tourist-
information@rottweil.de).

HEIDELBERG

Heidelberg's romantic setting, beneath wooded hills along the banks of the River
Neckar and overlooked by castle ruins, makes it a magnet for tourists and movie-
makers. The town has a long history and is home to Germany's oldest university,
founded in 1386, but there's little that's ancient in the centre, as most of it was rebuilt
in the 18th century following wholesale destruction by Louis XIV's troops in 1693.
In high summer, there's pretty much a non-stop procession of tourists through the
central streets.

The city's most famous sight is the part-ruined pink sandstone castle, high above
the town. From its terraces, you get a beautiful view over the red rooftops and gently flowing river.

HEIDELBERG'S CASTLE EVENTS

The highlight of summer is the castle festival (early July–early Sept), when opera performances are staged outdoors in the cobbled courtyard; Romberg's romantic operetta 'The Student Prince' is the permanent fixture. For tickets, ☎ (06221) 582000. Grand fireworks displays are held on the first Sat in June, July and Sept.

Many fine old mansions are scattered around the old town (**Altstadt**). The buildings around MARKTPL. include the Renaissance **Haus zum Ritter,** and the 14th-century **Heiliggeistkirche** (Church of the Holy Spirit). UNIVERSITÄTSPL., which has the **Löwenbrunnen** (Lion Fountain) in the centre, is the location of both the 'old' and 'new' universities. Until 1914, students whose high spirits had got out of hand were confined in the special students' prison round the corner in AUGUSTINERSTR. 2. Incarceration was regarded as an honour and self-portraits are common in the graffiti on the walls.

Across the river, over the *Alte Brücke*, the steep **Schlagenweg steps** zig-zag up through orchards to the **Philosophenweg** (Philosophers' Path). This is a scenic lane across the hillside, so-called because the views inspired philosophic meditation.

DAY TRIPS FROM HEIDELBERG

Summer **cruises** on the River Neckar depart from the quay by Stadthalle. Along the banks, half-timbered villages nestle in woods below old castles on rocky crags. Within a few minutes you reach **Neckargemünd** and then **Neckarsteinach**, which boasts four ruined castles.

Schwetzingen (served by a frequent train service) is renowned for the 18th-century **Schwetzinger Palace**. The building itself is not vastly interesting, but its extensive gardens (at their colourful best in May) are an amazing Rococo wonderland of statues, follies, mock ruins, tricks of perspective and fountains.

🚆 10-mins walk to the edge of the pedestrian district, or take 🚌 nos. 1/2; or 20 mins to the heart of the old Altstadt (or 🚌 no. 33).

ℹ️ **Tourist Office**: WILLI-BRANDT-PL. 1, directly in front of the rail station, ☎ (06221) 19433, fax (06221) 142222 (www.cvb-heidelberg.de; info@cvb-heidelberg.de). Accommodation booking service. The **Heidelberg Card** is valid for city travel, castle admission and various discounts (for 1–2 days including funicular ride to the Schloss). Guided walking tours in English, Thur–Sun at 1000 (Apr–Oct) from UNIVERSITÄTSPL. There are also themed guided tours, such as *Heidelberg in the Time of Romanticism*, or *Student Life in Heidelberg*: check with the Tourist Office for details.

🚌 A network of buses and trams serve the pedestrianised Altstadt, where a funicular ride saves the 300-step climb up to the Schloss. It's also possible to tour by bike (rentals available from **Per Bike**, BERGHEIMER STR, ☎ (06221) 161148), particularly pleasant for exploring the banks of the Neckar.

🏨 Heidelberg is a prime tourist destination, so the later you book during the summer, the further from the centre you will find yourself staying. The **Goldener Hirsch**, KLEINGEMUNDER STR 27, ☎ (06221) 800211, €, is a bit away from the Altstadt, but has simple rooms. **Am Kornmarkt**, KORNMARKT 7, ☎ (06221) 24325, fax (06221) 28218, €€, is central. **Youth**

GERMANY

hostel: TIERGARTENSTR. 5, ☎ (06221) 412066, fax (06221) 402559 (🚌no. 33 from the station). **Campsite**: **Camping Heidelberg**, SCHLIERBACHER LANDSTR. 151, ☎/fax (06221) 802506 (🚌no. 35 from the station, 20 mins).

🔆 The **Altstadt** is very touristy and its restaurants lively with a student atmosphere. Many spill out onto the traffic-free streets. This is also where most of the nightlife goes on. You are spoilt for choice along HEILIGGEISTR. and UNTERE-STR. *Kneipen* (taverns) are an important part of Heidelberg life and in term-time they fill up with students.

WHERE NEXT FROM HEIDELBERG?

*Heidelberg is served by trains to **Frankfurt** (55 mins, ETT table 910), where you can join the **Cologne–Passau** route (p. 272).*

KARLSRUHE

A major industrial and university city, Karlsruhe's most interesting sight is the huge **Schloss**, home of the Margraves and Grand Dukes of Baden until 1918. Built in 1715 by Margrave Karl Wilhelm, it's an enormous neo-classical pile with extensive formal gardens. From the tower, you see clearly how he designed the city to spread out from.it like a fan, with 32 streets.

Inside the Schloss, the wonderfully eclectic **Badisches Landesmuseum** covers prehistory to the present day. The Orangerie (free entry), merits a look for its 19th- and 20th-century European art. You'll need more time for the **Kunsthalle**, HANS-THOMA-STR. 2–6, a wide-ranging collection ranging from the 15th to 19th centuries and notable above all for its German primitives, among them Grünewald's astonishingly powerful Crucifixion; later German works include a fine set of paintings by the Black Forest artist Hans Thoma.

Marktplatz, the enormous central square near the *Schloss*, is dominated by a pyramid of red sandstone, under which Karl Wilhelm is buried.

The ZKM (*Zentrum furKunst und Medientechnologie Karlsruhe*: Centre for Art and Media Technology), LORENZSTR. 19 (tram no. 6 or 🚌no. 55 from the station), is an experience-oriented centre, media museum and interactive art gallery. There's enough for a full day's visit.

Directly across from the rail station and right next to the Tourist Office is the **Stadtpark-Tiergarten**. The park provides a respite from traffic and is a very pleasant way to cross town (particularly handy for getting to the Schloss). There is a boating lake and in season, outdoor cafés and a blaze of flowers. The small, modern zoo has a refreshing lack of cages for the most part.

🚆 25-min walk south of the centre (tram nos. 3/4).

ℹ️ **Tourist Office**: BAHNHOFPL. 6, ☎ (0721) 35530, fax (0721) 35534399 (www.karlsruhe.de;

vv@karlsruhe.de), opposite the rail station. Free room-booking service. There are good bus and tram services. Rhine cruises operate Easter–Nov from the western edge of town.

Internet Cafés
webSPIDERcafé,
Moltkestr. 28,
☎ (0721) 292 3745;
**Internetcafe am
Kronenplatz**, Kronenstr.
30, ☎ (0721) 338533.

🛏 **Pension Stadtmitte**, Zähringer Str. 72, ☎/fax (0721) 389637, €, and **Pension am Zoo**, Ettlingerstr. 33, ☎ (0721) 33678, €, both offer rooms from around €120 and €140 respectively. **Youth hostel**: Moltkestr. 24, ☎ (0721) 28248, fax (0721) 27647, west of Schlossgarten (tram nos. 3/S1-S11 to Moltkestr.).

BADEN-BADEN

Fashionable in the 19th century for gambling, particularly among Russian aristocrats, Baden-Baden soon became a major spa resort, thanks to its health-promoting hot mineral springs. The spa continues to this day, and it's extremely upmarket, with elegant promenades surrounding the pedestrian shopping area, while the Casino rakes in money. Even if you've no intention of either taking a Kur (spa treatment) or gambling your money away, it remains a compelling place for people-watching.

A long, manicured park with an avenue of plane trees known as the **Lichtentaler Allee** forms the heart of the resort. At the renovated art nouveau **Trinkhalle** (pump-room), Kaiserstr. 3, romantic murals depict the town's history as a spa; here you will find the tourist office and a bistro. There is a small well inside where you can try the saline waters.

Indulging in a spa treatment is a memorable experience that won't break the bank; at the historic **Friedrichsbad** you get a 3-hour session (whirlpools, saunas, steam rooms and hot and cold baths), massages extra. It has a marvellous Romanisches-Irisches Bad (Roman-Irish Bath, which combines bathing in thermal spring water with exposing the body to warm dry air), nudity mandatory. Underneath the building you can see traces of the original Roman baths. The **Caracalla-Therme**, Römerpl. 11, is a complex with currents, whirlpools and hot and cold grottos; upstairs (nudity mandatory) has saunas, steam rooms and suntan areas. Inside, the huge pool is under a Roman-style dome and outside, both hot and cold pools are embellished by fountains. Take your own towel.

The Casino in the neo-classical **Kurhaus**, Kaiserallee 1, is Germany's oldest and biggest. Redecorated in French style in 1853, it is promoted as one of the world's most beautiful casinos. There are daily tours 1000–1200 (no dress code). Gambling starts at 1400, dress code (jackets and ties available for hire). Over 21s only.

🚉 This is at **Oos**, 12 km north-west of town; 🚌 no. 201 runs every 10 mins 0500–2000, then every 20 mins until 2300.

ℹ️ **Tourist Office**: Schwarzwald Str. 52 (at the entrance to the city by road); **Trinkhalle** (Pump

Room), KAISERALLEE (city centre); both 🏨(07221) 275200, fax (07221) 275202 (www.baden-baden.com; online hotel reservations).

🛏 As the baths and casino attract many wealthy visitors, most hotels are glossy and expensive. Two cheaper options, are **Hotel Deutscher Kaiser**, LICHTENTALER HAUPTSTR. 35, 🏨(07221) 72152, €, (🚌no. 201 to ECKERLESTR. from the rail station or town centre), and **Am Friedrichsbad**, GERNSBACHER STR. 31, 🏨(07221) 271046, fax (07221) 38310, €€. There are also **private rooms** available. **Youth hostel**: **Jugendherberge**, HARDBERGSTR. 34, 🏨(07221) 52223, fax (07221) 60012 (🚌no. 201 to GROSSE DOLLENSTR., then a 7-min walk). The closest **campsite** is at **Campingplatz Adam**, 77815 BUHL-OBERBRUCH, 🏨(07223) 23194, approximately 12 kms from Baden – the site also does bike rentals.

OFFENBURG

Change here for trains to **Basel** (p. 321) via Freiburg.

FREIBURG

Placed at the western edge of the Black Forest, the city spreads around its Gothic cathedral. With most sights in the Altstadt (old town), it's very walkable so long as you don't fall into the numerous *Bächle* (gulleys) that run along the streets. This old drainage system was used as a fire precaution and for watering livestock and often still has water flowing along it. Freiburg's famously easy-going atmosphere is immediately apparent; the university is very much the life and soul of the city.

Topped by a 116-m spire, the red sandstone **Münster** (cathedral) has a Romanesque-Gothic interior illuminated by 13th- to 16th-century stained glass – many sections depicting the guilds who paid for them. From the tower, 331 steps up, you get a vertigo-inducing panorama.

On MUNSTERPL., the **Historisches Kaufhaus**, an arcaded merchants' hall, is flanked by two handsome baroque palaces, **Erzbischofliches Palais** and **Wenzingerhaus**. The latter was the house of the 18th-century artist Christian Wenzinger. A short stroll away, RATHAUSPL. is notable for the **Neues Rathaus**. A bridge links **Altes** and **Neues Rathaus** (old and new town hall). The nearby red and gold **Haus zum Walfisch** (FRANZISKANERSTR.) is a recreation of the elegant house (bombed in World War II) where Erasmus lived for two years. The **Augustiner**, SALZSTR., the town's best museum, contains religious and folkloric art from the Upper Rhine area.

WHERE NEXT FROM BADEN-BADEN?

It is easy to get to Switzerland or France from here, with 5 direct trains per day to Strasbourg (40 mins) and trains every 2 hrs to Basel (1 hr 30 mins; ETT table 910), at the end of the Cherbourg–Strasbourg route across central France (pp. 80–85); it's also easy to get to Switzerland, with hourly services to Basel (40 mins).

A good 10-min walk west of the centre.

i **Tourist Office**: Rotteckring 14, ☎ (0761) 3881880, fax (0761) 37003 (www.freiburg.de; touristik@fwt-online.de), is two blocks down Eisenbahnstr. Free accommodation booking service.

There are plenty of cheaper places (€–€€) to stay (and restaurants too) around the **Altstadt**, such as **Hotel Löwen**, Herrenstr. 47, ☎ (0761) 33161, fax (0761) 36238, €–€€, and **Hotel Schemmer**, Eschholzstr. 63, ☎ (0761) 207490, fax (0761) 207 4950, €. **Youth hostel**: **Jugendherberge**, Kartäuserstr. 151, ☎ (0761) 67656, at the extreme east of town (tram no. 1 to Römerhof). **Campsite: Hirzberg**, Kartäuserstr. 99, ☎ (0761) 35054, near the youth hostel.

TRIBERG

Cuckoo-clock shops have arrived here with a vengeance. At the heart of the **Schwarzwald** (Black Forest) and known for the purity of its air, the touristy spa town has been a centre for cuckoo clock-making since 1824, when Josef Weisser started his business in the **Haus der 1000 Uhren** (House of a Thousand Clocks). The **Schwarzwaldmuseum** is full of woodcarvings, some splendid local costumes and inevitably clocks. Apart from timepieces, **Triberg** is an appealing centre for walking; one walk is to the highest waterfall in Germany, which cascades down 163 m in seven stages and is floodlit at night.

1.5 km north-east of the town.

i **Tourist Office**: At the **Kurhaus**, Luisenstr. 10, ☎ (07722) 953 230, fax (07722) 953 236 (www.triberg.de; tourist-info@triberg.de). Accommodation reservation service.

Hotel Central, am Marktplatz, ☎ (07722) 4360, €. Just 4 km outside Triberg at Gremmelsbach is **Pension Schoch**, Untertal 13, ☎ /fax (07722) 4825, € (min stay 3 days). **Youth hostel**: Rohrbacher, ☎ (07722) 4110.

KONSTANZ

The Swiss border cuts through the southern part of this town on the **Bodensee** (Lake Constance). Leafy gardens extend along the water's edge and there's a pleasant old quarter, **Niederburg**, where alleys wind between half-timbered buildings with decorated façades. The harbour is the departure point for lake cruises and ferries. At the mouth of the marina is the 9-m high Imperia, a controversial statue built in 1993, allegedly depicting a famous courtesan of the past. In one hand she holds the king (representing the state) and in the other, the pope (representing the church), thus questioning who has the real power. In the Marktstätte (Market Place), elaborate frescos on the Renaissance **Rathaus** depict the town's history, and children clamber on the bronze beasts of a decidedly jolly 19th-century fountain.

🚊 Between BAHNHOFPL., the eastern boundary of Altstadt, and the **Bodensee** (Lake Constance).

_i_ **Tourist Office**: BAHNHOFPL. 13, ☎(07531) 133030, fax 133060 (www.konstanz.de and www.bodensee-info.com; info@ti.konstanz.de). Accommodation service. Bicycles can be hired at **Kultur-Rädle Radverleih** next to the Tourist Office at the station, ☎(07531) 27310, or **Pro Velo**, KONZILSTR. 3, ☎(07531) 29329.

🛏 The centre of town is more expensive than the (very pleasant) outlying villages, with, for example, **Gasthof Zur Linde**, RADOLFZELLERSTR. 27, ☎(07531) 97420, fax (07531) 974255, €–€€, and **Hotel Sonnenhof**, O.-RAGGENBASS STR. 3, ☎(07531) 22257, fax (07531) 20358, €. Nearby in **Dingelsdorf**, 30 mins away via 🚌 no. 4, is the **Gasthaus Seeschau**, ZUR SCHIFFSLÄNDE 11, ☎(07533) 5190, fax (07533) 7894, €, and **Hotel Pension Rose**, WALLHAUSERSTR. 12, ☎(07533) 97000, fax (07533) 97002, €; the last two have the cheapest rooms. **Private rooms** are available from about €25. **Youth hostel**: **Otto-Moericke-Turm**, ALLMANNSHÖHE 16, ☎(07531) 32260 (🚌 no. 4). **Campsite**: **Campingplatz Klausenhorn**, FOHRENBÜHLWEG 45, ☎/fax (07537) 33057, open Apr–Sept, or **Litzelstetten-Mainau**, GROSSHERZOG-FRIEDRICHSTR. 43, ☎(07531) 943030 which is near the shore opposite the Mainau island, open Easter–Sept.

AROUND THE BODENSEE (LAKE CONSTANCE) The quay on the Bodensee (Lake Constance), behind the rail station, offers a wide choice of boat trips and cruises on the lake and the Rhine (into which it flows nearby). The service is seasonal. The main operator is **Bodensee-Schiffsbetriebe**, HAFENSTR. 6; ☎(07531) 281398 (www.bsb-online.com). DB rail passes are valid. **Lindau** (3 hrs 30 mins by ferry) has rail services to Ulm and Augsburg (ETT table 935). Other ferry destinations include **Meersburg**, an atmospheric hillside town with a picturesque _Markt_ and old inhabited castle; **Unteruhldingen**, which has an open-air museum (with re-creations of Neolithic dwellings) and a basilica that's fully worth the 20-min uphill walk; **Überlingen**, a strikingly attractive town with a Gothic _Münster_ and a fine Moat Walk; and the island of **Reichenau**, which has three 9th-century monasteries, each surrounded by a village. Linked by a footbridge to the mainland, and reached by boat services from Konstanz, **Mainau** is a delightful 110-acre island, where a lushly colourful garden surrounds an inhabited baroque palace that was used by the Teutonic Knights for more than five centuries.

KEY JOURNEYS

Munich–Dresden — ETT tables 880, 900

Type	Frequency	Typical journey time
Train	Every 2 hrs	6 hrs 19 mins (change at Nuremberg)

Munich–Weimar — ETT tables 850, 900

Type	Frequency	Typical journey time
Train	Every hr	4 hrs 46 mins (change at Fulda)

Weimar– Berlin — ETT table 850

Type	Frequency	Typical journey time
Train	Every 2 hrs	3 hrs 5 mins

Munich–Berlin — ETT table 850

Type	Frequency	Typical journey time
Train	Every 2 hrs	6 hrs 40 mins

Steinach bei Rothenburg–Würzburg — ETT table 905

Type	Frequency	Typical journey time
Train	Every hr	43 mins

Würzburg–Fulda — ETT table 900

Type	Frequency	Typical journey time
Train	Every hr	30 mins

Fulda–Eisenach — ETT table 850

Type	Frequency	Typical journey time
Train	Every hr	55 mins

Eisenach–Gotha — ETT table 850

Type	Frequency	Typical journey time
Train	2 per hr	15 mins

Gotha–Erfurt — ETT tables 850, 865

Type	Frequency	Typical journey time
Train	2–3 per hr	18 mins

Erfurt–Weimar — ETT tables 850, 851

Type	Frequency	Typical journey time
Train	2–3 per hr	15 mins

Weimar–Leipzig — ETT table 850

Type	Frequency	Typical journey time
Train	Every 2 hrs	50 mins

Leipzig–Dresden — ETT table 842

Type	Frequency	Typical journey time
Train	2 per hr	1 hr 8 mins

Dresden–Berlin — ETT table 843

Type	Frequency	Typical journey time
Train	Every 2 hrs	2 hrs

ROUTE DETAIL

Munich–Eichstätt — ETT table 905

Type	Frequency	Typical journey time
Train	Every hr	1 hr 20 mins

Eichstätt–Steinach bei Rothenburg — ETT table 905

Type	Frequency	Typical journey time
Train	Every 1–2 hrs	1 hr 33 mins

This route passes through northern **Bavaria**, and includes the appealing old town of **Eichstätt** in the delightful **Altmühl** valley, and equally pretty Ansbach (not included here), and the university town of Würzburg. The picture-book **Rothenburg ob der Tauber** is a major tourist attraction, while the rail route takes you into former East Germany, visiting **Weimar, Leipzig** and **Eisenach**. Elsewhere you can take your pick of lesser-known gems such as **Fulda, Gotha** and **Erfurt**. There's a lot to take in during this trip, and if you don't have time for all of it, take the detour to Rothenburg, then cut across from Ansbach to **Dresden**.

EICHSTÄTT

For a great view of the town, make the steep but pretty 15-min climb from the station up a wooded hillside to the **Willibaldsburg**, a splendid white palace built between the 14th and 18th centuries. A recent addition to this is the **Hortus Eystettensis**, a garden based on the plants documented in the definitive 16th-century illustrated horticultural work. The Burg also houses the **Jura-Museum** of natural history, with a notable collection of fossils from the Altmühl valley.

The bustling market square consists of pretty gabled buildings, shops and pavement cafés, while nearby the **Residenzplatz** is a serene complex of pale green and white 18th-century mansions in a semi circle around the imposing **Residenz**, the former bishops' residence, now used by the town council as offices and reception rooms (free guided tours Mon–Sat). The adjoining light and airy Gothic **Dom** (cathedral) is notable for its stained-glass windows by Hans Holbein and intricately-carved 500-year-old Pappenheim altar.

Eichstätt Stadt, ☎ (01805) 99 66 33, is served by a shuttle train from **Eichstätt Bahnhof** on the main line, a 9-min journey. The Tourist Office is a 3-min walk over the bridge from the station.

i **Tourist Office**: DOMPL. 8, ☎ (08421) 98800, fax (08421) 988030 (www.eichstatt.de; tourismus@eichstatt.btl.de). Information on the **Altmühl Nature Park**, the surrounding area, is at: NOTRE-DAME 1, ☎ (08421) 98760 (tourismus@naturpark-altmuehltal.btl.de).

🛏 Spaces in guesthouses are easy to find. **Pension Poseidon**, WESENSTR. 17, ☎ (08421) 2640, €; **Gasthof Ratskeller**, KARDINAL-PREYSINGPL. 8–10, ☎ (08421) 901258, €, is slightly more expensive. **Private rooms** are also available (pick up a brochure at the Tourist Office). **Youth hostel**: REICHENAUSTR. 15, ☎ (08421) 980410, 10 mins from the rail station (closed Dec–Jan).

STEINACH BEI ROTHENBURG

Change here for the 15-min train journey to **Rothenburg ob der Tauber**.

ROTHENBURG OB DER TAUBER

This little town probably justifies the title 'the Jewel of the Romantic Road' – the **Romantische Strasse** (ETT table 927 for Eurobus times; 60% discount for holders of Eurailpass, Europass, and DB Railcard) being the best known of Germany's themed routes, running from Würzburg to Füssen. Situated on a rocky outcrop surrounded by medieval walls, its pastel-coloured steep-gabled houses – some half-timbered – are the stuff of picture-books, especially in summer, when window boxes trail with flowers.

A great area for nightlife is the **Bermuda Dreieck** ('Bermuda Triangle)', between Ansbach-, Adam- and Horberstrasse, with two discos, a cocktail bar and a couple of *Kneipen* (pubs).

As early as 1902, the local council, showing commendable foresight, imposed a preservation order, so physically not much has changed since the 15th century – if you ignore all the tourist shops, galleries, restaurants and the packs of holiday visitors, which can dilute the atmosphere. One of the best walks is around the intact (and roofed) town walls, which are long enough for you to lose most of the hordes of visitors.

On **Marktplatz**, there is usually some entertainment, whether a musical concert or a theatrical performance. The glockenspiel on the 15th-century **Ratstrinkstube** (Councillors' Tavern), now the Tourist Office, re-enacts on the hour (1100–1500 and 2000–2200) the historic scene in 1631, during the Thirty Years War, when Mayor Nusch rose to the challenge of knocking back a gallon of wine to save the town from destruction. The **Meistertrunk** festivities at Whitsun commemorate his feat. Climb the 200 steps (very steep and narrow at the top) onto the **Rathaus tower's** roof for a dizzying view. Then walk down Schmiedgasse to the **Burggarten**; graced by a remarkable 15th-century backdrop of the town, these shaded gardens were the site of a castle destroyed in an earthquake in 1356.

Just off the Marktpl., **St Jakobskirche** is renowned for its intricately-carved wood altar (1504), the Heiligblut-Altar (in the first floor west gallery), by the great Würzburg sculptor Riemenschneider.

The town centre is a 10-min walk straight ahead, then follow '*Stadtmitte*' signs.

i **Tourist Office**: Marktpl. 2, ☎ (09861) 40492, fax (09861) 86807 (www.rothenburg.de; info@ rothenburg.de). Room availability hotline: ☎ (09861) 19412. **Guided tours** in English at 1100 and 1400 from Marktpl., Apr–Oct and Dec; evening tour at 2000.

There is plenty of choice, including **private houses**, both inside and outside the old town walls. These include **Gästehaus Victoria**, Klingenschütt 4, ☎ (09861) 87682, €, and **Gärtner Hedwig**, Krebengässchen 2, ☎ (09861) 3248, €. **Youth hostel: Rossmühle und Spitalhof**, Mühlacker 1, ☎ (09861) 94160, located in a former horse mill in the old town. **Campsite: Tauber-Romantik.**

WÜRZBURG

Würzburg is a university town where in autumn the *Winzerfest*, a traditional annual harvest festival, celebrates the (justly famous) Franconian wines.

The rebuilt domes, spires and red roofs are seen at their best from the terrace battlements of **Festung Marienberg**, an impressive white fortress on a wooded hill above the River Main. Converted to baroque style in the 17th century, little remains inside, though the **Mainfränkisches Museum** displays a large collection of works by Franconian artists, including superb 16th-century wood carvings by one of the city's most famous sons, Tilman Riemenschneider. The Festung is best reached by no. 9, a 10-min ride, otherwise it's a 40-min walk.

The market place is notable for the **Marienkapelle**, a 14th-century church with more Riemenschneider carvings, and the richly decorated 18th-century **Haus zum Falken**, which houses the Tourist Office.

The town's main sight is the massive sandstone **Residenz**, RESIDENZ-PL. Built as the new palace of the Prince-Bishops in the 18th century by Balthasar Neumann, it has been given World Heritage Site status. Statues line the roof façade, symbolising the church's wealth and power. The rooms are sumptuously decorated with frescos and sculptures by leading artists of their day, including the Venetian master Tiepolo. Nightlife revolves around SANDERSTR., popular with students.

> **INTERNET CAFÉS**
>
> **Café Cairo** (near the youth hostel); **Café Franz**, FRANZ LUDWIGSTR. 6.

 At the foot of vineyards on the northern edge of the town centre, a 15-min walk.

i **Tourist Offices: Congress & Tourismus Zentrale**, AM CONGRESS CENTRUM, ☎(0931) 372335, fax (0931) 373652 (www.wuerzburg.de; tourismus@wuerzburg.de). **Offices**: In front of **rail station**: ☎(0931) 373436. Two-hour guided walks around the town in English start from the Haus Zum Falken Tourist Office at 1100, daily (May–Oct).

There is no shortage of hotels in all categories. Handy for the station and moderately priced is **Pension Spehnkuch**, RÖNTGENRING 7, ☎ (0931) 54752, fax (0931) 54760, €; the **Pension Siegel**, REISGRUBENGASSE 7, ☎(0931) 52941, fax (0931) 52967, €, is similarly priced. **Youth hostel**: **DJH Jugendgästehaus**, BURKARDER STR. 44, ☎(0931) 42590, fax (0931) 416862, on the bank of the Main, below Festung. **Campsite**: **Camping Canoe Club**, MERGENHEIMERSTR. 13B, ☎(0931) 72536 (tram no. 5 to JUDENBÜHLWEG).

> **WHERE NEXT FROM WÜRZBURG?**
>
> *Würzburg is on the Cologne–Passau route (p. 272).*

FULDA

Baroque sets the theme for much of the centre, although the town goes back 1,250 years. A modern fountain plays in the rose garden outside the twin-towered Italianate 18th-century **Dom** (cathedral), where pilgrims come to see the revered tomb of St Boniface within the crypt; the dagger that killed him and the codex with which he tried to shield himself are exhibited in the crypt museum.

Adjacent is 9th-century **Michaelkirche**, one of the oldest churches in Germany. It's somewhat reminiscent of an Arabic bath, with a circular theme running through it, an overhead dome and a barrel-vaulted crypt supported by a single pillar. Faint traces of a few of the original frescoes remain.

In the **Stadtschloss** (castle), the private apartments of the prince-abbots who once lived there are open to visitors and an impressive array of Fulda porcelain is on show. In front of the Orangery (now a convention centre) is the famous Floravase, an ornately sculptured vase nearly 7 m high.

7 mins' walk from the centre.

Tourist Office: Schloss Strasse 1, (0661) 1021814, fax (0661) 1022811 (www.fulda.de; tourismus@fulda.de).

Cheaper guesthouses near the station include **Pension Wenzel**, HEINRICHSTR. 38–40, (0661) 75335, €, and **Gasthof Hodes**, PETERSTOR 14, (0661) 72862, €. **Youth hostel**: SCHIRRMANNSTR. 31, (0661) 73389.

EISENACH

Though still a bit run-down as a legacy of its recent East German past, there are plentiful splashes of modern architecture as the town undergoes a facelift. The glory of the town is the splendid **Wartburg** on a hill on its south-west edge (12 mins by no. 10 from the rail station, and then 227 steps), the seat of the Landgraves of Thuringia. A medieval castle dating from 1067 with many later additions, it's an attractive complex where half-timbered buildings surround two courtyards. Wagner stayed there and used it as the setting for his opera *Tannhäuser*, and Martin Luther translated the New Testament into German there – in just 10 weeks – while being held in secret for his own protection in 1521–22 after being excommunicated.

The 15th-century **Lutherhaus**, LUTHERPL., is where Martin Luther lodged as a boy; the present half-timbered structure encloses the original house. **Bachhaus,** FRAUENPLAN 21, the former Bach family home is furnished in period style with documents and old musical instruments. A large statue of Bach stands just inside the big triple-galleried **St Georgenkirche**, MARKT, where he was christened.

Eisenach was where East Germany's second most famous car (after the notoriously unrobust Trabant), the **Wartburg**, was manufactured, until 1991. The **Automobilbau-museum** (the Museum of Car Building), RENNBAHN 6–8 (in SPARKASSENGEBÄUDE), ☎(03691) 743232, commemorates 100 years of its production (together with the occasional BMW).

🚃 Turn right outside for the town centre, a 5-min walk.

ℹ️ **Tourist Office**: MARKT 2, ☎(03691) 79230, fax (03691) 792320 (www.eisenach-tourist.de; tourist-info@eisenach-tourist.de).

🏠 There is a reasonable selection of both **Pensionen** and **Gasthöfe** starting from about €25, such as **Gasthof 'Storchenturm'**, GEORGENSTR. 43, ☎0700 40404050, €, or **Pension St Peter**, AM PETERSBERG 7, ☎(03691) 890401, fax (03691) 872831, €. The **youth hostel**: **Artur Becker**, MARIENTAL 24, ☎(03691) 743259, is about 1 km from the city centre. The **campsite**: **Altenberger See**, WILHELMSTHAL, ☎(03691) 215637, is some 10 km away, but is accessible by bus to BAD LIEBENSTEIN, from the bus station next to the rail station. It is on a lake, in the middle of the Thuringian Forest.

GOTHA

This attractive little town, gateway to the Thüringer Wald (Thuringian Forest), was the home of the Saxe-Coburg-Gotha dynasty, ancestors of the British royal family. It's also known as the 'Residence City'– a label dating from the mid-17th century, when Duke Ernst I chose the duchy of Gotha as his residence.

The main **market square** is surrounded by immaculately restored and colourful Renaissance and half-timbered buildings, among them the 16th-century terracotta Rathaus. The plain white exterior of **Schloss Friedenstein**, on a hill overlooking the town centre, gives no hint of the ornate décor inside. Built by Duke Ernst I in 1634, after the Thirty Years War, it now houses the municipal museum. The **Ekhof-Theater** is Germany's oldest baroque theatre in its original state, and aptly hosts an annual summer baroque music festival.

DAY TRIP FROM GOTHA

Tram no. 4 (the **Thüringerwaldbahn**) from the rail station goes to **Tabarz** in the Thüringer Wald (Thuringian Forest), a 1-hr ride past **Marienglashöhle**, which has lovely crystalline caves. From Tabarz, a road-train called 'Inselsberg Express' (Apr–Nov) goes most of the way up **Grosser Inselsberg** (916 m).

🚃 At the southern end of town (tram nos. 1/2/4 to the centre; alight at HUTTENSTR., then walk up ERFURTERSTR).

ℹ️ **Tourist Office**: BLUMENBACHSTR. 1–3, ☎(03621) 854036 (www.gotha.de; info@gotha.de). For the Thuringian Forest: **Tourismusverband Thüringer Wald**, MARGARETENSTR. 2, ☎(03691) 402921.

🏠 The modern **Waldbahn Hotel**, BAHNHOFSTR. 16, ☎(03621) 2340, €€, is a 400-m walk from the rail station. There are a fair amount of private rooms at lower prices.

ERFURT

Sited on the river Gera, the Thuringian capital has shot to prominence as a tourist attraction, with its substantial variety of attractive old buildings from mills to monasteries, much spruced up since German reunification. A flight of 70 steps leads up to **Dom St Marien**, the hilltop Gothic cathedral beside the Dompl., a large market place and useful tram stop. Stained-glass windows and carved choir stalls (above which choirboys have carved graffiti over the centuries) are highlights of the cathedral; in the middle of its three steeples hangs one of the world's largest bells, the Gloriosa, cast in 1497.

An array of decorative building surround **Fischmarkt**. Markstr. leads off it to **Krämerbrücke**, a 14th-century river bridge lined with old houses and shops, best seen from the river itself.

In the 15th century, Erfurt was noted for its altar pieces and a superb example can be seen in **Reglerkirche**, Bahnhofstr. To find out more on local traditions, check out the **Museum für Thüringer Volkskunde**, 140a Juri-Gagarin-Ring (closed Mon).

A 10-min walk along Bahnhofstr., or tram nos. 3/4/5, to the centre.

Tourist Office: Benedikts-Pl. 1, ☎ (0361) 66400, fax (0361) 6640290 (www.erfurt-tourist-info.de). Hotel booking service: ☎ (0361) 6640110. The **Classic-Card Erfurt** provides free transport, a complimentary city tour, and entry to many attractions.

The Etap Hotel, In den Weiden 11, ☎ (0361) 4232899, €, offers relative simplicity. Smaller pensions include **Pension Reuss**, Spittelgasse 15, ☎ (0361) 7310344, €. **Youth hostel**: Hochheimer Str. 12, ☎ (0361) 5626705, fax (0361) 5626706, 15-mins by tram no. 5.

WEIMAR

Smart shops, pavement cafés and a lively **Onion Fair**, which takes over the town for a weekend in Oct, are outward signs of Weimar's vitality. But, famously, Weimar is steeped in German culture, having been the home of two of the country's greatest writers, Goethe and Schiller, as well as the composers Bach, Liszt and Richard Strauss, the painter Lucas Cranach and the philosopher Nietzsche. It was also where the ill-fated pre-Nazi Weimar Republic was founded. Horse-drawn carriages offer 45-min rides (Apr–Oct) round the main centre of interest, **Altstadt**.

The entire town centre, with its wide tree-lined avenues, elegant squares and fine buildings, is officially listed as a historical monument. After decades of neglect, extensive renovation for its role as European City of Culture in 1999 – coinciding with the 250th anniversary of the birth of Goethe – has revived its gracious character.

The baroque mansion where Goethe lived, **Goethehaus**, FRAUENPLAN 1, displays furniture, personal belongings and a library of 5400 books. A stroll across the little River Ilm in the peaceful **Park an der Ilm** leads to the simple **Gartenhaus**, his first home in town and later his retreat (closed Tues). Goethe himself became a tourist attraction: people travelled from afar to glimpse the great man.

In the **Marktplatz** a plaque marks the house in the south corner where Bach lived when he was leader of the court orchestra. Close by, the spectacularly ornate **Cranachhaus** was where the painter Cranach spent the latter part of his life and produced the bulk of his work.

The **Liszthaus**, on the town side of the park, is the beautifully maintained residence of the Austro-Hungarian composer Franz Liszt. He moved to Weimar in 1848 to direct the local orchestra and spend the last 17 summers of his life: his piano and numerous manuscripts are on display.

Schiller spent the last three years of his life at **Schillerhaus**, SCHILLERSTR., and his rooms are much as they were then. Statues of Schiller and Goethe stand in the nearby THEATERPL. outside the imposing **Deutsches National Theater**, where many of their plays were first performed.

North of Weimar by 10 km is the memorial museum and site of **Buchenwald concentration camp**, a grim reminder of the horrors of the Nazi regime during the Second World War.

The **Weimar Card** gives 3 days' worth of free or reduced transport, admission to the 12 most important museums in the city, a 50% reduction on City Tours and a 10% discount on tickets for the German National Theatre.

RAIL 20-min walk north of the centre (🚌 nos. 1/7)

i **Tourist Office:** At the **station. Main office:** MARKT 10, ☎ (03643) 24000, fax (03643) 240040 (www.weimar.de; tourist info@weimar.de). Can arrange hotel and private accommodation. City tours 1100 and 1400 (in German only).

🏠 **Café, Restaurant, Pension 'Hainfels'**, BELVEDERER ALLEE 65, ☎ (03643) 850116, fax (03643) 850118, €, and **Zum Alten Gasthof**, WOHLSBORNER STR. 2, ☎ (03643) 437300, fax (03643) 437399, €, are some of the cheaper guesthouses in town (prices are lower at weekends). There are four **youth hostels**, including **Germania**, CARL-AUGUST-ALLEE 13, ☎ (03643) 850490, 2 mins from the station, and **Am Poseckschen Garten**, HUMBOLDTSTR. 17, ☎ (03643) 850792, in the centre.

LEIPZIG

Leipzig has been a cultural centre for many centuries, famous particularly for its music: numerous great 19th-century works were premiered at the **Gewandhaus**. AUGUSTUS-PL., beside the broad ring road encircling the **Innenstadt**, makes a good starting point for a stroll around the pedestrianised centre, whose streets of long-neglected buildings and arcades are fast acquiring rows of smart shops, restaurants and offices – yet Leipzig retains some of the grace of an old European city.

In 1989, the mass demonstrations and candlelit vigils in **Nikolaikirche**, NIKOLAISTR., were the focus for the city's brave peaceful revolt against communism. The **Stasi 'Power and Banality' Museum**, DITTRICHRING 24, in the former Ministry of State Security, covers the years of communist oppression.

Marktplatz is the centre for many of Leipzig's outdoor activities, including free concerts and impromptu beer fests. The fine Renaissance **Altes Rathaus** has survived and now houses the **Stadtgeschichtliches Museum**, covering the city's history.

Leipzig is second only to Vienna for its musical tradition, being the home of Bach, Mendelssohn and Schumann. The **Gewandhaus Orchestra, Opera House** and **Thomasaner-chor** (St Thomas's Church Choir), which was conducted by Bach for 27 years, have a worldwide reputation. Performances of all kinds of music take place throughout the year.

From Leipzig a trip can be made to **Colditz**, an attractive little town dominated by its castle (youth hostel: HAINGASSE 42, ☎(034381) 43335) – made notorious as a prisoner-of-war camp in World War II.

🚉 On the edge of the Innenstadt (city centre), a 10-min walk to the middle. Known as the **Hauptbahnhof Promenaden Leipzig** and built in 1915, the station is an attraction in its own right, and is one of Europe's biggest and most impressive, recently refurbished and attired with a glossy shopping mall, with its restaurants, cafés and supermarkets. Also part of the facelift is the magnificent *Deutsche Bahn* waiting room, complete with bar, stained-glass overhead ceiling and rich wooden interior.

ℹ️ **Tourist Office**: RICHARD-WAGNERSTR. 1, ☎(0341) 704260, 710 4260, fax (0341) 710 4271 (www.leipzig.de; lipsia@aol.com). Just inside the Innenstadt, a 2-min walk from the rail station. On-line free accommodation booking service, or phone ☎(0341) 7104255; no extra fee.

🚋 There's a good tram network from the rail station, but most things of interest are within the pedestrianised Innenstadt, which is encircled by a ring road. A **day card**, including travel and museum discounts is available, for 3 days also).

🛏️ Ask the Tourist Office for a list of local pensions; these include **Pension Preussenstrasse**, PREUSSENSTR. 1D, ☎(0341) 868800, fax (0341) 8688088, €, and **Herberge Zur Alten Bäckerei**, AN DER MÜHLE 12, ☎(0341) 415300, fax (0341) 4153030, €. **Youth hostel: Hostel Sleepy Lion,** Käthe-Kollwitz-Str. 3, ☎(0341) 993 9480, fax (0341) 993 9482 (info@hostel-leipzig.de): (non HI) clean, friendly, central, open 24 hrs; singles, doubles and dorms; bike hire. **Campsite: Am Auensee**, GUSTAV-ESCHE STR. 5, ☎(0341) 465 1600, fax (0341) 465 1617 (tram nos. 10/11 to ANNABERGER STR. and 🚌 no. 80 to AUENSEE).

🍽️ Restaurants crowd the pavements around KLEINE FLEISCHERGASSE, such as **Zill's Tunnel**, BARFÜSSGASSE 9, ☎(0341) 960 2078, a typical Saxon beerhouse serving traditional dishes. Famed

GERMANY

because Goethe featured it in *Faust*, having dined there as a student, is the 16th-century wood-panelled **Auerbachs** cellar restaurant in the exclusive Mädler shopping arcade off GRIMMAISCHESTR., ☎(0341) 21600. Lots of cafés crowd around the MARKTPL., with music spouting out of most of them. **Spizz** does jazz nights, as well as an excellent breakfast. **Internet café**: **Lebit**, KOHLGARTENSTR. 2, ☎(0341) 9982020 (www.wilder.osten.de/le-bit; lebit@img-net.de).

DRESDEN

The capital of Saxony for four centuries, Dresden will forever be remembered as one of the great tragedies of World War II: on 13–14 February 1945, the whole centre was carpet-bombed by the Allies, and some 35,000 people perished. Europe had lost one of its most beautiful cities.

Despite the devastation, the city has risen from the ashes, and is once again a major cultural centre. What is immediately impressive is the extent to which the baroque magnificence of the centre has been restored: from the **Brühlsche Terrasse** ('Europe's Terrace'), a raised terrace by the banks of the Elbe, you overlook the **Stadtschloss** (the tower of which gives another good view), and the spire of the early 18th-century **Hofkirche** (Royal Cathedral). Close by the cathedral is the **Semper Opera House**, also painstakingly restored to its former glory and reopened in 1985. A few steps away is the **Zwinger** (keep), the finest example of baroque Saxon architecture, a gracious complex of baroque pavilions, fountains and statuary: it is free to walk around the grounds, though there is admission to the Zwinger's world-famous museums.

One of the greatest art collections anywhere, the **Gemäldegalerie Alte Meister** (Old Master Gallery; closed Mon), has many instantly familiar works (among them, Raphael's *Sistine Madonna* with its immortal cherubs, and *Picture of a Young Man* by Dürer). The **Porzellansammlung** (closed Thur) showcases Dresden porcelain, including choice examples from nearby Meissen. In the 16th-century **Albertinum** (Arsenal), the **Gemäldegalerie Neue Meister** (Gallery of Modern Masters, closed Thur) is a superb collection of modern art, with works by German Expressionists and French Impressionists.

A particularly poignant reminder of the war destruction is the **Frauenkirche**, which the morning after the bombing miraculously still stood, but then abruptly collapsed. However, it has become a symbol of the city, and the whole building is being reassembled: completion is due in 2006.

Out of the main centre, Dresden really is a mixed bag. During the Communist era, it was rebuilt in dreary Stalinist style. However, the suburbs harbour a remarkable variety of Jugendstil (art nouveau) mansions: the eastern part of the city is particularly rewarding, and best explored by bicycle. The **River Elbe** (which has a riverside-cycle path as well as steamer cruises) also gives some gorgeous views of grand villas perched on the hillside on the opposite bank, and within moments of the centre you're virtually into countryside as you head east. Further on, **Schloss Pillnitz** was the only baroque building in Dresden to have escaped bombing; entry into the grounds is free. You can cycle on a couple of hours past the Königstein fortress into **Sächsige Schweitz** (Swiss Saxony), where huge, bizarre sandstone outcrops tower above the river; many of them can be climbed by stairs; alternatively you can take the train to Kurort Rathen, cross the river by ferry and walk up the obvious summit.

You can also take river cruises or an S-Bahn train to the porcelain-making town of **Meissen**, which has a superb and virtually pristine Altstadt (old town), and offers tours around the porcelain works.

Main rail station: left luggage (PASSAGE 4), exchange facilities, hotel information (main hall). Follow signs for PRAGER STR. – the old town is directly at the end of this street. **Neustadt station** is to the north.

The excellent value 48-hr **Dresden-Card** allows free public transport, admission to 11 main museums, and bus, boat and tram city tours.

Tourist Offices: PRAGER STR. (near the rail station), and SCHINKELWACHE (Old City Guard House), THEATERPL. Both ☎ (0351) 491920, fax (0351) 4919 2116 (www.dresden-tourist.de).

Hostels include **Rudi Arndt**, HÜBNER STR. 11, ☎ (0351) 4710667, tram no. 5 to NÜRNBERGER PL.; **Radebeul**, WEINTRAUBENSTR. 12, ☎ (0351) 838 2880, 300 m from Radebeul-Weintraube station; **Die Boofe**, LUISENSTR. 20, ☎ (0351) 8013361, fax (0351) 8013362, at the Neustadt, lots of 'Kneipen' (pubs) and restaurants around (tram no 7 from the station); and **Jugendgästehaus Dresden**, MATERNISTRASSE 22 ☎ (0351) 492 620, 800 m from the station, tram nos 7, 8; **Mondpalast**, KATHERINENSTR. 11–13, ☎ (0351) 804 6061. Cheap, central **hotels** include the **Stadt Rendsburg**, KAMENZER STR. 1, ☎ (0351) 804 1551, fax (0351) 802 2586.

WHERE NEXT FROM DRESDEN?

Trains to Prague (p. 534) take 3 hrs for the 191 km journey; there are six services a day.
ETT tables: 60, 1100.

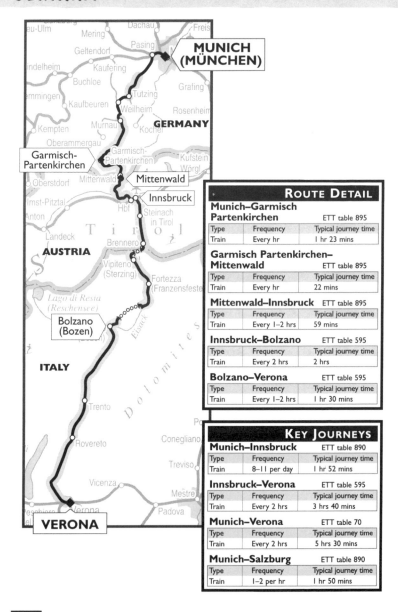

ROUTE DETAIL		
Munich–Garmisch Partenkirchen		ETT table 895
Type	Frequency	Typical journey time
Train	Every hr	1 hr 23 mins
Garmisch Partenkirchen–Mittenwald		ETT table 895
Type	Frequency	Typical journey time
Train	Every hr	22 mins
Mittenwald–Innsbruck		ETT table 895
Type	Frequency	Typical journey time
Train	Every 1–2 hrs	59 mins
Innsbruck–Bolzano		ETT table 595
Type	Frequency	Typical journey time
Train	Every 2 hrs	2 hrs
Bolzano–Verona		ETT table 595
Type	Frequency	Typical journey time
Train	Every 1–2 hrs	1 hr 30 mins

KEY JOURNEYS		
Munich–Innsbruck		ETT table 890
Type	Frequency	Typical journey time
Train	8–11 per day	1 hr 52 mins
Innsbruck–Verona		ETT table 595
Type	Frequency	Typical journey time
Train	Every 2 hrs	3 hrs 40 mins
Munich–Verona		ETT table 70
Type	Frequency	Typical journey time
Train	Every 2 hrs	5 hrs 30 mins
Munich–Salzburg		ETT table 890
Type	Frequency	Typical journey time
Train	1–2 per hr	1 hr 50 mins

Despite its relatively short distance, this journey through **Germany**, **Austria** and **Italy** and across the **Alps** packs in astonishing variety. **Munich** and **Verona**, each worth at least a few days to explore, could hardly be more different, and the Alps change in character almost from one valley to the next.

MUNICH (MÜNCHEN)

See p. 257.

GARMISCH-PARTENKIRCHEN

Once two quiet Bavarian villages at the foot of the 2962-m **Zugspitze**, Germany's highest mountain, **Garmisch** and **Partenkirchen** were officially united to host the 1936 Winter Olympics. Though now separated only by the railway line, they retain individual personalities. **Partenkirchen** is more modern and upmarket while **Garmisch** has much more of a traditional Bavarian character – the most appealingly rustic part is around FRÜHLINGSTR.

Garmisch is Germany's most popular ski resort and has 52 lifts (13 open in summer), with downhill and cross-country skiing on offer. In summer, it's a centre for mountain walking, climbing and biking. The **Olympic Ice Stadium**, OLYMPIASTR., built in 1936, stays open virtually year-round.

The **Zugspitzbahn** cog railway goes from beside the main rail station to a point near the summit of the Zugspitze, a 75-min journey. On the way, it stops at **Eibsee**, an idyllic mountain lake, where you can transfer to the **Eibseebahn** cable car (often appallingly crowded) to reach the summit; alternatively, take the easy 7-km path round the lake itself, which has a pleasant beer garden. Meanwhile, the train continues up through a winding 4.5-km tunnel to **Sonnalpin** (2600 m), from where the **Gletscherbahn** cable car goes the final stage to the summit. The views are impressively far-ranging in decent weather.

Several other summits around are accessible by chair lifts or cable cars from the town, giving plenty of scope for walks. These include **Eckbauer** (1238 m), from where you can follow a path down through the woods to the entrance to the **Partnachklamm**, one of the most dramatic of all Alpine gorges, and descend to the ski stadium.

Centrally located between Garmisch and Partenkirchen.

Tourist Office: RICHARD-STRAUSS PL., (08821) 180700, fax (08821) 180755 (www.garmisch-partenkirchen.de).

This is a popular ski resort, with plenty of pensions and hotels. Least expensive options are private rooms, such as **Hildegard Huber**, SCHWALBENSTR. 4, (08821) 3443, €, and **Martin Maurer**, TORLENSTR. 5, (08821) 2994, €. **Youth hostel**: JOCHSTR. 10, (08821) 2980, 4 km from town, in **Burgrain** (nos. 3/4/5). **Campsite**: ZUGSPITZE, (08821) 3180, west, near **Grainau** village.

Partenkirchen has plenty of typically Bavarian bar-restaurants.

MITTENWALD

Close to the Austrian border, **Mittenwald** is perhaps the most attractive town in the German Alps, with an abundance of character in its gabled, whitewashed houses, hung with green shutters and sporting creaky wooden balconies. Elaborate outside murals are another striking feature, but the town's main claim to fame is in its violins. Matthias Klotz (1653–1743), a pupil of the great Amati, began Mittenwald's tradition of high-quality violin-making that continues to this day.

⊞ 5 mins east of the town centre.

i **Tourist Office**: Dammkarstr. 3, ☎(08823) 33981, fax (08823) 2701 (www.mittenwald.de).

⊟ **Youth hostel**: Buckelwiesen 7, ☎(08823) 1701.

INNSBRUCK, AUSTRIA

See p. 350.

BOLZANO (BOZEN), ITALY

Although in Italy and with street names in Italian, **Bolzano** looks decidedly Austrian, with its pastel-coloured baroque arcades and Austrian menu items; for centuries Bolzano was in the possession of Austria. Set beneath Alpine slopes in a deep valley, it's handy for exploring the **Dolomites**. Piazza Walther is the focus of the town's outdoor life.

⊞ 5 mins from the town centre. Buses stop from an area by a small park, reached by crossing the main road outside the station and turning left.

i **Tourist Office: Municipal**: Piazza Walther 8, ☎(0471) 975 6561. **Regional**: Piazza Parrochia 11/12, ☎(0471) 993 808.

⊟ Reasonable range, starting from moderately priced.

WHERE NEXT FROM BOLZANO?

Buses from Bolzano climb eastward into the Dolomites for some of the most stunning scenery in the Alps. It's a virtually unbeatable region for walking, with paths to suit all abilities. A good centre to head for is **Ortisei** (St Ulrich in German), reached by direct bus twice daily from Bolzano. Famed for its woodcarving tradition, this pleasantly set small town at the meeting of valleys has plenty of accommodation and walkers are spoilt for choice. A cable car takes you onto the **Seiseralm**, said to be the largest of all Alpine pastures, and abundant in very easy strolls with strategically sited cafés.

VERONA

See p. 400.

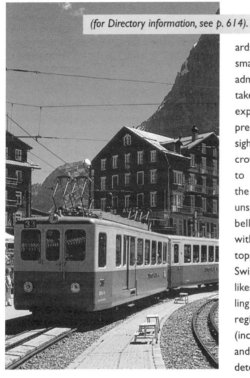

(for Directory information, see p. 614).

Even by European standards, Switzerland packs a lot into a small space, and, even with its admirable transport system, it can take a surprisingly long time to explore thoroughly, though it's predominantly scenery rather than sights that attracts the appreciable crowds. For once, reality lives up to the common preconception: the **Swiss Alps** have idyllically unspoilt Alpine pastures, grazed by bell-wearing cattle and backed with improbably perfect snow-topped pointy mountains, and the Swiss are still into traditions of the likes of alpenhorn-blowing, yodelling and folk music, as well as regional specialities, festivals (including classical music and jazz) and local pageantry. Costs can deter budget travellers from lingering, though it's not too bad if you use the hostels and mountain huts. Don't expect to find dazzling nightlife: a lot of it is decidedly peaceful after dark, although there's quite a bit happening in **Zürich**. Souvenir shopping can be rewarding, with numerous items special to certain areas, such as hand-woven linen, country crafts, painted pottery and wood carving.

There are marked regional differences, and four separate languages. Although most of the population lives outside the Alps in cities such as **Geneva** and **Basel**, it is still easy to find pockets of rustic and architecturally varied picture-book charm, with quaint wooden chalets and traditional farmhouses scattered around the landscape (to a much greater extent than you'll find in neighbouring Austria). Some of the best areas to visit include the dramatic valley of the **Engadine** in such resorts as St Moritz, the majestic **Bernese Oberland** around Kandersteg and in the side valleys of the **Valais** region (in the south-west).

Some of the most majestic scenery is in the **Bernese Oberland**, around the relaxed, provincial-feeling capital, **Berne**, and on the doorsteps of the pretty towns of **Interlaken** and **Grindelwald**. Less of a scenic jaw-dropper, central Switzerland does have some delicious lake scenery, notably around **Lake Lucerne** and **Lake Geneva** (*Lac Léman*). **Lugano**, in the south, is unmistakably Italian in feel.

ACCOMMODATION Swiss hotels have high standards but are expensive, and you'll be very lucky to get anything for less than SFr.75 for a single or SFr.120 for a double. In rural areas and Alpine resorts, it is often possible to get rooms in **private houses** (look for *Zimmer frei* signs posted in windows and gardens), but these are few and far between in cities. Budget travellers (unless they are camping) rely heavily on **youth hostels** – so book these as far ahead as possible. Every major town and major station has a **hotel-finding service**, sometimes free and seldom expensive. Prices vary widely according to season. **Switzerland Tourism (ST)** can provide information on accommodation, but does not make bookings.

YOUTH HOSTELS These cost SFr.20–40, including linen and breakfast (but excluding breakfast in group hostels). Self-caterers pay a small fee for use of fuel. Most hostels have family rooms. The hostelling headquarters is **Schweizer Jugendherbergen**, SCHAFFHAUSERSTR. 14, POSTFACH 161, CH-8042 ZÜRICH, ☎(01) 360 14 14, fax (01) 360 14 60 (www.youthhostel.ch; bookingoffice@youthhostel.ch).

BACKPACKERS' ACCOMMODATION Mountain backpackers can stay at **Swiss Alpine Club (SAC)** huts (**Schweizer Alpenclub**, MONBIJOUSTR. 61, CH-3000 BERNE 23, ☎(031) 370 1880, fax (031) 370 1890); these are primarily climbing huts based at the start of climbing routes, but walkers are welcome. There are also (in more accessible locations) mountain inns known as *Berghotels* or *Auberges de Montagne*, with simple dormitory accommodation as well as private rooms ranging from basic to relatively luxurious.

CAMPING There are hundreds of **campsites** in Switzerland (most open summer only). They are graded on a one to five star system. International *carnets* are required at many campsites. 'Rough' camping is not officially permitted, though it does happen. Guides are available from specialist bookshops or **Camping TCS**, TCS, CH BLANDONNET 4, CH-1214 Geneva, ☎(022) 417 2520 (www.tcs.ch) or **Verband Schweizer Campings**, SEESTR. 119, CH-3800 INTERLAKEN, ☎(033) 823 3523, fax (033) 923 2991 (www.swisscamps.ch).

FOOD AND DRINK

Portions tend to be ample, and pork and veal are common menu items, but in the lake areas you'll also find fresh fish. Swiss cheese is often an ingredient in local dishes; the classic *Swiss fondue*, for instance, is bread dipped into a pot containing melted cheese, garlic, wine and kirsch. *Raclette*, a speciality of the canton of Valais, is simply melted cheese, served with boiled potatoes, gherkins and silverskin onions. The ubiquitous meal accompaniment in German-speaking areas is *Rösti*, fried potatoes and onions, while French Switzerland goes in for stronger tastes, such as smoked sausages. In the Grisons, *Bündnerfleisch* is a tasty raw smoked beef, sliced very thin. Swiss wines are also excellent and very difficult to get in other countries.

There is a wide range of both food and eating-places. The cheapest are supermarket or department store cafeterias, such as those housed in the ubiquitous **Migros** outlets. Look out too for **EPA**, **Co-op** and, in Ticino, **Inova**. At lunch time (and quite often in the evenings), most resturants have a fixed-price dish-of-the-day menu *(Tagesteller, plat du jour, piatto del giorno)*, which is good value. Tipping in Swiss restaurants is not the norm.

EDITOR'S CHOICE

Berne; Château de Chillon (near Montreux); Interlaken; Lucerne; Lugano; Sion; St Moritz; Zermatt; Zurich. Scenic rail journeys: Chur–St Moritz (Bernina Express, p. 317); Berne–Geneva via Interlaken (p. 325); St Moritz–Zermatt (Glacier Express; see Where Next from Brig?, p. 330); Jungfraujoch and other funiculars from Interlaken (see p. 329); Gornergrat mountain railway from Zermatt (see p. 330); Lucerne–Lugano (p. 335).

Virtually any list of the world's top ten rail journeys would include at least one trip in Switzerland. As well as the breathtakingly engineered routes over countless viaducts and through scores of tunnels, such as the **Glacier Express** from Zermatt to St Moritz, rack railways edge their way up improbable gradients to stunning viewpoints such as the **Jungfraujoch**.

BEYOND THE BORDER

Basel–Brussels via Strasbourg (ETT table 40); Basel–Milan (table 82); Zurich–Vienna (table 86); Zurich–Stuttgart (table 82); Basel–Hamburg via Cologne (table 73); Geneva–Avignon via Lyon (tables 348, 351); Sion–Chamonix Mont Blanc (see Where Next from Sion?, p. 331).

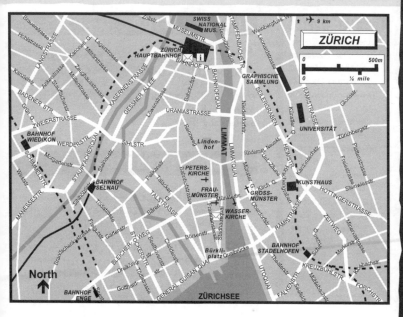

Switzerland's largest city (though not its capital), publicised as the 'little big city', comes as a surprise. Despite a stern reputation as one of the world's major financial centres, it has a picturesque setting on the River Limmat beside Lake Zürich (Zürichsee), a mountain backdrop, immaculate quayside parks, smart shops, open-air cafés, chic shopping and ancient squares. With its sizeable immigrant population, the city wears a distinctly cosmopolitan air. The best view of the lake and city is from Quaibrücke, which crosses the Limmat where the lake flows into it.

ARRIVAL AND DEPARTURE

Zürich Hauptbahnhof (HB), is on the west side of River Limmat and leads out onto BAHNHOFSTR., the main shopping street.

Zürich-Kloten Airport is 12 km north-east of the city centre; information, ☎(01)157 10 60. There are eight trains an hour from the rail station; journey time 10 mins.

SWITZERLAND

TOURIST OFFICE

On the station concourse,
HAUPTBAHNHOF,
☎ (01) 215 40 00,
fax (01) 215 40 44
(www.zurichtourism.ch;
information@
zurichtourism.ch). This
efficient, well-stocked
office sells a street map,
provides a free
accommodation service
(☎ (01) 215 40 40, fax
(01) 215 40 44), and the
free 2-week listing, *Zürich
News*, and monthly
Zürich' Guide.

INFORMATION

PHONES To phone **Zürich
from abroad:** ☎
00 (011 from US/Canada) +
41 (Switzerland) + 1
(Zürich); to phone **Zürich
from elsewhere in
Switzerland:** ☎ 01.

INTERNET CAFÉ
Internet Café, URANIASTR. 3,
☎ (01) 210 33 11,
fax (01) 210 33 13.

PUBLIC TRANSPORT

 The centre of Zürich is small enough to explore on foot. All
buses and trams, run by **VBZ Züri-Linie** (☎ 0848 80 18 80)
leave the terminal outside the HB every 6–12 mins
0530–2400. Buy your ticket from machines at stops before
boarding; 1 hr costs SFr.3.60, 24 hrs SFr. 7.20 or 6 days SFr. 36.
Taxis: ☎ (01) 222 22 22, or hail one in the street. **Bikes** can
be hired (free) at the main rail station and, from May–Oct, at
Altstetten, Enge, Oerlikon and Stadelhofen rail stations and
near Globus department store.

ACCOMMODATION

The **Aparthotel**, KARLSTR. 5, ☎ (01) 422 11 75, €, is central and near the lake. The **St
Josef**, HIRSCHENGRABEN 64–68, ☎ (01) 251 27 57, €€, is between the rail station and university. **Hotel Biber/City Backpacker**, NIEDERDORFSTR. 5, ☎ 251 90 15, €, is in the lively
Niederdorfer area and has dorms and private rooms.

The **youth hostel** is in MUTSCHELLENSTR. 114, ☎ (01) 482 35 44, south of the city in
Wollishofen (tram no. 7 to MORGENTAL, then 5-min walk).

Campers can try the **Campingplatz Zürich-Seebucht**, SEESTR. 559, ☎ (01) 482 16 12
(☐ nos. 161/165 from BÜRKLIPL.)

FOOD AND DRINK

Zürich has a large selection of restaurants of most nationalities, as well as its own
local cuisine. The Tourist Office issues the fortnightly *Zürich News*, which includes
many affordable restaurants. Local specialities include *Kalbgeschnetzeltes* (veal in
cream sauce) and the less expensive pork version, *Schweingeschnetzeltes*. There are
numerous fast-food and conventional restaurants around the huge station complex.

The largest selection of eating places is on or just off NIEDERDORFSTR., the main nightlife area, which stretches for about 1 km on the east side of the river, a block back from it. Fierce competition keeps prices at a relatively reasonable level.

HIGHLIGHTS

On the west bank of the Limmat, just behind the station, is the **Schweizerisches Landesmuseum** (Swiss National Museum), housed in a 19th-century mock castle, and giving an excellent cross-section of Swiss history. Reconstructed rooms depict different periods and there are displays of costumes, weapons and medieval art. A stroll away, the city's highest spot, LINDENHOF, is a wide terrace of lime trees with good views over the river. It's a favourite with local people who come to play chess – three sets of giant pieces are for all to use. The nearby 13th-century **St Peterskirche** is remarkable for its 16th-century clock tower, the largest in Europe; each of the four faces is 8.7 m wide.

Near MÜNSTERBRÜCKE, the 13th-century **Fraumünster** has outstanding stained-glass windows by Chagall. Across the bridge, the twin towers of the Romanesque **Grossmünster** (cathedral), offer great views from the top. It has stained glass by Giacometti and a statue of Charlemagne in the crypt. Nearby, **Wasserkirche** (Water Church), on LIMMATQUAI, is attached to the 18th-century **Helmhaus**, cloth market hall, where contemporary art exhibitions are staged.

Other old **Zunfthäuser** (guild halls) line LIMMATQUAI, some now converted to restaurants. **Kunsthaus** (Fine Arts Museum), HEIMPL., is Switzerland's premier art gallery, with works ranging from late Gothic to contemporary. Details of regularly changing exhibitions as well as the permanent exhibition are posted on the website (www.kunsthaus.ch). On the east bank, in the heart of the **Niederdorf** area, take a stroll along the quiet and narrow SPIEGELGASSE to see the house where Lenin once lived (no. 14).

By tram no. 2 or 4, at ZOLLIKERSTR. 172, the **Sammlung Bührle** (Bührle Collection) is a treasure-trove of art displayed in the villa of the industrialist who collected it; Emil Bührle had a taste for Impressionist paintings, and the means to acquire them, resulting in a rich show of works by Manet, Sisley and Van Gogh, as well as earlier masters such as Delacroix and Hals.

DAY TRIPS FROM ZÜRICH **Lake Zurich** (Zürichsee) is the obvious starting point for short excursions, with cruises offered by Zürichsee-Schiffahrtsgesellschaft (there are also 1-hr trips along the River Limmat from outside the rail station by the Schweizerisches Landesmuseum). **Rapperswill**, a small and very pretty town with a castle, is the most worthwhile place on the lake (reached by boat or in 40 mins by S-Bahn no. 5 or 7), and is famed for its roses.

For a high-level view from the city's own mountain, take the **Uetliberg Railway** (reached by S-Bahn no. 10 to Uetliberg) up to the 871-m summit of Uetliberg itself. There's a fine panorama of the Alps from the top, and you can walk a high-level path to Felsenegg (about 1 hr 30 mins), on a trail modelled somewhat unusually on the solar system (with the 'planets' spaced proportionately to show how far apart they really are. From Felsenegg a cable car takes you down to Adliswil for S-Bahn no. 4 back to Zurich.

Just within the Swiss side of the German border is the 150-m wide and 23-m high **Rheinfall** – the dramatic start of the same Rhine that ends in the North Sea, having wound its way gently through the castles of middle Germany from Basel. Taking 40 mins from Zürich to Schaffhausen (ETT table 940), you can then continue by train to the base of the falls themselves, a journey of only 3 mins. The walk down from **Schloss Laufen** (which is a youth hostel, ☎(052) 659 6152) skirts the water, leading to dramatic views. Halfway down, a tunnel opens out into the middle of the cascade, granting a spectacular, if damp, prospect. Continuing along the cliff and down to the water level, it's possible to take a boat trip to the tiny Swiss-flag adorned island in the middle of the stream (for boat information: **Rhyfall Mändli**, ☎(052) 672 48 11).

SHOPPING

The main shopping street is Bahnhofstr. Look out particularly for **Franz Karl Weber** at no. 62, which sells toys of all sorts, including a big selection of model trains, and cuckoo clocks. **Sprüngli** is arguably the best *Konditorei* in town and sells superb chocolate, some not sold outside Zürich. **Jelmoli Department Store**, just off Bahnhofstr., has the best selection and prices for Swiss souvenirs. Augustingasse, off it, is charming and has buildings dating from the 14th century as well as several very smart boutiques.

NIGHT-TIME AND EVENTS

Zurich has plenty going on at night. In summer there are a number of outside bars, particularly by the lake. After midnight, the city keeps going: around 300 venues stay open into the small hours, with an eclectic range catering for most tastes. There's no shortage of bars, clubs and street performers on and around **Niederdorfstrasse**, a lively – and safe – area for tourists, despite its reputation as the city's red light district.

Zürich's acclaimed opera company performs at the **Opernhaus Zürich**, FALKENSTR. 1, ☎(01) 268 66 66; concerts are given at the **Tonhalle**, CLARIDENSTR. 7. In mid-April is the **Sechseläuten**, the city's spring festival, when its guild members celebrate the end of winter by parading in historic costumes before burning Böögg, a huge snowman, on an enormous bonfire. July sees the Zürich **Festspiele**, a three-week music festival. In August there is a **Street Parade** of young people and deafening music to celebrate love, peace and tolerance.

WHERE NEXT FROM ZÜRICH?

Two trains an hour to **Lucerne** *(50 mins; ETT table 555) join the* **Berne–Lugano** *route (p. 335).*

ROUTE DETAIL

Lausanne—Neuchâtel   ETT table 500

Type	Frequency	Typical journey time
Train	Every hr	41 mins

Neuchâtel—Biel   ETT table 500

Type	Frequency	Typical journey time
Train	2 per hr	18 mins

Biel—Basel   ETT table 500

Type	Frequency	Typical journey time
Train	Every hr	1 hr 07 mins

Basel—Zürich   ETT table 510

Type	Frequency	Typical journey time
Train	3 per hr	1 hr

Zürich—Chur   ETT table 520

Type	Frequency	Typical journey time
Train	Every hr	1 hr 34 mins

Chur—St Moritz   ETT table 540

Type	Frequency	Typical journey time
Train	Every hr	2 hrs

St Moritz—Poschiavo   ETT table 547

Type	Frequency	Typical journey time
Train	Every hr	1 hr 45 mins

Poschiavo—Tirano   ETT table 547

Type	Frequency	Typical journey time
Train	Every hr	42 mins

Tirano—Milan   ETT table 593

Type	Frequency	Typical journey time
Train	7–10 per day	2 hrs 30 mins

Note

Lausanne to Poschiavo: change trains at Zürich, Chur and St Moritz.

KEY JOURNEYS

Geneva—Zurich   ETT table 500

Type	Frequency	Typical journey time
Train	2 per hr	2 hrs 54 min

Zurich—Milan   ETT table 82

Type	Frequency	Typical journey time
Train	9 per day	4 hrs 28 min

Vineyards cling to the hilly shores of **Lac Neuchâtel**, where **Yverdon** and **Neuchâtel** are pleasantly set lakeside towns, and lake views are a feature from the right (south) side of the train as far as **Biel**. Beyond the watch-and clock-making town of **Delmont**, the scenery is less remarkable between the cities of **Basel** and **Zürich**. Thereafter, things step up a couple of gears, with **Lake Zürich** and the **Walensee** immediately on the left, and beyond **Sargans** you pass within a stone's throw of the tiny prinicipality of **Liechtenstein**. **Chur** lies at the foot of an astonishing climb high up into the **Alps**, a section covered by the **Bernina Express** service (reservation compulsory and supplement payable), where the finely set resort of **St Moritz** is at the heart of the **Engadine**, the huge straight valley of the **Inn** that cuts across the **Grisons** (Grishun or Graubünden) Switzerland's canton in Romansch-speaking south-eastern corner. **Poschiavo**, on the other hand, is distinctly Italian both in character and language, and from there you can cross into Italy via the **Bernina Pass**, along the shore of **Lake Lecco** to end at **Milan**.

LAUSANNE

Half Alpine and half Riviera, this university town, both a commercial centre and resort, has a hilly setting, with some of the best views from the cathedral and old town, perched 130 m above **Lake Geneva**. The steepness of the place is part of its appeal, and if you don't fancy the trudge up from the lakeshore suburb of **Ouchy**, with its grand hotels and large park, to the station and up to the old town, there's a useful Metro (actually a funicular) linking all three in a few mins. The partly pedestrianised old town is small enough to be explored on foot.

The upper Metro terminal (Flon), Pl. St-François, just south of the main area of interest and dominated by the 15th-century steeple of the 13th–14th-century **Église St-François** (St Francis' Church). The **Cathédrale de Notre-Dame**, a 10-min walk up into the town, was consecrated in 1275. Italian, Flemish and French craftsmen all had a hand in its construction, and it is accepted as a perfect example of Gothic architecture. The night watch is still called from the steeple every hour from 2000 to 0200.

The **Musée Historique de Lausanne**, Pl. de la Cathédrale 4 (closed Mon), in the **Ancien-Evêché** (the bishops' palace until the early 15th century), exhibits a large-scale model of 17th-century Lausanne. Also by the cathedral is another fortified bishops' residence, the **Château St-Maire**, now the seat of the cantonal government (part open to the public). **Escaliers-du-Marché**, a wooden-roofed medieval staircase, links the cathedral square to Pl. de la Palud, an ancient square surrounded by old houses.

Day Trip from Lausanne

requent **SBB** service links the waterfront towns. **Compagnie Générale de Navigation (CGN),** Av. de Rhodanie 17, ☎0900 573 900, operate ferries from Ouchy (and paddle-steamers in summer) to **Geneva** (western end of the lake), **Evian** (in France, southern shore), **Montreux** and **St Gingolph**.

West of the cathedral, the Florentine-style **Palais de Rumine**, Pl. de la Riponne, was built by a Russian family at the turn of the century. It now houses a number of museums. Take a 10-min walk north-west (or 🚊no. 2) to the **Collection de l'Art Brut**, Av. des Bergières 11, housed in the **Château de Beaulieu**. This compelling post-war gallery was founded by a local collector, who sought the works of anyone who was not a trained or formal painter, from amateur dabblers to the criminally insane.

North of the centre is the **Fondation de l'Hermitage**, Rte du Signal 2, an early 19th-century villa full of period fixtures and fittings, which hosts top-quality touring exhibitions of contemporary art. The view from the villa gardens, over the city and the lake to the Alps, is magnificent. For more lake views, take 🚊no. 16 to the **Forêt de Sauvabelin**, 150 m above the city centre. This 140-acre beech forest offers a choice of walking paths and encompasses a deer reserve around a small lake.

The **quai de Belgique** is a shady, flower-lined, waterside promenade, looking towards the Savoy Alps. The 13th-century keep of **Château d'Ouchy** is now a hotel. Baron Pierre de Coubertin, founder of the modern Olympics in 1915, chose Lausanne as the headquarters of the International Olympic Committee. The unique **Musée Olympique**, quai d'Ouchy 1, is a large modern complex, cleverly designed to retain the natural beauty of its surrounding park. Boats can be hired near the 'cruise' pier.

Between the centre and Ouchy, connected by the Metro. Left luggage facilities and bike rental available.

Tourist Office: 2 Av. de Rhodanie, ☎(021) 613 7321 (www.lausanne-tourism.ch; information@lausanne-tourism.ch). **Vaud Regional Tourist Office:** av. d'Ouchy 60, ☎(021) 613 2626 (www.lake-geneva-region.ch). A walking tour (not always in English) of the old town leaves from the Town Hall at 1000 and 1500, Mon–Sat.

There's plenty of budget accommodation. The one-star **La Croisée**, Av. M. Dufour 15, ☎(021) 321 09 09, €, is in the middle of town, not far from the station. **Lausanne Guest House & Backpacker**, Epinettes 4 ☎(021) 601 8000, fax (021) 601 8001 (www.lausanne-guesthouse.ch), €, has twins and dorms, all facing the lake; electric bike rental, internet. **Youth hostel:** **Jeunotel**, Chemin du Bois-de-Vaux, ☎(021) 626 0222 (lausanne@youthhostel.ch), on the lakeside west of Ouchy, has 300 beds and offers simple modern rooms and dormitories (🚊no. 2 from Ouchy metro station to Bois-de-Vaux then 5-min walk). **Campsite: Camping de Vidy,** Chemin du Camping 3, ☎(021) 624 20 31, fax (021) 624 41 60.

NEUCHÂTEL

Set steeply beside the 38-km-long lake of the same name, **Neuchâtel** slopes down from its castle to its old town, and down to the busy quays. At the heart of the old town, itself characterised by Renaissance fountains and defensive towers, is **Place Pury**; markets are held in the adjacent **Place des Halles**. It's well worth the walk up to the top of town, past the **Tour des Prisons** (prison tower), used as a dungeon until 1848, for the views from the town's monumental set pieces: the imposing **Château**, built from the 12th to 16th centuries, now functions as the cantonal office; free guided tours take you within, though there's not much of historical interest inside nowadays. A walkway leads from there to the **Église Collégiale** (collegiate church), founded in the 12th century and featuring a splendid 14th-century monument to the Counts of Neuchâtel. The town's museums include the **Musée d'Art et d'Histoire**, boasting three fascinatingly intricate 18th-century automata – a draughtsman, a writer and a musician – the latter representing a lady harpsichordist.

I km north of the centre.

i **Tourist Office**: Hôtel des Postes, ☎ (032) 889 68 90, fax (032) 889 62 96 (www.neuchatel.ch).

BIEL (BIENNE)

Beside **Lake Biel**, the busy clock-making town (home to Omega watches since 1879) is unique in Switzerland in that French and German share equal billing – you can even hear one person talking in French and the other answering in German; French speakers know it as Bienne. Its old town has a wealth of medieval architecture, with turrets and arcades characteristic of the Bernese style, and prettily painted wrought-iron signs. Some of the best of it is along Burggasse and the Ring, a fine old square with a 16th-century fountain in the middle.

Hauptbahnhof, town centre. The old town is a 10-min walk via Bahnhofstr. and Nidaugasse, while the lake is 5 mins away, behind the station via Badhausstr.

i **Tourist Office**: Bahnhofpl. 12, ☎ (032) 322 75 75, fax (032) 323 77 57.

WHERE NEXT FROM NEUCHÂTEL?

*Twice-hourly trains, taking 41 mins (ETT table 511), link Neuchâtel with **Berne**, where you can join the **Berne–Geneva** (p. 325) or **Berne–Lugano** (p. 335) routes.*

LAKE BIEL AND ST PETERSINSEL

Lake Biel (Bielersee or lac de Bienne) has a nearby bathing beach, but its chief interest derives from **St Petersinsel** (St Peter's Island), a nature reserve reached by a 50-min boat trip from Schifflände, just west of Biel station. A monastery on the island has been tastefully converted into the **Restaurant-Hotel**, St Petersinsel, ☎ (032) 338 11 14; here in 1765 the Swiss-born French philosopher Jean-Jacques Rousseau spent a blissful time, which he recorded in his *Confessions* and in the *Reveries of the Solitary Walker.*

BASEL (BÂLE, BASLE)

Wedged into the corners of Switzerland, France and Germany, this big, working city (the second largest in the country after Zürich) has long been a crossroads for European culture, with many museums and other sights. If you are making day-trips to Basel it's worth considering the Basel Card. This gives free admission to museums, the zoo, sightseeing tours and ferries, plus discounts at shops, theatres, concerts, clubs, boat trips and taxis (SFr.25 for 24hrs, SFr.33 for 48hrs and SFr.45 for 72 hrs). Visitors staying in a hotel or youth hostel receive a mobility ticket which gives free bus and tram travel during your visit.

Of the six bridges across the River Rhine, **Mittlere Brücke** offers the best views. The medieval centre is on the south bank, in Grossbasel. Kleinbasel is the small modern area on the north bank. Admission to most museums generally costs around SFr.8, with some, such as the **Basel Museum of Ancient Art** and the **Historisches Museum**, offering free entry on the first Sun of the month.

> **BASEL'S CARNIVAL**
> The **Basel Fasnacht** is the country's most riotous carnival, taking over the town at 0400 on the Mon after Ash Wednesday and lasting for three days of noisy colourful fancy-dress fun.

Just south of the Rhine, Münsterpl. is dominated by the 12th-century red sandstone **Münster** (cathedral), which has decorative twin towers, a Romanesque portal surrounded by elegant carvings, and a rose window featuring the wheel of fortune. Housed within a Gothic church in Barfüsserpl., the **Historisches Museum** (closed Tues) has 13th–17th-century artefacts, including Luther's chalice; the 18th–19th-century sections of the collection are in the **Haus zum Kirschgarten**, Elisabethenstr. 27, about 300 m north of the SBB station.

> **TINGUELY IN BASEL**
> **Tinguely** is the Basel-born sculptor whose works typically resemble parodies of machines, manically juddering into action, seemingly against the odds. His **Fasnacht-Brunnen/Tinguely-Brunnen**, Theaterpl., is an extraordinary fountain (1977) that resembles a watery scrapyard. A museum dedicated to Tinguely, the **Museum Jean Tinguely**, Grenzacherstr. 210, celebrates his life and work (closed Mon and Tues).

The one sight not to miss is the world-class **Kunstmuseum** (Fine Arts Museum; closed Mon; tram no. 2 from the SBB rail station), St-Alban-Graben 16, in a building constructed in 1932–36 to house the art treasures the town had been accumulating since the 17th century, including important works by the 15th-century Basel master Konrad Witz, the world's largest collection of works by the Holbein family, and modern contributors such as Van Gogh, Picasso, Braque and Dalí.

> **GETTING AROUND BASEL**
> Most of the old centre is pedestrianised. Elsewhere a frequent tram service is supplemented by buses. Information and tickets are available from machines at every stop.

The permanent collection of the **Museum für Gegenwartskunst** (Museum of Contemporary Art), St-Alban-Rheinweg 60, includes pieces by Stella, Warhol and Beuys.

The recently restored 16th-century **Rathaus** (Town Hall) has an ornate and very picturesque red façade that includes an enormous clock. It towers over Marktplatz, the long-standing heart of Basel. Of the two main surviving medieval city gates, **St-Alban-Tor**, St-Alban-Graben, takes second place to the splendid 14th-century **Spalentor**, Spalengraben. Near here, on Spalenvorstadt, is the pick of the town's older fountains, the **Holbeinbrunnen**, based partly on a Holbein drawing and a Dürer engraving.

The **Zoologischer Garten**, Binningerstr. 40, west of the SBB station, has gained a reputation for breeding armoured rhinos, but is also known for its collections of pygmy hippos, gorillas and penguins.

▢ Basel is a frontier town for both France and Germany. The main station, **Bahnhof SBB**, is a 10-min walk south of the city centre (5 mins on tram nos. 1/8 from the terminus in front of the station), and handles Swiss and principal German services. Facilities include left luggage, bike rental, showers, a post office and a supermarket with extended opening hours. The **SNCF** station provides French services and boasts a large, suspended and animated Tinguely sculpture. Both stations evoke the heady old days of train travel, owing to the city's location at the 'Triangle' of Europe.

ⓘ **Tourist Office**: Schifflände 5, ▢ (061) 268 68 68, fax (061) 268 68 70, near the Mittlere Brücke, and at the SBB rail station (www.baseltourismus.ch; incomingsales@baseltourismus.ch).

▢ Moderate hotels in the old town include the **Rochat**, Petersgraben 23, ▢ (061) 261 81 40, fax (061) 261 64 92, €€, with prices beginning around SFr.100 (without private facilities), and the **Steinschanze**, Steingraben 69, ▢ (061) 272 53 53, fax (061) 272 45 73, €€, starting at SFr.120, including shower. The **youth hostel (Auberge de Jeunesse Bâle)** is at St Alban-Kirchrain 10, ▢ (061) 272 05 72, fax (061) 272 08 33, a 15-min walk from the SBB station or tram no. 2, then a 5-min walk. **Camping Waldhort**, Heideweg 16, Reinach, ▢ (061) 711 64 29, is 20–30 mins' south of the Bahnhof SBB rail station, via tram no. 11 to Landhof.

> **INTERNET CAFÉS**
> **Manor Warenhaus**,
> beim Kundendiensnst,
> Greifengasse 22, ▢ (061)
> 685 4618, Mon–Fri
> 0830–1900, Sat 0830–2100,
> Sun 0800–1700.

ZÜRICH

See p. 313.

CHUR

A cathedral city as well as capital of the canton of Grisons (population 32,000), **Chur** (pronounced Koohr) has an appealing old town. Green and red footprints mark recommended walking tours of the town (details from Tourist Office). With a fair range of places to eat and stay, it makes a feasible stopover. Its Romanesque-Gothic cathedral, built 1150–1272, has a dark, impressive interior with an exceptional Gothic triptych of carved and gilded wood, made by Jakob Russ 1486–92. In Postpl. in the **Kunstmuseum** has works by artists associated with Grisons.

In the town centre; cycle hire and left-luggage facility.

i **Tourist Office**: Grabenstr. 5, ☎ (081) 252 18 18, fax (081) 252 90 76 (www.churtourismus.ch; info@churtourismus.ch).

SIDE TRIP FROM CHUR TO DAVOS Retrace the route back to **Landquart**, and change for Davos (two stations: **Davos Dorf** and **Davos Platz**, the latter being the main place for activity, 69 mins by narrow-gauge railway, hourly (ETT table 545). This ski resort (**Tourist Office**: Promenade 67, Davos Pl., ☎ (081) 415 21 21, fax (081) 415 21 00 (www.davos.ch; davos@davos.ch.) is on yet another scenic line, between Landquart and **Filisur** – both ends connecting with the main **Lausanne–Poschiavo** route. **Davos** is the highest town in Europe (1560 m), and though it's rather dominated by modern purpose-built blocks and lacking in genuine Alpine atmosphere, it is an excellent centre for walking: a favourite easy excursion is to take the funicular up to the Alpine Garden at **Schatzalp**, where 800 plant species flourish. Schatzalp has a summer toboggan run and toboggans are for hire. Alternatively, take the cable car to **Jakobshorn** for superlative views along way-marked paths from the top.

LIECHTENSTEIN

The Principality of **Liechtenstein**, independent since 1719, is a green, mountainous little country covering just 158 square km; the train passes very close to it at **Sargans**, from where buses go to the capital, **Vaduz** (Swiss Passes valid). Apart from giving the chance to pick up a passport stamp of an obscure country, there isn't much to attract visitors, though the **Liechtensteinische Staatliche Kunstsammlungen** (State Art Collection) has some fine works (including a dazzling golden carriage) from the private collection of the Prince, who lives with his family in **Schloss Vaduz** (not open). Liechtenstein issues its own postage stamps, and philatelists may like to pay a visit to the **Briefmarkenmuseum** (Postage Stamp Museum).

ST MORITZ

Even in the face of opposition from the likes of Zermatt and Davos, **St Moritz** still pretty much leads the way as a Swiss sports resort, with a breathtaking location and a sunshine record (322 sunny days a year) unrivalled elsewhere in the country.

St Moritz divides into **Dorf** (village) on the hill, and **Bad** (spa) 2 km downhill around the lake; in St Moritz-Dorf lie the main hotels, shops and museums (including the **Engadine Museum**, offering an absorbing look at the furniture and house interiors of the Engadine). The centre for downhill skiing is **Corviglia** (2486 m), but even if you're not skiing it's worth the 2-km funicular trip for the views and a glimpse of the 'beautiful people' at play. From there, it's worth taking the cable car up to **Piz Nair** (3057 m) for a panorama of the Upper Engadine.

Near the centre of the town.

i **Tourist Office**:Via Maistra 12, (081) 837 33 33, fax (081) 837 33 77 (www.stmoritz.ch; information@stmoritz.ch).

Accommodation and food are generally less expensive in St Moritz Bad than in St Moritz Dorf. **Youth Hostel St Moritz Bad**:Via Surpunt 60, St Moritz Bad, (081) 833 39 69, fax (081) 833 80 46 (postbus to Hotel Sonne then 5-min walk).

POSCHIAVO

Tucked just inside the Swiss-Italian border, **Poschiavo** is distinctly southern in appearance, with a lovely central piazza surrounded by dignified Italianate houses. A wander round town reveals the 17th-century **town hall**, the Lombardian-style Gothic **church of San Vittore** and the 17th–18th-century **church of Santa Maria Presentata**, with its glorious ceiling. Spanish settlers in the 19th century built colourful houses in the Spaniola quarter.

In the town centre.

i **Tourist Office**: Piazza Communale, (081) 844 05 71, fax (081) 844 10 27 (www.valposchiavo.ch; valposchiavo@gr-net.ch).

MILAN (MILANO), ITALY

See p. 365.

WHERE NEXT FROM ST MORITZ?

*Take the **Glacier Express** (see p. 330), one of the great scenic rail journeys of the Alps from **St Moritz** to **Zermatt** via **Andermatt** and **Brig** (p. 330, ETT tables 540, 575, 579).*

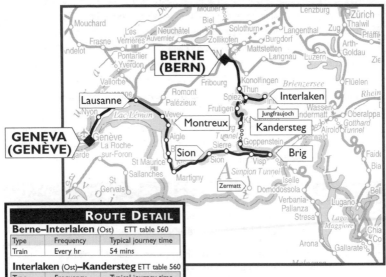

ROUTE DETAIL

Berne–Interlaken (Ost)   ETT table 560

Type	Frequency	Typical journey time
Train	Every hr	54 mins

Interlaken (Ost)–Kandersteg   ETT table 560

Type	Frequency	Typical journey time
Train	Every hr	1 hr 45 mins

Kandersteg–Brig   ETT table 560

Type	Frequency	Typical journey time
Train	Every hr	35 mins

Brig–Sion   ETT table 570

Type	Frequency	Typical journey time
Train	Every hr	37 mins

Sion–Montreux   ETT table 570

Type	Frequency	Typical journey time
Train	2 per hr	39 mins

Montreux–Lausanne   ETT table 570

Type	Frequency	Typical journey time
Train	2 per hr	21 mins

Lausanne–Geneva   ETT table 500/570

Type	Frequency	Typical journey time
Train	3 per hr	36 mins

Notes

Interlaken to Brig: change trains at Spiez. Trains also run directly from Berne to Brig (1 hr 38 mins) via Kandersteg (1 hr 3 mins).

KEY JOURNEYS

Geneva–Milan   ETT table 82

Type	Frequency	Typical journey time
Train	6 per day	4 hrs 32 mins

B E R N E – I N T E R L A K E N – G E N E V A

Berne, the easy-going city Swiss capital, is the prelude to the dramatic heights of the Bernese Oberland, a long-established area for tourism, then continuing along the partly industrialised Rhône Valley to end along the vineyards above Lake Geneva. It's well worth exploring the side trips, such as the expensive but spectacular mountain railway from Interlaken up **Jungfraujoch**, Europe's highest railway station; or explore the paths around **Kandersteg**. At **Brig** you can leave the route and go eastwards on the spectacular **Alpine Express** route (which in its entirety is Zermatt to St Moritz; Eurail/Inter-rail not valid; for a taster go up the **Goms valley**, with its quaint wooden villages, as far as Oberwald), or carry on and take the optional detour into **Zermatt**, a mountain resort near the Matterhorn. At **Martigny** choose between venturing into France and taking an exciting route past **Chamonix** and **Mont Blanc**, or passing Château Chillon beside **Lac Léman (Lake Geneva)**, the largest of all the Swiss lakes.

BERNE (BERN)

One of Europe's more relaxed capitals and much less international than Zürich or Geneva, Berne is pleasant for wandering around, with its harmonious medieval houses of yellow sandstone, its irregular roofscape, its ancient arcaded streets that make up Europe's largest covered shopping promenade (all 6 km of it) and its numerous fountains. The Alps are often visible in the distance, though the immediate surroundings are unremarkable.

From the main station, the first of 11 monumental fountains is the **Pfeiferbrunnen**, on Spitalgasse, a flamboyant 16th-century creation with technicolour carvings and flowers around the base.

Münsterpl. is home of the Gothic **Münster** (cathedral). There's been a cathedral here since 1200, but the building you see today was begun in 1421 and completed in 1520. It has a magnificent depiction of the *Last Judgment* above the main entrance, elaborate carvings on the pews and choir stalls, and superb 15th-century stained glass. The 100-m steeple (Switzerland's highest) provides a good view if you feel like climbing its 270 steps.

Berne was founded in 1191 by Berchtold V, Duke of Zähringen, who supposedly declared he would name his new city after the first creature he killed while hunting. The unfortunate victim, a bear, thus became the town's mascot.

Back on the main street (by now Gerechtigkeitsgasse), you pass Gerechtigkeitsbrunnen, where the blindfolded Goddess of Justice stands over the severed heads of historical figures. Cross the river by the 15th-century **Nydeggbrücke** and climb the hill facing you to look back on the picture-postcard view of the city.

The **Kunstmuseum** (Fine Art Museum), Hodlerstr. 8–12 (near Lorrainebrücke, north of the station), has a fine display of works by the Swiss artists Ferdinand

Hodler and Paul Klee (of whom this is the world's largest collection). Look too for exhibits by such diverse artists as Fra Angelico, Matisse, Kandinsky, Cézanne and Picasso. The other major museums are around Helvetiapl., south of the River Aare, across the Kirchenfeldbrücke (tram nos. 3/5). **Kunsthalle**, Helvetiapl. 1, hosts temporary exhibitions of contemporary art. Opposite, **Schweizerisches Alpines Museum** contains an interesting assem-

> ### Zytgloggeturm Clock Tower
> The clock tower, which was the original western gate, was first built in the 12th century. In the 16th century, an astronomical clock was added on its Kramgasse face. At exactly 4 mins to each hour, a mechanical jester summons a lion, a rooster and a procession of bears.

blage of items connected with the history of mountaineering. Close by, the **Naturhistorisches Museum** (Bernastr. 15) features Barry, the St Bernard dog, that rescued over 40 people, as well as African animals and the inevitable bears. The apartment and **workplace of Albert Einstein**, a resident of Berne, is at Kramgasse 49.

Getting around Berne

Berne's main thoroughfare runs east–west through the town centre, linking the station and Nydeggbrücke, and changes name four times: Spitalgasse, Marktgasse, Kramgasse, Gerechtigkeitsgasse. Other than the museums, much of interest is on or just off this street. There's an excellent tram and bus network. 🚊nos. 9A/15 and trolleybus 12 cover this street, as well as the Bärengraben, on the other side of the river. Departures from track 1 in the Vorpl. outside the station. The Tourist Office has details of city tours.

🚉 **Hauptbahnhof (Hbf)** is at the western end of the old centre.

ℹ️ **Tourist Office**: Hauptbahnhof, ☎(031) 328 12 12, fax (031) 328 12 33 (www.bernetourism.ch; info-res@bernetourism.ch). Its brochure *Bern Information* covers almost everything you're likely to need to know.

🛏️ Cheap accommodation is not plentiful but at least most of it is quite central. The two-star **Arabelle**, Mittelstr. 6, ☎(031) 301 03 05, fax (031) 302 42 62, €€, offers rooms with a shower beginning at SFr.90 (🚊no. 2, Mittelstr.). The **Isola**, Nissenweg 10, ☎(031) 302 17 11, fax (031) 302 41 65, €€, near the railway station, has rooms from SFr.100. **Youth Hostel Bern**: Weiherg. 4, ☎(031) 311 63 16, fax (031) 312 52 40, 10-mins' walk from the rail station, just below Bundeshaus. **Campsites: Eichholz**, Wabern, ☎(031) 961 26 02, 3.5 km south-east of centre (tram no. 9 to Wabern), open May–Sept, also **camping and bungalows: Eymatt**, Hinterkappelen, ☎(031) 901 10 07, 5 km north-west of the centre (Postbus to Eymatt from rail station).

🍴 The area around Spitalgasse, Bärenpl. and Zeughausgasse is good for menu browsing. The best-value lunch is at the pleasant self-service restaurant of the **EPA** department store, which straddles Zeughausgasse and Marktgasse. On Gerechtigkeitg, at no. 62, is the **Klötzlikeller**, Berne's oldest wine cellar (dating from 1635) serving snacks and full meals. For a picnic with a view, cross the Nydeggbrücke and walk to the lovely **Rose Garden**, or cross the Lorrainebrücke to the **Botanical Gardens**.

INTERLAKEN

This distinctly lively resort boomed in the 19th century when it became popular with British visitors as a base for exploring the mountains, and fanciful hotels sprang up along the Höheweg, the town's principal avenue (which links the two stations). It's still virtually unrivalled in the country as a centre for scenic excursions. You don't need transport for getting around town, but hiring a bike to explore the adjacent lakesides can be fun. Horse-drawn carriages (at a price) are available for hire outside both stations.

From the Höheweg a wonderful, uninterrupted view extends across the undeveloped meadow where the original 12th-century monastic site of the town once stood, to Jungfrau (4158 m) and other peaks looming beyond – especially magnificent in the later afternoon Alpenglow.

One of the period pieces in town is the distinctive 19th-century **Kursaal** (Casino), which in addition to gambling (high rollers should note that the ceiling for bets is only SFr.5) stages concerts and folklore evenings. Across the River Aare is the old part of town known as **Unterseen**, with the oldest buildings in the region. Cross the bridge and walk along the river to **Marktplatz**, with its 17th-century town hall and palace, 14th-century church and **Touristik Museum** (charting the rise and rise of Interlaken's tourist industry).

[RAIL] **Ostbahnhof** is on Lake Brienz, a 10-min walk from the centre. **Westbahnhof**, by Lake Thun, is central. The two stations are 15 mins apart on foot, 3 mins by rail. It is the Ostbahnhof that connects with the railway to Jungfraujoch. From Berne, Westbahnhof is the first stop and the journey, by hourly trains, averages 50 mins – sit on the left as you head south.

[i] **Tourist Office**: Höheweg 37, [fax](033) 826 53 00, fax (033) 826 53 75 (www.interlakentourism.ch; mail@interlakentourism.ch).

[hotel] There's no shortage of hotels, many catering largely for tour operators, but private rooms can be better value. **Backpackers Villa**, Alpenstr. 16, [fax](033) 826 7171, fax (033) 826 7172 (www.villa.ch; backpackers@villa.ch), €–€€, has twins, triples, quads and dorms; online reservation; 10 mins from station or [bus] no. 2. Other reasonably priced hotels include **Arnold's Bed & Breakfast**, Parkstr. 3, [fax](033) 823 6421, fax (033) 823 34 78, €€, and **Backpackers Villa Sonnenhof**, Alpenstr. 16, [fax](033) 826 71 71, fax (033) 826 71 72, €€. **Youth Hostel Bönigen bei Interlaken**: Aareweg 21, am See, [fax](033) 822 43 53, fax (033) 823 20 58, 20 mins' walk east from **Ostbahnhof**, in the village of **Bönigen** on Lake Brienz ([bus] no. 1). There's also an excellent private **hostel: Balmer's Herberge**, Hauptstr. 23, [fax](033) 822 19 61, fax (033) 823 32 61 (www.balmers.ch), 15 mins' walk from both stations, in the suburb of **Matten** ([bus] nos. 5/15). Seven **campsites** are within easy walking distance, so ask the Tourist Office for details.

[TO] Interlaken doesn't offer a wide choice of interesting cheap eats, though there are the usual fast food outlets (including McDonald's). In the summer, spontaneous outdoor restaurants and grills sprout, offering cheaper fare. Internet Café: **The Wave**, Rosenstr. 13, ☎ (033) 823 40 32 (www.thewave.ch), Mon–Sun 1400–2300.

Day Trips from Interlaken Interlaken's most popular excursion is the 2hr 10-min journey – each way – to **Jungfraujoch**, the highest railway station in Europe (3454 m). Services are hourly, and changes of train may be necessary in **Lauterbrunnen** or **Grindelwald** and **Kleine Scheidegg**. The earlier you start the better to increase the chance of clear views. Ostbahnhof has weather reports (see right). It's best to dedicate a whole day to the trip, if the weather warrants it, as stops can be made en route.

This trip is undeniably breathtaking, but also very expensive (currently SFr.159, passes not valid), although you can save about a quarter by taking the (very early) first train. (0635; ETT table 564). On a good day, you'll see the best of Switzerland, including phenomenal glaciers. At **Kleine Scheidegg**, the stop is directly in front of the magnificent triumvirate, the **Eiger**, the **Mönch** and the **Jungfrau**. The little rack-and-pinion railway then goes into the face of the Eiger, emerging from the long tunnel at the 3454-m summit. As well as the Jungfraujoch there are other, cheaper funicular rides up **Harder Kulm** (1320 m) and **Heimwehfluh** (669 m); both are close to town.

A **boat or bus ride** will take you to the **Beatushöhlen** – dramatic cliff caves along the Thunersee. For the best views of **Interlaken** and the **lakes of Thun and Brienz**, from which the towns take their names, catch a train to **Wilderswil** for the rack railway to **Schynige Platte**, its summit adorned with an Alpine garden. Beyond **Lauterbrunnen**, a bus ride to **Trummelbach waterfalls** (actually inside the mountain face) is a good afternoon's trip. The cliff steps are not for the infirm, though. Also from Lauterbrunnen, it's possible to take a cable car up to the revolving restaurant on the 2970 m **Schilthorn**, better known for its James Bond film connections, (*On Her Majesty's Secret Service*) and which offers views of more than 200 Alpine peaks.

KANDERSTEG

With its excellent train and bus links, and chair lifts up into the mountains, this large, old-fashioned village is perfectly sited for exploring the Bernese Oberland. Everything's geared to outdoor activities, with year-round walking trails and winter sports. Pick of the walks is up to the **Oeschinensee**, a stupendously sited mountain lake (walk up or take the chair lift), or take the Sunnbüel cable car and walk up to the Gemmi Pass. Other options include **Adelboden** (another pleasant old village, reached by train to Frutigen then post bus; ETT table 560) or the deeply traditional villages of the **Lötschental** (train to Goppenstein for connecting post bus to Blatten, where you can walk down to the valley to another village such as Kippel and pick up the bus back).

3 mins from the village centre.

Tourist Office: 3718 Kandersteg, ☎ (033) 675 80 80 (www.kandersteg.ch; info@kandersteg.ch). From the station take the road into the village centre, turn left along main street; Tourist Office is on the right.

⌂ Wide choice in the village, with bed and breakfast from around SFr50. Cheaper places include the **Edelweiss**, ☎ (033) 675 11 94, €, a centrally placed wooden chalet in the village centre, and on the edge of the village the more modern **Erika**, ☎ (033) 675 11 37 (hotelerika@datacom.ch), €, owned by an Anglo-Swiss couple.

BRIG

The town stands at a major meeting of rail routes, where you can change for trains to Zermatt. Now home to municipal offices, the vast Italianate palace of **Stockalper Castle** is the largest private building ever erected in Switzerland. It was constructed 1658–68 by Kaspar Stockalper, a merchant who made a fortune controlling the flow of goods between France, Lombardy and Switzerland.

 Near the town centre.

i **Tourist Office**: Verkehrsverein, ☎ (027) 921 60 30, fax (027) 921 60 31 (www.brig-tourismus.ch; info@brig-tourismus.ch)

SIDE TRIP FROM BRIG TO ZERMATT Served by narrow-gauge railway (1hr 20 mins from Brig, hourly; ETT table 575), **Zermatt** is a major ski centre and car-free. In summer it's a superb place for hiking. The little town's popularity largely rests on its proximity to the 4477-m **Matterhorn**, one of the best-known mountain profiles in the world, best appreciated by walking a little out of town. Zermatt is very touristy, but nothing (except the frequent clouds) can detract from the glory of its magnificent jagged peak. The **Gornergrat mountain railway** and a network of cable cars provide superb views of the whole area. The **Kleiner Matterhorn Cable Car** makes a three-stage ascent up to 3828 m, giving an extremely dramatic, and very different, view of the Matterhorn, as well as the Alpine range; Mont Blanc in France is prominent on aclear day. The journey to Zermatt is the westernmost stage of the famous **Glacier Express** route (see right: Where Next from Brig?). **Tourist Office**: Bahnhofpl., ☎ (027) 967 01 81, fax (027) 967 01 85 (www.zermatt.ch; zermatt@wallis.ch).

WHERE NEXT FROM BRIG?

From Brig you can continue south through the **Simplon Tunnel** *(one of the world's longest rail tunnels at 20 km) and into Italy, proceeding along the shores of* **Lake Maggiore** *(p. 339) to* **Milan** *(p. 365) (a 1 hr 50 min–2 hr 15 min trip – see ETT table 590).*

One of the great scenic Alpine routes is east on the **Glacier Express** *(narrow-gauge line) to* **St Moritz**; *the full Glacier Express route begins from Zermatt. There are some through services; for others change at* **Andermatt** *(takes 8–8hrs 30 mins; ETT tables 575 and 579; reservations recommended). At St Moritz you can join the* **Lausanne–Milan** *route (p. 317). In its entirety, from Zermatt to St Moritz, the route crosses 291 bridges and passes through 91 tunnels and many hairpin bends.*

SION

Though the area's a bit marred by industrial development, the attractive old centre of Sion looks terrific from a distance, with two hills popping up beside it, both excellent viewpoints in themselves. One is crowned by the scant ruins of **Château Tourbillon**, the other by a strange fortified church called the **Basilique de Valère**. As capital of the Valais canton, the town has provincial **museums** covering fine arts, archaeology and natural history.

Near the town centre.

Tourist Office: Pl de la Planta, ☎ (027) 322 85 86, fax (027) 322 18 82 (www.siontourism.ch; info@siontourism.ch).

Youth hostel: Auberge de Jeunesse, R. de l'Industrie 2, ☎ (027) 323 74 70, fax (027) 323 74 38, 350 m from station. There is a riverside **campsite**: **Camping des Îles**, ☎ (027) 346 43 47, fax (027) 346 68 47, 4 km west of the centre

WHERE NEXT FROM SION?

*Cross into **France** in style by taking the route via Chamonix–Mont Blanc and St Gervais, and re-entering **Switzerland** to end at **Geneva**, getting stunning mountain views most of the way. ETT tables 572, 367 and 363.*

*The **Mont Blanc Express** train grinds up an incredible one-in-five gradient to the French border village of **Vallorcine**; some trains run through, though others require a change here or at Le Châtelard Frontière. At **Chamonix Mont Blanc**, you have the option of taking the **Montenvers** rack railway up to Europe's biggest glacier.*

MONTREUX

The best-preserved of the **Lake Geneva** resorts, Montreux is blessed with a mild climate, with palm trees, magnolias and cypresses along its 10-km waterside promenade – a lovely place for strolling. Smart hotels make the most of the views, while the rest of the town rises in tiers up the hillside. The effect is slightly spoiled by a garish casino.

In the centre of town.

Tourist Office: R. du Théâtre 5, ☎ (021) 962 84 84, fax (021) 963 78 95 (www.montreux.ch; tourism@montreux.ch).

Youth Hostel: Passage de l'Auberge 8, ☎(021) 963 49 34, fax (021) 963 27 29 (montreux@youthhostel.ch). Just 150 m from Territet rail station (2 km from Montreux station); 🚃no. 1 from Montreux's main station.

DAY TRIPS FROM MONTREUX Take the funicular up to the 2042-m summit of **Rochers de la Naye** (55 mins), or about 3 hrs' walk. There are a couple of wonderfully sited restaurants at the top. Reached by 🚃no.1 train or a pleasant walk of 3 km south from Montreux, **Château de Chillon** is as impressive and well-preserved a medieval castle as you could hope to see. Famously, the Reformationist Bonivard was chained to a pillar in the dungeon here for four years, an event immortalised in verse by Byron; the poem itself brought the castle to public notice, and it's become the most visited attraction in Switzerland. A computer-aided display in the chapel projects representations of icons of the saints on the walls, giving an idea of how the original must have appeared.

WHERE NEXT FROM MONTREUX?

An even more scenic option from the main route is to divert from Montreux to Zweisimmen, then to Spiez where you rejoin the main route (ETT tables 565, 566). This is truly one of Switzerland's great train rides; there are ordinary trains as well as Golden Pass observation trains.

LAUSANNE

See p. 318.

GENEVA (GENÈVE)

With a dual role as a banking centre and a base for many international organisations, Geneva is a cosmopolitan, comfortably prosperous place, with promenades and parks beautifying the shores of **Lac Léman** (**Lake Geneva**). The River Rhône splits the city into two distinct sections, with the international area on the Rive Droite (right bank, to the north) and the compact old town on the Rive Gauche (left bank, to the south).

On Rive Droite (🚃nos. 5/8/14/F/Z) is Pl. des Nations, near which most of the international organisations are grouped. The **Musée International de la Croix-Rouge**, Av. de la Paix 17, is a stern building with high-tech exhibits tracing the history of the Red Cross and its Islamic offshoot, the Red Crescent. Profoundly moving, it covers man's inhumanity to man and natural disasters. Close by, the **Palais des Nations**, Av. de la Paix 14, is home to the European headquarters of the United Nations, which replaced the League of Nations in 1945; there are guided tours. Between here and the lake is the lovely **Jardin Botanique**, a perfect place for a quiet stroll (once you're away from the main road) and featuring a rock garden, a deer and llama park, and an aviary.

On Rive Gauche, south of the centre, the **Jardin Anglais**, on the waterfront, is famous for its **Horloge Fleurie** (floral clock), while the city's trade mark, the 140-m high fountain (**Jet d'Eau**), spouts from a nearby pier.

Getting Around Geneva

Geneva's sights are fairly scattered and a bit of route-planning is worthwhile. There is a good network of buses and one tram route. From May to Sept, **Compagnie Générale de Navigation de Lac Léman (CGN)** operate regular lake ferries from Quai du Mont-Blanc and Jardin Anglais, 10 mins' walk straight ahead out of the station subway down R. des Alpes; ☎ 0848 822 8488. Tramway and little train tours through the city operate in season.

At the heart of the old town is the lively Place du Bourg-de-Four, Geneva's oldest square. Take rue de l'Hôtel de Ville to the 15th-century Hôtel de Ville (town hall), where the first Geneva Convention was signed in 1864. Adjacent is the former arsenal and the 12th-century **Maison Tavel**, Geneva's oldest house and now an evocative museum, with several period rooms and exhibits covering the 14th–19th centuries.

The original 12th–13th-century Gothic façade of the **Cathédrale de St-Pierre** has incongruous 18th-century additions. Most interior decorations were stripped out in the Reformation, but there are some frescos in the neo-Gothic Chapelle des Maccabées. Calvin preached here and his chair has been saved for posterity. The north tower, reached by a 157-step spiral staircase, offers a great view of the old town. Beneath the cathedral is the **Site Archéologique**, where catwalks allow you to see the result of extensive excavations, including a 4th-century baptistery and a 5th-century mosaic floor.

Two blocks south, the vast marble **Musée d'Art et d'Histoire**, R. Charles-Galland 2, has several rooms in period style, Hodler landscapes and the famous painting *The Fishing Miracle*, by Witz, which portrays Christ walking on the water – of Lake Geneva.

The 19th-century **Petit Palais**, Terrasse St-Victor 2, has an impressive array of modern art and includes works by Cézanne, Renoir and the Surrealists. Nearby, the **Collection Baur**, R. Munier-Romilly 8, contains some lovely Japanese and Chinese objets d'art, ranging from Samurai swords to jade and delicate porcelain.

West of the cathedral, **Parc des Bastions** houses the university (founded by Calvin in 1559) and the vast **Monument de la Réformation** (erected in 1909), a 90-m-long wall featuring four central characters – Farel, Calvin, Bèze and Knox – each over 4.5 m high.

Gare de Cornavin is the main terminal, 10-min walk north of the centre (🚌 nos. 5/6/9). **Gare Genève Eaux-Vives**, on the eastern edge of the city, is the terminal for SNCF trains from Annecy and St Gervais (30-min walk from Cornavin station or 🚌 no. 12). **Metro Shopping**, a large complex that includes the 'Alimentation Automatique', is open Sun. The Aperto supermarket is open 0600–2200 every day.

The airport has its own station (Genève Aéroport), with frequent trains into central Geneva taking 9 mins; many services from Geneva to other points in Switzerland stop here.

[i] **Tourist Office**: R. de Mont-Blanc 18, ☎(022) 909 70 00, fax (022) 909 70 11 (www.geneve-tourisme.ch; info@geneve.tourisme.ch). A smaller central office is at Pont-de-la-Machine 1, ☎(022) 311 99 70. Traveller's information office also at Gare de Cornavin, ☎(022) 732 00 90. For hotel reservations ☎(022) 909 70 20, fax (022) 909 70 21. *Genève Guide pratique* and *Info-Jeunes* are free guides definitely worth picking up. *Genève Agenda* is the free weekly city entertainment guide.

🏨 Most hotels are expensive, but there are plenty of hostels and private rooms. Ask at the Tourist Office for a copy of *Info-Jeunes*, which lists useful information. From 15 June to 15 Sept, the **CAHJ (Centre d'Accueil d'Herbergement des Jeunes)**, located in a trailer in the pedestrian area opposite the station, offers accommodation booking and other advice to young people. There are at least a dozen hotels listed which are within walking distance of the centre, offering a room with shower from around SFr.50 including **Beau-Site**, Pl. du Cirque 3, ☎(022) 328 10 08, €, and **De la Cloche**, R. de la Cloche 6, ☎(022) 732 94 81, €. Just as cheap are the many university and religious institution lodgings on offer, including the **Cité Universitaire**, Av. Miremont 46, ☎(022) 839 22 22, fax (022) 839 22 23, €, and, with the most attractive and central location, **Centre Universitaire Catholique**, R. de Candolle 30, ☎(022) 329 70 56, fax (022) 320 12 38, €. In addition there's the **Youth Hostel: Auberge de Jeunesse Genève**, R. Rothschild 30, ☎(022) 732 62 60, fax (022) 738 39 87, in the Paquis area close to the main rail station. **Campsites: Camping Pointe-à-la-Bise**, Chemin de la Bise, Vésenaz, ☎(022) 752 12 96, fax (022) 752 36 67, open Apr–Oct, 7 km north-east, close to Lac Léman (🚌 no. E); **Camping d'Hermance**, R. du Nord 44, Hermance, ☎(022) 751 14 83, open Apr–Sep, 14 km north-east (🚌 no. E).

🍽 Because of its French influence and cosmopolitan nature, Geneva claims to be the culinary centre of Switzerland. The majority of places, however, cater for international business people. Good places to look for reasonably priced restaurants are on the R. de Lausanne (turn left out of Gare de Cornavin) and around Pl. du Cirque (Blvd Georges-Favon). Try **Sherlock's Café**, R. de la Servette 6 (behind Gare de Cornavin) or **Cafétéria de l'UOG**, Pl. des Grottes 3. Consult *Info-Jeunes* (see Accommodation above) for a list of university restaurants and for other cheap eats. **Parc des Bastions** is also great for picnics.

WHERE NEXT FROM GENEVA?

*Trains cross the border to France, where you can take TGV services to **Paris** and **Mâcon** (ETT table 347), **Lyon** (ETT table 348) and **Marseille**, **Nice** and **Montpellier** (ETT tables 350, 355, 360). Geneva to Paris takes 3 hrs 30 mins, Geneva to Lyon 1 hr 50 mins.*

ROUTE DETAIL		
Berne–Lucerne		ETT table 515
Type	Frequency	Typical journey time
Train	Every 1-2 hrs	1 hr 20 mins
Lucerne–Brunnen		ETT table 550
Type	Frequency	Typical journey time
Train	Every 2 hrs	47 mins
Brunnen–Lugano		ETT table 550
Type	Frequency	Typical journey time
Train	Every hr	2 hrs 15 mins

KEY JOURNEYS		
Berne–Milan		ETT table 560
Type	Frequency	Typical journey time
Train	3 per day	3 hrs 45 mins

Lake **Lucerne** is the outstanding scenic feature of central Switzerland, an irregularly shaped body of water encompassed by flattish land around the dignified old resort of **Lucerne** itself, as well as picture-book snowy mountains dotted with wooden chalets to the south. Beyond the **Gothard Tunnel**, the landscape changes abruptly, as you enter the canton of **Ticino**, to an emerald-green valley dotted with rustic granite houses and tall campaniles as you head towards the Italian border. **Lugano** has the atmosphere of a smart Italian provincial town, and makes a good base for excursions.

BERNE (BERN)

See p. 326.

LUCERNE (LUZERN)

This resort straddles the River Reuss, itself crossed by quaintly roofed medieval footbridges, at the end of Lake Lucerne. Old-fashioned hotels attest to the town's long standing as a holiday place. There's a major music festival mid-Aug to Sept.

Old Lucerne is characterised by its many elaborately painted houses, its cobbled squares, its fountains, its Renaissance town hall by the Kornmarkt, and the two bridges over the Reuss. As you cross the 14th-century **Kapellbrücke**, a wooden-roofed footbridge that straggles crookedly over the river, you pass under a succession of 111 triangular-shaped paintings depicting local and national history. Halfway across, the bridge goes through a sturdy 13th-century octagonal **Water Tower**, which has undergone several changes of function over the centuries, including use as a prison. A little further down the river is the other medieval roofed bridge, the **Spreuerbrücke**, also lined with 17th-century paintings, in this case depicting the macabre *Dance of Death*. Near the south end of Kapellbrücke, the **Jesuit Church** is plain from the outside, but has a gorgeous pink-and-white baroque interior dating from 1677. **Nolliturm**, near the north end of Spreuerbrücke, is a fortified gate at one end of a well-preserved stretch of **Musegg Wall**, the old fortifications. You can follow this all the way (and climb three of its nine surviving towers) as it curves east to end just off Löwenpl.

The **Luzern Museum Pass**, SFr.25, is good for one month and gives free entry to all the museums in town, including the **Verkehrshaus** (transport museum).

The graceful twin-spired **Hofkirche**, (Cathedral), off Schweizerhofquai, has an organ with 4950 pipes and a 10-ton bell. The city's mascot, the **Löwendenkmal** (Lion Memorial), Löwenstr., is a massive but movingly portrayed dying lion carved in the cliff-side, commemorating the Swiss Guards massacred at the Tuileries in Paris during the French Revolution. Nearby is the **Gletschergarten** (Glacier Garden), Denkmalstr. 4, a bed of smooth rocks pitted with holes, created by glacial action. There's an ingenious mirror-maze here too.

Anyone with an interest in transport in all its guises and vintages should make for the **Verkehrshaus** (Swiss Transport Museum), Lidostr. 5, 2 km east of town (near the campsite), reached by a pleasant lakeside walk (or 🚌 nos. 6/8); it's one of Europe's leading museums on the theme, with exhibits covering locos, vintage cycles, space rockets and more, plus an IMAX movie theatre (with a huge, almost vertigo-inducing screen), a 360-degree cinema.

PICASSO AND WAGNER IN LUCERNE

The Picasso Museum, Am Rhyn-Haus, Furrengasse 21, just off the old Kornmarkt square, contains a small collection of his later paintings and photographs of the great man. The local Rosengart family commissioned Picasso to paint a portrait of their daughter; they were so pleased with it that they bought several of his paintings, eight of which they donated to set up this museum. The **Richard Wagner Museum**, Wagnerweg 27, by the lake, 1.5 km south-east of the centre (🚌 nos. 6/8 or walk east along the lake from the station), occupies the house where the German composer lived during the time he wrote the scores for *Siegfried* and *Die Meistersinger von Nürnberg*. There's a collection of his memorabilia and original scores.

🚂 On the south bank of the River Reuss, where it meets Lake Lucerne, a few mins' walk over the bridge to the old town. In the basement is the '24-hr shopping' automat, for emergency rations.

ℹ️ **Tourist Office**: Zentralstr. 5 (in station); ☎ (041) 227 17 17, fax (041) 227 17 18 (www.luzern.org; luzern@luzern.org). Also in the station basement. Accommodation booking service. The *Luzern City Guide* is free and full of useful information.

🏨 Lucerne is a popular tourist destination, so advance booking is advisable for its limited range of cheap options, especially in summer; some of the 19th-century hotels surrounding the old town can be noisy.
The **Tourist Hotel**, St Karliquai 12, ☎ (041) 410 24 74, fax (041) 410 84 14, €€ (www.touristhotel.ch; info@touristhotel.ch), has rooms beginning at SFr.60, The **Pickwick**, Rathausquai 6, ☎ (041) 410 59 27, fax (041) 410 51 08, €€, and the **Derby**, Falkengasse. 6, ☎ (041) 410 26 62, fax (041) 410 42 82, €€, both have prices starting around SFr.75. **Backpackers Lucerne**, Alpenquai 42, ☎ (041) 360 04 20, fax (041) 360 04 42 (www.backpacker.ch), €, offers student-style accommodation by the south shore of the lake (10-min walk from the station).
Youth hostel: Am Rotsee, Sedelstr. 12, ☎ (041) 420 88 80, fax (041) 420 51 16 is situated by the lake north-west of town (🚌 no. 18 to Jugendherberge or no. 19 to Rosenberg).
Campsite: **Camping International Lido**, Lidostr. 19; ☎ (041) 370 21 46, fax (041) 370 21 45 (🚌 nos. 6/8 to Verkehrshaus), on the north shore of the lake.

🍽️ There are reasonably priced restaurants and cafés all round Lucerne's many squares and waterside promenades. The town's speciality is *Kügelipasteti*, a large meat and mushroom vol-au-vent covered in rich sauce.

DAY TRIPS FROM LUCERNE

You can get to most of the settlements around Lake Lucerne, which covers 114 square km, by regular local boat services, as well as excursion cruises in summer; contact **Schiffahrtgesellschaft** des **Vierwaldstättersees**, ☎(041) 367 67 67, fax (041) 367 68 68 (www.lakelucerne.ch; info@lakelucerne.ch), or book through the Tourist Office. These boats combine nicely with walks as well as rack railway and cable car trips. From **Alpnachstad** (reached by steamer), south of Lucerne, take the world's steepest rack railway (climbing a 48% gradient) up **Mt Pilatus** (2132 m). Supposedly haunted by the spirit of Pontius Pilate, the summit is also accessible by cable car from **Kriens** (🚌no. 1), on the southern out-skirts of Lucerne – giving scope for a circular tour of the mountain. From Vitznau, on the eastern shore, Europe's oldest rack railway ascends **Mt Rigi** (1800 m), where the summit view from **Rigi-Kulm** at sunrise (including the Jungfrau and Titlis) has attracted generations of tourists, including Victor Hugo. There's also a cable car from the sunny waterside resort of **Weggis**; if you prefer to walk, there's a 4-hr route from Weggis, or you can take the cable car up from **Küssnacht** to within a 2-hr hike of the summit. At **Engelberg**, 16 km south of the lake and 1 hr from Lucerne by train (hourly; ETT table 552), the huge **Rotair**, the world's first rotating cable car, gives an unparalleled view of the permanently snow-capped **Mt Titlis** (3020 m).

BRUNNEN

You may like to pause here to enjoy the site, at the meeting of **lakes Uri** and **Lucerne**. The bustling resort is well set-up for most watersports, as well as walking on Lake Uri's shores. Brunnen can claim to be the cradle of the nation's history. Here the for-est states of Unterwalden, Uri and Schwyz were sworn together as the Confederation in a declaration on Aug 1, 1291 in Rütli Meadow by the lake, an event immortalised in the legend of William Tell as told by Schiller in 1804; Aug 1 is Swiss National Day, celebrated nationwide with bonfires lit on high spots and the **Rütli Meadow** floodlit. The **Swiss Way** is a 22-km walkers' route round the lake, divided into 26 sections; each section represents a canton or half-canton, with the length of each determined by the proportionate populations of each canton.

🚆 Close to the town centre.

i **Tourist Office**: Bahnhofstr. 32, ☎(041) 825 00 40, fax (041) 825 00 49 (www.brunnentourismus.ch; info@brunnentourismus.ch).

LUGANO

Lugano, the largest town in the Italian-speaking canton of Ticino, is a handsome, sophisticated resort of Lombardic arcades and piazzas beside **Lake Lugano**. It climbs the hillside around a horseshoe bay surrounded by verdant mountains, so is an ideal base for walking as well as watersports. The lakeside promenade is a pop-ular place to stroll or roller-blade in July and Aug, when vehicles are banned from it. At its eastern end is the **Parco Civico** (Municipal Park), the pleasant setting for summer concerts and graced with fountains, statues and trees. Swimmers can head for the lido (to the east of the river), with its pool and sandy beaches.

Funiculars climb the two mountains guarding the bay: up **Monte Brè** (930 m) from **Cassarate** and up **San Salvatore** (912 m) from **Paradiso**, both 20-min walks from the centre or take 🚃 no. 1.

The arcaded Via Nassa is the main pedestrianised shopping street, where you can take your pick of such Swiss specialities as expensive wristwatches or chocolate in all its national varieties. There's more worthwhile art in **Thyssen-Bornemisza**, a collection of 19th- and 20th-century paintings and watercolours housed in the **Villa Favorita**, Riviera 14 (Fri–Sun, Easter–Oct), while the **Cantonal Art Museum**, Via Canova 10, also has many 20th-century works.

At the top of the town. From it a funicular descends to the middle (otherwise a 6-min walk), half-way down to the lake.

Tourist Office: Palazzo Civico, Riva Albertolli, 🕿 (091) 913 32 32, fax (091) 922 76 53 (www.lugano-tourism.ch; info@lugano-tourism.ch); on the lakeside opposite the central landing stage. Accommodation booking service.

The **Rosa**, V. Landriani 2–4, 🕿 (091) 922 92 86, fax (091) 923 42 70, €€, and the **Selva**, V. Tesserete 36, 🕿 (091) 923 60 17, fax (091) 923 60 09, €€, offer rooms beginning around SFr.55 and SFr.60 respectively. **Youth Hostel: Lugano-Savosa**, V. Cantonale 13, 🕿 (091) 966 27 28, fax (091) 968 23 63 (🚃 no. 5 from station to Crocifisso then a 3-min walk). Generally, **Paradiso** (the southern part of Lugano) is slightly better value.

There are several restaurants along the lakeside, as well as around the main square, the Piazza Riforma.

The Italian Lakes

WHERE NEXT?

*Hourly trains to **Milan** (p. 365) take 1 hr–1 hr 30 mins (ETT tables 82, 550), for connections with **Florence, Rome** and other Italian cities.*

Locarno on **Lake Maggiore** is 50 mins by train from Lugano (change at Bellinzona) (ETT table 550). From it, the scenic **Centovalli** (Hundred Valleys) route runs to **Domodossola** in Italy. The 53-km line clings to dramatic hillsides, soars across dozens of steep valleys (hence its name) over spectacular bridges and viaducts to **Santa Maria Maggiore**. Afterwards, continue exploring Switzerland via the major rail junction at **Brig**, 42 km north of Domodossola through the **Simplon Tunnel**.

North-east of Lugano, just beyond Gandria, is the Mediterranean-flavoured **Menaggio**. In Italy, this Lake Como town provides lovely views over the water. To get to the other bank, there are frequent trains from Lugano to Como (about 50 mins). Continuing on the Italian side, the train skirts the shore, providing views of Italian villages on both sides of the lake.

AUSTRIA

(for Directory information, see p. 586).

Sharing borders with Germany, Switzerland, Liechtenstein, Italy, the Czech Republic, Slovakia, Slovenia and Hungary, Austria feels very much at the centre of Europe. Its capital, **Vienna**, a greyish, stately affair of boulevards, parks and palaces, has a poignant air of once being at the centre of bigger things – harking back to the era of the great Habsburg empire. The rest of the country is quite different. **Salzburg**, the city indelibly associated with Mozart (though he hated the place), has bags of charm with its baroque squares. The Alps, which dominate the map of Austria, cover much of the country, and, though not as consistently dramatic as the Swiss Alps, have enough diversity to make them well worth exploring. There's little in the way of old-fashioned rural buildings in the mountain areas, though: the ubiquitous item is the immaculate white chalet with balconies full of geraniums, and onion-domed church towers preside over postcard-pretty scenes. Some may find that the neat, groomed appearance of Austria almost verges on the monotonous.

Tyrol and **Vorarlberg**, in western Austria, include the country's highest mountains and are dramatic indeed, with villages to match; **Innsbruck** and **Kitzbühel** are among the larger places worth seeing. The **Salzkammergut** is the obvious upland to venture into from Salzburg, where pleasant resorts lie scattered beside lakes under miniature limestone mountains. Further south are the lesser known areas of **Carinthia**, with more lake resorts, and the peaks of **Styria**, not quite as breathtaking as the Tyrol but very fine in their own right.

ACCOMMODATION

Hotels are graded on the usual five-star system, but even one-star establishments are pricey. *Gasthaus/Gasthof* indicates an **inn** and *Frühstückspension* a **bed and breakfast** place. The best value is usually a **private room** (look for signs), but many require stays of several nights and some charge extra for short stays. *Jugendherberge* is the word for a **youth hostel**; few of them are self-catering but most serve meals. They cost around €11–18. For details of hostels contact the **Österreichischer Jugendherbergsverband**, Hauptverband, 1010 Wien, Schottenring 28, ☎ (01) 533 5353, fax (01) 535 0861 (www.oejhv.or.at; oejhv-zentrale@oejhv.or.at). In summer, some universities let rooms.

ACCOMMODATION **341**

AUSTRIA

GUEST CARDS

Several resorts issue a guest card to visitors in higher quality accommodation. The cards entitle holders to anything from free escorted mountain hikes to discounts for ferries or museums. The cards are generally issued by *Gasthofs* or **hotels**.

Camping is popular and there are lots of sites, mostly very clean and well run, but pricey. Many sites are open summer only. In Alpine areas, there are also **refuge huts** – details from the local Tourist Office. For all accommodation it is advisable to book ahead for July, Aug, Christmas and Easter.

FOOD AND DRINK

Food tends towards the hearty, with wholesome soups and meat-dominated main courses (famously *Wiener Schnitzel* – a thin slice of veal fried in egg and breadcrumbs), while *goulasch* (of Hungarian origin) and dumplings are also prevalent. Cakes are sinfully cream-laden and high-cholesterol, including the amazingly rich *Sachertorte*, an iced chocolate cake invented in Vienna.

A filling snack, sold by most butchers, is *Wurstsemmel* – slices of sausage with a bread roll.

Lunch is usually more expensive in cafés than in restaurants. Drinks in bars and clubs cost more than in eating-places.

The Austrian pattern is: continental breakfast, lunch (1200–1400), coffee and cake mid-afternoon, then dinner (1800–2200). Beer is the most popular drink, but Austrian wine is good and there are numerous varieties of *Schnapps*. A service charge of 10–15% is included in restaurant bills. It is the custom to leave a further 5% if you're happy with the service.

EDITOR'S CHOICE

Innsbruck; Salzburg; Tyrol Alps around Kitzbühel; Vienna. Scenic rail journeys: Swiss border–Vienna via Innsbruck and Salzburg (p. 349 and Where Next from Innsbruck?, p. 351); Innsbruck-Spittal Millstättersee via Fortezza (Italy; ETT tables 596, 970).

BEYOND THE BORDERS

From Vienna to: Budapest (ETT table 61); Munich (table 67); Cologne via Würzburg (table 66); Prague (table 59); Bratislava (table 996); Rome via Venice (table 88); Warsaw (table 95). From Innsbruck to: Munich (table 70); Rome via Verona (table 70); Zürich (table 86).

CITIES: VIENNA (WIEN)

Austria's capital is one of Europe's great cultural centres, revered worldwide for its **music**. The waltz was born here in 1820 and virtually every great musician of the classical period is linked with the city, from Mozart and Gluck to Schubert, Brahms, Beethoven and Mahler. Operetta had its heyday with Johann Strauss and Lehar. For centuries the city was the cultural entrepôt between Eastern and Western Europe. Much of it wears a grand, old-fashioned, rather melancholy air, evoking its heyday as the centre of the **Habsburg empire** for 600 years, with such imperial hangovers as the massive Hofburg palace. Around 100 years ago Vienna became a leading architectural exponent of *Jugendstil* – the Austrian Art Nouveau – examples of which dot the city. The centre is largely pedestrianised, with cobbled streets, old merchants' houses, spacious gardens and hundreds of atmospheric places to eat and drink. A visit to one of the classic **coffee-houses** for coffee and home-made cake is *de rigueur*. Most sights are on or inside the famous **Ringstrasse**, which encircles the city centre. For architectural splendours of the late 19th century, take trams no. 1 or 2, passing the neo-Gothic **Rathaus** (City Hall), **Burgtheater**, **Parliament** and **Staatsoper**.

ARRIVAL AND DEPARTURE

Vienna has three main stations; for information: ☎1717 for all stations. All three are 3–4 km outside the Ringstr., connected to the centre by underground or tram, and have left-luggage and accommodation services. **Westbahnhof**, Europapl., serves the west, Germany, Switzerland and Hungary. **Südbahnhof**, Wiedner Gürtel/Arsenalstr., serves the south and east, including Italy, former Yugoslavia, the Czech Republic and Hungary. **Franz-Josefs-Bahnhof**, Julius-Tandler-Pl., serves the north, plus Berlin and the Czech Republic.

Vienna International Airport is 19 km south-east of the city at *Schwechat*. Flight information, ☎7007 22233 (24 hrs). Express bus transfers (Vienna Airport Lines: ☎93000 2300) run from the airport to City Air Terminal (U-Bahn and S-Bahn station: Lanstrasse/Wien Mitte) and back and to Westbahnhof and Südbahnhof (journey time 20 mins). There are also S-Bahn trains to Wien Mitte.

INFORMATION

Pick up the free city map from the Tourist Office: **Vienna Tourist Board**, Albertinapl. (corner of Maysedergasse), ☎(01) 211 14-222; fax (01) 216 84 92 (www.info.wien.at; info@info.wien.at), the *Vienna Scene* for an overview of the city and the monthly *Programm* which lists events for that month. Information and accommodation bureaux are also at Westbahnhof, Südbahnhof and Schwechat Airport. In addition, visit **wienXtra jugendinfo (youth information)**, Babenbergerstr. 1 (U2 Babenbergerstrasse and trams 1, 2, D); ☎1799, fax (01) 585 24 99 (www.jugendinfowien.at; jugendinfo.wien@wienxtra.at) for brochures *time4vienna* and *Camping & Youth Hostels* and information on the 'alternative' Vienna. The **central post office**, Fleischmarkt 19, has poste restante facilities (open 24 hrs) and money exchange. **Phone cards** are available from tobacconists and post offices. **To phone Vienna** from abroad,

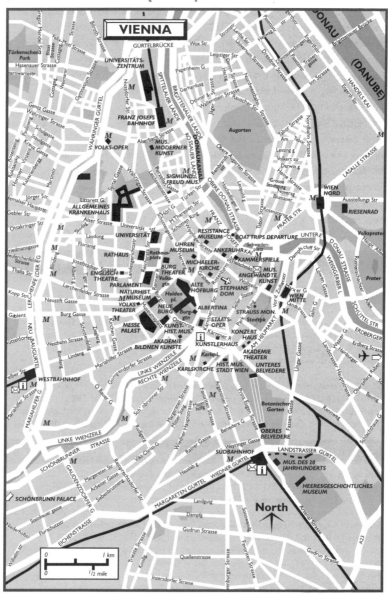

VIENNA

☎00 (or 011 from the US or Canada) +43 (Austria) +1 (Vienna) + number; to phone the city from elsewhere in Austria: ☎01 + number.

PUBLIC TRANSPORT

The **U-Bahn** has five lines, 0500–2400. **Trams**: run on 33 radial routes as well as in both directions round the Ringstr., 0500–2400. **Buses**: include 22 night routes (0030–0430), marked by a green N symbol. **Taxis**: not cheap; hail one with a 'frei' sign, or ☎(01) 31 300, (01) 40 100, (01) 60 160 or (01) 81 400. **Cycling**: fun, as the city is largely flat with many marked

TICKETS

U-Bahn (underground trains), **S-Bahn** (suburban trains) inside city limits, **trams** and **buses** all use the same tickets, with transfers allowed. Single tickets are sold in blocks of 4 (under-6s travel free, under-15s and students under 19 travel free on Sundays, public holidays and school holidays; photo ID required). You can get a 24-hour or 72-hour **rover ticket**; there are also 8-day **network tickets** (which can be used by several people travelling together). Just before travelling, validate (time-stamp) the ticket.
Another option is the **Wien-Karte** (Vienna Card, from hotels, Vienna Transport ticket offices and Tourist Offices), valid for 72 hrs' transport, plus 4 days' discounts on popular museums, sights, shops, restaurants, concert and theatre tickets and so on.

paths. The Tourist Office has a free booklet (*Tipps für Radfahrer*) with route maps. Hire bikes from stations: **Westbahnhof** (0400–2400), **Wien Nord** (0715–2200) and **Südbahnhof** (0500–2400); discount with same-day rail ticket. **Pedal Power** deliver bikes to your hotel, ☎(01) 729 72 34.

ACCOMMODATION

There are lots of options, and takers, so book ahead for May–Oct. Email hotel booking service: rooms@info.wien.at. Expect to pay €30–50 per person for a cheap hotel, including breakfast. Moderately priced guesthouses include **Apartment-Pension Sacher**, Rotenturmstr. 1, ☎(01) 533 32 38, €€, on a central 7th floor next to the cathedral. Southwest of the cathedral, near the museum quarter, are **Pension Mozart**, Theobaldgasse 15, ☎/fax (01) 587 85 05 (office@pension-mozart.at), €€ (14 rooms); and **Pension Quisisana**, Windmühlegasse 6, ☎(01) 587 33 41, fax (01) 587 71 56, €€.

Youth hostels: **Jugendherberge Myrthengasse/Neustiftgasse**, Myrthengasse 7, ☎(01) 523 63 16, fax (01) 523 58 49 (hostel@chello.at), U2 to Lerchenfelder Str., then short walk; **Jugendgästehaus Brigittenau**, Friedrich-Engels-Pl. 24, ☎(01) 332 82 94, fax (01) 330 83 79 (jgh.1200wien@chello.at), north of centre, U6 to Handelskai, 500m; **Jugendgästehaus Hütteldorf-Hacking**, Schlossberg 8, ☎(01) 877 15 01, fax (01) 87 702 632, Hüttledorf-Hacking U-bahn station 500m; **Schlossherberge am Wilhelminenberg**, Savoyenstr. 2, ☎(01) 485 85 03 (shb1@wigast.com), U-bahn to Thaliastrasse by U6; **Turmherberge Don Bosco**, Lechnerstr. 12, ☎(01) 713 14 94 (closed Dec–Feb), U3 to Kardinal Nagl Platz, 500 m; **Hostel Ruthensteiner**, Robert-Hamerling-Gasse 24, ☎(01) 893 42 02 (hostel.ruthensteiner@telecom.at); **Jugengästehaus Wien-Hütteldorf**, Schlossberggasse 8, ☎(01) 877 15 01 (jgh@wigast.com); **Wombat's City Hostel**, Grangasse 6, ☎(01) 897 23 36 (wombats@chello.at), near Westbahnhof. **Camping**: **Aktive Camping Neue Donau**, Kaisermülendamm 119, ☎/fax (01) 202 40 10, fax 203 28 23 (mid-May–mid-Sept) is across the Danube Canal.

FOOD AND DRINK

Vienna has given the gastronomic world *Wiener Schnitzel* (veal in breadcrumbs), *Sachertorte* (rich chocolate cake) and *Kaiserschmarrn*, the dessert of emperors. You'll find typically Viennese dishes in low-priced *Beisel*, which are pubs-cum-brasseries, or *Kellern*, wine cellars. *Konditoreis* (cake shops/cafés) offer a tempting array of home-made cakes and pastries. Coffee also comes in many varieties, from *melange* to *grosser Brauner*. **Café Central** in the Herrengasse and **Demel** by the Hofburg stand as tourist attractions as well as places to have coffee, for their extraordinary décor and design. Look out also for the numerous other exotic cafés around the centre, many of which provide live music. Every *Kaffeehaus* serves hot dishes too. And don't miss the sausages on sale from street vendors! The wide, pedestrianised Graben near the cathedral is just one source of cafés, while the area around the university (U2/4 to Schottentor) is good for budget meals. Bächerstr. is a good place to look for a moderately priced traditional meal. There are also plenty of *Würstelstände* (hot-dog stalls), sandwich bars and fast-food stalls at the Naschmarkt.

HIGHLIGHTS

The Tourist Office runs specialist walking tours (on such themes as art nouveau and food and drink (www.wienguide.at); reduction for holders of Vienna Cards, but finding your own way around the compact city centre is easy.

An ornately carved spire soars over **Stephansdom** (St Stephen's Cathedral), U1/3 to Stephanspl., Austria's greatest Gothic building. Its colourful roof, tiled in jazzy stripes, is best seen floodlit at night. The magnificent 14th-century **Südturm** (South Tower), known locally as the *Steffl*, is climbed by 343 steps for a terrific city view, while a lift whisks you up the (considerably lower) North Tower, the **Pummerin**. Interior highlights include the Albertine Choir, the pulpit and organ loft by Anton Pilgrim, and the tomb of Friedrich III.

The **Hofburg**, the Habsburgs' winter residence until 1918, occupies a prime position on the edge of the Ring overlooking formal gardens. Altogether, it comprises 18 wings, 54 stairways and 2,600 rooms, and now houses several museums. The **Imperial Apartments** have been preserved as they were in Emperor Franz Josef I's time, while the **Schatzkammer** (Treasury) displays the crown of the Holy Roman Empire.

The **Burgkapelle** is the chapel where the **Vienna Boys' Choir** sing mass on Sun morning (mid-Sept–June) at 0915 (charge for sitting but standing room free;

SPANISH RIDING SCHOOL
The famous Lippizzaner horses perform on Sun and some Sats (Mar–June and Aug–Nov; U1/3: Stephanplatz).
Tickets can be bought from **Spanische Hofreitschule**, Hofburg, A-1010 Vienna, fax (01) 535 01 86 (www.spanische-reitschule.com; office@srs.at). Or queue at the door (gate 2) of the **Redoute**, Josefspl., to see 'morning training' without music, usually Tues–Sat 1000–1200 (mid-Feb–late June and late Aug–early Nov).

TOURS

A sedate 40-min tour by *Fiaker* (horse-drawn carriage) leaves from Heldenpl. (next to the cathedral) and outside the Hofburg and Albertina. Bus tours of the city are operated by several companies, including **Vienna Line**, Stelzhamergasse 4/11, ☎(01) 712 46 83, fax (01) 714 11 41 (www.viennasightseeingtours.com; vst@viennasightseeingtours.co) whose hop-on, hop-off multi-lingual service stops at 13 places of interest; half-hourly or hourly 0900–1700. For a 1 hr 15-min boat trip on the River Danube/Danube Canal, start from Schwedenpl. (May–Oct; **DDSG-Blue Danube**, ☎(01) 588 80-0 (www.ddsg-blue-danube.at).

bookings fax (01) 533 99 27; hofmusikkapelle@asn-wien.ac.at). For afternoon concerts at the **Musikverein**, ☎(01) 588 04 (ticket@mondial.at).

Vienna has roughly 100 museums (most open Tue–Sun, 1000–1800; some open late on Thur). The major museum, the **Kunsthistorisches Museum** (Museum of Fine Arts), Maria-Theresien-Platz 1, is based on the Habsburgs' collection.

The superb 18th-century baroque **Belvedere Palace**, Prinz-Eugen-Str. 27, has two galleries and delightful gardens; its **Österreichische Galerie** (Austrian Gallery) contains world-famous works by Klimt, Schiele and 19th-century artists.

The **Akademie der bildenden Künste** (Academy of Fine Arts), Schillerpl. 3, includes Flemish works, while museums with a distinctive local flavour include the **Historisches Museum der Stadt Wien** (Historical Museum of the City of Vienna), Karslpl. The original entrance to **Karlsplatz Station** is one of the city's finest examples of *Jugendstil*.

One of the most enjoyable of Vienna's museums is the **Naturhistoriches Museum** (Natural History Museum), in the Museums Quarter on Maria-Theresien Platz opposite the Kunsthistorisches Museum. The high-ceilinged rooms are painted with wonderful 19th-century themed friezes – dinosaurs in the dinosaur galleries and so on. The archaeology galleries have fascinating displays from the pre-historic Hallstatt culture in the Salzkammergut, including a saltminer's rucksack that looks as if it is still serviceable.

The **Pasqualati Haus**, Mölker Bastei 8, is one of Beethoven's many lodgings; museum at **Heiligenstadt Testament Haus**, Probusgasse 6, in Heiligenstadt. Mozart's lodging, the **Figaro House**, Domgasse 5, contains memorial rooms, including the one in which he wrote *The Marriage of Figaro*. The **Schubert Museum** is at the composer's birthplace, Nussdorferstr. 54 (tram nos. 37/38), while Haydn's house in Haydngasse, off Mariahilferstr., is also a museum.

The **Sigmund Freud Museum**, Berggasse 19; (U2/U4: Schottenring, tram nos. D/37/38/40/41/42), is where the great psychoanalyst lived and worked from 1891 until his expulsion by the Nazis in 1938.

An architecture leaflet from the Tourist Office highlights interesting 20th-century build-ings, including the anarchic, ecological **Hundertwasserhaus** (Lowengasse/Kegelgasse), named after the painter-architect who redesigned this municipal housing estate in 1985, transforming the vicinity into an astonishing riot of colours and textures.

Further out, the palace of **Schönbrunn**, Schönbrunner Schlosstr. (U4: Schönbrunn, tram nos. 10/58/60); is a grand palace with fabulously baroque decoration, built as the Habsburgs' summer residence (guided tours of 40 rooms, or see 20 on your own).

The legendary **Prater Park** (U1 to Praterstern, tram nos. O/5/21) was originally the imperial hunting grounds. Riding the giant ferris wheel (famously filmed in the movie *The Third Man*), which has been turning there since 1897, provides a great view – but take care in the park at night. Vienna has several *Jugendstil* and art deco baths, such as **Amalienbad**, Reumannpl. 23 (baths, showers, saunas, steam rooms, swimming pools).

SHOPPING

Kärntnerstr. is the busiest shopping street and, together with Graben, is the place to promenade. The nearby **Ringstrasse Galerien**, Kärtner Ring 5–7, is a smart modern mall, open until 1900 (1700 Sat). Department stores are in Mariahilferstr., outside the Ring leading to the Westbahnhof. Flea market: **Flohmarkt**, U4: Wienzeile/Kettenbrückengasse, by station, open Sat (except public holidays) 0600–1800.

NIGHT-TIME AND EVENTS

Programm (monthly), listing all entertainment except cinemas (detailed in newspapers), is free from Tourist Offices. Festivals abound: the May–June festival features classical music and jazz, while the **Danube Island Festival** (June) is an open-air event with rock, pop and fireworks. In July–Aug, the **Mozart in Schönbrunn** festival features open-air Mozart concerts in front of the Roman ruins. In July–Aug, there's the free **Festival of Music Films**, shown on a giant screen in Rathauspl., which also hosts a great **Christmas market** from mid-Nov to Christmas.

> To avoid high agency commissions, apply for tickets to **Österreichische Bundestheater**, A-1010 Wien, Hanuschgasse 3, ☎ (01) 513 15 13, fax (01) 514 29 69 at least 3 weeks in advance; standing tickets sold 1 hr before the performance.

Night owls focus on the **'Bermuda Triangle'** (so called because people go into it and disappear), an area of lively bars, discos and pubs around Ruprechtspl., particularly Judengasse and Sterngasse. The **Staatsoper** (Vienna State Opera), Opernring 2, stages operas Sept–June. The **Volksoper**, Währingerstr. 78, offers operettas and musicals. The **Vienna Philharmonic Orchestra** can be heard in concerts at the **Musikverein**, and first-class musicians give concerts there and at the **Konzerthaus** throughout the year.

ROUTE DETAIL		
Innsbruck–Kitzbühel		ETT table 960
Type	Frequency	Typical journey time
Train	Every 2 hrs	1 hr 2 mins
Kitzbühel–Salzburg		ETT table 960
Type	Frequency	Typical journey time
Train	Every 2 hrs	2 hrs 26 mins
Salzburg–Linz		ETT table 950
Type	Frequency	Typical journey time
Train	1–2 every hr	1 hr 19 mins
Linz–Vienna		ETT table 950
Type	Frequency	Typical journey time
Train	2 every hr	1 hr 57 mins

KEY JOURNEYS		
Zürich–Innsbruck		ETT table 86
Type	Frequency	Typical journey time
Train	3 per day	3 hrs 46 mins
Innsbruck–Salzburg		ETT table 950
Type	Frequency	Typical journey time
Train	10 per day	2 hrs
Salzburg–Vienna		ETT table 950
Type	Frequency	Typical journey time
Train	Every hr	3hrs 18 mins

Austria's elongated shape permits few long journeys within its borders, but this is one well worth seeking out, making a trans-Alpine experience from the heart of the Tyrol to Salzburg, famed as Mozart's birthplace, before ending up at the Austrian capital (see p. 343). The most scenic route between Salzburg and Linz is via Bischofshofen and Selzthal (ETT tables 960, 975).

INNSBRUCK

The 800-year-old Tyrolean capital on the River Inn is a bustling, amiable city over-looked by the Karwendel mountains to the north and the Patscherkofel mountains to the south – making it an excellent starting point for walks and other activities in the Alps (guided hikes start daily June–Oct, meeting 0845 at the Congress Hall; free with Club Innsbruck Card, which you get when you stay overnight anywhere in Innsbruck – not to be confused with the Innsbruck Card). The Hungerburgbahn cog railway ascends from the Alpenzoo on the edge of the city on to the Hungerburg plateau – a superb place for walks and views.

The **Altstadt** area is dotted with 15th- and 16th-century buildings, many with elaborate stucco decorations and traditional convex windows to catch extra light on the narrow streets. Its most famous sight is the 15th-century **Goldenes Dachl**, Herzog-Friedrich-Str. 15, a roof of 2738 gilded copper tiles covering a balcony, which Emperor Maximilian I (the subject of an exhibition inside) added in 1500 to the **Neuhof**, the residence of the Tyrolean princes. The **Stadtturm** (City Tower) opposite the balcony offers views across the rooftops to the mountains. Nearby is the **Dom zu St Jakob**, a striking baroque cathedral.

The **Hofburg** (Imperial Palace), Rennweg, has a sumptuous ballroom lined with portraits of Empress Maria Theresa's family, who also feature in 28 larger-than-life bronze statues on Emperor Maximilian's grand tomb in the 16th-century **Hofkirche**, the court church. Wander round the **Hofgarten** (Court Gardens). The neighbouring **Tiroler Volkskunst Museum** concentrates on Tyrolean culture, displaying traditional costumes and wood-pan-elled rooms. The **Ferdinandeum**, Museumstr. 15, is more diverse, with beautiful old stained glass, medieval altars and works by Cranach and Rembrandt.

[RAIL] Left luggage, showers, tourist information. Walk down Salurner Str. and then right at the 1765 triumphal arch into Maria-Theresastr. (10 mins).

[+] [icon] (0512) 22525, 4 km west ([icon]F from the station).

[i] **Tourist Office**: Burggraben 3, [icon] (0512) 5356, edge of the Altstadt (www.tiscover.com/innsbruck; info@innsbruck.tvb.co.at);

INNSBRUCK CARD

All-inclusive **Innsbruck Card**, covering local transport (including some cable cars) and entrance to 36 museums and attractions plus reductions on tours and other attractions; valid 24, 48 or 72 hours; from Tourist Offices, cable cars and museums. Children: 50% off.

branch at the station. Accommodation booking service; money exchange, concert tickets, ski/cable car passes and Innsbruck Cards.

WHERE NEXT FROM INNSBRUCK?

Innsbruck *is on the* **Munich–Verona** *route (p. 306). You can also continue west to* **Liechtenstein,** *then enter Switzerland at* **Sargans** *to join the* **Lausanne–Milan** *route (p. 317; ETT tables 530, 547, 950).*

🚌 24-hr ticket available for **tram, bus** and **trolley bus** system. Bikes can be hired from the station: ☎(0512) 5305-0.

🛏 Budget rooms are scarce in June, when only three hostels are open, but 'summer hotels' usually open in university accommodation July and Aug. The family-run four-star **Sailer**, Adamgasse 6–10, ☎/fax (0512) 5363 (www.sailer-innsbruck.at), €, notable for its Tyrolean restaurant and décor, is handy for the station. Relatively central **youth hostels** are **Fritz Prior-Schwedenhaus**, Rennweg 17B, ☎(0512) 585814 (youth.hostel@tirol.com), summer only, and **Studentenheim**, Reichenauer Str. 147, ☎(0512) 346179 (yhibk@tirol.com). **Campsite: Camping IBK Kranebitten**, Kranebitter Allee 214, ☎/fax (0512) 284180 (www.cda.at/tourismus/campibk; campinnsbruck@hotmail.com), is west of town (🚌O).

🍴 The **Altstadt** area is generally expensive. **Café Munding**, Kiebachgasse 16, is the oldest Tyrolean café and pastry-shop, and serves fabulous cakes. Try the young, friendly pub, **Elferhaus**, Herzog-Friedrich-Str. 11.

KITZBÜHEL

With its mountain backdrop, this pleasant old town, with tree-lined streets of steeply gabled pastel-coloured buildings, is one of Austria's prettiest and largest ski resorts (though the snow's not that reliable; main season Christmas–Easter). The **Kitzbühel Museum**, Hinterstadt 32, occupies the town's oldest house and displays paintings by Alfons Walde (a contemporary of Klimt). Don't miss the **Kitzbüheler Horn** cable car to the summit of the Horn; near the top, some 120 species of flowers bloom in an **Alpine flower garden**, 1880 m high (free guided tours 1100 and 1330, July and Aug).

The ski élite arrive in Jan for the **Hahnenkamm Ski Competition**, a World Cup leg down one of the world's trickiest ski runs. At the top of the Hahnenkamm lift, the **Bergbahn Museum** reveals the history of skiing in Kitzbühel since 1893 (free entry).

The Tourist Office organises free guided hiking, bike and mountain bike trips (register one day before). A 2.5-km walk leads to the **Schwarzsee**, a good bathing lake. In summertime, hikers can buy lift passes valid for any three days in a week or six days in a ten-day period.

🚉 Bahnhofpl. 2. A 10-min walk to town centre; go straight across the River Ache, left along Achenpromenade, then follow signs right for centre. Bike hire at station: rates for 1, 3 or 7 days (reduction with rail ticket).

AUSTRIA

🛏 The *Frühstückpensionen* (bed and breakfast) are cheap, such as **Pension Hörl**, Josef-Pirchl-Str. 60, ☎/fax (05356) 63144, €. **Youth hostel: Café Pension Noichl**, Aurach 34, Aurach, ☎(0664) 173 2028; **Seereith**, Kirchberger Str. 67, ☎(0664) 173 2028. **Campsite: Bruggerhof**, Reitherstr. 24, Schwarzsee, ☎(05356) 62806, fax (05356) 64479-30 (hotel.bruggerhof@camping.netwing.at), near Schwarzsee station.

> Keep hold of **guest cards** from your accommodation, as these give discounts on lifts, cable cars, etc.

SALZBURG

Wonderfully sited between the Alps and the lakes of the Salzkammergut, Salzburg is renowned as Mozart's birthplace and is where *The Sound of Music* was filmed in 1964. Much of the city's appearance dates from the 17th century, when most of the old buildings were pulled down to make way for Italian-style squares with spectacular fountains. Salzburg's entire **Old City** (Altstadt) is designated a UNESCO World Heritage Site. Most of the centre is pedestrianised and its compactness makes it a delightful place to explore on foot.

The main shopping street is narrow Getreidegasse, always oozing tourists and bordered by elegant old houses, decorative wrought-iron signs and medieval arcades. **Mozarts Geburtshaus**, no. 9, where the composer was born in 1756 and spent most of his first 17 years, is now a museum. The family subsequently lived in the **Mozart-Wohnhaus**, Makartpl. 8, across the river, recently rebuilt in its original style following World War II destruction, and with its rooms furnished in period style; concerts are held there. In nearby Residenzpl. is the **Residenz** (hourly tours), the former Prince Archbishop's palace, built after the need for fortification had passed. Mozart conducted in its grand rooms.

The **cathedral**, in adjacent Dompl., is considered to be the finest early baroque church north of the Alps. A magnificent light-filled building, it has four domes and space inside for 10,000 people. Mozart worked there as *Konzertmeister* and court organist.

On **Mönchsberg** (Monk's Mountain), high above the Altstadt, looms the formidable **Festung Hohensalzburg**, Mönchsberg 34, once the stronghold of the Archbishops of Salzburg. Built over six centuries, it's almost perfectly preserved, with medieval torture chambers, early Gothic state rooms, and a 200-pipe barrel organ that booms out once the 7th-century 35-bell

Colour Section
(i) St Moritz, Switzerland (pp. 323–324)
(ii) The Forum, Pompei (pp. 375–376); volcanic scenery at Mount Etna, Sicily (p. 415); mosaics in St Vitalis church, Ravenna, Italy (p. 407)
(iii) Milan central railway station (p. 365); café in Il Campo, Siena, Italy (pp. 396–397)
(iv) View of Lake Bled (p. 428); countryside near Bled, Slovenia (p. 428)

DAY TRIPS FROM SALZBURG

Just south of town (5 km) is the ornate 17th-century **Schloss Hellbrunn** (🚌 no. 55 from station or Mirabellpl.). The gardens of this Italian-designed pleasure-palace are famous for their lovely sculptures and fountains, especially those that squirt unexpectedly from stone stools to surprise drunken guests (guided tours, Apr–Oct; evening tours, July–Aug).

carillon of the **Glockenspiel**, Mozartpl., has pealed (at 0700, 1100 and 1800). The castle can be reached on foot from Festungsgasse behind the cathedral, or by the **Festungsbahn**, Austria's oldest cable railway dating from 1892 (included in entry fee to the castle). Alternatively, the **Münchsbergaufzug** (Münchsberg Lift) operates from Gstättengasse 13 (by Museumpl.) and takes you to Winkler Terrace, where paths lead across to the castle.

Across on the other side of the river is **Schloss Mirabell**, Mirabellpl., which was originally built in the 17th century for Prince-Archbishop Wolf Dietrich's mistress, Salome Alt, who bore him 15 or 16 children. It houses the **Marble Hall**, a magnificent venue for chamber music concerts; its Angel Staircase sports marble cherubs. The **Mirabellgarten**, former royal pleasure gardens, is a tranquil oasis of late Baroque gardens, terraces and statuary (free).

🚉 Südtiroler Pl. 1, 20 mins' walk from the old centre (🚌 nos. 1/2/5/6/51 to Staatsbrücke, the main bridge). Tourist information, accommodation service, left luggage (by platforms 4 and 5, daily 0600–2200), money exchange, shops.

✈ 4 km west of the city; ☎ (0662) 8580. 🚌 no. 77 every 15 mins connects station with airport; journey time about 25 mins. Taxis to the city centre: ☎ (0662) 8111.

ℹ **Tourist Offices:** Auerspergstr. 7, ☎ (0662) 889 87-0, fax (0662) 889 87-32 (www. salzburginfo.at; tourist@salzburginfo.at); accommodation service (fee). Branch at the **station**.

🛏 During festivals, it pays to book early as accommodation often gets very scarce. Cheaper options, near the rail station, include **Hotel Sandwirt**, Lastenstr. 6a, ☎ /fax (0662) 874 351, €€. Centrally located are **Junger Fuchs**, Linzer Gasse 54, ☎ (0662) 875 496, €, and **Schwarzes Rössl**, Priesterhausgasse 6, ☎ (0662) 874 426, fax (0662) 874 426 (schwarzesroessl@telering.at), €€; summer only. **Youth hostels:** Aigner Str. 34, ☎ (0662) 623 248, fax (0662) 623 248-4 (hostel.aigen@salzburg.co.at), 🚌 no. 49; Eduard-Heinrich-Str. 2, ☎ (0662) 625 976, fax (0662) 627 980 (hostel.eduard-heinrich@salzburg.co.at); 🚌 nos. 51/95; Haunspergstr. 27, ☎ (0662) 875 030, fax (0662) 883 477 (Jul and Aug only; 5-min walk from station); Josef-Preis-Allee 18, ☎ (0662) 842 670-0, fax: (0662) 841 101 (jgh.salzburg@jgh.at); 🚌 nos. 5/51 to Justizgebäude. **Campsites:** include **Camping Nord-Sam**, Samstr. 22a, ☎ /fax (0662) 660 494 (www.camping-nord-sam.com); open Easter and May–Sept (🚌 no. 33).

Salzburg Card
Provides free admission to most of Salzburg's attractions, free public transport and other discounts; valid 24, 36 or 72 hrs.

Salzburgerland Summer Joker Card
Free access to over 130 attractions in the region for 15 days (12 May–26 Oct).

Bus and trolley tickets
From automatic vending machines or tobacconists; more expensive from driver (punch ticket immediately after boarding). Day passes also available.

🖭 **Café Tomaselli,** Alter Markt 9, is where the elegant have sipped coffee for the last two centuries. Also worth trying are beer gardens, especially the **Augustiner-Bräu,** Augustinerg. 4, where beer is brewed by the monastery.

NIGHT-TIME AND EVENTS The big event is the **Salzburg Festival,** mid-July–late Aug. For major performances, tickets must be booked months ahead from **Kartenbüro der Salzburger Festspiele,** Postfach 140, A-5010 Salzburg, 🖀 (0662) 8045-579, fax (0662) 8045-760 (www.salzburgfestival.at). Last-minute standing tickets sometimes available in the **Kleine Festspielhaus.** Events linked to the festival include an opening *Fackeltanz* (torch-dance) in the Residenzpl. (free) and performances of '*Jedermann*' ('Everyman'); standing tickets only sold at the Dompl. door 1 hr before start. Other events include **Mozart Week** in late Jan, a Nov **Jazz Festival** and an **Easter Music Festival.** In addition, there's always a concert on somewhere in the city. The **Marionettentheater,** Schwarzstr. 24, 🖀 (0662) 872 406, fax (0662) 882 141, presents operas 'performed' convincingly by puppets that 'sing' to recordings.

THE MOUNTAINS OF THE SALZKAMMERGUT

Salzburg is ideally placed for exploring the Salzkammergut, an area of Alpine peaks and glimmering lakes. You get tremendous views of it by taking a circular rail tour south-east of Salzburg: go east on the main route from Salzburg (towards Linz), but change at Attnach-Pucheim for Stainach-Irdning, and change for Salzburg (ETT tables 950, 960, 961). You can do the whole trip without stopping in under 6 hrs, but it's worth having a break along the way at Hallstatt (one stop north of Obertraun; Tourist Office: www.hallstatt.net), from where a passenger ferry connects with the train and takes you across the Hallstätter See to Hallstatt itself. This is an absolutely enchanting lakeside-village with plenty of inexpensive accommodation (including the characterfully old-fashioned Haus Sarstein, on the lake just to the right of the ferry; 🖀 (06134) 217, €); walk uphill or take the cable car to the Salzberg salt mines, worked since prehistoric times and the oldest in the world to be still mined; there's often a queue to get in, but for your money you get a train ride into the mountain, two descents down wooden slides and a view of a beautiful, improbably clear underground lake.

LINZ

As Austria's third city, Linz's prosperity is based on its position as a Danube port. **Hauptplatz,** a huge 13th-century closed square just off the river, blends colourful baroque and rococo façades around the baroque marble **Trinity column.** In 1938, Hitler stood on the balcony of No. 1 (now the Tourist Office) to inform the Austrians that the Nazis had annexed their country. Starting from Hauptpl., the dinky yellow Linz City Express 'road-train' provides a 25-min city introduction (May–Sept); alternatively, follow the free 'Linz geht rund' guided walk brochure from the Tourist Office. Linz's hottest attraction is the **Ars Electronica Center,** Europe's only museum dedicated to the 21st century (Wed–Sat 1000–1800), Hauptstr 2. The 17th-century Alter Dom, Domgasse, one of the city's two cathedrals, is simple outside, restrained baroque within. The other, the huge neo-Gothic Neuer Dom, Herrenstr., can hold 20,000 people. Landhaus, Promenade 24, is where the astronomer Johann Kepler developed the third law of planetary motion. Across the river, the Pöstlingbergbahn, the world's steepest rack railway, chugs from tram no. 3 terminus at Landgutstr. 19 to a fortress and pilgrimage church (Mon–Sat 0520–2000 every 20 mins; Sun 0715–1115 every 30 mins, 1115–2000 every 20 mins).

DANUBE STEAMBOAT

Trips and cruises are operated from the quay by **Donauschiffahrt Wurm & Köck**, Ernst-Koref-Promenade, ☎(0732) 783 607.

Linz City Ticket gives unlimited travel on public transport, the road-train and *Pöstlinberg* train, vouchers for visits to Linz's most important sights, plus a restaurant voucher.

Public transport 'MAXI' day ticket also available.

[i] Electronic information service, left-luggage lockers (24 hrs), shops. For centre, take tram no. 3 to Hauptpl. (10 mins).

[RAIL] **Tourist Offices**: Hauptpl. 1, ☎(0732) 7070 1777, fax (0732) 772 873 (www.tiscover.com/linz; tourist.info@linz.at). **Branch**: Urfahrmarkt 1.

[🏨] Near the station is the **Hotel Zur Locomotive**, Weingartshofstr. 40, ☎(0732) 654 554, fax (0732) 658 337 (office@hotel-lokomotive.at), €€€. More central is the **Goldenes Dachl**, Hafnerstr. 27, ☎/fax (0732) 775 897. **Youth hostels**: Kapuzinerstr. 14, ☎(0732) 778 777, fax (0732) 781 728-94 (zentrale@ooejugendherbergswerk.at); Stanglhofweg 3, ☎(0732) 664 434, fax (0732) 664 434-75 (jgh.linz@oejhv.or.at), just west of station; **Landesjugendherberge**, Blütenstr. 23, Lentia ☎(0732) 737 078, fax (0732) 737 078-15. The nearest **campsite** is **Campingplatz Pichlingersee**, Wiener Str. 937, ☎(0732) 305 314, fax (0732) 305 314-4 (tram no. 3 from station to Rudolfstr. across the river, then 🚌 no. 32).

[🍴] The pedestrian zone around Hofgasse is busy at night and has plenty of reasonable eateries. **Klosterhof**, Landstr. 30, boasts Austria's biggest beer garden. Sample *Linzer Torte* (almond cake topped with redcurrant jam).

WHERE NEXT FROM LINZ?

Join the **Cologne–Passau** route (p. 272) by taking the train over the German border to **Passau** (ETT table 920; 1 hr 15 mins).

VIENNA (WIEN)

See p. 343.

(for Directory information, see p. 599).

The cornerstone of Western civilisation, **Italy** has been firmly on the tourist map since the days of the 18th-century 'Grand Tour'. There is so much to experience that it isn't necessary to make a literal grand tour of the entire country at one go. You can get a good sample by, for instance, keeping to the hills and medieval cities of Tuscany, or heading down from **Rome** to **Sicily**, or combining **Lake Como** and **Lake Garda** with the **Dolomites** – which include some of the most astonishing mountain shapes in the Alps – plus maybe **Verona** and **Venice**. The rail network covers all of this, except for the Dolomites, which can be visited by taking a bus from Bolzano.

The sheer quantity and quality of historic stuff can be hard work, with oppressive crowds (and debilitating heat in high summer) and often incessant traffic in the bigger cities. You'd be better off mixing the major attractions such as **Florence**, **Herculaneum**, **Pompeii** and **Rome** with some less hectic spots such as **Lucca** or **Orvieto**.

Although virtually surrounded by sea, Italy lacks decent mainland beach resorts: the Neapolitan Riviera has great scenery around **Sorrento** and **Amalfi**, and small beaches, while the Adriatic (eastern) coast has the best beaches but the resorts are anonymous, dull, high-rise concrete affairs. By contrast, the islands of **Elba**, **Ischia** and **Sardinia** have much more scope for a beach holiday, though they do get packed in summer. The island of **Sicily** has some great beaches, ancient sites and volcanic scenery, and is excellent for combining sightseeing and a seaside holiday.

Drop into any street café for a snapshot of Italian life, where locals discuss the news or the football.

Around dusk the whole town meets during the evening stroll, or *passeggiata*, in the main street or square, and the Italian knack of chic dressing and looking good comes to the fore.

RURAL ACCOMMODATION

Agriturismo, Agriturist, Corso V Emanuele 101, 00186 Roma, ☎ (06) 685 2342, fax (06) 685 2424, has information about staying in rural cottages and farmhouses.

MOUNTAIN HUTS

Club Alpino Italiano, Via Fonseca Pimental 7, 20121 Milano, ☎ (02) 26 141 378, can supply details of mountain refuge huts.

ACCOMMODATION

All **hotels** are classified according to a five-star system and inspectors set a maximum (seasonal) rate that must be displayed in each room. It does not necessarily include showers or breakfast, but extras must be listed separately, so complain (to the Tourist Office if all else fails) if your bill does not agree with the rates listed. You must, by law, obtain a receipt from all hotels. **Venice** and **Capri** are particularly expensive for accommodation. Prices are often for rooms rather than per person. Most establishments now term themselves **hotel** or *albergo*, but some are still called *pensione* (one-, two- or three-star) or *locande* (one-star). **Bed and breakfast** accommodation is fast catching on in Italy. Most Tourist Offices have authorised lists of local B&Bs but you need to check their location carefully. Unofficial B&B networks are often better but need to be booked in advance via the internet. *Alberghi diurni*, near stations or in the centre, are day rooms: you can have a wash without taking a room for the night. **Cheaper hotels** may require you to stay at least three nights and take half board.

There is no shortage of **youth hostels**, but relatively few (just over 50) are members of the **HI** and the standard varies considerably; expect to pay €7–15.50 including sheets and breakfast for HI hostels. It is often just as cheap and more convenient to stay at a one-star hotel. The youth hostel headquarters is the **Associazione Italiana Alberghi per la Gioventù (AIG)**, Via Cavour 44, 00184 Roma, ☎ (06) 4871152, fax (06) 488 0492 (www.hostels-aig.org; aig@uni.net).

Camping is popular and there are over 1700 sites (all **Tourist Offices** have information about their area), but they are often fairly expensive and/or difficult to reach without a car. There are few places where you can camp rough without asking permission. **Touring Club Italiano (TCI)**, Corso Italia 10, 20122 Milano, ☎ (02) 85 261, fax (06) 852 6362 (www.touringclub.it), publishes an annual camping guide, *Campeggi in Italia*. Alternatively, you can get a free list, or the publication *Guida Camping d'Italia*, from **Federcampeggio**, Casella Postale 23, 50041 Calenzano, Firenze, ☎ (055) 882 391, fax (055) 882 5918 (www.federcampeggio.it), who can also make bookings.

FOOD AND DRINK

Look for **cover charges** (*coperto*) and **service** (*servizio*), both of which will be added to your bill. Prices on **Menu Turistico** include taxes and service charges.

Mealtime is an important social event for Italians, and there's a wide variety of food available everywhere, with pasta just one of many options. A full meal will consist of *antipasti* (cold meats etc.), pasta, a main course, and fruit or cheese. Italian ice-cream (*gelato*) is among the world's best. Much of the pleasure of eating in Italy is derived from the sheer freshness and quality of the ingredients.

Trattorie are simple establishments and are cheaper than *ristoranti*. For drinking, try an *enoteca*, a wine bar, or an *osteria*, which is more downmarket and also serves plain food. *Alimentari* stores often prepare excellent and interesting sandwiches and rolls. *Rosticcerie* sell good, hot takeaways, while *tavole calde* are cheap self-service, sit-down places. Smaller establishments seldom have menus: just ask for the dish of the day if you want something that is reasonably priced. Menus are displayed by the entrance.

Dishes vary enormously from region to region. For example in the **Trentino Alto Adige** up in the Alps the fare is Austrian, with smoked hams and sausages perhaps followed by fruit strudel while in the south of Italy, fish and shellfish predominate.

Coffee (*caffè*) takes many forms, from *espresso* to *liqueur*. It tends to come in small shots of *espresso*; if you want a larger cup of white coffee ask for *cappuccino* or *caffè-latte*. There are many fine Italian wines, though Italian beer tends to be bottled. Bars are good places to get a snack, such as a roll or toasted sandwich, as well as to sample the local 'fire waters' such as grappa.

If you're gathering picnic items, beware that food shops close for a lengthy lunch break.

BEYOND THE BORDER
Ventimiglia–Menton–Marseille (p. 113); Verona–Munich (p. 306); Milan–Stuttgart via Zürich (ETT table 82); Milan–Paris (table 44); ferry Livorno–Bastia (table 2580); ferry Genova–Bastia (table 2540). See also Where Next? panels for Milan (p. 369); Naples (p. 376); Rome (p. 382); Venice (p. 388); Trieste (p. 404); Palermo (p. 417).

EDITOR'S CHOICE
Assisi; Bologna; Dolomites (bus from Bolzano to Ortisei; or train to Toblach); Florence; Milan; Naples; Orvieto; Pisa; Pompeii and Herculaneum; Ravenna; Rome; San Gimignano; Sardinia; Sicily (Palermo, Taormina, etc); Siena; Venice; Verona. Scenic rail journeys: Ventimiglia–Pisa (p. 389); Arezzo–Assisi (p. 405); Messina–Palermo (p. 413); Circumetnea railway around Etna (see Side Trips from Messina, p. 415); lines in Sardinia to Arbatax (p. 420), Nuoro (p. 421) and Palau (p. 422); Cosenza–Castiglione Cosentino (ETT table 631).

ITALY: FLORENCE (FIRENZE)

One of the greatest of Italy's old city-states, Florence has one of the richest legacies of art and architecture in Europe. It is so popular that its narrow streets are tightly crammed from Easter to autumn and major sights get extremely crowded during this period. Be prepared to wait in line to enter the **Galleria Uffizi** – Italy's premier art gallery – or to see Michelangelo's *David* in the **Galleria dell'Accademia**. Nevertheless, few would omit Florence from a tour of Tuscany, and it's supremely rewarding providing you don't overdo the sightseeing, have an afternoon siesta, and keep your valuables well out of the reach of pickpockets and bag-snatchers.

There are plenty of other galleries of world status if you don't feel able to cope with the Uffizi crowds. Try the **Museo dell'Opera del Duomo,** the **Palazzo Pitti** museums or the **Bargello**. Enjoy the city by walking around: take in the **Ponte Vecchio,** the **Duomo** (cathedral) or the huge piazza by the Gothic church of **Santa Maria Novella**.

You pay an entrance fee for every building you visit in Florence – even some of the churches have instituted small admission fees for tourist visits. **Combined entrance tickets** are available for some museums, and queues can be avoided at the state museums (for a small fee) by reserving visiting times in advance through **Firenze Musei,** ☎ (055) 294 883. Most museums close on Mon, and some are closed Sun as well. The **Uffizi** is quietest an hour or so before it closes at 1900.

ARRIVAL AND DEPARTURE

🚆 **Santa Maria Novella (SMN)** is Florence's main rail hub. It is a short walk from the city centre; facilities include left luggage, currency exchange and an accommodation service. The fast **ETR 500** Milan/Florence/Rome express service stops at Santa Maria Novella.

✈ **Amerigo Vespucci Airport**, 4 km north-west of the city, ☎ (055) 373 498, handles mainly domestic and some European services. The airport bus is operated by **SITA**, Via Santa Caterina da Siena 157, ☎ (800) 373 760 (information). Pisa's **Galileo Galilei Airport** (84 km) is the main regional hub for international flights, ☎ (050) 500 707. There are 10–12 trains daily between the airport and Florence's **Santa Maria Novella** rail station (75 mins).

INFORMATION

CITY MAP
– inside back cover

MONEY Eurocheques are widely accepted, but credit cards are useful only in the more expensive shops and restaurants. Banks that change money usually display the sign *Cambio* (Exchange). There are also exchange kiosks at **SMN** station and at numerous city centre locations. ATM machines accept most major credit cards, and have user instructions in English.

TOURIST OFFICES

The **Azienda Promozione Turistica (APT)** has its head office at Via Manzoni 16, 50121 Firenze, ☎ (055) 23 320, fax (055) 234 6286 (www.firenze.turismo. toscana.it; info@firenze. turismo.toscana.it).

The **City of Florence** has tourist information offices at Borgo Santa Croce 29R, ☎ (055) 234 0444, and at Pza Stazione 4, just across the street from the train station, ☎ (055) 212 245. There is a combined **City and Province of Florence** office at Via Cavour 1r, ☎ (055) 290 832/3, fax (055) 276 0383 (www.regione.toscana.it; infoturismo@provincia.fi.it).

POST AND PHONES The main **post office** is at Via Pelliceria 53, open Mon–Fri 0815–1800, Sat 0815–1230. To phone **Florence from abroad**: ☎00 (international) + 39 (Italy) + 55 (Florence) + number; to phone **Florence from elsewhere in Italy**: ☎055 (Florence) + number.

INTERNET There are many internet points located around the historical centre. Most offer student discounts, and you can buy short amounts of time in many of the smaller shops around the station. **Internet Train**, a chain of internet points, sells credit on magnetic cards that can be used at outlets throughout Italy (www.internettrain.it); branch at Via Guelfa 24/a, in the city centre.

PUBLIC TRANSPORT

Most sights are in the compact central zone and the best way to see them all is on foot. You can cover much of the city in two days. You can also rent bicycles from the municipal rental location at Pza della Stazione, next to the SMN station, and at several other outlets around the city. Town maps are available from Tourist Offices and from ATAF (see below).

BUSES Florence's buses **Azienda Trasporti Autolinee Fiorentine (ATAF)** municipal run from 0515 to 0100. There is an **ATAF information office** opposite the main entrance of SMN rail station, ☎800 424500. Buy tickets for 1 trip or 4 trips (*biglietto per quattro corsi*) from the ATAF office at the station, from ticket machines at the main stops, or from newsstands, tobacconists, or bars displaying the ATAF logo. Validate them in the machine immediately upon boarding. People caught with non-validated tickets are fined more than 50 times the value of the ticket.

Bus tickets last for one hour from the time the machine stamps them, and you may change buses on the same ticket. A 24-hr pass costs less than the price of five single tickets, while multi-day passes are worthwhile if you take more than three trips a day.

TAXIS Licensed taxis are white with a yellow stripe. Prices are high (minimum fare is about six times the cost of a one-hour bus ticket). Avoid unlicensed cabs, which can be even more expensive.

ACCOMMODATION

Florence is Europe's busiest tourism city as well as a major venue for trade fairs and for business travel, and has some magnificent luxury properties, such as the exquisite **Villa Cora**, Via Machiavelli 18, ☎ (055) 229 8451, €€€. At the other end of the scale, accommodation pickings for the budget traveller are slim. Whichever rung of the accommodation ladder you plan to alight on, try to book well ahead. Very near the station and family run is the **Hotel Nuova Italia**, Via Faenza 26, ☎ (055) 268 430. The cheapest accommodation, though not the most appealing, is near the SMN station. Elsewhere, lodgings outside the city centre and south of the Arno are cheaper than those in the city's historic heart. The **Informazione Turistiche Alberghiere** (**ITA**) booth at the SMN station may be able to find you a room if you arrive without a booking (small commission charged); open 0830–2030, prepare to wait in a long queue.

Florence has three **youth hostels**: advance booking is recommended at all three. They are: **Ostello Villa Camerata**, Viale A Righi 2/4, ☎ (055) 601 451, fax (055) 610 300; **Ostello Santa Monaca**, Via Santa Monaca 6, ☎ (055) 268 338, fax (055) 280 185 (www.ostello.it); and **Archi Rossi**, Via Faenza 94r ☎ (055) 290804, fax (055) 230 2601, closed Dec. There are **campsites** at **Italiani e Stranieri**, Viale Michelangelo 80, ☎ (055) 681 1977 (Apr–Oct), and in the grounds of the **Villa Camerata youth hostel** (see above). A further list of campsites in and around Florence is available from **Federcampeggio** (see p. 358).

FOOD AND DRINK

Florence has a good supply of reasonably priced eating places. You can cut costs by opting for fixed-price (*prezzo fisso*) meals, which give you a choice of first courses, a choice of main courses, and fruit or cheese. Since one of the first course choices is always pasta, this makes a filling meal. **S. Spirito** and **S. Frediano** are good regions to get inexpensive food in **Oltrarno**, south of the river. An even cheaper option is the *tavola calda*, a buffet-style self-service restaurant where you can choose a single dish or a full meal. These are found all over town, and cover and service charges are included in the price displayed for each dish.

As in other Italian towns, drinks taken standing or sitting at the bar are a great deal cheaper than those consumed at a table, and restaurants outside the main sight-seeing semicircle are usually cheaper than those close to the main sights. For picnic ingredients try an *alimentari* (grocery shop) – but remember that they shut for lunch.

HIGHLIGHTS

The city is divided by the **River Arno**, with most of its glorious medieval heart on the north bank. South of the river, the **Oltrarno** district is packed with artisans' workshops; this is the traditional 'working' Florence, largely untouched by the major tourist sights at its heart across the river. Five bridges cross the Arno. The most central, the **Ponte Vecchio**, is lined with shops specialising in jewellery. Built in 1345, it is Florence's oldest bridge.

NORTH OF THE ARNO Most of the important sights lie in a semicircle north of the Arno, within a 2-km radius of the **Uffizi**. These include Florence's 'musts'. The **Galleria Uffizi** itself, Pzle degli Uffizi 6, contains works by many of the Renaissance greats, such as Giotto, Cimabue, Botticelli, Michelangelo and Raphael. The **Duomo** (Cathedral) of **Santa Maria del Fiore** is topped by Brunelleschi's dome. At the base of the **Campanile** (Bell Tower), designed by Giotto in 1334, are sculpted relief panels by Andrea Pisano. The **Baptistery** (Battistero di San Giovanni) is the oldest building in Florence, 5th–8th-century, famed for its 14th–15th-century bronze doors, known as the 'Gates of Paradise'.

The **Museo dell'Opera del Duomo**, Pza del Duomo 9, houses works taken from the **Duomo** for safe-keeping. Highlights are Michelangelo's *Pietà* and sculptures by Donatello and Della Robbia. The **Bargello**, Via del Proconsolo 4, possesses Italy's finest collection of Renaissance sculpture, including works by Michelangelo, Donatello and Cellini. **Piazza della Signoria** has a wonderful array of statuary and is dominated by the medieval **Palazzo Vecchio**, which provides an inside look at the rooms occupied by the city's rulers since the 14th century. Michelangelo designed the New Sacristy – and the Medici Tombs housed there – in Pza Madonna degli Aldobrandini, next to the church of San Lorenzo. He also designed the Laurentian Library and its magnificent staircase, entered from Pza San Lorenzo. **Santa Maria Novella**, at Pza di Santa Maria Novella, contains many important Renaissance treasures, including a fresco of the Trinity by Masaccio and frescos in the chancel by Ghirlandaio.

Outside the semicircle, 3 km north-east of the centre, the **Galleria Accademia** (Via Ricasoli 60) contains Michelangelo's *David* and other masterpieces by the artist. There's more world-famous art at the **Museo di San Marco** (Pza di S Marco 1), notably Fra Angelico's frescos, including the *Annunciation*.

SOUTH OF THE ARNO: THE OLTRARNO

Cross the **Arno** by the Ponte Vecchio to reach the main attractions south of the river: the grandiose 15th-century **Palazzo Pitti**, Pza Pitti, housing the wealth of the Medicis, a fine gallery of modern art, and the huge collection of paintings from the Renaissance

SHOPPING

Florence offers some of the finest quality products in leatherwork (particularly shoes and accessories), linen and jewellery. Cheaper souvenirs include hand-made paper and pottery. See where the supremely wealthy shop, on Via Tornabuoni and Via della Vigna Nuova, where prices range from unaffordable upwards. Then visit the Pza Ciompi flea-market (open daily, go early), the **Mercato Nuovo** on Via Calimala, the daily market in the Pza di San Lorenzo (for cheap clothing, silks, belts and food), or the vast Tuesday-morning market in the **Cascine** park for more affordable buys. Hand-made perfumes, herbal remedies and soaps can be had from the frescoed **Farmacia di Santa Maria Novella**, Via della Scala 16R; prices vary from inexpensive to outrageous. In general, olive oil, aromatic vinegars, cheese and dried mushrooms, neatly packaged, are good buys.

and the Baroque in the Palatine Gallery. The home of Elizabeth Barrett Browning and Robert Browning, **Casa Guida**, is on Pza San Felice 8. Further south, behind the Palazzo Pitti, lies the city's landscaped green gardens, the **Giardino di Boboli**, a park laid out for the Medicis in the 16th century.

NIGHT-TIME AND EVENTS

Florence offers plenty to do and see, especially out on the street. On summer evenings, street performers and fortune-tellers take over the Pza della Signoria, the Pza del Duomo and the Via Calzaiuoli, which connects the two squares. Alternatively, opera is as popular as anywhere in Italy, though it is an expensive way to spend an evening. The English-language listings guide *Florence: Concierge Information* can be picked up at most hotel desks. *Firenze Spettacolo*, the monthly listings guide available at newspaper stands and bookshops, has a section in English. A lively, local youth culture boosted by a large, summer, floating population ensures that there are plenty of clubs and discos. Admission prices are high, however, and drinks are usually expensive. The scene changes in the summer when many locales move their operations outdoors to the city squares, which become venues for recorded and live music of all kinds, as well as dance and other kinds of performance art. Admission is free, though consumption of at least one drink is expected.

There are numerous theatres, the most important of which is the **Teatro Comunale**, the venue for most opera and classical concerts. There is a big music and opera festival in May–July. **Cinema Astro**, Pza S Simone, shows English-language films a few nights a week. The **Odeon**, 1 Via Sassetti, a cinema of the old, grand style (balcony, velvet curtains, and all) shows English-language films every Mon and Tues.

VIEWS OF FLORENCE
Despite the crowds, the view of the old city straddling the banks of the **Arno** from the **Ponte Vecchio** is still much as the Florentines' ancestors knew it, while from the top of the cathedral dome there's a magnificent view across the city's rooftops. A wider view of the city can be had from **San Miniato al Monte**, the church facing the city from the hill to the south, behind the **Boboli Gardens**. Alongside it, the wide Piazzale Michelangelo is a popular place for night views of the city.

FIESOLE
Fiesole, set on a hill 8 km north-east, makes a handy escape from the summertime heat of Florence (🚌 no. 7 from city centre) and provides excellent views of its larger neighbour. Also founded by the Etruscans, **Fiesole** was once an independent city-state at war with Florence. Its main sights are the **Roman Theatre** and its attendant museum, and the **Monastery of San Francesco**.

Italy's second largest city is Italy's first commercial, industrial and banking city. With much of its centre rebuilt after bombing in 1943, Milan is not as architecturally attractive as Florence, Rome or Venice, but is cosmopolitan, with a rich legacy of art and architecture, including Romanesque churches, Neoclassical boulevards, Renaissance treasures (notably in the **Pinacoteca di Brera**) and a **cathedral** that is of one of the most majestic in Christendom. A street network of concentric circles radiates outwards: within the central circle are the main sights.

Milan is the commercial hub of Italy: exciting, fashionable and prosperous, its industrial and commercial acumen played a major role in the Italian post-war miracle. Today the city is deeply style-conscious, as befits one of Europe's top fashion centres, and its shops are strikingly upmarket. Be prepared for correspondingly inflated prices.

A Celtic and Roman settlement, Milan gained importance during medieval times. The Visconti and Sforza families ruled Milan between the 13th and 16th centuries. The Viscontis started construction on the Duomo (cathedral) while the Sforzas built the **castle** and brought to Milan many of the talented artists and thinkers of the time, including Leonardo da Vinci.

ARRIVAL AND DEPARTURE

The vast majority of trains serve the monumental and fully equipped **Stazione Centrale**, Pza Duca d'Aosta (Metro lines 2/3) and **Stazione Nord** (**Cadorna**) served by Metro lines 1/2. Some trains stop instead at **Stazione Porta Garibaldi**, served by Metro line 2.

There are two airports serving Milan, Malpensa, about 50 km north-west, and Linate, 7 km from the city. All intercontinental flights land at Malpensa while they share international, charter and domestic air travel. The new Malpensa Express train is a shuttle service to Malpensa from Stazione Nord (Cadorna) and back (Metro: Cadorna); every 30 mins (takes 40 mins). Travellers flying Alitalia travel free. Air Pulman buses (☎ 0331 230830) operate a shuttle service to and from both airports from Pza Luigi Di Savona (Stazione Centrale). Buses leave for Malpensa every 20 mins and for Linate every 1 hr 30 mins. Public transport 🚌 no. 73 leaves from Corso Europa (S.Babila) for Linate every 20 mins. For information on flights from either airport, ☎ (02) 7485 2200.

TOURIST OFFICES

Main APT office:
Palazzo del Turismo,
Via Marconi 1,
☎ (02) 725 24301,
fax (02) 7252 4350, to the right
of the cathedral; free maps and
guides to Milan in English.
Branch: Stazione Centrale
☎ (02) 725 24360.

CITY MAP
– inside back cover

INFORMATION

MONEY There are many **bureaux de change** in Milan. At weekends, exchange facilities are available in Pza

ITALY

Duomo and **Stazione Centrale**, and in both airports. Automatic machines that convert cash are located in the town centre and in **Stazione Centrale** and ATMs/cash machines (bancomat) can be found at almost all banks.

POST AND PHONES The **central post office**, Via Cordusio 4, ☎ (02) 869 2069, is open 24 hrs for telexes, faxes and telegrams. **Public telephone offices** can be found at **Galleria V Emanuele II**, Via Cordusio 4, and **Stazione Centrale**. Public phones take either coins or phonecards, the latter available from automatic cash dispensers and kiosks. The dialling code for Milan is 02. To phone **Milan from abroad**: ☎ 00 (011 from US/Canada) + 39 (Italy) + 02 (Milan) + number; to phone **Milan from throughout Italy, including from Milan**: ☎ 02 (Milan) + number.

TICKETS

The same tickets are used for all public transport. **Single tickets** are good for 75 mins' travel on public transport, including one metro journey. Tickets are available from machines in metro stations or from *tabacchi* (tobacconists) and newspaper kiosks. **Passes** for **one day** or **two days** are sold at underground stations.

PUBLIC TRANSPORT

METRO **Metropolitana Milano (MM)**, is clean, efficient and easy to use. There are three colour-coded lines. Validate tickets in the gates at station entrances.

BUSES AND TRAMS The bus and tram systems are more comprehensive and more complicated, but stops have details of each route serving them. Buy tickets in advance and validate them in the machines on board.

TAXIS Milan's taxis are yellow or white and can be expensive. There's a substantial flat fare to start with, and extra charges are applied for baggage and travel on holidays or late at night. There are large ranks at **Stazione Centrale** and Pza Duomo, and cabs can also be booked by phone or hailed on the street. Avoid touts offering unofficial taxis.

ACCOMMODATION

Accommodation in Milan is expensive, but there are plenty of pensions around the station and in the town centre. **Hotel Gelsomina**, Via Pier della Francesca 4/7, Ang. Via Mantegna, ☎ (02) 349 1742, €€, has ensuite doubles and is clean and friendly; reached by tram, 3 km from the city centre. The Tourist Office will provide a full list of accommodation.

Youth hostel: **Ostello Piero Rotta**, Viale Salmoiraghi 1, ☎ (02) 3926 7095 (metro line 1 to QT8 station).

Camping: **Campeggio Città di Milano**, Via G Airaghi 61, ☎ (02) 4820 0134 (closed Dec-Jan), 🚌 no. 244. Also 30 cabins.

HOTEL RESERVATIONS
Contact **Centro Prenotazioni Hotel Italia** at the following numbers: ☎ 800 015772 from Italy, or ☎ (00 (or 011 from US/Canada) 39) (02) 2953 1605 from abroad.

FOOD AND DRINK

The Milanese take their food seriously and are prepared to pay substantial sums for their meals, so restaurants are generally expensive. Better value eateries include the lunch spots catering for office workers, with many reasonable self-service restaurants around the centre. Away from the city centre, there are family-run *trattorie* and a variety of other inexpensive places. At lunch-time, customers often eat standing up. *Pizzerie* and Chinese restaurants offer reasonably priced evening meals. Bars tend to serve more coffee than alcohol, along with *panini* – rolls with a multitude of fillings.

Regional specialities include *cotoletta alla milanese*, an Italian version of *Wiener Schnitzel*, *risotto alla milanese* (a rice dish), and the filling vegetable and pork stew served with polenta (*casoeùla*). Despite being inland, Milan has excellent fish, fresh from the coast.

HIGHLIGHTS

If a city can have such a thing as a 'signature building', then Milan's is undoubtedly the **Duomo** (Cathedral), in the pigeon-populated Pza Duomo (Metro: DUOMO). Work started in 1386, at the behest of Gian Galeazzo Visconti. Wanting a son, and finding his prayers granted, he built this remarkable edifice as a tribute to the Virgin Mary.

The Duomo is a magical and extravagant Gothic structure, overflowing with belfries, statues and 135 pinnacles in white marble. It shimmers in the sunlight and glows in the winter fog. The stark interior contains fine stained glass and works of art dating back to before the cathedral's construction. Stairs (73 to the dome; 139 to the tower) lead up to the roof, from which there are fine views.

> Note that museums (including the Brera) are closed on Mon.

On the north side of Pza Duomo is the **Galleria Vittorio Emanuele II**, a monumental 19th-century iron and glass shopping arcade known as the **Salon de Milan**, where there are elegant cafés.

The Galleria leads through to Pza Scala, home of **La Scala** (more properly the Teatro alla Scala), probably the most famous opera house in the world. **La Scala Theatre Museum**, in the building, exhibits a huge array of opera memorabilia. It also provides the opportunity to see into the opera house itself.

The **Pinacoteca di Brera**, 28 Via Brera (Metro: LANZA), is Milan's finest art gallery. Its collection concentrates on Italian artists of the 14th–19th centuries, although foreign schools of the 17th–18th centuries are also represented. Notable works here are Raphael's *Marriage of the Virgin*, Mantegna's *Dead Christ* and works by Bramante, Carpaccio, Bellini and Veronese. The gallery is housed in part of the **Palazzo di Brera**.

In the **Pinacoteca Ambrosiana**, 2 Pza Pio XI (Metro: DUOMO or CORDUSIO), you will see works by Leonardo da Vinci, including the portrait of the musician Caffurio. Caravaggio's *Basket of Fruit* and Raphael's cartoons for the Vatican are other star attractions. Milan's most famous painting, and one of the great works of the Renaissance, is Leonardo da Vinci's *Last Supper* (1495–7), painted in tempera on a wall in the old Dominican monastery refectory next to **Santa Maria Delle Grazie** (Metro: CADORNA). It has been fully restored after years of deterioration and attracts large crowds. Tickets can be booked ☎ (02) 498 7588 or bought at the entrance.

The **Basilica di Sant'Ambrogio** (Metro: SANT'AMBROGIO) was built in the late 4th century by St Ambrose, patron saint of the city and former Bishop of Milan. So eloquent and smooth in speech was St Ambrose that his name was given to honey liqueur. Most of what is standing today dates from the 12th century. The saint's remains lie in the crypt.

The **Basilica of San Lorenzo**, 39 Corso di Porta Ticinese, has a similar history to Sant'Ambrogio, having been built around AD 500 and reconstructed some 700 years later. A notable portico of 16 columns from a Roman temple stands in front.

Sforza Castle, Pza Castello, at the end of Via Dante (Metro: CAIROLI), is a distinctive, solid fortress, built by Francesco Sforza, Duke of Milan in the 15th century, on top of an earlier Visconti fortress. It now houses an encyclopaedic collection of galleries and museums, displaying everything from arms to furniture and from Egyptian art to musical instruments, and including the **Museum of Antique Art**, with some valuable works by Michelangelo. It also houses the **Museum of Musical Instruments**, which contains a spinet on which Mozart played. Behind the castle is **Sempione Park**, the largest green space in central Milan. At the far end is the **Arco Della Pace** (Arch of Peace).

The **Poldi-Pezzoli Museum**, Via Manzoni 12 (Metro: MONTENAPOLEONE), was originally assembled by Gian Giacomo Poldi-Pezzoli, a well-to-do Milanese collector. It is yet another of the city's great collections and includes Botticelli and Mantegna paintings. The **Leonardo da Vinci**

SHOPPING

Milan is the prime place in Italy to buy clothes, accessories, modern furniture or jewellery – not necessarily practical or affordable! The image the Milanese present to the outside world is that of *la bella figura* ('looking good'), and the most chic shops are within the Quadrilatero a fashion district with four sides, Via Manzioni, Via Montenapoleone, Via Sant'Andrea and Via della Spiga. (Metro: SAN BABILA). Good value **clothing** can be found in the department stores **La Rinascente**, **Coin** and **Upim**. The Naviglio district hosts lots of young designer shops and boutiques. A huge open **market** in Viale Papiniano operates on Tuesday mornings and all day Sat (Metro: S. AGOSTINO). The Naviglio Grande is the scene of the monthly **Antiques Fair** (last Sunday of each month) and the Brera district is full of antique and household accessory stores.

National Museum of Science and Industry, Via San Vittore 21 (Metro: S'AMBROGIO), exhibits displays of Leonardo's own ideas, including a model of his famous air-screw, the precursor of the helicopter. In the western suburbs stands the architecturally curious **G. Meazza Stadium**, home to Milan's two successful football teams, Inter Milan and AC Milan, this futuristic construction of steel lattices and huge concrete cylinders holds more than 80,000 spectators. Stadium tours are given daily (☎ (02) 4870 7123) and matches are played most Sundays (Metro: LOTTO or LAMPUGNANO).

NIGHT-TIME AND EVENTS

Milan's daily newspapers, *La Repubblica* and *Corriere della Sera*, produce weekly supplements detailing Milan's entertainment, events and nightlife.

The city's most famous institution is the grand **La Scala** opera house. Tickets are extremely elusive, but you may be able to get them on Mon, for performances of classical music rather than opera. For information, ☎ (02) 7200 3744. In summer the repertoire extends to ballet and concerts too. The **Conservatorio** also hosts concerts.

Cinemas cluster around Corso Vittorio Emanuele (Metro: DUOMO). Movies in their original language are shown at the **Odeon** in Via Santa Radegonda and the **Anteo** in Via Milazzo (Mon), at the **Arcobaleno** in Via Tunisia (Tues) and the **Mexico** in Via Savona (Thurs). **Nightclubs** tend to close around 0200–0300; **Le Scimmie** (Monkeys), Via A Sforza, is a historic club restaurant with live music, **Shocking Club** (Pza XXV Aprile), **Old Fashion** (Viale Alemagna) and **Propaganda** (Via Castelbarco) are popular discos. Two of the more trendy areas of town are **Porta Ticinese** and **Brera**. The **Porta Ticinese** and the **Navigli** ('canals') district are home to a high concentration of bars and venues (the actual Porta Ticinese is a remnant of the 14th-century city ramparts). **Cafés and bars** also dot the small streets around **Brera**.

Via Brera is the showcase of Milan's fashion industry. The Milanese care about their clothes, and smart dress is the norm for almost all nightlife throughout the city, even informal promenading.

WHERE NEXT FROM MILAN?

Join the **Milan–Trieste** route (p. 399), or head south-east to **Bologna** (ETT tables 611, 620 and 630) for the **Bologna–Rome** route (p. 405). Alternatively head west through Turin (Torino) and the Alps into France (ETT table 585) and take the scenic mountain route via **Modane** and **Aix-les-Bains** to Lyon. There's an equally stunning ride northwards into Switzerland via **Como** on Lake Como (Lago Como) to **Lugano** (ETT table 550), from where you can take the **Berne–Lugano** route (p. 335) in reverse. Or take the **Lausanne–Milan** route (p. 317) in reverse.

ITALY: NAPLES (NAPOLI)

There's nowhere quite like **Naples** – the unruly, raucous, run-down capital of the South. It might have a notorious reputation as a city of crime and incredible traffic jams, but its ebullience, history, cuisine and sheer range of treasures make it a compelling place to visit on a southern Italian journey. The main highlight is the **National Archaeological Museum,** whose glories include its Greek sculptures, mosaics and artefacts. For many, however, their abiding memory will be of dark, crumbling, medieval alleys, with washing lines strung above and assorted cooking smells emanating from within, where housewives haul up bucketfuls of shopping by ropes linked to high tenement windows. Out on the streets, you can wander for hours in the city's various districts, such as the **Sanità,** and be entertained by the ebullience of daily life. Behind the Pza del Plebiscito is the ironically named Via Solitaria, a long, busy, local street.

Originally the Greek colony of Neapolis, Naples became a desirable winter resort for wealthy Romans. Of the many families that later ruled Naples, the Anjou and Aragon dynasties of the 13th–16th centuries were among the most influential, and many remains from that era dot the city.

Naples is somewhat upstaged by its surroundings, notably the Neapolitan Riviera – including the ultra-scenic resorts of **Sorrento, Positano** and **Amalfi,** and the island of **Capri,** just a short boat ride away – as well as the astonishing Roman remains of **Herculaneum** and **Pompeii.** All can be reached in a day trip from Naples, though you might prefer to base yourself on the Riviera for exploring the area fully.

ARRIVAL AND DEPARTURE

Most long-distance trains use **Stazione Centrale.** Some use **Stazione Pza Garibaldi** which is also the metro station directly beneath **Centrale. Mergellina** and **Campi Flegrei,** also terminals for some trains, are further west. The metro links all three stations. **Stazione Circumvesuviana** handles trains to **Pompeii** (see pp. 375–376) and **Sorrento;** it is adjacent to **Centrale** and is well signposted.

Capodichino, to the north, is reasonably close to the centre, so taxi fares are not exorbitant. There is a daily bus service to **Stazione Centrale.** For **airport information,** ☎(081) 789 6259.

INFORMATION

Pick up a town map at the city Tourist Office and a copy of the monthly listing *Qui Napoli.* **Ente Provinciale per il Turismo (EPT)** provides information about hotels; its **main office** is at Pza dei Martiri 58, ☎(081) 4051 311, and it maintains a spartan but helpful office in the **Stazione Centrale,** ☎(081) 268 779, and in the **Stazione di Mergellina,** ☎(081) 761 2102.

TOURIST OFFICES

The city Tourist Office is at **Palazzo Reale**, Pza del Plebiscito, ☎(081) 252 5711, with branches at Pza Gesù Nuovo 28 (it may be closed in the afternoon despite the official opening hours).

Youth information (CTS): Via Mezzocannone 25, ☎(081) 552 7960.

There is a 'Hello Napoli' freecall number for tourists, ☎ 800-251 396 (toll-free; English, French and German spoken).

PUBLIC TRANSPORT

The metro runs west to **Pozzuoli** and **Solfatara**. Trains can be infrequent and stations quiet out of peak hours. **Buses** and **trams** are more frequent and more extensive.

Frequent **hydrofoils and ferries** ply across the bay and out to Sicily and the other islands. Most leave from **Molo Beverello** (by **Castel Nuovo**) but some go from Mergellina. Three funicular railways (**Funicolare Montesanto**, **Centrale** and **Chiaia**) link the old city with the cooler **Vomero Hill**.

TICKETS

Trains: Buy tickets at kiosks and validate them in the machines near each platform.

Buses: Buy tickets from news kiosks, tobacconists and bars. Day passes available.

A local **transit ticket** is valid for 90 mins, and good for three trips on any metro, tram or bus (or one funicular ride and two other trips).

ACCOMMODATION

The Tourist Office has a list of hotels and can occasionally help in finding a place to stay, but confirm prices with the hotel before committing yourself. Cheap hotels cluster in and around the noisy, and not particularly salubrious, Pza Garibaldi. **Hotel San Pietro**, Via San Pietro ad Aram 18, ☎(081) 286 040, €€, is a large block just west of Pza Garibaldi (with the station behind you, take Corso Umberto leading diagonally left; the hotel is signed off to the right). Good value, with a big street market close by (so can be noisy). Also west of Pza Garibaldi is **Pensione Mancini**, Via Pasquale Stanislao Mancini 33, ☎(081) 553 6731, fax (081) 554 6675, €, a fair budget option which also has dorm facilities. The **Astoria**, Via Santa Lucia 90, ☎(081) 764 9903, €, is a friendly, small pension in an excellent, untouristy location ideal for exploring the city (🚌no. 152 from the station). **Le Fontane al Mare**, Via Nicolò Tommaseo 14, ☎(081) 764 3811, fax (081) 764 3470, is one of the cheapest and most central (near the Royal Palace) options if seafront accommodation is what you are after. Some rooms have a private bathroom but not those with a sea view.

The **youth hostel**, **Ostello Mergellina**, 23 Salita della Grotta, ☎(081) 761 2346, fax (081) 761 2391, is behind the Stazione Mergellina. **Campsites** are mainly in Pozzuoli (on the metro), west of Naples. **Campeggio Vulcano La Solfatara**, Via Solfatara 161, ☎(081) 526 7413, is the nearest.

FOOD AND DRINK

Naples is the birthplace of the pizza, the city's main contribution to the culinary world – authentically served with a fresh tomato sauce. The city's food is among Italy's best, healthiest and cheapest. Pasta is the staple ingredient, as are deep-fried vegetables and seafood. There are plenty of inexpensive places to eat – try the area just to the west of Via Toledo or the many open-air food stalls around the station and Pza Mercato.

HIGHLIGHTS

Modern Naples is hectic, crowded and noisy. Petty crime is rife, notably pickpocketing and bag-snatching, so be very careful, especially after dark.

Set in an imposing 18th-century Royal Palace and huge shady park, the **Museo di Capodimonte**, Via Miano 2 (take a bus from Pza Garibaldi to Porta Grande or Porta Piccola) also houses one of Italy's largest and richest collections of art – including important works by Italian masters such as Titian and Botticelli, art from Naples from the 13th to the 19th centuries, and modern paintings.

Do not miss the world-class **Museo Archeologico Nazionale** (National Archaeological Museum), Pza Museo Nazionale 19 (Metro: PZA CAVOUR; free for under 18s and over 65s; closed Tues), which contains an unparalleled collection from Pompeii and Herculaneum: bronzes, sculptures, mosaics, glass and, most interesting of all, mundane everyday objects.

South of the museum is the heart of medieval Naples, Spaccanapoli, centred around Via Benedetto Croce and Pza Gesù Nuovo, where you'll find the **Gesù Nuovo**, a 16th-century church whose façade, originally part of a palace, is studded with peculiar basalt diamond-shaped extrusions. Within, it is one of the extreme expressions of the ebullient Neapolitan baroque style.

A NIGHT AT THE OPERA
The best entertainments in Naples are culinary, operatic, or just strolling the streets. If you like opera and ballet, the Teatro San Carlo is well worth a visit (tickets on line at www.teatrosancarlo).

Not far away, **Santa Chiara**, Via Benedetto Croce, dates from the 14th century. In it are some exceptionally fine medieval tombs. Attached to it and bright with roses, marguerites and geraniums, the gently decaying **Cloister of the Clarisse** is notable for its walks, which are lined with decorative majolica tiles dating from the 18th century. Further east, the cavernous **Duomo** (Cathedral), Via Duomo, is dedicated to Naples' patron saint, San Gennaro. Housed here is a phial of his blood, which allegedly liquefies miraculously twice every year.

The massive **Castel Nuovo** (or Maschio Angioino) guards the port. The castle, begun in 1279, is chiefly recognisable for its massive round towers. The nearby **Palazzo**

Reale was the seat of the Neapolitan royalty. Vast and handsome, within it are acres of 18th- and 19th-century rooms. The adjacent **Teatro di San Carlo**, begun in 1737, ranks second only to **La Scala**, in Milan, in the Italian opera league.

Santa Lucia, the waterfront district to the south, is where **Castel dell'Ovo**, built by Frederick II, sticks out into the bay. The third major castle in Naples, **Castel Sant'Elmo**, occupies a peak high above the city – alongside the **Certosa di San Martino**. Inside the latter, whose courtyard is one of

SHOPPING

Shopping in Naples is rather specialised. Crib figures and accessories are available in the streets around the church of **S. Gregorio Armeno**, while **Capodimonte** figures and miniature tableaux are available citywide, particularly in the centre. Shopping for unfamiliar herb-infused oils and vinegars, salamis and other easily portable foodstuffs in the markets and delicatessens is a must. The shopping mall **Galleria Umberto I**, a real showcase, was built in 1887.

the masterpieces of the local baroque style, is **Museo Nazionale di San Martino** which contains an important collection of Neapolitan paintings and Christmas cribs, the *presepi*. The **Museo Principe di Aragona Pignatelli**, Riviera di Chiaia, contains salons decorated entirely in **local ceramics**. This gallery houses one of the greatest of European art collections.

SIDE TRIPS FROM NAPLES

In some ways, the surroundings of Naples offer more than the city itself. Your first impressions of the Naples area are likely to be mixed: it's a strange blend of immense physical majesty, with the still-active Mount Vesuvius rising massively over the bay itself, and the distant limestone peaks looming mysteriously beyond Sorrento. Meanwhile a vast industrial zone sprawls gracelessly along the shores, westwards almost as far as Sorrento and southwards to Salerno and beyond.

Exploring the area is easily done by train, bus and ferry. The **Circumvesuviana** is an extremely cheap private railway (half-hourly service) linking Naples, Sorrento, Pompeii and Herculaneum, and there are regular trains and buses (the latter from the main station in Pza Garibaldi) to Salerno (see p. 414), from where you can take a bus to Paestum or a bus or ferry to Amalfi.

Don't try to cover both Pompeii and Herculaneum in a day – Herculaneum and Vesuvius can be done together though.

THE SORRENTINE PENINSULA This is an unbeatable area if you like beaches, ancient sites, boat trips and stunning coastal scenery. Not many places in the world have all such features right on the doorstep. The best approach is by ferry – from Salerno to Amalfi, or from Naples to Sorrento and on to

Capri, for instance: here you will see villages and towns perched beneath towering limestone cliffs that will have you wondering how anyone ever managed to build on them. Virtually every accessible patch is either built on or cultivated with olives or lemons. The settlements are linked by a myriad network of tiny stepped paths, making it outstanding terrain for walking. If you want to try the walks in this region, purchase Julian Tippett's excellent *Landscapes of Sorrento and the Amalfi Coast* (published in English by Sunflower, and available locally).

Scenically, the Amalfi area has the edge over Sorrento. Because of the tortuous nature of the roads, driving or cycling here is not recommended; fortunately the bus network is excellent and cheap, and the ferries are even better.

Sorrento (Tourist Office: Via de Maio Luigi 35, ☎ (081) 807 4033) is the biggest resort on the Neapolitan Riviera, a limestone peninsula, easily reached by frequent trains from Naples on the (remarkably inexpensive) Circumvesuviana. Curiously, it has no beach, but is perched on cliffs, with a concentration of upmarket hotels in the centre (there's less pricey accommodation up the hill on the west side; **Hotel Elios**, Via Capo 33, ☎ (081) 878 1812, is quiet, with sea views from some rooms). Sorrento is well served with ferries, to Naples, Capri and Amalfi. If you have a choice, take the ferry rather than the jetfoil – which confines you indoors and can be bumpy.

A superb place to base yourself for a few days is **Amalfi** (Tourist Office: ☎ (089) 871 107) – also reached by bus or ferry from Salerno – which has considerably more charm than Sorrento. It's squeezed at the mouth of a beautiful limestone gorge, with lemon groves spread over the surrounding slopes. Beaches are small and grey-sanded, but the water in summer is clean and warm. Just east of Amalfi, **Atrani** is remarkably unspoilt, and less busy than neighbouring Amalfi; on its sole, tiny square – Pza Umberto 1 – is the hostel/hotel **A Scalinatella** ☎ (089) 871 492, excellent value and very friendly; it also rents out apartments and is adjacent to a beach.

There are some great walks here, along stepped paths and tiny lanes. Take the frequent bus from Amalfi up to **Ravello** and return by one of several very attractive paths. This delicious hilltop village has stupendous views and extraordinarily numerous semi-feral cats. The Villa Cimbrone has an incomparably romantic terraced garden (open to the public) overlooking the sea. Wagner set part of his opera *Parsifal* here, and classical music is still very much the thing in Ravello with a long summer music festival based at the Villa Rufolo.

CAPRI Lying just off the Sorrento Peninsula, the island of Capri is renowned for its wonderful setting, with bougainvillea, cacti and jasmine growing everywhere around the Greek-looking dome-roofed white houses. Don't be too put off by the crowds that descend on the main town (itself reached by funicular from the ferry, though to avoid the queues you may prefer to walk up), which is crammed full of expensive boutiques.

It's a much better option to leave town straight away and to explore the traffic-free lanes and paths eastwards to Villa Jovis, the villa of Emperor Tiberius, who used to get his less-favoured guests drunk and then have them hurled off the cliffs. From here, carry on southwards: a path leads down past a cliff cave to a viewpoint above a fantastic natural arch. It proceeds high above an idyllic beach to re-enter the town. For the best view on the island head up to the 589-m summit of Monte Solaro. A chair lift operates from May–Oct from Anacapri if you don't fancy the walk.

Capri is not thick on formal sights, but a good visit is to the Villa San Michele. This is the highly idiosyncratic former home of the Swedish doctor and author Axel Munthe. The Blue Grotto is a rip-off boat trip – the water colour is incredible but you get only a few minutes in the cave; longer cruises round the island may be well worthwhile, however.

ISCHIA The fertile island of **Ischia**, less well known than Capri, also has a remarkable setting, with spa resorts offering cures in radioactive waters, and some excellent beaches for lingering. There are about nine sailings daily from Naples to Capri and Ischia departing from Molo Beverello (40 mins to Capri, 80 mins to Ischia). Hydrofoils depart hourly from Mergellina (journey time 35 mins for both islands).

HERCULANEUM (ERCOLANO) AND VESUVIUS The Museo Archeologico Nazionale (National Archaeological Museum) in Naples (see p. 372) has the bulk of the finds from this famous Roman site.

Herculaneum (Station: Ercolano ; 10 mins' walk downhill to the site) was a wealthy Roman subtopia that was buried in AD 79 by the eruption of Mount Vesuvius, though it was engulfed by mud rather than ash. Excavations have revealed an astonishing time capsule, with many house façades virtually intact. Unlike Pompeii some upper storeys are in evidence; you can see half-timbered buildings and even the balconies, and some remarkable bathhouses – men's and women's – still roofed and with benches in position.

You enter the site through a tunnel piercing the mud that engulfed the town; originally this was the shore, and you get a further idea of the sheer scale of the disaster at the edge of the excavated town, where classical columns disappear upwards; the modern town lies on top, concealing much more. On your way back to the station, keep to the left of the main street for the fascinating (easily missed) medieval town – strikingly decayed and atmospheric, with a food market and crowded alleys.

Several buses a day zigzag up from the station (most leave in the morning, so it's best done before you visit Herculaneum) to within a 30-min walk of the summit of **Vesuvius**, where in addition to enjoying the view over the bay you can peer into the crater; there's no smoke or molten lava to be seen, but the volcano is still active.

POMPEII (POMPEI) Also on the Circumvesuviana railway and a short ride from Naples, **Pompeii** (Station: Pompei, adjacent to the site); is much the larger and more touristy site, its ruins mesmeric and eerie, though things aren't quite as well preserved here and packs of stray dogs roam the streets. This substantial Roman town, excavated from the volcanic ash that buried it, gives a real feel for life at the time: you can see original graffiti on the walls and chariot ruts in the road, wander into houses and courtyards, identify shop counters and even lose the crowds in some of the more remote areas. Indeed the scale of the place is almost daunting.

Highlights include the Forum, the Forum Baths, the Villa of the Mysteries, the outdoor and indoor theatres, the House of I Caius Secundus and the house of the Vettii (both with marvellous wall paintings), and the Lupanar (a brothel). On arrival at the site you can join guided tours, which can be worthwhile as nothing's explained once you're inside. As with Herculaneum, most of the best sculptures, mosaics and paintings have ended up in the National Archaeological Museum in Naples (see p. 372).

PAESTUM   There are a few trains every day from Naples' Central staton to Paestum station, a 10-min walk from the ruins. Otherwise get one of the frequent trains or buses from Naples to Salerno, where there are buses to **Paestum** (annoyingly the buses are operated by more than one company and tickets aren't interchangeable; the easiest ticket booth to find is by the rail station). However you decide to get there, it's definitely worth the effort, as Paestum (or Poseidonia as it was known in ancient times) is quite different from Pompeii and Herculaneum and far less overrun.

It was founded by Greeks from Sybaris in the 6th century BC and later colonized by the Romans. What remains are three magnificent Greek Doric temples, a good deal better preserved than most ruins in Greece itself. Most notable is the Temple of Neptune, dating from about 450BC, standing to its original height. The outline of the surrounding ancient town is still in evidence, with the weed-grown foundations of buildings and the original main street, and the museum has finds from the site, including a famous tomb fresco of a diving swimmer.

WHERE NEXT FROM NAPLES?

You can take the train via **Foggia** to **Brindisi**; journey time 2 hrs 12 mins–3 hrs 12 mins by daytime service (direct route via Bari); ETT tables 626 and 630. An alternative (and extremely attractive) route goes via **Battipaglia** to **Taranto** (table 640). Despite the heavy industry when approaching **Taranto**, there is an archaeological museum, **Museo Nazionale**, which is beginning to rival that in Naples with its excellent collection of ancient Greek artefacts. From **Taranto**, continue to **Bari** or **Brindisi** (table 630).

From **Brindisi** you can take ferries to **Corfu** and **Patras**.

There is also a nightly ship from **Naples** to **Palermo** (table 2625) and a weekly ship to **Cagliari** (table 2620).

The 'Eternal City', dominated by its seven hills (Aventine, Capitoline, Celian, Esquiline, Palatine, Quirinal and Viminal), is cut by the fast-flowing River **Tiber**. Filled with museums and galleries, and with churches and ruins redolent of the Caesars and the creative genius of Michelangelo, Rome spans 2000 years. There's an immense amount here: don't try to see too much, and make plenty of stops for ice-cream and espresso. Heading most people's list of attractions are likely to be the **Colosseum**, the **Forum**, **St Peter's Cathedral**, the **Sistine Chapel** in the Vatican, **Piazza Navona**, the **Pantheon**, **Trevi Fountain** and **Spanish Steps** in the historic centre and the **Catacombs** further out on the Via Appia Antica.

In August, the city empties a little as the Romans escape the heat and go on holiday. Be extra vigilant with your belongings, as thieves are abundant.

A good way of orientating yourself is to walk along the river: while this is rather noisy it clearly shows how the city is packed with history and it gives a sense of its being at the centre of the civilised world.

ARRIVAL AND DEPARTURE

There are four main railway stations. **Termini**, Pza dei Cinquecento, is Rome's largest, handling all the main national and international lines; bureaux de change, tourist and hotel information; well served by taxis, buses and night buses, and at the hub of the metro system. **Tiburtina** serves some long-distance north–south trains. Services to Bracciano (1 hr 30 mins) and Viterbo (1 hr 45 mins) depart from **Ostiense**. There are ATMs in the stations.

Leonardo da Vinci (Fiumicino) is 36 km south-west of Rome, ☎ (06) 65 951. **Taxis** into the centre are hassle-free, but expensive. Much cheaper is the 45-min train service, every 15 mins (every 30 mins late evenings, Sundays and holidays; 0627–2127), to **Tiburtina** station. There's an express rail link (30 mins) to **Termini** (0637–2237). **Aeroporto Ciampino**, ☎ (06) 794 941, is closer to town, 16 km to the south-east. A bus service (**COTRAL**) runs at irregular intervals to **Anagnina Metro Station** (underground to **Termini** every 30 mins, 0530–2230). **Airport Connection Services**, ☎ 3383221, has private taxis serving both airports.

INFORMATION

CITY AND TRANSPORT MAP
– inside back cover

MONEY **Banks** open 0830–1330 and 1500–1600, and **bureaux de change** generally open 0830/0900–1300 and 1530/1600–1930/2000; **hotels** will also change money. Major credit cards and Eurocheques are widely accepted (though not in all cheaper restaurants and places to stay; check beforehand).

ITALY

TOURIST INFORMATION

Main Tourist Office, APT (Rome Provincial Tourist Board): Via Parigi 5 (near Via XX Settembre), (Metro: Repubblica); hotel listings, maps and itineraries.

Other branches: Leonardo da Vinci Airport, Stazione Termini (arrivals hall).

Private Tourist Office: **Enjoy Rome**, Via Varese 39, ☎ (06) 445 1843, fax (06) 445 0734 (www.enjoyrome.com; info@enjoyrome.com), near Termini station, is packed with information and provides free hotel reservation.

POST AND PHONES The main **post office**, Pza San Silvestro 20, has 24-hr phones, fax and poste restante (address letters c/o Fermo Posta, Roma Centrale, 00186 Roma – put the surname first, underlined). Stamps are available from post offices and tobacconists displaying a black and white T. To be sure of a prompt delivery, use *posta prioritaria* stamps. Letters posted at the main post office, or anywhere within the **Vatican City** (use Vatican stamps in blue post boxes), arrive faster than those posted in the red pavement boxes.

To phone **Rome from abroad**: ☎00 (011 from US/Canada) + 39 (Italy) + 06 (Rome) + number. To phone **Rome from anywhere in Italy (including Rome)**: ☎06 (Rome) + number.

PUBLIC TRANSPORT

The *centro storico* (historic centre) is fairly compact, traffic-free and easy to see on foot. However, many of the most important sights lie outside this area. The main arteries are well served by buses, but stick to those and you miss Rome's ebullient streetlife, medieval alleys and baroque squares. Most hotels supply a basic street map. For more details, and bus and metro maps, ask at newsstands, tobacconists and Tourist Offices. Romans are very willing with directions.

METRO The Metropolitana has only two lines – A and B – and is not much use in the centre. Line A (red) is open 0530–2400; Line B (blue) is open 0530–2100, Mon–Fri. For ticket information see panel, p. 379.

BUSES AND TRAMS Rome's excellent bus service is centred on Pza dei Cinquecento, with major stops *(fermate)* in Pza Venezia, Largo Argentina and Pza del Risorgimento. Buses are orange, the number is at the front and they generally stop without your having to flag them down. Only one (☐no. 119, a small electric bus) is able to enter the narrow streets of the *centro storico* and does a useful round trip of most of the major sights in the centre.
Night buses run from 2400–0800. Buy tickets from the conductor on board.

TAXIS There are plenty of metered taxis, available from ranks or by phone: **Radiotaxi**, ☎(06) 3570; **Capitale**, ☎(06) 4994. There are surcharges for luggage, at night (2200–0700) and on Sun and holidays.

CITY TRANSPORT TICKETS

In order to save time and money, tourists should buy a 1-day pass, called a *BIG* ticket, or a 1-week pass, called a *Carta Settimanale per Turisti*, or a 1-month pass, called a *tessera mensile intera rete integrato*. These are valid for **all** forms of transport (bus, metro and tram) in Rome. You can also buy individual combined bus/metro tickets, called B.I.T. (*biglietto integrato a tempo*). These are valid for 75 mins with one metro ride only. All types of ticket and pass can be bought at most newsstands and tobacconists or at kiosks and ticket machines at railway and underground stations and bus termini. You need to validate (time stamp) individual tickets in the machine as you enter the bus (there are on-the-spot fines if you are caught ticketless). The *BIG* ticket needs to be validated once only. The 1-week pass just needs your name and the starting date. The 1-month pass needs your name only.

ACCOMMODATION

There are plenty of **hotels**, from the opulent – mainly located close to the **Spanish Steps** and the Via Veneto – to the basic, largely clustered around the Via Nazionale and Termini station.

Moderately priced centrally located hotels are generally very popular, and you should book up to two months ahead in high season. For the cheaper hotels, expect to pay around €40–45 per night, even without a private bathroom. Some do not take credit cards.

Tourist Offices will provide lists of residential hotels and make bookings. **Hotel Reservations (HR)**, at Leonardo da Vinci airport, Termini station and on Autostrada A1, ☎(06) 699 1000, is a free hotel booking service. **Enjoy Rome** (see p. 378) also make free hotel bookings.

If you don't mind the idea of a night-time curfew and pilgrims, several religious institutions offer cheap accommodation: try **Domus Mariae**, ☎(06) 66 27 758, and **Istituto Madri Pie**, ☎(06) 631 967, fax (06) 631 989 – both near the Vatican.

Youth hostels: **Associazione Italiana Alberghi per la Gioventù (AIG)**, see p. 358. Only holders of **AIG** or **HI** cards can use the **Ostello del Foro Italico**, Viale delle Olimpiadi 61, ☎ (06) 323 6267, fax (06) 32 42 613 (www.hostels-aig.org). The **YWCA** is at Via C Balbo 4, ☎(06) 48 80 056.

Camping: There are no sites in central Rome; although there are ten within a 45-min bus ride away.

FOOD AND DRINK

Italian **cafés and bars** have hefty seating charges, so most Romans eat their breakfast, and often lunch, standing up at the bar. You generally pay first and take your receipt to the counter. **Picnics** are a good alternative. Some **delicatessens** or **grocery stores** (*alimentari*) will fill a roll with the ingredients of your choice and slices of takeaway pizza are always available in *Pizza Rustica* outlets and often in bakeries.

ITALY

Restaurants are more expensive than *trattorie*, which offer substantial amounts of simple, robust Roman-style food, washed down with local wine. Some have no name, their purpose defined only by cooking smells, loud chatter and paper table-cloths. Some don't even have menus, so just point to whatever seems delicious on the next table. *Pizzerie* are a cheap alternative, while you can taste different wines and have delicious tiny snacks at an *enoteca*. **Vegetarian** restaurants are rare but most Italian menus are adaptable.

The Campo dei Fiori neighbourhood is best for alfresco dining, while the streets off the nearby Pza Farnese have stylish but reasonably cheap venues. **Trastevere** has boisterous, crowded, rough-and-ready eateries, which may involve queuing but are worth the wait. Other popular places are around Pza Navona and the **Pantheon**, while the **Ghetto** and the old slaughterhouse area of **Testaccio** offer some of the best traditional Roman cooking. Read the menu in the window to gauge price.

HIGHLIGHTS

The APT publishes *Musei e Monumenti di Roma* giving details of current changes and closures. Most museums are closed on Mon (the Vatican closes on Sun). Most places charge an entrance fee with admission free for under-16s and over 65s and reduced for 18–25s, teachers and students. A special **5-day sightseeing ticket** gives entry to six Roman museums/archaeological sites including the Colosseum.

The **Capitoline** hill is occupied by Michelangelo's Pza del Campidoglio, which is dominated by Rome's town hall, the **Palazzo Senatorio**. On either side of this, the magnificent Capitoline Museums in **Palazzo Nuovo** and, opposite it, **Palazzo dei Conservatori** house important collections of classical sculpture. In addition, the **Palazzo dei Conservatori** also contains the **Pinacoteca Capitolina**, an art gallery with paintings by, amongst others, Rubens, Caravaggio and Titian.

> ### EXPLORING THE VATICAN
> The **Vatican City**, a state within a city and home of the Pope and the Catholic Church, houses numerous treasures. The **Basilica di San Pietro** (St Peter's Cathedral), worked on by, amongst others, Bramante, Michelangelo and Bernini (whose immense colonnade precedes it), dominates the Vatican. The vast and elaborate **Vatican Museum**, Viale Vaticano, and the recently cleaned **Sistine Chapel** (enter from the museum), with Michelangelo's *Last Judgement*, considered his masterpiece, and his ceiling frescos depicting scenes from the Old Testament, draw in the crowds. Nearby is the **Castel Sant' Angelo**, built as a Roman tomb, converted into a fortress, used as a palace, and now a museum, Lungotevere Castello.

The great basilica of **Santa Maria Maggiore**, Pza di Santa Maria Maggiore, dominates the **Esquiline** hill. Nearby, **San Pietro in Vincoli**, Pza San Pietro in Vincoli, houses the chains with which St Peter was imprisoned, and Michelangelo's superb statue of Moses. Beyond it, **Trajan's Market** (the world's first shopping mall; Via 4 Novembre) and **Trajan's Column** face the **Forum**, site of the temples and basilicas of Imperial Rome.

The **Celian** hill is quiet, covered mainly by the gardens of the **Villa Celimontana**, Pza della Navicella. In front of it, the formal **Farnese Gardens** on the **Palatine** are filled with the ruins of Imperial palaces. Below lies Rome's most famous landmark, the **Colosseum**, Pza del Colosseo, built by Emperor Vespasian in AD 72. It held over 55,000 spectators and was the scene of the Roman games and gladiatorial combats.

At the base of the **Quirinal** hill is the **Trevi Fountain**, Pza Fontana di Trevi – into which, to ensure your return, you must throw a coin – while on its summit sits the president of Italy's residence, the **Palazzo del Quirinale**. Also on the Quirinal is the **Palazzo Barberini**, Via delle Quattro Fontane 13, which contains many important works of the Renaissance and baroque periods.

The **Campo dei Fiori**'s vegetable market adds life and colour to the district near **Palazzo Farnese**, Pza Farnese, and **Santa Andrea della Valle**, Corso Vittorio Emanuele. The **Palazzo Spada**, Via Capo di Ferro 13, includes paintings by Titian and Rubens.

The old Jewish **Ghetto** is one of Rome's quaintest neighbourhoods. It faces the district of Trastevere, on the far side of the Tiber. On the **Janiculum**, the hill that dominates Trastevere, **San Pietro in Montorio**, Pza San Pietro in Montorio, is adjacent to Bramante's Tempietto – one of the greatest buildings of the High Renaissance. Below it is the riverside **Villa Farnesina**, Via della Lungara 230, which was decorated in part by Raphael.

The **Spanish Steps** link the Pza di Spagna with the **Pincio** hill and the **Villa Borghese** gardens, which contain the **Villa Giulia Etruscan Museum** (Museo Nazionale Etrusco), Pzale di Villa Giulia 9, and the **Galleria e Museo Borghese**, in Villa Borghese – unmissable if you like Bernini. At the base of the Pincio, **Santa Maria del Popolo** contains important Caravaggio paintings.

TOURS

Sightseeing tours are provided by **ATAC**.
Tickets and information: **ATAC**, Pza dei Cinquecento, CIT,
☎ (06) 4695 2252
and **Ciao Roma**,
☎ (06) 474 3795.

A ride in a *carrozzella* (open carriage) can be fun, but agree a price with the driver beforehand.

DAY TRIPS FROM ROME

The **EUR** complex (monumental architecture of the Fascist era, but also a funfair and a good Museum of Roman Civilisation) is on metro line B, as is **Ostia Antica** (24 km south-west) with the sizeable remains of the ancient Roman port.

Trains from **Termini** run south-east to the **Castelli Romani** (Alban Hills), which include the wine areas of **Frascati** and **Castelli Romani,** and the papal residence of **Castel Gandolfo**. One of the highlights of this area is the little town of **Tivoli**, with the magnificent imperial Roman **Hadrian's Villa** (*Villa Adriano*) and the charmingly eccentric **Villa d'Este**, its garden flowing with fountains.

SHOPPING

Best buys are from the **delicatessens** and **grocery stores** – olive oil, fragrant vinegars, dried *funghi* (mushrooms), packets of dried herbs – in and around Via della Croce and the Campo dei Fiori. In Via del Corso you can buy cheaper versions of the designer clothing, from hats to shoes, on sale in the Via dei Condotti (big names like Gucci and Prada) and its parallel streets, while cheaper still are the clothes stalls of the Porta Portese and Via Sannio markets (Metro: San Giovanni), with their astonishing arrays of second-hand hand-me-downs. Rome has a strong artisan goldsmith and silversmith tradition (Ghetto, Via dei Coronari, Via dell'Orso), and is fairly well served by antiques shops (Via dei Coronari, Via Giulia, Via del Babuino). Take-home items might include terracotta from southern Italy, kitchen equipment made by Alessi, chunks of parmesan or pecorino cheese, ex-reliquaries from the flea market or bottles of heart-stopping grappa from a liquor store.

NIGHT-TIME AND EVENTS

Trovaroma (published with *La Repubblica* on Thurs), *Wanted in Rome* and *Metropolitan* (both published fortnightly in English) are very comprehensive what's on guides, available from newsstands.

Nightlife is limited. Most Italians like nothing better than to while away the evening in a restaurant. However, there are good venues for dancing, vibrant clubs (jazz, salsa, African, Latin) and overflowing, noisy bars. There is also a thriving gay scene.

The summer is Rome's liveliest season for **theatres** and **concerts**, with many performances set beneath the stars, possibly within some ancient ruin or Renaissance garden. As a rule, tickets for these events (apart from opera) cannot be booked in advance. There are also many choral concerts in the churches – watch the billboards outside for details.

WHERE NEXT FROM ROME?

Join the **Rome–Palermo** route (p. 413) or head north on the **Bologna–Rome** route (p. 405), branching off if desired at **Orte** to pick up the **Pisa–Orvieto** route (p. 393). You can also head northwards to **Pisa** to take the **Ventimiglia–Pisa** route (p. 389) in reverse to the French border, from where you can head on through the **French Riviera** (see **Marseille–Menton**, p. 113).

Few places merit the description 'unique', but **Venice** – as romantic a spot for a get-away as anywhere in the world – is definitely one of them. Built on 118 tiny islands, with gondolas and boats providing the only transport, and endowed with a stunning legacy of notable architecture, it formerly commanded an empire stretching from northern Italy to Cyprus. Rising dreamily out of the Lagoon, it looks magnificent at any time of year and at any time of day. No matter that the plasterwork has faded and the paint is peeling off many of the tall terracotta buildings or that the canals can look dark and dirty.

Sadly, Venice is gradually sinking, and no one knows how to solve the problem; in the meantime the mild sense of doom only adds to the poignancy of this marvellous place. As the city is very compact, the highlights can be absorbed in two or three days, though there's enough to fill a lifetime of sightseeing.

As Europe's only roadless city, Venice is a joy to explore, with its great public buildings and magnificent palaces bordering canals, narrow alleys and tiny squares. Much of it exudes a village-like calm once you're away from the main tourist drags, such as the **Rialto**, **St Mark's Square** and the **Accademia**. Prepare yourself for plenty of walking – there are 400 bridges over 177 canals – and expect to get lost fairly often (it must rank among the world's most confusing places; a compass is useful). However, you're never far from the **Grand Canal**, which snakes through the centre.

The best way to sightsee is simply to wander the narrow streets and canalsides at random, popping into churches as you pass and pausing to window-shop or sit at a pavement café whenever the whim takes you.

ARRIVAL AND DEPARTURE

To get to Venice itself, take a train to **Santa Lucia** station as some terminate 10 mins earlier at **Mestre** on the mainland. A frequent local service operates between **Mestre** and **Santa Lucia**. **Santa Lucia** has its own *vaporetto* (waterbus) stop, outside it, at the north-west end of the Grand Canal.

Marco Polo International Airport is 13 km north-east of Venice; **flight information**, (041) 260 9260. **Buses**: ACTV no. 5 and blue ATVO operate half-hourly (hourly in winter) between the airport and Ple Roma. To continue into Venice, transfer onto a **waterbus**. The regular motorboat service of **Alilaguna** operates from the airport (from 0600–2400 year-round) via the Lido to the Pza San Marco in the heart of Venice.

INFORMATION

Tourist Offices: Main Office, Pza San Marco 71, also at Santa Lucia station and, in summer, at Lido di Venezia, Gran Viale 6a. Central: ☎(041) 529 8711, fax (041) 523 0399 (www.turismovenezia.it; apt-06@mail.regione.veneto.it). The free *A Guest in Venice* guide lists what's on. For **youth information**, contact **Assessorato alla Gioventù**, San Marco, ☎(041) 274 7645; the free Mappa Sconti/Discount Guide maps locations of restaurants, hotels, hostels, internet points, cycle hire points etc. Most of these have discounts for holders of **Rolling Venice** rover tickets (ages 14–29 only), which give 72 hours' travel on all ACTV boats and buses; also available from ACTV ticket offices. Even if you don't qualify for a pass it's worth picking up the guide anyway.

MONEY When changing money, always ask for a supply of small denomination notes as every shop and café always seems to be short of change. There are exchange offices throughout the city.

POST AND PHONES **Main post office**: **Poste Centrali**, Rialto, Fontego dei Tedeschi. To phone **Venice from abroad** the code is 00 (011 from US/Canada) + 39 (Italy) + 041 (Venice; include the 0 of the city code); to phone **Venice from elsewhere in Italy**, it is 041.

PUBLIC TRANSPORT

VAPORETTO (WATERBUS) Other cities have the bus, train, tram or metro, but Venice has the *vaporetto*. These sturdy waterbuses, operated by the ACTV transport authority, run at 10–20min intervals in daytime and approximately hourly from midnight to 0600. Lines 1 and 82 run the length of the **Grand Canal**, connecting **Santa Lucia** station to Pza San Marco. Piers bear the line numbers – but make sure you go in the right direction. Lines 41 and 42 are round-the-islands services taking in **Murano**. The youth hostel on the Isola del Giudecca has its own stop on line 82.

A 24-hr *turistiche* (tourist ticket) allows you to use all *vaporetto* routes, and is especially useful if you plan to explore some of the city's outlying islands; **3-day tickets** and **7-day tickets** are also available. A ticket for the Grand Canal lasts 12 hours.

WATER TAXIS These are sleek but expensive.

RADIO TAXIS ☎522 2303.

GONDOLAS The city's 400 gondolas, which can take up to six passengers each, provide a costly, but definitely the most romantic, means of getting around. Rates are fixed. If you decide to treat yourself, go in the evening when the canals are at their most magical. There are 'stands' on several canals.

The cheapest gondola ride in Venice is on the *traghetto* (ferries), which cross the Grand Canal at eight points (signposted **Traghetto**).

ACCOMMODATION

Private bed and breakfast places are now common across the city; ask at tourist offices for details. There are clusters of hotels and pensions near the station: turn left (where you'll find several, including the pension **Alloggi Gerotto**, Cannaregio, Campo S. Geremia 283, ☎(041) 715361, €; and **La Gondola**, Cannaregio, 180, ☎(041) 715206), or cross the bridge and turn right along the water front (the second turn on the left leads to the 1-star **Marin**, S Croce, Calle del Traghetto 670/b, ☎(041) 718022, €€). If you want to be really central, there are some 1-star and 2-star hotels between the Rialto and the Piazza San Marco; or go further east to the **Foresteria Valdese**, Castello, Calle Lunga, S. Maria Formosa 5170, ☎(041) 528 6797, €, which has dormitories as well as doubles. Other reasonably priced hotels include **Al Gambero**, C. dei Fabbri 4687, ☎(041) 522 4384, fax (041) 520 0431, €€, just north of Pza San Marco, and **Hotel Ai Do Mori**, C. Larga San Marco 658, ☎(041) 520 4817, fax (041) 520 5328, €€. **AVA (Venetian Hotel Association)** has **reservation desks** at Santa Lucia station, ☎(041) 715 288, open daily 0800–2200 (Apr–Oct) and 0800–2100 (Nov–Mar), and at Marco Polo International Airport.

The main **youth hostel** is **Albergo per la Gioventù**, on Isola del Giudecca, ☎(041) 523 8211, fax (041) 523 5689 (Vaporetto line 82: Zitelle). Ten minutes from the railway station is **Santa Fosca Hostel** (Fondamenta Canal Diedo, Cannaregio 2372), ☎/fax (041) 715 775. **Azienda Promozione Turistica di Venezia (APT)**, ☎(041) 529 8711, fax (041) 523 0399 (www.turismovenezia.it; apt-06@mail.regione.veneto.it) has a list of hostels.

The nearest **campsites** are on the mainland or on the beach **Litorale del Cavallino**.

FOOD AND DRINK

Like all Italian cities, Venice takes pride in its distinctive regional cuisine which, as you would expect, leans heavily towards seafood. Rice and beans are also staple ingredients of local dishes.

Many of the **restaurants** around touristy areas like Pza San Marco and Rialto charge premium prices, but you only have to stroll a bridge or two away to find quieter streets and more affordable *trattorie* and *pizzerie*. Several atmospheric restaurants of varying price ranges are clustered around the Rialto market area, such as the lively **Osteria Sora al Ponte** (medium prices). For reasonably priced canalside eating try **Pizzeria da Crecola** in Campo S Giacomo dell'Orio.

Bacari, the typically Venetian wine bars, are ideal for budget travellers as they sell plates of pasta or risotto as well as sandwiches. **Cafés** sell delicious slices of pizza and, if you want to save money as well as time, stand at the bar where drinks cost a third as much as at a table. **Bar Foscarini**, Rio Terra Foscari, tucked beside the Grand Canal near the **Accademia** gallery, is well placed for people-watching and for gazing over the water.

ITALY

The city's most atmospheric bar is **Florian**, in one of the arcades around Pza San Marco. It occupies a series of small, beautifully decorated 'drawing rooms', which are still just as they were in the 18th century when Floriano Francesconi opened it. Expect to pay as much for a cappuccino as for a pizza elsewhere, but it's worth it for the surroundings and the opportunity to listen to the orchestra, which strikes up in the square outside in the evenings.

The **Rialto** market is a great place to pick up picnic items.

HIGHLIGHTS

Most of the major sights charge a steep entrance fee, but many of the city's art treasures can be seen for free, adorning church walls and altars.

A *vaporetto* ride along the Grand Canal – sit at the front – is among the greatest sight-seeing journeys in the world. Dodging gondolas, water taxis and delivery boats, it takes you past a succession of grand palaces and churches, and under the decorative white arch of the famous **Rialto** bridge.

PIAZZA SAN MARCO (ST MARK'S SQUARE) This piazza is the hub of the city, close to the mouth of the Grand Canal. Surrounded by arcades of exclusive shops and cafés, the huge square echoes with the chatter and footsteps of crowds of tourists while pigeons flap at their feet. Begin by taking the lift up the **Campanile di San Marco** for a panoramic view of the city and lagoon. The slender red brick tower itself is a 20th-century reconstruction of a 1000-year-old bell-tower that fell down in 1902.

Next to the Campanile di San Marco, the **Museo Correr**, occupying the south side of the square, traces the history of Venice and displays 14th–19th-century paintings.

The **Basilica di San Marco**, consecrated in 1094, was built to house the bones of St Mark the Evangelist. It has five impressive domes, each heavily encrusted with gold mosaics, that recount stories from the New Testament. The floor, too, is elaborately patterned in marble.

Its museum, in the galleries above the church, contains the gilded bronze *Horses of St Mark*, believed to date from the 2nd century and stolen from Byzantium by the Venetians in 1204. Don't miss the panoramic loggia overlooking the square.

Next to the Basilica along the waterfront stands the icing-white **Palazzo Ducale** (Doge's Palace). It contains important Venetian works of art, which provide a glimpse of the lifestyles of the city's former rulers. Stairs from it lead down to the **Ponte dei Sospiri** (Bridge of Sighs), which crosses a narrow canal to the **Palazzo delle Prigioni,** the former prison for petty offenders. Prisoners were led across the bridge – hence the name. However, the best view of it is from another bridge, **Ponte** della Paglia, on the busy promenade between the Lagoon and St Mark's Square.

CANALE GRANDE (GRAND CANAL): EAST BANK Following the canal around from St Mark's, you pass the baroque church of San Moisé and its neighbour Santa Maria del Giglio before coming to the handsome white **Ponte di Rialto** (Rialto Bridge) at the geographic heart of the city. Beyond it, the **Ca'd'Oro**, the most lavish of all Venice's aristocratic palaces, now houses **Galleria Franchetti**, a magnificent collection of paintings (including works by Mantegna and Guardi), Renaissance bronzes and medallions.

CANALE GRANDE: WEST BANK Standing guard at the beginning of the canal's west bank is the domed **Santa Maria della Salute**, the greatest baroque church in Venice. Nearby, the **Palazzo Venier dei Leoni**, the palace that Peggy Guggenheim bought specially in 1949, houses her remarkable cubist, abstract and surrealist collection. Yet another of the city's great art galleries, **Galleria dell'Accademia**, is only a short stroll away; it features works by Venetian artists such as Bellini, Canaletto, Carpaccio, Guardi, Titian, Tintoretto and Veronese, as well as Florentine Renaissance artists such as Piero della Francesca.

A short walk west of the canal, between the Rio della Frescada and the Campo San Polo, the **Scuola di San Rocco** guildhall contains a magnificent collection of Tintoretto's works. Nearby, the huge red-brick Gothic church of **Santa Maria Gloriosa dei Frari** looks almost like a factory from the outside, but contains paintings by Bellini, Donatello and Titian, amongst others. Both Titian and the composer Monteverdi are buried there.

THE ISLANDS

Organised sightseeing tours depart to the outlying **Murano** island and its neighbours, **Burano** and **Torcello**. Murano has glass factories and a fine church, Santissimi Maria e Donato, with Byzantine paving and 13th-century mosaics, while Burano is generally more pleasant, with a lively little fishing community and brightly coloured houses. You can visit these and other islands just as easily – and much more cheaply – on an ordinary *vaporetto* no. 12. The **Lido** is a glamorous (though, it must be admitted, overrated) bathing and sunbathing haunt, made famous during the *belle époque*.

NIGHT-TIME AND EVENTS

The entertainment calendar is busier in summer than winter, with events such as the annual ten-day **Venice Film Festival** (in Sept). **Palazzo Grassi** is the venue for many of the exhibitions that the city stages. The International Art Exhibition, reputedly the largest modern art event in the world is held at the Castello Giardini from June–Oct on even-numbered years.

The city's biggest event is **Carnival**, ten days of masked balls and street celebrations immediately before Lent. **La Vogalonga** ('The Long Row') on Ascension Sunday is a marathon regatta around the Lagoon – any sort of oar-powered craft can take part. Historic **Regata Storica** (first Sun in Sept) begins with a magnificent procession of veteran boats rowed by costumed crews along the Grand Canal. The main venue for opera, **La Fenice**, destroyed by fire in 1996, has not yet been rebuilt. Meanwhile, performances take place in a marquee erected on the parking area of **Tronchetto** island. Numerous concerts are held in the city's churches. The **Palazzo del Cinema** on the Lido is the venue for the annual film festival and shows international films year round. Throughout the city, bars and clubs offer live music and late-night drinking, but the streets are safe for quiet strolls throughout the night and there's no red-light area.

SHOPPING

The Venetians' aptitude for commerce has been sharpened by more than eleven centuries of international trade and 200 years of tourism. The main shopping streets are between Pza San Marco and the **Rialto,** particularly **Mercerie**. However, bargains are thin on the ground. If shopping for clothes, look out for *saldi* (sales) signs and never hesitate to bargain. Manufacturers of the city's famous glass include **Cenedese** and **Salviati**, both of which have shops on Pza San Marco. More affordable, and uniquely Venetian, are the painted papier-maché carnival masks sold in many small stores.

Colourful marbled paper printed from old blocks is the most inexpensive local souvenir. Typical Venetian jewellery is made from thin gold chain called *la manina*, but plenty of imitations are on sale as well as the genuine article, particularly around Pza San Marco. It's worth a trip to the neighbouring islands in the Lagoon, such as Murano where the glass is made. A free demonstration of skilful glass-making in the large furnaces is an interesting way to spend an hour or two; afterwards you're ushered into the showroom, but there's no obligation to buy.

WHERE NEXT FROM VENICE?

*Venice is on the **Milan–Trieste** route (p. 399). Ferries to **Patras** via **Corfu** take 35–38 hrs (ETT table 2875). A scenic route over the Alps into Austria via **Villach** (table 88) joins the **Innsbruck–Vienna** route (p. 349) at **Linz**, or you can change at **Villach** and join the same route further west at **Schwarzach-St Veit** (table 970).*

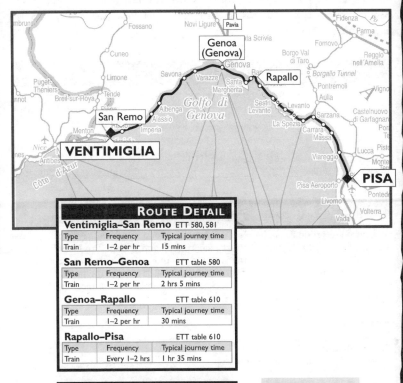

ROUTE DETAIL

Ventimiglia–San Remo ETT 580, 581

Type	Frequency	Typical journey time
Train	1–2 per hr	15 mins

San Remo–Genoa ETT table 580

Type	Frequency	Typical journey time
Train	1–2 per hr	2 hrs 5 mins

Genoa–Rapallo ETT table 610

Type	Frequency	Typical journey time
Train	1–2 per hr	30 mins

Rapallo–Pisa ETT table 610

Type	Frequency	Typical journey time
Train	Every 1–2 hrs	1 hr 35 mins

KEY JOURNEYS

Nice–Genoa ETT tables 360, 580

Type	Frequency	Typical journey time
Train	Every hr	3 hrs 05 mins

Nice–Pisa ETT tables 360, 580, 610

Type	Frequency	Typical journey time
Train	Every 1–2 hrs	5 hrs 30 mins

Notes

For the key journey Nice–Genoa, change at Ventimiglia.
For the key journey Nice–Pisa change at Ventimiglia and Genoa.

ITALY

From the French border (you can join this journey on to the **Marseille–Menton** route, p. 113), the line along the **Italian Riviera** has a wonderful sequence of coastal views. Against mountain backdrops, the vineyards, olive trees and palms flourish in the mild climes that attracted English visitors to the **Liguria** region in the 19th century. **Genoa** is less pretty but has its fascinations, and **Pisa** (see p. 394) is a fine introduction to **Tuscany**.

VENTIMIGLIA

The railway line runs between the town and the beach of this resort, which is situated right on the French/Italian border. It's a rather untidy and traffic-ridden place, but there is a Roman theatre and an attractive, steeply built old town, with a 12th-century cathedral. There is a thriving olive oil industry.

RAIL In the town.

i **Tourist Office:** Via Cavour 61, ☎/fax (0184) 351 183 (www.aptrivieradeifiori.it).

SAN REMO

The prime resort on the Italian Riviera stretches around an 8-km bay. It has a pleasant old town, with its narrow streets, steep steps and arches. The **Nobel Villa**, C. Cavalotti 112, was the house of the Swedish inventor Alfred Nobel, who established the series of international prizes named after him; it is open to the public. Early risers can visit the incredible flower market that takes place every morning June–Oct (0600–0800) in C. Garibaldi.

RAIL In the town.

i **Tourist Office:** Largo Nuvoloni 1, ☎ (0184) 571 571, fax (0184) 507 649 (www.apt.rivieradeifiori.it; aptfiori@sistel.it).

🏠 Modest rooms can be found at **hotels** like the **Morandi**, Corso Matuzia 51, ☎ (0184) 667 641, fax (0184) 666 567 (www.hotelmorandi.com; info.@hotelmorandi.com), and the **Villa Maria**, Corso Nuvoloni 30, ☎ (0184) 531 422, fax (0184) 531 425.

GENOA (GENOVA)

Noisy and sprawling, **Genoa**, 'La Superba', is Italy's foremost seaport and was once, like Venice, a proud maritime republic ruled by a doge or elected ruler. The city's grandeur has faded, but there is an interesting old town, with a maze of tiny alleys and many old palaces and mansions. It is centred on the port, to the south and south-west of the modern city, where stands the **Lanterna** (1544), the nation's oldest lighthouse. Guided tours of the port by boat start from **Ponte Spinola**.

The old part of town is easily explored on foot (during the day: it's not safe at night). Elsewhere, there's a good bus service. There is also a funicular from Pza del Portello to Sant'Anna, high on the hill on which the town is built. There's a great view from the top and the journey is worthwhile in itself.

The **Palazzo Ducale**, Pza Matteotti, was once the seat of the doge. Across the street is the **church of the Gesù,** which contains two Rubens and a Guido Reni. The nearby **Cattedrale di San Lorenzo** houses the **Museo del Tesoro di San Lorenzo**, containing reliquaries such as the plate on which John the Baptist's severed head is reputed to have rested and a dish said to have been used at the Last Supper.

Pza Caricamento, on the waterfront, is always a hive of activity, with market stalls and many cafés. Pza Banchi was the heart of the old city and is now the commercial centre. To the north is Via Garibaldi, home to several Renaissance palaces. Two of these, **Palazzo Bianco** (no. 11) and **Palazzo Rosso** (no. 18), are now galleries with excellent collections, including Flemish and Dutch masterpieces. Both palaces are worth a visit to see the incredible décor.

If you fancy a swim, the suburb of **Albaro** (🚌no. 41 from **Principe**) has a beach with showers.

Genoa's **Aquarium**, Porto Antico, is the largest in Europe and is truly mesmerising – the harbour seals are adorable. **Nervi**, a few stops along the line from **Brignole** station, has a beautiful promenade and a dramatic coastline.

🚆 There are two main stations. **Piazza Principe**; take 🚌no. 41 from here to get to the city centre. **Stazione Brignole** is further east; take 🚌no. 40 from here to get to the city centre. Trains to the north use both stations; use 🚌no. 37 to transfer between them.

ℹ️ **Tourist Offices: City centre**, Porto Antico, ☎(010) 248 711, fax (010) 246 76 58 (www.apt.genova.it). There are also offices at **Stazione FS Principe**, Pza Acquaverde, and at **Aeroporto**, C. Colombo-Sestri Ponente.

Special combined tickets are on sale at ticket offices to visit two of the civic museums/palazzi of your choice and two of the galleries. Automatic kiosks sell tickets giving unlimited bus travel for a day.

🛏️ Cheap accommodation is easy to find, but some of it is very tacky. Try the roads on the outskirts of the old town and (near **Brignole**) Via XX Settembre and Pza Colombo. **Youth hostel**: Via Costanzi, ☎(010) 242 24 57 (hostelge@iol.it), 🚌no. 40 from Brignole; it has (deservedly) been voted one of the top ten hostels in the world.

🍽️ The cheapest eating places for lunch are in the dock area, but most close in the evening. Street stalls all over the city sell fried seafood and chickpea pancakes.

SIDE TRIP TO PAVIA   **Pavia**, north of **Genoa** on the line to **Milan**, is reached by train in about 1 hr 15 mins (hourly; ETT table 610; station 10-min walk from centre, or take 🚌 nos. 3/6). It's a quietly attractive old town, known for its medieval towers, churches and peaceful squares. The pick of the churches is the 12th-century Romanesque **church of San Michele**, Via Cavallotti, with a yellow sandstone façade and friezes depicting mythical creatures that symbolise the struggle between good and evil. The huge 14th-century **Castello Visconteo** (Castle of the Visconti), Strada Nuova, houses the **Museo Civico**, which contains an absorbing archaeological section and some Venetian paintings. The highlight of the area and one of the great buildings of Italy is the **Certosa di Pavia**, a Carthusian monastery, 8 km north of town. It has an incredible façade, including Carrara marble transported from 250 km away. Cistercian monks now live there and maintain a vow of silence. The interior of the church is Gothic, as elaborately decorated as the flamboyant exterior. The rest of the monastery can be seen by joining a guided tour. Buses from Pavia are frequent (from Pza Piave), then there's a 1.5-km walk to the entrance. **Tourist Office**: Via Fabio Filzi 2, ☎(0382) 22 156, fax (0382) 32 221 (www.apt.pavia.it); near station. There's a shortage of budget accommodation. Try the **Hotel Aurora**, Via Vittorio Emanuele II 25, ☎(0382) 23 664. **Camping** (May–Sept): **Ticino**, Via Mascherpa 10, ☎(0382) 527 094 (camping.ticino@libero.it); 🚌 no. 4.

PISA

See p. 394.

RAPALLO

A once-beautiful resort haunted by writers, **Rapallo** is now hectically chic and expensive, with a large marina, but there is an attractive old area with cobbled streets and a castle. Menus offering fresh fish are everywhere. Walkers can enjoy the scenery by following footpaths up to the hill village of **Montallegro** (600 m above sea-level), with its 16th-century **Santuario**, a religious foundation, while the less energetic can ride the cablecar up from Via Castagneto.

🚉 Near the old town.

ℹ️ **Tourist Office**:V. Diaz 9, ☎(0185) 230 346, fax (0185) 63 051.

WHERE NEXT FROM PISA?

Either venture into **Tuscany** *on the* **Pisa–Orvieto** *route (p. 393) or carry on along the coast to* **Rome** *(p. 377) – see ETT table 610.*

On the way to Rome you can visit the island of **Elba**; *change at* **Campiglia** *for* **Piombino** *(table 609), then take the 25-min ferry crossing to* **Elba** *(table 2699).* **Elba** *has clear waters, fine beaches and a ragged coastline of capes and bays, though in summer it gets impossibly tourist-ridden; there are paths and attractive villages to explore, plus Napoleon's villa and a cable car up to a 1019-m summit.* **Buses** *serve the island's villages and resorts.* **Accommodation** *is plentiful (with lots of campsites), but it gets heavily booked in July and Aug; contact the* **Tourist Office** *at Calata Italia 26, Portoferraio (in the dilapidated ten-storey block near the ferry port),* ☎*(0565) 914671 (www.aptelba.it).*

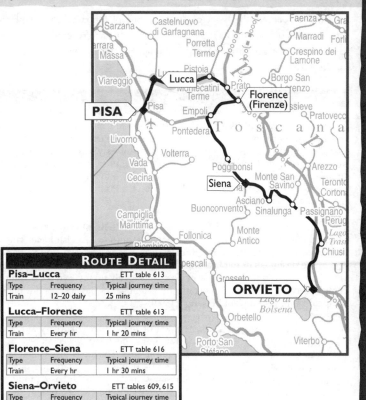

ROUTE DETAIL		
Pisa–Lucca		ETT table 613
Type	Frequency	Typical journey time
Train	12–20 daily	25 mins
Lucca–Florence		ETT table 613
Type	Frequency	Typical journey time
Train	Every hr	1 hr 20 mins
Florence–Siena		ETT table 616
Type	Frequency	Typical journey time
Train	Every hr	1 hr 30 mins
Siena–Orvieto		ETT tables 609, 615
Type	Frequency	Typical journey time
Train	Every 2 hrs	2 hrs 5 mins

KEY JOURNEYS		
Pisa–Florence		ETT table 614
(via Empoli)		
Type	Frequency	Typical journey time
Train	2 per hr	1 hr 17 mins
Pisa–Florence		ETT table 613
(via Lucca)		
Type	Frequency	Typical journey time
Train	4 per day	1 hr 40 mins
Florence–Rome		ETT table 620
(by Eurostar Italia)		
Type	Frequency	Typical journey time
Train	1–2 per hr	1 hr 35 mins

Notes

Pisa to Orvieto: change at Florence.

Siena to Orvieto: change at Chiusi.

ITALY

This trip encounters the heart of **Tuscany**, one of the culturally richest and most unspoilt parts of Italy, with its green hills striped with olive groves and vineyards, as well as historic towns and cities boasting astonishingly rich legacies of Renaissance art and architecture.

PISA

The **Leaning Tower of Pisa** rates among the world's most familiar landmarks, part of a magnificent triumvirate of buildings around the **Campo dei Miracoli** (Field of Miracles), by the Cathedral and Baptistry. Some of Italy's finest medieval sculptures are here, many by Nicola and Giovanni Pisano (father and son) and other Pisano (unrelated). The unusual architecture, characterised by distinctive stripes of marble and blind arcades, is thought to emanate from the Pisans' contact with the Moslems of North Africa and Spain.

The 11th-century, four-tiered **Duomo**, one of Italy's finest cathedrals, was the first Tuscan building to use marble in horizontal stripes (a Moorish idea). The original bronze entrance, **Portale di San Ranieri**, was cast around 1180 and is by Bonanno, one of the designers of the Leaning Tower itself. A fire destroyed much of the interior in the 16th century, but some of Cosmati's lovely floor survived, as did the 14th-century mosaic of Christ Pantocrator by Cimabue, in the apse, and a magnificent sculpted pulpit by Giovanni Pisano (c1300).

Construction of the circular **Baptistry** stopped when money ran out. The three lower storeys consist of Romanesque arcades. The top half, in Gothic style, with pinnacles and a dome, was added later (again by the prolific Pisanos, in the 1260s). It has a pulpit superbly carved by Nicola Pisano, whose design produced a whole series of similar pulpits during this period.

The **Leaning Tower** (Torre Pendente) began life in 1173, as a campanile for the Duomo. When it was 10 m high it began to tilt and the architect fled. Construction continued, however, with successive architects trying unsuccessfully to restore the balance.

A special 1-week ticket covers entry to the major museums and monuments in Pisa.

Centrale, south of the River Arno and 20 mins' walk from the Leaning Tower, or **CPT** nos.1/3.

Pisa's **Galileo Galilei Airport** is the main regional hub for international flights, ☎(050) 500 707. Frequent buses run to the city centre and rail station.

Tourist Offices: Via Carlo Cammeo 2, ☎(050) 560 464 (www.turismo.pisa.it), and Pza Stazione, ☎(050) 42 291. Free booking service, ☎(050) 830 253.

There are several good budget hotels around Campo dei Miracoli, but they are popular and in term time students fill the best. **Hostel**: **Centro Turistico Madonna dell'Acqua**, Via Pietrasantina 15, ☎(050) 890 622, ☐no. 3. **Campsite**: **Campeggio Torre Pendente**, Viale Cascine 86, ☎(050) 561 704, fax (055) 561 734, 1 km west of the Leaning Tower, signposted from Pza Manin.

Day Trip from Pisa

Certosa di Pisa, 12 km to the east and served by regular CPT buses, is an enormous 14th-century Carthusian monastery with a frescoed church where all 11 chapels are painted in pastel colours. Each three-room cell has its own little patch of garden.

LUCCA

Despite its considerable beauty, **Lucca** never feels overrun with tourists, and bicycles are more in evidence than cars. The tranquil streets are dotted with palaces, towers and handsome early churches, most of them dating from the city's heyday (11th–14th centuries). Start with a stroll around part of the 4 km of ancient walls – the most complete in Italy – that enclose the old city and are themselves encircled by a green belt, a buffer between the medieval and modern towns. Some bastions have been restored and you can get a good idea of the town's original layout.

The Romanesque **Duomo di San Martino**, in the south of the centre, has individually designed columns and loggias: look out for an exquisite early 15th-century **Tomb of Ilaria del Carretto** (by Jacopo della Quercia) and Tintoretto's *Last Supper*.

The central **church of San Michele** is in Foro, which takes its name from its position in the midst of what was once the ancient Roman forum. The church has a multi-tiered façade of striped marble loggias with a diversity of supporting pillars, either inlaid with mosaic or carved and twisted, and, at the top, a huge bronze of Archangel Michael. Funds ran out before the interior could be completed.

Near the western city wall is the **Pinacoteca Nazionale**, housed in **Palazzo Mansi**, Via Galli Tassi 43. The 17th-century palace is of rather more interest than the pictures it displays, and the overdecorated interior includes a particularly spectacular gilded bridal suite.

Further south-east is **Palazzo Guinigi**, Via Sant' Andrea, a rambling complex of interconnected

LUCCA'S AMPHITHEATRE
The Pza Anfiteatro is an oval of medieval tenements clustered round the site of a Roman amphitheatre. Parts of the original arches and columns are visible in the buildings themselves, and the shape of the oval is effectively a fossilisation of the theatre.

ITALY

medieval buildings. A climb of 230 steps leads up a turreted tower with an oak sprouting from the top, giving a fascinating view over the city's rooftops.

The city's main museum, **Museo Nazionale Guinigi**, east of the centre on Via della Quarquonia, contains a huge and varied collection of local Romanesque and Renaissance art.

🚊 Just outside the city walls, an easy walk to the centre. There are frequent trains from **Pisa** (25 mins), **Viareggio** (20 mins) and **Florence** (1 hr 20 mins).

ℹ️ **Tourist Office:** Vecchia Porta San Donato, Piazzale Verdi, 📞 (0583) 491 206, fax (0583) 469 964 (www.lucca.turismo.toscana.it; influcca@lucca@lucca.turismo.toscana.it).

🏠 Finding space is always a problem, so book ahead. An accommodation service for 35 hotels in Lucca and environs is provided by **Hotel Reservation**, 📞 (0583) 312 262. **Youth hostel:** Via del Brennero 673, 📞 (0583) 341 811. Open Mar–Oct. **Camping** is possible behind the hostel.

FLORENCE (FIRENZE)

See p. 360.

SIENA

Spread over low hills and filled with robust terracotta-coloured buildings, **Siena** is not much changed since medieval times. Indeed, this most beautiful of Tuscan cities has contracted inside its walls in places – look out from just behind the **Campo**, the main square, and there's a vista down a green, rural valley, as pretty as a wine label. The city was Florence's most tireless enemy for much of the Middle Ages, competing with it for supremacy politically, economically and artistically. Now it's a delightful place to visit, for its artistic treasures as well as just for the pleasures of discovering its myriad sloping alleys.

The fan-shaped Campo dates from 1347 and is regarded as the focus of the city's life. The arcaded and turreted **Palazzo Pubblico**, on the south side, still performs its traditional role as the town hall, and its bell-tower, the 102-m **Torre del Mangia**, soars above the town. The views from the top are dizzying in the extreme. Part of the **Palazzo Pubblico** houses the **Museo Civico**, whose Sala della Pace and Sala del Mappamondo contain treasures of Lorenzetti and Martini amongst others.

To the west stands the **cathedral**, its striped marble exterior featuring notable Renaissance sculpture by masters. Inside, the floor comprises 56 separate sections, on which over 40 artists worked for nearly two centuries, including an elaborate pulpit by Nicola Pisano and a notable Donatello bronze. The **Museo dell'Opera del Duomo** contains many Sienese masterpieces of painting and sculpture.

Terzo di Città (south-west of the Campo), has some of the city's finest private palaces, such as the **Palazzo Chigi-Saracini**, Via di Città 82.

SAN GIMIGNANO

San Gimignano (32 km north-west, half-hourly buses from Siena, via Poggibonsi) is a typical medieval hill town, which originally sported 70 towers, partly defensive and partly status symbols, of which 14 survive. Pza del Duomo has some of the finest medieval buildings, while the frescos by Gozzoli in the **church of Sant'Agostino** and the four fresco cycles in the **Collegiata** (cathedral) stand out among the town's notable art heritage. The **Tourist Office** is on the main square.

In the past, the city was divided into 60 *contrade* (wards named after animals), of which 17 remain, each with its own church, museum and central square with a fountain featuring the relevant animal. Rivalry between wards is strong, reaching a head in the famous twice-yearly **Palio**, a no-holds-barred horse race around the Campo (which is regarded as neutral territory) on 2 July and 16 Aug. Only ten horses can participate, so lots are drawn to decide which wards will be represented; the whole event is regarded as a matter of honour by the locals, with rehearsals for days beforehand and excitement mounting to fever pitch. Races last only 70 seconds or so, but are preceded by a two-hour procession. Get there early if you want to watch – standing in the centre is free, if crowded.

🚉 2 km north-east (in valley below town). It is a tedious 45-min walk uphill to the centre, but there are regular shuttle buses (tickets from machine by entrance).

🚌 **Long-distance buses** (covering all Tuscany), run by **Sena**, **Lazzi** and **Train**, leave from Pza Gramsci bus station.

Tourist Office: Pza del Campo 56, ☎ (0577) 280 551, fax (0577) 270 676 (www.siena.turismo.toscana.it; aptsiena@siena.turismo.toscana.it). This office has good maps and the useful booklet *Tourist Information*. There are also booths in the train and bus stations.

Private rooms are best value, but you often have to stay at least a week and they can be full of students in term time. The relatively few hotels are often full. For the **Palio** (early July and mid-Aug), either book well ahead or stay up all night (many do). At other times, if the Tourist Office can't help, try the **Cooperativa Siena Hotels** promotion booth opposite **San Domenico**, Pza San Domenico, ☎ (0577) 288 084. One of the cheapest hotels is **Tre Donzelle**, Via delle Donzelle 5, ☎ (0577) 280 358, fax (0577) 223 933. **Youth hostel**: Via Florentina 89, ☎ (0577) 52 212, 2 km north-west of centre (🚌 nos. 15/35/36/4/10). **Campsite: Campeggio Colleverde**, Strada di Scacciapensieri 47, ☎ (0577) 280 044, fax (0577) 333 298, 2 km north (🚌 nos. 8/3, both from Piazzade/Sale).

ORVIETO

Orvieto's setting on a raised plateau of volcanic tufa makes a striking impact amid a valley of vines. Dominating the town is the vividly striped **Duomo**, Pza Duomo, built in honour of a 13th-century miracle. With its triple-gabled exterior of gilded mosaics, bronze doors and bas-reliefs by Lorenzo Maitani, as well as its outstanding interior frescos by Luca Signorelli depicting the *Last Judgement* (in the **Cappella di San Brizio** in the right transept), it is one of the great churches of Umbria. Several grand buildings near the Duomo now contain museums.

The **Pozzo di San Patrizio**, Pza Cahen, near the funicular terminal, is an astonishing cylindrical well with a diameter of 13 m and a depth of 62 m. A double-helix mule-ramp runs around the interior. The well was completed in 1537 to provide an emergency water supply for the city.

COMBINED ENTRY TICKETS IN ORVIETO
A combined ticket, the **Carta Orvieto Unica**, allows access to four sights: the **Cappella di San Brizio**, the **Museo Claudio Faina**, Orvieto Underground and the **Torre del Moro** (a clock tower on Corso Cavour). It can be bought at any of the sights, or at the Tourist Office. Another cumulative ticket includes entrance to the **Pozzo di San Patrizio** and the **Museo Greco**.

By the bus station and connected by funicular to Pza Cahen in the old town (takes 2 mins; every 15 mins weekdays 0715–1230, Sun and public holidays 0800–2030), from where you can then walk or take any of the frequent buses (Line A or B) to the centre.

⌐i⌐ **Tourist Office**: Pza Duomo 24, ☎(0763) 341 772 or 341 911, fax (0763) 344 433 (www.umbria2000.it). Local bus tickets and the combined sightseeing ticket, **Orvieto Unica**, can be purchased here. Pick up the current version of *Welcome to Orvieto* for useful listings. The Tourist Information Point on Via Duomo is privately run and charges for most of its services.

If you want to experience the atmosphere of Orvieto at night, the best located central hotels (both inexpensive) are **Virgilio**, Pza del Duomo 5, ☎(0763) 341 882 (only a few rooms have views), or **Duomo**, Via Maurizio 7, ☎(0763) 341 887. The **Maitani**, V. Maitani 5, ☎(0763) 342 011, offers more luxury in a 17th-century palace with a garden.

Orvieto is famous for its wines: best known are the crisp fruity whites made from Trebbiano grapes, but reds and sweet wines are also produced. *Orvieto Classico* wines come from a specific area immediately around the city. They are fermented and stored in the underground passages and caves that honeycomb the soft local tufa, and are widely on sale throughout the region, many under the Cardeto label (the largest Umbrian wine cooperative). Bars and *enotecas* offer a chance to taste before you buy. **La Bottega del Buon Vino**, Via della Vaca 26, is an atmospheric place with good prices. Orvieto is full of good eating places, though prices are on the high side. There are picnic facilities in the **Parco delle Grotte** near the Pza Duomo; the public gardens of the **Rocca**, near the funicular terminal, can be enjoyed free, and have fine views over the **Paglia Valley**.

WHERE NEXT FROM ORVIETO?

Carry on to **Rome** *(p. 377); this route goes via* **Orte**, *where you can change for trains to* **Spoleto**. *See ETT tables 615 and 625.*

ROUTE DETAIL

Milano (Centrale)**–Verona**   ETT table 600

Type	Frequency	Typical journey time
Train	1–2 per hr	1 hr 26 mins

Verona–Vicenza   ETT table 600

Type	Frequency	Typical journey time
Train	1–2 per hr	30 mins

Vicenza–Padua   ETT table 600

Type	Frequency	Typical journey time
Train	1–2 per hr	22 mins

Padua–Venice (Sta Lucia)   ETT table 600

Type	Frequency	Typical journey time
Train	1–2 per hr	30 mins

Venice (Sta Lucia)**–Trieste**   ETT table 605

Type	Frequency	Typical journey time
Train	Every hr	2 hrs

Note

A change of train is
required at Venezia Mestre.

KEY JOURNEYS

Milan–Venice   ETT table 600

Type	Frequency	Typical journey time
Train	1–2 per hr	2 hrs 52 mins

Venice–Ljubljana   ETT table 89b

Type	Frequency	Typical journey time
Train	3 per day	5 hrs 26 mins

Venice–Zagreb   ETT table 89b

Type	Frequency	Typical journey time
Train	3 per day	8 hrs 20 mins

ITALY

The places rather than the views are of primary interest on this trip from **Lombardy**, Italy's busiest and most prosperous region, to **Trieste** in the east, with the foothills of the **Alps** to the north. **Verona** and **Venice** are among Europe's most romantic cities.

MILAN (MILANO)

See p. 365.

VERONA

ARENA TICKET OFFICE
☎ (045) 800 5151
(www.arena.it for on-line information and booking).
The cheap seats are unreserved and you sit on the stone terraces; bring or hire a cushion, and take along plenty of liquids.

Placed on an S-bend of the river **Adige** and best explored on foot, this beautiful city of pastel-pink marble thrives on the story of *Romeo and Juliet* (see below), but the real attractions are its elegant medieval squares, fine Gothic churches and massive Roman amphitheatre, the **Arena**, which comes alive during the annual opera festival in July and Aug. Dominating the large Pza Bra, it has 44 pink marble tiers that can accommodate 20,000 people – incredibly, the singers and orchestra are perfectly audible. Out of concert times, you can explore the arena by yourself for a small fee and imagine the feeling the gladiators must have had while waiting in the entrance tunnels.

Via Mazzini, which leads off Pza Bra, is one of Italy's smartest shopping streets. This leads to Pza delle Erbe, which is surrounded by Renaissance palaces, their burnt-orange façades now rather worn. Originally the Roman forum, the square is now covered each day by market stalls under giant white umbrellas. An archway leads to a much serener square, Pza dei Signori, centre of medieval civic life. Among its treasures is the graceful 15th-century **Loggia del Consiglio** and the **Palazzo del Capitano**, which has a crenellated tower. Be sure to pause for coffee at the **Dante**, the most celebrated café in town.

The ornate Gothic tombs of the Scaligeri family are in the grounds of the small Romanesque **church of Santa Maria Antica**. The Scaligeris ruled Verona when the city was at its peak in the 13th century and commissioned many of its finest buildings. An equestrian statue that once topped one of them stands outside their castle beside the river, now the **Castelvecchio Museum**, which displays weapons, jewellery and religious

ROMEO AND JULIET IN VERONA
A delicate bronze statue of Juliet stands in the small cobbled courtyard beneath the famous balcony of her supposed house, Via Cappelio. This restored 13th-century building was once an inn but the balcony was not added until 1935. The Montagues and Capulets on whom Shakespeare's play was based were real Veronese families. But the house is all a bit bogus, and you may be content just to poke your head into the courtyard and skip the tour. Romeo is said to have lived around the corner at Via Arche Scaligere 4 and Juliet's tomb to be in the crypt of a pretty Romanesque cloister, now the Museo degli Affreschi, off Via del Pontiere, a 10-min walk south.

paintings. Beyond it, **San Zeno Maggiore**, a superb Romanesque church, has a notable Madonna altarpiece by Mantegna and magnificent 11th–12th-century bronze doors.

Verona's striped red and white marble **cathedral**, Pza Duomo, is a blend of Romanesque and Gothic. Among its treasures is Titian's *Assumption*. Across the river, there are good views from the terraces of another Roman theatre on a wooded hillside.

Apart from the amphitheatre, the city has numerous other Roman remains, including the excavated **Porta Leona** and the exquisitely carved **Porta Borsari**, each a short walk from **Piazza Erbe** (itself the former Roman forum, or main square). Go across the river, over the partly Roman **Ponte Pietra**, Verona's best-known bridge. On the opposite bank are the appreciable remains of the **Roman theatre** (where plays were performed – as opposed to the amphitheatre, which was for coarser public entertainments); although smaller than the amphitheatre, there's rather more to see here, as entrance includes admission to the **Archaeological Museum**, housed in an atmospheric old convent placed on a cliff-like site just above the theatre itself, and there are great views of the city as well as collections of Roman statuary and bronze figurines. Part of the museum is off an exquisite palm-shaded cloister.

WHERE NEXT FROM VERONA?

Venture north into the Dolomites from Bolzano, or head via Innsbruck to Munich; see Munich–Verona, p. 306. Services (ETT table 595; 1 hr 30 mins) to Bologna link with the Bologna–Rome route (p. 405) via Florence, where you can join the Pisa–Orvieto route (p. 393).

The **Verona Card** is a 3-day combined sightseeing/travel card valid for public transport and entry to the major sights in Verona. Available at ticket offices.

Stazione Porta Nuova, 15–20-min walk south of the centre (🚌 nos. 11/12/13/14 from stop A). Bike hire available.

i **Tourist Offices:** Via Degli Alpini 9; ☎ (045) 806 8680, fax (045) 800 3638 (www.tourism.verona.it). Also at the station.

🏨 One of the best-value cheap options for centrally located hotels is **Locanda Catullo**, Via Valerio Catullo 1, ☎ (045) 8002786, fax (045) 596987 (locandacatullo@tiscalinet.it), €–€€, graciously old-fashioned but clean and friendly. A bit more expensive but also central are the 2-star **Sanmicheli**, Via Valverde 2, ☎ (045) 8003479, fax (045) 8004508, €€ (south-west of Piazza Bra, on the way to the station) and (a bit further east) **Armando**, Via Dietro Pallone 1, ☎ (045) 8000206, fax (045) 8036015, €€. There is plenty of **budget** student accommodation (booking essential for the opera season, July–Aug). **Youth hostel: Della Gioventù**, Salita Fontana del Ferro 15, ☎ (045) 590 360, 3 km from the station, 🚌 no. 73 (🚌 no. 90 on Sun) to Pza Isolo, from which the hostel is a short walk; camping in the grounds. **Campsite:** Castel San Pietro 2, ☎/fax (045) 592 037, open mid-June–mid-Sept, walkable from the centre (🚌 no. 41).

🍴 For reasonably priced **restaurants**, look around Pza delle Erbe or the Veronetta district on the east bank of the Adige. The Pza delle Erbe's **food market** is useful.

VICENZA

This prosperous city was largely rebuilt in the 16th century to designs by Andrea di Pietro della Gondola, better known as Palladio, who moved here from Padua at the age of 16 to become an apprentice stonemason. He gave his name to the Palladian style of architecture, which applied elegant Romanesque concepts to classical forms. His first public commission was the imposing Basilica, on Pza dei Signori, hub of the city. This medieval palace was in danger of collapsing until he shored it up brilliantly with Ionic and Doric columns.

Corso Palladio, the long, straight, main street, is lined with palaces. The **Teatro Olimpico** at the eastern end was Palladio's last work. Based on the design of ancient Roman theatres and opened in 1585, it is the oldest indoor theatre in Europe and still in use from May to early July, and from Sept to early Oct. The acoustics are superb. **Palazzo Chiericati**, Pza Matteotti, houses the well-stocked **Museo Civico**, which contains paintings by such masters as Tintoretto and Memling.

Palladio's most famous villa, **La Rotonda**, is on a hillside about 1.5 km south-east of the centre (🚌 nos. 8/13). It has a round interior under a dome set in a cube of classical porticoes, a design often copied. Nearby is the **Villa Valmarana**, an 18th-century country house notable for its Tiepolo frescos and dwarfs on the garden wall.

RAIL 10-min walk south of the centre (🚌 nos. 1/7).

i **Tourist Office**: Pza Matteotti 12, ☎ (0444) 320 854, fax (0444) 327 072 (www.ascom.veneziaimola.it/aptvicenza); branch at rail station. The **Vicenza Card** (available from Teatro Olimpico's ticket office) gives free admission to the city's main museums and monuments for a month.

🛏 The cheapest **hotels** are away from the centre or in noisy locations, so it's worth considering two-star places like **Hotel Vicenza**, Strada dei Nodari 5–7, ☎/fax (0444) 321 5121. Book ahead for summer and autumn. **Campsite**: **Campeggio Vicenza**, Strada Pelosa 241, ☎ (0444) 582 311 (20 mins by 🚌 no. 1 to Torri di Quartesolo from the station).

TO For eating out, look around Pza dei Signori.

PADUA (PADOVA)

Home of one of Europe's oldest universities, **Padua** is a busy, down-to-earth town with plenty of shops and several large daily markets, while an abundance of artistic treasures fill its churches and museums. Though the northern parts are modern, following World War II destruction, the old town has attractive arcaded streets and squares, now traffic-free. South of the centre is Prato della Valle, the largest square in Italy. A market is held there on Sat.

In the **University**, Via VIII Febbraio, founded in 1222, you can see the wooden desk used by Galileo, who taught natural philosophy here, and visit the old anatomical theatre.

One work of art alone is reason enough to visit Padua – the glorious depiction of the lives of Mary and Jesus in the **Cappella degli Scrovegni** (Scrovegni Chapel), Corso Garibaldi. This Giotto masterpiece, which took three years to complete, has 38 panels in three tiers and is in virtually perfect condition.

Padua's other major attraction is **Il Santo** – the **Basilica di Sant'Antonio** – Pza del Santo, which is visited by some 5 million pilgrims each year, St Anthony being one of Italy's best loved saints. The building is a mixture of styles (with a distinctly oriental flavour). The chapel contains 16th-century panels about the saint's life, but more notable are Donatello's bronze sculptures on the high altar and marble reliefs by Lombardo. Donatello's superb monument to Gattamelata, a famous medieval *condottiere*, or mercenary leader, is the central point of the square outside, and was the first major bronze of the Renaissance.

The **Oratorio di San Giorgio** is home to some fine frescos, while the works in the nearby 15th-century **Scuola del Santo** include early Titians. Just to the south is the **Orto Botanico** (Botanic Garden). Established in 1545, it was originally the university's herb garden and has changed little since. Pza dei Signori has some attractive 15th–16th-century buildings, while to the south an unexciting cathedral adjoins the Romanesque Baptistery, which is lined with lovely14th-century frescos.

At the northern edge of town, 15-min walk to centre or 🚌 nos. 3/8/12/18.

i **Tourist Office (APT)**: Stazione Ferroviaria (in the station), ☎ (049) 875 2077, fax (049) 875 5008 (www.padovanet.it; apt@padovanet.it). Another **branch**: Piazza del Santo, ☎ (049) 875 3087. *Padova Today* is a monthly mini-guide to what's on.

There is a wide choice of places to stay (try around Pza del Santo), though booking is advisable. Three-star **Hotel Al Cason**, Via Fra Paolo Scarpi 40, ☎ (049) 662 636, is handy for the station. **Youth hostel**: **Centro Ospitalita**, CittÀ di Padova, Via Aleardi 30, ☎ (049) 875 2219, fax (049) 654 210 (www.ctgveneto.it); 🚌 nos. 3/8/12/18. **Campsite**: **Montegrotto Terme**, Strada Romana Apponese, ☎ (049) 793 400 (15 mins by train, then 1-km walk); it has a pool and thermal baths.

You should find a reasonably priced *trattoria* around Pza del Santo, where the local specialities include *piperata* (mutton in wine sauce). Don't miss **Caffè Pedrocchi**, Pza Cavour, one of Italy's most famous cafés, where writers and artists used to meet during the 19th century, when it stayed open all night. A grand staircase leads to a series of fabulous rooms where you can sip your cappuccino.

VENICE (VENEZIA)

See p. 383.

TRIESTE

This city, on the border with Slovenia, once the chief port of the Austro-Hungarian Empire (up to 1918), is also the **Istrian** hinterland's window on the western world. Rebuilt in the 19th century, it is today a stately, solid place that relishes its role as a crossroads between East and West.

At Trieste's heart, the Borgo Teresiano is a stately grid of regular streets that identify this city more with its central European counterparts than with anything Italian. Here, the Corso Cavour straddles the **Canal Grande**, an urban waterway where boats are moored. Beside it, in Pza Ponterosso, is the daily market. Trieste's civic heart lies in Pza dell'Unita d'Italia: you can't miss the vast **Palazzo del Comune del Governo** beside it, aglow with its mosaic ornamentation. Also in the piazza is one of Trieste's oldest cafés, the **Caffè degli Specchi** (1839). There is another, **Caffè San Marco**, on the other side of town, at Via Cesare Battisti 18.

The **Capitoline hill** formed the heart of Roman and medieval Trieste, and it is here that its oldest surviving buildings are to be found. Apart from the surviving remains of the ancient **Forum** (ancient Trieste was called Tergeste), there is the 11th-century Cathedral of San Giusto (beside the Forum), founded in the 5th century on the site of a Roman temple; there are splendid early medieval mosaics and frescos. Still on the Capitoline, the 15th-century Venetian-built **Castello** houses the Museo Civico in which can be seen a collection of weaponry and armour. Still close to the cathedral, the Museo di Storia ed Arte houses important Roman artefacts, as does the Orto Lapidario. In V. Teatro Romano are the ruins of a Roman theatre.

🚆 **Stazione Centrale**, Pza della Libertà 8.

ℹ️ **Tourist Offices**: the central office is at Via San Nicolò 20, ☎ (040) 3478 312, fax (040) 3478 320 (www.triestetourism.it; apt@iol.it), and there is a second, smaller one in the station. The regional information office is at Via Rossini 6, ☎ (040) 363 952.

🏠 Accommodation is not a problem. **Pensione Centro**, Via Roma 13, ☎ (040) 634 408, is reasonable and central. **Hostel**: Ostello Tergeste, Viale Miramare 331, ☎/fax (040) 224 102, is 5 km from train and bus stations, take 🚌 no. 36.
Campsite: **Obelisco**, Strada Nuova per Opiciana 47, Villa Opiciana, is the nearest, take tram no. 2 or 🚌 no. 4 from Pza Oberdan.

'T FOR YOU' CARD

This card, available from hotels, gives considerable discounts in Trieste hotels, restaurants and some shops. Two-night weekend stay required. Ask for it when booking.

WHERE NEXT FROM TRIESTE?

Continue over the border into Slovenia to the caves at **Postojna**, and to **Llubljana**; see the **Llubljana–Dubrovnik** route p. 426.

ROUTE DETAIL

Bologna–Florence		ETT table 620
Type	Frequency	Typical journey time
Train	1–3 each hr	1 hr

Florence–Arezzo		ETT tables 615, 620
Type	Frequency	Typical journey time
Train	Every hr	38 mins

Arezzo–Perugia		ETT table 615
Type	Frequency	Typical journey time
Train	Every 2 hrs	1 hr

Perugia–Assisi		ETT table 615
Type	Frequency	Typical journey time
Train	Every hr	20 mins

Assisi–Spoleto		ETT table 625
Type	Frequency	Typical journey time
Train	Every hr	37 mins

Spoleto–Rome		ETT table 625
Type	Frequency	Typical journey time
Train	Every hr	1 hr 45 mins

KEY JOURNEYS

Florence–Rome		ETT tables 615, 620
(by Eurostar Italia)		
Type	Frequency	Typical journey time
Train	2–3 per hr	1 hr 35 mins

ITALY

From the graceful old university town of **Bologna** at the threshold of the **Apennines**, you venture into **Umbria**, with its ancient hilltop towns – the garden of Eden to Dante. Art and history are intermingled in such places as the great pilgrimage city of **Assisi**, the Umbrian capital of **Perugia** and the old Roman town of **Spoleto**. **Florence** and **Rome** demand at least a few days each.

BOLOGNA

The capital of Emilia-Romagna, Bologna is home to Europe's oldest university, founded in 1088. It has all you'd expect of a civilised, affluent university seat: the streetscape has real dignity in its arcades, red- and ochre-coloured buildings, stucco façades, greatly varied porticoes, church spires, palaces and medieval towers, the latter built as status symbols by the city's wealthy nobles.

The university's first permanent home is today in **Palazzo Poggi**, Via Zamboni. The two adjoining 13th-century squares, Pza Maggiore and Pza Nettuno, make the obvious central starting point. Around them lie the **Palazzo Comunale** (the town hall, which now houses Bologna's modern art collection), the 15th-century **Palazzo del Podestà, the Palazzo dei Banchi** and the **Basilica of San Petronio**. The Fountain of Neptune (1564) spouts in the north-west corner. At Pza San Stefano, the churches of **San Stefano** (**Crocifisso, Santo Sepolcro, Trinità, San Vitale** and **Sant'Agricola**) make up a complex, complete with cloisters and courtyards, that has retained its ancient atmosphere.

The two most distinctive towers still standing are the 98-m **Asinelli** (with a wonderful, if dizzying, panorama from the top, 486 steps up) and its inferior partner, the **Garisenda**, by Pza di Porta Ravegnana. A row of 666 arcaded porticoes ascends a hillside to the 18th-century **Basilica de San Luca**, a 35-min walk from **Meloncello** (reached by 🚌 no. 20 from Pza Maggiore), for a splendid vista of the city and the Apennines that adjoin it. Another great place for views is the Parco de Villa Ghigi, an area of Apennine foothills given to the city by a former rector of the university. Walk up from the Pza Maggiore and step out from city centre to a wild, open expanse with vineyards and cattle.

Bologna, famous for its *tortellini*, has a gastonomic reputation in Italy second to none. For good cheaper eateries (*trattorie* and *pizzerie*) try around the small streets near Pza Verdi, the hub of student life.

Stazione Centrale, 1 km north of Pza Maggiore; walk along Via del'Indipendenz (🚌 nos. 25/30). A memorial to casualties of the 1980 station bombing stands by the renovated station entrance.

i **Tourist Offices: railway station**, 🖂 (051) 246 541, fax (051) 421 1367 (www.comune.bologna.it/bolognaturismo); **airport**; and Pza Maggiore 6.

🛏 The Tourist Office has a wide-ranging list of **hotels** and **pensioni** in all categories. **Youth hostels**: Via Viadagola 5, 🖂 (051) 501 810 (6 km from the centre); and **Due Torri**, San Sisto 2. **Camping**: **Città di Bologna**, 🖂 (051) 325 016, fax (051) 325 318 (www.hotelcamping.com; info@hotelcamping.com), open all year.

SIDE TRIPS FROM BOLOGNA **Bologna** is on the line from **Naples** (p. 370) to **Venice** (p. 383), via **Florence** (p. 360); see ETT table 620.

Ravenna (1 hr 20 mins; ETT table 621) was the centre of Byzantine rule in Italy during the 6th and 7th centuries AD. The most impressive reminders of these periods are Ravenna's famed **mosaics** (the major sights cluster in the north-west corner of the old town). The 6th-century octagonal **Basilica of San Vitale** features depictions of the Byzantine Emperor Justinian and Empress Theodora. **Sant'Apollinare Nuovo** dates from the same period; its walls are lined with green and gold mosaics showing processions of saints and virgins. In the grounds are the **Mausoleum of Galla Placidia**, lined with richly coloured mosaics, and the **National Museum**. The station is about 500 m east of town. **Tourist Office**: Via Salaria 8/12, 🖂 (0544) 35 404, fax (0544) 35 094 (www.turismo.ravenna.it); in the centre of town.

You can also take the line along the Adriatic coast to **Brindisi** (ETT table 630), though this trip isn't Italy at its best. On the way you could pause at **Rimini**, a somewhat charmless resort but with an excellent beach and a 20-min bus trip from the tiny independent republic of **San Marino** (just 60 sq km of it), memorably perched on the slopes of **Monte Titano**. Other worthwhile detours include **Peschici Calenella**, east of **San Severo** on the **Gargano massif** (a rugged limestone coast), and the area around **Monópoli** (notable for its trulli – curious drystone, white-domed structures of feudal origins). **Brindisi**, the port near the 'heel' of Italy, has a useful ferry to **Patras** in Greece (ETT table 2770).

The **Bologna–Milan** service (ETT tables 611, 620, 630; 2 hrs 30 mins) runs via **Modena** (a quietly attractive old town with a Romanesque cathedral and with a fine collection of art and illuminated manuscripts within the Palazzo dei Musei) and **Parma** (a household name for its ham and cheese, worth a stop for the frescos by Correggio in the cathedral and the church of San Giovanni Evangelista).

FLORENCE (FIRENZE)

AREZZO

Arezzo was a major settlement in Etruscan, Roman and medieval times. Always a wealthy city, today its economy rests on jewellers, goldsmiths and antiques. Much of the centre is modern, but there are still attractive winding streets in the hilltop old town, with its Renaissance houses and the handsome Pza Grande.

> **AREZZO'S ANTIQUES FAIR**
> Don't expect to find a bargain by attending the **Fiera Antiquaria** (Antiques Fair), in Pza Grande on the first Sun of every month. Hugely popular with an ever more international clientele, it's the place to buy serious antique furniture, terracotta, linen and, of course, jewellery. Accommodation gets very heavily booked up.

One of the masterpieces of Italian Renaissance painting and the city's major attraction is Piero della Francesca's brilliant fresco cycle of the *Legend of the True Cross* (1452–66), on display in the 14th-century **church of San Francesco**, Via della Madonna del Prato, in the centre of the old town.

The spacious **cathedral**, begun in 1278 and lit by 16th-century stained glass, is adorned by Piero della Francesca's fresco of Mary Magdalene, near the organ. The **Galleria e Museo Medioevale e Moderno**, Via di San Loretino 8, contains an exceptional collection of majolica as well as sculpture dating from the 10th–17th centuries. **Santa Maria delle Grazie**, Via di Santa Maria, is a particularly fine 15th-century church that contains a high altar by Andrea della Robbia.

There's less to detain you in the lower town, though you may like to pause at the **Museo Archeologico**, Via Margaritone 10, in an old monastery not far to the east of the station; it has a collection of Roman Aretine ware (50 BC to AD 60–70 terracotta with a shiny red glaze and adorned with bas-reliefs), Etruscan bronzes and 1st-century BC vases. Nearby is a ruined Roman amphitheatre, the **Anfiteatro Romano**.

In the modern sector, west of the centre: walk up the hill to the old town.

i **Tourist Office**: Piazza della Repubblica 28 (by the station), /fax(0575) 20 839 (info@arezzo.turismo.toscana.it). The latest information on accommodation is posted outside the **APT office**, Pza Risorgimento 116.

Rooms are difficult to find over the first weekend of every month, but you should have few problems at other times. There are several budget options near the station. **Private hostel**: **Villa Severi**, Via F Redi 13, (0575) 299 047 (no. 4).

PERUGIA

Warlike and belligerent, the splendid capital of Umbria was smitten by strife almost until the 19th century and has a host of monuments bearing an undeniably martial face. Ignore the unattractive modern suburbs and head straight for the almost intact medieval centre, by bus or escalator. From Pza Italia the pedestrianised Corso Vannucci, lined with fortified palaces, cafés and shops – the centre of activities for a cosmopolitan crowd almost around the clock – runs north to the city's heart in Pza IV Novembre, where the **Duomo** (cathedral) is located. All the other major sights are within easy walking distance of here.

The **Duomo**, Pza IV Novembre, is a large, plain, medieval building, supposedly home to the Virgin Mary's wedding ring. In the centre of the square, but undergoing restoration, is the 13th-century Fontana Maggiore, a fountain that's a triumph of decoration by Nicola and Giovanni Pisano. Facing the fountain, somewhat forbidding **Palazzo dei Priori**, Corso Vannucci, Perugia's civic headquarters since 1297, has a great Gothic portal and long rows of windows. Fan-like steps lead up to the Sala dei Notari, covered with an entertaining array of frescos. **The Galleria Nazionale dell'Umbria**, on the 4th floor, contains works notably by Pinturicchio and Perugino, and is Italy's most important repository of Umbrian art; it also has a few Tuscan masterpieces, including Piero della Francesca's *Madonna and Saints with Child* and a triptych by Fra Angelico. See also **Collegio della Mercanzia**, with its magnificent 15th-century carvings, while the restored frescos of the **Collegio del Cambio** (the Bankers' Guild) are considered to be Perugino's finest works.

San Domenico, Pza G Bruno, is an enormous church with several outstanding works of art. Authorship of the 14th-century **Tomb of Pope Benedict XI** is unknown, but it's clearly the work of a master sculptor. Here, too, is a magnificent 15th-century, stained-glass window. The **Museo Archeologico Nazionale dell'Umbria**, in the monastery alongside San Domenico, includes Etruscan and Roman artefacts.

Don't miss the 10th-century **church of San Pietro**, south-east of the centre (Borgo XX Giugno). The decorations, dating from the Renaissance, are unbelievably rich, with scarcely an unadorned patch. The paintings were executed by a host of artists, including Perugino. A highlight is the magnificently carved choir.

GUBBIO

Gubbio (ten buses a day run from Perugia's Pza dei Partigiani, by the FCU station) is a typical Umbrian hill town, largely medieval, with steep narrow streets, grey and tiered. The huge Pza Grande della Signoria, home of the turreted **Palazzo de Consoli**, provides superb views, while the **Museo Civico** contains the most complete extant record of the ancient Umbrian language, in seven bronze tablets – the **Tavole Eugubine** (300–100 BC). A funicular climbs to the pink-brick **Basilica of Sant'Ubaldo** from Porta Romana, wherein lies St Ubaldo, Gubbio's bishop saint. **Tourist Office**: Pza Oderisi 6, (075) 922 0693, fax (075) 927 3409 (www.umbria2000.it; info@iat.gubbio.pg.it).

FS (State Railway), 4 km south-west of the centre (an uphill walk) or 15 mins by bus (📟nos. 6/7/8/9/11/15/130/135) to Pza Italia. Tickets from a forecourt booth or machine by the entrance. The private **FCU** (Ferrovia Centrale Umbria) railway terminal is **Stazione Sant'Anna**, from which you can get a *scala mobile* (escalator) to Pza Italia. There is an ATM in the station.

i **Tourist Office: Palazzo dei Priori**, Pza IV Novembre 3, ☎(075) 572 3327, fax (075) 573 9386 (www.umbria2000.it; info@iat.perugia.it). Get the monthly listing *Viva Perugia – What, Where, When* for detailed information.

🛏 There is plenty of cheap, central accommodation, but book ahead if you're coming during the international jazz festival (ten days every July). **Youth hostel**: 2 mins from the Duomo: **Centro Internazionale per la Gioventù** (non-HI):Via Bontempi 13, ☎(075) 272 3880 (closed mid-Dec–mid-Jan). **Campsite: Il Rocolo**, Colle della Trinità Str Fontana, ☎(075) 517 8550 (open mid-June–mid-Sept), or you can rough camp by **Lago Trasimeno**, reached by bus and train.

St Francis and the Basilica di San Francesco

San Francesco (St Francis) expressed the wish to be buried simply, but the news of his death (in 1226) brought a flood of donations from all over Europe and construction of the **Basilica di San Francesco**, at the western end of the old town, began in 1228. It has a choice collection of masterpieces, making it something of an art gallery in itself; several great artists were employed, inspiring each other into innovative forms of painting that departed from the rigid Byzantine conventions. The basilica consists of two churches: the **lower church**, designed for peaceful meditation by the saint's tomb, and the soaring **upper church**, intended to mollify the faction who wanted a glorious monument.
The upper church suffered severe damage during the 1997 earthquake, but has been completely restored.

ASSISI

One name is irrevocably linked with **Assisi** – S Francis. Born here in 1182, he practised what he preached: poverty, chastity and obedience leading to love of God and appreciation of al living things. He founded the Franciscan order and his home town became (and remains) major pilgrimage centre, with the action con centrated around the **Basilica di San Francesco** erected in his memory at the western end of th old town and adorned with some of the mos magnificent frescos in Italy (see panel).

St Francis's life initiated a wealth of art and architecture in Assisi. Still largely medieval and clinging to a side of **Monte Subasio** high above the green Umbrian countryside, the town is instantly familiar from the landscape in the frescos of the Umbrian painters.

The Pza del Comune, in the centre of the old town, is dominated by the 1st-century AB **Tempio di Minerva** – a Roman temple partly incorporated into what is now the church o Santa Maria.

To the east of the centre, below the cathedral, i the **Basilica di Santa Chiara**. Santa Chiara (St Clare) was an early friend of St Francis and with his guidance, established the Order of the Poor Clares, the female equivalent of the Franciscans.

The old fortress, known as **Rocca Maggiore**, towers dramatically above the northern edge of the city, providing panoramic views of the town and surrounding countryside.

The **Basilica di Santa Maria degli Angeli**, near the station, surrounds a chapel used by St Francis and the spot where he died. Much more evocative, if you fancy a 4-km forest walk to the north-east, is **Eremo delle Carceri**, on the slopes of Monte Subasio. It was here, in caves, that the original Franciscans lived. You can see the cell used by St Francis and the altar from where he addressed the birds.

This is not in Assisi proper, but in **Santa Maria degli Angeli**, about 5 km south-west and uphill all the way. Buses run to the centre every 30 mins.

Tourist Office: Pza del Comune 12, ☎ (075) 812 534, fax (075) 813 727 (www.umbria2000.it). It provides a map in English and has information about accommodation, including pilgrim hostels.

DAY TRIP FROM ASSISI

Spello (10 mins by train; ETT table 615) is the epitome of an Umbrian hill town, with tiers of pink houses, cobbled alleys and churches, and Roman gateways. The 13th-century **church of Santa Maria Maggiore** contains a chapel full of brilliantly restored frescos by Pinturicchio and a 15th-century ceramic floor. Spello is far from overrun with tourists and is generally much quieter than Assisi. From the station it's a short walk up to the old town.

Tourist Office: Pza Matteotti 3. Open only in summer, ☎ (0742) 301 009.

There is plenty of accommodation of every grade, but booking is advisable – essential for Easter, the **Feast of St Francis** (3–4 Oct) and **Calendimaggio** (a medieval celebration of spring held in early May). **Youth hostel**: Via di Valecchie 177, ☎/fax (075) 816 767, 10-min walk from Pza San Pietro. **Campsite: Fontemaggio**, ☎ (075) 813 636, 4 km east of town and uphill. Take a taxi or follow the signs from **Porta Cappuccini**.

SPOLETO

Founded by Umbrians in the 6th century BC, **Spoleto** has an interesting mix of Roman and medieval sights, the most spectacular being the cathedral, adorned on its entrance façade with eight rose windows of differing sizes. Its campanile, propped up by a flying buttress, was constructed from various bits of Roman masonry and other un-medieval elements – and yet still manages to present itself as a perfect blend of Romanesque and Renaissance styles. Within, a baroque makeover rather ruined the effect, though Fra Filippo Lippi's magnificent frescos depicting the life of the Virgin are timeless. Also of interest is **Cappella Eroli**, with a *Madonna and Child* by Pinturicchio, and the Cosmati marble floor.

After several centuries of power the town fell into obscurity until being chosen (in 1958) to host Italy's leading performing arts festival in June/July, the **Spoleto**

Festival, which transforms the tranquil town into an unrecognisably invigorated place; prices, inevitably, soar.

Part of the small **Roman Amphitheatre**, Pza Libertà, at the southern end of the old centre, has been carefully restored and is now used for festival performances. Another section is occupied by the **convent of Sant'Agata**, which houses a small collection of Roman artefacts. A walk through the **Arco di Druso** (AD 23), 100 m north, leads to Pza del Mercato, which was the Roman forum and is still a marketplace and the hub of Spoleto's social life. It's a great place to linger, surrounded by attractive old streets and overlooked by the huge hulks of medieval buildings.

Nearby, the small **Pinacoteca Comunale** is housed in the **Palazzo del Municipio**, a visit to which requires a guide. The décor is magnificent and some of the paintings are outstanding, especially in the Umbrian section. **Sant'Eufemia**, above the **Duomo**, is a lovely 12th-century Romanesque church remarkable for its early capitals and columns, and for the matroneum, the upper gallery where the women worshipped, segregated from the men below.

The **Rocca**, a huge 14th-century castle to the south-east of town, guards one of the finest engineering achievements of medieval times, the **Ponte delle Torri**: a 240-m-long bridge, supported by ten arches 80 m high. From it there are magnificent views of the gorge below and there's a pleasant 2-km walk (turn right) leading to **San Pietro**, with a façade adorned by some of the region's finest Romanesque sculpture.

🚉 In the lower town, with a long uphill walk south to the medieval town (or orange bus to Pza Libertà – tickets from the station bar). Free city map from the station newsstand.

ℹ️ **Tourist Office**: Pza LibertÀ 7, ☎ (0743) 220 311, fax (0743) 46 241(www.umbria2000.it; info@iat.spoleto.pg.it).

🏠 Book well ahead during the **summer arts festival**. At that time accommodation can be very pricey. At other times, look in the lower town. Alternatively, try **Foligno**, 26 km north-east and linked by trains that run until late; it has a **youth hostel** at Via Pieranton 23, ☎ (0742) 342 566, fax (0742) 343 559. **Campsites**: **Camping Monteluco**, ☎ (0742) 220 358, 15-min walk south from Pza Libertà, is very small and opens only Apr–Sept. **Camping Il Girasole**, ☎ (0742) 51 335, in the village of **Petrognano**, is larger and has a pool (hourly bus from station).

ROME (ROMA)

See p. 377.

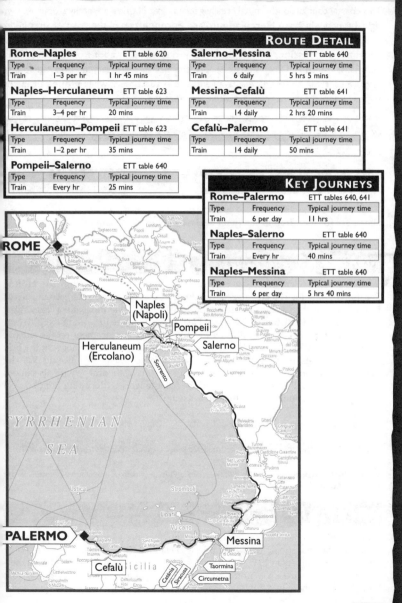

ROUTE DETAIL

Rome–Naples — ETT table 620

Type	Frequency	Typical journey time
Train	1–3 per hr	1 hr 45 mins

Naples–Herculaneum — ETT table 623

Type	Frequency	Typical journey time
Train	3–4 per hr	20 mins

Herculaneum–Pompeii — ETT table 623

Type	Frequency	Typical journey time
Train	1–2 per hr	35 mins

Pompeii–Salerno — ETT table 640

Type	Frequency	Typical journey time
Train	Every hr	25 mins

Salerno–Messina — ETT table 640

Type	Frequency	Typical journey time
Train	6 daily	5 hrs 5 mins

Messina–Cefalù — ETT table 641

Type	Frequency	Typical journey time
Train	14 daily	2 hrs 20 mins

Cefalù–Palermo — ETT table 641

Type	Frequency	Typical journey time
Train	14 daily	50 mins

KEY JOURNEYS

Rome–Palermo — ETT tables 640, 641

Type	Frequency	Typical journey time
Train	6 per day	11 hrs

Naples–Salerno — ETT table 640

Type	Frequency	Typical journey time
Train	Every hr	40 mins

Naples–Messina — ETT table 640

Type	Frequency	Typical journey time
Train	6 per day	5 hrs 40 mins

ITALY

This coastal tour of southern Italy really gets going at **Naples**, a worthy stop in its own right, beyond which are **Herculaneum** and **Pompeii**, two of the greatest sites in the ancient world. At the 'toe' of mainland Italy, you board a train ferry from **Villa San Giovanni** to **Messina**, on the isle of Sicily. Successive invasions of Romans, Arabs, Normans, French and Spanish have shaped the Sicilian character; the land is a strange mixture of fertile plains, volcanic lava fields and virtual desert, while **Mount Etna**, the great volcano, threatens to erupt within the next ten years.

ROME (ROMA)

See p. 377.

NAPLES (NAPOLI)

See p. 370.

See p. 373 for the **Circumvesuviana** to **Herculaneum** and **Pompeii**.

SALERNO

Spread around a crescent bay, Salerno is recommended as a stop for visiting Paestum or Amalfi. The city goes back a long way; it belonged to Greece in ancient times, and was then a Roman settlement, while in medieval times it was celebrated for its School of Medicine – the Code of Health, written here in verse in the 12th century – was for some time held to be the definitive pronouncement on the subject. Unfortunately, World War II devastation left it a shadow of its former self, the best of what remains being the atmospherically dilapidated centre around Via dei Mercanti, spanned by an 8th-century arch, and the cathedral – with its superb mosaic-covered 12th-century pulpit and the Salerno ivories (depicting Bible scenes) from the same period in the Cathedral Museum.

🚆 South of the old centre (turn right out of the station); 10-min walk.

ⓘ **Tourist Office**: near the station, 📠/fax (089) 231 432 (www.crmpa.it/ept; eptinfo@xcom.it).

🛏 **Youth Hostel**: Via Luigi Guerico, 📞 (089) 790 251. Plus a number of inexpensive pensions in the old part of town.

MESSINA

Messina, Sicily's nearest port to the mainland, was the victim of a massive earthquake in 1908 that shook for two months and claimed 84,000 lives, and of a massive attack by US bombers in 1943. But even those events can't take away its glorious setting beneath the massive, unmistakable form of Mount Etna, the volcano that brought about the city's downfall. Much has been rebuilt in a stable, squat style.

The well-reconstructed **cathedral**, Pza del Duomo, has an ornate Gothic central entrance portal and mosaics in the three apses: try to catch the moving figurines on the clock as it chimes at midday, and climb the tower for the view.

Trains from the mainland arrive on **FS** ferries at **Stazione Marittima**, and continue to **Stazione Centrale** – departure point for city and long-distance buses.

Tourist Office: Via Calabria 301, ☎ (090) 674 236, fax (090) 674 271.

There's limited accommodation, and the only **youth hostel** is at Ali (25 km) – Pza Spirito Santo, open May–Oct. The nearest **campsite**, **Dello Stretto**, is remotely situated on the city's northern edge at Punta del Faro.

SIDE TRIPS FROM MESSINA To the south, trains serve two of Sicily's most interesting places: Taormina and Siracusa (ETT table 641; 40 mins to Taormina, 2 hrs 45 mins to Siracusa), with the chance to ride round the base of Mount Etna. **Taormina** (Tourist Office: Pza Vittorio Emanuele, ☎ (0942) 23 243, fax (0942) 24 941; plus at the station) is a touristy and prosperous-looking Italian fleshpot, beautifully draped over the cliffs above the Ionian Sea in the shadow of Mount Etna. Of chief interest is the Teatro Greco, the Greek Theatre (3rd century BC, rebuilt 1st century AD). Accommodation is expensive, but cheaper, clean rooms can be found at Il Leone, Via Bagnoli Croci 126, ☎ (0942) 23878; they also have a great view from their (free) terrace. **Catánia** (Tourist Office: at central rail station, ☎ (095) 531 802; branch at Corso Italia 30, ☎ (095) 373 084), despite its 18th-century core, is scruffy and industrial. The Roman theatre, Teatro Romano, is in Via Vittorio Emanuele, while the remains of the lava-built Anfiteatro Romano, the 3rd-century AD Roman amphitheatre, are in Pza Stesicoro. The chief scenic interest of this stretch of coast is **Mount Etna**, the 3323-m volcano that is still very much active and threatens to engulf the towns in the ultra-fertile plain beneath it. For a superb scenic route round the mountain, take the Ferrovia Circumetnea from Catania Borgo station on Corso Italia (note this is not the same station as you stop at on the line from Messina and Taormina), and ride 4 hrs to Randazzo and back (2 hrs each way; some trains continue to join the main line at Riposto; see ETT table 644). Enquire at Catania about excursion buses to the summit of Mount Etna (via cable car for part of the way); although you're not allowed to stand at the very top of the crater for safety reasons, it's an amazing trip up for views and close-ups of lava flows. **Siracusa** (Syracuse), the power base in Sicily from the 5th century BC up to 878, has masses of early sites to visit, notably **Neapolis**, with its supremely preserved Greek and Roman theatres, man-made grotto (called the Ear of Dionysius), 3rd-century BC sacrificial altar (Hieron's Altar) and quarries that were used as outdoor prisons during the war with Athens in 413 BC. Elsewhere there are early Christian catacombs by the church of San Giovanni, and on the finest square in the town is a cathedral built out of an ancient Doric temple, nine columns of which are visible on the northern side. The Museo Archeologico Nazionale is a treasure house of Greek antiquities, including vases and statuary. Syracuse has good beaches. (Tourist Office: Via San Sebastiano 45, ☎ (0931) 67 710, fax (0931) 468 287; www.apt-siracusa.it; info@apt-siracusa.it).

CEFALÙ

Crammed between a rocky promontory and the sea, this idyllically attractive little fishing port and beach resort is a great place to rest, with plenty of restaurants, walks and views, and characterful corners, particularly in Corso Ruggero. The Arabo-Norman **cathedral**, a twin-towered, fortified medieval structure, dominates the town from its position just beneath the **Rocca**, the rock that protects it. It contains some of Sicily's best preserved – and earliest (1148) – mosaics. Dating from the time of the Norman kings, these are the work of Byzantine craftsmen. See the *Christ Pantocrator* in the main apse: it's one of the great works of medieval Sicily.

The **Museo Mandralisca**, Via Mandralisca 13, contains, along with a variety of arte-facts including some Greek ceramics, an important painting by Antonello da Messina, *Portrait of an Unknown Man* (c1460). Above the town, on the Rocca – ascend from Pza Garibaldi – a ruined medieval fortification provides magnificent views out over **Cefalù** and the coast. The attractive beach offers shallow bathing.

🚆 Via Moro, 10-min walk from Corso Ruggero.

ℹ️ **Tourist Office**: Corso Ruggero 77, ☎ (0921) 421 050, fax (0921) 422 386 (www.cefalu-tour.pa.it; info@cefalu-tour.pa.it).

🛏️ There is a variety of **hotel** accommodation here in all categories. **Campsites: Costa Ponente Internazionale**, ☎ (0921) 420 085 and, beside it, **Sanfilippo**, ☎ (0921) 420 184 – both about 3 km west of town at Contrada Ogliastrillo (🚌 heading for La Spisa).

PALERMO

With huge **Monte Pellegrino** to the north and an arc of mountains behind the city to the west, this somewhat undervisited and picturesquely decaying port looks tremendous from the ferries that arrive from **Naples**, **Genoa** and **Sardinia**. Wartime bombing, severe neglect and a bad criminal record have left their mark on **Palermo**, but it has great atmosphere, with an ancient-feeling labyrinth of narrow alleys and streets, hidden squares and timeless souk-like markets. More North African than Italian, the **Vucciria** in Via Maccheronai, or the excellent **Ballaro** in Pza Ballaro (near the station), signal Palermo's status as a meeting of two continents.

The rich legacy of the ancient Greeks can be studied in one of southern Italy's best museums, the **Museo Archeologico Regionale**, at Pza Olivella; highlights include the panels of relief sculpture from temples at **Selinunte**. Deep inside the **Palazzo dei Normanni** are the lavishly ornamental mosaics by Arab and Byzantine craftsmen (1150). Its ceiling is the finest surviving

GETTING AROUND PALERMO

Walking is the best way of getting around, but you might want to consider the buses. You can buy a **Palermo City Pass** lasting either for an hour or a day.

example of **Fatamid** architecture anywhere. Other mosaics in the city can be seen in the **Martorana** in Pza Bellini (12th century).

The other great milestone of Sicilian style is the baroque: the local Palermitan baroque is ornate and ebullient. The richest examples of it can be seen in the interiors of the little oratories of **Rosario di San Domenico** at Via Bambinai 2, and of **Santa Zita**, behind the **church of Santa Zita** at Via Valverde 3. In both, the stuccatore Giacomo Serpotta (1656–1732) unleashed the full throttle of his exuberance. His remarkably realistic stucco figures run riot around the walls. The Quattro Canti (1611) is Palermo's finest piazza, with a statue of a Spanish king in each corner and a fountain in the middle.

Stazione Centrale, in Pza Giulio Cesare, is at the southern end of the city. Located in the same square, and in the streets around it, are some of the termini of local, provincial and long-distance bus services. **Stazione Marittima**, Via Francesco Crispi, in the east, by the port, is the focus of ferry services (mostly **Tirrenia Shipping Line**) from **Naples**, **Cagliari** (Sardinia), **Genoa**, **Ustica**, and occasional hydrofoil connections to the Aeolian Islands. There is an ATM in the station.

Tourist Office: in the station, ☎ (091) 616 5914. The main office is at Pza Castelnuovo 34, ☎ (091) 583 847, fax (091) 586 338 (www.aapit.pa.it; aapit@aapit.pa.it). Ask for the *Palermo Flash Guide* booklet.

Cheap accommodation is easy to find, though much of it is tacky. The mid-range is well catered for. Away from the city, at **Sferracavallo** (🚌 no. 101) near the sea, are two **campsites**: **Camping Trinacria**, Via Barcarello 23, ☎ (091) 530 590, and **Camping degli Ulivi**, Via Pegaso 25, ☎ (091) 533 021. The only youth hostel is open from the end of July through Aug: **Pensionato San Saverio**, Via Di Cristina. Call in at **Albergherie Viaggi**, Pza San Saverio 3, ☎ (091) 651 8576, to make a reservation and to get directions.

WHERE NEXT FROM PALERMO?

*Ferries (ETT table 2655; once a week; 13 hrs 30 mins) depart to **Cágliari** (see p. 419), capital of the island of Sardinia, as well as to **Naples** (table 2625; daily; 11 hrs), **Livorno** (table 2588; three days a week; 17 hrs) and **Genoa** (table 2547; daily; 20 hrs).*

*Served by the ferry from **Palermo** and **Naples** as well as shorter 50-min hydrofoil crossings from **Milazzo** (west of Messina), the **Aeolian Islands** (also known as the **Eolian Islands** or the **Lipari Islands**) rise dramatically from warm, azure waters north of Sicily. Thought by the ancients to be the home of Aeolus, the God of the Winds, the volcanic archipelago has wonderful scenery and rich marine life including turtles, hammer-fish and flying-fish. **Lipari**, the main island, has an old walled town, while the isles **Vulcano** and **Strómboli** each have extremely active volcanos.*

DAY TRIPS FROM PALERMO

Mondello (about 10 km), is Palermo's beach resort, while **Monreale** (about 8 km to the south-west), is the focus of a splendid medieval cathedral containing a great series of Byzantine-style mosaics. **Monreale** also affords a **stunning view** over the city. At **Segesta** (about 65 km), to the north west, a near-complete Greek temple survives, while at **Bagheria** (about 14 km), in the south-east, the quirky baroque **Villa Palagonia** is an oddity in an area once renowned for the holiday homes of the 17th- and 18th-century nobility. All of these places are accessible by bus.

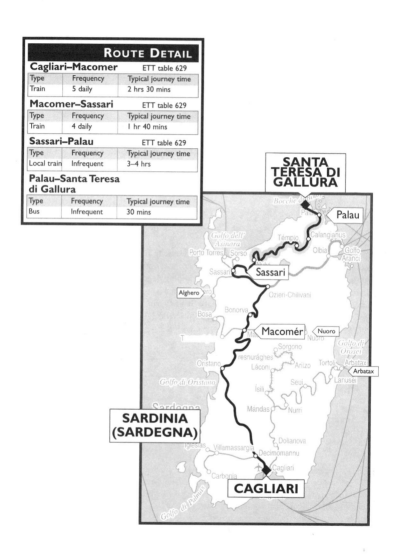

ROUTE DETAIL

Cagliari–Macomer — ETT table 629

Type	Frequency	Typical journey time
Train	5 daily	2 hrs 30 mins

Macomer–Sassari — ETT table 629

Type	Frequency	Typical journey time
Train	4 daily	1 hr 40 mins

Sassari–Palau — ETT table 629

Type	Frequency	Typical journey time
Local train	Infrequent	3–4 hrs

Palau–Santa Teresa di Gallura

Type	Frequency	Typical journey time
Bus	Infrequent	30 mins

This trip through the Mediterranean island of **Sardinia** allows some rewarding side visits to such coastal gems as **Alghero**, and to **Arbatax** via a railway that twists through the mountains. Resorts here are low-key, and nightlife is not that busy, except in July and Aug, when half of Europe seems to converge on it: June and Sept are much better. Some 7000 ancient **Nuraghic** fortress houses (or *nuraghi*), dating back to 1600 BC, dot the island.

CAGLIARI

The largest and most modern-looking city on the island, **Cagliari** is nevertheless thought to be of Phoenician origin. Much was rebuilt following wartime bomb damage, but there's a compact old city, inside the imposing 13th-century **Pisan** walls, with a warren of brick-paved lanes leading to the tree-lined piazzas. Seek out the two Pisan towers – the **Torre San Pancrazio** and **Torre delle Elefante** – and stroll the medieval quarter around the Bastione di Saint-Remy and the Porte di Leoni. The **National Archaeology Museum** in the Pza Arsenale contains an expansive and well-documented collection of **Nuraghi** artefacts. The Romanesque **cathedral**, built by Pisa, is inside the massive walls. On the north-west side of the citadel is the Roman **amphitheatre**, hewn from the rock in the 3rd century AD;

> ### ENTERTAINMENT AND EVENTS IN CAGLIARI
>
> The bi-monthly magazine *Appuntamenti Culturali*, available in hotels and at the tourist offices, provides listings for cinemas, concerts and cultural events. The annual **Festival of Sant'Efisio** (from 1 May), honouring the saint martyred under the Emperor Diocletian, features a solemn procession with horse-borne participants attired in traditional red costumes.

summer performances are staged here. The 5th-century Byzantine **church of San Saturno** is just off the busy Viale Cimitero. Visit the beach at **Poette** and the **Sella del Diavolo** stone formation in the bay, and wander to the salt marshes beyond the dunes to observe cranes and pink flamingos.

The modern **FdS Railway Museum** (at Monserrato in the northern suburbs) should interest railway enthusiasts, while the **botanical gardens**, Via Ignazio, make a pleasant retreat from the summer heat.

> ### FERRIES TO CAGLIARI
>
> All ferries are operated by Tirrenia Shipping Lines. There's a daily service from **Civitavecchia**, north-west of Rome (12 hrs 30 mins; ETT table 2525); weekly from **Palermo** and **Trápani** (both on Sicily) and **Genoa**; 2 weekly (weekly in winter) from **Naples**.

🚢 **Maritime Station**, Pza Matteotti, for all ships. **Tirrenia** bookings at 1 Via Campidano c/o Agenave, ☎ (070) 666 065. The **FS** stately 19th-century marble station, served by mainline trains to **Sassari** and the northern ports of **Porto Torres** and **Olbia**, is on Pza Matteotti, Via Sassari side.

The **Cagliari FS** station has a bank with ATM inside the main information/ticketing lobby. **FdS** tiny corner station is 3 km away at the Pza Repubblica on Via Dante side. Information through **ESIT** or at the station.

🚌 **Buses: ARST** ☎(070) 409 8324. Intercity buses out of Cagliari are run by ARST. Local Cagliari buses are run by CTM. CTM buses have daily and weekly tickets as well as the standard 90-min ticket. Intercity and Cagliari city transit buses use the newish station on Pza Matteotti.
All main urban sights are within a 20-min walk, but some steep hills could be an incentive to taking a city bus. Local buses terminate at the bus station on Pza Matteotti. Urban buses are needed to reach beaches (🚌 PF or PQ to **Poetto**).

ℹ️ **Tourist Offices**: For Cagliari tourist information, use the very helpful **Cagliari AAST** (Azienda Autonoma di Soggiorno e Turismo) on the Via Roma side of Pza Matteotti, ☎(070) 669 255, fax (070) 658 200 (www.tiscalinet.it/aast-ca). There is also a new AAST office in the port, ☎(070) 668 352. For Sardinia-wide tourist information, use the ESIT (Ente Sardo Industrie Turistiche) office next door to the AAST office, ☎(070) 60 231.

🛏️ A wide range of accommodation exists but prices rise in July and Aug. Budget **hotels** and **pensioni** cluster on the Via Roma between the Pza Matteotti and the **Palazzo Consiglio Regionale**, such as **Locanda Miramare**, Via Roma 59, ☎/fax (070) 664 021, but similar and much quieter places line the Via Sardegna paralleling Via Roma one block behind it. **Camping**: 45 mins east on the **Costa Rei** at **Villasimius** is **Camping Spiaggia del Riso**, ☎(070) 791 052, fax (070) 797 150 (open Apr–Oct and Christmas holidays). At 1 hr to the west on the Costa del Sud, just past **Porto di Teulada**, is **Camping Comunale Portu Tramatzu**, ☎(070) 928 3027 (open Apr–Oct).

🍽️ As the capital of Sardinia, **Cagliari** offers the greatest opportunity to sample the fine cuisine and wines specific to the island. Excellent and inexpensive seafood restaurants are located on the Via Sardegna and Via Cavour just off the port. Try the Pza Yenne for relaxed cafés and snackbars serving a variety of *panini* and *focaccia*.

SIDE TRIP FROM CAGLIARI TO ARBATAX The FdS narrow-gauge train runs once daily to **Arbatax** on the east coast, with a change of trains at Mandas. It allows access to the following towns, as well as spectacular mountain views from both sides of the train. Inland, **Seui** gives access to the **Barbagia** and some of Sardinia's highest and wildest peaks through the **Gennargentu** mountain range. Accommodation (**Hotel Moderno**, ☎(0782) 54 621) and tourist services are available in the compact little mountain town.

Arbatax has bright red (porphyry) cliffs and many isolated coves with sandy beaches. **Tourist information** is available through the **FdS office**, ☎(0782) 667 285. This tortuous rail line includes a unique full circle as it descends from **Barbagia** through tunnels and stone viaducts into the plateau town of **Tortoli**. Note the many large prickly pear cactuses along the rail line after **Tortoli**. Their fruit is cherished as a delicacy by locals. From **Tortoli**, an **ARST** bus runs to **Nuoro**, to make a very scenic link (check connections) back to the mainline.

MACOMÉR

Macomér is the mainline junction, with **FdS** lines for **Nuoro** and the **Barbagia** to the east and **Bosa** and its coast to the west. Occasional **FdS** steam excursions operate from **Macomér** towards the sea at **Tresnuraghes**.

[RAIL] The FdS Station is 200 m across the railway square from the **FS** station, but many **FdS** rail cars shuttle around the square to meet **FS** trains.

SIDE TRIPS FROM MACOMÉR The FdS line to **Nuoro** (east of **Macomér**; 6 trains daily except Sun, taking 1 hr 30 mins) passes many groves of cork trees, whose trunks are characteristically stripped of bark. The small town of Nuoro, set on a high granite plateau on the slopes of Mount Ortobene (itself bearing the vast statue, *Christ the Redeemer*), is disappointingly ugly, with high-rise development, but is a useful starting point for the exploration of the villages and rough country in the **Barbagia**. There is no budget accommodation, but if you need to stay overnight, **Mini Hotel**, Via Brofferio 13, ☎ (0784) 33 159, is quite pleasant. A compact, attractive old quarter radiates out from the pedestrianised Corso Garibaldi. Traditional Barbagia costumes and masks are on display in the wonderful **Regional Ethnographic Museum**, Via Antonio Mereu 56. **Tourist Office**: Pza Italia 19, ☎ (0784) 30 083, fax (0784) 33 432.

SASSARI

Sardinia's second city, founded in the 12th century, **Sassari** is the capital of the province of the same name and is a busy, modern commercial, administrative and university town. While it's not exactly a tourist hot spot you can experience real Sardinian life here in the knot of medieval streets. Near the station are the 13th-century **cathedral**, on Pza del Duomo, and the **Piazza Italia**, the town's most lively evening spot, with its monumental statue of Vittorio Emanuele II, as well as **Palazzo Giordano** and **Palazzo del Governo**. The Genoese **Rosello fountain** near the **Rosello Bridge** in the northern part of the centre is the symbol of the city.

[RAIL] The combined monumental **FS/FdS** rail station is on Via XXV Aprile, about 15 mins from the old city around the Pza Castello.

[i] **Tourist Offices: Main Office,** Viale Caprera 36, ☎ (079) 299 544, fax (079) 299 415. A **Regional Office** is at Viale Umberto 72, ☎ (079) 233 534, fax (079) 237 585.

[🛏] **Hotels** and **pensioni** are plentiful. **Hotel Giusy**, Piazza Sant' Antonio 21, ☎ (079) 233 327, near the station, is inexpensive.

SIDE TRIP FROM SASSARI TO ALGHERO Alghero (up to 11 trains daily; 35 mins) is a bewitching, bustling and unsophisticated west coast seaside resort. Much of the present city (as well as the local dialect) within the sturdy Genoese walls dates to the Catalan era: the **cathedral** (1552) in Pza Duomo, the **churches of San Francesco** (late 14th-century) in the Via Carlo Alberto, **Misericordia** (1662), Via Misericordia, **San Michele** (1612), Via Carlo Alberto, and the entire **Piazza Civica** contain striking Catalan influences. Walking along the narrow, cobblestone streets around the three bastions or in the centre is the best way to soak up the ambience. Excursion boats make the trip to the towering cliffs of **Capo Cáccia**, beneath which is the **Grotte di Nettuno**, bristling with stalagmites and stalactites.

The most appealing accommodation within the city is the restored convent of San Francesco, now the **Hotel San Francesco**, Via Ambrogio Machin 2, ☎(079) 980 330. **Youth Hostel**: **Ostello di Giuliani**, Via Zara 1, ☎(079) 930 353, is in Fertilia (6 km north of town). **Camping**: also in Fertilia is **Camping Calik**, ☎(079) 930 111. **Tourist Office**: Piazza Porta Terra 9, ☎(079) 979 054, fax (079) 974 881. The **FdS** railway station is in the **Lido** area 3 km from the centre, but **ARST** buses call in at the city park on Via Catalogna.

PALAU

This peaceful little port serves the small islands of **Caprera** – where the hero of Italian unification, Giuseppe Garibaldi, lived out his life – and **Maddalena**, the resort and naval base island.

i **Tourist Offices: Maddalena**, Cala Gavetta, ☎(0789) 736 321, fax (0789) 736 655. **Palau**, Via Nazionale 94, ☎(0789) 709 570, fax (0789) 709 570.

⌂ There is a good choice of hotel rooms in **Palau**. **Hotel Sierra**, Via Nazionale 7, ☎(0789) 709 519, is an option, or in **Maddalena** there is **Hotel Il Gabbiano**, Via Giulio Cesare 20, ☎(0789) 722 507.

SANTA TERESA DI GALLURA

This pleasantly uneventful town on the northern tip of the island, cited by the Romans and still called Portolongone by locals, sits on a rocky promontory, with a 16th-century Spanish tower looking out to the white cliffs of Corsica. It is a discreet summer tourism resort with all the expected facilities (ATM, bur-eau de change, hotels and pensioni) and a wide variety of isolated beaches accessible on foot or in one of the many small motor boats anchored in the harbour. The small town's limited hotels tend to fill in July–Aug.

i **Tourist Office: AAST**, Pza Vittorio Emanuele 24, 07028 Santa Teresa di Gallura, ☎(0789) 754 127, fax (0789) 754 185, a helpful office in the main square. It will respond to written queries in English and offers a free booklet on accommodation.

CROATIA AND SLOVENIA

(for Directory information, see pp. 589 and 610). **Croatia** and **Slovenia** emerged as independent countries following the break-up of Yugoslavia in 1991. Tiny Slovenia developed rapidly into an efficient and prosperous nation. Croatia was more traumatised by the war that ensued, but since 2000 things have been looking up and the country is now set to welcome back the tourists who once flocked to the shores of the beautiful Adriatic and its countless islands.

CROATIA

Croatia takes up a vast stretch of the Adriatic Coast. Travelling southwards the landscape becomes increasingly dramatic, culminating in Dalmatia with spectacular rugged mountains, sea and islands. Coastal towns such as Split, Hvar and Korčula spent several centuries under Venetian rule: traces remain in local architecture, customs and dialects. Inland Croatia is more Central European. The rather austere buildings, food and manners of the capital, Zagreb, remind one of the other grand cities that passed under Austro-Hungary.

YOUTH HOSTELS

The booking/travel section of the **Croatian Youth Hostel Association**: HFHS Travel Section, Dežmanova 9, 10000 Zagreb, Croatia, ☎ (385) (1) 484 7474 (hfhs-cms@zg.tel.hr).

ACCOMMODATION

Massive amounts of money have gone towards revitalizing Croatian tourism and many hotels have been totally refurbished. However, prices are not cheap. **Private accommodation** is generally the best-value option and can be arranged through local Tourist Offices. Owners usually live on the ground floor and let rooms or apartments upstairs. Prices vary depending on location and season: expect to pay between Kn60 and Kn100 per person per night. For stays of less than three nights you may have to pay a 30% surcharge. There are excellent **youth hostels** in Dubrovnik and Pula, and a cheap but poorly maintained hostel in Zagreb.

FOOD AND DRINK

Along the Dalmatian coast, fish and other seafood predominate. Many dishes are prepared Mediterranean-style, using large amounts of olive oil, garlic and parsley. Locals say that fish should swim three times: in the sea, in olive oil and in wine. Specialities include *lignje* (squid), *crni rižot* (rice in cuttlefish ink) and *škampi* (scampi). Inland, meat and dairy produce are more popular. Some of the best restaurants have gardens, where they serve *janjetina* (lamb) roast whole on a spit. Another traditional method of preparing meat is in a *peka*, a large iron pot with a dome shaped lid, which is buried to cook under glowing embers.

Tap water is safe and drinkable throughout both countries.

Top of the range wines are pricey. The cheapest solution is to buy wine 'on tap': look for the sign '*točno vino*' and bring an empty bottle with you. When staying on the coast try a herb brandy, *travarica*; when staying inland ask for a grape brandy, *lozovača*. Coffee (*kava*) is often served as espresso or cappuccino in bars, though most families prepare it Turkish style at home. Tea (*čaj*) is normally made from rosehip (*šipak*) and served with sugar and lemon.

SLOVENIA

Slovenia, a land of beautiful alpine mountains and lakes, undulating farmland and vineyards, blends Mediterranean charm with Austrian efficiency. Many Slovenes love hiking and skiing, and Triglav National Park offers ideal conditions for both. The country now looks set to be one of the first Eastern European nations to enter the EU.

YOUTH HOSTELS

Head office:
Bled Youth Hostel,
Grajska Cesta 17, 4260
Bled, Slovenia,
☎ (386) (4) 574 5250

ACCOMMODATION

Bookings for all types of accommodation can be made through Tourist Offices. Many hotels have been fully refurbished, standards are high and prices comparable to those of EU countries. Prices are higher in July and Aug, when accommodation may be in short supply. Tourist offices have lists of private rooms for rent, categorized I and II – category I having private shower and toilet, while you have to share the bathroom and toilet for category II. A 30% surcharge is sometimes made for stays of less than three nights. There is still a shortage of youth hostels, however, in **Ljubljana** and **Maribor** it is possible to stay in **university halls of residence** during the summer break (details from Tourist Offices). There are numerous mostly small but well equipped **campsites**, many with sports facilities.

FOOD AND DRINK

Places to eat go by many different names in Slovenia. A restaurant where you are served by a waitress is a *restauracija*, while a *gostilna* is an inn which typically serves national dishes in a rustic setting. Both sometimes have a set menu (*dnevno kosilo*) at lunch, which is usually the least expensive option. There are also a variety of self service places (*samopostrezna restauracija*) where you can eat standing up. Slovenian cuisine reflects historic ties with Vienna. Meat and dairy products predominate: *Wiener schnitzel* (veal in breadcrumbs) is a speciality, as is *pohana piska* (breaded fried chicken). There's a tasty range of smoked sausages, salamis and cured hams. Coffee shops offer a wide range of pastries, cakes and ice-creams. A *zavitek* is a light pastry filled with cream cheese, either sweet or savoury.

EDITOR'S CHOICE

Dubrovnik; Ljubljana;
Postojna Caves;
Slovenian Alps (around
Bled); Split; Zagreb.
Ferry trips: Rijeka–Split
(ETT table 2855);
Split–Dubrovnik
(p. 426).

BEYOND THE BORDERS

Ljubljana–Venice
via Trieste (ETT
table 89b);
Ljubljana–
Schwarzach
(table 62) to join
Innsbruck–Vienna route
(p. 349); Ljubljana–Budapest
(table 92).

LJUBLJANA

SLOVENIA

Lesce-Bled

Postojna

Zagreb

CROATIA

BOSNIA

Split

DUBROVNIK

Many lines marked ▬▬▬▬▬ in Croatia, Bosnia & Yugoslavia are currently being rebuilt and may re-open at any time.

ROUTE DETAIL

Ljubljana–Zagreb — ETT table 1320

Type	Frequency	Typical journey time
Train	7 daily	2 hrs 20 mins

Zagreb–Split — ETT table 1330

Type	Frequency	Typical journey time
Train	2–4 per day	7 hrs 25 mins

Split–Dubrovnik — ETT table 2855

Type	Frequency	Typical journey time
Ship	4 per week	9 hrs

KEY JOURNEYS

Ljubljana–Vienna — ETT table 89a

Type	Frequency	Typical journey time
Train	3 per day	6 hrs 35 mins

Zagreb–Budapest — ETT table 92

Type	Frequency	Typical journey time
Train	4 per day	7 hrs 15 mins

Zagreb–Vienna — ETT table 89a

Type	Frequency	Typical journey time
Train	2 per day	6 hrs 30 mins

This is a route with many alternatives, giving a choice between rail, ferry and bus. From Llubljana, at the heart of Slovenia, you can either go via **Zagreb** or by **Postojna** (home to some of Europe's finest caves) to the Adriatic coast at **Rijeka** for ferries to **Split**, or carry on by train from Zagreb to Split (be sure to go via Karlovac and avoid Bosnia, where lines are closed). Split itself has a Roman palace and is a good base for ferry excursions to islands; from here take the bus or the ferry to the wonderfully preserved town of Dubrovnik, one of the wonders of the Adriatic. Alternative starting points leading to Llubljana include Venice/Trieste (see Milan–Trieste, p. 399; 3 hrs from Trieste to Llubljana, ETT table 1300); or Vienna via Graz and the old university town of Maribor (ETT tables 980, 1305; or from Villach via Bled, an attractive lake resort in the Slovenian Alps (ETT table 1315).

LJUBLJANA, SLOVENIA

The capital of Slovenia, Ljubljana is a lively university town dominated by a hilltop fortress. The River Ljubljanica divides the city into two parts, joined in the city centre by an attractive and unique triple bridge, the **Tromostovje**. This links the city's old heart, **Stari Trg**, on the right bank, built below the hilltop castle, to **Novi Trg** on the left bank.

The old town, on the **right bank**, is an inviting maze of cobbled streets with historic buildings. Recent years have witnessed a renaissance with the opening of numerous shops, restaurants and bars, many with river views and generally reasonably priced. It is a gentle stroll up to the **castle**, which gives a good view of the city below. Baroque **St Nikolas's Cathedral**, Ciril-Metodov Trg, abuts the Bishop's Palace. Beyond, on Vodnikov Trg, lies the **central food market** (Mon–Sat 0600–1800), good for picnic shopping. Going south from the cathedral, a baroque fountain by the Italian architect and sculptor Francesco Robba stands opposite the Magistrat (Town Hall) on Mestni Trg.

On the river's **left bank**, the 17th-century Franciscan **church** dominates **Prešernov Trg**. Within, the high altar is the work of Robba. The left bank of the city also contains a conglomeration of museums, including the **National Museum**, the **National Gallery** (13th–20th-century works) and the **Museum of Modern Art**. Close by, the green expanse of **Tivoli Park** offers a welcome retreat from the bustle of city life. Within the grounds stands the recently opened **Museum of Modern History**, offering a lively portrayal of Slovenia through the 20th century, complete with the sound of gunfire and a video presentation. Antiques enthusiasts should visit the **flea market** at Cankarjevo Nabrežje, Sun 0800–1300.

> **SUMMER FESTIVAL**
> The annual International Summer Festival takes place in Plečnik's open-air Križanke Theatre, attracting well known musicians, actors and dancers from all over the world (July–Aug).

Trg Osvobodline Fronte (Trg OF), a 15-min walk from the main street, Slovenska Cesta.

Tourist Offices: Stritarjeva Ulica, ☎ (01) 306 1215, fax (01) 306 1204 (www.ljubljana.si; pcl.tic-lj@ljubljana.si); branch in station, ☎ (01) 433 9475. Guided tours of the city meet at the Magistrat, Mestni Trg 1, every day 1700 (June–Sept), Sun 1100 (Oct–May).

Private rooms are available for rent through the Tourist Office, but may be in short supply during the summer. You can stay in university halls of residence during the summer break; for details enquire, in advance, at the Tourist Office.

The riverside zone between Stari Trg and Novi Trg is the centre for friendly bars and reasonably priced eating places.

SIDE TRIPS FROM LJUBLJANA Postojna (1 hr; ETT table 1300). A 2-km walk from the station lies the spectacular Postojna Cave, one of the largest cave systems in the world, with 23 km of underground passages adorned with stalactites and stalagmites. A miniature railway guides visitors through the chambers, where temperatures average 8°C the year through (woollen cloaks are available for rent at the entrance). Visitors can marvel at the bizarre 'human fish', a family of eyeless and colourless amphibians, found nowhere else in the world. Tours leave every half-hour in summer, hourly the rest of the year. Tourist information: **Postojnska Jama Turizem**, Jamska Cesta 30, ☎(05) 7000 100, fax (05) 7000 130 (www.postojnska-jama.si; postojnska.jama@siol.net).

Bled (45 mins; ETT table1315; alight Lesce-Bled), on the lake of the same name, is a magnificently situated mountain resort. Lying on the edge of Triglav National Park, Bled offers excellent boating and walking in summer, and ice-skating and skiing in winter. Perched above the lake, on a steep cliff, stands **Grad**, a stately 16th-century castle (great views; exhibition of archaeological finds and period furniture). **Tourist Office**: Cesta Svobode 15, ☎(04) 5741 122, fax (04) 5741 555 (www.bled.si; info@dzt.bled.si). There is an excellent **youth hostel**, Grajska Cesta 17, ☎(04) 574 5250, just a 5-min walk from the lake. From Bled Jezero station you can head on to Bohinj Lake (Bohinjska Bistrica station; ETT table 1307).

Bohinj lies within Triglav National Park and makes an ideal base for walking and mountain biking (cycle hire: **Alpinum**, Ribčev Laz 50, ☎(04) 572 3441). The resort is less developed than Bled, but the landscape even more stunning. **Tourist Offices**: Ribčev Laz 48, ☎(04) 572 3370, and Bohinjsko Jezero, ☎(04) 572 3370, fax (04) 572 3330 (www.bohinj.si; tdbohinj@bohinj.si).

ZAGREB, CROATIA

Zagreb has a distinctly Austro-Hungarian flavour, both in the style of its buildings and the restrained manners of its citizens. Its most beautiful quarter, **Gornji Grad** (Upper Town) has the oldest and best-preserved monuments. To reach it, begin from Trg Bana Jelačića, the main square, and follow Ilica, to reach Tomičeva, where you can take the funicular up to Strossmayer promenade for one of the best views over the city. A cannon is fired daily at 1200 from Lotrščak Tower. Next take Cirilometodska to **St Mark's Church**, noted for its extraordinary red, white and blue tiled roof, and follow Kamenita to pass through an archway, housing a shrine complete with altar, flowers and flickering candles. Turn left up Radićeva, and take one of the series of steep wooden stairways to your right, which link the upper town to Kaptol. In the cathedral look for the inscription of the ten commandments on the northern wall, written in 12th-century Glagolithic characters unique to the old Slavic language. Zagreb's fine art collection is in the **Mimara Museum,** Rooseveltov Trg 4 (closed Mon). Outdoor strolling areas include **Maksimir Park** (tram nos. 11/12 from the main square), and the Mirogoj Cemetery (frequent bus service from Kaptol in front of the Cathedral). The city is served by an excellent tram network.

In the centre of town. Left luggage and exchange offices. Bar and newspaper kiosks.

Tourist Offices: Trg Bana Jelačića 11, ☎ (01) 48 14 051 or (01) 48 14 052. A 10-min walk from the station, over the three squares, keeping to Praška on the left, to arrive in Trg Bana Jelačića, the main town square. Alternatively, take tram nos. 6/13 which follow the same route. Trg Nikole Subica Zinjskog 14, on the third square in front of the station, is responsible for guided tours. Pick up a copy of the free monthly pamphlet, *Events and Performances*, published in English.

Generally expensive (around Kn170 for a single); private rooms can be booked through the Tourist Office or various agencies. **Youth hostel**: Petrinjska 77, ☎ (01) 484 1261, out of the station turn right off the square and take the first road to the left. A 100-m walk from the station; conveniently situated but in dire need of refurbishment. You can stay at **university halls of residence** during the summer break: contact the Tourist Office for details.

The best area for eating and drinking is Tkalčićeva, a lively street leading from Trg Bana Jelačića up to Gornji Grad. The nearby **market** at **Dolac**, overlooking Trg Bana Jelačića is the best place to shop for a picnic. For a dinner in a typical Central European beer hall, visit **Medvedgrad Pivnica**, Savska Cesta 56, close to the Cibona Stadium.

SPLIT

A useful transit point for ferries, Split is also a delightful coastal town. Its historic seafront area known as **Grad** lies within the walls of the **Roman palace** built in the 3rd century by Emperor Diocletian. Traffic-free Grad consists of narrow paved alleys, opening out onto ancient piazzas. From here the Tourist Office's self-guided walk leads through town; a series of information boards highlight Split's Roman roots, the **Cathedral of St Duje**, and the various buildings dating back to periods of Venetian and Austro-Hungarian domination. Climb the cathedral bell tower for fine views. Continue through the area of **Varoš**, where steep winding steps take you to the wooded Marjan peninsula. Split's best museums are the **Museum of Croatian Archaeological Monuments** and the **Meštrović Gallery**, both in Šetalište Ivana Meštrovića. There's a festival of music, opera and theatre, mid-July–mid-Aug.

The train station, bus station and ferry port are all next to each other, overlooking Gradska Luka, the town harbour. Left luggage; supermarket. The historic centre is just 100 m away.

Tourist Office: Obala Hrvatsog Narodnog Preporoda 12, ☎ (021) 342 142. Situated on the seafront (or Riva).

Accommodation is scarce, especially in Aug. Try the Tourist Office for private rooms. Expect to pay Kn150 single, Kn230 double. Upon arrival at the port, you may approached by locals offering *sobe* (rooms) for rent – these are cheaper but standards vary dramatically.

Locals eat out primarily at **merenda**, a hearty fisherman's brunch served between 0900–1130. Simple eating places offer a fixed menu at budget prices. For typical Dalmatian food try **Kod Jose**,

Sredmanuska 4, behind the market. For a cheap stand-up lunch with locals try **ribice**, tiny fishes deep fried and served with a glass of white wine, in a canteen-style establishment opposite the fish market (**Ribarnica**), Kraj Sv. Marije 8. Nearby, the best pizza in town is served at **Galija**, Tončiceva 12. To shop for a picnic visit **Pazar**, the colourful open-air market held just outside the main walls, Mon–Sat 0700–1330. Just across the road from here the **all-night bakery** provides for midnight snacks.

Split is packed with bars, which are busy the year through. Café life centres around **Luxor** on Peristil, amid a theatrical setting of Roman ruins floodlit by night. In summer, the centre of gravity shifts to the coast, with numerous bars and clubs overlooking Bačvice Bay staying open well into the early hours.

SIDE TRIPS FROM SPLIT

Trogir: The tiny city stands on a small island with a 13th-century cathedral. Easily reached by bus.

Brač (13 ferries a day in summer, journey time 1 hr): best known for the spectacular sandspit, Zlatni Rat, near Bol; expensive and crowded in summer. **Tourist Offices**: (in Supertar), Porat 1, ☎ (021) 630 551; (in Bol) Uz Pjacu 4, ☎ (021) 635 122.

Hvar (three ferries a day, journey time 2 hrs; the more regular service, Split–Stari Grad, involves a bus transfer to Hvar town): an island famed for its wines, lavender, pretty fishing villages and unspoilt coastline. Hvar town is one of the finest island settlements, with buildings dating back to the 15th century planned around the harbour, backed by a hilltop castle. **Tourist Office**: (in Hvar town), Trg Sv Stjepana 16, ☎ (021) 741 059.

DUBROVNIK

Dubrovnik is one of the most impressive medieval fortified cities on the Mediterranean. The best way to get a feel of the place is to walk the full 2 km circuit of the walls (open summer 0900–1930, winter 1000–1500; admission Kn10), which give a series of vantage points over the terracotta rooftops, the churches, the sea and the islands. For centuries Dubrovnik was a refined and prosperous trading port, which managed to keep its independence by paying off various would-be conquerors. Fine buildings such as the Rector's Palace, the Sponza Palace and Jesuit Church still bear witness to this glorious past. There's a major festival, mid-July–mid-Aug, with outdoor theatre, opera, jazz and classical music.

🚌 Put Republike 19, 24-hr left luggage.

🛳 Gruž Port, Obala S. Radića, ☎ (020) 418 000. The Jadrolinija coastal service runs Split-Dubrovnik, 4 times per week in summer, journey time 7–10 hrs depending on number of stops, Kn72.

ℹ️ **Tourist Office**: Placa 1, ☎ (020) 426 354 or (020) 426 355. Pick up a copy of the free monthly *Tourist Guide of Dubrovnik*.

🛏 **Youth Hostel**, Ulica Bana Jelačica 15–17, ☎ (020) 423 241; 100 m from the coach station and 300 m from the city walls. Clean and friendly.

🍴 Try along Prijeko, a picturesque narrow street running parallel to the central street, Placa, is the main area for eating out within the city walls. However, cheaper and less commercial restaurants can be found in Gunduljićeva Poljana, behind the cathedral.

(for Directory information, see pp. 591, 593, 604 and 612).

DENMARK, FINLAND, NORWAY AND SWEDEN

Scandinavian countries have much in common, with histories dominated by Viking exploits and political upheavals, as Denmark and Sweden sought to impose their authority over the Baltic and national boundaries changed many times.

English is widely spoken, making communication easy, aided by the natural friendliness of Scandinavians. All these countries are expensive by European standards, with costs particularly high in Norway. Scandinavian towns and buildings tend to have a neat, tidy look that's appealing to some, and dull to others. Queuing systems apply to train and hotel reservations, currency exchange offices, tourist offices and post offices throughout Scandinavia: collect a number on entry (make sure it's the right machine otherwise you may have to queue up again) and then wait your turn. At busy times, queues can be very long, particularly for train reservations, where you may have to wait a couple of hours. In the summer, the main train routes in Scandinavia (particularly Copenhagen to Oslo) are very busy and advance reservation is strongly advised.

FOOD AND DRINK

While each country has its own specialities, the Scandinavians share a love of fish – herring, sole and dried cod in particular. Meat can include reindeer or elk, and there is the open sandwich *smørrebrød* which, topped with meat, fish or cheese, can be a meal in itself. Eating out is quite expensive but there are good supermarkets where you can buy sandwiches and pastries. Coffee, tea and hot chocolate are widely available: a second cup of coffee is often free or half price. Alcohol is expensive, and you have to be over 18 or in some cases over 20 to buy it. See country specialities below. *Dagens Ret* is the day's special menu which is generally good value.

DENMARK

Protruding between the Baltic and the North Sea, **Denmark** incorporates some 400 islands, 90 of which are inhabited, as well as the peninsula of **Jutland**. It's low-lying and undramatic terrain, where you sense you're never far from the sea. With its 7000 km of coast, it has a long maritime tradition going back to the Vikings. Along the coast you'll also find quaint centuries-old fishing communities. **Copenhagen** is the brightest, liveliest spot in the nation, accounting for more than a quarter of the country's 5 million population. The island of **Fyn** (Funen) has some of the most attractive of Danish landscapes, and its main city, **Odense**, is celebrated as the birthplace of Hans Christian Andersen. Some of the nearby islands, such as **Ærø**, have an aptly fairy-tale prettiness and are tailor-made for exploring on foot or by cycle. **Århus**, in Jutland, is the most vibrant place outside Copenhagen.

ACCOMMODATION
Local Tourist Offices have brochures and booklets (mostly free) listing all types of accommodation, and they can make same-day bookings if you turn up in person (rooms in private homes are usually without breakfast).

HOTELS Branches of the **Danish Tourist Board** have the free annual *Denmark Accommodation Guide*. This covers **hotels**, **holiday centres** and **inns**, together with details of various discount schemes. In Copenhagen, expect to pay from DKr.400 for a double, without facilities but including breakfast. Elsewhere expect to pay from DKr.350. In rural areas the old inns, known as *kros*, are characterful places to stay. Hotel standards are good and the choice and price range are wide. Hotels affiliated to **Horesta**, the Danish hoteliers' association, are classified by one to five stars.

BED & BREAKFAST Dansk Bed & Breakfast publish a brochure of around 300 bed & breakfast establishments throughout Denmark (from DKr.150 per person per night); it can also make bookings. **Dansk Bed & Breakfast,** PO Box 53, Bernstorffsvej 71A, DK-2900, Hellerup, Denmark, ☎ (45) 39 61 04 05, fax (45) 39 61 05 25 (www.bbdk.dk; bed@bbdk.dk).

HOSTELS There are around 100 official (HI) **Danhostels** (*vandrerhjem*), graded one to five stars, and the general standard is excellent; most have private rooms (sleeping 2–6; DKr.200–600) as well as dormitories (sleeping bags usually not allowed; about DKr.100). Hostel cards can be bought on the spot for DKr.160. Hostelling headquarters: **Danhostel**, Vesterbrogade 39, DK-1620, Copenhagen V, Denmark, ☎ (45) 33 31 36 12, fax (45) 33 31 36 26 (www.danhostel.dk; ldv@danhostel.dk).

CAMPING The Camping Pass, available from any campsite, costs DKr.75. Camping/caravan sites are graded from one to five stars and cost from around DKr.50 a night per person. Many camps also have attractive self-catering cabins, costing DKr.2000–4500 a week for 2–6 people. Wild camping is permitted in designated areas only (details from Tourist Offices). **Campingrådet**, Hesseløgade 16, DK-2100 Copenhagen Ø, Denmark, ☎ (45) 39 27 88 44, fax (45) 39 27 80 44 (www.campingraadet.dk; info@campingraadet.dk).

SLEEP-INS For cheap, city-centre sleeping, try **Sleep-Ins** (high season only). Basic facilities (bring a sleeping bag) but clean and safe. Some have an upper age limit (usually 35). Average price DKr.100.

FOOD AND DRINK

Look for *Dagens Ret* (today's special), which is cheaper than à la carte. Open sandwiches (*smørrebrød*) are served on *rugbrød* (rye bread) or *frankskbrød* (wheat bread). *Sild* (herring), *rejer* (prawns) or *gammel ost* (a strong cheese) are typical and tasty lunchtime toppings. *Frikadeller* are meatballs and *wienerbrød* are real, flaky Danish pastries. The local spirit is *akvavit*, drunk ice-cold and down in one.

FINLAND

Tucked up into Scandinavia's north-eastern corner and stretching well into the Arctic, **Finland** is a relatively new country, having gained independence in 1917, and is probably the least-known Scandinavian nation. It formerly belonged to its neighbours, first Sweden in the Middle Ages, then after 1808 it became an autonomous Grand Duchy of tsarist Russia. There are cultural overtones to be found from both these countries, but Finland also has a strong identity of its own.

The south-western corner is the most populous region by far and includes **Turku**, the country's long-standing spiritual and cultural hub, as well as the rewarding industrial city of **Tampere**. The capital, **Helsinki**, is especially striking for its 19th- and 20th-century architecture. Glaciers gouged out huge trenches that became thousands of lakes, making up the **Finnish Lake District** that, together with the vast forests, covers much of southern Finland. Comfortable trains link the major towns, which, like the lines themselves, are virtually all confined to the south. For scenic rail routes, head for the lake regions, notably from **Helsinki** to **Oulu**, and from **Pieksämäki** to **Tampere**.

Like the rest of Scandinavia, Finland is an easy place to meet people and the Finns are friendly and receptive.

You can mitigate the cost by buying vouchers (valid mid-May–Sept) on the **Finncheque hotel discount scheme** from local travel agencies or specialist Finland tour operators in your own country.

ACCOMMODATION

Some Tourist Offices **book accommodation** for a small fee.

HOTELS Hotels tend to be quite luxurious and expensive. Better for budget travellers are **kesähotelli** or **sommarhotellen** (summer hotels, open June–Aug, in student accommodation) and **matkustajakoti** (the relatively cheap tourist hotels). Ask at Tourist Offices for the free brochures *Hotels in Finland* (not graded, but standards are high) or *Camping and Hostels*.

As is traditional in Scandinavia, **saunas** are pretty universal, even on ferries and in hostels; **M** is for men, **N** for women.

HOSTELS The 105 **hostels** (*retkeilymajat*; pronounced ret-kay-loo-mayat) are well spread across the country and 50 are open year-round. They're graded from two to four stars, all with dormitories sleeping 5+ as well as singles, doubles and rooms for 3–4; prices are around €10–45 without sheet sleeping bag (€3.50 extra); discount of around €2.60 per night for HI members. It's advisable to book ahead in July and Aug, and to warn if you will be arriving after 1800; booking is mandatory in winter. Many hostels have activity programmes, plus canoes, skis, boats and cycles. The Finnish hostelling association headquarters is **Suomen Retkeilymajajärjestö (SRM),** Yrjönkatu 38 B 15, FIN-00100 Helsinki, Finland, ☎(358) (9) 565 7150, fax (358) (9) 565 71510 (www.srmnet.org; info@srm.inet.fi).

CAMPING Campsites are widespread too (about 350; 200 belong to the **Finnish Travel Association's** national network). Sites are currently being reclassified from one to five stars; five-star sites typically have **camping cottages** sleeping up to five and are sometimes very well appointed (maybe including a sauna). Rough camping is generally allowed providing you keep 150 m from residents and remove any trace of your stay.

FOOD AND DRINK Fixed-price menus in a *ravintola* (upmarket restaurant) are the best value, or you may want to try a *grilli* (fast-food stand), *kahvila* (self-service cafeteria) or a *baari* (snack bar). For self-caterers, try **Slepa, Siwa, Saastari** or **Valintatalo** supermarkets. Some specials are *muikunmati* (a freshwater fish roe served with onions and cream and accompanied by toast or pancakes) and for dessert *kiisseli* (berry mousse). **ALKO** is the state-owned outlet that sells alcohol.

NORWAY

Stretching 1800 km, far above the Arctic Circle, **Norway** is one of Europe's great natural wonderlands. Its majestic fjords – massive watery corridors created by glacial action – make up one of the finest coastlines in the world, among a wild mountainous terrain that includes **Jostedalsbreen**, mainland Europe's largest glacier. **Bergen** makes the ideal access point for taking a cruise or a ferry to see the fjords at close range. The majestic scenery continues far north beyond the Arctic Circle.

The downside of visiting Norway is the cost: prices are higher than most of the rest of Europe, and even by camping or hostelling and living frugally, you'll inevitably notice the difference. Be sure to stock up on the essentials before going.

ACCOMMODATION **HOSTELS** Because Norway is so expensive, the **youth hostel** network is indispensable if you don't want to break the bank. There are some 90 hostels (*vandrerhjem*), many of which unfortunately open only mid-June–mid-Aug. The standard of hostel accommodation is very high, with singles, doubles and dormitories, and there's a good geographical spread. Booking ahead is highly recommended, and mandatory Oct–Apr. The Norwegian **HI** logo is a variation on the usual theme: a stylised green tree and blue hut with a yellow sun. The charge is NKr.100–300, excluding linen. The hostelling headquarters, **Norske Vandrerhjem**, are at Dronningensgate 26, N-0154, Oslo, ☎(47) 23 13 93 00, fax (47) 23 13 93 50 (www.vandrerhjem.no; hostels@online.no).

Private houses offering rooms can be quite good value, and in some cases almost the same price as hostels, with the advantage of greater privacy. Moving up the price scale, there are **guesthouses** and **pensions**.

HOTELS Generally very pricey, but many cut rates at weekends and in summer. Advance booking is important, especially in **Oslo**, **Bergen** and **Stavanger**, which are popular towns for conferences as well as tourists. Local Tourist Offices provide lists of all types of accommodation; most will make bookings for a small fee.

CAMPING Many of the 1500 official **campsites** (with 5-star classification) have pre-bookable **log cabins** for two or four people. Campsites nearly always have cabins (*hytter*), sleeping 2–4 people and equipped with kitchen and maybe a bathroom. Rough camping is permitted as long as you don't intrude on residents (you must be 150 m from them) or leave any trace of your stay. Never light fires in summer.

FOOD AND DRINK Specials here include *gravetlaks* (marinated salmon cured in dill) and *fiskesuppe* (a satisfying fish and vegetable soup. Meat can be hearty stew, sausages or meatballs. You may see heads of fish and animals – these are eaten by the locals. State-owned shops for wines and spirits are known as **Vinmonopol** but lagers are sold inexpensively in supermarkets. Bars may restrict the drinking age to over 21.

SWEDEN

Scandinavia's largest country includes huge tracts of forest and thousands of lakes, with mildly rolling, fertile terrain to the south, and excitingly rugged uplands spilling over the Norwegian border and beyond the Arctic Circle into **Lappland**. The sheer amount of space is positively exhilarating. The beaches (including naturist ones) compare with the finest in Europe, and in summer the climate of the south is much like that of Central Europe, except with longer days. Mosquitoes can be a problem, so take a strong repellent.

Sweden has a conspicuously comfortable standard of living: owing to its tax and social welfare system you won't see much poverty – conversely, few are ostentatiously rich either; equality is the buzz word. For all their sophistication, Swedes are very aware of their country origins, and walking, nature and village life are close to their hearts. National costume is accepted as formal wear, and there's a thriving tradition of handicrafts, particularly woodcrafts.

ACCOMMODATION

You can sleep in fair comfort at a reasonable price in Sweden. Tourist Offices have listings of places to stay and charge a small booking fee. **The Swedish Travel & Tourism Council** (see p. 614) can provide a national list of hotels (*Hotels in Sweden*). Local Tourist Offices have listings for their area, including farmhouse accommodation. You can also get brochures of individual chains, such as **Sweden Hotels** (hotels with individual character). **Bed and Breakfast Service Stockholm** can provide rooms and flats in the capital.

HOTELS Hotel standards are high and the cost usually includes a sauna and breakfast (prices from SKr.400–600 for a single/SKr.700–900 for a double).

HOSTELS There are more than 300 HI hostels (*vandrarhem*) about half of which open only in summer (most do not allow sleeping bags); some are extremely characterful places and include castles and boats. Family rooms are available. Most hostels are shut 1000–1700, and charges are about SKr.75–180 (additional Skr.40 for non-HI members). Hostels are run by **Svenska Turistföreningen** (**STF**). There are also 135 independent hostels operated by **SVIF**, Makrillviken, SE-450 43 Smögen (www.svif.se). Room-only accommodation in **private houses** is a good budget alternative.

CAMPING **Sveriges Campingvärdars Riksförbund** (**SCR**, Swedish Camping Site Owners' Association) lists around 650 campsites. You can rough camp for one night if you keep more than 150 m from the nearest house and leave no litter.

FOOD AND DRINK

Hearty buffet breakfasts are a good start to the day. Some cheap eateries for later on are the *konditori* (cafés) and fast-food outlets. *Pytt i panna* is a hearty fry-up and other traditional dishes are pea soup served with pancakes, and *Jansson's temptation* (potatoes, onions and anchovies). **Systembolaget** is the state-owned outlet for alcohol – shoppers must be over 20 but you can buy alcoholic drinks in pubs and cafés at 18.

Sweden Hotels, Sveavägen 39, Box 3377, S-103 67 Stockholm, ☎ (46) (8) 701 7900, fax (46) (8) 701 7910 (www.swedenhotels.se).

Svenska Turistföreningen (**STF**), Stureplan 4C, PO Box 25, 101 20 Stockholm, ☎ (46) (8) 463 21 00, fax (46) (8) 678 19 58 (www.stfturist.se).

Bed and Breakfast Service Stockholm, Sidenvägen 17, SE-178 37 Ekerö, ☎ (46) (8) 660 55 65, fax (46) (8) 663 38 22 (www.bedbreakfast.a.se).

Sveriges Campingvärdars Riksförbund (**SCR**), PO Box 255, SE-451 17 Uddevalla, ☎ (46) (522) 393 45, fax (46) (522) 64 24 30 (www.camping.se).

EDITOR'S CHOICE

Bergen (and surrounding fjords); Copenhagen; Geirangerfjord from Åndalsnes (p. 478); Gothenburg; Helsinki; Kuopio; Legoland (near Århus); Linköping (museum village); Lofoten Islands (near Bodø); Lund; Malmö; Odense (Hans Christian Andersen museum); Oslo; Savonlinna; Stockholm; Turku; Uppsala. Scenic rail journeys: Oslo–Bergen (p. 470); Stavanger–Kristiansand (p. 470); Oslo–Boden (p. 476); Norway in a Nutshell (p. 474); Stockholm–Gällivare (Inlandsbanan; p. 481); Helsinki–Oulu (p. 495).

BEYOND THE BORDERS

See Where Next? panels for Copenhagen (p. 443) and Helsinki (p. 448).

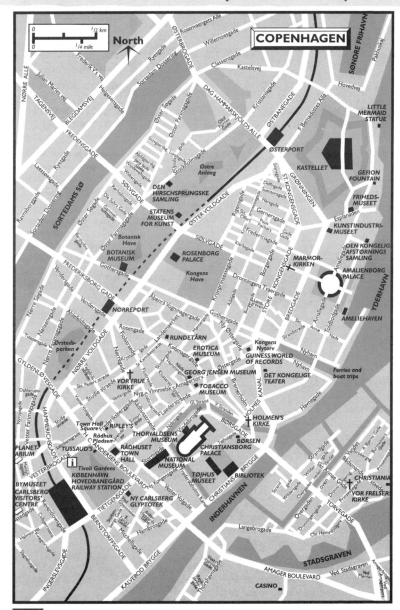

COPENHAGEN

North

½ km
¼ mile

NØRRE ALLÉ
TAGENSVEJ
BLEGDAMSVEJ
FREDENSGADE
Julian Maries vej
Frederik V's vej
Helgesensgade
Ryesgade
Sortedam Dossering
Ryesgade
Willemoesgade
ØSTERBROGADE
Rosenvængets Alle
Classensgade
Kastelsvej
Sortedam Dossering
DAG HAMMARSKJOLDS ALLE
Kristianiagade
F. Bernadottes Alle
Hovedvej
SØNDRE FRIHAVN
Pakhusvej

LITTLE MERMAID STATUE

ØSTBANEGADE
ØSTERPORT

KASTELLET

GEFION FOUNTAIN

FRIHEDS-MUSEET

KUNSTINDUSTRI-MUSEET

Laessegade
Ryesgade
Rantzausgade
Rosenørns Alle
Sortedam Dossering
SØLVGADE
Kerteholmsgade
Ole Suhrs Gade
Øster Farimagsgade
ØSTER VOLDGADE
ØSTER FARIMAGSGADE

SORTEDAMS SØ

Øster Søgade
Abildgaards
Jens gade
Wiedeweltsgade

Øste Anlæg

DEN HIRSCHSPRUNGSKE SAMLING

STATENS MUSEUM FOR KUNST

ST GRØNNINGEN
Dalingade
Svanensgade
Hærøgade
Gernersgade
Pauls Gade
Olfert Fischers Gade
Gadet
SØLVGADE
Fredericiagade
Klerkegade

STORE KONGENSGADE

Esplanaden

DEN KONGELIG AFSTØRNINGS SAMLING

AMALIENBORG PALACE

Botanisk Have

BOTANISK MUSEUM

ROSENBORG PALACE

Kongens Have

Gotherggade

Borgergade

MARMOR-KIRKEN

AMELIEHAVEN

YDERHAVN

FREDERIKSBORG GADE
Nørre Søgade
Vendersgade

NØRREPORT

Åbenrå
Vognmagergade
Gothersgade
Landemærket
Øster
Dronningens Tværgade
BREDGADE
Sankt Annæ Plads
Sankt Annæ Plads
Toldbodgade
Nyhavn

Nansensgade
Tullinsgade
Nørre Voldgade
Rosengade
Frolandt

Ørsteds-parken

RUNDETÅRN

EROTICA MUSEUM

Kongens Nytorv

GUINESS WORLD OF RECORDS

Nyhavn

Ferries and boat trips

GYLDENLØVESGADE
NØRRE VOLDGADE
Ahlefeldtsgade

Dahlerups-gade
Skt. Peders stræde
Studie stræde
VOR FRUE KIRKE
Nyg
Vimmelsk
Amagertorv
Skindergade
Købmagergade
Klosterstr
Niels Hemmingsensgade
Østergade

GEORG JENSEN MUSEUM

DET KONGELIGE TEATER

TOBACCO MUSEUM

Bremerholm

HOLMES KANAL

HAMMERICHSGADE
VESTERBROGADE
Vester Farimagsgade
Studie stræde
Lavendelstræde
Nørregade
Vestergade
Gl Strand
V.Stranden

Town Hall Square
RIPLEY'S
Rådhus Pladsen

BORSGADE

HOLMEN'S KIRKE

PLANET-ARIUM

TUSSAUD'S

THORVALDSENS MUSEUM

RÅDHUSET TOWN HALL

NATIONAL MUSEUM

CHRISTIANSBORG PALACE

BØRSEN

Strandgade

CHRISTIANIA

VOR FRELSERS KIRKE

HANS ANDERSENS BOULEVARD

Tivoli Gardens

KØBENHAVN HOVEDBANEGÅRD RAILWAY STATION

TØJHUS MUSEET

DET KONGELIGE BIBLIOTEK

CHRISTIANS BRYGGE

INDERHAVNEN

TORVEGADE

BYMUSEET
CARLSBERG VISITORS' CENTRE

TIETGENSGADE
VESTERBROGADE
Reventlowsgade
Colbjørnsgade

NY CARLSBERG GLYPTOTEK

BERNSTORFFSGADE

Hambrosgade

Langebrogade

INGERSLEVSGADE

KALVEBOD BRYGGE

AMAGER BOULEVARD

STADSGRAVEN

Ved Stadsgraven

CASINO

Copenhagen manages to be civilised, refined and vibrant, all at the same time: its easy-going, friendly atmosphere is perhaps its greatest draw. Cruise boats tour the canals that thread through a historic core revealing an appealing diversity of open spaces, spires, towers and statuary. Cycling is encouraged here, and the outdoor, almost Mediterranean, feel is compounded by an effervescent street life.

ARRIVAL AND DEPARTURE

The main rail station is **København Hovedbanegården (København H;** www.dsb.dk), with an S-train (local train) station of the same name. There are dozens of shops and cafés in the large, bright concourse, including a supermarket, a post office, a **bureau de change** and a newsagent that stocks English-language newspapers. There is a left luggage office (*bagagebokse*) and toilets and showers.

Buses to districts in and around Copenhagen stop right outside and the city centre is a 5-min walk away.

Take the train to **Helsingør** and catch the 20-min **Scandlines** ferry (which leaves every 20 mins; less often at night) to **Helsingborg** on the Swedish side. Note that there are also trains every 20 mins to Malmö (much quicker than the ferry).

Copenhagen Airport Kastrup, 📞 32 31 32 31 (www.cph.dk), is 8 km south-east of town. There is a tourist information desk, car hire desk, train ticket office, bank and hotel reservations desk in the arrival hall. Trains to København H every 20 mins, taking 12 mins, for DKr.19.50 if you buy the ticket before boarding the train but DKr.25 on the train. 🚌 no. 250S also runs every 10 mins to the city centre and takes 40 mins.

INFORMATION

The Tourist Office has information covering all of Denmark. Get the *Copenhagen Map* and a copy of *Copenhagen This Week* (published monthly; also at www.ctw.dk), both of which are free and incorporate masses of useful information. Also try to get hold of *The Copenhagen Post*, a weekly newspaper (out Fri) in English, for recent news and more listings.

THE LITTLE MERMAID
Combine a visit to this little statue (of Hans Christian Andersen fame) with other sights. From Kongens Nytorv walk along Bredgade to the **Marble Church** (Marmor Kirken), the **Gefion** fountain, the **Fortress** (Kastellet) and the **Little Mermaid** (Den Lille Havfrue).

For budget travellers, the first port of call should be the youth tourism service **USE IT**, Rådhusstræde 13, 📞 33 73 06 20, fax 33 73 06 49 (www.useit.dk; useit@ui.dk). All of its services are free and include internet access, short-term left luggage, poste-restante, a share-a-car notice board and free condoms. They can book you a room in a private home or ring around hostels to check availability. Make sure you get a copy of the free *Playtime* magazine, an excellent (annually updated) guide to Copenhagen on a tight budget.

DENMARK

TOURIST OFFICE

WONDERFUL COPENHAGEN

Postal address: Gammel
Kongevej 1, DK-1610,
København V, ☎ 70 22 24 42
(Mon–Fri 1000–1630),
fax 70 22 24 52
(www.visitcopenhagen.dk;
touristinfo@woco.dk).
Personal visits: Bernstorffsgade
1, opposite the station, by
Tivoli's main entrance.

MONEY In København H are **Den Danske Bank**, open daily 0800–2000 and **Forex**, open daily 0800–2100.

POST AND PHONES **Central Station Post Office** has the longest opening hours, Mon–Fri 0800–2100, Sat 0900–1600, Sun 1000–1600. Unless otherwise specified, poste restante mail goes to **Fisketorvet Posthus**, Kalvebod Brygge 59, 1560 København V, open Mon-Fri 1000–1800, Sat 1000–1400.

PUBLIC TRANSPORT

Buses and trains (0500–0030 and nightbuses) all form part of an integrated system in the Copenhagen area and tickets are valid on both. Nightbus fares are double. Most attractions are central, so for a single journey you will probably only need the cheapest ticket, DKr.13, which covers travel in two zones for 1 hr. Alternatively, buy either an all-zone 24-hr transport pass (DKr.75), or a **klippekort** ten-ride ticket covering two or three zones (DKr.90 or DKr.120). These tickets must be validated in the machines on board buses and on S-train platforms. Bus route maps available at HT info bureau on Rådhuspladsen (☎ 36 13 14 15; www.ht.dk). The **Copenhagen Card** (www.copenhagencard.dk) can be valid for 24 hrs (DKr.175), 48 hrs (DKr.295) or 72 hrs (DKr.395). It provides free public transport in Copenhagen and the surrounding region, gives free entrance to most attractions (including Tivoli), discounts on some ferries to Sweden and some attractions in southern Sweden. It is on sale at the airport, DSB stations, HT ticket offices, hotels, hostels, campsites, travel agents and Tourist Offices. For longer stays (fortnight plus) and frequent travel, consider buying a monthly pass (**Pendlerkort**); see p. 591. The first phase of a (driverless) metro stytem, known as the 'Mini Metro', opened in 2002, with further sections to open during 2003. There will be three lines, running east to west with an extension south.

ACCOMMODATION

Booking ahead is advisable although some hostels don't take advance bookings. The Tourist Office (see above) has a same-day booking service for most types of accommodation but you must turn up in person. You pay a DKr.50 fee but they can often get you a good discount. Tourist Office's free advance booking service (hotels only): ☎70 22 24 42 (Mon–Fri 1000–1630 only), fax 70 22 24 52 (booking@woco.dk).

See also **USE IT** (Information, p. 439).

An area in which the downmarket hotels tend to cluster is **Istedgade** (to the side of the station, away from the centre). In the summer months, when demand is high, Copenhagen offers a good choice of **hostel accommodation**, but you must arrive early if you have not booked. There are three HI hostels, all a fair distance out: **Copenhagen Amager**, Vejlands Allé 200, ☎32 52 29 08 (copenhagen@danhostel.dk), is 4 km southeast of the centre (Metro: SUNDBY or BELLA CENTER, both 1km away) but right beside the

stops for 🚌 nos. 37/46/100S; **Copenhagen Bellahøj**, Herbergvejen 8, ☎38 28 97 15 (bellahoej@danhostel.dk), is 4 km north-west of the centre in the opposite direction – 20 mins on 🚌 nos. 2/11, or nightbus no. 82N; and **Lyngby-Tårbæk Vandrerhjem**, Rådvad 1, Lyngby, ☎45 80 30 74, S-train to Lyngby, change to 🚌 nos. 187 (Mon–Fri), 100 m from hostel, and 182, 183 (Sat–Sun), 2 km from hostel, direction Hjortekjaer, is about 15 km from Copenhagen (open Apr–late Oct). The two hostel-style **Sleep-Ins** are more conveniently located, **Sleep-In**, Blegdamsvej 132, ☎35 26 50 59 (copenhagen@sleep-in.dk); open late June–Aug (🚌 nos. 1/6/14 or nightbus 85N/95N) and **Sleep-In Green**, Ravnsborggade 18, ☎35 37 77 77; open July–Aug (🚌 nightbus 81N/84N).
The **City Public Hostel**, Vesterbro Ungdomsgård, Absalonsgade 8, ☎ 33 31 20 70, fax 33 55 00 85, open mid-May–late Aug (6-min walk from København H), is another good option. The most central **campsite** is **Bellahøj Camping**, Hvidkildevej 66, ☎ 38 10 11 50, fax 38 10 13 32, open June–Aug (🚌 no. 11 or nightbus 81N/82N).

FOOD AND DRINK

Copenhagen This Week and *Playtime* have listings for all sorts of eating; the latter is full of tips for doing so on a budget. **Nyhavn** with its outdoor tables is pretty at night, but expensive. Traditional Danish fare is not cheap, but it's worth visiting one of the cellar restaurants (off Strøget) to sample the mainly Danish specialities.

There are many good cafés and take-aways in the smaller streets around **Vor Frue Kirke** including Turkish, Greek and Italian restaurants offering good-value buffet menus. **Vesterbro** and **Nørrebro** (Skt Hans Torv) are good areas for lively, cheap eateries. The best foodies' shopping street, Vaernedamsvej, has all manner of exotic groceries, delis, bakers, cheesemongers and a celebrated chocolatier, **Bo Bojesen**.

HIGHLIGHTS

Punctuated with pretty squares and invariably full of shoppers and strollers, **Strøget** is the pedestrian-only zone at the heart of the city.

On the far side of Gothersgade, the green-roofed Dutch Renaissance-style **Rosenborg Slot** (Rosenborg Palace) sits majestically in the **Rosenborg Have** (Rosenborg Garden), a tempting spot for sunbathing and picnics. The palace, no longer home to the royals, is now a museum of sumptuous palace furnishings and portraits of Danish Royalty from Christian IV onwards. The Crown Jewels are displayed in the basement along with the elaborate riding gear of Christian IV, who built the palace. From here, beaver-hatted soldiers march east for the **Changing of the Guard** at the current royal domicile, **Amalienborg** (accompanied by a band when the Queen is in residence; closed Mon). This consists of a quartet of rococo palaces near the quay, framing a courtyard that's overlooked by an equestrian statue of Frederick V. Especially photogenic is the nearby 300-year-old **Nyhavn** (New Harbour), bordered by picturesque 18th-century townhouses, cafés and masts of restored sailing vessels.

DENMARK

By contrast, in south-east Copenhagen lies **Christiania** – a self-governing, alternative society, which started in the 70s when homeless people and political activists took over the disused naval warehouses. It's a fun place to wander in: a maze of graffiti-encrusted alternative housing, cafés, bars and workshops. Cannabis is sold openly in 'Pusher Street' but be aware that it is illegal in Denmark.

Photography is not welcomed. There are several lively bars and cheap places to eat and **Den Grå Hal** is an excellent concert venue; 15 mins walk, or 🚌 no. 8 from the centre or take the harbour bus.

Other uniquely Danish attractions include **Kunstindustrimuseet** (Museum of Decorative Art), with a vast worldwide selection of applied art, including the pinnacles of Danish design (closed Mon); the **Carlsberg Visitors' Centre** at the brewery at Gamle Carlsbergvej 11 (closed Mon); the **Black Diamond**, Søren Kierkegaards Plads 1, an immense granite and glass extension to the Royal Library that reflects spectacularly from its waterside site; and the **Rundetårn** (Round Tower) in Købmagergade, built as an observatory and offering great views of the city (closed Sun).

Most museums and galleries are closed on Monday. An exception is the **Hirschprungske Samling** (Hirschprung Collection), a small gallery near the Botanical Gardens, showing Danish 19th and early 20th-century paintings including works by the famous Skagen painters.

Several **museums** are free on Wednesday, including the **Nationalmuseet** (closed Mon; with Viking treasures and ancient and Renaissance collections); the **Statens Museum for Kunst** (National Gallery; Danish and international paintings, sculptures and installations); and the **New Carlsberg Glyptotek** (closed Mon; also free on Sun; probably the best gallery in Copen-hagen; don't miss Rodin's sculptures, the Roman collection and the French

SHOPPING

Prices are somewhat higher than in other western European capitals. Design plays an important part in Danish living and many ordinary household objects are worth buying for that alone. Streets around **Vesterbro**, **Nørrebro** and **Studiestrœde** have many trendy boutiques, as well as shops selling second-hand books, records and so forth. **Ravnsborggade** and **Ryesgade** are two streets that make up the city's antiques quarter. Keep a look out for posters/ signs for flea markets (*loppemarked*), usually held at weekends.

mpressionists' works). Devotees of the philosopher Søren Kierkegaard and the fairy-tale writer Hans Christian Andersen should seek out their graves in **Assistens Cemetery** in Nørrebro.

For clean, sandy **beaches** take the S-train, line C from København H to Klampenborg; **Charlottenlund** and **Bellevue beaches** are close to the station, and the age-old **Bakken amusement park** in **Dyrehaven** (the Deer Park) is nearby.

NIGHT-TIME AND EVENTS

There are comprehensive listings in *Copenhagen This Week*, *The Copenhagen Post* and *Playtime*. Copenhagen's night scene is lively, and dress is almost always informal. There is no shortage of cafés and bars with live music. Discos and clubs tend to get lively around midnight and stay open until 0500 (the bakeries open at around 0600). The admission charge is usually not very high and prices for drinks are seldom loaded.

Alternatively, the city has a long theatrical tradition. Among some 160 stages, **Det Kongelige Teater** (Royal Theatre), Kongens Nytorv, reigns supreme. See *Copenhagen This Week* for listings. Films are almost invariably shown in the original language and subtitled. Film buffs should visit the **Danish Film Institute** on Gothersgade (opposite Rosenborg Slot).

The hip music venue is **Vega**, with two concert halls and a dance bar called Ideal. **Base Camp** is a superclub in a former cannon foundry near to Christiania, with space for 3000. **Pan Disco** at 3 Knabrostræde is a popular gay venue.

Annual events include the Fashion Design Festival in May, the Copenhagen International Jazz Festival in July and Copenhagen Mermaid Pride (gay parade) in August. Out of town, the July rock festival in Roskilde features many international stars.

LIGHTING UP THE TIVOLI

Best seen at night, when 100,000 fairy lights are switched on, Tivoli amusement park (founded 1843) is Copenhagen's playground, with everything from fairground rides to ballet – and dozens of eateries. Tivoli is open mid-Apr–late Sept and mid-Nov–late Dec for the Christmas Market. Two nights a week, fireworks are let off just before midnight. Entrance is quite expensive.

WHERE NEXT FROM COPENHAGEN?

*Southwards to **Hamburg** (p. 252) via the train ferry between Rødby and Puttgarten (five per day; 4 hrs 30 mins journey time; ETT tables 50 and 720). Trains to **Malmö** and beyond in Sweden cross on the new Øresund Fixed Link (ETT tables 701, 727, 730, 735 and 737. Booking strongly recommended, especially at weekends.).*

FINLAND: HELSINKI (HELSINGFORS)

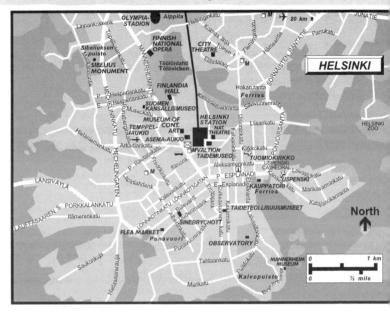

Built on a series of peninsulas and distinctly a city of the sea, Helsinki (Helsingfors) is perhaps something of an acquired taste, with a gritty, northern flavour, and both small and relatively modern as European capitals go. It became the capital of Finland in 1812 while under Russian influence and was rebuilt in a grand grid in the 19th century. With its public buildings standing proud on great granite steps, it has a distinctively Russian air, having been modelled on St Petersburg. The streets exude an exhilarating sense of space, while in the midst of it all rears the onion dome of the Russian Orthodox cathedral. Many buildings have sunny yellow walls, countering the slightly forbidding look.

ARRIVAL AND DEPARTURE

Helsinki, open Sun–Thurs 0515–0130; Fri–Sat 0515–0100. An amazingly innovative art nouveau structure of 1916 by Eliel Saarinen, a sight in itself, foreshadowing the art deco style that was to emerge later; as a station it is central and reasonably well-equipped. English newspapers are available at R-kioski, a Forex office converts currency, the **VR** (Finnish Railways; ☎0100 121; www.vr.fi) information offices open 0600–2200 daily, and there are several eateries. Lockers and a lost-property office are in the wing near platform 11 (open 0630–2200). The station is linked to the labyrinthine metro stop at **Rautatientori** (Railway Square) and is the terminal for many local buses, while a number of trams have stops in front of the station.

TOURIST OFFICE

Pohjoisesplanadi 19, (09) 169 3757, fax (09) 169 3839 (www.hel.fi/tourism; tourist.info@hel.fi); five blocks from the station, south on Keskuskatu, left on Pohjoisesplanadi).

Most leaflets are free and include a street map. Get the free leaflet *Helsinki on Foot*, which describes six separate walks, and *Helsinki This Week* (www.helsinkiexpert.fi).

For nationwide information, cross the road to the **Finnish Tourist Board: MEK (Matkailun edistämiskeskus)**, Eteläesplanadi 4, (09) 4176 9300 (www.mek.fi).

There are many **cruises**, both within Scandinavia and to **Tallinn (Estonia)** and **Germany**: check whether a visa is needed for your destination. The big companies are: **Silja Line**, (0203) 74 552 (www.silja.fi), and **Viking Line**, (09) 12351 (www.vikingline.fi). **Tallink**, (09) 2282 1277 (www.tallink.fi), has the cheapest ferries and catamarans to Tallinn (see p. 512). Buses to the city centre go from the ferry terminal (which has only limited currency exchange facilities, so come prepared with plenty of Euros).

Long-distance buses: (09) 6136 8433. The main terminal is off Mannerheimintie, just west of the post office. Tickets can be purchased at the terminal or on board.

Helsinki–Vantaa, (09) 82 771, 20 km north; has a Thomas Cook exchange bureau. **Finnair buses** depart (every 20 mins 0545–0110) from their office, Asema–Aukio 1 (Station Yard); 0800 140 160 (freephone) (www.ilmailulaitos.com). The journey takes about 30 mins. no. 615 (from the railway station, platform 10) takes 35 mins and operates 0520–2220.

INFORMATION

Budget travellers should drop in at **Kompassi Youth Information and Counselling Centre**, Lasipalatsi, Simonkatu 1, (09) 3108 0080 (www.hel.fi/nk/kompassi); Tue–Thur and Sun 1100–1800, Fri 1100–1600. Get *Helsinki Guide* and *Helsinki This Week*, for every conceivable listing and event. 'Helsinki Helps' (students wearing green and carrying green bags with an 'i') wander round the centre 0800–2000 (June–Aug) to provide general guidance. They know more about youth activities than Tourist Officers.

The **Helsinki Card** (www.helsinkicard.com) is available from the Tourist Office, **Hotellikeskus** (Hotel Booking Centre), travel agents and R-kioskis in the city centre, and provides free public transport (including some ferry trips), free or discounted tourist sight or museum entrance and many other discounts: 24, 48 or 72 hrs (around €24–38). **TourExpert**, in the City Tourist Office, 0600 02 288 (premium rate) sells airline, boat, bus, train and sightseeing-tour tickets.

MONEY **Banks** open Mon–Fri 0915–1615. **Forex** in the station (daily 0700–2100); cash exchange counter at the airport (daily 0600–2300). **Thomas Cook**: Aleksanterinkatu 9 and at the airport.

POST AND PHONES The **main post office**, Mannerheiminaukio 1A, (020) 451 4400 (open Mon–Fri 0900–1800), has a poste restante section open Mon–Fri 0700–2100, Sat–Sun 1000–1800, (020) 451 4921 (entrance Asema–Aukio), and phone and fax services. **Helsinki telephone code**: 09 (9 from outside Finland).

FINLAND

PUBLIC TRANSPORT

Many of the sights are in the area between the station and Kauppatori, and trams are a quick way of reaching most of the others.

METRO The Metro was designed primarily for commuters. The only line serves the north and east, but it is spreading. It operates 0533 (Sun 0638)–2323 and tickets are obtained from vending machines. Single tickets for city centre travel are sold on the tram or bus but are cheaper if bought from HKL offices and R-kiosks (the same applies for tram tickets), from where ten-trip tickets are also available. Tickets are valid for one hour.

PUBLIC TRANSPORT A good network of **buses** and **trams** runs approximately 0600–2300 (a few continue until 0130). The public transport company is **HKL (Helsingin Kaupungin Liikennelaitos)**, ☎(09) 0100 111 (www.hel.fi.hkl), with offices in Rautatientori metro station. The best way to get around is by tram. Tram no. 3T is frequent, 0600–0130, and has a figure-of-eight route, going to, or near, most of the city's main attractions. Many tram numbers are followed by a letter that denotes the direction. For taxis try **Helsinki Taxi Center,** ☎700 700.

FERRIES Most local **cruises and ferries** leave from **Kauppatori**.

> **City tourist tickets** (from the Tourist Office and HKL offices) give unlimited city travel on buses, trams, metro and local trains for one day, three days or five days.

ACCOMMODATION

Hotelliskus (Hotel Booking Centre), ☎(09) 2288 1400, fax (09) 2288 149 (www.helsinkiexpert.fi; hotel@helsinkiexpert.fi), is at the railway station (wes wing), open Mon–Sat 0900–1900, Sun 1000–1800 (June–Aug); Mon–Fri 0900–170 (Sept–May). They also book motels, inns, youth hostels and apartments.
Good value are **Hotel Anna**, Annankatu 1, ☎(09) 616 621, fax (09) 602 66 (info@hotelanna.com), €€, and **Hotel Arthur**, Vuorikatu 19, ☎(09) 173 441, fax (09 626 880 (sales.department@hotelarthur.fi), €€.
Hostels: HI hostels are **Eurohostel**, Linnankatu 9, ☎(09) 622 0470, fax (09) 655 04 (eurohostel@euroshostel.fi); 2 km east of the station (tram no.4 goes within 100 m) **Erottajanpuisto**, Uudenmaankatu 9, ☎(09) 642 169, fax (09) 680 2757. **Stadion Hostel** Pohjoinen Stadiontie 3b, ☎(09) 477 8480, fax (09) 4778 4811 (stadion@hostel.inet.fi trams 3b and 7 stop 500 m away. **Hostel Academica**, Hietaniemenkatu 14, ☎(09) 131 4334, fax (09) 441 201 (hostel.academica@hyy.fi), 700 m from station; open June–Sep **Kesähotelli Satakunta**, Lapinrinne 1a, ☎(09) 6958 5231, fax (09) 6958 5233 (e-mail ravintola.satakunta@sodexho.fi), 200 m from KAMPPI Metro station; open June–Aug.
Private hostels (non-HI): Omapohja, Itäinen Teatterikuja 1, ☎(09) 666 211, an **Hostel Paalupaikka**, Vilhonkatu 6B, ☎(09) 630 260, both centrally located.
Camping: Rastila Camping, Karavaanikatu 4, ☎(09) 321 6551, fax (09) 344 157 (rastilacamping@rastilacamping.fi), opens all year and also has cottages for two t six people. It's 14 km east (Metro: RASTILA).

Helsinki This Week gives a listing of eating places. Students can take advantage of the exceptionally low-priced **university cafés**: Fabianinkatu 33 and **Porthania, Hallituskatu 6**. Fried fish is available in abundance around the port. You can also pick up smoked salmon and reindeer sandwiches here, at the **Kauppahalli**. For fast food try the Mannerheimintie area – **Forum** offers a good choice.

Finland's remarkably numerous 20th-century architects of international stature have graced the city with some of the most elegant modern architecture you could find anywhere.

The **harbour** is a good place to start, with pleasant views and a market selling trinkets. To the east is the Byzantine **Uspenski Cathedral**, Kanavakatu 1, a magnificent reminder of Finland's Russian past, which still serves the Orthodox community. To the west, **Esplanadi** is a boulevard busy with street musicians in summer. To the north, grand-scale **Senaatintori** (Senate Square) is dominated by **Tuomiokirkko**, the domed Lutheran Cathedral designed by Engel. The recently renovated interior is plain but elegant. Also flanking the square are the **Government Palace**, **Helsinki University** and the **University Library**: an impressive group. The **City Museum**, just south of Senate Square, is a high-tech survey of Helsinki's growth from a seaside village to the national capital.

Valtion taidemuseo (Finnish National Gallery), Kaivokatu 2–4, incorporates the **Ateneum** (Museum of Finnish Art), Finland's largest collection of paintings, sculptures and drawings from the 18th century to the 1960s, with **Kiasma** (Museum of Contemporary Art) next to the post office at Mannerheimaukio 2 (www.kiasma.fi). In Mannerheimintie is the 1970s **Finlandia Hall**, whose designer, Alvar Aalto, plays on his surname, which means 'wave', in the asymmetrical pattern. Further north is the **Olympic Stadium**, worth the traipse out, if only to take in the immense view from the stadium tower (closed during competitions); there's also a sports museum here.

Other attractions include the Sibelius monument in **Sibeliuksen puisto** (Sibelius Park), ▣ no. 18, and the wonderful **Temppeliaukiokirkko** (Church in the Rock), Lutherinkatu 3, blasted out of solid rock. The highly worthwhile **Taideteollisuusmuseo** (Museum of Applied Arts), Korkeavuorenkatu 23, shows off the design by which Finland sets such high standards.

Four main islands hug the Helsinki peninsula, linked to Helsinki, and each other, by ferries and/or bridges. The first is **Suomenlinna** (15-min ferry trip from the South Harbour), endowed with a fine fortress and a World War II U-boat, *Vesikko*. There are good beaches – ideal for a picnic on a fine day. The island of **Korkeasaari**

FINLAND

TOURS

Boat trips and **bus tours** are available, and for the **walking tour** – get the free leaflet *See Helsinki on Foot* from the Tourist Office.

(🚌 no. 16 to Kuolosaari or Metro to HERTTONIEMI station, then 🚌 no. 11 – weekends only) is home to **Helsinki Zoo**, which specialises in species from the Arctic. **Seurasaari** (5 km from city centre; 🚌 no. 24 from Erottaja) is the site of Finland's largest and oldest **open-air museum** (closed winter), with 80 historic buildings, including peasant huts and Same (Lapp) tents; the island has several naturist beaches (emphatically single sex). **Pihlajasaari** is a recreation centre, popular with walkers and home to the area's best beaches.

NIGHT-TIME AND EVENTS

The Tourist Office has free entertainment guides and some hotels dispense copies. *Helsinki This Week* contains monthly listings May–Aug and 2 months listings Sept–April. For recorded programme information in English, ☎ 058. Reservations for all events are handled by **Lippupalvelu**, Stockmann department store, Mannerheimintie 1, ☎ 0600 10 495 (premium rate). Cultural events can also be booked with **Tiketti**, Forum Shopping Centre, Kukontori, ☎ 0600 11 616 (premium rate).

SHOPPING

Mannerheimintie, Helsinki's main artery, is home to countless shops, including the vast **Stockmann** department store (good selection of English-language publications) and **Forum**, a complex with over 150 shops. In the **Tunneli** (the tunnel underneath the station), shops open until about 2200 and many open Sun. **Kauppatori** (Market Square), by the port, has colourful waterside displays of freshly caught fish. This is where you get the best food buys. In season, look for *suomuuraimet* (cloudberries), which grow under the midnight sun.

Finlandia Hall, Karamzininkatu 4, is the main centre for classical music. It's next door to the new **Opera House**.

Evenings are lively; options range from discos to sophisticated nightclubs – more and more now open till 0400, and are often linked to big hotels, such as the **Sokos Vaakuna**. Most have a minimum age of 20 or 24. The best areas for bars are around the station, or further south around Uunenmankatu and Iso Roobertinkatu. In summer there's a tram carriage converted into a pub which travels around town: you can hop on, have a beer and hop off again after a pleasant tour.

WHERE NEXT FROM HELSINKI?

Ferries serve **Stockholm** (p. 454), **Tallinn** (p. 512) and **St Petersburg** (p. 501).

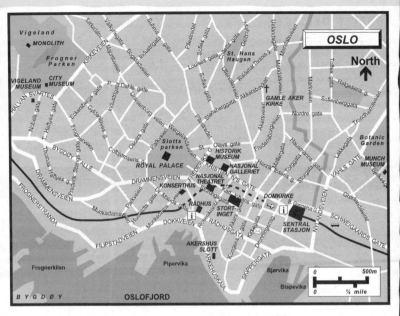

Hemmed in by water and forests, the former Viking capital is now a pleasant and laid-back modern-looking city. It is not a big place, more somewhere to look in on before venturing to the wilds of Norway, rather than a destination in its own right. There are watery views from the fortress of Akershus, while the harbour area merits a brief exploration, and there are some enjoyable boat trips. An outstanding list of museums offers the best possible insight into Norwegian culture.

ARRIVAL AND DEPARTURE

The main rail station is the very central **Oslo Sentralstasjon** (known as **Oslo S**). All long-distance trains stop here, as well as some local services. Crammed with facilities of every kind, the Central Station has been refurbished as a harmonious airport-lounge-style steel and glass construction. The long-distance ticket office opens daily 0630–2300. There are backpack-size lockers available for NKr.25. The T-bane (metro) is to the right as you leave the station.

There are daily sailings by **Color Line,** 81 00 08 11, to Germany (**Kiel**) and Denmark (**Hirtshals**); **DFDS Seaways,** 22 41 90 90, to Denmark (**Copenhagen**) and Sweden (**Helsingborg**); and **Stena Line,** 23 17 90 00, to Denmark (**Frederikshavn**) – not Mon.

NORWAY

TOURIST OFFICE

Brynjulf Bull's Plass 1
(at the west end of the
harbour), ☎23 11 78 80
(www.visitoslo.no;
oslo@oslopro.no). This is the
Tourist Office for Oslo as
well as selected parts of
Norway.

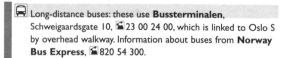 Long-distance buses: these use **Bussterminalen**, Schweigaardsgate 10, ☎23 00 24 00, which is linked to Oslo S by overhead walkway. Information about buses from **Norway Bus Express**, ☎820 54 300.

✈ All flights are now to and from **Gardermoen** (50 km north). This is a stunning example of Scandinavian modern architecture. Airport express trains take 19 mins to Oslo, NKr.120; buses take 45 mins, NKr.80. You can also travel north from here to Lillehammer and Trondheim (ETT table 785).

INFORMATION

Get *The Official Guide for Oslo*, *What's On* and a map, all free. There is a small information office in Oslo S station, open daily. The youth tourism information service **USE IT** is at Møllergata 3; ☎22 41 51 32 (www.unginfo.oslo.no); it has free internet access. Make sure you get their (free) *Streetwise* magazine – an excellent guide to Oslo on a shoestring, and probably the most up-to-date guide you'll get. Hikers should visit **DNT**, Storgate 3; ☎22 82 28 00.

The widely available **Oslo Card**, valid for 24 hrs (NKr.180), 48 hrs (NKr.290) or 72 hrs (NKr.390), provides free city transport, free admission to most attractions and various discounts. The **Oslo Package** provides hotel room and breakfast and the Oslo Card from NKr.450 per person in a double room – including children under 16 in their parents' room. Valid early June–mid-Aug and weekends year-round.

MONEY **Post offices** (most open Mon–Fri 0900–1700, Sat 1000–1400) take least commission. The **bank** in Oslo S opens Mon–Fri 0700–1900, Sat–Sun 0800–1700.

POST AND PHONES **Oslo Sentrum Postkontor** (the main post office), Dronningensgt 15, opens Mon–Fri 0800–1800, Sat 1000–1500. The post office in Oslo S opens Mon–Fri 0700–1800, Sat 0900–1500.

PUBLIC TRANSPORT

The centre's small and it's easy to reach outlying attractions on the excellent public transport system.

Trafikanten (the tower-like construction outside Oslo S), Jernbanetorget, ☎815 00 176 (open Mon–Fri 0700–2000, Sat–Sun 0800–1800), handles transport queries, timetables and tickets. Get the (free) public transport map, *Sporveiskart Oslo*. Single tickets, valid for 1 hr, cost NKr.20. Multi-ride tickets include day cards (*Dagskort*; NKr.50) and 7-day cards (*Syv-Dagerskort*; NKr.150).

Metro: T-lines converge at Stortinget. There are maps on the platforms and trains have a destination board. Most trams converge at Oslo S and most city buses at Oslo M (on Vaterland, by Oslo S). Most westbound buses and trams (including those to **Bygdøy** and **Vigelandsparken**) stop at the south side of Nasjonalteateret.

Taxis: ☎02323, or use the strategically positioned ranks. If you use an unregistered 'pirate taxi', agree a price beforehand and don't go alone.

Ferries to **Bygdøy** leave (Apr–Sept) from quay 3 on Rådhusbrygge, near the Tourist Office, as do sightseeing boats. Ferries to **Hovedøya**, **Langøyene** and other islands in the Oslofjord leave from Vippetangen (🚌 no. 60).

ACCOMMODATION

The Tourist Office at Oslo S will book hotel accommodation and rooms in private houses (NKr.30 fee charged). It will also supply a list of cheap accommodation (pensions, hostels), but does not book this kind of lodging. USE IT book rooms for a smaller fee. Book in advance in high season (May–Sept). A good-value option is in private accommodation (bookable in person through USE IT), typically Nkr.125–150 per person. Hotels start at around Nkr.300 for a single and Nkr.500 for a twin room. There are also some bed and breakfast operations, charging typically around Nkr.275 for a single and Nkr.475 for a double.

City Hotel, Skippergt 19, ☎22 41 36 10, fax 22 42 24 29, is a moderate, low-budget bed-and-breakfast hotel (two blocks from Oslo S), with comfortable old-style furniture and décor.

There are three **HI hostels**. **Haraldsheim**, Haraldsheimvn 4, Grensen, ☎22 22 29 65, is 5 km from Oslo S: tram 15 Kjelsås or 🚌 nos. 31/32 to Sinsenkrysset. The other two hostels are open summer only: **Frikirkens Studiesenter Ekeberg**, Kongsvn. 82, ☎22 74 18 90 (4 km from Oslo S; trams 18 and 19 stop 100 m away; 1 June–15 Aug only); and **Holtekilen**, Michelets vei 55, ☎67 51 80 40 (10 km from Oslo S, 1 km from Stabekk station). The **YMCA** (near USE IT at Grubbegata 4; July and Aug only) is really central. Bring a sleeping bag for both these.

Campsites: **Bogstad Camping**, Ankerveien 117, Holmenkollen, ☎22 51 08 00, open all year (🚌 no. 32 from Oslo S, 32 mins). **Ekeberg Camping**, Ekebergveien 65, ☎22 19 85 68, is closer (about 3 km: 10 mins on 🚌 nos. 34A/34B/45/46: Ekeberg), but open only June–Aug. You can camp in the forest north of town if you avoid public areas (head into the trees for about 1 km). **Langøyene island** has good beaches (boat from Vippetangen pier, departing 5 mins past each hour, 1100–2000. The campsite here is **Langøyene Camping**, ☎22 11 53 21.

FOOD AND DRINK

Eating out in Oslo is expensive. For restaurant listings, see *The Official Guide for Oslo*. There are a number of pricey options for good Norwegian food, while eating on a budget is tricky but possible if you stock up on hotel buffet breakfasts and shop at a supermarket (e.g. **Kiwi**, Storgaten 33, open until 2100) or cheap delis on the east side of town, and picnic in one of the parks. Try fresh (boiled) prawns from the harbour, on a fresh roll, with a dash of mayonnaise.

HIGHLIGHTS

A pleasant boat trip across the bay is to the mostly boat-related attractions at **Bygdøy**. Ferries leave from quay 3 every 40 mins (every 20 mins at peak times in summer); they take 10 mins. There are also beaches and picnic spots.

The first group of museums is right next to the closer of the two quays, and is dominated by the glass tent of the **Frammuset** (Fram Museum), which houses in its entirety *Fram*, the Arctic exploration ship built in 1892 and used by Amundsen and two other explorers. The **Kon-Tiki Museum** displays the late Thor Heyerdahl's raft *Kon-Tiki*, a replica of the kind of vessel on which he believed ancient civilisations migrated across the Atlantic from South America to Polynesia; he made the voyage himself to give credence to his theory (although DNA evidence now suggests otherwise). There are also Easter Island statues and film shows about his expedition.

Walk up the hill (bear right) to the second, and even more impressive group of museums (which are closer to Bygdøy's second quay).

DAY TRIP FROM OSLO

Tusenfryd, Amusement Park at Vinterbro (30 mins south by shuttle bus from the centre). With the Thunder Coaster – one of the world's largest wooden roller coasters.

FOR FREE

Botanisk Hage (botanical gardens), **Nasjonalgalleriet** (National Gallery, closed Tues), **Domkirke** (cathedral), **Sculpture Park** in Vigelandsparken, **National Museum of Contemporary Art**, park around Akershus, **museums** of geology, palaeontology and zoology (by Munchmuseet), **Post Museum** (in main post office).

The breathtaking **Vikingskiphuset** (Viking Ship Museum) houses three 9th-century ships, once buried fully equipped for the voyage to Valhalla in the afterlife, now resurrected and reassembled. Many beautifully worked and well-preserved iron, wood and leather artefacts are on display. Some 150 Nordic buildings, including an ancient stave church, have been collected to form the nearby **Norsk Folkemuseum**, worth allocating a day to see to the full.

Back at Oslo harbour, the fortress-palace complex of **Akershus** looms to the east; entry from Akersgt or over a drawbridge from Kirkegt. Several museums are in the extensive grounds, notably **Hjemmefrontmuseet**, a fascinating place devoted to the history of the Norwegian Resistance. The huge **Forsvarsmuseet** (Defence Museum) goes back as far as the Vikings.

The **Domkirke** (cathedral), Stortorget 1, dates from 1697, but only the baroque carved altarpiece and pulpit survive from the original cathedral. The stained-glass windows are by Vigeland, but the most striking feature is the vast ceiling painting.

Nasjonalgalleriet (National Gallery), Universitetsgt 13 (metro: Nasjonalteatret), houses a huge collection of Norwegian art and has a room dedicated to Edvard Munch, displaying *The Scream*.

CITIES: OSLO

The sculpture-filled **Vigelandsparken/ Frognerparken**, in northwest Oslo (main entrance from Kirkevn) – 🚌no. 20; tram no. 12: Frognerparken – is one of Oslo's most impressive sights. Life-size or larger, the statues both stand out from and fit into the landscape of the huge park. The display culminates in a phallic 15-m column of writhing bodies, which

SHOPPING

The most attractive buys are those reflecting Norwegian craftsmanship, such as crystal, leather goods, silver and knitwear, but nothing is cheap. **Karl Johans Gate** is the city's main street – part pedestrian and loaded with shops, restaurants, bars and street performers. **Basarhallene** (behind the cathedral) is an art and handicraft boutique centre, while the **Aker Brygge** complex stays open late and is a good place to browse. Other major complexes are **Paléet**, Karl Johansgt 37–43, and **Oslo City**, across from the station.

form the monolith of life. Edvard Munch gave much of his art to the city, most of it housed in the **Munchmuseet** (Munch Museum), Tøyengt 53 (Metro: TØYEN/ MUNCHMUSEET), east of the centre. The museum adjoins the extensive **Botanisk Hage** (botanical gardens). **Tryvannstårnet** TV/observation tower, 20-min walk north (or Metro: VOKSENKOLLEN), is a prominent landmark and offers unparalleled views.

NIGHT-TIME AND EVENTS

See *Streetwise, The Official Guide for Oslo* and *What's On* for listings. Oslo has a well-developed café culture, rather than big bars and clubs. The focus is the stretch between the station and the palace. The current trendy area is the **Grünerløkka** suburb to the north-east; a bit yuppie, but still atmospheric and lively. The scene is rapidly evolving. The **Aker Brygge**, by the harbour, has waterfront bars, but is more touristy and expensive. Drinking anywhere in Oslo is expensive; alcohol is cheaper from supermarkets, but they can't sell it after 2000 and you can only get wine and spirits from special **Vinmonopolet** shops, e.g. Møllergata 10/12. The drinking age is 18, but bars only serve 21+, and check ID rigorously. Most places stay open until 0300 or 0330.

Well-known operas are performed at **Den Norske Opera**, Storgt 23C, while the **Konserthus**, Munkedamsvn 14, stages folklore events in midsummer. Most movies are shown in their original language.

SWEDEN: STOCKHOLM

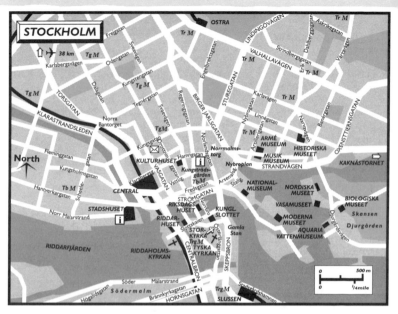

Spread over 14 islands with countless inlets, Stockholm has a stunning waterfront setting on a par with the likes of San Francisco and Sydney, and most visitors would probably rate it the most rewarding of the Scandinavian capitals. At the heart of it is the impressively intact original part of the city, **Gamla Stan**, with an enticing blend of dignified old buildings, cafés, and craft and designer shops; in contrast, the **Djurgården** is a huge natural park where the city comes to swim, canoe, fly kites, visit the zoo and the superb outdoor museum, or just admire the views.

Stockholm is airy with a whiff of the sea, a lovely place to be outdoors in summer (it can in winter seem a tad austere) whether listening to an outdoor concert or taking a cruise, but there are plenty of superb indoor attractions, such as the **Nationalmuseum** and the historic **Vasa** warship, a significant component of the city's rich maritime heritage. It's also a clean, safe and friendly place, and you get the feeling that everything works.

ARRIVAL AND DEPARTURE

 The labyrinthine and confusing **Stockholm C** – or Stockholm Centralstationen (0400–2400) – has showers (on the lower level), a bus information/ticket office and the city's longest opening

TOURIST OFFICE

Stockholm Information Service: Sverigehuset (Sweden House), Hamngatan 27, Kungsträdgården; Box 7542, SE-103 93 Stockholm, ☎ (08) 789 24 90, fax (08) 789 24 91 (www.stockholmtown.com; info@stoinfo.se). From Centralstationen, walk up Klarabergsg. to Sergels Torg (marked by an oddly-shaped pillar), then right on Hamngatan for the Tourist Office.

hours for postal services and currency exchange; good food stalls (if you can locate them!). Anything you need should be in (or adjoining) the main hall. If not, try the nearby Cityterminalen (see Buses, below). For domestic train information, ☎ (020) 75 75 75 (24 hrs); for international information, ☎ (08) 696 7540.

🚌 **Cityterminalen** (long-distance bus station, ☎ (08) 762 59 97), Klarabergsviadukten: across the road from Stockholm Centralstationen, but linked by tunnels. **Swebus** is the largest domestic company, ☎ (08) 655 00 90 (www.swebus.se).

⛴ Ferries from Helsinki: the overnight ships to Finland (see feature, p. 460) are run by **Silja Line**, with offices at Kungsgatan 2, ☎ (08) 22 21 40 (www.silja.com), and **Viking Line**, office at the Cityterminalen, ☎ (08) 452 40 00 (www.vikingline.se).

✈ **Stockholm Arlanda,** ☎ (08) 797 60 00, is 45 km north of Stockholm. The **Arlanda Express** (airport rail link to Centralstation), ☎ (08) 5951 1440, takes 20 mins, departures every 15 mins (every 15 mins, daily, 0535–0005) 0435–0035; SKr.120. The **Flygbuss** (airport bus), ☎ (08) 600 10 00 takes about 45 mins from **Cityterminalen** and runs every 10 mins 0640–2400 plus through the night in connection with flights; SKr.60.

INFORMATION

Small city maps are freely available, but a larger-scale one is useful. A wealth of free English-language literature includes the useful *What's On Stockholm* (free bi-monthly tourist and events guide), *Stockholm This Week* and *Hotels Stockholm* (free hotel and youth hostel guide).
The **Stockholm Card** (**Stockholmskortet**, SKr.220 for 24 hrs, SKr.380 for 48 hrs or SKr.540 for 72 hrs) from Tourist Offices, stations, the Silja Line terminal and most hotels, youth hostels and campsites, provides free public transport, free street parking, free boat tour, free entrance to 70 museums and attractions and wide-ranging discounts.

MONEY **Forex** branches include Centralstationen (ground level and metro station); Cityterminalen; Sweden House (Tourist Information Centre), NK department store (Hamngatan), Vasagatan 14, Götgatan 94, Sveavägen 24, Kungsgatan, Arlanda Express Terminal (Stockholm) and Arlanda Airport (Terminal 2).

POST AND PHONES The **main post office**, Drottninggatan 53, Stora Nygatan, Gamla Stan opens Mon–Fri 0930–1800, Sat 1000–1300. **Centralstationen** branch opens Mon–Fri 1000–2200, Sat–Sun 1000–1900. **Telecenter**, Centralstationen, opens daily 0800–2100. Buy phonecards here or from newsagents (eg. Pressbyrån) or vending machines in the station. The telephone code for Stockholm is 08.

DAY TRIPS FROM STOCKHOLM

Björkö (an island in Lake Mälaren) is the site of the **Birka Vikingstaden** (Birka Viking Town; open May–Sept), Sweden's oldest city, accessible by ferry from Stadshusbron. Excavations have unearthed remains of ancient houses and a cemetery. The island has good beaches for swimming.

PUBLIC TRANSPORT

Storstockholms Lokaltrafik (SL) runs the excellent bus and metro network. Main office: lower level of Sergels Torg; 📞600 10 00. There's a branch in Centralstationen.

Single tickets (from drivers: SKr.7 to board, plus SKr.7 per zone) are valid for 1 hr. **Rabattkuponger** provide 20 tickets for SKr.95 and **Turistkorten** (Tourist Cards) provide unlimited travel for 24 hrs (SKr.70) or 3 days (SKr.135); the 3-day card includes free admission to Gröna Lund and Kaknäs Tower and reduced admission to Skansen. There are reductions for under 18s and seniors. Multi-ride tickets are available from **SL**, **Pressbyrån** and the **Tourist Office**.

The metro, **Tunnelbana (T-bana)**, has three lines (red, green and blue). Trains are fast and frequent, 0500–0100. Metro stations display a blue 'T' on a white background. The décor on some lines is among the most imaginative in Europe: walls are moulded to look like caves and painted strident colours, with original murals.

🚌City buses are frequent, 0500–2400, and there's a night service *(nattbus).* 🚌nos. 47 (to Gröna Lund, Skansen and Vasa Museum) and 69 (to Kaknästronet) are most useful.

The larger taxi companies, **Taxi Stockholm**, 📞(08) 15 00 00, **Taxi Kurir**, 📞(08) 30 00 00, and **Taxi 020,** 📞(020) 93 93 93, are usually cheapest and rarely cost more than SKr.200 for journeys within city limits and SKr.435 to/from Arlanda Airport. If you take an independent 'Fritaxi' cab, make sure you agree the fare before setting out.

⛴The main local operator is **Waxholmsbolaget**, Strömkajen; 📞(08) 679 58 30. A **Båtluffarkort** allows 16 days of travel (SKr.300 from the Excursion Shop or Waxholmsbolaget offices). Single tickets can be purchased when you board. See also Tours, p. 458.

ACCOMMODATION

Hotellcentralen (Hotel Centre), the official accommodation booking service, is in the main hall of Centralstationen; 📞(08) 789 24 90, fax (08) 791 86 66 (www.stoinfo.se; hotels@stoinfo.se). Advance bookings are free, but there's a fee for same-day bookings. Pick up a (free) copy of *Hotels Stockholm* (including youth hostels). A useful booking service for private rooms is **Bed and Breakfast Agency Sweden (BBA)**, Mariatorget 8; 📞(08) 643 80 28, fax (08) 643 80 78 (www.bba.nu; info@bba.nu).

Youth Hostels: Try **AF Chapman & Skeppsholmen**, Flaggmansvägen 8, Skeppsholmen, 📞(08) 463 22 66, fax (08) 611 71 55 (info@chapmanstfturist.se), 🚌no. 65, a tall ship moored in the harbour; or **Långholmens**, Gamla Kronohäktet, Långholmsmuren 20, 📞(08) 668 05 10, fax (08) 720 85 75 (vandrarhem@langholmen.com), once a prison (nearest Metro: HORNSTULL).

The most central **campsite** is **Östermalm Citycamping,** Fiskartorpsvägen 2, Östermalm, ☎(08) 10 29 03, fax (08) 21 44 12, 1.5 km from city centre at Östermalm sports ground, 🚇no. 55, (open late June–mid-Aug). **Bredäng Camping,** Stora Sällskapetsväg, Skärholmen, ☎(08) 97 70 71, fax (08) 708 72 62 (bredangcamping@swipnet.se), 10 km south-west of the city (Metro: BREDÄNG), open mid-Apr–late Oct; there's a **youth hostel** here too (open all year).

FOOD AND DRINK

Although not exactly the culinary capital of Europe, Stockholm has a good range of cuisine. Budget options are limited: by eating a main meal at lunchtime you can take advantage of the best offers. Small, inexpensive places are more abundant south of the water.

HIGHLIGHTS

Many museums are closed on Mon; most are open 1100–1600, with longer hours in summer. See *Stockholm This Week* or *What's On Stockholm* for details. On limited time or cash, head for the pleasant and atmospheric Gamla Stan, then take the ferry from there to the Djurgården.

GAMLA STAN Joined to the mainland by bridges, **Gamla Stan** is the immaculately preserved old quarter of Stockholm, with old merchants' houses, boutiques and craft shops to browse in. Seek out the main square, **Stortorget**, with its colourful façades, gabled roofs and rococo **Börsen** (Stock Exchange), and the timewarp street of **Prästgatan**. Conspicuous both for its size and its splendour is **Kungliga Slottet** (Metro: GAMLA STAN), the former royal palace of 1760, whose royal apartments, treasury, armoury and palace museum can be visited (separate entrance for each), and where the royal palace guard changes at noon each day. Next to it, the **Storkyrkan** (cathedral) hosts royal marriages and has an exuberant baroque interior as well as a fine 15th-century wooden sculpture of St George and the Dragon. The royal burial place is the 13th-century former monastery of **Riddarholmskyrkan**, which is adorned with ornate sarcophagi and colourful coats of arms.

In the 1970s, the remains of the old town wall were discovered and incorporated into **Stockholms Medeltidsmuseet** (Museum of Medieval Stockholm). On a small island accessible from **Norrbro** (one of the

DAY TRIPS FROM STOCKHOLM

For details get the leaflet *Run Away For A Day* from the Tourist Office. Probably the most impressive is **Drottningholms Slott** (Drottningholm Palace), home of the royal family and sometimes called 'Sweden's Versailles'. It is 11 km west of the city, and best reached by boat from Stadshusbron, taking an hour, or Metro: BROMMAPLAN, then 🚇nos. 301/323. Several rooms are on view and there are tours of the 18th-century theatre. **Kina Slott** (the Chinese pavilion and a World Heritage Site), at the far end of the gardens, was a summer cottage.

TOURS

Strömma Kanalbolag,
Skeppsbron 22, ☎ (08)
587 140 00 (www.
strommakanalbolaget.com)
operate boat excursions in the
archipelago and on Lake
Mälaren.

Cinderellåbatarna
(Cinderella Boats),
Skeppsbron 22, ☎ (08)
587 140 50 (www.
cinderellabatarna.com),
offer boat excursions to the
outer archipelago.

FOR FREE

Tours of **Riksdagshuset**
(Swedish parliament);
Changing the Guard at
Kungliga Slottet (Royal
Palace); **Storkyrkan** (main
church in Gamla Stan);
**Bergianska Botaniska
Trädgården** (Bergius
Botanic Garden).

bridges linking Norrmalm and Gamla Stan, Metro: GAMLA STAN, ☐nos. 43/62), it presents an imaginative reconstruction of medieval life. In front of the museum stands the **Riksdagshuset**, where the Swedish parliament meets; there are free guided tours from the rear of the building in early afternoon (weekdays in summer; weekends Jan–May and Sept).

North of the centre (Metro: UNIVERSITETET), the **Bergianska Botaniska Trädgården** (Bergius Botanic Garden) includes **Victoriahuset**, home of the world's largest water-lily, while at **Fjärils Och Fågelhuset** (Butterfly House), Hagaparken, you can see tropical butterflies and birds in a natural environment.

NORRMALM AND BLASIEHOLMEN

Norrmalm is the bland centre of modern Stockholm, an area of 1960s office blocks and shopping malls near the main rail station, with the glass obelisk of **Sergels Torg** (where the **Kulturhuset,** Cultural Centre, Metro: CENTRALEN, is home to changing exhibitions of Swedish contemporary arts and crafts). Things get better around the leafy park of **Kungsträdgården**, the foremost meeting place in the city, lined with cafés and full of street life.

Close by, **Medelhavsmuseet** (Museum of Mediterranean and Near Eastern Antiquities), Fredsg. 2 (Metro: KUNGSTRÄDGÅRDEN), is a wonderful treasure house of the ancient world, with a particularly striking Egyptian section. On **Kungsholmen** (immediately west of Centralstationen), the 1920s **Stadshuset** (City Hall), Hantverkargatan 1 (Metro: CENTRALEN/RÅDHUSET), hosts the annual Nobel Banquet (Dec); daily guided tours. Of particular note are the 19 million mosaics in the Golden Room and royal murals in the Prince's Gallery.

The peninsula of **Blasieholm**, to the east, is home to the superb **Nationalmuseum** (National Swedish Museum of Fine Arts), Blaisieholmshammen (Metro: KUNGSTRÄDGÅRDEN), with a choice collection of Swedish applied art, including furniture, as well as worldwide pieces, notably Russian Orthodox art. Linked to Blasieholmen by bridge, Skeppsholmen has a host of museums, including an outstanding gallery of modern art (**Moderna Museet**). Further east from Norrmalm, **Östermalm** is a residential area with supremely elegant streets such as Strandvägen.

Historiska Museet (Museum of National Antiquities), Narvavägen 13–17 (Metro:

KARLAPLAN/ÖSTERMALMSTORG), is famous for the Guldrummet (Golden Room), an underground chamber that contains one of Europe's richest collections of prehistoric and medieval gold and silver jewellery.

DJURGÅRDEN 🚌nos. 44/47 stop near each of the main attractions in the city's island pleasure garden. There are ferries, operator **Waxholmsbolaget** (see p. 456), from NYBROPLAN (in Gamla Stan) in summer, and from Skeppsbron (east of Kungsträdgården) year-round, as well as a private tram from Norrmalmstorg.

The eastern section of this large island, together with **Ladugårdsgärdet** (to the north), forms **Eko Park**, a 56-sq km-nature reserve.

Along the western side are various attractions. Don't miss **Vasamuseet** (Vasa Museum), built to house *Vasa*, a 17th-century warship that was well preserved in mud dredged up in 1961 from the harbour where she sank on her maiden voyage.

SHOPPING

The main areas are Hamngatan, Drottninggatan, Sergels Torg and Gamla Stan. **NK**, Hamng. 18–20, and **Åhléns**, Klarabergsg. 50, are well-stocked department stores. Specialities include Swedish crystal, handmade paper, textiles and ceramics. **Æter & Essencefabriken**, Wallingatan 14, is a highly fragrant spice shop, while **Stockholms Läns Hemslöjdförening**, Drottningg., is one of a number of places for Swedish handicrafts, which can also be found at numerous places in Gamla Stan. The most popular markets, a mixture of stalls and indoor food halls, are **Östermalmstorg**, **Hötorget** and **Söderhallarna**.

The **Nordiska Museet** (Nordic Museum) is a great way to put Sweden's life and culture in perspective, with exhibits including Sami (Lapp) artefacts. The **Thielska Galleriet** (Thiel Gallery) is a turn-of-the-century mansion, interesting architecturally in itself, which houses a tremendous collection of Scandinavian art, including works by Munch and the Swedish artist Carl Larsson, whose poignantly attractive tableaux of childhood have suddenly risen to international fame.

Aquaria Vattenmuseum (Aquaria Water Museum) is a high-tech complex that enables you to experience 24 hours in a rain-forest and get close to marine creatures (entrance fees help to save endangered rain-forest).

For something more frivolous, **Gröna Lund Tivoli** offers live entertainments and rides.

Skansen, Stockholm's most popular attraction, is an unmissable open-air museum consisting primarily of over 150 historical buildings – including houses, period shops, farms and workshops – and a large zoo specialising in Nordic fauna such as bears and wolves. Its highest point, Solliden, gives an impressive view over the city. There's easily enough going on here to fill a whole day. Another excellent viewpoint is the immense TV tower known as **Kaknästornet**. It is Scandinavia's tallest building, with a viewing platform at 128 m (headphones give a commentary on what you can see).

NIGHT-TIME AND EVENTS

Stockholm This Week and *What's On Stockholm* carry listings. There are around 70 theatres and concert halls and, in summer, you can enjoy free concerts in the parks. Most films are shown in the original language. **Cosmonova Omnitheatre** (in Naturhistoriska Riksmuseet) offers highly advanced planetarium performances and Omnimax films.

Södermalm, south of the water, is the best area for pubs (open till 0100), and is more bohemian and cheaper than the glitzy north side – a good place to wander around too. Clubs are centred around **Stureplan** and **Norrmalm**; some stay open till 0500, but some don't admit under-25s.

EVENTS

A major event is **Archipelago Boat Day** (June); a parade of old steamboats from Stockholm to the island of Vaxholm and back. Other regular events include a **kite festival** (May), **National Day** (6 June) and a **beer festival** (late Sept). **Regattas** are held frequently in the summer.

WHERE NEXT? FERRIES TO HELSINKI

Departing from Stockholm, the immense Viking and Silja ferries (ETT table 2465; see p. 455) that make the journey across the Baltic are a popular institution with the locals. There's a great view of the archipelagos at the Swedish end, and the food and drink are tax-free, a difference you are certain to notice in Scandinavia. Each has pubs and clubs which stay open and distinctly active until 0500, especially at weekends; some say it's the best night out around. This journey is surprisingly cheap, especially if you don't take a cabin. Seats are cheaper than cabins but still need to be booked; cheaper cabins have four beds and en-suite toilets/showers. Generally late bookings are more expensive and mid-week is cheaper than weekends. Book a sitting for the all-you-can-eat buffet as soon as you get on board. The boats take about 16 hrs, leaving Stockholm 1700, arriving in Helsinki 0930–1000, and you can sleep off your night's entertainment for a while before getting booted off. Travellers have been known to spend all their nights on the boat, touring Helsinki and Stockholm on alternate days. The operators sometimes run even cheaper 20-hr sailings which just cruise out of harbour, drop anchor and open the bar.

ROUTE DETAIL		
Copenhagen–Roskilde ETT table 700		
Type	Frequency	Typical journey time
Local train	Frequent	20 mins
Roskilde–Odense	ETT table 700	
Type	Frequency	Typical journey time
Train	Every 30 mins	1 hr 10 mins
Odense–Århus	ETT table 700	
Type	Frequency	Typical journey time
Train	Every hr	1 hr 37 mins
Århus–Aalborg	ETT table 700	
Type	Frequency	Typical journey time
Train	Every hr	1 hr 25 mins
Aarlborg–Frederikshavn ETT table 700		
Type	Frequency	Typical journey time
Train	Every hr	1 hr 10 mins
Frederikshavn–Gothenburg ETT 2320		
Type	Frequency	Typical journey time
Ferry	5–6 daily	3 hrs 15 mins

Notes

There are also 2–3 HSS Fast Ferry services daily between Frederikshavn and Gothenburg, taking 2 hrs.

KEY JOURNEYS		
Copenhagen–Gothenburg ETT 735 (via Malmö)		
Type	Frequency	Typical journey time
Train	6–9 daily	3 hrs 25 mins

SCANDINAVIA

This journey takes in the dramatic 18-km **Store Bælt (Great Belt)** tunnel and bridge combination linking Denmark's two largest islands – **Zealand** and **Funen** – as well as the opportunity to visit some of northern Denmark's lesser-known yet highly attractive towns. **Odense** makes a particularly useful base for exploring the area.

COPENHAGEN (KØBENHAVN)

See p. 438.

ROSKILDE

Roskilde was Denmark's first capital. Its cathedral is the traditional burial place of Danish royalty. The **Viking Ship Museum** exhibits remains of original ships and shows a film about their excavation process in the 1960s. Nearby is the museum harbour where, in the summer months, visitors are allowed in to the workshops to try their hand at maritime crafts. The famous open-air **rock festival** is in late June/early July (www.roskilde-festival.dk).

ODENSE

Odense, a busy manufacturing city, is the largest settlement on the island of **Fyn** *(Funen)* and the third largest in the country. Throughout Denmark it's known as the birthplace of Hans Christian Andersen, who turned to writing fairytales after failing in his ambitions to be an actor and playwright.

Hans Christian Andersen's childhood home from the age of two, **Barndomshjem**, Munkemøllestræde 3–5, has a couple of rooms crammed with his belongings (closed Mon), but there's far more material in the **H C Andersen Museum**, Hans Jensens Stræde 37–45, the tumbledown cottage where he was born in 1805, including manuscripts and his celebrated top hat (closed Mon).

Two excellent art museums are **Fyns Kunstmuseum** (Funen Art Gallery; closed Mon), a superb collection of Danish art, and the **Museet for Fotokunst** (Museum of Photographic Art), featuring permanent and temporary exhibits (closed Mon, Sept–June). Carl Nielsen, Denmark's greatest composer, was born near Odense in 1865, and is commemorated by the **Carl Nielsen Museum** at Claus Bergs Gade 11 (by the concert hall; closed Mon–Wed).

RAIL The railway forms the northern boundary of the city centre.

i **Tourist Office**: Rådhuset, Jernbanegade, ☎ 66 12 75 20, fax 66 12 75 86 (www.odenseturist.dk; otb@odenseturist.dk).

An **Odense Adventure Pass** is available for 24 hrs (DKr.85) or 48 hrs (DKr.125), giving free public transport, entrance to swimming pools, free admission at many attractions and reductions

at others including a cruise on the Odense River (available from the Tourist Office and transport ticket offices).

Youth hostels: Danhostel Odense City, Østre Stationsvej 31, ☎ 63 11 04 25, fax 63 11 35 20 (www.cityhostel.dk). **Danhostel Odense Vandrerhjem**, Kragsbjergvej 121, ☎ 66 13 04 25, fax 65 91 28 63 (www.odense-danhostel.dk).

ÅRHUS

Denmark's second city is a large port and commercial and cultural centre, but even so most places are within walking distance. Old Århus has the monopoly of nightspots and several museums, including three on one site – the **Kvindemuseet** (Woman's Museum), examining the lot of women through history, the **Besættelsesmuseet** (free but open weekends only), paying homage to the Danish Resistance in World War II, and the free **Vikingemuseet** (Viking Museum). Close by, the vast **Domkirke** (cathedral) has a 93-m nave – Denmark's longest – and contains several restored, pre-Reformation frescos as well as an altar triptych by Bernt Notke.

DAY TRIP FROM ÅRHUS

An hour's journey away in **Billund** is the **Legoland** park, a showpiece of this Danish invention: ☎ 75 33 13 33 (www.legoland.dk).

Next to the **botanical gardens** to the west of the centre, the city's major attraction is **Den Gamle By**, Denmark's national museum of urban living. This delightful open-air complex consists of some 70 buildings from around Denmark, depicting 400 years of life in the city. Located 5 km south of the city the superb **Moesgård Museum** is home to the 2000-year-old **Grauballe man**, discovered in a bog in 1952; ☐ no. 6 passes by.

🚊 The station is just south of the centre.

Tourist Office: Rådhuset, Park Allé, ☎ 89 40 67 00, fax 86 12 95 90 (www.aarhus-tourist.dk; info@visitaarhus.com). An **Århus Pas** (Århus Pass), available for 24 hrs (DKr.88), 48 hrs (DKr.110), or 7 days (DKr.155), gives free public transport, entry to all attractions and sightseeing trips (on sale at tourist offices, hotels, campsites, marinas and major newsagents).

Youth hostel: Danhostel Århus Vandrerhjem, Marienlundsvej 10, Risskov, ☎ 86 16 72 98, fax 86 10 55 60 (danhostel.aarhus@get2net.dk); closed late Dec–late Jan. **City Sleep-In**, Havnegade 20, ☎ 86 19 20 55, fax 86 19 18 11 (sleep-in@citysleep-in.dk)

AALBORG

The humble herring brought prosperity to the town in the 17th century, and the legacy of that boom is the handsome old quarter, with fine old merchants' houses, such as the spectacularly ornate **Jens Bang's Stenhus**. **Nordjyllands Kunstmuseum** (Museum of Modern Art, closed Mon, Sept–June) is home to one of the nation's foremost collections of 20th-century art – and has a sculpture garden. The **Zoo** at Mølleparkvej 63 contains animals in a near-natural environment. After the sun goes down, Jomfru Ane Gade is the street for bars (maybe to sample the local spirit, Akvavit), nightlife and eateries. The Aalborg Carnival takes place in May every year and throughout the summer open-air rock concerts are held in Mølle Park and in Skovdalen.

🚂 A short walk south down Boulevarden from the town centre.

ℹ️ **Tourist Office**: Østerågade 8, ☎98 12 60 22, fax 98 16 69 22 (www.aalborg-tourist.dk; info@aalborg-tourist.dk).

🏠 **Youth hostel: Aalborg Vandrerhjem and Chalet Island**, Skydebanevej 50, ☎98 11 60 44, fax 98 12 47 11 (www.danhostelnord.dk/aalborg), 3km from Aalborg centre, close to the marina (🚌 nos. 2/8). Accommodation in 4-bed rooms or in one of 30 cabins sleeping 5–7.

GOTHENBURG (GÖTEBORG), SWEDEN

The huge cranes and shipyards that greet visitors arriving at Scandinavia's prime port mask Sweden's second largest and most attractive old city (with a population approaching half a million), created by Dutch merchants in the early 17th century. Boat tours take in the best of the waterside views from the old canals, while elsewhere there's stacks of atmosphere in the squares and in the numerous leafy parks that earn Gothenburg the nickname of the Garden City. Much of the city centre is traffic-free and easily managed on foot, though the trams that clatter around the streets are part of its charm too.

In summer there are English-language tours on **Ringlinien**, *a vintage open-air tram (weekends Apr–June and Aug–Sept, daily July) from Centralstation to Liseberg (see panel on next page).* **Paddan sightseeing boats**, ☎*(031) 60 96 70, depart from Kungsportsbron (late Apr–late Sept; first departure 1000, then up to 4 times per hour, lasting 50 mins): their harbour cruise is recommended, but be prepared to duck low under one or two of the bridges. Paddan also run dry-land tours on a 'convertible bus'. A range of summer cruises are also available, around the harbour and further afield. Ask the Tourist Office for details.*

To get your bearings, go up **Skanskaskrapan** (Skanska Skyscraper), a striking red and white skyscraper, 86 m, which has a lookout (**Götheborgs Utkiken**; closed weekdays Sept–Apr) with a small café near the top, giving superb harbour views. It's situated in **Lilla Bommen**, itself a charming area, with shops and craft workshops. Dominating the whole scene here, however, is the spectacular modern waterside **Göteborgs Operan** (Gothenburg Opera House) with performances of opera, ballet and concerts from Aug–May.

Kungsportsavenyn, usually known simply as 'Avenyn' (The Avenue), is the hub of the city, a 50-m wide boulevard lined with lime trees and endowed with shops and eateries, further enlivened by buskers and impromptu street stalls. It leads up to **Götaplatsen**, the city's cultural centre, fronted by the fountain of **Poseidon** by the Swedish sculptor

Carl Milles. Just off Avenyn is **Trädgårdsföreningen**, Nya Allén, a park full of fragrance, flora and birdsong, dotted with works of art and other attractions.

The city's oldest secular building (1643) is **Kronhuset** (Crown Arsenal), Postgasse 6–8. Around it is **Kronhusbodarna**, a courtyard bounded by handicraft boutiques in 18th-century artisans' dwellings. Other good places for browsing are the **Antikhallarna** antique market in Västra Hamngatan, and **Haga Nygata**, a renovated historical area of cobbled streets, lined with craft, second-hand, antique, and design shops, as well as cafés and restaurants. Opposite, the **Feskekörka** resembles a 19th-century church, but is a thriving fish market, open Tues–Sat, also Mon in summer, and has a good fish restaurant.

> **BOCKKRANEN ERIKSBERG**
> *Bungee jumping takes place from the huge gantry crane visible from the ferry on the way into Gothenburg,*
> 📱*(0771) 12 12 12.*

Most city museums open Tues–Sun 1100–1600 (Sept–Apr) and daily 1100–1600 (May–Aug), but some open earlier and close later. Details, including those of special exhibitions, are given in the multi-lingual leaflet, *Göteborgs Museer*. Of special interest are the **Göteborgs Maritima Centrum** (Gothenburg Maritime Centre), Packhuskajen (open Mar–Nov), the **Konstmuseet** (Art Museum), Götaplatsen and the **Universeum** (the national science centre), Korsvägen. In the large nature park of **Slottsskogen** (outside the city: tram nos. 1/2: Linnéplatsen) are an observatory, a children's zoo and the **Naturhistoriska Museet** (Natural History Museum).

Göteborg C (Central), at the north-east edge of the centre, compact and with many amenities. Facilities include **Forex** foreign exchange (open daily), **Pressbyrån** (a chain selling papers, snacks etc.), lockers, showers and reasonably priced eateries. Most buses stop at Nils Ericsonsplatsen, next to the station. There's a branch of **Nordstan** (eateries etc.) in the centre of the huge complex opposite the station, to which it's linked by a foot tunnel.

*The popular **Liseberg Amusement Park,** Örgrytevägen 5 (tram no. 5), Scandinavia's largest amusement park, is dominated by the 150-m-high **Spaceport**, which offers panoramic views. Among the 30 or so gut-wrenching rides is one of Europe's longest rollercoasters. Open late Apr–late Sept and Christmas.*

🚢 To/from the UK (**Newcastle**), and Norway (**Kristiansand**); **DFDS Seaways**, 📱(031) 65 06 50, sail from Frihamnen, 5 mins from the city centre, tram nos. 2/5. The bus leaves from stop U on Nils Ericsonsplatsen 1hr 30mins before each ferry departs. **Stena Line**, 📱(031) 704 00 00, fax (031) 85 85 95, to/from Germany (**Kiel**) sail from Manjabbehamnen, 15 mins west of town; Stena ships to/from Denmark (**Frederikshavn**) sail from Masthuggskajen, at the west end of the centre.

Tourist Offices: Kungsportsplatsen 2; 📱(031) 61 25 00, fax (031) 61 25 01 (www.goteborg.com; turistinfo@gbg-co.se). There is another branch at Nordstadstorget. Pick up the *Göteborg Guide*, a booklet containing listings and tips, and with a good town map. Also get a copy of *What's On*, a monthly guide to culture and events.

**ENTERTAINMENT AND
EVENTS**

There is a wide selection
of lively bars and clubs,
centred around **Avenyn**;
things hot up around mid-
night, and keep going until
0500. At the
Göteborgskalaset
(Gothenburg Festival) in
early Aug the town goes
mad and there is all-night
partying in the streets.

$\boxed{i}$ The centre's attractions are quite close together, but there's an excellent **tram** network if you don't feel like walking. Lines are colour-coded, so it's easy to see the stop and vehicle you need. Tram and bus stops show the numbers and destinations of lines using them. Tickets can be bought from the driver. You can save by buying a multi-ride **Magnet Kort** (must be pur-chased in advance at **Pressbyrån**), giving ten city rides on trams, buses and city boats. **TidPunkten** supply information about routes, times and fares; ☎ (031) 80 12 35. **Main office**: Nils Ericson Terminalen (bus station). Others: Drottningtorget, Brunnsparken and Folkungabron.

$\boxed{\boxminus}$ The Tourist Offices will book private rooms, as well as hotels, for a small fee. **Hotel Lorensberg**, Berzeliig 15, ☎ (031) 81 06 00, fax (031) 20 50 73 (www.hotel-lorensberg.se; info.lorensberg@ swedenhotels.se), €€€, is part of Sweden Hotels chain. For something a little different, try **M/S Seaside**, a hostel on a boat semi-permanently docked at Packhuskajen 8; ☎ (031) 10 59 70, fax (031) 13 23 69 (www. gmtc.se; seaside@gmtc.se), €. It offers 2–4-berth cabins and pri-vate cabins, and supplies equipment for evening deck barbecues. There are three **HI hostels** (and dozens of others). **Torrekulla Turiststation**, Kållered, ☎ (031) 795 14 95, fax (031) 795 51 40 (www.stfturist.se/torrekulla); **Slottsskogens**, Vegagt 21, ☎ (031) 42 65 20, fax (031) 14 21 02 (mail@slottskogenvh.se); and **Stigbergsliden**, Stigbersliden 10, ☎ (031) 24 16 20, fax (031) 24 65 20 (www.hostel-gothenburg.com). An independent hostel is **Kårralunds Vandrarhem**, **Liseberg**, Olbersg, ☎ (031) 84 02 00, fax (031) 84 05 00 (www.liseberg.se), tram no. 5. This last hostel is near the closest **campsite** to town: **Lisebergs Camping & Stugbyar Kårralund**, Olbergsg 1 (same ☎, fax, email and website), which has **cottages** as well as camping and is open all year.

Göteborg Pass
The Gothenburg Pass is
obtainable from Tourist
Offices, Pressbyrån, stations,
hotels, youth hostels, campsites, museums. This gives
free use of the city's public
transport and parking
meters as well as free or
discounted entrance to most
museums and attractions
(including Liseberg amusement park and the boat to
Elfsborg Fortress), plus offers
on shopping, dining and
entertainment.

$\boxed{\text{IO}}$ The **seafood** is excellent, most restaurants clustering along the waterfront. For other types of cuisine, try around Avenyn. The **Nordstan** complex offers a lot of eateries, including familiar fast-food outlets and a good supermarket, **Hemköp**, which has a deli section in the basement of the big store known as **Åhléns City**. For picnic items, the indoor **Storr Saluhallen market**, Kungstorget, has a tempting range of goodies.

WHERE NEXT?

The **Copenhagen–Oslo** (p. 467) route passes through Gothenburg. Services run north-east to **Stockholm**; for a longer route to the Swedish capital via the southern shore of Lake Vänern use the **Herrijunga–Hallsberg** service via **Mariestad** (ETT table 741).

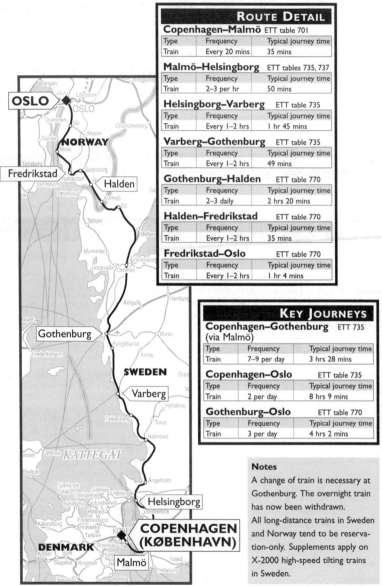

ROUTE DETAIL

Copenhagen–Malmö ETT table 701

Type	Frequency	Typical journey time
Train	Every 20 mins	35 mins

Malmö–Helsingborg ETT tables 735, 737

Type	Frequency	Typical journey time
Train	2–3 per hr	50 mins

Helsingborg–Varberg ETT table 735

Type	Frequency	Typical journey time
Train	Every 1–2 hrs	1 hr 45 mins

Varberg–Gothenburg ETT table 735

Type	Frequency	Typical journey time
Train	Every 1–2 hrs	49 mins

Gothenburg–Halden ETT table 770

Type	Frequency	Typical journey time
Train	2–3 daily	2 hrs 20 mins

Halden–Fredrikstad ETT table 770

Type	Frequency	Typical journey time
Train	Every 1–2 hrs	35 mins

Fredrikstad–Oslo ETT table 770

Type	Frequency	Typical journey time
Train	Every 1–2 hrs	1 hr 4 mins

KEY JOURNEYS

Copenhagen–Gothenburg ETT 735 (via Malmö)

Type	Frequency	Typical journey time
Train	7–9 per day	3 hrs 28 mins

Copenhagen–Oslo ETT table 735

Type	Frequency	Typical journey time
Train	2 per day	8 hrs 9 mins

Gothenburg–Oslo ETT table 770

Type	Frequency	Typical journey time
Train	3 per day	4 hrs 2 mins

Notes

A change of train is necessary at Gothenburg. The overnight train has now been withdrawn.

All long-distance trains in Sweden and Norway tend to be reservation-only. Supplements apply on X-2000 high-speed tilting trains in Sweden.

From the Danish capital, the route crosses over to **Malmö** in Sweden via a huge tunnel and bridge link (opened in 2000), then heads along the coast to the Swedish port of **Helsingborg** – in the Middle Ages this was in Danish hands, and the Sound was jealously guarded and tolls demanded from every ship that made its way in or out of the Baltic. If you prefer, you can head instead from Copenhagen to **Helsingør**, and cross by ferry to Helsingborg. Sweden's western seaboard has superb sandy beaches. Later you reach the impressive historic city of **Gothenburg**. There is plenty of potential to stop off at lesser known fortress towns. You cross into Norway just before **Halden**.

COPENHAGEN (KØBENHAVN), DENMARK

See p. 438.

MALMÖ, SWEDEN

See p. 484.

HELSINGBORG

During much of the Middle Ages, Helsingborg was Danish and functioned as an important garrison town; the massive fortified keep, the **Kärnan**, still dominates the place. The bustling port is a pleasant enough base, with an old quarter to explore, as well as the rewarding 15th-century **church of St Maria** and an entertainingly eclectic **Stadsmuseet** (town museum). On the east side of town **Frederiksdal** is an open-air museum of reconstructed buildings.

RAILS Next to the ferry terminal.

i **Tourist Office**: Stortorget/Södra Storgatan 1, ☎ (042) 10 43 50, fax (042) 10 43 55 (www.helsingborg.se; turistbyran@helsingborg.se).

⌂ **Youth hostel: Helsinborg/KFUM Nyckelbo**, Scoutstigen, ☎ (042) 920 05, fax (042) 910 50 (open May–Aug).

WHERE NEXT?

*Continue southwards for **Lund**, joining with the **Copenhagen–Stockholm** route (p. 483). You can also take the ferry across to Denmark to Helsingør (itself served by frequent trains for Copenhagen, taking 1 hr 5 mins; ETT table 701), best known for Kronberg Slot, the Elsinore of Shakespeare's Hamlet.*

VARBERG

Varberg was discovered in the late 19th century as a **bathing station**, and has some appealing period survivals, notably the **wooden pavilion** (Societeshuset) in the **park**, and the rectangular bathing section of 1903, with changing rooms and sun-loungers ranged around a tamed expanse of sea water. The dominant feature of this spa-like port is the moated 13th-century **castle**, which doubles as a youth hostel, with plenty of idyllic beaches (including naturist ones) within close range. Within walking distance from the centre is **Apelviken Bay** popular with surfers.

Tourist Office: Brunnsparken, ☎(0340) 887 70, fax (0340) 61 11 95 (tourist@varberg.se).

Youth hostel: Vareberg, Vare 325, ☎(0340) 411 73, fax (0340) 416 00 (vare.vandrarhem@swipnet.se), open Apr–Sept; 7 km south of the centre.

GOTHENBURG

See p. 464.

HALDEN, NORWAY

Halden is another old border post, on the attractive **Iddefjord** and overlooked by **Fredriksten Fort**, a huge star-shaped 17th-century castle just south-east of the town. Other historical highlights include the **Frederikshalds Theater**, with its fully restored baroque stage and old scenery, and **Rød Herregard**, a furnished 18th-century manor house.

On the south bank of the river.

Tourist Offices: Gjesthavn (Visitors' Marina), south of the station, ☎69 18 14 78; Langbrygge 3, north of the station in the main town (over the bridge), ☎69 19 09 80.

Youth hostel: Halden Vandrerhjem, ☎69 18 00 77, open late June–early Aug.

FREDRIKSTAD

With three sides still bordered by fortified walls, Fredrikstad guarded the southern approaches to Oslo and has survived as one of the best-preserved fortress towns in Scandinavia, owing to its continuous military use. It's conducive for wandering, particularly around the walls and along the cobbled alleys of **Gamlebyen** (the old town) over on the east bank. **Fort Kongsten** is a pleasant 15–20-min stroll.

5 mins' walk south-east of the centre.

Tourist Office: Nygaardsgaten 26, ☎69 39 65 04 (www.borgdest.no).

OSLO

See p. 449.

WHERE NEXT?

Follow the routes to **Malmö** *(p. 484) or* **Stockholm** *(p. 454), or the* **Oslo–Bergen–Oslo** *circuit (p. 470).*

ROUTE DETAIL

Oslo–Voss   ETT table 780

Type	Frequency	Typical journey time
Train	4–5 daily	5 hrs 20 mins

Voss–Bergen   ETT table 780

Type	Frequency	Typical journey time
Train	9–15 daily	1 hr 15 mins

Bergen–Stavanger   ETT table 2270

Type	Frequency	Typical journey time
Ship	2–3 daily	4 hrs 10 mins

Stavanger–Kristiansand   ETT table 775

Type	Frequency	Typical journey time
Train	7 Mon–Fri and Sun; 4 on Sat	3 hrs

Kristiansand–Kongsberg   ETT table 775

Type	Frequency	Typical journey time
Train	3–5 daily	3 hrs 25 mins

Kongsberg–Oslo   ETT table 775

Type	Frequency	Typical journey time
Train	1–2 per hr	1 hr 25 mins

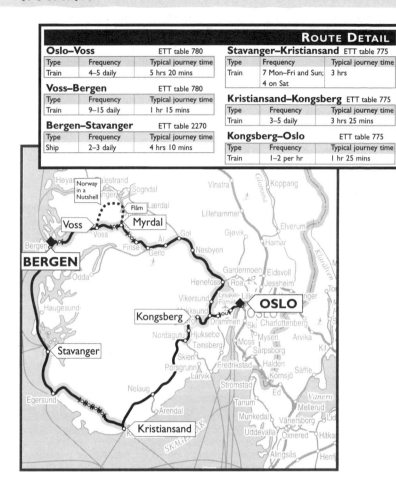

Notes

New tilting 'Signatur' trains are being introduced on these routes. These trains travel faster around curves and enable journey times to be reduced. As with all Norwegian long-distance services, reservation is compulsory.

Undoubtedly one of Europe's most spectacular train journeys, this circuit encounters some of the most stunning of Norwegian landscapes. The trip incorporates two lines, connected by a catamaran voyage between Bergen and Stavanger. From Oslo the route steadily climbs, past the year-round resorts of **Gol** and **Geilo**, and up to the holiday centre of Ustaoset (990 m), followed by a bleak but magnificent mountainscape of icy lakes and rocky, snow-capped ridges. Shortly after leaving Finse, the train enters a 10-km tunnel to emerge near Hallingskeid. The next stop is **Myrdal**, where you can divert to the hugely popular loop via train, boat and bus to the north via **Flåm** dubbed *Norway in a Nutshell* and offering a glimpse of a superb fjord. The main line then descends to the lakeside town of **Voss**. Thereafter, the scenery's a little less wild, although still impressive.

After you've had a look around the quaint harbour city of Bergen, the catamaran to Stavanger is fast and enjoyable. Even the last leg back to Oslo passes consistently pleasant countryside, lakes and forest, and gives access to the cities of **Kristiansand** and **Kongsberg**.

If the Oslo–Bergen train is booked up, make Bergen–Oslo reservations and do the circuit in reverse, which has the advantage of saving the really dramatic stuff for later on.

OSLO

See p. 449.

VOSS

Mountains rise straight out of the lakeside resort, itself just 56 m above sea level. Sights are pretty much limited to the 13th-century baroque-embellished **church**, as most of the town is modern and geared towards winter sports; its après-ski atmosphere is distinctly lively. A cable car, **Hangursbanen**, runs up to 1100 m, covering a height difference of about 570 m in 4 mins. For water sports, contact the Voss Rafting Senter, ☎56 51 05 25 (www.bbb.no/rafting; voss.rafting@online.no).

5 mins' walk from town centre

Tourist Office: Hestavangen 10, ☎56 52 08 00 (www.voss-promotion.no; vossn@online.no), a 3-min walk from the railway station, has plenty on hiking.

Youth hostel, Vanger, ☎56 51 20 17, fax 56 51 08 37 (Jan–Oct) 10 mins from centre.

WALKING TRIPS

You can get almost everywhere on foot in Bergen, but take the **Fløibanen** (funicular) from the centre up Mt Fløyen (320 m), for a panoramic view. At the top there's scope for pleasant picnics and walks in the woods.

BERGEN

An old Hanseatic port, Norway's extremely appealing second city is the gateway to some of the country's most magnificent fjords. Placed on a peninsula and surrounded by mountains, Bergen has meandering cobbled streets lined with gabled weatherboard houses and dignified old warehouses.

The city centres on the waterfront **Fisketorget** open Mon–Fri 0700–1600, Sat 0800–1500, a working fish (and various other things) market.

At the centre of the old quarter, **Bryggen** contains a fine row of medieval houses deemed worthy of UNESCO World Heritage Site listing.

Tiny **Theta Museum**, Enhjørningsgården Bryggen, was the clandestine one-room centre for Resistance operations in World War II, until it was discovered by the Nazis in 1942. When the **Bryggens Museum** was being constructed, the remains of the original city of 1050–1500 were discovered and incorporated.

Other museums in town are the art museums and those housed in the university Christiesgt, which also runs the botanical garden.

Gamle Bergen (Old Bergen), at **Sandviken**, is an open-air museum of some three dozen 18th- and 19th-century wooden houses and shops, many furnished in period style, ranged around cobbled paths and streets. You can wander round for nothing, but have to join a tour if you want to see the interiors. Yellow buses 🚌 nos. 9/ 20/22/50 take 10 mins: from the east side of Vågen, direction Lønborg.

EDVARD GRIEG'S HOME

Classical music lovers may like to pay a visit to **Troldhaugen**, home of Edvard Grieg, Norway's greatest composer. Crammed with memorabilia, it is little altered since his death in 1907, and is open daily in summer; the site includes a museum and concert hall. There are buses from the main bus station to Hopsbroen, from where it's a walk of 15–20 mins.

🚃 **Strømgaten**; 10 mins' walk east of the centre; walk straight ahead down Marken and keep going.

ℹ️ **Tourist Office**: (the best outside Oslo) Vågsalmenning 1; 📞 55 32 14 80 (www.visitbergen.com; info@vistbergen.com). International and local ferries mostly leave from **Vågen**, the inner harbour. International sailings use Skoltegrunnskaien, on the north side, including **Fjord Line** ferries from Newcastle, England (via Stavanger and Haugesund), 📞 (0191) 296 1313 in the UK. **Flaggruten** catamarans to **Stavanger** leave from Strandkaien, on the east side. Their office is in Strandkeiterminalen, 📞 55 23 87 00 (www.hsd.no). Pick up a boarding-pass 30 mins before departure; be certain to book ahead in July. The **Bergen Card** (Nkr.150 for 24 hrs, Nkr.230

for 48 hrs, from Tourist Offices, station, hotels and campsites) offers free local transport, free or discounted admission to most of the attractions, and 'a surprise in the menu' at selected restaurants. If you want to wander further afield on foot, or even on skis, **Bergen Turlag** (Bergen Touring Association), in DNT office, Tverrgt 4–6, ☎55 32 22 30, fax 55 32 81 15, can provide walking maps for the surrounding mountains.

Advance booking recommended – Bergen is often chock full of tourists and conference-goers. **Youth hostel: Montana**, Johan Blyttsvei 30; ☎55 20 80 70, is on Mt Ulriken (☐no. 31, open all year. The **YMCA/Interrail Centre**, Nedre Korskirkealmenning 4; ☎55 60 60 55, is conveniently located, within sight of the Tourist Office. Open May–Sept. The most central **campsite** (open 2 July–end Aug) is **Bergenshallen**, Vilh. Bjerknesvei 24, Landås, ☎55 27 01 80, 10 mins on ☐no. 90.

Bergen has plenty of nightlife. **Ole Bulls Plass**, south-east of the quay, is good for bars, as is the area behind Torget. There are more student-frequented bars and cafés up towards the university. Look out for events at the **Kulturehuset**, on an old wharf to the south.

There's a cheap **supermarket** next to the YMCA on Nedre Korskirkealm. Buy fruit and cheap (and delicious) smoked salmon or prawn sandwiches from the **fish market**. The large red and white building on Zachariasbryggen contains several mid-market restaurants.

DAY TRIPS TO THE FJORDS Three fjords near Bergen are among the deepest and most popular in the country: the **Hardangerfjord** (south of Bergen) is a major target for tourists, alternating verdant lowlands and precipitous cliffs scattered with waterfalls; **Nordfjord** (north of Bergen) twists over 100 km to the foot of the **Briksdal glacier**; the **Sognefjord** (north of Bergen) is the longest (205 km) and deepest (1300 m) in Norway; in some places the shoreline is gentle, in others it soars straight up to 1000 m. Two of its most spectacular arms are the **Nærøyfjord** and **Aurlandsfjord** (see *Norway in a Nutshell*, p. 474). Several boat tours, including day trips, depart from Bergen.

STAVANGER

The centre is small and easily walkable, with an excellent pedestrianised cobbled shopping area, and there's a good bus network to reach outlying attractions.

Gamle Stavanger (the old town) is the area on the west side of the harbour. Lovely for a stroll, with cobbled walkways and rows of early 18th-century wooden houses at crazy angles. The impressive medieval centre has retained the **Domkirke** (St Svithun's Cathedral).

You can also enter **Ledaal**, a mansion of 1800 that is used by the royal family when visiting the town, and **Breidablikk**, a 19th-century ship owner's house. **Valbergtårnet**, a 19th-century watchtower perched on top of a hill in the centre, provides an excellent view of the harbour.

🚆 Jernbanevej, 10 mins from the harbour and Tourist Office; round the left side of the lake and straight on.

⛴ **Flaggruten,** ☎51 86 87 80, catamarans for Bergen leave from Fiskepiren, 5 mins' walk east. **Fjord Line** international sailings leave from **Strandkaien**, to Newcastle, England, ☎(0191) 296 1313 in the UK.

i **Tourist Office**: Rosenkildetorget 1; ☎51 85 92 00, fax 51 85 92 02 (www.destinasjon-stavanger.no; info@destinasjon-stavanger.no). Exchange, cash machine next door.

🏨 Essential to book in advance – Stavanger is often booked out for conferences and is short on cheap hotels. The only **youth hostel** is **Stavanger Vandrerhjem Mosvangen**, Henrik Ibsensgt 21, ☎51 87 29 00, south of the centre. Otherwise, try the **Lille Hotel**, Madlavn. 7, ☎51 53 43 27, or **Havly Hotel**,Valberggt. 1, ☎51 89 67 00.

NORWAY IN A NUTSHELL This hugely popular circuit from **Myrdal** via **Flåm** and the **Sognefjord** uses the main rail line to Myrdal and rejoins it at Voss (or vice versa), combining a train, bus and ferry to link them. You can do it as a day excursion from Bergen, or en route to or from Oslo; the mainline trains must be booked in advance. It's not an escorted tour: you simply buy a ticket and follow the relevant timetable. Rail passes are not valid between Myrdal and Flåm, but rail-pass holders do receive a 30% discount. At **Myrdal**, you board a local train for a breathtaking journey down the branch to **Flåm**, taking about an hour. The descent covers 866 m in 20 km (at a gradient of up to 1:18), with superb views of towering cliffs, chasms and cascades. There are 16 tunnels on the route, including one 'turn around', in which the line makes a 360° turn completely within the mountain.The train stops at the particularly spectacular **Kjosfossen waterfall** for photographers to descend.

The railway ends at **Flåm**, a tiny village at the head of the **Aurlandsfjord,** accessible by rail on the **Sognefjord**. There are at least a couple of hours to relax, lunch, shop before boarding a 2-hr ferry journey (refreshments available) along the Aurlandsfjord and **Nærøyfjord**.

Disembarking at **Gudvangen** (accommodation available here also), the bus back to Voss follows an incredibly steep and breathtakingly dramatic road out of the fjord.

KRISTIANSAND

Ferries from Newcastle in England and Hirtshals in Denmark serve this bustling port and resort at the southern tip of Norway. In summer, the town's pleasant beaches get are busy. Much of the town was laid out in the 17th century by Christian IV, after whom it is named. His plan included the **Christiansholm Festning**, Strand-promenaden, built to guard the eastern approach to the harbour; the circular fortress is now the major sight with views to match. Forming the north-eastern part of the old quarter, **Posebyen** has many carefully preserved little wooden houses, while the neo-Gothic **Domkirke** (cathedral), Kirkegt, of 1885 asserts a massive presence. The **fish market** on the quay is a good place to pick up some smoked salmon or prawns for a picnic lunch.

On the west side of the centre, a few blocks from the Tourist Office, along Vestre Strandgate.

Tourist Office: Vestre Strandgate 32, ☎ 38 12 13 14 (www.sorlandet.com; destinasjon@sorlandet.com).

Youth hostel: Skansen 8, ☎ 38 02 83 10, (hostlkrs@online.no)

DYREPARKEN

(15 mins from the centre of Kristiansand by 🚌 no. 1) is a virtually cageless zoo and Norway's most visited attraction. There is also an amusement park with a special children's area (Cardomon Town).

KONGSBERG

Silver put the town on the map following the discovery of silver deposits of unique purity in the early 17th century in the nearby mountains. Kongsberg also established Norway's National Mint.

DAY TRIP FROM KONGSBERG TO THE SILVER MINES

Highly recommended is the trip to the disused **silver mines** at **Saggrenda** (8 km south, 🚌 no. 410). **Tours** (mid-May–Sept) feature a train ride through the heart of the mountain. The shafts go 560 m below sea-level and it's definitely chilly at 6°C.

On the west side of the river, next to the Tourist Office.

Tourist Office: Storgate 35, ☎ 32 73 50 00 (office@kongsberg-turistservice.no).

Youth hostel: Vinjesgate 1, ☎ 32 73 20 24 (vh.bergm@online.no).

ROUTE DETAIL

Oslo–Hamar   ETT table 785

Type	Frequency	Typical journey time
Train	every 1–2 hrs	1 hr 26 mins

Hamar–Lillehammer   ETT table 785

Type	Frequency	Typical journey time
Train	every 1–2 hrs	45 mins

Lillehammer–Dombås   ETT table 785

Type	Frequency	Typical journey time
Train	3–4 daily	1 hr 57 mins

Dombås–Trondheim   ETT table 785

Type	Frequency	Typical journey time
Train	3–4 daily	2 hrs 25 mins

Trondheim–Bodø   ETT table 786

Type	Frequency	Typical journey time
Train	2 per day	9 hrs 48 mins

Bodø–Narvik   ETT table 786

Type	Frequency	Typical journey time
Bus	2 daily	6 hrs 35 mins

Narvik–Gällivare   ETT table 760

Type	Frequency	Typical journey time
Train	2 daily	4 hrs

Gällivare–Boden   ETT table 760

Type	Frequency	Typical journey time
Train	3 daily	1 hr 50 mins

KEY JOURNEYS

Oslo–Boden   ETT tables 750, 760
(via Stockholm)

Type	Frequency	Typical journey time
Train	1 per day	22 hrs 55 mins

Boden–Stockholm   ETT table 760

Type	Frequency	Typical journey time
Train	2 per day	13 hrs

Boden–Helsinki   ETT tables 760, 769, 794
(via Luleå and Kemi; by bus Luleå–Kemi)

Type	Frequency	Typical journey time
Train	1–2 per day	15 hrs

Notes

The direct route between Oslo and Boden includes a change of train at Stockholm. Travellers from Trondheim to Narvik not wanting to visit Bodø can connect into the Bodø to Narvik bus at Fauske (55 km south of Bodø).

The real attraction of this extremely popular route into the **Arctic Circle** is the scenery itself, giving the opportunity to experience the Midnight Sun in summer. Gradually the scene evolves from gentle and bucolic in the area north of Oslo to breathtakingly dramatic in the northern reaches, which are inhabited by reindeer and by the Sami, or Lapps – one of the oldest peoples in Europe. Distances here are serious: Norway is a big country and sections of the route take as long as 10 hours. In particular, the recommended side trip ride from **Dombås** to **Åndalsnes** is an epic one, plunging through tunnels, over bridges, and past waterfalls and Europe's highest vertical canyon. From **Narvik**, you can continue on the scenic Ofoten line to **Boden** in Sweden, or change at **Gällivare** and take the equally fine **Inlandsbanan** to Mora, and then on to Stockholm. An equally thrilling and less touristy trip is the four-hour ferry (not covered by rail passes but inexpensive) from **Bodø** to **Moskenes** in the Lofoten Islands, where jagged peaks and homely fishing villages await. You can opt to cover the Bodø to Narvik section by boat, via **Svolvær** in the Lofoten Islands.

OSLO

See p. 449.

HAMAR

A 2-km walk northwards along the lakeside from the peaceful small town on Lake Mjøsa leads to Domkirkeodden peninsula, home to the **Hedmarksmuseet**, a regional museum, with some 50 historic buildings. The herb garden recreates a medieval monastery garden and there's an art centre where you can watch traditional skills. On the same site are the ruins of the medieval cathedral, which had been under cover for a decade to protect them from pollution, are now on display under the Hamardomen, a huge glass and steel tent.

On the southern edge of the centre.

Tourist Office: Torggata 1, ☎ 62 51 02 26 (www.hamarregionen.net). Just opposite the railway station.

Youth hostel: Vikingskipet Vandrerhjem, Åkersvikveien 24, ☎ 62 52 60 60. **Seiersted Pensjonat**, Hoelsgate 64, ☎ 62 52 12 44.

LILLEHAMMER

Lillehammer is a major skiing centre as well as an appealing lakeside town with wooden houses clinging to a hillside. It hosted the 1994 Winter Olympics and many of the facilities can be visited – and in some cases used (see Day Trips). In winter, the downhill and cross-country ski trails and skating rinks are open. Many are open in summer too – including chair lifts and summer ski-jumping, and the surrounding area is laced with paths. The Tourist Office has details.

DAY TRIPS FROM LILLEHAMMER At **Hunderfossen**, 15 km north (10 mins by train), you can try out the 1994 Olympic luge and bobsleigh tracks (up to 60 mph; on wheels in summer), or 'play, learn and experience' at the **Hunderfossen Family Park**. Worth it for the highly surreal 12-m model trolls.

Several operators run rafting and canoeing trips in the **Gundbrandsdal valley**, ranging from a half-day taster to an epic two-day voyage down the river Sjoa. Ask for details at Tourist Offices in **Lillehammer** or **Dombås**. **Sjusjoen**, reached by regular buses from Lillehammer, is a sports village by a lake, high up on a plateau where the snow stays till late in the year. A couple of ski rental shops can kit you out for cross-country skiing, and a map of the vast network of prepared tracks (*loype*) is on sale. In summer, it's a good place for water sports.

[RAIL] West of the centre.

[i] **Tourist Offices:** Turistkontor: Elvegate 19; walk straight out of the station to Storgata and turn left, ☎ 61 25 92 99 (www.lillehammerturist.no). **Skysstasjon**, in the station. *Lillehammer This Month* lists events and opening times.

[▣] **Gjestebu**, Gamleveien 110, ☎ 61 25 43 21, is central and comfortable. **Gjestehuset Ersgaard**, Nordseterveien 201, ☎ 61 25 06 84, another pension-type. **Youth hostel:** Jernbanetorget 2, ☎ 61 26 25 66. Next to the railway station.

DOMBÅS

The branch line to **Åndalsnes** diverges here. The journey itself is one reason for a visit. Another is the **Geirangerfjord,** arguably the most stunning of all the fjords. The green-blue water winds for 16 km between cliffs (up to 1500 m) and past cascading waterfalls. Get a bus from Åndalsnes to **Hellesylt** or **Geiranger** (at opposite ends of the fjord) and take the ferry between them (70 mins), then bus back to Åndalsnes – or on to **Ålesund**, a trip offering a mix of architectural styles. **Station:** a few mins' walk from the centre. **Tourist Office**: in the station, ☎ 71 22 16 22.

TRONDHEIM

Norway's first capital was founded in 997 by the Viking king, Olav Tryggvason, whose statue tops a column in the market square. Trondheim still has royal connections – monarchs are crowned in the cathedral and it has been the seat of the monarchy since the 12th century – and is now Norway's third largest city and a major university town, with more than 20,000 students. The narrow streets and alleys of the compact old centre make a pleasant strolling ground.

The **Nidaros Domkirke** (cathedral), Bispegata, is cavernously Gothic, worth seeing for its decorative stonework and sumptuous stained-glass windows. Northwards from the cathedral lies **Torvet**, the main square, and further on by the water's edge is **Ravnkloa**, home to a fish market. From here there are hourly boats to the island of **Munkholmen**, a monastery turned fortress standing on the site of an execution ground; it's a popular place for swimming.

Trondhjems Kunstforening (Trondheim Art Gallery), Bispegata 7, exhibits some of Norway's greatest art, while the **Nordenfjeldske Kunstindustrimuseum** (Museum of Applied Art), Munkegata 5, has a collection of contemporary arts and crafts. Other sights include the **Gamle Bybro** (Old Town Bridge), with views of the wharf.

North of the centre; also the bus station, and contains a Tourist Office; 15-min walk to the Tourist Office (cross the bridge, after three blocks turn right on to Olav Tryggvasonsgata and left down Munkegata).

Tourist Office: Munkegata 19, ☎ 73 80 76 60; entrance from Torvet – market square (www.taas.no; touristinfo@taas.no). **Taxis**: ☎ 73 50 50 73 (24 hrs).

Youth hostel: Rosenborg, Weidemannsvei 41, ☎ 73 87 44 50, 2 km east (🚌 no. 3; infrequent Sat–Sun). **Pensjonat Jarlen**, Kongensgt. 40, ☎ 73 51 32 18, is the cheapest pension in town. **Munken Hotel**, Kongensgt. 44, ☎ 73 53 44 50, is cheap (for Norway) and comfortable.

Day Trips from Trondheim Don't miss **Ringve Museum**, Lade Allé 60, 3 km east of town: 🚌 nos. 3/4: Fagerheim (from Munkegata towards Lade). The couple who donated their farm as a music museum began the extraordinary collection. You must join a tour, but it's thoroughly enjoyable. Some rooms are dedicated to composers, furnished in period and containing everything from letters to death masks; the guides play short samples of their music on antique instruments. Buildings at **Trondelag Folkemuseum**, Sverresborg, include turf huts and a small stave church dating from 1170 (buses from Dronningsgata (D1): 🚌 no. 8 towards Stavset or no. 9 towards Heimdal/Sjetnemarka; 10 mins).

Scandinavia

BODØ

Badly damaged by bombing in World War II, Bodø was largely rebuilt and has little to detain you, but is the departure point for ferries to the Lofoten Islands. The **Domkirke** (cathedral), unusual in having its spire detached from the main building, has rich modern tapestries.

🚉 300 m further east of town than the Tourist Office.

ℹ️ **Tourist Office**: Sjogata 21, ☎ 75 54 80 00 – called Destinasjon Bodø (www.bodoe.com; destinasjon.bodo@nl.telia.no).

⚓ **Ferries**: Hurtigruten and ferries to the islands leave from quays on the road beside the station.

🚌 Long-distance bus station is 300 m further along Sjogata.

🏨 For central budget accommodation, try **Opsahl Gjestegård**, Prinsengata 131, ☎ 75 52 07 04, € **Norrøna Hotel**, Storgate 4B, ☎ 75 52 55 50, €€. **Youth hostel**: Jernbanetorvet, ☎ 75 52 11 22 (claim to be open all year, but call ahead). **Camping**: 3 km south-east of town. ☎ 75 56 36 80.

THE LOFOTEN ISLANDS Bodø is the best place from which to take a ferry to the spectacular Lofoten Islands (www.lofoten-tourist.no), a chain of improbably jagged glacier-carved mountains sheltering fishing villages, farms, sheep and thousands of birds (including puffins). This is really Norwegian outdoors at its best – amazing scenery and still comparatively uncrowded. The islands are blessed with a surprisingly mild gulf stream climate. It's excellent terrain for walking, riding (horses available at Lofoten Leisure Farm, near Hol Church in Vestvågøy, between Leknes and Mortsund), canoeing and cycling (cycle hire in Svolvær and Moskenes), and there are some highly scenic boat trips – including to the cliffside bird colonies of **Værøy** and to **Trollfjord**, the best-known beauty spot in the archipelago. **Røst** and Værøy are tiny and support colonies of puffins. Both have hostels. You can also rent a motorised boat or join a fishing trip.

The main town is **Svolvær** (pop. 4000), on Austvågøy. Tourist Office: ☎ 76 06 98 00, fax 76 07 30 01, by the harbour; open until 2200 every night in summer. (Svolvær is actually much better reached from Skutvik, which is midway between Narvik and Bodø.) Ferries link Svolvær with Skutvik, Fiskebøl with Melbu, Moskenes with Bodø, and with Værøy and Røst in the far south. There are also flights from Bodø (including helicopter flights to Værøy). The main islands are linked by bridges and tunnels. There's a picturesque fishing village called **Å**, 5 km south of Moskenes, with cottages and a hostel (☎ 76 09 11 21), and a campsite. Fishing, caving and hiking trips can all be arranged here. There is also an express boat service from Svolvær to Narvik, taking 3 hrs 30 mins.

Colour Section

(i) Lofoten Islands, Norway (see left); Norwegian Folk Museum, Oslo (p. 452)

(ii) Tramcars, Stockholm, Sweden (p. 456); Orthodox cathedral and old town, Tallin, Estonia (pp. 512–515); Catherine Palace, St Petersburg, Russia (p. 501)

(iii) Vltava River, Charles Bridge, Castle and St Vitus Cathedral, Prague (pp. 537–539); Old Town Square; Old Town Clock, Prague, Czech Republic (p. 537)

(iv) Fisherman's Bastion, Budapest (p. 564); street minstrel; inset: Gellért Bath, Budapest, Hungary (p. 563)

NARVIK

Endowed with fine views by virtue of its hilliness and with a mild climate owing to the Gulf Stream, this small, modern port was invaded in 1940 by the Germans in a bid to control shipments of iron ore; within days the British destroyed the German fleet and the allies recaptured the town. The first section of the **Nordland Røde Kors Krigsminnemuseum** (Red Cross War Museum), commemorates the town's role in World War II as well as the work of the Norwegian resistance.

Narvik's prosperity owes virtually everything to the Ofoten railway line, which carries iron ore from Sweden and ships it out from here; these aspects are explained in the **Ofoten Museum**. For panoramic views towards the Lofoten Islands, take the *gondolbaner* (cable car) up **Fagernesfjellet** – a popular place for hang-gliding and paragliding; allow at least 2 hrs if you wish to walk up.

RAIL 900 m from the Tourist Office.

Bus station: in the city centre, ☎76 96 35 10.

i **Tourist Office**: Kongensgata 66, ☎76 94 33 09, fax 76 94 74 05.

Breidablikk Gjestehus, Tore Hundsgate 41, ☎76 94 14 18, €, up the hill from the main road, is an inexpensive pension. **Norlandia Narvik**, Skistuaveien 8, ☎76 94 75 00, €€, is upmarket, but cheaper than others and has great views. **Youth hostel: Nordkalotten**, Tiurveien 22, ☎76 96 22 00, (postmottak@ssin.no), open mid-June–mid-Aug.

GÄLLIVARE, SWEDEN

Iron and copper ore mining dominates the scene, and tours (Mon–Fri mid June–mid Aug) enter the opencast copper mine and the underground iron mine. In Malmberget (the site of the mines north of town) are the museum village, **Kåkstan**, and the **Mining Museum**. Gällivare's also a good place to immerse yourself in the Sami (Lapp) culture, whose heritage is reflected in the (current) name of its mid-18th-century church, **Lappkyrkan**. There's a small museum of Sami history in the Tourist Office building, and about 2 km from the centre of town, up the road to Dundret, **Vägvisaren** is a small open-air museum based on Sami culture, with a traditional hut (similar to a teepee) and live reindeer.

INLANDSBANAN

Gällivare is the northern end of the superbly scenic Inlandsbanan, that runs 1067 km through central Sweden from **Mora** (summer-only service; change at Östersund; ETT tables 761, 762). For a 100 km sample, ride from Gällivare to Jokkmokk (2 hrs). There's only one train a day in each direction, giving you rather longer than you might need there; alternatively, daily buses from Gällivare allow you a 5-hr stay. **Jokkmokk** grew from a Sami mission into a sizeable town and its prime role today is to keep the Sami culture alive. **Tourist office**: Stortoget 4, ☎(0971) 121 40, fax (0971) 171 89 (www.jokkmokk.se; jokkmokk.turistbyra@ jokkmokk.se)

The top of Dundret, the 820-m hill that looms to the south of the town, is a **nature reserve** with panoramic views. It's 7 km to the top and you should allow at least 3 hrs for the full return hike (many people take twice as long), but you can get great views by going only as far as 4 km. When the **Midnight Sun** is visible there are special bus tours to the top of Dundret.

[RAIL] On the western edge of town.

[i] **Tourist Office**: Storgatan 16, ☎ (0970) 166 60, fax (0970) 147 81 (www.gellivare.se; turistinfo@gellivare.se).

[🛏] **Gällivare Värdshus**, Vid Bradhuset, ☎ (0970) 162 00, fax (0970) 155 45. **Youth hostel**: **Gällivare Vandrarhem**, Andra Sidan, ☎ (0970) 143 80.

BODEN

See p. 490.

The **Aurora Borealis**, or **Northern Lights**, is a stunning natural spectacle of glowing light in the sky, an atmospheric phenomenon caused by collisions between air molecules and charged particles from the sun that have entered the earth's magnetic field. It occurs sporadically in winter throughout northern Scandinavia. More visitors have a chance to experience the Midnight Sun of the far north in summer.

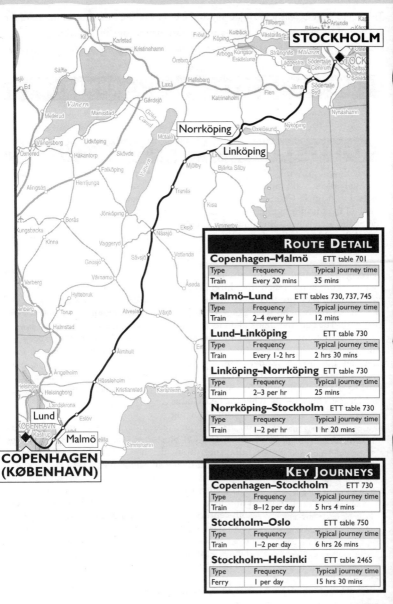

STOCKHOLM

Norrköping

Linköping

COPENHAGEN (KØBENHAVN)

Lund

Malmö

ROUTE DETAIL

Copenhagen–Malmö ETT table 701

Type	Frequency	Typical journey time
Train	Every 20 mins	35 mins

Malmö–Lund ETT tables 730, 737, 745

Type	Frequency	Typical journey time
Train	2–4 every hr	12 mins

Lund–Linköping ETT table 730

Type	Frequency	Typical journey time
Train	Every 1-2 hrs	2 hrs 30 mins

Linköping–Norrköping ETT table 730

Type	Frequency	Typical journey time
Train	2–3 per hr	25 mins

Norrköping–Stockholm ETT table 730

Type	Frequency	Typical journey time
Train	1–2 per hr	1 hr 20 mins

KEY JOURNEYS

Copenhagen–Stockholm ETT 730

Type	Frequency	Typical journey time
Train	8–12 per day	5 hrs 4 mins

Stockholm–Oslo ETT table 750

Type	Frequency	Typical journey time
Train	1–2 per day	6 hrs 26 mins

Stockholm–Helsinki ETT table 2465

Type	Frequency	Typical journey time
Ferry	1 per day	15 hrs 30 mins

SCANDINAVIA

This route is an excellent introduction to the beauty of the landscape of the southern portion of Sweden, yet it also allows the opportunity to visit three historical Swedish cities. Forests and countless numbers of picturesque lakes are visible on the journey.

COPENHAGEN (KØBENHAVN), DENMARK

See p. 438.

MALMÖ, SWEDEN

Sweden's fast-growing third city, with a population of around quarter of a million, is a lively place, with plenty of good bars, clubs and coffee houses, and an excellent festival in August. Capital of the Skåne province, Malmö was part of Denmark for much of the Middle Ages and came under Swedish sovereignty in 1658: even today the Skåne accent has something of a Danish tinge. Enclosed by a canal that loops round through a park and doubles as the castle moat, the city's well-groomed historic centre dates back to Danish times and features two fine cobbled squares.

Leaving the station southwards along Hamngatan, you soon reach the huge central square, Stortorget, presided over by the statue of Carl X Gustav, who won Skåne back from Denmark. The square is flanked on its east side by the statue-embellished **Rådhuset** (town hall) of 1546 (with 19th-century alterations), itself on the line of **Sodergatan**, the main pedestrianised street. Just behind stands **St Petri Kyrka** (St Peter's church) – Sweden's second largest church – its whitewashed Gothic interior showing off its baroque altar and medieval frescos to best advantage. Off Stortorget's south-western corner lies **Lilla Torg**, a smaller and infinitely more charming square with medieval, sometimes lopsided, brick and timber façades, outdoor cafés and restaurants; live music adds to the atmosphere on summer evenings. From here a short walk west leads to the formidable 15th-century fortress, **Malmöhus Slott**, open daily 1200–1600, with its circular towers and assorted buildings containing a set of museums covering a range of themes – including city history, military exhibits, art and natural history – with real flair.

> If the weather's set fair, lounge in one of the three great parks, **Kungsparken, Slottsparken** and **Pildammsparken**; or head down to the 3 km-long **Ribersborg beach**, within walking distance. You can pick up the basics for a picnic at the excellent **Saluhallen** covered market in **Lilla Torg**.

> Consider getting the **Malmökortet** (Malmö Card), valid for 1 adult and 2 children (SKr.150 for 24 hrs) for free local buses, free parking, free admission to all of Malmö's museums, and savings on sightseeing, trips, shopping, entertainment and eating out. Available from the Tourist Office and Forex Offices.

🚆 **Malmö C**, just north of the old town.

$\boxed{i}$ **Tourist Office: Centralstation**; ☎(040) 34 12 00, fax (040) 34 12 09 (www.malmo.se; malmo.tourism@malmo.se). Get the useful free *Malmö This Month* 2-monthly guide for events and listings. For information on the August festival contact the website (www.festival.malmo.se).

🏨 **Hotellcentralen**, ☎(040) 10 92 10, fax (040) 10 92 19 (hotel@malmo.se) make hotel bookings. **City Room**, S. Forstadg. 31, ☎(040) 795 94, fax (040) 12 36 63 (cityroom@telia.com), supply lists of private rooms. **Hotel Formule 1**, Lundvägen 28, ☎(040) 93 05 80, fax (040) 18 36 40, €, is a cheap chain hotel. **Youth hostel: Vandrarhem**, Backavägen 18, ☎(040) 822 20, fax (040) 51 06 59 (🚌no. 36). **Campsite: Sibbarps Camping & Stugby**, Strandgatan 101, ☎(040) 15 51 65, fax (040) 15 97 77 (sibbarps.camping@swipnet.se); open all year.

WHERE NEXT?

Malmö to Gothenburg X2000 trains taking 2 hrs 45 mins – supplement payable – slower trains taking 3 hrs 20 mins run from Malmö to Gothenburg, see Copenhagen–Gothenburg (p. 461).

LUND

The handsome ancient university town is one of the most rewarding places in southern Sweden. A religious centre in the 12th century, much of medieval Lund is still extant. There's a decent range of accommodation and plenty of studenty eating haunts.

🚉 5 mins' walk west of the centre.

$\boxed{i}$ **Tourist Office: Stadshuset**, Kyrkogatan 11, ☎(046) 35 50 40, fax (046) 12 59 63 (www.lund.se; turistbyran@lund.se). Get the free brochure *i Lund* for listings and info.

🛏 **Youth hostel:** Tåget Väveregatan 22, Bjeredsparken, ☎(046) 14 28 20 (300 m from the station).

LINKÖPING

The town's prime attraction is **Gamla Linköping**, Malmslättsvägen (5 mins on 🚌nos. 203/205/207, or 20 mins' walk), an ambitious lived-in museum village recreating the 19th century Linköping, much of which was painstakingly removed piece by piece and rebuilt here – it includes a small chocolate factory, as well as working craft shops, houses, street lamps and old signs. Try to go when the individual buildings will be open; otherwise you may have to be content with walking round and viewing from the outside.

Linköping's **Domkyrkan** is one of Sweden's oldest cathedrals, with a 107 m green spire visible from far around, and contains fine stone carving around the south doorway and elsewhere; the north doorway is a survival of the original Romanesque building that was later Gothicised. It is a magnificent structure with a fascinating crypt resplendent with ancient carved tombstones, and an intricate **astronomical clock** that springs into action twice a day (1200 and 1500; Sun and holidays 1300 and 1500), with an entire miniature theatre's worth of moving figurines.

Flygvapen Museum (Airforce Museum), next to Malmen military airfield, 6 km west of Linköping (⊟no. 213 from Resecentrum, the central train/bus station), is an assemblage of some 60 military aircraft dating from 1912 – some of which you can sit in the cockpit of (closed Mon, Sept–May).

🚆 5 mins' walk east of the centre.

ℹ️ **Tourist Office: Quality Hotel Ekoxen**, Klostergatan 68, 📞 (013) 20 68 35, fax (013) 12 19 03 (www.linkoping.se; turism@ekoxen.se). Get *Linköpings Guiden* and *Next Stop Linköping*.

🏨 **Youth hostel: Linköpings Vandrahem**, Klostergatan 52A, 📞 (013) 14 90 90, fax (013) 14 83 00 (www.linkopingsvandrahem.se) also has apartments, central.

NORRKÖPING

Norrköping is a prosperous textile centre, with a museum celebrating the town's industrial legacy. For most visitors, however, the main reason for a stop is **Kolmårdens Djur och Naturpark** (Kolmården Zoo and Safari Park; www.kolmarden.com), open Easter and May–Sept. The zoo is said to be Europe's largest and is in three separate sections: the main zoo, a safari park and a dolphinarium. A cable car offers the best view of many animals. It's 30 km north-east of town: ⊟no. 432 (roughly hourly) takes about 50 mins; ⊟no. 481 runs 10 km to **Löfstad Slott** (Löfstad Castle), a sumptuous 17th/18th-century mansion amid spreading grounds, totally unchanged since the last owner died some 60 years ago (📞 (020) 75 75 75).

🚆 Norrköping C, 5 mins' walk north of the centre.

ℹ️ **Tourist Office ('Destination Norrköping')**: Dalsgt 16, 📞 (011) 15 50 00, fax (011) 15 50 74 (www.destination.norrkoping.se; info@destination.norrkoping.se); open April–Oct.

🏨 **Hotel and youth hostel: Turistgården**, Inglestadgatan 31, 📞 (011) 10 11 60, €.

Rock carvings depicting beasts, ships and human figures – and dating from 1500 to 500BC – can be seen at **Himmelstalund**, 2 km west of Norrköping.

STOCKHOLM

See p. 454.

ROUTE DETAIL		
Stockholm–Uppsala		ETT tables 760, 761
Type	Frequency	Typical journey time
Train	2–3 per hr	40 mins
Uppsala–Sundsvall		ETT table 760
Type	Frequency	Typical journey time
Train	5–8 daily	2 hrs 40 mins
Sundsvall–Umeå		ETT table 768
Type	Frequency	Typical journey time
Bus	5 daily	4 hrs
Umeå–Luleå		ETT tables 760, 768
Type	Frequency	Typical journey time
Bus	4–5 daily	4 hrs 25 mins
Train	2 daily	4 hrs 15 mins
Luleå–Kemi		ETT table 769
Type	Frequency	Typical journey time
Bus	4–8 daily	4 hrs 20 mins
Kemi–Oulu		ETT table 794
Type	Frequency	Typical journey time
Train	5 daily	1 hr 10 mins
Oulu–Tampere		ETT table 794
Type	Frequency	Typical journey time
Train	6 daily	5 hrs
Tampere–Turku		ETT table 795
Type	Frequency	Typical journey time
Train	6 daily	2 hrs
Turku–Helsinki		ETT table 791
Type	Frequency	Typical journey time
Train	Every 1–2 hrs	2 hrs

Notes

Buses between Sweden and Finland now operate from Luleå. There are direct buses from Umeå to Luleå; from Luleå to Kemi, change at Haparanda. Trains from Umeå to Luleå go via Boden.

Sweden's coastal towns north of **Stockholm** offer a variety of attractions, from the lively university town of **Uppsala** to the clean refinement of **Gävle** (pronounced 'Yervle'). A long but enjoyable bus ride connects **Sundsvall** with **Umeå** (no rail pass discounts). The northern stretch of the route runs above the **Arctic Circle**, where reindeer roam and local Sami peoples retain their traditional, if modernised, ways. Later, you cross over into the wild northern territories of **Finland** and head south past the strongly contrasting cities of **Tampere** and **Turku**.

STOCKHOLM

See p. 454.

UPPSALA

No visitor to Sweden should miss out on the former capital, home of the country's oldest university as well as its religious centre. The 16th-century **Uppsala Slott** (Red Castle), overlooking the town, was built by King Gustaf Vasa, who broke ties with the Vatican and pointed his cannons directly at the archbishop's palace. Beneath the castle is the surviving part of the old city: it's all instantly familiar to anyone who has seen Ingmar Bergman's movie masterpiece *Fanny and Alexander*, set here in Bergman's birthplace. The central sights are walkable if you don't want to wait for a bus. Furthest from the station are two gardens (the Botanical Garden and Linnaeus' Garden; see below) in different directions: 30 mins at a slow pace. On summer weekends, **Lennakatten vintage railway** runs on a narrow-gauge line from Östra station (behind Uppsala C).

Dominating the skyline are the twin towers of Scandinavia's biggest church, the French-Gothic **Domkyrka**. It took 175 years to build and was consecrated in 1435, but there were major restorations in the 18th and 19th centuries. Virtually every inch of the side chapels is covered by tapestries or wall and ceiling paintings. The impressive side chapels include those of St Erik, Gustaf Vasa and the botanist Linnaeus (see below).

Founded in 1477, the **old university building** (**Gustaviauum**) features an anatomical theatre where public dissections of executed convicts were a 17th-century tourist attraction, and is open to visitors. Books, manuscripts and maps are on display in **Carolina Rediviva Universitetsbiblioteket** (library), corner Övre Slottsg/Drottningg, notably half of a 6th-century Silver Bible – a rare example of the extinct Gothic language, written on purple vellum – and the manuscript of Mozart's *Die Zauberflöte* (*The Magic Flute*).

The great 18th-century professor of botany, Linnaeus (Carl von Linné), developed the definitive system of plant and animal classification. His former residence is now a museum, **Linnéanum**, in the small **Linnéträdgården** (Linnaeus' Garden), Svartbäcksg 27. His **Botaniska Trädgården** (Botanical Garden), Thunbergsv 2–8, is much larger.

Gamla Uppsala (Old Uppsala), 5 km north, was the cradle of Swedish civilisation and likely the centre of a pre-Christian cult. Hundreds of tombs are dominated by huge grassy mounds, thought to be the resting-places of three 6th-century kings. Alongside them are the rebuilt Uppsala Kyrka (church) and a small museum village.

Uppsala C. East of the centre, 5-min stroll to the Tourist Office: walk straight up Bangårdsg to the river, turn right and cross the second bridge – the Tourist Office is halfway along the block.

Tourist Office: Fyristorg 8, ☎ (018) 27 48 00, fax (018) 13 28 95 (res.till.uppland.nu).

Uppsala Room Agency: ☎ (018) 10 95 33, fax (018) 12 82 42 (Mon–Fri 0900–1700, Sat, Jul and Aug 0900–1200), can book private rooms. **Samariterhemmets Gästem**, Samaritergränd 2, ☎ (018) 10 34 00, fax (018) 10 83 75 (www.svkyrkan.se/samariterhemmet), €€, is probably the cheapest hotel. **Basic Hotel**, Kungsgt 27, ☎ (018) 480 50 00, fax (018) 480 50 50 (www.basichotel.com; reception@basichotel.com), €€, is just what it says it is, and cheap. **Grand Hotel Hörnan**, Bangårdsgt 1, ☎ (018) 13 93 80, fax (018) 12 03 11 (www.eklundshof.se; info@eklundshof.se), €€, is old-style classy and more expensive. **Youth hostel: Sunnersta Estate**, Sunnerstav 24, ☎ (018) 32 42 20, fax (018) 32 40 68, 5 km south (🚌 nos. 20/25/50 to Herrgårdsvägen). **Camping: Fyrhishovs Camping**, Idrottsg 2, ☎ (018) 27 49 60, fax (018) 24 43 33 (www.fyrishov.se; info@fyrishov.se) by the river, 2 km north (🚌 nos. 4/6/20/24/25/50/54). Open all year.

SUNDSVALL

Spread over the mainland and onto the island of Alnö, the town is primarily a timber port, though despite the place's preoccupation with wood, the centre is dominated by late 19th-century limestone and brick structures erected on a grand scale after a disastrous fire in 1888 destroyed most of Sundsvall's wooden buildings. The **Kulturmagasinet** is an interesting complex of restored warehouse buildings, now housing a small local museum and gallery. For a look at an unusual modern church interior, look inside the red-brick **Gustav Adolfs Kyrkan**. Otherwise, head out of the centre to medieval **Alnö gamla kyrka** (🚌 no. 1 to Alnö), a church containing well-preserved 16th-century frescos; or to **Norra Bergets Hantverks och Friluftsmuseum**, an open-air museum with an eclectic mix of handicrafts and panoramic views, reached by a 3km climb up Gaffelbyn.

10-min walk from the main square.

Tourist Office: Stora Torget, ☎ (060) 61 04 50, fax (060) 12 72 72 (www.sundsvall.se)

Continental, Rådhusgatan 13 (in the centre), ☎ (060) 15 00 60, fax (060) 15 00 60 (hotell.continental@spray.se), €€, an old sweet factory, now a lovely, homely and inexpensive hotel. **Youth hostel: Vandrarhem Sundsvall**, Norra Berget, ☎ (060) 61 21 19, fax (060) 61 78 01 (stf.vandrarhem.sundsvall@telia.com), next to Norra Berget outdoor museum, 20-min walk from centre or 🚌 Plus Bus (☎ (060) 18 27 99 one hour in advance).

UMEÅ

Umeå is a rapidly growing university town with a youthful population. You can shoot nearby rapids in rubber rafts (mid-May–mid-Sept). One place really worth lingering is **Gammlia**, a complex with seven museums, including a **Ski Museum** and an excellent **open-air museum** with buildings brought from all over the region; most sections open only in summer. For students and young people, nightlife revolves around the university campus.

5-min walk north of the centre. Luggage lockers.

i **Tourist Office**: Renmarkstorget 15, ☎(090) 16 16 16, fax (090) 16 34 39 (www.umea.se; umeturist@umea.se). Free hotel reservation service.

Strand Hotell,Västra Strandgatan 11, ☎(090) 70 40 00, fax (090) 70 40 90 (strand@linfors.se), €€, has a central riverfront location. Cheaper options are **Pensionat Pendlaren**, Pendelgatan 5, ☎(090) 12 98 55, €, and **Vandrarhemmet Statarlängan**, south-west of Umeå in Hörnefors, ☎(0930) 210 81.

BODEN

Primarily a rail junction and garrison town, Boden is a pleasant enough place to wait between trains. Fearing attack by Russia after the 1809 invasion of Finland, the Swedes erected a mighty complex of fortresses, among them the **Rödbergsfortet**, whose mighty ramparts date from 1900–1910. Boden is the main centre of the Swedish army; the **Garnisonsmuseet** (Garrison Museum), on the south-western edge of town, is chock-full of militaria.

WHERE NEXT FROM BODEN?

For those with a real taste for epic journeys, carry on far into **Lappland** and the Arctic Circle, by taking the **Oslo–Boden** route in reverse (p. 476), or by returning to **Stockholm** via Gällivare and taking the Inlandsbanan (p. 481; ETT table 762). Between Boden and Kemi are **Haparanda** and **Tornio** – effectively one town but in two time zones, linked by bridges. There is a border post, as Haparanda is in Sweden and Tornio in Finland, but no formalities to observe.

Boden C. 20 mins' walk north-west of centre.

i **Tourist Office**: Kungsgatan 40, ☎(0921) 624 10, fax (0921) 138 97 (www.turistbyran.com; info@turistbyran.com). Pick up a copy of the mostly Swedish-language Bodenturist.

Hotell Standard, opposite station, Stationsgatan, ☎(0921) 160 55; mid-range rooms, plus dorm beds in basement.

KEMI, FINLAND

One thing to head for here is the **Jalokivigalleria** (Gemstone Gallery), at the end of Kauppakatu (open daily; also home to the Tourist Office). The ground floor has excellent displays of stones, while upstairs you'll find copies of some famous diamonds and royal regalia, as well as the genuine – but never worn – Finnish royal crown. From Feb–mid-April (weather permitting) every year the three-storey **Kemi Snowcastle** is open to the public for exhibitions and events, even restaurants and accommodation. Ask for details at the Tourist Office.

A 5-min walk east of the centre: straight along Kauppakatu.

Asemakatu, 0200 4069. Walk round the Medivire office building in front of the rail station and it's on the far side. It's better equipped than the rail station. **Information office**; when it's closed, get tickets on board – you don't need them if you have a valid rail pass. Booking is not necessary.

Tourist Office: Kemin Kaupungin Matkailutoimisto, Kauppakatu 29, (016) 259 690, fax (016) 259 675 (www.kemi.fi; kemin.matkailu@kemi.fi), in the Gemstone Gallery (open Mon–Fri 0800–1600, also Sat–Sun 1000–1800 Feb–mid-Apr and in summer).

Two Finnish chain hotels: **Cumulus Kemi Hotel** (Restel), Hahtisaarenkatu 3, (016) 22 831, fax (016) 228 299 (kemi.cumulus@restel.fi), €€, and **Hotel Palomestari** (Finlandia), Valtakatu 12, (016) 257 117, fax (016) 257 118 (hotelli.palomestari@pp.inet.fi), €€.

SIDE TRIP TO ROVANIEMI Helsinki-bound trains from Kemi come down from Rovaniemi, giving you the option of catching a train for the 1 hr 30 mins' northward trip to see Rovaniemi itself, the capital of the Finnish province of Lappland. Thoroughly destroyed in 1944 and subsequently rebuilt, its Sami roots seem far removed, but it has the impressive **Arktikum** (science centre and museum of the Arctic regions) at Pohjoisranta 4. The station is south-west of the centre and a 20-min walk to the main city Tourist Office: Koskikatu 1, (016) 346 270, fax (016) 342 4650 (www.rovaniemi.fi). Accommodation: **Outa,** Ukkoherrantie 16, (016) 312 474, €; **youth hostel: Tervashonka,** Hallituskatu 16, /fax (016) 344 644.

OULU

High-tech industries are in evidence here, and the mostly modern town (population 120,000) is home to **Science Centre Tietomaa**, Nahkatehtaankatu 6, an interactive science and technology centre – completely non-esoteric and great fun. A few older buildings such as the city hall recall the 19th-century tar boom – in which Oulu did pretty well – and there's an assemblage of Sami artefacts and other local miscellania at the absorbing **Pohjois–Pohjanmaan Museo** (North Ostrobothnia Provincial Museum; closed until autumn 2002 for refurbishment), Ainola Park. The seashore looks out to the town's islands, joined by bridges.

Rautatienkatu, east of centre. From Kemi there are about 6 trains daily, taking around I hr 15 mins.

i **Tourist Office**: **Olun Kaupungin Matkailupalvelut**, Torikatu 10, ☎ (08) 5584 1330, fax (08) 5584 1771 (www.oulutourism.fi). Take Asemakatu for six blocks, left on Torikatu. Get *Oulu This Week* and *Look at Oulu* (plus free map).

🛏 **Hotelli Turisti**, Rautatienkatu 9, ☎ (08) 375 233, fax (08) 3110 755, €€: small family-run hotel opposite the railway station. **Youth hostel**: **Uni Hostel Välkkylä**, Kajaanintie 36, ☎ (08) 8803 311, fax (08) 8803 754 (kuntopalatsi@oyy.fi), 20-min walk from the station; open June–Aug.

WHERE NEXT?

An alternative, but longer, way to Helsinki is by taking the **Helsinki–Oulu** *journey (p. 495) in reverse.*

TAMPERE (TAMMERFORS)

Finland's second city was once the country's major industrial base, but the red-brick factory buildings and warehouses have been converted into museums, galleries and shopping centres, etc. and Tampere is a surprisingly attractive place, flanked by lakes and graced with abundant green spaces.

A few streets to the right as you exit the station is **Tuomiokirkko** (cathedral), Satakunnankatu, built of granite in 1907 and resplendent with frescos and stained glass. From the station, Hämeenkatu leads across the **Tammerkoski**, a series of rapids that connect the city's two largest lakes and provide a source of eco-friendly hydro-electric energy for Tampere.

To the north you'll see the former **Finlayson factory**, whose workers were housed in the Amuri district, built in the 1880s. **Amurin työläismuseokortteli** (Museum of Workers' Housing; open early May–mid-Sept), Makasiininkatu 12, preserves 32 of these houses and shops, which manage still to have a genuinely lived-in feeling. Close by, the city library (1986) in Hämeenpuisto, is a curvaceous masterpiece of modernism by Reima and Raili Pietilä. There's also a **Lenin Museum** in Hämeenpuisto, near the end of Hämeenkatu. This is where Lenin met Stalin in the early 1900s – Lenin lived in Tampere after the 1905 revolution.

Two of Tampere's galleries give an excellent survey of Finnish art: the **Hiekka Art Museum**, Pirkankatu 6, contains earlier works amassed by goldsmith Kustaa Hiekka include some of his jewellery, while the lakeside **Sara Hildén Art Museum** (20 mins' walk or 🚌 no. 16 north-west of the centre) displays some of the nation's finest modern art. The latter is in **Särkänniemi**, an amusement park encompassing a children's zoo, an aquarium, a dolphinarium, a planetarium and the Näsinneula tower – at 168 m the country's tallest structure and which provides a magnificent view.

Towards the surreal end of the scale is **Moominvalley**, Hämeenpuisto 20 (Tampere City Library, separate entrance), dedicated entirely to Moomins, the characters of Tove Jansson's wonderfully innovative children's books.

The **Nukke-ja pukumuseo** (Doll and Costume Museum), Hatanpään Kartno, Hatanpään Puistokuja 1 (3 km south of the centre, 15 mins on 🚌 no. 21; open Mar–Sept), is beautifully sited, within a 19th-century building amid gardens on the tip of a small peninsula. It contains some 4000 dolls and puppets – the oldest a 12th-century Incan rag doll – and a wide range of traditional Finnish and other costumes. The basement concentrates on exotic exhibits, from costumed fleas and rude wooden carvings to meticulously executed Balinese-dancer dolls.

A 5-min walk east of the centre; left luggage office (Mon–Sat 0730–1900, Sun 0815–1900).

Tourist Office: Verkatehtaankatu 2, 📠 (03) 3146 6800, fax (03) 3146 6463 (www.tampere.fi; touristbureau@tampere.fi). Walk up Hämeenkatu and turn left just before the bridge: it's on the riverside. *Tampere* is a free comprehensive listing that includes a map; there's also a self-guided walking tour.

Hotelzon (hotel booking centre): 📠 (09) 5840 9100, fax (09) 5840 9111 (www.hotelzon.fi; hotellit@hotelzon.fi). The three **HI hostels** include **Uimahallin Maja**, Pirkankatu 10–12, 📠 (03) 222 9460, fax (03) 222 9940 (aris@sci.fi), a hostel and hotel with reasonably priced rooms. Open all year, comfortable and central. It is 1 km from the station, straight up Hämeenkatu, turn right and Pirkankatu is on the left. The other two hostels open June–late Aug: **Hostel Tampereen**, Tuomiokirkonatu 12A, 📠 (03) 254 4020, fax (03) 254 4022, and **Kesähotelli Härmälä**, Nuolialantie 50, 📠 (03) 265 1355, fax (03) 266 0365 (myyntipalvelu@lomaliitto.fi). **Camping: Camping Härmälä**, 📠 (03) 265 1355, fax (09) 713 713 (myyntipalvelu@lomaliitto.fi), km south of the centre (🚌 no. 1 to within 200 m). Open mid-May–late Aug.

TURKU (ÅBO)

Finland's oldest city and until 1812 its capital, Turku is home to Finland's oldest university and is a vibrant commercial and cultural centre, with a pulsating nightlife. Its cathedral is very much the nation's spiritual heart.

Turku's much-rebuilt but impressive **Tuomiokirkko** (cathedral) is easily spotted by the tower's distinctive face, the result of several fires over the centuries, which has become the city's symbol; look out for some intriguing tombs, including those of **Karin Mansdotter**, a local flower girl who became Queen of Sweden in 1568.

Turku Castle, Linnankatu 80, 3 km from the centre near the ferry terminal, is not very appealing from the outside, but the interior is a wondrous maze of passageways and halls. These fortifications were the seat of Finland's government for over 500 years.

Close by, beside the river, the **Sibelius Museo** (Sibelius Museum), Piispankatu 17, displays over 350 musical instruments, as well as memorabilia of the great composer revered throughout Finland (not that he had any connection with Turku itself; the most famous house connected with him is Ainola, at Järvenpää, north of Helsinki); concerts are sometimes given here.

South of the cathedral, **Luostarinmäki**, near Vartiovuori Hill, is an 18th-century area of town that has been turned in its entirety into a highly recommendable open-air museum, busy with artisans' workshops. A recent addition to the city's museums is **Aboa Vetus/Ars Nova**, Itäinen Rantakatu 4–6. In 1992, excavations for the **art museum** (Ars Nova) revealed extensive remains, parts dating from the 15th century. They were left in situ and form the basis of 'Aboa Vetus', so history and contemporary art rub shoulders.

Apteekkimuseo (Pharmacy Museum), Läntinen Rantakatu 13, consists of a restored 18th-century home and an old pharmacy that looks ready to re-open for business.

WHERE NEXT?
*Turku is served by ferries to **Stockholm** (10 hrs 30mins, ETT table 2480), some of which stop at **Mariehamn** or **Långnäs** in the **Åland islands**, an archipelago of 6000 low-lying, forested isles belonging to Finland.*

At **Forum Marinum**, Linnakatu 72, a trio of historic ships are open as attractions *Suomen Joutsen* (a 96-m full-rigger built in 1902), *Keihässalmi* (a World War II mine carrier), and *Sigyn* (a 19th-century wooden 3-masted barque); in summer take ferry Pikkuföri.

[RAIL] **Turku** is north-west of the centre, 15-min walk from the Tourist Office. One or two trains continue to **Satama** (*Hamnen*; the harbour). **Kupittaa** is also fairly central, but not as well equipped as Turku.

[ferry] **Ferries:** At the south-west end of town. [bus] no. 1 (to the main square) is more frequent than the trains, and also goes to the airport.

[i] **Tourist Office:** Aurakatu 4, [tel] (02) 262 7444, fax (02) 262 7674 (www.turku.fi). The free full-colour brochure *Fun Times and Joy for All: Welcome to Turku and Southwest Finland* has everything you need.

[hotel] **Scandic Hotel Marina Palace**, Linnankatu 32, [tel] (02) 336 300, fax (02) 251 6750 (www.scandic-hotels.com), €€€, is pricey but has an unbeatable riverside location. **Turun Karina**, Itäinen Pitkäkatu 30B, [tel] (02) 265 7911, fax (02) 265 7919 (hotelli@issy.fi), €€, has the cheapest hotel rooms in town. The **youth hostel** is near the Scandic Hotel at Linnankatu 39, [tel] (02) 262 7680, fax (02) 262 7675 (hosteltk@saunalahti.fi). **Bed and breakfast: Vaahtera**, Kielokuja 2, [tel] (02) 242 1207 is good value, as is **Majatalo Kultainen Turisti**, Käsityöläisenkatu 11, [tel]/fax (02) 250 0265.

HELSINKI

See p. 444.

ROUTE DETAIL

Helsinki–Parikkala
ETT table 797

Type	Frequency	Typical journey time
Train	4–5 per day	4 hrs 10 mins

Parikkala–Retretti

Type	Frequency	Typical journey time
Train	2–3 per day	26 mins

Retretti–Savonlinna

Type	Frequency	Typical journey time
Train	2–3 per day	25 mins

Parikkala–Joensuu
ETT table 797

Type	Frequency	Typical journey time
Train	4–5 per day	1 hr 25 mins

Joensuu–Kuopio
ETT tables 799, 798

Type	Frequency	Typical journey time
Train	1–2 per day	3 hrs 20 mins

Kuopio–Oulu
ETT table 798

Type	Frequency	Typical journey time
Train	2–3 per day	4 hrs 55 mins

KEY JOURNEYS

Helsinki–Stockholm
ETT table 2465

Type	Frequency	Typical journey time
Ship	2 daily	17 hrs 15 mins

Helsinki–Oulu
ETT tables 790, 794

Type	Frequency	Typical journey time
Train	6 daily	6 hrs 50 mins (day)
		8 hrs 55 mins (night)

Helsinki–Tallinn
ETT table 2410

Type	Frequency	Typical journey time
High-speed craft	20 daily	1 hr 35 mins

Notes

Helsinki to Oulu: 4–5 day trains and 2–5 night trains via Kokkola; 1–2 day trains and 1–2 night trains via Kuopio.

Parikkala to Retretti to Savonlinna: additional buses run throughout the day.

Joensuu to Kuopio: change trains at Pieksämäki.

FINLAND

This satisfying trip takes in all that is quintessential about Finland, from the rolling farm-lands of the south to the untamed swathes of forest and thousands of lakes in the north, with **Kuopio** one of the main highlights. The spur from **Parikkala** to **Savonlinna** via the **Punkaharju** causeway has far from frequent services but is especially rewarding, so it is included as part of the main route.

HELSINKI

See p. 444.

PARIKKALA

Change here for trains on the spur to **Savonlinna** (buses also available). Trains from Parikkala to Savonlinna call at **Retretti** on request.

RETRETTI

Retretti, 33 km from Parikkala (buses when the train isn't running and the option of a cruise in summer), is a spectacular arts complex (**Taidekeskus**) housed partly in man-made caverns in **Punkaharjuesker**, a 7-km-long ridge of pine-crowned rocks, but also spreads into the surrounding woodlands. In addition to the many paintings and sculptures, attend summer concerts underground for great acoustics.

SAVONLINNA

Sited on a group of bridge-linked lake islands, this spa resort, fashionable with the tsars in the mid 19th century, has a number of attractions, but there are two which make it unmissable. **Olavinlinna**, the best-preserved medieval castle in the northern countries, was built in 1475. It's largely intact and retains a medieval character. The courtyard is the venue for the other major draw, the annual international **opera festival**. It's staged in July: tickets go on sale the previous Nov and it's essential to book months in advance (☎(015) 476 7515, fax (015) 476 7540; operafestival.ltd@operafestival.fi), for accommodation as well as tickets.

🚋 **Savonlinna–Kauppatori** station is the first stop and more central than the main one. Two trains (47 mins) and 2–3 buses (1 hr 20 mins) make the trip from **Parikkala**, serving **Retretti** en route. Turn left out of the station, then left again onto Olavinkatu to get to the centre.

ℹ️ **Tourist Office**: Puistokatu 1, ☎(015) 517 510, fax (015) 517 5123 (www.savonlinna.fi; savonlinna@touristservice-svl.fi).

🏨 **Kesähotelli Vuorilinna**, Kylpylaitoksentie, just north of the rail station, ☎(015) 739 5494, fax (015) 272 524 (casino.myynti@svlkylpylaitos.fi), €, open early June–late Aug. Or try **Savonlinnan Kristillinen Opissto (Savonlinna Christian College)**, Ritalanmäki 1, ☎(015) 572 910, fax (015) 572 9121 (slnkris@kolumbus.fi), €, 6 km from the centre with regular bus connections.

JOENSUU

Worthy of a few hours' stop, Joensuu is the capital of Finnish Karelia (what is left of it after parts were ceded to the Russians in 1944), and although much expanded, a fair number of its 19th-century wooden buildings survive. It also has the worthwhile **North Karelian Museum**, an art nouveau **town hall**, Lutheran and Orthodox **churches**, the university's **botanical gardens** and a **tropical butterfly and turtle garden**. Try to be there for the **street festival** in mid-July.

KUOPIO

The main reason to stop here is the outstanding **Suomen Ortodoksinen Kirkkomuseo** (Finnish Orthodox Church Museum), Karjalankatu 1 (closed Mon), about 1 km north-west of the centre (🚃 no. 7). The Russian Orthodox religion once flourished in this area and in 1939, to safeguard them from the Nazis, precious 18th-century icons and other sacred objects were gathered together from all over the country. The result is an eclectic and fascinating collection. The sights include a pretty Lutheran **cathedral**, **Old Kuopio Museum** (an open-air ethnographic museum), and a harbour with summer festivals when it's light all night. All are in the centre.

On the northern edge of town, about 500 m from the central market square.

Tourist Office: Haapaniemenkatu 17 (by the market square), 🕿 (017) 182 584, fax (017) 261 3538 (www.kuopioinfo.fl; tourism@kupio.fi).

Hermannin Salit, Hermanninaukio 3A, 🕿 (017) 364 4961, fax (017) 364 4911, €, is 10 mins' walk south of the centre and has both cheap rooms and dorm beds. Another budget option is **Matkakoti Souvari**, Vuorikatu 42, 🕿 (017) 262 2327, €. **Youth hostel**: **Puijon Maja**, Puijontornintie, 🕿 (017) 255 5250, fax (017) 255 5266 (hotelli.puijo@pspt.fi).

SIDE TRIP FROM KUOPIO TO LAKE LADOGA On an island in Lake Ladoga, the 800-year-old **Valamon Luostari** (Monastery of Valamo, 🕿 (017) 570 111, 🚃 daily to within 4 km), at Heinävesi is the centre for the Russian Orthodox religion in Finland (guided tours 1000–1700 in summer). You can stay at the hostel on the island, 🕿 (017) 570 1504, fax (017) 570 1510 (valamo@valamo.fi), but wearing shorts is not acceptable and photographs are not permitted. The Orthodox **Lintulan Luostari** (Convent of Lintula), 🕿 (017) 563 106 (lintulan.luostari@ort.fi), 20 km away in Palokki, also offers accommodation. A full-day excursion that operates mid-June–Aug is the easiest way to visit both briefly. If you want to stay longer, there are various options: ask the Tourist Office for details.

OULU

See p. 491. The Stockholm–Helsinki trip passes through here.

BALTIC STATES

(for Directory information, see pp. 592, 600 and 601).
The landscape of the Baltic states (**Estonia**, **Latvia** and **Lithuania**) belongs to the northern European plain, which might seem at first monotonous, but which has its distinctive charms. Forests of birch give way to low, rolling hills, scattered woods, lakes, great lazy rivers, and rocky outcrops with ruined castles.

Ruined castles and 18th-century estates, largely unknown to outsiders, dot the territory. Much of the coast is studded with islands.

Estonia and Latvia are both very Germanic in character – the dominant religion and architecture being Protestant. Lithuania was historically part of Poland and differs strongly in its Catholic mood. All three countries have coped quite successfully with the transition from a Soviet planned economy – although some relics of the Soviet past are in evidence – to a Western market-oriented economy. There may still be occasional shortcomings but few places in Europe have changed at such a pace. The Baltic States have strongly asserted their independence from Russia, attracting intensive foreign investment and aligning themselves closely with the European Union. Nonetheless, you will find them still relatively cheap. For general information on the Baltic States, check out the websites: www.balticsww.com and www.ciesin.ee.

ESTONIA

YOUTH HOSTELS

Estonian Youth Hostel Association, Tatari 39–310, Tallinn, ☎ (02) 646 14 55, fax (02) 646 15 95 (eyha@online.ee), will make reservations at 40 hostels throughout Estonia from 150EEK. It is conveniently linked: www.balticbudgettravel.com (Balti Puhkemajad) at the same address. Also check out www.baltichostels.net.

ACCOMMODATION

There should be no problem with accommodation in Estonia, which has a variety of hostels and inexpensive hotels. **Home stays** offer accommodation in farmhouses, summer cottages, homes and small boarding houses.

FOOD AND DRINK

As elsewhere in the Baltic States, starters are varied and plentiful and are eaten in quantity, while the main course may be more modest. The most popular drink is beer (*õlu*), and Estonian beers (both dark and light) have a growing reputation – try **Saku**, **Tartu** and **Saaremaa**. In winter, try mulled wine or the excellent Estonian liqueur, **Vana Tallinn** (great in tea or in cocktails).

Baltic States

LATVIA

ACCOMMODATION

The more sophisticated accommodation tends to cluster around **Riga** and the seaside resort **Jurmala**, once one of the Soviet Union's most fashionable holiday places. Most camping facilities are in the area of Jurmala and the coastline. **Latvian Youth Hostels Association**, Aldaru 8, Riga LV 1050; ☎921 8560, fax 722 4030 (lyha@navigators.lv), or for budget guesthouses try **Latvia Country Tourism Association**, Kugu 11, Riga LV 1048, ☎761 7600, fax 783 0041 (www.celotajs.lv; lauku@celotajs.lv).

FOOD AND DRINK

Many Latvian dishes are accompanied by a richly seasoned gravy, and are usually eaten with superb rye bread. Latvian beer (*alus*) is good and strong – try **Aldaris**, **Bauskas** or **Piebalgas**. The spicy Riga **balsam** is famous throughout the former Soviet Union and is considered very good for health. Add it to tea, champagne and cocktails, or just drink it on its own, whether you're ailing or not.

INFORMATION

Lithuanian Hotels Reservation Centre Service (www.lithuanianhotels.com).
Bed & Breakfast: Litinterp, Bernardinu 7/2, Vilnius, ☎ (02) 22 38 50 or (02) 22 32 91, fax (02) 22 35 59 (www.litinterp.lt; vilnius@litinterp.lt). Can arrange accommodation with local families.
Lithuanian Youth Hostels Association
PO Box 12, Filaretų 17, Vilnius, ☎/fax (02) 26 26 60 (filaretai@post.omnitel.net).

LITHUANIA

ACCOMMODATION

If you have no luck with any of the agencies listed on the left, Lithuania has an extensive system of tourist information offices which cover all the main towns (for Vilnius see p. 506) and can help you find accommodation of all kinds.

FOOD AND DRINK

Local specialities include: *cepelinai* (the national dish – meatballs in potato), *blynai* (mini pancakes) and *kotletas* (pork cutlets). Fish and dairy products are common in all dishes. Lithuanians eat their **evening meal** early and you should aim to order by 2000; service is leisurely, so relax and make an evening of it. Vodka (the best is **Kvietine**) and very sweet liqueurs are the main spirits. Lithuanian beer (**Utena**, **Svyturys** and other brands) is easily available. The beer bars in **Vilnius** are worth a visit if you want to see 'the other side' of Lithuania; here, watered-down beer is sold to sometimes belligerent hard drinkers.

EDITOR'S CHOICE: Riga; St Petersburg (Russia); Tallinn; Vilnius.

BEYOND THE BORDERS: Vilnius–Warsaw (ETT table 1040); Tallinn–Helsinki ferry (tables 2410, 2412).

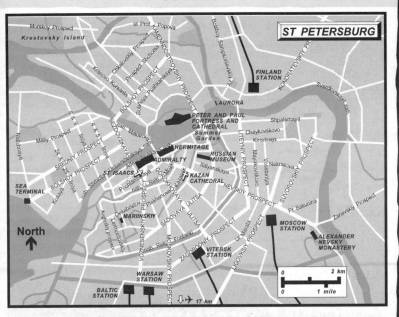

ST PETERSBURG

We have included Russia's second city in this chapter on the Baltic States as it's very much dominated by the Baltic itself and is a tremendously atmosphere-laden city. You'll need to obtain a Russian visa in advance; the journey from Berlin or Warsaw involves transit through Belarus, but the visa allows for this. There are direct services to Moscow, 650 km away (shortest journey by high-speed ER200 train, which runs four times a week, taking under 5 hrs; ETT table 1900). St Petersburg (formerly Leningrad), capital of Russia 1712–1918, was the brainchild of the westernising Tsar, Peter the Great. Almost every other building, lining broad avenues and vast expanses of water, seems to be a palace or architectural monument of some kind. There are more than 8000 listed buildings here. Despite crumbling façades and peeling paintwork, St Petersburg is blindingly beautiful summer or winter.

ARRIVAL AND DEPARTURE

Moscow Station (Moskovskiy vokzal; Metro: MAYOKOVSKAYA PLOSHCHAD VOSSTANIYA) for trains to Moscow and onwards to the south. **Vitebsk Station** (Vitebskiy vokzal; Metro: PUSHKINSKAYA) for trains to **Belarus**, **Poland** and the **Baltic States**.

Finland Station (Finlyandskiy vokzal; Metro: PLOSHCHAD LENINA) for trains to **Helsinki**. Tickets can be bought at stations for roubles only, or with a card via travel agencies (check Sindbad at 3-ya Sovetskaya, ☎ 327 8384, www.sindbad.ru), hotels or the Central Railway Booking Office (**Tsentralny Zheleznodorozhnye Kassy**), (**Griboedova**) **kanala naberezhnaya** 24 at windows 100–4, 2nd floor. Metro: NEVSKIY PROSPECT.

Sea Terminal, **Morskoy Vokzal**, MORSKOY SLAVY PLOSHCHAD 1, ☎ (812) 322 6052 (numerous buses, trolleybuses and commercial minibuses). Boats from Moscow arrive at the River Passenger Terminal, Obukhovskoy oborony 195 (Metro: LOMONOSOVSKAYA), ☎ 262 0239.

Pulkovo, ☎ (812) 104 34 34. St Petersburg's international airport is located 17 km south of the city centre. The currency exchange office has limited opening hours and is generally unreliable. Route Taxis (minibuses) link both terminals (domestic flights: Pulkovo 1; international flights: Pulkovo 2) to MOSKOVSKAYA metro station 0700–2200, taking 10–15 mins.

Tickets for all local surface transport (buses, trams, trolleybuses and commercial minibuses) are sold on board by conductors or the driver. There are ticket inspectors (not in uniform), so make sure you buy your ticket immediately. A *yedinyy bilet* covers all state transport for a calendar month and is good value if you are staying a long time. For the metro, **tokens** (*jetony*) must be dropped into the turnstiles, but most people buy magnetic cards, valid for a set number of journeys.

TOURIST INFORMATION

City information office at Nevskiy prospect 41, ☎ 311 2843, fax 311 2943. The useful *St Petersburg Official City Guide* (quarterly) is available online (www.cityguide.spb.ru). Events listings are available weekly in the *St Petersburg Times* (www.sptimes.ru) and the monthly glossy paper, *Pulse*.

INFORMATION

POST AND PHONES — **Central Post Office**, Pochtamtskaya Ulitsa 9 (Mon–Sat 0900–1930). Faxes and express post can be sent from here. **Westpost** (Nevskiy prospect 86, ☎ 275 07 84) offer 5-day postal services via Finland at quite moderate rates, or for American destinations try Post International at Nevskiy prospect 20.

The local phone area code is 812. Phone cards (for green city PTS phones) offer the cheapest alternative for both local and international dialling (dial 8 – dial tone – 10 then international code etc). Blue BCL phones in hotels and airports, etc. take credit cards.

INTERNET ACCESS — Westpost and Rednet (Central Railway Booking Office) offer Internet.

MONEY — Hard currency is no longer an option when paying for services, so always have plenty of roubles. ATMs are fairly common in Nevskiy prospect, in hotels and the metro, but some offer only extremely limited sums. Best deal is offered by **Sberbank** at Dumskaya 3 (opposite Gostiny Dvor, just off Nevskiy prospect) and Malaya Sadovaya 9.

PUBLIC TRANSPORT

Public transport is comprehensive and startlingly cheap. It runs 0530–2400, but is infrequent after 2300. Official transport maps abound, and are available in English (try Dom Knigi at Nevskiy prospect 28).

METRO The metro is cheap and reliable, although not comprehensive. All four lines are colour coded, but you'll need basic knowledge of the Cyrillic alphabet. Two intersecting stations on different lines will have different names. Stations are indicated by a large blue M.

BUSES Look out for the signs: Red T for trams, A on yellow for buses, flat-topped M for trolleybuses. Still incredibly cheap and much less crowded are the commercial buses and minibuses which cover all main routes and some more unusual areas.

TAXIS Official cabs are mostly yellow and have an orange light on top. If you order a cab from a hotel the cost will be extortionate. Flag a cab down on the street, but remember that drivers often hope for two or three times as much from foreigners.

BRIDGES
From 0150 to around 0445, May–Oct, St Petersburg's bridges are raised to let ships pass up and down the river. Think it may not affect you? Well, many visitors spend at least one night on the WRONG bank of the river.

RIVER TOURS

It would be a sin to visit St Petersburg and not take a canal or river tour. Or take a hydrofoil (*raketa*) service (0900–1830 in summer, 30 mins) to the 18th-century palace and gardens at Peterhof, departing outside the Hermitage Museum.

ACCOMMODATION

As in Moscow, there is a distinct shortage of medium-price and budget accommodation, but the adventurous can always get a good deal. Still, a number of highly select, tiny apartment-cum-hotels offer cosy intimacy and independence at very central locations. Try **Turgeniev** off season, Bolshaya Konyushennaya 13, 314 4529, fax 311 5180, or **Vergaz** on 7-ya Liniya, Vasilyevskiy ostrov, /fax 327 8883/4.

At the cost of some minor inconvenience, go for the **Oktyabrskaya Hotel**, Ligovsky prospect 10, 277 6330, fax 315 7501, Metro: PLOSHCHAD VOSSTANIYA, just across the road from the Moscow Station. Insist on the upgraded rooms (they have nice bathrooms). Some St Petersburg regulars go for **Neva Hotel** at Chaykovskovo 17, 278 0504, fax 273 2593, right by the Summer Garden.

The **St Petersburg Youth Hostel**, 3-ya Sovetskaya ulitsa 28, 329 8018, fax 329 8019 (ryh@ryh.ru), Metro: PLOSHCHAD VOSSTANIYA, is surely one of the most successful ventures of its kind in Russia. It provides excellent back up in all situations, and has an attached student/youth travel agency, Sindbad, which can book onward journeys. If that's booked up, try **Holiday Hostel** at Mikhailova 1, 327 1070, fax 327 1033 (info@hostel.spb.ru), Metro: PLOSHCHAD LENINA.

RUSSIA

For **bed and breakfast**, go for the long-established **HOFA** (Host Families' Guest Association), ☎/fax 275 1992 (russianstay@yahoo.com). They can do visas and find a room with ordinary families in St Petersburg and the Baltic States.

FOOD AND DRINK

There's no need to spend the earth on dining in St Petersburg. Most places offer excellent food, although on Nevskiy prospect itself cafés are thin on the ground. Take a hop and a skip off the main road, however, and if you're paying more than €8 a head without drink you're not really on a budget.

HIGHLIGHTS

Whether seen under a sheen of snow, or in the summer sun, St Petersburg is a seductive place with countless beautiful grand old buildings set on seemingly endless French-style boulevards, or lining intricate canalways, and museums galore. For the best view, get out and walk, winter, summer, rain or shine, it's what the locals do.

St Petersburg's elegant main avenue, **Nevskiy prospect**, extends 5 km eastwards from Palace Square to the Alexander Nevsky Lavra (monastery). Shops, clubs and museums are clustered in the near reaches of this avenue, and it has some striking palaces and bridges to keep bringing you back to it.

The **State Hermitage** is not only one of the world's largest and most magnificent museums, but it incorporates the **Winter Palace**, former residence of the Russian imperial family. Take a tour of the blindingly rich state apartments, and don't forget to go upstairs to see works by Matisse, or down to the gold collection – everything from Greek gold to Chinese, Indian and Iranian treasures (closed Mon; students free).

Although 19th-century novelist **Fyodor Dostoevsky** is most closely associated with the Haymarket, the setting for *Crime and Punishment*, it is his last home in the city that has been refurbished as a **museum** (Kuznechnyy Pereulok 5/2). You should also visit the **apartment** of Russia's greatest poet, **Alexander Pushkin** (Naberezhnaya reki Moyki 12).

If you want to go to the **Mariinsky Theatre** (known as the **Kirov** abroad), but cannot afford the price, check out the ticket touts out front, or get a Russian to buy a ticket for local prices and dress down when you go in.

WHERE NEXT?

Ferries serve *Tallinn* (p. 512).

ROUTE DETAIL

Vilnius–St Petersburg   ETT table 1820

Type	Frequency	Typical journey time
Train	1 daily	14 hrs

Vilnius–Riga   ETT table 1810

Type	Frequency	Typical journey time
Train	2 daily	7 hrs

Riga–Tartu   ETT table 1800

Type	Frequency	Typical journey time
Bus	1 a day	4 hrs 45 mins

Tartu–Tallinn   ETT table 1880

Type	Frequency	Typical journey time
Train	2 daily	3 hrs 15 mins

Tallinn–St Petersburg   ETT table 1870

Type	Frequency	Typical journey time
Bus	6 daily	9 hrs

KEY JOURNEYS

Warsaw–Vilnius   ETT table 1040

Type	Frequency	Typical journey time
Train	alternate days	9 hrs

Riga–Tallinn   ETT table 1800

Type	Frequency	Typical journey time
Bus	7 daily	5 hrs 30 mins

Tallinn–Helsinki   ETT table 2410

Type	Frequency	Typical journey time
High-speed craft	20 daily	1 hr 35 mins

Note

Estonia and Latvia put their clocks forward in summer, while Lithuania does not. So in summer when the time is 2200 in Latvia and Estonia, it is 2100 in Lithuania.

Baltic States

This intriguing route crosses the frontiers of the three independent Baltic Republics of **Lithuania**, **Latvia** and **Estonia**, and of Russia. The through journey can be performed by bus or a combination of bus and rail, with ample time to absorb a landscape of dense forest of pine and silver birch, gently undulating verdant uplands, and isolated farmsteads. Extend the journey by beginning from **Warsaw** (p. 518), or omit **St Petersburg** and take the ferry from **Tallinn** across the **Gulf of Finland** to **Helsinki** (p. 444). There are more buses if you skip Tartu and go directly from Riga to Tallinn.

VILNIUS, LITHUANIA

Lithuania and its capital Vilnius are less colourful, less visited and less tourist-friendly than their Baltic rivals, Latvia and Estonia. Nevertheless, the cobbled winding streets of the old part of the town are attractive and Vilnius' appeal can partly be said to rest in its comparative obscurity. The main street which bisects the town, Gedimino, could be a useful place to start and return to as it connects the old and new parts of Vilnius.

> Avoid the districts of **Uzupio** and **Kalvariju** late at night.

> Note that **museums and galleries** are usually closed on Mon.

The cathedral square, the focal point of the city, witnessed mass anti-Soviet demonstrations in the run-up to independence in 1991. The **cathedral** was built on an ancient site dedicated to the God of thunder. Re-built eleven times, it received its classical façade in 1777–1801. Within its **Kazimieris Chapel** are the splendid tombs of the members of the Polish-Lithuanian royal dynasty. **St John's Church**, the university church, has the striking Observatory Tower of 1659. The **Gedimino tower** is all that remains of the royal castle and now contains the **Vilnius Castle Museum**. Adjacent to the cathedral is **Kalnu Park**, a shady streamside sanctuary. T Kosciuskos leads eastwards from the north side of the park to the **Church of St Peter and St Paul**, the finest baroque church interior in Vilnius, with over 2000 stucco figures. The **Tuskulenai Estate** opposite was a burial place of Stalin's victims. Gedimino leads westwards from the square into modern Vilnius, terminating at the Parliament Building. Adjacent to the **Music Academy** may be found the old KGB headquarters, now home to the **Lithuanian Museum of Genocide Victims**, Gedimino 40 (entrance from Avku 2A; conducted tours of the cells, sometimes by former inmates, Tues–Sun). **Vilnius Picture Gallery** can be found at Didzioju 4, where tickets for all the branch galleries can be purchased (student and other concessions available).

🚂 Currently being rebuilt.

🚌 **Buses**: Sodu 2, information ☎ 26 24 82. Left luggage office. Most express buses do not pass through Vilnius and you need to pick them up at Kaunas. Eurolines Baltic International, however (☎ 251 377) run to most cities in Europe.

Tourist Offices: Pilies 42, ☎ 62 07 62. They will book accommodation and arrange guides. Branch at Vilniaus 22, ☎ 62 96 60. Buy *Vilnius in Your Pocket*, an objective guide to the sights, hotels, restaurants and bars. Go for the local **website**: www.vilnius.lt, which covers local history and all the sites, complete with plentiful colour images to help you choose your route.

Medical care: Baltic-American Medical & Surgical Clinic in Vilnius University Hospital at Antakalnio 124, (☎ 34 20 20).

Money: Plentiful cash machines around town. Visa: Gedimino 10–12 and Savanoviu 19.

Post and phones: The **Central Post Office**, Gedimino 7, ☎ 61 67 59. Buy phone cards from post offices or Spauda kiosks. The **Vilnius area code** is 370 2.

Internet: Not many cybercafés in Vilnius, but try Ralinga at Pylimo 20, ☎ 61 19 66.

Shopping: Markets (haggling permitted!) may be found at Pilies 23 (souvenirs) and Gedimino (general). Gift shops selling handicrafts and amber proliferates in the old town.

Public transport: The most attractive part of the city, the old town, is best explored on foot (easy walking distance from bus and train stations.) Public transport runs 0500–2300.

The Lithuanian Youth Centre Hostel, Ukmerges 25, ☎ 25 46 27, is a modern upmarket hostel. The **Filaretai Hostel**, Filaretu 17, ☎ 24 46 27, is now home to the Lithuanian Youth Hostels Association and can book accommodation for the whole of the Baltics (🚌 no. 34 from the station). **Litinterp Agency**, Bernardinu 7–2, ☎ 22 38 50, books bed and breakfast accommodation.

The cheapest food is from street stalls and the colourful food market at **Hales Turgaviete** on the corner of Pylimo and Bazilijonu. Some restaurants close early.

SIDE TRIPS FROM VILNIUS **Museum of Genocide**, Agrastu 15 (frequent bus services) marks the site where 100,000 people (mostly Jews) were murdered by the Nazis in the Paneriai Forest, 10 km from Vilnius. Grassed over pits in the forest serve as a chilling reminder (1100–1800, closed Tues).

Trakai, the old medieval capital of Trakai (Tourist Office: Vytauto 69, ☎ 51 934), has an impressive (restored) castle, dating from the 14th century, on a picturesque lake (open daily). Frequent buses and trains; just under 1 hr.

Kaunas (Tourist Office: A. Mickeviciaus 36, ☎ 7 32 34 36, turizmas@takas.lt; buy *Kaunas in Your Pocket*) was the pre-war capital, and retains an air of elegance as Lithuania's second city. Laisves, the city's pride and joy, is a pedestrianised, tree-lined boulevard, bordered with shops and cafés that reflect increasing prosperity. Next to the **Military Museum of Vytautas the Great**, Vienybës Square, **MK Ciurlionis State Art Museum**, houses a vast collection of modern Lithuanian and folk art. The famous **Devil's Museum** is a collection of over 2000 devils from all over the world, including Hitler and Stalin dancing upon Lithuania. A walk eastwards, along **Putvinskio**, leads to the funicular, which ascends the 'green hill' for a fine view over the city; you can pay using a trolleybus ticket. **Perkunas House** is the finest example of late Gothic architecture in the town, and houses handicraft displays at weekends.

Youth hostel: Lytagra, Ateities 50, ☎73 78 27. **Litinterp Agency**, Kumeliu 15-4, ☎22 87 18 (kaunas@litinterp.lt), will find you somewhere for bed and breakfast (closed Sun).

Šiauliai, en route north of Vilnius, is worth visiting for its extraordinary **Hill of Crosses** – 80,000 crosses of all sizes, the first of which appeared in the mid-19th century. From Šiauliai, visit **Klaipeda**, the old port city (ETT table 1850) with its aquarium and dolphinarium and the Maritime Museum in the old fort (closed Mon).

RIGA, LATVIA

Of the Baltic Republics, Latvia has the strongest remaining links with Russia and over 30% of its inhabitants are Russians. You'll hear Russian being spoken on the streets of Riga. Nevertheless, the country and its capital have asserted their independence from Russia and Riga has witnessed an upsurge in tourism. Celebration of the city's 800th anniversary in 2001 led to an upsurge in national pride and the further revitalisation of the city. Riga has three cities – a 17th century Hanseatic town preserved as the historic core, a large monumentally Parisian-feeling quarter of boulevards, parks and art nouveau architecture and the odd Stalinist building beyond the fortifications, and a modern, more industrial and ugly part of the city on the other side of the river. There is no need to stray from the northern shore unless you want to cross the bridge to look at the old town's church spires from a distance. You can walk the old town but you might need public transport for the Parisian-feeling area.

The nightlife is active with many bars and nightclubs. In the summer, there are numerous live bands playing in the centre of town with packed outdoor cafés selling local beers.

Old town Riga is a mass of winding streets, attractive old buildings and a great number of worthwhile churches. Don't miss the **cathedral** and the other large churches of the old town, the **Central Market** or **Riga Castle**.

Adjacent to the rail and bus stations is the eye-opening **Central Market** on Negu Iela. Housed in three huge former Zeppelin hangars, it's a mixture of meat, varieties of bread, dairy products, vegetables and anything else edible. The approaches often consist of lines of women selling things like used shoes to make a bit of money.

Cross the road by the subway and proceed up Aspazijas Bulv. On the right is the newly restored National Opera, and the old moat, set in a linear park on the site of the old fortifications. The wide expanse of the **Brivibas** on the right, leads to the **Freedom Monument**. A guard is mounted (and changed) every hour by the new Latvian Army. Turn left down Torna Lela. The **Pulvertonis** (Powder tower) on the left is now part of the **Latvian War Museum**. The road continues past the surviving (but

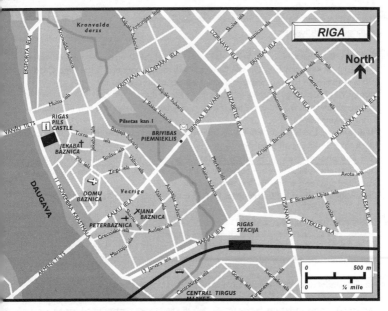

much restored) section of the old town wall, dating from the 13th century. It ends with the picturesque **Swedish Gate**, built in 1698.

Riga Castle dates from 1330 and contains the official residence of the President of Latvia and **museums of Latvian history, foreign art** and **Latvian culture**. On the cobbled cathedral square, the **cathedral** is the largest place of worship in the Baltics, and is famous for its organ. In M. Pils Iela, **Three Brothers** are the most famous of Riga's old houses, dating from the 15th century. For an excellent view of the city, ascend the tower of the **Church of St Peter**, Skarnu 19 (closed Mon). On **Rifleman Square** (named after the Latvian Red Rifleman who played a heroic part in the first World War and later aided the Bolsheviks) is the medieval **House of the Blackheads**, a lay order of bachelor merchants, now the central tourist centre. The **Occupation Museum** (free) displays the sufferings of the Latvian people under the Nazi and Soviet regimes, and tells of the recent struggle to regain independence.

immediate departure tickets from windows 3–9. **International booking office**: walk through the subway, then left across car park; purchases in cash until 2000 (information ☎ 583 2134 and 583 3095). Left luggage in the station basement, plus lockers off the subway (0400–0100). **Tourist bureau** arranges cheap international travel. **Parex Bank** (Smilpu 3) cashes travellers' cheques 0830–2130. There is a 24-hr supermarket opposite the station.

🚌 **Bus station**: Near the rail station, adjacent to the Central Market, ☎900 0009. Currency exchange and left luggage.

ℹ️ **Tourist Office**: Ratslaukums 6, ☎704 4377 (tourinfo@riga800.lv); buy *Riga in Your Pocket* (quarterly) or *Riga This Week*. On sale here (and in hotels, airport etc) is the **Riga Card**, including admission to major sights and unlimited city transport journeys.
Money: Visa/MasterCard machine at post office next to the station. Cash machines/ATMs are increasingly plentiful around town, but travellers cheques are changeable only in banks (i.e. during banking hours).
Medical care: Latvia is a little behind in international health care, but try ARS Clinic at Skolas 5, which has a 24-hr English telephone service, ☎720 1001.
Post and phones: **Main post office**: Brivibas 19, open 24 hrs. It has a number of phone cabins (pay after call). There are numerous digital phone boxes and cards are available at any post office and most shops. The **telephone code** is (371).
Cybercafés: The best is **Elektroniska Kafehnica** at Elizabetes 83/85, ☎724 2826.

🚌 **Public transport**: Buses, trams and trolleybuses operate 0530–0030, with some all-night services. Buy separate tickets for each mode of transport from conductor/kiosk. **Taxibuses** charge 15–25 Santîmi. Avoid **taxis**, except for long distances, and stick to the orange and black vehicles (insist the meter is turned on).

🛏️ **Placis**, Laimdotas lela 2A, ☎/fax 755 1271, offers self-catering dormitories (🚌no. 1 or trolleybus no. 4 to Teika). On the edge of Old Riga is **Bastejs**, Basteja Bulvaris 10, ☎755 1271. **Patricia Accommodation**, Elizabetes 22, ☎728 4868 (www.rigalatvia.net) has a tourist office, its own hostel on the site, and booking for home stays all over the Baltics, as well as offering excellent backup service if you run into trouble.

🍽️ As Riga has grown in popularity, the streets of the Old Town have seen a rapid increase in the number and variety of bars and restaurants. There are eating places to suit all pockets from Russian fast food joints (seving *pelmeni*, a Russian-style ravioli) to local specialities and branches of familiar Western chains. The **buffet bars** in the Riga meat market offer bargain price and filling fare. The local speciality is *Rigas Balzam*, a mix of cognac, ginger and oak bark, drunk with vodka or coffee; a shop opposite the station sells a wide variety. Try also the local bread, known as *Rupjmaize*, sometimes used with cream to make tomato soup.

Side Trips from Riga   **Jurmala** is a 30-km-long string of seaside resorts, west of Riga, a popular holiday destination since the 19th century. It's a continuous length of beach, sand dunes, and fragrant pines between the Baltic and the Lielupe river. The best place to visit is **Majovi** and its vicinity. The **Tourist Office** at Jomas 42, ☎776 4276 (jurmalainfo@mail.bkc.lv), has English-speaking staff, and will organise accommodation. **Frequent trains** from Riga, taking less than 1 hr. **Kuldiga** is probably the most perfectly preserved Latvian town; four to six buses a day, taking 4 hrs.

A visit to the Livonian Switzerland is an excellent day out. Head straight for the ruins of **Sigulda Castle**, dating from 1207, and including an auditorium for cultural events. The **New Castle** is a 19th-century structure, and contains a moderately priced restaurant. Continue to the cable-car station and cross the beautiful **Gauga National Park** – 40 km from one side of the valley to the other. Bungee jumpers launch themselves from here at weekends.

From the far side of the valley, find the path to the right to the ruins of **Kimulda Castle**, where it veers left; then look for the path on the right, signposted for **Gutman's Cave**, dropping steeply via steps to the valley floor, where the path veers to the left (with the river on the right) to reach the celebrated cave. Gutman was a Latvian Robin Hood and his sandstone cave has graffiti dating back to the 17th century. Where the path ends at a roadside picnic area, carry on along the road, looking for a path on the right that ascends steeply up the opposite side of the valley and to **Tuvaida Castle**, one of the most attractive in Latvia; there's a great view from the tower. Here you can hire horses, take a carriage ride or use the bobsleigh track at Sveices 13, ☎297 2008; in summer, try a wheeled sledge.

Tourist offices: **Sigulda Tourist Information Centre**, Pils 4A, ☎297 1335 (sigulda@rrp.lv). **Gauga National Park Information Centre**, Raina 15, ☎297 1345.

TARTU, ESTONIA

Tartu is Estonia's University town, built into a wooded hill, with picturesque views. The concrete river bridge replaces the original stone bridge of 1784 which symbolised Tartu. There is a fund to reconstruct it, hence the donation boxes all over the town. The **Tartu Citizens' Museum**, Jaani 16, is a reconstructed 1830s home (closed Mon and Tues). **St John's Church** is being reconstructed bit by bit, including its remarkable terracotta. The **University** was founded by the King Gustav Adolphus of Sweden in 1632 (statue behind) but the classical university building dates from 1809. The **Town Hall Square** is probably the most photographed spot in Tartu. At one end is the bridge and at the other, the fine neo-classical **Town Hall**, built in 1778–84. Notice the leaning house (No.18) – one wall is built on the foundation of the town wall, the other isn't. Take time out to explore **Toomemägi**. You can cross the 'sighing bridge' to ascend 'kissing hill'. Look out for the sacrificial stone upon which Tartu students burn their notes at the end of final exams. The excellent **Estonian Folk Museum**, Kuperjanovi 9, has Estonian customs, traditions and costumes (closed Mon and Tues; free Fri).

Vaksali. Left luggage, international booking office. The simplest way into the town centre is right along Vaksali, and left along Riia.

Bus station: Junction of Riia and Turu.

Tourist Office: Raekoja Plats 12, ☎43 21 41 (www.tartu.ee/english; info@tartu.tourism.ee).

Kooli, at Pülli 11, ☎7 400 252, fax 7 400 275, is very cheap, or you can go for the more expensive **Tartu**, Soola 3, ☎7 43 30 41 (tarhotel@server.ee).

AROUND TALLINN

Kadriorg Palace of 1718 (tram to the **Kadriorg** terminus) was created for Peter the Great and is in itself well worth a visit. It also houses the **Museum of Foreign Art** (closed Mon). The nearby **Peter the Great House Museum** at Mäekalda 2 is open in summer.

In the district of **Pirita** (buses; or, better, walk from **Kadriorg**), where there's a beach and a yacht marina. The graceful **Rusalka** (mermaid) monument stands by the sea, commemorating the loss of a Tsarist warship in a storm. Walk along Pirita Tee, to the great concrete complex built by the Soviets as a monument to all those who fought for Soviet power. You can continue past **Marjamäe Palace**, home to the modern section of the **Estonian History Museum**, from 1918 to the present day (closed Mon and Tues). The oldest attraction in Pirita is the **Convent of St Bridget**, an impressive and most romantic ruin. You can also visit the British-built submarine *Lembit* (1936) in the harbour (closed Mon and Fri).

Rocca-al-Mare, the open-air **Ethnographical Museum**, is beside the sea at Vabaohumuseumi 12, ☎ 654 91 00 (www.evm.ee). There's a host of reconstructed buildings from all over Estonia, plus folk performances at weekends in summer (🚌 no. 21 from the rail station).

TALLINN

Over the past few years, Tallinn has become something of a tourist mecca both for Finns on booze-cruises and western Europeans exploring further afield. Said by some to be the Prague of the Baltic States, the old parts of the town are compact, manageable and a delight to explore on foot both in the day and at night. Nightlife in Tallinn goes on into the small hours particularly on the long summer nights (the summer season is very short so the locals and visitors need to take advantage of it whilst it is there). Live music is common and there is a vibrant atmosphere on the streets.

The increase in tourist traffic has led to a sharp rise in the number of shops with good quality local goods (linen, leather, suede and woollen products) and a wide variety of craft stalls and stores selling local specialities. The old part of Tallinn is thick with attractive cobbled streets, picturesque painted houses, medieval churches and fortifications. Against a stretch of the medieval wall surrounding the old city which can be entered through a number of gates, there is a **craft market**, specialising in traditionally patterned fishermen's knitwear and multi-bobbled hats. Katariina Käik is a medieval alley tenanted by craftswomen and is lined with ancient gravestones. **Tallinn Town Museum**, Vene 17, has a section on modern history (English tour available; closed Tues). From here it's a short walk through the **Vana Turg** (Old Market) into the **Raekoja Plats** (Town Hall Square), with its outdoor cafés on the cobbles, and watched over by the Gothic town hall of 1404 (sporting **Vana Toomas**, or Old Thomas, the city guardian, on its tower – which can be climbed).

St Nicholas Church houses medieval art, including a striking 15th-century *Dance of Death*, while the **Orthodox Cathedral of Alexander Nevsky** of 1900 is worth a look if you've never seen the interior of a Russian church. Behind the church is a stretch of wall with the **Virgins Tower** and museum of fortification. Across Lossi Plats is **Toompea Castle**, the seat of government: it's not open, but you can walk

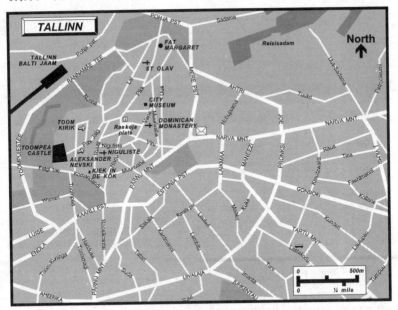

round its 18th-century façade (hiding the medieval structure) and see **Tall Herman**, the tower from which the Estonian flag now flies.

From here Toom Kooli leads to the cathedral, Tallinn's oldest church, founded by the Danes and much rebuilt. It contains fine gravestones and crests of Swedish and German noblemen, plus a memorial to one of many Scottish Jacobite naval officers who left Britain and joined the Russian service (closed Mon). Nearby **Tompea Hill** has two good viewpoints, one over the old town and the other looking towards the harbour.

Returning to the **Orthodox Cathedral**, Pikk Valg (long leg) drops between the walls of **Toompea** and **Tallinn** proper (the two communities didn't get on). The charming gate leads to Pikk. On the corner is the **Church of the Holy Ghost**, with a beautiful altarpiece (1483), while at Pikk 17 is the **Estonian History Museum**, housed in the **Great Guild Hall** (1407–1410) and with captions in English (closed Wed). Pikk terminates at the **Coastal Gate** by the **Three Sisters**, a perfectly preserved range of medieval houses. Alongside the gate is the **Fat Margaret tower**, which contains the excellent **Estonian Maritime Museum** (closed Mon and Tues).

The most old-fashioned and backward of all means of transport in Estonia, as reflected in the run-down station. Booking hall at east end for local trains; main building for long distance travel

within **Estonia**; upstairs for international/advance tickets and customs declaration forms for
Russian trains. Left luggage, currency exchange, Visa cashpoint.
Bus station: Lastekodu 46, ☎601 03 86, some distance from centre (take a tram). Obtain
tickets before travel; destination board is arranged in direction of travel, not alphabetically, with
international buses listed last. For Estonia use **Ekspress** buses. Eurolines have a separate office.

🚢 Enquiries: ☎631 85 50; main terminal has full facilities, plus summer tourist information desk.

ℹ️ **Tourist Office**: Raekoja Plats 10, ☎645 77 77 (turismiinfo@tallinnlv.ee), one of the best in the
Baltic States. On sale here (also at harbour, station and airport, plus some hotels and ferries) is
the **Tallinn Card**: includes admission to major sights,
unlimited city transport journeys, a boat trip in **Pirita
Harbour**, a city tour and discounts in some restaurants.
Medical care: Recognising international insurance policies is
Medicover, Gonsiori 33, ☎605 15 00.
Money: Plenty of cash machines and exchange bureaux.
Post and phones: The main post office is at Narnu Mantee 1,
☎641 13 33, closed Sun; telephone office 0800–1900, Sat
0900–1600, closed Sun. Long-distance/international calls ordered
at the counter are 30% cheaper than from the public phone. To
call abroad from a phone box, dial 8, wait for the dial tone,
then dial 00. All public phones now take cards, which are
widely available. The area code is 372 (for 7-figure numbers
beginning with 6) and 372-2 (for the few remaining 6-digit numbers).
Cybercafé: The best is easily **Enter**, located at Gonsior 4, or try the **Internet Café @5** in
Tallinn Department Store next door at Gonsiori 2.

TICKETS
Buy tickets from a kiosk or
from the driver with the
right change (not coins and
remember tickets are more
expensive bought this way).
Cancel tickets on board.
White minibuses can be
flagged down at stops.

🚍 **Public transport:** Trams connect harbour, rail and bus stations with Vivu Valjak (Vivu Square);
also buses and trolleybuses.

🏨 **Eeslitau:** Dunku 4, ☎631 37 55. Centrally located in the old town; popular, so book early.
Hostels: **Vana Tom**, Väike Karja 1, ☎631 32 52; **Merevaik**, Sopruse 182, ☎655 37 67, bare
and simple and cheap. **Bussiterminal**, Öömaja, ☎655 26 79, above the bus station and
extremely simple (trolleybus from rail station). **Rasastra**, Mere 4, ☎641 22 91.

🍴 A plethora of bars, liquor shops, night clubs, coffee shops and restaurants have opened in the
wake of the tourist invasion. There are prices to suit all budgets and many branches of familiar
American fast food outlets as well as countless pizzerias which offer filling fare.

SIDE TRIPS FROM TALLINN **Pärnu** (ETT table 1805; 3 hrs 45 mins; take bus from
station to town centre) is a pleasant and historic resort
town (a good break if you're making the journey from **Riga** to **Tallinn** by bus).
Tourist Office: ☎447 30 00 (info@parnu.tourism.ee). Within the old town you can
explore a stretch of the old fortifications overlooking the former moat. The pre-1914
wooden bandstand and mud baths are features of the sea front; a short walk along
Ranna Puisti reveals two pre-war architectural treasures – the **Rannahoon Beach**

Pavilion and the **Rannahotel**, both art deco gems. Supeluse (bathing street) commences at the mud bath, and runs through the attractive parkland back to town. From **Pärnu** excursions include by local bus to the narrow-gauge railway museum at **Lavasaare** (steam days from time to time). **Narvu-Joesu** is a (decayed) resort, with a great deal of tourist potential. Frequent buses and trains from **Tallinn**.

Haapsalu is Estonia's second seaside resort (**Tourist Office** at Posti 37, ☎473 32 48, info@haapsalu.tourism.ee). Look for the remains of the **Bishops Castle and Church**. The old resort area and spa building have been restored, although the modern beach is to the west of the town. The old station (specially built to receive the Tsar) is now the home of the **National Railway Museum**, complete with historic locomotives and rolling stock. Estonians regard the islands of **Kuressaare** and **Saarema** (the Western Islands) as the most unspoilt part of their country – the true heartland of the people. Kuressaare is the capital of Saavema, the largest island (**Tourist Office** at Tallinna 2, ☎453 31 20, info@oesel.tourism.ee). To see the island fully, stay overnight, but book the accommodation ahead from **Tallinn**. The castle at Kuressaare is the best preserved in Estonia, and the rest of the island boasts historic churches, windmills and a meteorite crater. Frequent buses from **Tallinn** (which go on the ferries) take about 4 hrs.

ST PETERSBURG

See p. 501. Visa required.

MOSCOW

If you want to venture further into Russia from St Petersburg (and already have your visa sorted out) Moscow is the obvious next stop. The noisy, bustling, thrusting hub of Russia, it is still emerging from the shadow of its Communist past, but hums with the energy of change. Many of the older buildings have been restored to their former pastel shades of yellow, blue and pink. However, most striking for visitors are the large buildings of all styles which dominate the Moscow skyline, from the many glittering onion-shaped cathedral domes within the Kremlin to the overpowering Stalinist-Gothic towers. There are a host of unmissable attractions including the whole **Kremlin** complex of museums and churches, the **Red Square** and **St Basil's Cathedral**, the restored **GUM department store**, the **Bolshoi Theatre**, several excellent **art galleries**, the often beautiful **metro stations** and the numerous second-hand **street markets**. There are countless other grand old buildings plus the infamous headquarters of the KGB, the **Lubyanka**. Whilst central Moscow is relatively safe to walk around (not the case further out), you should be extra careful with valuables. It is not a cheap city. Accommodation can be very pricey and restaurants range from reasonable to extortionate.

With sandy beaches, ancient lakes, dense forests and (for Directory information, see p. 606). alpine mountains, Poland is a surprisingly varied country. Don't miss the rich architecture and culture in the many historic towns, castles, shrines and palaces that have managed to survive centuries of strife, but also make time for its sober monuments to the devastation of the last war. There is much that is unique here: the Wieliczka salt cathedral, the Jaskinia Niedźwiedzia caves and Malbork's vast Teutonic fortress.

Although many older folk and 90% of station staff don't speak English, Poles are friendly, good-natured people who are only too happy to help travellers.

Youth Hostels

The hostelling organisation is **Polskie Towarzystwo Schronisk Młodzieżowych (PTSM)**, 00–791 WARSZAWA, UL. CHOCIMSKA 28, POLAND, ☎ (48) (22) 8498128 (hostellingpol.ptsm@pvo. onet.pl).

ACCOMMODATION

Orbis runs a chain of pricey international and tourist hotels across the country, and some less expensive motels. Otherwise there's a choice between cheaper hotels, pensions, private rooms, university halls of residence (during summer vacations) and youth hostels (which tend to have lockouts and curfews). Most tourist information centres will arrange accommodation for you. There are good deals for hotels on the net – eg www.hotelsinpoland.com. Beware higher prices during trade fairs and look out for weekend reductions.

FOOD AND DRINK

Simple meals and snacks can easily be obtained at cafés and fast-food outlets, while *zajazdy*, reasonably priced roadside inns and cafés, serve typical Polish food and pastries. Opening hours and dishes are varied enough to suit all tastes in the major cities. Classic national dishes include beetroot soup, herrings in soured cream, potato pancakes, stuffed cabbage leaves, *bigos* (cabbage and sausage stew), *pierogi* (large-scale ravioli), baked cheesecake and doughnuts. A wide variety of Polish mineral waters are drunk in preference to tap water, though the latter is safe now in major cities. The vast range of clear and flavoured vodka is excellent and inexpensive.

EDITOR'S CHOICE Auschwitz–Birkenau; Kraków; Poznań; Toruń; Wieliczka Salt Mines; Zakopane (for Tatra Mountains).

BEYOND THE BORDERS Warsaw–Vilnius (ETT table 93); Poznań–Berlin (table 56); Warsaw–Prague (table 95); Warsaw–Vienna (table 95); Kraków–Budapest via Slovakia (table 95).

POLAND: WARSAW (WARSZAWA)

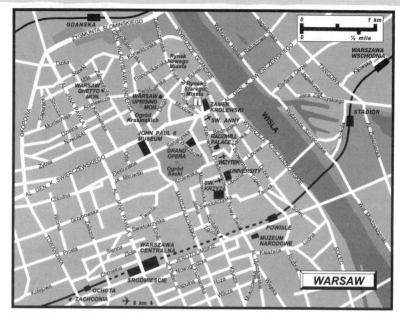

While **Warsaw** has its fair share of post-war concrete blocks, there are also areas of beauty and historic significance, including its parks, palaces and old town that were meticulously rebuilt after complete devastation in the Second World War. Having suffered under communism, Warsaw is now thriving under democracy: entertainment, restaurants and shopping are coming into their own, and fast approaching the standards of major Western cities.

If you're in a hurry, the places to head for are the **Royal Castle, Łazienki Palace and Park,** the **Old Town Square** and **Warsaw Historical Museum.** The **River Vistula** divides Warsaw, with most sights on the west bank. Most attractions are walkable.

ARRIVAL AND DEPARTURE

 Warszawa Centralna is the central rail station at AL. JEROZOLIMSKIE 54 (www.pkp.com.pl); a crime hotspot, so avoid at night. Some 30 mins' walk to the old town (with Hotel Marriott in front of you, turn left along AL. JEROZOLIMSKIE, then walk or take any tram two stops to the bottom of NOWY ŚWIAT, for numerous buses to the old town). Left luggage (counter 0700–2100, lockers 24 hrs); tourist information (0800–1800), rail information (24 hrs), post office, bus

TOURIST OFFICES

☎ (022) 656 6584 (www.msiwarszawa.com; mit@mufa.pl). Offices with English-speaking staff which will help with accommodation (all open daily, until 1800): **Okecie Airport** (open until 2000 at weekends); **Warszawa Centralna** (central rail station), main hall upstairs; **Pl. Zamkowy 1/13** (Castle Square); **Pl. Defilad 1**. (MSI), inside the Palace of Culture; **Rynek Starego Miasta 28** (in the Historical Museum of the City of Warsaw in the Old Town Square).

information, currency exchange (24 hrs) and ticket office (0600–2000). Other large stations in the city are: **Warszawa Wschodnia** on the east bank of the Wisla (Vistula) River, and the western suburban station, **Warszawa Zachodnia**, 3 km west of **Centralna**, opposite the PKS bus station.

✈ **Okecie Airport**, UL. ŻWIRKI I WIGURY 1, ☎ (022) 846 1731 (international flights), ☎ (022) 650 4100 (national flights), lies 10 km south of the city, with two terminals (arrivals and departures). **Airport City Bus** no. 175 (611 at night) every 20 mins (30 mins on Sat and holidays), stopping at major hotels and **Warszawa Centralna** rail station.

INFORMATION

The monthly *Warsaw Insider* magazine, (4zł) is an expat publication full of useful tips. *Warsaw in Your Pocket* is another useful guide, available on the net at www.inyourpocketcom/poland/warsaw. Monthly magazines available in the pricier hotels, like *Welcome to Warsaw* and *Warszawa: What, Where, When* are less useful as they are aimed at business tourists, but have handy maps. *The Warsaw Voice*, an English-language newspaper, has useful features and local news items.

MONEY Cashpoint machines and credit-card facilities are widespread in all tourist areas. Some **bureaux de change** *(kantor)* will not cash traveller's cheques (try **Orbis Travel**, large hotels or the larger banks instead).

POST AND PHONES The **Main Post Office**, UL. ŚWIĘTOKRZYSKA, 31/33, is open 24 hrs. **Phone cards** are needed to operate most public telephones – the cards are available from kiosks and other outlets. Cost ranges from 7.32zł (25 units) to 24.28zł (100 units). A one-minute call abroad will consume about 50 units. **To phone Warsaw:** ☎ 00 48 (Poland) + 22; **to phone Warsaw from elsewhere in Poland:** ☎ 022.

PUBLIC TRANSPORT

Trams and buses operate on a grid system. Buses, which are generally crowded, run from 0430–2300 on weekdays. Night buses operate every 30 mins and cost three times the normal fare. The useful PPWK-published Warsaw map (about 5zł) shows bus routes. The limited underground service (Metro) runs from the south to the centre of the city (red 'M' on yellow background denotes a Metro station); trains run every six minutes, 0430–2330. You can pick up taxis easily, but the reliable ones have a number on the roof. Alternatively ring for one – eg ☎ 919, 9628 or 9622.

ACCOMMODATION

Hotels: Check www.hotelsinpoland.com for reduced rates which can make even the normally pricey hotels affordable, especially at weekends. Some good moderate options are: **Harenda,** UL. KRAKOWSKIE PRZEDMIEŚCIE 4/6, ☎(022) 826 0071, €–€€: good central location with a 'ranch' underneath that's a favourite with drinkers; **Maria,** AL. JANA PAWŁA II, ☎(022) 838 4062 (hotmaria@optimus.waw.pl), €€: central, small, very comfortable, family-run; **Praski,** AL. SOLIDARNOŚCI 61, ☎(022) 818 4989, €–€€: over the river in the Praga district, but only one tram stop from underneath the Royal Castle and located next to an excellent Lebanese restaurant; **Saski,** PLAC BANKOWY 1, ☎(022) 620 4611, fax (022) 620 1115, €–€€: central; **Wileński,** UL. KŁOPOTOWSKIEGO 36, ☎(022) 818 5317, €: clean, cheap, friendly, and 5 mins' walk from the Praski in the Praga district.

Budget options: For a selection of **private rooms** (about 50–70zł. per night) contact the Syrena office at UL. KRUCZNA 17 (Mon–Sat 0900-1900, Sun 0900–1700, ☎(022) 628 7540, www.syrena.hotel.pl), next to the Lokomotyva pub not far from the Central Station. **Student halls** are available during summer vacations (late June–mid-Sept) and can be booked through Almatur Student Travel at UL. KOPERNIKA 23, ☎/fax (022) 826 4592. They are the same cost as youth hostels without the hassle of lock-outs and curfews. The main **hostels** are at UL. SMOLNA 30, ☎(022) 827 8952 (central) and UL. KAROLKOWA 53A, ☎(022) 632 8829 (tram nos. 1/13/20/24 to AL SOLIDARNOŚCI). **Campsites:** the site at UL. ZWIRKI I WIGURY 32, ☎(022) 825 4391, offers cheap bungalows as an alternative to renting tentspace. The campsite at UL. BITWY WARSZAWSKIEJ 1920R, ☎(022) 823 3748, has the same alternative but is pricier.

PUBLIC TRANSPORT IN POLAND Always buy an extra ticket for large luggage items such as rucksacks or suitcases (over 60 x 40 x 20 cm). Tickets are sold at RUCH kiosks or any corner shop with Bilety MZK on it (or from the driver at slightly higher cost, but don't expect change); punch tickets once on board and when changing vehicles.

FOOD AND DRINK

Privatisation has revolutionised eating out, with **restaurants** spanning Asian, European and South American food. Traditional Polish food has been joined by 'new wave' Polish, featuring lighter versions of classic dishes. 'New wave' pioneers include the **Malinowa** and **Restauracja Polska**. Snacks and fast food can easily be found, with plenty of alfresco cafés, particularly in the Old Town.

HIGHLIGHTS

RYNEK STAREGO MIASTA (OLD TOWN MARKET SQUARE) AND AREA Very much a focal point, this square is lined with painstaking reconstructions of the original burghers' houses. At no. 28 is the **Muzeum Historyczne Warszawy** (Warsaw Historical Museum, Tues–Sun; Sun free) which chronicles the city's turbulent history. A short film, *Warsaw After All*, includes footage shot by the Nazis, documenting their systematic destruction of the city (screenings in English at 1200).

Continue along ŚWIĘTOJAŃSKA to PL. ZAMKOWY, dominated by **Zamek Królewski** (Royal Castle; closed Mon). Restored after the war, the castle's mixed architecture and stylised interiors are a showcase for furniture, tapestries, paintings and more. Tickets (12zł; free Sun) are sold from the souvenir shop opposite the castle on the corner of ŚWIĘTOJAŃSKA.

NORTHWARDS AROUND THE BARBAKAN AND KRAŚINSKI PARK

The 16th-century **Barbakan** (Barbican) was once part of the city walls, but is now a haunt of artists out to make a quick złoty or two. From here UL. FRETA which at no. 16 has a museum dedicated to Maria Skłodowska (the woman who discovered radioactivity) leads to 18th-century RYNEK NOWEGO MIASTA (New Market Square), less flamboyant than its Old Town counterpart, with the **Church of the Blessed Sacrament**, founded in 1688 by Queen Maria in memory of her husband (King Jan III Sobieski), who defeated the Turks at Vienna. From RYNEK NOWEGO MIASTA, UL. DŁUGA leads to PL. KRASIŃSKICH, site of a monument and museum to the 63-day-long Warsaw Uprising, and **Kraśinski Palace** (now a library), fronting the **Kraśinski Park**.

MUSEUMS

Pride of place amongst the many museums (closed Mon unless mentioned) goes to **Muzeum Narodowe** (National Museum), AL. JEROZOLIMSKIE 3 (Sat free), which has an impressive collection of paintings, successfully hidden during the war. The **Ethnographic Museum**, UL. KREDYTOWA 1 (Wed free), has a collection of Polish folk art and world-wide tribal art. The **Pope John Paul II Museum**, PL. BANKOWY 1 (free), has a huge collection of art including works by Titian, Breughel, Rembrandt and Rodin. The **Frederic Chopin Museum**, UL. OKÓLNIK 1 (1000–1400; closed Tues) has an interesting but smallish collection of the great Polish composer's memorabilia. Every five years Warsaw hosts the prestigious Chopin Piano Competition, which next takes place in 2005.

THE ROYAL ROUTE

The city's main thoroughfare is the **Royal Route**, which starts at KRAKOWSKIE PRZEDMIEŚCIE by the **Stare Miasto** (Old Town) and heads south, along NOWY ŚWIAT and AL. UJAZDOWSKIE, 10 km to Wilanów, the royal summer palace, taking in 15th-century **Kościół Sw. Anny** (St Anne's Church), the **Adam Mickiewicz Monument** and finally **Radziwiłł Palace**, where the Warsaw Pact was signed in May 1955. Just off KRAKOWSKIE PRZEDMIEŚCIE, in the **Ogród Saski** (Saxon Gardens), the Tomb of the Unknown Soldier is guarded around the clock. Dominating PL. PIŁSUDSKIEGO is the neoclassical **National Theatre** (1825–33). Returning to KRAKOWSKIE PRZEDMIEŚCIE, Chopin played the organ in the **Kościół Wizytek** (Church of the Visitation), while **Kościół Sw. Krzyża**, is a masterpiece of baroque, and also the resting place of Chopin's heart (in an urn on the left column by the nave).

POLAND

PALACES Surrounded by water, the late-18th-century **Łazienki Palace** (Palace-on-the-Isle), UL. AGRYKOLA 1, ☎ (022) 625 7944, was the classical summer residence of Stanislaus Augustus Poniatowski, Poland's last king. Its park contains the **Chopin monument**, plus smaller palaces, pavilions, a moated amphitheatre, an Egyptian temple, an orangery and the Biały Dom (White House), with its Chinoiserie interiors.

Some 10 km from the centre of town stands the extravagantly baroque **Wilanów Palace**, UL. WIERTNICZA 1 (closed Tues; free Thur), the former residence of King Jan III Sobieski; the grounds include a baroque chapel, an orangery and a museum of modern poster art; park open daily until dusk; 🚌 nos.130/116/522.

JEWISH WARSAW Before World War II, Warsaw had one of Europe's largest Jewish communities. During the Nazi occupation, the population fell from 380,000 to just 300. There are two great monuments: to the **Heroes of the Warsaw Ghetto**, UL. ZAMENHOFA, and the white marble monument to Concentration Camp Victims, at the point where hundreds of thousands of Jews were herded onto trains bound for the concentration camps. The 'Our Roots' agency at UL. TWARDA 6 next to the restored Nożyk Synagogue organises tours of Jewish Warsaw, ☎ (022) 620 0556. Boat trips leave from **Poniatowski Bridge** for a leisurely view of Warsaw.

TOURS

For a more leisurely view of Warsaw, tour the city by boat on the River Vistula: the **WARS** ship sails daily from the passenger marina near **Poniatowksi Bridge** on WYBRZEŻE KOŚCIUSZKOVSKIE.

SHOPPING

Local specialities include silver, leather, crystal and amber, with **Cepelia** stores having the best selection of folk art. **Desa** is a chain of antique shops (there are restrictions on what can be exported). Some of the best shopping is in the Old Town, KRAKOWSKIE PRZEDMIEŚCIE (for books), UL. NOWY ŚWIAT and UL. CHMIELNA. Try **Wola antique market**, KOŁO BAZAR, UL. OBOZOWA, for clothes, furniture and books (Sat–Sun 0800–1300; 🚌 no. 159 or tram nos. 13/20/24). Warsaw has many shops open non-stop or at least every day until well into the evening (e.g. the **Empik** chain of general stores). For late or weekend shopping try **Marszalkowska** opposite the Palace of Culture.

NIGHT-TIME AND EVENTS

There is a good range of entertainment, with pubs and discos, and live music, including rock, jazz, and classical music. Chopin concerts are held every Sun at 1200 and 1600 in Jul–Aug by Chopin's monument in **Łazienki Park**. Cinemas often show foreign films, usually subtitled. The imposing **Pałac Kultury i Nauki** (Palace of Culture and Science) houses **shops, museums, theatres** and a **multiplex cinema**.

Worth visiting also for the panoramic rooftop view, reached in 20 seconds by express lift.

There are opera and ballet at the **National Theatre** (Teatr Narodowy), PL. TEATRALNY 1, while the **National Philharmonic** (Filharmonia Narodowa) is at UL. JASNA 5. Many of the performances at **Buffo Theatre**, UL. KONOPNICKIEJ 6, ☎ (022) 625 4709, have gained cult status with young Poles.

NARROW-GAUGE RAILWAYS IN POLAND

Poland has 10 historic narrow-gauge lines with steam locos, running along 12 to 55 km of track (linked to the national rail network). The railways date from the mid-19th century, though nowadays they mostly operate as tourist attractions or even as party locations. The longest is at Gryfice near the coast towards the German border, with a rail museum en route; other lines visit a reconstructed prehistoric Slav settlement, the Bieszczady Mountains and the historic former capital, Gniezno. See www.cleeve.com/poland/ for comprehensive information and illustrations.

WHERE NEXT FROM WARSAW?

Warsaw is on the **Poznań–Zakopane** route (p. 524); if you just want to see one Polish city take this to **Kraków**. Alternatively head north-east to **Vilnius** to join the **Vilnius–St Petersburg** route (p. 505).

ROUTE DETAIL

Poznań–Toruń   ETT table 1020

Type	Frequency	Typical journey time
Train	2 daily	2 hrs 15 mins

Toruń–Warsaw   ETT table 1020

Type	Frequency	Typical journey time
Train	4 daily	3 hrs

Warsaw–Kraków   ETT table 1065

Type	Frequency	Typical journey time
Train	Every 1-2 hrs	2 hrs 50 mins

Kraków–Zakopane   ETT table 1066

Type	Frequency	Typical journey time
Train	14 daily	3–4 hrs

KEY JOURNEYS

Berlin–Poznań   ETT table 1001

Type	Frequency	Typical journey time
Train	3 daily	3 hrs 15 mins

Poznań–Kraków
(via Wkrocław)   ETT table 1075

Type	Frequency	Typical journey time
Train	4 daily	5 hrs 45 mins– 6 hrs 30 mins

This succinct exploration of the best of Poland encounters its two finest cities – **Kraków** and **Toruń** – as well as the Polish capital, and ends up at the foot of the majestic **Tatra** mountains. The earlier parts of the journey are low-lying and unspectacular, but the cultural highlights more than compensate. **Poznań** can easily be reached by train from **Berlin**, and from **Kraków** you can venture out to **Auschwitz** – a grim reminder of the atrocities of the Third Reich – or see the extraordinary **Royal Wieliczka Salt Mine**; it's also feasible to extend the journey into **Slovakia**.

POZNAŃ

The provincial capital of **Wielkopolska** became one of the two main centres of Poland as well as the seat of its first bishop in the 10th century. A long-held status as a great trade centre (it's still an important place for trade fairs) has contributed to the architectural heritage of its old town.

The city's focal point is STARY RYNEK, a spacious square with gabled burghers' houses and a grand 16th-century Renaissance **Town Hall**, where at midday two mechanical goats emerge from above the clock to lock horns. Inside lie the **Chamber of the Renaissance** with its beautifully painted, coffered ceiling (1555) and the **Historical Museum of the City of Poznań**. Also on STARY RYNEK, at no. 45, is the **Muzeum Instrumentów Muzycznych** (Museum of Musical Instruments), housing some 2000 instruments, and with a room dedicated to Chopin. In the partly reconstructed **Royal Castle** on Przemysław Hill is the **Museum of Applied Arts**, with a wide-ranging collection through the ages, and a cellar full of poster art.

> Almost all museums are closed Mon and most are free on Fri.

Several churches form an outer ring around the market square. One of the finest can be found on GOŁĘBIA, south of the square, the baroque **Poznań Parish Church** (Kosciół Farny) dedicated to St Mary Magdalene. The **Jesuit College** next door, once Napoleon's residence, now hosts Chopin concerts. A short walk to the east is **Ostrów Tumski**, the original part of the city, an island in the middle of the River **Warta**; here stands the **cathedral**, heavily restored after World War II.

Poznań has two zoos and a vast palm house (part of Poland's largest botanical garden). On the edge of the city is the 100 square km **Wielkopolski Park Narodowy** (a national park), easily accessible by train.

Poznań Główny, 24-hr rail information office, tourist information, cash machines, currency exchange, left luggage and shops; 10-min walk to centre or take tram 5 to the centre from the western exit beyond platform 5. Buy tickets from the MKP kiosk at the western exit. Most international trains stop here, although some use **Starołęka Station**, 5 km south-east.

Tourist Offices: The most central is at STARY RYNEK 59, ☎ (061) 852 6156, fax (061) 852 6964.

Glob-Tour office at the station, ☎/fax (061) 866 0667 (24 hrs). **City information centre**, ARKADIA SHOPPING CENTRE, UL. RATAJCZAKA 44, ☎(061) 851 9645 (www.cim.poznan.pl). Get the blue map of Poznań, plus *Welcome to Poznań* and the bi-monthly *Wielkopolska* magazine (information in English). The PPWK-published map of Poznań is useful for travel outside the centre (shows bus routes).

🏨 Poznań has a number of trade fairs (the main one being in June) during which hotel prices double: at such a time ask at tourist information offices such as Glob-Tour (at the Central Station) about renting private rooms or staying in university accommodation.
The central **Tourist Guest House**, STARY RYNEK 91, ☎/fax (061) 852 8893, €, has rooms and dormitories. Try also the **Lech Hotel**, UL. ŚW. MARCIN 74, ☎(061) 853 0151, €€; **Rzymski Hotel**, AL. MARCINKOWSKIEGO 22, ☎(061) 852 8121, fax (061) 852 8983, €€, or **Wielkopolska Hotel**, UL. ŚW. MARCIN 67, ☎(061) 852 7631, fax (061) 851 5492, €€. There are a number of **motels** on the edge of the city which also offer cheap accommodation, such as **Strzeszynek**, at UL. KOSZALIŃSKA 15, ☎(061) 848 3145, fax (061) 848 3145 (also runs a nearby campsite next to a lakeside recreation centre; buses). The most central **campsite** is **Lake Malta**, KRAŃCOWA 98, ☎(061) 876 6203, fax (061) 876 6283. **Youth hostels** at UL. BERWIŃSKIEGO 2/3, ☎(061) 866 4040; GŁUSZYNA 127, ☎(061) 878 8461; UL. DRZMAŁY 3, ☎(061) 848 5836; and UL. BISKUPIŃSKA 27, ☎(061) 822 1063. Glob-Tour has private rooms for rent.

🍴 There are plenty of eateries on STARY RYNEK, many with menus in English. For something different try the African dishes at Africana, UL. ZAMKOWA 3.

TORUŃ

Pomerania's capital is an almost perfectly intact medieval city on the river **Wisła** (Vistula), second only to Kraków in terms of Polish architectural heritage. **Toruń** has two diverse claims to fame: one is its elaborately iced gingerbread, the other the great astronomer Nicolaus Copernicus (1473–1543), who broke new ground in arguing that the Sun, and not the Earth, is the centre of the solar system. All sights are closed on Mon.

The obvious starting point is the RYNEK STAROMIEJSKI (Market Square). Its main building, the 14th century **Ratusz** (Town Hall) – with 12 halls, 52 small rooms and 365 windows – houses the **Muzeum Okręgowe** (Regional Museum) and has panoramic views from the tower. Copernicus's house at UL. KOPERNIKA 17 is now the **Nicolaus Copernicus Museum**, its interior recreated as it was in his day.

Don't miss the **Leaning Tower of Toruń** on KRZYWA WIEŻA.

Toruń hosts many annual international festivals, including **Probaltica** (music festival) early May; **Kontakt** (theatre festival) last week in May; a **June folk festival**, a **street theatre festival** (July–Aug), and a **'Cameraimage'** festival in Nov.

BOAT TRIPS

These go along the **Wisła** from the landing stage in BULWAR FILADEFIJSKI.

ain station: **Toruń Główny**, left luggage (main hall, window 10), restaurant; 🚌 nos. 22/27 to
d town – get off at 2nd stop; buy tickets at kiosks/on bus. Exit beyond platform 4, not by the
ain hall, which is for taxis only.

ourist Office: Inside the Town Hall in the Old Town Square (STARY RYNEK), ☎ (056) 621 0931,
x (056) 621 0930 (www.it.torun.com).

otel **Trzy Korony**, RYNEK STAROMIEJSKI 21, ☎ (056) 6260 31; **Hotel Polonia**, PL. TEATRALNY 5,
☎ (056) 6230 28 (both €€, central). **Youth hostel: Schronisko Młodzieżowe**, UL. ŚW. JÓZEFA
, ☎ (056) 654 4580 (cheap, bring bedding; 🚌 nos. 6/11 from main station); **Fort IV**, SCHRONISKO
JRYSTYCZNE, UL. CHROBREGO/RÓG MLECZNEJ, ☎ (056) 655 82 36 (18-bed rooms in old fort).
ampsite: **Tramp**, UL. KUJAWSKA 14, near the train station, ☎ (056) 622 4187 (huts available),
en May–mid-Sept. Student dorms available (€) in summer: ask at tourist information.

WARSAW (WARSZAWA)

ee p. 518.

KRAKÓW

Kraków is Poland's cultural and spiritual centre and the most beautiful city in the country. The city entered a golden age in the 14th century but lost its capital atus to **Warsaw** in 1596. When Poland was partitioned at the end of the 18th century, Kraków was part of the Austro-Hungarian Empire. During the Nazi occupation, served as headquarters for the General Government, then was liberated by Soviet rces in 1945.

's a great place for strolling the old town, looking in designer boutiques, antique ops and old pharmacies that boast original fittings.

RYNEK GŁÓWNY Lively with flower stalls and alfresco cafés, this is one of the largest and most beautiful medieval market places in Europe. While the riginally 13th-century RYNEK GŁÓWNY is never entirely swamped by the crowds, try isiting late at night or early in the morning for the full impact. The size of the **ukiennice** (Cloth Hall), which stands centre-stage, and the surrounding burghers' ouses create a unique setting. The Cloth Hall started as a Gothic roof over trading talls, enlarged during the reign of Casimir the Great. Following a 1555 fire, it was econstructed in the Renaissance style, and remains a thriving commercial concern, acked with stalls selling amber, silver and upmarket souvenirs and an art gallery n the first floor (closed Mon; www.muz-nar.krakow.pl).

ll that remains of the Gothic town hall is the **Ratusz** (City Hall Tower), RYNEK ŁÓWNY 1 (closed Mon and Tues), which has a fine view from the top and contains basement café. In the opposite corner of the square, **St Adalbert's**, in Romanesque tyle, is the oldest and smallest church in Kraków. Within the vaults is the **Historical Museum of the Rynek** (Tues–Fri).

POLAND

Further north, **Mariacki** (St Mary's Church) has a wooden Gothic altar, 13 m high and adorned by 200 figures, created by Wit Stwosz, the 15th-century master carver of Nuremberg. Legend has it that a watchman was shot down from the church tower by Tartar invaders. The *hejnał*, the melody he trumpeted to sound the alarm, is repeated hourly. For military architecture explore the **Floriańska Gate,** three towers and barbican.

THE UNIVERSITY DISTRICT Central Europe's second oldest university was founded in 1364. Distinguished students include the Polish astronomer Nicolaus Copernicus and Pope John Paul II. **Collegium Maius,** UL JAGIELLOŃSKA 15, is the oldest college, a magnificent example of Gothic architecture in which 35 globes are on display, one dating from 1510 and featuring the earliest illustration of America, marked 'a newly discovered land'. Tours (1100–1700, no Sun) take in the alchemy rooms (supposedly Dr Faustus's laboratory), lecture rooms, the assembly hall and professors' apartments.

WAWEL Kraków's most important sites are the dramatic **cathedral** and fortified **Royal Castle** (both built by King Casimir the Great), high on **Wawel Hill** and bordered by the **Wisła** (Vistula) river. The Gothic cathedral of 1320–64 replaced an 11th-century church, whose relics are displayed in the castle's west wing. The most striking of the 19 side chapels is the gold-tiled, domed Renaissance **Zygmuntowska** (Sigismund's Chapel), built 1519–31. Climb the tower for a great view plus the 2.5-m diameter **Zygmunt Bell,** rung on church or national holidays.

The Royal Castle, chiefly a Renaissance structure of 1502–36, has a superb courtyard with three-storey arcades. Displayed in the Royal Chambers you can see 142 exquisite **Arras tapestries,** commissioned in the mid-16th century. Both are closed Mon.

Kraków Główny (main station) is a short walk from the centre. Currency exchange, accommodation information, left luggage (0500–2300), showers, restaurant. Head left from station, turn right down BASZTOWA STREET, enter the large underpass and head for *Planty/Basztowa* exit to right. **Główny** has a service to **Auschwitz. Płaszów Station** serves **Wieliczka,** has some night services and is about 30 mins from centre by tram no. 13.

i **Tourist Office:** UL. PAWIA 8, ☎ (012) 429 1768, fax (012) 422 0471, near **Główny** station. Branches at RYNEK GŁÓWNY 1/3 and UL. DŁUGA 9. Full information, tickets and a monthly listings magazine (English supplement) can be obtained from **Centrum Informacji Kulturalnej** (Cultural Information Centre), UL. ŚW JANA 2, ☎ (012) 421 7787, fax (012) 421 7731.

Krakow can be busy in summer, so it's wise to plan ahead. See www.hotelsinpoland.com for bargains and www.jordan.krakow.pl for specific details from an accommodation and tourist office in the city. It's common to be approached by individuals at the station – check location and price; pay only when you've seen the place. Hotels: **Saski,** UL. SLAWKOWSKA 3, ☎ (012) 421 4222 (www.hotelsaski.com.pl; info@hotelsaski.com), €€, centrally located (note the antique lift). **Wawel Tourist,** UL. POSELSKA 22, ☎ (012) 424 1300 (www.wawel-tourist.com.pl; hotel@wawel-tourist.com.pl), €€, group rates, centrally located; **Kazimierz,** UL. MIODOWA 16, ☎ (012) 421

6129 (hotel@hk.com.pl), €€, is located in the heart of the Jewish district. Bargains at pricier hotels can often be netted via the web or tourist offices in the city.

There are plenty of student rooms available during the summer. Try **Bydgoska,** UL. BYDGOSKA 19, ☎ (012) 636 8000, fax (012) 630 7786 or **Żaczek,** AL. 3 MAYA 5 (www.zaczek.com.pl; zaczek@zaczek.com.pl) or ask at tourist offices. The best **hostel** is the **Express** at UL. WROCŁAWSKA 91, ☎ (012) 633 8862 (www.express.91.pl); the largest is at UL. OLEANDRY 4, ☎ (012) 633 8822, fax (012) 633 8920, with an early curfew. The **Krak campsite** is at UL. RADZIKOWSKIEGO 99, ☎ (012) 637 2122.

🍴 **Rynek Główny** and the surrounding streets are packed with inexpensive restaurants.

DAY TRIPS FROM KRAKÓW **Auschwitz**, synonymous with the atrocities of the Holocaust, was the largest Nazi concentration camp. Between 1.5 and 2 million mainly Jewish men, women and children were transported here in cattle trucks from across Europe to meet brutality and death. Piles of spectacle frames, shoe-polish tins, baby clothes and monogrammed suitcases confiscated from the victims are displayed. Screenings of liberators' films are regularly shown in several languages. Nearby Birkenau was an even more 'efficient' Nazi death factory. National Museum of Auschwitz–Birkenau, UL. WIĘŹNIÓW OŚWIECIMIA 20, ☎ (033) 843 2022, www. auschwitz-museum.oswiecim.pl (daily, free). Trains to **Oświecim** (1 hr 20 mins; ETT table 1099) leave from Kraków Główny or Płaszów stations; frequent buses from PKS station (11 daily, take 1 hr 40 mins). Tours are organised by tourist information centres and many hotels. Accommodation: International Youth Meeting House and Education Centre, UL. LEGIONÓW 11, Auschwitz, ☎ (033) 843 2107, fax (033) 843 1211 (www.mdsm.pl).

Kazimierz Reached by trams nos. 3, 9, 11, 13 (get off at PL. WOLNICA), this district of Kraków is the former Jewish quarter and location depicted in the film *Schindler's List*. The many places worth visiting here include the the Old Synagogue at UL. SZEROKA 2 (open till 1530, Wed–Sun), the Jewish Cultural Centre at UL. MEISELSA 17 and UL. SZEROKA 2 (exhibition, bookshop, a restaurant with Jewish food and music; organises guides to Auschwitz).

> **One-day ticket:**
> 6zł; **single journey:** 2zł.
> **Taxis** are quite cheap;
> ☎ (012) 919 or 9666.

The **Royal Wieliczka Salt Mine**, PARK KINGI I, ☎ (012) 278 7302 (www.kopalnia.pl). Mined for over 700 years, it has 560 km of tunnelling. It's a dazzling spectacle, with 40 chapels carved entirely from salt, larger-than-life salt statues and an underground lake. Guided tours in English. Hop on the LUX minibus just right of Główny, departs every 15 mins (very cheap, 30 mins), stops below the mine. Entry pricey at 29zł.

WHERE NEXT FROM KRAKÓW?

*Join the eastern end of the **Prague–Poprad Tatry** route by travelling to **Poprad Tatry** and changing at **Plaveč** (3 services daily taking 6–7 hrs; ETT tables 1078 and 1182).*

ZAKOPANE

Endowed with ornate wooden houses and churches, Zakopane is the base from which to tackle the Tatra mountains, either for skiing/sleigh rides in winter or hiking/climbing in summer. Information from the PTTK office (UL. KRUPOWKI 12), Tatra Tours and Travel (UL. KOŚCIELISKA 1; www.tatratours.pl) or the less central Tatra National Park Information Centre (UL. CHALUBINSKIEGO 44). If you're hiking into the mountains, book mountain huts ahead (or end up sleeping on the stairs), and take your own food. August is the busiest month for walking and September is said to be the best (for good weather and relatively uncrowded conditions). As for day hikes from Zakopane, one of the best is to the summit of Giewont (7 hrs round walk); there's also a cable car up to Kasprov (1985 m), from where there's a ridge path into the centre of things.

From Zakopane you can also venture to the **Pieniński National Park**, with its time-warp villages and castles. A great favourite is to go rafting in the Dunajec River Gorge here (see www.flisacy.com.pl). The tourist office (Biuro Uslug Turystycznych) at UL. KOŚCIELISKA 11B organises rafting trips and excursions by bus to places of interest such as the spa town of **Szczawnica**, which makes a good base and has accommodation.

Left luggage, currency exchange. Short walk to town centre.

| *i* | **Tourist Office:** UL. KOŚCIUSZKI 17, (018) 201 2211, fax (018) 206 6051 (arranges accommodation and has useful maps).

Book ahead. **Dom Turysty PTTK**, UL. ZARUSKIEGO 5, (018) 206 3207, fax (018) 206 3281, €, (informacja@domtuvysty.zakopane.pl). **Youth hostel: Szarotka Schronisko PTSM**, UL. NOWOTARSKA 45, (018) 206 6203 (one of the largest hostels in Poland). **Sabala,** UL. KRUPÓWKI 11, (018) 201 5092 (www.sabala.zakopane.pl), €€.

(for Directory information, see pp. 590 and 609).

In the bloodless Velvet Revolution of 1989, Czechoslovakia defiantly broke away from the Soviet bloc, and the **Czech Republic** and **Slovakia** went their separate ways in 1993. The Czechs fared better economically, and **Prague,** one of the most gracious of old European capitals, a city that survived the world wars virtually unscathed, has emerged as a major tourist destination.

Industrialisation has left its mark on the two countries, but there's plenty to enjoy. The many swathes of forest are already recovering from acid rain and the extensive reconstruction and renovation work is making its mark on many towns and cities. You'll find some extremely pretty hills and mountain ranges (laced with trails; walking is a national pastime) and delightful old town squares and imposing castles. In the Czech Republic, **Bohemia** conjures up romantic visions; the south is extraordinarily beautiful, containing medieval carp ponds, moated castles, walled Renaissance towns and national parks. The **Krkonoše mountains** harbour some good hiking country and the lesser-known hills of **Beskydy** in **Moravia** have idyllic meadows and woodlands. **Western Bohemia**, home to several big and astonishingly elegant spas, is distinctly Germanic in feel.

Slovakia has a deeply traditional rural hinterland and a characterful capital in **Bratislava**, and though it's not quite as well-endowed with historic buildings, has the most dramatic scenery in the **High Tatra** mountains (shared with Poland), a compact range of Alpine-like peaks, the highest summits in the Carpathian Mountains. They get very busy in high season; the less spectacular but rewarding **Low Tatra** and **Fatra** mountains might be better if you want to escape the crowds.

ACCOMMODATION

There is a wide choice of one- to five-star **hotels**, **private rooms** and **pensions**, and, at a much more basic level, old-style **tourist hotels**, **hostels** and **inns** with a few spartan rooms, plus *chaty* (simple chalets) and *chalupy* (traditional cottages) in the countryside. However, quality (once outside the top range) can sometimes leave a lot to be desired, despite relatively high prices, so if you are on a budget, it can still make more sense to look at private rooms rather than cheap hotels. Credit cards are accepted in bigger hotels, though some places insist on payment in cash. The Czech Republic is the most popular of the former Eastern bloc countries and the deluge of tourists has resulted in a real shortage of beds, so always book ahead (directly or through Tourist Offices). There are plenty of **campsites** (usually May–Oct only), most of which cater for caravans as well. Rough camping is forbidden.

YOUTH HOSTELS

In the **Czech Republic**, the organisation to contact is the **KMC Club of Young Travellers**, KAROLÍNY SVETLÉ, 11000 PRAHA 1, CZECH REPUBLIC, ☎ (420) (2) 2222 0081, fax (420) (2) 2222 0347.

On arriving at a station, you're often greeted by locals offering rooms. This can be a good way to find somewhere to stay, but be sure to ask the price first. Note that **youth hostels** are not very common in Slovakia, only in bigger towns, although student dormitories are available in larger towns and cities in both countries in June–Sept, during the summer break.

FOOD AND DRINK

Lunch is around 1130–1400 and dinner 1700–2200. Czech cuisine is rich and meat-based, but vegetarian options include fried cheese (*smažený sýr*), risotto and salads. Pork with cabbage and dumplings (*vepřo–knedlo-zelo*) is on virtually every menu, as is *guláš*, a bland beef stew. Try goose (*husa*) and potato soup (*bramborová polévka*). Slovak food is very similar to Hungarian; a typical dish is *Bryndzové halušky*, gnocchi with grated sheep's cheese.

> Drink mineral rather than tap water.

The cost of eating and drinking is reasonable, especially in a self-service *bufet* (where you stand while eating). *Kavárny* and *cukrány* serve coffee and very sweet pastries. Pubs (*pivnice*) and wine bars (*vinárny*) are good places to eat. Czech and Slovak beers are excellent, and Moravian wine and the sweet *Tokaj* from South Slovakia are worth a try. Beers include **Pilsner**, **Budvar** and black beer (*černé pivo*), spirits include herb-based **Becherovka** or **Fernet**.

EDITOR'S CHOICE

Bratislava; High Tatra mountains near Poprad Tatry; Prague; Trnava.

BEYOND THE BORDERS

Poprad Tatry–Kraków (ETT tables 1182, 1078; Prague–Hamburg via Berlin and Dresden (table 60); Prague–Cologne via Würzburg and Frankfurt (table 57); Prague–Warsaw (table 95); Prague–Vienna (table 59).

CZECH REPUBLIC: PRAGUE (PRAHA)

A major tourist destination since the fall of the Iron Curtain, Prague is one of Europe's most beautiful capitals, with an exceptional and architecturally rich centre (baroque, medieval and Renaissance, although it's said that every form of architecture can be found somewhere within the city, from Cubist to Romanesque) of cobbled streets, pastel buildings and fine squares, plus abundant green space. In turns laid back, elegant and charged with creative energy, the city is full of buskers and artists, and notices everywhere advertising meetings and theatrical or musical events. May to Aug is very touristy with long sunny days; spring sees a wonderful array of cherry blossom on the hills embracing the Castle district, as well as the arrival of the renowned Prague Spring international music festival. Winter months have their charms, with snug cafés, opera and jazz festivals, snowy lanes and jolly Christmas markets selling mulled wine, wooden toys and iced gingerbread – although the cold can be severe.

ARRIVAL AND DEPARTURE

RAIL TICKETS can only be purchased in Czech currency at ticket office windows. Credit card and cheque purchases can be made at **Czech Railways** travel agencies at Holešovice and Hlavní railway stations or at **Čedok**, NA PŘÍKOPĚ 18.

Praha Hlavní Nádraží (Main Railway Station), WILSONOVA 2, is the main station (rail reservations 0800–1800; often long queues; English spoken). To reach the centre of town, either hop one stop (direction HÁJE) on the Metro, which you will find clearly signed at basement level within the station concourse, to Muzeum or turn left out of the main station entrance, passing through the park. Both routes will take you to the top of Wenceslas Square in about five minutes although the park route is unsafe outside daylight hours. Some long-distance and international services also use **Nádraží Praha-Holešovice**, in PRAGUE 7 (a little way out). Take the Metro, a few metres from the railway station, for four stops to Muzeum (direction HÁJE) – this is far quicker than travelling by any of the trams from across the station car-park and buses from here are normally destined for the suburbs. Both stations are on Metro Line C and have exchange bureaux, left luggage and accommodation services. **Rail information service**, (02) 2461 4030-32. Avoid **taxis** (extortionate fares). **Masarykovo** (HYBERNSKÁ, PRAGUE 1) and **Smíchovské** (NÁDRAŽNÍ, PRAGUE 5) stations cover many local trains.

Central Bus Station (long-distance services): KŘIŽÍKOVÁ 4, (02) 10 34 (www.infos.eunet.cz/svt/abus_e) Metro: FLORENC. Take Metro line C two stops to MUZEUM (direction HÁJE) or Metro line B two stops to MŮSTEK (direction ZLIČÍN) to reach the centre of town.

Ruzyně Airport, 15 km north-west of the city centre (flight enquiries, (02) 2011 1111). Accommodation desks and 24-hr currency exchange. no. 119 (every 10 mins; 12Kč) from DEJVICKÁ metro; **Czech Airlines (ČSA) bus service** every 30 mins 0530–2400 to DEJVICKÁ metro

CITIES: PRAGUE (PRAHA)

TOURIST OFFICES

Prague Information Service (PIS)
(www.pis.cz): in the **Old Town Hall** (STAROMĚSTSKÁ RADNICE), STAROMĚSTSKÉ NÁMĚSTÍ 1 at the **Praha Hlavní Nádraží rail station** and, in the summer months, in the **Malá Strana Bridge Tower** (MALOSTRANSKÁ MOSTECKÁ VĚŽ) and at NA PŘÍKOPĚ 20. Free brochures, accommodation services, information about cultural events, tickets, tours, trips, transport and travel cards.
For information:
☎ 12444 (Mon–Fri), reservation service, ☎ (02) 2171 4130.

and to its terminal in the STARÉ MĚSTO (Hotel Renaissance, near Masarykovo rail station). **Cedaz's** excellent mini-bus service runs door-to-door (0600–2200) and to NÁMĚSTÍ REPUBLIKY, but costs more. Fixed price taxis should charge 550 Kč to the centre, but often demand far more. Alternatively, order a taxi from **Taxi AAA** (English spoken) ☎ 14014.

CITY AND METRO MAP – inside back cover | INFORMATION

MONEY Banks open Mon–Fri 0900–1800. There are plenty of automatic cash dispensers. **Thomas Cook bureau de change**; KARLOVA ST. 3. Travellers cheques, Eurocheques and credit cards are widely accepted.

POST AND PHONES The **Central Post Office** and Poste Restante are at JINDŘIŠSKÁ 14 (daily 0700–2000). The non-stop post office is close by, at HYBERNSKA 15, with fax, telegram and phone services. Stamps and phone-cards from post offices/newsagents. The older, coin-operated telephones are unreliable (local calls 4Kč), but modern phone booths accept phone cards and have instructions in English. **English-speaking operator,** ☎ (02) 0135. Collect calls, ☎ (02) 0132. Prague area code: 02.

A **Prague Card**, from **Čedok travel agency** (NA PŘÍKOPĚ 18) combines a 3-day transport ticket with free entry to major sights.

PUBLIC TRANSPORT

Metro, trams and buses: All public transport runs from about 0500 to 2400; there are also night services, at approximately 40-min intervals. Efficient metro (3 lines; red, yellow and green) plus good tram network (buses mostly serve suburbs and are little use for

TICKETS

A **12Kč single ticket** (jízdenka) allows 1hr on all forms of public transport (Mon–Fri 0500–2200) (90 mins all weekend, plus Mon–Fri 2200–0500); an **8Kč single ticket** gives up to 15 mins, no transfers, (30 mins off peak). A better buy are **1, 3, 7** or **15-day** (70Kč, 200Kč, 250Kč or 280Kč) **tourist tickets** (denní jízdenka), valid on all forms of public transport. Tickets from Tabák or Trafika tobacconists/ newsagents or from metro stations; also available from the Čedok desk at the airport. Punch your ticket in the yellow machines at the metro station entrances or inside trams and buses. Plain-clothes inspectors often flash their badge and ID – fines are 400–800Kč, and should be paid on the spot. Children aged up to 5 travel free; those aged 6–15 half price.

visitors); beware pickpockets on popular tourist routes (especially no. 22). Night trams all stop at LAZARSKÁ, just off VODIČKOVÁ. A funicular runs up Petřín hill between 0915 and 2045 daily (tram 9/12/22).

Taxis: Avoid if possible – over-charging of foreigners is endemic. Always agree a fare before getting in. Reputable services include **AAA**, ☎ 14014 (English-speaking), PROFI, ☎ 1035. They should, theoretically, charge a flat rate of 30Kč per ride plus 22Kč per km within Prague.

ACCOMMODATION BUREAUX

AVE, Hlavní nádraží, ☎ (02) 2422 33226 or ☎ (02) 2422 3521 or **reservations**, ☎ (02) 2461 7113; **Čedok**, NA PŘÍKOPĚ 18, ☎ (02) 2419 7632; PAŘÍŽSKÁ 6, ☎ (02) 2314 302; and RYTÍŘSKÁ 16, ☎ (02) 26 27 14 (www.travelguide.cz) provides detailed information about over 3000 hotels and hostels and 140 campsites in the Czech Republic – and can also book these for you.

YOUTH-ORIENTED INFORMATION

CKM, JINDŘIŠSKÁ 28, ☎ (02) 26 05 32/26 85 07 (daily 0900–1800), or the **Junior Hotel (Youth Hostel) reservation office**, ŽITNÁ 12, ☎ (02) 29 29 84 (open 24 hrs). **Student Hostel Booking Office**, ☎ (02) 53 99 51/59.

CAMPSITE

Camp Sokol Troja, TROJSKA 171A, PRAHA 7, ☎ (02) 8385 0486 and (02) 8542 908 (Apr–Nov).

ACCOMMODATION

Hotels are often pricey. In July, Aug and Sept, **CKM** also lets cheap rooms in student hostels. You can call the **Student Hostel Booking Office** (see left). Accommodation hawkers offering private apartments/rooms wait for visitors arriving by train – agree a price first. There are several **campsites** within the city boundary (camping rough is forbidden).

Hotels: Dům U Krále Jiřího, LILIOVÁ 10, ☎/fax (02) 242 219 83, €€, in the old town. **U Zlatého Stromu**, KARLOVA 6, ☎ (02) 242 213 85, €€€, moderate and ideally located. **Hotel u staré paní**, MICHALSKÁ 9, ☎ (02) 2422 8090, €€, friendly, very central with a great jazz bar.

Hostels: Hostel Imperial Kavárna, NA POŘÍČÍ 15, ☎/fax (02) 231 6012 (www.hostelimperial.cz; hostelimperial@razda.cz), spotless rooms in an art nouveau hostel with jazz café. **Travellers' Hostel**, DLOUHA 33, ☎ (02) 2482 6662-3 (www.travellers.cz; hostel@travellers.cz), 3 mins' walk from the old town square; laundry, bar, kitchen, internet and e-mail service, luggage room, parking, plus super-trendy nightclub, Roxy. **Hostel Junior**, SENOVAZNE NAM. 21, ☎ (02) 2423 1754, fax (02) 2422 1579, cheap, cheerful, buffet breakfast included, 5 mins' walk from WENCESLAS SQUARE.

FOOD AND DRINK

There are three main categories of eating house: *restaurace* (restaurant), *vinárna* (wine-bar/restaurant) and *pivnice* (pub).The Old Town, Lesser Quarter and Castle district are all groaning with places to eat of all shapes and sizes, but bear in mind that, the nearer the major sights, the higher the price although not necessarily the quality. It is well worth wandering even fractionally off the beaten track to find cheaper grub in more plentiful portions, washed down with a range of beers and spirits – restaurants with menus only in Czech are normally a safe bet. The Prague Žižkov district, for example, is blessed with the city's largest collection of authentic pubs. In addition to Czech and international style dishes, Italian cuisine is becoming increasingly popular here and almost every street in the centre now boasts its pizzeria. WENCESLAS SQUARE is the home of fast-food joints, both home-grown and household-name, as well as booths offering grilled sausage, roast chicken and clammy sandwiches. To find out more about the latest and best local eateries, try the listings in the weekly English-language broadsheet, *The Prague Post* (www. praguepost.cz) or take a look at www.gurman.cz.

HIGHLIGHTS

NATIONAL JEWISH MUSEUM
One timed ticket for all sights: 480Kč (students 340Kč). Closed Sat. See www.jewishmuseum.cz.

Old Prague is divided into **Staré Město** (Old Town), **Nové Město** (New Town) and **Josefov** (the Jewish Quarter) to the east, and **Malá Strana** (Lesser Quarter) and **Hradčany** (Castle District) to the west of the **River Vltava**.

STARÉ MESTO, NOVÉ MESTO AND JOSEFOV At the heart of **Staré Město** is the picturesque **Staroměstské náměstí** (Old Town Square; tram nos. 17/18; metro: STAROMĚSTSKÁ, line A). Here, visit the **Staroměstská Radnice** (Old Town Hall), with its astronomical clock and fabulous views over the Old Town, the baroque **Kostel Sv. Mikuláše** (St Nicholas Church), the baroque **Kinský Palace**, and the Romanesque **Dům U kamenného zvonu** (House of the Stone Bell), which hosts art exhibitions and classical concerts. The dramatic 1915 monument to Jan Hus in the middle of the square is a traditional rallying point for Czechs.

The Prague castle area is open daily 0500–2400, castle gardens daily 1000–1800, castle buildings open daily, Changing of the Guard at castle gates, on the hour.

The old Jewish ghetto of **Josefov** (metro: A/tram no. 17: STAROMĚSTSKÁ) was cleared in 1893, leaving behind the only functioning medieval synagogue in Central Europe (the Old-New Synagogue) and a haunting **Old Jewish Cemetery**. The surrounding buildings (which include the **Pinkas Synagogue**, with a Holocaust memorial, among others) constitute a **National Jewish Museum**.

For further information on the **castle district**, ☎ 2437 3368 (www.hrad.cz) obtainable at the information centre in the third courtyard. You can buy a 120Kč **3-day ticket**, 60Kč for students, covering the entire district.

Nové Město is a sprawling area with fewer sights, but all visitors spend time in the lively **Václavské náměstí** (Wenceslas Square) (metro: MŮSTEK or MUZEUM), which witnessed the climax of the 'Velvet Revolution' in 1989. At the top end is a shrine to **Jan Palach**, who burned himself to death on 16 Jan 1969 in protest at the Warsaw Pact invasion. Just off NA PŘÍKOPĚ is the excellent **Mucha Museum** (PANSKÁ 7, open daily) featuring works by the famous Art Nouveau artist and illustrator.

> The beautiful sandstone **Charles Bridge**, commissioned by Charles VI in 1357, is now the standard image of Prague. At each end are high towers, and the parapet is lined by 31 statues (mainly 1683–1714, with a few copies and later works) – some cleaned up, others stained black with pollution.

> All museums are open Tues–Sun 1000–1800 unless stated

MALÁ STRANA

This area is a picturesque town of narrow cobbled streets of orange/yellow-rendered houses, with diminutive squares squeezed between the river and the wedge-shaped plateau of Hradčany. Here, **Malostranské náměstí** (Lesser Quarter Square) is particularly worth visiting (tram nos. 12/22/23: MALOSTRANSKÉ NÁMĚSTÍ), dominated by the **Sv. Mikuláše** (Church of St Nicholas) – Prague's finest church – and ringed with baroque palaces. The **Waldštejn gardens** on LETENSKÁ, north-east of the square, contain exquisite gardens (open 1000–1800). Not far away are the even more delightful **Velkopřevorské náměstí** (Grand Prior's Square) and the adjoining **Maltézské náměstí** (Square of the Knights of Malta), which contain churches, embassies and palaces, together with the celebrated John Lennon Wall, a pop-art folly (tram nos. 12/22/23: HELLICHOVA). Visit the **Church of our Lady Victorious** (Panna Marie Vítězná) at KARMELITSKÁ 9, to see the wax effigy of Baby Jesus, still an object of pilgrimage. Further east, off VALDŠTEJNSKÉ NÁMĚSTÍ, the baroque Ledeburské gardens zig-zag up the terraces below the castle.

HRADCANY

The huge hilltop castle district is the focal point of Prague (tram no. 22: MALOSTRANSKÉ NÁMĚSTÍ/PRAŽSKÝ HRAD; metro: HRADČANSKÁ, line A). Dominating the whole complex is the magnificent **Katedrála Svatého Víta** (St Vitus Cathedral), the core of which was commenced in 1344, but completed in 1929. Highlights include the St Wenceslas Chapel, the late Gothic Royal Oratory, the fabulous baroque tomb of St John Nepomuk and the oak-panel relief in the ambulatory.

Nearby, much of the **Starý Královský Palác** (Old Royal Palace) was built for King Vladislav Jagello in the 15th century. Don't miss the magnificent late Gothic **Vladislav Hall**, the so-called **Riders' Stairs**, the **Spanish Hall** (built by Rudolf II and the **Bohemian Chancellery**, where the most famous of Prague's four defenestrations occurred, when Protestant nobles threw Frederick II's ambassadors from the window in 1618. The castle is now the seat of the President of the Republic.

Beyond the Castle area lies an imposing district, beginning with **Hradčanské náměstí** (Hradcany Square). If you walk up LORETÁNSKÁ, you come to the **Černín Palace** (no 5), from whose window Foreign Minister Jan Masaryk plunged to his death in 1948. A short stroll away is the Strahov Monastery, STRAHOVSKÉ NADV. 1, the star attraction of which is the historic library with ancient tomes, frescoed walls and an eccentric collection of paraphernalia (tram no 22: POHOŘELEC). The **Belvedere** (Summer Palace), Prague's finest Renaissance building (tram no. 22: BELVEDER), houses exhibi ions – don't miss the 'singing fountain' in the gardens. South of the castle, wander through **Petřínské sady** (Petřín Hill), a traditional lovers' spot with its lush woods, orchards, 1891 model of the Eiffel Tower and funicular to Malá Strana.

The absorbing National Gallery collection is scattered round four main venues: **Sternberg Palace**, HRADČANSKÉ NÁMĚSTÍ 15, contains a collection of European art; **St George's Convent**, JIŘSKÉ NÁMĚSTÍ 33, houses old Bohemian art; **St Agnes' Convent**, U MILOSRDNÝCH 17 (tram nos. 5/14/26: REVOLUČNÍ) is devoted to 19th-century artists of the Czech national revival; the **Veletržní palác**, DUKELSKYCH HRDINU 47, houses the collection of contemporary and 19th- and 20th-century art; and **Zámek Zbraslav** (Zbraslav Castle), ZBRASLAV NAD VLTAVOU (metro: SMÍCHOVSKÉ NÁDRAŽÍ, then nos. 129/241), has a remarkable display of 19th- and 20th-century Czech sculpture.

At **Vyšehrad** (metro C: VYŠEHRAD), south of Nové Město, is the ancient citadel where the Slavs first settled. Sights include the Slavín Pantheon with 600 leading Czechs buried in the cemetery next to the Church of St Peter and St Paul, plus St Martin's rotunda, pleasant gardens and breathtaking views over the Vltava from the bastions.

The free, monthly *Prague Cultural Events*, available at all Tourist Offices, lists all museums and galleries.

NIGHT-TIME AND EVENTS

Consult the English-language newspaper *The Prague Post* for weekly listings. *Kultura v Praze* (monthly, also issued in English) details what's on. There's an excellent array of classical music, opera and theatre (in Czech), plus numerous puppet and mime shows.

ADVANCE TICKETS

Prague enjoys an extraordinary number of concerts, festivals, exhibitions and other events, year-round. Either contact **Ticketpro** at PIS, STAROMĚSTKÉ NÁMĚSTÍ I ☎ (02) 14051 (www.ticketpro.cz), or try - www.prague-info.cz for both details and tickets to the latest events.

SHOPPING

The Czech speciality is crystal glass. (Fiendishly expensive) **Moser**, NA PŘÍKOPĚ 12, ☎ (02) 24 21 12 93, and MALÉ NÁMĚSTÍ 11, offers a mailing service. In the narrow streets and *pasáže* (covered arcades) of Malá Strana, Nové Mesto and Staré Mesto are small souvenir shops, selling glass, ceramics, wooden toys and puppets; try **Česka lidová remesla** at MELANTRICHOVÁ 17, for local handicrafts, or the museum shops at Prague Castle, the Jewish Museum and the Decorative Arts Museum. The four main department stores are: **Kotva**, NÁMĚSTÍ REPUBLIKY 8; **Bílá Labut'**, NA POŘÍČÍ 23; **Julius Meinl**, VÁCLAVSKÉ NÁMĚSTÍ 21; and **Tesco**, NÁRODNÍ 26.

CZECH REPUBLIC AND SLOVAKIA

ROUTE DETAIL

Praha–Brno
ETT table 1150

Type	Frequency	Typical journey time
Train	14 daily	3 hrs 20 mins

Brno–Bratislava
ETT table 1150

Type	Frequency	Typical journey time
Train	8 daily	2 hrs

Bratislava–Trnava
ETT table 1180

Type	Frequency	Typical journey time
Train	Every 1–2 hrs	40 mins

Trnava–Piešt'any
ETT table 1180

Type	Frequency	Typical journey time
Train	Every 1–2 hrs	28 mins

Piešt'any–Trenčín
ETT table 1180

Type	Frequency	Typical journey time
Train	Every 1–2 hrs	32 mins

Trenčín–Žilina
ETT table 1180

Type	Frequency	Typical journey time
Train	Every 1–2 hrs	1 hr 10 mins

Žilina–Poprad-Tatry
ETT table 1180

Type	Frequency	Typical journey time
Train	Every 1–2 hrs	2 hrs 05 mins

KEY JOURNEYS

Prague–Munich
ETT table 57

Type	Frequency	Journey Time
Train	3 daily	4 hrs 56 mins

Prague–Vienna
ETT table 59

Type	Frequency	Journey Time
Train	4 daily	4 hrs 35 mins

Prague–Berlin
ETT table 60

Type	Frequency	Journey Time
Train	5 daily	5 hrs 30 mins

Prague–Hamburg
ETT table 60

Type	Frequency	Journey Time
Train	5 daily	8 hrs 30 mins

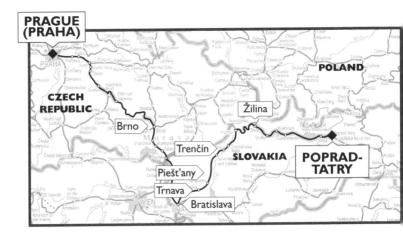

From the Czech capital, the train heads past Kolín (the connection for Kutná Hora, with its old medieval town huddled around a superb Gothic church), through the Bohemian–Moravian uplands to **Brno**, in the centre of South Moravia, a land of rolling hills, dotted with elegant châteaux and medieval castles where many Czech and foreign films are set, peaceful nature reserves and areas with karst limestone scenery and underground caves. It's also the main Czech wine-growing region (with attractively-painted wine cellars dotting the hills) and features a range of folk festivals and charming village traditions.

Bratislava, served by trains to Vienna and Budapest, deserves a few days' exploration; beyond lies the finest part of the route, rounding the spectacular Fatra and **Tatra** mountains, amid the bear country of the Carpathians. Bear in mind that it can take far longer than expected to explore the mountainous regions as the trains meander between the endless mountain ranges. Slovakia, although less explored by tourists, nonetheless has more than its fair share of attractions. These include spas (including cave therapy, fresh air and mud cures and potent waters), Renaissance towns almost untouched by time, deeply rural areas with folk architecture and striped fields, breathtaking national parks and craggy castles that used to guard the trade routes between Poland and Hungary. Beyond **Poprad Tatry**, it's feasible to continue into Poland, most easily by bus.

DAY TRIPS FROM BRNO

The **Moravský Kras** (*Moravian Karst*) limestone caves form a series of dramatic underground rivers, stalagmites and stalactites in the middle of a forest (daily 0800–1530, cheap). There are several trains a day to nearby **Blansko** (35 mins). Take the frequent bus from **Zvonařska** central bus station to explore **Mikulov**, a lovely hill-top town with a castle (rebuilt in the 1950s, but it still looks impressive from afar), charming old houses and noted wine-cellars, overlooking the Austrian border (40 mins).

PRAGUE (PRAHA)

See p. 534.

BRNO

High-rise blocks and an unmistakably industrial look might tempt you to skip Brno, which expanded in the 19th century as a textile making centre, but it does

En route to Brno is the stunning town of **Kutná Hora** with an ancient silver mine, the lovely Gothic church of **Sv. Barbora**, endless Renaissance and mediaeval architecture and also an extraordinary 'bone church' 2 km from the centre in Sedlec (just by the train station) richly and gruesomely decorated with the bones of long-expired nobles.

have a scattering of good sights (most close Mon, and are either cheap or free) within 1 km of the station in the largely traffic-free centre. The neo-Gothic **Chrám sv. Petra a Pavla**, (Cathedral of Sts Peter and Paul), crowns Petrov Hill, while the 13th-century **Spilberk Castle** was the most notorious prison in the Austro-Hungarian empire – you can visit the horrifying prison cells (Tues–Sun). A little way south-west is the **Augustinian Monastery**, where in 1865 the monk Mendel studied genetics breeding pea plants in the garden. Garden and plants remain, and there's also a small museum, the **Mendelianum**, Mendlovo náměstí 1 (Mon–Fri).

The **Old Town Hall**, Radnická 8, is Gothic-, Renaissance- and baroque-style and displays a 'dragon', a stuffed crocodile from 1608. Brno's most bizarre sight is the crypt of the **Kapučínský Klášter** (Capuchin Monastery), containing 150 mummified bodies, air-dried since 1650 (closed Mon).

🚉 (Exchange facilities, left luggage). For town centre, head across the road in front of the station and up Masarykova street.

ℹ️ **Tourist Office**: Old Town Hall, Radnická 4, 8, 10, ☎(05) 4221 1090/3267 (www.brno.cz).

🏨 Book well in advance as Brno is a trade fair city and its hundreds of hotels and pensions tend to book up months ahead. **YMCA**: Stamicova 11, ☎(05) 381 314 and (05) 6722 0963; **Pension Venia**, Riegrova 27, ☎(05) 4121 3290. The helpful staff at the Tourist Office can provide you with comprehensive accommodation info, and are happy to arrange this for you.

Day Trip from Bratislava

Towering above the Danube and Morava rivers, **Devín castle** is a picturesque ruined fortress at the edge of the Little Carpathian mountains. There are frequent buses (🚌 no. 29) and boats (from Fajnorovo nábr., ☎(07) 5923 2226, cheap). **Pezinok** (25 mins by bus, ten daily) is a pretty vintner's town in the wine-growing region, boasting a Renaissance castle and centre. Don't miss the **wine festivals** at the end of Aug and early Sept.

BRATISLAVA, SLOVAKIA

For four centuries Bratislava was a strategic part of the *Limes Romanus*, the Roman frontier. In the 16th century, when much of Hungary lay under Turkish occupation, it became the Hungarian capital, remaining in this position for almost 250 years. Now, as the Slovak capital since 1993, the city is slowly re-establishing itself.

Within particularly hideous outskirts of grey tower blocks (and one of Europe's largest housing estates), it has a charming and relaxed old centre, free from the tourist crowds and peppered with cafés (though it suffers in comparison with Prague). Many of its older and more distinguished buildings and squares have been renovated. The castle dominates the town – although dating from the 9th century, most of the current structure is 1960s vintage (closed Mon). During Bratislava's period as Hungarian capital, 11 kings were crowned in **St Martin's Cathedral**, across Staromestska from the

...stle. The attractive, fountain-filled old centre, largely pedestrianised, contains the glo-rious **Mirbach Palace**, RADNIČNÁ ST, the **Primacialne Palace**, 1 PRIMACIALNE SQ., and the Gothic **Franciscan Church**, FRANTIŠKÁNSKÉ NÁMĚSTÍ, one of Bratislava's oldest surviv-ing structures. Clamber up the medieval **St Michael's Tower**, MICHALSKA 22 (Wed–Mon), for a bird's-eye view over the old town, and visit the **Town Hall**, HLAVNÉ NÁMĚSTÍ, (Tues–Sun), a gorgeous hotch-potch of buildings housing a surpris-ingly interesting municipal museum. It's well worth trying out a boat or hydrofoil trip down the Danube, to Passau, Vienna or Budapest (☎(07) 5923 2226) – boats depart from FAJNOROVO NABREŽIE 2.

Most trains serve the main station, **Hlavná stanica**, 1.5 km north of old town. **Tourist/accommodation office**: ☎(07) 5249 5906, exchange facilities, café, left luggage and showers. Tram no.1 to old town. **Nové Mesto** station is 3 km north-east of the centre. The new **Petržalka** station (for trains to Vienna via Kittsee) is in the suburbs south of the river.

Tourist Office: BIS, KLOBÚČNICKÁ 2, ☎(07) 5443 3715 (bis@isnet.sk). BIS also arranges all categories of accommodation, but only if you present yourself at the office at KLOBÚČNICKA 2.

Budget accommodation is hard to find here. Student accommodation is only possible during July and Aug – the best all round is **Youth Hostel Bernolák**, BERNOLÁKOVA 1, ☎(07) 524 977 23, not far fom the centre, but you can also try **Belojanis**, WILSONOVA 6 (very basic, no phone). Other cheap and cheerful accommodation includes **Hostel Izov**, NOBELOVA 16, ☎(07) 444 570 7, €€, or **Hotel Plus**, BULHARSKA 72, ☎(07) 432 933 78, €€. Ask the English-speaking staff at the BIS office and at the railway station Tourist Office for help, as they maintain a large database of hotels, hostels and pensions. The website (www.hotel.sk) also provides a large database of pensions, hotels and hostels.

WHERE NEXT FROM BRATISLAVA?

It's just over 1 hr to **Vienna** *(ETT table 996), and just over 2 hrs 30 mins to* **Budapest** *(table 1170).*

🍴 Head for the old heart of town to find decent places to eat – MICHALSKA and HLAVNÉ NÁMĚSTÍ are lined with lively cafés, pubs and bars serving snacks, wine, coffee and sticky cakes. PANSKÁ and the charming streets and squares close by boast some good restaurants, pizzerias and gallery cafés. Check out the latest eateries in *The Slovak Spectator* (www.slovakspectator.sk), the weekly English-language newspaper or browse www.gurmania.sk.

TRNAVA

Dubbed somewhat ludicrously the 'Slovak Rome', Trnava is a picturesque walled university town boasting 12 churches and unspoiled, cobbled lanes. It's an easy day trip from Bratislava. While you're there don't miss TROJIČNÉ NÁMĚSTÍ, with its fine houses and public buildings and plague column. The huge Rococo **Univerzitný kos-tol**, on HOLLÉHO street, is one of the town's most interesting and elegant churches, but it's just as rewarding to wander the town's sleepy, leafy alley-ways and squares.

The centre is 10 mins' walk up Hospodárska st., then right down Bernolákova brana st.

Tourist Office: **TINS**, Trojičné Námestí 1, ☎(0805) 5501 391.

Cheap accommodation is thin on the ground: if you are travelling in a group, try the **Hotel Inka**, UL Vladimira Klementisa, ☎(0805) 590 5111, €€–€€€, or the cheaper **Hotel Micron**, UL Jana Bottu, ☎(0805) 552 1095, €.

PIEŠŤ'ANY

Slovakia's biggest, grandest spa, built at the turn of the century, Piešť'any offers cures, elegant cafés and peaceful, riverside parks, and is just over an hour's spa ride from the capital. Recently renovated, its smartest spa hotels (€€€) are now largely populated with holidaying well-heeled Russians, Germans and Austrians taking the mud and water treatments. Take a leisurely swim in the **Eva** pool, sample the granny-filled cafés on Winterová and explore the tranquil parks on **Kúpeln island**. This is one of the most relaxing places in Slovakia.

15 mins' walk west of the centre (signposted).

Tourist Office: **Informačné stredisko Piešť'any** (in the Hotel Eden), Winterová 60, ☎(0838) 762 4709/5009/4691. The Tourist Office at Hotel Eden also arranges all categories of accommodation and has some reasonably-priced rooms of its own €€–€€€.

TRENČÍN

Trenčín, dwarfed by a towering castle on a crag, is a charming old town on the river Váh. The massive reconstructed castle is open daily for guided tours and provides spectacular views particularly at night. Mierové Námestí (the main square), lined with trees and pastel-coloured houses, includes some cafés, pubs and a pizzeria. Trenčín also makes a good base for hiking in the **Povarsky Inovec woods**. There is a branch line from Trenčianska Teplá (8 km from Trenčín) to **Trenčianske spa** (with pseudo-Turkish baths) on the narrow-gauge railway. Try the Hammam bath (men only) and the Zelená žaba spring-water baths, the marked walks up to Krájove and, if you're in town in the summer, the international art film and music festivals.

Walk 10 mins east through the park for the centre.

Tourist Office: **Kultúrno-informačné centrum mesta Trenčín**, Štúrovo Námestí 10, ☎(0831) 186 or (0831) 533 505.

The best source of accommodation is via the helpful Tourist Office – booking ahead is strongly recommended. Cheap accommodation includes student accommodation at the **Domov Mladeze**, Stanicna 6 (by the railway station), ☎(0831) 6522 380, €, open July–Aug, or the **Autocamp** in Ostrov, ☎(0831) 743 4013, €, some 10–15 mins' walk from the railway station.

Day Trip from Žilina

Four trains per day make the short run through from Žilina to Martin, taking 45 mins (ETT table 1185). Plenty more journeys are possible by changing at **Vrútky**. **Martin** is an outstanding base for walking or skiing in the Malá and Velká Fatra mountains, and for visiting the **Slovak Village Museum** (at Jahodnicke haje), 3 km away.

ŽILINA

Although the town isn't much to write home about, it's worth taking a look at the Renaissance arcades in the town centre on Mariánské náměstí. A sprinkling of cafés, restaurants and pubs can be found on the square or nearby. Budatín chateau (incorporating the regional museum) is almost on the doorstep; Orava castle is further afield. The train journey to both Banská Štiavnica and Kremnica, charming former Hungarian/German mining towns with exquisite architecture, is spectacular. Žilina is an ideal base for exploring the Malá Fatra and Velká Fatra mountain ranges and the **Kysuce Nature Reserve**. As a well-known Slovak holiday area, the region is crisscrossed with well-marked paths of varying lengths and difficulty. The **Vratná Dolina valley** is one of the most renowned beauty spots – take the chairlift to Snilovské Sedlo for stunning views. Stop-offs on the way to Poprad Tatry include **Liptovský Mikuláš**, for its beautiful lake and connections to the Low Tatra mountains. Part of the Slovak karst system, **Demänovská Dolina** boasts some astonishing underground stalactite and stalagmite caves (hourly bus from Liptovský Mikuláš).

North-east of the centre, on Národná ulica.

i Tourist Office: **Selinan Travel Agency**, Burianova medzierka 4, ☎ (089) 621 478.

Camping is one possibility in Žilina, if you have your own tent – try the tourist office for further details (they can also arrange accommodation) or you can stay cheaply at **Penzión Majovej**, Jána Mlca 3, ☎ (089) 624 152, €€.

POPRAD TATRY

Poprad, sandwiched between the High and Low Tatra mountain ranges, is undistinguished, but **Spišská Sobota** (3 km east of the station) has Renaissance houses and exquisite church carvings.

1 km north of the town centre. Catch the frequent TEZ train for the mountains – it departs from the upper north-facing station concourse at regular intervals.

i Tourist Office: **Popradská informačná agentúra**, Nám. sv. Egídia 2950/114, ☎ (092) 16186 or (092) 721 700.

Tatranská informačná kancelária, ☎ (0969) 442 3440, can arrange accommodation, and the **Popradská informčná agentúra**, ☎ (092) 16186 or (092) 721 700, has information about chalets, pensions and hotel accommodation. The High Tatras are very popular in the summer and ski seasons, so booking ahead is essential.

Eating out well is something of a challenge as the spas and hotels are almost dead to the world at night – try some of the larger hotel restaurants or the occasional pub which can be found in the main resorts.

Side Trips from Poprad Tatry From Poprad and Strba, the TEZ railway (ETT table 1182) climbs into the stunning alpine **High Tatra** mountains, stopping at **Starý Smokovec, Štrbské Pleso** and **Tatranská Lomnica** for spas, hiking and skiing. Although the Alpine mountain range is only 25 km long, paths of varying difficulty provide a wealth of choice for walkers – and skiers in the winter.

Ždiar ia a pretty Goral village, with a small folk museum and traditional wooden architecture, on the bus route to Poland.

Buses also cover the Spiš region – unspoilt Renaissance villages amongst rolling hills, striped fields and tiny white churches: the town of **Levoča** and **Spišský Hrad (Spiš castle)** are unmissable UNESCO World Heritage sites. **Stará L'ubovna** (reached by train), although pretty dull in itself, is home to a fascinating regional **open-air museum**. The bus from here takes you to the **Pieniny National Park** and the chance to float down the River Dunajec by raft at Červený Kláštor, also the site of a 14th-century monastery (open Tues–Sun) and a camping and caravan site on the river banks.

WHERE NEXT
FROM POPRAD TATRY?

*It's feasible to continue into Poland by heading on east to **Plaveč** then north to **Kraków**, joining the **Poznań–Zakopane** route (p. 524); (ETT tables 1182 and 1078).*

SOUTH-EAST EUROPE

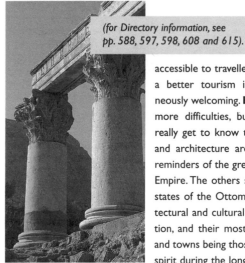

(for Directory information, see pp. 588, 597, 598, 608 and 615).

Of the countries covered in this section, **Greece**, **Turkey** and **Hungary** are the most accessible to travellers, more cosmopolitan and with a better tourism infrastructure, yet less spontaneously welcoming. **Bulgaria** and **Romania** present more difficulties, but also more opportunities to really get to know the people. Hungary's traditions and architecture are central European, with many reminders of the great days of the Austro-Hungarian Empire. The others share a history of being subject states of the Ottoman Empire (Turkey), their architectural and cultural high points coming with liberation, and their most revered buildings, monasteries and towns being those which maintained the national spirit during the long centuries of subjugation.

Nowadays, the young in all these countries have a social life to rival that of their counterparts in western Europe. Cafés are lively and stimulating meeting places. Head for Hungary for its elegant capital and fine towns; to Greece for its vibrant light and relaxing beach life, with archaeological treasures always within reach; to Romania for a country with rural beauty but dilapidated cities and a capital trying to recapture its role as the Paris of the East; to Bulgaria for magnificent scenery and wildlife, inexpensive skiing, quality wine at bargain prices, some fine cities and great beaches; and to Istanbul, at the very edge of Europe, for a taste of Asia beyond.

BULGARIA

This small, comparatively little-known country on the eastern side of the Balkan Peninsula has beautiful mountain scenery, rich in wild flowers and birds. There are cities like **Plovdiv** and **Veliko Târnovo** (both accessible by train), with picturesque old quarters built during the 19th-century National Revival. Monasteries like Rila and Bachkovo, both on UNESCO's World Heritage List, have stunning frescos and impressive buildings. They can be reached by bus from **Sofia** and **Plovdiv** respectively. The large resorts on the Black Sea coast are gradually being improved, but much of the coast is still largely agricultural, and there are some pretty villages as well as the more cosmopolitan charms of Varna, the largest port. Folk traditions still play a part in rural life, and hospitality to visitors is warm and friendly.

ACCOMMODATION

In **Sofia** (particularly at the airport, railway station and in the city centre) various agencies offer accommodation booking and information. Small private hotels and bed and breakfast type accommodation are increasingly available and good value. The main hotels also have information desks, often useful for maps and a monthly free city information guide in English.

FOOD AND DRINK

Bulgaria produces a wide variety of excellent fruits and vegetables. Soups are popular all the year round, with yoghurt-based cold ones on offer in summer. Meat is generally pork or lamb, either cooked slowly with vegetables or grilled. Desserts include seasonal fruit, ice-cream, gateaux and sweet pastries. Vegetarians can go for the varied and generally excellent salads, and dishes such as stuffed peppers or aubergine dishes like *kyopolou*.

Tea is often herbal or Chinese and served without milk. Coffee is normally espresso. Bottled fruit juices are cheap and readily available, as are imported soft drinks in cans. Local beers are European lager style and good value. **Grozdova, slivova** and **mastika** are strong drinks, served in large measures, traditionally accompanying cold starters. Tap water is safe to drink and there are many good local mineral waters. Bulgarian wine is often of high quality, and very good value.

GREECE

Inexpensive, sunny, friendly and beautiful, with a wonderful array of archaeological sites, Greece offers a seductive mix of culture and idling around, with plenty of opportunity to linger in tavernas or relax on a beach as well as visiting ancient ruins. Wild flowers make a colourful spectacle in spring – an ideal time for travelling – while in summer it's often too hot to do more than flop in the shade (Aug can be really crowded as most Greeks take the month off), and by autumn the landscape is parched and past its prime but is still excellent for swimming and sightseeing.

Most visitors will probably at least pass through **Athens**, and spare more than a fleeting glance at the famous classical remains. From there you can escape the noise and pollution of the capital by taking ferries out to the islands of the Aegean Sea. Close by are the **Saronic Gulf Islands**, farther east are the **Cyclades**, while farther

PELOPONNESE PENINSULA

A particularly idyllic area for exploring is the Peloponnese peninsula, with the seaside town of Nafplion and some impressive classical sights and scenic treats. The rail network is sparse, and many services are erratic, but buses are generally efficient and plentiful.

east still, towards Turkey, lie the **Dodecanese**. Within these archipelagos the islands are strongly contrasting, some ruggedly mountainous such as **Náxos, Santorini** and **Kárpathos**, some good for nightlife and beaches such as **Íos** and **Mykonos**, others peaceful and uncrowded such as **Iraklia**. Further afield are the major resort islands of **Corfu, Rhodes** and **Crete** (the most southerly and largest of all the islands, with superb ancient remains and astonishingly diverse scenery). The islands are covered in great detail in *Greek Island Hopping* by Frewin Poffley (Thomas Cook Publishing).

ACCOMMODATION

Greece is over-supplied with accommodation, from deluxe hotels to pensions, village rooms, self-catering apartments, dormitories and youth hostels. You should have no problem finding a bed in **Athens, Patras** or **Thessaloniki (Salonika)** even in high summer (though the very cheapest Athens dorms and pensions are often very crowded in July and Aug). Rooms are hardest to find over the Greek Easter period (note this date is different from Easter elsewhere, as it's based on the Orthodox calendar), so try to book ahead. Outside the Easter and July–Sept peaks, accommodation costs up to 30% less. You should also get a 10% discount if staying three or more nights. Cheaper places will keep your passport overnight unless you pay in advance. Youth hostels are not good value and are being phased out by the government. **Campsites** at major sights (including **Delphi, Mistra** and **Olympia**) can be good value, with laundries, hot showers, cafés and even swimming pools. You can get a list of sites from the national tourist office, the Hellenic Tourism Organisation (EOT; see p. 554).

FOOD AND DRINK

Greeks rarely eat breakfast (many get up at dawn and start the day with coffee and a cigarette) but cafés in tourist areas advertise 'English breakfast'. Traditional Greek meals are unstructured, with lots of dishes brought at once or in no particular order. Lunch is any time between 1200 and 1500, after which most restaurants close until around 1930. Greeks dine late, and you will find plenty of restaurants open until well after midnight.

The best Greek food is fresh, seasonal and simply prepared. Seafood dishes are usually the most expensive. Pork, chicken and squid are relatively cheap, and traditional salad – olives, tomatoes, cucumber, onions, peppers and feta cheese drowned in oil, served with bread – is a meal in itself. The majority of restaurants in touristy areas have a bilingual Greek and English menu. In smaller places, visit the kitchen to choose what you want, or in more expensive establishments choose dishes from a display cabinet.

Coffee is easier to find than tea; iced coffee (**frappé**) is now more popular than the tiny, strong cups of old-fashioned Greek coffee. Aniseed-flavoured **ouzo** is a favourite aperitif. **Retsina** (resinated wine) is an acquired taste. Greek brandy, **Metaxa**, is on the sweet side. Draught lager is not widely available and is neither as good nor as cheap as bottled beer: Amstel, Henninger, Heineken and Mythos, brewed in Greece and sold in half-litre bottles. Tap water is safe but heavily chlorinated.

HUNGARY

The **Great Plain**, Alföld, extends across more than half this landlocked country, with the most appreciable hills rising in the far north. Hungary's most scenic moments occur along **Lake Balaton** (much developed with resorts, one of the pleasantest being **Keszthely**) and the **Danube Bend** (or Dunakanyar), north of Budapest, with a trio of fine towns – **Szentendre** (with its ceramics museum), **Visegrád** (with its ruined palace) and **Esztergom** (dominated by a huge basilica). **Budapest** is the obvious highlight, exuding the grace of an old middle European city, memorably placed on the Danube.

ACCOMMODATION There is a wide range of accommodation, with some superb **hotels** of international standing in the capital. Some castles are being turned into hotels of varying standards. **For the medium to lower price bracket**, **private rooms** are very good value as is the small pension. Steer clear of the old Soviet-style tourist hotels and youth hostels as they are very basic with limited facilities. **Spas** offer good weekend packages. **Campsites** are, on the whole, very good and can be found near the main resorts. Many have cabins to rent, but contact the authorities first in order to book. Camping 'rough' is not permitted and could net a hefty fine. Information on accommodation addresses, phone numbers and services: **Tourinform:** ☎(1) 438-8080 (www.hungarytourism.hu).

FOOD AND DRINK Cuisine has been much influenced by Austria, Germany and Turkey. Portions are generous and most restaurants offer a cheap fixed-price menu. Lunch is the main meal of the day, and a bowl of *gulyás* (goulash) laced with potatoes and spiced with paprika is a 'must'. Try smoked sausages, soups (sour cherry soup is superb) and paprika noodles or pike-perch. Dinner is early and you should aim to begin eating well before 2100. In order to avoid the pitfalls of phrase book ordering, try eating in an **Önkiszolgáló** or **ételbár** (inexpensive self-service snack bars). **Csárda** are folk restaurants usually with traditional music, but menus can be limited and slightly more expensive. Still in the moderate range are the **Vendéglő**, where home cooking often features. **Étterem** are larger restaurants with a more varied menu. Leave a tip, generally equivalent to 10% of the total. Hungary has some very decent wines, such as **Tokaji** and **Egrí Bikavér** (Bulls Blood), while **pálinka** is a fiery schnapps.

ROMANIA

The lofty **Carpathian Mountains** snake through the heart of the country, rising to over 2500 m in the region of **Transylvania**, the terrain of the original Count Dracula. Much of the countryside is rugged and remote, and travel can be a real adventure, though be warned that standards for tourism are not on a par with Western countries'. The brutal dictator Ceauşescu, before his demise and assassination in 1989, destroyed many villages and re-housed large communities in hastily erected apartment blocks; **Bucharest** has many legacies of his era and is not the most appealing of European capitals, and many other towns suffered a similar fate. If you really want to get off the beaten track by rail, venture into **Maramures** in the country's north-western corner, or go to the **Republic of Moldavia**, or explore the churches and monasteries of **Bucovina** in the north-east. Prices are low and you'll still find places where tourists are rare, and the reception from locals is almost universally warm despite the obvious poverty of the inhabitants.

ACCOMMODATION

Hotels vary a great deal in quality, even within each category (one to five stars). At the bottom end they can be basic and inexpensive, while some match the highest international standards and prices. **Private rooms** may be booked at Tourist Offices in some towns, and in a few tourist areas touts will meet trains at the station to offer their rooms – which may be centrally located in attractive old houses, or far out in grim suburban tower blocks, so make sure you know what you're agreeing to. **Campsites** should generally be avoided, as standards of cleanliness and hygiene can be appalling. Book in advance for hotels on the **Black Sea coast** in summer and in **mountain ski resorts** at winter weekends. It's well worth using an **accommodation agency** to book – try www.rotravel.com for details of the best – or **Touring Europabus Romania**, ☎(01) 21 17 19 3 (touring@rotravel.com) for accommodation throughout Romania. For **youth hostels** throughout Romania browse www.dntcj.ro/yrh.

FOOD AND DRINK

There are many restaurants in the main cities, offering a variety of foods, in principle. In practice you often end up with pork, plus potato and vegetables. Chicken, beef, veal and lamb are also available, and fish can be delicious, especially Danube carp (termed, unfortunately, *crap*). The traditional accompaniment is *mămăligă*, a polenta-like purée of maize flour. Unsmoked frankfurters *(pariser)* and light liver sausages *(cremwurst)* are tasty, as are stews such as *tachitura moldoveneasca*. Other local specialities are *sarmale*, stuffed cabbage leaves (sometimes without meat), *ciorba*, a sour soup, and *mititei*, herby meatballs grilled in beer gardens in summer. There's a plethora of takeaway stalls and some pizzerias.

Cafés serve excellent cakes *(prăjitură)*, soft drinks, beer and coffee; *turceasca* is Turkish-style ground coffee, while *Ness* is instant coffee. Wines are superb and very cheap. Try the plum brandy known as *tuică* (pronounced 'tswica'), or its double-distilled version *palinca*. Tap water is safe to drink.

EDITOR'S CHOICE

Athens; Bran Castle (near Braşov); Budapest; Delphi; Istanbul; Peloponnese (including Nafplion; Epidavros; Korinthos and Olympia); Plovdiv; Sighişoara; Veliko Târnovo. Scenic rail journeys: Athens–Olympia; including side trip to Kalávrita (ETT tables 1450/5); Sighişoara–Braşov (p. 572); Veliko Târnovo–Sofia (table 1525).

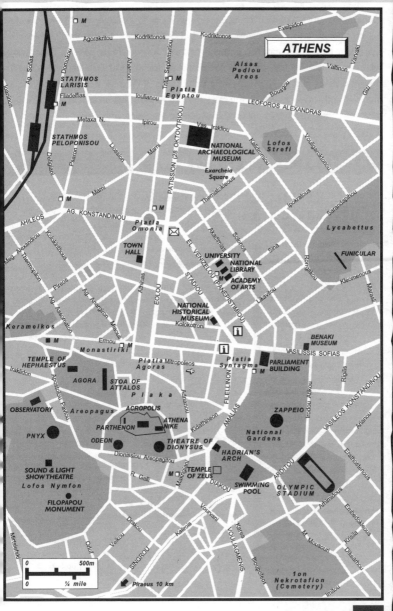

ATHENS

GREECE: ATHENS (ATHINAI)

Modern **Athens** is a noisy, bustling, exhausting and badly polluted city of more than four million people. Yet many Athenians live a laid-back, village-style life amid the concrete apartment blocks, and hardly a corner is without a tiny café or taverna. Street crime rates are remarkably low and it's a conspicuously friendly place. Its enduring draw are the great sights of the ancient city where the seeds of Western democracy, philosophy, medicine and art were planted. You can visit most of the sights on foot as it is quite compact and best seen early in the morning to avoid the worst of the heat and crowds.

ARRIVAL AND DEPARTURE

TOURIST INFORMATION

Greek national tourist office: **Hellenic Tourism Organisation (EOT)**, 2 AMERIKIS ST, ATHENS, ☎(00 30) (1) 3310 692, 3310 565 or 3310 561/2, fax (00 30) (1) 3252 895 (www.gnto.gr); sightseeing information leaflets, fact sheets, local and regional transport schedules and up-to-date opening times of sights. There are also **EOT offices** in the **Eleftherios Venizelos Airport**, and in **Piraeus Zea Marina**. The **tourist police** in Athens, ☎ 171, can help with lists of licensed accommodation (DIMITRAKOPOULOU 77, KOUKAKI, ☎(01) 9242 700). **International Student and Youth Travel Services**, ☎(01) 3221 267 (isyts@travelling.gr).

Trains from **Thessaloniki (Salonika), Northern Greece, Bulgaria** and **Europe** use **Larissa Station** (*Stathmos Larisis*), THEODOROU DILIGIANI, ☎(01) 8237 741. Trains from **Patras** and the **Peloponnese** use **Peloponnese Station** (*Stathmos Peloponisou*), ☎(01) 5131 601. These small stations are only 200 yards apart: Peloponnese is behind Larissa over the metal footbridge. They are about 2 km north-west of **Syntagma** (metro: STATHMOS LARISIS). **International rail tickets** can be bought at Larissa station or **OSE offices** in Athens: 1 KAROLOU ST, ☎(01) 5297 777; 6 SINA ST, ☎(01) 3624 402-6. For **domestic rail timetable information**, ☎145; **international services**, ☎147.

The **Piraeus Port Authority** serves the Greek islands, ☎(01) 4226 000-4 or 143 for ferry timetables. The port itself, 8 km south-west of Athens, is served by **train** and **metro**. The **Tourist Office** has a monthly **all-island ferry timetable**. If you are island-hopping, Thomas Cook's guidebook *Greek Island Hopping* combines a guide to every Greek island with ferry timetable information.

The new **Eleftherios Venizelos Airport** is 20 km south-east of the city centre and served by both Olympic Airways and international airlines. For international flight information, ☎3530 000. 🚌 no. E95 runs to Syntagma, no. 94 to ETHNIKI AMYNA metro station and no. E96 to Piraeus (via Glyfada) every 15 mins 0600–2300 and then at 30-min intervals during the night (apart from the E94). Tickets valid for 24 hrs can be used on the metro, bus or trolleybus. **OA reservations**: ☎(01) 9666 666.

CITIES: ATHENS (ATHINAI)

INFORMATION

MONEY There is a **Thomas Cook bureau de change** at 4 KARAGEORGI SERVIAS ST., SYNTAGMA SQ.

POST AND PHONES The **main post office** is in **Syntagma**, MITROPOLEOS ST, Mon–Sat 0730–2000 and Sun 0730–1330. Another branch is at 100 EOLOU ST, Mon–Sat 0730–2000. The **Hellenic Telecommunications Organisation** (OTE) has an office open 24 hrs at 85 PATISSION ST, where **international calls** can be made. You can make **local calls** from phonecard boxes and international calls from those which bear the orange 'international' legend. You can also make calls from **metered phones** at *periptero* street booths all over the city. The **dialling code** for Athens is 01.

PUBLIC TRANSPORT

The **Athens Urban Transport Organisation**'s excellent free *Pocket Map to Athens* shows **metro, trolley-bus** and **bus routes**. Central Athens, from OMONIA to SYNTAGMA and then through the **Plaka** to the **Acropolis**, is increasingly walkable thanks to a ban on traffic in several core blocks.

Metro (0500–2400): There are three lines. The **M1** runs from **Piraeus** north to the centre of town, where there are stations at MONASTIRAKI (for the Plaka), OMONOIA (for the Archaeological Museum) and VICTORIA then on to **Kifissia**. The **M2** operates from SEPOLIA to DAFNI via OMONOIA and SYNTAGMA (eventually it will extend to AGIOS ANTONIOS). The **M3** runs from ETHNIKI AMYNA to SYNTAGMA (currently being extended to MONASTIRAKI).

Trolley-buses (0500–2400, Sun from 0530) and **buses** (0500–2330, Sun from 0530): the network is far more comprehensive than the metro. Most routes pass through either SYNTAGMA or OMONOIA.

Taxis: Hard to find, especially during the rush hour, around lunch time and early afternoon. Sharing a taxi is normal; all passengers pay full fare. Some airport taxi drivers will overcharge unwary visitors so agree a fare before getting in. From Syntagma to the airport it should cost approximately €10 in the daytime and €13 at night (2400–0500).

ACCOMMODATION

The **Hellenic Chamber of Hotels** provides a booking service for Athens hotels. They can be contacted before arrival at STADIOU 24, 10564 ATHENS, by correspondence, fax (01) 3225 449 or 3236 962 (users.otenet.gr/~grhotels;

Metro tickets (Covering 1 zone, 2 zones or all lines, valid 90 mins) are available from station kiosks or self-service machines; validate them in the machines at station entrances. **Trolley-buses** and **buses** – buy **tickets** from blue booths near bus stops or from kiosks throughout Athens. Validate tickets on board. Failure to validate any transport ticket incurs a fine of 40 times the ticket cost. The **24-hr ticket** is valid for the metro, trolley-buses and buses; validate ticket once only, on first use.

grhotels@otenet.gr), or upon arrival in Athens at 2 KARAGEORGI SERVIAS ST, of SYNTAGMA, ☎(01) 3237 193/3229 912, in the National Bank. The Tourist Office has details of class D and E hotels if you are seeking cheaper options. Athens has many private hostels for budget travellers. Standards vary widely.

Hostels cluster in the **Plaka** area, noisy but ideally located for the main sights, or between **Victoria** and the stations (where the tackiest accommodation is found). Some of the cheapest 'hostel' accommodation near the station is extremely overcrowded in high season with tight-budget travellers. However, except in the height of summer you should have plenty of options. The HI hostel, **Athens International Youth Hostel** 16 VICTOROS HUGO, ☎(301) 5234 170, fax (301) 5234 015, is further out than most of the private hostels. **Camping** is not a good idea; campsites are up to an hour from the centre by bus, dirty and poorly serviced, and not dramatically cheaper than hostels.

FOOD AND DRINK

On a tight budget, eat on the move: *giros*, a kind of *souvlaki* (kebab), slices of pork with onions, tomatoes, yoghurt and fries wrapped in flat bread, is a meal in itself and there are lots of other street snacks to choose from. Try *spanakopita* (spinach pie) and *frappé* coffee. **Plaka** restaurants tend to be touristy, but those at PLATEIA FILIK ETERIAS, off KIDATHINEON on the edge of the Plaka, are a little less so. Around EXARCHEIA SQUARE (behind the National Archaeological Museum), there are many *souvlaki* places. For even cheaper eats, go to the **Pankrati** suburb, north of the National Gardens and Stadiou.

HIGHLIGHTS

THE ACROPOLIS Occupied since neolithic times (5000 BC), the 'high city' was Athens's stronghold until it was converted into a religious shrine. What you see today dates from the 5th century BC. It's on a steep hill and can only be reached on foot: smog often limits the otherwise spectacular views.

The Tourist Office has fact sheets on the major sites – highlights are the **Parthenon** the **Temple of Athena**, the great gateway to the Acropolis, and **Propylaea**.

Pericles built the **Parthenon** (Home of the Virgin), between 447 and 432 BC. Designed by Iktinus and Phidias, it is the finest example of Doric architecture still in existence. Close examination of the temple reveals irregularities: columns are closer together at the corners, where light can shine between them; columns are of differing width and bulge one third of the way up; the roof line is curved. But it was designed to be seen from afar, giving an impression of perfect symmetry – one of the finest optical illusions ever devised. Most of the dramatic friezes (known as the **Elgin Marbles** that adorned the Parthenon's exterior are in London's British Museum (and Greece would dearly like them back), although the **Acropolis Museum** to the east of the Parthenon has some fragments.

The **Erechtheum**, north-west of the Parthenon, is most notable for its six caryatids – graceful sculptures of women. Due to the effects of air pollution, the originals have been removed and replaced by the replicas on display today. Four of the originals are on display in the **Acropolis Museum**.

The **Temple of Athena Nike** (Victory), with its eight small columns, stands on the south-west corner of the Acropolis. Built around 420 BC, during a pause in the Peloponnesian War, the temple was once the only place from where you could look out to sea over the defensive walls. It is considered one of the finest Ionic buildings left in Greece.

The bulky **Propylaea**, the great gateway to the Acropolis, takes up most of the western end of the hill and today welcomes thousands of visitors. Arrive early if you want any peace or uninterrupted photo opportunities.

> There is a fantastic view of the Acropolis and all of Attica from the **Monument of Filopapou**, though the site itself is unimpressive and sadly defaced by graffiti.

BEYOND THE ACROPOLIS Most of the city suburbs are anonymous concrete swathes distinguished only by dark green awnings, but in areas close to the Acropolis you can pick out many other ancient ruins. Just below the Acropolis hill, on the south side, are two ancient theatres. Now scant ruins, the **Theatre of Dionysius**, built in the 4th century BC, is the earliest such structure in the Western world. The **Roman Odeon of Herodes Atticus** has been reconstructed and is once again in use.

The remains of the **Temple of Olympian Zeus** are also clearly visible east of the Acropolis. There are only a few surviving columns, but you can still absorb the grandeur of what was the largest temple in Greece. Next to it is **Hadrian's Arch**, constructed by the enthusiastic Roman emperor-builder to mark where the ancient Greek city ended and his new city began.

MUSEUMS AND CHURCHES Entrance to state-run museums is free on Sun. For an incomparable collection of relics from Athens and many other Greek sites, head to the **National Archaeological Museum** (closed during 2003), 44 PATISSION: allow a full day. Exhibits range through Minoan frescos, Mycenaean gold, a collection of over 300,000 coins, sculptures, *kouroi* and much more.

Plenty of other museums offer insights into ancient and modern Greek life. These include the **Museum of Cycladic and Ancient Greek Art**, 4 NEOFITOU DOUKA ST.; the **Benaki Museum**, KOUMPARI ST. and VASILISSIS SOFIAS AV.; and **the Byzantine Museum**, VASILISSIS SOFIAS 22, which houses icons from this later glory of Greek culture. The website www.culture.gr has information on museums in Greece.

From **Lycabettus Hill**, the highest in Athens at 278 m, the view surpasses even that from the Acropolis. There's a little church and café at the summit. Take the **funicular railway** up and the path down for the best round-trip.

SHOPPING

For gold and silver jewellery, ceramics, leather goods and fashion with a Greek slant – lots of linen and cotton in bright colours – try **Pandrossou Flea Market**, between **Monastiraki** and MITROPOLEOS SQ. For antiques, bric-a-brac, army surplus, antique clothing and camping gear, the original flea market on IFESTOU, on the opposite side of MONASTIRAKI, is a better bet. Streets such as ADRIANOU and PANDROSSOU in the **Plaka** quarter have plenty of tourist-oriented shops and stalls, with clothes, leather, pottery and marble on offer. Other crafts include lace making, needlepoint and crochet.

NIGHT-TIME AND EVENTS

The Plaka is where most of the night scene happens. Most **cinemas** show the latest English language movies with original soundtrack and Greek subtitles; see the English-language weekly *Athens News* for listings. See traditional music and dance with the **Dora Stratou Dance Theatre** in the Filopapous Theatre; ☎(01) 9226 141. The **Sound and Light** show on PNYX HILL, ☎(01) 3221 459, is not to be missed. For clubs and bars, head for the Thisseio area: **+SODA**, ERMOU 161, ☎(01) 3456 187 and **Stavlos**, IRAKLEIDON 10, ☎(01) 3452 502 are popular with the young and trendy.

During the **Athens Festival** (June–Sept), events staged in the Odeon of Herodes Atticus and Megazon, as well as Lycabettus Hill Theatre, include **ancient Greek drama** plus **classical music** and **ballet**, performed by Greek and international companies and orchestras. For information, ☎(01) 3221 459.

WHERE NEXT FROM ATHENS?

*Athens is well placed for beginning a trip to the **Kiklades** (Cyclades) archipelago and other islands. For full descriptions consult **Greek Island Hopping** by Frewin Poffley, published annually by Thomas Cook.*

*The other main area to head for is the **Peloponnese** (south-west of Athens; ETT tables 1450, 1455), a largely unspoilt peninsula ringed by railways, and with limestone peaks, sandy bays and a stunning heritage of ancient and medieval sites. **Korinthos** (Corinth) is the first place across the gorge-like Corinthian Canal; Old Corinth (7 km away) features the columns of the 6th-century BC **Temple of Apollo** – a huge central forum flanked by the odd row of crumbling ancient shop buildings, plus the Fountain of Peirene – and the fortress of Akrokorinth on a crag high above the old city. You can continue by train to **Nafplion**, the prettiest town in the Peloponnese, set on a little rocky peninsula beneath a huge Venetian fortress: a great place to stay. From here and Athens excursion buses visit **Epidavros** (Epidauros), site of the most famous of all ancient Greek amphitheatres – its acoustics as perfect as ever. **Mycenae** (Mikines) is the other nearby must-see, the 1600-year-old royal residence of the kingdom of Agamemnon.*

Budapest always was the most westernised of the Warsaw Pact capitals, and with the all of the Iron Curtain it rapidly demolished many of its communist monuments though the Liberation Monument survives and others have been assembled in a Statue Park) and embraced capitalism. It's a place to indulge yourself in spas, Hungarian cuisine and thriving cultural life. The grey-green Danube splits the city into **Buda**, on the west bank, and **Pest** on the east. Buda is the photogenic, hilly old town, with its pastel-coloured baroque residences, gas-lit cobblestone streets and hilltop palace, while Pest is the thriving, mostly 19th-century commercial centre, with the imposing riverside State Parliament building, its wide boulevards and **Vörösmarty tér**, the busy main square. Between Buda and Pest, Margit Bridge gives access to the island of **Margit** (**Margit sziget**), a green oasis and venue for alfresco opera and drama in summer.

ARRIVAL AND DEPARTURE

There are three major stations: **Nyugati pályaudvar** (Western Station), designed in 1877 by the Eiffel firm from Paris (tourist office; accommodation; exchange; left luggage); **Keleti pályaudvar** (Eastern Station; accommodation; exchange; K&H Bank Mon–Sat; left luggage 24 hrs); and **Déli pályaudvar** (Southern Station; electronic information system; post office; accommodation; exchange; left luggage). All three stations are fairly central, close to hotels and on the metro: KELETI and DÉLI on line 2, NYUGATI on line 3, trams 4 and 6. International services and fares, ☎(1) 461 5500; local train information, ☎(1) 461 5400. Rail tickets can also be bought from the MÁV offices, ANDRÁSSY ÚT 35, Mon–Fri 0900–1800 (Oct–Mar: 0900–1700), ☎(1) 322 8082; at **Wasteels**, at Platform 9 in Keleti station (Mon–Fri 0800–1900, Sat 0800–1300, closed Sun); or at **American Express** near VÖRÖSMARTY TÉR at DEÁK FERENC U. 10. (Mon–Fri 0900–1730) and at the stations. A rail-bus minibus service runs between the stations. Pre-booking necessary at the railbus offices in the stations; passes are not valid.

Ferihegy Airport has two terminals. For the centre, there's an extortionate taxi service or the cheap ☐Reptér-busz (every 10–20 mins, 0455–2320), which connects passengers from Terminal 2 with Kőbánya-Kispest, the terminus of the metro line 3 (pre-purchased ticket Ft.100, ticket from the bus driver Ft.120). The airport coach service links both terminals with Erzsebet tér (0530–2100 daily, every 30 mins, Ft.600). Some hotels have collection services. There's also an airport minibus service taking visitors directly to their destination (Ft.1500), ☎(1) 296 8555.

INFORMATION

MONEY Only change currency in official places such as banks (**Erste Bank**, near Western Station, BAJCSY-ZS. ÚT, 74 (ATM), or **OTP Bank**, DEÁK F.U. 5–7 (ATM).

POST AND PHONES The main **post office** is next door to the main telephone office; the post offices near **Nyugati**, TERÉZ KÖRÚT 61, and **Keleti** stations, BAROSS TÉR 11/C, are open daily 0700–2100. The code for Budapest is 1.

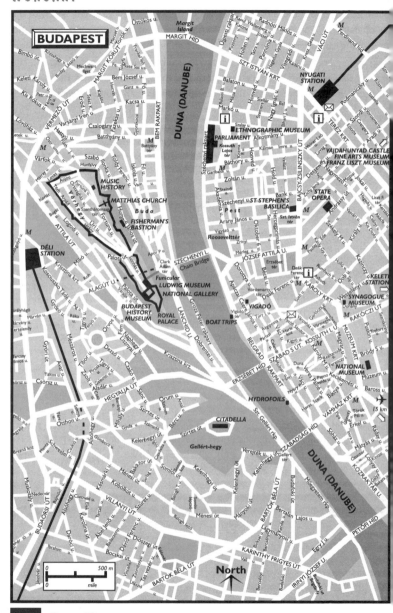

BUDAPEST

TOURS

Legenda, VIGADÓ TÉR, (1) 266 4190 (www.legenda.hu), offer river cruises. Boats leave Budapest (Vigadó tér ship station, (1) 318 1223; 1–3 times daily Apr–Sept) for the charming town of **Szentendre** and follow the Danube bend to **Visegrád** and **Esztergom**. **Mahart Passnave**, (1) 484 4010 (www.mahartpassnave.hu), run trips from the International Boat Station (BELGRÁD RAKPART, (1) 318 1704) and hydrofoils to **Vienna** and **Bratislava** (Pozsony in Hungarian). Book well ahead (at least 3 days).

TOURIST INFORMATION

The nationwide Tourinform tourist bureaux are an excellent source of information. **Tourinform**, VÖRÖSMARTY TÉR (open 24 hrs daily, metro: VÖRÖSMARTY TÉR); branch at SÜTŐ UTCA. 2, (1) 317 9800 (Metro: DEÁK TÉR) are helpful, with multilingual staff (www.hungary-tourism.hu). Their hotline (from abroad) is (+36) 60 55 00 44 or (in Hungary, toll free) 06 80 66 00 44, Tourinform call centre (1) 438 8080 (hungary@tour-inform.hu). **Budapest Tourist Office**: branches at Nyugati rail station, SZENTHÁROMSÁG TÉR and LISZT FERENC TÉR 11; open 0800–2000 Apr–Oct, 0900–1800 winter, (1) 302 8580 (www.budapestinfo.hu). **Ibusz** books accommodation and organises tours, VÖRÖSMARTY TÉR 6; branches at Nyugati and Keleti rail stations. **Program & Hotel Service Office** (1) 317 0532 (www.ibusz.hu).

PUBLIC TRANSPORT

Night lines run 2300–0500 on the most popular routes. There are also 82 km of **cycle lanes**. **Public transport information**, (1) 317 1173 (www.bkv.hu).
Metró: Fast and inexpensive; runs 0430–2310; just **three lines**, all intersecting at DEÁK TÉR. These include M1 (the yellow line), M2 (the red line) and M3 (the blue line). Line M1 was the first continental metro, built in 1896.

Metró tickets are available from kiosks in stations or from machines that require coins. All tickets must be stamped in the machines at the station entrance. A one-ride fare is Ft.100, the ticket (vonaljegy) is valid for all kind of public transport. Transfer for two rides (átszállójegy) Ft.180: validate on both vehicles. Metro-only transfer ticket (metróátszállójegy) Ft.150: validate once only. One-day, three-day and seven-day travel passes, valid for all kinds of public transport, are available (Ft.850, Ft.1700 and Ft.2100), as are packs of ten tickets for the price of nine. For visitors staying longer, consider weekly passes.

Buses, trams and **suburban trains**: For areas not on the metro, the bus, trolleybus and tram system is very useful as it covers the city extensively. A similar method for ticket stamping exists, with machines on board. Ticket inspectors wearing red armbands can fine Ft.1500 on the spot. The suburban network of HÉV trains travel several kilometres out of the city boundary, as well as embracing the ruins of **Aquincum** and the old town of **Óbuda**. Local tickets and passes (but not European rail passes) are valid to the city limit on the HÉV.

Taxis: Abundant at all times. Remember to check that the meter is running, have the address of where you are going written down and negotiate the fare before setting off. It may be easier to use public transport. Taxis are forbidden in the castle area. Reputable firms include: **City Taxi**, (1) 211 1111, **Főtaxi**, toll free: 06 80 222 222 and **Buda Taxi**, (1) 233 3333. From May to Aug, boat services operate from the southern end to the northern end of Budapest, from BORÁROS TÉR to Pünkösdfürdő, Thur–Sun, 0900–1620; local passes not valid. The **Funicular (Sikló)** from the Buda side of the Chain Bridge to Buda Castle Palace runs daily; passes not valid.

The **Budapest card**, available at hotels, tourist offices and main underground stations, allows free travel by public transport, ample discounts in restaurants, bars and shops, airport minibus discounts, and reductions on more than 80 sights throughout Budapest (Ft.3700 for two days, Ft.4500 for three days – cost includes one adult accompanied by a child under 14).

You can explore the Buda Hills around the city on three different forms of transport:
Cogwheel Railway (Fogaskerekű) from Városmajor (two stops from Moszkva tér on trams 18 or 56) to Széchenyi Hill, local tickets, passes are valid. **Chair-lift (Libegő)** from Zugliget (🚌no. 158 from MOSZKVA TÉR) to the lookout on János Hill (Budapest's highest point at 526 m), local tickets, passes not valid, special fare, operates daily except every 2nd Mon. **Children's Railway (Gyermekvasút)**, with children on duty, from Hűvösvölgy (tram 56 from MOSZKVA TÉR) to Széchnyi Hill. The narrow-gauge railway travels at 20 km/h for roughly 11 km through the Buda forests (allow 45 mins). Special pedal-operated vehicles for 2–6 persons (called *bringó–hintó*) are for hire in Margit sziget (Margaret Island) and Városliget (City Park).

ACCOMMODATION

The city offers a wide choice of one- to five-star hotels, pensions and hostels (in summer heat air-conditioned rooms are advisable). **Advance booking** is strongly recommended, particularly in early Aug during the Hungarian Grand Prix. Spa hotels generally offer competitive weekend packages.

Buda Center is basic but has air-conditioning and is ideally located below Castle Hill, CSALOGÁNY U. 23, 📠(1) 207 6333 (holtelbch@euroweb.hu), €€€. **City Panzio Pilvax**, PILVAX KÖZ 1–3, 📠(1) 266 7660, €€, is very centrally located by the river. Basic and centrally located near the Opera-House by the ANDRÁSSY ÚT is **Hotel Medosz**, JÓKAI TÉR 9, 📠(1) 374 3000, €€. The **Caterina** hostel, ANDRÁSSY·ÚT 47, 3rd floor 18, 📠 (1) 342 0804 (caterina@mail.inext.hu), is also right in the centre of town and has an excellent reputation. The **Citadella** hostel, CITADELLA SETANY, 📠(1) 466 5794, is perched on Gellért with wonderful views.

Private rooms are less expensive than hotels. Rooms are usually a few stops away from the centre of town. These, as well as hotel and pension accommodation, are bookable at **Tourinform** and **Ibusz,** or through **Vista**, a Budapest-based travel agency whose helpful staff speak fluent English (📠(1) 267 8603, at PAULAY EDE U. 7), Mon–Fri 0800–2000, Sat 0900–1900, Sun 1000–1900 (www.vista.hu; incoming@vista.hu) and can obtain very reasonable rates. Outside the main offices and at railway stations, you may well find people offering private accommodation; make sure you know the price and location – usually the rooms they offer will be safe and clean, as the Hungarians are excellent hosts. Ibusz can also book apartments. Booking websites include www.hotelshungary.com, www.budapestinfo.hu, www.travelport.hu and www.budapesthotels.com.

Youth hostel and **student accommodation** is plentiful. Hostel organisations advertise widely at the stations and often offer free transport to hostels. **Camping** places at the

ROMAIFÜRDŐ stop of the HÉV and at the ZUGLIGET LIBEGŐ (🚌no. 158 from MOSZKVA TÉR). Camping at unregistered sites is forbidden.

FOOD AND DRINK

Rich, spicy and meat- or fish-based, Hungarian cuisine is delicious. Cold fruit soups make wonderful starters, followed by game, goose, pike, perch, pork, goulash soup or paprika chicken, washed down with sour cherry juice, *pálinka* spirit or **Tokaji aszú** wine. Budapest's elegant coffeehouses offer irresistible cakes, pastries and marzipans. Check local listings and websites (such as www.travelpot.hu) for the latest recommendations. However, you can be sure of finding a lively café, bar or restaurant on or near VÁCI UTCA and ANDRÁSSY ÚT, all of which compare very favourably with Western prices. There are plenty of eateries in the Castle district, too, although this can get a bit more pricey. Finally, ask your hotel staff for their recommendations – they will also make reservations for you.

HIGHLIGHTS

BUDA The Buda hills offer marvellous views of the city and the Danube. To the west lie woods and paths, circumnavigated by a cogwheel railway from **Városmajor** to **Széchenyi** hill. On **Gellért-hegy** (Gellért Hill), surveying the city and the Royal Palace, is the gigantic **Liberation Monument**, which commemorates the Soviet liberation of Budapest (🚌no. 27 from MÓRICZ ZS. KÖRTÉR, VILLÁNYI ÚT to BÚSULÓ JUHÁSZ, and then 400 m walk up). **Várhegy** (Castle Hill) was first built in the 13th century and is the prime historic feature in Budapest; its streets have retained their medieval form. **Budavári Palota** (Buda Palace), a vast neo-baroque edifice, was originally built as part of the fortifications of the city during the Middle Ages and remained a royal residence for 700 years, but was virtually destroyed during World War II and then rebuilt. There are three museums in the palace: **Budapest History Museum**, **Museum of Contemporary History** and **Hungarian National Gallery** (Tues–Sun, free concerts every Tues). Walk up the hill from DÉLI or MOSZKVA metró stations, or catch the **Budavári sikló** funicular (daily) from CLARK ÁDÁM TÉR at the foot of the Chain Bridge or take 🚌Várbusz (bus) from MOSZKVA TÉR (VÁRFOK UTCA) via the Várhegy to the BUDAVÁRI SIKLÓ upper station; or 🚌 no. 16 from DEÁK FERENC TÉR to DÍSZ TÉR. It's possible to visit the **Castle**

SPAS

Budapest boasts ten spas, offering mixed and segregated bathing, endless treatments and often stunning architecture at affordable prices. Just south of Buda Palace, the art nouveau **Gellért** has a much-photographed 'champagne' bath (KELENHEGYI ÚT 2–4), and nearby the **Rudas fürdő (Rudas Baths)** (DÖBRENTEI TÉR.), are an amazing time warp (men only). Further north the **Király fürdő (Király Baths)** (FŐ UTCA 84) were built in the 16th century – their green cupolas are a reminder of the Turkish occupation. For further details ask **Tourinform**, or see the booklet *Budapest Baths* (Hungarian National Tourist Office).

HUNGARY

caverns at the corner of DÁRDA and ORSZÁGHÁZ ÚT. (open daily).

Look out for **Halász bástya** (Fisherman's Bastion), with its seven conical turrets connected by a walkway, built mainly for decoration and presenting a perfect river panorama, and the nearby square (SZENTHÁROMSÁG TÉR), always filled with tourists, street entertainers and market stalls.

The **statue to St Stephen** (Szent István), legendary king of Hungary, is overlooked by the neo-Gothic **Mátyás templom** (Matthias Church), the coronation church of Hungarian kings, and resplendent with its multicoloured roof tiles. The surrounding streets are cobbled, below fine baroque and Gothic buildings and façades. It's worth wandering down TÁNCSICS MIHÁLY UTCA, TÁRNOK UTCA, TÓTH ÁRPÁD SÉTÁNY and ÚRI UTCA to explore.

Do visit the picturesque **Margit Island** (Margit sziget). Vehicles are allowed only as far as the Thermal and Grand hotels: the kilometres of walks along the river are delightful, as are the Japanese garden, open-air theatre, cinema and two 13th-century ruins (trams nos. 4, 6 or 🚌no. 26).

PEST This is the city's busy commercial sector, built in two semicircular avenues with broad tree-lined boulevards radiating from it, and home to the elegant shopping street VÁCI UTCA and the street cafés of VÖRÖSMARTY TÉR, the artists' haunt.

The imposing **Parliament**, KOSSUTH LAJOS TÉR, has a richly ornate interior and was built in

SHOPPING

The main shopping streets are VÁCI UTCA, including **folk art** and **black ceramics** at VÁCI UTCA 14, PETŐFI SÁNDOR UTCA and ANDRÁSSY ÚT. Best buys include Zsolnay and Herend **porcelain** (SZENTH ÁROMSÁG U. 5), **glass**, **antiques**, **wine**, salami and **leather**. Try the **Wine Society**, BATTHYÁNYI U. 59 and the **Hungarian Wine Shop**, RÉGIPOSTA UTCA 7–9. **Markets** abound, some open-air, others flea markets (the best is **Ecseri Piac**, NAGYKŐRÖSI ÚT 156; Mon–Sat. until 1500, 🚌no. 54 from BORÁROS TÉR to FIUME UTCA). The huge **Western City Center** at the left side of the Nyugati (Western) Railway Station is the biggest and most centrally located mall.

One thousand years of Hungarian existence in the Carpathian basin are commemorated by statues of rulers and princes in the **Millenary Monument** in HŐSÖK TERE (Heroes' Square), built in the 19th century. This opens onto leafy **Városliget** (City Park), with its zoo, **Közlekedési Múzeum** (Transport Museum; free for Inter-railers), boating lake-cum-ice rink and the romantic **Vajdahunyad vára** (Vajdahunyad Castle), replicating sites from pre-Trianon Hungary and built around the 1890s. Don't miss ANDRÁSSY ÚT., Budapest's most famous avenue, home of the **Opera House** (metro M1 OPERA or 🚌no. 4). Close by is the **Liszt Museum**, 35 VÖRÖSMARTY UTCA (open Mon–Fri 1000–1800, Sat 0900–1700), where the composer lived. There are also museums to the Hungarian composers Bartók and Kodály.

1904 in Gothic style (highly reminiscent of London's Palace of Westminster), and can be visited by pre-arranged guided tour (book through Tourinform).

NIGHT-TIME AND EVENTS

There is always plenty for all tastes in Budapest. Check monthly listings guides and English-language newspapers such as the *Budapest Sun* (www.budapestsun.com) or *Where Budapest*, a free monthly info guide, for the latest information.

Music has always been popular in Hungary. Opera, recitals and cinema shows can be checked in the *Budapest Sun*. The stunning neo-Renaissance **Opera House**, ANDRÁSSY ÚT. 22, ☎(1) 353 0170 (www.opera.hu), now 115 years old, was the first modern theatre in the world (guided tours daily 1500 and 1600). Operetta, too, has its place, and the less ornate building nearby at NAGYMEZŐ U. 17, ☎(1) 269 3870, is usually packed for patriotic programmes of light music. Organ recitals are often given at **Matthias Church** (Mátyás templom), VÁRHEGY, and at **St Stephen's Basilica** (Szent István Bazilika). The **Academy of Music**, LISZT FERENC TÉR 8, ☎(1) 342 0179, and the **Vigadó Concert Hall**, VIGADÓ TÉR 2, ☎(1) 327-4322 (www.vigado.hu), frequently host classical concerts. Another concert venue is the **Arany Janos Theatre**, a wonderful art nouveau building; there are cheap standing tickets.

Many cinemas show English-language movies. Bars are to be found all over the city; the nightclubs in the red-light area in district VII are only for the extremely broad-minded.

EASY DAY TRIPS FROM BUDAPEST

Don't let the opportunity to explore outside the capital pass you by. Take the slow river boat to **Szentendre** (1 hr 30 mins by boat, 40 mins by HÉV suburban train from BATTHYÁNY TÉR M2 metro station running every 10–30 mins, or 30 mins by the yellow Volánbusz bus from ÁRPÁD HÍD bus station at the ÁRPÁD HÍD M3 metro station, running every 20–60 mins), a touristy but enticing town with exquisite architecture, street cafés and a marzipan museum; or drift up the Danube towards **Esztergom's** massive Catholic basilica, palace ruins and museums (5 hrs by boat, 1 hr 30 mins by train). Halfway between Esztergom and Szentendre in the Danube bend (Dunakanyar) is **Visegrád's** lofty citadel and ruined palace.

Vác is another captivating medium-sized town with a baroque main square; it's less touristy than Szentendre and lies on the other bank of the Danube; you can easily manage both in one day by visiting Szentendre first and then take the hourly bus from Szentendre bus station at the HÉV terminus to VÁCI RÉV, where a ferry takes you to the centre of Vác. Vác has frequent trains to Nyugati until 2230.

Wine lovers should head for **Tokaj's** vineyards and wine cellars (3 hrs by train), home to golden Tokaji wine, known as the 'wine of kings and the king of wines'. If you are pushed for time, check out details of guided tours operated by Tourinform, among other agencies (see p. 561), for organised trips to the Hungarian plains.

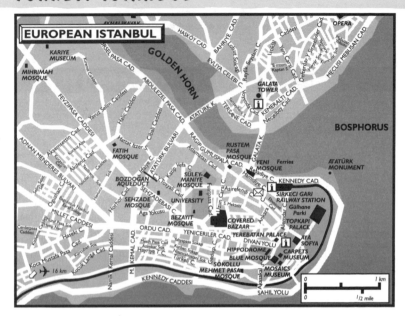

Istanbul is unique in being a city on two continents, with the Bosphorus dividing Europe from Asia, and the European side itself (shown on the map) split by the Golden Horn. Istanbul is a fascinating, complex melting pot in which a multitude of different cultures co-exist.

To the ancient Greeks it was Byzantium. The Emperor Constantine christened it Constantinople, relocating his capital here from Rome in AD 330. Constantinople it remained until renamed by Kemal Atatürk, father of modern Turkey, in 1923. In 1453 it fell to the Ottoman Sultan Mehmet II, and became the glittering, cosmopolitan capital of an even greater empire stretching from the Danube to the Red Sea – the city was as much Greek, Armenian and Balkan as Turkish.

The Asian side is usually called **Anadolu Yakasi**. The European side is itself split by the Golden Horn (Haliç), an estuary off the Bosphorus. Most of the historic tourist sights are in **Sultanahmet**, south of the Golden Horn. Places not to be missed include **Topkapi Palace**, **Aya Sofya museum** and the **Covered Bazaar**; also try to visit one of the mosques (such as the **Suleimaniye** and the **Blue Mosque**) and to take a boat trip on the Bosphorus. Nationals of Australia, Canada, Ireland, the UK and the USA need visas for Turkey; these can be obtained on entry.

TOURIST OFFICES

Main Office: 57 MEŞRUTIYET CAD., BEYOĞLU, ☎ (0212) 243 3731 or 243 2928, fax (0212) 252 4346.
Branches: Atatürk Airport; **Karakoy Maritime Station**; **Hilton Hotel,** CUMHURIYET CAD., HARBIYE; **Sultanahmet Meydani; Taksim Meydani Maksem**; and **Sirkeci Station**.
Tourist police ☎ (0212) 527 4503 or 512 7676.

ARRIVAL AND DEPARTURE

RAIL There are two rail terminals. **Sirkeci Station**, near the waterfront at Eminönü (express tram or 10 mins' walk beside tram line to SULTANAHMET) serves trains to **Europe via Greece or Bulgaria**. The bureau de change in the station will exchange only cash, but there are others immediately outside and automatic cash dispensers in the forecourt. Rail services to **Asian Turkey** and beyond use **Haydarpaşa Station**, across the Bosphorus (by ferry). Note that in **Greek rail timetables**, Istanbul is still referred to (in Greek script) as **Constantinopolis**.

✈ **Atatürk Airport,** ☎ (0212) 663 6400, is in **Yeşilköy**, 15 km west of Istanbul. **Buses** run every hour between Atatürk and the Marmara Hotel in TAKSIM SQ. between 0600 and 2400. The Havaş bus service to the airport departs from TAKSIM SQ. in front of the THY Sales Office at 0600, 0700 and then every half hour until 2230.

INFORMATION

MONEY There are plenty of bureaux de change around. Dövis bureaux have almost exactly the same rates. Banks usually have poor exchange rates. Traveller's cheques are difficult to cash – some banks and post offices accept them but charge commission. Owing to extremely high inflation, exchange rates date rapidly, although prices stay reasonably constant in terms of Western currencies. Automatic cash dispensers are common and convenient.

POST AND PHONES The **main PTT office** is at 25 YENI POSTANE CAD., near Sirkeci Station. However, there are many branches throughout Istanbul which generally have shorter queues, both for postal services and for making telephone calls. You can make **international calls** at all the major PTT offices. Avoid places on the street that allow you to make calls on a unit price basis. **Card phones** are very common (cards available from PTT offices). The **dialling code** for Istanbul is 0212 (European side of the Bosphorus), or 0216 (Asian side of the Bosphorus).

PUBLIC TRANSPORT

Trams: There is one express tram line, running from **Sirkeci station** west along **DIVAN YOLU** and **MILLET CAD.**, out to the **old city walls**. Buy tickets from kiosks by the stops: place them in the metal containers at the entrance to the platforms. Istanbul's oldest trams and tramline, dating from the turn of the century, have been reprieved and refurbished, and run down the 1.2 km length of ISTIKLAL CAD., the Beyoğlu district's fashionable pedestrianised shopping street.

TURKEY

They connect with the *Tünel*, a short, steep, underground railway built in 1875 to connect the hilltop avenue – then the main thoroughfare of the smart European quarter called Pera – with the warehouses and docks of the Golden Horn waterfront.

Buses: Large fleets of buses cover most of Istanbul, but routes can be confusing and there is no bus map, so ask for details at major stops or Tourist Offices. The major departure points are TAKSIM SQUARE, EMINÖNÜ (near the Galata Bridge) and BEYAZIT.

Taxis: The yellow taxis offer a simpler alternative to the buses. Fares are cheap, but ensure that the driver starts the meter when you get in. Fares double between midnight and 0600. The unique *dolmuş* (shared taxis) are minibuses that run on set routes and drop off or pick up passengers anywhere along the way.

Ferries: These run regularly across the Bosphorus, between **Karaköy** on the European side and **Haydarpaşa** and **Kadiköy**; and between **Eminönü** on the European side and **Üsküdar**. Schedules can be confusing and piers chaotic, so ask for details at the Tourist Office, or consult Thomas Cook's *Greek Island Hopping*.

Akbil are magnetic travel counters sold for a small deposit at Eminönü and Taksim. You buy as many units as you wish, which can be used on all forms of public transport. Akbil can be refilled and each unit costs less than a full-price fare.

Bus tickets are sold from kiosks or from street vendors and are surrendered into machines on board.

ACCOMMODATION

Most **budget accommodation** lies in the Sultanahmet district (the area behind Aya Sofya), in the back streets between SULTANAHMET SQUARE and the water and especially in YEREBATAN CAD. **Youth hostel: Yücelt Inter Youth Hostel**, 6 CAFERIYE SOK, ☎ (0212) 513 6150. There is also a collection of similarly priced **private hostels**. Although basic and often crowded, these are cheap and marvellously placed for Istanbul's main sights, only 2 mins' walk to the Blue Mosque. There are often a few people hawking rooms to arriving rail passengers, but they are usually touting for establishments far from the centre. Make sure you know where they are and how to get there before accepting. It is best to ask the Tourist Office.

Most of Istanbul's **top-range hotels** congregate north of the Golden Horn around Taksim and Harbiye, areas of less historical interest, which are a considerable distance from the main sights. There are, however, plenty of hotels south of the Golden Horn, so it is possible to stay in this more atmospheric part of the city without having to slum it, with a particular concentration of hotels of all categories in **Sultanahmet**, from the Four Seasons Hotel (a former prison) and good three-star hotels to youth hostels.

An architecturally beautiful 5-star hotel worth visiting just for a drink beside the Bosphorus is the **Çırağan Palace Hotel Kempinski Istanbul**, ÇIRAĞAN CADDESI, €€€.

A cheaper option in Sultanahmet is **Hotel Antique** (KÜÇÜK AYASOFYA CAD., OĞUL SOK 17, ☎ (0212) 516 49 36 or (0212) 516 09 97, fax (0212) 517 63 70, €€.

On Büyük Ada, an island in the Sea of Marmara some 40 mins away by fast catamaran, is the magnificently ramshackle **Splendid Otel**, in a domed 19th-century wooden building.

There are **campsites** around Istanbul, all a long way from the centre.

FOOD AND DRINK

Istanbul's eating options are as varied and colourful as the city itself. Surprisingly, though, Sultanahmet is a restaurant desert. In the daytime, head for the **Grand Bazaar**, where there are lots of indoor and outdoor cafés, the **Laleli** district around the university or **Istiklal Caddesi** and the streets off it.

Located near two seas, Istanbul is naturally a great place for **seafood,** though it is relatively expensive. It's also a great place for vegetarians, with plenty of meat-free dishes and wonderful fresh fruit. The best place to eat is in **Çiçek Paşaji** (Flower Passage), off pedestrianised ISTIKLAL CAD., where a covered arcade and the alleys around it are packed with restaurant tables. The cheapest places are in the lane behind the arcade, called **Nevizade**.

HIGHLIGHTS

Memorable landmarks surround **Sultanahmet**, where the **Aya Sofya museum** and the **Blue Mosque** sit squarely opposite one another, with the **Topkapi Palace** nearby. These, with many others, create a memorable skyline, best seen from the Bosphorus at dawn, or from the top of the **Galata Tower**, north of the Golden Horn (daily 0900–2000), built in 1348 by the Genoese.

TOPKAPI This is a sightseeing 'must', spectacular both outside and in, with glowing displays of jewels and cloth. If you see nothing else in Istanbul, see the amazing contents of *Topkapi Palace* (closed Tues), seat of the Ottoman Sultans from the 15th to the 19th centuries. The complex, at the tip of the old city peninsula, has now been converted into an all-embracing collection of the Imperial treasures, stretching through three courtyards. Allow at least a half day to take in the cream of the exhibits, which include Islamic armour, imperial robes, jewellery and precious objects, porcelain and miniatures. One of the most fascinating parts of the Topkapi is the extensive **Harem** area, which housed the wives, concubines and children of the sultans, with their attendant eunuchs. You can only visit the harem on scheduled tours. Book as soon as you get to Topkapi.

TURKEY

AYA SOFYA Aya Sofya (closed Mon) was the largest domed structure in the world until St Peter's in Rome was built. Inside, massive marble pillars support a vaulted dome 31 m in diameter and 55 m high, and around the gallery (up the sloped flagstone walkway) are some outstanding mosaics. The interior is an uneasy mixture; the Christian frescos which adorned the dome in Byzantine times were covered and, ironically, preserved by abstract patterns while Aya Sofya was a mosque; the décor that remains is an intriguing harmony of religions.

MOSQUES AND MUSEUMS Undoubtedly the most beautiful of Istanbul's many mosques is the **Suleimaniye**, built between 1550 and 1557 for Sultan Suleiman the Magnificent by his court architect Mimar Sinan. Seen from the banks of the Golden Horn, the complex of domes and spires is the most striking sight in the old city.

Opposite Aya Sofya, the **Blue Mosque** or Sultanahmet Mosque was built in 1609–16, its exterior almost mesmeric with its sequence of nested half-domes. Thousands of turquoise Iznik tiles pick up the gentle washed light that filters in through the windows. The interior is open outside prayer times and contrary to what the many touts and hustlers say you don't have to pay admission, join an expensive tour or to have your shoes looked after (carry your own footwear in).

> All mosques are open daily except during prayer times. Take your shoes off when you enter, and dress modestly. If you're female, cover your shoulders, arms and preferably head (a shawl is useful).

West of the Blue Mosque are the remains of the **Hippodrome,** with three columns dating from the early centuries of the Byzantine era: the 4th-century Column of Constantine, the 6th-century Obelisk of Theodosius, and the bronze Serpentine Column. A few fragments of the Hippodrome wall can be seen nearby. Across from the Hippodrome, the *Ibrahim Paşa Palace* houses the **Museum of Turkish and Islamic Art** (closed Mon), including some priceless ancient Persian carpets.

The **Yeni Mosque** (meaning 'new', although built between 1597 and 1633) is unmissable to those arriving at Eminönü or crossing the *Galata Bridge*. There are a miserly two minarets here.

Some distance west of Sultanahmet, the **old city walls**, now partially restored, stretch across the landward end of the peninsula from the Sea of Marmara to the Golden Horn. Built at the command of the 5th-century Emperor Theodosius, they protected all the land approaches to the ancient city.

DAY TRIPS FROM ISTANBUL
Take a ferry from Sirkeci or Kabataş to the **Princes' Islands,** an archipelago of nine islands, where princes were sent into exile by paranoid Ottoman sultans. **Büyükada** is the largest, and is distinctive as it has outlawed all cars. Transport is by horse carriage. If you want a day on the beach, try **Kilyos** on the European side of the Black Sea coast.

The **Bosphorus strait**, leading north from the Sea of Marmara to the Black Sea, is sprinkled with impressive imperial palaces and pavilions built by a succession of sultans. The best way to see them is by boat; popular excursion trips run up to RUMELI KAVAĞI and ANADOLU KAVAĞI from Eminönü, pier 3. Two boats run each way. The most prominent palace en route – and the one not to miss – is the **Dolmabahçe** (closed Mon, Thur), which has a 600-m water frontage. Built in the 19th century, this served as the final seat of the Ottoman sultans – a compromise between what the sultans thought of as modern European style and their age-old love of lavish adornment. In the enormous reception room, the 4.5 ton chandelier is supported by 56 columns and glitters with 750 bulbs. Atatürk died here in 1938.

NIGHT-TIME AND EVENTS

Istanbul's thriving nightlife is to be found on the north side of the Golden Horn in the side streets off ISTIKLAL, in the **Beyoğlu** area, and in **Ortaköy**, which has a huge number of bars and restaurants, with the benefit of a Bosphorus view. At weekends, the streets are bursting with stalls selling jewellery, books and trinkets. If you prefer to have a leisurely walk, try a **Bosphorus walk** along from **Bebek** to **Rumeli Hisari** or the ancient city walls.

SHOPPING

The most famous of the markets is the **Kapali Carşı** (Covered Bazaar), Beyazıt: go along DIVAN YOLU from SULTANAHMET, with around 5 km of lanes, streets and alleys. Keep moving, because you'll be pressurised to buy if you pause to browse. There are thousands of shops and stalls here, roughly grouped according to merchandise, with whole alleys selling gold, silver, brass or leather. Also seek out the smaller **Spice Market** opposite the Yeni mosque near the Galata Bridge. If you are going to buy anything, bargain: this is a sport in itself.

The **International Music Festival** is in June and July. Its main venues are the Cemal Reşit Rey Hall, Harbiye, and the Atatürk Cultural Center, Taksim.

BRATISLAVA

SLOVAKIA

Budapest

HUNGARY

Sighişoara

ROMANIA Braşov

Bucharest
(Bucureşti)

Snagov

YUGOSLAVIA

Veliko Târnovo

BULGARIA

TURKEY

GREECE **ISTANBUL**

ROUTE DETAIL

Bratislava–Budapest   ETT table 1170

Type	Frequency	Typical journey time
Train	8 daily	2 hrs 40 mins

Budapest–Sighişoara   ETT table 1620

Type	Frequency	Typical journey time
Train	4 per day	10 hrs

Sighişoara–Braşov   ETT table 1630

Type	Frequency	Typical journey time
Train	8 daily	1 hr 40 mins

Braşov–Bucharest   ETT tables 1620, 1630

Type	Frequency	Typical journey time
Train	Every 1–2 hrs	2 hrs 45 mins

Bucharest–Veliko Târnovo   1500, 1525

Type	Frequency	Typical journey time
Train	1 daily	5 hrs 45 mins

Veliko Târnovo–Istanbul   ETT 1525, 1550

Type	Frequency	Typical journey time
Train	1 daily	12 hrs 40 mins

KEY JOURNEYS

Vienna–Budapest   ETT table 1250

Type	Frequency	Typical journey time
Train	7 per day	2 hrs 40 mins

Budapest–Bucharest   ETT table 60

Type	Frequency	Typical journey time
Train	6 per day	13 hrs 30 mins

Budapest–Istanbul   ETT table 61

Type	Frequency	Typical journey time
Train	1 per day	36 hrs 15 mins

This winding route through Slovakia, Hungary, Bulgaria, Romania, easternmost Greece and ending in the western tip of Turkey gives a fascinating insight into parts of Eastern Europe still unfamiliar to most Westerners.

In Romania the route includes the capital, Bucharest, another rapidly changing city, beautiful old towns and stunning mountain scenery, particularly in Transylvania, one of the most colourful and multi-ethnic areas in Europe – the rural land of Dracula (real and legendary), with Bran Castle the must-visit sight near **Braşov**. Sit on the west side of the train (the right side, heading south) for spectacular mountain views between Braşov and the Romanian capital, **Bucharest**, itself a bit blighted by petty crime and dominated by a charmless Communist palace, although it boasts some splendid, if decaying, architecture and a lively social scene. Beyond the Danube, you're into the wine-growing country of Bulgaria. The fortified town of **Veliko Târnovo** is worth leaving the train for; the bus from Gorna Orjahovitza can be more convenient than the through train (🚌nos. 10 and 14 leaving every 20 mins or so).

BRATISLAVA, SLOVAKIA

See p. 542.

BUDAPEST, HUNGARY

See p. 559.

SIGHIŞOARA, ROMANIA

Sighişoara (or Segesvár) is a wonderful Transylvanian town with winding streets, covered stairways and breathtaking architecture, set in spectacular medieval fortifications. It was one of the strongholds of the Saxon community, and also has large populations of Hungarians and gypsies. From the commercial centre, you enter the old town by the 14th-century Clock Tower, now a history museum. Beyond this is an ancient house where Vlad the Impaler (Dracula) was reputedly born about 1431, and to the right, the 15th-century church of the Dominican monastery, PIAŢA MUZEULUI 8, is famous for its bronze baptismal fonts dating back to 1440. At the highest point of the citadel and reached by a roofed wooden stairway is the **Bergkirche** (Church on the Hill), STR. ŞCOLII 7, built in Gothic style 1345–1525, adorned with some remarkable frescos.

km north of the centre. **CFR Agency**, STR. I DECEMBRIE 1918, 2, ☎ (065) 77 18 20.

Tourist Office: STR. I DECEMBRIE 1918, 10.

The basic state hotel, the **Steaua**, STR. I DECEMBRIE 1918, 12, ☎ (065) 77 15 94 or (065) 77 19 31, fax (065) 77 19 32, is the only central one; new private hotels include the **Chic**, STR. LIBERĂŢI 44, ☎ (065) 77 59 01, opposite the station. **Bobby's Youth Hostel**, STR. TACHE IONESCU 18, ☎ (065) 77 22 32, open in the summer holidays only. **Elvis's Villa Hostel**, STR. LIBERTATII ☎ (065) 772546 is 250 m west of station (www.elvisvilla.ro).

BRAŞOV

Baroque buildings dominate much of the beautiful centre of Romania's second city, also in Transylvania, while imposing gates guard the road into the Schei quarter to the south-west. In central PIAŢA SFATULUI (Council Square) stands the Town Hall, now the local History Museum; from its tower trumpeters sounded the warning of impending attack, by Tatars or Turks, for many centuries. Nearby, the Black Church overshadows the same square with its Gothic pinnacles. Dating from the 14th century, this is one of the greatest monuments of Transylvania's Saxon (German) community, and displays historic prints and fine carpets brought by merchants from Turkey. You can get great views of the city and surrounding mountains from the summit of **Mt Tîmpa**, reached by a cable car or by footpaths; the base of the hill is fortified with a wall and bastions.

About 2 km north of the old town. ☐ no. 4 runs from the station to PIAŢA SFATULUI and PIAŢA UNIRII in the old town. **CFR Agency**, STR. REPUBLICII 53, ☎ (068) 14 29 12.

i **Tourist Office**: STR. BALCESCU 12, ☎/fax (068) 41 67 11, can help find accommodation.

Hotels in the centre are expensive, and your best bet is either a private room (from people who meet trains at the station) or through the **EXO office**, STR. POŞTĂ varulu 6, ☎ (068) 14 4. 91. The budget hotel **Aro Sport**, STR. SFÂNTUL IOAN 3, ☎ (068) 41 28 40, a short distance from the main square is an option as is **Elvis's Villa Hostel**, STR. DEMOCRATIEI 2B (near PIAŢA UNIRII), ☎ (091) 844940 (www.elvisvilla.ro), ☐ no. 4 from station to last stop, or a taxi (about $1).

DAY TRIPS FROM BRAŞOV The ski resorts of **Sinaia** and **Predeal** lie on the main rail line from Bucharest to Braşov, and most trains call here, making it easy for you to break your journey (ETT tables 1620, 1630). One of the best hotels in Romania, although hardly expensive, is the **Palace**, STR. OCTAVIAN GOGA 4–11, SINAIA, ☎ (044) 31 30 51; there are plenty of other places to stay. **Bran Castle** has been associated by the tourist industry with **Count Dracula** and is visited by every coach tour to the area. Although there's no factual connection with Vlad the Impaler, the castle looks the part, bristling with medievalism (though it's largely renewed inside). It's 26 km from **Braşov**, with regular buses from **Livada Postei**, as well as tours laid on by the Tourist Office. There is a wealth of excellent **private accommodation** in Bran, easily found once you're there.

BUCHAREST (BUCUREŞTI)

Bucharest was once known as 'The Paris of Eastern Europe', for its decadent lifestyle and for the elegant mansions lining its 19th-century boulevards. However, the city has been vandalised over the years, above all by communist planners, perversely for many people and the city's main sight is the so-called **Ceauşescu's Palace**, now officially known as the Palace of Parliament, a huge edifice whose construction required the demolition of a quarter of the city's historic centre. B-DUL UNIRII, lined with fountains and trees, leads from PIAŢA UNIRII (hub of the Metro system), which offers the

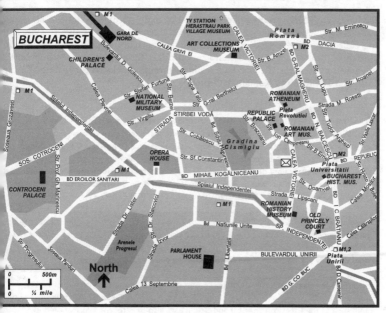

major vista of the Palace. Tours of the interior start from the south door; these pass through a succession of grandiose public halls with chandeliers, marble and mirrors. Its construction costs almost bankrupted the country. Most other sights are along CALEA VICTORIEI, the historic north–south axis, which is also lined with the smartest shopping street. Near its mid-point is PIAŢA REVOLUŢIEI, scene of the most dramatic events of Ceauşescu's overthrow during Christmas 1989; here the newly refurbished Atheneum concert hall faces the former Royal Palace, now the **National Art Gallery** (which may be closed for restoration). To the south along CALEA VICTORIEI, is the **National History Museum**, which houses Romania's finest archaeological collection and National Treasury. To the north of PIAŢA REVOLUŢIEI are the **Museum of Ceramics and Glass**, the **Museum of Arts Collections** and the **George Enescu Museum of Music**, all in former palaces.

The **History Museum of Bucharest**, housed in the 19th-century Sutu Palace on PIAŢA UNIVERSITAP II, forges some links with the legend of Dracula, in fact the local prince **Vlad Tepeş** (Vlad the Impaler). Protests against the hijacking of the 1989 revolution by the functionaries of the communist regime were centred on PIAŢA UNIVERSITAP II. You can still see political graffiti here, as well as memorials to those killed.

To the west of the city in a pleasant leafy suburb is **Cotroceni Palace**, home of the president of Romania. There is a medieval art collection here.

Bucharest has a large number of pleasant parks: to the north in the largest, Herăstrău Park, is the open-air **Village Museum**, OS. KISSELEFF 28–30, open daily. This fascinating collection of re-erected buildings brought from all over the country includes churches, houses, watermills and windmills. Elsewhere, the quintessential Bucharest experience is to be had walking through backstreets, visiting the tiny 15th- and 16th-century Romanian Orthodox churches.

Virtually all trains use the **Gara de Nord**, northwest of the city centre on CALEA GRIVIȚEI (952 for **general information**). This is chaotic and crowded, and it's teeming with pickpockets. It is served by the **Metro (Metrou)**, although you'll have to change trains to reach the city centre. Other stations are mostly for local or seasonal trains. The **Gara de Nord** currently has the only computerised ticket office in Romania, allowing you to join any queue and buy any ticket virtually until departure time. **Tickets and reservations** can also be purchased from one to ten days in advance at **Agenția de Voiaj CFR** (in Bucharest at: 10–14 DOMNIȚA ANASTASIA ST, (01) 313 26 42; and CALEA GRIVIȚEI 139, (01) 650 72 47).

Otopeni, (01) 230 00 22, 18 km north of the centre, handles almost all international flights. There is a good **bus service** (no. 783) to the city centre (PIAȚA UNIRII) every 15 mins (30 mins at weekends), costing about US$1. Try to agree a fare of US$10 (paid only in lei) – you should certainly pay no more than US$15 from the centre to Otopeni airport.

i **Romanian Tourist Promotion Office**, 17 APOLODOR ST, BUCHAREST 5, (01) 410 0491, fax (1) 410 05 79 (www.romaniatravel.com). There's a branch at **Otopeni Airport**, and major hotels, such as the **Intercontinental** and **București**, also have tourist information desks. ONT-Carpați can arrange tours and car hire, book hotels and private rooms, exchange money and supply maps.

Money: Always change your money at official exchange offices or banks and keep the **receipts**, as the more expensive hotels may require proof of legitimate exchange.

Post and phones: The main telephone and post office, CALEA VICTORIEI 37 (open Mon–Fri 0800–2000, Sat 0800–1400, closed Sun), is around the corner from the poste restante office at STR. MATEI MILLO 10 (open daily 0730–1930).

The **Metro** (0500–2330) is efficient and fast, linking central Bucharest to the **Gara de Nord** and the **suburbs**. There are three main lines and most city maps carry a metro plan. **Magnetic tickets** (for a minimum of two trips) must be bought as you enter a station and passed through a turnstile; there are also better-value 10-trip and day-tickets.
Buses, trams and **trolley-buses** run throughout the city, although it can be hard to work out their routes, as maps are rare. They are rundown and crowded, but very cheap. Buy any number of tickets before boarding from the **grey aluminium kiosks** by most stops. **Express buses**, including those to the airports, require special magnetic tickets.

Taxis are plentiful and inexpensive by Western standards. State-run cabs should have and use meters, but this is unlikely with the private ones; **agree on a price** before travelling. These cars may also be old and in poor condition. Taxi companies with English-speaking operators: Alfa

Taxi, ☎(01) 948 or Meridian Taxi, ☎(01) 944. Have a **street map** to hand and show the driver exactly where you want to go.

Accommodation: ONT (the tourist office) can arrange both hotel and private rooms, for a hefty commission or try www.bucharest-travel-guide.com for details of hotels and apartments in Bucharest (€€–€€€). Private rooms usually come with breakfast, but check first. Expect to pay US$15 (in dollars) a night for a double. Some hosts will also offer an evening meal, for about US$5. You may be offered a room by a tout at the Gara de Nord, but you should be very careful, as these will often be in outlying suburbs and of a very poor standard. Hot water may only be available morning and evening, or less frequently, and even cold water may be cut off at times. Another possibility that can be good value is to rent an apartment (€–€€€) on a nightly basis – try **B&D Apartments**, ☎(01) 320 09 55 (www.rotravel.com) – rates are usually set in US$.

Hotels are more central and have fewer problems with water supply, and those around the Gara de Nord are barely more expensive than those in the rest of the country; this is, however, a rough guide. The cheapest of these is the **Bucegi**, STR WITING 2, ☎(01) 637 52 25, fax (01) 637 51 15, €, followed by the **Cerna**, STR DINICU GOLESCU 29, ☎(01) 637 40 87, fax (01) 311 07 21, €; the best in the area is the **Astoria**, STR DINICU GOLESCU 27, ☎(01) 637 76 40, fax (01) 638 26 90, €€. Nearer the city centre, the best hotels in the budget price range are the **Muntenia**, STR ACADEMIEI 21–22, ☎(01) 314 60 10 or (01) 314 17 82, €, while the **Hanul lui Manuc**, STR IULIU MANIU 62–64, ☎(01) 313 14 11, fax (01) 312 28 11, €€, is less expensive than it looks (singles US$45, doubles US$52) and is a most attractive former caravanserai. Another cheaper option is **Căminul Mihail Kogălniceanu**, STR KOGĂLNICEANU 64, ☎(01) 310 42 70, fax (01) 313 17 40, €. **Elvis' Villa Hostel**, 5 AVRAM LANCU, ☎(01) 315 5273 (www.elvisvilla.ro), near PIATA PROTOPOPESCU, has all mod cons, 24-hr reception (🚌no. 85 from rail station to Calea Moilor).

There are no convenient campsites near Bucharest; student hostels can be used during the summer holidays; the most convenient is at the N. Balescu Agronomic Institute on BLVD MĂRĂȘTI (🚌no. 105 from the Gara de Nord, or tram nos. 41/42 from the centre). There's also a **youth hostel, Villa Helga**, at STR. SALCÂMILOR 2, ☎(01) 610 22 14 (helga@rotravel.com; 🚌no. 785 east from STR. ȘTEFAN FURTUNȘĂ, near the Gara de Nord, tram nos. 5/16 from the centre). **YMCA Hostel**, STR SIVESTRU 23, ☎/fax (01) 210 09 09.

You can afford to eat well in Bucharest, or opt for pizzas/hamburgers, or patisseries/cafés. **Panipat** is a chain of good if pricey takeaway bunshops (pizza and pastry), found in six locations in the city, the one at B-DUL MAGHERU 24 is open 24 hrs. The area around PIATA UNIVERSITĂTII has several cafés frequented by students and young people.

NIGHTLIFE English-language newspapers and magazines, distributed free in the better hotels, list what's on. Discos include **Vox Maris International**, CALEA VICTORIEI 155; and **Why Not?** STR. TURTURELELOR 11. Bars such as **Sydney Bar & Grill**, CALEA VICTOREI 224 and **The Dubliner**, B-DUL N. TITULESCU 18 are also very popular. There are no language difficulties at classical music concerts or the **Opera Română**, B-DUL KOGĂLNICEANU 70–72 (Metro: EROILOR). Many films are shown in English, for example at the **Cinematheca Română**, STR. EFORIE 2; there's live jazz in the bar here at weekends, and also at the **Green Hours 22 Club Jazz Café**, CALEA VICTORIEI 120.

Side Trip to Snagov Only 40 km from Bucharest lies the Snagov forest and lake. **Snagov** is the playground of Bucharest. Imposing villas surround the attractive lake, and on an island is a 15th-century monastery where Prince Vlad the Impaler (the original Dracula) is probably buried. There is only one train a day, but buses and tours operate at other times. The Romanian Railways-owned Complex CFR Snagov Sat, ☎(0179) 40460, has a restaurant, rooms and camping space directly on the lake, where you can also go swimming.

WHERE NEXT FROM BUCHAREST?

About 225 km east of Bucharest, (2 hrs 30 mins by train, ETT table 1680; book ahead in summer), **Constanţa** *on the Black Sea coast is a long-standing port dating from the 6th century BC (an excellent collection of Roman statues and mosaics, plus a display on the exiled poet Ovid in its archaeology museum), with a pleasant waterfront graced by 19th-century buildings, an aquarium and dolphinarium, an elegant promenade and a rococo-style casino. There is ready access to sandy beaches and a choice of resorts. Costinesti and Neptun are the favoured beaches for young Romanians, and these have the liveliest discos and nightlife as does the Tomis Boulevard.*

VELIKO TÂRNOVO, BULGARIA

Former capital 1185–1396, this spectacularly situated town perches on steep hills separated by the River Yantra. **Tsarevats Hill** (sometimes floodlit at night) has the restored ruins of the medieval citadel. Nearby are Byzantine churches and the **Samovodska Charshiya** (Bazaar), a photogenic area of restored workshops interspersed with modern jewellers, souvenir shops and cafés.

Neither the bus nor the rail station is central. 🚌nos. 4/13 run from the train station to the centre. Trolleybuses 1/21 and 🚌no. 12 go from the bus terminal to the centre. Trains from Sofia to Varna stop at Gorna Oriahovitsa just to the north of Veliko Târnovo (eight local trains per day connect to the town), or take the shuttle bus to Gorna Oriahovitsa bus station from which 🚌nos. 10/14 go into town every 15 mins.

Often booked up as the town is popular with Bulgarians. Possibilities include **Hotel Etur**, UL. Ivailo 2, ☎62 18 38, €, or **Hotel Trapezitsa**, St. Stambolov St 79, ☎62 20 61, €.

ISTANBUL, TURKEY

See p. 566.

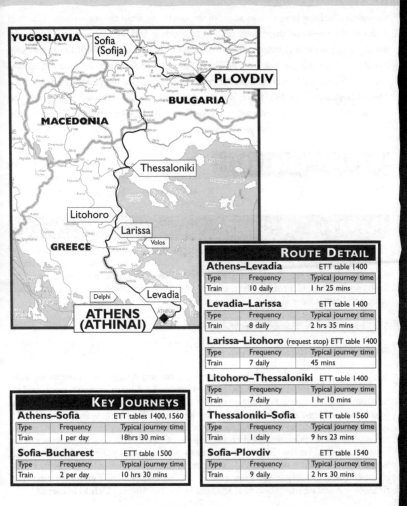

ROUTE DETAIL		
Athens–Levadia		ETT table 1400
Type	Frequency	Typical journey time
Train	10 daily	1 hr 25 mins
Levadia–Larissa		ETT table 1400
Type	Frequency	Typical journey time
Train	8 daily	2 hrs 35 mins
Larissa–Litohoro (request stop)		ETT table 1400
Type	Frequency	Typical journey time
Train	7 daily	45 mins
Litohoro–Thessaloniki		ETT table 1400
Type	Frequency	Typical journey time
Train	7 daily	1 hr 10 mins
Thessaloniki–Sofia		ETT table 1560
Type	Frequency	Typical journey time
Train	1 daily	9 hrs 23 mins
Sofia–Plovdiv		ETT table 1540
Type	Frequency	Typical journey time
Train	9 daily	2 hrs 30 mins

KEY JOURNEYS		
Athens–Sofia		ETT tables 1400, 1560
Type	Frequency	Typical journey time
Train	1 per day	18hrs 30 mins
Sofia–Bucharest		ETT table 1500
Type	Frequency	Typical journey time
Train	2 per day	10 hrs 30 mins

It's worth allocating time to take some of the diversions from the main route. North of **Athens**, the towns on the railway tend to be modern and unprepossessing, but nearby are some of the most wonderful ancient sites in Greece, including **Delphi**, near **Levadia** (itself a town in the cornfields of the Thessalian plain) and the extraordinary **Meteora** monasteries perched on crags beneath mountains a couple of hours away from **Larissa**. Near **Litohoro** rises **Mt Olympus**, marking the border between **Thessaly** and **Macedonia**, and its lofty summit, a demanding two-day hike. Beyond **Thessaloniki** (worth a stop for its archaeological museum), the route enters Bulgaria, passing through its fast-changing capital, **Sofia**, and ending at

ATHENS (ATHINAI)

See p. 553.

Plovdiv, its more appealing second city. From **Plovdiv**, you can head east to join the **Bratislava–Istanbul** route (p. 572).

LEVADIA

Overlooked by a 14th-century sandstone castle tower, the modern town is a common stopping point for travellers en route to Delphi, 56 km west. In ancient times those heading to the Oracle at Delphi could stop at Levadia's Oracle of Zeus Trofonios on top of **Profitis Ilias**, one of the two hills overlooking the town, on which the **castle** now stands.

RAIL 3 km from the centre, but **taxis** are available.

i **Tourist Police:** ☎(0261) 28 551.

SIDE TRIP TO DELPHI **Delphi** (buses from Levadia and Athens) is synonymous with its Oracle, the greatest spiritual power in ancient Greece, said to be situated over the centre of the world. This belief was aided by leaking volcanic gases which induced lightheadedness and trance-like stupors. People came from far and wide to seek wisdom; prophecies were given so ambiguously that they could never be proved wrong. The most dramatic aspect of the **Temple of Apollo** (the Oracle), however, is its location, perched on the cliffs of **Mt Parnassus** and reached by the paved, zigzagging **Sacred Way**. Delphi is one of the largest remaining ancient sites in Greece, with a host of other ruins, notably a **Stadium** and an **Amphitheatre**. The famous bronze of a charioteer is among many beautiful artefacts in the outstanding **Delphi Museum**.

Thousands of visitors make for Delphi, so come early (or out of season). **Accommodation** is a problem: in high season hotels and pensions are often full, while many of them are closed off season. The **Stadion Hotel**, ☎(0265) 82 251, €€€, just up from the Tourist Office, has great views. **Tourist office**: PAVLOU ST, ☎(0265) 82 900.

LARISSA

Larissa is the starting point for some outstanding day trips.

1 km from the centre of the town.

Tourist office: EOT, 18 KOUMOUNDOUROU ST, ☎(041) 534 369. **Police:** 86 PAPANASTASIOU ST, ☎(041) 623 158.

DAY TRIPS FROM LARISSA **Volos**: Apart from the waterfront **Archaeological Museum** there's little of note in this ugly industrial port (where Jason set sail in the Argo in search of the Golden Fleece), but it's the main base from which to explore the lush forests and charming old villages of the mountainous **Pilion peninsula** to the east (best done by hired car, or take either of two bus routes from Volos); or you can take a ferry to the **Sporades islands** (of which **Skiathos** is the most beautiful and most touristy). **Trains** run from Larissa to Volos every 1–2 hrs, taking about 1 hr (ETT table 1405). **Bus station info**, ☎(0421) 25 527. **EOT Office**: PLATIA RIGA FEREOU, ☎(0421) 36 233, fax (0421) 24 750. **Tourist Police**: 217 ODOS ALEXANDRAS, ☎(0421) 39 036.

Kalambaka and the **Meteora monasteries**: The major tourist attraction in northern Greece, **Meteora**, is reached by **bus** from Kalambáka, to which there are five **trains** a day from Larissa; a change may be necessary at **Paleofarsalos** (ETT table 1408). The journey takes about 1 hr 50 mins. Paleofarsalos is on the main rail route between **Athens** and **Salonika**, if you want to visit Meteora without going to Larissa.

LITOHORO

Litohoro is the access point for **Mt Olympus** (2917 m), home of the ancient gods: it actually has nine peaks. You don't need any special equipment (other than suitable footwear) for the full ascent, but it does demand real fitness and takes two days – and treat it with respect, as more people die here than on any other Greek mountain. Book a bunk in one of the mountain refuge dormitories (hot meals and drinks available) through the EOS office. Getting to the top involves taking a taxi or hitching a lift to the car park 6 km from Litohoro, at the 1000 m level; then hiking through wooded ravines to the refuge at around 2000 m. It is best to spend the night here before making the demanding trek to the tops. The final 100 m traverse to **Mitikas**, the highest peak, requires strong nerves.

Near the coast, 5 km east of town. Buses link the station to town.

Tourist Office: ODOS AG. NICOLAOU 15, ☎(0352) 84 700 or (0352) 81 111 (in the Town Hall).

Papanikolau Pension, NIKOLAU EPISKOPOU KITROUS 1, ☎(0352) 81 236, €€, has cosy furnished studios for 2–3 people.

DAY TRIP FROM LITOHORO **Dion**: This is a comparatively uncrowded archaeological site, not as spectacular as the likes of Delphi but still impressive. There are several **buses** daily from Litohoro village and station to Dion village, 8 km north of Litohoro and 2 km west of the site. Highlights are the **marble** and **mosaic floors**, the **Sanctuary of Isis**, the extensive **public bath complex**, and a length of the **paved road** which led to Olympus. The **museum**, in the centre of the village, has a fine collection of finds from the site.

THESSALONIKI (SALONIKA)

The second largest city in Greece was founded in 315 BC; many of the interesting sights are within 10–15 mins' walk of the Tourist Office. The old town was destroyed by fire in 1917 and suffered a severe earthquake in 1978. Thessaloniki today is a modern, busy city, laid out along a crescent bay – yet it's a worthwhile place to stop over, with some elegant corners and a lively night scene. A good area to eat and go out at night is **Ladadika**.

> Buses cover the city comprehensively. Buy bus tickets from the conductor, who sits at the rear, or from a kiosk.

Thessaloniki (Salonika) became strategically vital to the romans, straddling the Via Egnatia, their highway between Constantinople and the Adriatic, and later to the Byzantines and their Turkish conquerors. It was one of the greatest cities of the Ottoman Empire, rejoining Greece only in 1913.

A **Museum of Byzantine Art and History** is housed in the White Tower, the most prominent surviving bastion of the Byzantine-Turkish city walls. Opposite, the **Archaeological Museum** – the **city's top sight** – houses archaeological treasures from different parts of Macedonia. The **Folklore Museum**, VASSILISSIS OLGAS 68, has a fine series of exhibits on the vanished folkways of northern Greece. The city's Roman heritage includes remains of the **Forum**, ODOS FILIPOU, the **Palace of Galerius**, PLATIA NAVARINOU, the **Baths**, next to **Agios Dimitrios church**, and the **Arch of Galerius**, beside ODOS EGNATIA, near PLATIA SINTRIVANIOU. The city also has a fine collection of Byzantine churches the most notable of which are **Agios Georgios** and the restored 4th-century **Agios Dimitrios rotunda**.

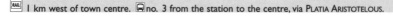

I km west of town centre. no. 3 from the station to the centre, via PLATIA ARISTOTELOUS.

i **Tourist Office**, 34 MITROPOLEOS ST, (031) 271 888 or 222 935, fax (031) 265 504.
Information desk at the station. **Tourist Police**: ODOS DODEKANISSOU, near PLATIA DIMOKRATIAS, (031) 554 871.
Main post office: 26 ARISTOTELOUS ST. **Phone office**: 27 KAROLOU ST (ERMOU ST).

Accommodation: The cheaper D and E class hotels mostly cluster along EGNATIA ST. – the continuation of MONASTIRIOU ST, east of the station. There's a fairly central **youth hostel**: 44 AL. SVOLOU ST, (031) 225 946.

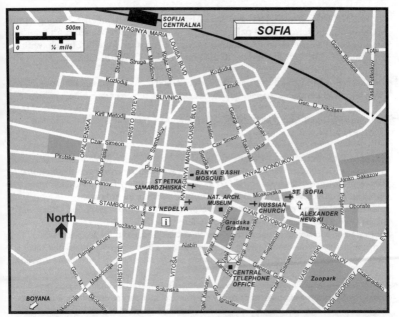

When Bulgaria was liberated from the Turks in 1878, Sofia became its capital, and imposing public buildings, squares and parks were created. Though Sofia is one of the oldest cities in Europe, it is still one of its least known capitals. Traces of Thracians, Romans, Byzantines, Slavs and Ottoman Turks can all be seen here. The city takes its name from the newly restored 6th-century basilica of St Sofia, which stands in a central square. The main sights are all in a comparatively small area, easily covered on foot. Sofia nowadays is a lively, changing city with many new cafés, bars, restaurants and small family-run hotels. Its excellent museums, art galleries and concerts, and the proximity of **Mt Vitosha** (about 30 mins from the centre by public transport) deserve a visit.

The **Alexander Nevski Memorial Church**, with its neo-Byzantine golden domes dominating the skyline, is the most photographed image of Sofia: don't miss the superb collection of Bulgarian icons in its crypt. Nearby, the tiny **Russian Church** is an exuberant, vividly decorated gem, its gold domes contrasting with its emerald-green spires. The 4th-century **St George's Rotunda** lies hidden in a courtyard behind the Sheraton Hotel.

If you only have time for one museum, visit the **National History Museum** (fixed route taxi 21 from the National Palace of Culture), which has the fabulous Thracian gold treasures. Nearby **Boyana Church**, with its sophisticated 13th-century frescoes, is on UNESCO's World Heritage list. Also worth a visit are the **Ethnographic Museum** (in the former royal palace) and the **Archaeological Museum** (in the 15th-century Great Mosque). In the foothills of Mount Vitosha, **Boyana Church**, with its sophisticated 13th-century frescos, is also on UNESCO's World Heritage list.

Central rail station, MARIA LUISA BLVD, 1.5 km north of the centre. **Buses, taxis, tourist information, currency exchange**. Be extra cautious here, as petty crime is not uncommon.

Sofia International, ☎(02) 88 44 33, is 11 km from the centre. **All flight information** ☎(02) 937 22 11.

i **National Information and Advertising Centre**, 1 SV. SOFIA ST., ☎(02) 987 97 78, is a useful first stop for information. **Tickets** are sold by the **Travel Centre**, underneath the **National Palace of Culture**, 1 BULGARIA SQ., ☎(02) 59 01 36. Expect to pay for printed information.
Post and phones: **Central Post Office**: 6 GURKO ST, opposite the **Rila** agency.
International phone calls can be dialled directly from the **Central Telephone Office** on STEFAN KARADZA ST, diagonally behind the post office.
Money: Some bureaux de change open 24 hrs on VITOSHA BLVD, and there are plenty of exchange facilities in the central station. Bureaux may give a better deal than banks (but check rates/commission). ATMs available. Changing money on the street is risky and should be avoided.

Central Sofia is fairly compact and most areas of interest can be reached on foot. Good network of **trams, trolleybuses** and **buses**; stops display the routes of each service using them. Buy **tickets** (single trip) from drivers, kiosks or street vendors near stops. A **one-day pass** is good value if you are planning more than three rides, but tickets are extremely cheap anyway. **Trams** (nos.1/7) run from the station along KNYAGINYA MARIA LOUISA BLVD and VITOSHA BLVD through the town centre.

Various agencies offer accommodation booking, information and exchange facilities.
Balkantours, 27 AL. STAMBOLIISKI BLVD, can book private rooms. For information on hiking and a variety of activity holidays, as well as reservations for private hotels and village houses, contact the specialist agency **Odysseia-In**, 20-V STAMBOLIISKI BLVD, ☎(02) 989 0538, fax (02) 980 3200.
Private rooms are good value (£10–£15 per person in a twin-bedded room), as are the many small **family-run hotels** in the foothills of **Mount Vitosha** at **Simeonovo** and **Dragalevtsi**.

TO Sofia's restaurants have increased in number and quality, but prices (for foreign visitors) remain low.

WHERE NEXT FROM SOFIA?

Join the Bratislava–Istanbul route by taking the train east to Tulovo (ETT table 1520).

Side streets off VITOSHA BLVD, particularly to the east, have a mixture of western fast-food outlets and **Bulgarian, Italian, Chinese** and **Indian** restaurants. In the foothills of **Mount Vitosha** are several traditional style **taverns** serving **local specialities**. Some of the more popular restaurants need to be booked ahead. **Street kiosks** have excellent coffee, very cheap fast food, sandwiches, cakes, pastries, nuts and seasonal offerings like corn on the cob.

Recommended places for **nightlife** include **Chervilo**, TSAR OSVOBODITEL BLVD; **La Corazon**, GRAF IGNATIEV; and **Mr Punch**, ST KARADJA/RAKOVSKI BLVD.

PLOVDIV

Plovdiv (Philippopolis to the Macedonians and Trimontsium to the Romans) was described by Lucian in the 2nd century AD as 'the largest and most beautiful of all cities in Thrace'. The unification of Bulgaria was announced here in 1885: Sofia became capital of the unified state and Plovdiv's influence slowly declined. As Bulgaria's second city, Plovdiv has uninspiring suburbs of industrial buildings and tower blocks, but the characterful **Old Town** is a different world, with coarsely cobbled streets full of National Revival period houses and dotted with Roman remains: it has a charm that Sofia lacks.

Buses and trolleybuses run throughout Plovdiv, but much of the hilly **Old Town** is only accessible on foot. It's a 10–15 min-walk north-east along tree-lined IVAN VAZOV ST, diagonally across from the station, to the central square. Here you will find **Hotel Trimontsium** and the main **post office** and telephone building. TSAR BORIS III OBEDINITEL ST, the pedestrianised main street, leads north towards the Old Town.

ETHNOGRAPHIC MUSEUM
Don't miss the Ethnographic Museum, Argit Koyumdjioglu House, with its wonderful wooden ceilings and interior; it also has interesting local history exhibits.

Archaeological finds date Plovdiv to around 4000 BC, and the city was occupied by Thracians and Macedonians before the Romans took over in 72 BC. Remains of Trimontsium, the city of the three hills, include the partially restored 2nd-century marble **Roman Theatre**, one of Bulgaria's most notable archaeological sites. The remains of the **Roman Forum**, including marble floors, can be seen in the central square near Hotel Trimontsium.

The city's most important contribution to recent Bulgarian culture is the National Revival period house. This refers not to a single house, but to many, scattered around the Old Town: The **Balabanov House** now hosts recitals and exhibits works by contemporary Bulgarian painters.

About 1 km south-west of the centre on HRISTO BOTEV BLVD. Exchange facilities. The city's two **bus stations** are immediately to the east.

Puldin Tours, 106 BULGARIA BLVD, ☎ (032) 95 28 07, provide **tourist information**. **Hotel Trimontsium**, 2 KAPITAN RAICHO ST, ☎ (032) 62 41 86, in the central square, is helpful with **tourist information** and sells reasonable **city maps**.

Puldin Tours (see *i* above) arrange **private rooms**. Other commercial **accommodation agencies** operate along TZAR BORIS III OBEDINITEL ST. Plovdiv has six major hotels, but even the cheaper ones cost more than a private room. You may also find locals offering **private accommodation**.

WHERE NEXT FROM PLOVDIV?

Join the **Bratislava–Istanbul** route by taking the train east to **Tulovo** (ETT table 1525).

AUSTRIA

CAPITAL	Vienna (Wien).
CLIMATE	Moderate Continental climate. Warm summer; high winter snowfall.
CURRENCY	**Euro (€).** I Euro = 100 cents. £1 = €1.59; $1 = €1.12.
CUSTOMS ALLOWANCES	Standard EU regulations apply (see pp. 19–20).
EMBASSIES AND CONSULATES IN VIENNA	**Aus**: MATTIELLISTR. 2–4, ☎ (01) 512 85 80. **Ire**: HILTON CENTER, LANDSTR./ HAUPTSTR. 2, ☎ (01) 715 4246. **SA**: SANDG. 33, ☎ (01) 320 64 93. **UK**: JAURÉSG. 12, ☎ (01) 716 13-0. **USA**: BOLTZMANNG. 16, ☎ (01) 313 39-0.
EMBASSIES AND CONSULATES OVERSEAS	**Aus**: 12 TALBOT ST, FORREST, ACT 2603, CANBERRA ☎ (06) 295 1533. **Can**: 445 WILBROD ST, OTTAWA, ONTARIO KIN 6M7, ☎ (613) 789 1444. **Ire**: 15 AILESBURY COURT APTS, 93 AILESBURY RD, DUBLIN 4, ☎ (01) 269 4577. **SA**: 1109 DUNCAN ST, PRETORIA 0002 (Postal address: PO BOX 851, PRETORIA 0001), ☎ (012) 46 2483. **UK**: 18 BELGRAVE MEWS WEST, LONDON SW1X 8HU, ☎ (020) 7235 3731. **USA**: 3524 INTERNATIONAL COURT N.W., WASHINGTON DC 20008, ☎ (202) 895 6775.
LANGUAGE	**German**; English is widely spoken in tourist areas.
OPENING HOURS	**Banks**: mostly Mon, Tues, Wed, Fri 0800–1230 and 1330–1500, Thur 0800–1230 and 1330–1730. **Shops**: Mon–Fri 0800–1830 (some closing for a 1- or 2-hr lunch), Sat 0800–1200/1300 (in larger towns often until 1700 on Sat). **Museums**: check locally.
POST OFFICES	Indicated by golden horn symbol; all handle poste restante (postlagernde Briefe). Open mostly Mon–Fri 0800–1200 and 1400–1800. Main and station post offices in larger cities open 24 hrs. Stamps (Briefmarke) also sold at Tabak/Trafik shops.
PUBLIC HOLIDAYS	1, 6 Jan; Easter Mon; 1 May; Ascension Day; Whit Mon; Corpus Christi; 15 Aug; 26 Oct; 1 Nov; 8, 25, 26 Dec.
PUBLIC TRANSPORT	Long-distance: bus system run by Bundesbus; usually based at rail stations/post offices. City transport: tickets cheaper from Tabak/Trafik booths; taxis: metered; extra charges for luggage (fixed charges in smaller towns).
RAIL PASSES	IR, ED, Eu, EP, European East valid (pp. 26–31). Visitor Card: unlimited travel on local transport, discounted museum entry; Vienna (€16.90; 3 days), Salzburg (€18, €26, €32), Innsbruck (€19, €24, €29). 1-Plus Ticket: 2–5 persons; journey over 101 km; 25–40% discount. Das Gruppen: 6 or more persons; discounts of 30–40%.
RAIL TRAVEL	Run by Österreichische Bundesbahnen (ÖBB) (www.oebb.at). Mostly electrified; fast and reliable, with IC trains every 1–2 hrs and regional trains connecting with IC services. Other fast trains: D (ordinary express trains); E (semi-fast/local trains); EC (with stops only in larger cities). Most overnight trains have sleeping-cars (up to three berths) and couchettes (four/six berths), plus 2nd-class seats. Seat reservations: 2nd class €3.50, 1st class free. Most stations have left luggage facilities.
TELEPHONES	Cheapest to phone long distance 2000–0600 and public holidays. Dial in: ☎ +43 and omit the initial 0 of the area code. Outgoing: ☎ 00 + country code. International enquiries and operator: ☎ 1613 (Europe); 1614 (outside Europe). National enquiries/operator: ☎ 1611. Police: ☎ 133; Fire: ☎ 122; Ambulance: ☎ 144.
TIPPING	Hotels, restaurants, cafés and bars: service charge of 10–15% but tip of around 10% still expected. Taxis 10%.
TOURIST INFORMATION	(Website: www.austria-tourism.at) Staff invariably speak some English. Opening times vary widely, particularly restricted at weekends in smaller places. Look for green 'i' sign; usually called a Fremdenverkehrsbüro.
TOURIST OFFICES OVERSEAS	**Aus**: 1ST FLOOR, 36 CARRINGTON ST, SYDNEY NSW 2000, ☎ (02) 9299 3621, fax (02) 9299 3808. **Can**: 2 BLOOR ST E., SUITE 3330, TORONTO, ONTARIO M4W 1A8, ☎ (416) 967 3381, fax (416) 967 4101. **SA**: CRADOCK HEIGHTS, corner of CRADOCK AVE/TYRWHITT AVE., ROSEBANK 2196, JO'BURG; PRIVATE BAG X18, PARKLANDS 2121, JO'BURG, ☎ (011) 442 7235, fax (011) 788 2367. **UK**: PO BOX 2363, LONDON W1A 2QB, ☎ (020) 7629 0461, fax (020) 7499 6038; Austrian rail enquiries 0906 851 7175; 60p/minute). **USA**: PO BOX 1142, NEW YORK, NY 10108–1142, ☎ (212) 944 6880, fax (212) 730 4568.

ABBREVIATIONS

IR	Inter-Rail Pass
EP	Eurail Pass
ED	Euro Domino Pass
Eu	Europass
Aus	Australia
Can	Canada
Ire	Republic of Ireland
SA	South Africa
NZ	New Zealand
UK	United Kingdom
USA	United States of America

EXCHANGE RATES
In this Directory we give **exchange rates** as they were in summer 2002; obviously they vary, but we include them to give you an idea of what currencies are worth. The latest rates are listed in the *Thomas Cook European Timetable*. **Cash machines** are a handy way of changing money, as you avoid commissions (though there is a smaller withdrawal charge); it's generally a good idea though to take some **traveller's cheques** in £, € or $ as backup – you get free replacements if you lose them.

VISAS	An EU National Identity Card or passport is sufficient. Visas are not needed by nationals of Australia, Canada, New Zealand or the USA.

BELGIUM

CAPITAL	**Brussels** (Bruxelles/Brussel)
CLIMATE	Rain prevalent at any time; warm summers, cold winters (often with snow).
CURRENCY	**Euro** (€). I Euro = 100 cents. £I = €1.59; $1 = €1.12.
CUSTOMS ALLOWANCES	Standard EU regulations apply (see pp. 19–20).
EMBASSIES IN CONSULATES IN BRUSSELS	**Aus**: R. GUIMARD 6, ☏ 02 231 05 00. **Can**: AV. DE TERVUREN 2, ☏ 02 741 06 11. **Ire**: R. FROISSART 98, ☏ 02 230 53 37. **NZ**: BLVD DU RÉGENT 47, ☏ 02 512 10 40. **SA**: 26 R. DE LA LOI, ☏ 02 230 68 45. **UK**: R. ARLON 85, ☏ 02 287 6343. **USA**: BLVD DU RÉGENT 27, ☏ 02 508 21 11.
EMBASSIES AND CONSULATES OVERSEAS	**Aus**: 19 ARKANA ST, YARRALUMLA, CANBERRA, ACT 2600, ☏ (06) 273 2501. **Can**: 80 ELGIN ST, OTTAWA, ONTARIO K1P 1B7, ☏ (613) 236 7267 **NZ**: WILLIS COROON HOUSE, 1–3 WILLESTON ST, WELLINGTON, ☏ (04) 472 9558. **SA**: 625 LEYDS ST, MUCKLENEUK, 0002 PRETORIA, ☏ (012) 44 3201. **UK**: 103–105 EATON SQ., VICTORIA, LONDON SW1 9AB, ☏ (020) 7470 3700. **USA**: 3330 GARFIELD ST N.W., WASHINGTON DC 20008, ☏ (202) 333-6900.
LANGUAGE	**Dutch** (north), **French** (south) and **German** (east). Many speak both French and Dutch, plus often English and/or German.
OPENING HOURS	Many establishments close 1200–1400. **Banks**: Mon–Fri 0900–1600. **Shops**: Mon–Sat 0900/1000–1800/1900 (often later Fri). **Museums**: vary, but most open six days a week: 1000–1700 (usually Tues–Sun, Wed–Mon or Thur–Tues).
POST OFFICES	*(Postes/Posterijen/De Post)* open Mon–Fri 0900–1700 (very few open Sat morning). Stamps also sold in newsagents.
PUBLIC HOLIDAYS	1 Jan; Easter Mon; 1 May; Ascension Day; Whit Mon; 21 July; 15 Aug; 1, 11 Nov; 25 Dec. Transport and places that open usually keep Sun times.
PUBLIC TRANSPORT	National bus companies: De Lijn (Flanders), Tec (Wallonia, i.e. the French areas); few long-distance buses. Buses, trams and metros: board at any door with ticket or buy ticket from driver. Fares depend on length of journeys. Tram and bus stops: red and white signs (all request stop – raise your hand). Taxis seldom stop in the street, so find a rank or phone; double rates outside city limits.
RAIL PASSES	IR, EP, Eu, ED, Benelux Tourrail Pass valid (pp. 26–31). Reductie Kaart: €16.30; half price tickets for one month. Weekend Ticket: 40% discount on return ticket (plus 60% discount for up to five other passengers) anywhere in Belgium at weekends.
RAIL TRAVEL	SNCB (French) or NMBS (Dutch). Website: www.b-rail.be SNCB/NMBS Information/Motorail, BLACKFRIARS FOUNDRY, 156 BLACKFRIARS RD, LONDON E1 8EN, ☏ (020) 7593 2332 (Mon–Fri 0900–1700). Rail information offices: 'B' in an oval logo. Seat reservations available for international journeys only. Refreshments not always available. Some platforms serve more than one train at a time; check carefully. Left luggage and cycle hire at many stations. Timetables usually in two sets: Mon–Fri and weekends/holidays.
TELEPHONES	Phonecards sold at rail stations, post offices, book shops, some tobacconists. Most international calls cheaper Mon–Sat 2000–0800, all day Sun. Dial in: ☏ +32; omit the initial 0 from the area code. Outgoing: ☏ 00 + country code. Police: ☏ 101. Fire/ambulance: ☏ 100. Note that you need to dial the area code (eg 02 for Brussels) even when calling from within that area.
TIPPING	Tipping in cafés, bars, restaurants and taxis not generally the norm, as service is supposed to be included in the price. Becoming expected in places where staff are used to receiving people from the international community (who often leave generous tips): 10 to 15%. Tip hairwashers in salons and delivery men €2.50–4, cloakroom attendants €1.25–2.50 and toilet attendants €0.25–0.50.

DIRECTORY

TOURIST INFORMATION	(Website: www.belgium-tourism.net) *Office du Tourisme* in French, *Toerisme* in Flemish and *Verkehrsamt* in German. Most have English-speaking staff and free English-language literature, but charge for walking itineraries and good street maps. Opening hours, especially in small places and off-season, are flexible.
TOURIST OFFICES OVERSEAS	**UK**: Belgian Tourist Office, Tourism Flanders-Brussels, 31 PEPPER ST, LONDON E14 9RW, ☎ 0900 302 0245 (premium rate), fax (020) 7458 0045 (www.belgium-tourism.net; info@flanders-tourism.org); Belgian Tourist Office Brussels-Wallonia, 217 MARSH WALL, LONDON E14 9FJ, ☎ 0906 3020 245 (premium rate), fax (020) 7531 0393 (www.belgiumtheplacetobe.be; info@belgiumtheplacetobe.be). Brochure request line for both: ☎ 0800 9545 245 (free phone). **USA** (and for **Can**): 780 THIRD AV., SUITE 1501, NEW YORK, NY 10017, ☎ (212) 758 8130, fax (212) 355 7675 (www.visitbelgium.com; info@visitbelgium.com).
VISAS	Same requirements as The Netherlands (see p. 604).

BULGARIA

CAPITAL	**Sofia** (Sofija)
CLIMATE	Hot summers; wet spring and autumn; snow in winter (skiing popular).
CURRENCY	**Leva** (Lv.); 1 Lev = 100 stotinki (st), obtainable only in Bulgaria; re-exchanged for hard currency before leaving. Credit cards increasingly accepted. £1 = 3.10Lv; $1 = 2.18Lv; €1 = 1.95Lv.
CUSTOMS ALLOWANCES	200 cigarettes, or 50 cigars, or 250g of tobacco products, 1 litre of spirits, 2 litres of wine, and 50ml of perfume. Declare amounts above US$1000. Some goods, such as antiques, liable for export duty; check with vendors. Keep receipts *(borderaux)* for exchange transactions and accommodation.
EMBASSIES AND CONSULATES IN SOFIA	**UK**: 9 MOSKOVSKA STR., ☎ (02) 933 9222. **USA**: 1 SUBORNA, ☎ (02) 980 5241. Citizens of Canada, Australia and New Zealand: use UK Embassy.
EMBASSIES AND CONSULATES OVERSEAS	**Aus**: 1/4 CARLOTTA RD, DOUBLE BAY, SYDNEY NSW 2028, ☎ (02) 9327 7581. **Can**: 325 STEWART ST, OTTAWA, ONTARIO K1N 6K5, ☎ (613) 789 3215. **SA**: 1071 CHURCH ST, PRETORIA 0083, ☎ (012) 342 3720. **UK**: 186/188 QUEEN'S GATE, LONDON SW7 5HL, ☎ (020) 7584 9433. **USA**: 1621 22ND STREET N.W., WASHINGTON DC 20008, ☎ (202) 483 5885.
LANGUAGE	**Bulgarian** (Cyrillic alphabet); English, German, Russian and French in tourist areas . Nodding the head indicates 'no' *(ne)*; shaking it means 'yes' *(da)*.
OPENING HOURS	**Banks**: Mon–Fri 0900–1500. Some exchange offices open longer hours and weekends. **Shops**: Mon–Fri 0800–2000, closed 1200–1400 outside major towns, Sat open 1000–1200. **Museums**: vary widely, but often 0800–1200, 1400–1830. Many close Mon or Tues.
POST OFFICES	Stamps *(marki)* sold only at post offices *(poshta)*, usually open Mon–Sat 0800–1730. Some close 1200–1400.
PUBLIC HOLIDAYS	1 Jan; 3 Mar; Orthodox Easter Sunday and Monday, dates variable; 1, 24 May; 6, 22 Sept; 1 Nov; 24, 25, 26 Dec.
PUBLIC TRANSPORT	Buses (good network) slightly more expensive than trains; both very cheap for hard currency travellers. Sofia: buses and trams use same ticket; punch it at machines inside, get new ticket if you change. Daily/weekly cards available.
RAIL PASSES	IR, ED, Balkan Flexipass valid (pp. 26–31). Domestic rail fares are cheap.
RAIL TRAVEL	IR, EP, ED valid. Bulgarian State Railways (BDŽ) run express, fast and slow trains. Quickest on electrified lines between major cities. Often crowded; reservations recommended (obligatory for express). All medium- and long- distance trains have 1st and 2nd class, plus limited buffet service. Overnight trains between Sofia and Black Sea resorts have 1st- and 2nd-class sleeping cars and 2nd-class couchettes. One platform may serve two tracks, platforms and tracks both numbered. Signs at stations are in Cyrillic.
TELEPHONES	Use central telephone offices in major towns for long-distance calls. Dial in: ☎ +359 and omit the initial 0 of the area code. Outgoing: ☎ 00 + country code. Police ☎ 166.

Fire ☎160. Ambulance ☎150.

TIPPING
Waiters and taxi drivers expect a tip of about 10%.

TOURIST INFORMATION
National Information and Advertising Centre, ST. SOFIA ST 1, SOFIA 1000, ☎(02) 987 97 78 or (02) 989 50 72, fax (02) 987 9778.

TOURIST OFFICES OVERSEAS
Not official tourist offices but helpful are: **UK**: Tourism Section, Bulgarian Embassy, 186–188, QUEEN'S GATE, LONDON SW7 5HL, ☎(020) 7584 9400, fax (020) 7589 4875. **USA**: BALKAN HOLIDAYS, SUITE 508, 317 MADISON AVE., NEW YORK, NY 10017, ☎(212) 573 5530, fax (212) 573 5538.

VISAS
Passports must have 6 months validity remaining. Visas not required for EU citizens for stays up to 30 days, or for nationals of Aus, NZ, Can and SA if on package holidays or if with Travel Agency vouchers on arrival for pre-paid accommodation and tourist services in Bulgaria. Visitors staying with friends or family (i.e. not in paid accommodation) need to register on arrival.

CROATIA

CAPITAL
Zagreb

CLIMATE
Continental on the Adriatic coast, with very warm summers.

CURRENCY
Kuna (Kn); 1 Kuna = 100 Lipa. Credit cards, Deutschmarks and US dollars widely accepted. £1 = 11.87Kn; $1 = 8.32Kn; €1 = 7.45Kn.

CUSTOMS ALLOWANCES
200 cigarettes, or 50 cigars, or 250 g tobacco products, 1 litre spirits.

EMBASSIES AND CONSULATES OVERSEAS
Aus: 14 JINDALEE CRESCENT, O'MALLEY ACT 2606, CANBERRA, ☎(6) 286 69 88. **Can**: 130 ALBERT ST, SUITE 1700, OTTAWA, ONTARIO, K1P 5G4, ☎(613) 230 73 51. **NZ**: 131 LINCOLN RD, HENDERSON, PO BOX, 83200 EDMONTON AUCKLAND, ☎(9) 83 65 581. **SA**: 1160 CHURCH ST, 0083 COLBYN PRETORIA, PO BOX 11335, 0028 HATFIELD ☎(12) 342 1206. **UK**: 21 CONWAY ST, LONDON, W1P 5HL, ☎(020) 7387 1790. **USA**: 2343 MASSACHUSETTS AV., N.W. WASHINGTON DC, 20008-2803, ☎(202) 588 5943.

LANGUAGE
Croatian. English, German and Italian spoken in tourist areas.

OPENING HOURS
Banks: Mon–Fri 0700–1900, Sat 0700–1300, but may vary, some banks may open Sun in larger cities. Most **shops**: Mon–Fri 0800–2000, Sat 0800–1400/1500; many shops also open Sun, especially in summer. Some shops close 1200–1600. Most open-air **markets** daily, mornings only. **Museums**: vary.

POST OFFICES
Usual hours: Mon–Fri 0700–1900 (some post offices in larger cities open until 2200), Sat 0700–1300. Stamps (*markice*) sold at news-stands (*kiosk*) or tobacconists (*trafika*). Post boxes are yellow.

PUBLIC HOLIDAYS
1 Jan, 6 Jan, Easter Mon, 1 May, 30 May, 22 Jun, 5 Aug, 15 Aug, 1 Nov and 25–26 Dec. Many local saints' holidays.

PUBLIC TRANSPORT
Jadrolinija maintains most domestic ferry lines; main office in Rijeka, ☎(051) 666 100; cheap and efficient. Buses and trams are cheap, regular and efficient.

RAIL PASSES
IR, ED valid. Domestic fares are cheap. (see pp. 26–31).

RAIL TRAVEL
National railway company: Hrvatske Željeznice (Hž), ☎(01) 45 73 253 (www.tel.hr/hz). Main intersection for international trains at Zagreb. Slow but efficient services and limited network, due in part to war damage; reconstruction has reopened some lines to passenger traffic. Zagreb–Rijeka and Zagreb–Split lines are efficient. Station amenities: generally left luggage, a bar, newspaper kiosk and WCs.

TELEPHONES
Make international calls from booths in post offices (HPT) – pay the clerk after the call; or from public telephone booths (only accept phonecards) – phonecards sold at post offices, news-stands and tobacconists. Dial in: ☎+385. Outgoing: ☎00 + country code. Police: ☎92. Fire: ☎93. Ambulance: ☎94.

TIPPING
Leave 10% for good service in a restaurant. It's not necessary to tip in bars.

TOURIST INFORMATION
Website: www.htz.hr.

DIRECTORY

TOURIST OFFICES OVERSEAS	**UK**: 2 THE LANCHESTERS, 162–164 FULHAM PALACE RD, LONDON, W6 9ER, ☎ (020) 8563 7979, fax (020) 8563 2616 (www.htz.hr; info@cnto.freeserve.co.uk). **USA**: 350 FIFTH AV., SUITE 4003, NEW YORK, NY 10118, ☎ (212) 279 8672, (212) 279 8674 or (800) 329 4416 (toll-free), fax (212) 279 8683 (www.htz.hr; cntony@earthlink.net).
VISAS	South African nationals need a 3-month tourist visa.

CZECH REPUBLIC

CAPITAL	**Prague** (Praha).
CLIMATE	Mild summers and very cold winters.
CURRENCY	**Czech Korunas** or Crowns (Kč); 1 Koruna = 100 Hellers. No restrictions on foreign currencies. Credit cards widely accepted. £1 = 53Kč; $1 = 37Kč; €1 = Kč33.
CUSTOMS ALLOWANCES	200 cigarettes or equivalent in tobacco, 1 litre spirits and 2 litres wine.
EMBASSIES AND CONSULATES IN PRAGUE	**Can**: MICKIEWICZOVA 6, 160 00 PRAHA 6, ☎ (02) 7210 1800. **Ire**: TRŽIŠTĚ 13, ☎ (02) 5753 0061. **SA**: RUSKÁ 65, 100 00 PRAHA 10, ☎ (02) 6731 1114. **UK**: THUNOVSKÁ 14, PRAHA 1, ☎ (02) 5740 211. **USA**: TRŽIŠTĚ 15, 110 00 PRAHA 1, ☎ (02) 5753 0663.
EMBASSIES AND CONSULATES OVERSEAS	**Aus**: 38 CULGOA CIRCUIT, O'MALLEY, CANBERRA, ACT 2606, ☎ (02) 2901 1386. **Can**: 541 SUSSEX DR., OTTAWA, ONTARIO, KIN 6Z6, ☎ (613) 562 3875. **Ire**: 57 NORTHUMBERLAND RD, BALLSBRIDGE, DUBLIN 4, ☎ (01) 668 1135. **SA**: P.O.B. 3326, 936 PRETORIUS ST, ARCADIA, PRETORIA 0083, ☎ (12) 342 3477. **UK**: 28 KENSINGTON PALACE GDNS, LONDON W8 4QY, ☎ (020) 7243 1115. **USA**: 3900 SPRING OF FREEDOM ST N.W., WASHINGTON DC 20008, ☎ (202) 274 9100.
LANGUAGE	**Czech**. Czech and Slovak are closely related Slavic tongues. English, German and Russian are widely understood, but Russian is less popular.
OPENING HOURS	**Banks**: Mon–Fri 0800–1800. **Shops**: Mon–Fri 0900–1800, Sat 0900–1200 (often longer in Prague Sat–Sun). **Food shops**: usually open earlier plus on Sun. **Museums**: (usually) Tues–Sun 1000–1800. Most castles close Nov–Mar.
POST OFFICES	Usual opening hours are 0800–1900. Stamps also available from newsagents and tobacconists. Erratic postal services. Post boxes: orange and blue.
PUBLIC HOLIDAYS	1 Jan; Easter Mon; 1, 8 May; 5, 6 July; 28 Oct; 24–26 Dec.
PUBLIC TRANSPORT	Good long-distance bus network, run by ČSAD or private companies. You can buy tickets from the driver; priority to those with reservations.
RAIL PASSES	IR, ED, European East, Czech and Slovak Rail Pass (pp. 26–31). Kilometrická banka 2000 (KMB); 2000 km or 6 months travel; minimum journey 100 km, maximum 400 km. Ordinary trains Kč1050, quality trains Kč1350. 20% discount on ČD fares; passport photo required. Rapid Integro-Doprava travelcard, valid for all public transport up to 50 km from Prague (24 hrs Kč70, 72 hrs Kč200, 7 days Kč250, 15 days Kč280).
RAIL TRAVEL	National rail company is České Dráhy (ČD). Network cheap and extensive, often crowded. Main lines: IC, EC and expresses (supplement payable), one Praha–Ostrava train classified SuperCity (SC), 1st class, special fare. Some branch lines have been privatised. Other trains: spešný (semi-fast), osobný (very slow). Some dining cars; sleepers and couchettes; seats for express trains may be reserved at least 1 hr before departure at counter marked R at stations.
TELEPHONES	Dial in: ☎ +420; omit the initial 0 of the area code. Outgoing: ☎ 00 + country code. Police: ☎ 158. Fire: ☎ 150. Ambulance: ☎ 155.
TIPPING	You should tip at pubs and restaurants, in hotels and taxis and hairdressers. In general, round up the nearest 10Kč unless you are somewhere upmarket, when you should tip 10%.
TOURIST INFORMATION	(Website: www.visitczech.cz) ☎ (02) 2481 0411 or (02) 2481 0412; or PIS offices ☎ (02) 544 444. Čedok Travel agency A.S., ☎ (02) 2419 7350.

TOURIST OFFICES OVERSEAS | Can: PO BOX 198, EXCHANGE TOWER, 2 FIRST CANADIAN PL., 14TH FLOOR, TORONTO, ONTARIO M5X 1A6, ☎ (416) 363 9928 (ctacanada@iprimus.ca). UK: 95 GREAT PORTLAND ST, LONDON WIN 5RA, ☎ (020) 7291 9925 (gillespie@czechcentre.org.uk). USA: 1109–1111 MADISON AVE, NEW YORK, NY 10028, ☎ (212) 288 0830 (travelczech@pop.net).

VISAS | Visas needed by nationals of Canada, Australia and New Zealand.

DENMARK

CAPITAL | **Copenhagen** (København).

CLIMATE | Maritime climate. July–Aug is warmest, May–June often very pleasant, but rainier; Oct–Mar is the wettest, with periods of frost.

CURRENCY | **Danish kroner** or **crown**, (DKK, DKr.). £1 = Dkr.11.86; $1 = Dkr.8.31; €1 = Dkr.7.44.

CUSTOMS ALLOWANCES | Standard EU regulations apply (see pp. 19–20).

EMBASSIES AND CONSULATES IN COPENHAGEN | Aus: STRANDBOULEVARDEN 122; ☎ 70 26 36 76. Can: KRISTEN BERNIKOWSGADE 1, ☎ 33 48 32 00. Ire: ØSTBANEGADE 21, ☎ 35 42 32 33. SA: GAMMEL VARTOVVEJ 8, HELLERUP, ☎ 31 18 01 55. UK: KASTELSVEJ 36–40, ☎ 35 44 52 00. USA: DAG HAMMARSKJÖLDS ALLÉ 24, ☎ 35 55 31 44.

EMBASSIES AND CONSULATES OVERSEAS | Aus: 15 HUNTER ST, YARRALUMLA, A.C.T. 2600, ☎ (02) 6273 2195. Can: 47 CLARENCE ST, SUITE 450, OTTAWA, ONTARIO K1N 9K1, ☎ (613) 562 1811. Ire: 121–122 ST. STEPHEN'S GREEN, DUBLIN 2, ☎ (01) 475 6404. NZ: CONSULATE: 273 BLEAKHOUSE RD, HOWICK, PO BOX 619, AUCKLAND 1, ☎ (09) 537 3099. SA: 8TH FLOOR, SANLAM CENTRE, CNR PRETORIUS AND ANDRIES STS, PO BOX 2942, PRETORIA 0001, ☎ (012) 322 0595. UK: 55 SLOANE ST, LONDON SW1X 9SR, ☎ (020) 7333 0200. USA: 3200 WHITEHAVEN ST N.W., WASHINGTON D.C. 20008-3683, ☎ (202) 234 4300.

LANGUAGE | **Danish**. English is almost universally spoken. *'Ikke'* translates as 'do not'.

OPENING HOURS | **Banks** (Copenhagen): Mon–Fri 0930–1600 (some until 1700; most until 1800 on Thur). Vary elsewhere. **Shops**: (mostly) Mon–Thur 0930–1730, Fri 0930–1900/2000, Sat 0900–1300/1400, though many in Copenhagen open until 1700 and may also open Sun. **Museums**: (mostly) daily 1000/1100–1600/1700. In winter, hours are shorter and museums usually close Mon.

POST OFFICES | Mostly Mon–Fri 0900/1000–1700/1800, Sat 0900–1200 (but opening times vary greatly). Stamps also sold at newsagents.

PUBLIC HOLIDAYS | 1 Jan, Maundy Thursday–Easter Monday; Common Prayer Day (4th Fri after Easter); Ascension Day (May); Whit Mon; 5 June, 24–26, 31 Dec.

PUBLIC TRANSPORT | Long-distance travel easiest by train. Excellent regional and city bus services (www.ht.dk), many dovetailing with trains. Ferries or bridges link all the big islands. Taxis: green *'Fri'* sign when available; metered and most accept major credit cards. Many cycle paths and bike hire shops. Free use of City Bikes in Copenhagen.

RAIL PASSES | IR, ED, EP, Scanrail Pass (pp. 26–31). Fares based on national zonal system. København 24-hr klippekort: DKr.85; trains and buses; also valid in North Zealand; one adult and two children (under 10); from stations or ticket offices. Pendlerkort 30-day all-zone 2nd-class ticket Dkr.2600 (photocard required). The Copenhagen Card provides free public transport in Copenhagen and the surrounding region (see Copenhagen: Public Transport, p. 440).

RAIL TRAVEL | Danish State Railways: Danske Statsbaner (DSB; www.dsb.dk); some private lines. IC trains reach up to 200 kph. Re *(regionaltog)* trains frequent, but slower. IR: slower and less frequent. Refreshment on most trains. Reservations recommended, not compulsory (DKr.15) except on InterCity trains across the Storebelt (supplement Dkr.30). Special rules apply during holidays. Nationwide reservations ☎ 70 13 14 15. Baggage lockers at most stations, usually DKr.20 per 24 hrs. Usually free trolleys, but you may need a (returnable) coin.

TELEPHONES | Most operators speak English. Phonecards (DKr.30–100) available from DSB kiosks, post offices and news-stands. Dial in: ☎ +45 + eight-digit number (no area code).

Outgoing: ☎00 + country code. Directory enquiries: ☎118. International operator/directory: ☎14. Emergency services: ☎112.

Tipping

At least DKr.20 in restaurants. Elsewhere (taxis, cafés, bars, hotels etc) tipping is not expected.

Tourist information

(Website: www.visitdenmark.com) Nearly every decent-sized town in Denmark has a tourist office (*turistbureauet*), normally found in the town hall or central square; they distribute maps, information and advice. Some also book accommodation for a small fee, and change money.

Tourist offices overseas

UK: Danish Tourist Board, 55 Sloane St, London SW1X 9SY, ☎(020) 7259 5959, fax (020) 7259 5955. **USA**: Danish Tourist Board, 655 Third Avenue 18th Floor, New York, NY 10017, ☎(212) 885 9700.

Visas

Citizens of South Africa need a visa.

Estonia

Capital

Tallinn

Climate

Warm summers, cold, snowy winters; rain all year, heaviest in Aug.

Currency

Kroon or **crown** (EEK); 1 Kroon = 100 Sents. Exchange facilities limited; carry spare cash. £1 = 24.92EEK; $1 = 17.47EEK; €1 = 15.64EEK.

Customs allowances

Although not a member state, standard EU regulations apply (see pp. 19–20).

Embassies and consulates in Tallinn

Aus: Kopli 25, ☎650 93 08. **Can**: Toomkooli 13, ☎627 33 11. **UK**: Kentmanni 20, ☎667 47 00. **USA**: Kentmanni 20, ☎668 81 00.

Embassies and consulates overseas

Aus: 86 Louisa Rd, Birchgrove, NSW 2041, ☎(02) 9810 7468. **Can**: 958 Broadview Av., Toronto, Ontario, M4K 2R6, ☎(416) 461 0764. **UK**: 16 Hyde Park Gate, London SW7 5DG, ☎(020) 7589 3428. **USA**: 2131 Massachusetts Av. N.W., Washington DC 20008, ☎(202) 588 0101.

Language

Estonian. Some Finnish is useful, plus Russian in Tallinn and the north-east.

Opening hours

Banks: Mon–Fri 0900–1600. **Shops**: Mon–Fri 0900/1000–1800/1900, Sat 0900/1000–1500/1700; many also open Sun. **Museums**: days vary (usually closed Mon and/or Tues); hours commonly 1100–1600.

Post offices

Stamps sold at large hotels, post offices, news-stands, tourist offices.

Public holidays

1 Jan; 24 Feb; Good Fri; Easter Mon (unofficial); 1 May; 23 June (Victory Day), 24 June; 20 Aug; 25, 26 Dec.

Public transport

Bus services often quicker, cleaner and more efficient than rail but getting pricier. Book international services in advance from bus stations. Pay the driver at rural stops or small towns.

Rail passes

IR, ED, EP not valid, but rail fares are cheap.

Rail travel

Most local services (except trains to the south and west and Tallinn suburbans) have been withdrawn. Comfortable overnight trains to Russia; best to take berth in 2nd-class coupé (compartment of four berths). Trains carry superior coupé with two berths. Reservations compulsory for all sleepers; entry visa to Russia may need to be shown when booking. Very little English spoken at stations.

Telephones

Dial in: ☎+372. Outgoing: ☎00 + country code. Local calls: ☎0 + area code (not initial 0) + number. Pay phones take phonecards (from hotels, Tourist Offices, post offices, news-stands). Police: ☎110. Fire and Ambulance: ☎112.

Tipping

Not necessary to tip service at the bar or counter, but tip 10% if served at your table. Round up taxi fares to a maximum of 10%.

Tourist information

Turismiamet (Estonian Tourist Board), Mündi 2, 10146 Tallinn, ☎699 04 20, fax 699 04 32 but try their excellent website first (www.tourism.ee), with links to other useful Baltic websites. **Ekspress Hotline**, ☎1182, is an English-speaking information service covering all Estonian towns.

TOURIST OFFICES OVERSEAS	**Can**: Orav Travel, 5650 YONGE ST, NORTH YORK, ONTARIO M2M 4G3, ☎ (416) 221 4164, fax (416) 221 6789. Estonian embassies and consulates abroad can help.
VISAS	Visas not needed by citizens of Australia, Ireland, Japan, New Zealand, UK and USA. Estonian visas also valid for Latvia and Lithuania. Regulations change constantly; check with the consulate/embassy. Canadian passport holders can enter with visa for other Baltic States or obtain visa on border.

FINLAND

CAPITAL	**Helsinki** (Helsingfors).
CLIMATE	Extremely long summer days; spring and autumn curtailed further north; continuous daylight for 70 days north of 70th parallel. Late June–mid-Aug best for far north, mid-May–Sept for south. Ski season: mid-Jan–mid-Apr.
CURRENCY	**Euro (€)**. I Euro = 100 cents; £1 = €1.59; $1 = €1.12.
CUSTOMS ALLOWANCES	EU regulations apply (pp. 19–20), but must be aged 20 or over to buy spirits and 18 or over for alcohol under 22% proof.
EMBASSIES AND CONSULATES IN HELSINKI	**Aus**: MUSEOHATU 25B, ☎ (09) 447 233. **Can**: POHJOISESPLANADI 25B, ☎ (09) 171 141. **Ire**: EROTTAJANKATU 7A, ☎ (09) 646 006. **SA**: RAHAPAJANKATU 1A, ☎ (09) 6860 3100. **UK**: ITÄINEN PUISTOTIE 17, ☎ (09) 2286 5100. **USA**: ITÄINEN PUISTOTIE 14A, ☎ (09) 171 931.
EMBASSIES AND CONSULATES OVERSEAS	**Aus**: 10 DARWIN AV., YARRALUMLA, CANBERRA ACT 2600, ☎ (02) 6273 3800. **Can**: 55 METCALFE ST, SUITE 850. OTTAWA, ONTARIO K1P 6L5, ☎ (613) 236 2389. **Ire**: RUSSELL HOUSE, STOKES PL., ST. STEPHEN'S GREEN, DUBLIN 2, ☎ (01) 478 1344. **SA**: 628 LEYDS ST, MUCKLENEUK, PRETORIA 0002 (Postal address: PO BOX 443, PRETORIA 0001), ☎ (012) 343 0275. **UK**: 38 CHESHAM PLACE, LONDON SW1X 8HW, ☎ (020) 7838 6200. **USA**: 3301 MASSACHUSETTS AV. N.W., WASHINGTON, D.C., 20008, ☎ (202) 298 5800.
LANGUAGE	**Finnish**, and, in the north, **Lapp/Sami**. Swedish, the second language, often appears on signs after the Finnish. Knowledge of English is scattered, but there's not much problem in Helsinki. German reasonably widespread.
OPENING HOURS	**Banks**: Mon–Fri 0915–1615, with regional variations. **Shops**: Mon–Fri 0900–2000, Sat 0900–1500, though many shops open Mon–Fri 0700–2100, Sat 0900–1800; many shops also open Sun, June–Aug. **Stores/food shops**: Mon–Sat 0900–1800/2000. **Museums**: usually close Mon, hours vary. Many close in winter.
POST OFFICES	Most *posti* open at least Mon–Fri 0900–1700. Stamps also sold at shops, hotels and bus and train stations. Yellow postboxes.
PUBLIC HOLIDAYS	1, 6 Jan; Good Fri; Easter Sun–Mon; 1 May; Ascension; Whit Sun; Midsummer's Day (Sat falling 20–26 June); All Saints Day (Sat falling 31 Oct–6 Nov); 6 Dec; 25–26 Dec.
PUBLIC TRANSPORT	Timetables for trains, buses and boats dovetail conveniently. *Suomen Kulkuneuvot/ Finlands Kommunikationer* (in Finnish and Swedish; €23) covers all in detail, available at bus and rail stations. Buses: stops are usually a black bus on a yellow background for local services; white bus on a blue background for longer distances. Cheaper to buy tickets from stations or agents than on board. At terminals, look for destination. Taxis: for hire when the yellow *'taksi'* sign is lit; hailing them in the street is acceptable; metered.
RAIL PASSES	IR, ED, EP, Scanrail Pass valid (see pp. 26–31). Finnrailpass: unlimited 2nd-class travel on VR for any 3, 5 or 10 days (2nd class: €114/154/208; 1st class: €174/232/312 respectively). Tourist Ticket (Helsinki): 1, 3 or 5 days consecutive travel on public transport; €22.50, €29.50, €34.50. Helsinki Card: unlimited travel on public transport (including some ferries), free entry to nearly 50 attractions; €22.50, €29.50, €34.50 for 24/48/72 hours.
RAIL TRAVEL	National rail company: VR (www.vr.fi); Pendolinos (up to 220 km/h) are being introduced. Fares depend upon train type – those for S220 (Pendolino), IC (InterCity) and P (express) trains include a seat reservation. Sleeping-cars: two or

DIRECTORY

TELEPHONES	three berths per compartment (2nd class), single compartment (1st class). Sleeping accommodation generally costs less Mon–Thur (winter). Station: 'Rautatieasema' or 'Järnvägsstation'; virtually all have baggage lockers.
	Phonecards sold by R-kiosks, Tourist Offices, Tele offices (Tele card used nationwide) and some post offices. Dial in: ☎+358 + area code (minus initial 0). Outgoing: ☎00 + country code. Emergency services: ☎112.
TIPPING	Service charge included in hotel and restaurant bills but leave coins for good service. Hotel and restaurant porters and sauna attendants expect a few markka or a Euro or two. Taxi drivers and hairdressers do not expect a tip.
TOURIST INFORMATION	(Website: www.finland-tourism.com) For Finnish Tourist Board national offices see p. 445. Every Finnish town has a tourist office (Matkailutoimistot) where staff speak English. English literature, mostly free.
TOURIST OFFICES OVERSEAS	**Aus:** LEVEL 4, 81 YORK ST, SYDNEY, NSW 2000, ☎(02) 9290 1950, fax (02) 9290 1981. **UK:** 177–179 HAMMERSMITH RD, LONDON W6, ☎(020) 7365 2512, fax (020) 7321 0696. **USA:** PO BOX 4649, GRAND CENTRAL STATION, NEW YORK, NY 10163-4649, ☎(212) 885 9700, fax (212) 885 9739.
VISAS	National identity cards or passports issued by EU countries, Iceland, Norway and Switzerland sufficient. Visas not required by those countries, nor by nationals of Australia, Canada, New Zealand or the USA. South Africans need visas.

FRANCE

CAPITAL	**Paris**, divided into arrondissements numbered 1 to 20 (1st, 2nd or 1er, 2e etc).
CLIMATE	Cool–cold winters, mild–hot summers; south coast best Oct–Mar, Alps and Pyrenees, June and early July. Paris best spring and autumn.
CURRENCY	**Euro** (€). 1 Euro = 100 cents. £1 = €1.59; $1 = €1.12.
CUSTOMS ALLOWANCES	Standard EU regulations apply (see pp. 19–20).
EMBASSIES AND CONSULATES IN PARIS	**Aus:** 4 R. JEAN REY, 15E, ☎01 40 59 33 00. **Can:** 35 AV. MONTAIGNE, 8E, ☎01 44 43 29 00. **Ire:** 12 AV. FOCH, 16E, ☎01 44 17 67 00. **NZ:** 7 TER R. L-DE-VINCI, 16E, ☎01 45 01 43 43. **SA:** 59 QUAI D'ORSAY, 7E, ☎01 53 59 23 23. **UK:** 35 R. FBG-ST. HONORÉ, 8E, ☎01 44 51 31 00. **USA:** 2 AV. GABRIEL, 1ER, ☎01 43 12 22 22.
EMBASSIES AND CONSULATES OVERSEAS	**Aus:** 6 PERTH AV., YARRALUMLA, CANBERRA, ACT 2600, ☎(02) 6216 0100. **Can:** 42 PROMENADE SUSSEX, OTTAWA, ONT. K1M 2C9, ☎(613) 789 1795. **NZ:** 34/42 MANNERS ST, WELLINGTON, ☎(04) 384 2555. **Ire:** 36 AILESBURY RD, BALLSBRIDGE, DUBLIN 4, ☎(01) 260 1666. **SA:** (Apr–Jan) 807 GEORGE AV., ARCADIA, PRETORIA 0083, ☎(012) 429 7000; (Feb–Mar) 78 QUEEN VICTORIA ST, CAPE TOWN, ☎(021) 422 1338. **UK:** 58 KNIGHTSBRIDGE, LONDON SW1X 7JT, ☎(020) 7201 1000. **USA:** 4101 RESERVOIR RD N.W., WASHINGTON DC 20007, ☎(202) 944 6000.
LANGUAGE	**French**; many people can speak a little English, particularly in Paris.
OPENING HOURS	**Paris and major towns**: shops, banks and post offices generally open 0900/1000–1700/1900 Mon-Fri, plus often Sat am/all day. Small shops can be open Sun am but closed Mon. **Provinces**: weekly closing is mostly Sun pm/all day and Mon; both shops and services generally close 1200–1430; services may have restricted opening times. Most **super/hypermarkets** open to 2100/2200. **Museums**: (mostly) 0900–1700, closing Mon or Tues; longer hours in summer; often free or discount rate on Sun. **Restaurants** serve 1200–1400 and 1900–2100 at least. Public holidays: services closed, food shops open am in general, check times with individual museums and tourist sights.
POST OFFICES	Called La Poste. Letter boxes are small, wall or pedestal-mounted, and yellow. The basic rate postage stamp (timbre) can also be bought from Tabacs or Café-Tabacs.
PUBLIC HOLIDAYS	1 Jan; Easter Mon; 1, 8 May; Ascension Day; Whit Sun–Mon; 14 July; 15 Aug; 1, 11 Nov; 25 Dec. If on Tues or Thur, many places also close Mon or Fri.
PUBLIC TRANSPORT	In Paris, use the Métro where possible: clean, fast, cheap and easy. For urban and peri-urban transport, enquire whether carnets (generally 10-ticket packs) are on

sale: cheaper than individual tickets. Some city transport passes combine discount entries to certain tourist attractions. Bus and train timetables available from bus and train stations and Tourist Offices; both free. Always ask if your rail pass is valid – it may be. Bus services infrequent after 2030 and on Sun. Sparse public transport in rural areas. Licensed taxis (avoid others) are metered; white roof-lights when free; surcharges for luggage, extra passengers and journeys beyond the centre.

RAIL PASSES

IR, ED, EP, Eu, France n' Italy Pass valid (pp. 26–31). Stamp all tickets (except Inter-Rail) in orange machines *(composteurs)* on platform. Two fare periods: blue (quiet) and white (peak). **France Railpass:** valid for 3 to 7 days within one month, available (e.g. from Rail Europe) to those resident outside France. Valid 3–7 days within a month, available (e.g. from Rail Europe) to those resident outside France. 3 days £119 first class £93 second class, 4 days £146/117, 5 days £170/137, 6 days £193/153, 7 days £213/170; youth (12–25) about 80% of adult rate, child (4–11) 50%. Senior version (1st class only) £106/130/153/173/193 respectively. Several regions have 1–2 day rovers or half-fare cards valid on Sats, Suns and public holidays (valid on local TER services only). Paris Visite: 1, 2, 3, or 5 consecutive days travel on public transport in Paris, free or discounted entry to 20 attractions. Zones 1–3: €8.35/13.70/18.25/26.65 for 1/2/3/5 days respectively.

RAIL TRAVEL

Société Nationale des Chemins de Fer Français (SNCF) www.sncf.com, ☎ 08 36 35 35 35 but French only. Overnight trains may carry sleeping-cars *(wagons-lits)* and/or *couchettes* and/or reclining seats and/or normal seats. If single traveller, request same-sex cabins for *wagons-lits* and *couchette* cabins. Whether day or night trains, they can get very full so avoid having to spend the journey standing, and book a seat (supplement). TGV obligatory reservation and supplement included in TGV tickets; check that your rail pass includes it. Minimal (and exorbitant) bar/trolley service on most long-distance trains. Most larger stations have 24-hr left-luggage coin-operated lockers, and possibly pay-showers.

TELEPHONES

Phone boxes: most with English instructions. Many post offices have metered phones: pay when you've finished. Restaurants etc have (more expensive) pay phones; avoid calling from your hotel. Different denomination phonecards *(télécartes)* on sale in post offices, some tobacconists and certain Tourist Offices; few phones still accept coins; some do credit cards. Dial in: ☎ +33 and knock off the initial zero from telephone number. Outgoing: ☎ 00 + country code and knock off the initial zero from telephone number. Police: ☎ 17. Fire: ☎ 18. Ambulance: ☎ 15. Emergency from a mobile phone: ☎ 112. Mobile phone rental: Ellinas (www.ellinas.com) offers good deals (free incoming calls; location at Charles de Gaulle airport).

TIPPING

Not necessary to tip in bars or cafés although it is common practice to round up the price. In restaurants there is no obligation to tip, but if you wish to do so leave €1–2.

TOURIST INFORMATION

Check out www.franceguide.com first; at a new destination call at the local Tourist Office: look for *Syndicat d'Initiative* or *Office de Tourisme*; staff generally speak English. Opening times seasonal. Many sell passes for local tourist sights or services and can organise accommodation (for a fee).

TOURIST OFFICES OVERSEAS

Aus: 25 BLIGH ST, SYDNEY, NSW200, ☎ (02) 9231 5244. **Can:** 1981 AV. MACGILL COLLEGE, SUITE 490, MONTREAL, QUE H3A 2W9, ☎ (514) 288 4264. **Ire:** 10 SUFFOLK ST, DUBLIN 2, ☎ (01) 679 0813. **SA:** CRAIGHALL, JOHANNESBURG 2024, ☎ (011) 880 8062. **UK:** 178 PICCADILLY, LONDON W1V 0AL, ☎ (020) 7399 3500. **USA:** 444 MADISON AVE, NEW YORK, NY 10020, ☎ (212) 838 7800. Also in Chicago, Beverley Hills and Miami.

VISAS

Visas needed by South Africans; but for others, only for stays of over 90 days (subject to change, so enquire before travelling).

GERMANY

CAPITAL

Berlin (the functions of the capital have been transferred from Bonn).

CURRENCY	**Euro** (€). I Euro = 100 cents. £1 = €1.59; $1 = €1.12.
CUSTOMS ALLOWANCES	Standard EU regulations apply (see pp. 19–20).
EMBASSIES AND CONSULATES IN BERLIN	**Aus**: FRIEDRICHSTR. 200, ☎ (030) 88 00 880. **Can**: IHZ BUILDING, FRIEDRICHSTR. 95, ☎ (030) 2031 2470. **NZ**: ATRIUM, 4TH FLOOR, FRIEDRICHSTR. 60, ☎ (030) 206 210. **UK**: WILHELMSTR. 70–71, ☎ (030) 204 570. **USA**: NEUSTÄDTISCHE KIRCHSTR. 4, ☎ (030) 83050.
EMBASSIES AND CONSULATES OVERSEAS	**UK**: EMBASSY, 23 BELGRAVE SQ., LONDON SW1X 8PZ, ☎ (020) 7824 1300. **USA**: EMBASSY, 4645 RESERVOIR RD N.W., WASHINGTON DC 20007-1998, ☎ (202) 298 8141.
LANGUAGE	**German**; English and French widely spoken in the west, especially by young people, less so in the eastern side.
OPENING HOURS	Vary; rule of thumb: **Banks**: Mon–Fri 0830–1300 and 1430–1600 (until 1730 Thur). **Shops**: Mon–Fri 0900–1830 (large department stores may open 0830/0900–2000) and Sat 0900–1600. **Museums**: Tues–Sun 0900–1700 (until 2100 Thur).
POST OFFICES	Mon–Fri 0800–1800, Sat 0800–1200. Main post offices have poste restante (*Postlagernd*).
PUBLIC HOLIDAYS	1, 6* Jan; Good Fri; Easter Sun–Mon; 1 May, Ascension Day; Whit Mon; Corpus Christi*, 15 Aug*; 3 Oct; 1 Nov*; 24 Dec (afternoon); 25 Dec; 26 Dec. (*Catholic feasts, celebrated only in the south.)
PUBLIC TRANSPORT	Most cities have U-Bahn (U) underground railway and S-Bahn (S) urban rail service. City travel passes cover both and other public transport, including ferries in some cities. International passes usually cover S-Bahn. Single fares are expensive; day card (*Tagesnetzkarte*) or multi-ride ticket (*Mehrfahrkarte*) pays its way if you take more than three rides.
RAIL PASSES	IR, ED, Eu, EP valid (pp. 26–31). More details on these and other discount tickets from **ServicePoint** at main stations (Hbf). DB Railcard: half-price 1st or 2nd-class travel; passport photo required. German Rail Pass (for people resident outside Europe and North Africa) 4–10 days unlimited travel within a month: 4 days $260/180 1st/2nd class; add approx $33/23 per day; not valid on Metropolitan business trains. German Rail Youth Pass (under 26), 2nd class only, 4 days $142; add approx $13 for each extra day. German Rail Twin Pass (non-European residents only), giving 50% discount for second adult over 5 or 10 days. Saver and Supersaver Tickets: discounts on ICE long-distance travel; stay must include Friday night. Regional Ticket: unlimited 2nd-class travel on DB local trains Mon–Fri off-peak (0900–1600, 1800–0300) in a number of states.
RAIL TRAVEL	**Deutsche Bahn** (DB), ☎ (01805) 99 66 33 for timetable or ticket information (www.bahn.de); also some privately owned railways. Buy tickets before you board, or pay a small supplement. Long-distance trains: ICE (modern high speed trains up to 186 mph/299 kph), IC, EC, EN, NZ, CNL, D. Regional: IRE, RB, RE (modern and comfortable; these link with long-distance services). Frequent S-Bahn services in major cities. Most offer 1st and 2nd class. Supplements charged on IC, EC trains; ICE have special fares. Overnight services: seating and sleeping-cars with up to three berths and/or couchettes with four or six berths. Seat reservations recommended for express trains, not local ones. Most long-distance trains have refreshments. Stations: well staffed, often with left luggage, refreshments, bicycle hire. Main station is *Hauptbahnhof* (Hbf).
TELEPHONES	Kartentelefon boxes take only cards (buy almost anywhere). Dial in: ☎ +49 and omit the initial 0 of the area code. Outgoing: ☎ 00 + country code (few exceptions, but kiosks give full information). Police ☎ 110. Fire ☎ 112. Ambulance ☎ 112.
TIPPING	Not a must but customary for good service. Small sums are rounded up, while for larger sums you could add a tip of €1, or up to 10% of the bill.
TOURIST INFORMATION	(Website: www.germany-tourism.de). Usually near station. English is widely spoken; English-language maps and leaflets available. Most offer room-finding service.
TOURIST OFFICES OVERSEAS	**Aus**: c/o GERMAN–AUSTRALIAN CHAMBER OF INDUSTRY AND COMMERCE, PO BOX A 980, SYDNEY SOUTH, NSW 1235, ☎ (02) 9267 8148, fax (020) 9267 9035 (gnto@germany.org.au). **Can**: 175 BLOOR ST EAST, NORTH TOWER, SUITE 604,

TORONTO, ONTARIO M4W 3R8, ☎ (416) 968 1570, fax (416) 968 1986
(gntoyyc@d-z-t.com). **UK:** PO BOX 2695, LONDON W1A 3TN, ☎ (020) 7317 0908
or (09001) 600 100, fax (020) 7495 6129 (gntolon@d-z-t.com). **USA:** 122 EAST
42ND ST, 52ND FLOOR, NEW YORK, NY 10168-0072, ☎ (212) 661 7200, fax (212) 661
7174 (gntonyc@d-z-t.com).

VISAS

EU National Identity Cards and ID cards acceptable for citizens of the Czech and
Slovak Republics, Hungary, Iceland, Liechtenstein, Malta, Monaco, Poland, and
Switzerland. Visas not needed by nationals of Aus, Can, NZ or the USA.

GREECE

CAPITAL	**Athens** (Athinai).
CLIMATE	Uncomfortably hot in June–Aug; often better to travel in spring or autumn.
CURRENCY	**Euro** (€). 1 Euro = 100 cents. £1 = €1.59; $1 = €1.12.
CUSTOMS ALLOWANCES	Normal EU regulations apply, see pp. 19–20.
EMBASSIES AND CONSULATES IN ATHENS	**Aus:** 37 D. SOUTSOU ST, ☎ 645 0404. **Can:** IOANNOU GENNADIOU 4, ☎ 727 3400. **Ire:** 7 VAS. KONSTANTINOU AV., ☎ 723 2771/2. **NZ:** 268 KIFISSIAS AV., ☎ 687 4701. **SA:** 60 KIFISSIAS AV., MAROUSI, ☎ 680 6645/9. **UK:** PLOUTARCHOU 1, ☎ 723 6211. **USA:** VASSILISSIS SOFIAS 91, ☎ 721 2951/9 or 721 8401.
EMBASSIES AND CONSULATES OVERSEAS	**UK:** CONSULATE GENERAL, 1A HOLLAND PARK, LONDON W11 3TP, ☎ (020) 7221 6467. **USA:** 2221 MASSACHUSETTS AV. N.W., WASHINGTON DC 20008-2873, ☎ (202) 939 5800.
LANGUAGE	**Greek;** English widely spoken in Athens and tourist areas (some German, French or Italian), less so in remote mainland areas.
OPENING HOURS	**Banks:** (usually) Mon–Thur 0800–1400, Fri 0830–1330, longer hours in peak holiday season. **Shops:** vary; in summer most close midday and reopen in the evening (Tue, Thu, Fri) 1700–2000. **Sites and museums:** mostly 0830–1500; Athens sites and other major archaeological sites open until 1900 or open until sunset in summer.
POST OFFICES	Normally Mon–Fri 0800–1300, Sat 0800–1200; money exchange, travellers cheques, Eurocheques. Stamps sold from vending machines outside post offices, street kiosks.
PUBLIC HOLIDAYS	1, 6 Jan; Shrove Mon; 25 Mar; Easter; 1 May; Whit Mon; 15 Aug; 28 Oct; 25, 26 Dec. Everything closes for Easter; Greeks use the Orthodox calendar and dates may differ from Western Easter.
PUBLIC TRANSPORT	KTEL buses: fast, punctual, fairly comfortable long-distance services; well-organised stations in most towns (tickets available from bus terminals). Islands connected by ferries and hydrofoils; see Thomas Cook guide *Greek Island Hopping*. City transport: bus or (in Athens) trolley-bus, metro and electric rail; services are crowded. Outside Athens, taxis are plentiful and good value.
RAIL PASSES	IR, EP, Eu, ED, Balkan Flexipass valid (pp. 26–31). Greek Flexipass: unlimited 1st-class rail travel for 3 or 5 days within a month. Hellenic Tourpass (only available from OSE Head Office – see below – or International window at Thessaloniki station) gives unlimited 2nd class rail travel €43.13/72.19/96.26 for 10/20/30 days; discounts for groups of 2–5 people. Greek Flexipass Rail 'n Fly (available from Rail Europe in the USA): 3 days' unlimited 1st class train travel within 1 month, plus two flight coupons for selected Olympic Airways flights: $222/ child $119; under 26 version also available. Further information: OSE Head Office, 1–3 KAROLOU ST, GR-10437 ATHENS, ☎/fax (1) 5240 996 (www.ose.gr).
RAIL TRAVEL	Trains run by Hellenic Railways (Organismós Sidiródromon tis Éllados; OSE), ☎ (01) 5297 777 (www.ose.gr): limited rail network, especially north of Athens. Sleepers/couchettes. Reservations essential on most express trains. IC trains (supplement payable) are fast and fairly punctual, other services are erratic. Stations: often no left luggage or English-speaking staff, but many have restaurants.

TELEPHONES	Dial in: ☎+30. Outgoing: ☎00 + country code. General emergency/police/operator: ☎100. Fire ☎199. Ambulance: ☎166. Tourist police (24 hrs; English): ☎171.
TIPPING	Not necessary for restaurants or taxis.
TOURIST INFORMATION	**Hellenic Tourism Organisation**; see p. 554.
TOURIST OFFICES OVERSEAS	**Aus**: 51–7 PITT ST, SYDNEY NSW 2000, ☎(02) 9241 1663/5. **Can**: 1300 BAY ST, MAIN LEVEL, TORONTO, ONTARIO M5R 3K8, ☎(416) 968 2220. **UK**: 4 CONDUIT ST, LONDON W1R 0DJ, ☎(020) 7734 5997, fax (020) 7287 1369 (www.tourist-offices.org.uk; eot-greektouristoffice@btinternet.com). **USA**: OLYMPIC TOWER, 645 FIFTH AV (5TH FLOOR), NEW YORK, NY 10022, ☎(212) 421 5777.
VISAS	Not needed for EU citizens; or for nationals of the USA, Canada, Australia and New Zealand for stays of less than three months.

HUNGARY

CAPITAL	**Budapest**
CURRENCY	**Forints** (Ft). You can buy your currency at banks and official bureaux. Credit cards/ Eurocheques/small denomination traveller's cheques widely accepted; Deutschmarks more useful than dollars or sterling. £1 = Ft401; $1 = Ft281; €1 = Ft252.
CUSTOMS ALLOWANCES	200 cigarettes or 50 cigars or 250 g tobacco; 2 bottles of wine, 0.25 litres of spirits and 250 ml cologne or perfume.
EMBASSIES AND CONSULATES IN BUDAPEST	**Aus**: KIRÁLYHÁGÓ TÉR 8–9, ☎201 8899. **Can**: BUDAKESZI ÚT 32, ☎275 1200. **NZ** (CONSULATE): TERÉZ KRT. 38, ☎331 4908. **Ire**: SZABADSÁG TÉR 7–9, ☎302 9600. **SA**: GÁRDONYI GÉZA ÚT 17, ☎392-0999. **UK**: HARMINCAD ÚT 6, ☎266 2888. **USA**: SZABADSÁG TÉR 12, ☎475 4400 and 475 4703.
EMBASSIES AND CONSULATES OVERSEAS	**Aus**: 17 BEALE CRESCENT, DEAKIN ACT., 2600 CANBERRA, ☎(02) 6282-3226. **Can**: 299 WAVERLEY ST, OTTAWA, ONTARIO K2P 0V9, ☎(613) 230 9614. **Ire**: 2 FITZWILLIAM PL., DUBLIN 2, ☎(01) 661 2902. **SA**: 959 ARCADIA ST, ARCADIA, PRETORIA (PO Box 27077, SUNNYSIDE 0132), ☎(012) 433 030. **UK**: 35 EATON PLACE, LONDON SW1X 8BY, ☎(020) 7235 5218. **USA**: 3910 SHOEMAKER ST N.W., WASHINGTON DC 20008-3811, ☎(202) 362-6730.
LANGUAGE	**Hungarian** (Magyar). Both English and German are widely understood.
OPENING HOURS	Food/tourist shops, markets, malls open Sun. **Banks**: commercial banks Mon–Thur 0800–1500, Fri 0800–1300. **Food shops**: Mon–Fri 0700–1900, others: 1000–1800 (Thur until 1900); shops close for lunch and half-day on Sat (1300). **Museums**: usually Tues–Sun 1000–1800, free one day a week, closed public holidays.
POST OFFICES	Mostly 0800–1800 Mon–Fri, 0800–1200 Sat. Stamps also sold at tobacconists. Major post offices cash Eurocheques and change western currency; all give cash for Visa Eurocard/Mastercard, Visa Electron and Maestro cards.
PUBLIC HOLIDAYS	1 Jan; 15 Mar; Easter Mon; 1 May; Whit Mon; 20 Aug; 23 Oct; 25, 26 Dec.
PUBLIC TRANSPORT	Long-distance buses (Volán busz, ☎(1) 318-2122), slow ferries along Danube.
RAIL PASSES	IR, ED, Eu, EP, European East valid (pp. 26–31). Budapest Card: 2 or 3 days unlimited travel on public transport, free/reduced entry to sights. Website information: www.budapestinfo.hu.
RAIL TRAVEL	Comprehensive rail system; most towns on the Hungarian State Railways (MÁV) network. Express services connect Budapest with major towns and Lake Balaton: EC, IC, ICR services require reservation and supplement. InterPici (IP) trains are fast railcars connecting with IC trains (reservation also compulsory). Other trains are without reservation or supplement, including gyorsvonat (fast trains) and sebesvonat (semi-fast). Local trains (személyvonat) are very slow. Book sleepers well in advance. (TrainsEurope can book for you, ☎(01354) 660222.)
TELEPHONES	Phonecards on sale at news-stands, tobacconists, post offices, supermarkets. Payphones take 10, 20 50 and 100 forint coins. Dial in: ☎+36. Outgoing: ☎00. Domestic long distance calls: ☎06. Police ☎107. Fire ☎105. Ambulance ☎104.

TIPPING	Round up by 5–15% for restaurants and taxis. People do not generally leave coins on the table; instead the usual practice is to make it clear that you are rounding up the sum. Service is included in some upmarket Budapest restaurants (where tipping is not necessary).
TOURIST INFORMATION	(Websites: www.hungarytourism.hu; www.gotohungary.com) **Tourinform** branches throughout Hungary; English-speaking staff. Hungarian Tourist Card, valid for 13 months, Ft.5992 (www.hungarycard.hu).
TOURIST OFFICES OVERSEAS	**UK**: 46 EATON PL., LONDON SW1X 8AL, ☎ (020) 7823 1032. **USA**: 150 E. 58TH ST, 33RD FLOOR, NEW YORK, NY 101 55-3398, ☎ (212) 355 0240.
VISAS	Not required by citizens of EU, Can, SA or USA. Nationals of Aus and NZ must obtain visas before travelling.

ITALY

CAPITAL	**Rome** (Roma).
CLIMATE	Very hot in July and Aug; May, June, Sept best for sightseeing. Holiday season ends mid Sept or Oct. Rome crowded at Easter.
CURRENCY	**Euro** (€). 1 Euro = 100 cents. £1 = €1.59; $1 = €1.12.
CUSTOMS ALLOWANCES	Standard EU regulations apply (see pp. 19–20).
EMBASSIES AND CONSULATES IN ROME	**Aus**: V. ALESSANDRIA, 215, ☎ (06) 85 27 21. **Can**: V. GB DE ROSSI, 27, ☎ (06) 44 59 81. **NZ**: V. ZARA, 28, ☎ (06) 441 71 71. **UK**: V. XX SETTEMBRE, 80A, ☎ (06) 482 54 41. **USA**: V. VITTORIO VENETO, 119A, ☎ (06) 467 41.
EMBASSIES AND CONSULATES OVERSEAS	**Aus**: 12 GREY ST, DEAKIN, CANBERRA 2600, ☎ (02) 6273 3333. **Can**: 21ST FLOOR, 275 SLATER ST, OTTAWA, ONTARIO K1P 5H9, ☎ (613) 232 2401. **NZ**: 34 GRANT RD, THORDON, WELLINGTON, ☎ (04) 473 5339. **UK**: 14 THREE KINGS YARD, LONDON W1Y 2EH, ☎ (020) 7312 2209. **USA**: 1601 FULLER ST N.W., WASHINGTON, DC 20009, ☎ (202) 328 5500.
LANGUAGE	**Italian**; standard Italian is spoken across the country though there are marked regional pronunciation differences. Some dialects in more remote areas. Many speak English in cities and tourist areas. In the south and Sicily, French is often more useful than English.
OPENING HOURS	**Banks**: Mon–Fri 0830–1330, 1430–1630. **Shops**: (usually) Mon–Sat 0830/0900–1230, 1530/1600–1900/1930; closed Mon am/Sat pm July/Aug. **Museums/sites**: usually Tues–Sun 0930–1900; last Sun of month free; most refuse entry within an hour of closing. Churches often close lunchtime.
POST OFFICES	Mostly Mon–Fri 0830–1330/1350, Sat 0830–1150. Some counters (registered mail and telegrams) may differ; in main cities some open in the afternoon. Send anything urgent via express. *Posta prioritaria* stamps also guarantee a faster delivery. Stamps *(francobolli)* available from tobacconists *(tabacchi)*. Poste restante *(Fermo posta)* at most post offices.
PUBLIC HOLIDAYS	All over the country: 1, 6 Jan; Easter Sun and Mon; 25 Apr; 1 May; 15 Aug (virtually nothing opens); 1 Nov; 8, 25, 26 Dec. Regional saints' days: 25 Apr in Venice; 24 June in Florence, Genoa and Turin; 29 June in Rome; 11 July in Palermo; 19 Sept in Naples; 4 Oct in Bologna; 6 Dec in Bari; 7 Dec in Milan.
PUBLIC TRANSPORT	Buses often crowded, but regular; serve many areas inaccessible by rail. Services drastically reduced at weekends; not always shown in timetables. Taxis: metered, can be expensive; steer clear of unofficial ones.
RAIL PASSES	EP, IR, ED, Eu, France n' Italy Pass valid (pp. 26–31). Biglietto Chilometrico: valid for 2 months; allows up to 20 journeys or 3000 km for up to 5 people; 1st class £150/€180.76, 2nd class £88, €116.67; supplements/reservations extra. Italy Flexi Railcard: 4, 8, or 12 days' consecutive travel on FS network within 1 month; 1st/2nd class 4 days €216/173, 8 days €302/242, 12 days €389/311.

RAIL TRAVEL

Italian rail times online: www.fs-on-line.com; national rail information ☎848-888088 (to talk to an operator say 'no' during the pause after the initial recorded message in Italian). National rail company: Trenitalia, a division of Ferrovie dello Stato (FS). High-speed express services between major cities. 'Eurostar Italia' requires payment of a higher fare and reservations are compulsory. Reservations also possible for IC and EC. IR trains: semi-fast expresses. Espresso: 1st-/2nd-class long-distance domestic trains; stop only at main stations. Diretto: stop frequently, very slow. Locale: stop almost everywhere. Services reasonably punctual. Some long-distance trains do not carry passengers short distances. Sleepers: single or double berths in 1st class, three (occasionally doubles) in 2nd. Couchettes: four berths in 1st class, six in 2nd. Refreshments on most long-distance trains. Queues at stations often long; buy tickets and make reservations at travel agencies (look for FS symbol).

TELEPHONES

Public phones take coins or phonecards (carte scheda telefoniche); good for international calls. Scatti (metered) phones common in bars; pay the operator after use. The area code must be included even within the code area; for instance you must dial 06 (code for Rome) even when calling within Rome. There are changes to telephone codes planned with a 4 to replace the initial 0. Dial in: ☎+39, include first 0 in area code. Outgoing: ☎00 + country code. English information for inter-continental calls: ☎170; for European and Mediterranean calls: ☎176. Police: ☎113. Fire: ☎115. Ambulance: ☎118.

TIPPING

In restaurants you need to look at the menu to see if service charge is included. If not, a tip of 10% is fine depending on how generous you feel like being. The same percentage applies to taxi drivers. A helpful porter can expect up to €2.50.

TOURIST INFORMATION

(Website: www.italiantourism.com) Most towns and resorts have Azienda Autonoma di Soggiorno e Turismo (AAST), many with their own websites, or Pro Loco.

TOURIST OFFICES OVERSEAS

Aus: ITALIAN GOVERNMENT TRAVEL OFFICE (ENIT) , C/O CAMERA DI COMMERCIO E INDUSTRIA ITALIANA IN AUSTRALIA, LEVEL 26, 44 MARKET ST, NSW 2000, SYDNEY, ☎(02) 9262 1666, fax (02) 9262 1667 (enitour@ihug.com.au). **Can**: ITALIAN GOVERNMENT TRAVEL OFFICE (ENIT), 17 BLOOR ST, SUITE 907, SOUTH TOWER, M4W 3R8 TORONTO, ONTARIO, ☎(416) 925 4882, fax (416) 925 4799. **UK**: ITALIAN STATE TOURIST BOARD, 1 PRINCES ST, LONDON W1R 8AY, ☎(020) 7408 1254, fax (020) 7493 6695 (enitlond@globalnet.co.uk). **USA**: ITALIAN GOVERNMENT TRAVEL OFFICE (ENIT), 630 FIFTH AV., SUITE 1565, ROCKEFELLER CENTER, NEW YORK, NY 10111, ☎(212) 245 4822, fax (212) 586 9249 (enitny@italiantourism.com).

VISAS

Visas not needed by EU or commonwealth citizens or nationals of USA.

LATVIA

CAPITAL

Riga

CLIMATE

Similar to Estonia.

CURRENCY

Lat. 1 Lat = 100 Santīmi. £1 = 0.89Lat; $1 = 0.62Lat; €1 = 0.56Lat.

CUSTOMS ALLOWANCES

200 cigarettes or 200g tobacco products, and 1 litre alcohol.

EMBASSIES AND CONSULATES IN RIGA

Aus: RAINA 3, ☎722 2388. **Can**: DOMA LAUKUMS 4, ☎722 6315. **UK**: ALUNANA IELA 5, ☎777 4700. **USA**: RAINA BULV 7, ☎721 0005.

EMBASSIES AND CONSULATES OVERSEAS

Aus: (honorary consulate in Sydney), ☎61 297 44 59 81. Consulates: **Can**: 280 ALBERT ST, SUITE 300, OTTAWA, ONTARIO, ☎(613) 238 6014. **UK**: 45 NOTTINGHAM PL., LONDON W1M 3FE, ☎(020) 7312 0040. **USA**: 4325 17TH ST N.W., WASHINGTON, DC 20011, ☎(202) 726 8213/4.

LANGUAGE

Latvian, spoken by over half the population. Russian understood all over Latvia. English and German often spoken.

OPENING HOURS

Banks: mainly Mon–Fri 0900–1600, some Sat 0900–1230. **Shops**: Mon–Fri 0900/1000–1800/1900 and Sat 0900/1000–1700. Many close on Mon. **Museums**: days vary, but usually open Tues/Wed–Sun 1100–1700.

POST OFFICES

Mon–Fri 0900–1800, Sat 0900–1300. In Riga (BRIVIBAS) open 24 hrs.

PUBLIC HOLIDAYS	I Jan; Good Fri; Easter Sun/Mon; I May; Mothers' Day (second Sun in May); 23 June (Midsummer), 24 June (St John's Day); 18 Nov; 25, 26, 31 Dec.
PUBLIC TRANSPORT	Very cheap for Westerners. Taxis generally affordable (agree fare first if not metered). Beware of pickpockets on crowded buses and trams. Long-distance bus network preferred to slow domestic train service.
RAIL PASSES	IR, ED, EP not valid, but rail fares are cheap.
RAIL TRAVEL	Comfortable overnight trains; best to take berth in 2nd-class coupé (compartment of four berths). Trains to Moscow etc also convey superior coupé with two berths. Reservations compulsory for all sleepers; Russian-bound ones may require proof of entry visa when booking. Very little English spoken at stations.
TELEPHONES	Phone cards for 2, 5 or 10 Lati sold at post offices, shops and kiosks. Dial in: ☎ +371; omit initial 0 from area code. Outgoing: ☎ 00 + country code. Police: ☎ 110. Fire and Ambulance: ☎ 112.
TIPPING	Not necessary to tip service at the bar or counter, but tip 10% if served at your table. Round up taxi fares to a maximum of 10%.
TOURIST INFORMATION	**Latvian Tourism Development Agency**, PILS LAUK 4, LV 1050 RIGA, ☎ 722 9945, fax 750 8468 (www.latviatravel.com).
TOURIST OFFICES OVERSEAS	**Finland: Latvian Tourism Information Centre**, MARIANKATU 8B, 00170 HELSINKI, ☎ (09) 278 4774 (latviatravel@kolumbus.fi); **Germany: Baltic Tourism Information Centre**, SALZMANSTR. 152, 48159 MÜNSTER, ☎ (251) 21 50 742 (info@baltic-info.de).
VISAS	Visas (not needed by Ire, UK, USA) obtainable by Australian, Canadian, New Zealand and most European nationals at airport and Riga passenger ports (not train border crossings), valid 10 days. Check at least 21 days before travelling.

LITHUANIA

CAPITAL	**Vilnius**
CLIMATE	Similar to Estonia.
CURRENCY	**Litas (Lt)**; I Litas = 100 Centų (singular: Centas) (ct). Travellers cheques and credit cards widely accepted. £1 = Lt5.70; $1 = Lt4.00; €1 = Lt3.58.
CUSTOMS ALLOWANCES	Allowances constantly changing. Currently: 200 cigarettes or 50 cigars or 250g tobacco, and 1 litre spirit or 2 litres wine or 2 litres champagne or 5 litres beer.
EMBASSIES AND CONSULATES IN VILNIUS	**Aus**: TOTORIU 15, ☎ (22) 22 33 69. **Can**: GEDIMINO 64, ☎ (22) 22 08 98. **UK**: ANTAKALNIO GATVE 2, ☎ (22) 22 20 70. **USA**: AKEMNU 6, ☎ (22) 22 30 31.
EMBASSIES AND CONSULATES OVERSEAS	**Can**: 130 ALBERT ST, SUITE 204, OTTAWA, ONTARIO K1P 5G4, ☎ (613) 567 5458. **UK**: 84 GLOUCESTER PL., LONDON W1H 3HN, ☎ (020) 7486 6401. **USA**: 2622 16TH ST NW, WASHINGTON DC, 20009, ☎ (202) 234 5860.
LANGUAGE	**Lithuanian**. Lithuanian and Latvian are both Indo-European in origin. Russian is helpful but unpopular.
OPENING HOURS	**Banks**: mostly Mon–Thur 0900–1600, Fri 0900–1500. **Shops**: (large shops) Mon–Fri 1000/1100–1900; many also open Sat until 1600. Some close for lunch 1400–1500 and also on Sun and Mon. **Museums**: days vary, most close Mon and sometimes Tues and open at least Wed and Fri; often free on Wed; hours usually at least 1100–1700, check locally.
POST OFFICES	All towns have post offices with an international telephone service.
PUBLIC HOLIDAYS	I Jan; 16 Feb; 11 Mar; Easter Sun and Mon; I May; the first Sun in May (Mothers Day); 6 July; 15 Aug; I Nov; 25, 26 Dec.
PUBLIC TRANSPORT	Similar to Latvia (see above).
RAIL PASSES	IR, ED, EP not valid, but rail fares are cheap.

Directory

RAIL TRAVEL	Major routes are to St Petersburg, Moscow and Kaliningrad (Russia), Warsaw (Poland), Riga (Latvia) and Minsk (Belarus). Warsaw trains have standard European couchettes and sleepers. Other overnight trains have 54-bunk open coaches (P), 4-bed compartments (K) and (on Moscow trains only) 2-bed compartments (M-2). International train reservations in Vilnius, ☎ (22) 62 69 47.
TELEPHONES	Phone cards sold at news-stands. Dial in: ☎ 370 + area code (minus initial 2). Outgoing: ☎ 8 10 + country code. Police: ☎ 02. Fire: ☎ 01. Ambulance: ☎ 03.
TIPPING	Not necessary to tip service at the bar or counter, but tip 10% if served at your table. Round up taxi fares to a maximum of 10%.
TOURIST INFORMATION	**Lithuanian State Department of Tourism**: VILNIAUS 4/35, LT-2600 VILNIUS, ☎ (2) 62 26 10, fax (2) 22 68 19. Another excellent website with links to other Baltic sites is www.tourism.lt; tb@tourism.lt.
TOURIST OFFICES OVERSEAS	**Germany:** Baltic Tourism Information Centre, SALZMANSTR. 152, 48159 MUENSTER, ☎ (251) 21 50 742 (info@baltic-info.de). **USA:** Vytis Tours, 40–24 235TH STREET, DOUGLASTON, NY 11363, ☎ (718) 423 6161, fax (718) 423 3979 (vyttours@earthlink.net).
VISAS	Not required by citizens of Aus, Can, Ire, NZ, UK, USA or most EU citizens. Many other nationalities can obtain a visa at the airport. Lithuanian visas valid in Latvia and Estonia; check first.

LUXEMBOURG

CAPITAL	**Luxembourg City** (Ville de Luxembourg).
CLIMATE	Similar to Belgium.
CURRENCY	**Euro** (€). 1 Euro = 100 cents. £1 = €1.59; $1 = €1.12.
CUSTOMS ALLOWANCES	Standard EU regulations (pp. 19–20). No checks at land borders (by train).
EMBASSIES AND CONSULATES OVERSEAS	**UK**: 27 WILTON CRESCENT, LONDON SW1X 8SD, ☎ (020) 7235 6961. **USA**: 2200 MASSACHUSETTS AV. N.W., WASHINGTON DC 20008, ☎ (202) 265 4171.
LANGUAGE	**Lëtzebuergesch** is the national tongue, but almost everybody also speaks fluent French and/or German, plus often at least some English.
OPENING HOURS	Many establishments take long lunch breaks. **Banks**: usually Mon–Fri 0830–1200 and 1400–1630 or later. **Shops**: Mon 1300/1400–1800; Tues–Sat 0800/0900–1800. **Museums**: most open six days a week (usually Tues–Sun).
POST OFFICES	Usually open Mon–Fri 0800–1200 and 1400–1700.
PUBLIC HOLIDAYS	1 Jan; Feb (Carnival); Easter Mon; 1 May; Ascension; Whit Mon; Corpus Christi; 23 June; 15 Aug; 3 Sept (Luxembourg City Fête); 1 Nov; 25, 26 Dec. When holidays fall on Sun; the Mon usually becomes a holiday but only twice in one year.
PUBLIC TRANSPORT	Good bus network between most towns. Taxis not allowed to pick up passengers in the street; most stations have ranks.
RAIL PASSES	IR, EP, ED, Eu Benelux Tourrail Pass valid (pp. 26–31). Billet Réseau: day card €4.40; unlimited 2nd-class travel on all public transport; carnet of 5 day cards costs €17.60; from CFL offices. Luxembourg Card: unlimited transport on all trains and buses, free entry to more than 40 attractions within the Duchy of Luxembourg; 1 day (€9), 2 days (€16), 3 days (€22); family pass for 2–5 people (maximum of 3 adults) at twice one person rate; available from Tourist Offices, hotels, youth hostels, campsites, stations etc.
RAIL TRAVEL	Rail services converge on Luxembourg City. National rail company: CFL, also runs long-distance buses; these and city buses covered by multi-ride passes. Stations: most are small, few facilities.
TELEPHONES	*Télécartes*, available from post offices or stations. Dial in: ☎ +352. Outgoing: ☎ 00 + country code. There are no area codes in Luxembourg. Police ☎ 113. Emergency services (fire and ambulance): ☎ 112.

TIPPING	In restaurants, cafés and bars service charge is usually included, round up to nearest €1. Taxi drivers €2–5; porters €1–2; hairdressers €2; cloakroom attendants €0.50; toilet attendants €0.25.
TOURIST INFORMATION	Literature covering all of Luxembourg from any Tourist Office.
TOURIST OFFICES OVERSEAS	**UK:** 122 REGENT ST, LONDON W1B 5SA, ☎ (020) 7434 2800, fax (020) 7734 1205 (www.luxembourg.co.uk; tourism@luxembourg.co.uk). **USA:** 17 BEEKMAN PL., NEW YORK, NY 10022, ☎ (212) 935 8888, fax (212) 935 5896 (www.visitluxembourg.com; luxnto@aol.com).
VISAS	Visas are not needed by citizens of Australia, Canada, EU, New Zealand or the USA. South Africans do need visas.

THE NETHERLANDS

CAPITAL	Administrative capital: **Amsterdam**. Legislative capital: **The Hague** (Den Haag).
CLIMATE	Can be cold in winter; rain prevalent all year. Many attractions close Oct–Easter, while Apr–May is tulip time and the country is crowded; June–Sept can be pleasantly warm and is busy with tourists.
CURRENCY	**Euro (€).** 1 Euro = 100 cents. £1 = €1.59; $1 = €1.12.
CUSTOMS ALLOWANCES	Standard EU regulations apply (see pp. 19–20).
EMBASSIES AND CONSULATES IN THE HAGUE/AMSTERDAM	**Aus:** CARNEGIELAAN 4, THE HAGUE, ☎ (070) 310 8200. **Can:** SOPHIALAAN 7, THE HAGUE, ☎ (070) 311 1600. **NZ:** CARNEGIELAAN 10, THE HAGUE, ☎ (070) 346 9324. **Ire:** DR. KUYPERSTR. 9, THE HAGUE, ☎ (070) 363 0993. **SA:** WASSENAARSEWEG 40, ☎ (070) 392 4501. **UK:** LANGE VOORHOUT 10, THE HAGUE, ☎ (070) 364 5800 (consulate in Amsterdam ☎ (020) 676 4343). **USA:** LANGE VOORHOUT 102, THE HAGUE, ☎ (070) 310 9209 (consulate in Amsterdam ☎ (020) 575 5309).
EMBASSIES AND CONSULATES OVERSEAS	**Aus:** 120 EMPIRE CIRCUIT, YARRALUMLA, CANBERRA, ACT 2600, ☎ (06) 273 3111. **Can:** SUITE 2020, 350 ALBERT ST, OTTAWA, ONTARIO K1R 1A4, ☎ (613) 237 5030. **Ire:** 160 MERRION RD, DUBLIN 4, ☎ (01) 269 3444. **NZ:** PO BOX 840, WELLINGTON, ☎ (04) 477 6390. **SA:** PO BOX 117, PRETORIA 0001, ☎ (012) 344 3910. **UK:** 38 HYDE PARK GATE, LONDON SW7 5DP, ☎ (020) 7590 3200. **USA:** 4200 LINNEAN AV. N.W., WASHINGTON, DC 20008, ☎ (202) 244 5300.
LANGUAGE	**Dutch**; English widely spoken.
OPENING HOURS	**Banks:** Mon–Fri 0900–1600/1700 (later Thur or Fri). **Shops:** Mon–Fri 0900/0930–1730/1800 (until 2100 Thur or Fri), Sat 0900/0930–1600/1700. Many close Mon morning. **Museums:** vary, but usually Mon–Sat 1000–1700, Sun 1000–1700 (some close Mon). In winter many have shorter hours.
POST OFFICES	Logo is 'ptt post' (white on red). Most open Mon–Fri 0830–1700 and some Sat 0830–1200. Stamps also sold in many postcard shops. Post international mail in left slot of mailbox, marked *overige* (other) *postcodes*.
PUBLIC HOLIDAYS	1 Jan; Good Fri; Easter Sun–Mon; 30 Apr; 5 May; Ascension Day; Whit Sun–Mon; 25, 26 Dec.
PUBLIC TRANSPORT	Centralised (premium rate) numbers for all rail and bus enquiries (computerised, fast and accurate): national, ☎ 0900 9292 (www.9292ov.nl); international, ☎ 0900 9296 (www.ns.nl). Most vehicles/carriages have buttons inside and out for passengers to open doors. Taxis best boarded at ranks or ordered by phone as they seldom stop in the street. In many cities (not Amsterdam), shared Treintaxis have ranks at stations and yellow roof signs (€3.40 for anywhere within city limits; tickets from rail ticket offices). *Strippenkaarten* (from stations, city transport offices, post offices and sometimes VVV) are strip tickets valid nationwide on metros, buses, trams and some trains (2nd class) within city limits; zones apply; validate on boarding; valid 1 hr; change of transport allowed.
RAIL PASSES	Benelux Tourrail Pass, IR, ED, EP, Eu valid (see pp. 26–31). Netherlands Rail offer range of tickets. Normal fares based upon distance travelled: day return costs on average 25% less than two singles. Holland Rail Pass (from International Rail and

Railchoice in the UK, plus NS stations): 3 or 5 days' unlimited travel within 1 month; 3 days £62/£41 (1st/2nd class), under 26/seniors £49/£34; 5 days £89/£61, under 26/seniors £72/£49; if 2 people travel together, 2nd person travels half price. Day rover €55.20/35.60 (1st/2nd). Zomertoer: 3 days' travel within 10 days 1 July–mid-Sept, €45 for 1 person, €59 for 2 people. Amsterdam Pass (3 days' public transport, plus various attractions) €29. Information: Holland Rail, CHASE HOUSE, GILBERT ST, ROPLEY, HANTS SO24 0BY, ☎ (01962) 773646, fax (01962) 773625 (www.hollandrail.com; sales@hollandrail.com).

RAIL TRAVEL	National rail company: **Nederlandse Spoorwegen** (NS). ICs and Sneltreins call at principal stations and stoptreins at all stations. Seat reservations only available for international journeys. Credit cards not accepted at rail stations. Most stations have GWK banks (daily; credit cards accepted), plus cycle hire and baggage lockers.
TELEPHONES	Booths have instructions in English. Booths are green and take only *telefoonkaarten* cards – available from post offices, VVV, NS, Primafoon (Dutch Telecom) shops and some shops; some phone booths take credit cards. International calls cheapest Mon–Fri evenings and all day Sat, Sun. Most numbers requesting information are prefixed 0900 and are at premium rates. Dial in: ☎ +31, and omit initial 0 from area code. Outgoing: ☎ 00 + country code. Operator: ☎ 118. International directory: ☎ 0900 8418. National directory ☎ 0900 8008. Emergency services: ☎ 112.
TIPPING	Although service charges are included, it is customary in restaurants, bars and cafés to leave a tip of 5–10% if you are satisfied. Taxi drivers expect a 10% tip.
TOURIST INFORMATION	(Website: www.vvv.nl) Tourist bureaux are VVV *(Vereniging voor Vreemdelingenverkeer)*: signs show a triangle with three Vs. All open at least Mon–Fri 0900–1700, Sat 1000–1200. Museumjaarkaart (€32, aged under 25 €14, from VVV and participating museums) is valid for one year; free entry to most museums nationwide; Kortingkaart is less comprehensive; CJP (Cultureel Jongeren Paspoort), for those under 26.
TOURIST OFFICES OVERSEAS	**Can**: SUITE 710, 25 ADELAIDE ST E., TORONTO, ONTARIO M5C 1Y2, ☎ 1 888 GO HOLLAND. **UK**: EGGINTON HOUSE, 18 BUCKINGHAM GATE, LONDON SW1E 6NT (no personal callers), ☎ 0906 871 777 (premium rate), fax (020) 7828 7941 (hollandinfo-uk@nbt.nl). **USA**: SUITE 1854, 225 N. MICHIGAN AV., IL 60601, CHICAGO, ☎ 1 888 GO HOLLAND.
VISAS	Visas are needed by citizens of South Africa, but not of Australia, Canada, EU, New Zealand or USA.

NORWAY

CAPITAL	**Oslo**.
CLIMATE	Surprisingly mild considering it's so far north; can be very warm in summer, particularly inland; the coast is appreciably cooler. May and June are driest months, but quite cool; summer gets warmer and wetter as it progresses, and the western fjords have high rainfall year-round. Days are very long in summer: the sun never sets in high summer in the far north. July and Aug is the busiest period; Sept can be delightful. Winter is the time to see the Northern Lights *(Aurora Borealis)*. Excellent snow for skiing Dec–Apr.
CURRENCY	**Norwegian kroner** (Nkr./NOK); 1 krone = 100 øre. On slot machines, *femkrone* means a NKr.5 coin and *tikrone* a NKr.10 coin. £1 = Nkr.12.74; $1 = Nkr.8.93; €1 = Nkr.8.00.
CUSTOMS ALLOWANCES	EU residents aged 18 or more: 200 cigarettes or 250g tobacco, 2 litres of beer, 1 litre of spirits (up to 60% and only if aged over 20) and 1 litre of wine etc (up to 22%), or 2 litres wine if no spirits. All limits doubled for non-EU residents.
EMBASSIES AND CONSULATES IN OSLO	**Can**: WERGELANDVN 7, ☎ 22 99 53 00. **SA**: DRAMMENSVN 88C, ☎ 22 44 79 10. **UK**: THOMAS HEFTYESGT 8, ☎ 23 13 27 00. **USA**: DRAMMENSVN 18, ☎ 22 44 85 50.
EMBASSIES AND CONSULATES OVERSEAS	**Aus**: 17 HUNTER ST., YARRALUMLA, CANBERRA ACT 2600, ☎ (02) 6273 3444. **Can**: ROYAL BANK CENTER, 90 SPARKS ST (SUITE 532), OTTAWA, ONT. K1P 5B4, ☎ (613) 238 6571. **Ire**: 34 MOLESWORTH ST, DUBLIN 2, ☎ (01) 662 1800. **SA**: PARIOLI BUILDING

A2, 1166 PARK ST, HATFIELD 0083, ☎ (027) 342 6100. **UK**: 25 BELGRAVE SQUARE, LONDON, SW1X 8QD, ☎ (020) 7591 5500. **USA**: 2720 34TH ST N.W., WASHINGTON D.C. 20008, ☎ (202) 333 6000.

LANGUAGE

Bokmål and **Nynorsk** are both variants of Norwegian. Almost everyone speaks English; if not, try German. Norwegian has three additional vowels: æ, ø and å, which (in that order) follow z.

OPENING HOURS

Banks: Mon–Wed and Fri 0815–1500 (1530 in winter), Thur 0815–1700. In Oslo, some open later, in the country some close earlier. Many have minibank machines that accept Visa, MasterCard (Eurocard) and Cirrus. **Shops**: Mon–Fri 0900–1600/1700 (Thur 0900–1800/2000), Sat 0900–1300/1500, many open later, especially in Oslo. **Museums**: usually Tues–Sun 1000–1500/1600. Some open Mon, longer in summer and/or close completely in winter.

POST OFFICES

Usually Mon–Fri 0800/0830–1700, Sat 0830–1300. Postboxes: red posthorn and crown on yellow boxes for local mail; reversed colours for elsewhere.

PUBLIC HOLIDAYS

1 Jan; Maundy Thur–Good Fri; Easter Sun–Mon; 1 May; Ascension Day (40th day after Easter); 17 May; Whit Sun–Mon; 25–26 Dec.

PUBLIC TRANSPORT

Train, boat and bus schedules linked to provide good connections. Often worth using buses or boats to connect two dead-end lines (e.g. Bergen and Stavanger), rather than retracing your route. Rail passes sometimes offer good discounts, even free travel, on linking services. NorWay Bussekspress, BUSSTERMINALEN, GALLERIET, SCHWEIGAARDSGT 8, N-0185 OSLO, ☎ 23 00 24 00, fax 23 00 24 49 (www.norway.no; ruteinformasjon @norway.no), has the largest bus network, routes going as far north as Kirkenes. Long-distance buses: comfortable, with reclining seats, ample leg room. Tickets: buy on board or reserve, ☎ 81 54 44 44 (premium-rate number). Taxis: metered, can be picked up at ranks or by phoning; treat independent taxis with caution.

RAIL PASSES

Scanrail, IR, ED, EP valid (see pp. 26–31). Norway Rail Pass: (for non-Europeans), 3, 4 or 5 days' travel within one month; 1st class $190/236/264, 2nd class $146/182/202; 20% reduction for seniors; seat reservations extra; 30% discount on Flåm Railway and reduced supplement in Signatur 1st-class coaches; not valid on Oslo airport trains; available from major NSB stations. Oslo Kortet/Card: free transport on buses, trams, underground and NSB local trains (up to Zone 3), free entry to attractions, discounts on sightseeing buses/boats; 1 day NKr.180, 2 days NKr.290, 3 days NKr.390, 1 day family card (2 adults, 2 children) NKr.395; available from most hotels, campsites and Tourist Offices.

RAIL TRAVEL

National rail company: Norges Statsbaner (NSB), ☎ 23 15 00 00, fax 23 15 31 75 (www.nsb.no). Fast trains: Signatur (tilting trains), Ekspresstog (Et) and Agenda. 2nd-class seating is comfortable and far more plentiful than 1st-class. Sleeping cars have one-, two- and three-berth compartments (passengers may reserve a berth in any category with either a 1st- or 2nd-class ticket). Long-distance trains carry refreshments. Reservations required for express and many other fast trains, ☎ 81 50 08 88. Reserved seats not marked, but your confirmation specifies carriage and seat/berth numbers. Carriage numbers are shown by the doors at the ends, berth numbers outside compartments, seat numbers on seat-backs or luggage racks. Stations: most have baggage lockers, larger stations have baggage trolleys. Narvesen chain (at most stations; open long hours) sells English-language publications and good range of snacks.

TELEPHONES

Telekort (phonecards) available from Narvesen, news stands and post offices. Card phones spreading fast, some accept credit cards. Coin and card boxes usually together, green marking the ones for cards. Overseas calls cheapest 2200–0800 and weekends. Dial in: ☎ +47. Outgoing: ☎ 00 + country code. Directory enquiries: ☎ 180 for Nordic countries, ☎ 181 for other countries. Local operator: ☎ 117. International operator: ☎ 115. Operators speak English. These are all premium-rate calls. Emergencies: Police: ☎ 112. Fire: ☎ 110. Ambulance: ☎ 113.

TIPPING

Tip 10% in restaurants (but not bars/cafés), if you are satisfied with the food, service etc. Not necessary for taxis.

TOURIST INFORMATION

(Website: www.visitnorway.com) Tourist Offices: *Turistinformasjon;* tourist boards: *Reiselivslag.* To be found in virtually all towns; free maps, brochures etc. available.

DIRECTORY

TOURIST OFFICES OVERSEAS

Aus: (see Embassies Overseas). **UK:** Norwegian Tourist Board, CHARLES HOUSE, 5 REGENT STREET (LOWER), LONDON SW1 4LR, ☎ (020) 7839 2650, fax (020) 7839 6014 (www.visitnorway.com; greatbritain@ntr.no). **USA:** Norwegian Tourist Board, 655 THIRD AVE, NEW YORK, NY 10017, ☎ (212) 885 9700.

VISAS

National identity cards issued by EU countries, Iceland and Switzerland are sufficient. Visas not needed by Nationals of Australia, Canada, New Zealand and the USA. South Africans need Schengen visas.

POLAND

CAPITAL

Warsaw (Warszawa).

CLIMATE

Temperate, with warm summers and cold winters; rain falls throughout year.

CURRENCY

Złoty (Zł.), divided into 100 Groszy. British pounds, American dollars and German marks are useful. Kantor exchange offices sometimes give better rates than banks and opening hours are longer. Credit cards increasingly accepted but not universal. £1 = 5.78Zł; $1 = 4.05Zł, €1 = 3.63Zł.

CUSTOMS ALLOWANCES

Visitors aged 18 or over: 250 cigarettes or 50 cigars or 250 g tobacco, 0.25 litre pure alcohol or 1 litre spirits or 5 litres wine. Taking out books and antiques pre-1945 requires authorisation. Ask in the bookshops or gallery at time of purchase.

EMBASSIES AND CONSULATES IN WARSAW

Aus: UL. NOWOGRODZKA 11, ☎ (022) 5213444. **CAN:** AL. JEROZOLIMSKIE 123, 10TH FLOOR, ☎ (022) 5843100. **IRE:** UL. HUMAŃSKA 10, ☎ (022) 8496655. **NZ:** UL. MIGDAŁOWA 4, ☎ (022) 6451407. **UK:** AL. RÓŻ. 1, ☎ (022) 6281001. **USA:** AL. UJAZDOWSKIE 29/31, ☎ (022) 6283041.

EMBASSIES AND CONSULATES OVERSEAS

Aus: 7 TURRANA ST, YARRALUMLA ACT, 2600 CANBERRA, ☎ (02) 62 73 12 08. **Can:** 443 DALY AV., OTTAWA 2, ONTARIO K1N 6H3, ☎ (613) 789 04 68. **Ire:** 5 AILESBURY RD, DUBLIN 4, ☎ (01) 283 08 55. **NZ:** 17 UPLAND RD, KELBURN, WELLINGTON, ☎ (4) 475 94 53. **SA:** 14 AMOS ST, COLBYN, PRETORIA 0083; ☎ (012) 43 26 31. **UK:** 47 PORTLAND PL., LONDON W1N 3AG, ☎ (020) 7580 0475. **USA:** 2640 16TH ST N.W., WASHINGTON DC 20009, ☎ (202) 234 3800.

LANGUAGE

Polish; many older Poles speak German; younger Poles (particularly students) may understand English. Russian widely understood, but unpopular.

OPENING HOURS

Banks: Mon–Fri 0800–1600/1800, Sat 0800–1300. **Shops:** Mon–Fri 0800/1100–1900, Sat 0900–1300. **Food shops:** Mon–Fri 0600–1900, Sat 0600–1600. Many stores are now open daily or round the clock in major cities. **Museums:** usually Tues–Sun 1000–1600; often closed public holidays and following day.

POST OFFICES

Known as *Poczta*; Mon–Fri 0700/0800–1800/2000, Sat 0800–1400 (main offices). City post offices are numbered (main office is always 1); number should be included in the post restante address. Post boxes: green (local mail), red (long-distance).

PUBLIC HOLIDAYS

1 Jan; Easter Sun–Mon; 1, 3 May; Corpus Christi; 15 Aug; 1, 11 Nov; 24, 25, 26 Dec.

PUBLIC TRANSPORT

PKS buses: cheap and often more practical than trains. Tickets normally include seat reservations (seat number is on back), bookable from bus station. In rural areas, bus drivers often halt between official stops if you wave them down.

RAIL PASSES

IR, ED, European East valid (see pp. 26–31). Polrail Pass: unlimited 1st and 2nd class travel on PKP network for 8 people (£103/69), 15 (£123/82), 21 days (£138/92) or 1 month (£175/116); ages 11–25 £73/48, £86/58, £97/64, £122/81 respectively; available from Railchoice and TrainsEurope.

RAIL TRAVEL

Cheap and punctual, run by Polskie Koleje Państwowe (PKP). At stations, departures *(odjazdy)* are on yellow paper, arrivals *(przyjazdy)* on white. IC, express *(ekspres* – prefixed Ex) and semi-express trains *(pospieszny)* are printed in red (all bookable). Black *osobowy* trains are the slowest. About 50% more for 1st class, but still cheap by Western standards and probably worth it. Overnight trains usually have 1st/2nd-class sleepers, plus 2nd-class couchettes and seats. Most long-distance trains have refreshments. Left luggage and refreshments in major stations. Few ticket clerks speak English.

TELEPHONES	Older public telephones take tokens but almost all the ones that work now take phonecards available from kiosks and tobacconists (ask for 'Karta Telefoniczna'. Dial in: ☎ +48. Outgoing: ☎ 901. English-speaking operator: ☎ 903. Police: ☎ 997. Fire: ☎ 998. Ambulance: ☎ 999.
TIPPING	An older system of rounding up has now been largely superseded by a flat rate 10% for table service in bars and restaurants, hairdressers, taxis and guides.
TOURIST INFORMATION	(Website: www.inyourpocket.com/poland/) IT tourist information office can usually help with accommodation. Also Orbis offices, for tourist information, excursions and accommodation (www.hotelsinpoland.com has info/bargains).
TOURIST OFFICES OVERSEAS	**UK**: Polish National Tourist Office, REMO HOUSE, 310–312 REGENT ST, LONDON W1R 5AJ, ☎ (020) 7580 8811, fax (020) 7580 8866 (www.pnto.dial.pipex.com; pnto@dial.pipex.com). **USA**: Polish National Tourist Office, 275 MADISON AV, SUITE 1711, NEW YORK, NY 10016, ☎ (212) 338 9412, fax (212) 338 9283.
VISAS	No visas needed for stays of up to 90 days for citizens of Ireland, UK or USA (but passports must be valid for at least six months after planned departure date from Poland). Nationals of Australia, Canada, New Zealand and South Africa need visas. For travellers in Germany, visas are obtainable from the Polish consulate in Leipzig (TRUFANOW-STR. 25, 04105 LEIPZIG, ☎ (0341) 5623300, www.botschaft-polen.de); open Mon, Tues, Thur and Fri, 0900–1200.

PORTUGAL

CAPITAL	**Lisbon** (Lisboa).
CLIMATE	Hotter and drier as you go south; southern inland parts very hot in summer; spring and autumn milder, but wetter. Mountains are very cold in winter.
CURRENCY	**Euro (€)**. 1 Euro = 100 cents. £1 = €1.59; $1 = €1.12.
CUSTOMS ALLOWANCES	Standard EU regulations apply (see pp. 19–20).
EMBASSIES AND CONSULATES IN LISBON	**Aus**: no embassy; nearest contact MADRID, SPAIN ☎ (00 34) 91 441 93 00. **Can**: 4TH FLOOR, AVENIDA DA LIBERDADE 144–156; ☎ 21 316 46 00. **Ire**: R. DA IMPRENSA À ESTRELLA 1–4; ☎ 21 392 94 40. **NZ**: UK Embassy handles New Zealand business. **UK**: RUA S. BERNARDO 33; ☎ 21 392 40 00. **USA**: AVENIDA DAS FORÇAS ARMADAS; ☎ 21 727 33 00.
EMBASSIES AND CONSULATES OVERSEAS	**Aus**: 33 CULGOA CIRCUIT, PO BOX 92, DEAKIN ACT, 2600 CANBERRA, ☎ (02) 6262 901 733. **Can**: 645 ISLAND PARK DR., OTTAWA, ONTARIO, K1Y OB8, ☎ (613) 729 0883. **Ire**: KNOCKSINNA HOUSE, KNOCKSINNA, FOXROCK, DUBLIN 18, ☎ (01) 289 4416. **NZ**: DELEITE TOUCHE TOHMATSU, 61 MOLESWORTH ST, WELLINGTON, ☎ (04) 644 472 1677. **SA**: 599 LEYDS ST, MUCKLENEUK, 0002 PRETORIA, ☎ (012) 341 2340. **UK**: 11 BELGRAVE SQ., SW1X 8PP, ☎ (020) 7235 5331. **USA**: 2125 KALORAMA RD N.W., WASHINGTON, DC 20008-1619, ☎ (202) 328 8610.
LANGUAGE	**Portuguese**; English, French, German in some tourist areas. Older people often speak French as second language, young people Spanish and/or English.
OPENING HOURS	**Banks**: Mon–Fri 0830–1445/1500. **Shops**: Mon–Fri 0900/1000–1300 and 1500–1900, Sat 0900–1300. City shopping centres often daily 1000–2300 or later. **Museums**: Tues–Sun 1000–1700/1800; some close for lunch and some are free on Sun. Palaces and castles usually close on Wed.
POST OFFICES	*Correio* indicates both post boxes and post offices. Most post offices open Mon–Fri 0900–1800, Sat 0900–1300; smaller ones close for lunch and Sat. Most large post offices have poste restante. Stamps *(selos)* on sale at places with sign depicting red horse or white circle on green background.
PUBLIC HOLIDAYS	1 Jan; National Carnival – end Feb/beginning March; Shrove Tues; Good Fri; 25 Apr; 1 May; 10 June; Corpus Christi; 15 Aug; 5 Oct; 1 Nov; 1, 8, 25 Dec. Many local saints' holidays.

PUBLIC TRANSPORT	Usually buy long-distance bus tickets before boarding. Bus stops: *paragem*; extend your arm to stop a bus. Taxis: black with green roofs or beige; illuminated signs; cheap, metered in cities, elsewhere fares negotiable; drivers may ask you to pay for their return journey; surcharges for luggage over 30 kg and night travel; 10% tip. City transport: can buy single tickets as you board, but books of tickets or passes are cheaper; on boarding, insert 1–3 tickets (according to length of journey) in the machine behind driver.
RAIL PASSES	IR, EP, ED, Eu valid (pp. 26–31). Heavy fines if you board train without ticket bought in advance. Bilhetes turisticos: unlimited 1st and 2nd class travel on CP network; 7 days (€100), 14 days (€170) or 21 days (€250); available from major stations.
RAIL TRAVEL	National rail company: Caminhos de Ferro Portugueses (CP); cheap (rail passes probably not worth it), but not always punctual; 1st/2nd class on long-distance. Trains: Suburbano or Regional (local, slow); IR, IC and Alfa Pendular (modern, fast; supplement payable; and seat reservations compulsory for IC and Alfa, which have buffet cars). CP information in Lisbon; ☎ 21 888 40 25. Lockers in most stations.
TIPPING	Not necessary in hotels; customary to round up taxi fares and bills in cafés/bars, though not essential. Tip 10% in restaurants.
TELEPHONES	Phonecards (from post offices and some tobacconists), plus coin-operated and (erratic) credit card phones. Surcharge for phones in hotels etc. International calls best made at post offices; pay after the call. Dial in: ☎ +351. Outgoing: ☎ 00. Operator: ☎ 118. Emergency services: ☎ 112. Area code must be used even when phoning from inside that area.
TOURIST INFORMATION	Multi-lingual telephone information service for tourists, based in Lisbon, ☎ 21 970 6341. The police (dark blue uniforms in towns, brown in rural areas) wear red arm bands if they are bi-lingual.
TOURIST OFFICES OVERSEAS	**Can**: 60 BLOOR ST W., SUITE 1005, TORONTO, ONTARIO, M4W 3B8, ☎ (613) 921 7376. **Ire**: 54 DAWON ST, DUBLIN 2, ☎ (01) 670 9133. **SA**: DIAMOND CORNER, 8TH FLOOR, 68 ELOFF ST, JOHANNESBURG 2000, ☎ (011) 33 74775. **UK**: 22/25A SACKVILLE ST, LONDON W1X 1LY, ☎ (020) 7494 1441. **USA**: 590 FIFTH AV. (4TH FLOOR), NEW YORK, NY 10036-4704, ☎ (212) 354 4403/4.
VISAS	Visas required by Nationals of South Africa and Australia. Nationals of Canada and USA may stay for up to 2 months without a visa.

ROMANIA

CAPITAL	**Bucharest** (Bucureşti).
CLIMATE	Hot inland in summer, coast cooled by breezes; milder in winter, snow inland, especially in the mountains.
CURRENCY	**Leu** (plural: Lei). Carry pounds, Euros or, ideally, dollars, in small denominations, plus traveller's cheques; change cash (commission-free) at exchange kiosks or banks; as rates can vary it's wise to check a few places first. Keep hold of your exchange vouchers; avoid black market exchange (risk of theft). Credit cards needed for car rental, accepted in better hotels and restaurants. Bancomats (automatic cash dispensers; accept most cards at good rates) in most cities. £1 = 44,974 Lei; $1 = 31,538 Lei; €1 = 28,237 Lei.
CUSTOMS ALLOWANCES	200 cigarettes or 300 g of tobacco, 1 litre of spirits and 4 litres of wine or beer, one video, two cameras. The latest information can be found at www.customs.ro. It's forbidden to export items with historic, cultural or artistic value.
EMBASSIES AND CONSULATES IN BUCHAREST	**Aus**: B-DUL UNIRII 16; ☎ 320 98 02 **Can**: STR. NICOLAE IORGA 36; ☎ 222 98 45. **Ire**: (Consulate): STR. V LASCAR 42; ☎ 211 39 67. **UK**: STR. JULES MICHELE 24; ☎ 312 03 03. **USA**: STR. TUDOR ARGHEZI 79; ☎ 210 40 42.
EMBASSIES AND CONSULATES OVERSEAS	**UK**: ARUNDEL HOUSE, 4 PALACE GREEN, LONDON W8 4QD, ☎ (020) 7937 9666/8. **USA**: 1607 23RD ST N.W., WASHINGTON DC, 20008-2809, ☎ (202) 332 4848.

DIRECTORY

LANGUAGE	Romanian; English understood by younger people, plus some German, and Hungarian throughout Transylvania.
OPENING HOURS	Banks: Mon–Fri 0900–1200/1300; private exchange counters open longer. Shops: usually 0800/0900–1800/2000, plus Sat morning or all day; often close 1300–1500. Local food shops often 0600–late. Few except in Bucharest open Sun. Museums: usually 0900/1000–1700/1800; open weekends, closed Mon (and maybe Tues).
POST OFFICES	Mail usually takes five days to reach Western Europe and up to two weeks to reach North America. Post offices in every town, open Mon–Fri, plus Sat morning.
PUBLIC HOLIDAYS	1–2 Jan; Easter Mon (Romanian Orthodox); 1 May; 1 Dec (National Unity Day); 25–26 Dec.
PUBLIC TRANSPORT	Buy bus/tram/metro (metrou) tickets in advance from kiosks (as a rule) and cancel on entry. Taxis inexpensive; if meter not in use agree a price first and always pay in lei, not foreign currency. Trains are best for long-distance travel, although bus routes are expanding and connect important towns and cities.
RAIL PASSES	Balkan, IR, ED, Balkan Flexipass valid (see pp. 26–31).
RAIL TRAVEL	Rail company: Compania Naţională de Căi Ferate (CFR). Network links major towns; main lines mostly electrified and quite fast, but branch lines very slow. Service fairly punctual and very inexpensive. Buy tickets in advance from Agenţia de Voiaj CFR, or at the station from 1 hr before departure. Except local trains, reserve and pay a speed supplement in advance (tickets issued abroad include supplement): cheapest are *tren de persoane* (very slow), then *accelerat* (still cheap), *rapid* and finally IC trains (prices approaching Western levels). Food usually only available on IC and some *rapids*; drinks sold on other trains. Couchette (*cuşeta*) or sleeper (*vagon de dormit*) inexpensive.
TELEPHONES	Operator-connected calls by telephone offices in post offices, or use Direct Access number to reach operator at home, or buy telephone card (20,000 or 50,000 Lei) for use in orange phones all over the country. Calls through hotel operators/domestic phones: ☎971 (international), ☎991 (long-distance). Dial in: ☎+40. Outgoing: ☎00 + country code. Police: ☎955. Fire: ☎981. Ambulance: ☎961.
TIPPING	Small tips are appreciated for good service at restaurants, hotels and in taxis. Only tip 10% at top-notch restaurants.
TOURIST INFORMATION	(Website: www.romaniatravel.com) Local tourist offices are not particularly helpful; most of the time you are better off asking at a travel agency.
TOURIST OFFICES OVERSEAS	UK: 22 NEW CAVENDISH ST, LONDON W1M 7LH, ☎ (020) 7224 3692, fax (020) 7935 6435 (uktouroff@romania.freeserve.co.uk). USA: 14 EAST 38TH ST, 12TH FLOOR, NEW YORK 10016, ☎ (212) 545 84 84, fax (221) 251 0429 (www.rezq.com/ronto; ronto@erols.com).
VISAS	Tourist visas are not required by EU or US citizens. Other nationals should check if they need a visa. Make sure you keep your visa papers when you enter – you'll pay a large fine if you don't have them when you leave Romania.

SLOVAKIA

CAPITAL	Bratislava.
CLIMATE	Similar to Czech Republic.
CURRENCY	Slovak Korunas or Crowns (SK or Kč); 1 Koruna = 100 Hellers. Credit cards becoming more widely accepted. £1 = 69.12Kč; $1 = 48.47Kč; €1 = 43.40Kč.
CUSTOMS ALLOWANCES	200 cigarettes, or 50 cigars, or equivalent in tobacco, 1 litre spirits and 2 litres wine.
EMBASSIES AND CONSULATES OVERSEAS	Aus/NZ: 47 CULGOA CIRCUIT, O'MALLEY, CANBERRA ACT 2606, ☎(061) 62 90 1516. Can: 50 RIDEAU TERRACE, OTTAWA, ONTARIO K1M 2AL, ☎(613) 749 4442. Ire: 107 THE SWEEPSTAKES, BALLSBRIDGE, DUBLIN 4, ☎(01) 660 0270. SA: 930 ARCADIA ST, ARCADIA 0083, PRETORIA, ☎(012) 342 2051-2. UK: 25 KENSINGTON PALACE GARDENS, LONDON W8 4QY, ☎(020) 7313 6470/0803. USA: 2201 WISCONSIN AV., N.W., SUITE 250, WASHINGTON DC 20007, ☎(202) 965 5160-5.

Directory

LANGUAGE	**Slovak**, a Slavic tongue closely related to Czech. Some Russian (unpopular), German, Hungarian (especially in the south), plus a little English and French.
OPENING HOURS	**Banks:** Mon–Fri 0800–1800. **Shops:** Mon–Fri 0900–1800, Sat 0800–1200. **Food shops** usually open 0800 and Sun. **Museums:** (usually) Tues–Sun 1000–1700. Most castles close national holidays and Nov–Mar.
POST OFFICES	Erratic post service. Usually post office hours: 0800–1900. Stamps also available from newsagents and tobacconists. Post boxes are orange.
PUBLIC HOLIDAYS	1, 6 Jan; Good Fri; Easter Mon; 1 May; 5 July; 29 Aug; 1, 15 Sept; 1 Nov; 24–26 Dec.
PUBLIC TRANSPORT	Comprehensive long-distance bus network, often more direct than rail in upland areas. Buy tickets from driver; priority given to those with bookings.
RAIL PASSES	European East, Czech and Slovak Railpass, ED, IR valid (see pp. 26–31). Fares based upon distance travelled; supplements for travel on R, EC/IC and IC air-conditioned trains. Kilometrica Banka (KMB): you purchase 2000 km of travel (1700Kč); minimum journey 100 km; 1st class travel 1½ times 2nd class price.
RAIL TRAVEL	National rail company: **eleznice Slovenskej Republiky** (ŽSR). Trains cheap, but often crowded. Apart from a small number of EC and IC trains, fastest trains are *expresný* (Ex). *Rýchlik* (R) trains cost as much as express; cheaper are *zrýchlený* (semi-fast) and *osobný* (very slow). At stations, departures *(odjezdy)* are on yellow posters, arrivals *(prijezdy)* on white. Sleeping cars/couchettes (reserve at all main stations, well in advance in summer) on most overnight trains. Seat reservations recommended (at station counters marked R) for express trains. Reservation agency: MTA, PÁRIĖKOVA 29, BRATISLAVA, ☎(07) 526 9311.
TELEPHONES	Slowly improving phone connections. Dial in: ☎+421, omit initial 0 from area code. Outgoing: ☎00. Bratislava code: ☎07. Information: ☎120 (national), ☎0149 (international). Police: ☎158. Fire: ☎150. Ambulance: ☎155.
TIPPING	Tipping is expected at hotels, hairdressers, in eateries and taxis. In general, round up to the nearest 10Kč, unless you are somewhere very upmarket, where you should tip 10%.
TOURIST INFORMATION	Bratislava Information Service (BIS), KLOBUCNICKA 2, ☎(07) 533 3715/4370; staff speak English and can arrange accommodation. SACR (Slovak Tourist Board) Head Office: BANSKA BYSTRICA: SACR, NAM. SLOBODY 2, PO BOX 497, 974 01 BANSKA BYSTRICA, ☎(088) 4142 860, fax (088) 4146 626 (www.sacr.sk). Satur (Slovak Tours and Travel Company), MILETICOVA 1, 824 72 BRATISLAVA, ☎(07) 542 2828.
TOURIST OFFICES OVERSEAS	**USA**: VICTOR INTERNATIONAL TRAVEL SERVICES, 10 EAST 40TH ST, 3604 NEW YORK, NY 10016, ☎(212) 6800 730.
VISAS	Not needed by nationals of EU, Canada, South Africa or USA. Nationals of Australia and New Zealand need visas and passports valid for at least six months.

SLOVENIA

CAPITAL	Ljubljana.
CLIMATE	Warm summers, cold winters; Mediterranean climate along coast; snow in the mountains in winter.
CURRENCY	Tolar (SIT); 1SIT = 100 stotins. £1 = 349SIT; $1 = 245SIT; €1 = 219SIT.
CUSTOMS ALLOWANCES	200 cigarettes, or 50 cigars, or 250g tobacco products, 1 litre spirits.
EMBASSIES AND CONSULATES OVERSEAS	**Aus**: LEVEL 6, ADVANCE BANK CENTER, 60 MARCUS CLARKE ST, CANBERRA ACT 2601, PO Box 284, ☎(06) 243 48 30. **Can:** 150 METCALFE ST, SUITE 2101, OTTAWA, K2P 1P1, ☎(613) 565 57 81. **UK:** SUITE ONE, CAVENDISH COURT, 11–15 WIGMORE ST, LONDON, W1H 9LA, ☎(020) 7495 77 75. **USA**: 1525 NEW HAMPSHIRE AV. N.W., WASHINGTON DC 20036, ☎(202) 667 53 63.
LANGUAGE	**Slovenian**; English, German and Italian often spoken in tourist areas.
OPENING HOURS	**Banks**: vary, but mostly Mon–Fri 0830–1230 and 1400–1630, Sat 0830–1200. **Shops**: mostly Mon–Fri 0800–1900, Sat 0830–1200. **Museums**: larger ones 1000–1800, many smaller ones 1000–1400; some close Mon.

POST OFFICES
Mon–Fri 0800–1800, Sat 0800–1200. Main post offices in larger centres may open evenings and on Sun. Ljubljana's main post office, TRG OSVOBODILNE FRONTE 5, by station, open 24 hrs. Efficient postal service.

PUBLIC HOLIDAYS
1–2 Jan; 8 Feb; Easter Sun–Mon; 27 Apr; 1–2 May; 25 June; 15 Aug; 31 Oct; 1 Nov; 25–26 Dec.

PUBLIC TRANSPORT
Long-distance bus services frequent and inexpensive; usually buy ticket on boarding. Information: TRG OSVOBODILNE FRONTE 5, next to Ljubljana station, ☎ (01) 2344 606. City buses have standard fare, paid with correct change into box by driver; cheaper to buy tokens from news-stands/post offices. Daily or weekly bus passes in main cities.

RAIL PASSES
ED, IR valid (see pp. 26–31).

RAIL TRAVEL
National rail company: Slovenske Železnice (Sž). Information: Ljubljana station; ☎ (01) 2913 332, or Slovenijaturist, SLOVENSKA 58, LJUBLJANA, ☎ (01) 2913 071.

TELEPHONES
International calls best made in post offices (pay afterwards). Phone booths: buy phonecards from post offices or tokens from post offices/news-stands. Dial in: ☎ +386. Outgoing: ☎ 00 + country code. Police: ☎ 113. Fire/ambulance: ☎ 112.

TIPPING
No need to tip bar staff or taxi drivers, although you can round sums up as you wish. In restaurants add 10%.

TOURIST INFORMATION
(Website: www.slovenia-tourism.si; info@slovenia-tourism.si) Slovenian Tourist Board, DUNAJSKA 156, SI-1000 LJUBLJANA, ☎ (01) 5891 858.

TOURIST OFFICES OVERSEAS
UK: 49 CONDUIT ST, LONDON W1R 9FB, ☎ (020) 7287 7133, fax (020) 7287 5476. **USA:** 345 E. 12TH ST, NEW YORK, NY 10003, ☎ (212) 358 9686, fax (212) 358 9025 (slotouristboard@sloveniatravel.com).

VISAS
Not generally needed, but South Africans need 3-month tourist visa and return ticket.

SPAIN

CAPITAL
Madrid.

CURRENCY
Euro (€). 1 Euro = 100 cents. £1 = €1.59; $1 = €1.12.

CUSTOMS ALLOWANCES
Standard EU regulations apply (see pp. 19–20).

EMBASSIES AND CONSULATES IN MADRID
Aus: PLAZA DEL DESCUBRIDOR DIEGO DE ORDÁS, 3 ☎ 91 441 93 00. **Can:** C. NÚÑEZ DE BALBOA 35, ☎ 91 423 32 50. **Ire:** PASEO DELA CASTELLANA, ☎ 91 436 40 93. **NZ:** PLAZA LEALTAD 2 (3RD FLOOR); ☎ 91 523 02 26. **SA:** C. CLAUDIO COELLO 91, ☎ 91 436 37 80. **UK:** C. FERNANDO EL SANTO 16, ☎ 91 700 82 00. **USA:** C. SERRANO 75, ☎ 91 587 25 10.

EMBASSIES AND CONSULATES OVERSEAS
Aus: LEVEL 24 ST MARTIN'S TOWER, 31 MARKET ST, SYDNEY NSW 2000, ☎ (612) 9 26 24 33. **SA:** 169 PINE ST, ARCADIA, PRETORIA 0083, ☎ (012) 34 43 875. **UK:** 20 DRAYCOTT PL., LONDON SW3 2RZ, (020) 7589 8989; **USA:** 2375 PENNSYLVANIA AV. (NW. WASHINGTON, DC) 20037, ☎ (202) 728 23 30.

LANGUAGE
Castilian Spanish most widely spoken. Three other official languages: Catalan, spoken in the east; Galego, spoken in Galicia (north-west), and Euskera, common in the Basque country, Navarra, even across the Pyrénées into France. English is fairly widely spoken in tourist areas. In Spanish listings 'CH' comes at the end of the 'C' section, 'LL' at the end of the 'L' section.

OPENING HOURS
Banks: Mon–Thur 0930–1630; Fri 0830–1400; Sat 0830–1300 (winter); Mon–Fri 0830–1400 (summer). **Shops:** Mon–Sat 0930/1000–1400 and 1700–2000/2030; major stores do not close for lunch, food shops often open Sun. **Museums** (www.mcu.es/nmuseos): vary; mostly open 0900/1000, close any time from 1400 to 2030. Few open Mon and some also close (or open half day) Sun. Expect to find most places closed 1300–1500/1600, esspecially in the south.

POST OFFICES
Most *correos* open 0800–1400 and 1700–1930. Larger ones offer poste restante (*lista de correos*). Stamps (*sellos*) also sold at tobacconists (*estancos*). Post boxes: overseas mail in slot marked *extranjero*. Postal system very slow.

Directory

PUBLIC HOLIDAYS	1, 6 Jan; several days at Easter; 1 May; 25 July; 15 Aug; 12 Oct; 1 Nov; 6, 8 Dec and several days at Christmas. Each region has at least four more public holidays, usually local saints' days.
PUBLIC TRANSPORT	Numerous regional bus companies *(empresas)* provide fairly comprehensive, cheap (if confusing) service. City buses are very efficient.
RAIL PASSES	IR, ED, EP, Eu valid (pp. 26–31). Fares based upon date and time of travel. Tarjeta Turística: 3–10 days unlimited 2nd-class travel within 2-month period, sold by RENFE (holders must purchase discount ticket for AVE, Talgo 200 and Euromed trains); prices unconfirmed but Euro Domino is a better bet. Spain FlexiPass: for non-European residents, 3–10 days unlimited travel within 2-month period; 3 days $200 (1st class), £155 (2nd class) – add $35 1st class/$30 2nd class for each extra day; supplement on AVE/Talgo 200 trains.
RAIL TRAVEL	General information: www.renfe.es or ☎ 902 24 02 02; FEVE: ☎ 902 100 818; AVE: ☎ 91 506 63 29; Grandes Líneas: ☎ 902 105 205; international: ☎ 93 490 11 22. National rail company: Red Nacional de los Ferrocarriles Españoles (RENFE). FEVE and a number of regionally-controlled railways operate lines in coastal regions. Long distance: AVE (Alta Velocidad Española: high-speed line) and Grandes Líneas (all other express services). RENFE offer money back if their AVE trains arrive more than 5 mins late! Premier Grandes Líneas services include Talgo (light articulated train) Euromed, Alaris (Madrid–Valencia), and IC expresses. *Diurno:* ordinary long-distance day train; *Estrella* is night train (including sleeper and/or couchette cars). Pricier alternative for night travel is the *Trenhotel* (train-hotel), offering sleeping compartments with their own shower and WC. All convey 1st- and 2nd-class accommodation *(Preferente* and *Turista;* AVE also have a 'super-first' class: *Club)* and require advance reservation. *Regionales:* local stopping service; *Cercanías:* suburban trains. *Regional Exprés* (not express in English sense of word) is gradually being introduced. In remoter parts of the country, services may be very infrequent. Compulsory reservations for all services for which a train category is shown in the timing column of the European Timetable (Talgo, IC etc).
TELEPHONES	At least one Telefónica office (the former state telephone company) in every large town: use a booth to make a call and pay the clerk afterwards. Public telephone booths *(teléfono público* or *locutorio)* usually have English instructions. Accept credit cards, money or *Teletarjeta* (phonecard – sold in tobacconists, post offices, some shops). Pay phones in bars are usually more expensive. Dial in: ☎ +34. Outgoing: ☎ 08. Police: ☎ 091 everywhere. Fire: ☎ 080 in most towns, can vary. General emergency number: ☎ 112. Area code must be used even when phoning from inside that area.
TIPPING	Not necessary to tip in bars and taxis; tipping is more common in restaurants but by no means obligatory. If you want to tip for good service, add around 5%.
TOURIST INFORMATION	(Websites: www.tourspain.es, www.okspain.org). *Oficinas de Turismo* (Tourist Offices) can provide maps and information on accommodation and sightseeing, and generally have English-speaking staff. Regional offices stock information on the whole region, municipal offices cover only that city; larger towns have both types of office.
TOURIST OFFICES OVERSEAS	**UK**: 22 MANCHESTER SQ., LONDON W1M 5AP, ☎ (020) 7486 8077. **USA**: 666 FIFTH AV, NEW YORK, NY 10103, ☎ (212) 265 8822.
VISAS	Visas not needed by citizens of Aus, Can, EU, NZ, USA for visits of up to 90 days. Non-EU nationals must hold onward or return tickets plus a minimum of £25 (sterling) per day of their intended stay, or a minimum of €301.20.

SWEDEN

CAPITAL	**Stockholm.**
CLIMATE	Often warm (especially in summer; continuous daylight in far north). Huge range between north and south; it can be mild in Skåne (far south) in Feb, but spring comes late May in the north. Winter generally very cold everywhere.

CURRENCY	**Kronor** or crowns. (SEK or SKr.); 1 krona = 100 öre. Växlare machines give change. The best exchange rate is obtained from Forex, which has branches at many stations. Keep receipts so that you can re-convert at no extra cost. £1 = Skr.15.24; $1 = Skr.10.68; €1 = Skr.9.57.
CUSTOMS ALLOWANCES	EU regulations apply (pp. 19–20); must be aged 20 or over to import alcohol.
EMBASSIES AND CONSULATES IN STOCKHOLM	**Aus:** SERGELS TORG 12, 11TH FLOOR, ☎ (08) 613 29 00. **Can:** TEGELBACKEN 4; ☎ (08) 453 30 00. **SA:** LINNÉGATAN 76, ☎ (08) 24 39 50. **UK:** SKARPÖGATAN 6–8, ☎ (08) 671 30 00. **USA:** DAG HAMMARSKJÖLDS VÄG 31, ☎ (08) 783 53 00.
EMBASSIES AND CONSULATES OVERSEAS	**Aus:** 5 TURRANA ST, YARRALUMLA, ACT 2600, CANBERRA, ☎ (02) 6270 2700. **Can:** 377 DALHOUSIE ST, OTTAWA, ONTARIO K1N 9N8, ☎ (613) 241 8553. **Ire:** 13–17 DAWSON ST, DUBLIN 2, ☎ (01) 671 5822. **NZ:** (see Australia); Consulate: VOGEL BUILDING, 13TH FLOOR, AITKEN ST, WELLINGTON, ☎ (04) 499 9895. **SA:** OLD MUTUAL BUILDING, ANDRIES ST 167, 9TH FLOOR, PRETORIA, ☎ (12) 321 1050. **UK:** 11 MONTAGU PL., LONDON W1H 2AL, ☎ (020) 7917 6400. **USA:** 1501 M ST N.W. WASHINGTON, D.C., 20005-1702; ☎ (202) 467 2600.
LANGUAGE	**Swedish.** English is widely spoken. Useful rail/bus/ferry words include *daglig* (daily), *Vard./Vardagar* (Mon–Sat), *helg./heldagar* (Sun and holidays).
OPENING HOURS	**Banks:** Mon–Fri 0930–1500 (Thur. and Mon–Fri in some cities, until 1730). Some, especially at transport terminals, have longer hours. **Shops:** mostly Mon–Fri 0900/0930–1700/1800, Sat 0900/0930–1300/1600. In larger towns department stores open until 2000/2200; also some on Sun 1200–1600. **Museums:** vary widely. In winter, many attractions close Mon and some close altogether.
POST OFFICES	Generally Mon–Fri 0900–1800, Sat 1000–1300, but there are local variations. Stamps also sold at newsagents and tobacconists. Post boxes: overseas mail are yellow; blue are local.
PUBLIC HOLIDAYS	1, 6 Jan; Good Friday; Easter Sun–Mon; Labour Day (1 May); Ascension Day; Whit Sun–Mon; Midsummer's Eve–Day; All Saints Day; 24–26 Dec. Many places close early the previous day, or Fri if it's a long weekend.
PUBLIC TRANSPORT	Transport system is highly efficient; ferries covered (in whole or part) by rail passes and city transport cards. Biggest operator of long-distance buses is Swebus ☎ (08) 655 00 90 (www.swebus.se). Advance booking is required on some routes and always advisable in summer; bus terminals usually adjoin train stations.
RAIL PASSES	IR, ED, EP, Scanrail valid (pp. 26–31).
RAIL TRAVEL	National rail company: Statens Järnvägar (SJ); some local lines run by regional authorities, or private companies and services in the far north are operated by Svenska Tågkompaniet. Central information line, ☎ (020) 75 75 75 or for reservations ☎ (0498) 20 33 80, both from anywhere in Sweden (www.sj.se). Supplement required on X2000 train (up to 200 kph); smaller supplements for CityExpress trains. Sleeping-cars: one or two berths in 2nd class; couchettes: six berths; female-only compartment available. 1st-class sleeping-cars (ensuite shower and WC) on many overnight services; 2nd-class have wash-basins, shower and WC and are at end of carriage. Long-distance trains have refreshment service. Many trains have family car, with a playroom, and facilities for the disabled. Seat reservations compulsory on X2000, night trains and through journeys to Copenhagen. X2000 services operate between Sweden and Copenhagen via the Öresund bridge and tunnel. Better to use local trains for short journeys. A big town's main station shows 'C' (for Central) on platform boards. Stations: *Biljetter* indicates the rail ticket office. Large, detailed timetables are displayed for long-distance trains: yellow for departures, white for arrivals, and there's usually a plan showing train composition. Pressbyrån (at most stations): sell English-language publications and snacks.
TELEPHONES	Coin-operated phones decreasing in number; most card phones accept credit cards and *Telia* phonecards (*telefonkorten*, from most newsagents, tobacconists, Pressbyrån kiosks. Dial in: ☎ +46. Emergency services (police, fire, ambulance): ☎ 112.
TIPPING	Restaurants include a service charge but a tip of 10–15% is appreciated. Taxis 10%. Tip hotel staff, porters, cloakroom attendants etc. at your discretion.
TOURIST INFORMATION	(Website: www.visit-sweden.com) Swedish Travel & Tourism Council. Tourist offices called *Turistbyrå*. Often a numerical queuing system in public places.

DIRECTORY

TOURIST OFFICES OVERSEAS	**UK**: Swedish Travel & Tourism Council, 11 MONTAGU PL., LONDON W1H 2AL; ☎ (020) 7870 5600, fax (020) 7724 5872. **USA**: Danish & Swedish Tourist Boards, PO Box 4649, GRAND CENTRAL STATION, NEW YORK, NY 10163-4649, ☎ (212) 885 9700, fax (212) 885 9710.
VISAS	Visas not required by citizens of Australia, Canada, EU, New Zealand and the USA. South Africans need visas.

SWITZERLAND

CAPITAL	**Bern** (Berne).
CLIMATE	Rainfall spread throughout the year. May–Sept are best in the mountains. June or early July best for the wild flowers. Snow at high altitudes even in midsummer. Season in the lakes: Apr–Oct. July and Aug get very busy.
CURRENCY	**Swiss Francs** (SFr.); £1 = Sfr.2.35; $1 = Sfr.1.65; €1 = Sfr.1.47.
CUSTOMS ALLOWANCES	Visitors aged 17 or over: 200 cigarettes or 50 cigars or 250 g tobacco, 2 litres alcohol up to 15% volume, and 1 litre over 15% volume. Residents outside Europe are entitled to twice the tobacco allowance.
EMBASSIES AND CONSULATES IN BERNE	**Aus**: ☎ 0900 57 80 13 (visa information only); **Can**: KIRCHENFELDSTR., 88 ☎ (031) 357 3200; **UK**: THUNSTR., ☎ (031) 359 7700. **USA**: JUBILÄUMSSTR. 93, ☎ (031) 357 70 11.
EMBASSIES AND CONSULATES OVERSEAS	**UK**: 16/18 MONTAGU PL., LONDON W1H 2BQ, ☎ (020) 7616 6000. **Ire**: 6 AYLESBURY RD, BALLSBRIDGE, DUBLIN 4, ☎ (01) 269 2515. **USA**: 2900 CATHEDRAL AVE N.W., WASHINGTON, DC 20008, ☎ (202) 745 7900.
LANGUAGE	**German, French, Italian** and **Romansch** are all official languages. Most Swiss people are at least bilingual. English is widespread.
OPENING HOURS	**Banks**: Mon–Fri 0800–1200 and 1400–1700. Money change desks in most rail stations, open longer hours. **Shops**: Mon–Fri 0800–1200 and 1330–1830, Sat 0800–1200 and 1330–1600. Many close Mon morning. In stations, shops open longer hours and on Sun. **Museums**: usually close Mon. Hours vary.
POST OFFICES	Usually Mon–Fri 0730–1200 and 1345–1830, Sat 0730–1100; longer in cities. Poste restante (*Postlagernd*) facilities available at most post offices.
PUBLIC HOLIDAYS	1–2 Jan; Good Fri; Easter Mon; Ascension Day; Whit Mon; 1 Aug; 25, 26 Dec. Also 1 May; Corpus Christi in some areas.
PUBLIC TRANSPORT	Swiss buses are famously punctual. Yellow postbuses stop at rail station; free timetables from post offices. Swiss Pass valid (see below), surcharge (SFr.5) for some scenic routes. Best way to get around centres is on foot.
RAIL PASSES	IR, ED, Eu valid (pp. 26–31). Swiss Pass: consecutive days on Swiss Railways, boats and most alpine postbuses and city buses, plus discounts on mountain railways; 4, 8, 15, 22 days or 1 month (1st class £151/214/258/300/332, 2nd £101/143/172/200/221); under 26 deduct 25%. Swiss Flexi Pass: as above but valid 3, 4, 5, 6 or 8 days within 1 month; 1st/2nd class from 3 days (£145/97) to 8 days (265/176; no youth version. Swiss Transfer Ticket: 1 month return from any airport/border station to any Swiss station (£76/48); Swiss Card additionally offers half-fares for rest of month, (£101/69). 13 regional passes covering 7 areas.
RAIL TRAVEL	Principal rail carrier is Swiss Federal Railways; plus many small, private lines. Services are fast and punctual, trains spotlessly clean. Express trains stop only at major cities. *Regionalzüge*, slow local trains, stop more frequently on same routes. Some international trains have sleepers (3 berths) and/or couchettes (up to 6 people). Sleepers can be booked up to 3 months in advance, couchettes/seats up to 2 months ahead. Reservations required on some sightseeing trains (e.g. Glacier Express and Bernina-Express). Information: ☎ 0900 300 300 (www.rail.ch), English-speaking operator. All main stations have information offices (and usually Tourist Offices), shopping and eating facilities. Provincial stations display train schedules. Cycle hire at most stations.

TELEPHONES	Swisscom offices sell phonecards (taxcard; also available from post offices, newsagents and most rail stations for SFr.5, 10 and 20). All operators speak English. Dial in: ☎+41; omit initial 0 from area code. Outgoing: ☎00 + country code. Police: ☎117. Fire: ☎118. Ambulance: ☎144 (most areas).
TOURIST INFORMATION	(Website: www.switzerlandtourism.ch). Tourist Offices in almost every town or village. The standard of information is excellent.
TIPPING	Not necessary or expected in restaurants or taxis.
TOURIST OFFICES OVERSEAS	**Can**: Switzerland Tourism (ST), 926 THE EAST MALL, ETOBICOKE, TORONTO, ONT., M9B 6K1, ☎(416) 695 2090, fax (416) 695 2774. **UK**: Switzerland Tourism (ST), SWISS CENTRE, SWISS COURT, LONDON W1V 8EE, ☎00800 100 200 30, fax 00800 100200 31 (stc@stlondon.com). **USA**: Switzerland Tourism (ST), SWISS CENTER, 608 FIFTH AVE, NEW YORK, NY 10020, ☎(212) 757 5944, fax (212) 262 6116 (stnewyork@switzerlandtourism.com). **Worldwide**: Switzerland Travel Centre (information, reservations, sales): ☎(00800) 100 200 30 (worldwide freephone), fax (00800) 100 200 31 (worldwide freefax) (www.myswitzerland.com)
VISAS	Valid passport required. Visas required for stays of more than 3 months. For shorter stays, visas not needed by citizens of EU, Australia, countries of the American continents (except Belize, Dominican Republic, Haiti and Peru), Japan and New Zealand.

TURKEY

CAPITAL	**Ankara.**
CLIMATE	Very hot summers, more manageable in spring or autumn. Cool Nov–Mar.
CURRENCY	**Turkish Lira** (TL). Credit cards widely accepted. £1 = TL2,109,000; $1 = TL1,479,000; €1 = TL1,324,000.
CUSTOMS ALLOWANCES	10 rolls of unused film; 200 cigarettes and 50 cigars; 200 gs of tobacco and 200 cigarette papers. (Plus you can buy 400 cigarettes, 100 cigars, and 500 gs of pipe tobacco from duty-free shops on entering.) Mobile phones to be accompanied by a certification form showing ownership. Tax refunds for larger purchases available on departure.
EMBASSIES AND CONSULATES OVERSEAS	**Aus**: 60 MUGGA WAY, RED HILL ACT 2603, ☎(06) 295 0227. **Can**: 197 WURTEMBURG ST., OTTAWA ONTARIO ON K1N 8L9, ☎(613) 789 4044. **Ire**: 11 CLYDE RD, BALLSBRIDGE, DUBLIN 4, ☎(01) 668 5240. **SA**: 199 CANOPUS ST, WATER KLOOF RIDGE, PRETORIA, ☎(012) 342 6053. **UK**: 43 BELGRAVE SQ., LONDON SW1X 8PA, ☎(020) 7393 0202. **USA**: 1714 MASSACHUSETTS AV, NW WASHINGTON, DC 20036, ☎(202) 659 8200.
LANGUAGE	**Turkish**, written in Latin alphabet. English and German often understood.
OPENING HOURS	**Banks**: 0830–1200, 1300–1700, Mon–Fri (some private banks are open at lunchtime). **Shops** 0930–1900; until around 2400 in tourist areas. **Government offices**: 0830–1230, 1300–1700 (closed Sat and Sun). In Aegean and Mediterranean regions, many establishments stay open very late in summer. **Museums**: many close on Mon.
POST OFFICES	Post offices have PTT signs. Major offices: Airport, Beyoğlu and Sirkeci open 24 hrs all week (limited services at night). Small offices: 0830–1700 (some close 1230–1300).
PUBLIC HOLIDAYS	1 Jan; 23 Apr; 19 May; 30 Aug; 29 Oct.
PUBLIC TRANSPORT	Excellent long-distance bus system (generally quicker than rail), run by competing companies (the best are Varan and Ulusoy). Shorter rides via dolmuş (shared taxis) that pick up passengers like a taxi, but only along a set route and much cheaper. TML run the ferries. Istanbul has a modern metro line, as well as a light-rail and tram route.
RAIL PASSES	IR, ED, Balkan Flexipass valid (pp. 26–31).
RAIL TRAVEL	Routes are tortuous and slow. Run by TCDD (Turkish State Railways). Beyond Istanbul, consult the Thomas Cook Overseas Timetable for Asian Turkey.

DIRECTORY

TELEPHONES	Telephone offices have Türk Telekom signs. Telephone cards (available in 30, 60 and 100 units) are the best way to make calls. Dial in: ☎ +90.
TIPPING	A 10% tip is usual in restaurants, unless service is included. Do not tip barmen directly. 10–20% is customary at hair salons. Do not tip taxi drivers.
TOURIST INFORMATION **TOURIST OFFICES OVERSEAS**	(Website: www.tourismturkey.org). **UK**: 170 D3 PICCADILLY, LONDON W1V 9DD, ☎ (020) 7734 8681; **USA**: 821 UNITED NATIONS PLAZA, NEW YORK, NY 10017, ☎ (212) 949 0160, fax (212) 983 1293 (tcbkny@wolrnet.att.net); 2525 MASSACHUSETTS AVE., WASHINGTON, DC 20008, ☎ (202) 612 6700, fax (202) 612 6744 (www.turkey.org; info@turkey.org).
VISAS	Required by nationals of Australia, Canada, Ireland, UK and USA. Obtainable at the border (fee).

UNITED KINGDOM

CAPITAL	**London.**
CLIMATE	Cool, wet winters, mild spring and autumn, winter can be more extreme. Wetter in the west. Aug and Bank Holiday weekends busiest in tourist areas.
CURRENCY	**Pounds Sterling** (£). $1 = £0.70; €1 = £0.64.
CUSTOMS ALLOWANCES	Standard EU regulations apply (see pp. 19–20).
EMBASSIES AND CONSULATES IN LONDON	**Aus**: AUSTRALIA HOUSE, STRAND, WC2B 4LA, ☎ (020) 7379 4334. **Can**: 1 GROSVENOR SQ., W1X 0AB, ☎ (020) 7258 6600. **Ire**: 17 GROSVENOR PL., SW1X 7HR, ☎ (020) 7235 2171. **NZ**: NEW ZEALAND HOUSE, 80 HAYMARKET, SW1Y 4TQ, ☎ (020) 7930 8422. **SA**: SOUTH AFRICA HOUSE, TRAFALGAR SQ., WC2N 5DP, ☎ (020) 7451 7299. **USA**: 24 GROSVENOR SQ., W1A 1AE, ☎ (020) 7499 9000.
EMBASSIES AND CONSULATES OVERSEAS	**Aus**: COMMONWEALTH AVE, YARRALUMLA, CANBERRA, ACT 2600, ☎ (06) 270 6666. **Can**: 80 ELGIN ST, OTTAWA, ONTARIO K1P 5K7, ☎ (613) 237 1530. **Ire**: 29 MERRION RD, DUBLIN 4, ☎ (01) 205 3742. **NZ**: 44 HILL ST, WELLINGTON 1, ☎ (04) 472 6049. **SA**: 255 HILL ST, PRETORIA 0002, ☎ (021) 483 1200. **USA**: 3100 MASSACHUSETTS AV. N.W., WASHINGTON, DC 20008, ☎ (202) 588 6500.
LANGUAGE	**English**, plus, in a very small way, Welsh and Gaelic.
OPENING HOURS	**Banks**: Mon–Fri 0930–1530. Some open Sat morning. **Shops**: Mon–Sat 0900–1730. Many supermarkets and some small shops open longer, plus Sun. **Museums**: usually Mon–Sat 0900/1000–1730/1800, half-day Sun.
POST OFFICES	Usually Mon–Fri 0930–1730, Sat 0930–1300; stamps sold in newsagents etc.
PUBLIC HOLIDAYS	England and Wales: 1 Jan; Good Fri; Easter Mon; May Day (first Mon May, may change): Spring Bank Holiday (last Mon May); Summer Bank Holiday (last Mon Aug); 25, 26 Dec. Variations in Scotland and Ireland.
PUBLIC TRANSPORT	Inter-city buses are cheaper, but slower, than trains. Main operator: National Express (www.gobycoach.com). Most town networks are good, but rural services patchy.
RAIL PASSES	(pp. 26–31). Rover/Ranger Ticket: almost unlimited travel within defined area; All-Line Rail Rover covers whole country; rovers valid 3–15 days, rangers 1 day. Saver/SuperSaver: reduced fare tickets; some time restrictions; purchase day of travel or shortly before.
RAIL TRAVEL	Passenger services run by private sector companies; booking office staff will give cheapest fare if asked. National enquiry number ☎ 08457 484 950. Fast trains, comfortable and frequent; 1st and standard class. Other long- and medium-distance regional services, usually standard class only. Refreshments available on board. Sleepers: cabins are two-berth or (higher charge) single. Reservation (essential for sleepers) available for most long-distance services; free when compulsory, else £1–2. Travel between Sat evening and Sun afternoon is often interrupted by engineering works; buses may replace trains. Online booking up to 3 days before departure, and timetable information: www.thetrainline.com and www.qjump.co.uk.

TELEPHONES	Phonecards sold at newsagents; pay phones take coins, phonecards or credit cards. Dial in: ☎ +44; omit initial 0 from code. Outgoing: ☎ 00 + country code. Emergency services: ☎ 999 or 112.
TIPPING	Tip 10% in restaurants, but not in pubs, self-service restaurants or bars; there is no need to tip in restaurants where the service is included (this is becoming increasingly common). Tip taxis (10%) hailed in the street, but you do not need to tip minicab drivers (where you order a cab by phone and agree a price).
TOURIST INFORMATION	Best to contact local Tourist Offices. For details of any tourist information centre, ☎ 0800 192192, toll-free (www.visitbritain.com or www.travelengland.org.uk).
TOURIST OFFICE OVERSEAS	**Aus:** 1 MACQUARIE PL., SYDNEY, NSW 2000, ☎ (02) 9377 4400. **Can:** 5915 AIRPORT RD, SUITE 120, MISSISSAUGA, ONTARIO L4V 1T1, ☎ (905) 405 1840, or toll free: 1 888 VISIT UK. **Ire:** 18-19 COLLEGE GREEN, DUBLIN 2, ☎ (01) 670 8000. **NZ:** 151 QUEEN ST, AUCKLAND 1, ☎ (09) 303 1446. **SA:** LANCASTER GATE, HYDE PARK LANE, HYDE PARK 2196 (visitors); PO Box 41896, CRAIGHALL 2024 (mail); ☎ (011) 325 0343. **USA:** 551 FIFTH AVENUE, NEW YORK, NY 10176-0799, ☎ (212) 986 2200, or toll free: 1 800 GO 2 BRITAIN; branches in Chicago and Los Angeles.
VISAS	Visas not needed by EU citizens, or by tourists from Australia, Canada, New Zealand, South Africa and USA.

CONVERSION TABLES

DISTANCES (approx. conversions)
1 kilometre (km) = 1000 metres (m) 1 metre = 100 centimetres (cm)

Metric	Imperial/US	Metric	Imperial/US	Metric	Imperial/US
1 cm	3/8 in.	10 m	33 ft (11 yd)	3 km	2 miles
50 cm	20 in.	20 m	66 ft (22 yd)	4 km	2½ miles
1 m	3 ft 3 in.	50 m	164 ft (54 yd)	5 km	3 miles
2 m	6 ft 6 in.	100 m	330 ft (110 yd)	10 km	6 miles
3 m	10 ft	200 m	660 ft (220 yd)	20 km	12½ miles
4 m	13 ft	250 m	820 ft (275 yd)	25 km	15½ miles
5 m	16 ft 6 in.	300 m	984 ft (330 yd)	30 km	18½ miles
6 m	19 ft 6 in.	500 m	1640 ft (550 yd)	40 km	25 miles
7 m	23 ft	750 m	1/2 mile	50 km	31 miles
8 m	26 ft	1 km	5/8 mile	75 km	46 miles
9 m	29 ft (10 yd)	2 km	1½ miles	100 km	62 miles

24-HOUR CLOCK
(examples)

0000 = Midnight	1200 = Noon	1800 = 6 pm
0600 = 6 am	1300 = 1 pm	2000 = 8 pm
0715 = 7.15 am	1415 = 2.15 pm	2110 = 9.10 pm
0930 = 9.30 am	1645 = 4.45 pm	2345 = 11.45 pm

TEMPERATURE
Conversion Formula: °C × 9 ÷ 5 + 32 = °F

°C	°F	°C	°F	°C	°F	°C	°F
-20	-4	-5	23	10	50	25	77
-15	5	0	32	15	59	30	86
-10	14	5	41	20	68	35	95

WEIGHT
1kg = 1000g 100 g = 3½ oz

Kg	Lbs	Kg	Lbs	Kg	Lbs
1	2¼	5	11	25	55
2	4½	10	22	50	110
3	6½	15	33	75	165
4	9	20	45	100	220

FLUID MEASURES
1 ltr.(l) = 0.88 Imp. quarts = 1.06 US quarts

Ltrs.	Imp. gal.	US gal.	Ltrs.	Imp. gal.	US gal.
5	1.1	1.3			
			30	6.6	7.8
10	2.2	2.6	35	7.7	9.1
15	3.3	3.9	40	8.8	10.4
20	4.4	5.2	45	9.9	11.7
25	5.5	6.5	50	11.0	13.0

MEN'S SHIRTS

UK	Europe	US
14	36	14
15	38	15
15½	39	15½
16	41	16
16½	42	16½
17	43	17

MEN'S SHOES

UK	Europe	US
6	40	7
7	41	8
8	42	9
9	43	10
10	44	11
11	45	12

MEN'S CLOTHES

UK	Europe	US
36	46	36
38	48	38
40	50	40
42	52	42
44	54	44
46	56	46

LADIES' SHOES

UK	Europe	US
3	36	4½
4	37	5½
5	38	6½
6	39	7½
7	40	8½
8	41	9½

LADIES' CLOTHES

UK	France	Italy	Rest of Europe	US
10	36	38	34	8
12	38	40	36	10
14	40	42	38	12
16	42	44	40	14
18	44	46	42	16
20	46	48	44	18

AREAS

1 hectare = 2.471 acres
1 hectare = 10,000 sq metres
1 acre = 0.4 hectares

INDEX

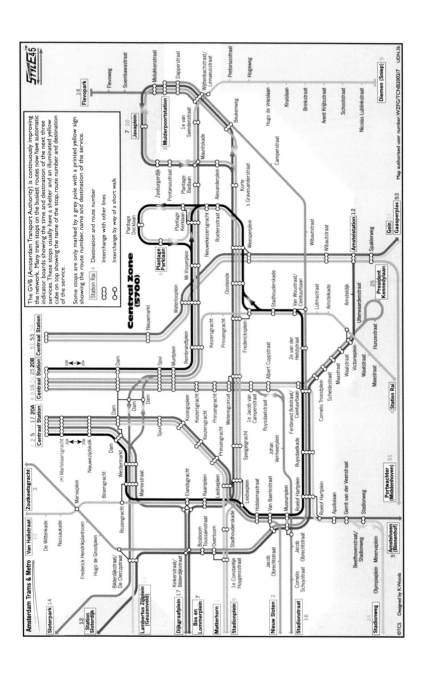

Amsterdam Trams & Metro

The GVB (Amsterdam Transport Authority) is continuously improving the network. Many tram stops on the busiest routes now have automatic indicator boards showing the time and destination of the next three services. These stops usually have a shelter and an illuminated yellow cube on top showing the name of the stop, route number and destination of the service.

Some stops are only marked by a grey pole with a printed yellow sign showing the route number, name and destination of the service.

Station Rai   4   Destination and route number

Interchange with other lines

Interchange by way of a short walk

Central Zone (5700)

©TCS   Designed by R.Woods

Map authorised user number: WZFG/TCNB2002/7   UDN.3b

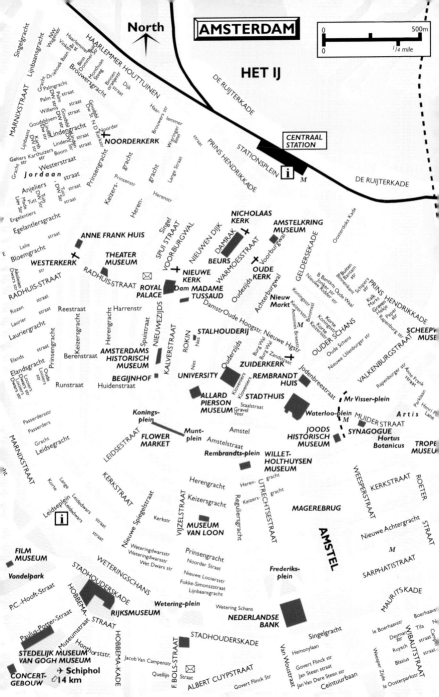

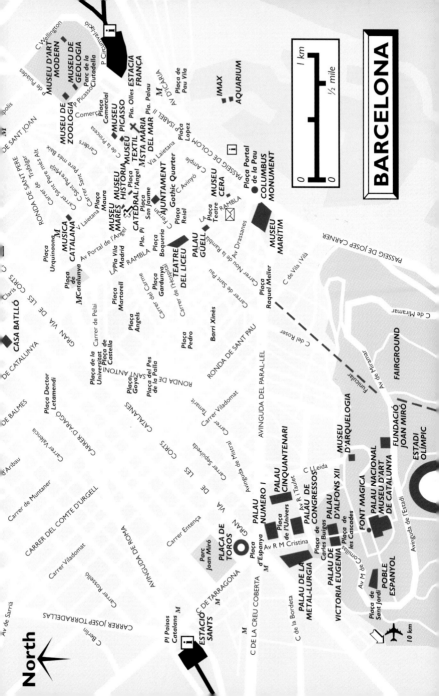

BARCELONA

0   ½ mile   1 km

North

C. Wellington
C. de Pujades
C. Berlín
Av de Sarrià
C de Ríos
Pl Països Catalans
CARRER JOSEP TORRADELLAS
ESTACIÓ DE SANTS
C DE LA CREU COBERTA
C de Tarragona
C de la Bordeta
C DE TARRAGONA
SANTS

MUSEU D'ART MODERN
MUSEU DE GEOLOGIA
Parc de la Ciutadella
Plaça Picasso
MUSEU DE ZOOLOGIA
Plaça Comercial
Comerç
MUSEU PICASSO
ESTACIÓ FRANÇA
AV D'ICÀRIA
Pla. Olles
Pla. Palau
Pla. del Palau
Pla. Isabel II
IMAX
AQUARIUM

Carrer de la Princesa
Carders
MUSEU TÈXTIL
MSTA MARIA DEL MAR
Plaça Lopez

RONDA DE SANT PERE
Carrer Sant Pere més Baix
Trafalgar
Carrer Sant Pere Mitja
Carrer Sant Pere més Alt
Plaça Moura
MUSEU MARÈS
MUSEU HISTÒRIA
CATEDRAL
Plaça de l'Àngel
AJUNTAMENT
Gothic Quarter
Plaça San Jaume
C Ample
Via Laietana
MUSEU CERA
Plaça Portal de la Pau
COLUMBUS MONUMENT

DE SANT JOAN
RONDA DE SANT PERE
Plaça Urquinaona
MÚSICA CATALANA
Av Portal de l'Àngel
Plaça Madrid
RAMBLA
Pla. Pi
Boqueria
C d'Avinyó
Plaça Reial
Plaça Teatre
RAMBLA
PASSEIG DE COLOM

Plaça Urquinaona
Plaça de Catalunya
Plaça Martorell
Carrer del Carme
Plaça Gardunya
Carrer de l'Hospital
PALAU GÜELL
TEATRE DEL LICEU
Carrer Nou de la Rambla
Av Drassanes
MUSEU MARÍTIM
Plaça Raquel Meller

CASA BATLLÓ
GRAN VIA DE LES CORTS
Claris
DE CATALUNYA
Carrer de Pelai
Plaça de la Universitat
Plaça Goya
SANT ANTONI
Plaça del Pes de la Palla
RONDA DE SANT PAU
Plaça Pedró
Barri Xinès
C de Sant Pau
C de Vila i Vilà
C. de Miramar

DE BALMES
Carrer Aribau
Carrer de Muntaner
Carrer València
CARRER D'ARAGÓ
Carrer de Balmes
Plaça Doctor Letamendi
Plaça de Castella
Plaça Àngels
Carrer de Pelai
Carrer Viladomat
RONDA DE SANT PAU
AVINGUDA DEL PARAL·LEL
C del Roser
PASSEIG DE JOSEF CARRER
FAIRGROUND
Av de Miramar
Funicular

CARRER DEL COMTE D'URGELL
Carrer Rosselló
Carrer Viladomat
CARRER DE ROMA
CATALANES
Carrer Tamarit
Carrer Viladomat
AVINGUDA DEL MARQUÈS DE MISTRAL
GRAN VIA
DE LES CORTS
Carrer Sepúlveda
Carrer Entença
PLAÇA DE TOROS
Parc Joan Miró
Plaça d'Espanya
Av R M Cristina
PALAU NÚMERO I
PALAU CINQUANTENARI
Plaça de l'Univers
PALAU DE CONGRESSOS
C Leida
Av R. I Taulet
PALAU D'ALFONS XII
PALAU VICTORIA EUGENIA
PALAU DE LA METAL·LÚRGIA
Plaça Carles Buïgas
Plaça de les Cascades
Av M de Conillola
FONT MÀGICA
MUSEU D'ARQUEOLOGIA
PALAU NACIONAL MUSEU D'ART DE CATALUNYA
FUNDACIÓ JOAN MIRÓ
ESTADI OLÍMPIC
Avinguda de l'Estadi
POBLE ESPANYOL
Plaça de Sant Jordi

10 km

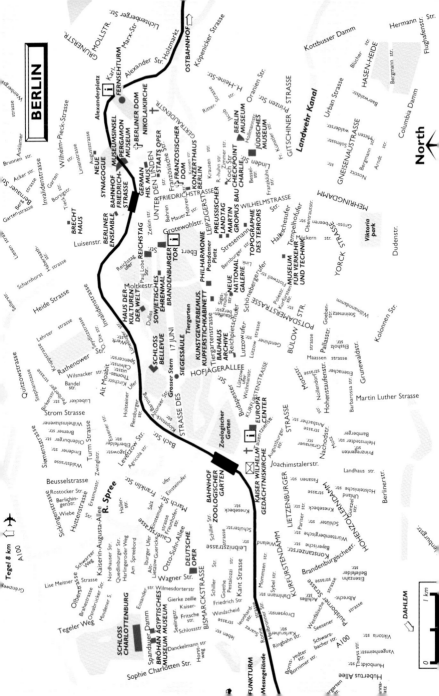

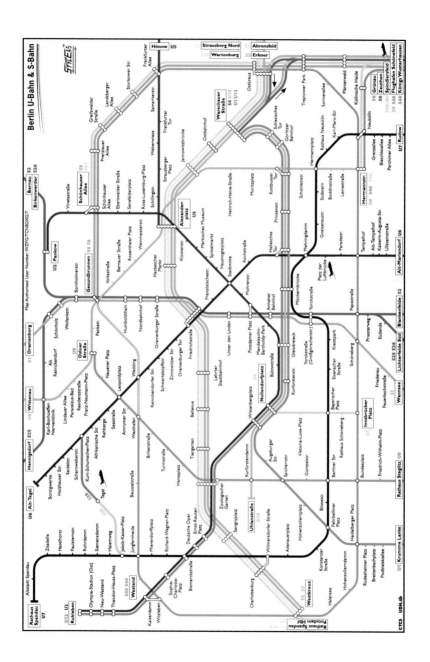

Berlin U-Bahn & S-Bahn

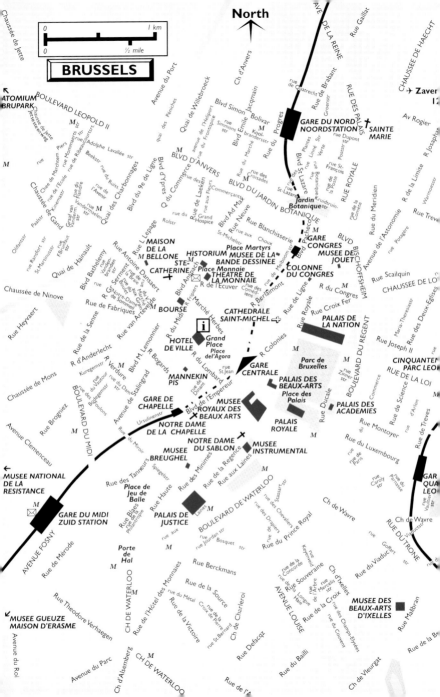

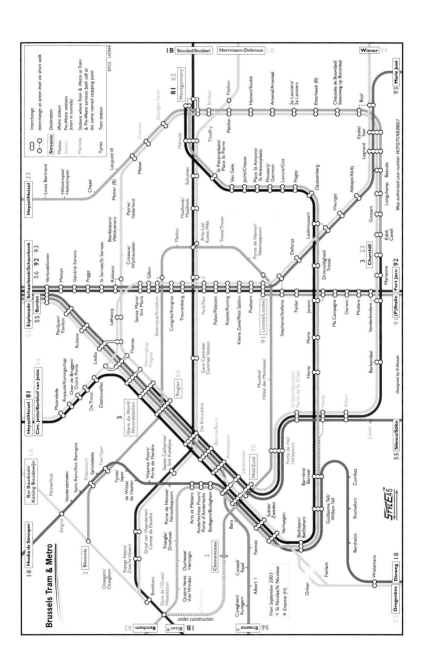

Brussels Tram & Metro

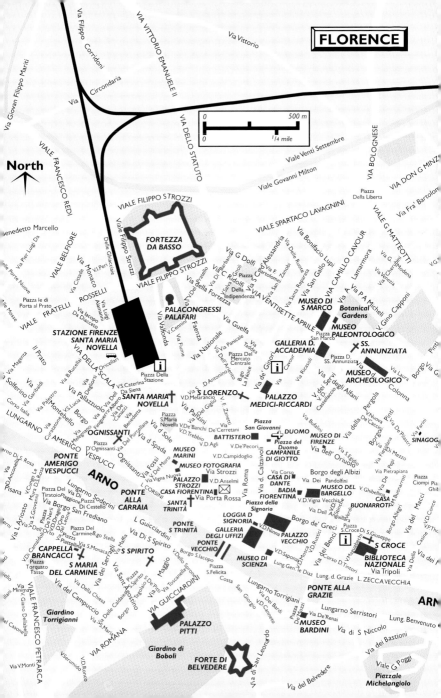

FLORENCE

North

500 m
1/4 mile

Via Giovan Filippo Mariti
Via Filippo Corridoni
VIA VITTORIO EMANUELE II
Via Vittorio
Via Circondaria
Via
VIA DELLO STATUTO
Viale Venti Settembre
Viale Giovanni Milton
VIA BOLOGNESE
VIA DON G MINZ
VIA FRA' Bartolom
Piazza Della Liberta
Via Fra' Bartolom
VIALE FRANCESCO REDI
Benedetto Marcello
Via Per Luigi Da
VIA BELFIORE
Viale Porte Nuove
Delle Ghiaccaie
VIALE FILIPPO STROZZI
VIALE FILIPPO STROZZI
Viale Filippo Strozzi
VIALE SPARTACO LAVAGNINI
Via Bonifacio Lupi
VIA G MATTEOTTI
VIA CAMILLO CAVOUR
Lamarmora
Via G. Orto
Via Venezia
Via A Via P A Micheli
Via Gino Capponi

FORTEZZA DA BASSO

VIA CITTADE
VIA MONACO
Via le di Porta al Prato
ROSSELLI
Via lacopo Da Diacceto
VIALE FRATELLI
Via Luigi Alamanni
PALACONGRESSI PALAFARI
Via G Dolfi
Via F Bartolomei
Via S Caterina d'Alessandria
Via Delle Ruote
Via Santa Reparata
Via San Gallo
MUSEO DI S MARCO
Botanical Gardens
MUSEO PALEONTOLOGICO
SS. ANNUNZIATA
MUSEO d ARCHEOLOGICO

Il Prato
Piazza le di Porta al Prato
STAZIONE FIRENZE SANTA MARIA NOVELLA
VIA CENNINI
Via C Ridolfi
Piazza Della Indipendenza
Via Della Fortezza
Via Faenza
VIA VENTISETTE APRILE
Via Guelfa
Via Panicale
Piazza San Marco
GALLERIA D. ACCADEMIA
Via degli Alfani
Via dei Servi
Borgo Via S

Piazza Della Stazione
VS.Caterina Da Siena
SANTA MARIA NOVELLA
S LORENZO
Via Nazionale
Piazza Del Mercato Centrale
Via Ricasoli
Via De' Ginori
Via Cavour
Colonna
Laura
Pergola

VIA DELLA SCALA
Il Prato
Via Magenta
S Solferino
Via Garibaldi
Corso Italia
LUNGARNO C AMERIGO
VS.Lucia
Via Palazzuolo
Via Montebello
VS.Lucia
Via Borgo Ognissanti
SANTA MARIA NOVELLA
V.D.Melarancio
Via Il Prato
S D'Antonino
PALAZZO MEDICI-RICCARDI
Via Bufalini
MUSEO DI FIRENZE
Via dell' Oriuolo
SINAGOG

OGNISSANTI
Piazza Ognissanti
Via del Moro
Via della Porcellana
Via d Spada
Piazza S.Maria Novella
V.D.Banchi
V.De'Cerretani
Piazza San Giovanni
DUOMO
BATTISTERO
Piazza del Duomo
CAMPANILE DI GIOTTO
Borgo degli Albizi
Via Pietrapiana
Piazza Ciompi

PONTE AMERIGO VESPUCCI
ARNO
Via Vigna Nuova
MUSEO MARINI
MUSEO FOTOGRAFIA
Via Strozzi
V.D.Agli
V.De'Pecori
V.D.Campidoglio
Via Corso
CASA DI DANTE
MUSEO DEL BARGELLO
V.Ghibellina
CASA BUONARROTI
Via del Macci

PONTE ALLA CARRAIA
ARNO
Lungarno Soderini
Via Dei Fossi
L CORSINI
PALAZZO STROZZI
CASA FIORENTINA
Via Porta Rossa
SANTA TRINITA
BADIA FIORENTINA
V.D.Vigna Vecchia
V.D.Vigna Vecchia
Via dell' Anguillara
Via Dei Pandolfini
S.Croce

PONTE ALLA CARRAIA
Lungarno Guicciardini
PONTE S TRINITA
GALLERIA DEGLI UFFIZI
LOGGIA D SIGNORIA
Piazza della Signoria
PALAZZO VECCHIO
V.D.Ninna
Borgo de' Greci
Via dei Benci
S CROCE
Piazza S.Croce
Di S.Giuseppe

CAPPELLA BRANCACCI
S MARIA DEL CARMINE
S SPIRITO
Via Maggio
Borgo S.Jacopo
PONTE VECCHIO
MUSEO DI SCIENZA
Lung.Gen.le Diaz
V.D.Saponai
V.D.Rustici
Via del Corso D.Tintori
BIBLIOTECA NAZIONALE
Via Tripoli
L. ZECCA VECCHIA

VIA GUICCIARDINI
Costa San Giorgio
Piazza S.Felicita
Lung. d. Grazie
PONTE ALLE GRAZIE
Lungarno Serristori
Lung. Benvenuto
ARN

VIALE FRANCESCO PETRARCA
Giardino Torrigianni
PALAZZO PITTI
Giardino di Boboli
FORTE DI BELVEDERE
Via di S Leonardo
Lungarno Torrigiani
Via de' Bardi
MUSEO BARDINI
Via di S Niccolo
Via dei Bastioni
Viale G Poggi
PIAZZALE Michelangiolo
Via del Belvedere

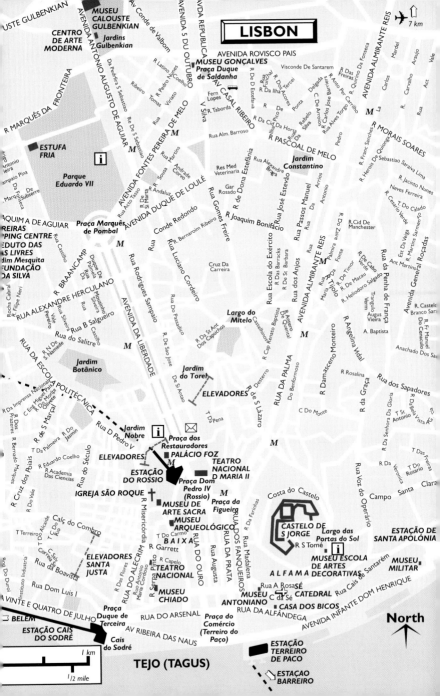

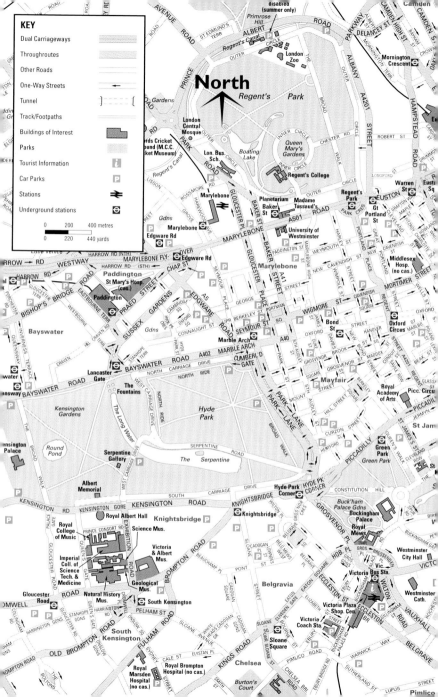

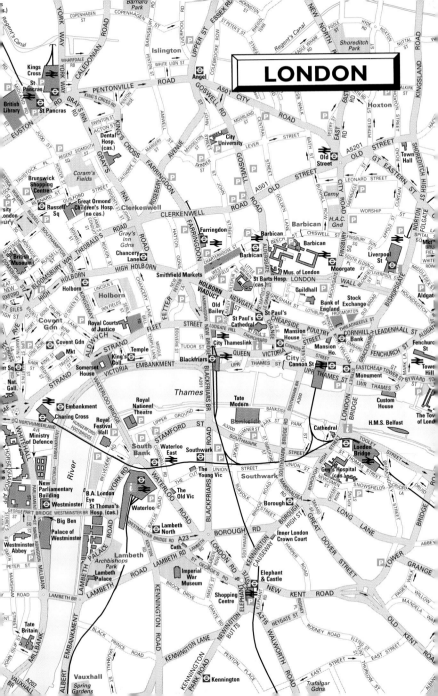

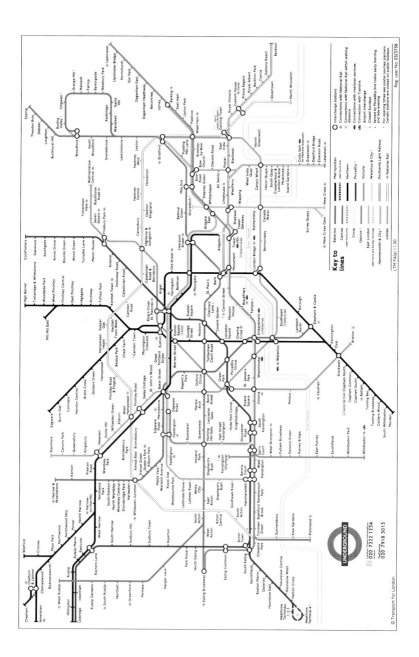

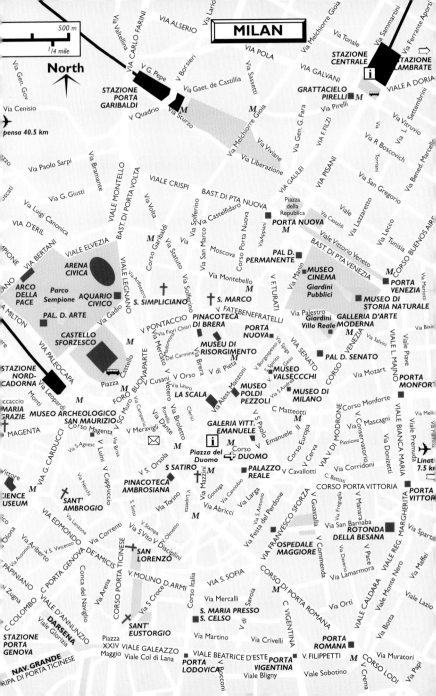

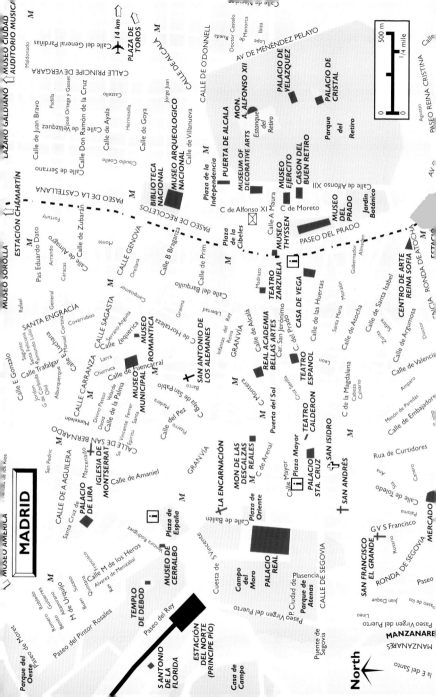

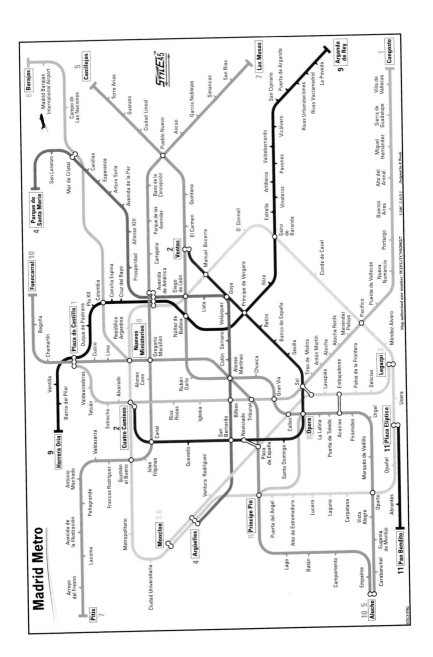

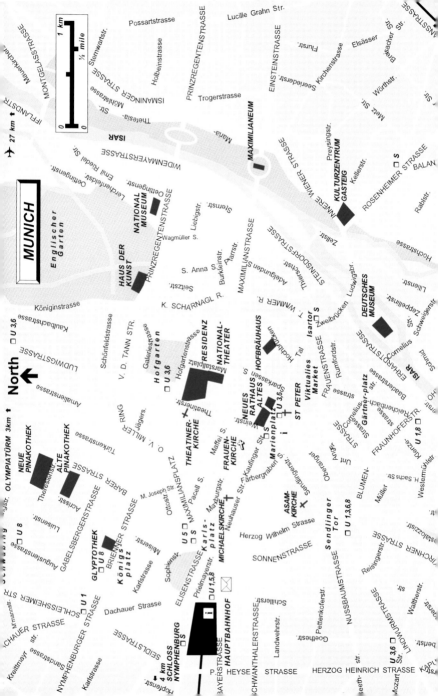

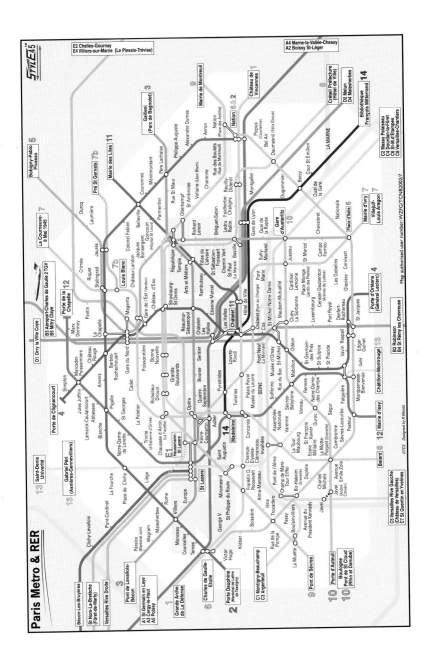

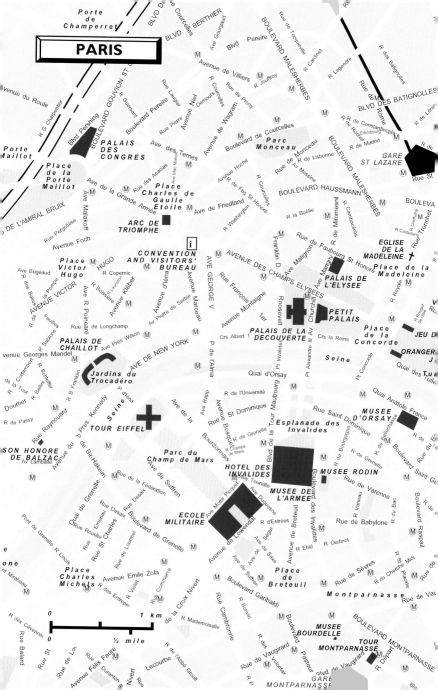

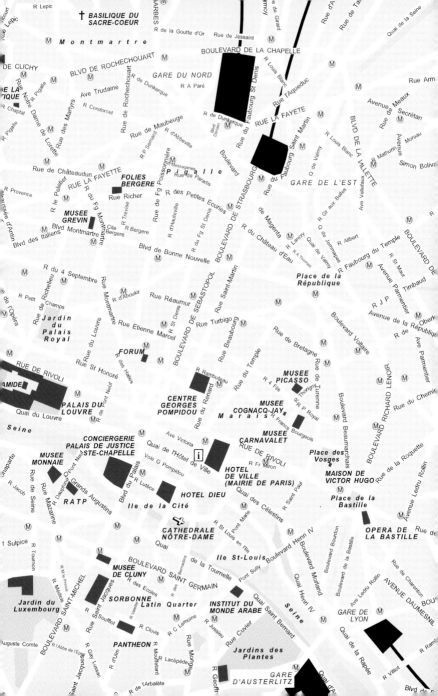

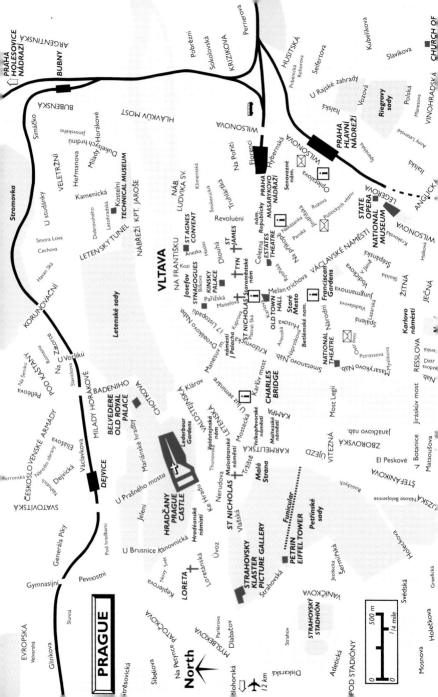

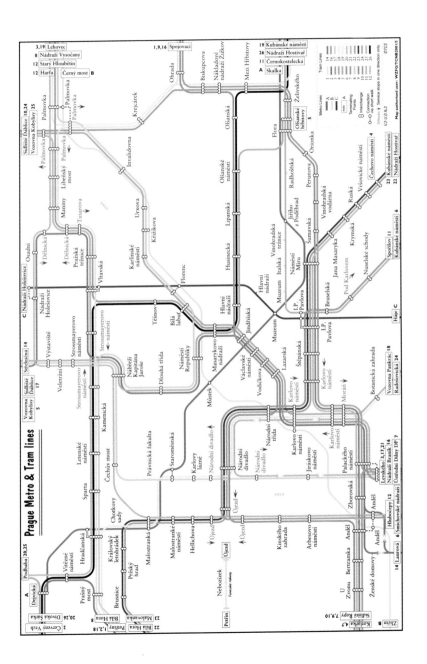

Prague Metro & Tram lines

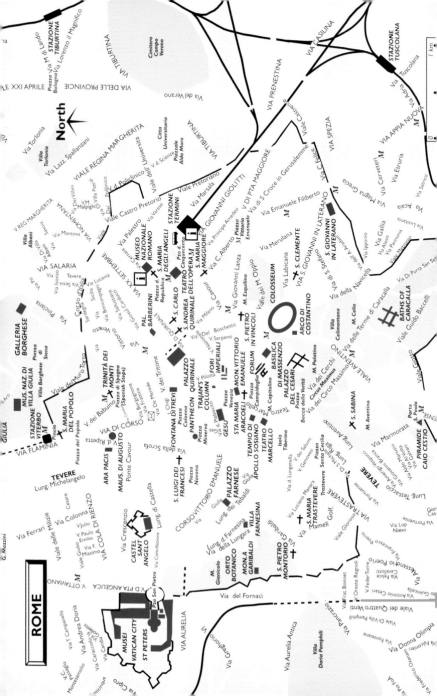

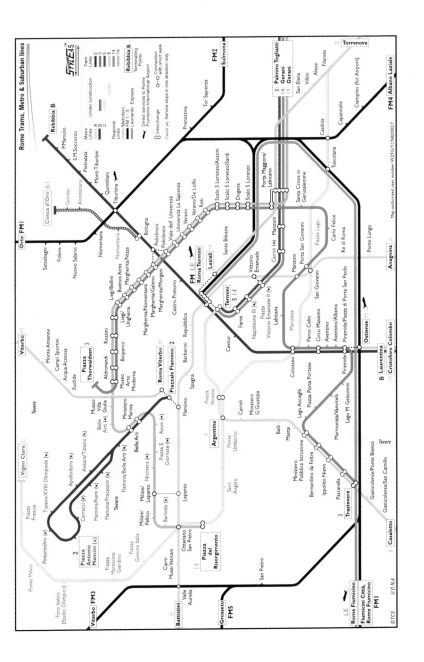

Rome Trams, Metro & Suburban lines

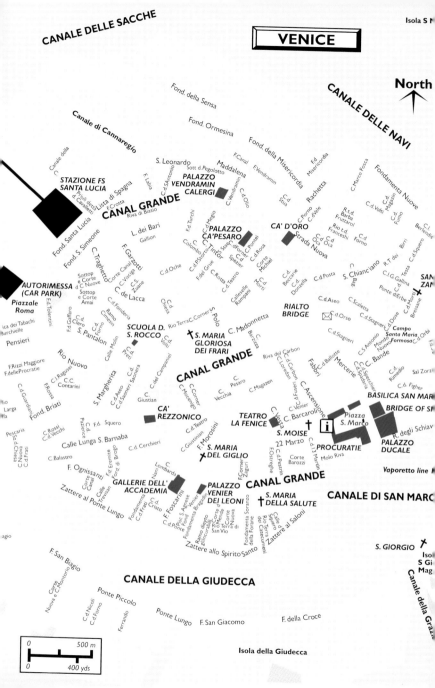

AFFIX
STAMP
HERE

Thomas Cook Publishing
PO Box 227, Units 19–21
The Thomas Cook Business Park
Peterborough
PE3 8XX

To claim your **free gift pocket atlas**, please help us improve future editions by taking part in our reader survey. Complete and return this card to the address on the reverse or e-mail your feedback to books@thomascook.com or visit www.thomascookpublishing.com. Any suggestions which are used for updating will be acknowledged in future editions.

1. Which Independent Traveller's title did you purchase?

....

2. Is this the first Independent Traveller's guidebook you have bought?

☐ YES   ☐ NO

3. Why is this your preferred choice of budget travel guide?

....

....

4. In your opinion, how could future editions of this book be improved?

....

....

5. What other titles would you like to see in this series?

....

Full Name ....

Age ☐ under 21   ☐ 21-30   ☐ 31-40   ☐ 41-50   ☐ over 50

Address ....

.... Postcode ....

Daytime telephone number ....

E-mail address ....

☐ Please tick here if you do not wish to receive details of products and services from Thomas Cook Publishing.